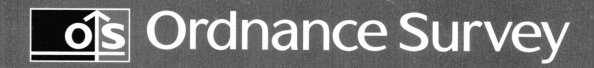

Ordnance Survey

STREET ATLAS
Cheshire

Contents

III Key to map symbols

IV Key to map pages

VI Administrative and post code boundaries

1 Street maps

237 Extra-large-scale map of Chester town centre

238 Town maps

    238 Altrincham
    239 Cheadle and Gatley
    240 Stockport
    241 Hyde
    241 Romiley
    242 Sale
    242 Stalybridge

243 Index of hospitals, railway stations, schools, shopping centres, street names and universities

PHILIP'S

First edition published 1995
First colour edition published 1998 by

Ordnance Survey®   and George Philip Ltd
Romsey Road   an imprint of Reed Consumer Books Ltd
Maybush   Michelin House, 81 Fulham Road,
Southampton   London SW3 6RB
SO16 4GU   and Auckland and Melbourne

ISBN 0-540-07507-8 (hardback)
ISBN 0-540-07508-6 (wire-o)

To the best of the Publishers' knowledge, the information in this
atlas was correct at the time of going to press. No responsibility
can be accepted for any errors or their consequences.

The representation in this atlas of a road, track or path is no
evidence of the existence of a right of way.

**The mapping between pages 1 and 237 (inclusive) in this atlas
is derived from Ordnance Survey® Large Scale and Landranger®
mapping; pages 238-242 (inclusive) are derived from Ordnance
Survey® OSCAR® and Land-line® data, and Landranger® mapping.**

Ordnance Survey, OSCAR, Land-Line and Landranger are registered
trade marks of Ordnance Survey, the National Mapping Agency of
Great Britain.

Printed and bound in Spain by Cayfosa

Digital Data

The exceptionally high-quality mapping
found in this book is available as digital
data in TIFF format, which is easily
convertible to other bit-mapped (raster)
image formats.

The index is also available in digital form
as a standard database table. It contains
all the details found in the printed index
together with the National Grid reference
for the map square in which each entry
is named and feature codes for places
of interest in eight categories such as
education and health.

For further information and to discuss
your requirements, please contact the
Ordnance Survey Solutions Centre on
01703 792929.

Symbol	Description
(22a)	**Motorway** (with junction number)
	Primary route (dual carriageway and single)
	A road (dual carriageway and single)
	B road (dual carriageway and single)
	Minor road (dual carriageway and single)
	Other minor road
	Road under construction
	Pedestrianised area
	County and Unitary Authority boundaries
	Railway
	Tramway, miniature railway
	Rural track, private road or narrow road in urban area
	Gate or obstruction to traffic (restrictions may not apply at all times or to all vehicles)
	Path, bridleway, byway open to all traffic, road used as a public path

The representation in this atlas of a road, track or path is no evidence of the existence of a right of way

160 38 237 Adjoining page indicators

The map area within the pink band is shown at a larger scale on the page indicated by the red block and arrow

Abbr	Full	Abbr	Full
Acad	Academy	Mon	Monument
Cemy	Cemetery	Mus	Museum
C Ctr	Civic Centre	Obsy	Observatory
CH	Club House	Pal	Royal Palace
Coll	College	PH	Public House
Ent	Enterprise	Recn Gd	Recreation Ground
Ex H	Exhibition Hall	Resr	Reservoir
Ind Est	Industrial Estate	Ret Pk	Retail Park
Inst	Institute	Sch	School
Ct	Law Court	Sh Ctr	Shopping Centre
L Ctr	Leisure Centre	Sta	Station
LC	Level Crossing	TH	Town Hall/House
Liby	Library	Trad Est	Trading Estate
Mkt	Market	Univ	University
Meml	Memorial	YH	Youth Hostel

Symbol	Description
	British Rail station
(M)	Metrolink station
	Underground station
D	Docklands Light Railway station
M	Tyne and Wear Metro
	Private railway station
	Bus, coach station
◆	Ambulance station
◆	Coastguard station
◆	Fire station
◆	Police station
+	Accident and Emergency entrance to hospital
H	Hospital
+	Church, place of worship
i	Information centre (open all year)
P P&R	Parking, Park and Ride
PO	Post Office
Prim Sch	Important buildings, schools, colleges, universities and hospitals
River Medway	Water name
	Stream
	River or canal (minor and major)
	Water
	Tidal water
	Woods
	Houses
House	Non-Roman antiquity
VILLA	Roman antiquity

■ The dark grey border on the inside edge of some pages indicates that the mapping does not continue onto the adjacent page
■ The small numbers around the edges of the maps identify the 1 kilometre National Grid lines

The scale of the maps is 5.52 cm to 1 km (3½ inches to 1 mile)

0 | ¼ | ½ | ¾ | 1 mile
0 | 250m | 500m | 750m | 1 kilometre

The scale of the map on page numbered in red is 11.04 cm to 1 km (7 inches to 1 mile)

0 | 220 yards | 440 yards | 660 yards | ½ mile
0 | 125m | 250m | 375m | ½ kilometre

Key to map pages

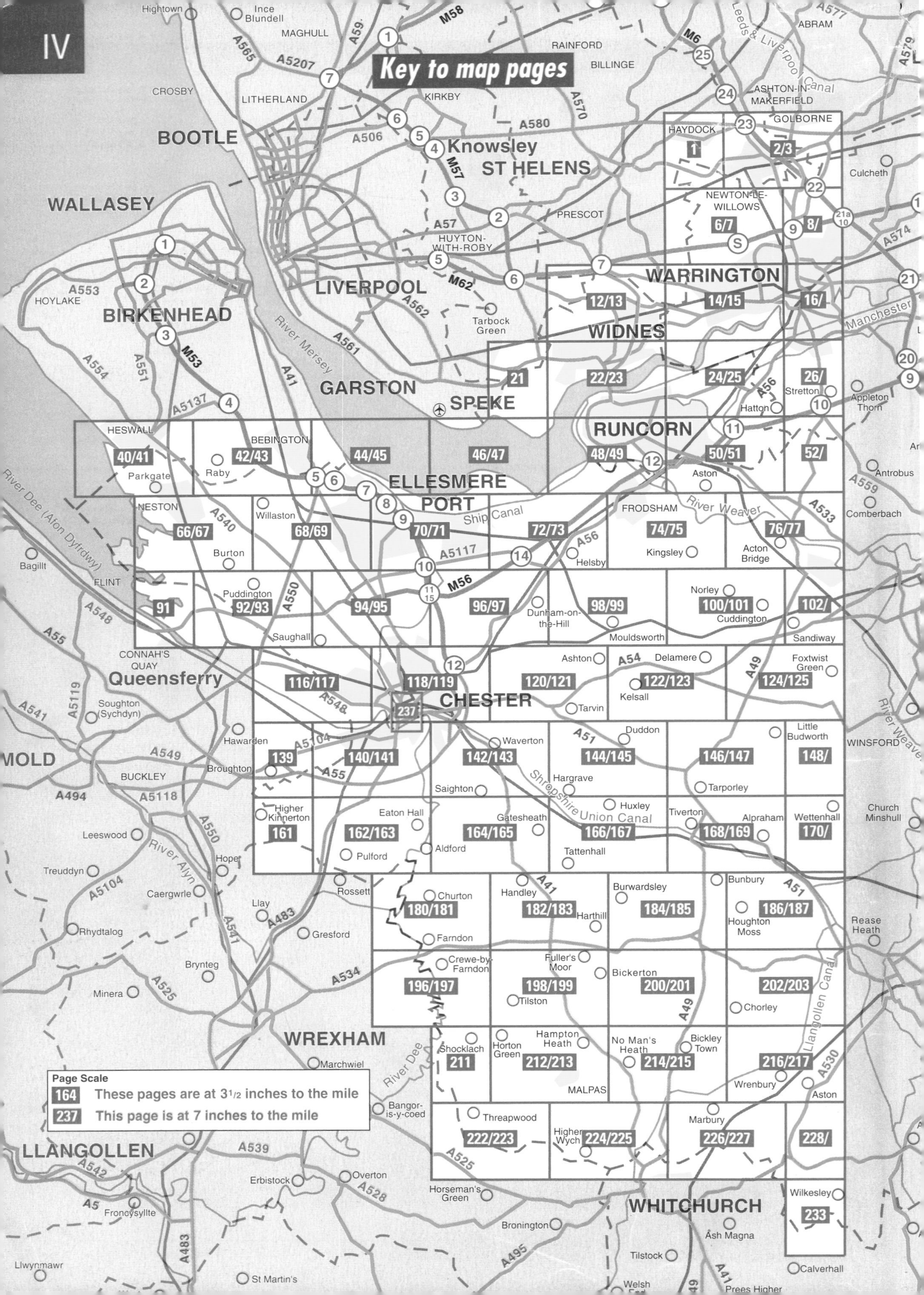

BOOTLE
Knowsley
ST HELENS
WALLASEY
BIRKENHEAD
LIVERPOOL
GARSTON
SPEKE
WARRINGTON
WIDNES
RUNCORN
ELLESMERE PORT
CHESTER
Queensferry
MOLD
WREXHAM
LLANGOLLEN
WHITCHURCH
Page Scale
164 These pages are at 3 1/2 inches to the mile
237 This page is at 7 inches to the mile

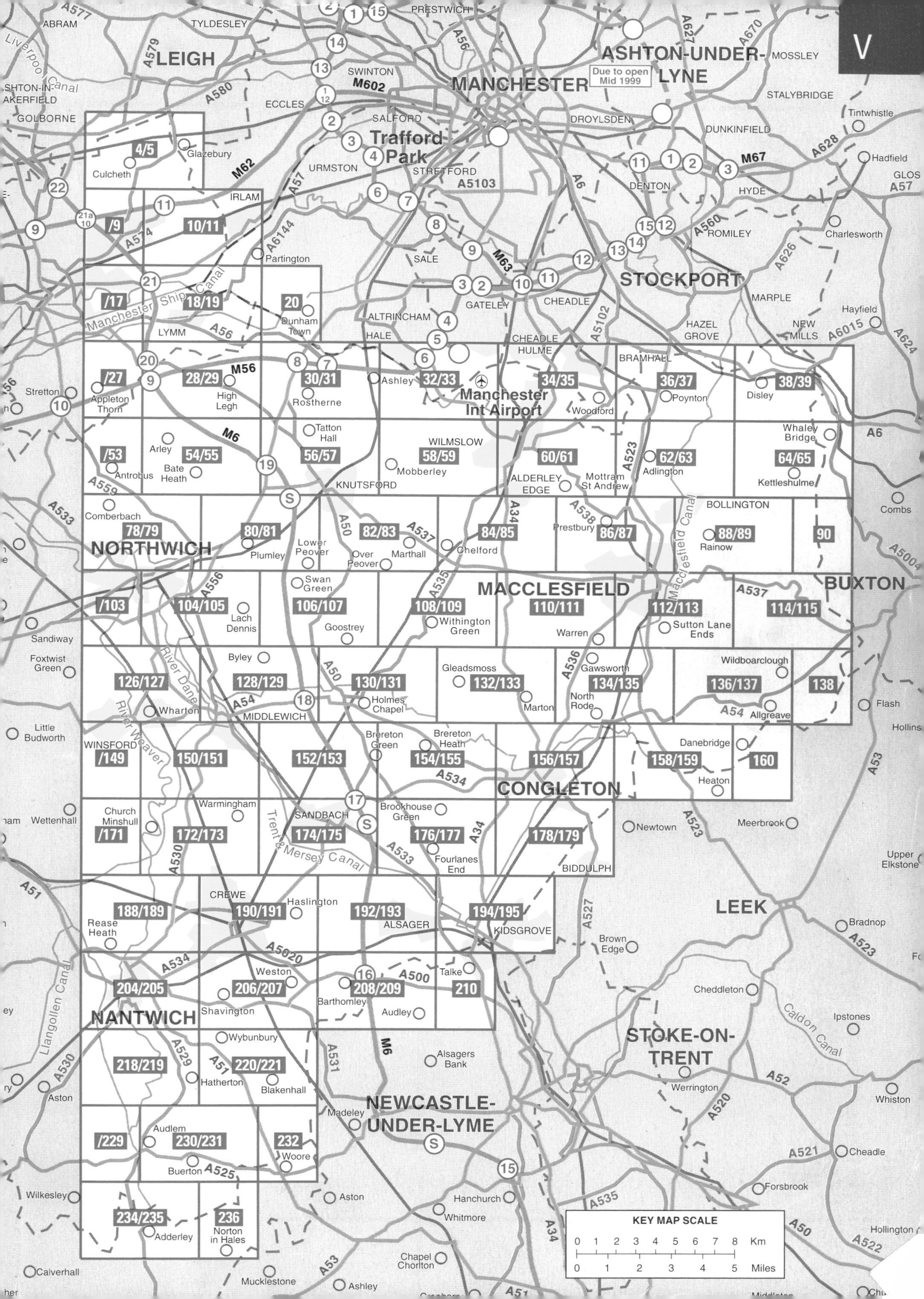

V
A577
ABRAM
TYLDESLEY
PRESTWICH
A56
A627
A670
LEIGH
A579
Liverpool Canal
SWINTON
MANCHESTER
ASHTON-UNDER-LYNE
Due to open Mid 1999
MOSSLEY
M602
A580
ECCLES
SALFORD
STALYBRIDGE
GOLBORNE
Trafford Park
DROYLSDEN
DUNKINFIELD
Tintwhistle
4/5
Glazebury
Culcheth
M62
URMSTON
STRETFORD
A5103
M67
A628
Hadfield
GLOS
A57
DENTON
HYDE
IRLAM
/9
10/11
A574
A6144
A57
A6
A560
ROMILEY
Charlesworth
Partington
SALE
M63
A626
STOCKPORT
/17
18/19
20
Manchester Ship Canal
Dunham Town
ALTRINCHAM
GATELEY
CHEADLE
MARPLE
Hayfield
LYMM
A56
HALE
CHEADLE HULME
A5102
HAZEL GROVE
NEW MILLS
A6015
A624
BRAMHALL
/27
28/29
M56
30/31
32/33
34/35
36/37
38/39
Stretton
Appleton Thorn
High Legh
Rostherne
Ashley
Manchester Int Airport
Woodford
Poynton
Disley
M6
Tatton Hall
WILMSLOW
Whaley Bridge
A6
/53
54/55
56/57
58/59
60/61
62/63
64/65
Arley
Antrobus
Bate Heath
Mobberley
ALDERLEY EDGE
Mottram St Andrew
A523
Adlington
Kettleshulme
A559
KNUTSFORD
A533
Comberbach
78/79
80/81
82/83
84/85
86/87
88/89
90
NORTHWICH
A50
A537
A34
A538
Prestbury
BOLLINGTON
Combs
Plumley
Lower Peover
Over Peover
Marthall
Chelford
Rainow
Macclesfield Canal
A5004
A556
MACCLESFIELD
BUXTON
/103
104/105
106/107
108/109
110/111
112/113
114/115
A535
A537
Sandiway
Swan Green
Lach Dennis
Goostrey
Withington Green
Warren
Sutton Lane Ends
Foxtwist Green
Byley
126/127
128/129
130/131
132/133
134/135
136/137
138
River Dane
A50
Gleadsmoss
A536
Gawsworth
Wildboarclough
A54
MIDDLEWICH
Holmes Chapel
Marton
North Rode
A54
Allgreave
Flash
Wharton
Little Budworth
River Weaver
Hollins
WINSFORD
/149
150/151
152/153
154/155
156/157
158/159
160
Brereton Green
Brereton Heath
A534
CONGLETON
Danebridge
Heaton
A53
Church Minshull
Warmingham
Wettenhall
/171
172/173
174/175
176/177
178/179
SANDBACH
Trent & Mersey Canal
Brookhouse Green
A34
A533
Fourlanes End
A530
BIDDULPH
Newtown
A523
Meerbrook
Upper Elkstone
A51
CREWE
188/189
190/191
192/193
194/195
Haslington
ALSAGER
KIDSGROVE
Rease Heath
A527
LEEK
Bradnop
A523
Brown Edge
A534
A5020
Weston
A500
Talke
204/205
206/207
208/209
210
Llangollen Canal
NANTWICH
Shavington
Barthomley
Audley
Cheddleton
Caldon Canal
Ipstones
Wybunbury
M6
A529
A51
A531
Alsagers Bank
STOKE-ON-TRENT
218/219
220/221
Hatherton
Blakenhall
A530
Aston
Werrington
A52
A520
Whiston
NEWCASTLE-UNDER-LYME
Madeley
Audlem
/229
230/231
232
Woore
Buerton
A525
A521
Cheadle
Wilkesley
Aston
Forsbrook
A535
234/235
236
Adderley
Norton in Hales
Hanchurch
Whitmore
KEY MAP SCALE
0 1 2 3 4 5 6 7 8 Km
0 1 2 3 4 5 Miles
A34
Hollington
A50
A522
Calverhall
Chapel Chorlton
A53
Mucklestone
Ashley
A51

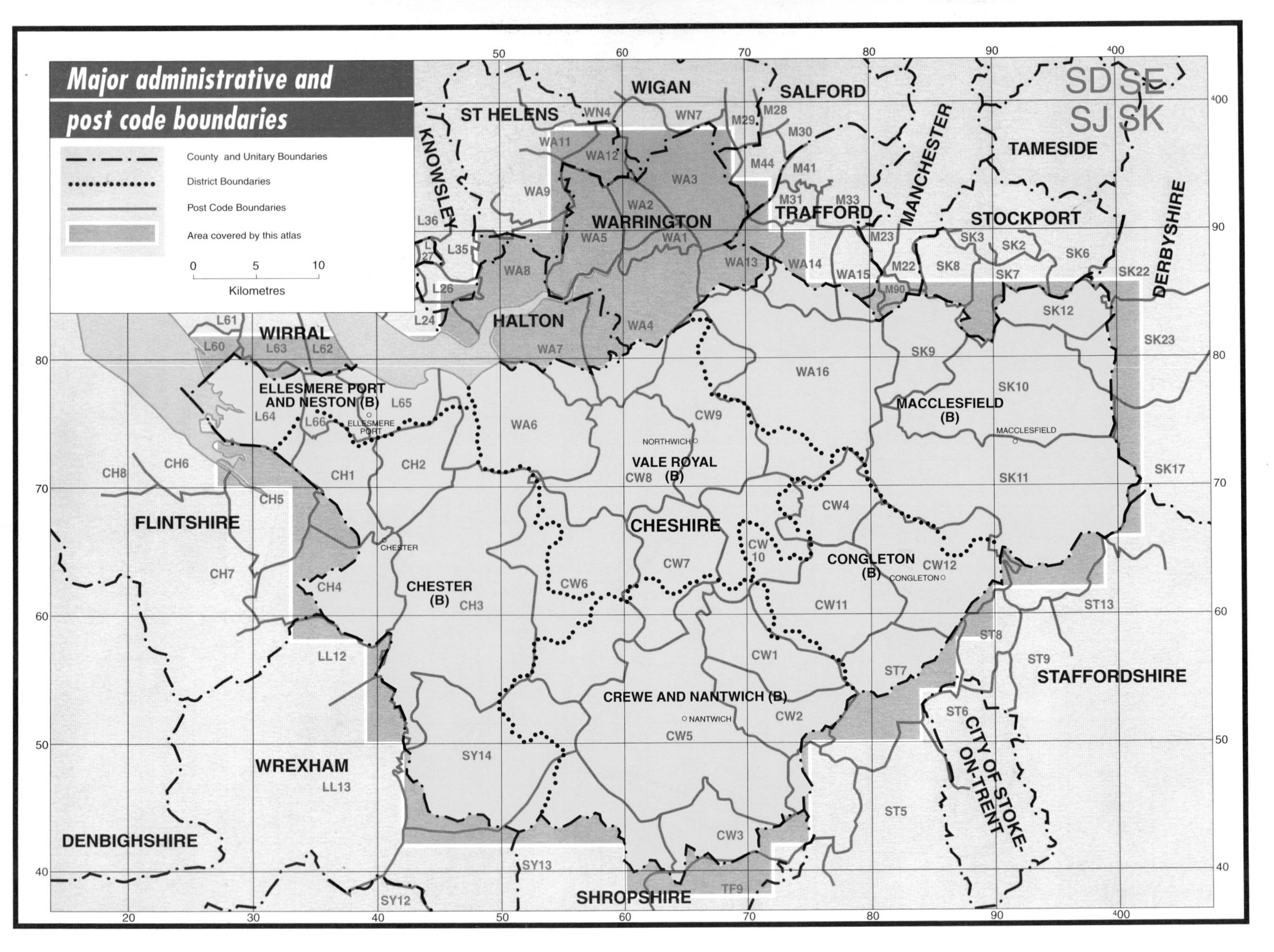

VI

Major administrative and post code boundaries

- — · · — County and Unitary Boundaries
- · · · · · · District Boundaries
- ——— Post Code Boundaries
- Area covered by this atlas

Kilometres

0   5   10

2

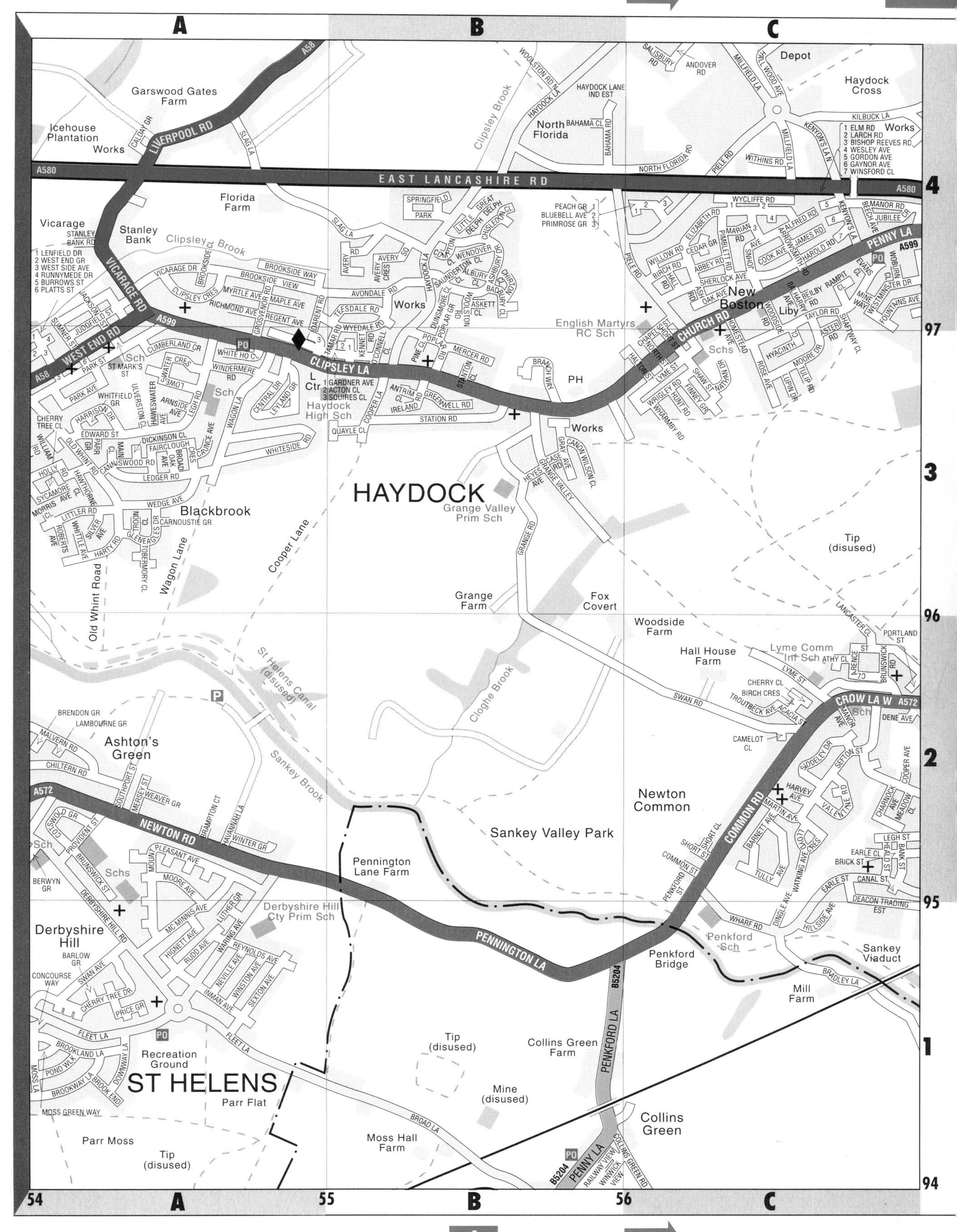
A
B
C
Garswood Gates
Farm
Icehouse
Plantation
Works
LIVERPOOL RD
A58
A580
EAST LANCASHIRE RD
Florida
Farm
Vicarage
Stanley
Bank
Clipsley Brook
VICARAGE RD
WEST END RD
A599
CLIPSLEY LA
HAYDOCK
Grange Valley
Prim Sch
Haydock
High Sch
Blackbrook
Cooper Lane
Wagon Lane
Old Whint Road
North
Florida
HAYDOCK LANE
IND EST
Depot
Haydock
Cross
Works
1 ELM RD
2 LARCH RD
3 BISHOP REEVES RD
4 WESLEY AVE
5 GORDON AVE
6 GAYNOR AVE
7 WINSFORD CL
PENNY LA
CHURCH RD
New
Boston
English Martyrs
RC Sch
Schs
PH
Works
1 LENFIELD DR
2 WEST END GR
3 WEST SIDE AVE
4 RUNNYMEDE DR
5 BURROWS ST
6 PLATTS ST
1 GARDNER AVE
2 ACTON CL
3 SQUIRES CL
PEACH GR
BLUEBELL AVE
PRIMROSE GR
Tip
(disused)
Grange
Farm
Fox
Covert
Woodside
Farm
Hall House
Farm
Lyme Comm
Inf Sch
St Helens Canal
(disused)
Cloghe Brook
Sankey Brook
Ashton's
Green
CROW LA W
A572
Newton
Common
Sankey Valley Park
NEWTON RD
Pennington
Lane Farm
Derbyshire Hill
Cty Prim Sch
Derbyshire
Hill
PENNINGTON LA
COMMON RD
Penkford
Sch
Penkford
Bridge
Sankey
Viaduct
Mill
Farm
B5204
PENKFORD LA
Tip
(disused)
Collins Green
Farm
Recreation
Ground
ST HELENS
Parr Flat
Mine
(disused)
Collins
Green
Parr Moss
Tip
(disused)
Moss Hall
Farm
BROAD LA
PENNY LA
97
96
95
94
3
2
1
4
54
55
56

6
2

1

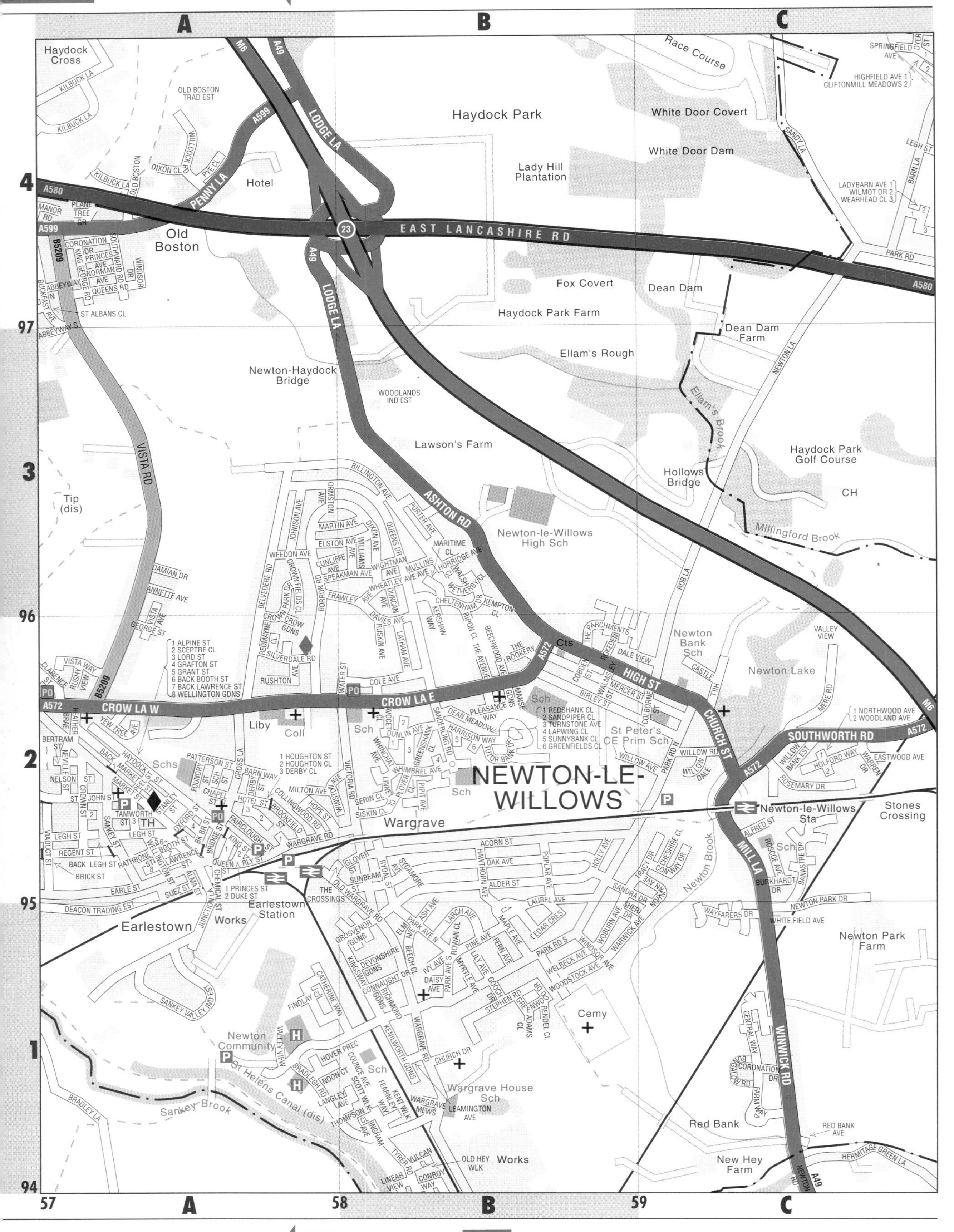
A
B
C
Haydock Cross
OLD BOSTON TRAD EST
Race Course
Haydock Park
White Door Covert
White Door Dam
Lady Hill Plantation
Hotel
Old Boston
EAST LANCASHIRE RD
A580
A599
A49
M6
LODGE LA
PENNY LA
Fox Covert
Dean Dam
Haydock Park Farm
Dean Dam Farm
Ellam's Rough
Newton-Haydock Bridge
WOODLANDS IND EST
Lawson's Farm
Ellam's Brook
Haydock Park Golf Course
Hollows Bridge
CH
VISTA RD
Tip (dis)
ASHTON RD
Newton-le-Willows High Sch
Millingford Brook
NEWTON LA
ROB LA
Newton Bank Sch
Newton Lake
VALLEY VIEW
HIGH ST
CHURCH ST
CROW LA W
CROW LA E
A572
B5209
Liby
Coll
Sch
Schs
St Peter's CE Prim Sch
SOUTHWORTH RD
NEWTON-LE-WILLOWS
Wargrave
Newton-le-Willows Sta
Stones Crossing
TH
Earlestown Station
THE CROSSINGS
Works
Earlestown
MILL LA
Newton Park Farm
Newton Brook
Cemy
Newton Community
St Helens Canal (dis)
Sankey Brook
Wargrave House Sch
Red Bank
New Hey Farm
WINWICK RD
Works
BRADLEY LA
HERMITAGE GREEN LA
4
3
2
1
97
96
95
94
57
58
59

1

7

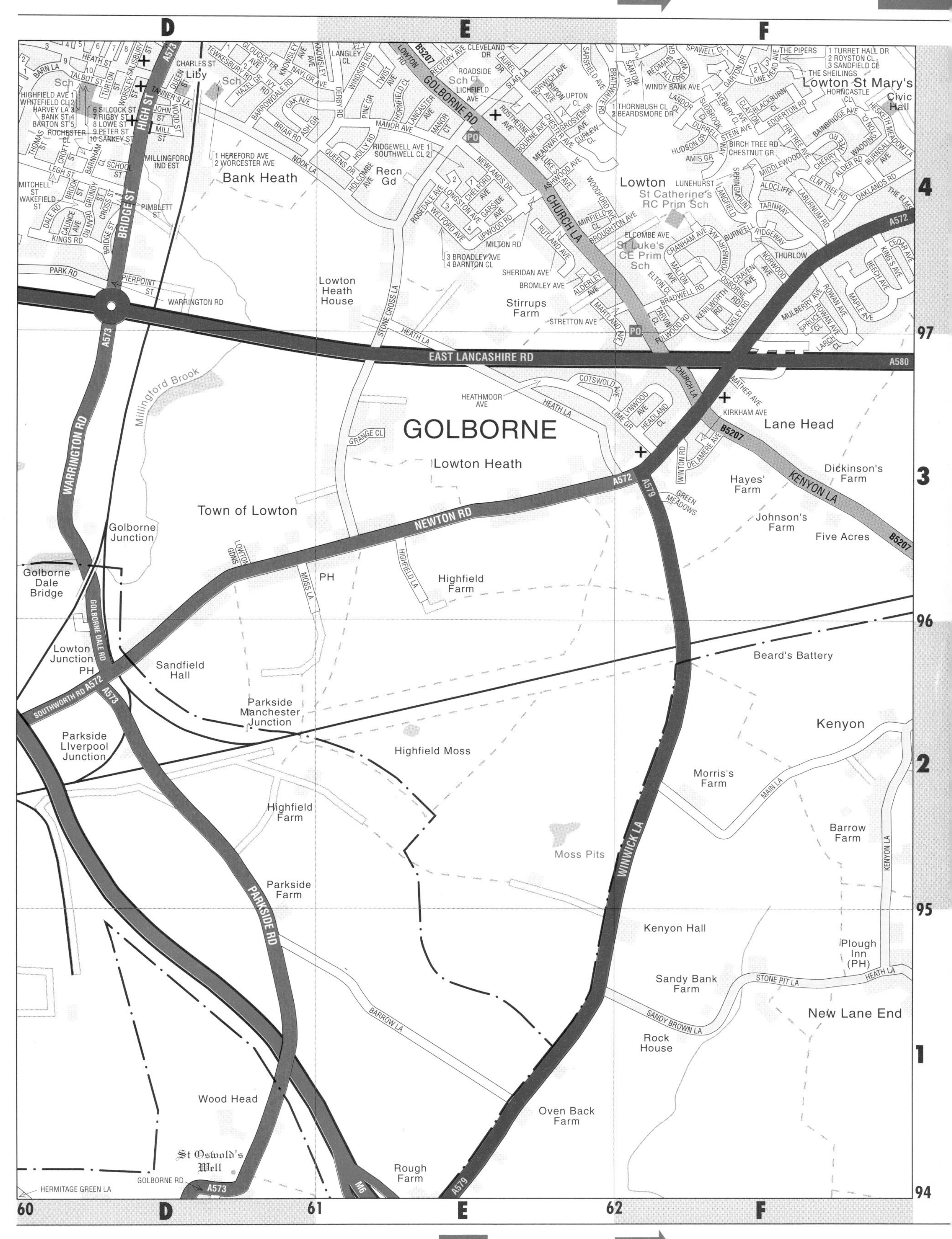
4
D
E
F
GOLBORNE
Lowton St Mary's
Civic Hall
Bank Heath
Recn Gd
Lowton
St Catherine's RC Prim Sch
St Luke's CE Prim Sch
Lowton Heath House
Stirrups Farm
EAST LANCASHIRE RD
A580
A572
A573
A579
B5207
Millingford Brook
Lowton Heath
Lane Head
Town of Lowton
Golborne Junction
NEWTON RD
WARRINGTON RD
HIGH ST
BRIDGE ST
CHURCH LA
GOLBORNE RD
KENYON LA
Hayes' Farm
Dickinson's Farm
Johnson's Farm
Five Acres
Golborne Dale Bridge
PH
Highfield Farm
Lowton Junction
Sandfield Hall
Parkside Manchester Junction
Beard's Battery
Kenyon
Highfield Moss
Parkside Liverpool Junction
Morris's Farm
Barrow Farm
Moss Pits
WINWICK LA
PARKSIDE RD
Parkside Farm
Kenyon Hall
Plough Inn (PH)
Sandy Bank Farm
STONE PIT LA
HEATH LA
SANDY BROWN LA
BARROW LA
New Lane End
Rock House
Wood Head
Oven Back Farm
St Oswold's Well
Rough Farm
HERMITAGE GREEN LA
M6
97
96
95
94
60
61
62
1
2
3
4

8
4

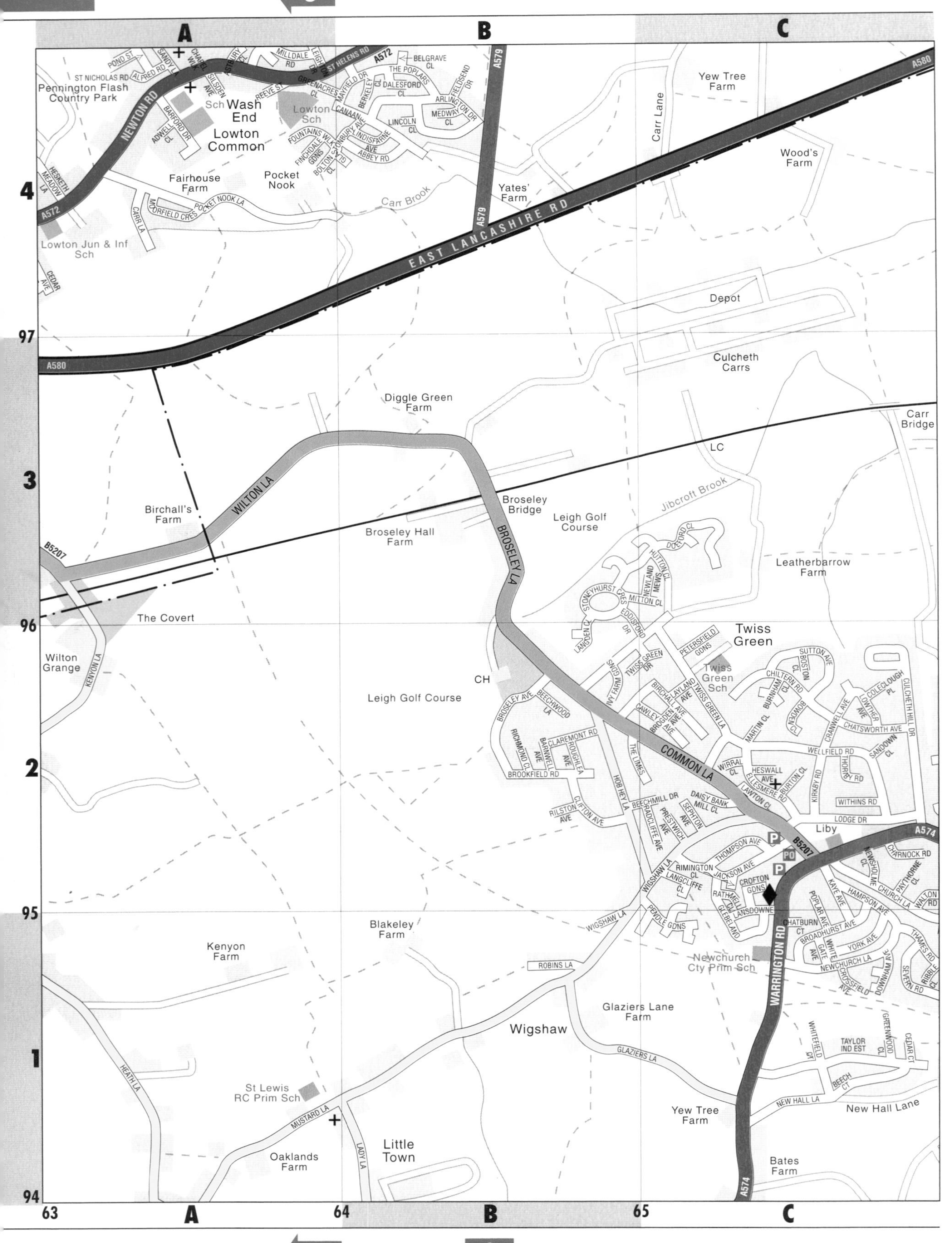

A   B   C

Pennington Flash
Country Park

St NICHOLAS RD
PORTBURY CL
POND ST
ALFRED RD
BARFORD CL
ADNELL CL
CHURCHILL WLK
CENTURY AVE
KELSALL AVE
GREENACRES
LEIGH LA
MILLDALE RD
MAYFIELD DR
ST HELENS RD
BERKELEY CL
THE POPLARS
BELGRAVE CL
DALESFORD CL
ARLINGTON DR
A572
A579
MEDWAY CL
LINCOLN CL

Sch

Wash
End
Lowton
Common

Lowton
Sch

FOUNTAINS WLK
FINCHDALE GDNS
BOLTON LVD
CANAANS
LINDISFARNE
ABBEY RD

Fairhouse
Farm

Pocket
Nook

HESKETH
MEADOW

A572

MORFIELD CRES
POCKET NOOK LA
CARR LA

Carr Brook

Yates'
Farm

Yew Tree
Farm

Carr Lane

Wood's
Farm

A580

4

Lowton Jun & Inf
Sch

CEDAR AVE

A580

Depot

97

Culcheth
Carrs

Carr
Bridge

Diggle Green
Farm

WILTON LA

Broseley
Bridge

Leigh Golf
Course

Jibcroft Brook

LC

Leatherbarrow
Farm

3

Birchall's
Farm

B5207

Broseley Hall
Farm

BROSELEY LA

STONEYHURST CRES
NEWLAND MEWS
WILTON CL
MILTON CL
EDGEFORD
DR
DORCHESTER
RD

Twiss
Green

PETERSFIELD
GDNS
TWISS GREEN
DR
SUTTON AVE
BOSTON
CL
CHILTERN RD
BURNHAM CL
CULCHETH HILL DR

The Covert

LARKS CL

CH

Twiss
Green
Sch

BIRCHALL
AVE
TWISS GREEN LA
CRANWELL AVE
CONIFER
WALK
COLCLOUGH
PL
CHATSWORTH AVE

96

Wilton
Grange

KENYON LA

Leigh Golf Course

BROSELEY AVE
BEECHWOOD
LA
CAWLEY AVE
BRIDGES LA
MARTIN CL
HESWALL
AVE
KIRKBY RD
THORBY RD
SANDOWN
CL
WELLFIELD RD
WITHINS RD

2

RICHMOND CL
CLAREMONT
AVE
BARNWELL
AVE
PUGH LA
WIRRAL CL
BURTON CL
ELLESMERE RD
LAWTON CL
LODGE DR

BROOKFIELD RD

RILSTON
AVE
CLIFTON AVE
HUB HEY LA
BEECHMILL DR
PRESTWICH
AVE
RADCLIFFE AVE
THE TIMBS
DAISY BANK
MILL CL
SEFTON
CL

Liby

A574

Kenyon
Farm

Blakeley
Farm

WIGSHAM LA
WIGSHAW LA
THOMPSON AVE
RIMINGTON
CL
JACKSON AVE
LANGCLIFFE
CL
PENDLE GDNS
RATHMELL CL
CROFTON
GDNS
LANSDOWNE
CHATBURN
CT
POPLAR AVE
KAYE AVE
HAMPSON AVE
KENSINGTON DR
CHARNOCK RD
HAWTHORNE
WALTON
CL
B5207

P
PO
P

95

ROBINS LA

Newchurch
Cty Prim Sch

WARRINGTON RD

BROADHURST AVE
WHITE
GATE
AVE
YORK AVE
NEWCHURCH LA
CROSSFIELD
AVE
THAMES RD
RIBBLE
CL
SEVERN RD

Wigshaw

Glaziers Lane
Farm

GLAZIERS LA

WHITEFIELD
GREENWOOD
CEDAR CT
TAYLOR
IND EST

1

HEATH LA

St Lewis
RC Prim Sch

MUSTARD LA

LADY LA

Yew Tree
Farm

New Hall Lane

NEW HALL LA
BEECH
CL

Oaklands
Farm

Little
Town

Bates
Farm

A574

94

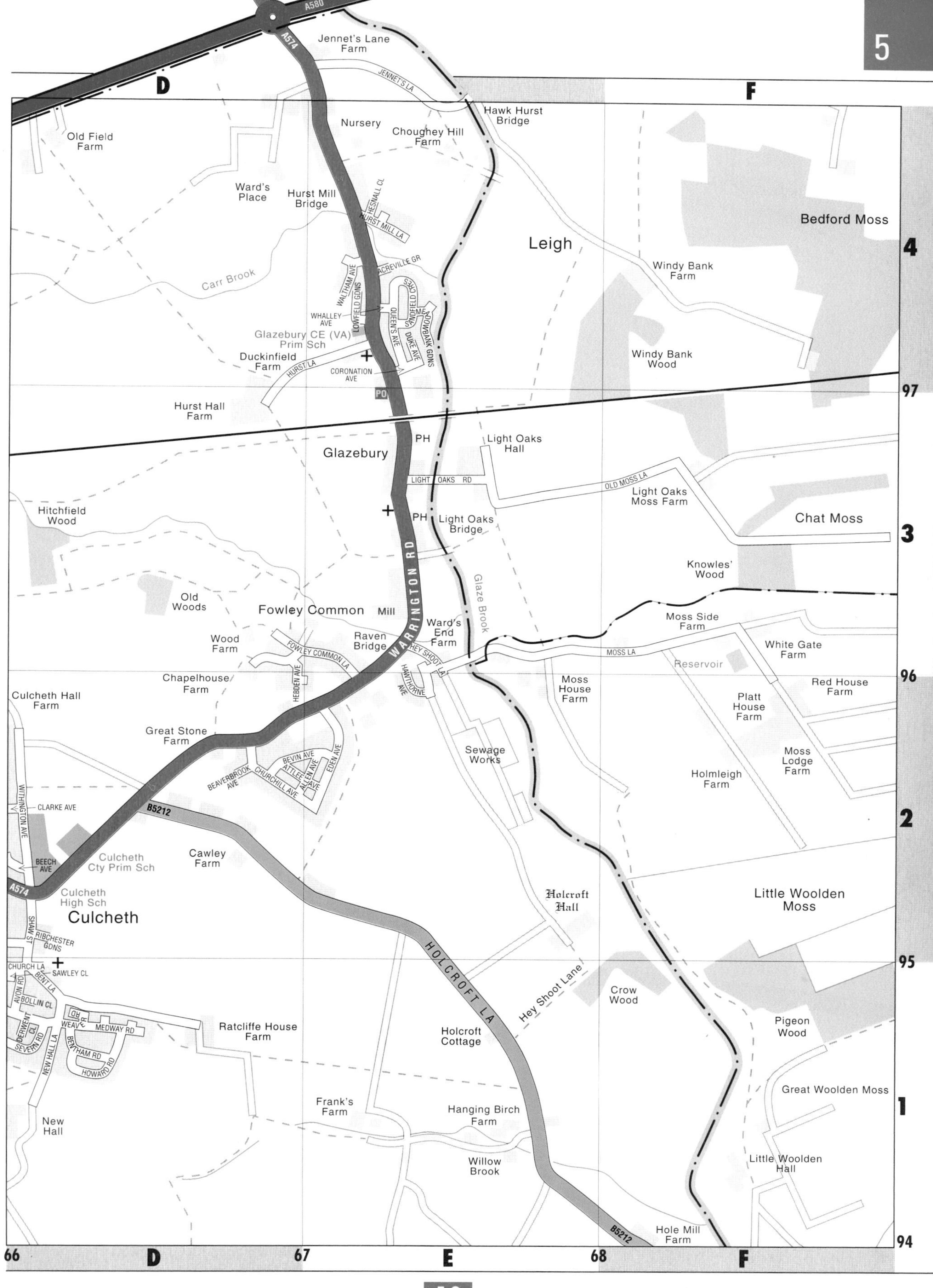

A580

A574

Jennet's Lane
Farm

JENNET'S LA

Hawk Hurst
Bridge

D

F

Old Field
Farm

Nursery

Choughey Hill
Farm

Ward's
Place

Hurst Mill
Bridge

HESNALL CL

HURST MILL LA

Leigh

Bedford Moss

Windy Bank
Farm

4

Carr Brook

WALTHAM AVE

ACREVILLE GR

LOWFIELD GDNS

GREENFIELD GDNS

MOORBANK GDNS

QUEEN'S AVE

DUKE AVE

WHALLEY
AVE

Glazebury CE (VA)
Prim Sch

Windy Bank
Wood

Duckinfield
Farm

HURST LA

CORONATION
AVE

PO

97

Hurst Hall
Farm

Light Oaks
Hall

Glazebury

PH

LIGHT OAKS RD

OLD MOSS LA

Light Oaks
Moss Farm

Chat Moss

3

Hitchfield
Wood

PH

Light Oaks
Bridge

WARRINGTON RD

Glaze Brook

Knowles'
Wood

Old
Woods

Fowley Common

Mill

Moss Side
Farm

White Gate
Farm

Wood
Farm

FOWLEY COMMON LA

Raven
Bridge

HEY SHOOT LA

Ward's
End Farm

MOSS LA

Reservoir

Red House
Farm

96

Chapelhouse
Farm

HEBDEN AVE

HAWTHORNE
AVE

Moss
House
Farm

Platt
House
Farm

Moss
Lodge
Farm

Culcheth Hall
Farm

Great Stone
Farm

BEVIN AVE

ATTLEE
AVE

EDEN AVE

Sewage
Works

Holmleigh
Farm

WITHINGTON AVE

CLARKE AVE

BEAVERBROOK
AVE

CHURCHILL AVE

B5212

Little Woolden
Moss

2

BEECH
AVE

Culcheth
Cty Prim Sch

Cawley
Farm

Holcroft
Hall

A574

Culcheth
High Sch

HOLCROFT LA

Culcheth

SHAW ST

RIBCHESTER
GDNS

Hey Shoot Lane

95

CHURCH LA

SAWLEY CL

Crow
Wood

Pigeon
Wood

HIGH
BOLLIN CL

BENT LA

WEAV

RD

MEDWAY RD

BENTHAM RD

Ratcliffe House
Farm

Holcroft
Cottage

Great Woolden Moss

DERWENT
CL

SEVERN RD

NEW HALL LA

HOWARD RD

Frank's
Farm

Hanging Birch
Farm

Little Woolden
Hall

1

New
Hall

Willow
Brook

B5212

Hole Mill
Farm

94

66

D

67

E

68

F

1

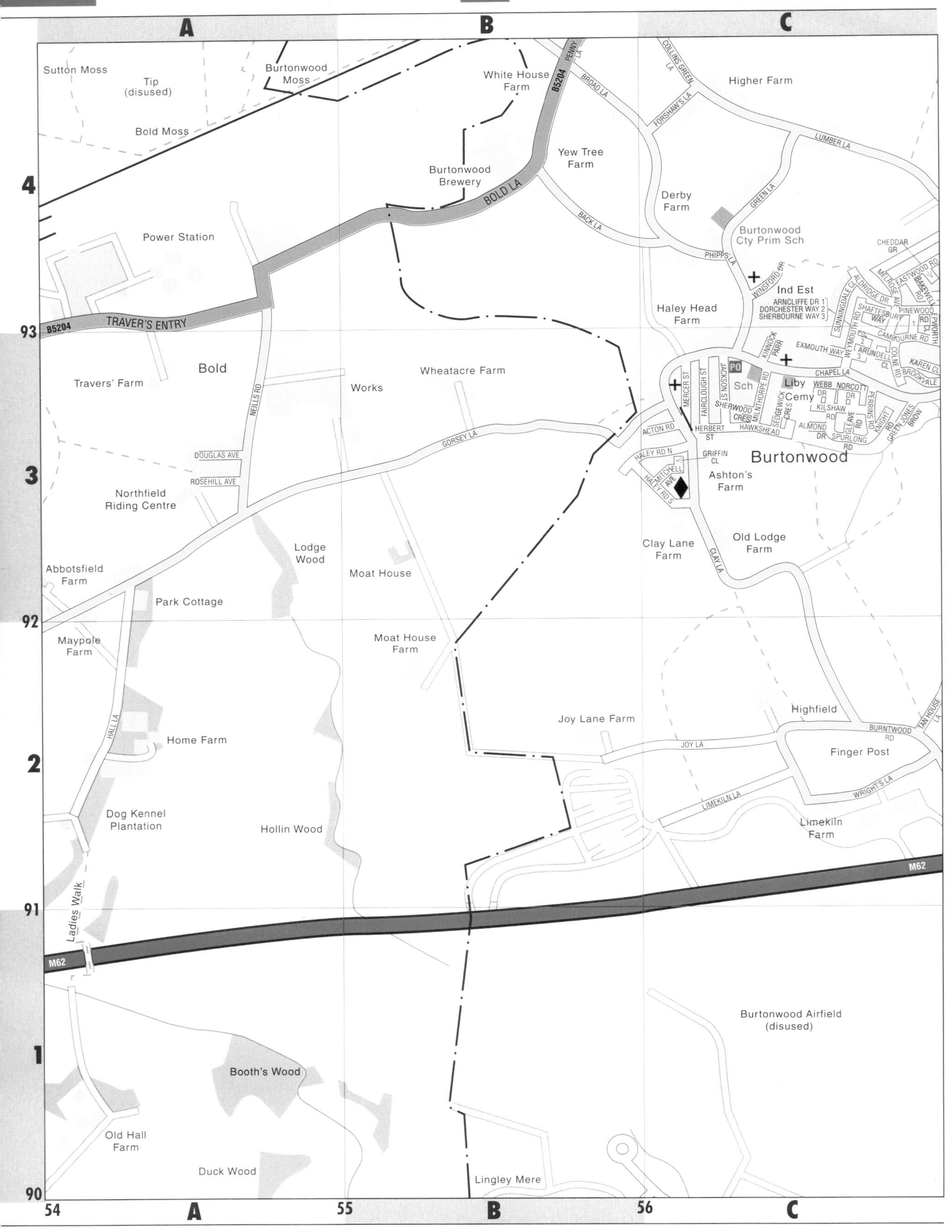

A
B
C
Sutton Moss
Tip (disused)
Burtonwood Moss
White House Farm
Higher Farm
Bold Moss
Yew Tree Farm
Burtonwood Brewery
Derby Farm
Power Station
Burtonwood Cty Prim Sch
Ind Est
Haley Head Farm
Bold
Travers' Farm
Works
Wheatacre Farm
Sch
Liby
Cemy
Burtonwood
Ashton's Farm
Northfield Riding Centre
Lodge Wood
Moat House
Clay Lane Farm
Old Lodge Farm
Abbotsfield Farm
Park Cottage
Maypole Farm
Moat House Farm
Highfield
Joy Lane Farm
Home Farm
Finger Post
Dog Kennel Plantation
Hollin Wood
Limekiln Farm
Ladies Walk
Burtonwood Airfield (disused)
Booth's Wood
Old Hall Farm
Duck Wood
Lingley Mere
B5204
TRAVER'S ENTRY
BOLD LA
PENNY LA
BROAD LA
COLLINS GREEN LA
FORSHAW'S LA
LUMBER LA
GREEN LA
BACK LA
PHIPPS' LA
WINSFORD DR
ARNCLIFFE DR 1
DORCHESTER WAY 2
SHERBOURNE WAY 3
CHEDDAR GR
EASTWOOD RD
SUNNINGDALE CL
ALDRIDGE DR
MELROSE AVE
SHAFTESBURY WAY
PINEWOOD
EPWORTH CL
CAMBOURNE RD
WEYMOUTH RD
EXMOUTH WAY
ARUNDELL CL
COLNE RD
KAREN CL
BROOKVALE
KINNOCK PARK
CHAPEL LA
MERCER ST
FAIRCLOUGH ST
JACKSON ST
SHERWOOD CRES
MILNTHORPE RD
SEDGEWICK CRES
WEBB DR
NORCOTT DR
KILSHAW RD
PERRINS RD
GLEAVE RD
KNIGHT RD
GREEN JONES BROW
ALMOND DR
SPURLONG RD
HAWKSHEAD
HERBERT ST
ACTON RD
HALEY RD N
GRIFFIN CL
MITCHELL AVE
HALEY RD S
NEILLS RD
DOUGLAS AVE
ROSEHILL AVE
GORSEY LA
CLAY LA
HALL LA
JOY LA
BURNTWOOD RD
TAN HOUSE LA
WRIGHT'S LA
LIMEKILN LA
M62
4
93
3
92
2
91
1
90
54
55
56

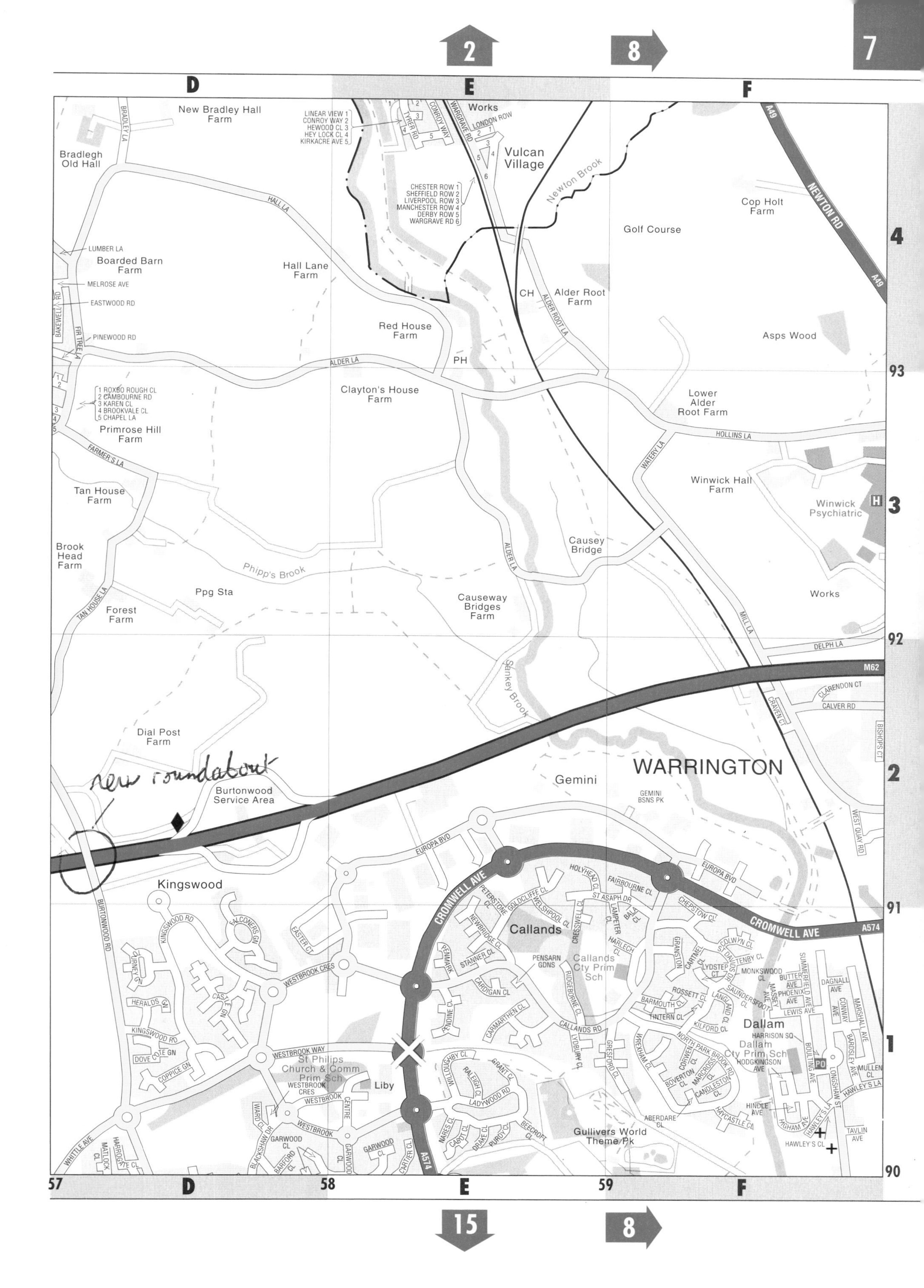

D   E   F

New Bradley Hall Farm

Bradlegh Old Hall

BRADLEY LA

Works

LINEAR VIEW 1
CONROY WAY 2
HEWOOD CL 3
HEY LOCK CL 4
KIRKACRE AVE 5

CONROY WAY

TYER RD

WARGRAVE RD

LONDON ROW

Vulcan Village

Newton Brook

Cop Holt Farm

Golf Course

NEWTON RD

A49

4

LUMBER LA

Boarded Barn Farm

MELROSE AVE

EASTWOOD RD

PINEWOOD RD

HALL LA

Hall Lane Farm

CHESTER ROW 1
SHEFFIELD ROW 2
LIVERPOOL ROW 3
MANCHESTER ROW 4
DERBY ROW 5
WARGRAVE ROW 6

CH

Alder Root Farm

ALDER ROOT LA

Asps Wood

BAKEWELL RD

FIR TREE LA

Red House Farm

ALDER LA

PH

93

1 ROXBO ROUGH CL
2 CAMBOURNE RD
3 KAREN CL
4 BROOKVALE CL
5 CHAPEL LA

Clayton's House Farm

Lower Alder Root Farm

HOLLINS LA

WATERY LA

Primrose Hill Farm

FARMER S LA

Tan House Farm

Winwick Hall Farm

Winwick Psychiatric

H

3

Brook Head Farm

TAN HOUSE LA

Phipp's Brook

ALDER LA

Causey Bridge

Forest Farm

Ppg Sta

Causeway Bridges Farm

Works

92

Senkey Brook

DELPH LA

M62

CLARENDON CT

CALVER RD

Dial Post Farm

new roundabout

Burtonwood Service Area

WARRINGTON

Gemini

GEMINI BSNS PK

BISHOPS CT

2

WEST QUAY RD

Kingswood

BURTONWOOD RD

EUROPA BVD

CROMWELL AVE

EUROPA BVD

CROMWELL AVE

A574

91

KINGSWOOD RD

FALCONERS GN

EASTER CT

WESTBROOK CRES

CARNEY GN

HERALDS GN

KINGSWOOD RD

CASY GN

DOVE CL

COPPICE GN

TE GN

HOLYHEAD CL
GOLDCLIFFE CL
WELSHPOOL CL
FAIRBOURNE CL
ST ASAPH DR
LAMPETER CL
BALA CL

PETERSTONE

NEWBRIDGE CL

STAINER CL

Callands

CRESSWELL CL

CHEPSTOW CL

COLWYN CL

GRANSTON

CARTMEL

LYDSTEP CT

MONKSWOOD CL

TENBY CL

PENSARN GDNS

Callands Cty Prim Sch

RIDGEBORNE CL

HARLECH

ROSSETT CL

LANGWOOD

SAUNDERSFOOT

BARMOUTH CL

TINTERN CL

KILFORD CL

SUMMERFIELD AVE

BUTTERFIELD AVE

MASSEY

PHOENIX AVE

LEWIS AVE

CONWAY AVE

DAGNALL AVE

MARSHALL AVE

Dallam

BARDSLEY AVE

WESTBROOK WAY

St Philips Church & Comm Prim Sch

WESTBROOK CRES

WESTBROOK CENTRE

Liby

PENDINE CL

ROBIN WALK

CARDIGAN CL

CARMARTHEN CL

CALLANDS RD

LYBURY CL

GRESFORD CL

WREXHAM CL

BOVERTON CL

MARGROSS

CANDLESTON CL

NORTH PARK BROOK

CORNWALL

HARRISON SQ

Dallam Cty Prim Sch

HODGKINSON AVE

BOLTON AVE

PO

LONGSHAW ST

BAYCASTLE CL

MULLEN CL

HAWLEY'S CL

WARD DR

GARWOOD CL

BARFORD CL

BLACKHEATH

GARWOOD CL

WESTBROOK

WILLOUGHBY CL

RALEIGH CL

LADYWOOD RD

GRANT CL

NARES CL

CARYL CL

DROAK CL

PURDY CL

BEECROFT CL

Gullivers World Theme Pk

ABERDARE CL

HATCASTLE CL

HINDLE AVE

HIGHAM CL

LINNET LA

TAVLIN AVE

WHITTLE AVE

MATLOCK CL

HARRODS GTE CL

A574

CARTER RD

GARWOOD

1

90

57   D   58   E   59   F   90

7 3

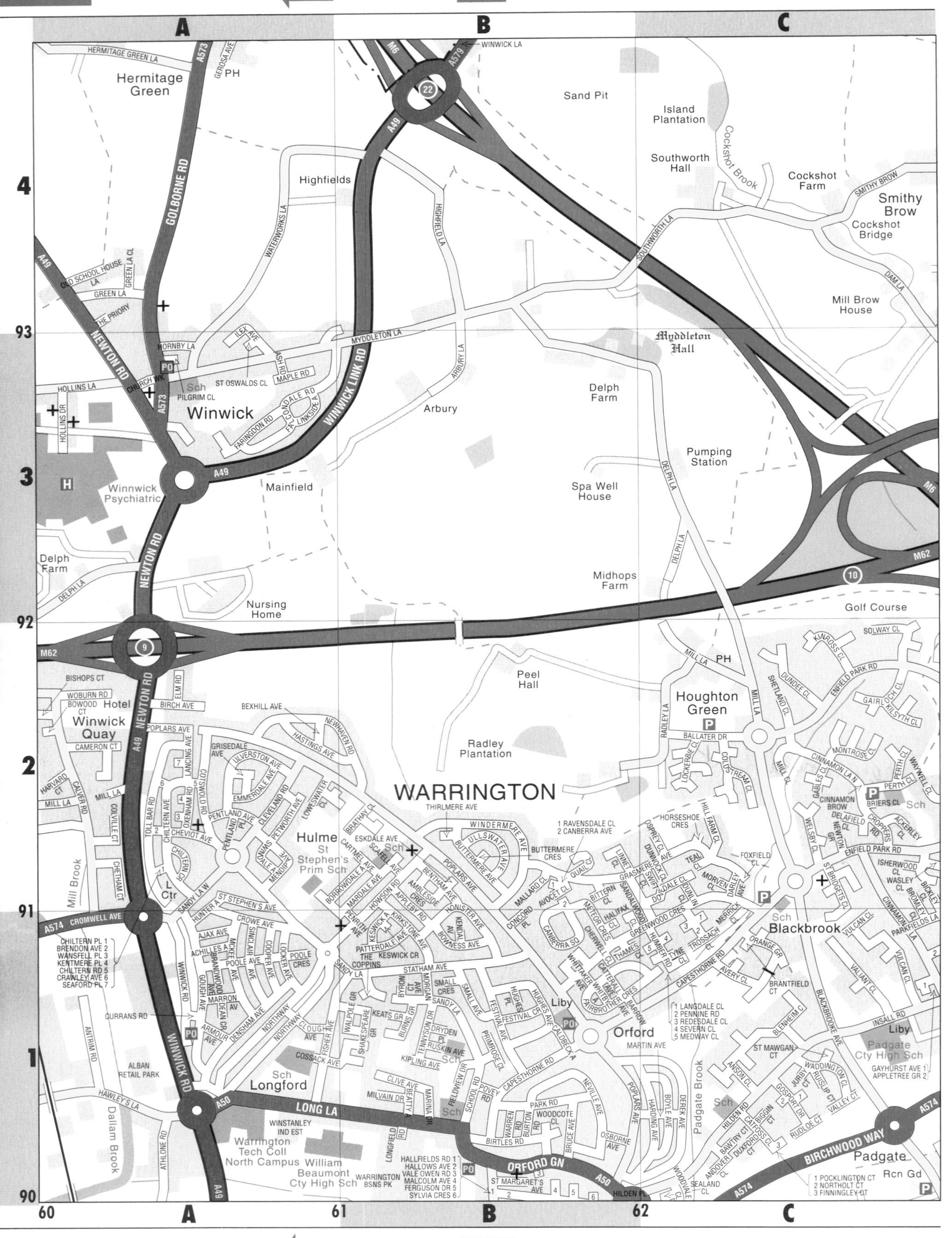
A
B
C
4
93
3
92
2
91
1
90
60
61
62
HERMITAGE GREEN LA
Hermitage Green
GEROSA AVE
PH
A573
M6
A579
WINWICK LA
22
A49
Sand Pit
Island Plantation
Southworth Hall
Cockshot Brook
Cockshot Farm
SMITHY BROW
Smithy Brow
Cockshot Bridge
GOLBORNE RD
Highfields
WATERWORKS LA
HIGHFIELD LA
SOUTHWORTH LA
DAM LA
Mill Brow House
OLD SCHOOL HOUSE LA
GREEN LA CL
GREEN LA
THE PRIORY
NEWTON RD
HORNBY LA
ILEX AVE
ASH RD
MYDDLETON LA
Myddleton Hall
ARBURY LA
MAPLE RD
ST OSWALDS CL
HOLLINS LA
CHURCH WK
PO
Sch
PILGRIM CL
Winwick
FARINGDON RD
FALCONDALE RD
LINKSIDE A
WINWICK LINK RD
Arbury
Delph Farm
Pumping Station
HOLLINS DR
H
Winnwick Psychiatric
A49
Mainfield
Spa Well House
DELPH LA
M6
M62
10
Delph Farm
DELPH LA
Nursing Home
Midhops Farm
Golf Course
92
9
M62
BISHOPS CT
WOBURN RD
BOWOOD CT
Hotel
Winwick Quay
ELM RD
BIRCH AVE
Peel Hall
MILL LA
PH
SOLWAY CL
KINROSS CL
DUNDEE CL
ENFIELD PARK RD
GAIRLOCH CL
KILSYTH CL
SHETLAND CL
Houghton Green
RADLEY LA
BALLATER DR
BEXHILL AVE
NEWHAVEN RD
HASTINGS AVE
POPLARS AVE
CAMERON CT
Radley Plantation
LOCKERBIE CL
COLDSTREAM CL
MONTROSE CL
PERTH CL
WAYWELL CL
CINNAMON LA N
GRISEDALE AVE
ULVERSTON AVE
EMMERDALE AVE
LANCING AVE
COTSWOLD RD
CLEVELAND RD
PETWORTH AVE
LOWESWATER CL
WARRINGTON
THIRLMERE AVE
HARVARD CT
CALVER RD
MILL LA
COLVILLE CT
MILL LA
TOLL BAR RD
CHILTERN AVE
OXENHAM RD
PENTLAND AVE
CHEVIOT AVE
Hulme
St Stephen's Prim Sch
ESKDALE AVE
SCAFELL AVE
BRATHAY CL
CARTMEL AVE
WINDERMERE AVE
ULLSWATER AVE
BUTTERMERE AVE
BUTTERMERE CRES
1 RAVENSDALE CL
2 CANBERRA AVE
HORSESHOE CRES
HILL FARM CL
FOXFIELD CL
Sch
BRIERS CL
CINNAMON BROW
DELAFIELD CL
CROPPERS RD
ACKERLEY CL
NEWTON GR
WELSBY CL
Mill Brook
CHETHAM CT
L Ctr
SANDY LA W
HUNTER AVE
ST STEPHEN'S AVE
BORROWDALE AVE
MARDALE AVE
PATTERDALE AVE
HOWSON RD
AMBLESIDE CRES
APPLEBY RD
BENTHAM AVE
POPLARS AVE
HONISTER AVE
MALLARD CL
CONCORD PL
AVOCET CL
QUAIL CL
BITTERN CL
HALIFAX CL
GRASMERE AVE
DUNNOCK CL
TEAL CL
MORVEN CL
DARLEY AVE
MERRICK CL
TROSSACH CL
ENFIELD PARK RD
ISHERWOOD CL
WASLEY CL
BICKLEY CL
BROMLEY CL
ST BRIDGETS CL
Blackbrook
PARKFIELDS LA
CINNAMON LA
VULCAN CL
91
A574
CROMWELL AVE
CROWE AVE
AJAX AVE
ACHILLES AVE
MCKEE AVE
SINCLAIR AVE
COOPER AVE
LOCKER AVE
POOLE CRES
POOLE AVE
KESWICK AVE
KIRKSTONE AVE
KENDAL AV
BOWNESS AVE
CANBERRA SQ
METEOR CRES
CHERWELL CL
GREENWOOD CRES
THAMES CL
HUMBER RD
TYNE CL
CAPESTHORNE RD
AVERY CL
ORANGE GR
BRANTFIELD CT
CHILTERN PL 1
BRENDON AVE 2
WANSFELL PL 3
KENTMERE PL 4
CHILTERN RD 5
CRAWLEY AVE 6
SEAFORD PL 7
BRANDWOOD AVE
GOUGH AVE
MARRON AV
DEAN CR
SANDY LA
THE COPPINS
THE KESWICK CR
STATHAM AVE
MORGAN AVE
SMALL CRES
SMALL AVE
HUGHES PL
HUGHES AVE
FESTIVAL CR
FESTIVAL AVE
WHITAKER AVE
CATTERALL AVE
FAIRBROTHER CRES
BARRON AVE
Liby
PO
1 LANGDALE CL
2 PENNINE RD
3 REDESDALE CL
4 SEVERN CL
5 MEDWAY CL
VALIANT CL
INSALL RD
Liby
Padgate Cty High Sch
CURRANS RD
WINWICK RD
ARMOUR AVE
DENSHAM AVE
NORTHWAY
CLOUGH AVE
FISHER AVE
WALPOLE GR
SHAKESPEARE GR
KEATS GR
BURNS GR
BYRON CT
TENNYSON DR
DRYDEN PL
RUSKIN AVE
KIPLING AVE
PRIMROSE CL
CALDBECK A
Orford
MARTIN AVE
BLACKBROOKE AVE
BLENHEIM CL
ST MAWGAN CT
WADDINGTON CL
GAYHURST AVE 1
APPLETREE GR 2
ANTRIM RD
ALBAN RETAIL PARK
COSSACK AVE
Sch
Longford
CLIVE AVE
MILVAIN DR
BEATTY AV
MARINA DR
FIELDVIEW DR
SCHOOL RD
POVEY RD
CAPESTHORNE RD
PARK RD
WOODCOTE CL
NEVILLE AVE
POPLARS AVE
HARDING AVE
BOYLE AVE
DEREK AVE
Padgate Brook
ANSON CL
JURBY CL
RUISLIP CT
VALLEY CT
GOSPORT DR
HAWLEY'S LA
A50
LONG LA
WINSTANLEY IND EST
Sch
WARREN RD
BURTON RD
BRUCE AVE
OSBORNE AVE
Sch
HILDEN RD
BAWTRY CT
CATFOSS CL
BIGGIN CT
DUXFORD CT
RUDLOE CT
A574
BIRCHWOOD WAY
Dallam Brook
ATHLONE RD
Warrington Tech Coll North Campus
William Beaumont Cty High Sch
LONGFIELD RD
HALLFIELDS RD 1
HALLOWS AVE 2
VALE OWEN RD 3
MALCOLM AVE 4
FERGUSON DR 5
SYLVIA CRES 6
WARRINGTON BSNS PK
PO
BIRTLES RD
ORFORD GN
ST MARGARET'S AVE
A50
HILDEN PL
WOODDALE CL
SEALAND CL
ANDOVER CL
A574
1 POCKLINGTON CT
2 NORTHOLT CT
3 FINNINGLEY CT
Padgate
Rcn Gd
P
A49

7 16

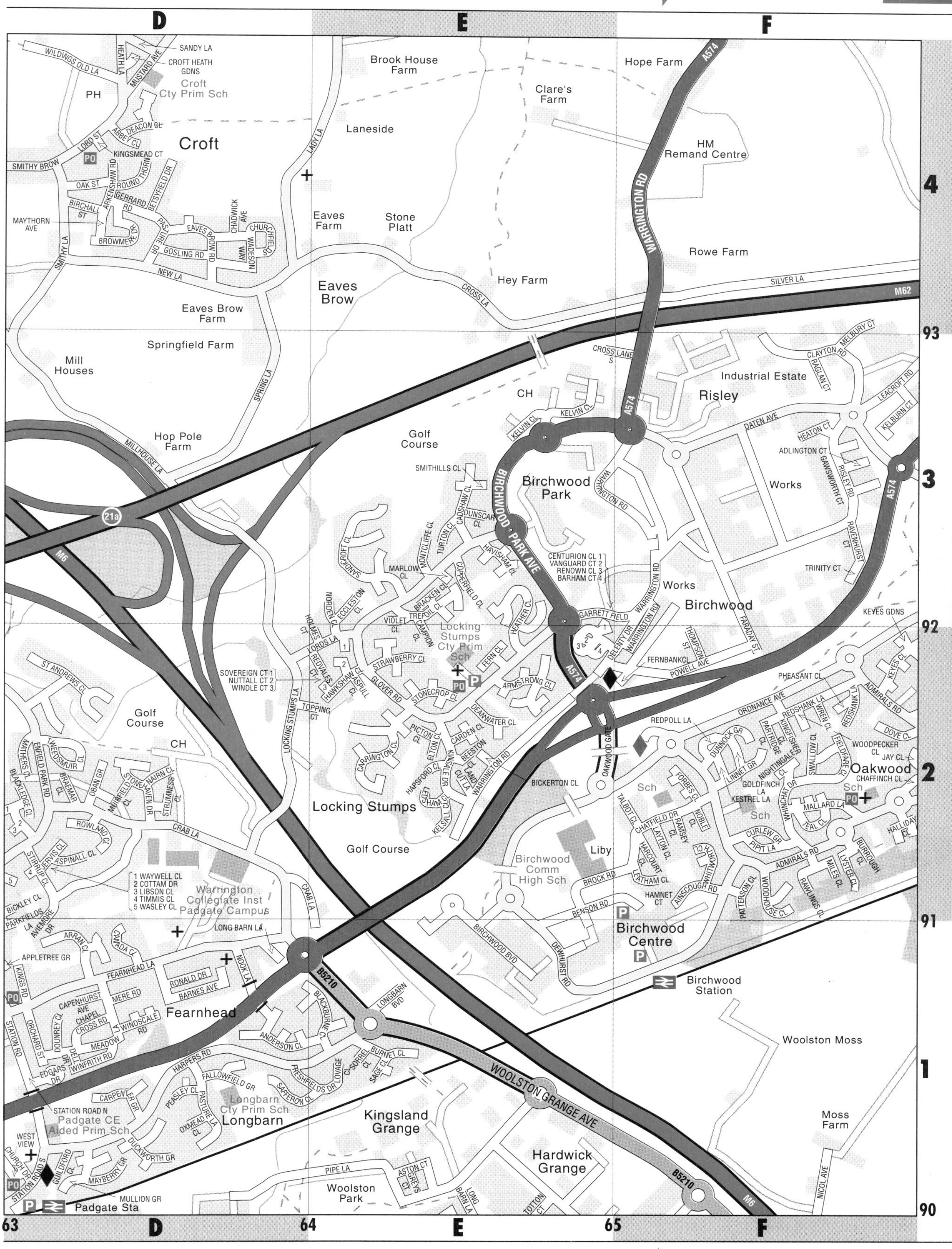
D
E
F
4
93
3
92
2
91
1
90
63
64
65
Croft
Croft Cty Prim Sch
PH
Brook House Farm
Hope Farm
Clare's Farm
Laneside
HM Remand Centre
Eaves Farm
Stone Platt
Rowe Farm
Hey Farm
Eaves Brow
Eaves Brow Farm
Springfield Farm
Mill Houses
Hop Pole Farm
Golf Course
Industrial Estate
Risley
CH
Birchwood Park
Works
Birchwood
Locking Stumps Cty Prim Sch
Locking Stumps
Golf Course
Oakwood
Sch
Liby
Birchwood Comm High Sch
Birchwood Centre
Birchwood Station
Woolston Moss
Moss Farm
Warrington Collegiate Inst Padgate Campus
Fearnhead
Longbarn Cty Prim Sch
Longbarn
Padgate CE Aided Prim Sch
Kingsland Grange
Hardwick Grange
Woolston Park
Padgate Sta
WARRINGTON RD
BIRCHWOOD PARK AVE
WOOLSTON GRANGE AVE
SILVER LA
CROSS LA
NEW LA
SMITHY LA
SMITHY BROW
WILDINGS OLD LA
SANDY LA
CROFT HEATH GDNS
DEACON CL
ABBEY CL
KINGSMEAD CT
OAK ST
BIRCHALL ST
MAYTHORN AVE
GERRARD RD
EAVES BROW RD
GOSLING RD
CHURCHFIELDS
LADY LA
SPRING LA
MILLHOUSE LA
CROSS LANE S
KELVIN CL
DATEN AVE
CLAYTON RD
MELBURY CT
RAGLAN CT
LEACROFT RD
KELBURN CT
HEATON CT
ADLINGTON CT
GAWSWORTH CT
RISLEY RD
RAVENHURST CT
TRINITY CT
KEYES GDNS
SMITHILLS CL
DUNSCAR CL
HAVISHAM CL
MARLOW CL
CENTURION CL 1
VANGUARD CT 2
RENOWN CL 3
BARHAM CT 4
GARRETT FIELD
FARADAY ST
THOMPSON ST
FERNBANK CL
POWELL AVE
PHEASANT CL
ORDNANCE AVE
REDPOLL LA
OAKWOOD GATE
BICKERTON CL
DUNNOCK GR
LINNET GR
GOLDFINCH LA
KESTREL LA
MALLARD LA
CURLEW GR
PIPIT LA
ADMIRALS RD
WOODPECKER CL
JAY CL
CHAFFINCH CL
DOVE CL
TALBOT CL
CHATFIELD DR
HARCOURT CL
LATHAM CL
BROCK RD
HAMNET CT
AINSCOUGH RD
BENSON RD
BIRCHWOOD BVD
DEWHURST RD
PATTERSON CL
WOODHOUSE CL
RAWLINGS CL
MILES CL
SOVEREIGN CT 1
NUTTALL CT 2
WINDLE CT 3
LOCKING STUMPS LA
TOPPING CT
STRAWBERRY CL
GLOVER RD
STONECROP CL
ARMSTRONG CL
DEANWATER CL
PICTON CL
CARRINGTON CL
HAPSFORD CL
KINSALE DR
BEESTON
ST ANDREWS CL
ENFIELD PARK RD
TWEEDSMUIR CL
BRAEMAR CL
OBAN GR
STRUMNESS CL
ROWLAND CL
CRAB LA
ASPINALL CL
1 WAYWELL CL
2 COTTAM DR
3 LIBSON CL
4 TIMMIS CL
5 WASLEY CL
BICKLEY CL
PARKFIELDS LA
AVIEMORE DR
ARRAN CL
CANADA CL
LONG BARN LA
APPLETREE GR
KINGS RD
FEARNHEAD LA
RONALD DR
BARNES AVE
NOOK LA
CAPENHURST AVE
CHAPEL CROSS RD
MERE RD
WINDSCALE RD
MEADOW LA
WINFRITH RD
ORCHARD ST
STATION RD
EDGARS DR
ANDERSON CL
BLACKBURN CL
LONGBARN BVD
BURNET CL
HARPERS RD
FALLOWFIELD GR
PEASLEY CL
PASTURE LA
CARPENTER GR
SAFFRON CL
FRESHFIELDS DR
OXMEAD CL
DUCKWORTH GR
MAYBERRY GR
MULLION GR
STATION ROAD N
STATION ROAD S
WEST VIEW
CHURCH DR
GUILDFORD CL
PIPE LA
ASTON CT
LONG BARN LA
TOTTON CT
NICOL AVE
A574
M62
M6
B5210
21a
PO
P

A B C

Old Abbey Farm

Moss Side Farm

B5212

Aikin Knowle's Bridge

Keeper's Cottage

Glaze Brook

HOLCROFT LA

M62

B5212

4

Ferndale Nurseries

Holcroft Moss

SILVER LA

M62

(11)

A574

Pestfurlong Hill

PRESTWOOD CT

93

Ind Est

LEACROFT RD

Pestfurlong Moss

Glazebrook Moss

BIRCHWOOD WAY

A574

COLUMBIA CL

SILVER LA

HAMPSTER LEY CL

GORSE COVERT RD

Hoyle's Moss Farm

ROCKINGHAM CL

ARDEN CL

STANMORE CL

FALSTON CL

WOOLMER CL

FISHERFIELD DR

RANGE CL

DARNAWAY CL

RENDLESHAM CL

Milverton Farm

MOSS LA

ALDERLEY CL

SECROSS

PO

Sch

HAZELBOROUGH CL

SCHOOL LA

3

BRAMS...CL

MOSS

WHITTLEWOOD

RINGWOOD CL

New Hall Farm

WESTWAY CRES 1
WIGMORE CL 2
DUNLEY CL 3
ROSENDALE DR 4
CULBIN CL 5

GATE

STANLEY CL

LANGWELL

ASHDOWN CL

ROWLAND

GILDERDALE CL

Gorse Covert

Omrod Farm

DALBY CL

P

KILLINGWORTH CL

CHARNWOOD CL

Birchwood Forest Park

ORDNANCE AVE

P

Visitors Centre

Risley Moss

DAM LA

Bridge Farm

DAM HEAD LA

92

KEYES CL

KEYES CL

Risley Moss Country Park

Land Fill Site

Moss Hall Farm

Hollingreave Farm

BIRCHWOOD BROOK

DANIEL CL

MANSFIELD CL

COLEBROOK CL

Moss Side

Ash Tree Farm

2

ADMIRALS CL

JAY CL

McCARTHY CL

PALLISER CL

PENNANT

ASHMORE CL

Prospect Farm

PROSPECT LA

Moss Side Farm No.2

MOSS SIDE LA

Moss Side Farm

Brick Works

91

HOLLY BUSH LA

Rixton Moss

WOODEND LA

Woodend Farm

Works

Woolston Moss

Rixton Clay Pits Nature Reserve

MOAT LA

Gas Compressor Station

CLAYTON GDNS

CHAPEL LA

1

Marshall's Farm

Moss Head

Rixton Firs

MANCHESTER RD

A57

BROOK LA

Moss Farm

90

66 A 67 B 68 C

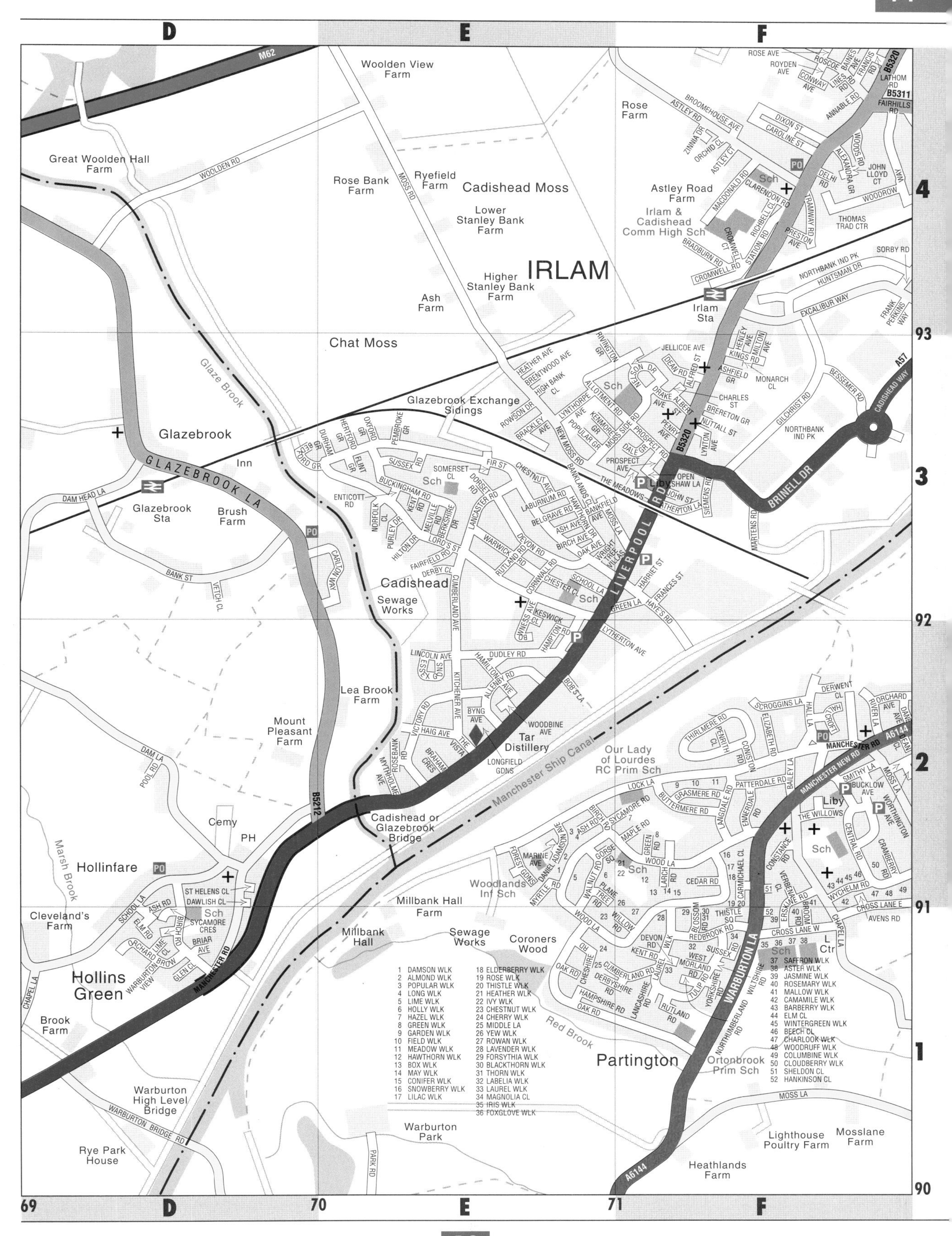

D | E | F

Woolden View Farm

Rose Farm

ROSE AVE
ROYDEN AVE
ROSCOE RD
BAINES AVE
FRANCIS RD
LATHOM RD
B5320
B5311
FAIRHILLS RD

BROOMEHOUSE AVE
ASTLEY RD
DIXON ST
CAROLINE ST
CONWAY AVE
ANNABLE RD
WOODS RD
DELHI RD
ALEXANDRA RD
JOHN LLOYD CT
WOODROW

Great Woolden Hall Farm

WOOLDEN RD

Rose Bank Farm
Ryefield Farm
MOSS RD

Cadishead Moss

Astley Road Farm

Irlam & Cadishead Comm High Sch

MACDONALD RD
CLARENDON RD
ORCHARD ST
ASTLEY CT
RIDGELL CL
STATION RD
Sch

RAMWAY RD
PRESTON AVE
THOMAS TRAD CTR

4

Lower Stanley Bank Farm

IRLAM

BRADBURN RD
CROMWELL RD
CROMWELL CT

NORTHBANK IND PK
HUNTSMAN DR

SORBY RD

Glaze Brook

Higher Stanley Bank Farm

Irlam Sta

EXCALIBUR WAY

FRANK PERKINS WAY

93

Ash Farm

Chat Moss

HEATHER AVE
BRENTWOOD AVE
HIGH BANK CL
JELLICOE AVE
RIVINGTON GR
RAVDEN CL
DEAN RD
ALFRED ST
KINGS RD
SHFIELD
MILTON AVE
MONARCH CL
BESSEMER RD
A57 CADISHEAD WAY

Glazebrook

Glazebrook Exchange Sidings

ROWSON DR
BRACKLEY AVE
NEW MOSS RD
ALLOTMENT RD
KENMORE RD
POPULAR GR
DRAKE AVE
CHARLES ST
BRERETON GR
NUTTALL ST
LYNTON AVE
GILCHRIST RD
NORTHBANK IND PK

BRINELL DR

Glazebrook Inn

GLAZEBROOK LA

DURHAM GR
HERTFORD GR
OXFORD GR
PEMBROKE GR
SUSSEX GR
LYNTHORPE GR
PROSPECT RD
DALE GR
PROSPECT AVE
THE MEADOWS
OPEN SHAW LA
B5320
LIVERPOOL RD
MARTENS RD

3

DAM HEAD LA

Glazebrook Sta

Brush Farm

CARR WAY

ENTICOTT RD
NORFOLK CL
PURLEY DR
KENT RD
MELVILLE RD
BERKSHIRE RD
BUCKINGHAM DR
HILTON DR
LORD'S ST
WARWICK RD
SOMERSET CL
Sch
DORSET RD
FIR ST
CHESTNUT AVE
LABURNUM RD
BELGRAVE RD
HAMPTON RD
ASH AVON RD
BIRCH AVE
MOSS LA
SIEMENS RD
ATHERTON RD
HARRIET ST
FRANCES ST

BANK ST
VETCH CL

Cadishead

Sewage Works

FAIRFIELD RD
DERBY CL
CUMBERLAND AVE
RUTLAND RD
DEVON RD
OAK AVE
CORNWALL RD
CHESTER CL
SCHOOL LA
Sch
GREEN CL
HAYES RD
WRIGHT ST

92

LINCOLN AVE
ESSEX ST
KESWICK DR
INVESS AVE
HAMILTON AVE
DUDLEY RD
ALLENBY RD
LYTHERTON AVE

Lea Brook Farm

KITCHENER RD
VICTORY RD
HAIG AVE
ALTRINCHAM
BYNG AVE
VISTA
BRAMHALL CRES

Mount Pleasant Farm

DAM LA
POOL RD

B5212

ROSEBANK RD
MYRTHOLME AVE
LONGFIELD GDNS
THE

Woodbine AVE
Tar Distillery

Our Lady of Lourdes RC Prim Sch

Manchester Ship Canal

DERWENT CL
ORCHARD AVE
RIVER LA
THIRLMERE RD
SCROGGINS LA
ELIZABETH RD
HALL LA
CONISTON RD
PENRITH CL
PATTERDALE RD
BAILEY RD
ENNERDALE RD
LANGDALE RD
BUTTERMERE RD
GRASMERE RD
LOCK LA
MANCHESTER NEW RD
A6144
MANCHESTER RD
BUCKLOW AVE
WORTHINGTON AVE

2

Cemy
PH
Cleveland's Farm

Hollinfare
PO

ST HELENS CL
DAWLISH CL
SYCAMORE CRES
SCHOOL LA
ELM RD
BIRCH RD
LIME CL
BRIAR AVE
MAY AVE
ORCHARD BROW
WARBURTON VIEW

MANCHESTER RD

Cadishead or Glazebrook Bridge

Millbank Hall Farm

Woodlands Inf Sch

MARINE AVE
DANIEL ADAMSON RD
WALNUT RD
MYRTLE RD
FOREST RD
GORSE RD
PLANE TREE RD
WILLOW RD
ASH RD
SYCAMORE RD
MAPLE RD
WOOD LA
LARCH RD
CEDAR RD
GREEN

Sch
THE WILLOWS
CONSTANCE RD
VERNON RD
CENTRAL RD
CRANBERRY RD
WYCHELM RD
CROSS LANE E

Liby

Sch

1

Marsh Brook

Hollins Green

Brook Farm

CHAPEL LA
GLEN CL

WARBURTON BRIDGE RD

Millbank Hall

Sewage Works

Coroners Wood

Partington

OAK RD
CHESHIRE RD
DERBYSHIRE RD
HAMPSHIRE RD
OAK RD
CUMBERLAND RD
LANCASHIRE RD
RUTLAND RD
WEST AVE
DEVON RD
KENT RD
BLOSSOM CL
THISTLE
REDBROOK RD
MORLAND
SUSSEX RD
Red Brook

Ortonbrook Prim Sch

WARBURTON LA
NORTHUMBERLAND RD
WILTSHIRE RD
YORKSHIRE RD

SAFFRON WLK
ASTER WLK
JASMINE WLK
ROSEMARY WLK
MALLOW WLK
CAMAMILE WLK
BARBERRY WLK
ELM CL
WINTERGREEN WLK
BEECH CL
CHARLOCK WLK
WOODRUFF WLK
COLUMBINE WLK
CLOUDBERRY WLK
SHELDON CL
HANKINSON CL
CROSS LANE W
CHAPELA
AVENS RD
L Ctr

Warburton High Level Bridge

WARBURTON BRIDGE RD

Rye Park House

Warburton Park

PARK RD

A6144

Heathlands Farm

Lighthouse Poultry Farm
Mosslane Farm

MOSS LA

90

1 DAMSON WLK
2 ALMOND WLK
3 POPULAR WLK
4 LONG WLK
5 LIME WLK
6 HOLLY WLK
7 HAZEL WLK
8 GREEN WLK
9 GARDEN WLK
10 FIELD WLK
11 MEADOW WLK
12 HAWTHORN WLK
13 BOX WLK
14 MAY WLK
15 CONIFER WLK
16 SNOWBERRY WLK
17 LILAC WLK
18 ELDERBERRY WLK
19 ROSE WLK
20 THISTLE WLK
21 HEATHER WLK
22 IVY WLK
23 CHESTNUT WLK
24 CHERRY WLK
25 MIDDLE LA
26 YEW WLK
27 ROWAN WLK
28 LAVENDER WLK
29 FORSYTHIA WLK
30 BLACKTHORN WLK
31 THORN WLK
32 LABELIA WLK
33 LAUREL WLK
34 MAGNOLIA CL
35 IRIS WLK
36 FOXGLOVE WLK

37 SAFFRON WLK
38 ASTER WLK
39 JASMINE WLK
40 ROSEMARY WLK
41 MALLOW WLK
42 CAMAMILE WLK
43 BARBERRY WLK
44 ELM CL
45 WINTERGREEN WLK
46 BEECH CL
47 CHARLOCK WLK
48 WOODRUFF WLK
49 COLUMBINE WLK
50 CLOUDBERRY WLK
51 SHELDON CL
52 HANKINSON CL

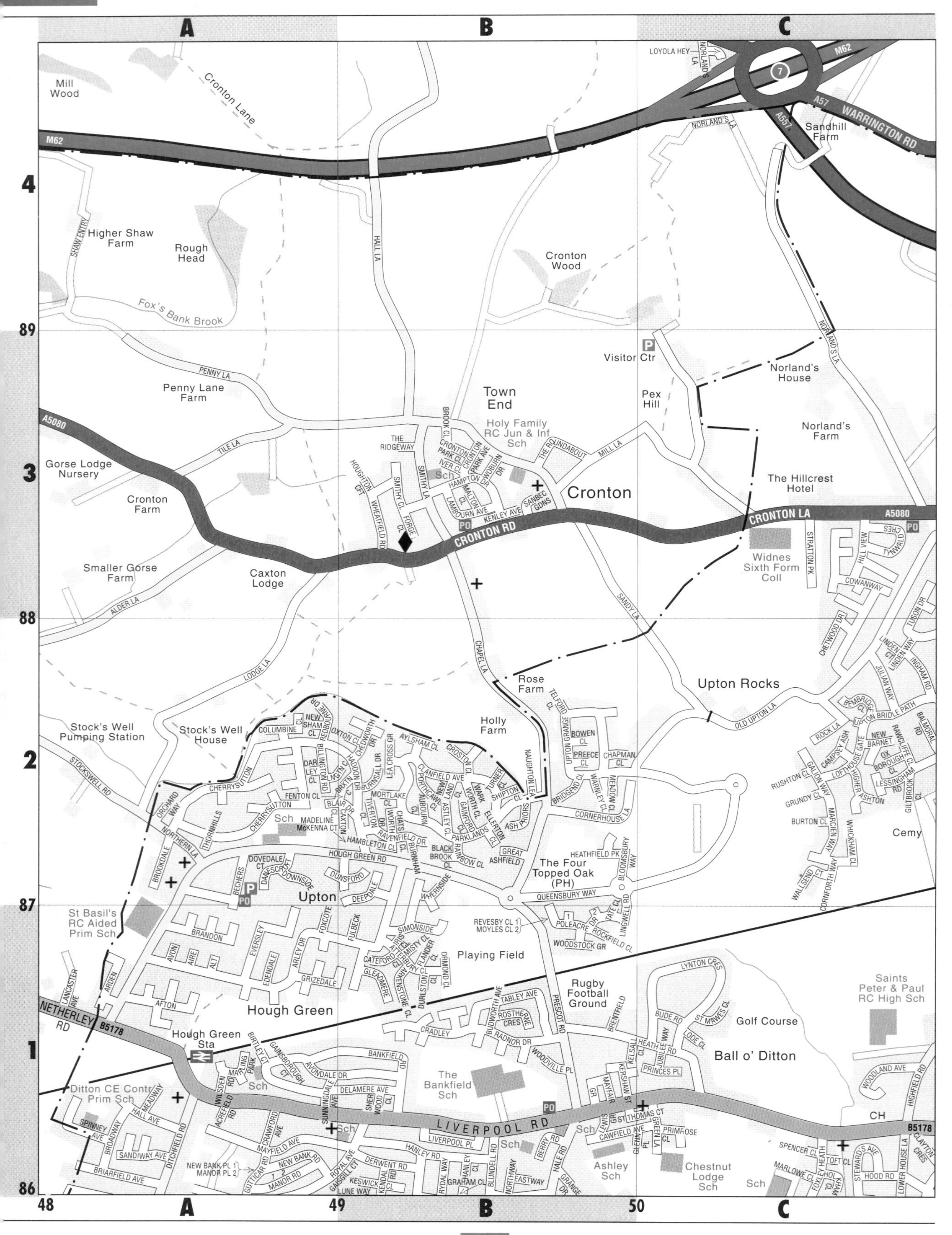
A
B
C
4
89
3
88
2
87
1
86
48
49
50
M62
Cronton Lane
Mill Wood
Higher Shaw Farm
Rough Head
Fox's Bank Brook
HALL LA
Cronton Wood
Visitor Ctr
Pex Hill
Town End
Holy Family RC Jun & Inf Sch
Norland's House
Norland's Farm
The Hillcrest Hotel
Sandhill Farm
A57 WARRINGTON RD
NORLAND'S LA
LOYOLA HEY
PENNY LA
Penny Lane Farm
A5080
Gorse Lodge Nursery
Cronton Farm
Smaller Gorse Farm
Caxton Lodge
Cronton
CRONTON RD
CRONTON LA
MILL LA
Widnes Sixth Form Coll
SANDY LA
CHAPEL LA
Rose Farm
Holly Farm
Upton Rocks
OLD UPTON LA
Stock's Well Pumping Station
Stock's Well House
STOCKSWELL RD
LODGE LA
ALDER LA
TILE LA
Upton
HOUGH GREEN RD
QUEENSBURY WAY
The Four Topped Oak (PH)
Playing Field
Rugby Football Ground
St Basil's RC Aided Prim Sch
Hough Green
Hough Green Sta
NETHERLEY RD
B5178
Ditton CE Contr Prim Sch
LIVERPOOL RD
The Bankfield Sch
Ashley Sch
Chestnut Lodge Sch
Golf Course
Ball o' Ditton
Saints Peter & Paul RC High Sch
Cemy
PRESCOT RD
LYNTON CRES
WOODLAND AVE
HIGHFIELD RD

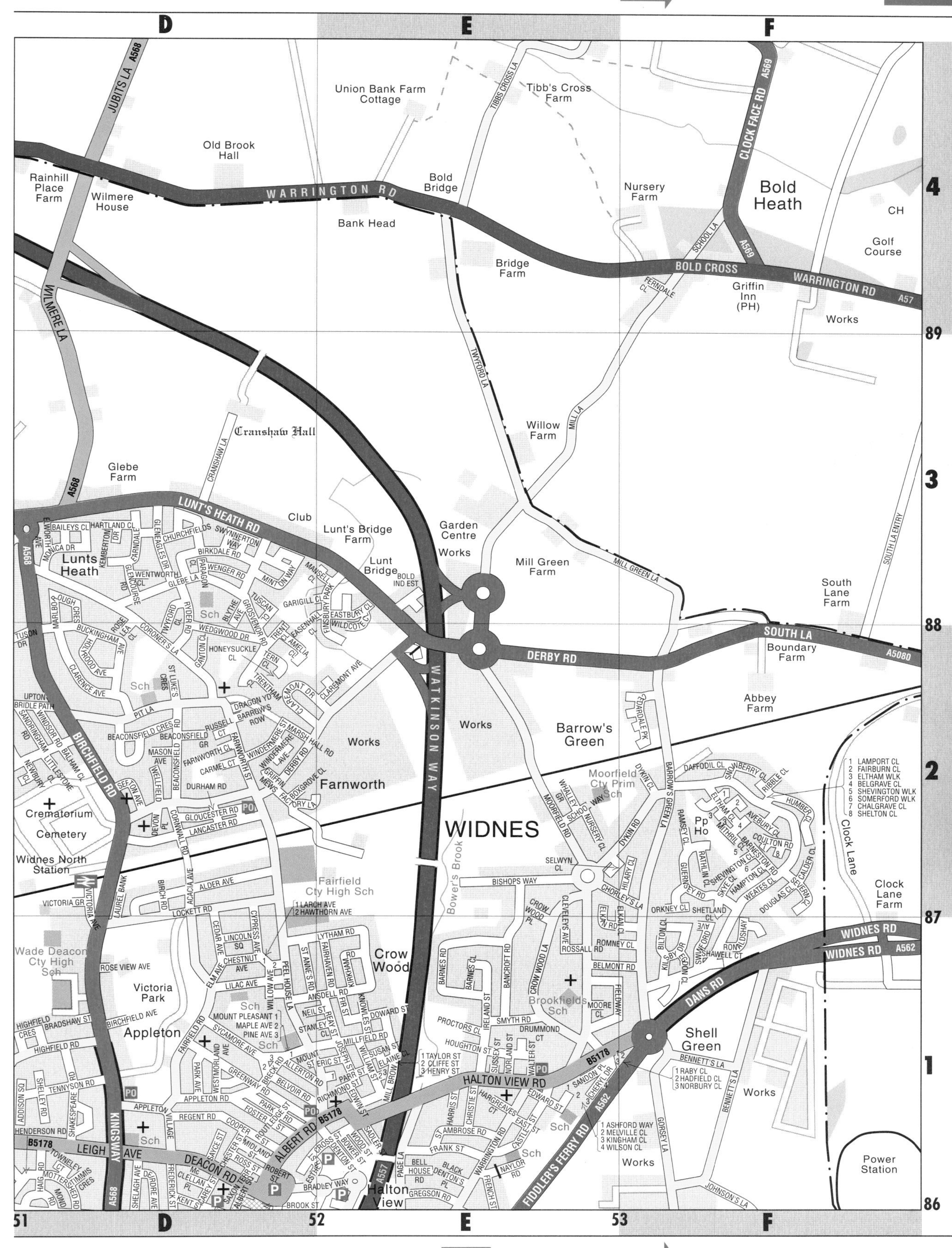

D   E   F

JUBIT'S LA A568

Union Bank Farm Cottage

Tibb's Cross Farm

CLOCK FACE RD A569

Old Brook Hall

Rainhill Place Farm

Wilmere House

Nursery Farm

Bold Heath

CH

WARRINGTON RD

Bold Bridge

Golf Course

4

Bank Head

SCHOOL LA

Bridge Farm

BOLD CROSS

A569

Griffin Inn (PH)

WARRINGTON RD A57

WILMERE LA

FERNDALE CL

Works

89

Cranshaw Hall

Willow Farm

MILL LA

A568

Glebe Farm

CRANSHAW LA

Garden Centre

Mill Green Farm

MILL GREEN LA

South Lane Farm

3

LUNT'S HEATH RD

Club

Lunt's Bridge Farm

Works

SOUTH LA ENTRY

Lunt's Heath

A568

Lunt Bridge

BOLD IND EST

South La

A5080

88

DERBY RD

SOUTH LA

Boundary Farm

Abbey Farm

1 LAMPORT CL
2 FAIRBURN CL
3 ELTHAM WLK
4 BELGRAVE CL
5 SHEVINGTON WLK
6 SOMERFORD WLK
7 CHALGRAVE CL
8 SHELTON CL

Works

Farnworth

WATKINSON WAY

Barrow's Green

2

Crematorium

Cemetery

Moorfield Cty Prim Sch

Clock Lane

Clock Lane Farm

WIDNES

Widnes North Station

Fairfield Cty High Sch

Bower's Brook

1 LARCH AVE
2 HAWTHORN AVE

SELWYN CL

BISHOPS WAY

87

WIDNES RD

BIRCHFIELD RD

Wade Deacon Cty High Sch

Rose View Ave

Crow Wood

Brookfields Sch

WIDNES RD A562

Victoria Park

Appleton

DANS RD

Shell Green

1 MOUNT PLEASANT
2 MAPLE AVE
3 PINE AVE

1 TAYLOR ST
2 CLIFFE ST
3 HENRY ST

1 RABY CL
2 HADFIELD CL
3 NORBURY CL

BENNETT'S LA

Works

1

KINGSWAY

LEIGH AVE

B5178

DEACON RD

ALBERT RD

HALTON VIEW RD

B5178

FIDDLER'S FERRY RD A562

1 ASHFORD WAY
2 MELVILLE CL
3 KINGHAM CL
4 WILSON CL

Works

Power Station

86

51   D   52   E   53   F

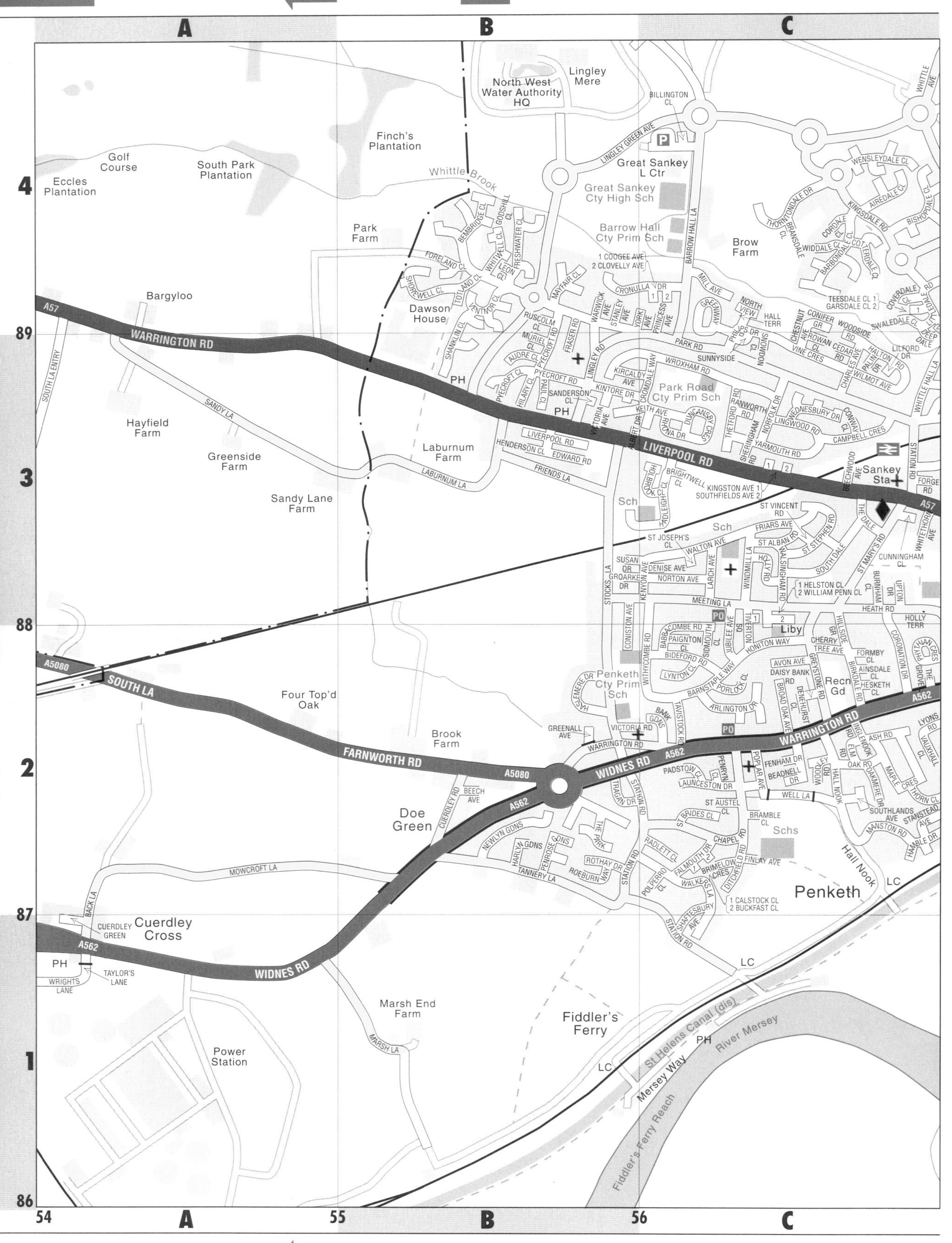

North West
Water Authority
HQ

Lingley
Mere

BILLINGTON
CL

Golf
Course

South Park
Plantation

Finch's
Plantation

Great Sankey
L Ctr

WHITTLE
AVE

Eccles
Plantation

4

Great Sankey
Cty High Sch

WENSLEYDALE CL

BISHOPDALE CL

Whittle Brook

Barrow Hall
Cty Prim Sch

Park
Farm

Brow
Farm

BARROW HALL LA

THORNTONDALE DR

BRANSDALE

KINGSDALE RD

AIREDALE CL

Bargyloo

1 COOGEE AVE
2 CLOVELLY AVE

WIDDALE CL

CORDALE

COTERDALE CT

BARDSDALE CL

A57

Dawson
House

MILL AVE

CRONULLA DR

WARRINGTON RD

NORTH
VIEW

CONIFER

WOODSIDE

TEESDALE CL 1
GARSDALE CL 2

COVERDALE

89

PH

WARWICK
AVE

STANLEY
AVE

YORK
AVE

PRINCESS
AVE

GREENWAY

HALL
TERR

CHESTNUT

ROWAN
GR

CEDARS

SWALEDALE RD

HALTON
RD

LILFORD

DEEPDALE

SOUTH LA ENTRY

PH

RUSCOLM
CL

LINGLEY
CL

KIRCALDY
AVE

PARK RD

SUNNYSIDE

PINCH DR

VINE CRES

CHARLES RD

WILMOT AVE

WHITTLE HALL LA

SANDY LA

MURIEL
CL

AUDRE
CL

FRASER RD

WROXHAM RD

Park Road
Cty Prim Sch

RANWORTH

LINGWOOD RD

NORFOLK RD

CONWAY

CAMPBELL CRES

Hayfield
Farm

PYECROFT CL

HILARY CL

PAUL CL

PYECROFT RD

SANDERSON
CL

KEITH AVE

CRANDALE WAY

HEDNESBURY DR

STATION RD

FORGE RD

Greenside
Farm

LIVERPOOL RD

HENDERSON CL

EDWARD RD

VICTORIA AVE

ALBERT RD

LIVERPOOL RD

SHERINGHAM RD

YARMOUTH RD

THETFORD

Sankey
Sta

A57

3

Sandy Lane
Farm

Laburnum
Farm

FRIENDS LA

BRIGHTWELL
CL

KINGSTON AVE 1
SOUTHFIELDS AVE 2

ST VINCENT
RD

FRIARS AVE

ST STEPHEN RD

ST MARY'S RD

THE DALE

WHITETHORN

CUNNINGHAM
CL

LABURNUM LA

Sch

ST JOSEPH'S
CL

ST ALBAN
CL

SUSAN
DR

GROARKEN
DR

DENISE AVE

NORTON AVE

LARCH AVE

WALTON AVE

WINDMILL LA

HOLT
AVE

ST STEPHEN RD

STAINBECK AVE

BURNHAM
CL

UPTON

HEATH RD

HOLLY
TERR

STOCKS LA

KENYON
CL

88

A5080

SOUTH LA

COMPTON AVE

BABBACOMBE RD

PAIGNTON
CL

SIDMOUTH
CL

TIVERTON

Liby

CHERRY
TREE AVE

FORMBY CL

AINSDALE CL

HESKETH CL

THE GROVE

THAMES CRES

Four Top'd
Oak

CONISTON AVE

WITHYCOMBE RD

Penketh
Cty Prim
Sch

JUBILEE AVE

HONITON WAY

AVON AVE

DAISY BANK
RD

Recn
Gd

A562

FARNWORTH RD

Brook
Farm

BIDEFORD RD

LYNTON
CL

PORLOCK CL

BROAD OAK AVE

DINGLEBANK
CL

GREYSTONE RD

DAIRE

WARRINGTON RD

ASH RD

LYONS
RD

VAUXHALL

Doe
Green

GREENALL
AVE

VICTORIA RD

BARNSTAPLE WAY

ARLINGTON AVE

BANK
GDNS

PO

FENHAM DR

PENMON

POPLAR AVE

ELM

HALL NOOK

OAK RD

MAPLE

OAKMERE

THORN CL

SOUTHLANDS
AVE

STANSTEAD

2

CUERDLEY RD

BEECH
AVE

WIDNES RD

A562

WARRINGTON RD

BEADNELL
DR

WELL LA

ST AUSTELL

Schs

MANSTON RD

CRES

HAMBLE CL

Hall Nook

LC

MOWCROFT LA

NEWLYN GDNS

HARTY
GDNS

PENROSE
GDNS

THE PARK

STATION RD

ST BRIDES CL

CHAPEL
LA

BRAMBLE
CL

Penketh

BACK LA

RADLETT CL

FALMOUTH DR

FINLAY AVE

1 CALSTOCK CL
2 BUCKFAST CL

87

CUERDLEY
GREEN

Cuerdley
Cross

ROTHAY DR

POLPERRO
CL

BRIMELOW
CRES

WALKER LA

STATION RD

LC

A562

TANNERY LA

ROEBURN

SHAFTESBURY
AVE

LC

PH

TAYLOR'S
LANE

WIDNES RD

WRIGHTS
LANE

Marsh End
Farm

Fiddler's
Ferry

St Helens Canal (dis)

PH

River Mersey

Power
Station

MARSH LA

LC

Mersey Way

Fiddler's Ferry Reach

1

86

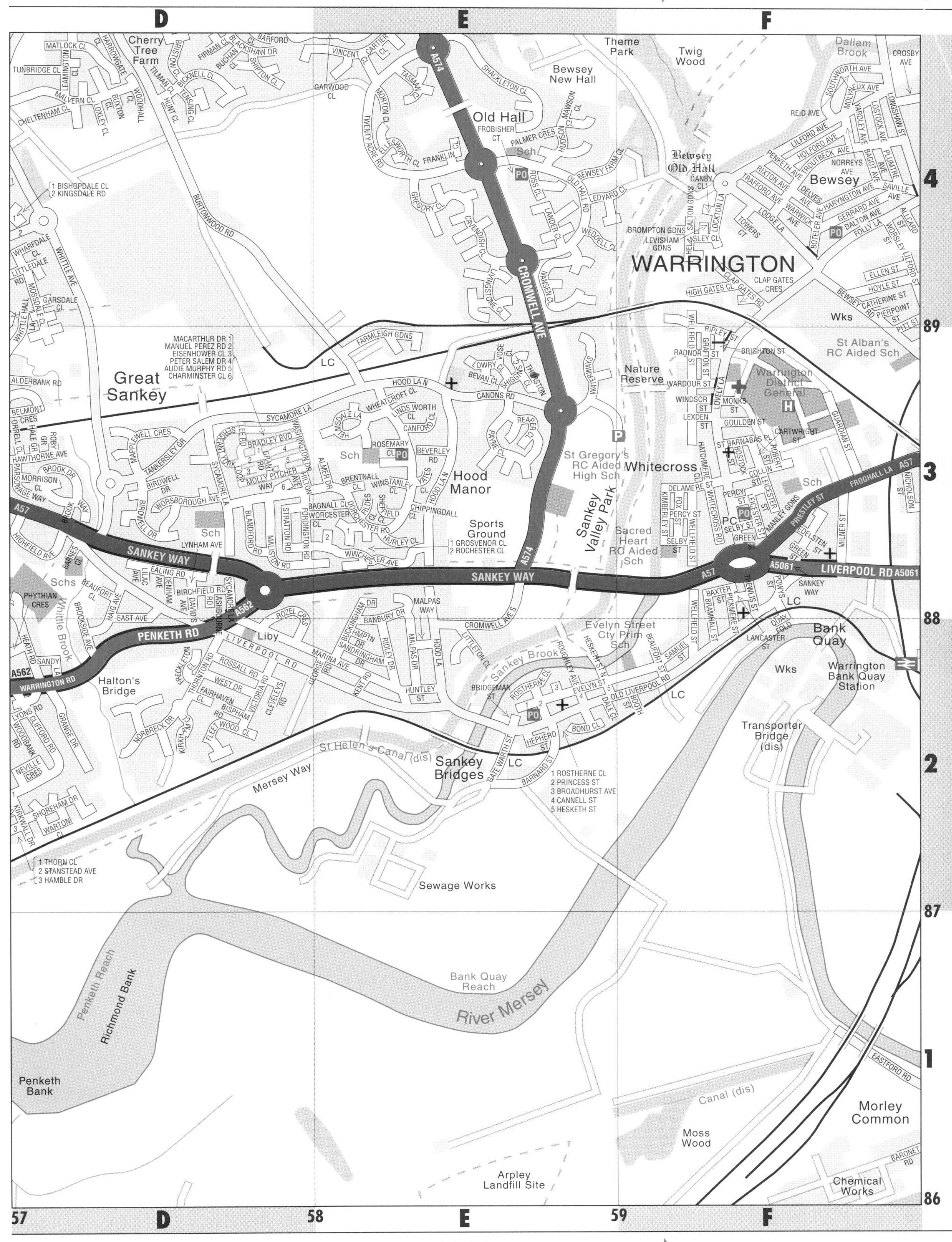

D   E   F

4

89

3

88

2

87

1

86

WARRINGTON

Great Sankey

Cherry Tree Farm

Old Hall

Theme Park

Twig Wood

Dallam Brook

Bewsey New Hall

Bewsey Old Hall

Bewsey

St Alban's RC Aided Sch

Warrington District General

Hood Manor

Nature Reserve

Whitecross

St Gregory's RC Aided High Sch

Sports Ground
1 GROSVENOR CL
2 ROCHESTER CL

Sankey Valley Park

Sacred Heart RC Aided Sch

SANKEY WAY

PENKETH RD

WARRINGTON RD

LIVERPOOL RD

Liby

Halton's Bridge

Evelyn Street Cty Prim Sch

Bank Quay

Warrington Bank Quay Station

Transporter Bridge (dis)

Sankey Bridges

1 ROSTHERNE CL
2 PRINCESS ST
3 BROADHURST AVE
4 CANNELL ST
5 HESKETH ST

St Helen's Canal (dis)

Mersey Way

Sewage Works

Bank Quay Reach

River Mersey

Penketh Reach

Richmond Bank

Penketh Bank

Canal (dis)

Morley Common

Moss Wood

Arpley Landfill Site

Chemical Works

1 THORN CL
2 STANSTEAD AVE
3 HAMBLE DR

1 BISHOPDALE CL
2 KINGSDALE RD

MACARTHUR DR 1
MANUEL PEREZ RD 2
EISENHOWER CL 3
PETER SALEM DR 4
AUDIE MURPHY RD 5
CHARMINSTER CL 6

57   58   59

15
8

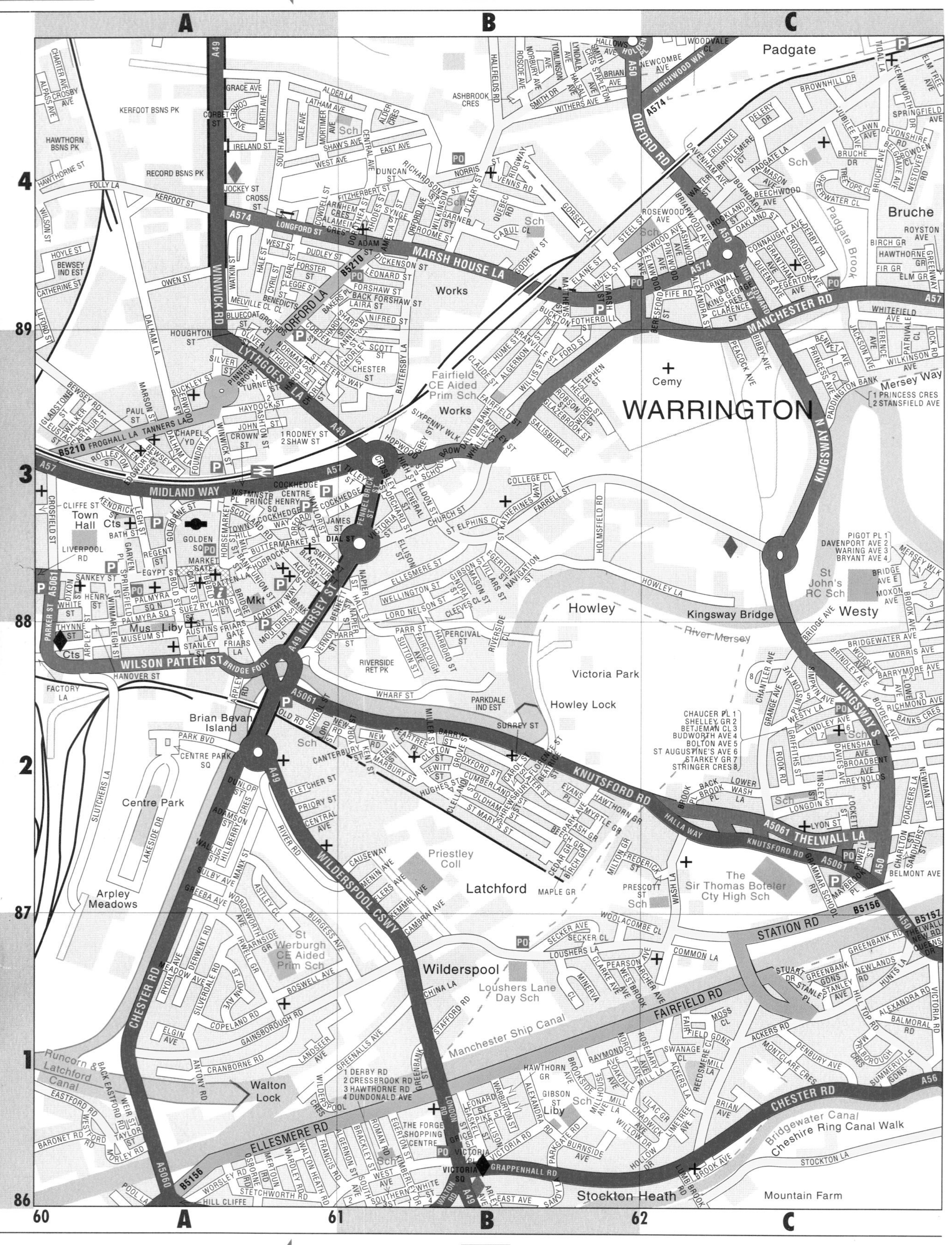
A
B
C
WARRINGTON
Padgate
Bruche
Westy
Howley
Latchford
Wilderspool
Stockton Heath
Mountain Farm
Victoria Park
Howley Lock
Kingsway Bridge
River Mersey
Mersey Way
Manchester Ship Canal
Runcorn & Latchford Canal
Bridgewater Canal
Cheshire Ring Canal Walk
Walton Lock
Brian Bevan Island
Centre Park
Arpley Meadows
Town Hall
Cemy
Works
Priestley Coll
The Sir Thomas Boteler Cty High Sch
St John's RC Sch
Fairfield CE Aided Prim Sch
St Werburgh CE Aided Prim Sch
Loushers Lane Day Sch
KERFOOT BSNS PK
HAWTHORN BSNS PK
RECORD BSNS PK
RIVERSIDE RET PK
PARKDALE IND EST
BEWSEY IND EST
MIDLAND WAY
MARSH HOUSE LA
MANCHESTER RD
KINGSWAY N
KINGSWAY S
KNUTSFORD RD
THELWALL LA
WILDERSPOOL CSWY
CHESTER RD
ELLESMERE RD
FAIRFIELD RD
STATION RD
WILSON PATTEN ST
MERSEY ST
WINWICK RD
LYTHGOES LA
ORFORD RD
GRAPPENHALL RD
LONGFORD ST
A49
A50
A57
A574
A5061
A5060
A56
B5156
B5157
B5210
4
3
2
1
89
88
87
86
60
61
62

15
26

9
18

D
E
F
Grange
Martinscroft Moss
HARDWICK GRANGE
CHESFORD GRANGE
B5210 WOOLSTON GRANGE AVE
M6
Woolston
Woolston CE Aided Prim Sch
Green Lane Sch
Spittle Brook
PADGATE BSNS CTR
Paddington
Schs
Woolston Cty High Sch
Liby
Woolston Cty Prim Sch
Sch
Leisure Centre
Martinscroft
CLARES FARM CL
B5210
A57
MANCHESTER RD
NEW MANCHESTER RD
HOLES LA
HILLOCK LA
WARREN LA
GIG LA
HAWTHORNE AVE
NEW CUT LA
BRIDGE RD
BRIDGE LA
WALNUT CL
MULBERRY CL
Mersey Way
SHROPSHIRE CL
Grey Mist
River Mersey
Woolston New Weir
Woolston Weir
The Eyes
WILKINSON AVE
MERSEY WLK
1 WARING AVE
2 BRYANT AVE
BRIDGEWATER AVE
GARNETT AVE
Works
Thelwall Ferry (P)
Laskey Lane Farm
Manchester Ship Canal
Latchford Locks
THELWALL NEW RD
THELWALL LA
THELWALL IND EST
Thelwall Cty Jun Sch
Thelwall
Chaigley Sch
LYMM RD
B5157
A56
BELL LA
STOCKPORT RD
WOODLANDS DR
KNUTSFORD OLD RD
CHESTER RD
KNUTSFORD RD
A50
Thelwall Heys
Cheshire Ring Canal Walk
Bridgewater Canal
Oak House
WEASTE LA
Highfields Farm
Thelwall Massey Hall Sch
Thelwall Grange
Grappenhall
Sch
PH
Liby
STOCKTON LA
CHURCH LA
Grappenhall Hall Sch
Canal Bank Farm
CANAL SIDE
CINDER LA
89
88
87
86
63
64
65
4
3
2
1
27
18

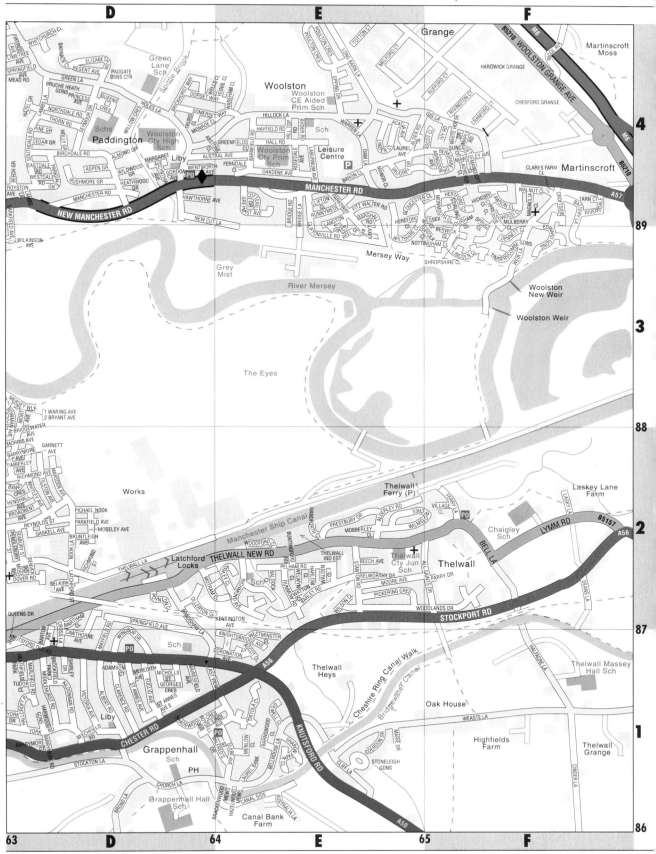

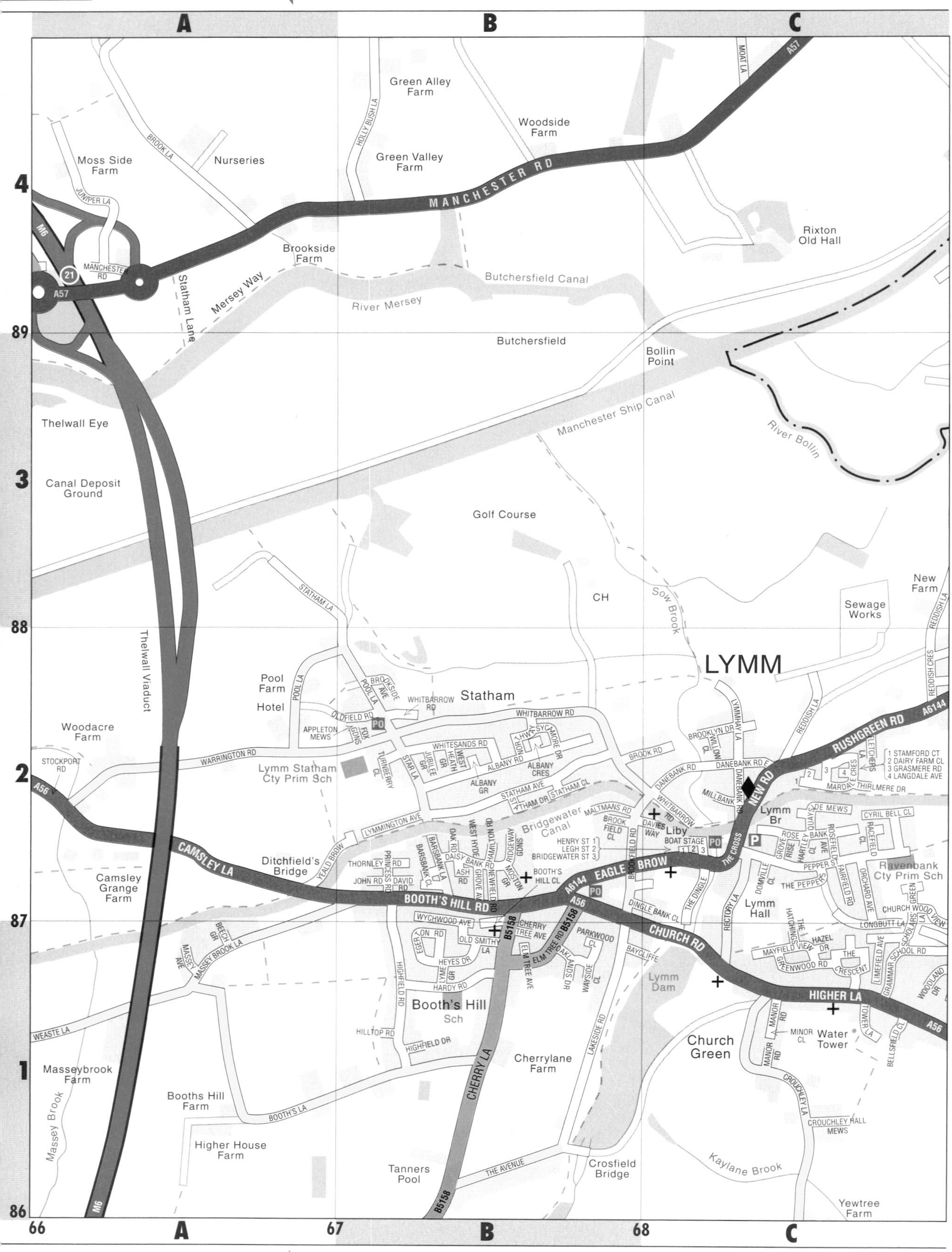

A   B   C

Green Alley Farm

Woodside Farm

Moss Side Farm

BROOK LA

Nurseries

Green Valley Farm

HOLLY BUSH LA

MANCHESTER RD

JUNIPER LA

4

M6

MANCHESTER RD

21

A57

Brookside Farm

Rixton Old Hall

Statham Lane

Mersey Way

Butchersfield Canal

A57

MOAT LA

89

River Mersey

Butchersfield

Bollin Point

Manchester Ship Canal

River Bollin

Thelwall Eye

3

Canal Deposit Ground

New Farm

Golf Course

CH

Sow Brook

Sewage Works

REDDISH LA

88

LYMM

Thelwall Viaduct

STATHAM LA

REDDISH CRES

Pool Farm Hotel

POOL LA

BROOKSIDE AVE

Statham

Whitbarrow RD

WHITBARROW RD

BROOKLYN DR

LYMMHAY LA

RUSHGREEN RD

A6144

Woodacre Farm

OLDFIELD RD

FOX COVERT

Lymm Statham Cty Prim Sch

APPLETON MEWS

WEST RD

WHITESANDS RD

JUBILEE GR

SYCAMORE DR

HEATH

ALBANY RD

BROOK RD

DANEBANK RD

New Rd

Lymm Br

BEECHERS RD

1 STAMFORD CT
2 DAIRY FARM CL
3 GRASMERE RD
4 LANGDALE AVE

STOCKPORT RD

A56

WARRINGTON RD

TURNBERRY

STAR LA

ALBANY CRES

ALBANY GR

STATHAM AVE

STATHAM DR STATHAM CL

DANEBANK RD E

2 3 4

MARDAL

THIRLMERE DR

2

CAMSLEY LA

Ditchfield's Bridge

TEAL BROW

LYMMINGTON AVE

WEST HYDE

NEWFIELD RD

OAK RD

DAISY BANK LA

ASH RD

GROVE AVE

Bridgewater Canal

BROOK FIELD CL

MALTMANS RD

HENRY ST 1
LEGH ST 2
BRIDGEWATER ST 3

DAVIES WAY

Liby

Lymm Br

CYRIL BELL CL

DE MEWS

GROVE

ROSE

RISE

HAZEL

PEPPER

CY PRIM SCH

Camsley Grange Farm

THORNLEY

PRINCESS RD

JOHN RD DAVID RD

Booth's Hill Cl

A6144 EAGLE BROW

BROOKFIELD RD

A56

BOAT STAGE

1 2 3

PO

THE CROSS

P

Lymm Hall

DOMVILLE CL

THE DINGLE

THE PEPPER

FAIRFIELD RD

ORCHARD AVE

Ravenbank Cty Prim Sch

LONGBUTT LA

SCHOOL RD

WOOD VIEW

87

WYCHWOOD AVE

LYON RD

Old Smithy

B5158

CHERRY TREE AVE

ELM TREE RD

PARKWOOD CL

DINGLE BANK CL

CHURCH RD

RECTORY LA

MAYFIELD VIEW

HATCHINGS

GREENWOOD RD

THE CRESCENT

HAZEL

LIMEFIELD AVE

GRAMMAR SCHOOL RD

CHURCH WOOD

WEASTE LA

MASSEY AVE

BELCH GR

MASSEY BROOK LA

EGER RD

HEYES DR

HARDY RD

HIGHFIELD RD

Booth's Hill Sch

BAYCLIFFE

Lymm Dam

HIGHER LA

A56

MANOR RD

Water Tower

BELLSFIELD CL

TOWER LA

1

Masseybrook Farm

Massey Brook

BOOTH'S LA

HILLTOP RD

HIGHFIELD DR

Cherrylane Farm

LAKESIDE RD

Church Green

MINOR AVE

MANOR RD

WOODLAND DR

Booths Hill Farm

CHERRY LA

THE AVENUE

Crosfield Bridge

Lymm Dam

CROUCHLEY LA

Higher House Farm

Tanners Pool

B5158

Kaylane Brook

CROUCHLEY HALL MEWS

Yewtree Farm

86

66   A   67   B   68   C

11

20

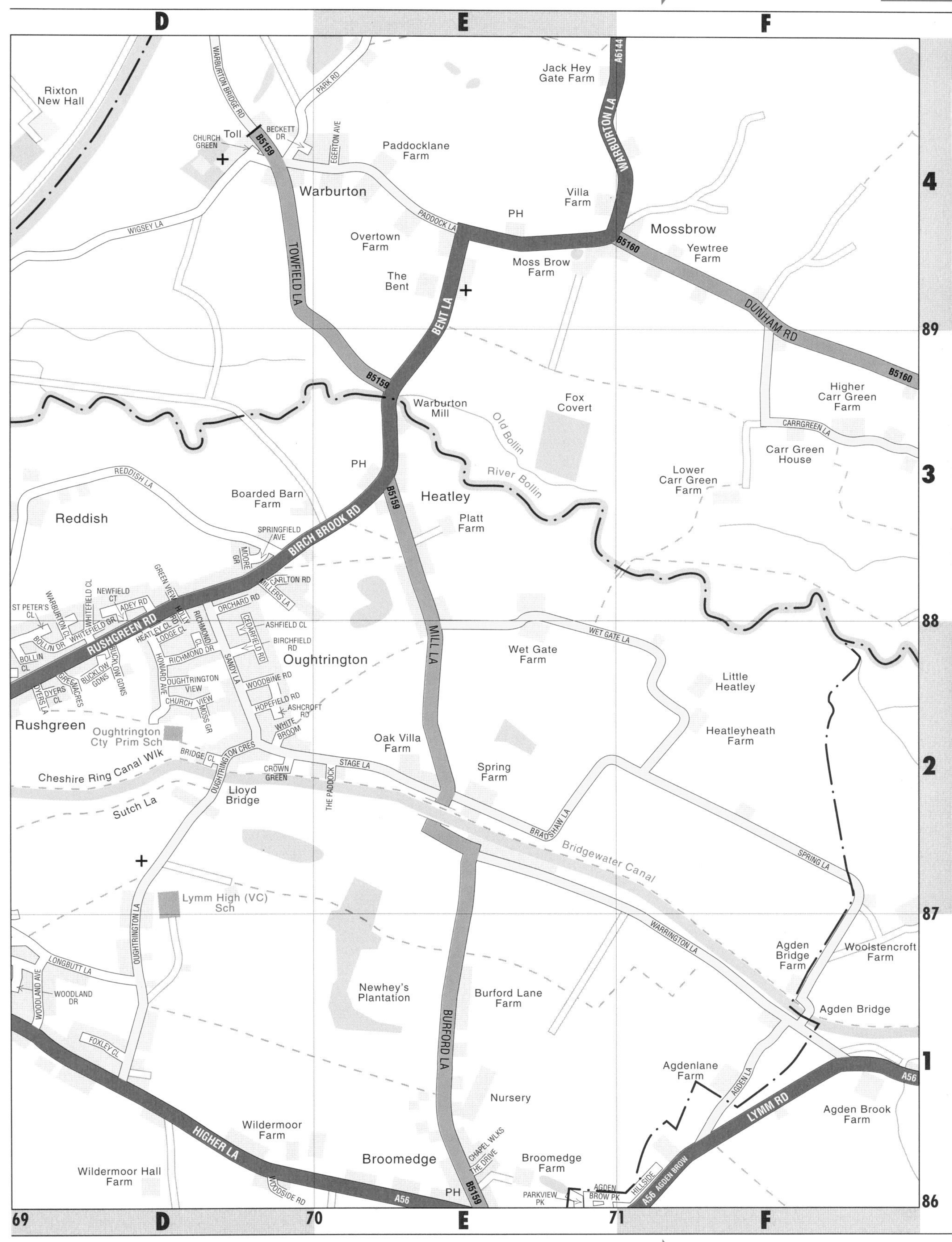

D
E
F
Rixton
New Hall
WARBURTON BRIDGE RD
PARK RD
Jack Hey
Gate Farm
A6144
WARBURTON LA
CHURCH
GREEN
Toll
BECKETT
DR
B5159
EGERTON AVE
Paddocklane
Farm
Warburton
Villa
Farm
4
WIGSEY LA
PADDOCK LA
PH
Mossbrow
Overtown
Farm
B5160
Yewtree
Farm
Moss Brow
Farm
TOWFIELD LA
The
Bent
BENT LA
DUNHAM RD
89
B5159
B5160
Higher
Carr Green
Farm
Warburton
Mill
Fox
Covert
Old Bollin
CARRGREEN LA
Carr Green
House
PH
River Bollin
Lower
Carr Green
Farm
3
REDDISH LA
Boarded Barn
Farm
B5159
Heatley
Reddish
BIRCH BROOK RD
Platt
Farm
SPRINGFIELD
AVE
MOORE
GR
CARLTON RD
GREEN VIEW
NEWFIELD
CT
WHITEFIELD CL
WARBURTON CL
ST PETER'S
CL
ADEY RD
MILLERS LA
ORCHARD RD
HOLLY
RD
RICHMOND
CL
WHITEFIELD GR
RUSHGREEN RD
ASHFIELD CL
MILL LA
88
HEATLEY CL
LODGE CL
BIRCHFIELD
RD
WET GATE LA
BOLLIN DR
CEDARFIELD RD
BOLLIN
CL
RICHMOND DR
Wet Gate
Farm
Oughtrington
Little
Heatley
HOWARD AVE
SANDY LA
BUCKLOW
GDNS
BUCKLOW GDNS
DYERS
CL
GREENACRES
OUGHTRINGTON
VIEW
WOODBINE RD
DYERS LA
CHURCH VIEW
HOPEFIELD RD
ASHCROFT
RD
MOSS GR
Rushgreen
WHITE
BROOM
Heatleyheath
Farm
Oughtrington
Cty Prim Sch
Oak Villa
Farm
BRIDGE CL
OUGHTRINGTON CRES
Cheshire Ring Canal Wlk
STAGE LA
Spring
Farm
2
CROWN
GREEN
THE PADDOCK
Lloyd
Bridge
Sutch La
BRADSHAW LA
Bridgewater Canal
SPRING LA
Lymm High (VC)
Sch
87
WARRINGTON LA
OUGHTRINGTON LA
Agden
Bridge
Farm
Woolstencroft
Farm
LONGBUTT LA
WOODLAND AVE
WOODLAND
DR
Newhey's
Plantation
Burford Lane
Farm
BURFORD LA
Agden Bridge
FOXLEY CL
1
Agdenlane
Farm
A56
AGDEN LA
Nursery
LYMM RD
HIGHER LA
Agden Brook
Farm
Wildermoor
Farm
CHAPEL WLKS
THE DRIVE
Broomedge
Broomedge
Farm
Wildermoor Hall
Farm
HILLSIDE
AGDEN BROW
WOODSIDE RD
A56
PH
B5159
PARKVIEW
PK
AGDEN
BROW PK
A56
86
69
70
71
D
E
F

29

20

19

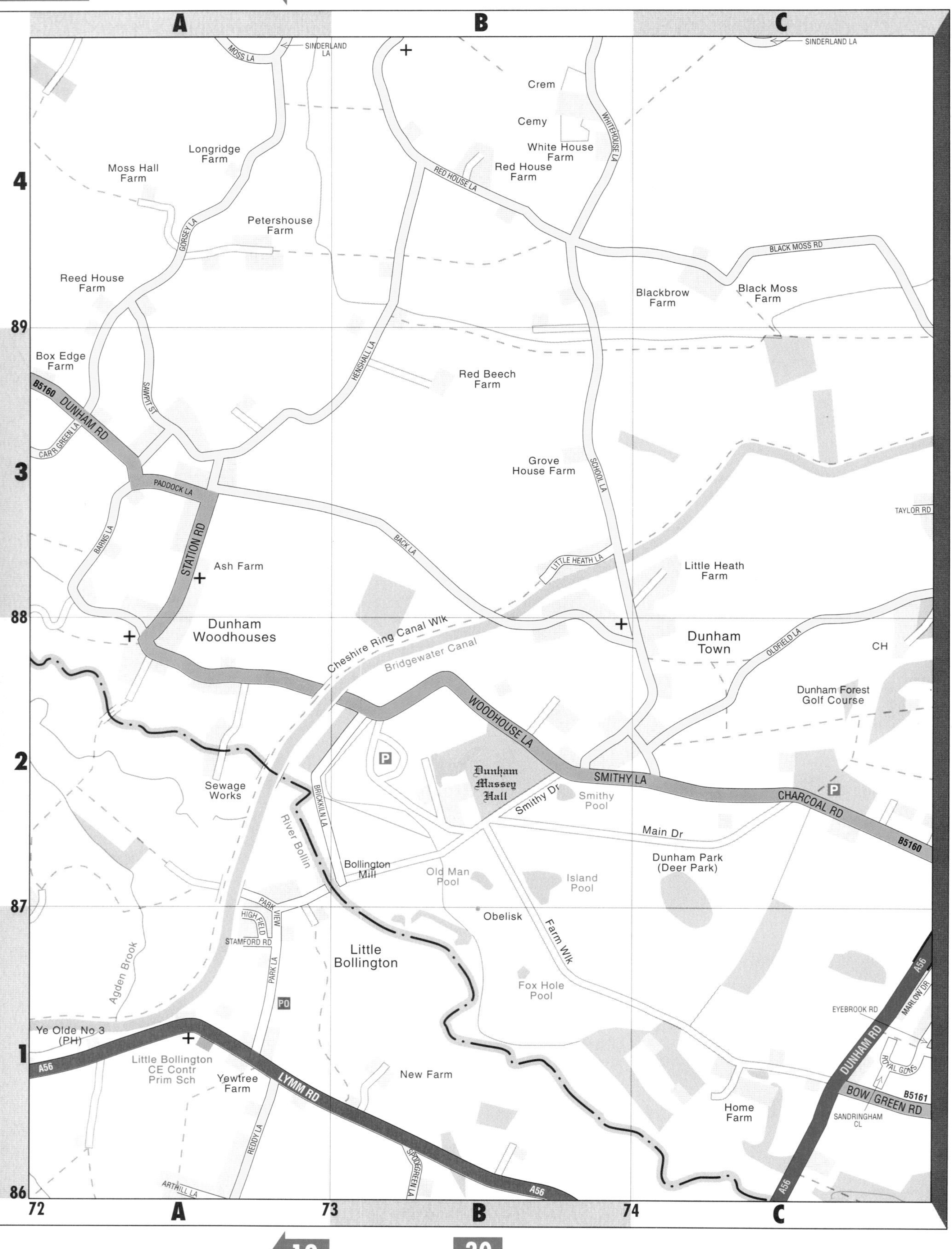
A
B
C
4
89
3
88
2
87
1
86
72
73
74
Sinderland La
Moss La
Crem
Cemy
White House Farm
Whitehouse La
Red House Farm
Red House La
Longridge Farm
Moss Hall Farm
Petershouse Farm
Gorsey La
Black Moss Rd
Reed House Farm
Blackbrow Farm
Black Moss Farm
Box Edge Farm
Henshall La
Red Beech Farm
B5160
Dunham Rd
Sawpit St
Carr Green La
Grove House Farm
School La
Paddock La
Back La
Taylor Rd
Barns La
Station Rd
Ash Farm
Little Heath La
Little Heath Farm
Dunham Woodhouses
Cheshire Ring Canal Wlk
Bridgewater Canal
Dunham Town
Oldfield La
CH
Dunham Forest Golf Course
Woodhouse La
Dunham Massey Hall
Smithy La
Smithy Dr
Smithy Pool
Charcoal Rd
Sewage Works
River Bollin
Bricklin La
Main Dr
B5160
Bollington Mill
Old Man Pool
Island Pool
Dunham Park (Deer Park)
Park View
High Field
Stamford Rd
Obelisk
Farm Wlk
Little Bollington
Agden Brook
Park La
PO
Fox Hole Pool
A56
Marlow Dr
Eyebrook Rd
Ye Olde No 3 (PH)
Dunham Rd
Royal Gdns
Little Bollington CE Contr Prim Sch
Yewtree Farm
Lymm Rd
New Farm
Home Farm
Bow Green Rd
B5161
Sandringham Cl
Reddy La
Spodegreen La
Arthill La
A56
72
A
73
B
74
C

19
30

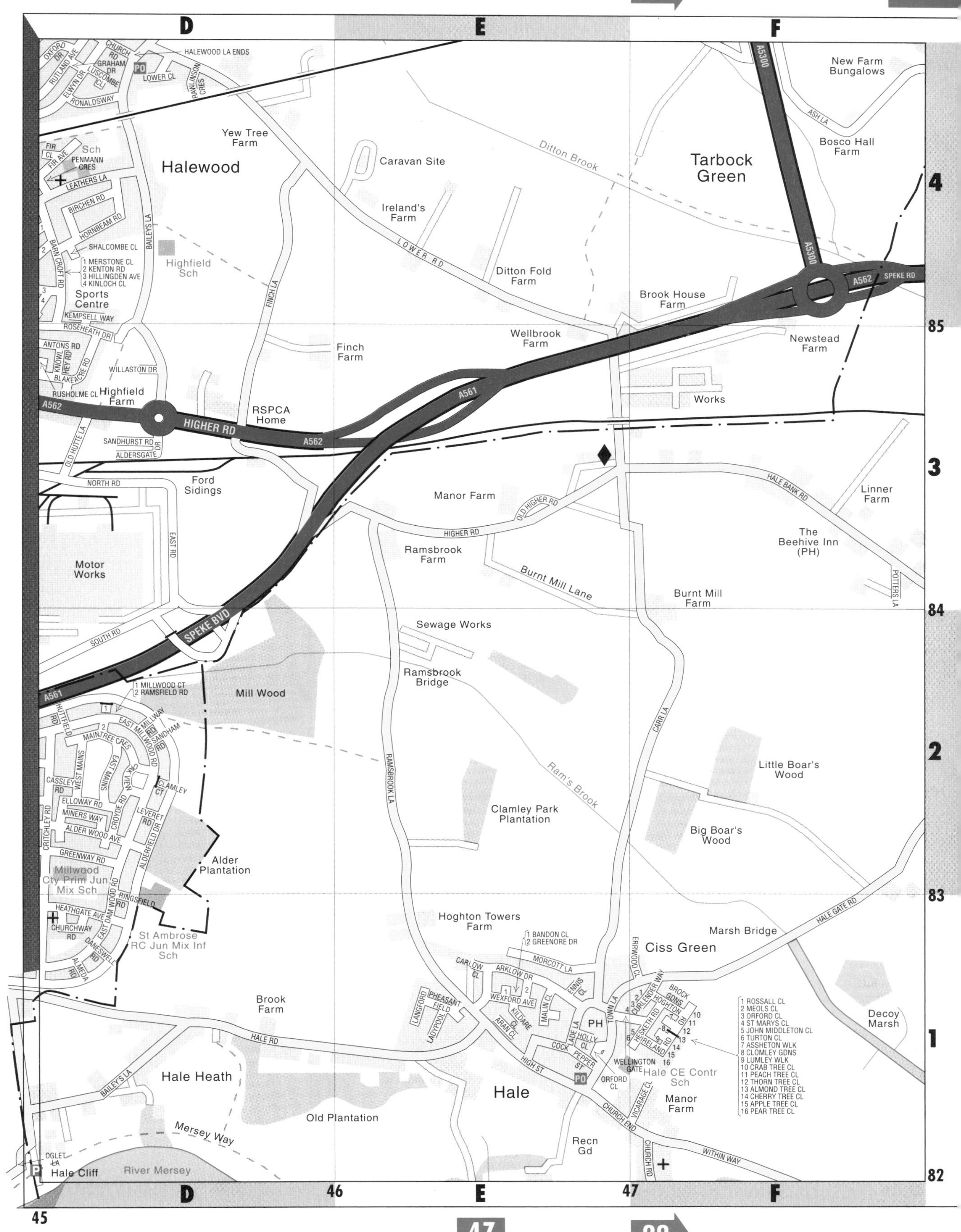

HALEWOOD LA ENDS

Halewood

Yew Tree Farm

Caravan Site

Ireland's Farm

Ditton Brook

Tarbock Green

New Farm Bungalows

Bosco Hall Farm

LOWER RD

Ditton Fold Farm

4

Finch Farm

Wellbrook Farm

Brook House Farm

Newstead Farm

85

SPEKE RD

A562

A5300

Sports Centre

Highfield Sch

Sch

FINCH LA

BAILEYS LA

RSPCA Home

Highfield Farm

HIGHER RD

A562

A561

Works

Ford Sidings

NORTH RD

Manor Farm

OLD HIGHER RD

HIGHER RD

HALE BANK RD

Linner Farm

The Beehive Inn (PH)

3

POTTERS LA

Motor Works

EAST RD

SOUTH RD

Ramsbrook Farm

Burnt Mill Lane

Burnt Mill Farm

84

SPEKE BVD

A561

1 MILLWOOD CT
2 RAMSFIELD RD

Mill Wood

Sewage Works

Ramsbrook Bridge

RAMSBROOK LA

CARR LA

Little Boar's Wood

2

Ram's Brook

Clamley Park Plantation

Big Boar's Wood

Alder Plantation

83

Millwood Cty Prim Jun Mix Sch

Hoghton Towers Farm

Marsh Bridge

HALE GATE RD

Ciss Green

Decoy Marsh

St Ambrose RC Jun Mix Inf Sch

1 BANDON CL
2 GREENORE DR

MORCOTT LA

ERRWOOD CL

CARLOW CL

ARKLOW DR

WEXFORD AVE

SINIS

TOWN LA

1 ROSSALL CL
2 MEOLS CL
3 ORFORD CL
4 ST MARYS CL
5 JOHN MIDDLETON CL
6 TURTON CL
7 ASSHETON WLK
8 CLOMLEY GDNS
9 LUMLEY WLK
10 CRAB TREE CL
11 PEACH TREE CL
12 THORN TREE CL
13 ALMOND TREE CL
14 CHERRY TREE CL
15 APPLE TREE CL
16 PEAR TREE CL

Brook Farm

PHEASANT FIELD

LANGFORD

LADYPOOL

KILLMORE

MALIN CL

HOLLY

PH

PEPPER ST

COCK LA

HIGH ST

Hale

ORFORD CL

PO

WELLINGTON GATE

Hale CE Contr Sch

Manor Farm

HALE RD

Hale Heath

Old Plantation

Mersey Way

Recn Gd

CHURCH END

VICARAGE CL

CHURCH RD

WITHIN WAY

1

P

OGLET LA

Hale Cliff

River Mersey

82

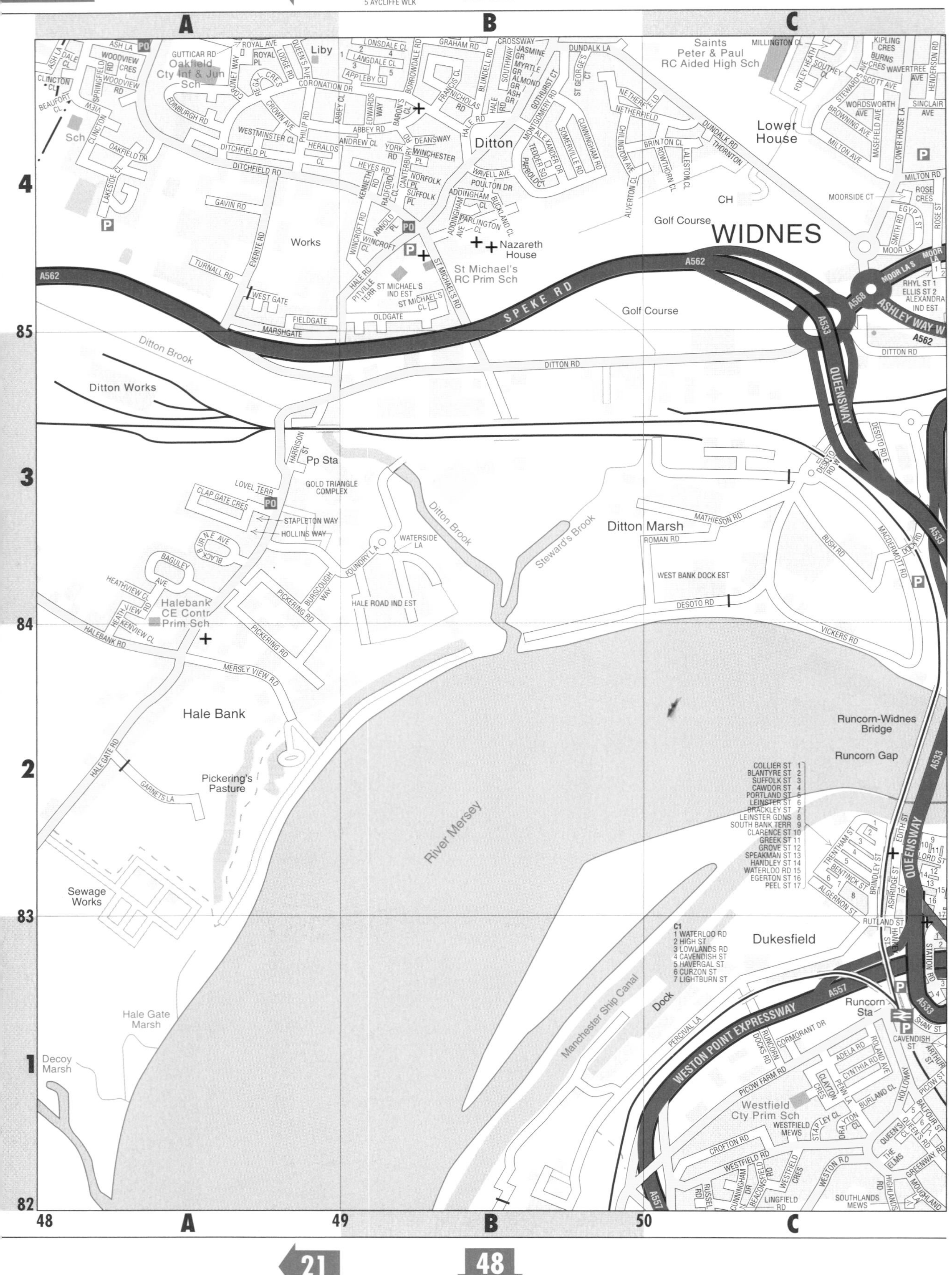

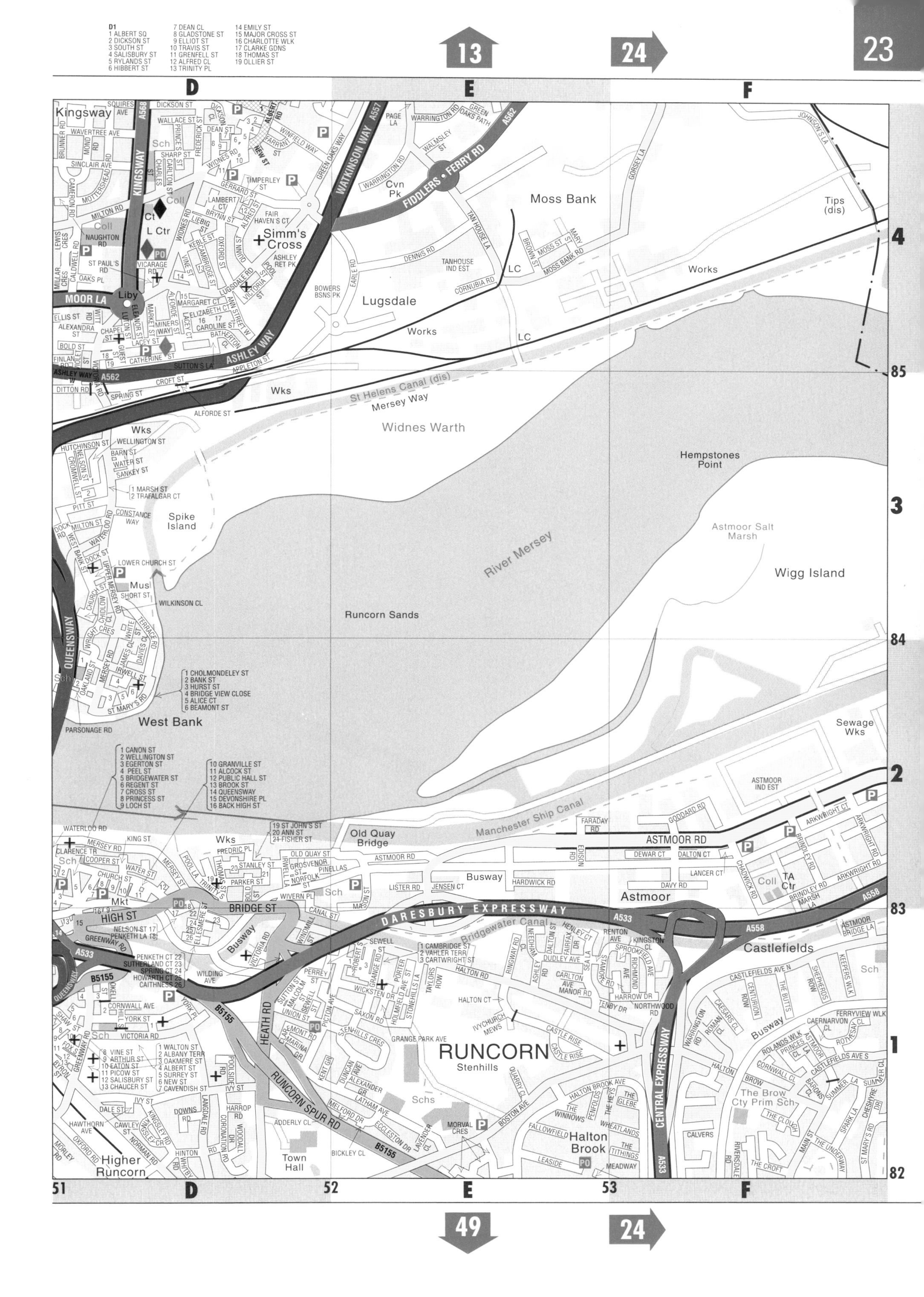

23
13
24
49
D1
1 ALBERT SQ
2 DICKSON ST
3 SOUTH ST
4 SALISBURY ST
5 RYLANDS ST
6 HIBBERT ST
7 DEAN CL
8 GLADSTONE ST
9 ELLIOT ST
10 TRAVIS ST
11 GRENFELL ST
12 ALFRED CL
13 TRINITY PL
14 EMILY ST
15 MAJOR CROSS ST
16 CHARLOTTE WLK
17 CLARKE GDNS
18 THOMAS ST
19 OLLIER ST
Kingsway
KINGSWAY
WATKINSON WAY
FIDDLERS FERRY RD
Moss Bank
Tips (dis)
Simm's Cross
Cvn Pk
Lugsdale
Works
Wks
MOOR LA
ASHLEY WAY
A562
A557
A568
St Helens Canal (dis)
Mersey Way
Widnes Warth
Hempstones Point
Spike Island
River Mersey
Astmoor Salt Marsh
Wigg Island
Runcorn Sands
West Bank
QUEENSWAY
Sewage Wks
ASTMOOR IND EST
Manchester Ship Canal
Old Quay Bridge
ASTMOOR RD
Astmoor
Busway
DARESBURY EXPRESSWAY
A533
A558
Bridgewater Canal
Castlefields
HIGH ST
BRIDGE ST
RUNCORN
Stenhills
CENTRAL EXPRESSWAY
RUNCORN SPUR RD
B5155
HEATH RD
Halton Brook
The Brow Cty Prim Sch
Town Hall
Higher Runcorn
D
E
F
1
2
3
4
51
52
53
82
83
84
85

23 14

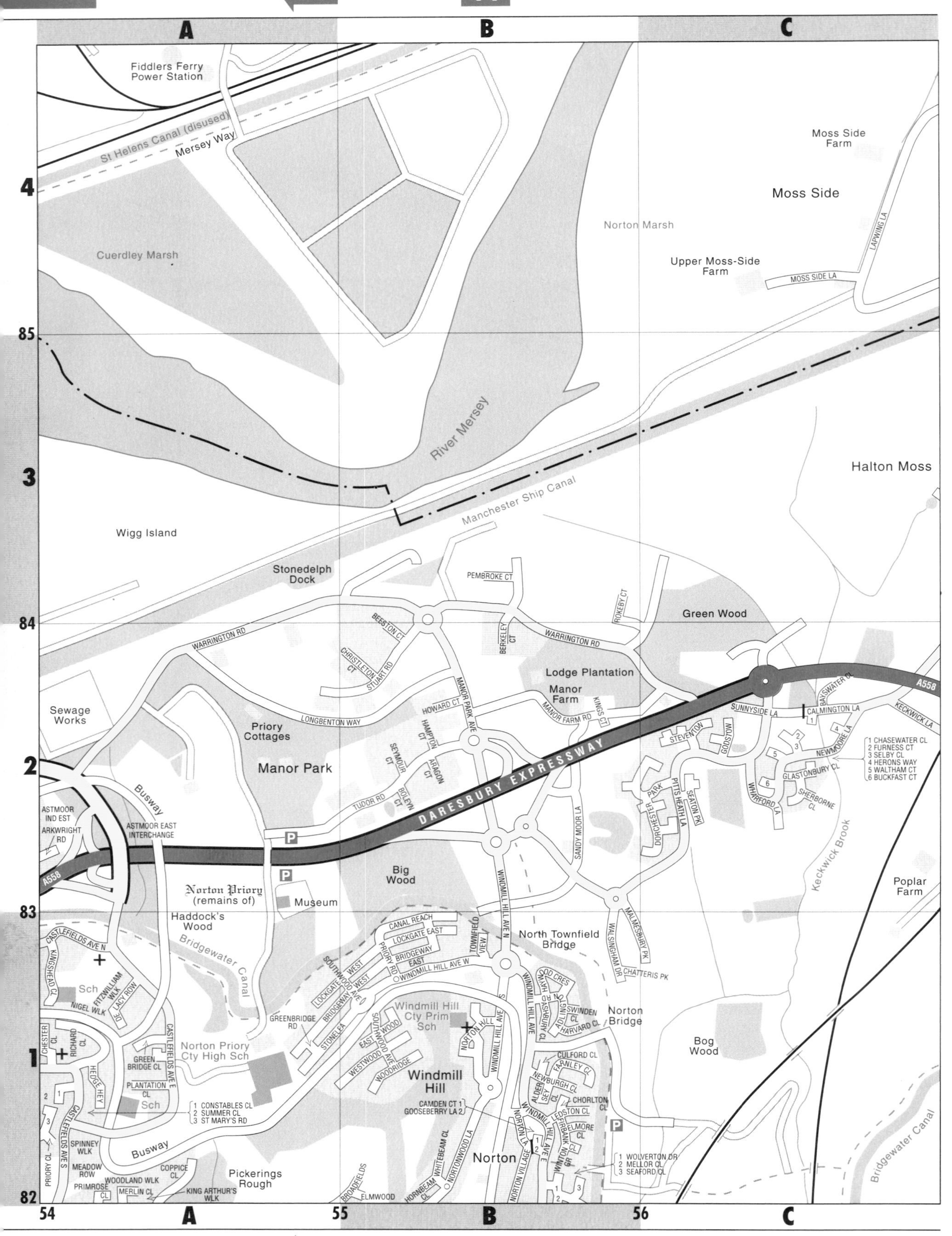
A
B
C
Fiddlers Ferry Power Station
St Helens Canal (disused)
Mersey Way
Moss Side Farm
Moss Side
Norton Marsh
Cuerdley Marsh
Upper Moss-Side Farm
MOSS SIDE LA
LAPWING LA
River Mersey
Halton Moss
Manchester Ship Canal
Wigg Island
Stonedelph Dock
PEMBROKE CT
Green Wood
WARRINGTON RD
BEESTON CT
BERKELEY CT
ROKEBY CT
CHRISTLETON CT
STUART RD
Lodge Plantation
Manor Farm
MANOR FARM RD
MANOR PARK AVE
HOWARD CT
KINGS CT
Sewage Works
LONGBENTON WAY
Priory Cottages
Manor Park
HAMPTON CT
SEYMOUR CT
ARAGON CT
TUDOR RD
BOLEYN CT
DARESBURY EXPRESSWAY
A558
SUNNYSIDE LA
CALMINGTON LA
BAYSWATER CL
KECKWICK LA
STEVENTON
GODSTOW
NEWMOORE LA
GLASTONBURY CL
WHARFORD LA
SHERBORNE CL
1 CHASEWATER CL
2 FURNESS CT
3 SELBY CL
4 HERONS WAY
5 WALTHAM CT
6 BUCKFAST CT
DORCHESTER PARK
PITTS HEATH LA
SEATON PK
SANDY MOOR LA
Busway
ASTMOOR IND EST
ARKWRIGHT RD
ASTMOOR EAST INTERCHANGE
Big Wood
Norton Priory (remains of)
Museum
Haddock's Wood
Keckwick Brook
Poplar Farm
Bridgewater Canal
CANAL REACH
LOCKGATE EAST
BRIDGEWAY EAST
TOWNFIELD VIEW
WINDMILL HILL AVE N
WINDMILL HILL AVE W
North Townfield Bridge
MALMESBURY PK
WALSINGHAM DR
CHATTERIS PK
CASTLEFIELDS AVE N
KINGSHEAD CL
FITZWILLIAM WLK
DE LACY ROW
NIGEL WLK
Sch
SOUTHWOOD AVE
LOCKGATE WEST
BRIDGEWAY WEST
PRIORY RD
GREENBRIDGE RD
STONELEA
Windmill Hill Cty Prim Sch
NORTON HILL
WINDMILL HILL AVE
Norton Bridge
SWINDEN CL
HARVARD CL
ASHBURY CL
ADLINGTON CL
CHESTER CL
RICHARD CL
Norton Priory Cty High Sch
GREEN BRIDGE CL
PLANTATION CL
HEDGE HEY
CASTLEFIELDS AVE E
EAST WOOD
WESTWOOD
WOODRIDGE
Windmill Hill
CULFORD CL
FARNLEY CL
NEWBURGH CL
Bog Wood
CAMDEN CT 1
GOOSEBERRY LA 2
1 CONSTABLES CL
2 SUMMER CL
3 ST MARY'S RD
CHORLTON CL
LEDSTON CL
ELMORE CL
WHITEBEAM CL
NORTONWOOD LA
NORTON LA
CASTLEFIELDS AVE S
SPINNEY WLK
MEADOW ROW
PRIORY CL
PRIMROSE CL
WOODLAND WLK
MERLIN CL
COPPICE CL
KING ARTHUR'S WLK
Pickerings Rough
Norton
1 WOLVERTON DR
2 MELLOR CL
3 SEAFORD CL
BROADFIELDS
ELMWOOD
HORNBEAM CL
NORTON VILLAGE
WINDMILL HILL AVE E
54
55
56
82
83
84
85
1
2
3
4

23 50

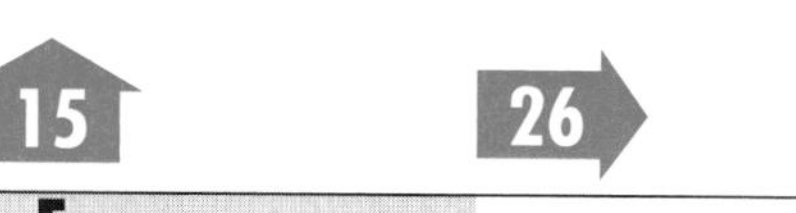

15
26

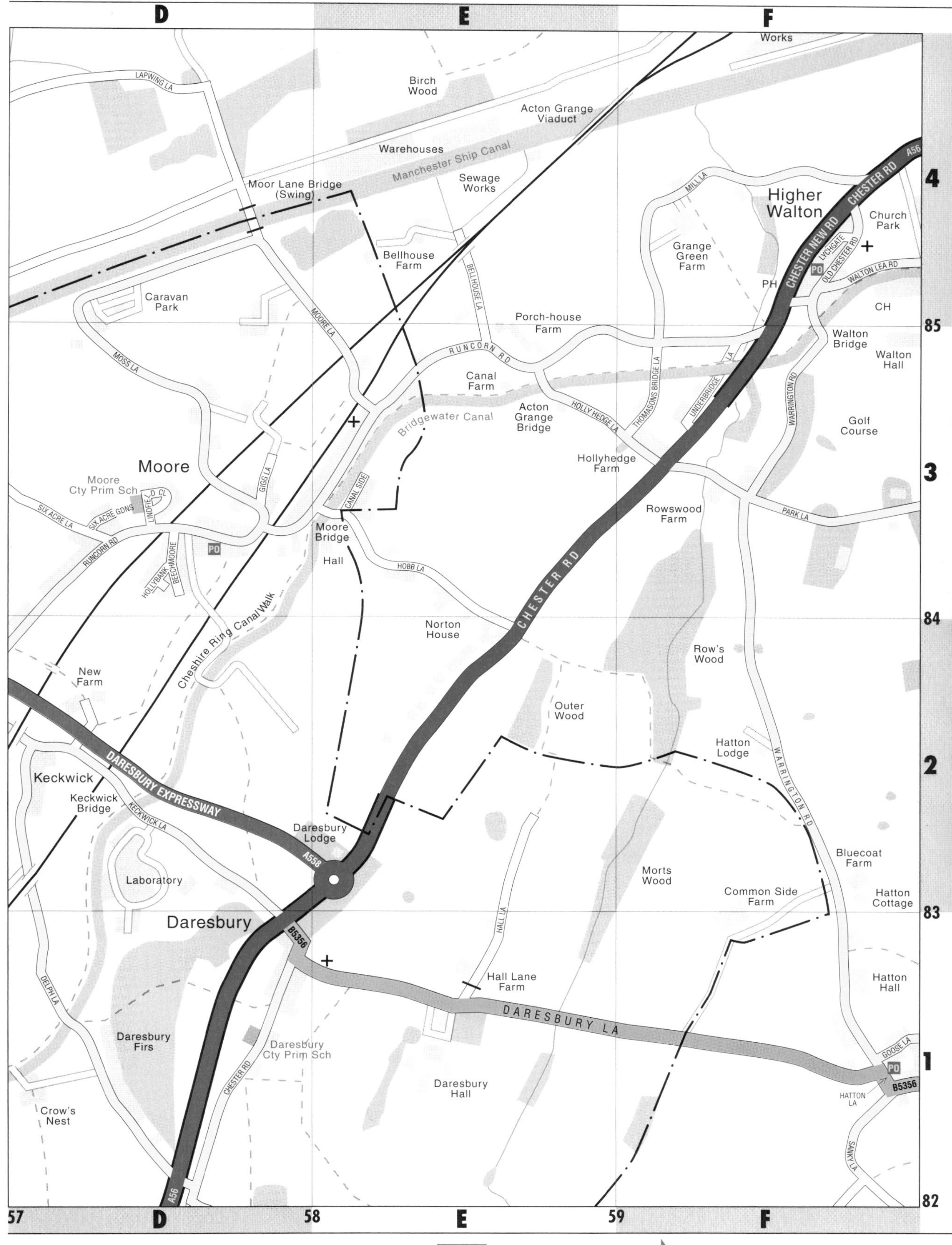

D
E
F
Works
Birch Wood
Acton Grange Viaduct
Warehouses
Manchester Ship Canal
Sewage Works
Moor Lane Bridge (Swing)
LAPWING LA
Higher Walton
CHESTER NEW RD
CHESTER RD
A56
Church Park
MILL LA
Grange Green Farm
LYCHGATE
OLD CHESTER RD
WALTON LEA RD
PO
PH
CH
Bellhouse Farm
BELLHOUSE LA
Caravan Park
MOORE LA
Porch-house Farm
RUNCORN RD
Walton Bridge
Walton Hall
MOSS LA
Canal Farm
THOMASONS BRIDGE LA
UNDERBRIDGE LA
WARRINGTON RD
Acton Grange Bridge
HOLLY HEDGE LA
Bridgewater Canal
Golf Course
Hollyhedge Farm
Moore
GIGG LA
Moore Cty Prim Sch
LINDFIELD CL
SIX ACRE LA
SIX ACRE GDNS
CANAL SIDE
Rowswood Farm
PARK LA
Moore Bridge
Hall
RUNCORN RD
PO
HOLLYBANK
BEECHMOORE
HOBB LA
CHESTER RD
Norton House
Cheshire Ring Canal Walk
Row's Wood
New Farm
Outer Wood
Hatton Lodge
WARRINGTON RD
Keckwick
DARESBURY EXPRESSWAY
Keckwick Bridge
KECKWICK LA
Daresbury Lodge
A558
Bluecoat Farm
Laboratory
Morts Wood
Common Side Farm
Hatton Cottage
Daresbury
B5356
HALL LA
Hatton Hall
Hall Lane Farm
DELPH LA
DARESBURY LA
Daresbury Firs
Daresbury Cty Prim Sch
CHESTER RD
GOOSE LA
PO
B5356
HATTON LA
Daresbury Hall
Crow's Nest
SANKEY LA
A56
4
85
3
84
2
83
1
82
57
58
59

25
16

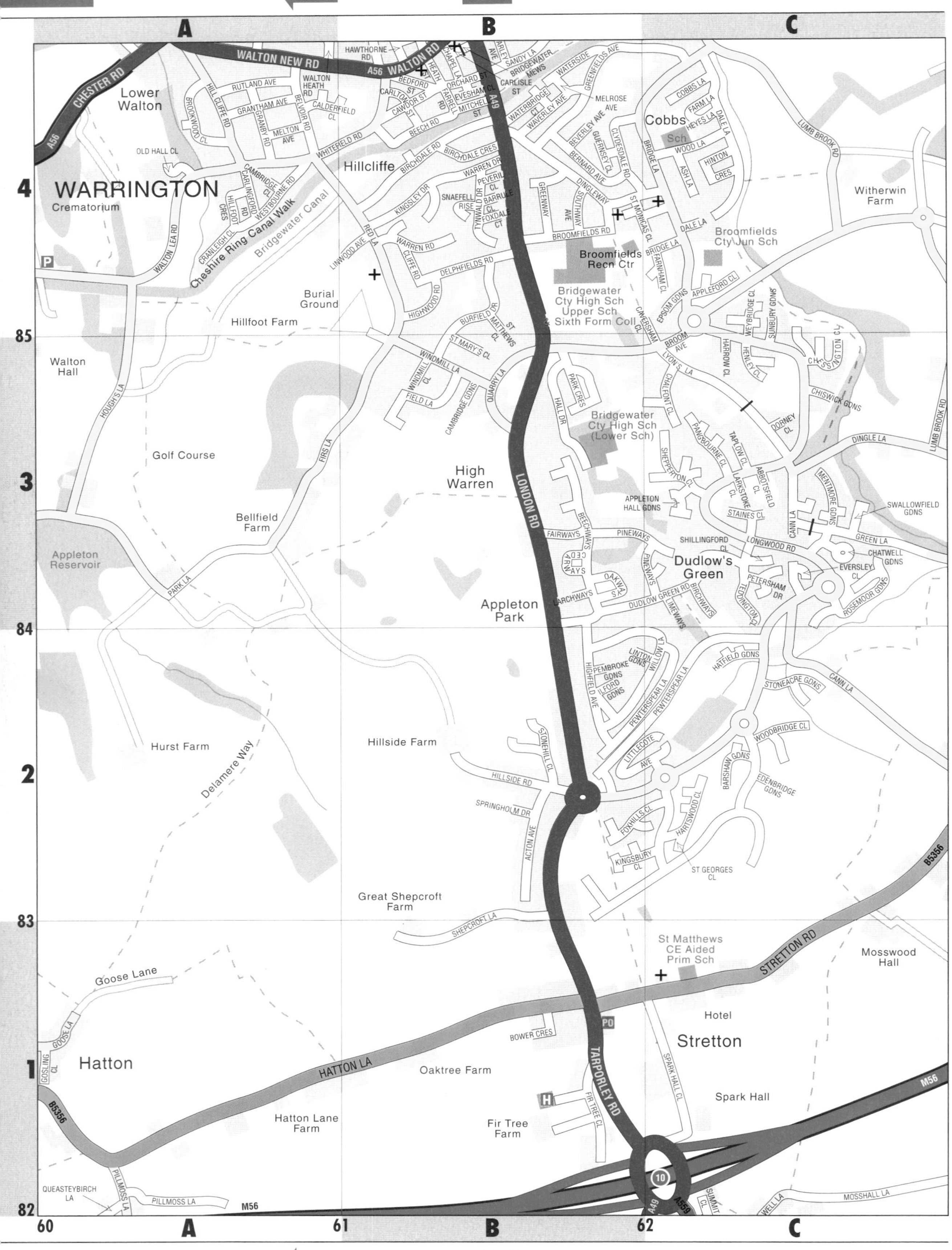
A
B
C
WALTON NEW RD
CHESTER RD
A56
WALTON RD
Lower Walton
WARRINGTON
Crematorium
Hillcliffe
Cobbs
Sch
Witherwin Farm
Broomfields Cty Jun Sch
Broomfields Recn Ctr
Bridgewater Cty High Sch Upper Sch & Sixth Form Coll
Bridgewater Cty High Sch (Lower Sch)
Cheshire Ring Canal Walk
Bridgewater Canal
Burial Ground
Hillfoot Farm
Walton Hall
Golf Course
High Warren
LONDON RD
A49
Bellfield Farm
Appleton Reservoir
Dudlow's Green
Appleton Park
Hurst Farm
Delamere Way
Hillside Farm
Great Shepcroft Farm
St Matthews CE Aided Prim Sch
STRETTON RD
Mosswood Hall
Goose Lane
Hotel
Stretton
Hatton
HATTON LA
Oaktree Farm
TARPORLEY RD
Spark Hall
Hatton Lane Farm
Fir Tree Farm
B5356
M56
A559
PILLMOSS LA
QUEASTEYBIRCH LA
MOSSHALL LA
LUMB BROOK RD
DINGLE LA
CANN LA
LONGWOOD RD
BROOM AVE
LYON'S LA
FIRS LA
PARK LA
HOUGH'S LA
WALTON LEA RD
RED LA
WINDMILL LA
HILLSIDE RD
SPRINGHOLM DR
ACTON AVE
SHEPCROFT LA
BOWER CRES
FIR TREE CL
SPARK HALL CL
GOSLING CL
GOOSE LA
PILLMOSS LA
SUMMIT CL
60
61
62
82
83
84
85
1
2
3
4

25
52

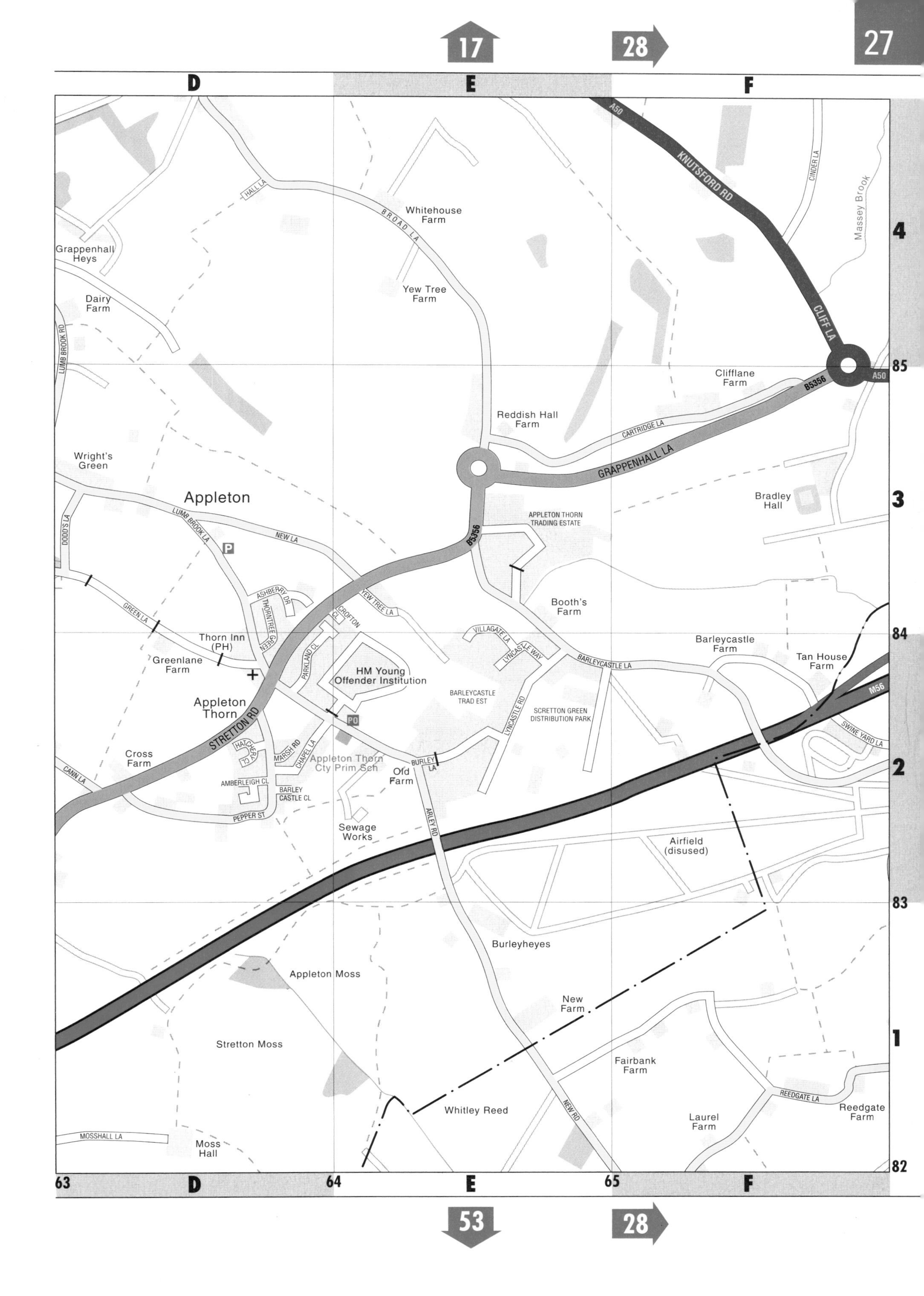
17
28
D
E
F
Grappenhall Heys
Dairy Farm
Whitehouse Farm
Yew Tree Farm
Reddish Hall Farm
Clifflane Farm
Wright's Green
Appleton
Bradley Hall
APPLETON THORN TRADING ESTATE
Booth's Farm
Thorn Inn (PH)
Greenlane Farm
HM Young Offender Institution
Barleycastle Farm
Tan House Farm
Appleton Thorn
BARLEYCASTLE TRAD EST
SCRETTON GREEN DISTRIBUTION PARK
Cross Farm
Appleton Thorn Cty Prim Sch
Old Farm
Sewage Works
Airfield (disused)
Burleyheyes
Appleton Moss
New Farm
Stretton Moss
Fairbank Farm
Whitley Reed
Laurel Farm
Reedgate Farm
Moss Hall
HALL LA
BROAD LA
KNUTSFORD RD
CLIFF LA
CINDER LA
Massey Brook
A50
B5356
CARTRIDGE LA
GRAPPENHALL LA
LUMB BROOK RD
LUMB BROOK LA
NEW LA
DODD'S LA
GREEN LA
ASHBERRY DR
THORNTREE GREEN
YEW TREE LA
CROFTON CL
PARKLAND CL
VILLAGATE LA
LYNCASTLE WAY
LYNCASTLE RD
BARLEYCASTLE LA
M56
SWINE YARD LA
STRETTON RD
HATCHERY CL
MARSH RD
CHAPEL LA
BURLEY LA
ARLEY RD
CANN LA
AMBERLEIGH CL
BARLEY CASTLE CL
PEPPER ST
REEDGATE LA
NEW RD
MOSSHALL LA
4
85
3
84
2
83
1
82
63
64
65
53
28

27
18

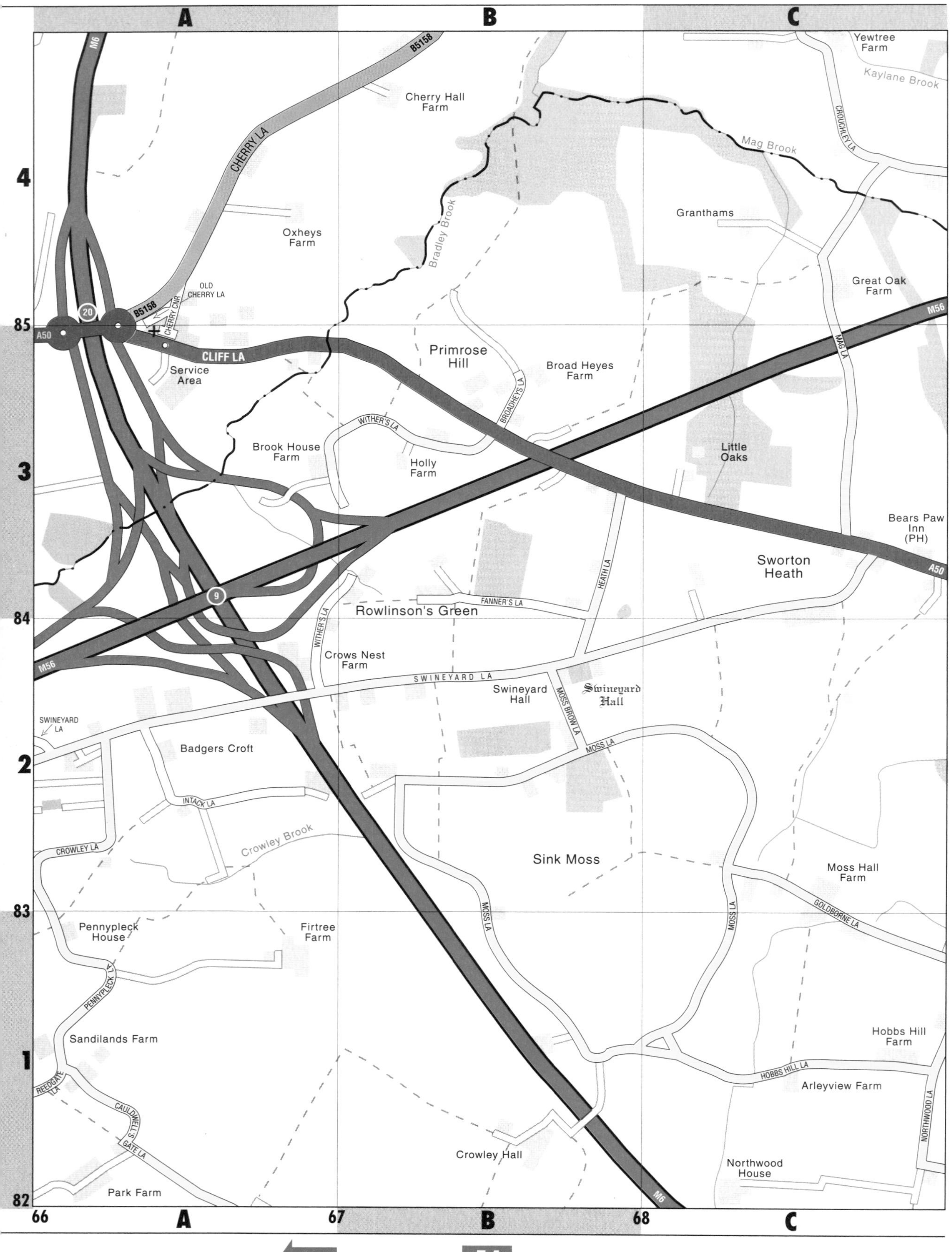
A
B
C
4
3
2
1
85
84
83
82
66
67
68
M6
B5158
CHERRY LA
Cherry Hall
Farm
Yewtree
Farm
Kaylane Brook
Mag Brook
CROUCHLEY LA
Bradley Brook
Oxheys
Farm
Granthams
Great Oak
Farm
OLD
CHERRY LA
CHERRY CNR
20
A50
CLIFF LA
Service
Area
Primrose
Hill
Broad Heyes
Farm
BROADHEYS LA
M56
MAG LA
WITHER'S LA
Brook House
Farm
Holly
Farm
Little
Oaks
Bears Paw
Inn
(PH)
Sworton
Heath
9
HEATH LA
FANNER'S LA
Rowlinson's Green
WITHER'S LA
Crows Nest
Farm
SWINEYARD LA
Swineyard
Hall
MOSS BROW LA
Swineyard
Hall
SWINEYARD
LA
Badgers Croft
MOSS LA
INTACK LA
Crowley Brook
CROWLEY LA
Sink Moss
Moss Hall
Farm
GOLDBORNE LA
Pennypleck
House
Firtree
Farm
MOSS LA
MOSS LA
PENNYPLECK LA
Sandilands Farm
Hobbs Hill
Farm
HOBBS HILL LA
Arleyview Farm
REEDGATE LA
CAULDWELL'S GATE LA
NORTHWOOD LA
Crowley Hall
Northwood
House
Park Farm

27
54

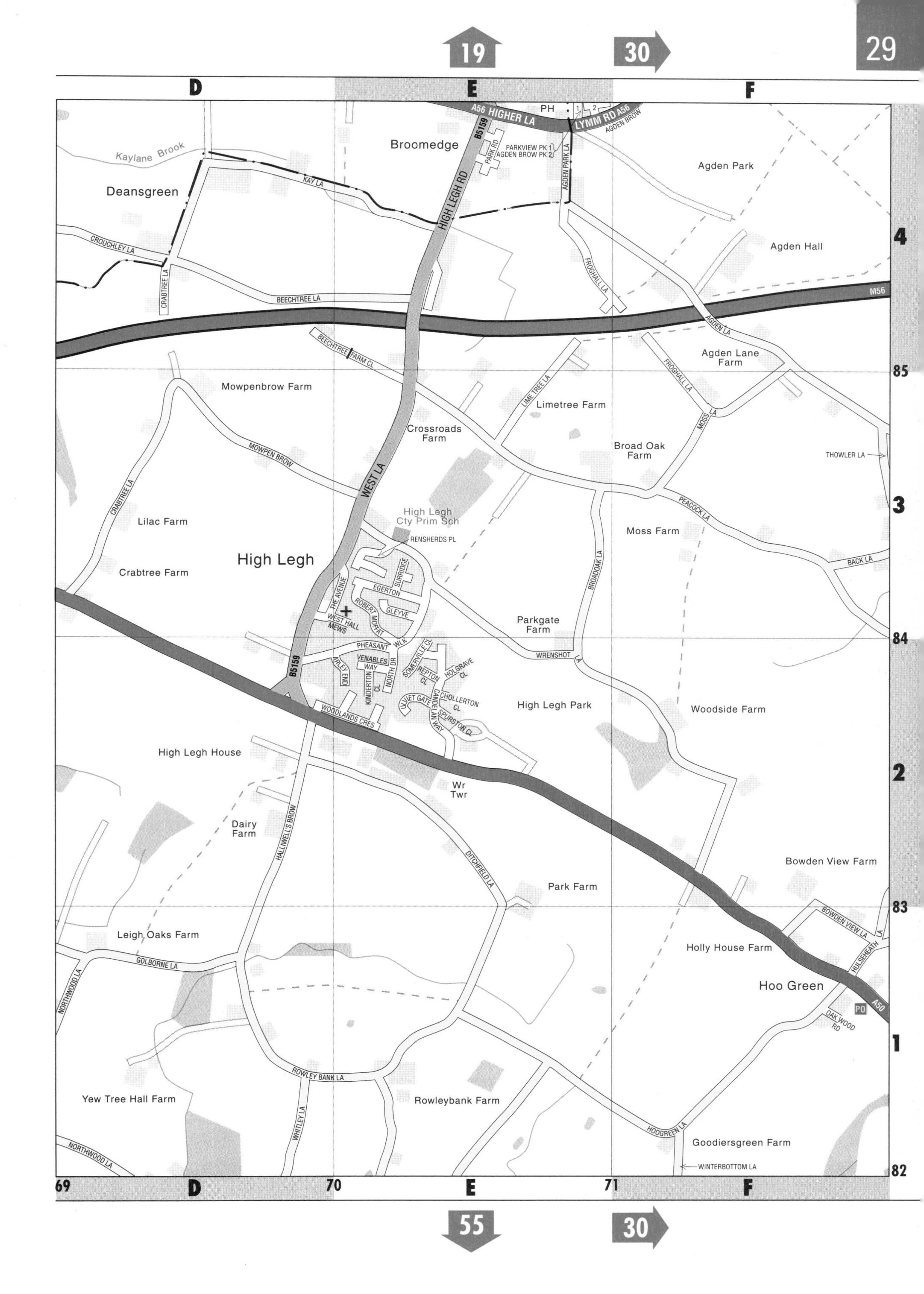

D

E

F

Kaylane Brook

Deansgreen

Broomedge

A56 HIGHER LA
PH
LYMM RD A56
AGDEN BROW

B5159

Park Rd

PARKVIEW PK 1
AGDEN BROW PK 2

Agden Park

Agden Brow

AGDEN PARK LA

KAY LA

HIGH LEGH RD

FROGHALL LA

Agden Hall

CROUCHLEY LA

CRABTREE LA

BEECHTREE LA

AGDEN LA

M56

BEECHTREE FARM CL

Agden Lane
Farm

FROGHALL LA

85

Mowpenbrow Farm

LIME TREE LA

Limetree Farm

MOSS LA

THOWLER LA

MOWPEN BROW

Crossroads
Farm

Broad Oak
Farm

CRABTREE LA

WEST LA

High Legh
Cty Prim Sch

PEACOCK LA

Moss Farm

BACK LA

3

Lilac Farm

High Legh

RENSHERDS PL

BROADOAK LA

SUNRIDGE

Crabtree Farm

EGERTON
THE AVENUE
ROBERT MOFFAT
GLEVVE
WEST HALL
MEWS

Parkgate
Farm

84

B5159

PHEASANT
VENABLES
WAY
ARLEY END
KINDERTON CL
NORTH DR

SOMERVILLE CL
REPTON CL
HOLGRAVE CL
CHOLLERTON CL
SPURSTON CL
VIOLET GATE
DELLAN WAY

WRENSHOT LA

High Legh Park

Woodside Farm

WOODLANDS CRES

High Legh House

HALLIWELLS BROW

Wr
Twr

2

DITCHFIELD LA

Bowden View Farm

Dairy
Farm

Park Farm

83

Leigh Oaks Farm

GOLBORNE LA

Holly House Farm

BOWDEN VIEW LA

HILLSIDE HEATH

NORTHWOOD LA

Hoo Green

PO
A50

OAK WOOD RD

1

ROWLEY BANK LA

WHITLEY LA

Yew Tree Hall Farm

Rowleybank Farm

HOOGREEN LA

Goodiersgreen Farm

NORTHWOOD LA

WINTERBOTTOM LA

82

29
20

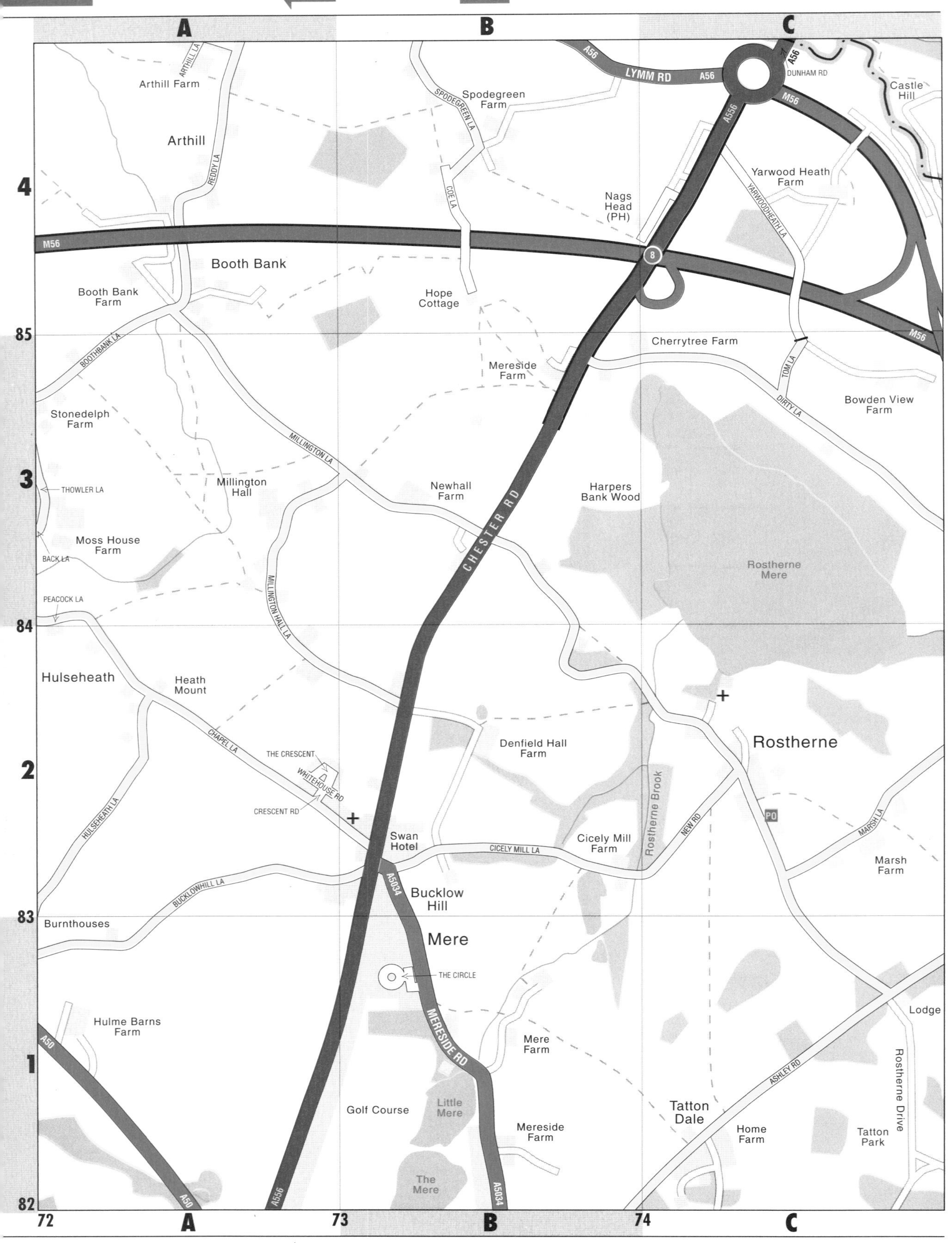
A
B
C
4
3
2
1
85
84
83
82
72
73
74
Arthill Farm
ARTHILL LA
Arthill
REDDY LA
Spodegreen Farm
SPODEGREEN LA
COE LA
LYMM RD
A56
M56
A556
DUNHAM RD
Castle Hill
Yarwood Heath Farm
YARWOODHEATH LA
Nags Head (PH)
Booth Bank
Booth Bank Farm
Hope Cottage
BOOTHBANK LA
Cherrytree Farm
TOM LA
DIRTY LA
Mereside Farm
Bowden View Farm
Stonedelph Farm
MILLINGTON LA
Millington Hall
THOWLER LA
Newhall Farm
Harpers Bank Wood
CHESTER RD
Moss House Farm
BACK LA
Rostherne Mere
PEACOCK LA
MILLINGTON HALL LA
Hulseheath
Heath Mount
CHAPEL LA
THE CRESCENT
WHITEHOUSE RD
CRESCENT RD
Denfield Hall Farm
Rostherne
Rostherne Brook
NEW RD
PO
MARSH LA
HULSEHEATH LA
Swan Hotel
CICELY MILL LA
Cicely Mill Farm
Marsh Farm
BUCKLOWHILL LA
A5034
Bucklow Hill
Burnthouses
Mere
THE CIRCLE
Hulme Barns Farm
A50
MERESIDE RD
Mere Farm
Lodge
ASHLEY RD
Rostherne Drive
Golf Course
Little Mere
Tatton Dale
Mereside Farm
Home Farm
Tatton Park
The Mere

29
56

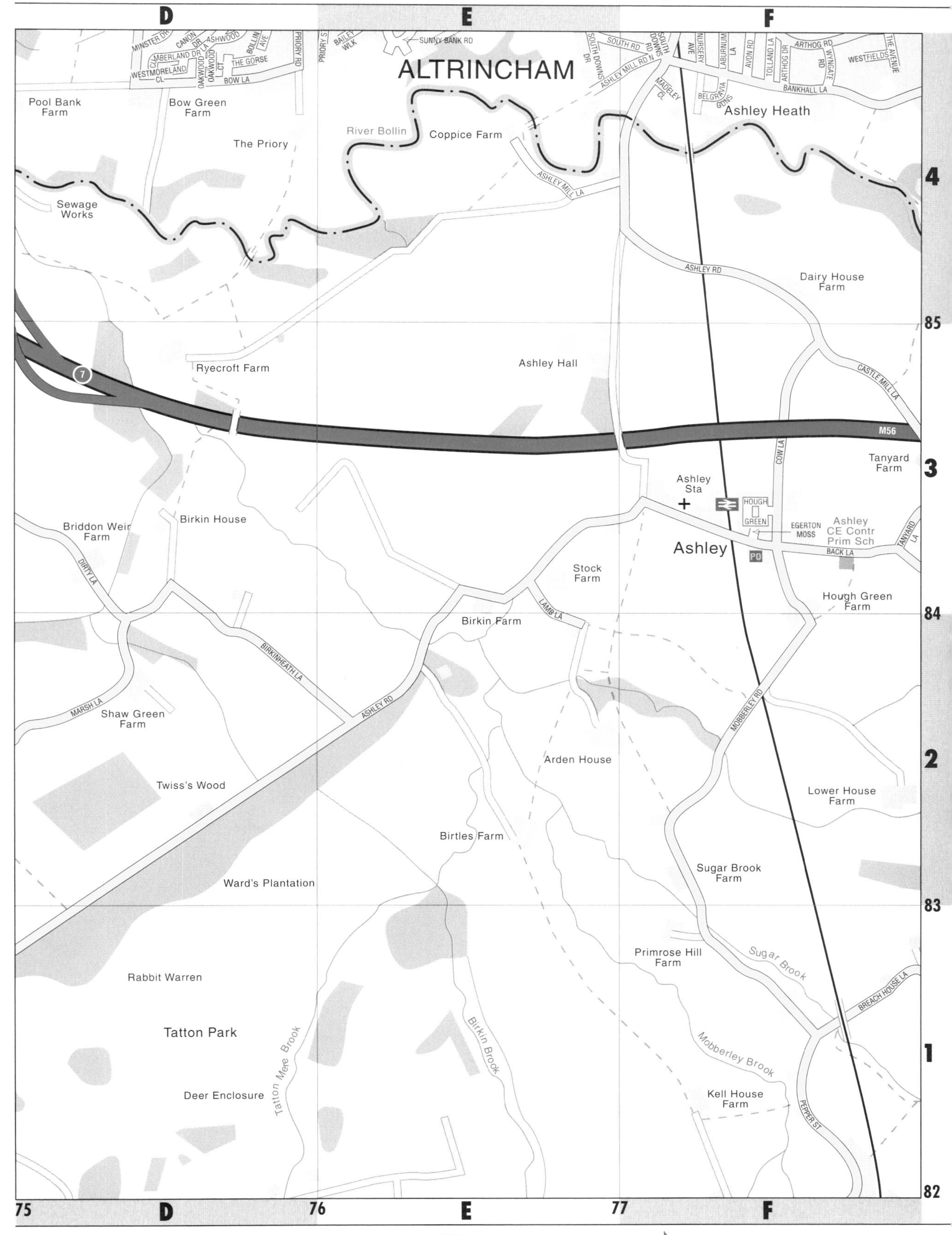

D **E** **F**

MINSTER DR
CANON
AMBERLAND DR
OAKWOOD
WESTMORELAND
CL
ASHWOOD
THE GORSE
BOW LA
PRIORY RD
BAILEY WLK
PRIORY S
BOLLIN AVE
OAKWOOD CT

SOUTH RD
SOUTH DOWNS DR
ASHLEY MILL RD N
SOUTH RD
NURSERY AVE
BELGRAVIA GDNS
LABURNUM
AVON RD
TOLLAND LA
ARTHOG DR
ARTHOG RD
WYNGATE
BANKHALL LA
WESTFIELDS
THE AVENUE

ALTRINCHAM

~~SUNNY BANK RD~~

Pool Bank
Farm

Bow Green
Farm

The Priory

River Bollin

Coppice Farm

Ashley Heath

MADLEY CL

4

Sewage
Works

ASHLEY MILL LA

ASHLEY RD

Dairy House
Farm

85

Ryecroft Farm

⑦

Ashley Hall

CASTLE MILL LA

M56

3

Briddon Weir
Farm

Birkin House

DIRTY LA

Ashley
Sta

✚   🚉   HOUGH
GREEN

COW LA

Tanyard
Farm

EGERTON
MOSS

Ashley
CE Contr
Prim Sch

TANYARD LA

Ashley

PO

BACK LA

Stock
Farm

LAMB LA

Birkin Farm

Hough Green
Farm

84

BIRKINHEATH LA

ASHLEY RD

MARSH LA

Shaw Green
Farm

Arden House

MOBBERLEY RD

Lower House
Farm

2

Twiss's Wood

Birtles Farm

Sugar Brook
Farm

Ward's Plantation

83

Primrose Hill
Farm

Sugar Brook

BREACH HOUSE LA

Rabbit Warren

Tatton Park

Tatton Mere Brook

Birkin Brook

Mobberley Brook

1

Deer Enclosure

Kell House
Farm

PEPPER ST

82

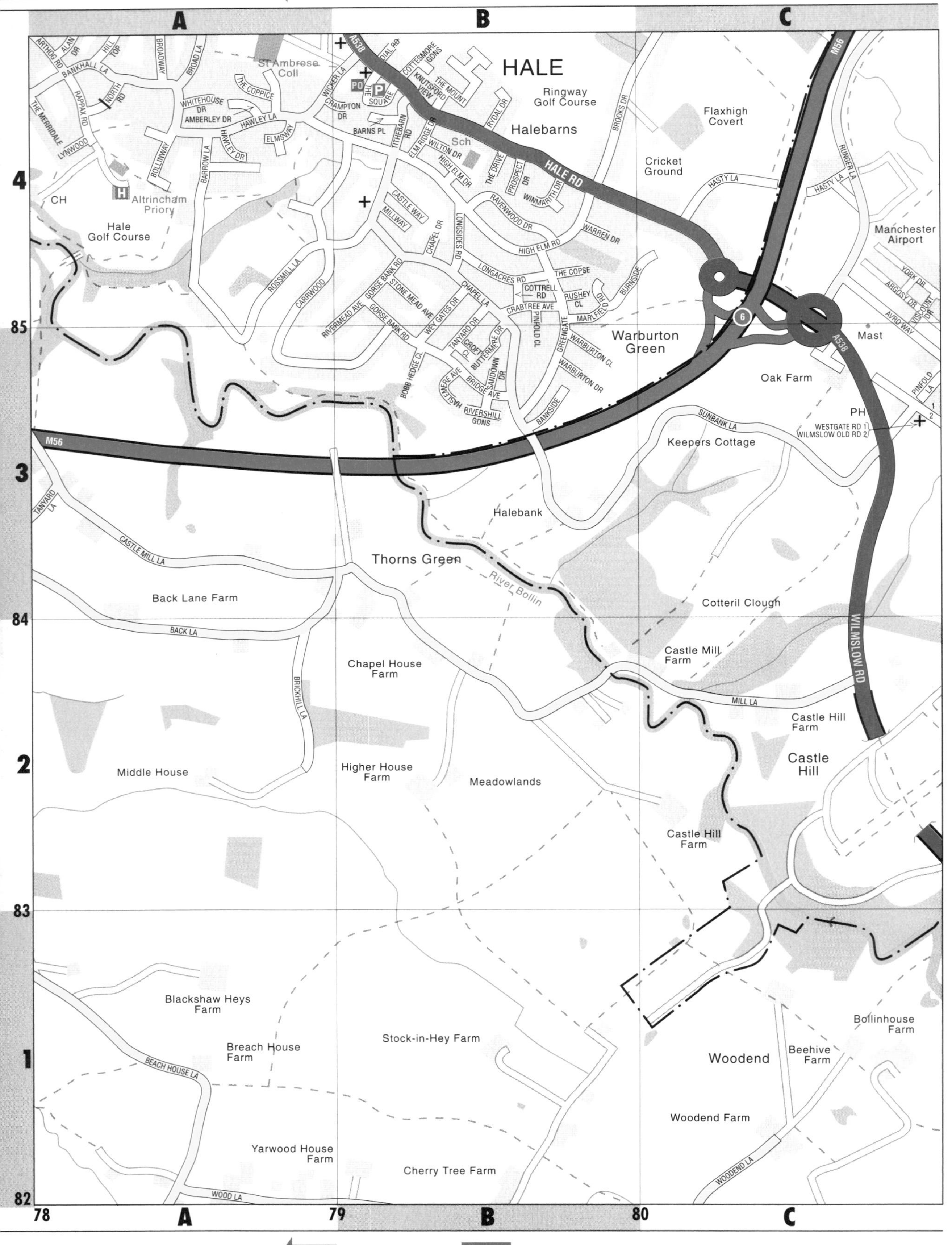

HALE

Ringway
Golf Course

Halebarns

HALE RD

Flaxhigh
Covert

Cricket
Ground

St Ambrose
Coll

CH

Altrincham
Priory

Hale
Golf Course

Manchester
Airport

Warburton
Green

Mast

Oak Farm

PH
WESTGATE RD 1
WILMSLOW OLD RD 2

Keepers Cottage

M56

Halebank

Thorns Green

River Bollin

Cotteril Clough

Back Lane Farm

BACK LA

Chapel House
Farm

Castle Mill
Farm

Castle Hill
Farm

Castle
Hill

Middle House

Higher House
Farm

Meadowlands

Castle Hill
Farm

WILMSLOW RD

MILL LA

Blackshaw Heys
Farm

Breach House
Farm

Stock-in-Hey Farm

Woodend

Bollinhouse
Farm

Beehive
Farm

BEACH HOUSE LA

Yarwood House
Farm

Cherry Tree Farm

Woodend Farm

WOODEND LA

WOOD LA

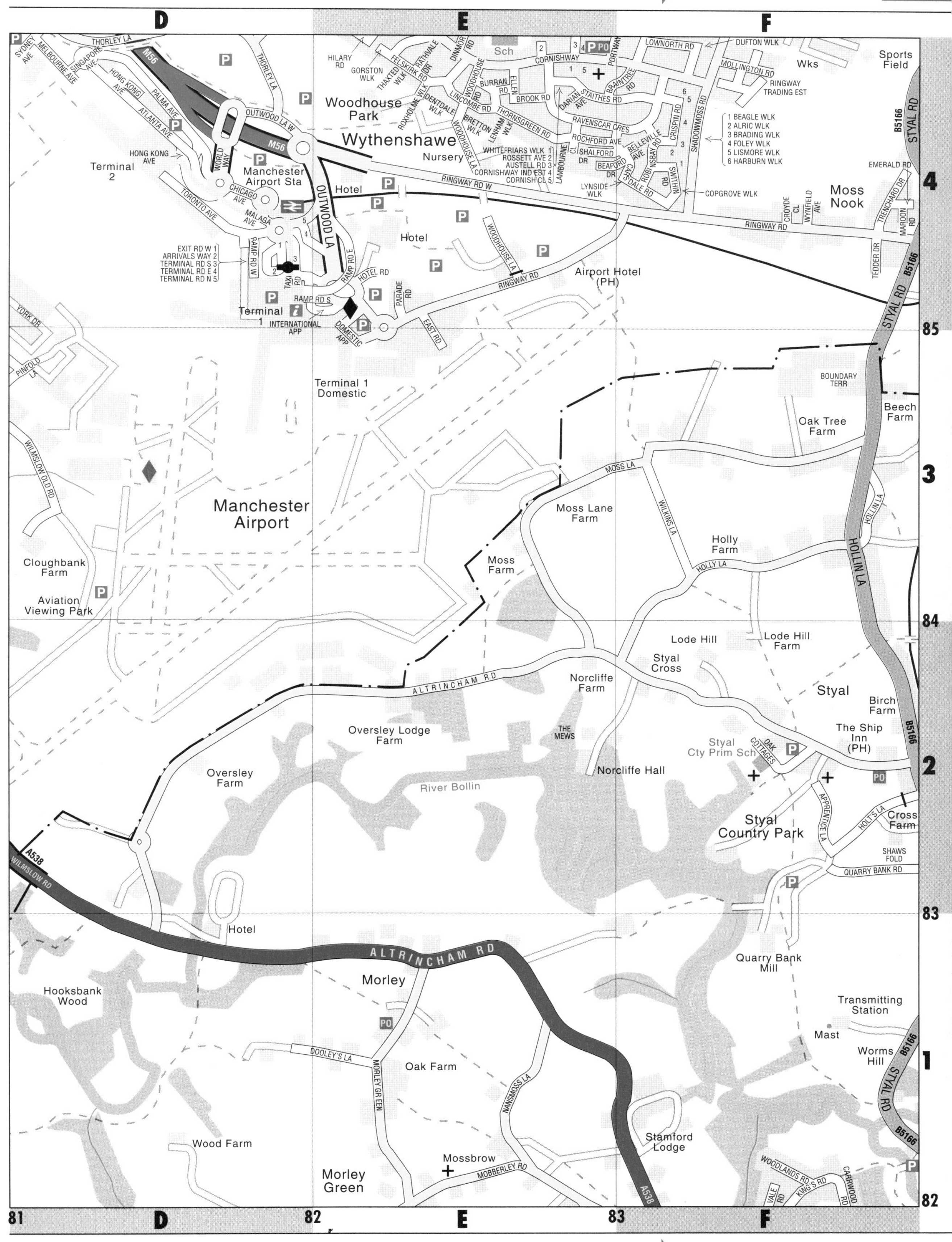

D

E

F

P SYDNEY AVE
P MELBOURNE AVE
SINGAPORE AVE
THORLEY LA
HONG KONG AVE
ATLANTA AVE
PALMA AVE
M56
OUTWOOD LA W
WORLD WAY

P

THORLEY LA
HILARY RD
GORSTON WLK
FELSKIRK RD
EATVALE
DINMORE
GODWARD
Sch
CORNISHWAY
2
3 4 P PO
LOWNORTH RD
DUFTON WLK
MOLLINGTON RD
Wks
Sports
Field

Woodhouse
Park
ROKDANK
WIDENTDALE WLK
THAXTED
THORNSGREEN RD
WOODHOUSE LA
BROOK RD
BURRAN
ELLEN
LINCOMBE RD
BRETTON WLK
LENHAM
1
RAVENSCAR CRES
DAMIAN
STAITHES RD
BRAINTREE
RINGWAY
TRADING EST
1 BEAGLE WLK
2 ALRIC WLK
3 BRADING WLK
4 FOLEY WLK
5 LISMORE WLK
6 HARBURN WLK

Wythenshawe
Nursery
WHITEFRIARS WLK 1
ROSSETT AVE 2
AUSTELL RD 3
CORNISHWAY IND EST 4
CORNISH CL 5
RINGWAY RD W
RAVENSCAR CRES
SHALFORD
BELLEVILLE
CRISPIN RD
SHADOWMOSS RD

Terminal
2
HONG KONG
AVE
CHICAGO
AVE
MALAGA
AVE
TORONTO AVE
Manchester
Airport Sta
OUTWOOD LA
P
Hotel
RINGWAY RD W
LAMBOURNE
RD
BEAFORD
DR
SMITH
DALE RD
LYNSIDE
WLK
COPGROVE WLK
CROYDE
CL
WYNFIELD
AVE
RINGWAY RD
EMERALD RD
Moss
Nook

EXIT RD W 1
ARRIVALS WAY 2
TERMINAL RD S 3
TERMINAL RD E 4
TERMINAL RD N 5
TAXI
RD
RAMP RD W
RAMP RD E
HOTEL RD
P
P
Hotel
WOODHOUSE LA
RINGWAY RD
B5166
STYAL RD
TEDDER DR
TRENCHARD DR
MARON RD
B5166

4

YORK DR
PINFOLD
LA
Terminal
1
i INTERNATIONAL
APP
RAMP RD S
P
DOMESTIC
APP
EAST RD
PARADE
RD
Hotel RD
Airport Hotel
(PH)

85

Terminal 1
Domestic
BOUNDARY
TERR
Beech
Farm

WILMSLOW OLD RD
Manchester
Airport
MOSS LA
Moss Lane
Farm
WILKINS LA
Oak Tree
Farm

3

Cloughbank
Farm
Moss
Farm
Holly
Farm
HOLLY LA
HOLLIN LA

P
Aviation
Viewing Park
Lode Hill
Styal
Cross
Lode Hill
Farm

84

ALTRINCHAM RD
Norcliffe
Farm
Styal
Birch
Farm
B5166

Oversley Lodge
Farm
THE
MEWS
Styal
Cty Prim Sch
OAK
COTTAGES
P
The Ship
Inn
(PH)
PO

2

Oversley
Farm
River Bollin
Norcliffe Hall
Styal
Country Park
APPRENTICE LA
HOLT'S LA
Cross
Farm
SHAWS
FOLD

A538
WILMSLOW RD
QUARRY BANK RD
P

83

Hotel
ALTRINCHAM RD
Quarry Bank
Mill

Morley
Transmitting
Station
Mast

Hooksbank
Wood
PO
Worms
Hill
B5166
STYAL RD

DOOLEY'S LA
MORLEY GREEN
Oak Farm
MAINSMOSS LA

1

Wood Farm
Stamford
Lodge
WOODLANDS RD
VALE
RD
KING'S RD
CARWOOD
RD
P

Morley
Green
Mossbrow
MOBBERLEY RD
A538

82

D

81

E

82

83

F

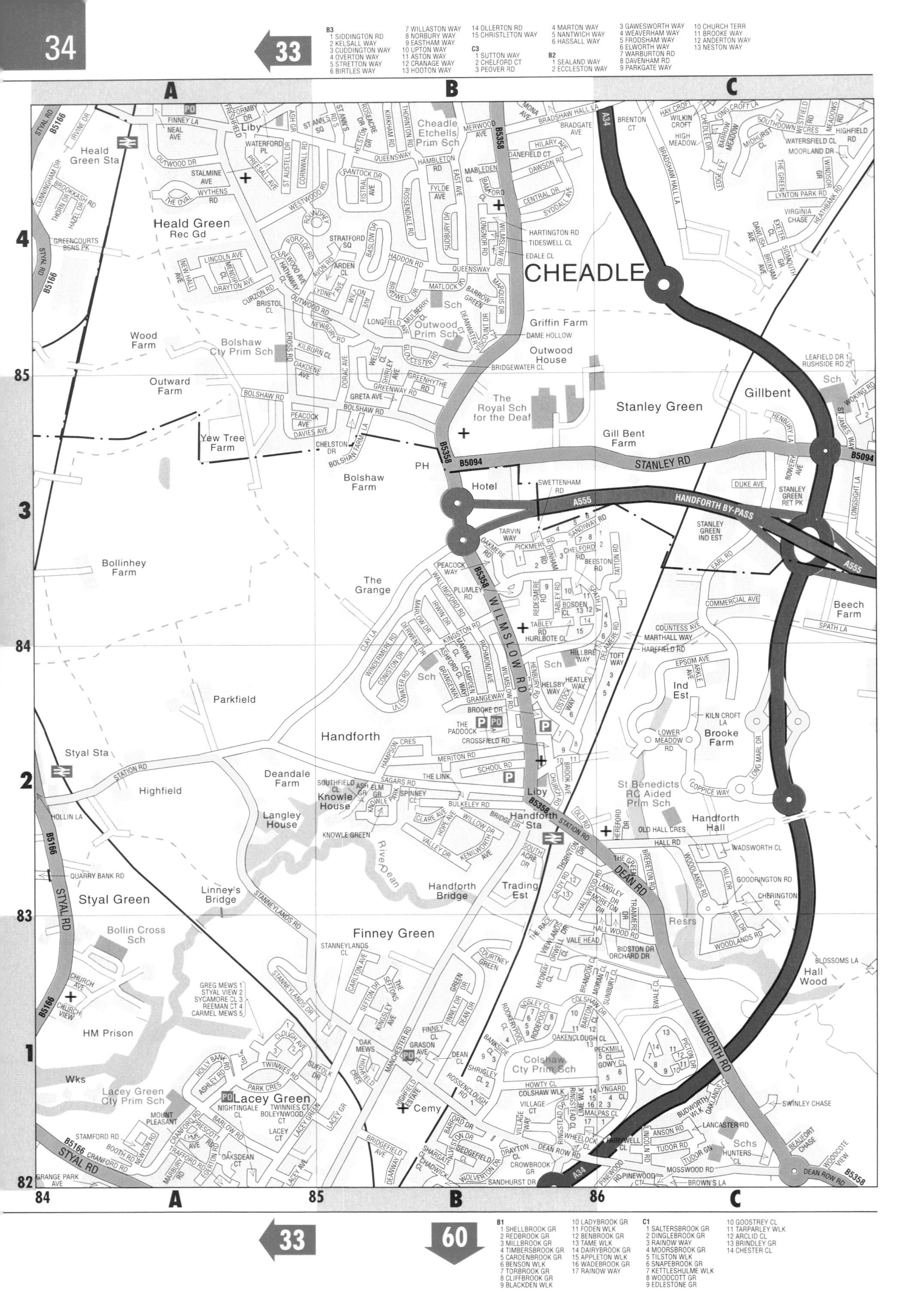

33

B3
1 SIDDINGTON RD
2 KELSALL WAY
3 CUDDINGTON WAY
4 OVERTON WAY
5 STRETTON WAY
6 BIRTLES WAY

7 WILLASTON WAY
8 NORBURY WAY
9 EASTHAM WAY
10 UPTON WAY
11 ASTON WAY
12 CRANAGE WAY
13 HOOTON WAY

14 OLLERTON RD
15 CHRISTLETON WAY

C3
1 SUTTON WAY
2 CHELFORD CT
3 PEOVER RD

4 MARTON WAY
5 NANTWICH WAY
6 HASSALL WAY

B2
1 SEALAND WAY
2 ECCLESTON WAY

3 GAWESWORTH WAY
4 WEAVERHAM WAY
5 FRODSHAM WAY
6 ELWORTH WAY
7 WARBURTON RD
8 DAVENHAM RD
9 PARKGATE WAY

10 CHURCH TERR
11 BROOKE WAY
12 ANDERTON WAY
13 NESTON WAY

B1
1 SHELLBROOK GR
2 REDBROOK GR
3 MILLBROOK GR
4 TIMBERSBROOK GR
5 CARDENBROOK GR
6 BENSON WLK
7 TORBROOK GR
8 CLIFFBROOK GR
9 BLACKDEN WLK

10 LADYBROOK GR
11 FODEN WLK
12 BENBROOK GR
13 TAME WLK
14 DAIRYBROOK GR
15 APPLETON WLK
16 WADEBROOK GR
17 RAINOW WAY

C1
1 SALTERSBROOK GR
2 DINGLEBROOK GR
3 RAINOW WAY
4 MOORSBROOK GR
5 TILSTON WLK
6 SNAPEBROOK GR
7 KETTLESHULME WLK
8 WOODCOTT GR
9 EDLESTONE GR

10 GOOSTREY CL
11 TARPARLEY WLK
12 ARCLID CL
13 BRINDLEY GR
14 CHESTER CL

36

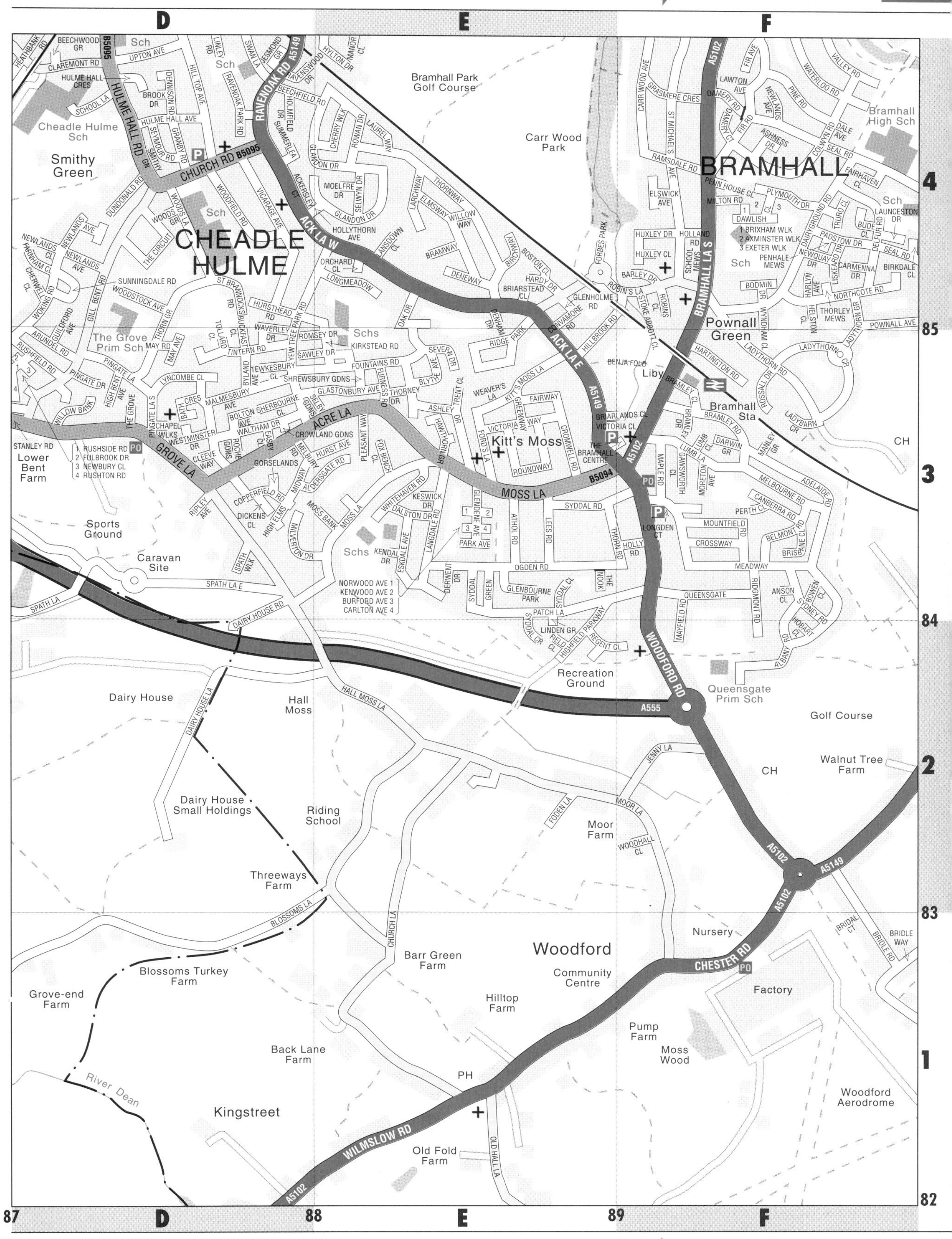
D
E
F
CHEADLE
HULME
BRAMHALL
Smithy
Green
Cheadle Hulme
Sch
Bramhall Park
Golf Course
Carr Wood
Park
Bramhall
High Sch
Pownall
Green
Bramhall
Sta
Kitt's Moss
The Grove
Prim Sch
Lower
Bent
Farm
Sports
Ground
Caravan
Site
Dairy House
Hall
Moss
Recreation
Ground
Queensgate
Prim Sch
Golf Course
Walnut Tree
Farm
Dairy House
Small Holdings
Riding
School
Moor
Farm
Threeways
Farm
Nursery
Woodford
Barr Green
Farm
Community
Centre
Blossoms Turkey
Farm
Grove-end
Farm
Hilltop
Farm
Factory
Pump
Farm
Moss
Wood
Back Lane
Farm
River Dean
Kingstreet
Woodford
Aerodrome
Old Fold
Farm
HULME HALL RD
CHURCH RD
RAVENOAK RD
ACK LA W
ACK LA E
BRAMHALL LA S
WOODFORD RD
ACRE LA
GROVE LA
MOSS LA
SPATH LA E
DAIRY HOUSE RD
DAIRY HOUSE LA
HALL MOSS LA
JENNY LA
MOOR LA
FODEN LA
WOODHALL CL
BLOSSOMS LA
CHURCH LA
CHESTER RD
WILMSLOW RD
OLD HALL LA
BRIDLE WAY
BRIDAL CT
A5149
A5102
A555
B5095
B5094
4
3
2
1
85
84
83
82
87
88
89
1 RUSHSIDE RD
2 FULBROOK DR
3 NEWBURY CL
4 RUSHTON RD
NORWOOD AVE 1
KENWOOD AVE 2
BURFORD AVE 3
CARLTON AVE 4
1 BRIXHAM WLK
2 AXMINSTER WLK
3 EXETER WLK

61

36

35

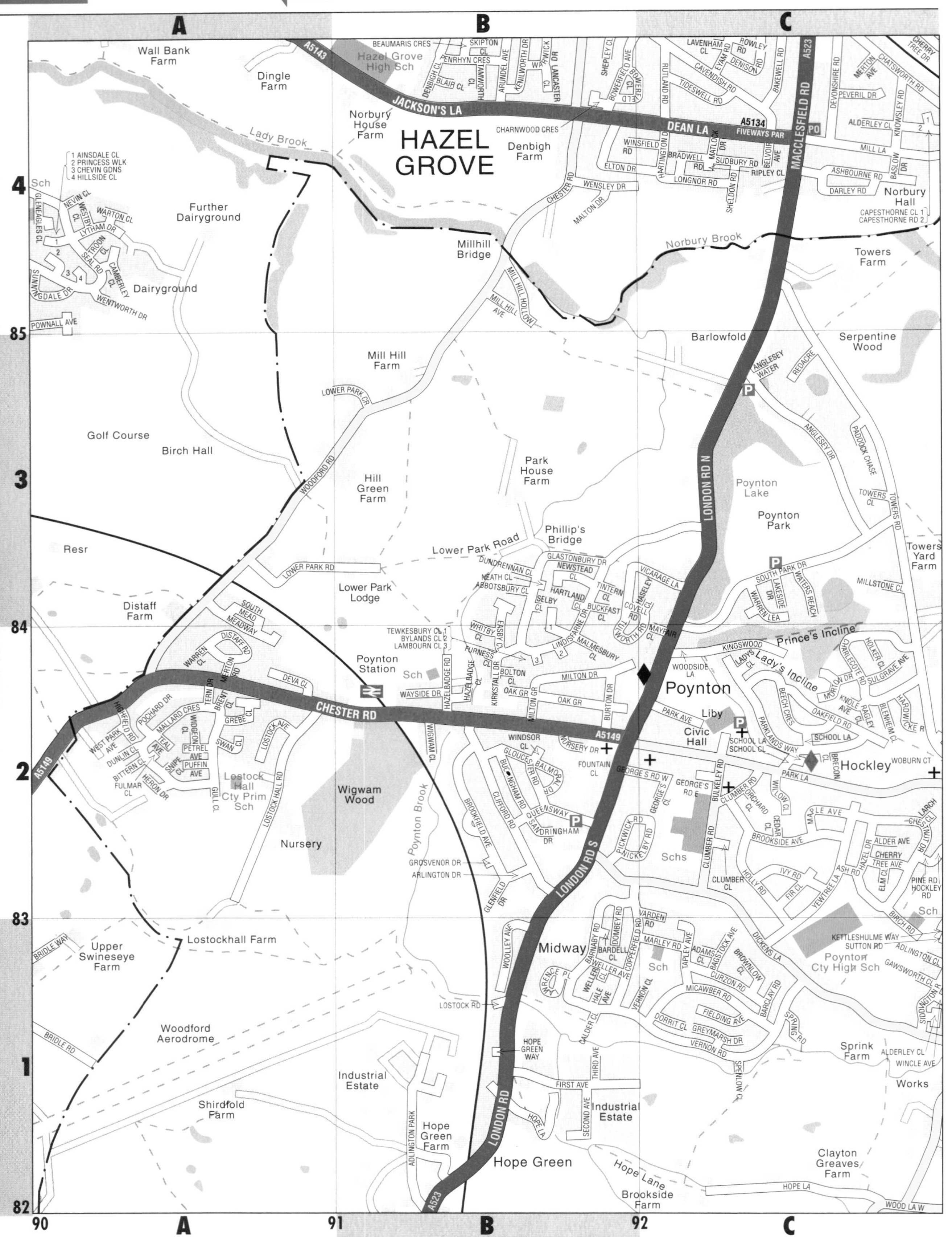

A
B
C
Wall Bank Farm
Dingle Farm
Hazel Grove High Sch
BEAUMARIS CRES
SKIPTON CL
PENRHYN CRES
BLAIR CL
DENBIGH CL
TAMWORTH CL
ARUNDEL AVE
KENILWORTH DR
WARWICK DR
LANCASTER CL
SHEPLEY CL
BOWERFIELD AVE
LAVENHAM CL
ROWLEY RD
EYAM RD
DENISON RD
RUTLAND RD
CAVENDISH RD
TIDESWELL RD
BAKEWELL RD
A5143
A523
JACKSON'S LA
DEAN LA
A5134
FIVEWAYS PAR
PO
MACCLESFIELD RD
DEVONSHIRE RD
MERTON AVE
CHATSWORTH RD
CHERRY TREE DR
PEVERIL DR
KNOWSLEY RD
ALDERLEY CL
MILL LA
ASHBOURNE RD
BASLOW DR
DARLEY RD
Norbury Hall
CAPESTHORNE CL 1
CAPESTHORNE RD 2
Norbury House Farm
Lady Brook
HAZEL GROVE
CHARNWOOD CRES
Denbigh Farm
WINSFIELD RD
HARTINGTON D
BRADWELL RD
MATLOCK DR
SUDBURY RD
BELVOIR AVE
RIPLEY CL
ELTON DR
LONGNOR RD
SHELDON RD
WENSLEY DR
CHESTER RD
MALTON DR
1 AINSDALE CL
2 PRINCESS WLK
3 CHEVIN GDNS
4 HILLSIDE CL
Sch
GLENEAGLES CL
NEVIN CL
WESTBY CL
WARTON CL
LYTHAM DR
TROON CL
SEAL RD
CAMBERLEY CL
SUNNINGDALE DR
WENTWORTH DR
POWNALL AVE
Further Dairyground
Dairyground
Millhill Bridge
Norbury Brook
Towers Farm
MILL HILL HOLLOW
MILL HILL AVE
Barlowfold
Serpentine Wood
Mill Hill Farm
ANGLESEY WATER
REDACRE
P
LOWER PARK CR
Golf Course
Birch Hall
WOODFORD RD
Hill Green Farm
Park House Farm
LONDON RD N
Poynton Lake
ANGLESEY DR
PADDOCK CHASE
TOWERS CL
TOWERS RD
Poynton Park
Resr
Lower Park Road
Phillip's Bridge
LOWER PARK RD
Lower Park Lodge
GLASTONBURY DR
DUNDRENNAN CL
NEWSTEAD CL
NEATH CL
ABBOTSBURY CL
SELBY CL
HARTLAND CL
TINTERN CL
BUCKFAST CL
COVELL RD
HASELEY CL
VICARAGE LA
SOUTH PARK DR
LAKESIDE DR
WARREN LEA
WATERS REACH
Towers Yard Farm
MILLSTONE CL
Distaff Farm
SOUTH MEAD
MEADWAY
DISTAFF RD
WARREN CL
MERTON RD
TEWKESBURY CL 1
BYLANDS CL 2
LAMBOURN CL 3
WHITBY CL
EASBY CL
FURNESS CL
LINDISFARNE DR
MALMESBURY CL
TUTWORTH RD
MAYFAIR CL
KINGSWOOD
Prince's Incline
Lady's Incline
HOLKER CL
CHARLECOTE RD
SULGRAVE AVE
Poynton Station
Sch
HAZELBADGE RD
HAZEL BADGE CL
KIRKSTALL DR
BOLTON CL
MILTON DR
OAK GR
MILTON GR
BURTON DR
WOODSIDE LA
Poynton
DEVA CL
WAYSIDE DR
CHESTER RD
TERN DR
BRENT CL
GREBE CL
POCHARD DR
MALLARD CRES
WIDGEON CL
HIGHFIELD RD
WEST PARK AVE
DUNLIN CL
TEAL AVE
PETREL AVE
SWAN CL
LOSTOCK AVE
SNIPE CL
PUFFIN AVE
BITTERN CL
FULMAR CL
HERON DR
GULL CL
Lostock Hall Cty Prim Sch
LOSTOCK HALL RD
A5149
WIGWAM CL
WINDSOR CL
GLOUCESTER RD
BALMORAL DR
BUCKINGHAM RD
NURSERY DR
FOUNTAIN CL
GEORGE'S RD W
GEORGE'S RD E
GEORGE'S CL
PARK AVE
Liby
Civic Hall
SCHOOL LA
SCHOOL CL
PARKLANDS WAY
BEECH CRES
KNOLE AVE
RAGLEY CL
OAKFIELD RD
BLENHEIM CL
HARDWICKE RD
BRECON
Hockley
WOBURN CT
PARK LA
BULKELEY RD
CLUMBER RD
ORCHARD CL
WILLOW CL
CEDAR CL
MAPLE AVE
LARCH CL
CHESTNUT DR
BROOKSIDE AVE
ALDER AVE
CHERRY TREE AVE
HAZEL DR
Wigwam Wood
Nursery
Poynton Brook
BROOKFIELD RD
CLIFFORD RD
QUEENSWAY
SANDRINGHAM DR
PICKWICK RD
NICKLEBY RD
Schs
CLUMBER CL
HOLLY RD
IVY RD
FIR CL
YEWTREE LA
ASH RD
ELM CL
PINE RD
HOCKLEY RD
GROSVENOR DR
ARLINGTON DR
BROOKFIELD AVE
GLENFIELD DR
LONDON RD S
BIRCH RD
Sch
Upper Swineseye Farm
Lostockhall Farm
BRIDLE WAY
WOOLLEY AVE
Midway
BARNABY RD
DOMBEY RD
COPPERFIELD RD
VARDEN RD
BARDELL CL
MARLEY RD
TAPLEY AVE
ADAMS CL
BAGSTOCK AVE
BROWNLOW CL
DICKENS LA
KETTLESHULME WAY
SUTTON RD
ADLINGTON CL
Poynton Cty High Sch
GAWSWORTH CL
LAWRENCE PL
WELLER CL
WELLER AVE
HALE AVE
VERNON CL
CURZON RD
MICAWBER RD
BARCLAY RD
FIELDING AVE
DORRIT CL
GREYMARSH DR
VERNON RD
SPRING RD
CALDER CL
LOSTOCK RD
SIDDINGTON R
Woodford Aerodrome
BRIDLE RD
HOPE GREEN WAY
Sprink Farm
ALDERLEY CL
WINCLE AVE
Works
Industrial Estate
THIRD AVE
FIRST AVE
SPENLOW CL
Shirdfold Farm
ADLINGTON PARK
Hope Green Farm
LONDON RD
HOPE LA
SECOND AVE
Industrial Estate
Hope Green
Hope Lane
Clayton Greaves Farm
HOPE LA
Brookside Farm
WOOD LA W
A523
4
85
3
84
2
83
1
82
90
91
92

35

62

38

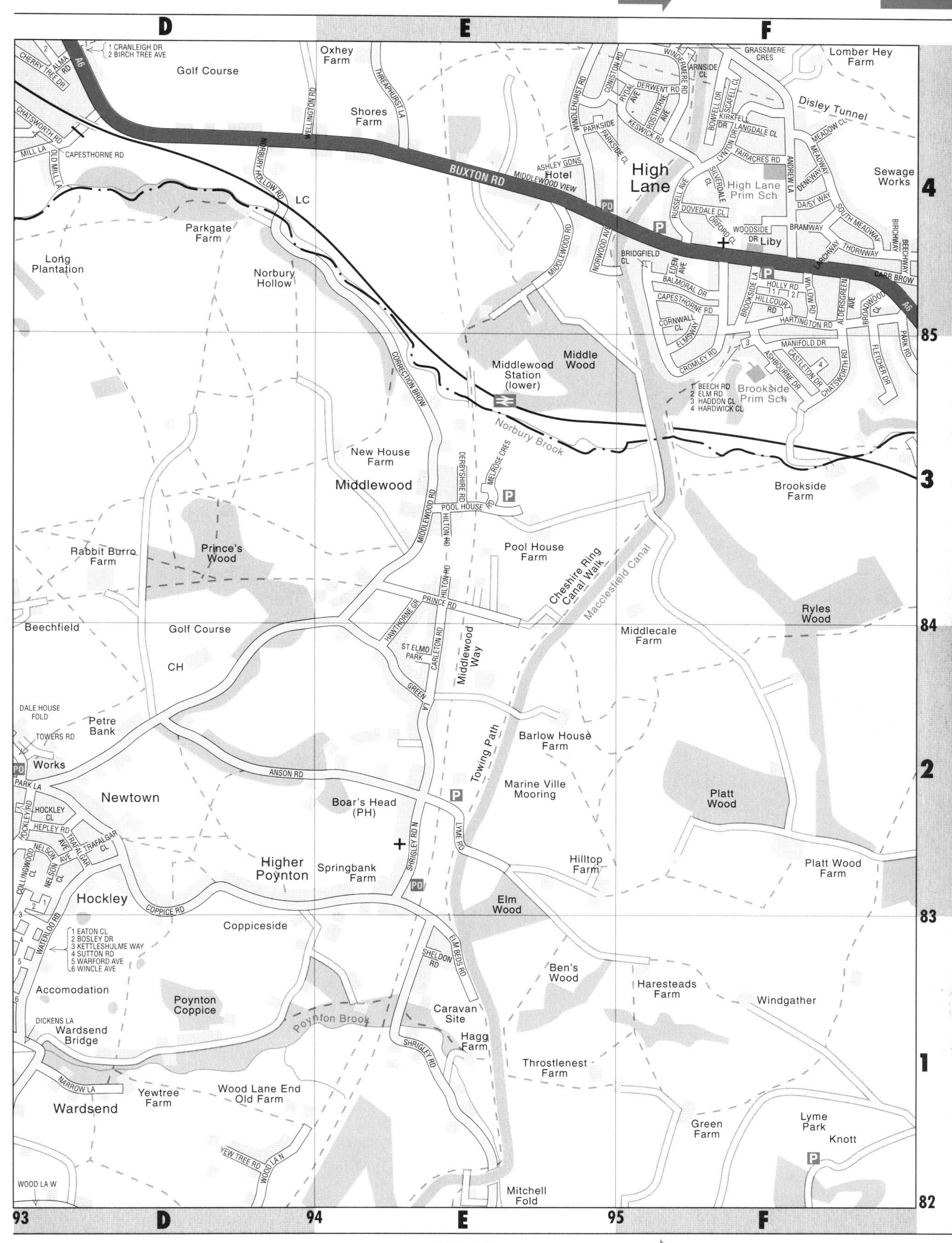
D
E
F
Golf Course
Oxhey Farm
Shores Farm
Lomber Hey Farm
Disley Tunnel
Sewage Works
BUXTON RD
A6
High Lane
High Lane Prim Sch
Hotel
Liby
LC
Parkgate Farm
Long Plantation
Norbury Hollow
Middlewood Station (lower)
Middle Wood
Brookside Prim Sch
Norbury Brook
New House Farm
Middlewood
Brookside Farm
Rabbit Burro Farm
Prince's Wood
Pool House Farm
Cheshire Ring Canal Walk
Macclesfield Canal
Ryles Wood
Beechfield
Golf Course
CH
Middlecale Farm
Middlewood Way
Petre Bank
Works
Barlow House Farm
Towing Path
Newtown
Marine Ville Mooring
Platt Wood
Boar's Head (PH)
Higher Poynton
Springbank Farm
Hilltop Farm
Platt Wood Farm
Hockley
Elm Wood
Coppiceside
Ben's Wood
Haresteads Farm
Windgather
Accomodation
Poynton Coppice
Caravan Site
Poynton Brook
Wardsend Bridge
Hagg Farm
Throstlenest Farm
Yewtree Farm
Wood Lane End Old Farm
Wardsend
Green Farm
Lyme Park
Knott
Mitchell Fold
1 CRANLEIGH DR
2 BIRCH TREE AVE
1 BEECH RD
2 ELM RD
3 HADDON CL
4 HARDWICK CL
1 EATON CL
2 BOSLEY DR
3 KETTLESHULME WAY
4 SUTTON RD
5 WARFORD AVE
6 WINCLE AVE
4
85
3
84
2
83
1
82
93
94
95

63

38

37

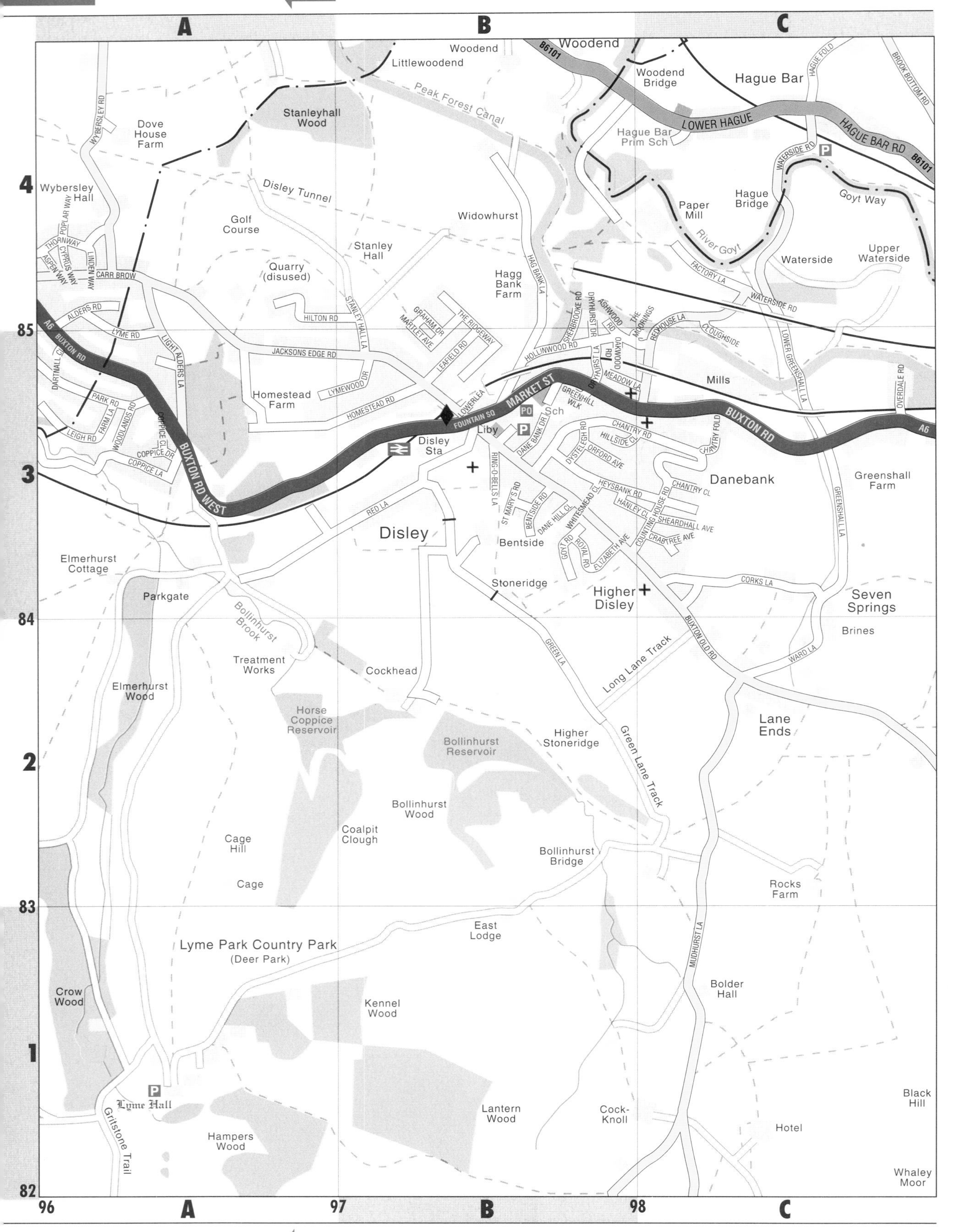
A
B
C
Woodend
Littlewoodend
Woodend Bridge
Hague Bar
Peak Forest Canal
Stanleyhall Wood
Dove House Farm
LOWER HAGUE
HAGUE BAR RD
B6101
Hague Bar Prim Sch
Wybersley Hall
Disley Tunnel
Paper Mill
Hague Bridge
Goyt Way
Golf Course
Widowhurst
River Goyt
Stanley Hall
Waterside
Upper Waterside
Quarry (disused)
Hagg Bank Farm
CARR BROW
HILTON RD
JACKSONS EDGE RD
WATERSIDE RD
FACTORY LA
Mills
Homestead Farm
MARKET ST
FOUNTAIN SQ
BUXTON RD
A6
Disley Sta
Liby
Sch
BUXTON RD WEST
Danebank
Greenshall Farm
RED LA
Disley
Bentside
Elmerhurst Cottage
Stoneridge
Higher Disley
Parkgate
Seven Springs
CORKS LA
Brines
Bollinhurst Brook
Treatment Works
Cockhead
Long Lane Track
Elmerhurst Wood
Horse Coppice Reservoir
Bollinhurst Reservoir
Higher Stoneridge
Lane Ends
Green Lane Track
Bollinhurst Wood
Cage Hill
Coalpit Clough
Bollinhurst Bridge
Cage
Rocks Farm
East Lodge
Lyme Park Country Park
(Deer Park)
Crow Wood
Kennel Wood
Bolder Hall
Lyme Hall
Lantern Wood
Cock-Knoll
Hotel
Black Hill
Hampers Wood
Gritstone Trail
Whaley Moor
MUDHURST LA
GREEN LA
BUXTON OLD RD
4
85
3
84
2
83
1
82
96
97
98

37

64

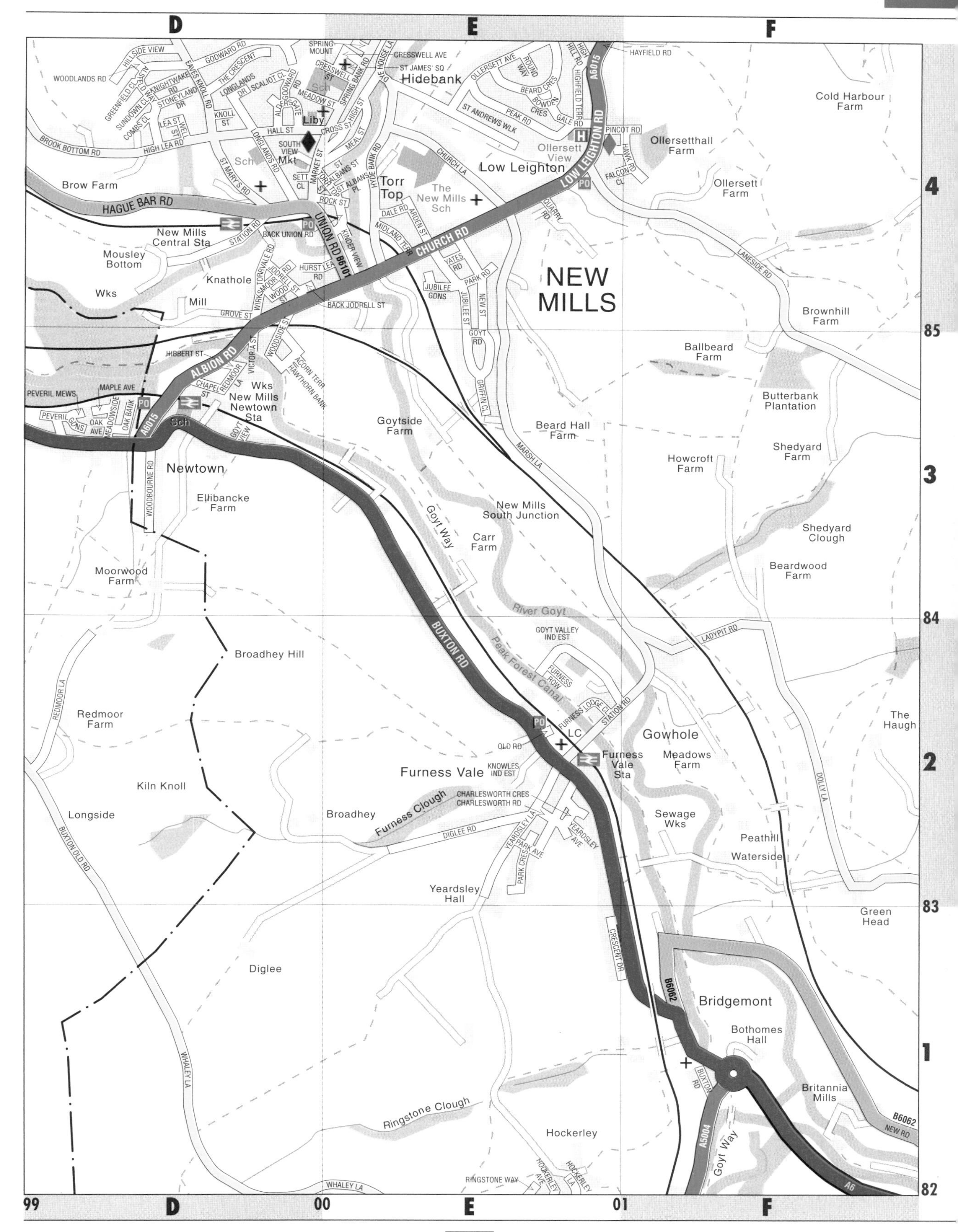
D
E
F
Hidebank
Cold Harbour Farm
Ollersetthall Farm
Ollersett Farm
Ollersett View
Low Leighton
Torr Top
The New Mills Sch
Brow Farm
HAGUE BAR RD
New Mills Central Sta
Mousley Bottom
Knathole
Wks
Mill
NEW MILLS
Brownhill Farm
Ballbeard Farm
Butterbank Plantation
Beard Hall Farm
Howcroft Farm
Shedyard Farm
Shedyard Clough
Beardwood Farm
Goytside Farm
New Mills Newtown Sta
Newtown
Ellibancke Farm
New Mills South Junction
Carr Farm
Goyt Way
Moorwood Farm
River Goyt
Peak Forest Canal
Broadhey Hill
GOYT VALLEY IND EST
Redmoor Farm
Gowhole
The Haugh
Furness Vale Sta
Meadows Farm
Furness Vale
Kiln Knoll
Longside
Broadhey
Furness Clough
Sewage Wks
Peathill
Waterside
Yeardsley Hall
Green Head
Diglee
Bridgemont
Bothomes Hall
Britannia Mills
Ringstone Clough
Hockerley
CHURCH RD
UNION RD B6101
ALBION RD
LOW LEIGHTON RD
A6015
BUXTON RD
B6062
A5004
A6
NEW RD
99
00
01
4
85
3
84
2
83
1
82

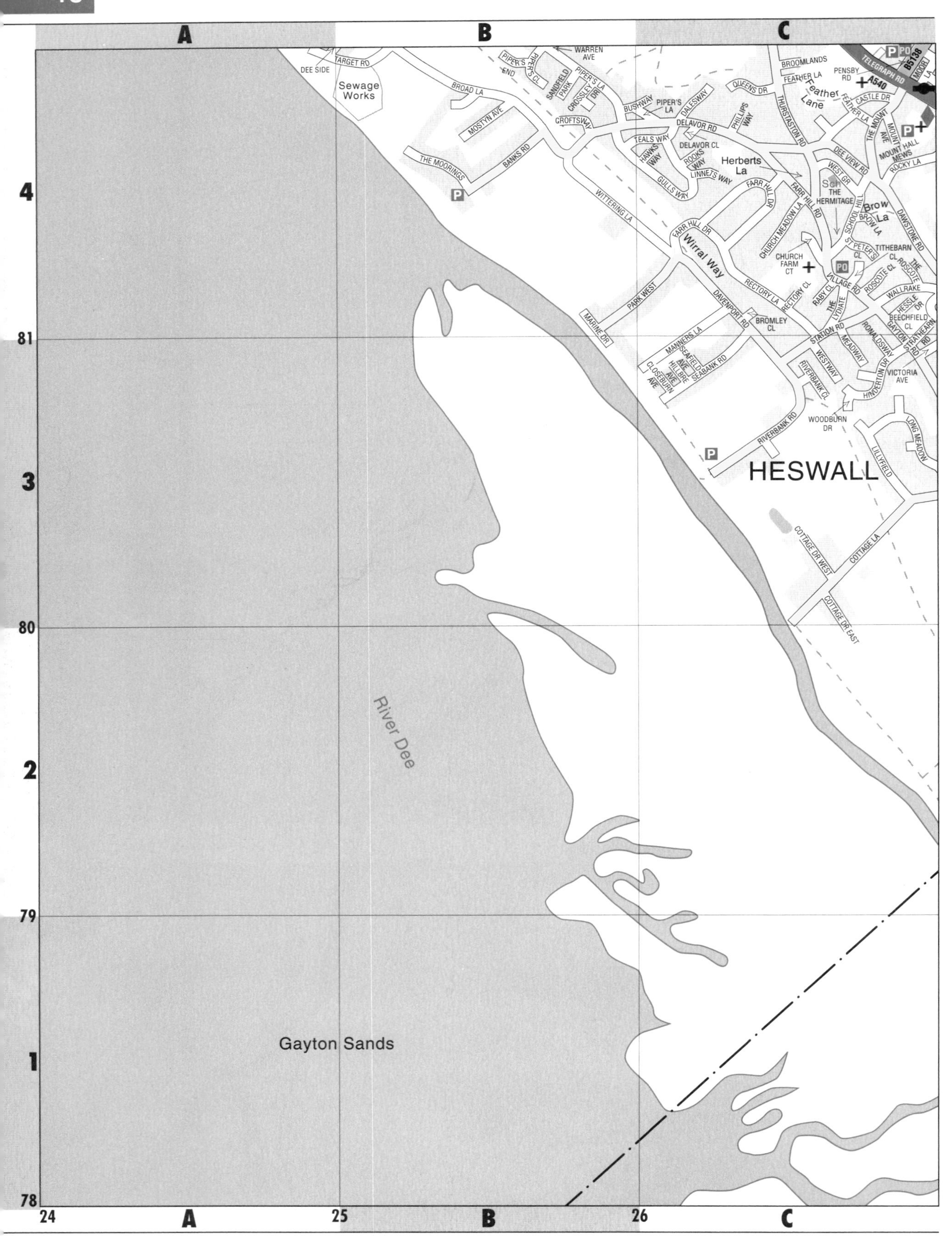
A
B
C
HESWALL
River Dee
Gayton Sands
Sewage Works
Wirral Way
Herberts La
Feather Lane
Brow La
TELEGRAPH RD
A540
B5138
4
3
2
1
81
80
79
78
24
25
26

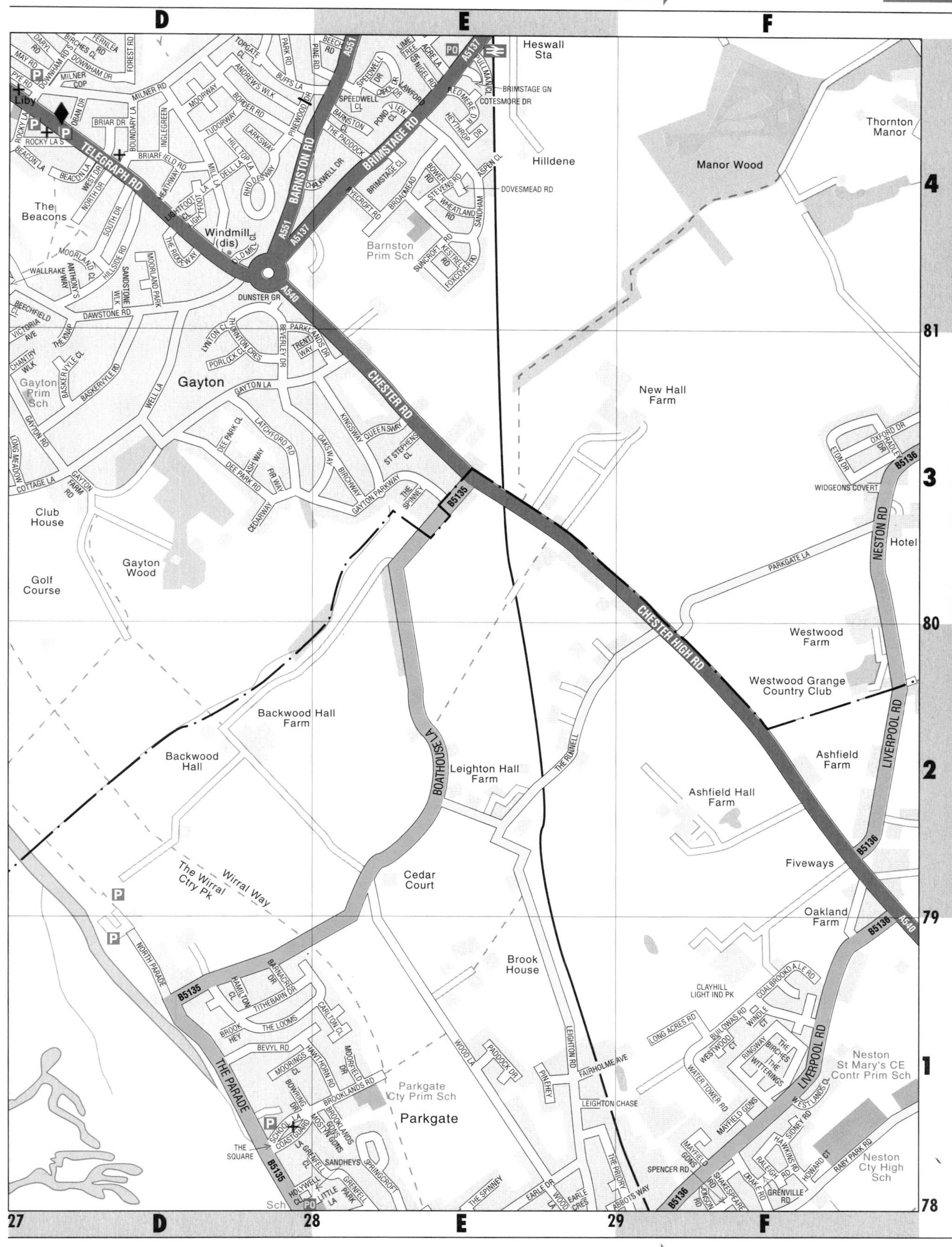

Heswall Sta

BRIMSTAGE GN
COTESMORE DR

Hilldene

Thornton Manor

Manor Wood

DOVESMEAD RD

4

The Beacons

Windmill (dis)

Barnston Prim Sch

81

New Hall Farm

Gayton Prim Sch

Gayton

WIDGEONS COVERT

Hotel

3

Club House

Gayton Wood

PARKGATE LA

Golf Course

Westwood Farm

80

Westwood Grange Country Club

Backwood Hall Farm

Leighton Hall Farm

Ashfield Farm

Backwood Hall

Ashfield Hall Farm

2

The Wirral Ctry Pk

Wirral Way

Cedar Court

Fiveways

Oakland Farm

79

Brook House

CLAYHILL LIGHT IND PK

Parkgate Cty Prim Sch

Parkgate

Neston St Mary's CE Contr Prim Sch

1

THE SQUARE

Neston Cty High Sch

SPENCER RD

78

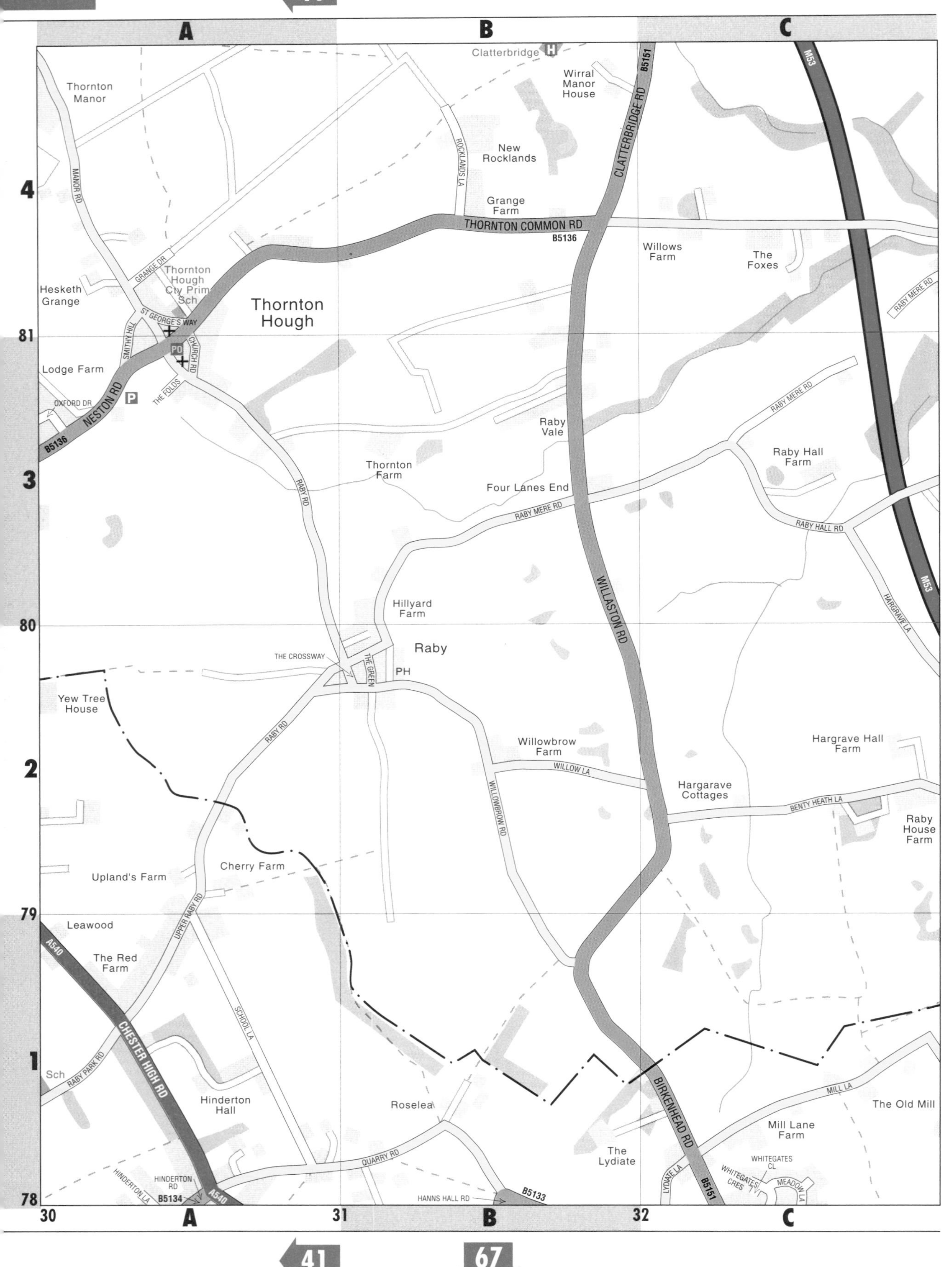

A   B   C

4

Thornton Manor

Clatterbridge H

Wirral Manor House

New Rocklands

ROCKLANDS LA

CLATTERBRIDGE RD

B5151

M53

Grange Farm

THORNTON COMMON RD

B5136

Willows Farm

The Foxes

RABY MERE RD

MANOR RD

GRANGE DR

Thornton Hough Cty Prim Sch

ST GEORGE'S WAY

Thornton Hough

81

SMITH HILL

PO

CHURCH RD

Raby Vale

RABY MERE RD

Raby Hall Farm

RABY MERE RD

Hesketh Grange

Lodge Farm

NESTON RD

OXFORD DR

P

THE FOLDS

Thornton Farm

Four Lanes End

RABY MERE RD

Raby Hall Farm

RABY HALL RD

3

B5136

RABY RD

HARGRAVE LA

M53

80

THE CROSSWAY

Hillyard Farm

THE GREEN

Raby

PH

Yew Tree House

RABY RD

Willowbrow Farm

WILLOW LA

Hargrave Hall Farm

2

WILLOWBROW RD

Hargarave Cottages

BENTY HEATH LA

Raby House Farm

Upland's Farm

Cherry Farm

UPPER RABY RD

79

Leawood

A540

The Red Farm

SCHOOL LA

CHESTER HIGH RD

BIRKENHEAD RD

MILL LA

The Old Mill

1

Sch

RABY PARK RD

Hinderton Hall

Roselea

The Lydiate

Mill Lane Farm

WHITEGATES CL

WHITEGATES CRES

MEADOW LA

LYDIATE LA

B5151

78

HINDERTON LA

HINDERTON RD

B5134

A540

QUARRY RD

HANNS HALL RD

B5133

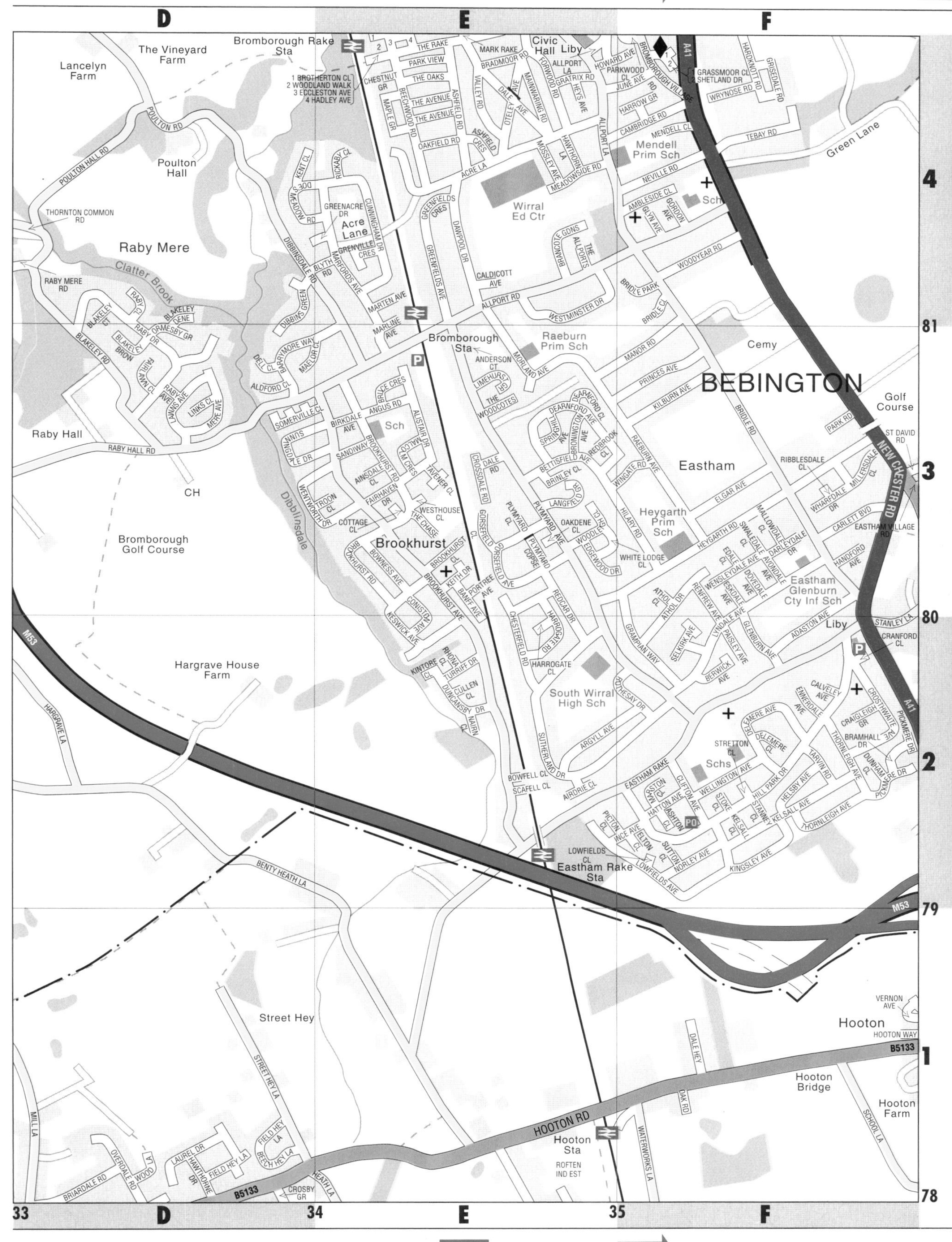
D
E
F
Lancelyn Farm
The Vineyard Farm
Bromborough Rake Sta
1 BROTHERTON CL
2 WOODLAND WALK
3 ECCLESTON AVE
4 HADLEY AVE
Civic Hall
Liby
THE RAKE
MARK RAKE
PARK VIEW
THE OAKS
THE AVENUE
BRADMOOR RD
CHESTNUT GR
MAPLE GR
BEECHWOOD RD
ASHFIELD RD
VALLEY RD
DALE AVE
OTELEY AVE
MAINWARING RD
FORWOOD RD
ALLPORT LA
GRATRIX RD
HEYS AVE
HOWARD AVE
PARKWOOD CL
JUNE AVE
BROMBOROUGH VILLAGE RD
A41
GRASSMOOR CL
SHETLAND DR
WRYNOSE RD
HARDKNOTT RD
GRISEDALE RD
TEBAY RD
Green Lane
HARROW GR
CAMBRIDGE RD
MENDELL CL
Mendell Prim Sch
NEVILLE RD
POULTON RD
POULTON HALL RD
Poulton Hall
THORNTON COMMON RD
Raby Mere
Clatter Brook
RABY MERE RD
KENT CL
RICKABY CL
MEADOW RD
GREENACRE DR
Acre Lane
CUNNINGHAM DR
GRENVILLE CRES
OAKFIELD RD
ASHFIELD CRES
ACRE LA
MOSSLEY AVE
HAWTHORN LA
ALLPORT LA
MEADOWSIDE RD
Wirral Ed Ctr
GREENFIELDS CRES
DAWPOOL DR
GREENFIELDS AVE
AMBLESIDE CL
GLYN AVE
GORDON AVE
Sch
BRANCOTE GDNS
THE ALLPORTS
WOODYEAR RD
DIBBINSDALE RD
BLYTH RD
MARFORDS AVE
MARTEN AVE
CALDICOTT AVE
ALLPORT RD
WESTMINSTER DR
BRIDLE PARK
BRIDLE CL
BLAKELEY CL
RABY CL
BLAKELEY DENE
RABY DR
ORMESBY GR
BLAKELEY BROW
BLAKELEY RD
FAIRLAWN CL
RABY AVE
LAWNS AVE
LINKS CL
MERE AVE
DIBBINS GREEN
BARRYMORE WAY
MAELOR CL
DELL CL
ALDFORD CL
MARLINE AVE
Bromborough Sta
P
ANDERSON CT
LIMEHURST GR
THE WOODCOTES
MORLAND AVE
Raeburn Prim Sch
MANOR RD
PRINCES AVE
KILBURN AVE
Cemy
BEBINGTON
Golf Course
PARK RD
ST DAVID RD
NEW CHESTER RD
Raby Hall
RABY HALL RD
SOMERVILLE CL
BRUCE CRES
ANGUS RD
BIRKDALE AVE
Sch
ALISTAIR DR
SANDIWAY
BROOKHURST RD
MALCOLM CRES
TAVENER CL
AINSDALE CL
FAIRHAVEN DR
TROON CL
WENTWORTH DR
COTTAGE CL
WESTHOUSE CL
THE CHASE
DALE RD
CROSSDALE RD
DEARNFORD AVE
DEARNFORD CL
SPRINGHILL AVE
BRONINGTON AVE
REDBROOK CL
BETTISFIELD AVE
BRINLEY CL
LANGFIELD GR
RAEBURN AVE
WINGATE RD
HILARY RD
Eastham
RIBBLESDALE CL
MILLERSDALE CL
WHARFDALE DR
CARLETT BVD
EASTHAM VILLAGE RD
ELGAR AVE
Heygarth Prim Sch
HEYGARTH RD
MALLOWDALE CL
SWALEDALE CL
AVONDALE AVE
DARLEYDALE DR
HANDFORD AVE
CH
Dibbinsdale
Bromborough Golf Course
Brookhurst
BROOKHURST CL
BROOKHURST AVE
KEITH DR
BOWNESS AVE
PORTREE AVE
BANFF AVE
GORSEFIELD CL
GORSEFIELD AVE
PLYMYARD CL
PLYMYARD AVE
PLYMYARD COPSE
OAKDENE CL
WOODLEE RD
EDGEWOOD DR
WHITE LODGE CL
EDALE CL
WENSLEYDALE AVE
ESKDALE AVE
DOVEDALE AVE
Eastham Glenburn Cty Inf Sch
CONISTON AVE
KESWICK AVE
REDCAR RD
HARROGATE RD
CHESTERFIELD RD
HARROGATE CL
ATHOL CL
ATHOL DR
RENFREW AVE
LYNDALE AVE
GLENBURN AVE
ADASTON AVE
Liby
STANLEY LA
CRANFORD CL
M53
Hargrave House Farm
HARGRAVE LA
KINTORE CL
RHONA CL
TURRIFF DR
CULLEN CL
DUNCANSBY DR
NAIRN CL
GRAMPIAN WAY
SELKIRK AVE
PAISLEY AVE
BERWICK AVE
South Wirral High Sch
ROTHESAY DR
CALVELEY AVE
EMBERDALE AVE
CROSTHWAITE AVE
CRAIGLEIGH GR
BRAMHALL DR
DELAMERE AVE
DELAMERE CL
STRETTON CL
Schs
THORNLEIGH AVE
TARVIN RD
DUNHAM CL
PICKMERE DR
ARGYLL AVE
SUTHERLAND DR
BOWFELL CL
SCAFELL CL
AIRDRIE CL
EASTHAM RAKE
CLIFTON AVE
WELLINGTON AVE
HILL PARK DR
HELSBY AVE
KELSALL AVE
HORNLEIGH AVE
HATTON AVE
STOKE CL
KELSALL CL
PICTON CL
INCE AVE
ELTON CL
SUTTON CL
NORLEY AVE
KINGSLEY AVE
LOWFIELDS CL
LOWFIELDS AVE
PO
Eastham Rake Sta
BENTY HEATH LA
VERNON AVE
Hooton
HOOTON WAY
B5133
Street Hey
DALE HEY
Hooton Bridge
Hooton Farm
SCHOOL LA
STREET HEY LA
MILL LA
OAK RD
HOOTON RD
Hooton Sta
ROFTEN IND EST
WATERWORKS LA
FIELD HEY LA
BEECH HEY LA
LAUREL DR
HAWTHORNE DR
FIELD HEY LA
OVERDALE RD
WOOD LA
BRIARDALE RD
HEATH LA
CROSBY GR
B5133
4
81
3
80
2
79
1
78
33
34
35
D
E
F

43

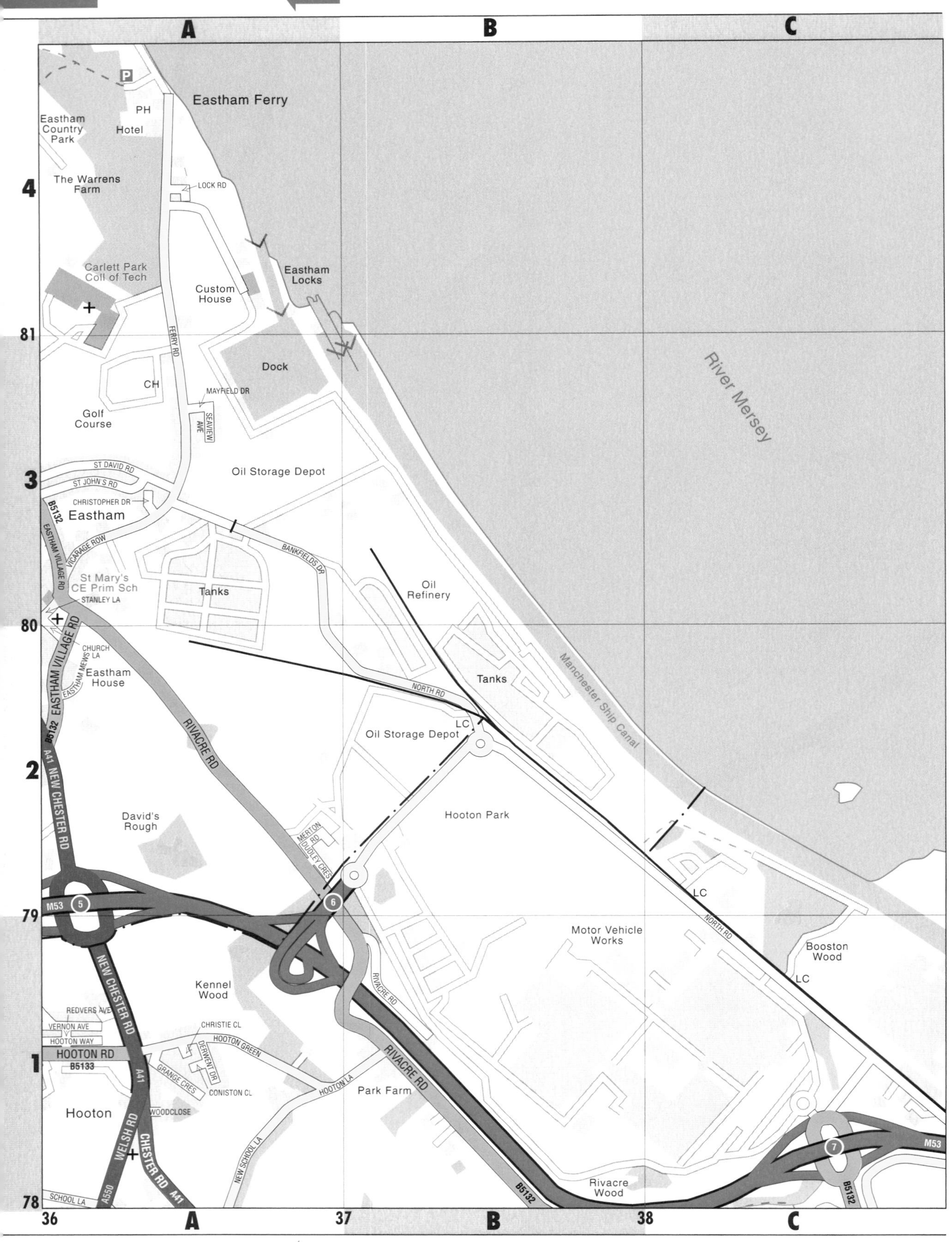

Eastham Ferry
Eastham Country Park
PH
Hotel
The Warrens Farm
LOCK RD
Carlett Park Coll of Tech
Custom House
Eastham Locks
FERRY RD
Dock
CH
MAYFIELD DR
Golf Course
SEAVIEW AVE
River Mersey
ST DAVID RD
ST JOHN'S RD
Oil Storage Depot
CHRISTOPHER DR
B5132
Eastham
EASTHAM VILLAGE RD
VICARAGE ROW
BANKFIELDS DR
St Mary's CE Prim Sch
Tanks
Oil Refinery
STANLEY LA
CHURCH LA
Eastham House
EASTHAM MEWS
NORTH RD
Tanks
Manchester Ship Canal
LC
Oil Storage Depot
RIVACRE RD
A41 NEW CHESTER RD
Hooton Park
David's Rough
MERTON RD
DUDLEY CRES
LC
M53
Motor Vehicle Works
Booston Wood
LC
Kennel Wood
REDVERS AVE
VERNON AVE
HOOTON WAY
CHRISTIE CL
HOOTON RD
B5133
HOOTON GREEN
DERWENT DR
GRANGE CRES
CONISTON CL
HOOTON LA
Park Farm
Hooton
WOODCLOSE
WELSH RD
CHESTER RD
NEW SCHOOL LA
A550
A41
SCHOOL LA
Rivacre Wood
B5132
M53

43
69

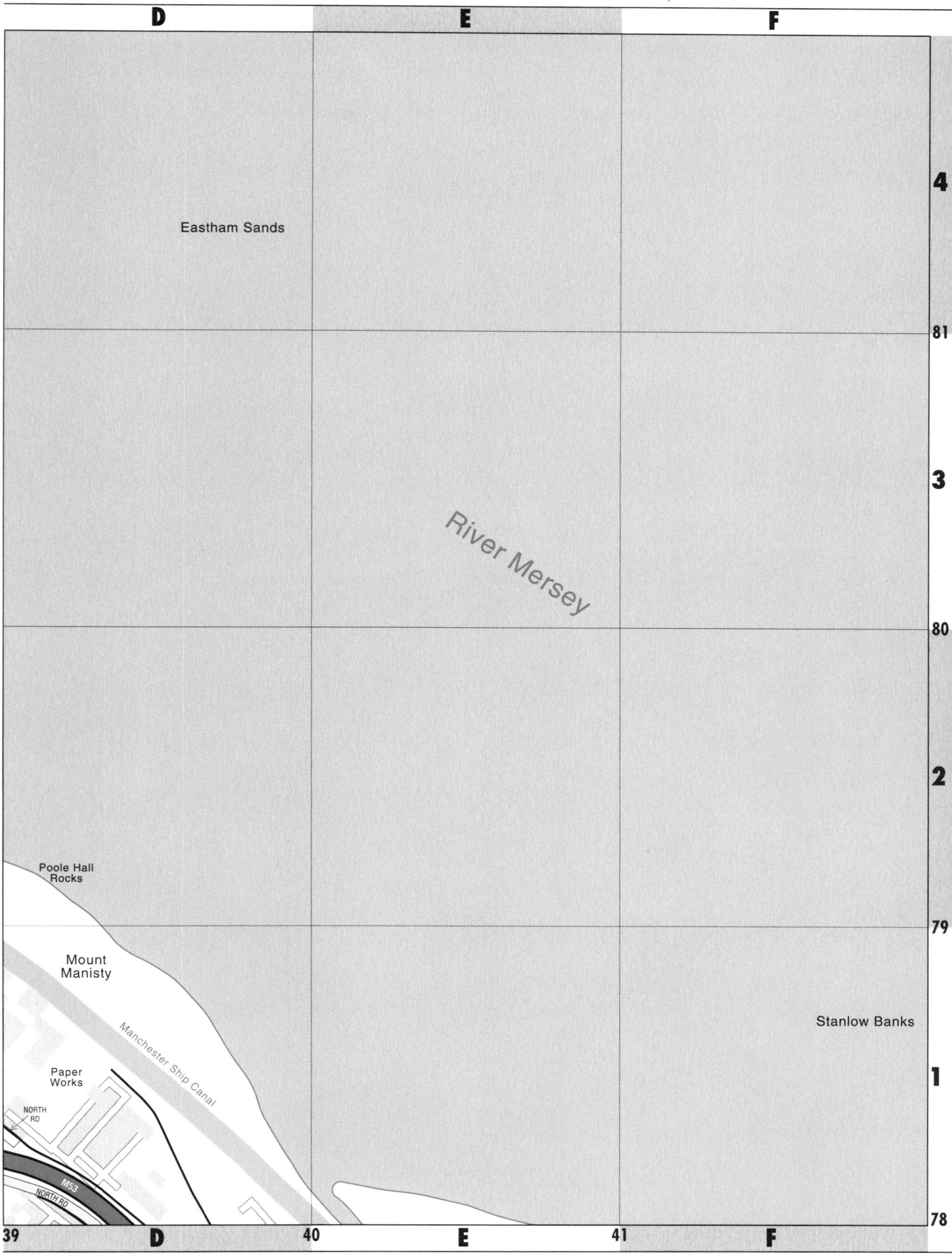

D **E** **F**

4

Eastham Sands

81

3

River Mersey

80

2

Poole Hall
Rocks

79

Mount
Manisty

Stanlow Banks

Manchester Ship Canal

Paper
Works

1

NORTH
RD

M53

NORTH RD

78

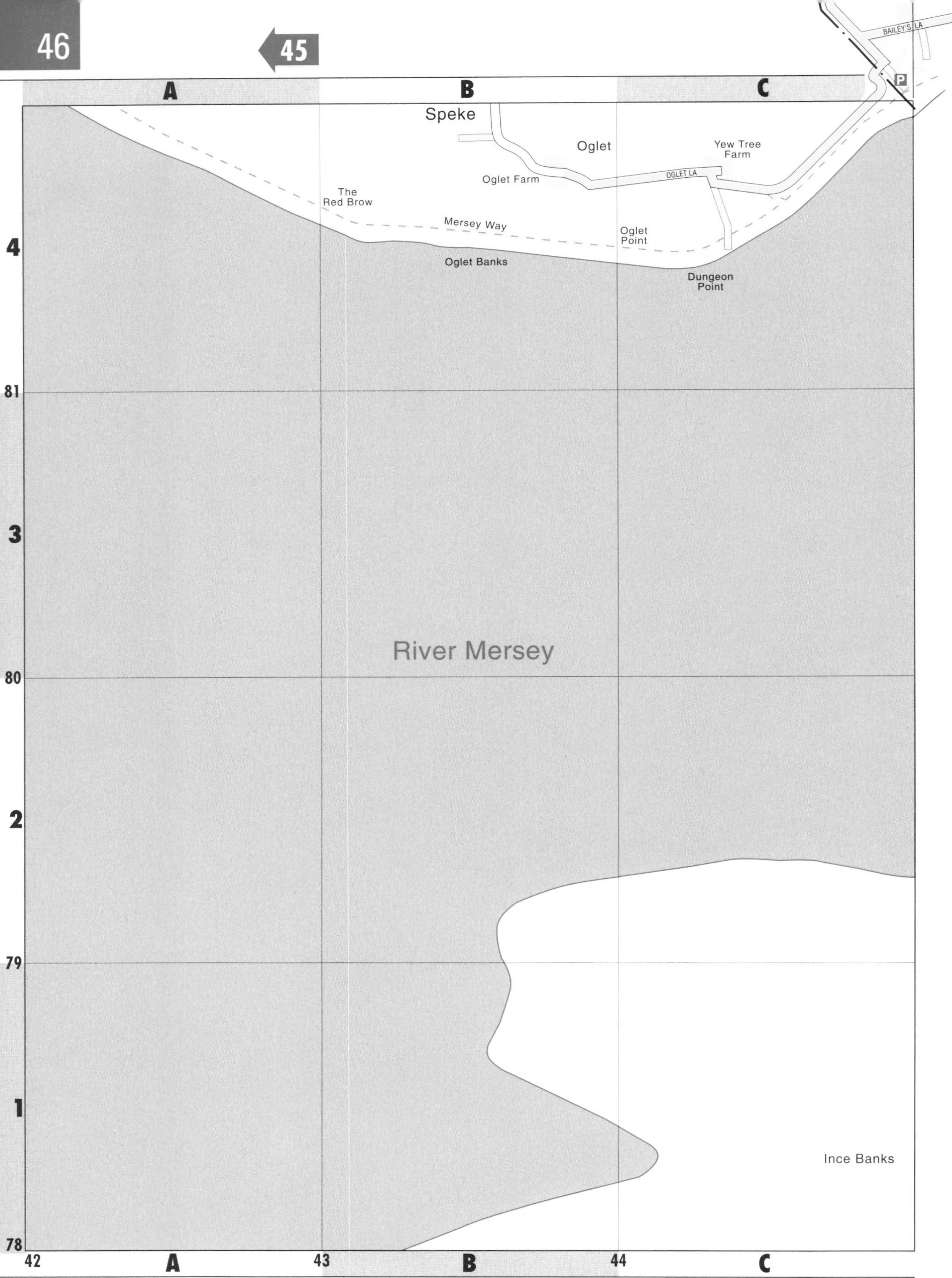

A B C

Speke

Oglet

Yew Tree
Farm

Oglet Farm   OGLET LA

The
Red Brow

Mersey Way

Oglet
Point

4

Oglet Banks

Dungeon
Point

BAILEY'S LA

P

81

3

River Mersey

80

2

79

1

Ince Banks

78

42   A   43   B   44   C

Icehouse
Plantation

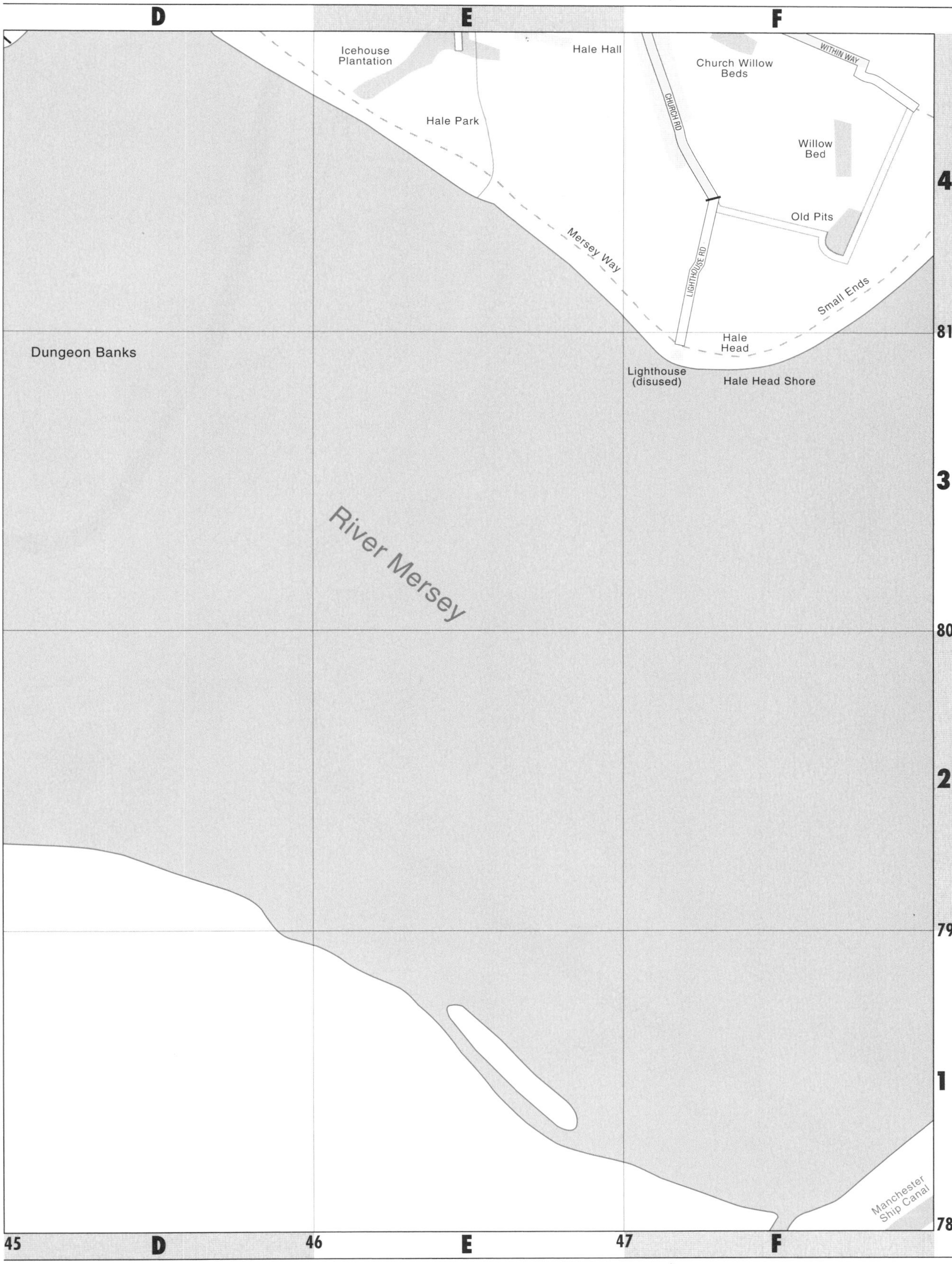

Hale Hall

Church Willow
Beds

WITHIN WAY

CHURCH RD

Hale Park

Willow
Bed

4

Mersey Way

LIGHTHOUSE RD

Old Pits

Small Ends

81

Dungeon Banks

Hale
Head

Lighthouse
(disused)

Hale Head Shore

3

River Mersey

80

2

79

1

Manchester
Ship Canal

78

A   B   C

4

81

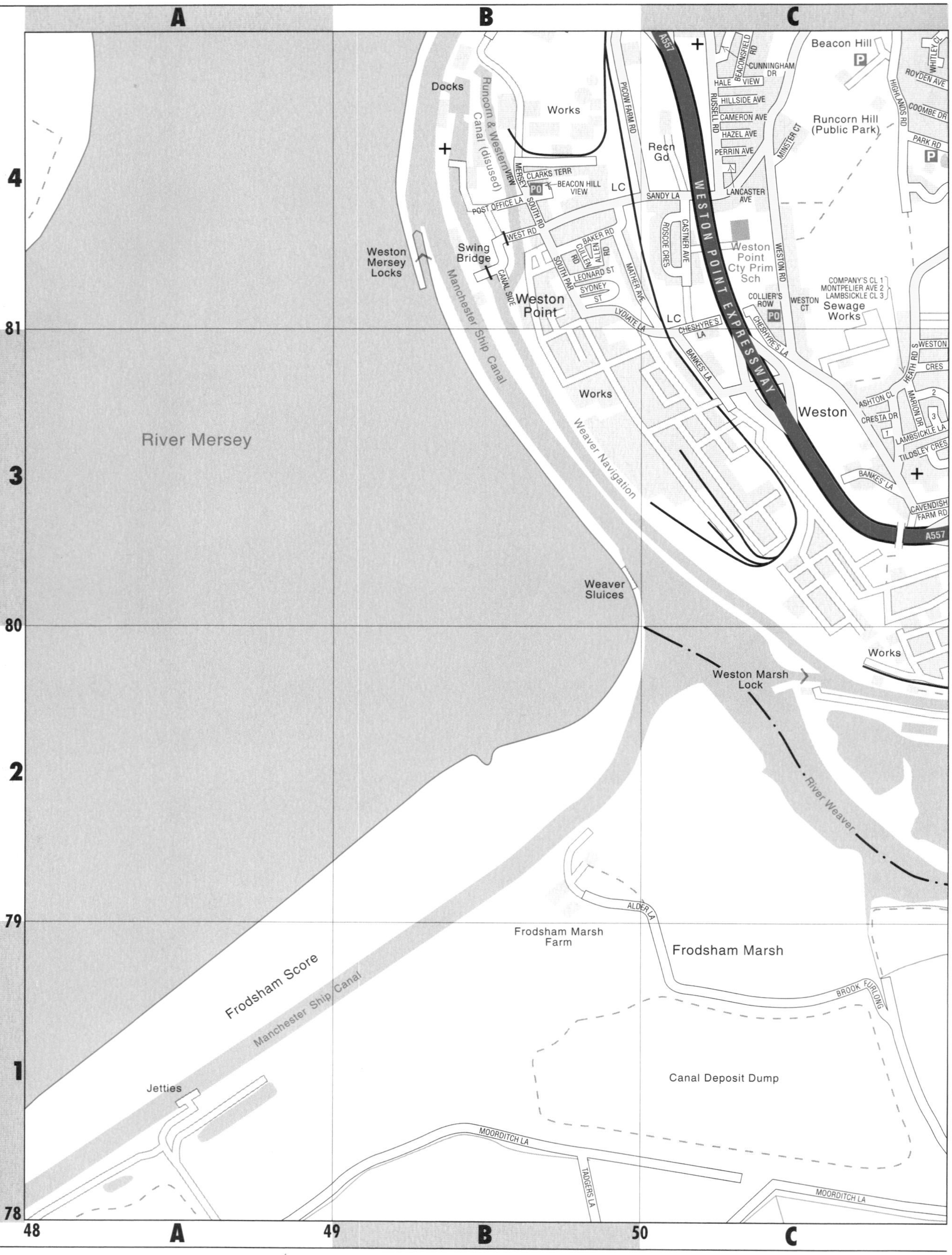

River Mersey

3

80

2

79

1

78

+

Docks

Works

Runcorn & Western
Canal (disused)

PICOW FARM RD

BEACONSFIELD
RD
CUNNINGHAM
DR
Beacon Hill
P
WHITLEY CT

HALE VIEW

HILLSIDE AVE

A557

CAMERON AVE

Runcorn Hill
(Public Park)

ROYDEN AVE

COOMBE DR

HIGHLANDS RD

PARK RD

P

RUSSELL RD

HAZEL AVE

MINSTER CT

PERRIN AVE

Recn
Gd

+

Weston Mersey
Locks

Manchester Ship Canal

MERSEY RD
SOUTH RD

CLARKS TERR

POST OFFICE LA

PO

BEACON HILL
VIEW

LC

SANDY LA

LANCASTER
AVE

Swing
Bridge

WEST RD

CASTNER AVE

ROSCOE CRES

Weston
Point Cty Prim
Sch

WESTON RD

COMPANY'S CL 1
MONTPELIER AVE 2
LAMBSICKLE CL 3

CANAL SIDE

BAKER RD

Weston
Point

SOUTH PM
CULLEN
RD
LEONARD ST

SYDNEY
ST

MATHER AVE

LYDIATE LA

LC

CHESHYRE'S
LA

COLLIER'S
ROW

PO

WESTON
CT

WESTON POINT EXPRESSWAY

Sewage
Works

HEATH RD S
WESTON
CRES

Works

CHESHYRE'S LA

BANKES LA

Weston

ASHTON CL

CRESTA DR

MARION DR

LAMBSICKLE LA

TILDSLEY CRES

2

3

1

+

Weaver
Sluices

Weaver Navigation

BANKES' LA

CAVENDISH
FARM RD

A557

Weston Marsh
Lock

Works

River Weaver

Frodsham Score

Manchester Ship Canal

Frodsham Marsh
Farm

ALDER LA

Frodsham Marsh

BROOK FURLONG

Jetties

Canal Deposit Dump

MOORDITCH LA

TADGERS LA

MOORDITCH LA

23

50

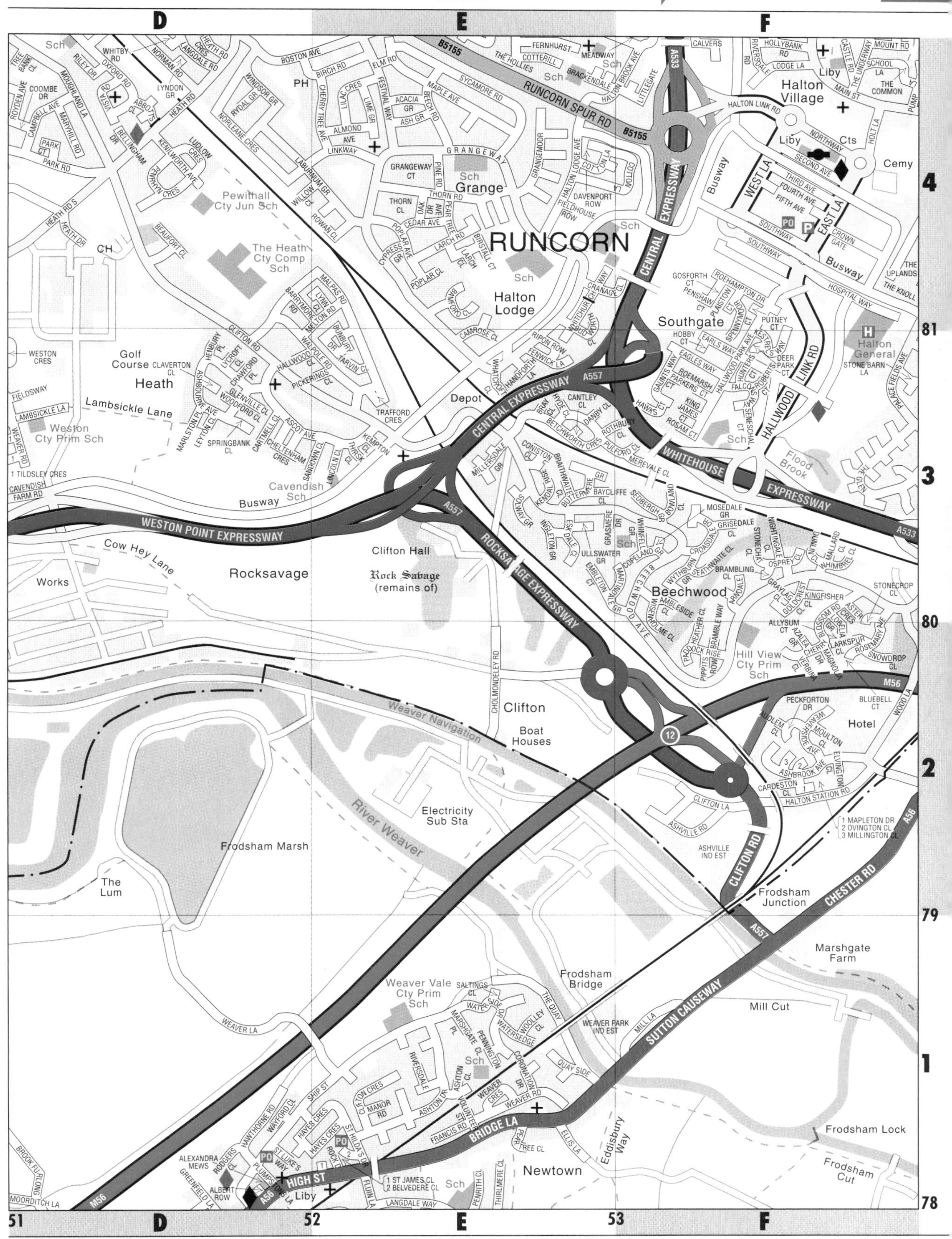

D
E
F
RUNCORN
Halton Village
Halton Lodge
Grange
Southgate
Heath
Golf Course
Pewithall Cty Jun Sch
The Heath Cty Comp Sch
Weston Cty Prim Sch
Cavendish Sch
Lambsickle Lane
Cow Hey Lane
Works
Rocksavage
Clifton Hall
Rock Savage (remains of)
Depot
Beechwood
Hill View Cty Prim Sch
Halton General
Clifton
Boat Houses
Hotel
Weaver Navigation
River Weaver
Electricity Sub Sta
Frodsham Marsh
The Lum
Frodsham Junction
Marshgate Farm
Frodsham Bridge
Weaver Vale Cty Prim Sch
Mill Cut
Frodsham Lock
Frodsham Cut
Newtown
Eddisbury Way
WESTON POINT EXPRESSWAY
CENTRAL EXPRESSWAY
ROCKSAVAGE EXPRESSWAY
WHITEHOUSE EXPRESSWAY
RUNCORN SPUR RD
HALLWOOD LINK RD
CLIFTON RD
CHESTER RD
SUTTON CAUSEWAY
BRIDGE LA
HIGH ST
Busway
Flood Brook
Cemy
Liby
Cts
A533
A557
A56
M56
B5155
4
81
3
80
2
79
1
78
51
52
53

49
24

A B C

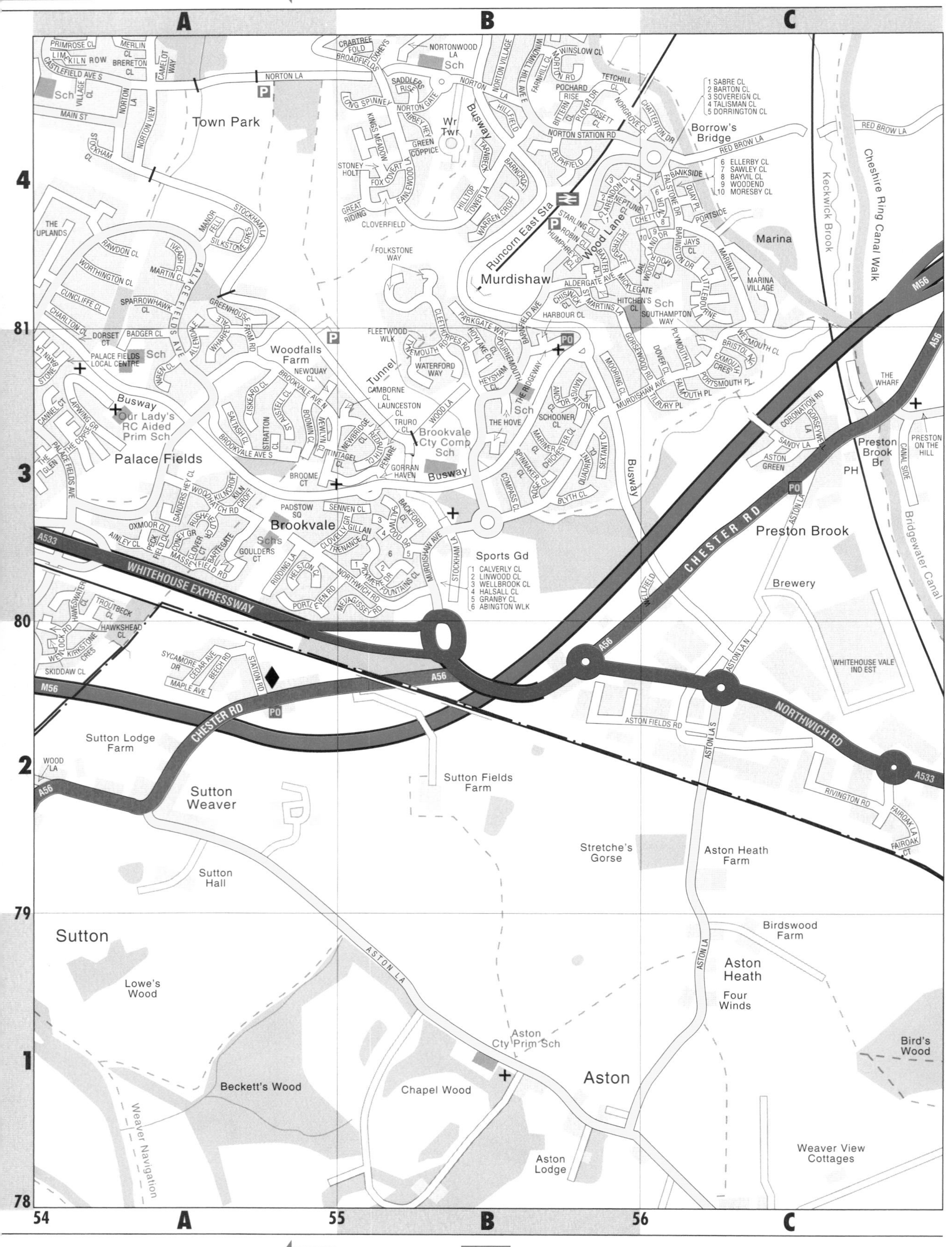
Town Park
Borrow's Bridge
Marina
Cheshire Ring Canal Walk
Keckwick Brook
Murdishaw
Runcorn East Sta
Wood Lane
Busway
Woodfalls Farm
Tunnel
Brookvale Cty Comp Sch
Palace Fields
Our Lady's RC Aided Prim Sch
Brookvale
Sports Gd
Preston Brook
Preston Brook Br
Brewery
Bridgewater Canal
CHESTER RD
WHITEHOUSE EXPRESSWAY
NORTHWICH RD
WHITEHOUSE VALE IND EST
Sutton Lodge Farm
Sutton Weaver
Sutton Fields Farm
Stretche's Gorse
Aston Heath Farm
Sutton Hall
Sutton
Lowe's Wood
Birdswood Farm
Aston Heath
Four Winds
Aston Cty Prim Sch
Bird's Wood
Beckett's Wood
Chapel Wood
Aston
Weaver Navigation
Aston Lodge
Weaver View Cottages
ASTON LA
1 SABRE CL
2 BARTON CL
3 SOVEREIGN CL
4 TALISMAN CL
5 DORRINGTON CL
6 ELLERBY CL
7 SAWLEY CL
8 BAYVIL CL
9 WOODEND
10 MORESBY CL
1 CALVERLY CL
2 LINWOOD CL
3 WELLBROOK CL
4 HALSALL CL
5 GRANBY CL
6 ABINGTON WLK
4
81
3
80
2
79
1
78
54
55
56

A B C

49
75

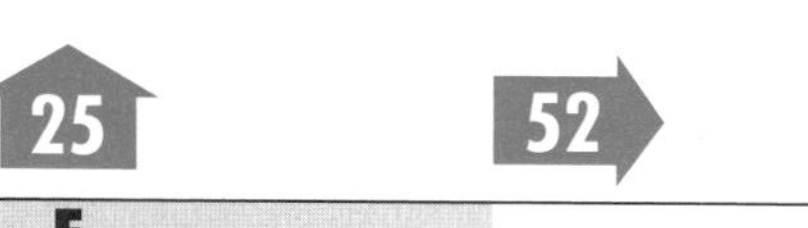

25
52

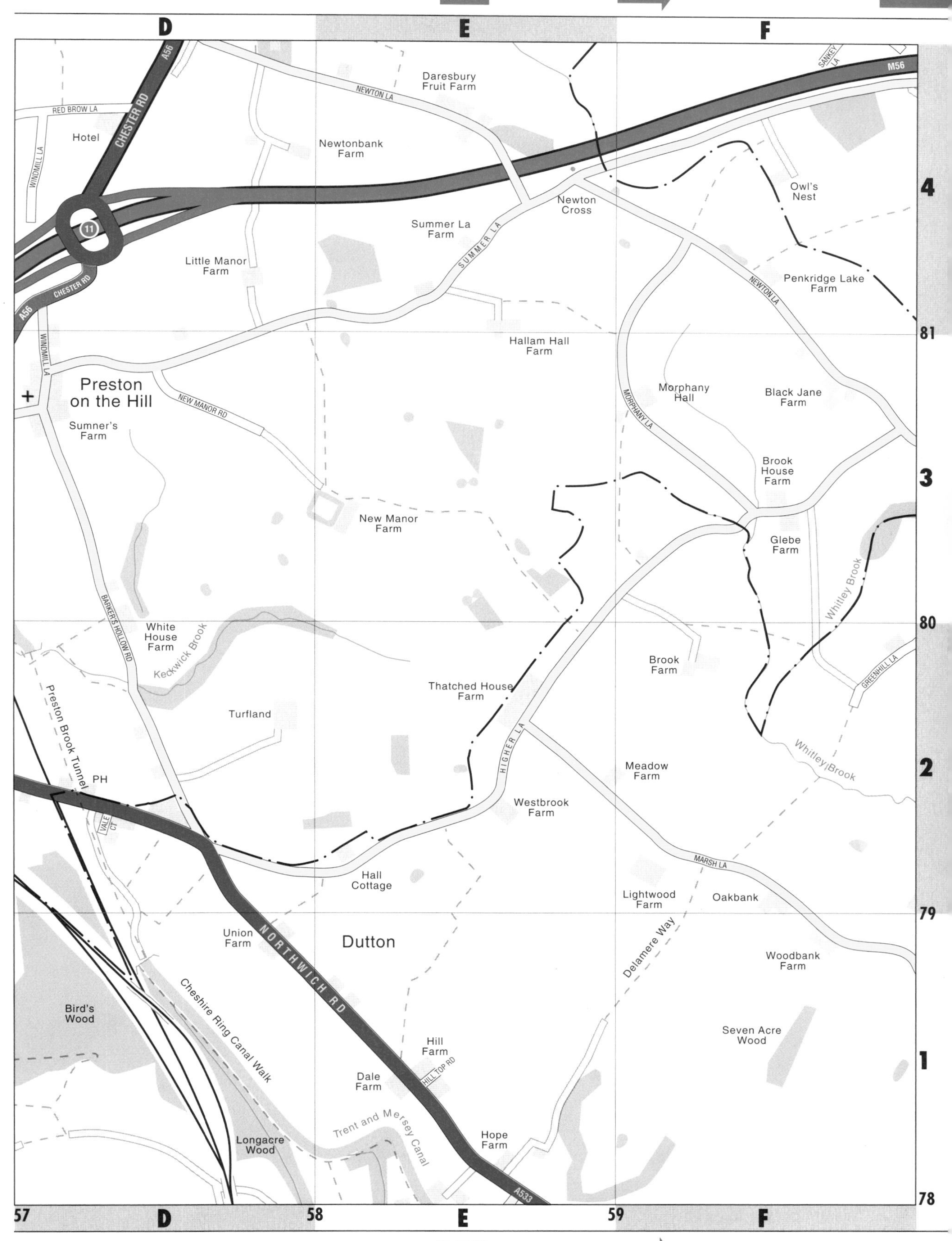

D
E
F
Daresbury Fruit Farm
NEWTON LA
Newtonbank Farm
RED BROW LA
Hotel
CHESTER RD
A56
WINDMILL LA
M56
SANKEY LA
Owl's Nest
Newton Cross
Summer La Farm
SUMMER LA
Little Manor Farm
CHESTER RD
Penkridge Lake Farm
NEWTON LA
Hallam Hall Farm
81
Preston on the Hill
NEW MANOR RD
Morphany Hall
Black Jane Farm
MORPHANY LA
Sumner's Farm
Brook House Farm
3
New Manor Farm
Glebe Farm
Whitley Brook
BARKER'S HOLLOW RD
White House Farm
Keckwick Brook
80
Brook Farm
GREENHILL LA
Thatched House Farm
Turfland
Preston Brook Tunnel
HIGHER LA
PH
Meadow Farm
Whitley Brook
2
Westbrook Farm
VALE CT
Hall Cottage
MARSH LA
Lightwood Farm
Oakbank
79
Union Farm
NORTHWICH RD
Dutton
Delamere Way
Woodbank Farm
Cheshire Ring Canal Walk
Bird's Wood
Seven Acre Wood
Hill Farm
HILL TOP RD
1
Dale Farm
Trent and Mersey Canal
Hope Farm
Longacre Wood
A533
78
57
58
59
76
52

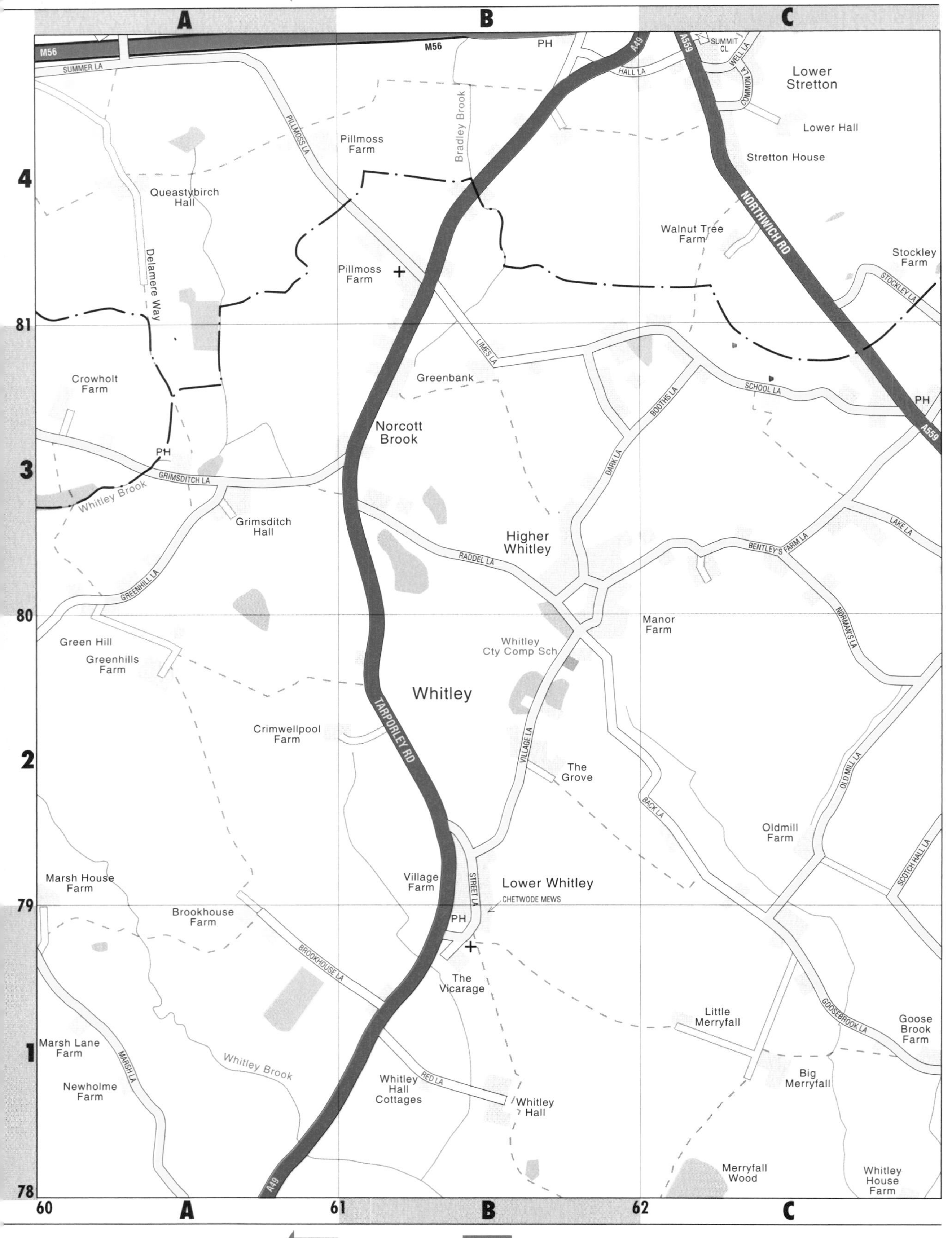

A   B   C

M56
SUMMER LA
M56
PH
A49
HALL LA
A559
SUMMIT CL
WELL LA
Lower Stretton
COMMON LA
Lower Hall

PILLMOSS LA
Pillmoss Farm
Bradley Brook
Stretton House

4
Queastybirch Hall
NORTHWICH RD
Walnut Tree Farm

Delamere Way
Pillmoss Farm
+
Stockley Farm

STOCKLEY LA

81
Crowholt Farm
Greenbank
LIMES LA
SCHOOL LA
PH
A559

3
PH
GRIMSDITCH LA
Norcott Brook
BOOTHS LA

Whitley Brook
Grimsditch Hall
DARK LA

RADDEL LA
Higher Whitley
LAKE LA

GREENHILL LA
BENTLEY'S FARM LA

80
Green Hill
Greenhills Farm
Whitley Cty Comp Sch
Manor Farm

NORMAN'S LA

Whitley
VILLAGE LA

Crimwellpool Farm
TARPORLEY RD
The Grove
BACK LA
OLD MILL LA
Oldmill Farm

2
SCOTCH HALL LA

Marsh House Farm
Village Farm
STREET LA
Lower Whitley
CHETWODE MEWS

79
Brookhouse Farm
PH
Little Merryfall
GOOSEBROOK LA
Goose Brook Farm

BROOKHOUSE LA
+
The Vicarage

MARSH LA
1
Marsh Lane Farm
Whitley Brook
RED LA
Big Merryfall

Newholme Farm
Whitley Hall Cottages
Whitley Hall

Merryfall Wood
Whitley House Farm

78
A49

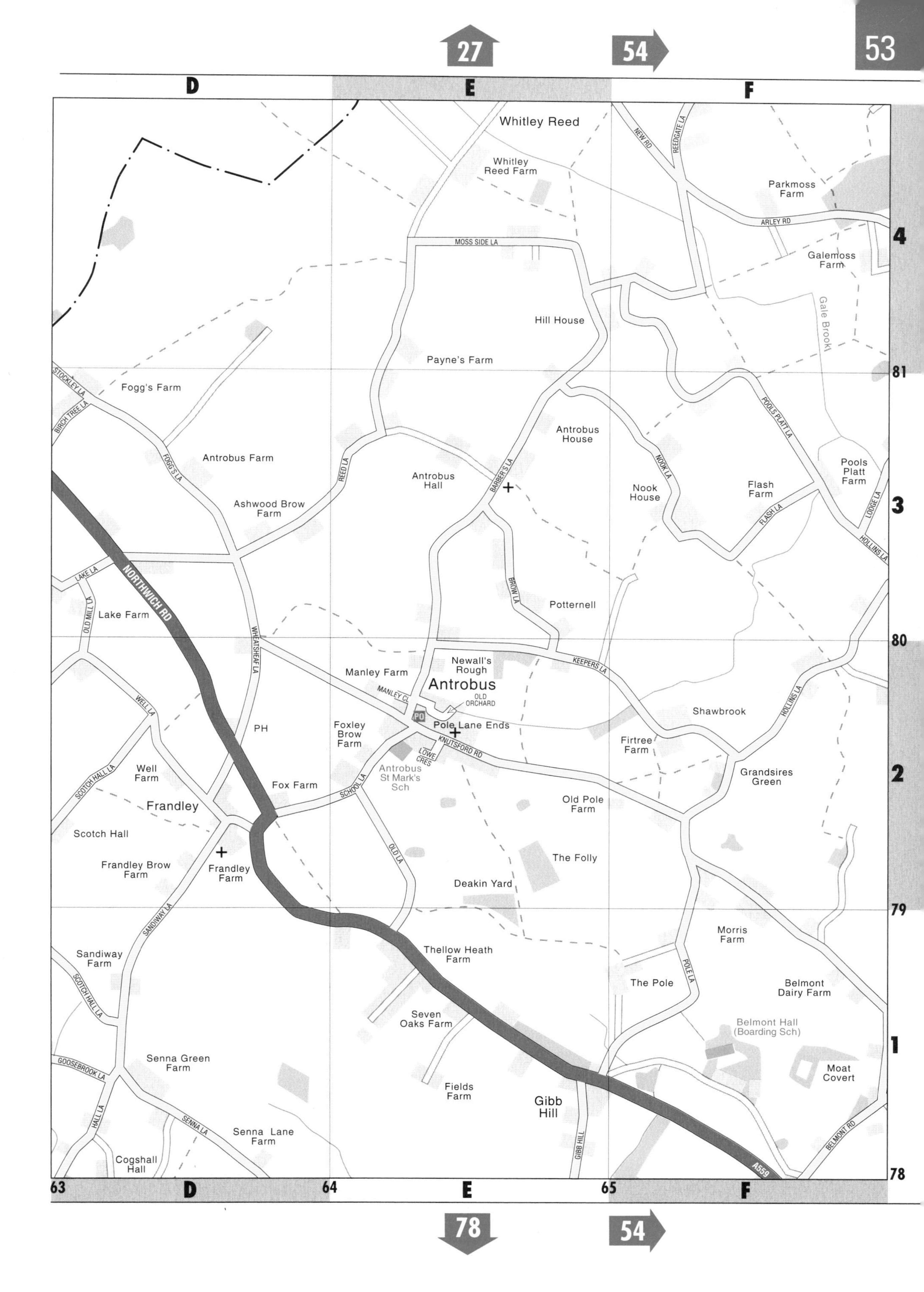

D · E · F

4

81

3

80

2

79

1

78

Whitley Reed

Whitley Reed Farm

NEW RD

REEDGATE LA

Parkmoss Farm

ARLEY RD

Galemoss Farm

MOSS SIDE LA

Gale Brook

Hill House

Payne's Farm

POOLS PLATT LA

Fogg's Farm

STOCKLEY LA

BIRCH TREE LA

Antrobus House

Pools Platt Farm

FOGGS LA

Antrobus Farm

REED LA

BARBERS LA

Antrobus Hall

Nook House

NOOK LA

Flash Farm

FLASH LA

HOLLINS LA

LODGE LA

Ashwood Brow Farm

NORTHWICH RD

LAKE LA

OLD MILL LA

Lake Farm

WHEATSHEAF LA

BROW LA

Potternell

KEEPERS LA

80

WELL LA

Manley Farm

MANLEY CL

Newall's Rough

Antrobus

OLD ORCHARD

Shawbrook

HOLLINS LA

PH

PO

Foxley Brow Farm

Pole Lane Ends

KNUTSFORD RD

LOWER CRES

Firtree Farm

Grandsires Green

SCOTCH HALL LA

Well Farm

Fox Farm

SCHOOL LA

Antrobus St Mark's Sch

Old Pole Farm

Frandley

Scotch Hall

OLD LA

The Folly

Frandley Brow Farm

Frandley Farm

Deakin Yard

Morris Farm

SANDIWAY LA

Thellow Heath Farm

POLE LA

Sandiway Farm

SCOTCH HALL LA

The Pole

Belmont Dairy Farm

Seven Oaks Farm

Belmont Hall (Boarding Sch)

Senna Green Farm

GOOSEBROOK LA

HALL LA

SENNA LA

Fields Farm

Moat Covert

Senna Lane Farm

Gibb Hill

GIBB HILL

BELMONT RD

Cogshall Hall

A559

A B C

The Firs

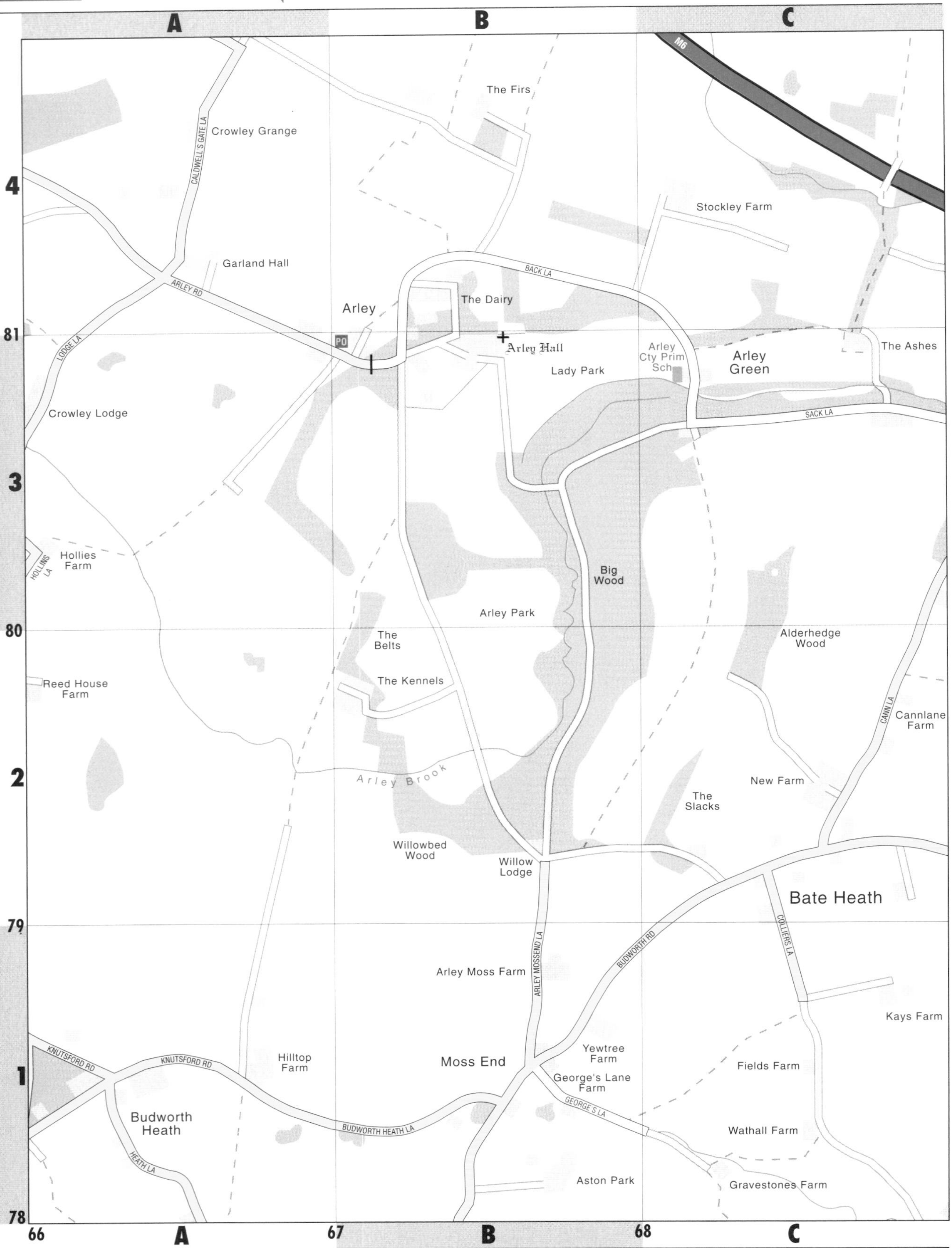

Crowley Grange

M6

CALDWELL'S GATE LA

Stockley Farm

4

Garland Hall

BACK LA

ARLEY RD

The Dairy

Arley

Arley
Cty Prim
Sch

LODGE LA

81 PO + Arley Hall

Lady Park

Arley
Green

The Ashes

SACK LA

Crowley Lodge

3

HOLLINS LA

Hollies
Farm

Big
Wood

Arley Park

Alderhedge
Wood

80

The
Belts

CANN LA

Cannlane
Farm

Reed House
Farm

The Kennels

New Farm

2

Arley Brook

The
Slacks

Willowbed
Wood

Willow
Lodge

Bate Heath

79

ARLEY MOSSEND LA

BUDWORTH RD

COLLIERS LA

Arley Moss Farm

Kays Farm

KNUTSFORD RD

KNUTSFORD RD

Hilltop
Farm

Moss End

Yewtree
Farm

George's Lane
Farm

Fields Farm

1

Budworth
Heath

BUDWORTH HEATH LA

GEORGE'S LA

Wathall Farm

HEATH LA

Aston Park

Gravestones Farm

78
66 A 67 B 68 C

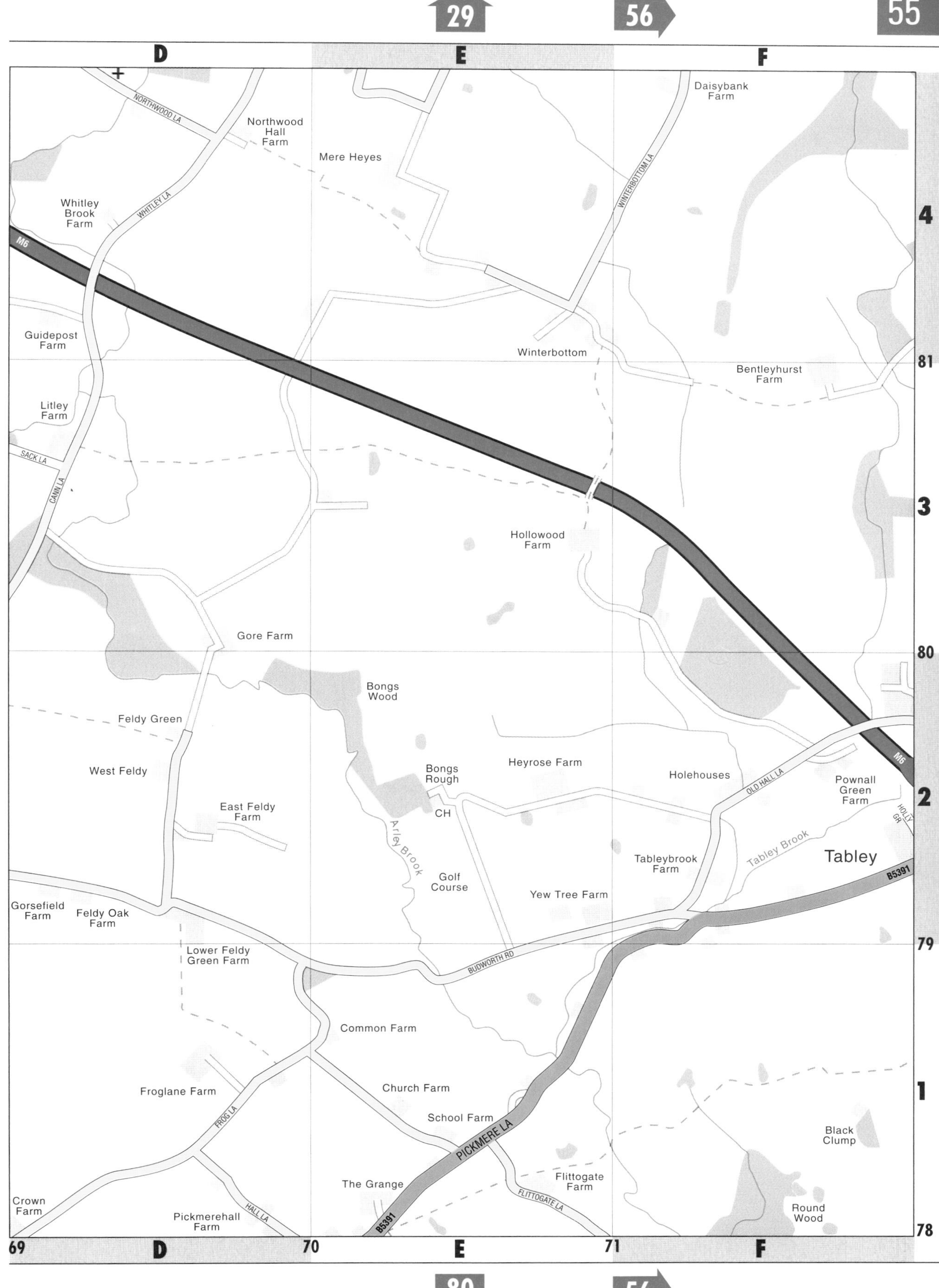
D
E
F
Daisybank Farm
Northwood Hall Farm
NORTHWOOD LA
Mere Heyes
WINTERBOTTOM LA
Whitley Brook Farm
WHITLEY LA
M6
4
Guidepost Farm
Winterbottom
Bentleyhurst Farm
81
Litley Farm
SACK LA
CANN LA
3
Hollowood Farm
Gore Farm
80
Bongs Wood
Feldy Green
West Feldy
Heyrose Farm
Bongs Rough
Holehouses
OLD HALL LA
Pownall Green Farm
2
East Feldy Farm
CH
HOLLY GR
Arley Brook
Tabley Brook
Tabley
Tableybrook Farm
Golf Course
B5391
Yew Tree Farm
Gorsefield Farm
Feldy Oak Farm
79
Lower Feldy Green Farm
BUDWORTH RD
Common Farm
Church Farm
1
Froglane Farm
FROG LA
School Farm
PICKMERE LA
Black Clump
The Grange
Flittogate Farm
FLITTOGATE LA
Crown Farm
HALL LA
Pickmerehall Farm
Round Wood
B5391
78
69
70
71

55 30

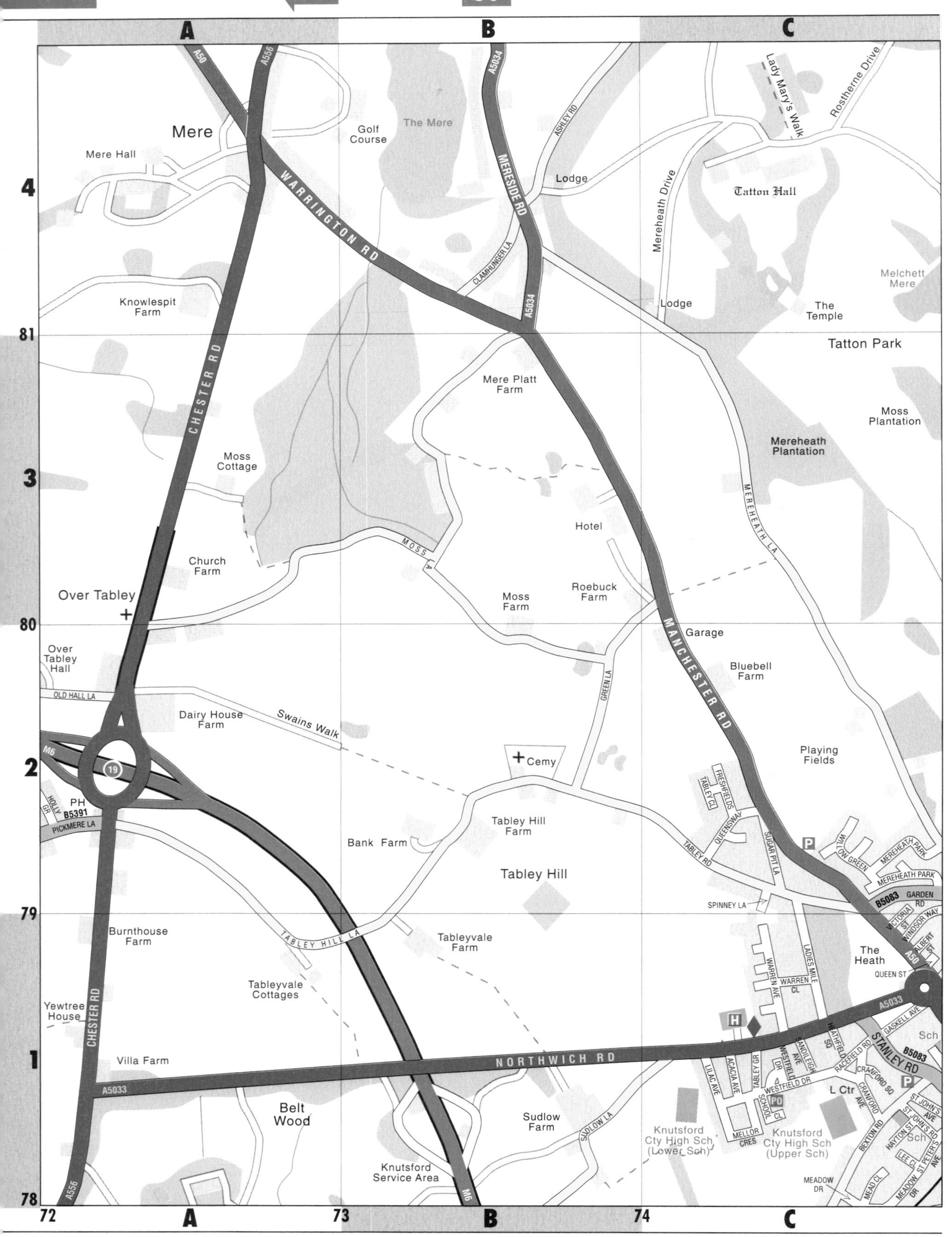
Mere
Mere Hall
Golf Course
The Mere
Lodge
Tatton Hall
Lady Mary's Walk
Rostherne Drive
Mereheath Drive
WARRINGTON RD
MERESIDE RD
ASHLEY RD
CLAMHUNGER LA
Knowlespit Farm
Lodge
Melchett Mere
The Temple
Tatton Park
CHESTER RD
Mere Platt Farm
Moss Plantation
Mereheath Plantation
Moss Cottage
MEREHEATH LA
Hotel
Church Farm
MOSS LA
Roebuck Farm
Over Tabley
Moss Farm
Garage
Over Tabley Hall
MANCHESTER RD
Bluebell Farm
OLD HALL LA
GREEN LA
Dairy House Farm
Swains Walk
Playing Fields
Cemy
M6
PH
B5391
PICKMERE LA
Tabley Hill Farm
Bank Farm
Tabley Hill
TABLEY RD
SUGAR PIT LA
SPINNEY LA
TABLEY HILL LA
Burnthouse Farm
Tableyvale Farm
The Heath
Tableyvale Cottages
Yewtree House
Villa Farm
NORTHWICH RD
A5033
STANLEY RD
B5083
Belt Wood
Sudlow Farm
SUDLOW LA
Knutsford Cty High Sch (Lower Sch)
Knutsford Cty High Sch (Upper Sch)
L Ctr
Sch
Knutsford Service Area
MEADOW DR
A B C
72 73 74
4 81 3 80 2 79 1 78

55 81

31

58

D E F

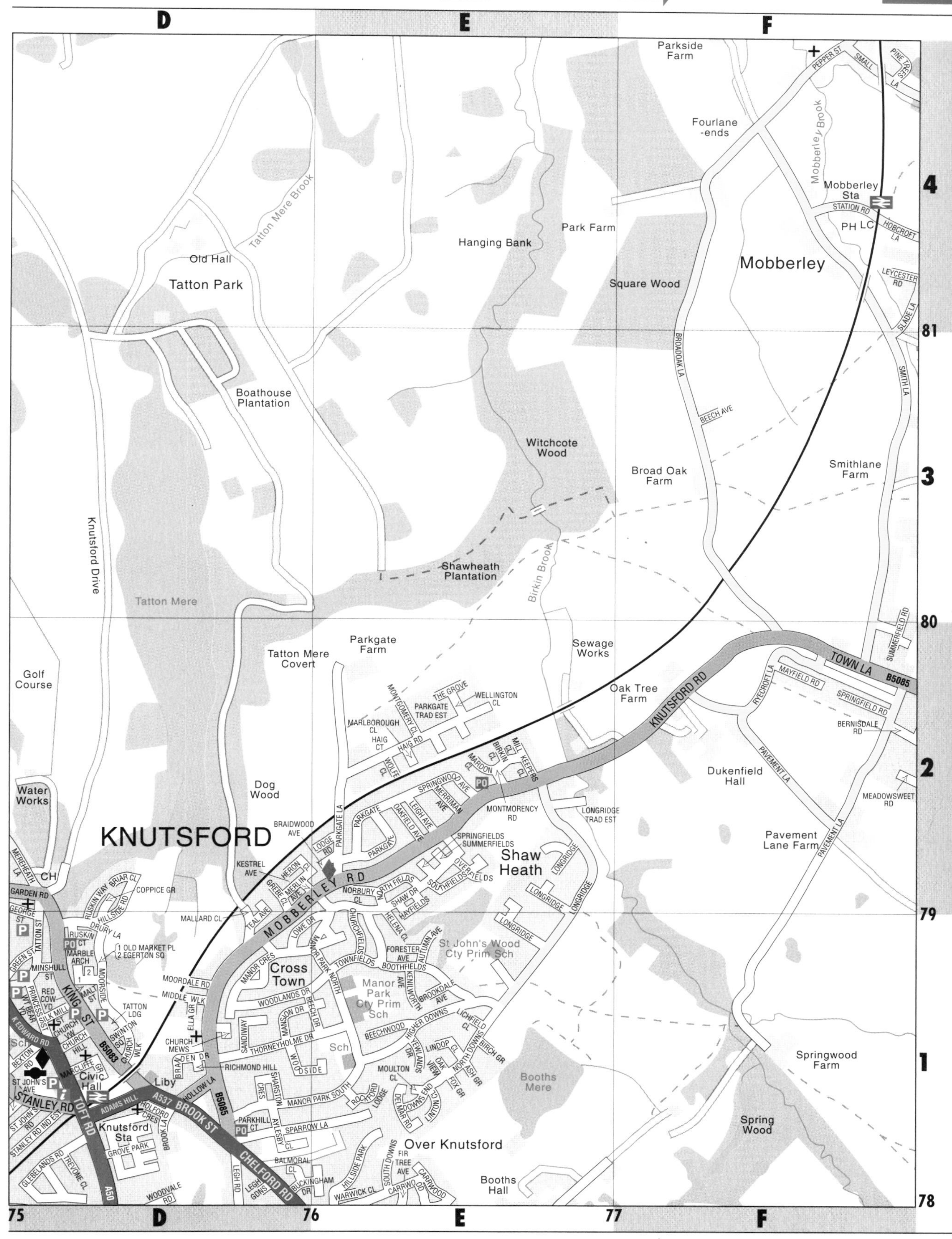

Parkside Farm
Fourlane -ends
Mobberley Brook
Mobberley Sta
STATION RD
HOBCROFT LA
PH LC
Mobberley
LEYCESTER RD
SLADE LA
SMITH LA
Tatton Mere Brook
Old Hall
Tatton Park
Hanging Bank
Park Farm
Square Wood
Boathouse Plantation
BROADOAK LA
BEECH AVE
Witchcote Wood
Broad Oak Farm
Smithlane Farm
Knutsford Drive
Shawheath Plantation
Birkin Brook
Tatton Mere
Golf Course
Parkgate Farm
Tatton Mere Covert
Sewage Works
SUMMERFIELD RD
TOWN LA
B5085
MAYFIELD RD
SPRINGFIELD RD
BERNISDALE RD
RYECROFT LA
Oak Tree Farm
KNUTSFORD RD
PARKGATE TRAD EST
THE GROVE
WELLINGTON CL
MARLBOROUGH CL
HAIG CT
HAIG RD
Dukenfield Hall
PAVEMENT LA
MEADOWSWEET RD
Water Works
Dog Wood
KNUTSFORD
BRAIDWOOD AVE
MONTMORENCY RD
LONGRIDGE TRAD EST
Pavement Lane Farm
Shaw Heath
MOBBERLEY RD
KESTREL AVE
GARDEN RD
COPPICE GR
MALLARD CL
LONGRIDGE
KING ST
Cross Town
St John's Wood Cty Prim Sch
Manor Park Cty Prim Sch
TOWNFIELDS
BOOTHFIELDS
BROOKDALE AVE
WOODLANDS DR
THORNEYHOLME DR
RICHMOND HILL
Sch
HIGHER DOWNS
LICHFIELD CL
BEECHWOOD
LINDOP CL
NORTH DOWNS
BIRCH GR
ASH GR
Booths Mere
Springwood Farm
Civic Hall
Liby
STANLEY RD
TOFT RD
ADAMS HILL
A537 BROOK ST
B5085
MANOR PARK SOUTH
Knutsford Sta
GROVE PARK
CHELFORD RD
SPARROW LA
Spring Wood
Over Knutsford
Booths Hall
A50
WOODVALE RD
LEGH RD
HILLSIDE PARK
SOUTH DOWNS
FIR TREE AVE
WARWICK CL
CARRWOOD
BUCKINGHAM DR
BALMORAL CL
75
76
77
78
79
80
81
1
2
3
4

D E F

82

58

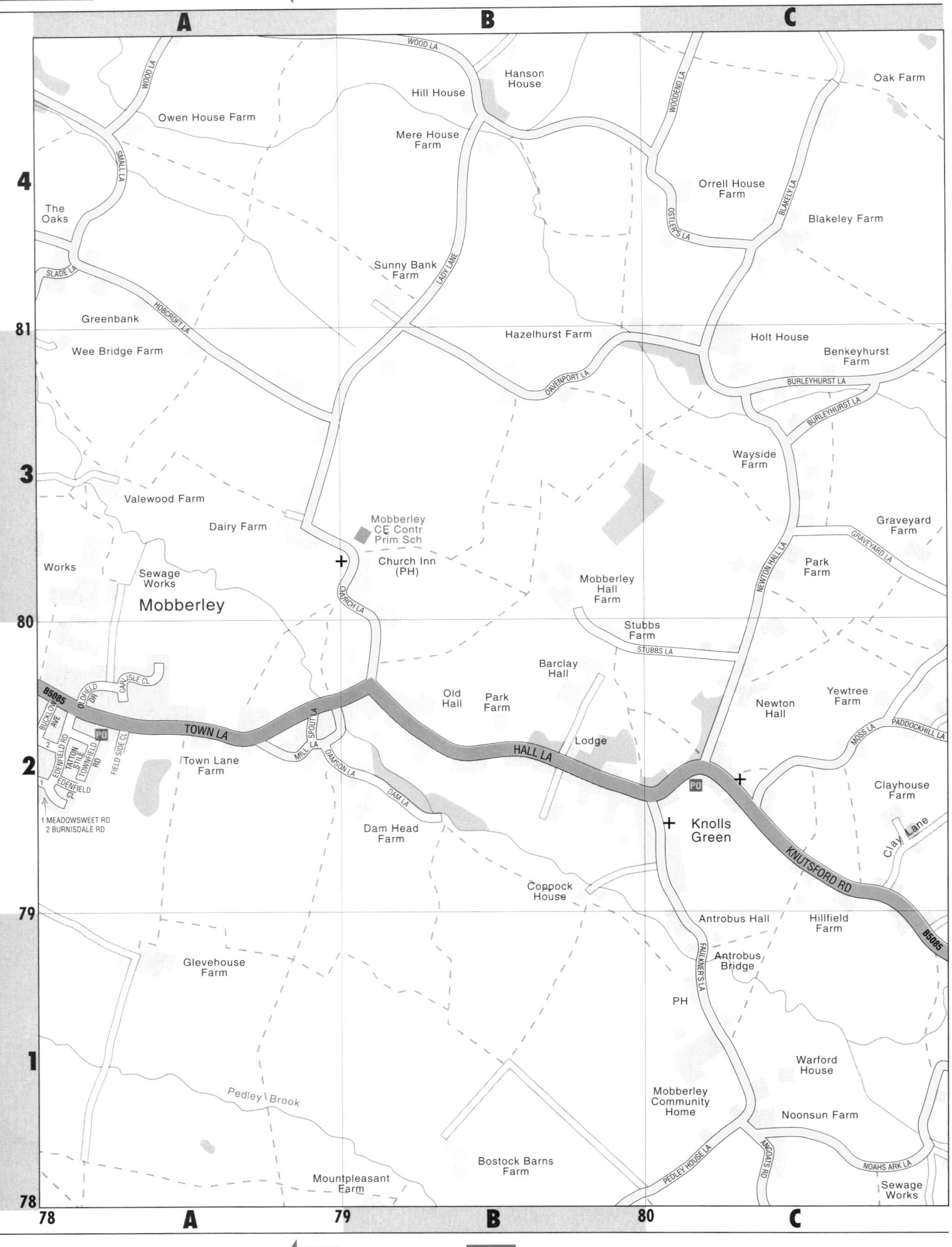

A B C

4

81

3

80

2

79

1

78

WOOD LA

Owen House Farm

Hill House

Hanson House

Mere House Farm

Oak Farm

The Oaks

SMALL LA

Orrell House Farm

OSTLER'S LA

WOODROW LA

Blakeley Farm

BLAKELY LA

SLADE LA

Greenbank

HOBCROFT LA

Sunny Bank Farm

LADY LANE

Hazelhurst Farm

Holt House

Benkeyhurst Farm

BURLEYHURST LA

Wee Bridge Farm

DAVENPORT LA

BURLEYHURST LA

Valewood Farm

Wayside Farm

NEWTON HALL LA

Graveyard Farm

GRAVEYARD LA

Dairy Farm

Mobberley CE Contr Prim Sch

Church Inn (PH)

Mobberley Hall Farm

Park Farm

Works

Sewage Works

Mobberley

MARCH LA

Stubbs Farm

STUBBS LA

Newton Hall

Yewtree Farm

MOSS LA

PADDOCKHILL LA

B5085

OLD FIELD DR

CARLISLE CL

TOWN LA

MILL SPOUT LA

Barclay Hall

Old Hall

Park Farm

Lodge

PO

Knolls Green

Clayhouse Farm

CLAY LANE

BUNGALOW AVE

EDENFIELD RD

TATTON STILE

TOWNFIELD RD

PO

FIELD SIDE CL

Town Lane Farm

DAMSON LA

HALL LA

KNUTSFORD RD

B5085

EDENFIELD CL

2

1

1 MEADOWSWEET RD
2 BURNISDALE RD

DAM LA

Dam Head Farm

Coppock House

Antrobus Hall

Hillfield Farm

Glevehouse Farm

FALKNER'S LA

Antrobus Bridge

PH

Warford House

Pedley Brook

Mobberley Community Home

Noonsun Farm

ANCOATS RD

NOAHS ARK LA

Mountpleasant Farm

Bostock Barns Farm

PEDLEY HOUSE LA

Sewage Works

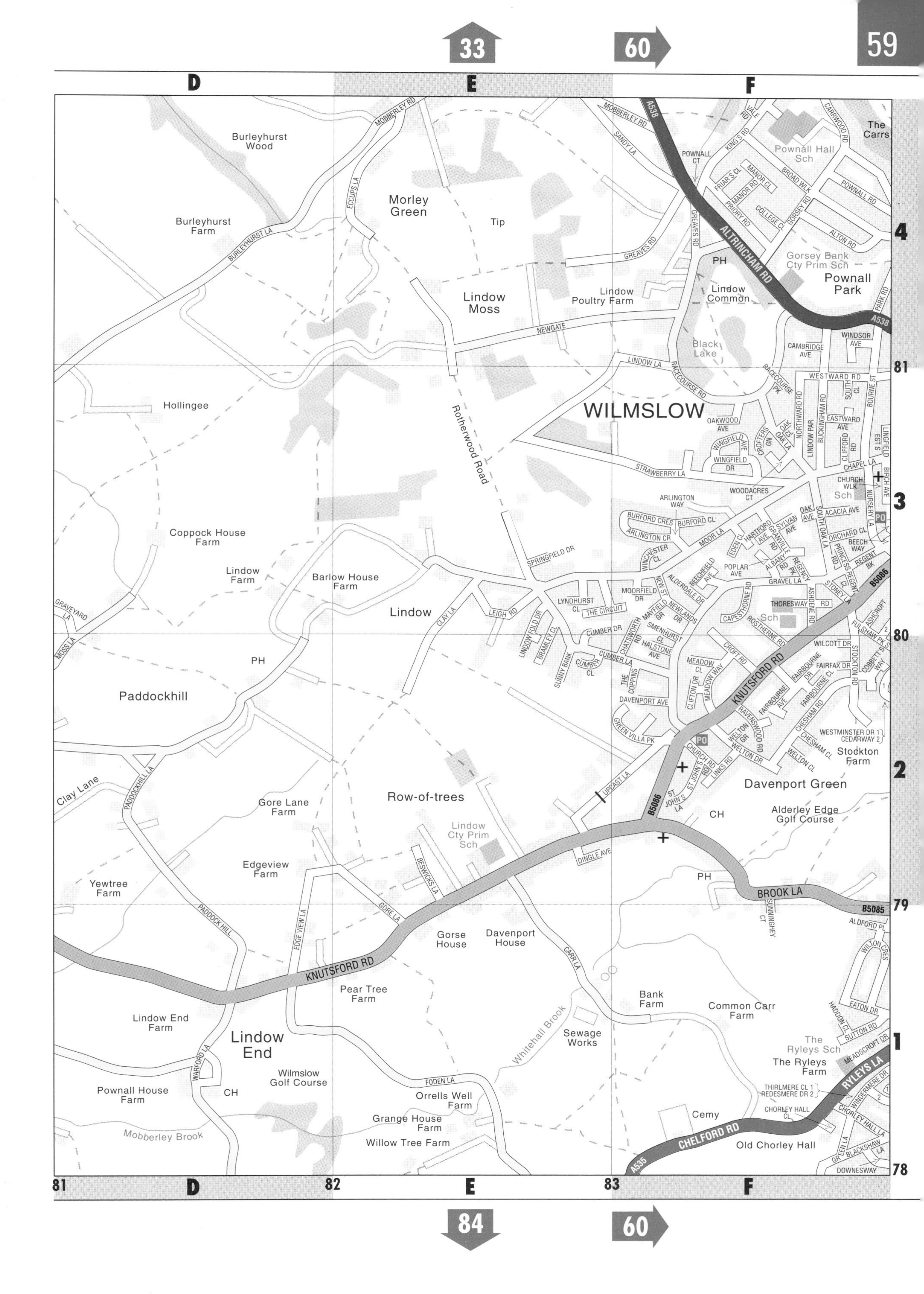

D   E   F

4

81

3

80

2

79

1

78

Burleyhurst Wood

Morley Green

Tip

Burleyhurst Farm

BURLEYHURST LA

ECCUPS LA

MOBBERLEY RD

MOBBERLEY RD

SANDY LA

A538

ALTRINCHAM RD

A538

The Carrs

VALE RD

KING'S RD

CARRWOOD

Pownall Hall Sch

BROAD WLK

PARK RD

POWNALL CT

GREAVES RD

GREAVES LA

FRIAR'S CL

MANOR CL

MANOR RD

PRIORY RD

COLLEGE CL

PH

POWNALL RD

ALTON RD

Gorsey Bank Cty Prim Sch

Lindow Common

Pownall Park

Hollingee

Lindow Moss

Lindow Poultry Farm

NEWGATE

Black Lake

Lindow La

RACECOURSE RD

RACECOURSE PK

WINDSOR AVE

CAMBRIDGE AVE

WESTWARD RD

SOUTH CL

LINGFIELD EST S

BOURNE S

BIRCH AVE

NURSERY LA

PO

Rotherwood Road

STRAWBERRY LA

WILMSLOW

OAKWOOD AVE

WINGFIELD AVE

WINGFIELD DR

CROFTERS GN

LINDOW PAR

NORTHWARD RD

BUCKINGHAM RD

EASTWARD AVE

CLIFFORD

CHAPEL LA

CHURCH WLK Sch

Coppock House Farm

Lindow Farm

Barlow House Farm

GRAVEYARD LA

MOSS LA

PH

Springfield Dr

Lindow

CLAY LA

LEIGH RD

LINDOW FOLD DR

BRAMLEY CL

SUNNY BANK

CUMBER CL

LYNDHURST CL

THE CIRCUIT

MOORFIELD DR

NEW'S LA

MAYFIELD DR

CHATSWORTH RD

CUMBER DR

CUMBER LA

SMENHURST CL

HALSTONE AVE

THE COPPINS

DAVENPORT AVE

GREEN VILLA PK

WOODACRES CT

ARLINGTON WAY

BURFORD CRES

BURFORD CL

ARLINGTON CR

WINCHESTER CL

ALDERDALE DR

NEWLANDS RD

EDEN CL

HARTFORD AVE

GRANVILLE RD

SYLVAN AVE

ALBANY RD

POPLAR AVE

GRAVEL LA

BEECHFIELD RD

OAK AVE

SOUTH OAK LA

ACACIA AVE

ORCHARD CL

PRINCESS RD

REGENT RD

REGENT PK

STONE'S

BEECH WAY

REGENT BK

THORESWAY

CAPESTHORNE RD

ROSTHERNE RD

Sch

ASHDENE RD

B5086

Paddockhill

PADDOCKHILL LA

Row-of-trees

Lindow Cty Prim Sch

MEADOW CL

OROFT RD

CLIFTON RD

MEADOW WAY

WILCOTT DR

RAVENSWOOD RD

KNUTSFORD RD

FAIRBOURNE CL

FAIRBOURNE AVE

FAIRBOURNE RD

FAIRFAX RD

STOCKTON RD

CHESHAM CL

CHESHAM DR

WELTON DR

WELTON GR

WELTON CL

COBBETT'S S

ASHCROFT

FULSHAM PK

WAY

WESTMINSTER DR 1

CEDARWAY 2

Stockton Farm

Clay Lane

Gore Lane Farm

Edgeview Farm

EDGE VIEW LA

Yewtree Farm

PADDOCK HILL

GORE LA

BENNICKS LA

DINGLE AVE

UPCAST LA

ST JOHN'S LA

ST JOHN'S RD

CHURCH RD

LINKS RD

B5086

PO

+

+

+

CH

Davenport Green

Alderley Edge Golf Course

PH

BROOK LA

B5085

SUNNINGHEY CT

ALDFORD PL

WILTON CRES

Gorse House

Davenport House

Pear Tree Farm

CARR LA

Whitehall Brook

Bank Farm

Common Carr Farm

EATON DR

HADDON CL

SUTTON RD

MEADSCROFT DR

RYLEYS LA

The Ryleys Sch

Lindow End Farm

Lindow End

WARFORD LA

Wilmslow Golf Course

FODEN LA

Orrells Well Farm

Sewage Works

The Ryleys Farm

THIRLMERE CL 1

REDESMERE DR 2

CHORLEY HALL CL

GREEN LA

WINDERMERE DR

CHORLEY HALL LA

Pownall House Farm

CH

Grange House Farm

Willow Tree Farm

Mobberley Brook

Cemy

Old Chorley Hall

A535

CHELFORD RD

GR BLACKSHAW LA

DOWNESWAY

59
34

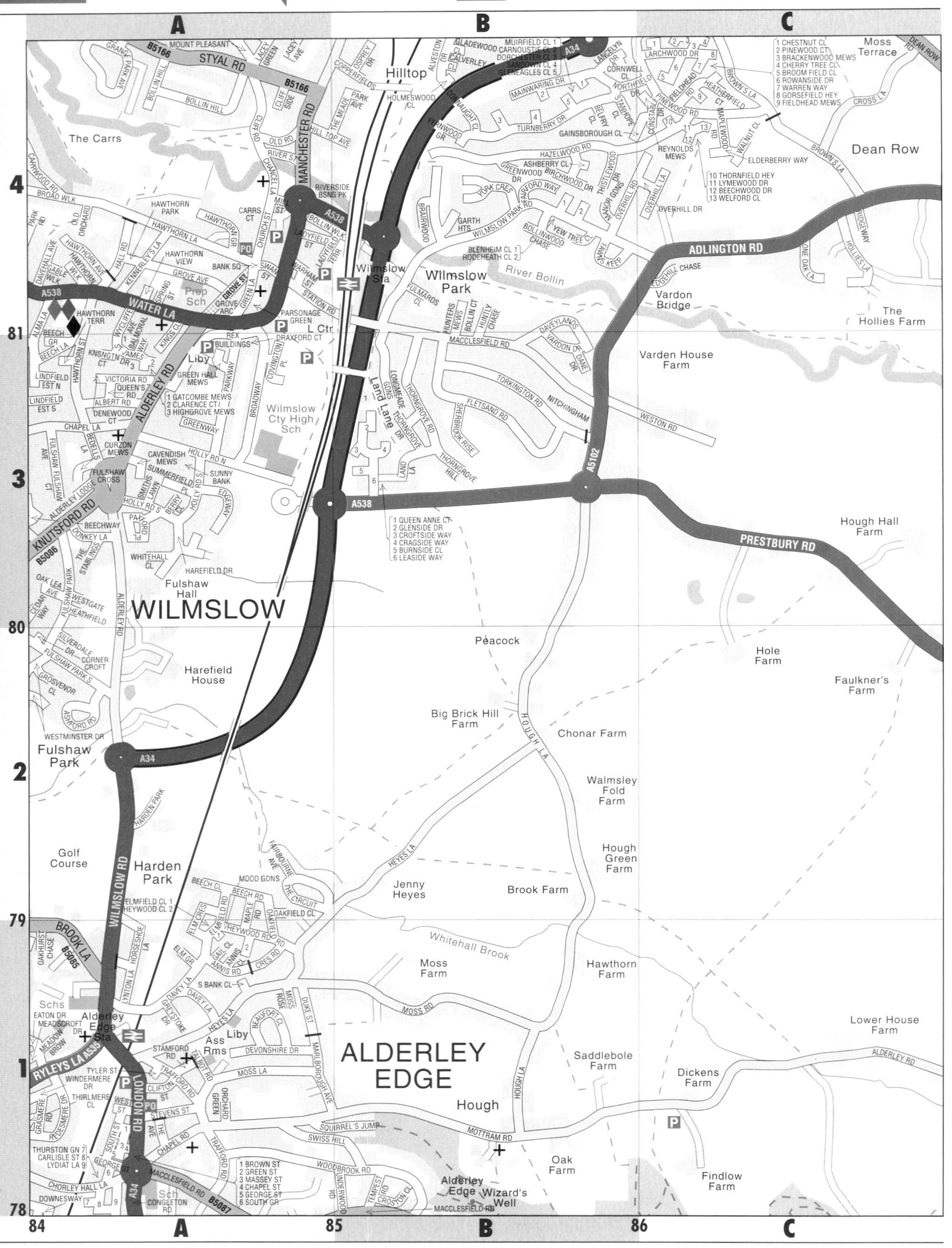
A
B
C
4
81
3
80
2
79
1
78
84
85
86
WILMSLOW
ALDERLEY EDGE
Wilmslow Park
Fulshaw Park
Harden Park
Dean Row
Hilltop
The Carrs
Moss Terrace
Vardon Bridge
The Hollies Farm
Varden House Farm
Hough Hall Farm
Peacock
Hole Farm
Faulkner's Farm
Big Brick Hill Farm
Chonar Farm
Walmsley Fold Farm
Hough Green Farm
Jenny Heyes
Brook Farm
Moss Farm
Hawthorn Farm
Lower House Farm
Saddlebole Farm
Dickens Farm
Hough
Oak Farm
Findlow Farm
Alderley Edge Wizard's Well
Fulshaw Hall
Harefield House
Golf Course
Wilmslow Cty High Sch
River Bollin
Whitehall Brook
ADLINGTON RD
PRESTBURY RD
STYAL RD
WATER LA
MANCHESTER RD
ALDERLEY RD
KNUTSFORD RD
WILMSLOW RD
LONDON RD
MACCLESFIELD RD
BROOK LA
RYLEYS LA
A34
A538
A5102
B5166
B5086
B5085
B5087
1 CHESTNUT CL
2 PINEWOOD CT
3 BRACKENWOOD MEWS
4 CHERRY TREE CL
5 BROOM FIELD CL
6 ROWANSIDE DR
7 WARREN WAY
8 GORSEFIELD HEY
9 FIELDHEAD MEWS
10 THORNFIELD HEY
11 LYMEWOOD DR
12 BEECHWOOD DR
13 WELFORD CL
1 GATCOMBE MEWS
2 CLARENCE CT
3 HIGHGROVE MEWS
1 QUEEN ANNE CT
2 GLENSIDE DR
3 CROFTSIDE WAY
4 CRAGSIDE WAY
5 BURNSIDE CL
6 LEASIDE WAY
1 BROWN ST
2 GREEN ST
3 MASSEY ST
4 CHAPEL ST
5 GEORGE ST
6 SOUTH GR
THURSTON GN 7
CARLISLE ST 8
LYDIAT LA 9
ELMFIELD CL 1
HEYWOOD CL 2
BLENHEIM CL 1
RODEHEATH CL 2
MUIRFIELD CL 1
CARNOUSTIE CL 2
DORCHESTER CL 3
SANDOWN CL 4
GLENEAGLES CL 5

59
85

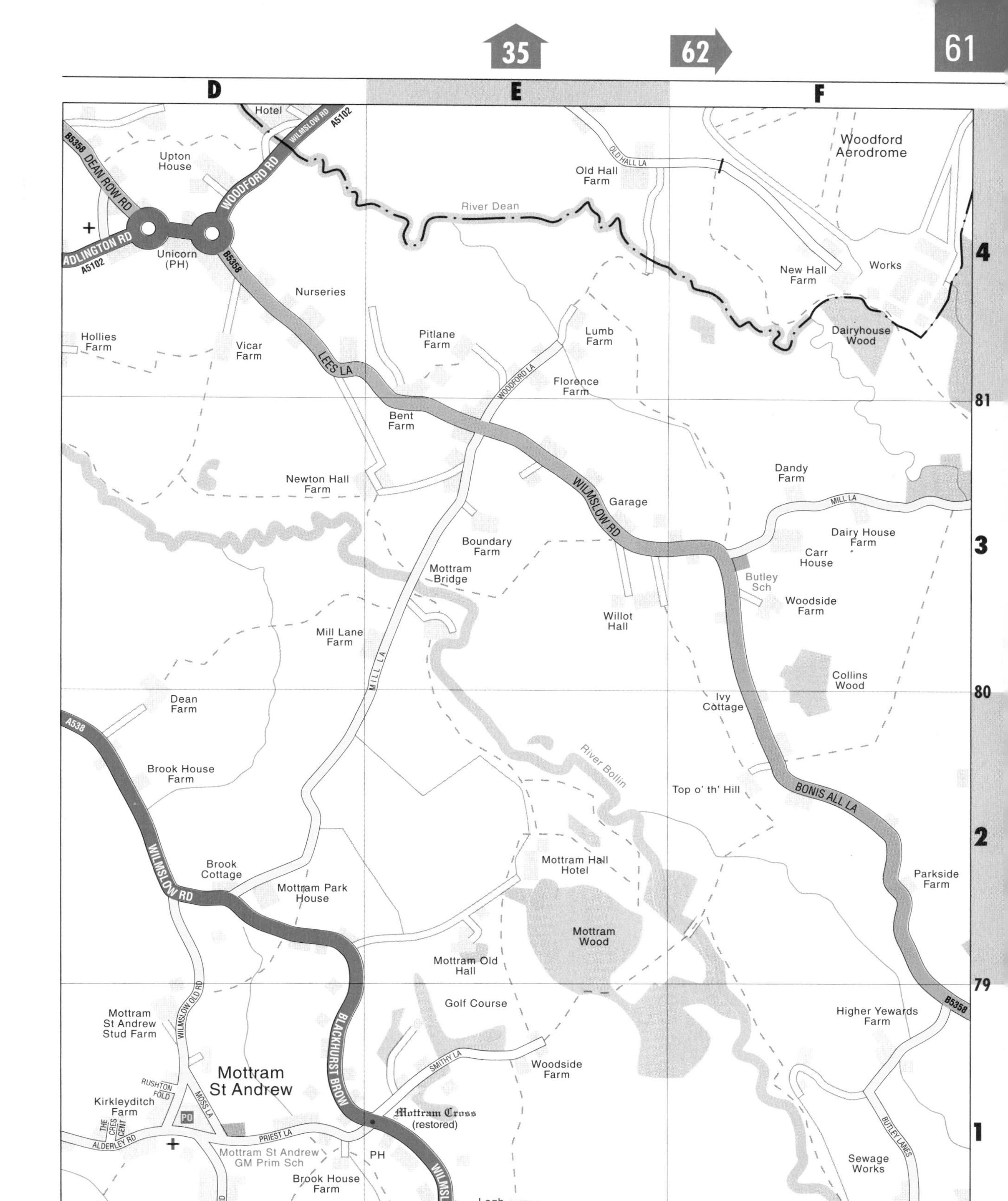

Hotel
Upton
House
B5358 DEAN ROW RD
WOODFORD RD
WILMSLOW RD
A5102
+
ADLINGTON RD
A5102
Unicorn
(PH)
B5358
Nurseries
Woodford
Aerodrome
OLD HALL LA
Old Hall
Farm
River Dean
New Hall
Farm
Works

4

Hollies
Farm
Vicar
Farm
LEES LA
Pitlane
Farm
Lumb
Farm
WOODFORD LA
Florence
Farm
Dairyhouse
Wood

Newton Hall
Farm
Bent
Farm
WILMSLOW RD
Garage
Dandy
Farm
MILL LA
Dairy House
Farm

81

Boundary
Farm
Mottram
Bridge
Carr
House
Butley
Sch
Woodside
Farm

3

Mill Lane
Farm
MILL LA
Willot
Hall
Collins
Wood

Dean
Farm
River Bollin
Ivy
Cottage

80

A538
Brook House
Farm
Top o' th' Hill
BONIS ALL LA

WILMSLOW RD
Brook
Cottage
Mottram Park
House
Mottram Hall
Hotel
Parkside
Farm

2

Mottram
Wood
B5358

Mottram
St Andrew
Stud Farm
WILMSLOW OLD RD
BLACKHURST BROW
Mottram Old
Hall
Golf Course
Higher Yewards
Farm

79

Mottram
St Andrew
RUSHTON
FOLD
MOSS LA
SMITHY LA
Woodside
Farm
BUTLEY LANES

Kirkleyditch
Farm
THE CRESCENT
PO
PRIEST LA
Mottram Cross
(restored)
Sewage
Works

1

ALDERLEY RD
+
Mottram St Andrew
GM Prim Sch
PH
OAK RD
Brook House
Farm
Legh
Hall
WILMSLOW RD
A538

78

61
36

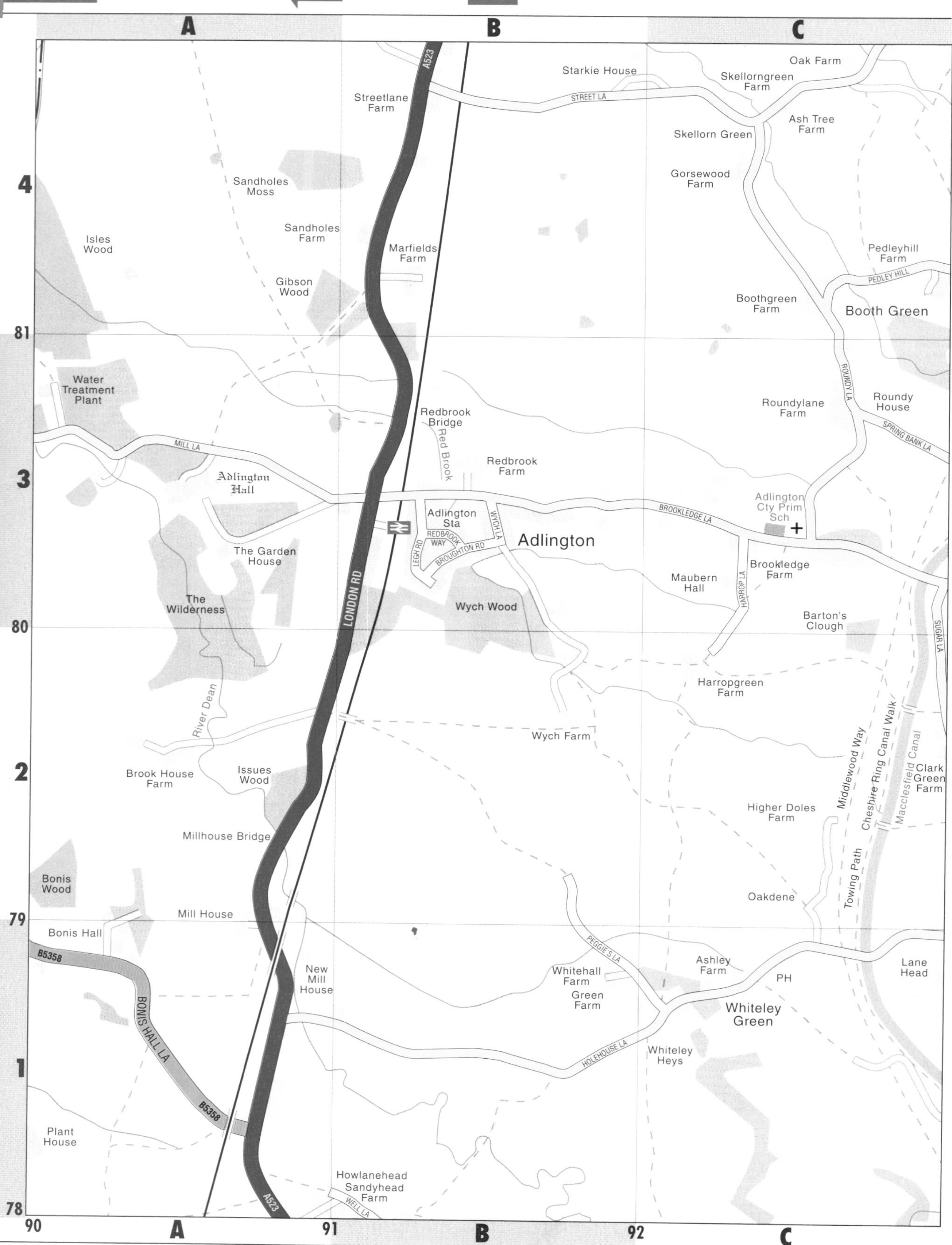

A
B
C
4
81
3
80
2
79
1
78
90
91
92
A523
Streetlane Farm
Starkie House
STREET LA
Oak Farm
Skellorngreen Farm
Skellorn Green
Ash Tree Farm
Gorsewood Farm
Sandholes Moss
Sandholes Farm
Isles Wood
Marfields Farm
Gibson Wood
Pedleyhill Farm
PEDLEY HILL
Boothgreen Farm
Booth Green
Water Treatment Plant
ROUNDY LA
Roundylane Farm
Roundy House
SPRING BANK LA
Redbrook Bridge
Red Brook
MILL LA
Redbrook Farm
Adlington Hall
Adlington Cty Prim Sch
BROOKLEDGE LA
Adlington Sta
WYCH LA
REDBROOK WAY
LEGH RD
BROUGHTON RD
Adlington
The Garden House
Brookledge Farm
Maubern Hall
HARROP LA
The Wilderness
Wych Wood
LONDON RD
Barton's Clough
SUGAR LA
Harropgreen Farm
River Dean
Wych Farm
Middlewood Way
Cheshire Ring Canal Walk
Macclesfield Canal
Clark Green Farm
Brook House Farm
Issues Wood
Higher Doles Farm
Millhouse Bridge
Towing Path
Bonis Wood
Oakdene
Mill House
Bonis Hall
B5358
PEGGIE'S LA
Ashley Farm
PH
Lane Head
New Mill House
Whitehall Farm
Green Farm
Whiteley Green
BONIS HALL LA
HOLEHOUSE LA
Whiteley Heys
B5358
Plant House
Howlanehead
Sandyhead Farm
WELL LA
A523

61
87

37

64

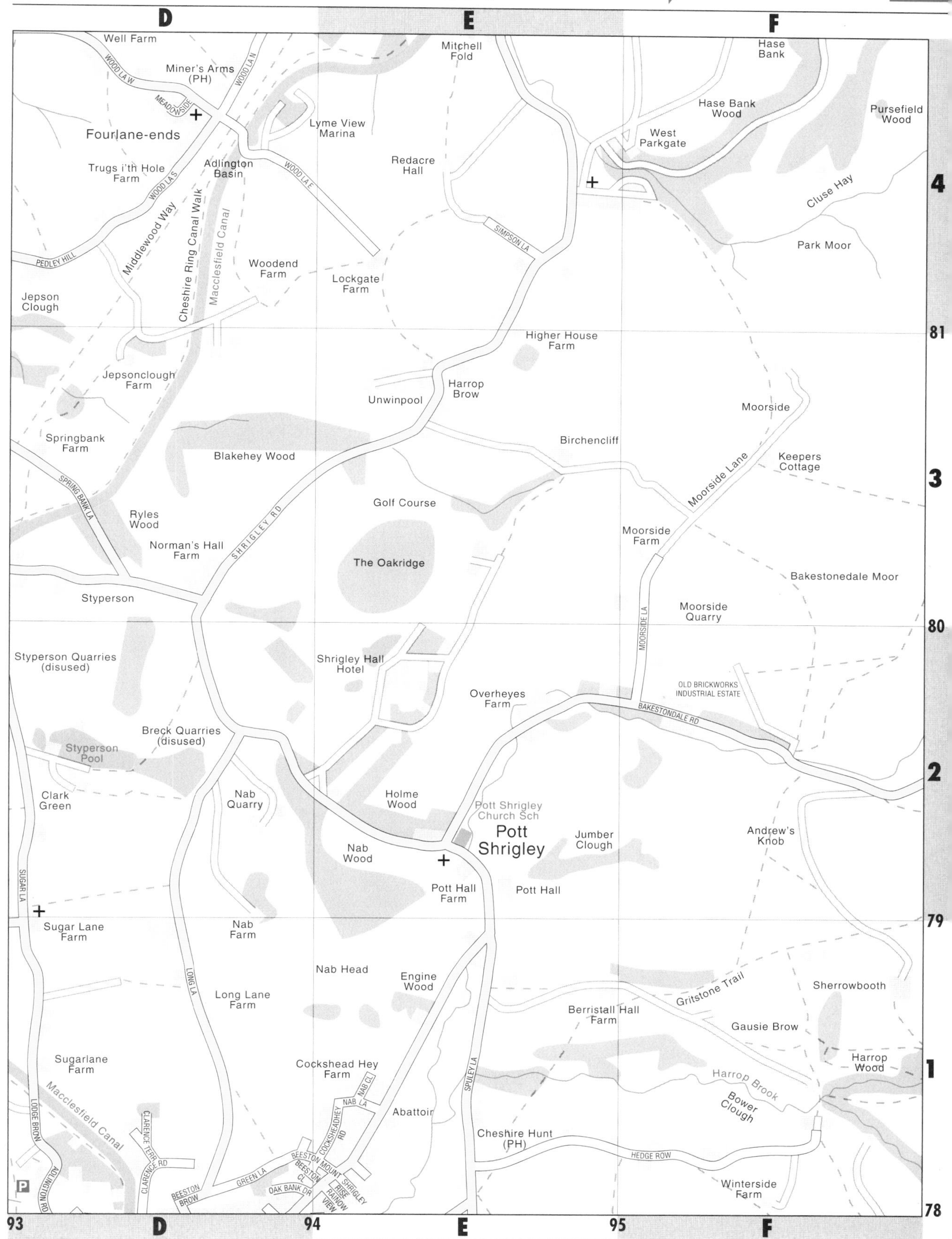

D
E
F
Well Farm
Mitchell Fold
Hase Bank
Miner's Arms (PH)
WOOD LA W
WOOD LA N
MEADOWSIDE
Fourlane-ends
Lyme View Marina
Hase Bank Wood
Pursefield Wood
West Parkgate
Trugs i'th Hole Farm
Adlington Basin
WOOD LA E
Redacre Hall
WOOD LA S
Cluse Hay
4
Middlewood Way
Cheshire Ring Canal Walk
Macclesfield Canal
SIMPSON LA
Park Moor
PEDLEY HILL
Woodend Farm
Lockgate Farm
Jepson Clough
Higher House Farm
81
Jepsonclough Farm
Harrop Brow
Unwinpool
Moorside
Springbank Farm
Blakehey Wood
Birchencliff
Keepers Cottage
Moorside Lane
SPRING BANK LA
3
Golf Course
Ryles Wood
SHRIGLEY RD
Moorside Farm
Norman's Hall Farm
The Oakridge
Bakestonedale Moor
Styperson
Moorside Quarry
MOORSIDE LA
80
Styperson Quarries (disused)
Shrigley Hall Hotel
OLD BRICKWORKS INDUSTRIAL ESTATE
Overheyes Farm
BAKESTONDALE RD
Breck Quarries (disused)
Styperson Pool
2
Clark Green
Nab Quarry
Holme Wood
Pott Shrigley Church Sch
Pott Shrigley
Jumber Clough
Andrew's Knob
Nab Wood
SUGAR LA
Pott Hall Farm
Pott Hall
Sugar Lane Farm
Nab Farm
79
Nab Head
Engine Wood
Sherrowbooth
LONG LA
Long Lane Farm
Gritstone Trail
Berristall Hall Farm
Gausie Brow
Sugarlane Farm
Cockshead Hey Farm
SPULEY LA
Harrop Wood
Harrop Brook
1
Macclesfield Canal
NAB CL
NAB LA
Bower Clough
LODGE BROW
CLARENCE TERR
COCKSHEADHEY RD
Abattoir
Cheshire Hunt (PH)
HEDGE ROW
CLARENCE RD
BEESTON MOUNT
BEESTON CL
SHRIGLEY RISE
Winterside Farm
ADLINGTON RD
BEESTON BROW
GREEN LA
OAK BANK DR
RAINOW VIEW
P
78
93
D
94
E
95
F

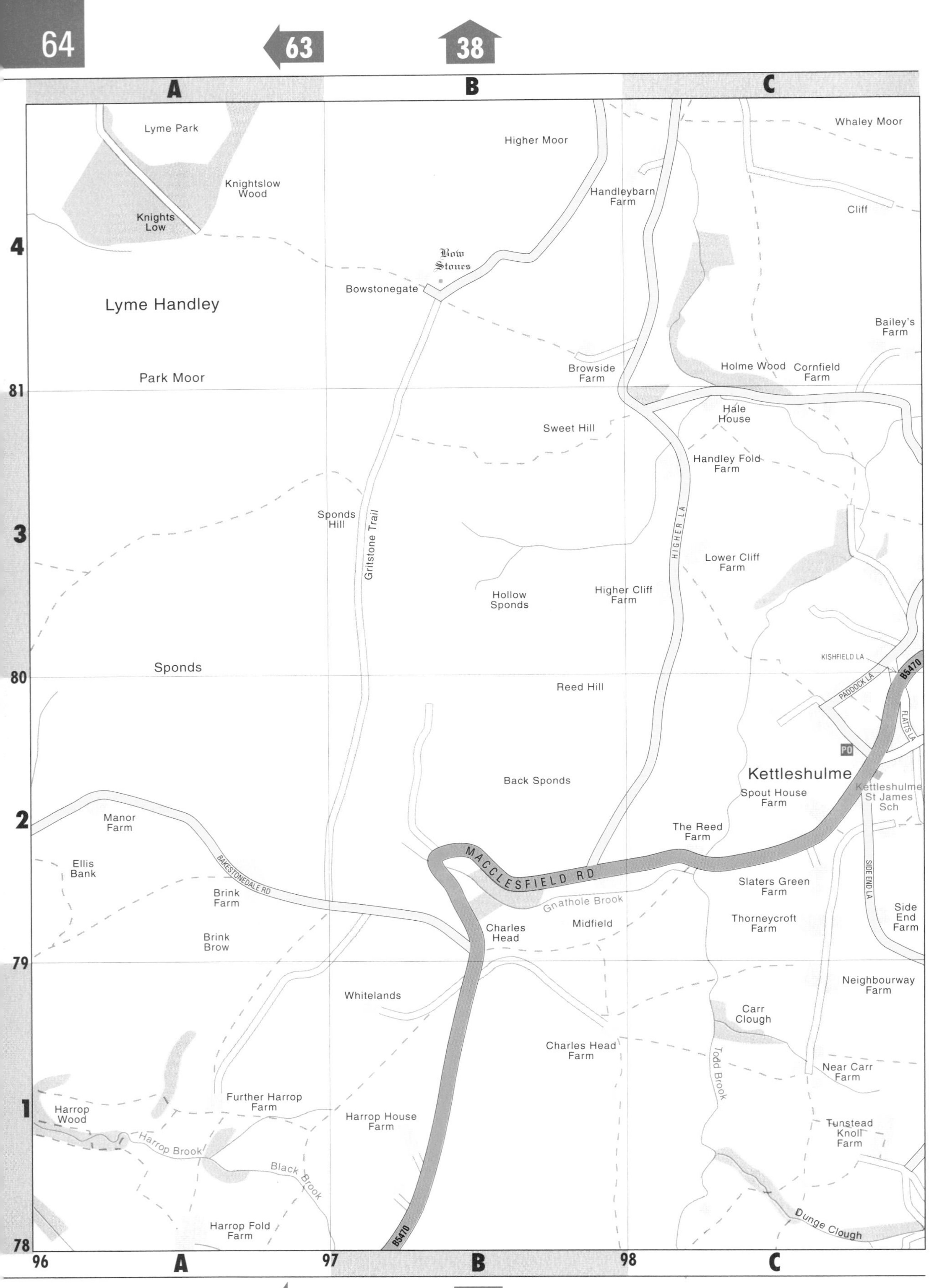

A   B   C

Lyme Park

Knightslow Wood

Knights Low

Higher Moor

Handleybarn Farm

Whaley Moor

Cliff

Bow Stones

Bowstonegate

4

Lyme Handley

Bailey's Farm

Browside Farm

Holme Wood

Cornfield Farm

Park Moor

81

Sweet Hill

Hale House

Handley Fold Farm

Sponds Hill

3

Gritstone Trail

Lower Cliff Farm

Hollow Sponds

Higher Cliff Farm

HIGHER LA

KISHFIELD LA

PADDOCK LA

B5470

Sponds

80

Reed Hill

FLATTS LA

PO

Back Sponds

Kettleshulme

Spout House Farm

Kettleshulme St James Sch

2

Manor Farm

The Reed Farm

Slaters Green Farm

SIDE END LA

Side End Farm

Ellis Bank

BAKESTONEDALE RD

Brink Farm

MACCLESFIELD RD

Gnathole Brook

Midfield

Thorneycroft Farm

Brink Brow

Charles Head

79

Whitelands

Charles Head Farm

Neighbourway Farm

Carr Clough

Todd Brook

Near Carr Farm

1

Harrop Wood

Further Harrop Farm

Harrop House Farm

Harrop Brook

Black Brook

Tunstead Knoll Farm

Harrop Fold Farm

B5470

Dunge Clough

78

96   A   97   B   98   C

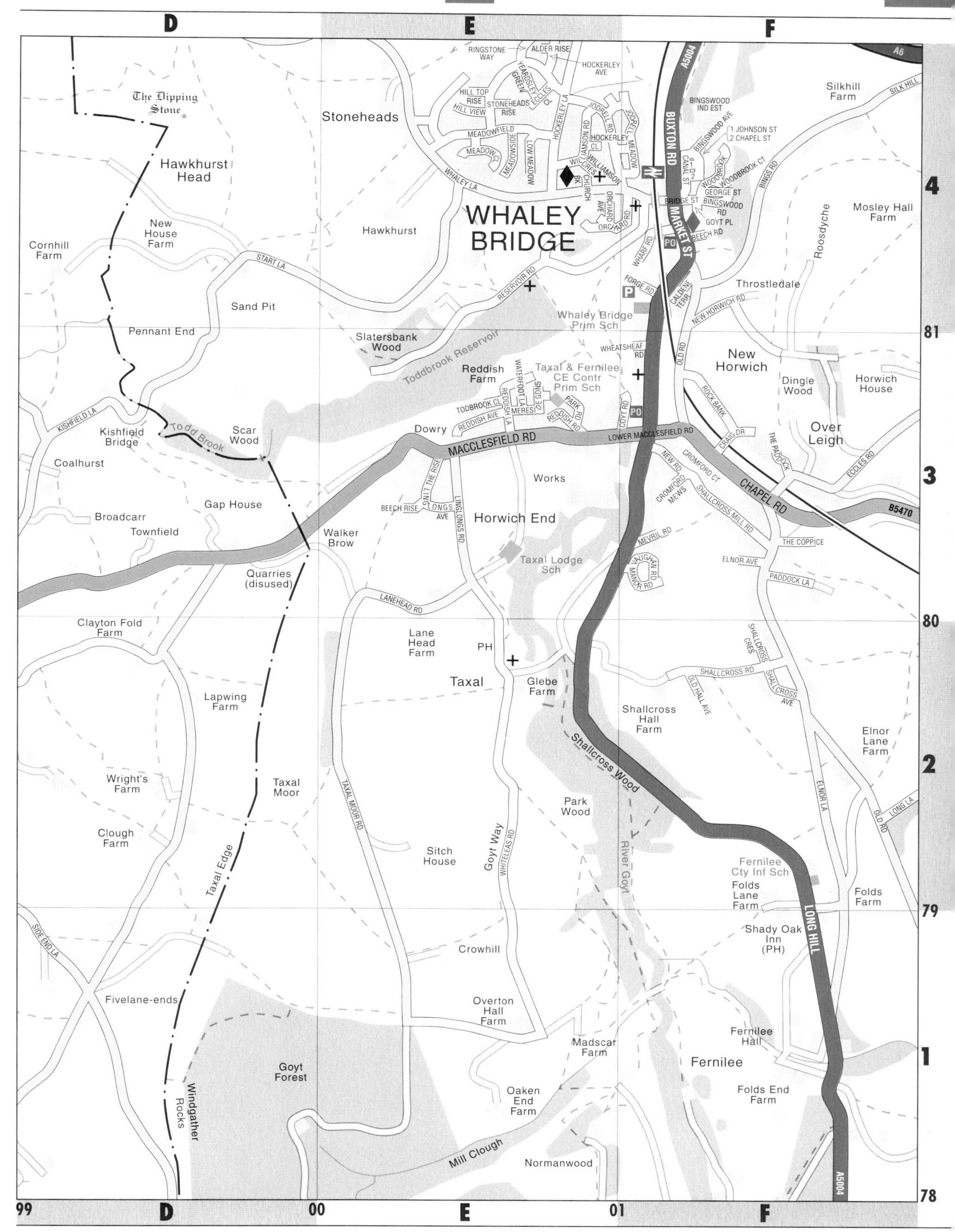
D
E
F
The Dipping Stone
Hawkhurst Head
Stoneheads
WHALEY BRIDGE
Hawkhurst
New House Farm
Cornhill Farm
Sand Pit
Pennant End
Slatersbank Wood
Toddbrook Reservoir
Reddish Farm
Whaley Bridge Prim Sch
Taxal & Fernilee CE Contr Prim Sch
Kishfield Bridge
Todd Brook
Scar Wood
Coalhurst
Dowry
MACCLESFIELD RD
LOWER MACCLESFIELD RD
Works
Gap House
Broadcarr
Townfield
Walker Brow
Horwich End
Taxal Lodge Sch
Quarries (disused)
Clayton Fold Farm
Lane Head Farm
PH
Taxal
Glebe Farm
Lapwing Farm
Shallcross Hall Farm
Shallcross Wood
Wright's Farm
Taxal Moor
Park Wood
Clough Farm
Taxal Edge
Sitch House
Goyt Way
River Goyt
Crowhill
Fivelane-ends
Overton Hall Farm
Madscar Farm
Goyt Forest
Windgather Rocks
Oaken End Farm
Fernilee
Mill Clough
Normanwood
Silkhill Farm
Mosley Hall Farm
Roosdyche
Throstledale
New Horwich
Dingle Wood
Horwich House
Over Leigh
CHAPEL RD
B5470
BUXTON RD
MARKET ST
A5004
A6
LONG HILL
Elnor Lane Farm
Fernilee Cty Inf Sch
Folds Lane Farm
Folds Farm
Shady Oak Inn (PH)
Fernilee Hall
Folds End Farm
1 JOHNSON ST
2 CHAPEL ST
BINGSWOOD IND EST
4
81
3
80
2
79
1
78
99
00
01

41

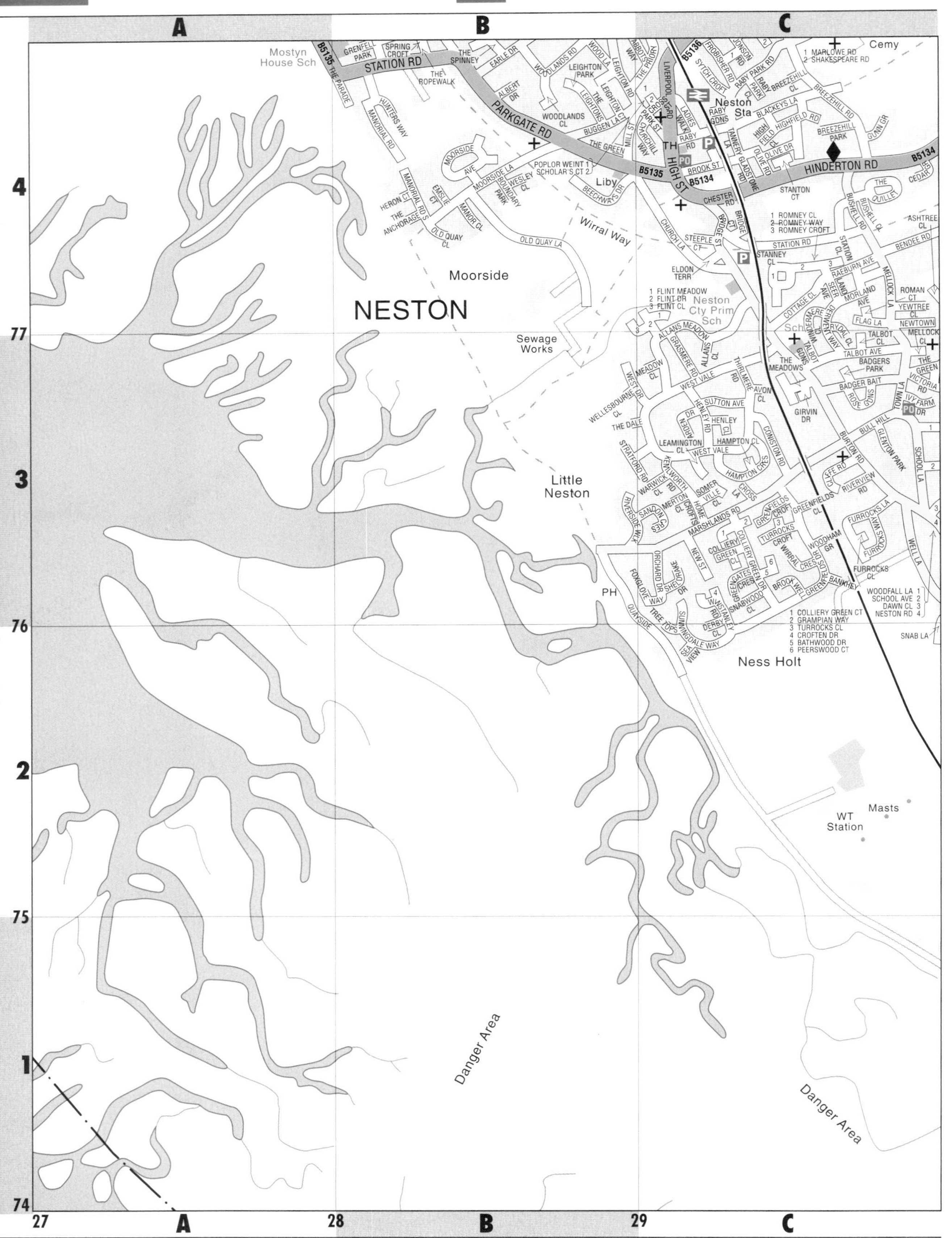
A
B
C
NESTON
Moorside
Little Neston
Ness Holt
Sewage Works
Wirral Way
Mostyn House Sch
Neston Cty Prim Sch
Neston Sta
STATION RD
PARKGATE RD
HINDERTON RD
HIGH ST
Cemy
WT Station
Masts
Danger Area
Danger Area
PH
27
28
29
74
75
76
77
1
2
3
4

91

42

68

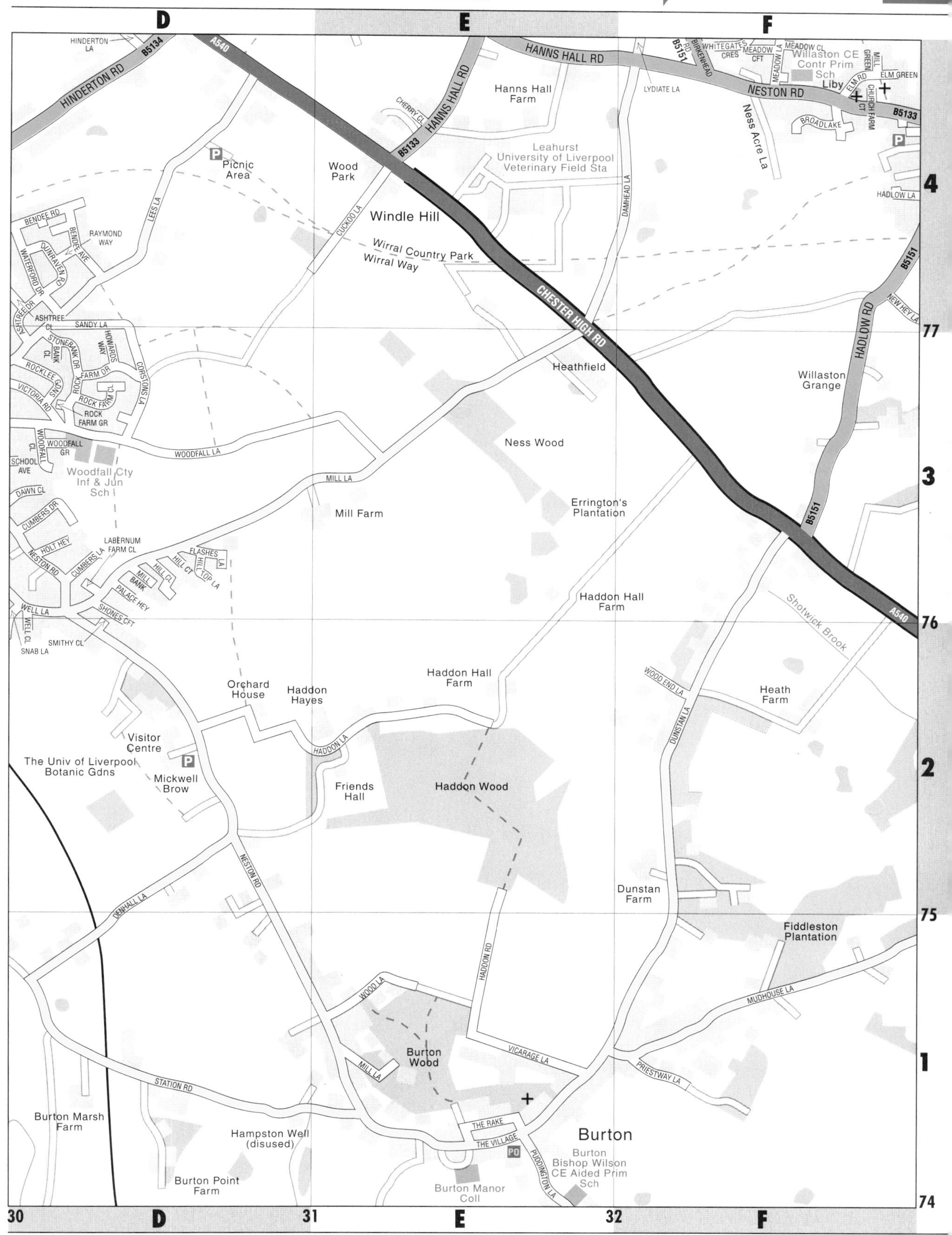

D
E
F
HINDERTON LA
B5134
A540
HINDERTON RD
HANNS HALL RD
B5151
RD
BIRKENHEAD
WHITEGATES CRES
MEADOW CFT
MEADOW LA
MEADOW CL
Willaston CE Contr Prim Sch
MILL GREEN
ELM GREEN
ELM RD
Liby
CHURCH FARM CT
LYDIATE LA
NESTON RD
B5133
Hanns Hall Farm
CHERRY CL
HANNS HALL RD
Ness Acre La
BROADLAKE
B5133
Leahurst University of Liverpool Veterinary Field Sta
Picnic Area
Wood Park
HADLOW LA
LEES LA
CUCKOO LA
DAMHEAD LA
Windle Hill
BENDEE RD
RAYMOND WAY
BENDEE AVE
DUNRAVEN RD
WATERFORD DR
Wirral Country Park
Wirral Way
B5151
ASHTREE DR
ASHTREE CL
SANDY LA
NEW HEY LA
CHESTER HIGH RD
STONEBANK DR
BANK CL
HOWARDS WAY
HADLOW RD
CORSTONS LA
ROCKLEE GDNS
ROCK FARM DR
Heathfield
Willaston Grange
VICTORIA RD
ROCK FARM CL
ROCK FARM GR
WOODFALL CL
WOODFALL GR
WOODFALL LA
Ness Wood
SCHOOL AVE
Woodfall Cty Inf & Jun Sch
MILL LA
DAWN CL
Errington's Plantation
Mill Farm
CUMBERS DR
B5151
HOLT HEY
LABERNUM FARM CL
FLASHES LA
NESTON RD
CUMBERS LA
HILL TOP LA
HILL CT
HILL CL
MILL BANK
Haddon Hall Farm
PALACE HEY
Shotwick Brook
WELL LA
SHONES CFT
A540
WELL CL
SMITHY CL
SNAB LA
WOOD END LA
Haddon Hall Farm
Orchard House
Haddon Hayes
Heath Farm
DUNSTAN LA
Visitor Centre
HADDON LA
The Univ of Liverpool Botanic Gdns
Mickwell Brow
Friends Hall
Haddon Wood
NESTON RD
Dunstan Farm
DENHALL LA
Fiddleston Plantation
HADDON RD
WOOD LA
MUDHOUSE LA
Burton Wood
VICARAGE LA
MILL LA
STATION RD
PRIESTWAY LA
Burton Marsh Farm
THE RAKE
Hampston Well (disused)
THE VILLAGE
Burton
PO
PUDDINGTON LA
Burton Bishop Wilson CE Aided Prim Sch
Burton Point Farm
Burton Manor Coll
4
77
3
76
2
75
1
74
30
31
32

92

68

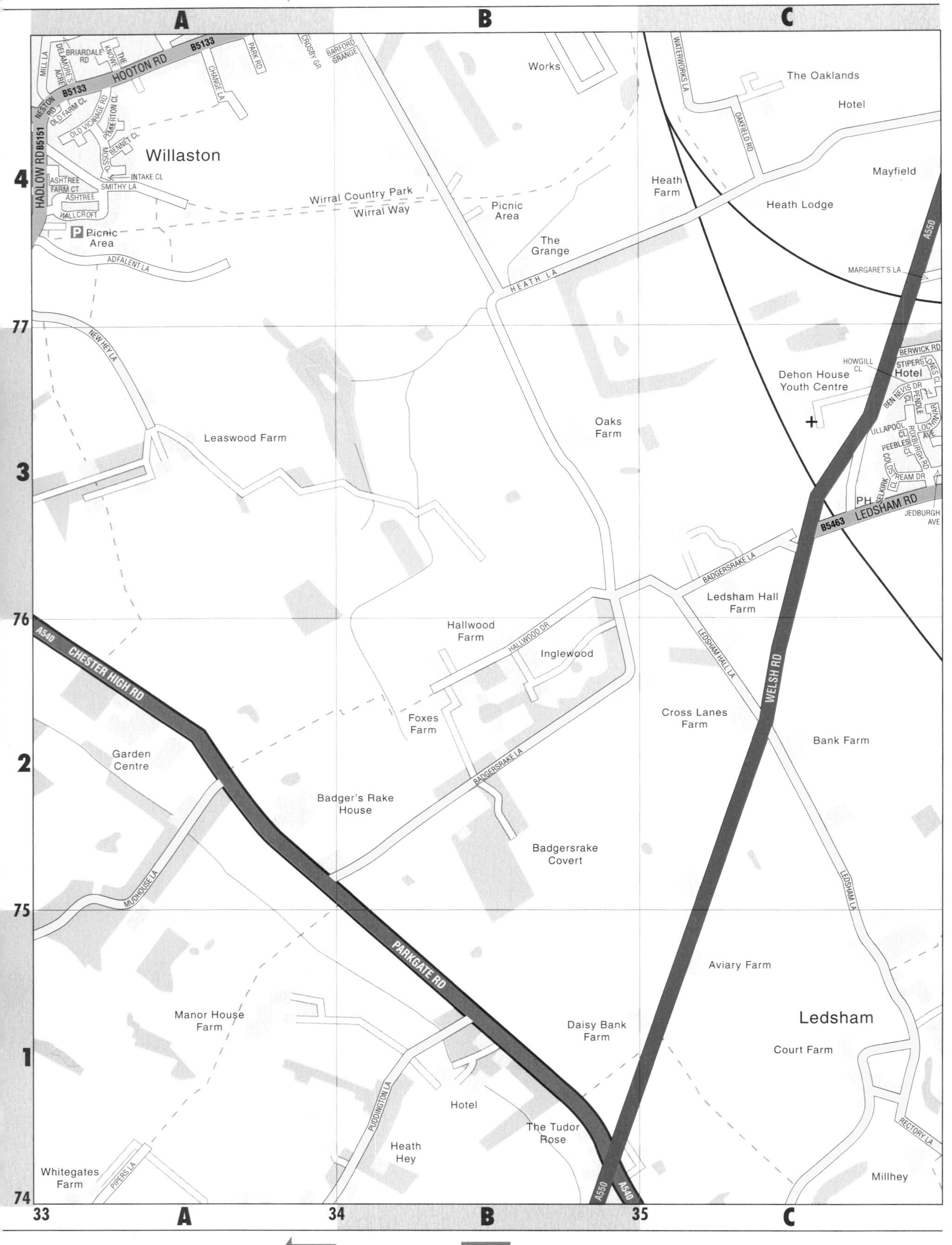

A B C

4

77

3

76

2

75

1

74

33 A 34 B 35 C

Willaston

Wirral Country Park
Wirral Way

Picnic
Area

Picnic
Area

ADFALENT LA

HOOTON RD
B5133

B5133

HADLOW RD B5151

MILL LA
BRIARDALE RD
THE KINE
ARCHER RD
PARK RD
CROSBY GR
BARFORD GRANGE
CHANGE LA
OLD VICARAGE RD
OLD FARM CL
EGERTON CL
NESTON RD
GLISSOW
BENNET CL
INTAKE CL
SMITHY LA
ASHTREE FARM CT
ASHTREE
HALLCROFT

NEW HEY LA

Leaswood Farm

Works

Heath
Farm

The Grange

HEATH LA

Picnic
Area

Oaks
Farm

Hallwood
Farm

Inglewood

HALLWOOD DR

Foxes
Farm

BADGERSRAKE LA

Badger's Rake
House

Badgersrake
Covert

CHESTER HIGH RD
A540

Garden
Centre

MUDHOUSE LA

PARKGATE RD

Manor House
Farm

PUDDINGTON LA

Heath
Hey

Hotel

The Tudor
Rose

Whitegates
Farm

PIPERS LA

Daisy Bank
Farm

The Oaklands

Hotel

Mayfield

Heath Lodge

WATERWORKS LA

OAKFIELD RD

MARGARET'S LA

A550

Dehon House
Youth Centre

HOWGILL CL
BERWICK RD
STIPERS CL
JONES CL
PENDLE
BEN NEVIS DR
ULLAPOOL CL
PEEBLES CL
COLD STREAM DR
SELKIRK
ROXBURGH RD
LOCHINVAR RD

PH.
LEDSHAM RD
B5463

JEDBURGH
AVE

BADGERSRAKE LA

Ledsham Hall
Farm

LEDSHAM HALL LA

WELSH RD

Cross Lanes
Farm

Bank Farm

LEDSHAM LA

Aviary Farm

Ledsham

Court Farm

RECTORY LA

Millhey

A550
A540

44

70

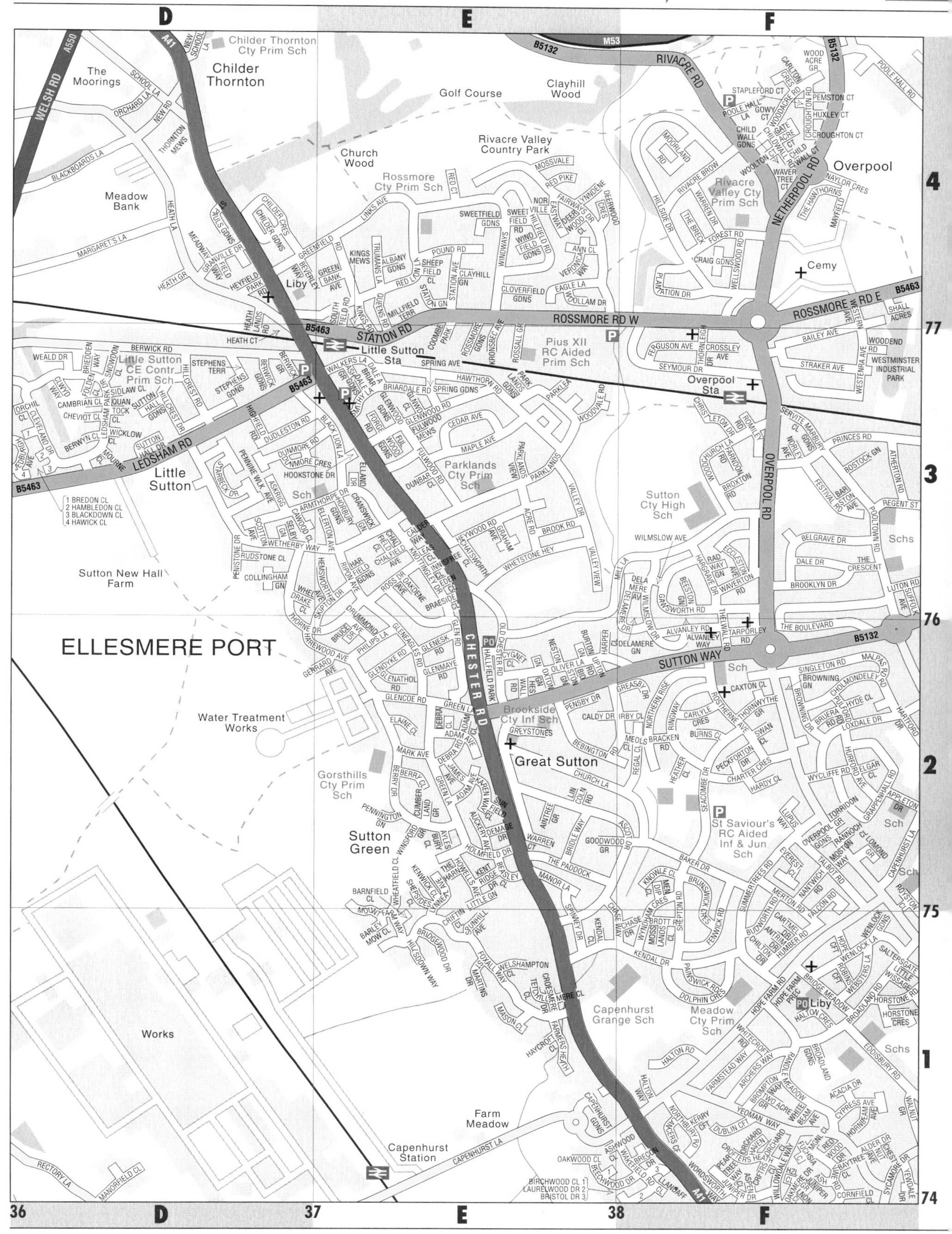

D
E
F
Childer Thornton Cty Prim Sch
Childer Thornton
The Moorings
Golf Course
Clayhill Wood
RIVACRE RD
M53
B5132
A41
A550
WELSH RD
SCHOOL LA
ORCHARD LA
NEW RD
THORNTON MEWS
BLACKBOARDS LA
Meadow Bank
HEATH LA
MARGARET'S LA
HEATH GR
Church Wood
Rivacre Valley Country Park
Rossmore Cty Prim Sch
MOSSVALE
RED PIKE
CHILDER CRES
CHILDER GDNS
LINKS AVE
SWEETFIELD GDNS
POUND RD
KINGS MEWS
TRUMANS LA
ALBANY GDNS
CLAYHILL GN
CLOVERFIELD GDNS
EAGLE LA
WOLLAM DR
Liby
GREEN BANK AVE
RED LION LA
STATION AVE
STATION GN
MILLFIELD TERR
HEATH CT
HEATHLANDS RD
STATION RD
B5463
Little Sutton Sta
SPRING AVE
ROSSMORE RD W
ROSSMORE RD E
Pius XII RC Aided Prim Sch
Overpool Sta
Overpool
Cemy
Rivacre Valley Cty Prim Sch
NETHERPOOL RD
MOORLAND RD
HILLSIDE DR
RIVACRE BROW
WARREN DR
FOREST RD
CRAIG GDNS
WELLSWOOD RD
PLANTATION DR
STAPLEFORD CT
POOLE HALL LA
POOLE HALL RD
PEMSTON CT
HUXLEY CT
CROUGHTON CT
NAYLOR CRES
THE HAWTHORNS
MAYFIELD
WOOD ACRE GR
FERGUSON AVE
SEYMOUR DR
THORNLEIGH DR
CROSSLEY AVE
BAILEY AVE
STRAKER AVE
WOODEND RD
WESTMINSTER INDUSTRIAL PARK
WESTENRA AVE
SHALL ACRES
WEALD DR
BERWICK RD
Little Sutton CE Contr Prim Sch
STEPHENS TERR
STEPHENS GDNS
HILLCREST RD
BERWICK GDNS
CAMBRIAN CL
CHEVIOT CL
SIDLAW CL
QUANTOCK CL
SUTTON HALL GDNS
WICKLOW CL
SUTTON HALL DR
BERWYN CL
MOURNE
ORCHIL CL
CLEVELAND DR
LEDSHAM RD
Little Sutton
1 BREDON CL
2 HAMBLEDON CL
3 BLACKDOWN CL
4 HAWICK CL
HIGHFIELD RD
DUDLESTON RD
DUNMORE RD
HOOKSTONE DR
BLACK LION LA
PARKBECK DR
PENNINE WALK
ASHRIGG
Sch
ARMTHORPE DR
ELLERTON AVE
SCOTTON AVE
WETHERBY WAY
RUDSTONE CL
COLLINGHAM GN
PENISTONE DR
Sutton New Hall Farm
BRIARDALE RD
SPRING GDNS
HAWTHORN RD
GLENWOOD RD
FULWOOD MEWS
CEDAR AVE
MAPLE AVE
Parklands Cty Prim Sch
PARKLANDS VIEW
PARKLANDS
DUNBAR CL
ELAND DR
CRANSWICK GN
CHALFIELD AVE
HEYWOOD RD
CHATSWORTH
GRAHAM AVE
ACRE RD
BROOK RD
WHETSTONE HEY
VALLEY DR
VALLEY VIEW
PARKLEA
WOODVALE RD
Sutton Cty High Sch
WILMSLOW AVE
ECCLESTON AVE
CHRISTLETON DR
FARNDON AVE
BROXTON RD
ROMILEY
OVERPOOL RD
SERVITE CL
MARBURY GDNS
PRINCES RD
BOSTOCK GN
ATHERTON RD
REGENT ST
POOLTOWN RD
BELGRAVE DR
DALE DR
THE CRESCENT
BROOKLYN DR
Schs
LUTON RD
SUFFOLK
THE BOULEVARD
ELLESMERE PORT
HAREWOOD AVE
THORNE DR
GERRARD AVE
PHILIPS LA
GLENEAGLES RD
GLENESK RD
GLENMAYE RD
GLENDYKE RD
GLENATHOL RD
GLENCOE RD
DRUMMOND AVE
ROSS DR
OAKDENE
BRAESIDE
CHESTER RD
OLD CHESTER RD
HALLFIELD PARK
CYGNET CL
NESTON GN
OLIVER LA
BURTON GN
UPTON DR
HARPER CL
DELAMERE AV
ALVANLEY RD
ALVANLEY WAY
TARPORLEY RD
SUTTON WAY
B5132
Sch
CAXTON CL
SINGLETON RD
BROWNING DR
MALPAS RD
CHOLMONDELEY RD
HYDE CL
LOXDALE DR
HARTFORD DR
Brookside Cty Inf Sch
GREYSTONES
Great Sutton
PENSBY DR
CALDY DR
IRBY CL
BEBINGTON RD
NORTHERN RISE
RINGWAY
CARLYLE CRES
BURNS CL
THORNWYTHE GR
SWAN CL
MEOLS CL
BRACKEN RD
REGAL CL
HEATHER CL
PECKFORTON DR
CHARTER CRES
HARDY CL
WYCLIFFE RD
ELGAR CL
Water Treatment Works
ELAINE CL
MARK AVE
ADAM AVE
DEBRA RD
JAMES AVE
GREEN LA
Gorsthills Cty Prim Sch
BERRY DR
CUMBERLAND GR
PENNINGTON GN
Sutton Green
CHURCH LA
AINTREE GR
BRIDLE WAY
ASCOT DR
WARREN CT
GOODWOOD GR
THE PADDOCK
MANOR LA
St Saviour's RC Aided Inf & Jun Sch
SEACOMBE DR
LUPUS WAY
OVERPOOL GR
TORRIDON
APPLETON DR
CAPENHURST LA
Sch
BAKER DR
KNOWLE CL
BRUNSWICK CRES
SUMMERTREES RD
EVEREST CL
NANTWICH RD
MERTON RD
FALCON RD
ROYSTON CL
HOLMFIELD DR
KENT RD
RIDGE DR
BEASLEY CL
LITTLE GN
HOWELLS AVE
BARNFIELD CL
WHEATFIELD CL
MOUNT FARM WAY
BARLEY MOW CL
SHEPSIDES
CRIFTIN CL
SUNHILL AVE
HILLSDOWN WAY
BRIDGEWOOD DR
SPINNEY DR
CHASE WAY
KENDAL DR
WYNDHAM CRES
SHEPTON RD
FENWICK RD
BUDWORTH RD
CARTMEL DR
HUMBER RD
CHILTON DR
WENLOCK LA
HOPE FARM RD
HOPE FARM PREC
Liby
HALTON CRES
BRIDGE MEADOW
BROADLAND RD
HORSTONE RD
HORSTONE CRES
SALTERSGATE
LITTLE WISSAGE
NELSHAMPTON
ST MARTINS DR
TETCHILL DR
CROESMERE DR
MERE CL
MASON CL
HAYCROFT CL
FARMERS HEATH
Capenhurst Grange Sch
PAINSWICK RD
DOLPHIN CRES
Meadow Cty Prim Sch
HALTON RD
WHITECROFT RD
FARMSTEAD WAY
ARCHERS WAY
Schs
EDDISBURY RD
ACACIA DR
CYPRESS AVE
WALNUT GR
Works
Farm Meadow
HALTON WAY
NORTHBURY RD
YEOMAN WAY
DUBLIN CFT
CAPENHURST GDNS
Capenhurst Station
CAPENHURST LA
ASHWOOD CL
OAKWOOD CL
BIRCHWOOD CL 1
LAURELWOOD DR 2
BRISTOL DR 3
LLANDAFF
WORDSWORTH WAY
CORNFIELD CL
SYCAMORE DR
YEWDALE DR
RECTORY LA
MANORFIELD CL
ALDER DR
BAYTREE CL
4
3
2
1
77
76
75
74
36
37
38

94

70

69
45

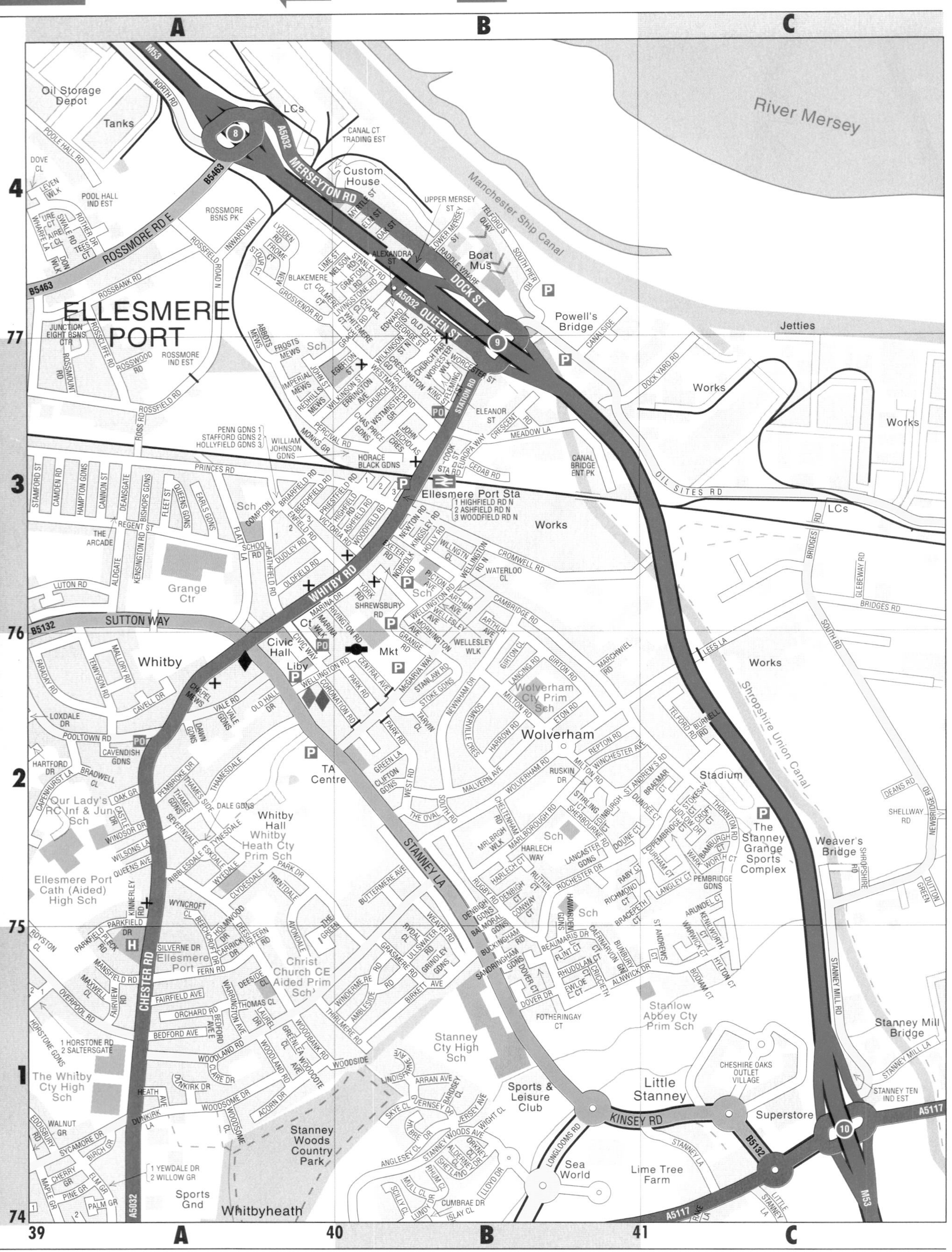
A
B
C
4
77
3
76
2
75
1
74
39
40
41
River Mersey
Manchester Ship Canal
Oil Storage Depot
Tanks
LCs
CANAL CT TRADING EST
Custom House
ELLESMERE PORT
ROSSMORE RD E
POOL HALL IND EST
ROSSMORE BSNS PK
JUNCTION EIGHT BSNS CTR
ROSSMORE IND EST
MERSEYTON RD
DOCK ST
QUEEN ST
Boat Mus
Powell's Bridge
Jetties
Works
OIL SITES RD
Ellesmere Port Sta
1 HIGHFIELD RD N
2 ASHFIELD RD N
3 WOODFIELD RD N
CANAL BRIDGE ENT PK
PRINCES RD
WHITBY RD
STATION RD
Grange Ctr
SUTTON WAY
Whitby
Civic Hall
Liby
Mkt
Wolverham Cty Prim Sch
Wolverham
Stadium
Shropshire Union Canal
The Stanney Grange Sports Complex
Weaver's Bridge
BRIDGES RD
LEES LA
TA Centre
Our Lady's RC Inf & Jun Sch
Whitby Hall
Whitby Heath Cty Prim Sch
Ellesmere Port Cath (Aided) High Sch
STANNEY LA
CHESTER RD
Ellesmere Port
Christ Church CE Aided Prim Sch
Stanlow Abbey Cty Prim Sch
Stanney Cty High Sch
Stanney Mill Bridge
STANNEY MILL RD
CHESHIRE OAKS OUTLET VILLAGE
Little Stanney
Sports & Leisure Club
KINSEY RD
Superstore
STANNEY TEN IND EST
The Whitby Cty High Sch
Stanney Woods Country Park
Sea World
Lime Tree Farm
Sports Gnd
Whitbyheath
A5117
A5032
M53
B5463
B5132

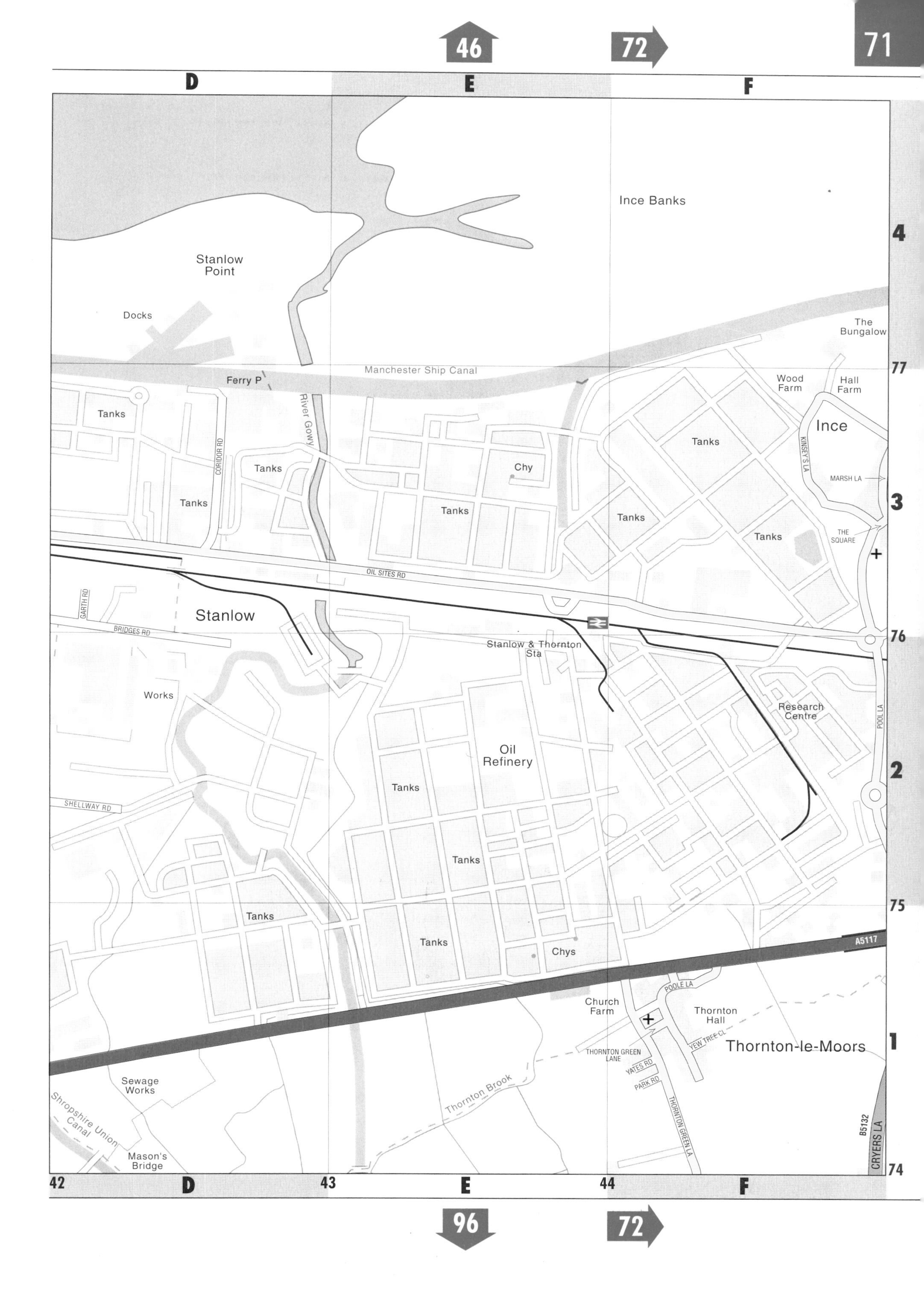

46
72

Ince Banks

4

Stanlow
Point

Docks

The
Bungalow

Manchester Ship Canal

Ferry P

River Gowy

77

Wood
Farm

Hall
Farm

Ince

Tanks

CORRIDOR RD

Tanks

Tanks

Chy

Tanks

KINSEY'S LA

MARSH LA →

Tanks

THE
SQUARE

3

Tanks

Tanks

+

OIL SITES RD

GARTH RD

Stanlow

BRIDGES RD

Stanlow & Thornton
Sta

76

Research
Centre

POOLE LA

Works

Oil
Refinery

2

Tanks

SHELLWAY RD

Tanks

75

Tanks

Tanks

A5117

Chys

Tanks

POOLE LA

Church
Farm

Thornton
Hall

YEW TREE CL

Thornton-le-Moors

1

THORNTON GREEN
LANE

YATES RD

PARK RD

Sewage
Works

Thornton Brook

THORNTON GREEN LA

B5132

CRYERS LA

Shropshire
Union
Canal

Mason's
Bridge

74

A **B** **C**

4

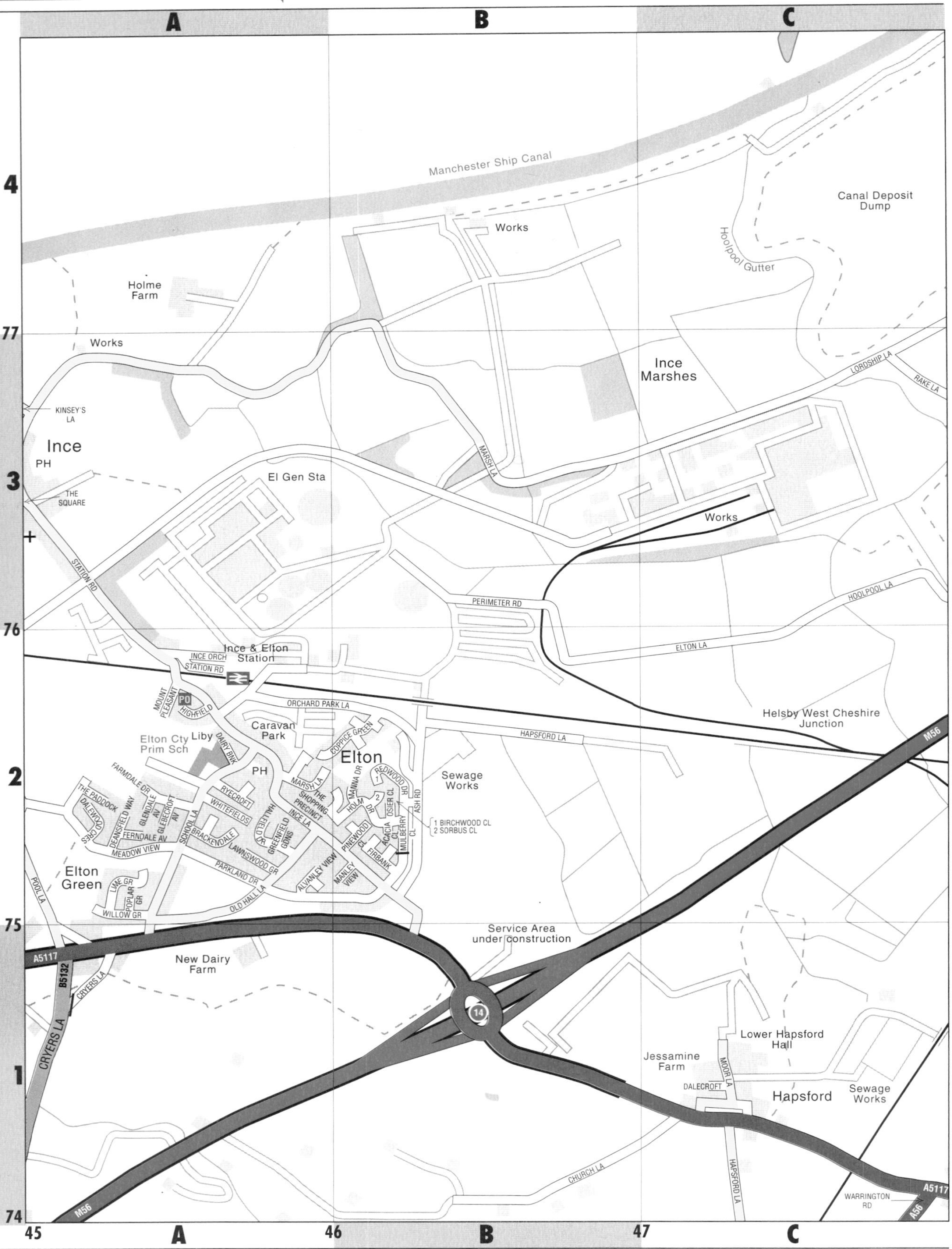

Manchester Ship Canal

Works

Canal Deposit
Dump

Hoolpool Gutter

77

Works

Ince
Marshes

KINSEY'S
LA

LORDSHIP LA

RAKE LA

Ince

PH

Holme
Farm

3

THE
SQUARE

El Gen Sta

Works

MARSH LA

HOOLPOOL LA

STATION RD

PERIMETER RD

76

ELTON LA

Ince & Elton
Station

INCE ORCH
STATION RD

Helsby West Cheshire
Junction

MOUNT
PLEASANT

PO

HIGHFIELD

ORCHARD PARK LA

M56

Caravan
Park

COPPICE GREEN

HAPSFORD LA

Elton Cty
Prim Sch

Liby

DAIRY BNK

Elton

2

FARMDALE DR

PH

MARSH LA

REDWOOD DR

Sewage
Works

THE PADDOCK

OAKWOOD

DEANSFIELD WAY

GLENDALE

FERNDALE AV

GLEBECROFT

SCHOOL LA

BYECROFT

WHITEFIELDS

HALLFIELD

GREENFIELD GDNS

THE
SHOPPING
PRECINCT

INCE LA

MARINA DR

HOLM DR

PINEWOOD CL

ACACIA CL

OSIER CL

MULBERRY CL

ASH RD

FIRBANK

1 BIRCHWOOD CL
2 SORBUS CL

1
2

CRES

BRACKENDALE

LAWNSWOOD GR

MEADOW VIEW

ALVANLEY VIEW

MATLEY VIEW

Elton
Green

PROLA

LIME GR

POPLAR GR

WILLOW GR

PARKLAND DR

OLD HALL LA

75

Service Area
under construction

A5117

B5132

CRYERS LA

New Dairy
Farm

14

Lower Hapsford
Hall

MOOR LA

Jessamine
Farm

1

DALECROFT

Hapsford

Sewage
Works

HAPSFORD LA

CHURCH LA

WARRINGTON
RD

A5117

A56

74

M56

45 **A** **46** **B** **47** **C**

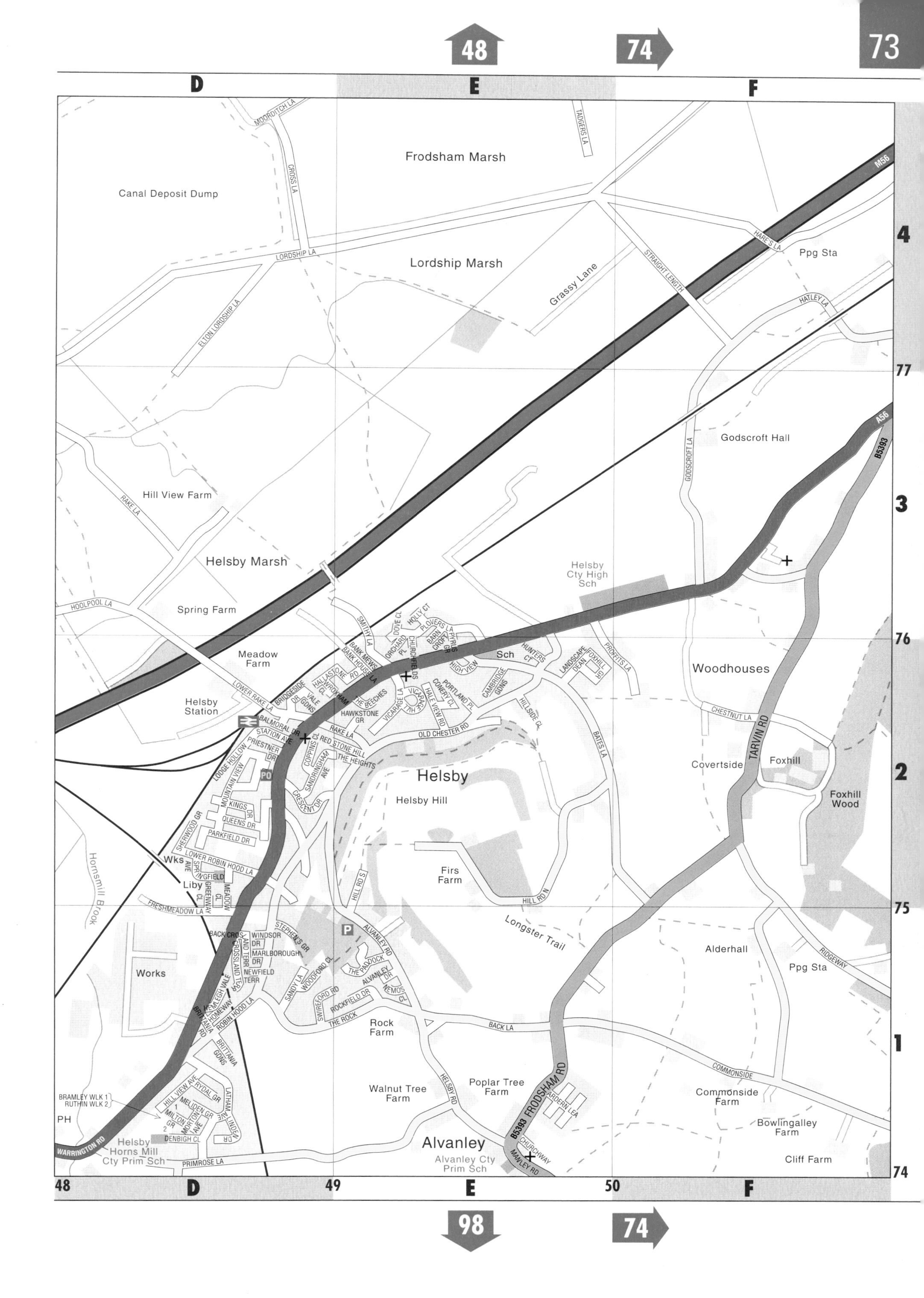
48
74
D
E
F
Frodsham Marsh
Canal Deposit Dump
Lordship Marsh
Grassy Lane
Ppg Sta
Godscroft Hall
Hill View Farm
Helsby Marsh
Spring Farm
Helsby Cty High Sch
Meadow Farm
Helsby Station
Woodhouses
Covertside
Foxhill
Foxhill Wood
Helsby
Helsby Hill
Wks
Liby
Hornsmill Brook
Firs Farm
Longster Trail
Alderhall
Ppg Sta
Works
Rock Farm
Walnut Tree Farm
Poplar Tree Farm
Commonside Farm
Bowlingalley Farm
Cliff Farm
Alvanley
Alvanley Cty Prim Sch
Helsby Horns Mill Cty Prim Sch
PH
Sch
M56
A56
B5393
TARVIN RD
FRODSHAM RD
WARRINGTON RD
LORDSHIP LA
MOORDITCH LA
CROSS LA
TADGERS LA
STRAIGHT LENGTH
HARE'S LA
HATLEY LA
GODSCROFT LA
ELTON LORDSHIP LA
RAKE LA
HOOLPOOL LA
LOWER RAKE LA
CHESTNUT LA
BATES LA
PROFFITS LA
HILLSIDE CL
OLD CHESTER RD
HILL RD N
HILL RD S
ALVANLEY RD
BACK LA
COMMONSIDE
RIDGEWAY
HELSBY RD
CHURCHWAY
MANLEY RD
ARDERN LEA
PRIMROSE LA
DENBIGH CL
BRAMLEY WLK 1
RUTHIN WLK 2
4
3
2
1
77
76
75
74
48
49
50
98

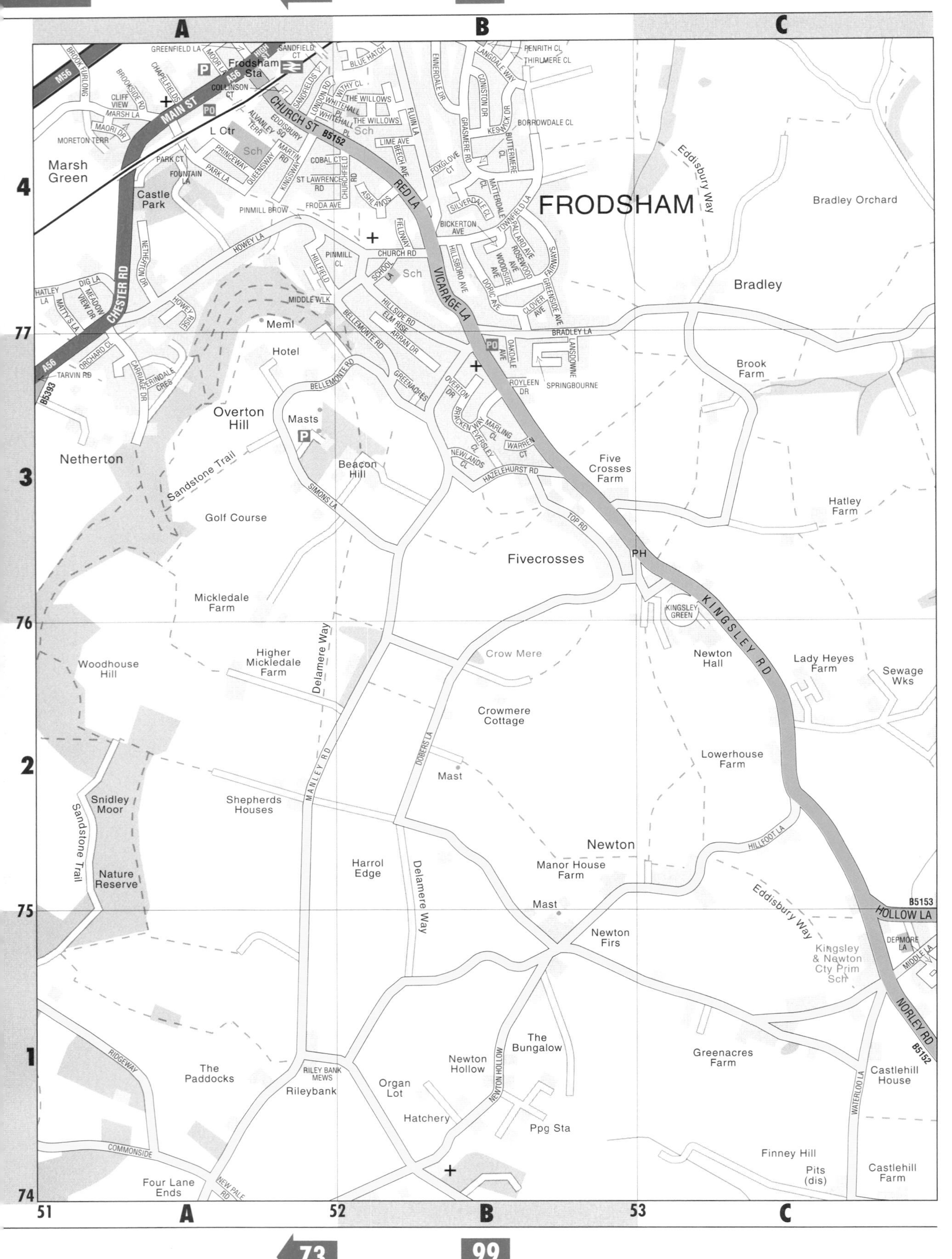

FRODSHAM

Marsh Green

Bradley Orchard

Bradley

Netherton

Overton Hill

Fivecrosses

Woodhouse Hill

Snidley Moor

Nature Reserve

Newton

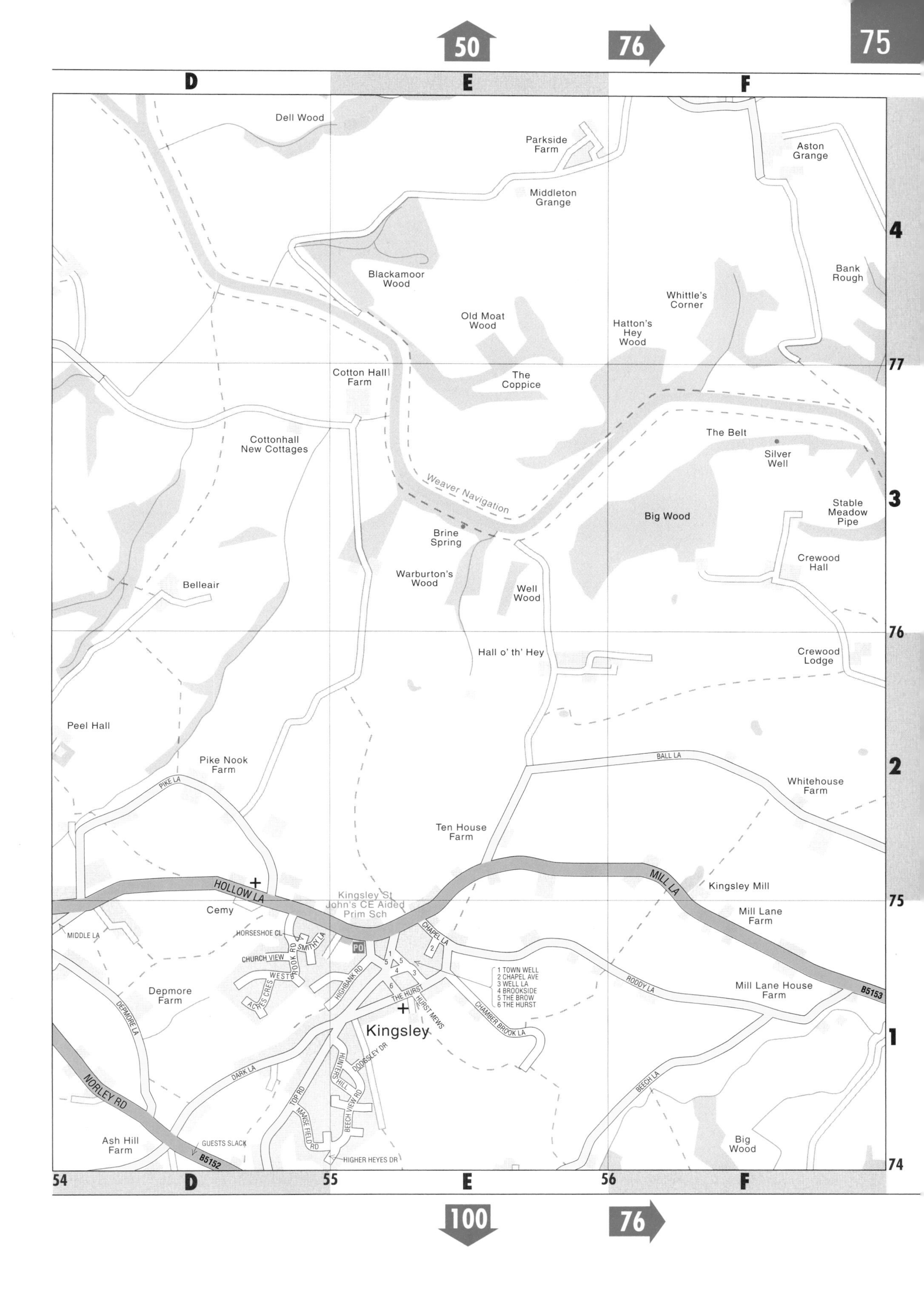

D
E
F

Dell Wood

Parkside Farm

Aston Grange

Middleton Grange

4

Blackamoor Wood

Bank Rough

Old Moat Wood

Whittle's Corner

Hatton's Hey Wood

77

Cotton Hall Farm

The Coppice

Cottonhall New Cottages

The Belt

Silver Well

Weaver Navigation

3

Big Wood

Stable Meadow Pipe

Brine Spring

Crewood Hall

Belleair

Warburton's Wood

Well Wood

Peel Hall

76

Hall o' th' Hey

Crewood Lodge

Pike Nook Farm

2

BALL LA

Whitehouse Farm

PIKE LA

Ten House Farm

MILL LA

Kingsley Mill

HOLLOW LA

Kingsley St John's CE Aided Prim Sch

Cemy

75

Mill Lane Farm

MIDDLE LA

HORSESHOE CL

CHAPEL LA

RODDY LA

Mill Lane House Farm

B5153

CHURCH VIEW

WEST S

HIGHBANK RD

SMITH LA

WEST BROOK RD

PO

1 TOWN WELL
2 CHAPEL AVE
3 WELL LA
4 BROOKSIDE
5 THE BROW
6 THE HURST

ACRES CRES

Depmore Farm

THE HURST

HURST MEWS

CHAMBER BROOK LA

DEPMORE LA

Kingsley

1

DARK LA

HILL

DODGSLEY DR

BEECH LA

Big Wood

NORLEY RD

TOP RD

SMITH LA

BEECH VIEW RD

MANSE FIELD RD

Ash Hill Farm

B5152

GUESTS SLACK

HIGHER HEYES DR

74

54
D
55
E
56
F

75
51

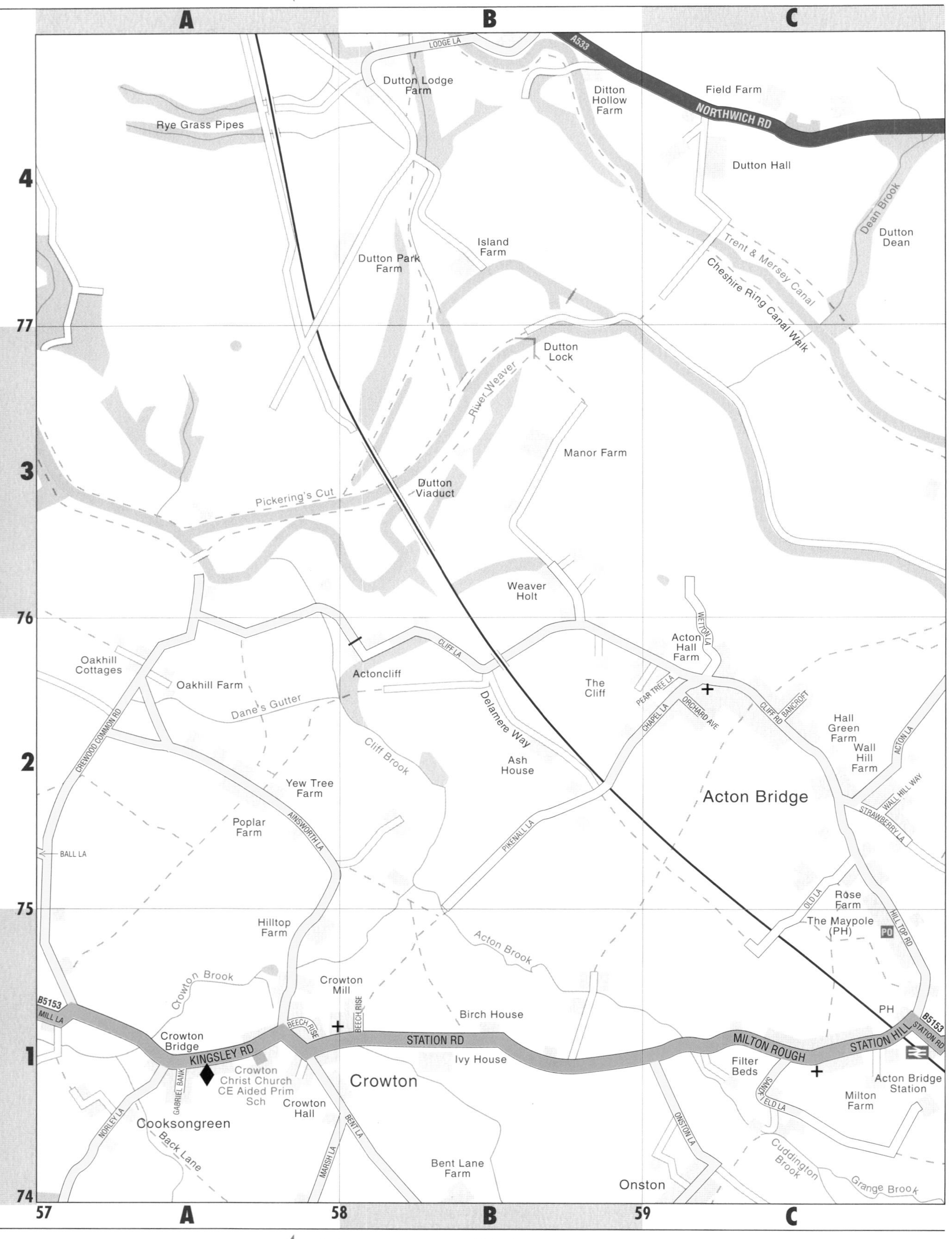
A
B
C
Dutton Lodge Farm
LODGE LA
A533
Ditton Hollow Farm
Field Farm
NORTHWICH RD
Rye Grass Pipes
Dutton Hall
Dean Brook
Dutton Dean
Island Farm
Dutton Park Farm
Trent & Mersey Canal
Cheshire Ring Canal Walk
Dutton Lock
River Weaver
Manor Farm
Pickering's Cut
Dutton Viaduct
Weaver Holt
Acton Hall Farm
WETTON LA
Oakhill Cottages
CLIFF LA
Oakhill Farm
Actoncliff
The Cliff
PEAR TREE LA
Dane's Gutter
CHAPEL LA
ORCHARD AVE
CLIFF RD
BANCROFT
Hall Green Farm
Delamere Way
Wall Hill Farm
ACTON LA
CREWOOD COMMON RD
Cliff Brook
Ash House
Yew Tree Farm
Acton Bridge
WALL HILL WAY
STRAWBERRY LA
Poplar Farm
AINSWORTH LA
PIKENALL LA
BALL LA
OLD LA
Rose Farm
The Maypole (PH)
PO
HILL TOP RD
Hilltop Farm
Acton Brook
Crowton Brook
Crowton Mill
B5153
MILL LA
Birch House
PH
BEECH RISE
STATION RD
MILTON ROUGH
STATION HILL
Crowton Bridge
KINGSLEY RD
Ivy House
Filter Beds
Crowton Christ Church CE Aided Prim Sch
GABRIEL BANK
Crowton
SANDFIELD LA
Acton Bridge Station
Milton Farm
Crowton Hall
NORLEY LA
Cooksongreen
BENT LA
ONSTON LA
Back Lane
Cuddington Brook
MARSH LA
Bent Lane Farm
Onston
Grange Brook
4
77
3
76
2
75
1
74
57
58
59

75
101

52
78

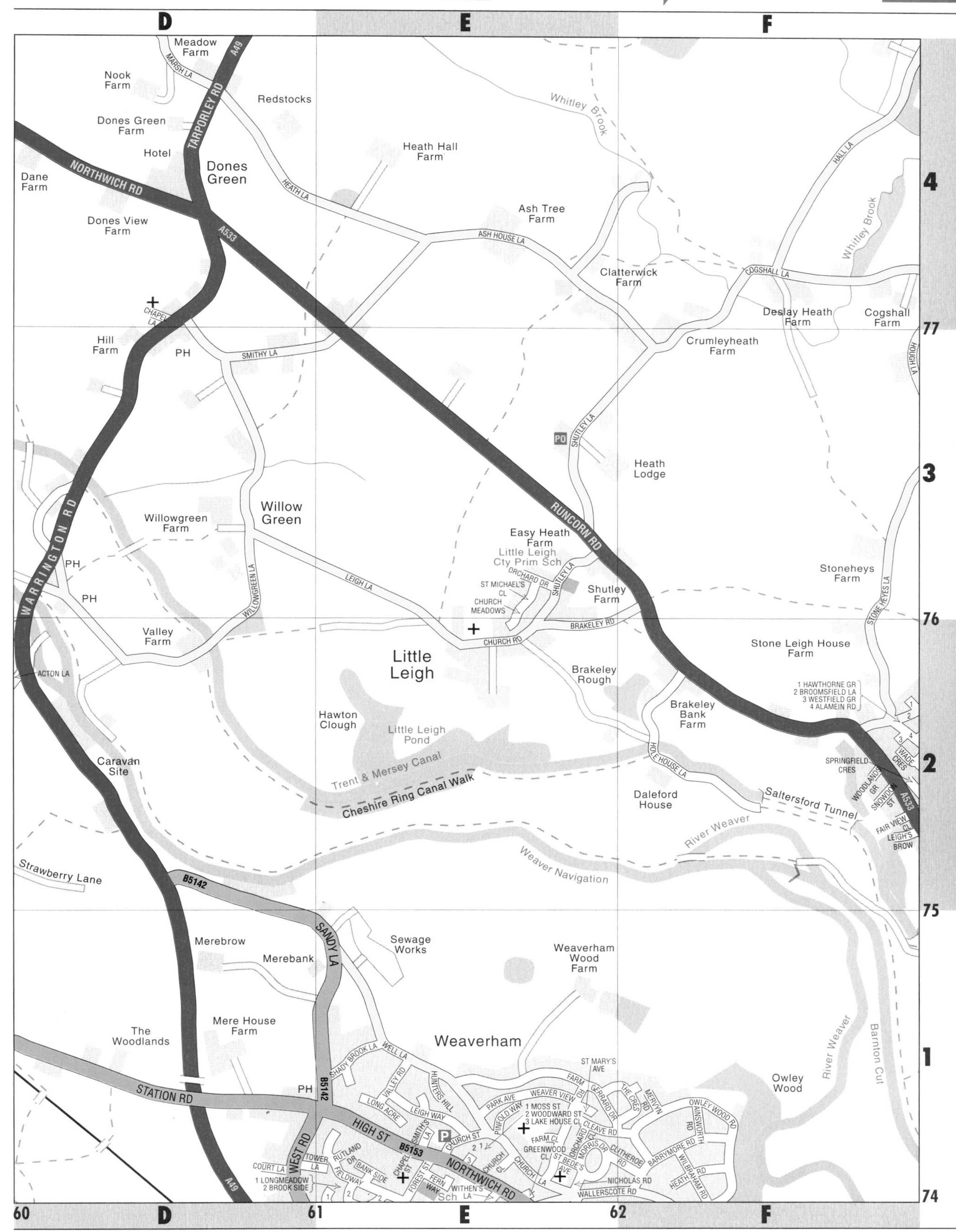
D
E
F
Meadow Farm
MARSH LA
A49
Nook Farm
Redstocks
Dones Green Farm
TARPORLEY RD
Whitley Brook
Hotel
Heath Hall Farm
Dane Farm
NORTHWICH RD
Dones Green
HEATH LA
HALL LA
4
Ash Tree Farm
Dones View Farm
A533
ASH HOUSE LA
Whitley Brook
Clatterwick Farm
COGSHALL LA
CHAPEL LA
Deslay Heath Farm
Cogshall Farm
77
Hill Farm
PH
SMITHY LA
Crumleyheath Farm
HOUGH LA
PO
SHUTLEY LA
Heath Lodge
3
Willow Green
RUNCORN RD
Willowgreen Farm
WARRINGTON RD
Easy Heath Farm
Little Leigh Cty Prim Sch
PH
ORCHARD DR
SHUTLEY LA
Stoneheys Farm
PH
LEIGH LA
ST MICHAEL'S CL
Shutley Farm
CHURCH MEADOWS
WILLOWGREEN LA
STONE HEYES LA
Valley Farm
BRAKELEY RD
76
CHURCH RD
Little Leigh
Stone Leigh House Farm
ACTON LA
Brakeley Rough
1 HAWTHORNE GR
2 BROOMSFIELD LA
3 WESTFIELD GR
4 ALAMEIN RD
Hawton Clough
Brakeley Bank Farm
Little Leigh Pond
Caravan Site
Trent & Mersey Canal
HOLE HOUSE LA
SPRINGFIELD CRES
WADE CRES
2
Cheshire Ring Canal Walk
Daleford House
Saltersford Tunnel
WOODLANDS GR
SNOWDON ST
A533
FAIR VIEW CL
LEIGH'S BROW
River Weaver
Strawberry Lane
Weaver Navigation
B5142
75
SANDY LA
Sewage Works
Merebrow
Weaverham Wood Farm
Merebank
Mere House Farm
River Weaver
Barnton Cut
The Woodlands
Weaverham
1
ST MARY'S AVE
SHADY BROOK LA
WELL LA
Owley Wood
VALLEY RD
HUNTERS HILL
FARM RD
GERRARD DR
THE CRES
MERYN RD
STATION RD
PH
B5142
LONG ACRE
PARK AVE
WEAVER VIEW
OWLEY WOOD RD
AINSWORTH RD
LEIGH WAY
PINFOLD WAY
1 MOSS ST
2 WOODWARD ST
3 LAKE HOUSE CL
CLEAVE RD
HIGH ST
SMITH'S LA
P
CHURCH ST
B5153
FARM CL
GREENWOOD CL
ORCHARD DR
MORRIS DR
CLITHEROE RD
BARRYMORE RD
WEST RD
TOWER LA
RUTLAND DR
BANK SIDE
NORTHWICH RD
CHURCH CL
CHURCH LA
ST BEDE'S AVE
WILBRAHAM RD
HEATH RD
COURT LA
1 LONGMEADOW
2 BROOK SIDE
FIELDWAY
CHAPEL ST
FOREST ST
FERN WAY
WITHEN'S LA
Sch
NICHOLAS RD
WALLERSCOTE RD
A49
74
60
D
61
E
62
F

102
78

77
53

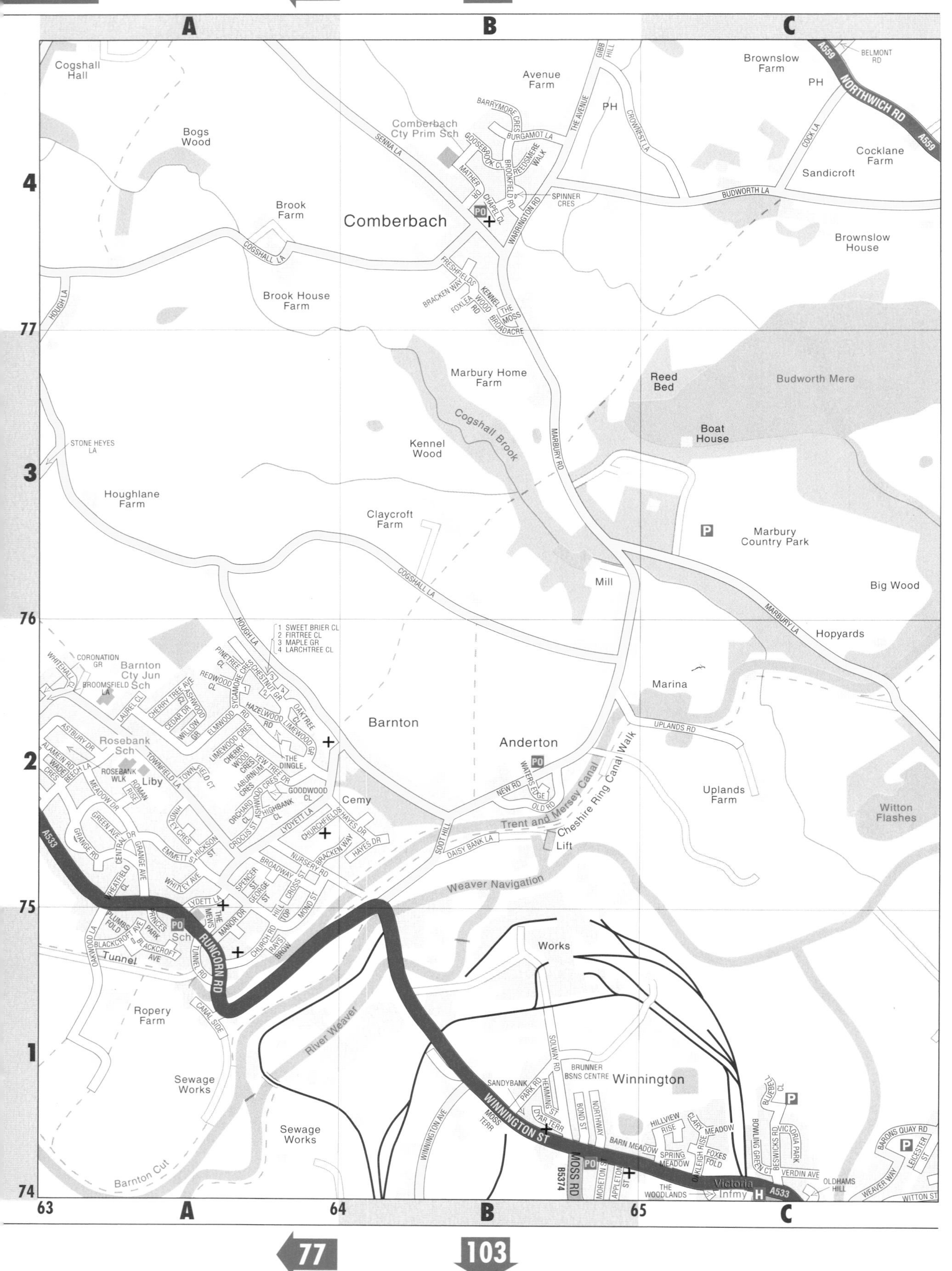
A
B
C
Cogshall Hall
Bogs Wood
Brook Farm
Comberbach
Comberbach Cty Prim Sch
Avenue Farm
Brownslow Farm
PH
Cocklane Farm
Sandicroft
Brownslow House
Brook House Farm
Budworth Mere
Reed Bed
Boat House
Marbury Home Farm
Kennel Wood
Cogshall Brook
Houghlane Farm
Claycroft Farm
Marbury Country Park
Mill
Big Wood
Hopyards
Marina
Barnton
Anderton
Uplands Farm
Witton Flashes
Barnton Cty Jun Sch
Rosebank Sch
Liby
Cemy
Trent and Mersey Canal
Cheshire Ring Canal Walk
Lift
Weaver Navigation
Works
Tunnel
Ropery Farm
River Weaver
Sewage Works
Sewage Works
Winnington
Barnton Cut
Victoria Infmy
NORTHWICH RD
A559
A533
RUNCORN RD
WINNINGTON ST
MOSS RD
B5374
BUDWORTH LA
MARBURY LA
MARBURY RD
COGSHALL LA
SENNA LA
HOUGH LA
WARRINGTON RD
UPLANDS RD
1 SWEET BRIER CL
2 FIRTREE CL
3 MAPLE GR
4 LARCHTREE CL
63
64
65
74
75
1
2
76
3
77
4

77
103

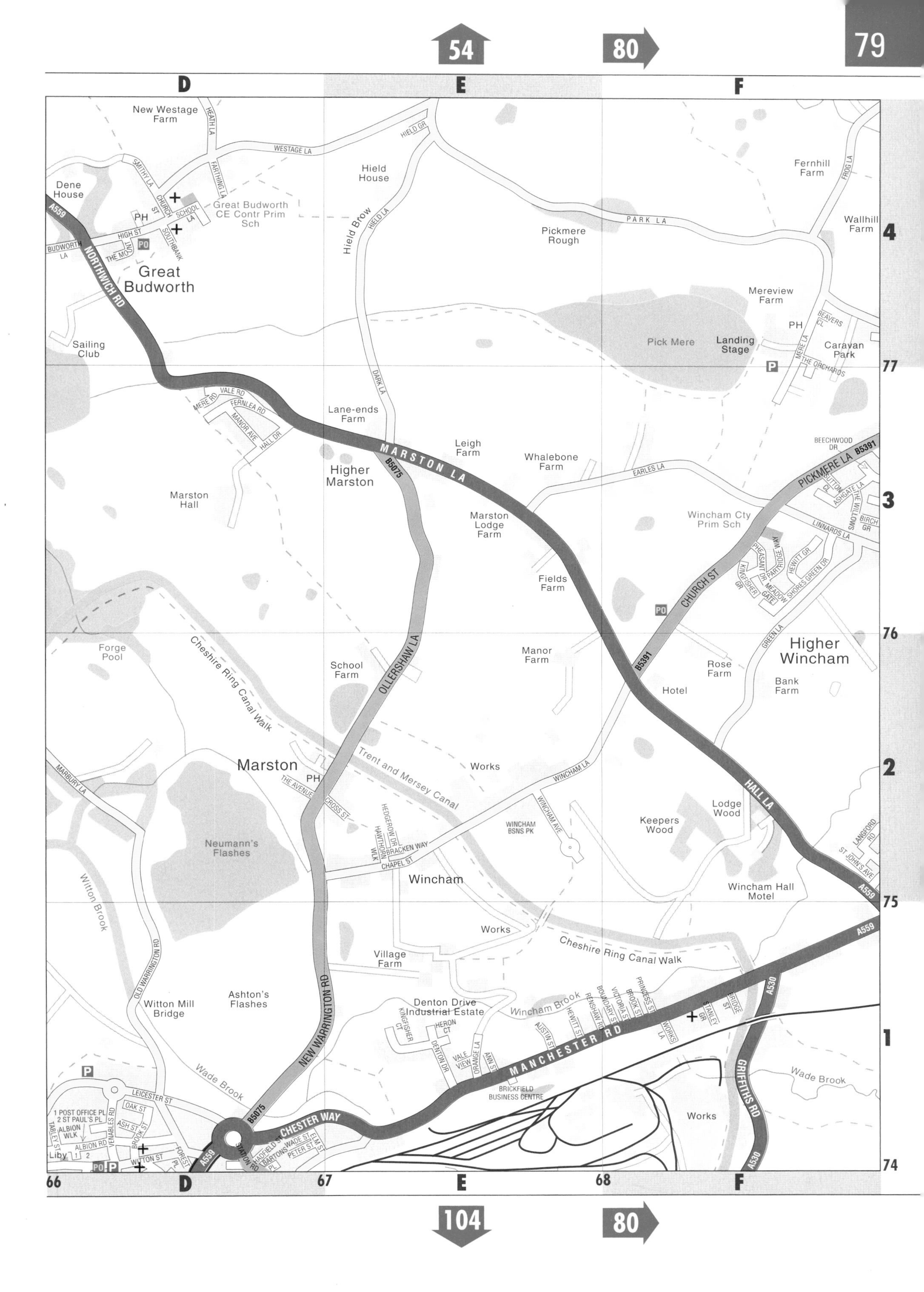
54
80
104
80
D
E
F
New Westage Farm
HEATH LA
WESTAGE LA
HIELD GR
SMITHY LA
FARTHING LA
Dene House
CHURCH ST
SCHOOL LA
Great Budworth CE Contr Prim Sch
Hield House
Fernhill Farm
FROG LA
A559
PH
HIGH ST
SOUTHBANK
PO
BUDWORTH LA
THE MOUNT
NORTHWICH RD
Great Budworth
HIELD LA
Hield Brow
PARK LA
Pickmere Rough
Wallhill Farm
4
Mereview Farm
BEAVERS CL
Sailing Club
Pick Mere
Landing Stage
Caravan Park
MERE LA
THE ORCHARDS
P
77
DARK LA
VALE RD
MERE RD
FERNLEA RD
MANOR AVE
HALL DR
Lane-ends Farm
Leigh Farm
Whalebone Farm
BEECHWOOD DR
B5391
PICKMERE LA
MARSTON LA
B5075
Higher Marston
EARLES LA
SUTTON CL
ASHGATE LA
THE WILLOWS
BIRCH GR
Marston Hall
Marston Lodge Farm
Wincham Cty Prim Sch
3
LINNARDS LA
PHEASANT DR
PARTRIDGE WAY
HEWITT GR
KINGFISHER GR
MEADOW GATE
SHORES GREEN DR
Fields Farm
CHURCH ST
76
GREEN LA
Forge Pool
Cheshire Ring Canal Walk
School Farm
OLLERSHAW LA
Manor Farm
Rose Farm
Higher Wincham
Bank Farm
Hotel
Marston
Trent and Mersey Canal
Works
2
MARBURY LA
PH
THE AVENUE
CROSS ST
WINCHAM LA
WINCHAM AVE
HALL LA
Lodge Wood
Keepers Wood
HEDGEROW DR
HAWTHORN WLK
BRACKEN WAY
CHAPEL ST
WINCHAM BSNS PK
LANGFORD RD
ST JOHN'S AVE
Neumann's Flashes
Witton Brook
Wincham
Wincham Hall Motel
75
Works
Cheshire Ring Canal Walk
Village Farm
OLD WARRINGTON RD
NEW WARRINGTON RD
Ashton's Flashes
Witton Mill Bridge
Denton Drive Industrial Estate
Wincham Brook
KINGFISHER CT
HERON CT
DENTON DR
VALE VIEW
ORANGE LA
ANN ST
AUSTIN ST
HEWITT ST
RENSHAW RD
BOUNDARY ST
VICTORIA ST
BROOK ST
PRINCESS ST
WORKS LA
STANLEY GR
BRIDGE ST
A530
MANCHESTER RD
1
Wade Brook
Wade Brook
GRIFFITHS RD
BRICKFIELD BUSINESS CENTRE
Works
LEICESTER ST
OAK ST
1 POST OFFICE PL
2 ST PAUL'S PL
ALBION WLK
TABLEY ST
VENABLES RD
ASH ST
BROOK ST
ALBION RD
CHESTER WAY
STATION RD
HADFIELD ST
BARTONS PL
WADE ST
PETER ST
ELM ST
FOREST PL
WITTON ST
Liby
74
66
67
68

79
55

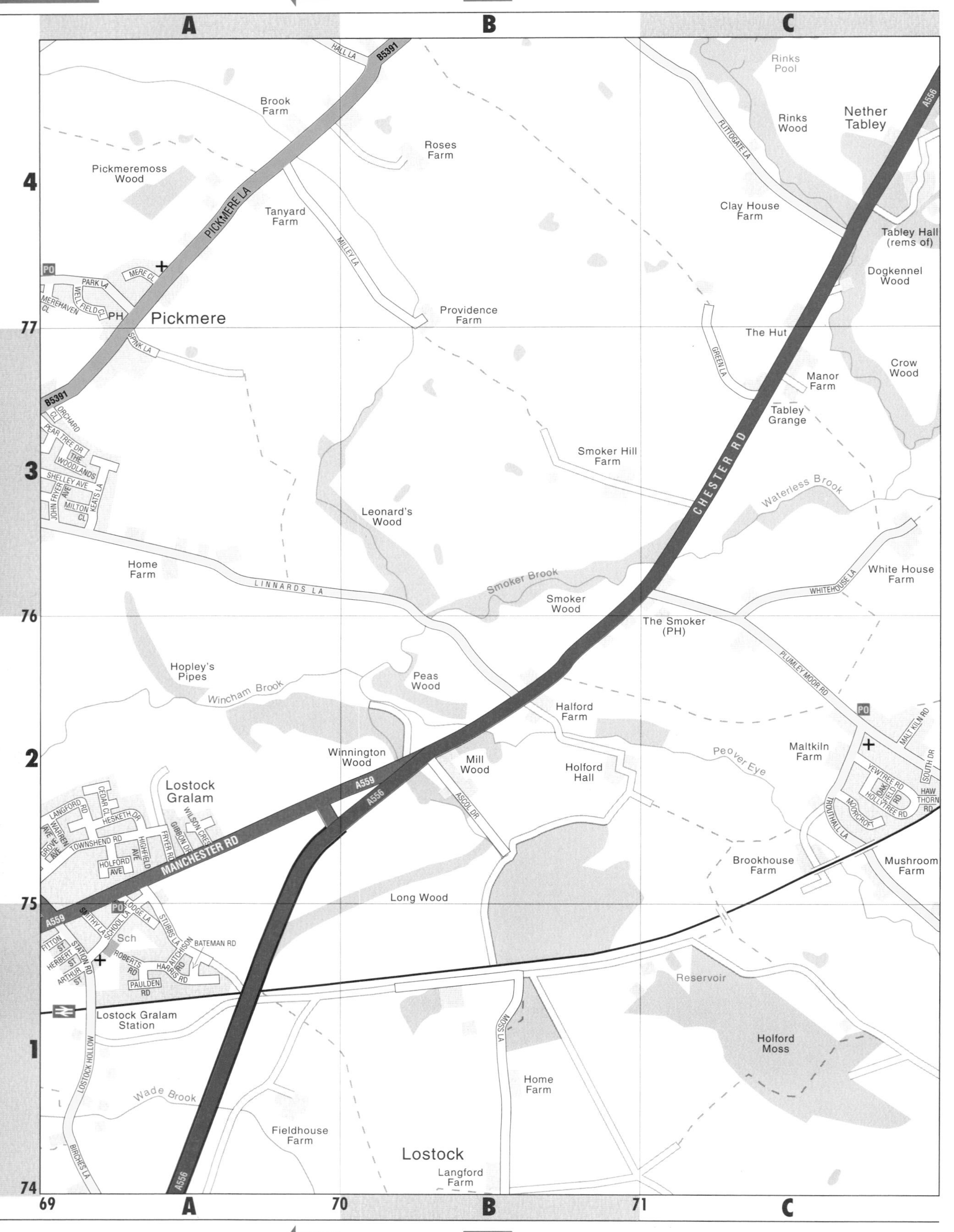
A
B
C
Rinks Pool
Rinks Wood
Nether Tabley
Brook Farm
Roses Farm
Pickmeremoss Wood
Tanyard Farm
PICKMERE LA
B5391
HALL LA
MILLEY LA
FLITTOGATE LA
Clay House Farm
Tabley Hall (rems of)
Dogkennel Wood
Providence Farm
Pickmere
PARK LA
MERE CL
WELLFIELD CL
MEREHAVEN CL
PH
PO
SPINK LA
The Hut
GREEN LA
Crow Wood
Manor Farm
Tabley Grange
ORCHARD CL
PEAR TREE DR
THE WOODLANDS
SHELLEY AVE
JOHN FRYER AVE
MILTON CL
KEATS LA
Smoker Hill Farm
CHESTER RD
Waterless Brook
Leonard's Wood
Home Farm
LINNARDS LA
Smoker Brook
Smoker Wood
WHITEHOUSE LA
White House Farm
The Smoker (PH)
PLUMLEY MOOR RD
Hopley's Pipes
Wincham Brook
Peas Wood
Halford Farm
Winnington Wood
Mill Wood
Holford Hall
Peover Eye
Maltkiln Farm
MALT KILN RD
SOUTH DR
Lostock Gralam
A559
A556
ASCOL DR
YEWTREE RD
OAK FIELD RD
HOLLYTREE RD
HAWTHORN RD
MOORCROFT
TROUTHALL LA
LANGFORD RD
CEDAR CL
HESKETH DR
WILSON CRES
WARREN AVE
GROVE AVE
TOWNSHEND RD
HIGHFIELD AVE
FRYER RD
GIBBON DR
HOLFORD AVE
MANCHESTER RD
Brookhouse Farm
Mushroom Farm
Long Wood
SMITHY LA
SCHOOL LA
LODGE LA
STUBBS LA
AITCHISON RD
BATEMAN RD
Sch
FITTON ST
HERBERT ST
STATION RD
ARTHUR ST
ROBERTS RD
HARRIS RD
PAULDEN RD
Reservoir
Lostock Gralam Station
MOSS LA
Holford Moss
LOSTOCK HOLLOW
Home Farm
Wade Brook
Fieldhouse Farm
Lostock
Langford Farm
BIRCHES LA
4
77
3
76
2
75
1
74
69
70
71

79
105

CHESTER RD A556

Tabley House

Top Willowbed Wood

Blockhill Farm

BEXTON RD
GLOUCESTER RD
MALVERN RD
MEADOW DR
ASHWORTH PARK
BLACKHILL LA

Bexton Cty Prim Sch

Bexton House

4

Island Wood

Serpentine Water

Parkgate Farm

SUDLOW LA

BEXTON LA

Yewtree Farm

Botany Bay Wood

Bexton Hall Farm

77

Tabley Mere

Black Clump

Royd Wood

Parkside Farm

Bexton Wood

3

Parkside Cottage

Diamond Farm

Ullardhall Farm

Ash Wood

Nursery

76

Wash Farm

Wood's Tenement

PINFOLD LA

Hucknall Farm

Bucklow Farm

Victoria Wood

2

Plumley Station

Beech House Farm

Plumleylane Farm

Inn

Pinfold Farm

Plumley

Holly Tree Farm

The Grange

Plumleymoor RD

Merry Farm

Smithy Green

MIDDLEWICH RD

B5081

75

Beech Farm

TROUTHALL LA

Plumley Moor

Lower Peover Hall

Heesom Green Farm

Moss Farm

Fields Farm

Brookfield House

BROOM LA

PO

1

CHEADLE LA

BACK LA

Peover Eye

Lower Peover

CROWN LA

PH
THE COBBLES
CHURCH WALK
BARROWS BROW

FREE GREEN LA

Red Brook

The Fields Farm

M6

Lower Peover CE Aided Prim Sch

B5081

74

81
57

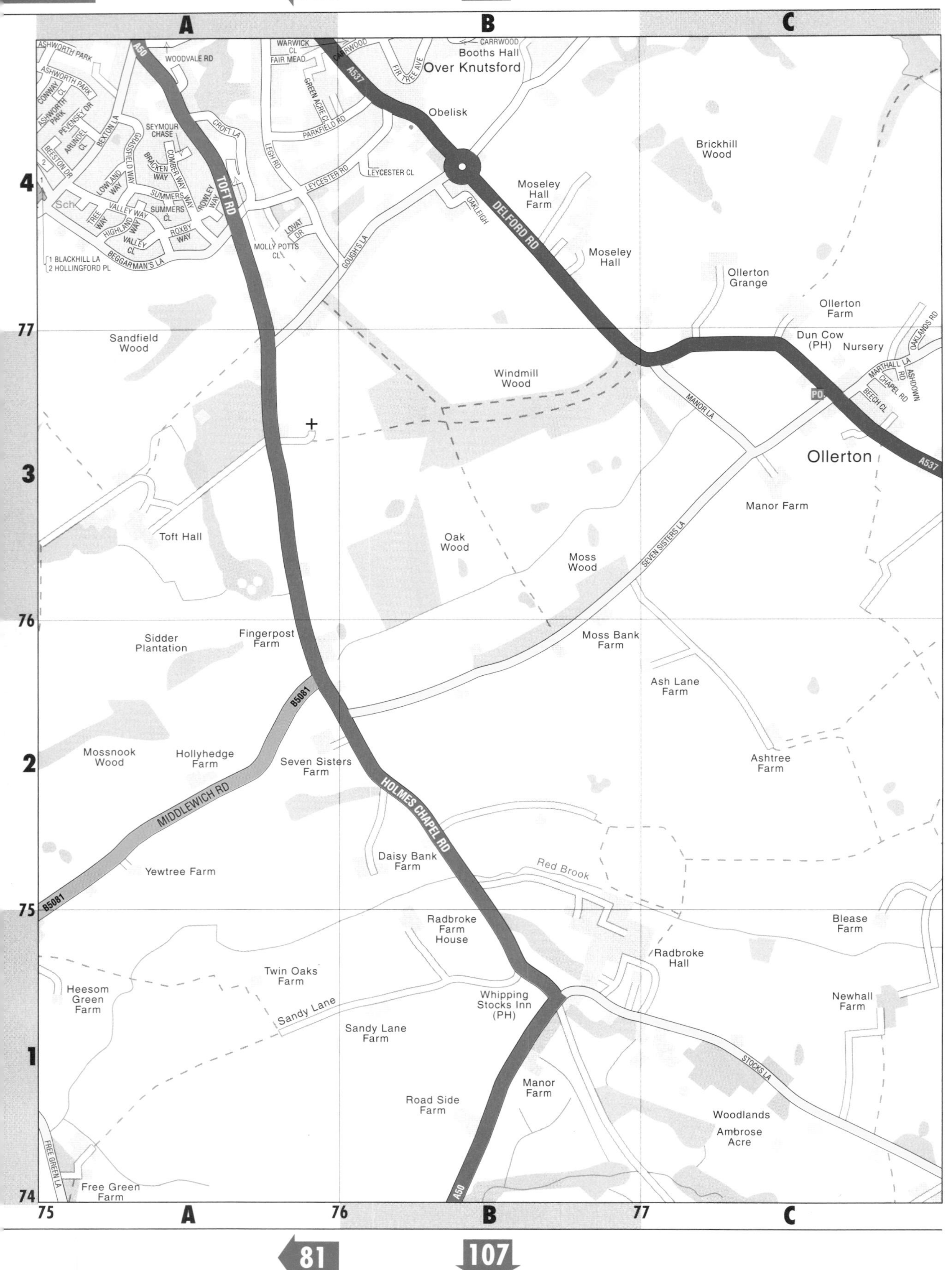
A
B
C
Over Knutsford
Booths Hall
Obelisk
Brickhill Wood
Moseley Hall Farm
Moseley Hall
Ollerton Grange
Ollerton Farm
Dun Cow (PH)
Nursery
Sandfield Wood
Windmill Wood
Ollerton
Manor Farm
Toft Hall
Oak Wood
Moss Wood
Sidder Plantation
Fingerpost Farm
Moss Bank Farm
Ash Lane Farm
Mossnook Wood
Hollyhedge Farm
Seven Sisters Farm
Ashtree Farm
Yewtree Farm
Daisy Bank Farm
Red Brook
Radbroke Farm House
Blease Farm
Radbroke Hall
Heesom Green Farm
Twin Oaks Farm
Whipping Stocks Inn (PH)
Newhall Farm
Sandy Lane
Sandy Lane Farm
Manor Farm
Road Side Farm
Woodlands
Ambrose Acre
Free Green Farm
TOFT RD
DELFORD RD
A537
A50
B5081
MIDDLEWICH RD
HOLMES CHAPEL RD
SEVEN SISTERS LA
MANOR LA
STOCKS LA
GOUGH'S LA
LEYCESTER RD
LEYCESTER CL
PARKFIELD RD
LEGH RD
CROFT LA
WOODVALE RD
ASHWORTH PARK
WARWICK CL
FAIR MEAD
GREEN ACRE CL
CARRWOOD
FIR TREE AVE
OAKLEIGH
LOVAT DR
MOLLY POTTS CL
BEGGARMAN'S LA
1 BLACKHILL LA
2 HOLLINGFORD PL
Sch
MARTHALL LA
CHAPEL RD
BEECH CL
ASHDOWN
OAKLANDS RD
PO
FREE GREEN LA
4
3
2
1
77
76
75
74

81
107

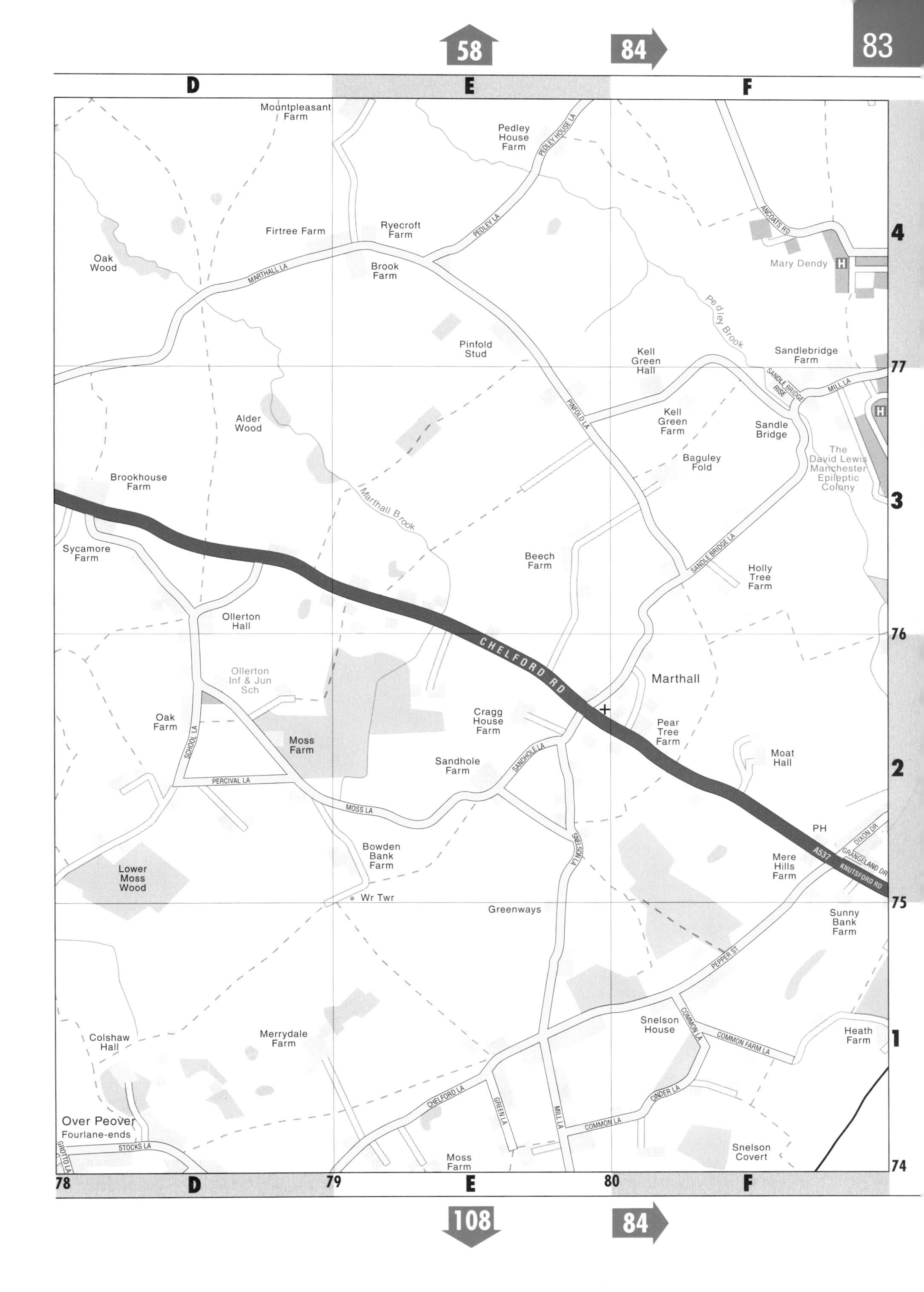

Mountpleasant Farm

Pedley House Farm

PEDLEY HOUSE LA

Ryecroft Farm

PEDLEY LA

ANCOATS RD

Firtree Farm

Brook Farm

Mary Dendy H

Oak Wood

MARTHALL LA

Pinfold Stud

Pedley Brook

Sandlebridge Farm

Kell Green Hall

SANDLE BRIDGE RISE

MILL LA

77

Alder Wood

PINFOLD LA

Kell Green Farm

Sandle Bridge

H

Baguley Fold

The David Lewis Manchester Epileptic Colony

Brookhouse Farm

Marthall Brook

Beech Farm

SANDLE BRIDGE LA

Holly Tree Farm

3

Sycamore Farm

Ollerton Hall

CHELFORD RD

76

Ollerton Inf & Jun Sch

Marthall

Oak Farm

SCHOOL LA

Moss Farm

Cragg House Farm

Pear Tree Farm

Moat Hall

PERCIVAL LA

Sandhole Farm

SANDHOLE LA

+

2

MOSS LA

PH

DIXON DR

Lower Moss Wood

Bowden Bank Farm

SNELSON LA

Mere Hills Farm

A537

GRANGELAND DR

KNUTSFORD RD

• Wr Twr

Greenways

75

Sunny Bank Farm

PEPPER ST

Colshaw Hall

Merrydale Farm

Snelson House

COMMON LA

COMMON FARM LA

Heath Farm

1

MILL LA

CINDER LA

Over Peover
Fourlane-ends

CHELFORD LA

GREEN LA

COMMON LA

Snelson Covert

GROTTO LA

STOCKS LA

Moss Farm

74

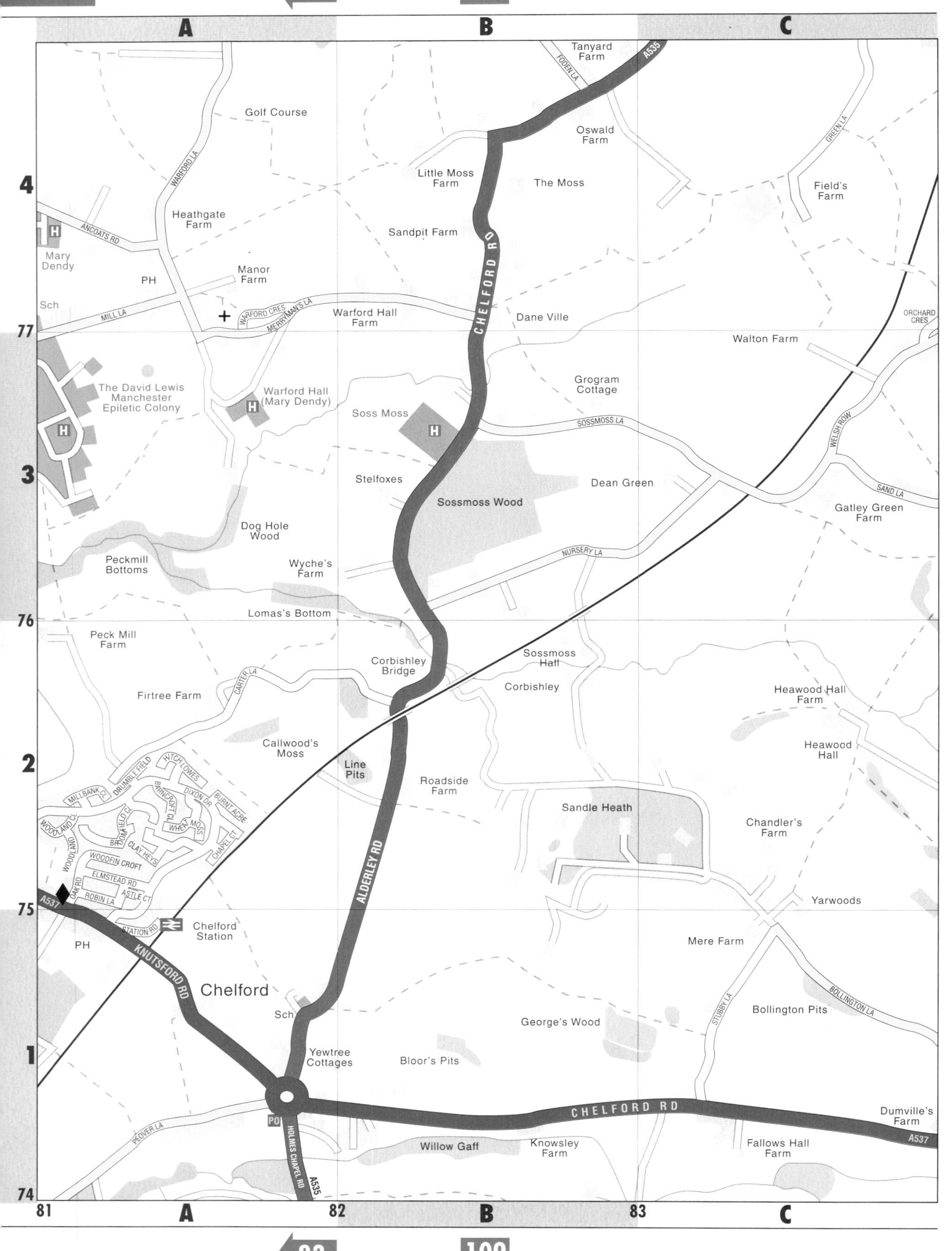

A
B
C

Tanyard
Farm

Golf Course

Oswald
Farm

Little Moss
Farm

The Moss

Field's
Farm

4

Heathgate
Farm

Sandpit Farm

H
Mary
Dendy

PH

Manor
Farm

CHELFORD RD

Dane Ville

Warford Hall
Farm

77

Sch

MILL LA

WARFORD CRES

MERRYMAN'S LA

Walton Farm

ORCHARD
CRES

The David Lewis
Manchester
Epiletic Colony

Warford Hall
(Mary Dendy)

H

Soss Moss

Grogram
Cottage

SOSSMOSS LA

WELSH ROW

H

H

Stelfoxes

Sossmoss Wood

Dean Green

SAND LA

3

Gatley Green
Farm

Dog Hole
Wood

Wyche's
Farm

NURSERY LA

Peckmill
Bottoms

Lomas's Bottom

76

Peck Mill
Farm

Corbishley
Bridge

Sossmoss
Hall

Corbishley

Heawood Hall
Farm

CARTER LA

Firtree Farm

Callwood's
Moss

Line
Pits

Heawood
Hall

MILL BANK

DRUMBLE FIELD

HTCH HOMES

BURNT ACRE

DIXON DR

BARNCROFT LA

WHEN MOSS

Roadside
Farm

2

Sandle Heath

Chandler's
Farm

WOODLAND

WOODFIN CROFT

CLAY HEYS

CHAPEL LA

ELMSTEAD RD

ASTLE CT

ALDERLEY RD

BROMFIELD

ROBIN LA

A537

75

Yarwoods

PH

STATION RD

KNUTSFORD RD

Chelford
Station

Mere Farm

STUBBY LA

BOLLINGTON LA

Chelford

Sch

George's Wood

Bollington Pits

1

Yewtree
Cottages

Bloor's Pits

HOLMES CHAPEL RD

PO

PLOVER LA

Willow Gaff

Knowsley
Farm

CHELFORD RD

Dumville's
Farm

A535

Fallows Hall
Farm

A537

74

81

A

82

B

83

C

60
86

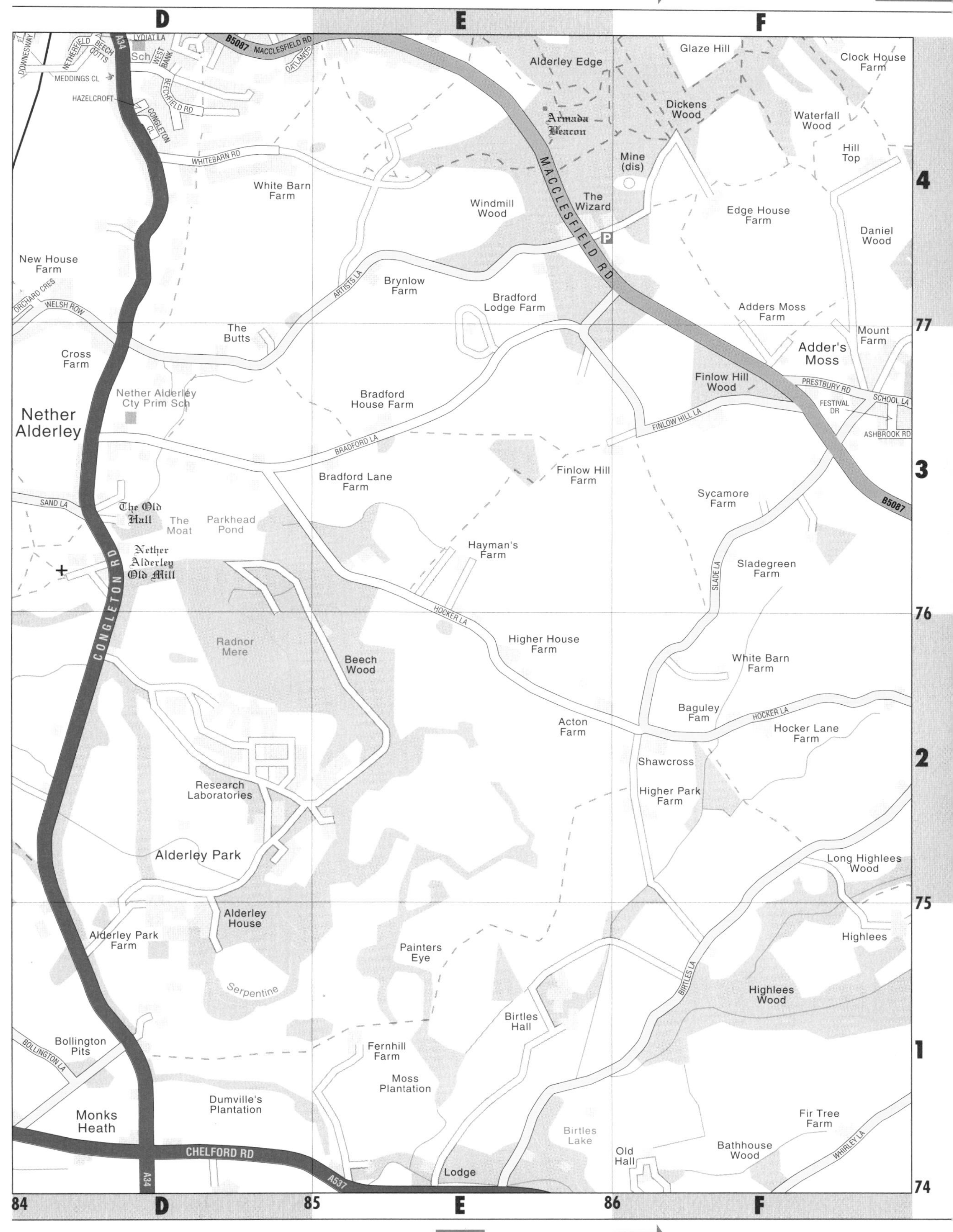
D
E
F
4
3
2
1
77
76
75
74
84
85
86
Glaze Hill
Clock House Farm
Alderley Edge
Dickens Wood
Waterfall Wood
Armada Beacon
Hill Top
Mine (dis)
White Barn Farm
Windmill Wood
The Wizard
Edge House Farm
Daniel Wood
New House Farm
Brynlow Farm
Bradford Lodge Farm
Adders Moss Farm
Mount Farm
Adder's Moss
The Butts
Cross Farm
Finlow Hill Wood
Nether Alderley Cty Prim Sch
Bradford House Farm
Nether Alderley
Finlow Hill Farm
Bradford Lane Farm
Sycamore Farm
The Old Hall
The Moat
Parkhead Pond
Nether Alderley Old Mill
Hayman's Farm
Sladegreen Farm
Radnor Mere
Higher House Farm
Beech Wood
White Barn Farm
Baguley Fam
Acton Farm
Hocker Lane Farm
Shawcross
Research Laboratories
Higher Park Farm
Alderley Park
Long Highlees Wood
Alderley House
Alderley Park Farm
Painters Eye
Highlees
Serpentine
Highlees Wood
Birtles Hall
Bollington Pits
Fernhill Farm
Moss Plantation
Dumville's Plantation
Monks Heath
Fir Tree Farm
Birtles Lake
Bathhouse Wood
Old Hall
Lodge
Sch
P
LYDIAT LA
B5087
MACCLESFIELD RD
DOWNESWAY
NETHERFIELD
BEECH COTTS
WEST BANK
OATLANDS
MEDDINGS CL
BEECHFIELD RD
HAZELCROFT
CONGLETON CL
WHITEBARN RD
ARTISTS LA
MACCLESFIELD RD
ORCHARD CRES
WELSH ROW
PRESTBURY RD
SCHOOL LA
FESTIVAL DR
ASHBROOK RD
FINLOW HILL LA
BRADFORD LA
B5087
SAND LA
SLADE LA
CONGLETON RD
HOCKER LA
HOCKER LA
BIRTLES LA
BOLLINGTON LA
CHELFORD RD
A34
A537
WHIRLEY LA

110
86

85
61

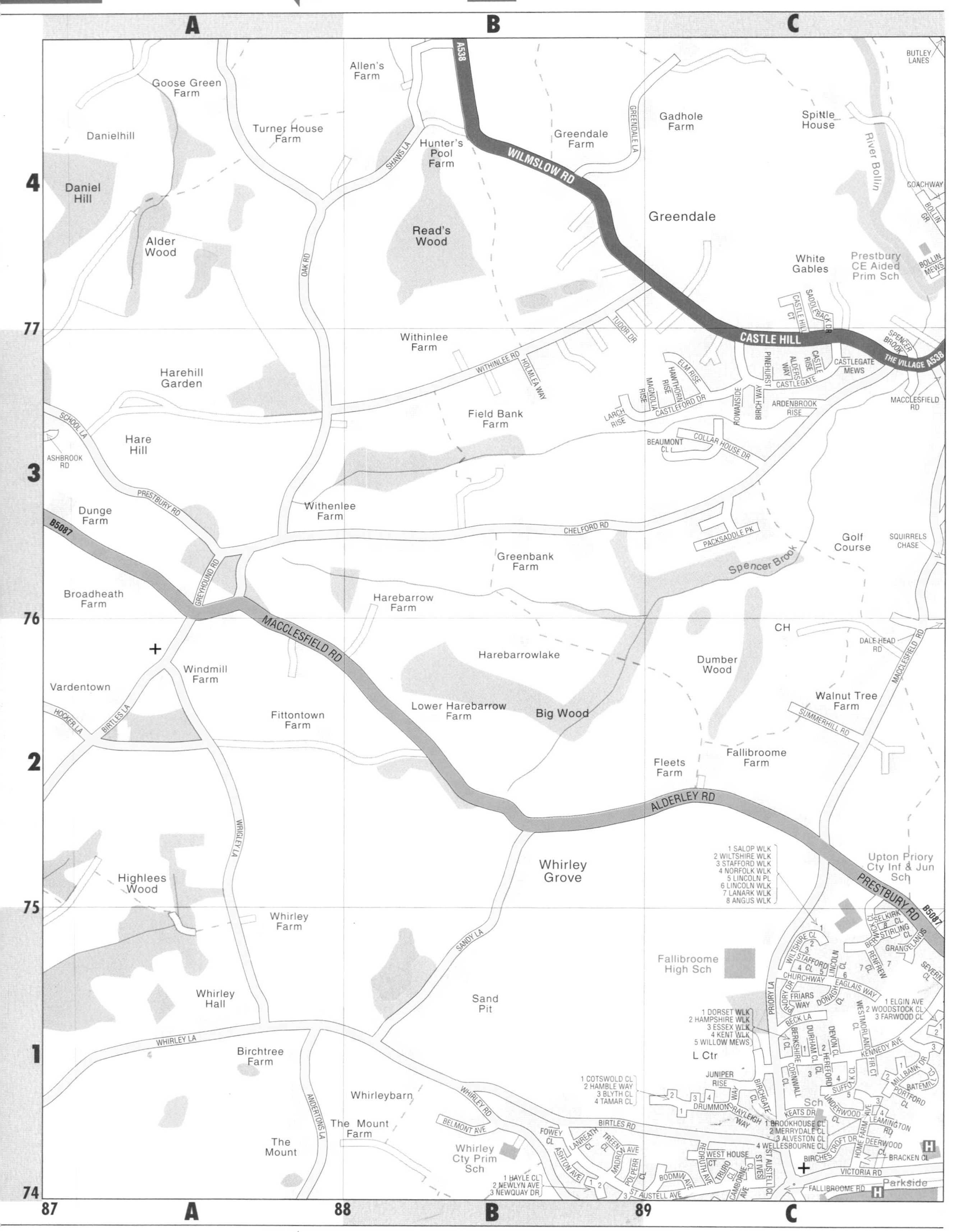
A
B
C
Allen's Farm
Goose Green Farm
Danielhill
Turner House Farm
Hunter's Pool Farm
Greendale Farm
Gadhole Farm
Spittle House
BUTLEY LANES
River Bollin
Daniel Hill
Alder Wood
Read's Wood
Greendale
White Gables
Prestbury CE Aided Prim Sch
A538
WILMSLOW RD
GREENDALE LA
SHAWS LA
OAK RD
COACHWAY
BOLLIN GR
BOLLIN MEWS
CASTLE HILL
TUDOR DR
SADDLEBACK DR
CASTLE HILL CT
SPENCER BROOK
THE VILLAGE
Withinlee Farm
WITHINLEE RD
HOLMLEA WAY
Harehill Garden
ELM RISE
HAWTHORN RISE
MAGNOLIA RISE
PINEHURST
ALDERS WAY
CASTLE RISE
CASTLEGATE MEWS
CASTLEGATE
ROWANSIDE
BIRCH WAY
ARDENBROOK RISE
LARCH RISE
CASTLEFORD DR
MACCLESFIELD RD
SCHOOL LA
ASHBROOK RD
Hare Hill
Field Bank Farm
BEAUMONT CL
COLLAR HOUSE DR
PRESTBURY RD
Dunge Farm
B5087
Withenlee Farm
CHELFORD RD
PACKSADDLE PK
Golf Course
SQUIRRELS CHASE
Greenbank Farm
Spencer Brook
GREYHOUND RD
Broadheath Farm
Harebarrow Farm
CH
DALE HEAD RD
MACCLESFIELD RD
Windmill Farm
Harebarrowlake
Dumber Wood
Vardentown
Fittontown Farm
Lower Harebarrow Farm
Big Wood
Walnut Tree Farm
SUMMERHILL RD
HOCKER LA
BIRTLES LA
Fleets Farm
Fallibroome Farm
ALDERLEY RD
WRIGLEY LA
Whirley Grove
Upton Priory Cty Inf & Jun Sch
PRESTBURY RD
B5087
Highlees Wood
1 SALOP WLK
2 WILTSHIRE WLK
3 STAFFORD WLK
4 NORFOLK WLK
5 LINCOLN PL
6 LINCOLN WLK
7 LANARK WLK
8 ANGUS WLK
Whirley Farm
SANDY LA
SELKIRK CL
STIRLING CL
GRANGELANDS
RENFREW
SEVERN CL
WILTSHIRE CL
STAFFORD CL
LINCOLN CL
Fallibroome High Sch
CHURCHWAY
EAGLAIS WAY
PRIORY LA
PRIORY DR
FRIARS WAY
DONAGH CL
1 ELGIN AVE
2 WOODSTOCK CL
3 FARWOOD CL
Whirley Hall
Sand Pit
1 DORSET WLK
2 HAMPSHIRE WLK
3 ESSEX WLK
4 KENT WLK
5 WILLOW MEWS
BECK LA
BERKSHIRE CL
DURHAM CL
DEVON CL
WESTMORLAND CL
KENNEDY AVE
WHIRLEY LA
Birchtree Farm
L Ctr
HEREFORD CL
CORNWALL CL
FIR CT
MILLBANK DR
BATEMILL CL
JUNIPER RISE
1 COTSWOLD CL
2 HAMBLE WAY
3 BLYTH CL
4 TAMAR CL
SUFFOLK CL
PORTFORD CL
Whirleybarn
ANDERTONS LA
WHIRLEY RD
DRUMMOND WAY
RAYLEIGH WAY
BIRCHGATE CL
Sch
KEATS DR
UNDERWOOD CL
HOME FARM AVE
LEAMINGTON RD
The Mount Farm
BELMONT AVE
BIRTLES RD
1 BROOKHOUSE CL
2 MERRYDALE CL
3 ALVESTON CL
4 WELLESBOURNE CL
FOWEY CL
LANREATH CL
TREEN CL
BIRCHES CROFT DR
DEERWOOD
The Mount
Whirley Cty Prim Sch
ASHTON AVE
MADRON AVE
POLPERR CL
REDRUTH AVE
WEST HOUSE CT
TRURO CL
CAMBORNE AVE
ST IVES CL
ST AUSTELL CL
BRACKEN CL
VICTORIA RD
1 HAYLE CL
2 NEWLYN AVE
3 NEWQUAY DR
BODMIN AVE
ST AUSTELL AVE
FALLIBROOME RD
Parkside
4
77
3
76
2
75
1
74
87
88
89

85
111

62

88

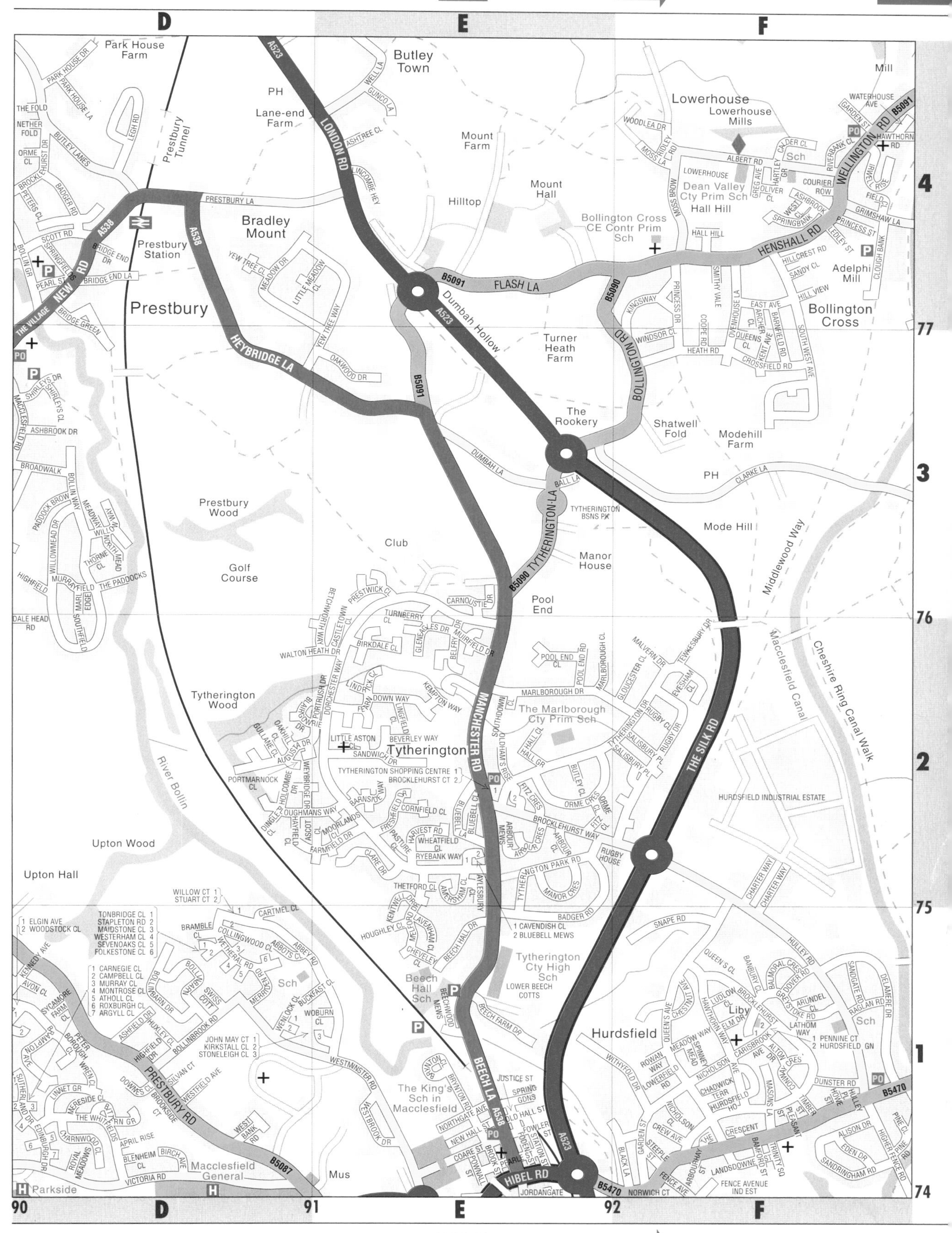

D
E
F
Park House Farm
Butley Town
PH
Lane-end Farm
Prestbury Tunnel
Mount Farm
Mount Hall
Hilltop
Lowerhouse
Lowerhouse Mills
Mill
Dean Valley Cty Prim Sch
Hall Hill
Bollington Cross CE Contr Prim Sch
Bradley Mount
Prestbury Station
Prestbury
Adelphi Mill
Bollington Cross
Turner Heath Farm
Dumbah Hollow
The Rookery
Shatwell Fold
Modehill Farm
Prestbury Wood
Club
Golf Course
Mode Hill
Manor House
Pool End
Middlewood Way
Macclesfield Canal
Cheshire Ring Canal Walk
Tytherington Wood
Tytherington
The Marlborough Cty Prim Sch
HURDSFIELD INDUSTRIAL ESTATE
River Bollin
Upton Wood
Upton Hall
Tytherington Cty High Sch
Beech Hall Sch
Hurdsfield
Liby
The King's Sch in Macclesfield
Macclesfield General
Parkside
Mus
LONDON RD
A523
A538
B5091
FLASH LA
B5090
BOLLINGTON RD
HENSHALL RD
WELLINGTON RD
HEYBRIDGE LA
NEW RD
PRESTBURY LA
TYTHERINGTON LA
MANCHESTER RD
THE SILK RD
BEECH LA
HIBEL RD
PRESTBURY RD
B5087
B5470
CHARTER WAY
TYTHERINGTON SHOPPING CENTRE
BROCKLEHURST CT
1 ELGIN AVE
2 WOODSTOCK CL
TONBRIDGE CL 1
STAPLETON RD 2
MAIDSTONE CL 3
WESTERHAM CL 4
SEVENOAKS CL 5
FOLKESTONE CL 6
1 CARNEGIE CL
2 CAMPBELL CL
3 MURRAY CL
4 MONTROSE CL
5 ATHOLL CL
6 ROXBURGH CL
7 ARGYLL CL
WILLOW CT 1
STUART CT 2
JOHN MAY CT 1
KIRKSTALL CL 2
STONELEIGH CL 3
1 CAVENDISH CL
2 BLUEBELL MEWS
1 PENNINE CT
2 HURDSFIELD GN
77
76
75
74
4
3
2
1
90
91
92

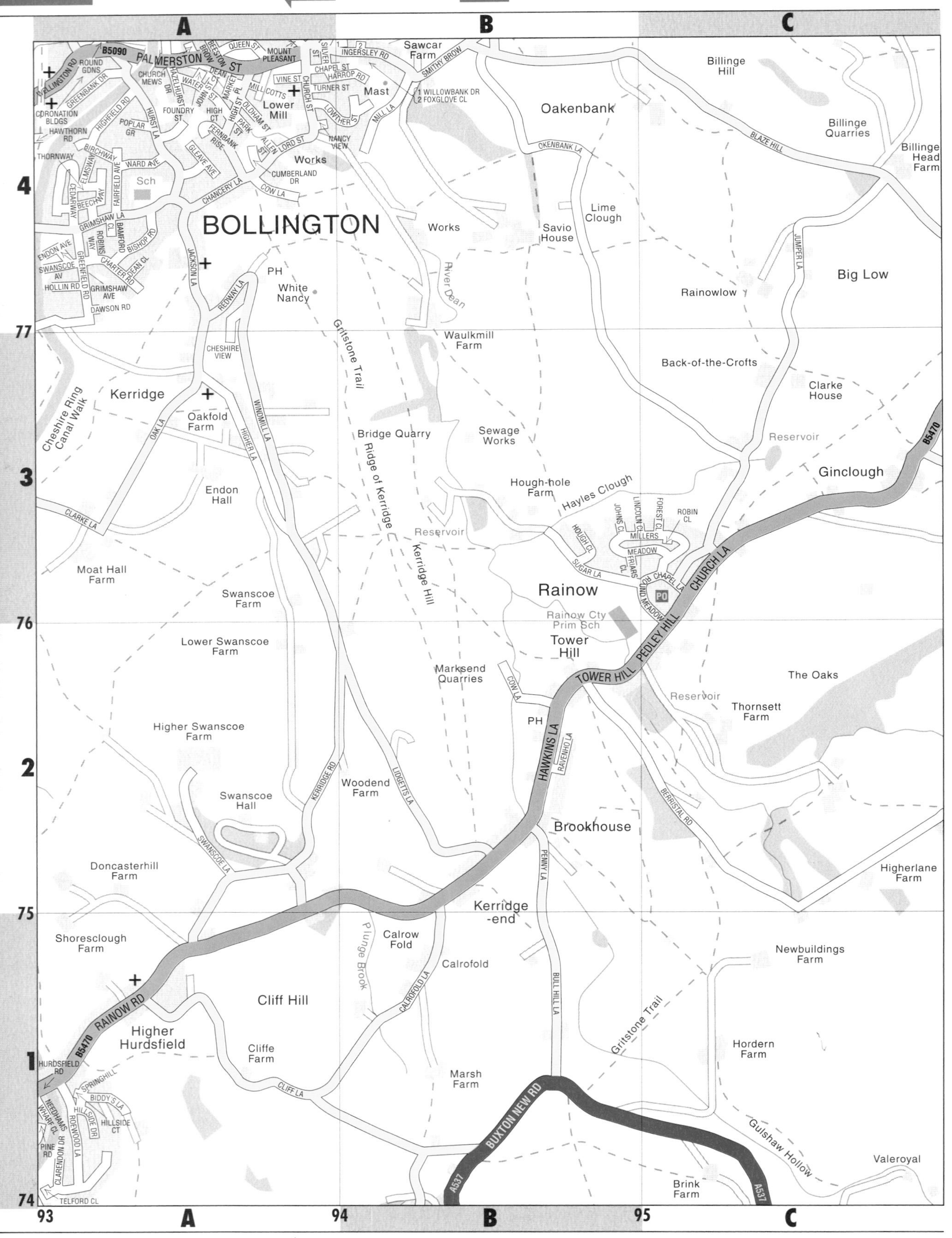

A   B   C

BOLLINGTON

B5090 PALMERSTON ST
ROUND GDNS
GREENBANK DR
CORONATION BLDGS
HAWTHORN RD
THORNWAY
BEECHWAY
CEDARWAY
ELMSWAY
Grimshaw La
BIRCHWAY
FAIRFIELD AVE
ROBINS WAY
BAMFORD
CHARTER RD
HOLLIN RD
SWANSCOE AV
GREENFIELD RD
BISHOP RD
DEAN RD
DAWSON RD
ENDON AVE
JACKSON LA
REDWAY LA

Queen St
Beeston Brow
Mount Pleasant
CHURCH MEWS
WATER ST
DEAN ST
MILL
JOHN ST
POPLAR GR
HIGH CT
FOUNDRY ST
HURST ST
HIGHFIELD RD
FERNBANK
HIGH ST
PARK
ALLEN
WARD LA
CHANCERY LA
COW LA
CUMBERLAND DR

SILVER ST
VINE ST
CHAPEL ST
TURNER ST
OLDHAM ST
LORD ST
NANCY VIEW
CORTHERS
MILL LA
Lower Mill
Mast

Sawcar Farm
Smithy Brow
INGERSLEY RD
HARROP RD
1 WILLOWBANK DR
2 FOXGLOVE CL

Works

Oakenbank

OKENBANK LA

Savio House

Lime Clough

Rainowlow

Back-of-the-Crofts

Billinge Hill

BLAZE HILL

Billinge Quarries

Billinge Head Farm

Big Low

JUMPER LA

B5470

Clarke House

Reservoir

Ginclough

Sch

White Nancy

PH

Gritstone Trail

River Dean

Waulkmill Farm

CHESHIRE VIEW
WINDMILL LA
HIGHER LA

Kerridge

Oakfold Farm

OAK LA

Cheshire Ring Canal Walk

CLARKE LA

Endon Hall

Moat Hall Farm

Swanscoe Farm

Lower Swanscoe Farm

Higher Swanscoe Farm

Swanscoe Hall

SWANSCOE LA

Bridge Quarry

Ridge of Kerridge

Kerridge Hill

Reservoir

Sewage Works

Hough-hole Farm

Hayles Clough

HOUGH LA
SUGAR LA
JOHNS CL
LINCOLN CL
MILLERS MEADOW
FRIARS CL
OLD CHAPEL CL
OLD MEADOW
CHAPEL LA
PEDLEY HILL
CHURCH LA
FOREST CL
ROBIN CL

Rainow

Rainow Cty Prim Sch

PO

Tower Hill

TOWER HILL

The Oaks

Thornsett Farm

Reservoir

KERRIDGE RD
LIDGETTS LA
Woodend Farm
Marksend Quarries
COW LA
PH
HAWKINS LA
RAVENHO LA
PENNY LA
Brookhouse
BERRISTAL RD
Higherlane Farm

Doncasterhill Farm

Shoresclough Farm

RAINOW RD
B5470
Higher Hurdsfield

HURDSFIELD RD
SPRINGHILL
BIDDY'S LA
HILLSIDE CT
HILLSIDE RD
NEEDHAMS
WHARF CL
ROEWOOD LA
PINE RD
CLARENDON DR
TELFORD CL

Cliff Hill

Cliffe Farm

CLIFF LA

Plunge Brook

Calrow Fold

Calrofold

CALROFOLD LA

Marsh Farm

BULL HILL LA

Kerridge -end

Gritstone Trail

Newbuildings Farm

Hordern Farm

Guishaw Hollow

Valeroyal

BUXTON NEW RD
A537

Brink Farm

A537

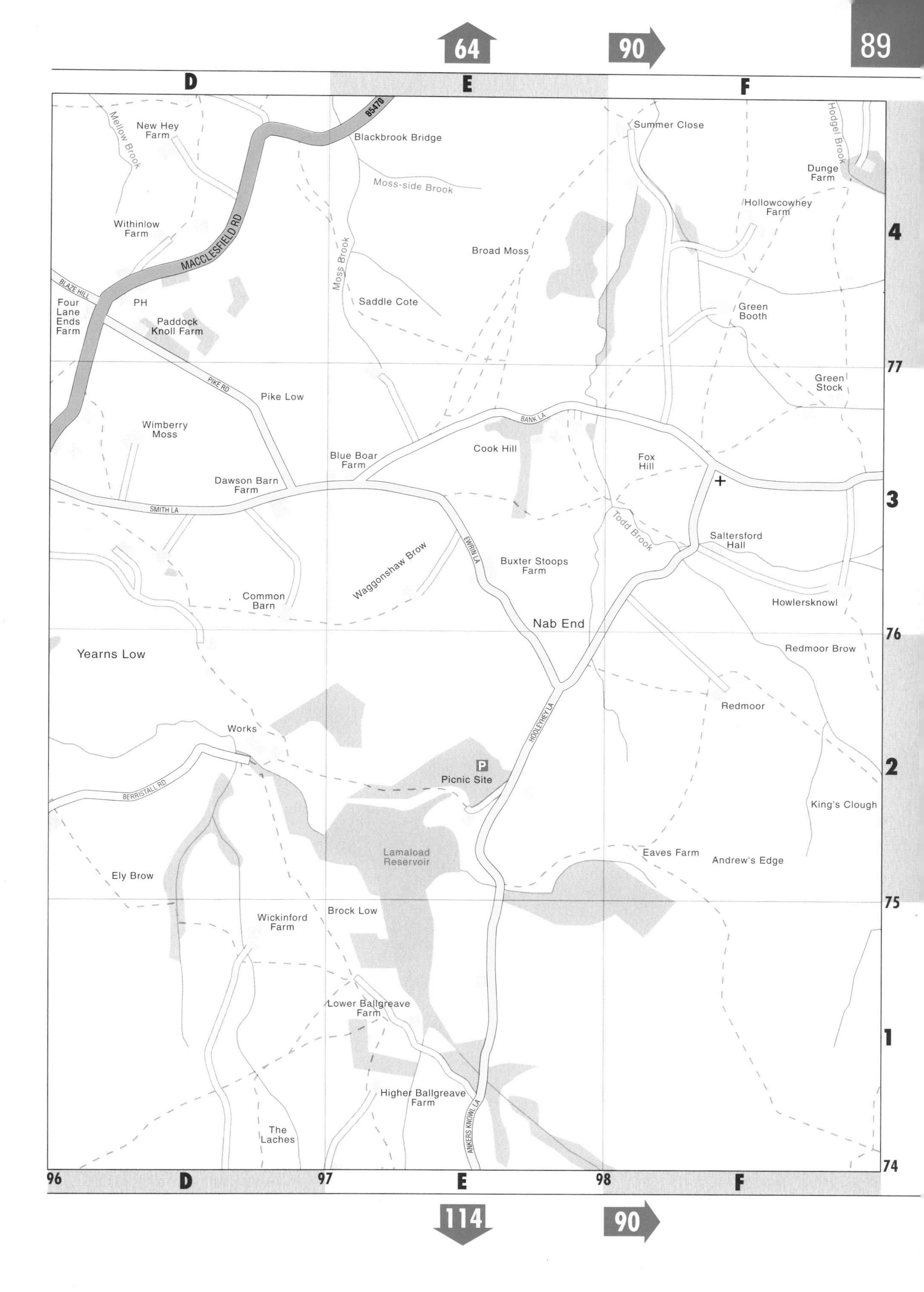

D   E   F

New Hey Farm

B5470

Blackbrook Bridge

Summer Close

Hodgel Brook

Mellow Brook

Moss-side Brook

Dunge Farm

Withinlow Farm

Hollowcowhey Farm

4

MACCLESFIELD RD

Broad Moss

Moss Brook

Green Booth

BLAZE HILL

Four Lane Ends Farm

PH

Saddle Cote

Paddock Knoll Farm

Green Stock

77

PIKE RD

Pike Low

BANK LA

Wimberry Moss

Blue Boar Farm

Cook Hill

Fox Hill

Saltersford Hall

3

Dawson Barn Farm

Todd Brook

+

SMITH LA

EWRIN LA

Buxter Stoops Farm

Howlersknowl

Common Barn

Waggonshaw Brow

Nab End

Redmoor Brow

76

Yearns Low

Redmoor

Works

HOOLEYHEY LA

2

BERRISTALL RD

P
Picnic Site

King's Clough

Ely Brow

Lamaload Reservoir

Eaves Farm

Andrew's Edge

75

Wickinford Farm

Brock Low

Lower Ballgreave Farm

1

Higher Ballgreave Farm

ANKERS KNOWL LA

The Laches

74

96   D   97   E   98   F

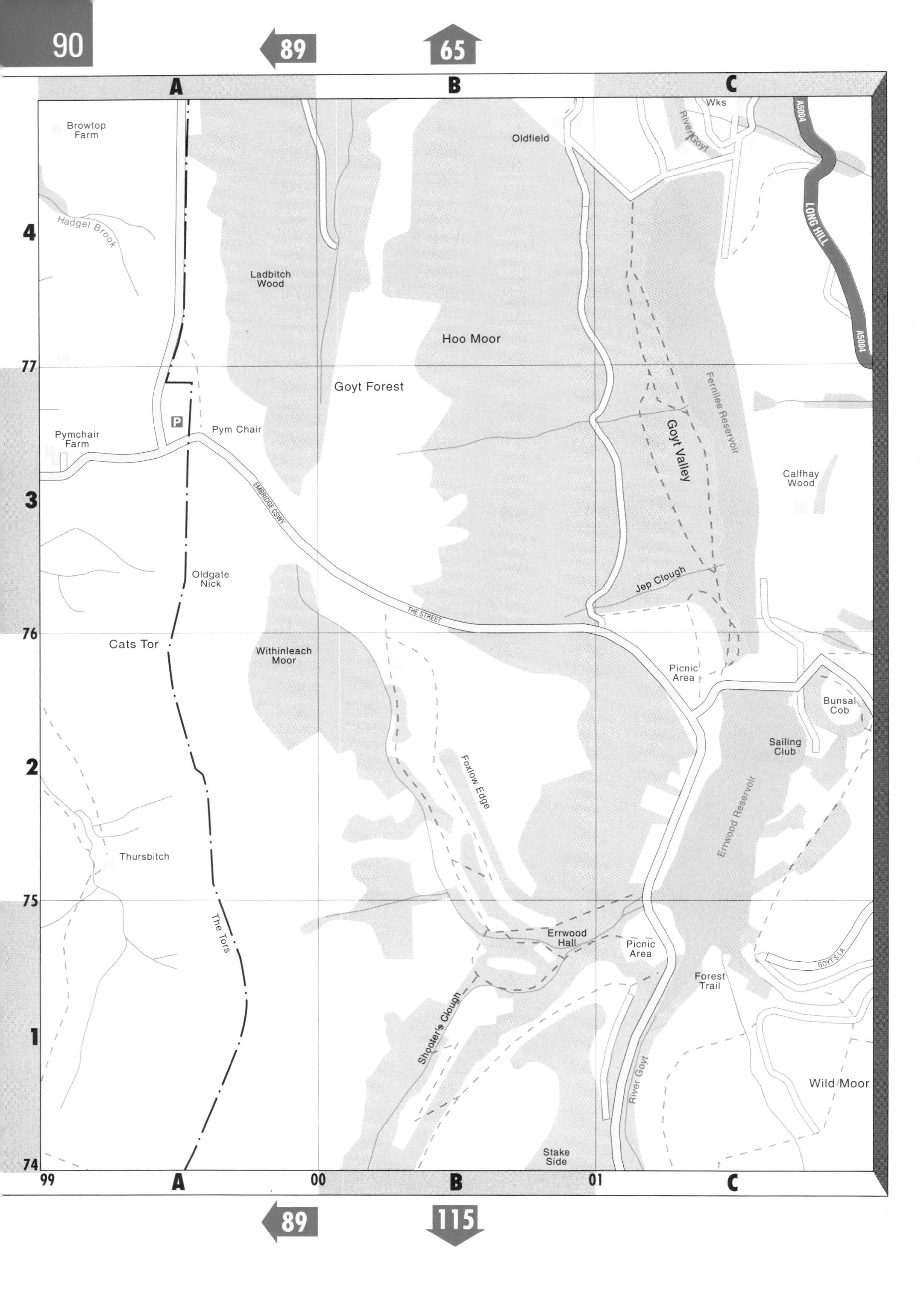
89
65
A
B
C
Browtop Farm
Hadgel Brook
Ladbitch Wood
Oldfield
Wks
River Goyt
A5004
LONG HILL
Hoo Moor
Goyt Forest
Pym Chair
Pymchair Farm
Fernilee Reservoir
Goyt Valley
Calfhay Wood
EMBRIDGE CSWY
Oldgate Nick
Jep Clough
THE STREET
Cats Tor
Withinleach Moor
Picnic Area
Bunsal Cob
Sailing Club
Foxlow Edge
Errwood Reservoir
Thursbitch
The Tors
Errwood Hall
Picnic Area
GOYT'S LA
Forest Trail
Shooter's Clough
River Goyt
Wild Moor
Stake Side
4
77
3
76
2
75
1
74
99
00
01
89
115

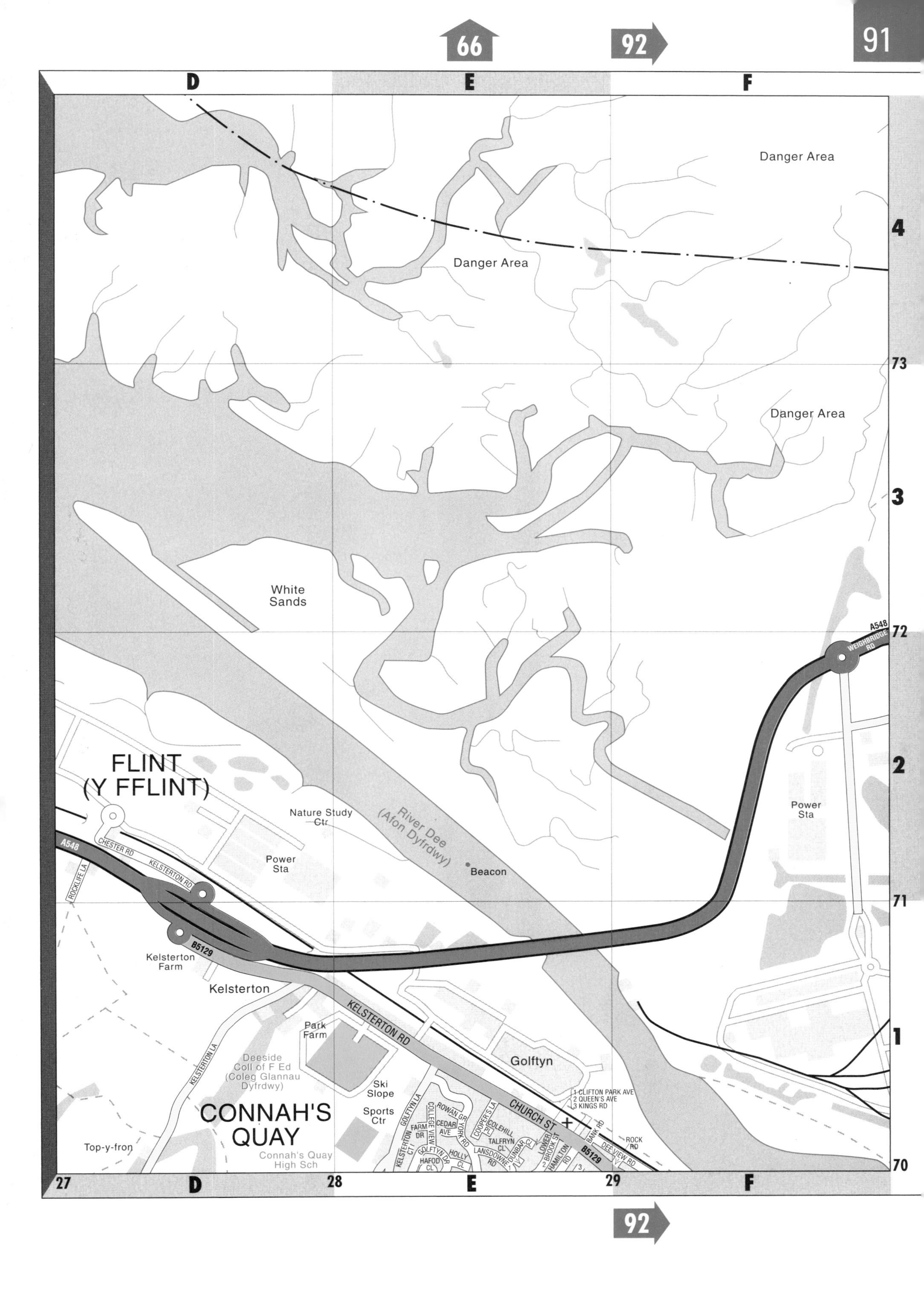

D
E
F

4

73

3

Danger Area

Danger Area

Danger Area

White
Sands

A548

WEIGHBRIDGE RD

72

2

Power
Sta

FLINT
(Y FFLINT)

Nature Study
Ctr

River Dee
(Afon Dyfrdwy)

Power
Sta

Beacon

71

A548

CHESTER RD

ROCKCLIFFE LA

KELSTERTON RD

B5129

Kelsterton
Farm

Kelsterton

KELSTERTON RD

Park
Farm

Golftyn

Ski
Slope

KELSTERTON LA

Deeside
Coll of F Ed
(Coleg Glannau
Dyfrdwy)

CONNAH'S
QUAY

Sports
Ctr

Top-y-fron

Connah's Quay
High Sch

CHURCH ST

1 CLIFTON PARK AVE
2 QUEEN'S AVE
3 KINGS RD

KELSTERTON CT I
GOLFTYN LA
COLLEGE VIEW
FARM DR
CEDAR AVE
ROWAN GR
YORK RD
GOLFTYN CL
HAFOD CL
HOLLY CL
LANSDOWNE RD
TALFRYN CL
COOPER'S LA
COLEHILL
FERNBANK CL
CL
HAMILTON RD
LOWER BROOK ST
BANK RD
DEE VIEW RD
ROCK RD
B5129

1

70

27
D
28
E
29
F

91
67

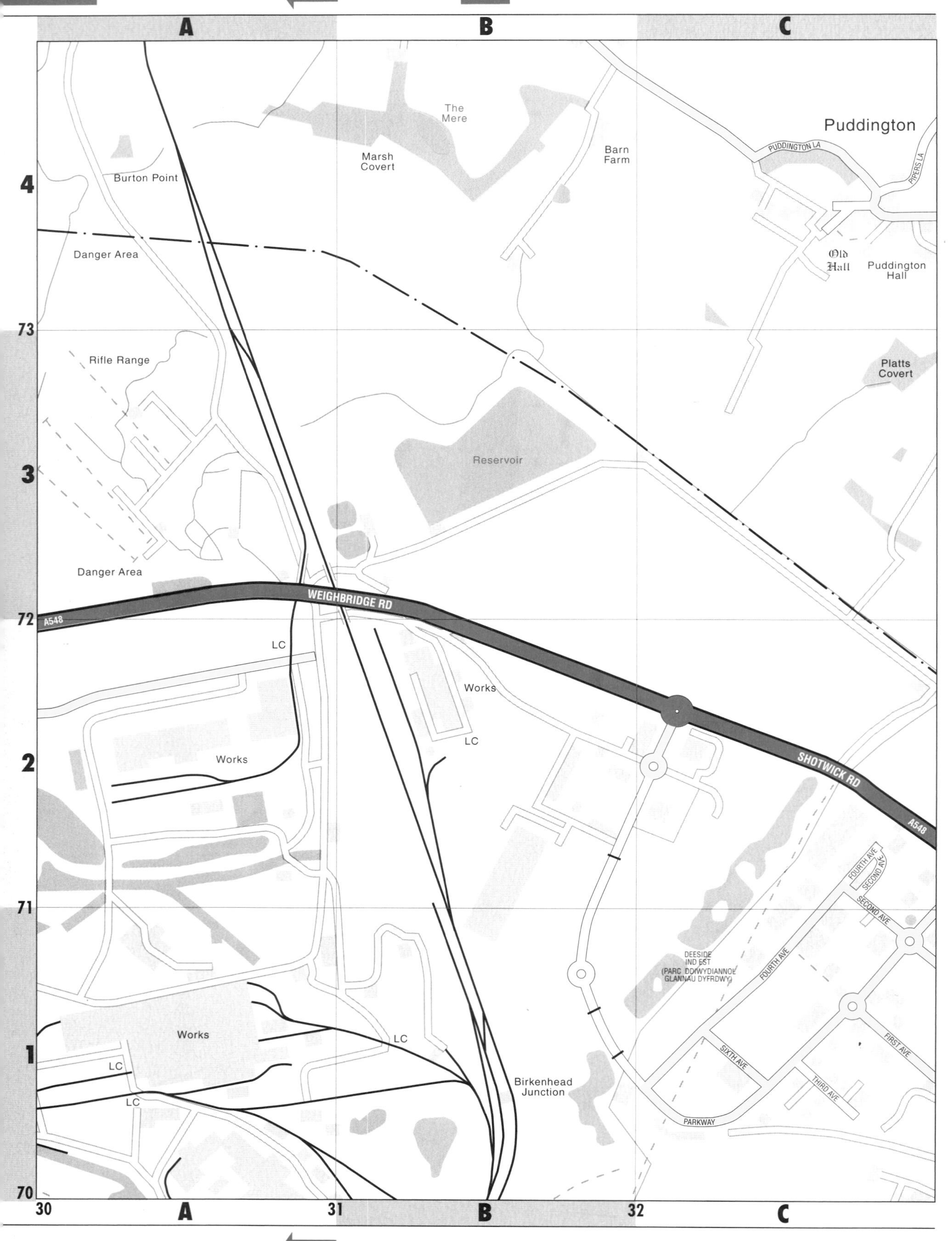
A
B
C
The Mere
Marsh Covert
Barn Farm
Puddington
PUDDINGTON LA
PIPERS LA
Burton Point
Danger Area
Old Hall
Puddington Hall
73
Rifle Range
Platts Covert
Reservoir
Danger Area
WEIGHBRIDGE RD
A548
72
LC
Works
LC
2
Works
SHOTWICK RD
A548
FOURTH AVE
SECOND AVE
SECOND AVE
71
DEESIDE IND EST
(PARC DDIWYDIANNOL GLANNAU DYFRDWY)
FOURTH AVE
Works
LC
1
LC
LC
SIXTH AVE
FIRST AVE
Birkenhead Junction
THIRD AVE
PARKWAY
70
30
31
32
4
3

91

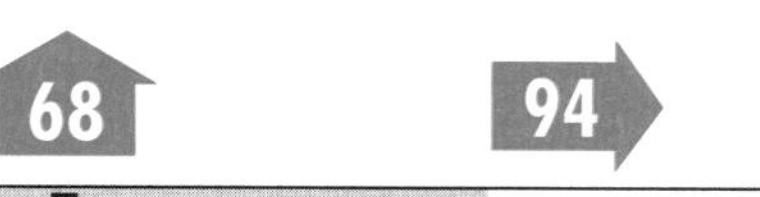
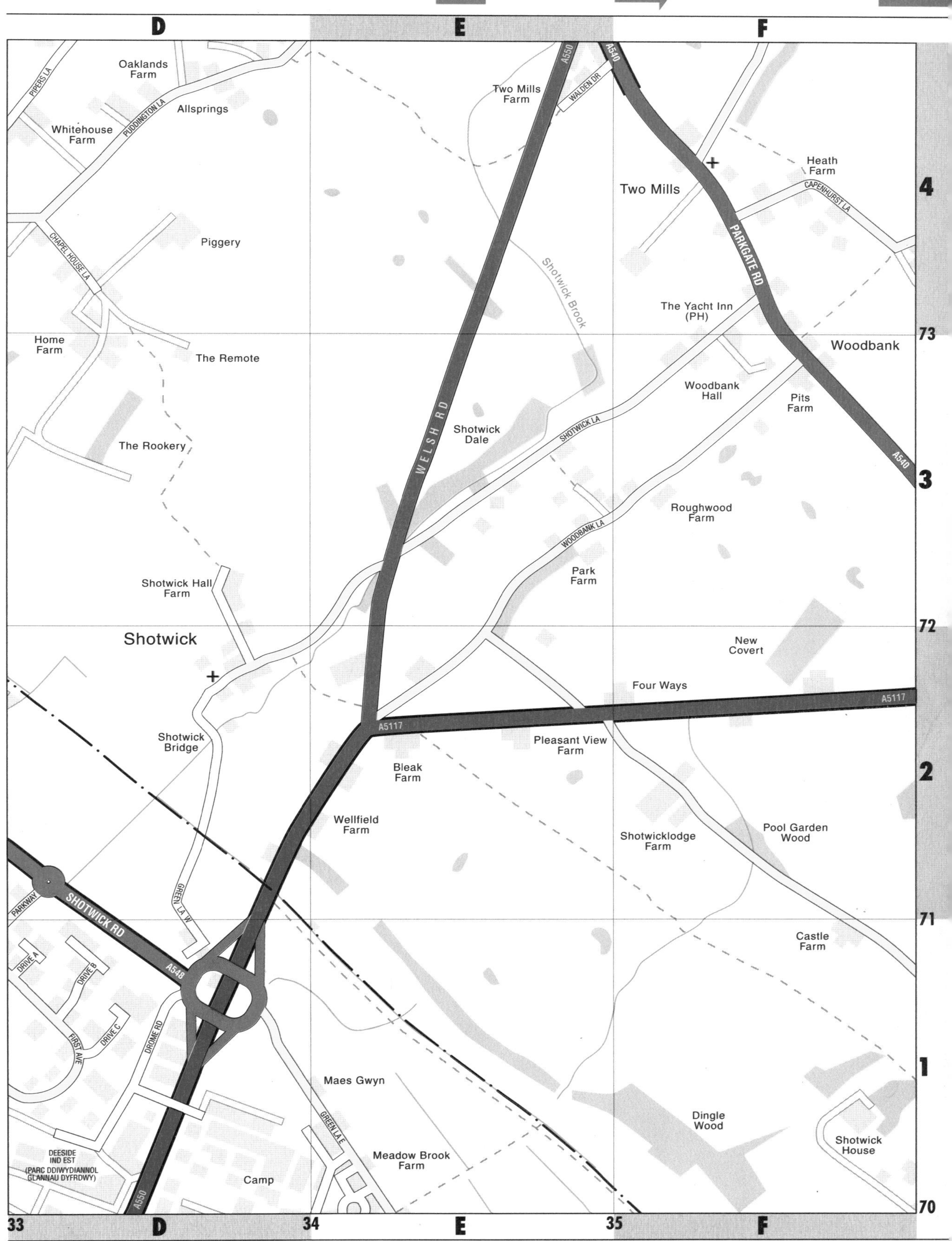

Oaklands Farm
Pipers La
Whitehouse Farm
Puddington La
Allsprings
Chapel House La
Piggery
Home Farm
The Remote
The Rookery
Shotwick Hall Farm
Shotwick
Shotwick Bridge
Parkway
SHOTWICK RD
A548
Green La W
Drive A
First Ave
Drive B
Drive C
Drome Rd
DEESIDE IND EST (PARC DDIWYDIANNOL GLANNIAU DYFRDWY)
Camp
A550

Two Mills Farm
A550
Walden Dr
A540
Two Mills
Heath Farm
Capenhurst La
Parkgate Rd
The Yacht Inn (PH)
Woodbank
Shotwick Brook
Welsh Rd
Shotwick Dale
Shotwick La
Woodbank Hall
Pits Farm
A540
Woodbank La
Roughwood Farm
Park Farm
New Covert
Four Ways
A5117
A5117
Pleasant View Farm
Bleak Farm
Wellfield Farm
Shotwicklodge Farm
Pool Garden Wood
Castle Farm
Maes Gwyn
Green La E
Meadow Brook Farm
Dingle Wood
Shotwick House

4
73
3
72
2
71
1
70

D E F

33 34 E 35 F

93
69

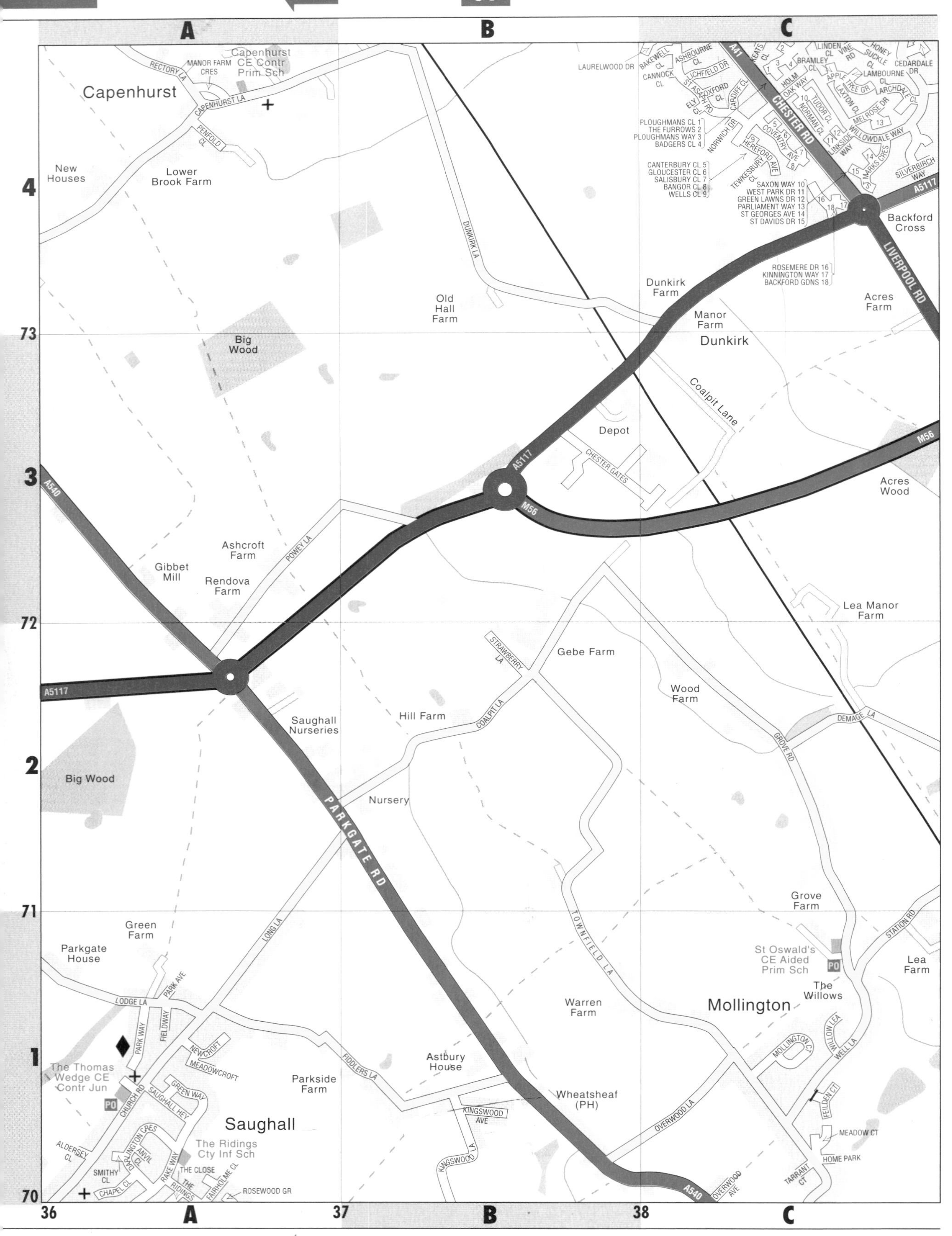
Capenhurst
Capenhurst CE Contr Prim Sch
MANOR FARM CRES
RECTORY LA
CAPENHURST LA
PENFOLD CL
New Houses
Lower Brook Farm
DUNKIRK LA
Old Hall Farm
Big Wood
Ashcroft Farm
Gibbet Mill
Rendova Farm
POWEY LA
A540
A5117
M56
Saughall Nurseries
Hill Farm
STRAWBERRY LA
COALPIT LA
Gebe Farm
Wood Farm
Big Wood
Nursery
PARKGATE RD
Depot
CHESTER GATES
Coalpit Lane
Dunkirk Farm
Manor Farm
Dunkirk
Acres Farm
Acres Wood
Backford Cross
LIVERPOOL RD
CHESTER RD
A41
LAURELWOOD DR
BAKEWELL CL
ASHBOURNE CL
CANNOCK CL
LICHFIELD DR
ST ASAPH RD
ELY CL
OXFORD CL
CARDIFF CL
NORWICH DR
KEATS CL
HOLM OAK WAY
BRAMLEY CL
LINDEN CL
VINE RD
HONEY SUCKLE CL
CEDARDALE DR
LAMBOURNE CL
APPLE TREE GR
LAXTON CL
LARCHDALE CL
TUDOR CL
NORMAN CL
MELROSE DR
WILLOWDALE WAY
LINKSIDE WAY
MARKS CRES
SILVERBIRCH WAY
COVENTRY AVE
HEREFORD AVE
TEWKESBURY CL
PLOUGHMANS CL 1
THE FURROWS 2
PLOUGHMANS WAY 3
BADGERS CL 4
CANTERBURY CL 5
GLOUCESTER CL 6
SALISBURY CL 7
BANGOR CL 8
WELLS CL 9
SAXON WAY 10
WEST PARK DR 11
GREEN LAWNS DR 12
PARLIAMENT WAY 13
ST GEORGES AVE 14
ST DAVIDS DR 15
ROSEMERE DR 16
KINNINGTON WAY 17
BACKFORD GDNS 18
Lea Manor Farm
DEMAGE LA
GROVE RD
Grove Farm
St Oswald's CE Aided Prim Sch
PO
The Willows
Lea Farm
STATION RD
Mollington
MOLLINGTON CT
WILLOW LEA
WELL LA
FEILDEN CT
MEADOW CT
HOME PARK
TARRANT CT
OVERWOOD AVE
OVERWOOD LA
TOWNFIELD LA
Warren Farm
Wheatsheaf (PH)
Astbury House
KINGSWOOD AVE
KINGSWOOD LA
FIDDLERS LA
Parkside Farm
LONG LA
Green Farm
Parkgate House
LODGE LA
PARK AVE
PARK WAY
FIELDWAY
NEWCROFT
MEADOWCROFT
GREEN WAY
SAUGHALL HEY
CHURCH RD
The Thomas Wedge CE Contr Jun
Saughall
The Ridings Cty Inf Sch
ALDERSEY CL
DARLINGTON CRES
ANVIL CL
SMITHY CL
CHAPEL CL
RAKE WAY
THE RIDINGS
THE CLOSE
FAIRHOLME CL
ROSEWOOD GR
A B C
36 37 38
70 71 72 73
1 2 3 4

93
117

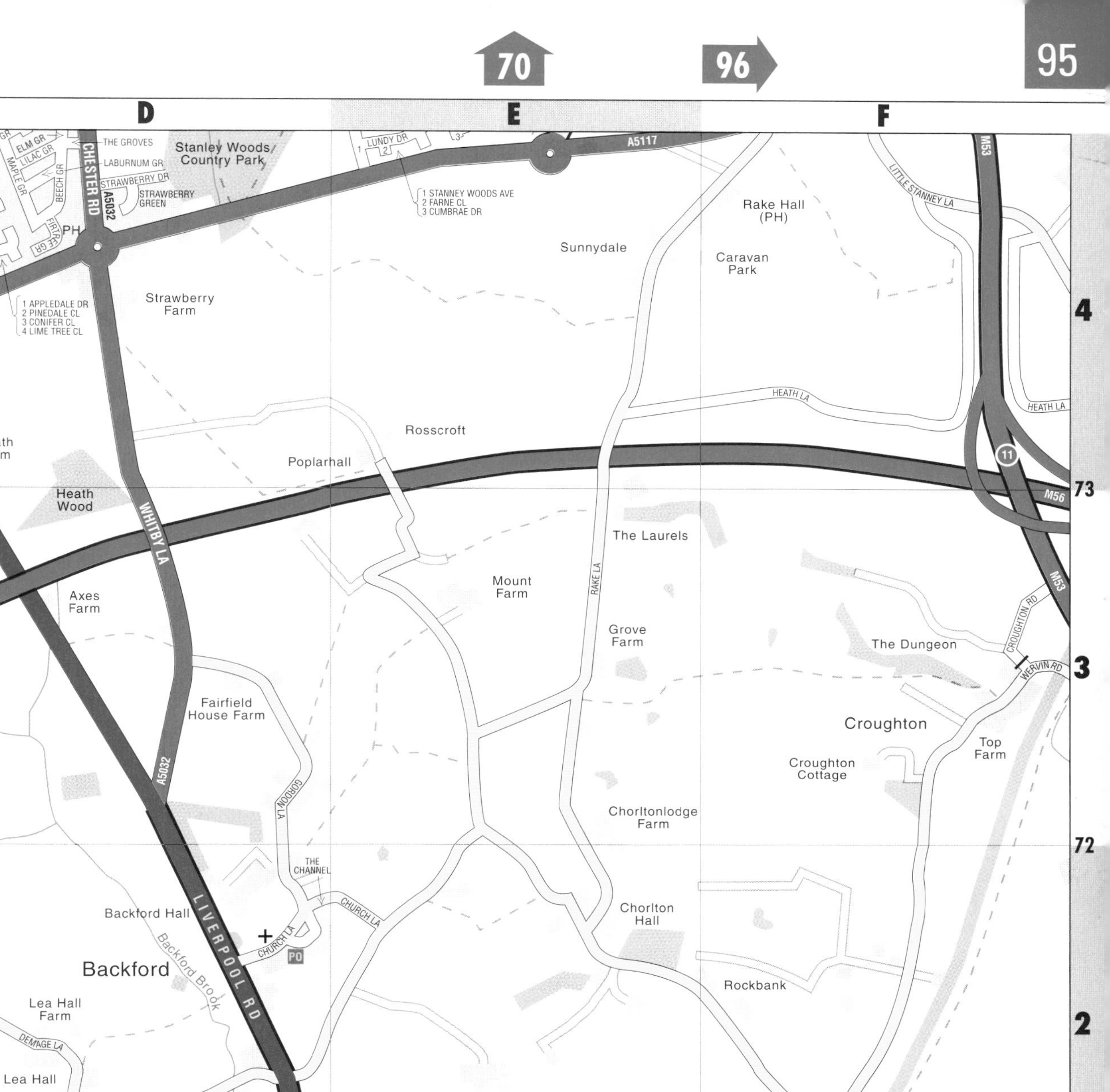
D
E
F
Stanley Woods/ Country Park
THE GROVES
LABURNUM GR
STRAWBERRY DR
STRAWBERRY GREEN
CHESTER RD
A5032
A5117
1 STANNEY WOODS AVE
2 FARNE CL
3 CUMBRAE DR
LUNDY DR
M53
LITTLE STANNEY LA
Rake Hall (PH)
Sunnydale
Caravan Park
1 APPLEDALE DR
2 PINEDALE CL
3 CONIFER CL
4 LIME TREE CL
Strawberry Farm
4
HEATH LA
Heath Farm
Rosscroft
Poplarhall
Heath Wood
A41
WHITBY LA
M56
73
The Laurels
Axes Farm
Mount Farm
RAKE LA
Grove Farm
The Dungeon
CROUGHTON RD
WERVIN RD
3
Fairfield House Farm
Croughton
Top Farm
Croughton Cottage
A5032
GORDON LA
Chorltonlodge Farm
72
THE CHANNEL
CHURCH LA
Backford Hall
LIVERPOOL RD
Chorlton Hall
Backford
Backford Brook
PO
Rockbank
Lea Hall Farm
DEMAGE LA
2
Lea Hall
Collinge Farm
STATION RD
Friars Park
Croughall Bridge
Collinge Wood
Shropshire Union Canal
71
Towing Path
Lea Farm
CAUGHALL RD
BADGERS WLK
Caughall Manor
Moston Hall
Butter Hill
Moston Hill Farm
Viaduct Wood
1
WERVIN RD
Moston
1 CROOKENDEN CL
2 SIMPSON CL
3 BRODIE CL
MALTA RD
The Dale
NORMANDY RD
Chester Zoological Gardens
MOSTON RD
PROSSER RD
A5116
ALAMEIN RD
SALERNO RD
CROOKENDEN RD
SIMPSON RD
CHARLES RD
4 DAUNCEY CL
5 HARINGTON CL
6 HARINGTON RD
FLAG LAN
ACRES LA
70
39
40
41

95
71

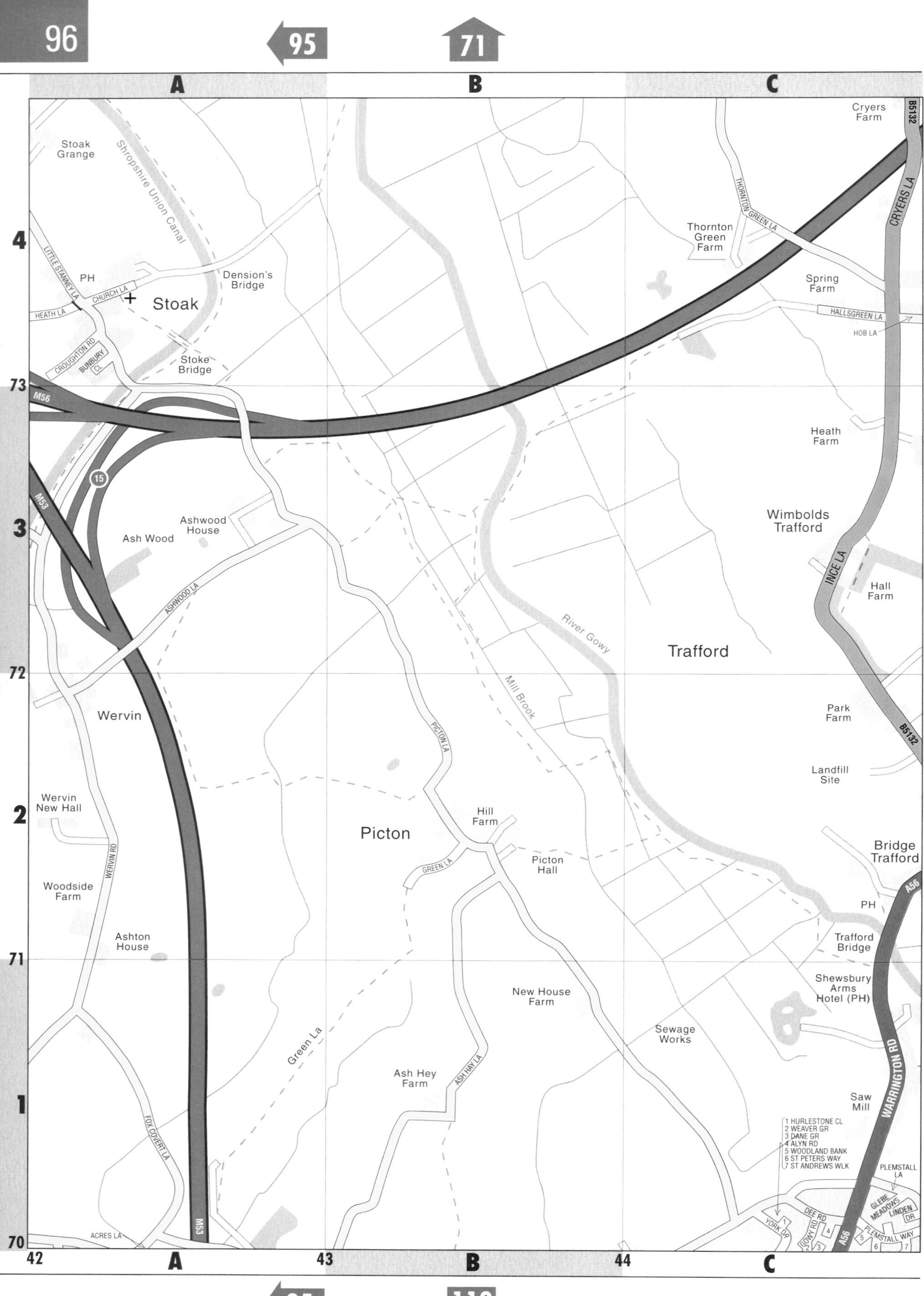
A
B
C
4
3
2
1
73
72
71
70
42
43
44
Cryers Farm
B5132
Stoak Grange
Shropshire Union Canal
Thornton Green Farm
THORNTON GREEN LA
CRYERS LA
LITTLE STANNEY LA
PH
Dension's Bridge
CHURCH LA
Stoak
Spring Farm
HEATH LA
HALLSGREEN LA
HOB LA
CROUGHTON RD
BUNBURY CL
Stoke Bridge
M56
Heath Farm
15
M53
Ashwood House
Ash Wood
Wimbolds Trafford
INCE LA
Hall Farm
ASHWOOD LA
River Gowy
Trafford
Mill Brook
Park Farm
Wervin
PICTON LA
Landfill Site
Wervin New Hall
Hill Farm
Picton
Bridge Trafford
Picton Hall
GREEN LA
Woodside Farm
WERVIN RD
A56
PH
Ashton House
Trafford Bridge
Shewsbury Arms Hotel (PH)
New House Farm
Sewage Works
Green La
WARRINGTON RD
Ash Hey Farm
ASH HAY LA
Saw Mill
FOX COVERT LA
1 HURLESTONE CL
2 WEAVER GR
3 DANE GR
4 ALYN RD
5 WOODLAND BANK
6 ST PETERS WAY
7 ST ANDREWS WLK
PLEMSTALL LA
GLEBE MEADOWS
LINDEN DR
DEE RD
YORK DR
GOWY RD
PLEMSTALL WAY
ACRES LA

95
119

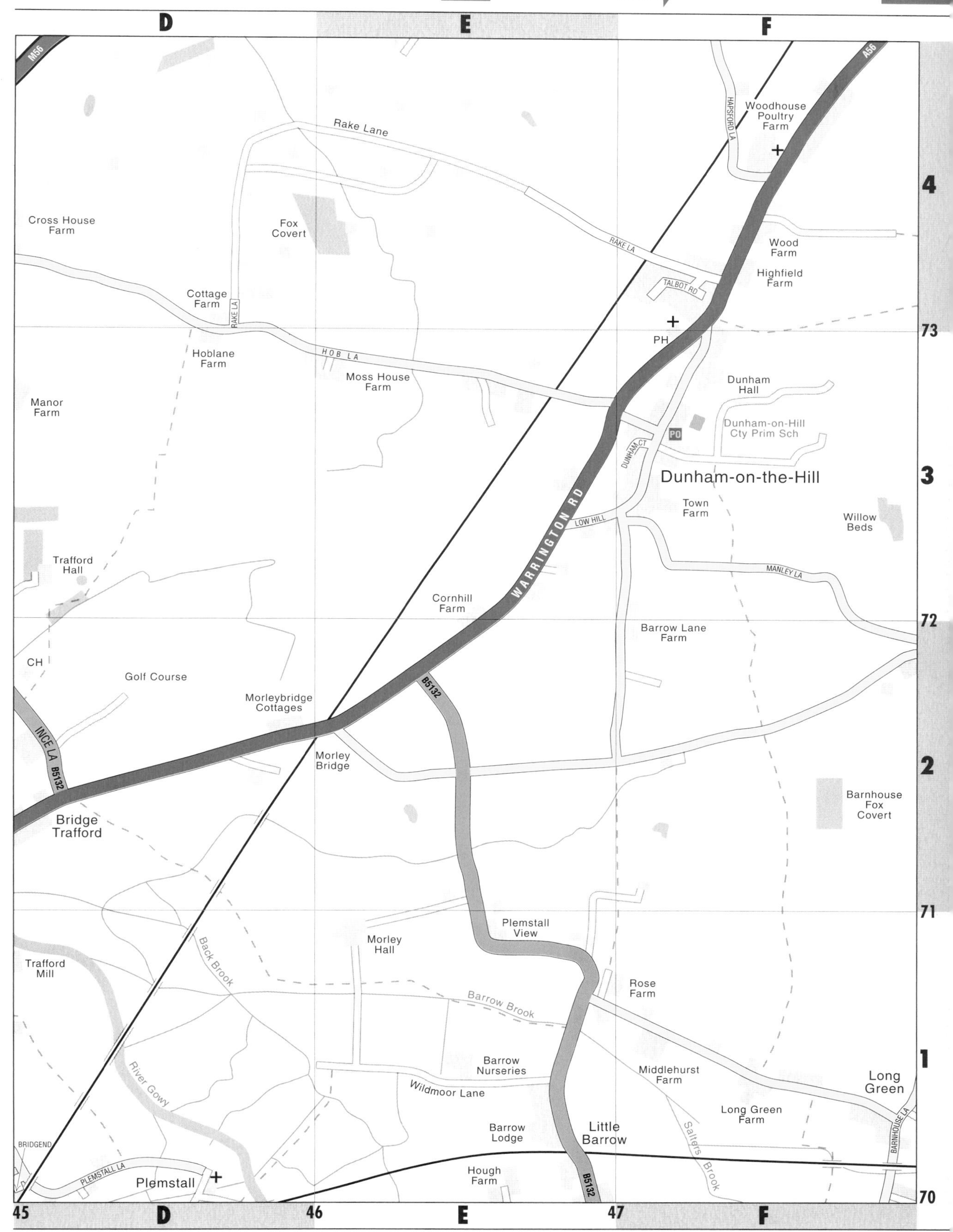

D
E
F

4

Cross House Farm

Rake Lane

Fox Covert

RAKE LA

Woodhouse Poultry Farm

HAPSFORD LA

A56

M56

Cottage Farm

RAKE LA

Wood Farm

Highfield Farm

TALBOT RD

Hoblane Farm

HOB LA

Moss House Farm

PH

73

Manor Farm

Dunham Hall

Dunham-on-Hill Cty Prim Sch

PO

DUNHAM CT

Dunham-on-the-Hill

3

Trafford Hall

Cornhill Farm

WARRINGTON RD

LOW HILL

Town Farm

Willow Beds

MANLEY LA

CH

Golf Course

Barrow Lane Farm

72

Morleybridge Cottages

INCE LA B5132

B5132

Morley Bridge

Barnhouse Fox Covert

2

Bridge Trafford

71

Back Brook

Morley Hall

Plemstall View

Rose Farm

Trafford Mill

Barrow Brook

River Gowy

Barrow Nurseries

Middlehurst Farm

Long Green

1

Wildmoor Lane

Long Green Farm

Salters Brook

BARNHOUSE LA

BRIDGEND

Barrow Lodge

Little Barrow

PLEMSTALL LA

Plemstall

Hough Farm

B5132

70

45
D
46
E
47
F

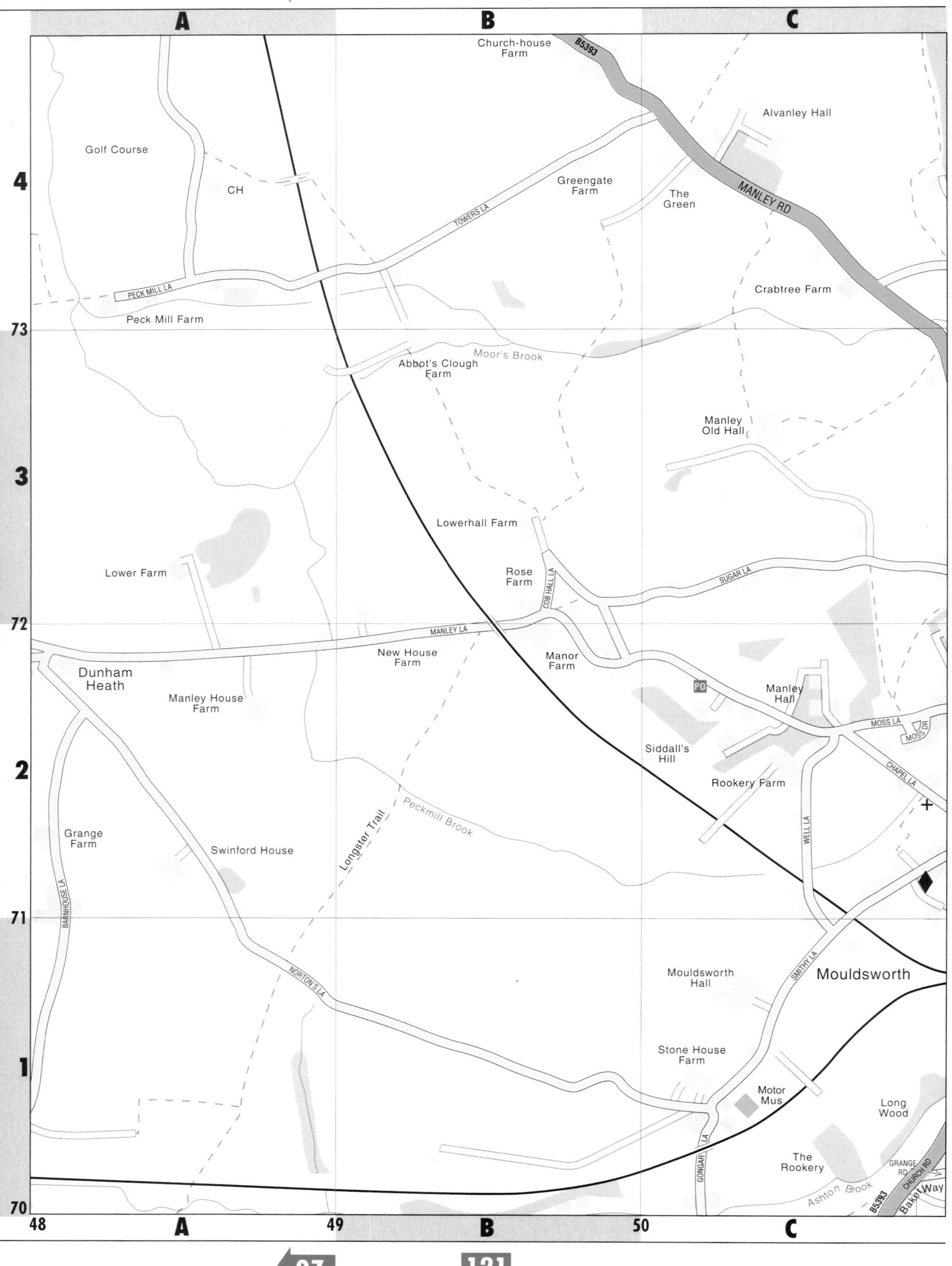

A   B   C

4

73

3

72

2

71

1

70

48   A   49   B   50   C

Golf Course

CH

PECK MILL LA

Peck Mill Farm

Church-house Farm

B5393

Alvanley Hall

TOWERS LA

Greengate Farm

The Green

MANLEY RD

Crabtree Farm

Moor's Brook

Abbot's Clough Farm

Manley Old Hall

Lowerhall Farm

Rose Farm

COB HALL LA

SUGAR LA

Lower Farm

MANLEY LA

New House Farm

Manor Farm

PO

Manley Hall

MOSS LA

MOSS DR

Dunham Heath

Manley House Farm

Siddall's Hill

Rookery Farm

WELL LA

CHAPEL LA

Grange Farm

Swinford House

Longster Trail

Peckmill Brook

BARN HOUSE LA

NORTON'S LA

SMITHY LA

Mouldsworth Hall

Mouldsworth

Stone House Farm

Motor Mus.

Long Wood

GONGAR LA

CHURCH RD

The Rookery

GRANGE RD

B5393

Baker Way

Ashton Brook

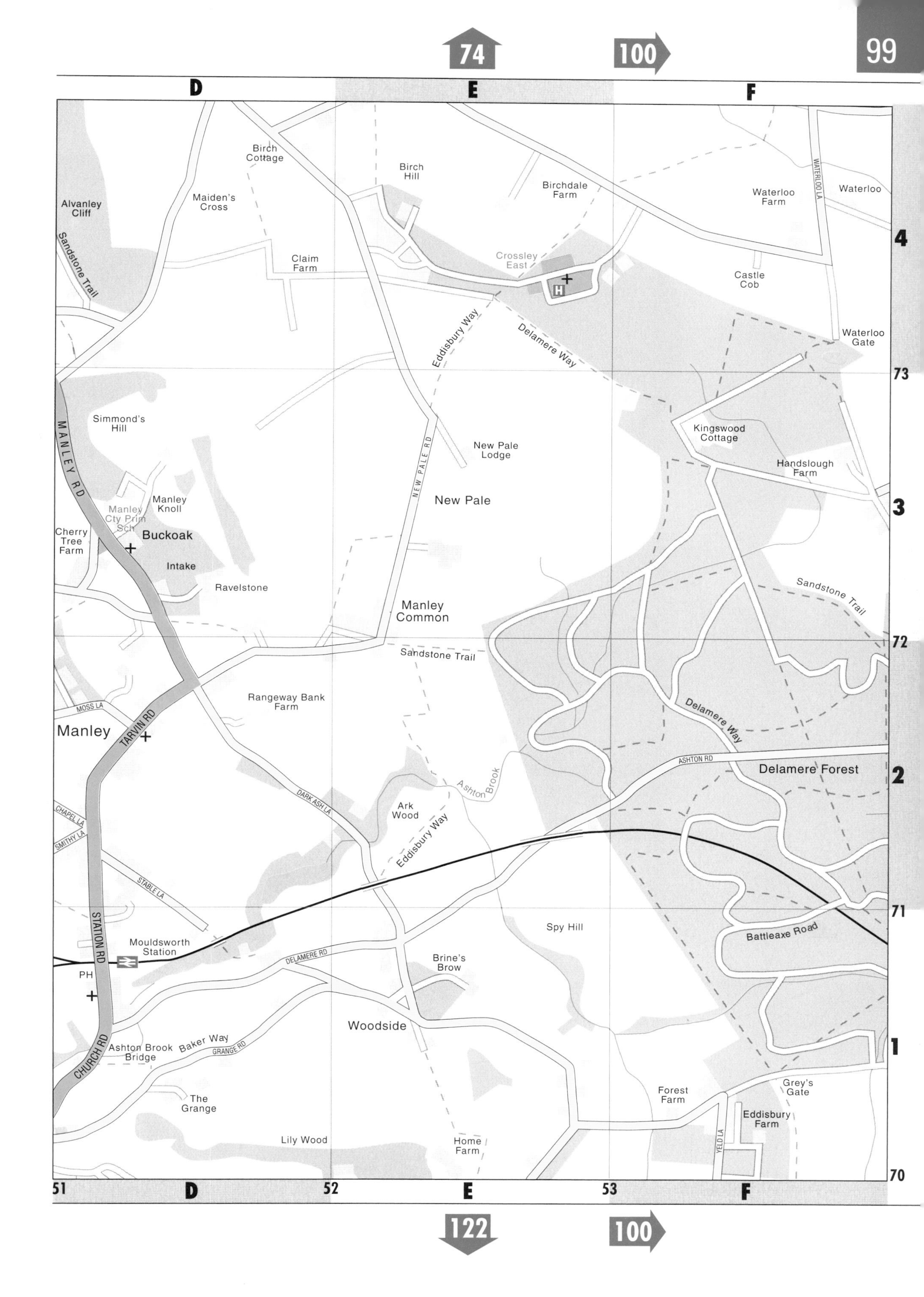
74
100
D
E
F
Birch Cottage
Birch Hill
Birchdale Farm
Waterloo Farm
Waterloo
WATERLOO LA
Alvanley Cliff
Maiden's Cross
Sandstone Trail
Claim Farm
Crossley East
H
Castle Cob
Eddisbury Way
Delamere Way
Waterloo Gate
4
73
Simmond's Hill
MANLEY RD
NEW PALE RD
New Pale Lodge
Kingswood Cottage
Handslough Farm
New Pale
Manley Knoll
Manley Cty Prim Sch
Cherry Tree Farm
Buckoak
Intake
Ravelstone
3
Manley Common
Sandstone Trail
72
Sandstone Trail
Rangeway Bank Farm
MOSS LA
Manley
TARVIN RD
Delamere Way
ASHTON RD
Delamere Forest
2
Ashton Brook
DARK ASH LA
Ark Wood
Eddisbury Way
CHAPEL LA
SMITHY LA
STABLE LA
STATION RD
71
Spy Hill
Battleaxe Road
Mouldsworth Station
DELAMERE RD
Brine's Brow
PH
Woodside
CHURCH RD
Ashton Brook Bridge
Baker Way
GRANGE RD
1
Forest Farm
Grey's Gate
Eddisbury Farm
The Grange
YELD LA
Lily Wood
Home Farm
70
51
D
52
E
53
F
122
100

99
75

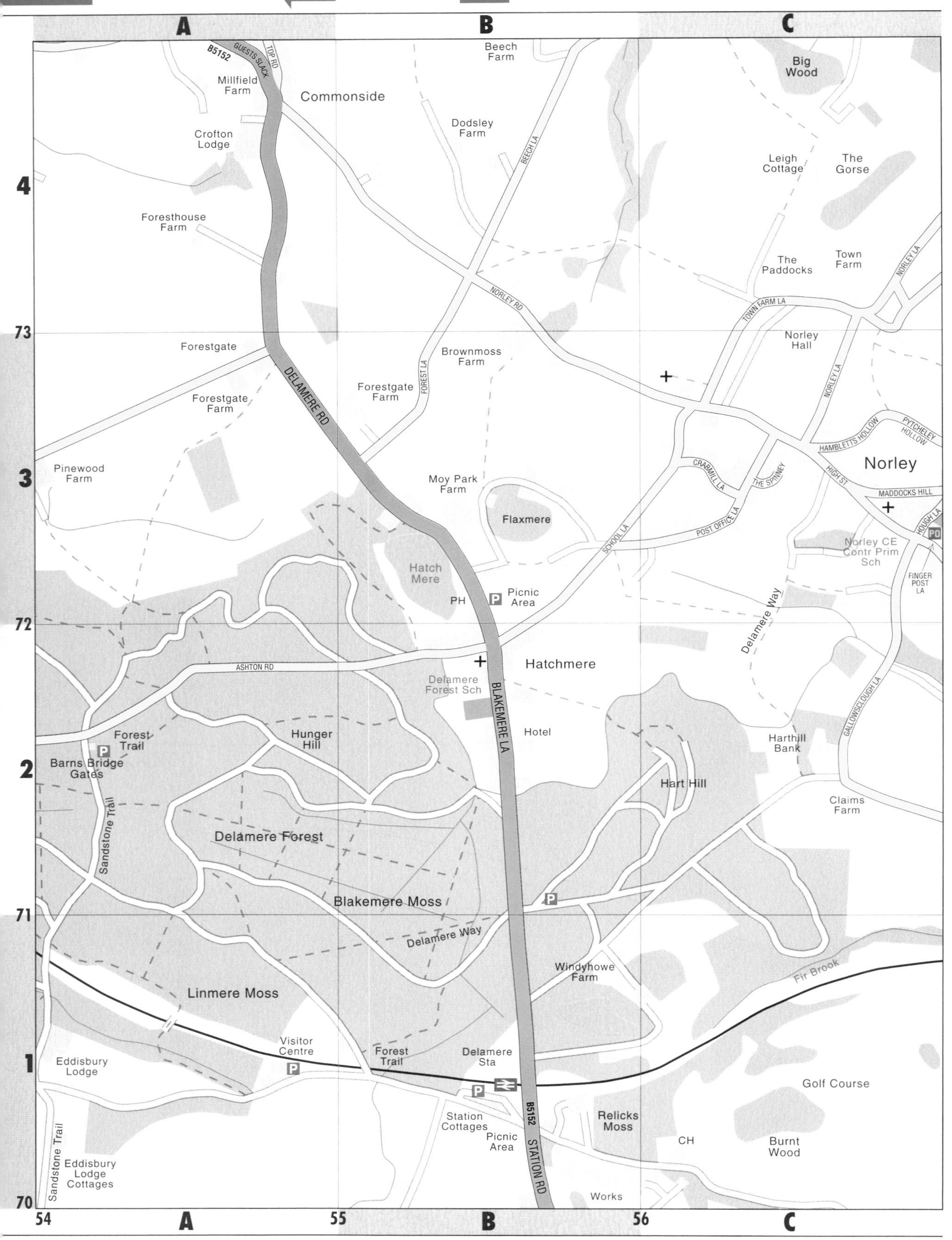
A
B
C
B5152
GUESTS SLACK
TOP RD
Beech Farm
Big Wood
Millfield Farm
Commonside
Dodsley Farm
Crofton Lodge
BEECH LA
Leigh Cottage
The Gorse
Foresthouse Farm
The Paddocks
Town Farm
NORLEY LA
NORLEY RD
TOWN FARM LA
Forestgate
Brownmoss Farm
Norley Hall
DELAMERE RD
Forestgate Farm
FOREST LA
Forestgate Farm
NORLEY LA
HAMBLETTS HOLLOW
PYTCHELEY HOLLOW
Pinewood Farm
Norley
HIGH ST
Moy Park Farm
CRABMILL LA
THE SPINNEY
MADDOCKS HILL
Flaxmere
POST OFFICE LA
SCHOOL LA
HOUGH LA
PO
Norley CE Contr Prim Sch
Hatch Mere
FINGER POST LA
PH
Picnic Area
Delamere Way
ASHTON RD
Hatchmere
Delamere Forest Sch
BLAKEMERE LA
Hotel
Forest Trail
Hunger Hill
Harthill Bank
GALLOWSCLOUGH LA
Barns Bridge Gates
Hart Hill
Claims Farm
Sandstone Trail
Delamere Forest
Blakemere Moss
Delamere Way
Windyhowe Farm
Fir Brook
Linmere Moss
Visitor Centre
Forest Trail
Delamere Sta
Eddisbury Lodge
Golf Course
B5152
Station Cottages
Relicks Moss
Picnic Area
STATION RD
CH
Burnt Wood
Sandstone Trail
Eddisbury Lodge Cottages
Works
4
73
3
72
2
71
1
70
54
55
56

99
123

76
102

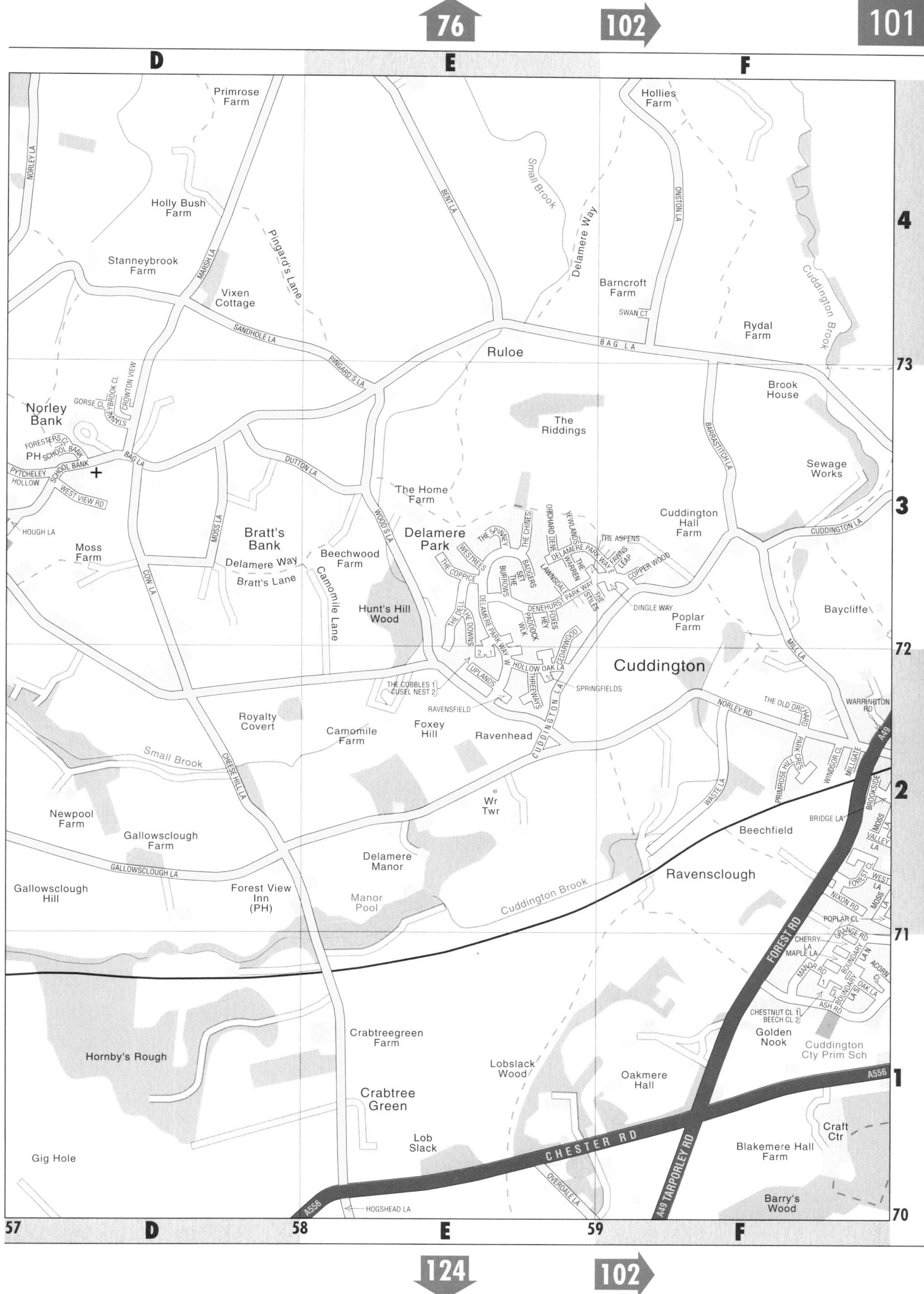
D
E
F
Primrose Farm
Hollies Farm
NORLEY LA
Holly Bush Farm
BENT LA
Small Brook
ONSTON LA
Delamere Way
Pingard's Lane
Stanneybrook Farm
MARSH LA
Vixen Cottage
Barncroft Farm
SWAN CT
Cuddington Brook
Rydal Farm
SANDHOLE LA
BAG LA
Ruloe
PINGARD'S LA
Norley Bank
GORSE CL
STANNEYBROOK CL
CROWTON VIEW
FORESTERS CL
PH
SCHOOL BANK
PYTCHELEY HOLLOW
WEST VIEW RD
HOUGH LA
Brook House
The Riddings
BARRASTITCH LA
Sewage Works
DUTTON LA
The Home Farm
Cuddington Hall Farm
CUDDINGTON LA
MOSS LA
Bratt's Bank
Moss Farm
Delamere Way
Bratt's Lane
Beechwood Farm
Camomile Lane
WOOD'S LA
Delamere Park
THE SPINNEY
WESTREES
THE COPPICE
THE CHINES
BADGERS SET
THE BURROWS
ORCHARD DENE
YEWLANDS
DELAMERE PARK WAY E
THE WARREN
LAWNSDALE
THE ASPENS
FAWNS LEAP
COPPER WOOD
DENEHURST PARK WAY
THE STILES
DINGLE WAY
Poplar Farm
Baycliffe
COW LA
Hunt's Hill Wood
THE DELL
THE DOWNS
DELAMERE PARK WAY W
PADDOCK WLK
FOXES HEY
CEDARWOOD
HOLLOW OAK LA
THREEWAYS
UPLANDS
SPRINGFIELDS
Cuddington
MILL LA
THE COBBLES 1
CUSEL NEST 2
RAVENSFIELD
CUDDINGTON LA
NORLEY RD
THE OLD ORCHARD
WARRINGTON RD
Royalty Covert
Camomile Farm
Foxey Hill
Ravenhead
A49
Small Brook
CHESE HILL LA
PARK CRES
WINDSOR CL
MILLGATE
PRIMROSE HILL
WASTE LA
BROOKSIDE
Newpool Farm
Wr Twr
BRIDGE LA
Gallowsclough Farm
Beechfield
MOSS VALLEY LA
Delamere Manor
GALLOWSCLOUGH LA
Ravensclough
Gallowsclough Hill
Forest View Inn (PH)
Manor Pool
Cuddington Brook
FOREST CL
WEST LA
NIXON RD
MOSS LA
POPLAR CL
FOREST RD
CHERRY LA
GRANGE RD
MAPLE LA
MANOR RD
BOUNDARY LA N
ACORN CL
OAK LA
BOUNDARY LA S
ASH RD
CHESTNUT CL 1
BEECH CL 2
Crabtreegreen Farm
Golden Nook
Cuddington Cty Prim Sch
Hornby's Rough
Lobslack Wood
Oakmere Hall
A556
Crabtree Green
Craft Ctr
Lob Slack
CHESTER RD
TARPORLEY RD
Blakemere Hall Farm
Gig Hole
OVERDALE LA
A556
HOGSHEAD LA
A49
Barry's Wood
4
3
2
1
73
72
71
70
57
58
59
D
E
F

124
102

101
77

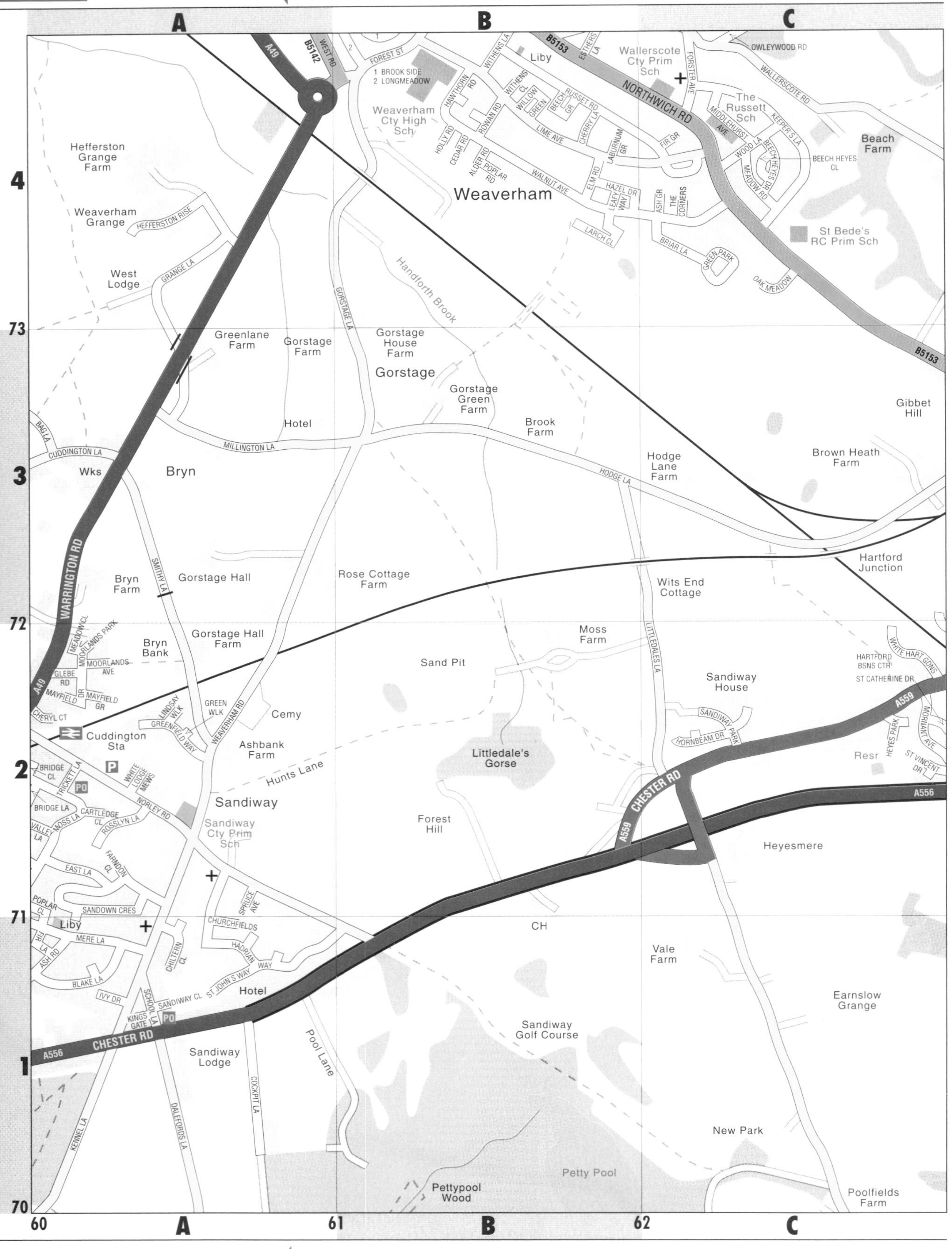
A
B
C
Weaverham
Gorstage
Bryn
Sandiway
Hefferston Grange Farm
Weaverham Grange
West Lodge
Greenlane Farm
Gorstage Farm
Gorstage House Farm
Gorstage Green Farm
Brook Farm
Hodge Lane Farm
Hotel
Wks
Bryn Farm
Gorstage Hall
Bryn Bank
Gorstage Hall Farm
Rose Cottage Farm
Wits End Cottage
Hartford Junction
Moss Farm
Sand Pit
Sandiway House
Cemy
Cuddington Sta
Ashbank Farm
Hunts Lane
Littledale's Gorse
Forest Hill
Sandiway Cty Prim Sch
Heyesmere
Liby
CH
Vale Farm
Earnslow Grange
Sandiway Golf Course
Sandiway Lodge
Pool Lane
New Park
Petty Pool
Pettypool Wood
Poolfields Farm
Weaverham Cty High Sch
Wallerscote Cty Prim Sch
The Russett Sch
Beach Farm
St Bede's RC Prim Sch
Gibbet Hill
Brown Heath Farm
Resr
Handforth Brook
NORTHWICH RD
CHESTER RD
WARRINGTON RD
A49
A556
A559
B5153
B5142
1 BROOK SIDE
2 LONGMEADOW
60
61
62
70
71
72
73

101
125

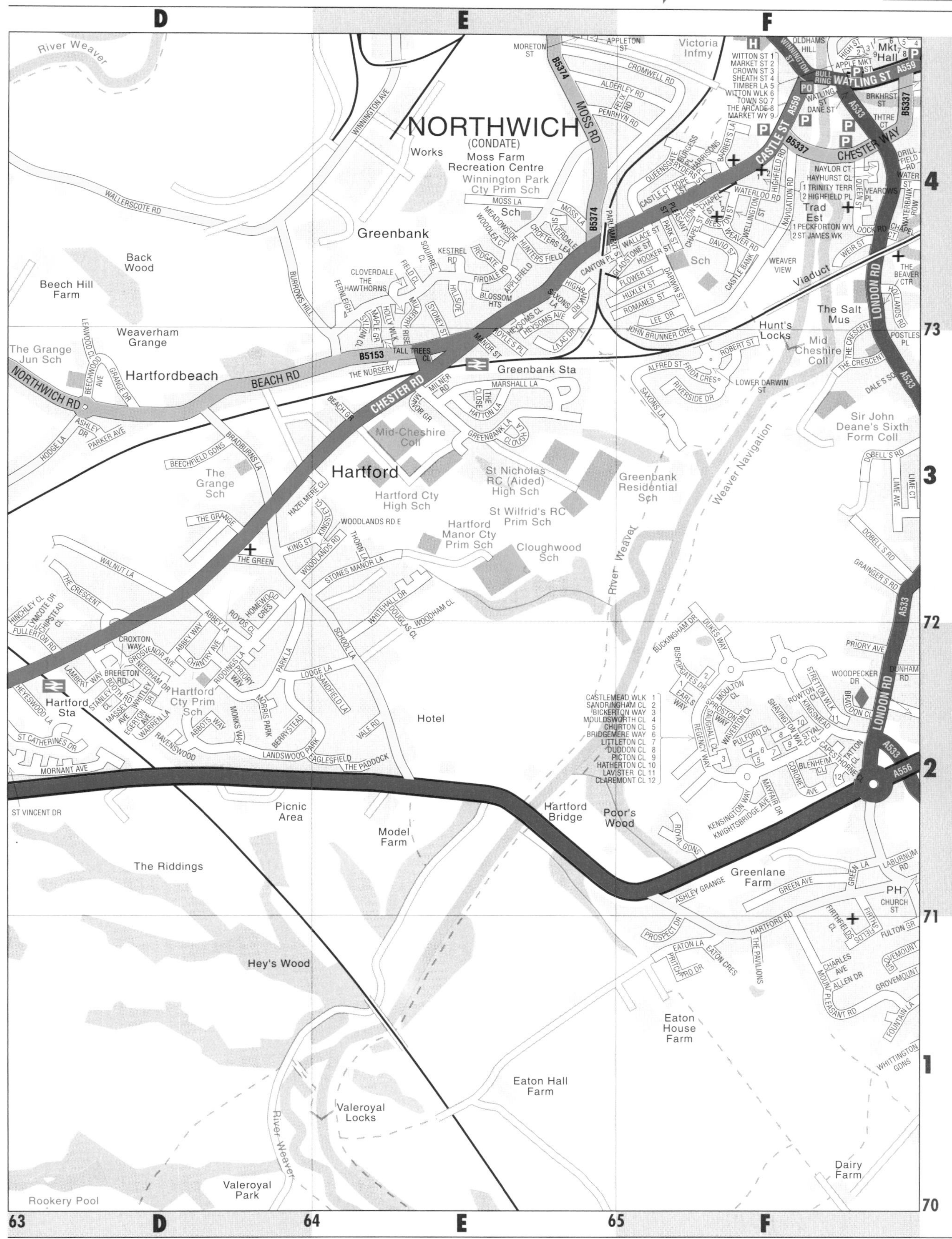

NORTHWICH
(CONDATE)

Moss Farm
Recreation Centre

Winnington Park
Cty Prim Sch

Works

Greenbank

River Weaver

WINNINGTON AVE

WALLERSCOTE RD

Back
Wood

Beech Hill
Farm

Weaverham
Grange

The Grange
Jun Sch

Hartfordbeach

NORTHWICH RD

BEACH RD

CHESTER RD

B5153

Tall Trees

The Nursery

Greenbank Sta

Mid-Cheshire
Coll

Hartford

The
Grange Sch

The Grange

The Green

Hartford Cty
High Sch

WOODLANDS RD E

Hartford
Manor Cty
Prim Sch

St Nicholas
RC (Aided)
High Sch

St Wilfrid's RC
Prim Sch

Cloughwood
Sch

Greenbank
Residential
Sch

River Weaver

Weaver Navigation

WALNUT LA

The Crescent

Croxton
Way

Hartford
Cty Prim
Sch

Hartford
Sta

Hotel

School La

Lodge La

Vale Rd

Landswood

Eaglesfield

The Paddock

Ravenswood

St Catherine's Dr

Mornant Ave

St Vincent Dr

Picnic
Area

Model
Farm

Hartford
Bridge

Poor's
Wood

CASTLEMEAD WLK   1
SANDRINGHAM CL   2
BICKERTON WAY   3
MOULDSWORTH CL   4
CHURTON CL   5
BRIDGEMERE WAY   6
LITTLETON CL   7
DUDDON CL   8
PICTON CL   9
HATHERTON CL   10
LAVISTER CL   11
CLAREMONT CL   12

Woodpecker Dr

Dunham Rd

Priory Ave

London Rd

Greenlane
Farm

Ashley Grange

Green La

Green Ave

Laburnum Rd

PH

Church St

Hartford Rd

The Riddings

Hey's Wood

The Pavilions

Eaton La

Eaton Cres

Eaton
House
Farm

Eaton Hall
Farm

Valeroyal
Locks

River Weaver

Valeroyal
Park

Rookery Pool

Dairy
Farm

Victoria
Infmy

WITTON ST   1
MARKET ST   2
CROWN ST   3
SHEATH ST   4
TIMBER LA   5
WITTON WLK 6
TOWN SQ   7
THE ARCADE 8
MARKET WY   9

Mkt
Hall

WATLING ST

CASTLE ST

CHESTER WAY

A559

A533

B5337

Trad
Est
1 PECKFORTON WY
2 ST JAMES WK

The Salt
Mus

Mid
Cheshire
Coll

Sir John
Deane's Sixth
Form Coll

Hunt's
Locks

The
Crescent

LONDON RD

A533

Viaduct

A556

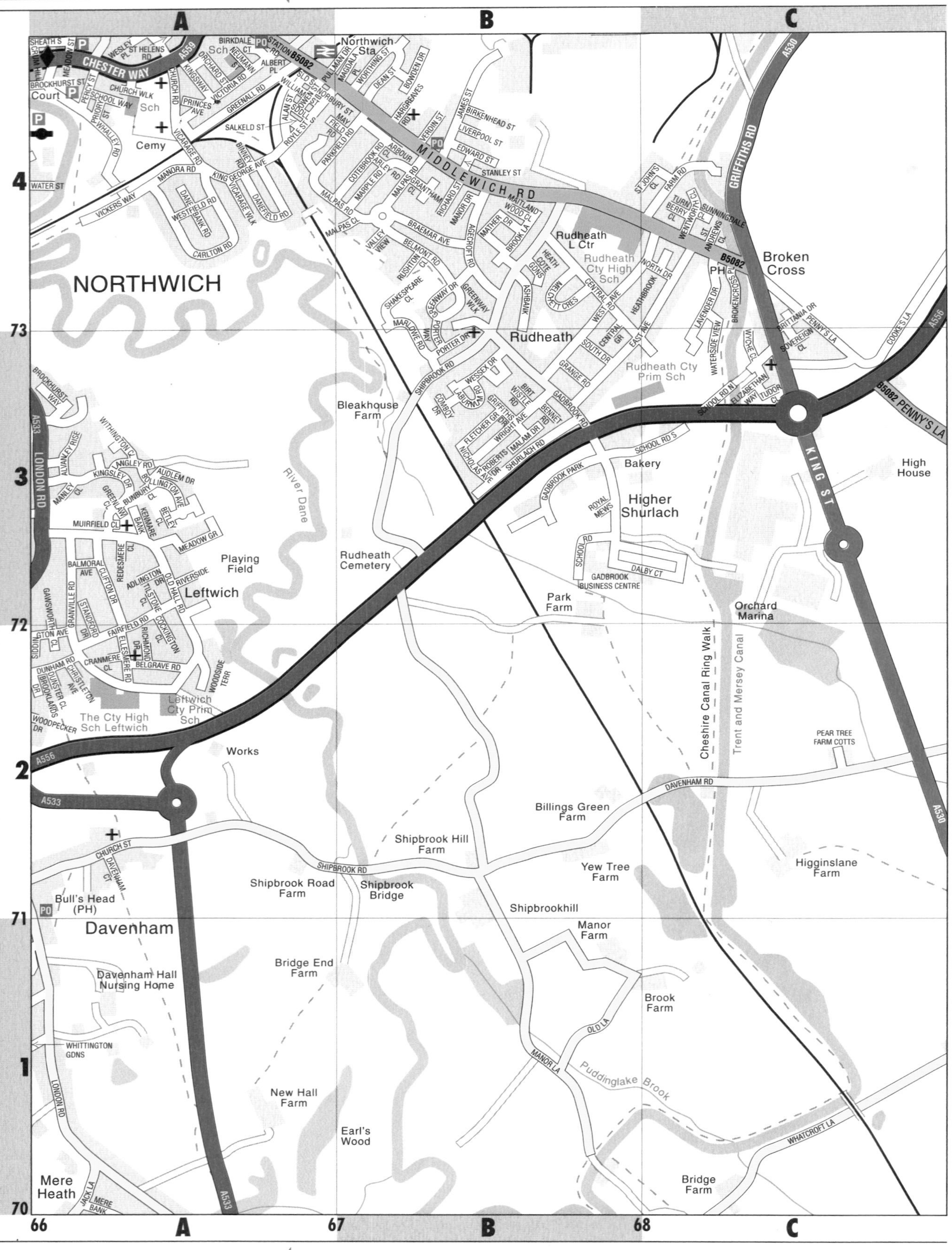

A   B   C

CHESTER WAY

Northwich Sta.

MIDDLEWICH RD

GRIFFITHS RD

4

NORTHWICH

Rudheath L Ctr

Broken Cross

Rudheath Cty High Sch

73

Rudheath

Bleakhouse Farm

Rudheath Cty Prim Sch

River Dane

KING ST

High House

3

Kingsley Rd

Leftwich

Playing Field

Rudheath Cemetery

Bakery

Higher Shurlach

Royal Mews

72

The Cty High Sch Leftwich

Leftwich Cty Prim Sch

Park Farm

Gadbrook Park

SCHOOL RD S

DALBY CT

GADBROOK BUSINESS CENTRE

Orchard Marina

Cheshire Canal Ring Walk

Trent and Mersey Canal

PEAR TREE FARM COTTS

Works

DAVENHAM RD

Higginslane Farm

2

Church St

Shipbrook Hill Farm

Billings Green Farm

Shipbrook Rd

Bull's Head (PH)

Davenham

Shipbrook Road Farm

Shipbrook Bridge

Yew Tree Farm

Shipbrookhill

71

Manor Farm

Davenham Hall Nursing Home

Bridge End Farm

Brook Farm

OLD LA

MANOR LA

Puddinglake Brook

1

WHITTINGTON GDNS

New Hall Farm

Earl's Wood

WHATCROFT LA

Mere Heath

Bridge Farm

70

66   A   67   B   68   C

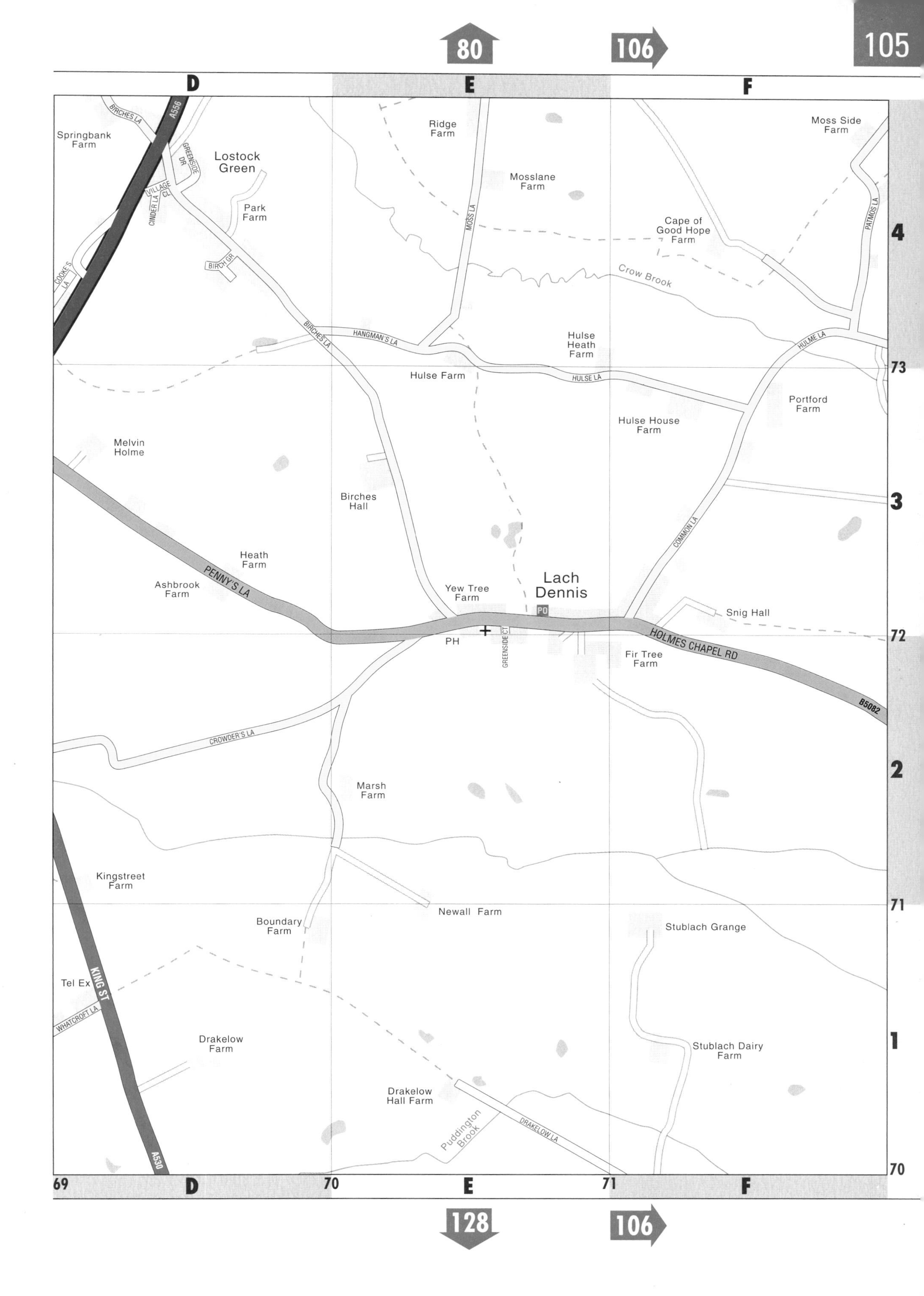

D

E

F

4

Springbank
Farm

Lostock
Green

Park
Farm

BIRCHES LA

GREENSIDE DR

CINDER LA

VILLAGE CL

COOKE'S LA

A556

BIRCH GR

Ridge
Farm

Mosslane
Farm

Moss Side
Farm

MOSS LA

PATMOS LA

Cape of
Good Hope
Farm

Crow Brook

HULME LA

73

BIRCHES LA

HANGMAN'S LA

Hulse
Heath
Farm

Hulse Farm

HULSE LA

Portford
Farm

Melvin
Holme

Hulse House
Farm

Birches
Hall

3

Heath
Farm

PENNY'S LA

COMMON LA

Ashbrook
Farm

Yew Tree
Farm

Lach
Dennis

PO

Snig Hall

72

PH

GREENSIDE CT

HOLMES CHAPEL RD

Fir Tree
Farm

B5082

CROWDER'S LA

Marsh
Farm

2

Kingstreet
Farm

Newall Farm

71

Boundary
Farm

Stublach Grange

Tel Ex

KING ST

WHATCROFT LA

Drakelow
Farm

Stublach Dairy
Farm

1

Drakelow
Hall Farm

Puddington Brook

DRAKELOW LA

A530

70

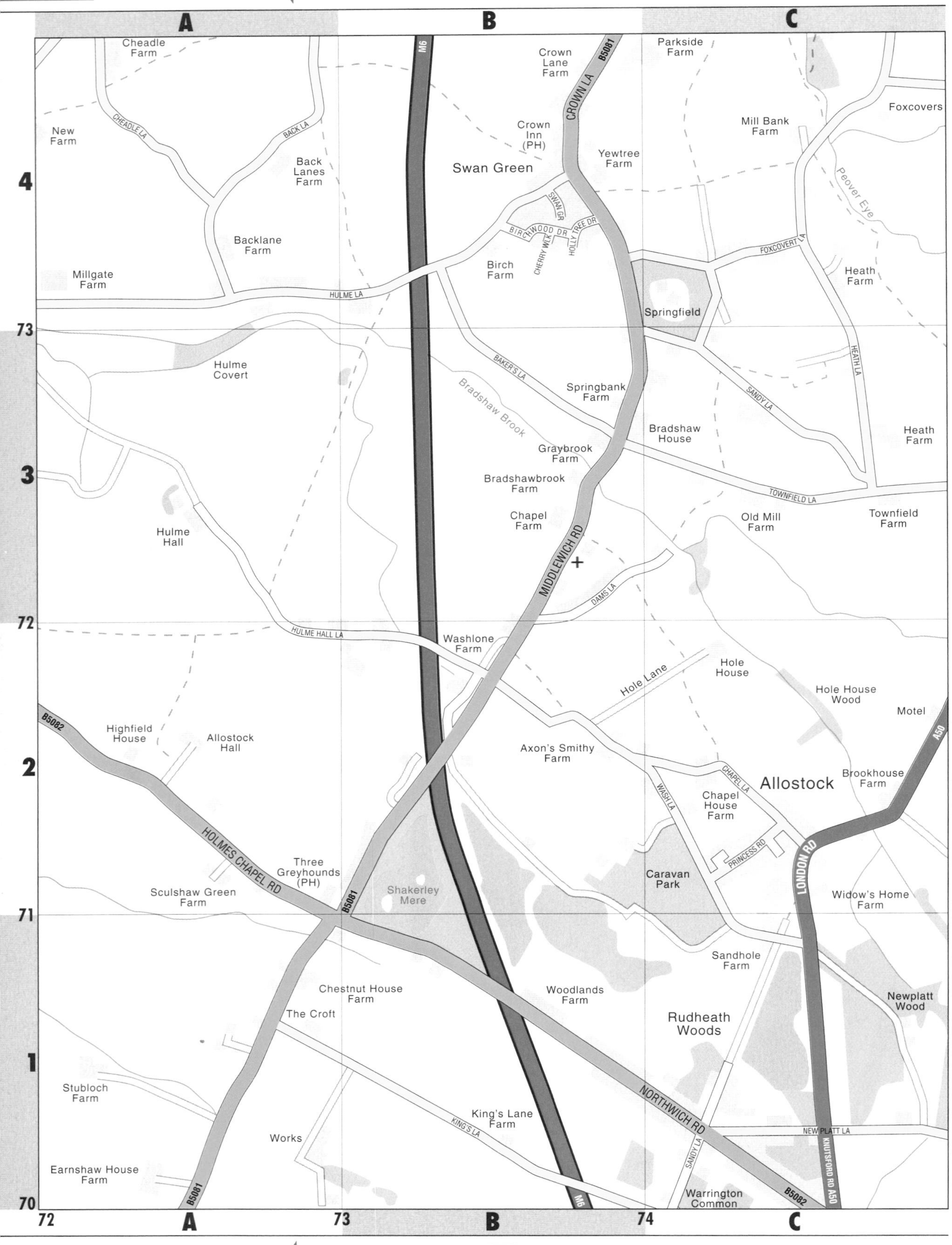

105
81

A   B   C

Cheadle
Farm

New
Farm

CHEADLE LA

BACK LA

Back
Lanes
Farm

Backlane
Farm

Millgate
Farm

HULME LA

Crown
Lane
Farm

CROWN LA

B5081

Parkside
Farm

Foxcovers

Crown
Inn
(PH)

Swan Green

Yewtree
Farm

Mill Bank
Farm

SWAN GR

BIRCHWOOD DR

CHERRY WLK

HOLLY TREE DR

Birch
Farm

FOXCOVERT LA

Peover Eye

Springfield

Heath
Farm

4

Hulme
Covert

BAKER'S LA

Bradshaw Brook

Springbank
Farm

SANDY LA

Bradshaw
House

HEATH LA

Heath
Farm

73

Hulme
Hall

Graybrook
Farm

Bradshawbrook
Farm

Chapel
Farm

MIDDLEWICH RD

+

DAMS LA

Old Mill
Farm

TOWNFIELD LA

Townfield
Farm

3

HULME HALL LA

Washlone
Farm

Hole Lane

Hole
House

Hole House
Wood

Motel

72

B5082

Highfield
House

Allostock
Hall

HOLMES CHAPEL RD

Axon's Smithy
Farm

WASH LA

CHAPEL LA

Chapel
House
Farm

Allostock

A50

Brookhouse
Farm

2

Sculshaw Green
Farm

Three
Greyhounds
(PH)

B5081

Shakerley
Mere

Caravan
Park

PRINCESS RD

LONDON RD

Widow's Home
Farm

71

Chestnut House
Farm

The Croft

Woodlands
Farm

Sandhole
Farm

Newplatt
Wood

1

Stubloch
Farm

Rudheath
Woods

NORTHWICH RD

KNUTSFORD RD A50

Works

King's Lane
Farm

KING'S LA

SANDY LA

NEW PLATT LA

B5082

Earnshaw House
Farm

B5081

M6

Warrington
Common

70

72   A   73   B   74   C

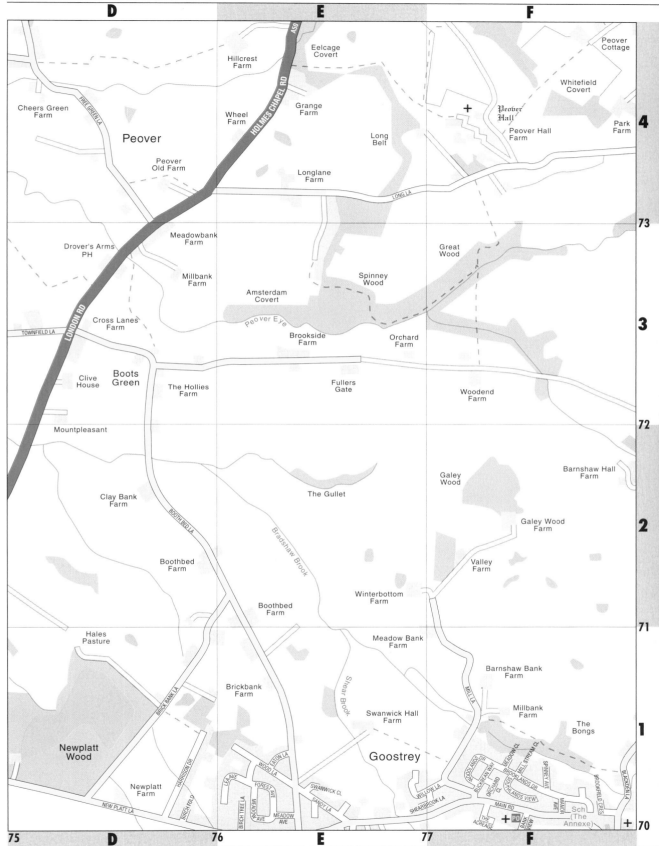

D E F

Peover Cottage

Whitefield Covert

Peover Hall

Peover Hall Farm

Park Farm

4

Hillcrest Farm

Eelcage Covert

A50

HOLMES CHAPEL RD

Wheel Farm

Grange Farm

Long Belt

Cheers Green Farm

FREE GREEN LA

Peover

Peover Old Farm

Longlane Farm

Long La

73

Meadowbank Farm

Great Wood

Drover's Arms PH

Millbank Farm

Spinney Wood

Amsterdam Covert

LONDON RD

Cross Lanes Farm

TOWNFIELD LA

Peover Eye

Brookside Farm

Orchard Farm

3

Clive House

Boots Green

The Hollies Farm

Fullers Gate

Woodend Farm

Mountpleasant

72

The Gullet

Galey Wood

Barnshaw Hall Farm

Clay Bank Farm

BOOTH BED LA

Boothbed Farm

Bradshaw Brook

Galey Wood Farm

Valley Farm

2

Boothbed Farm

Winterbottom Farm

71

Hales Pasture

BRICK BANK LA

Meadow Bank Farm

MILL LA

Barnshaw Bank Farm

Brickbank Farm

Shear Brook

Swanwick Hall Farm

Millbank Farm

The Bongs

1

Newplatt Wood

HARRISON DR

BIRCH FOLD

Newplatt Farm

NEW PLATT LA

LEA AVE

WOOD LA

EXTON LA

FOREST AVE

BIRCH TREE LA

MEADOW AVE

MEADOW AVE

SWANWICK CL

SANDY LA

Goostrey

WILLOW LA

SHEARBROOK LA

MAIN RD

THE ACREAGE

PO

BANK VIEW

WOODLANDS DR

BLACKBEAN WAY

ORCHARD CL

MEADOW CL

BROOKLANDS DR

WOODLANDS VIEW

MILL STREAM CL

SPINNEY AVE

MANOR AVE

BROOKFIELD CRES

BLACKDEN LA

Sch (The Annexe)

70

75 D 76 E 77 F

107 83

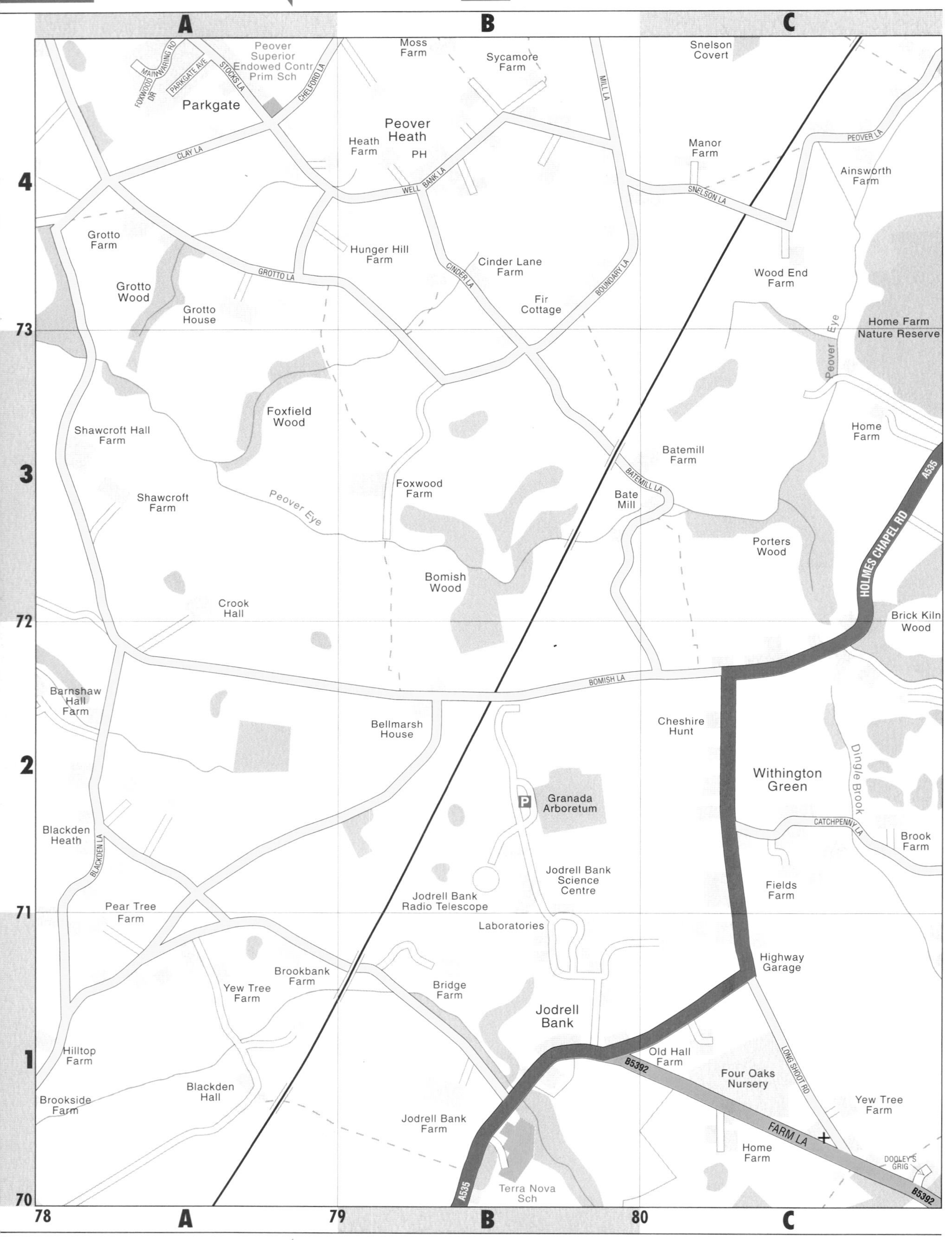
A
B
C
Peover Superior Endowed Contr Prim Sch
Moss Farm
Sycamore Farm
Snelson Covert
Parkgate
Peover Heath
Heath Farm
PH
Manor Farm
Ainsworth Farm
CLAY LA
WELL BANK LA
SNELSON LA
PEOVER LA
MILL LA
CHELFORD LA
STOCKS LA
PARKGATE AVE
MAINWARING RD
FOXWOOD DR
Grotto Farm
Hunger Hill Farm
Cinder Lane Farm
Wood End Farm
Grotto Wood
Grotto House
GROTTO LA
CINDER LA
Fir Cottage
BOUNDARY LA
Home Farm Nature Reserve
Peover Eye
Foxfield Wood
Shawcroft Hall Farm
Batemill Farm
Home Farm
BATEMILL LA
Foxwood Farm
Bate Mill
Shawcroft Farm
Porters Wood
Bomish Wood
HOLMES CHAPEL RD
A535
Crook Hall
Brick Kiln Wood
BOMISH LA
Barnshaw Hall Farm
Bellmarsh House
Cheshire Hunt
Withington Green
Dingle Brook
P
Granada Arboretum
Blackden Heath
CATCHPENNY LA
Brook Farm
BLACKDEN LA
Jodrell Bank Science Centre
Fields Farm
Jodrell Bank Radio Telescope
Pear Tree Farm
Laboratories
Highway Garage
Brookbank Farm
Yew Tree Farm
Bridge Farm
Jodrell Bank
Hilltop Farm
Old Hall Farm
B5392
LONG SHOOT RD
Four Oaks Nursery
Blackden Hall
Brookside Farm
Yew Tree Farm
Jodrell Bank Farm
FARM LA
Home Farm
DOOLEY'S GRIG
Terra Nova Sch
4
73
3
72
2
71
1
70
78
79
80

107 131

84

110

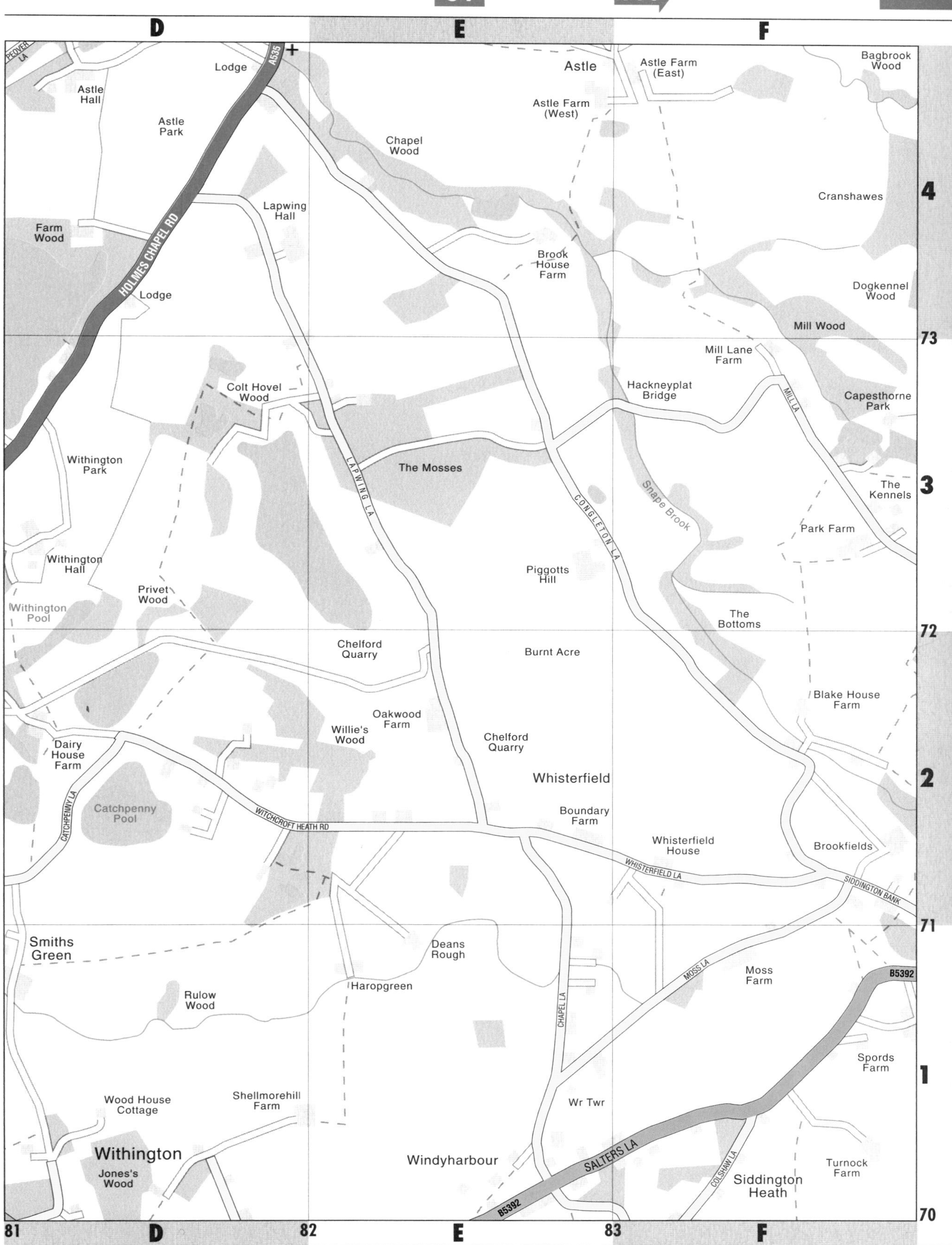

D
E
F
PEOVER LA
A535
Lodge
Astle
Astle Farm (East)
Bagbrook Wood
Astle Hall
Astle Farm (West)
Astle Park
Chapel Wood
Lapwing Hall
Cranshawes
Farm Wood
HOLMES CHAPEL RD
Brook House Farm
Dogkennel Wood
Lodge
Mill Wood
Mill Lane Farm
Colt Hovel Wood
Hackneyplat Bridge
MILL LA
Capesthorne Park
Withington Park
The Mosses
LAPWING LA
CONGLETON LA
Snape Brook
The Kennels
Park Farm
Withington Hall
Piggotts Hill
Privet Wood
Withington Pool
The Bottoms
Chelford Quarry
Burnt Acre
Blake House Farm
Oakwood Farm
Willie's Wood
Dairy House Farm
Chelford Quarry
Whisterfield
CATCHPENNY LA
Catchpenny Pool
WITCHCROFT HEATH RD
Boundary Farm
Whisterfield House
Brookfields
WHISTERFIELD LA
SIDDINGTON BANK
Smiths Green
Deans Rough
MOSS LA
Moss Farm
B5392
Haropgreen
Rulow Wood
CHAPEL LA
Spords Farm
Wood House Cottage
Shellmorehill Farm
Wr Twr
SALTERS LA
Withington
Windyharbour
Turnock Farm
Jones's Wood
COLSHAW LA
Siddington Heath
B5392
4
73
3
72
2
71
1
70
81
82
83

109
85

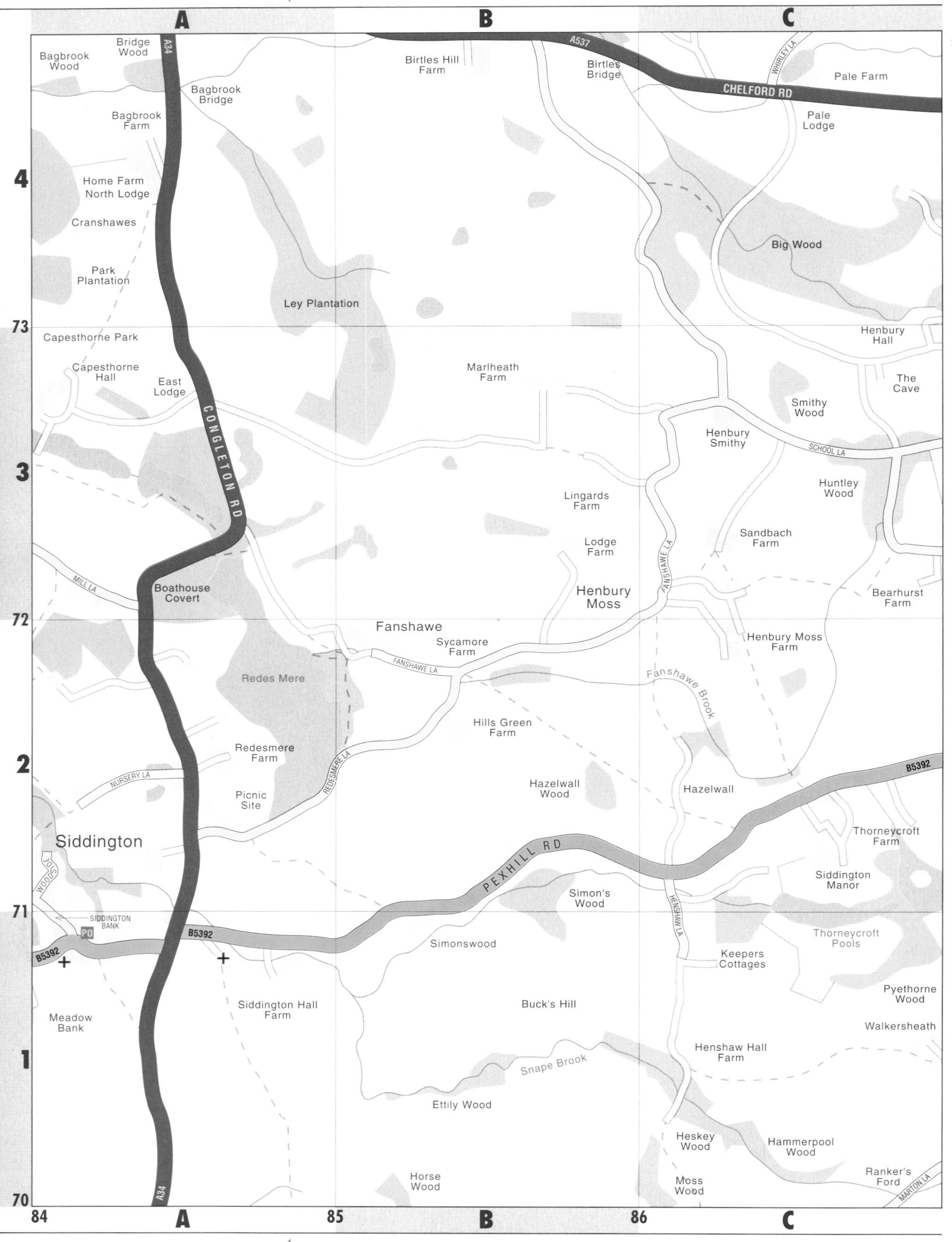
A
B
C
Bagbrook Wood
Bridge Wood
A34
Birtles Hill Farm
A537
Birtles Bridge
Pale Farm
CHELFORD RD
WHIRLEY LA
Bagbrook Bridge
Bagbrook Farm
Pale Lodge
4
Home Farm
North Lodge
Cranshawes
Big Wood
Park Plantation
Ley Plantation
73
Capesthorne Park
Henbury Hall
Capesthorne Hall
East Lodge
Marlheath Farm
The Cave
CONGLETON RD
Smithy Wood
Henbury Smithy
SCHOOL LA
3
Huntley Wood
Lingards Farm
Sandbach Farm
Lodge Farm
MILL LA
FANSHAWE LA
Boathouse Covert
Henbury Moss
Bearhurst Farm
72
Fanshawe
Sycamore Farm
Henbury Moss Farm
FANSHAWE LA
Redes Mere
Fanshawe Brook
Hills Green Farm
Redesmere Farm
2
B5392
NURSERY LA
REDESMERE LA
Hazelwall Wood
Hazelwall
Picnic Site
Thorneycroft Farm
Siddington
PEXHILL RD
WOODSIDE
Siddington Manor
Simon's Wood
HENSHAW LA
71
SIDDINGTON BANK
PO
B5392
B5392
Simonswood
Thorneycroft Pools
Keepers Cottages
Siddington Hall Farm
Pyethorne Wood
Meadow Bank
Buck's Hill
Walkersheath
1
Henshaw Hall Farm
Snape Brook
Ettily Wood
Heskey Wood
Hammerpool Wood
Horse Wood
Moss Wood
Ranker's Ford
MARTON LA
70
84
85
86

109
133

86
112

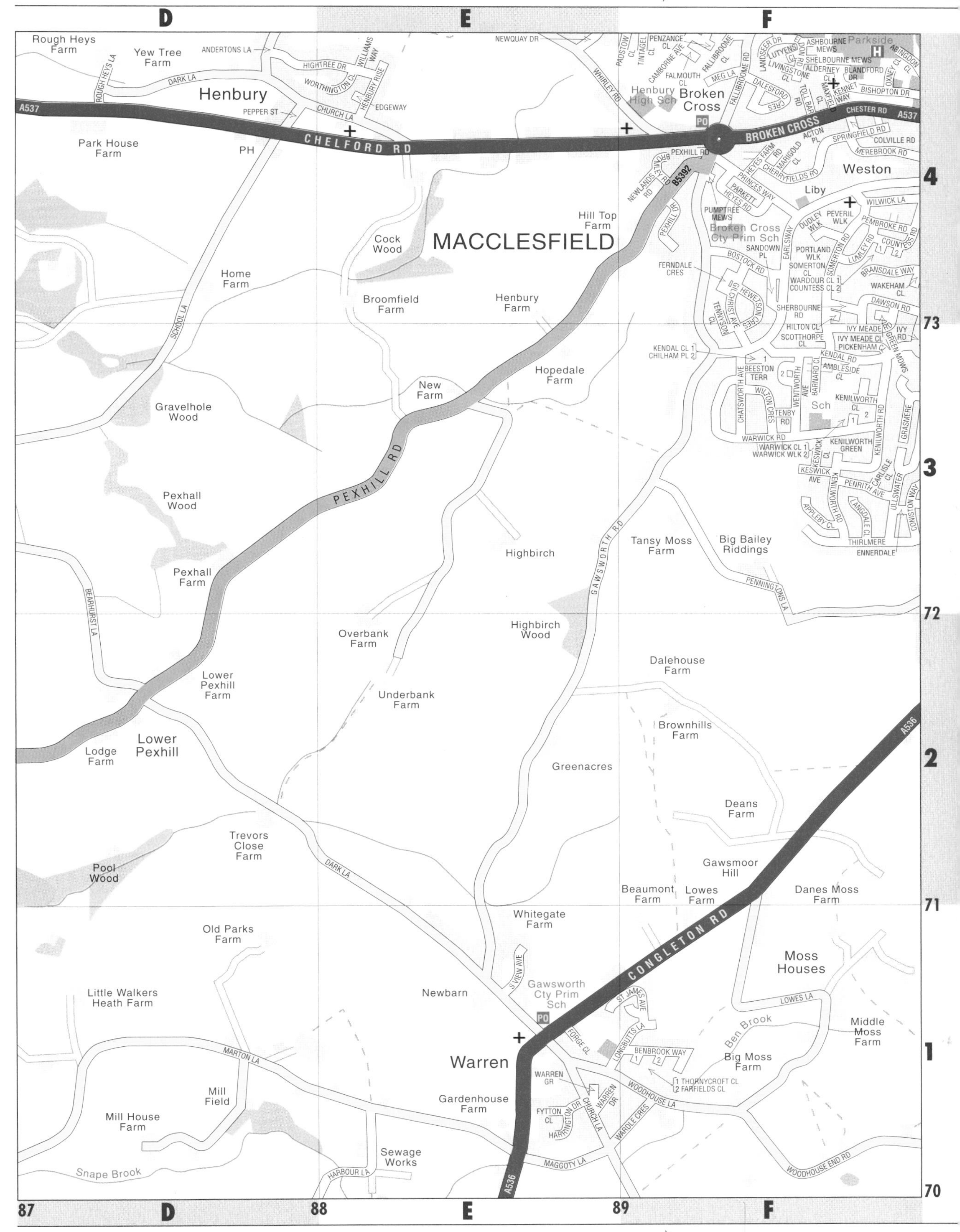
D
E
F
Rough Heys Farm
Yew Tree Farm
ANDERTONS LA
Henbury
DARK LA
ROUGH HEYS LA
A537
PEPPER ST
CHURCH LA
EDGEWAY
CHELFORD RD
Park House Farm
PH
NEWQUAY DR
WHIRLEY RD
Henbury High Sch
Broken Cross
PO
BROKEN CROSS
CHESTER RD
Weston
Liby
PEXHILL RD
B5392
Hill Top Farm
MACCLESFIELD
Cock Wood
Home Farm
Broomfield Farm
Henbury Farm
Broken Cross Cty Prim Sch
SCHOOL LA
Gravelhole Wood
New Farm
Hopedale Farm
Sch
Pexhall Wood
PEXHILL RD
Highbirch
Tansy Moss Farm
Big Bailey Riddings
GAWSWORTH RD
Pexhall Farm
BEARHURST LA
Overbank Farm
Highbirch Wood
PENNINGTONS LA
Dalehouse Farm
Lower Pexhill Farm
Underbank Farm
Brownhills Farm
Lower Pexhill
Lodge Farm
Greenacres
A536
Deans Farm
Trevors Close Farm
Gawsmoor Hill
Pool Wood
DARK LA
Beaumont Farm
Lowes Farm
Danes Moss Farm
CONGLETON RD
Whitegate Farm
Old Parks Farm
Moss Houses
Little Walkers Heath Farm
Newbarn
Gawsworth Cty Prim Sch
PO
LOWES LA
Ben Brook
Middle Moss Farm
MARTON LA
Warren
BENBROOK WAY
Big Moss Farm
Mill Field
Mill House Farm
Gardenhouse Farm
WOODHOUSE LA
CHURCH LA
Sewage Works
Snape Brook
HARBOUR LA
MAGGOTY LA
WOODHOUSE END RD
A536
87
88
89
70
71
72
73
4
3
2
1

134
112

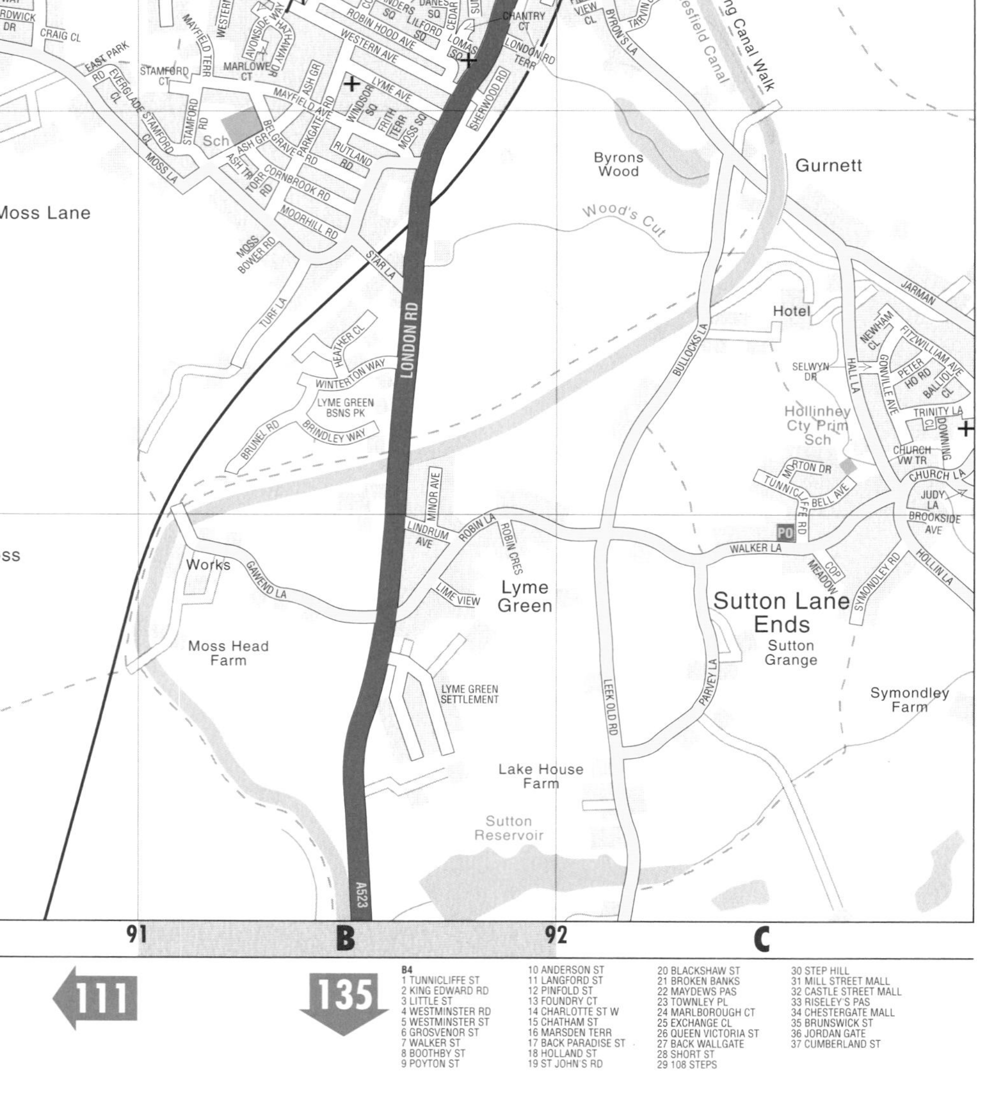

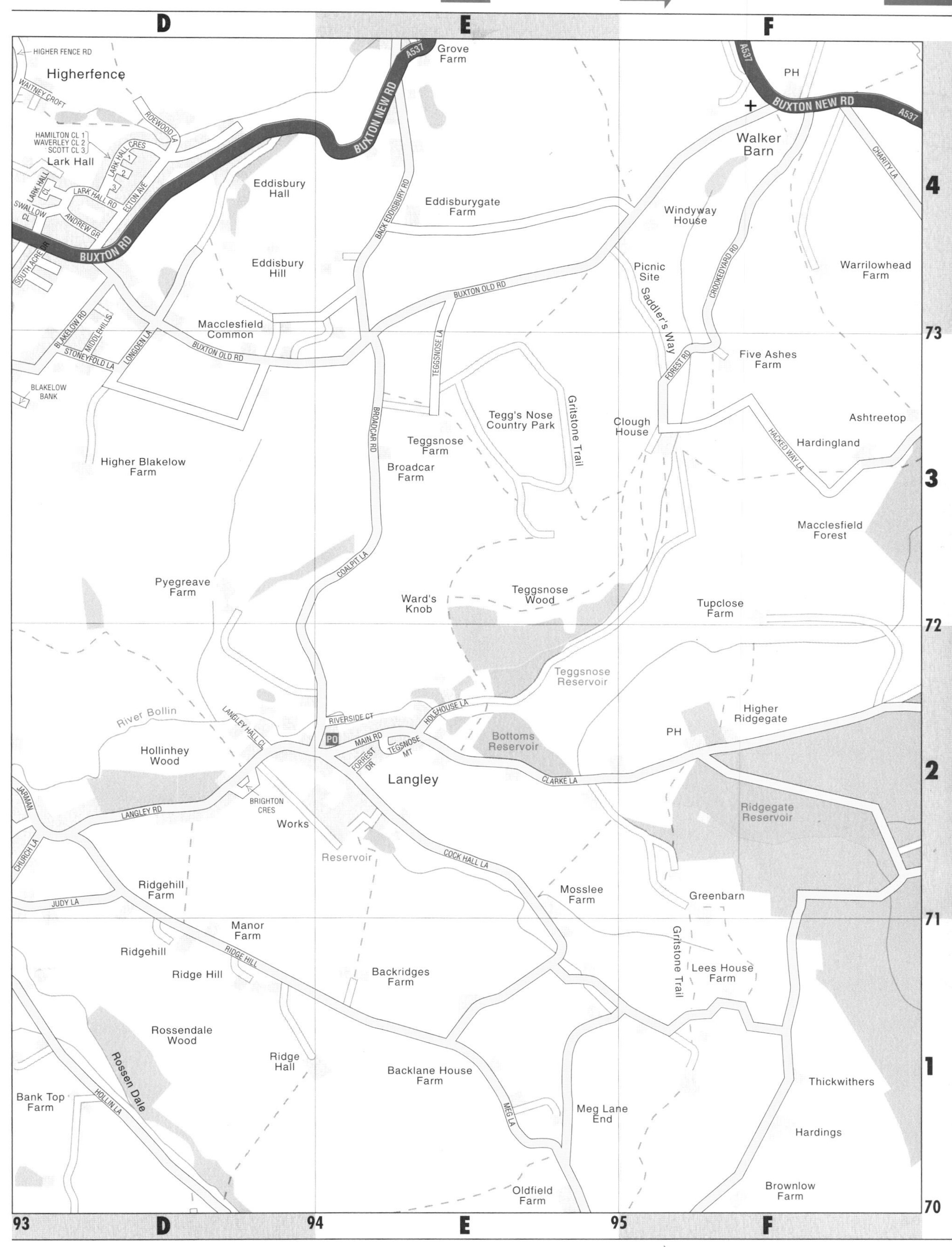
D
E
F
Higherfence
HIGHER FENCE RD
WAITNEY CROFT
ROEWOOD LA
HAMILTON CL 1
WAVERLEY CL 2
SCOTT CL 3
Lark Hall
LARK HALL CRES
LARK HALL RD
ECTON AVE
SWALLOW CL
ANDREW GR
SOUTH ACRE DR
BUXTON RD
BUXTON NEW RD
A537
Grove Farm
Eddisbury Hall
Eddisbury Hill
BACK EDDISBURY RD
Eddisburygate Farm
PH
Walker Barn
CHARITY LA
Windyway House
Picnic Site
Saddler's Way
CROOKEDYARD RD
Warrilowhead Farm
BUXTON OLD RD
Macclesfield Common
BLAKELOW RD
MIDDLEHILLS
STONEYFOLD LA
LONGDEN LA
BLAKELOW BANK
TEGGSNOSE LA
FOREST RD
Five Ashes Farm
Tegg's Nose Country Park
Gritstone Trail
Clough House
Ashtreetop
Hardingland
HACKED WAY LA
BROADCAR RD
Teggsnose Farm
Broadcar Farm
Higher Blakelow Farm
Macclesfield Forest
COALPIT LA
Pyegreave Farm
Ward's Knob
Teggsnose Wood
Tupclose Farm
Teggsnose Reservoir
River Bollin
LANGLEY HALL CL
RIVERSIDE CT
HOLEHOUSE LA
Higher Ridgegate
PH
PO
MAIN RD
TEGSNOSE MT
FORREST DR
Bottoms Reservoir
Hollinhey Wood
Langley
CLARKE LA
Ridgegate Reservoir
JARMAN
LANGLEY RD
BRIGHTON CRES
Works
CHURCH LA
Reservoir
COCK HALL LA
Ridgehill Farm
JUDY LA
Mosslee Farm
Greenbarn
Manor Farm
Ridgehill
RIDGE HILL
Ridge Hill
Backridges Farm
Lees House Farm
Rossendale Wood
Rossen Dale
Ridge Hall
Backlane House Farm
Thickwithers
Bank Top Farm
HOLLIN LA
MEG LA
Meg Lane End
Hardings
Oldfield Farm
Brownlow Farm
4
73
3
72
2
71
1
70
93
94
95

113
89

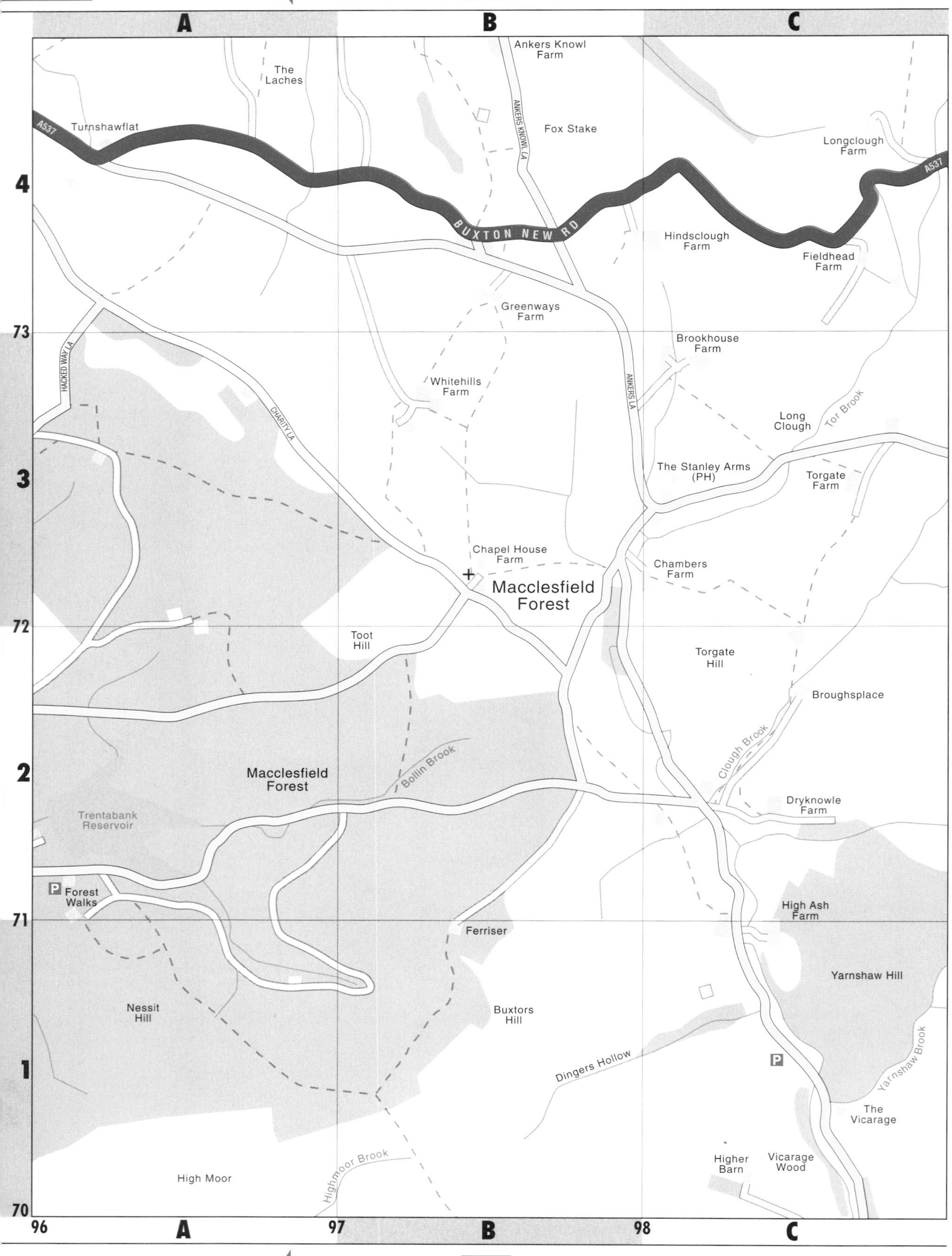
A
B
C
Ankers Knowl Farm
The Laches
Turnshawflat
A537
ANKERS KNOWL LA
Fox Stake
Longclough Farm
BUXTON NEW RD
Hindscloough Farm
Fieldhead Farm
Greenways Farm
Brookhouse Farm
HACKED WAY LA
Whitehills Farm
ANKERS LA
CHARITY LA
Long Clough
Tor Brook
The Stanley Arms (PH)
Torgate Farm
Chapel House Farm
Chambers Farm
Macclesfield Forest
Toot Hill
Torgate Hill
Broughsplace
Clough Brook
Bollin Brook
Macclesfield Forest
Trentabank Reservoir
Dryknowle Farm
Forest Walks
High Ash Farm
Ferriser
Yarnshaw Hill
Nessit Hill
Buxtors Hill
Dingers Hollow
Yarnshaw Brook
The Vicarage
Highmoor Brook
Higher Barn
Vicarage Wood
High Moor
4
73
3
72
2
71
1
70
96
97
98

113
137

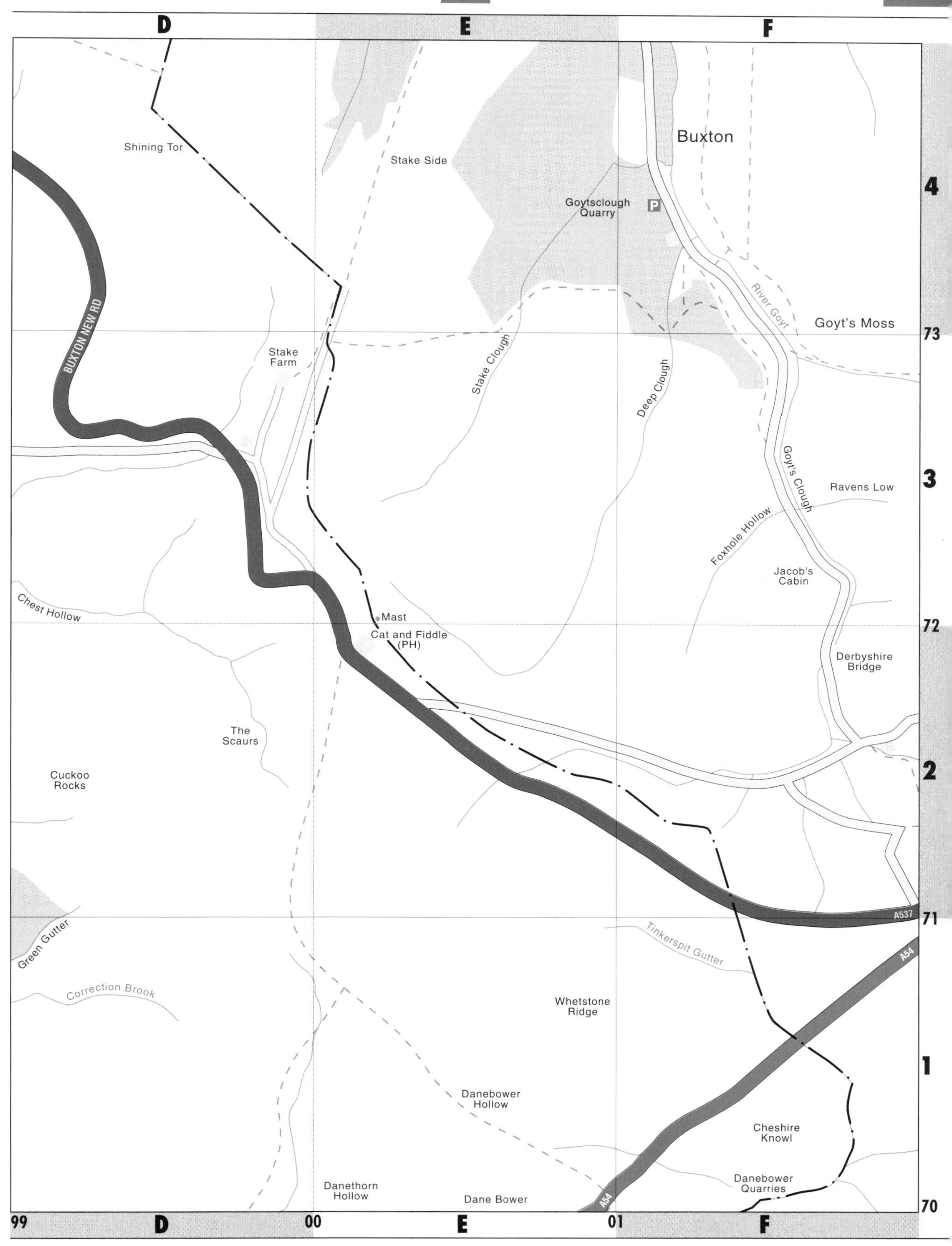

Shining Tor

Stake Side

Buxton

Goytsclough
Quarry

P

River Goyt

Goyt's Moss

4

BUXTON NEW RD

Stake
Farm

Stake Clough

Deep Clough

73

Goyt's Clough

Ravens Low

3

Chest Hollow

Foxhole Hollow

Jacob's
Cabin

Mast

Cat and Fiddle
(PH)

72

Derbyshire
Bridge

The
Scaurs

Cuckoo
Rocks

2

A537

71

Green Gutter

Tinkerspit Gutter

A54

Correction Brook

Whetstone
Ridge

1

Danebower
Hollow

Cheshire
Knowl

Danethorn
Hollow

Dane Bower

A54

Danebower
Quarries

70

93

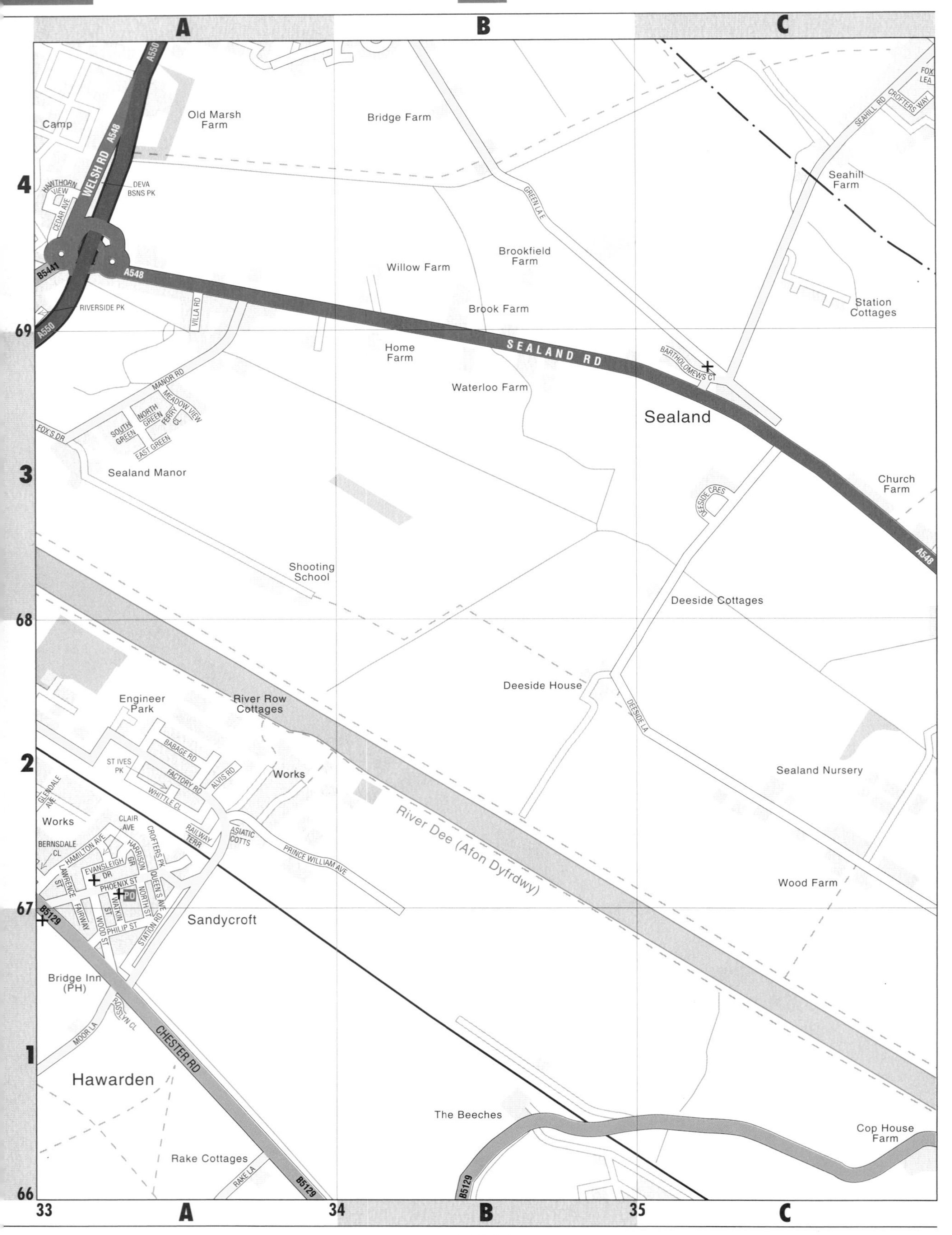

A
B
C
4
3
2
1
69
68
67
66
33
34
35
Old Marsh Farm
Camp
Bridge Farm
WELSH RD
A548
A550
DEVA BSNS PK
HAWTHORN VIEW
CEDAR AVE
B5441
RIVERSIDE PK
VILLA RD
Willow Farm
Brookfield Farm
Brook Farm
Home Farm
SEALAND RD
Waterloo Farm
GREEN LA E
BARTHOLOMEWS CT
Sealand
Seahill Farm
SEAHILL RD
CROFTERS WAY
FOX LEA
Station Cottages
Church Farm
MANOR RD
MEADOW VIEW
NORTH GREEN
SOUTH GREEN
EAST GREEN
FERRY CL
FOX'S DR
Sealand Manor
DEESIDE CRES
Shooting School
Deeside Cottages
Deeside House
DEESIDE LA
Engineer Park
River Row Cottages
BABAGE RD
FACTORY RD
ALVIS RD
WHITTLE CL
ST IVES PK
Works
Sealand Nursery
GLENDALE AVE
CLAIR AVE
BERNSDALE CL
HAMILTON AVE
HARRISON GR
CROFTERS PK
EVANSLEIGH DR
PHOENIX ST
LAWRENCE ST
QUEEN'S AVE
NORTH ST
RAILWAY TERR
ASIATIC COTTS
PRINCE WILLIAM AVE
River Dee (Afon Dyfrdwy)
Wood Farm
FAIRWAY
WOOD ST
WATKIN ST
PHILIP ST
STATION RD
Sandycroft
B5129
Bridge Inn (PH)
ROSLYN CL
CHESTER RD
MOOR LA
Hawarden
The Beeches
Cop House Farm
Rake Cottages
RAKE LA

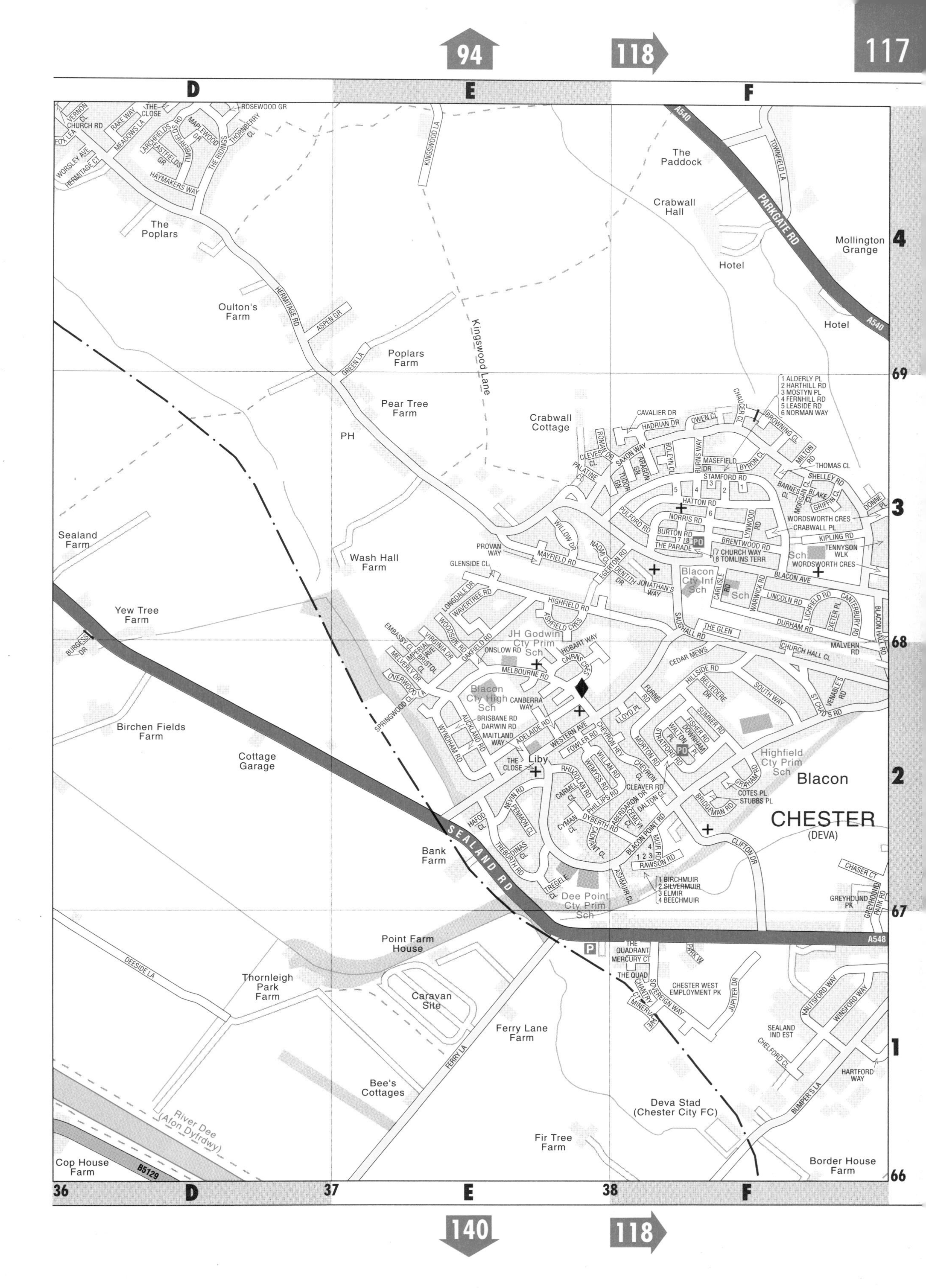
94
118
D
E
F
The Paddock
Crabwall Hall
Mollington Grange
Hotel
Hotel
PARKGATE RD
A540
The Poplars
Oulton's Farm
HERMITAGE RD
ASPEN GR
GREEN LA
Poplars Farm
Kingswood Lane
KINGSWOOD LA
Pear Tree Farm
PH
Crabwall Cottage
Sealand Farm
Wash Hall Farm
Yew Tree Farm
BURGESS DR
Birchen Fields Farm
Cottage Garage
JH Godwin Cty Prim Sch
Blacon Cty High Sch
Blacon Cty Inf Sch
Sch
Sch
Liby
Highfield Cty Prim Sch
Blacon
CHESTER
(DEVA)
Bank Farm
SEALAND RD
Dee Point Cty Prim Sch
Point Farm House
A548
Thornleigh Park Farm
Caravan Site
DEESIDE LA
Ferry Lane Farm
FERRY LA
Bee's Cottages
River Dee
(Afon Dyfrdwy)
Cop House Farm
B5129
Fir Tree Farm
Deva Stad
(Chester City FC)
Border House Farm
CHESTER WEST EMPLOYMENT PK
SEALAND IND EST
KNUTSFORD WAY
WINSFORD WAY
HARTFORD WAY
BUMPER'S LA
CHELFORD CL
GREYHOUND PK
CHASER CT
1 ALDERLY PL
2 HARTHILL RD
3 MOSTYN PL
4 FERNHILL RD
5 LEASIDE RD
6 NORMAN WAY
1 BIRCHMUIR
2 SILVERMUIR
3 ELMIR
4 BEECHMUIR
BLACON AVE
BLACON HALL RD
CHURCH HALL CL
SAUGHALL RD
HIGHFIELD RD
MAYFIELD RD
WESTERN AVE
CLIFTON DR
4
3
2
1
69
68
67
66
36
37
38
140
118

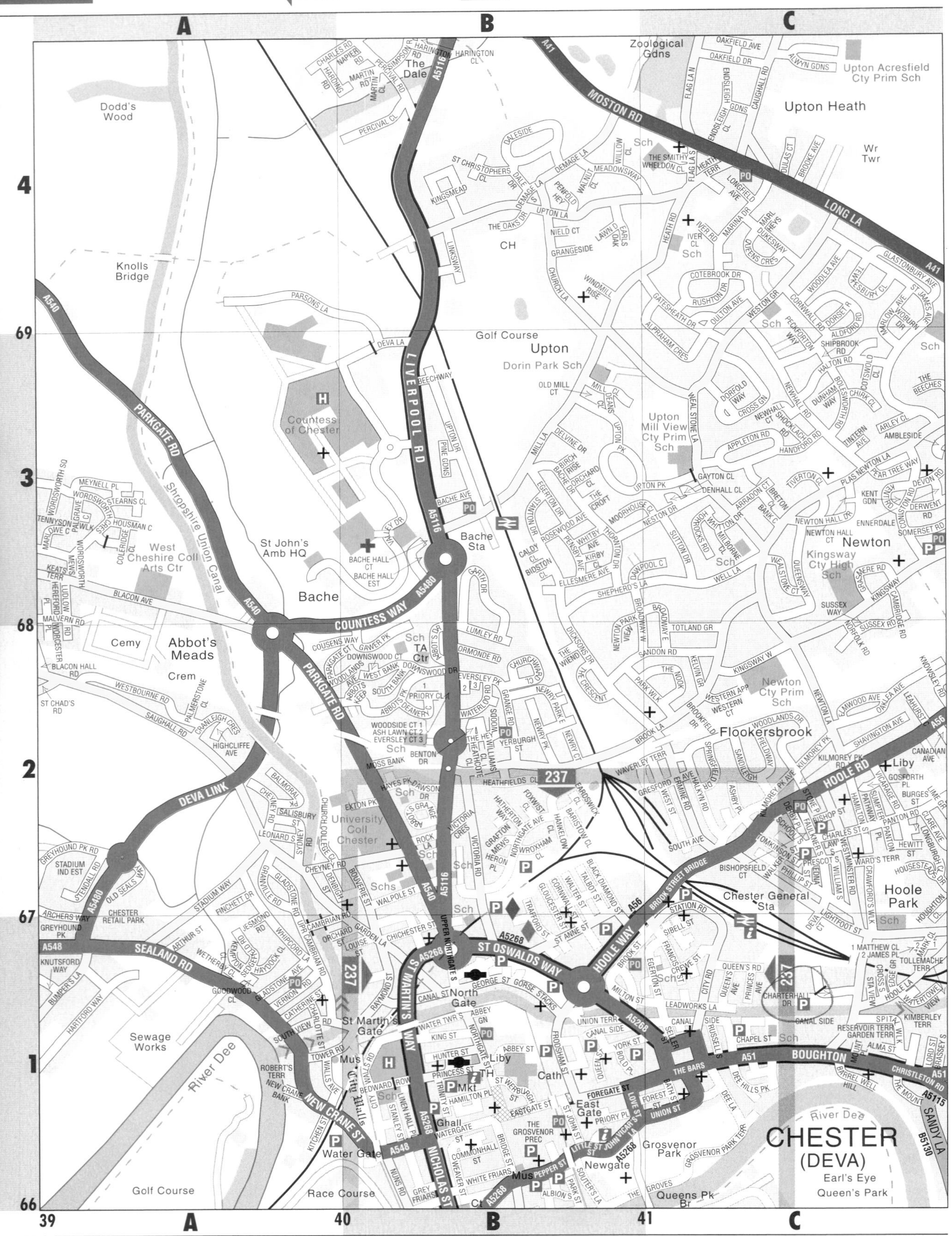

117
95

117
141

For full street detail of the
highlighted area see page
237.

CHESTER
(DEVA)

Earl's Eye
Queen's Park

96
120

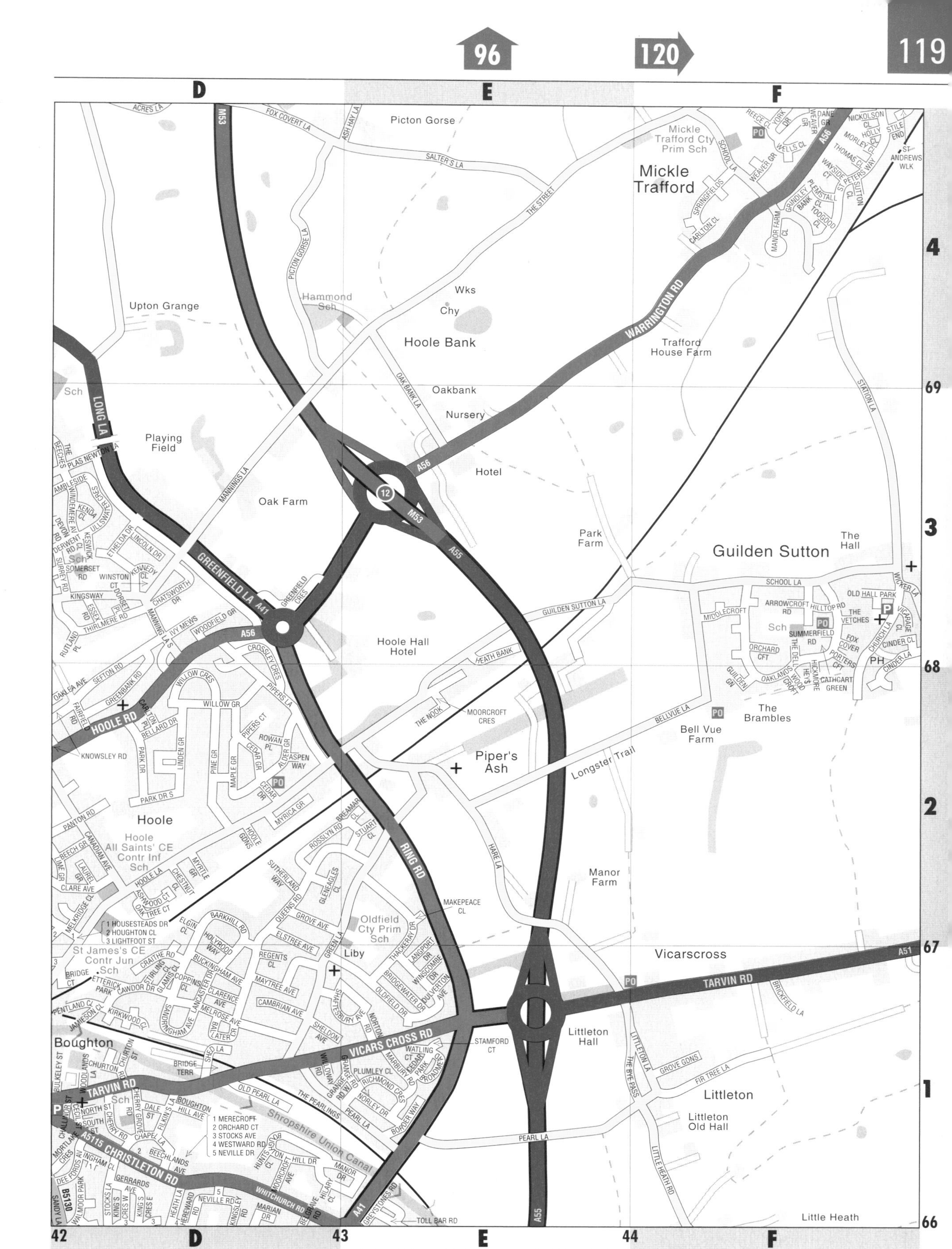
D
E
F
Picton Gorse
Mickle Trafford Cty Prim Sch
Mickle Trafford
Upton Grange
Hammond Sch
Wks
Chy
Hoole Bank
Trafford House Farm
Oakbank
Nursery
Playing Field
Hotel
Oak Farm
Park Farm
Guilden Sutton
The Hall
Hoole Hall Hotel
The Brambles
Bell Vue Farm
Piper's Ash
Longster Trail
Hoole
Hoole All Saints' CE Contr Inf Sch
Manor Farm
Oldfield Cty Prim Sch
Liby
Vicarscross
St James's CE Contr Jun Sch
Boughton
Littleton Hall
Littleton
Littleton Old Hall
Shropshire Union Canal
Little Heath
WARRINGTON RD
GREENFIELD LA
HOOLE RD
RING RD
TARVIN RD
VICARS CROSS RD
CHRISTLETON RD
LONG LA
M53
A56
A55
A41
A51
A5115
B5130
1 HOUSESTEADS DR
2 HOUGHTON CL
3 LIGHTFOOT ST
1 MERECROFT
2 ORCHARD CT
3 STOCKS AVE
4 WESTWARD RD
5 NEVILLE DR
42
43
44
66
67
68
69
1
2
3
4

142
120

119
97

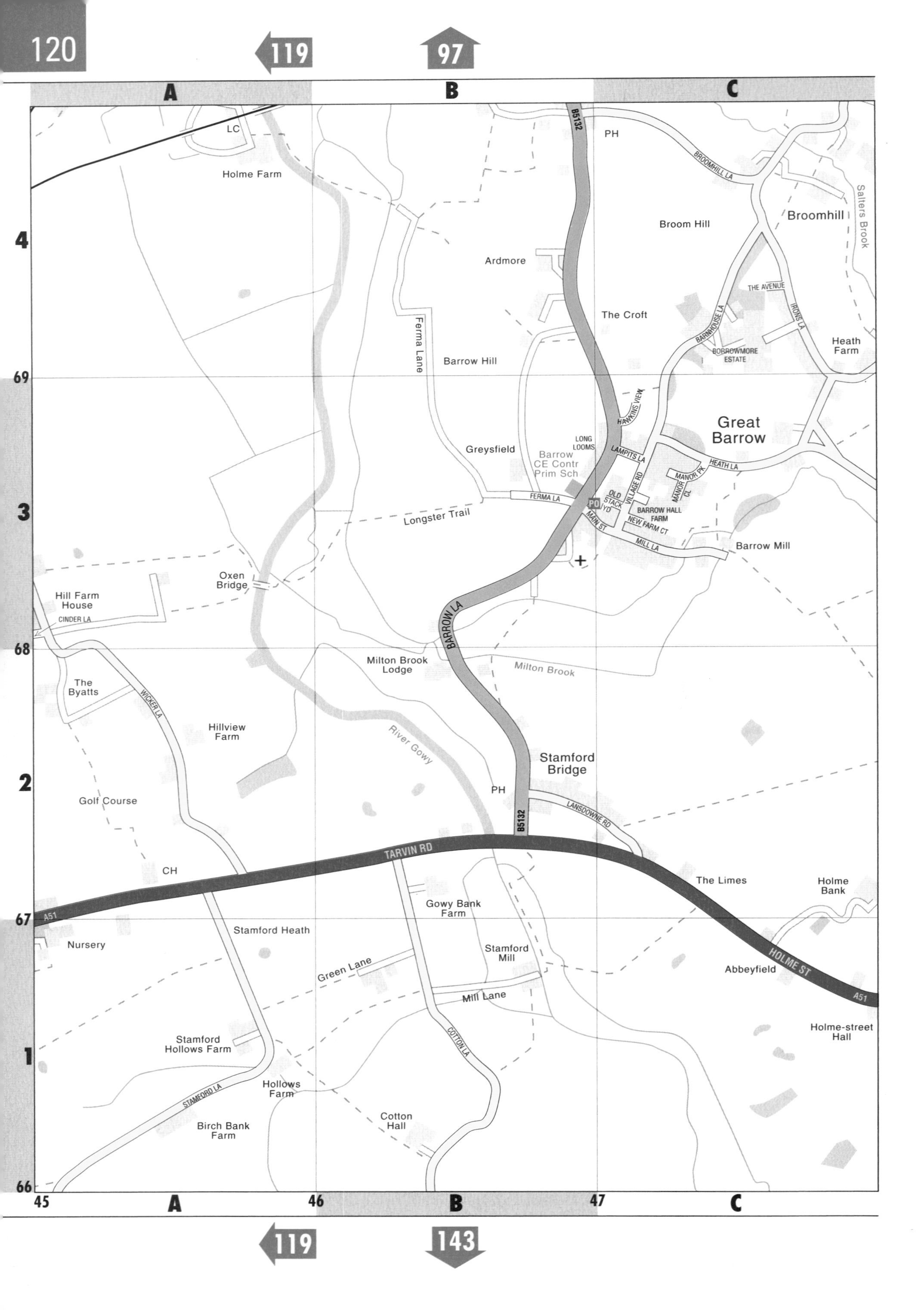
A
B
C
LC
Holme Farm
B5132
PH
Broomhill La
Broom Hill
Broomhill
Salters Brook
Ardmore
The Avenue
The Croft
Barnhouse La
Irons La
Borrowmore Estate
Heath Farm
Ferma Lane
Barrow Hill
Hawkins View
Great Barrow
Long Looms
Greysfield
Barrow CE Contr Prim Sch
Lampits La
Heath La
Manor Pk
Manor Cl
Village Rd
Ferma La
PO
Old Stack Yd
Barrow Hall Farm
New Farm Ct
Main St
Longster Trail
Mill La
Barrow Mill
Oxen Bridge
Hill Farm House
Cinder La
Barrow La
Milton Brook Lodge
Milton Brook
The Byatts
Wicker La
Hillview Farm
River Gowy
Stamford Bridge
Golf Course
PH
B5132
Lansdowne Rd
Tarvin Rd
CH
The Limes
Holme Bank
A51
Gowy Bank Farm
Nursery
Stamford Heath
Stamford Mill
Holme St
Abbeyfield
Green Lane
Mill Lane
A51
Holme-street Hall
Stamford Hollows Farm
Cotton La
Hollows Farm
Stamford La
Cotton Hall
Birch Bank Farm
4
69
3
68
2
67
1
66
45
46
47

119
143

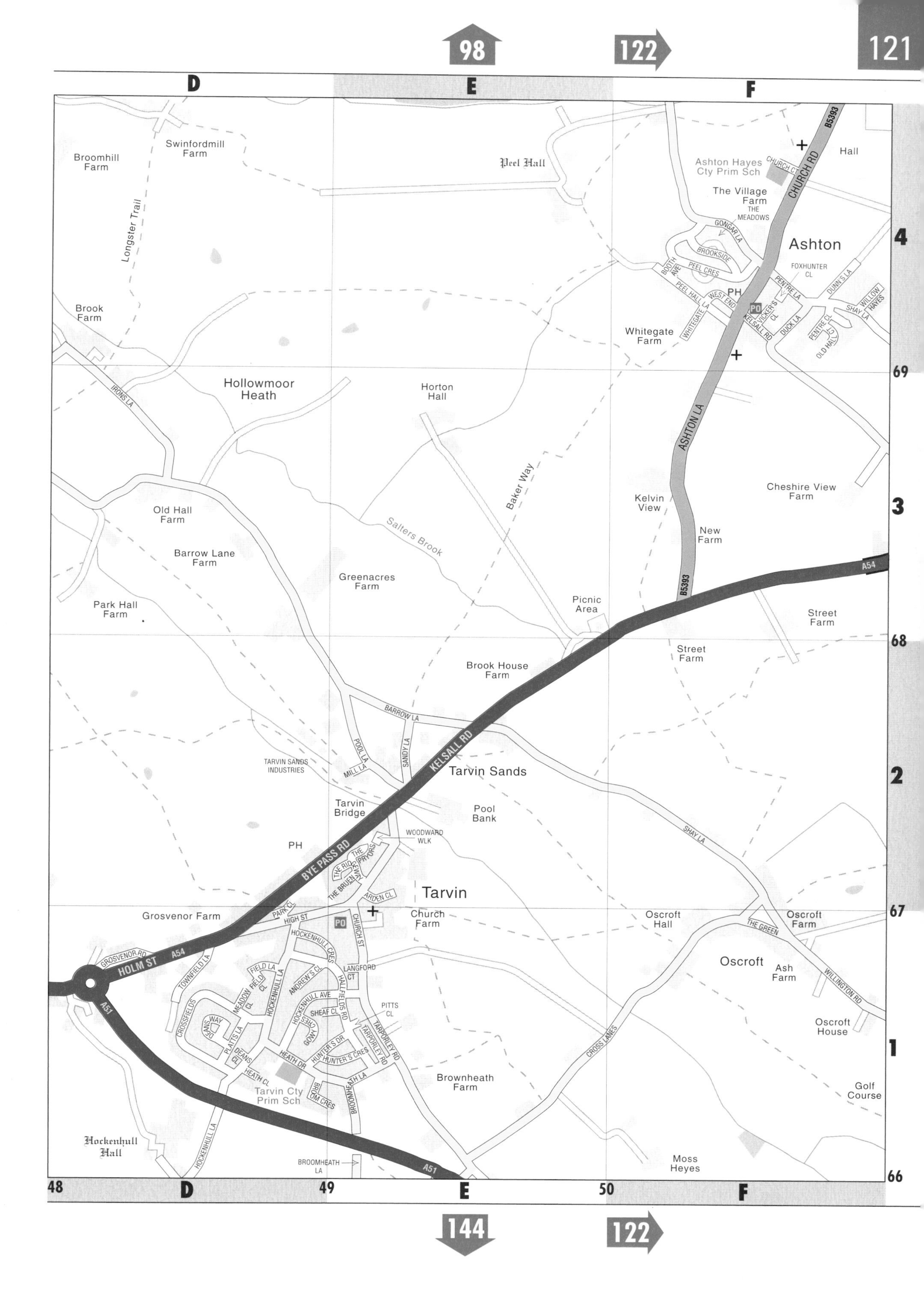

D
E
F

Broomhill Farm

Swinfordmill Farm

Peel Hall

Ashton Hayes Cty Prim Sch

Hall

CHURCH RD

B5393

The Village Farm

THE MEADOWS

Ashton

4

GONGAR LA

BROOKSIDE

FOXHUNTER CL

Longster Trail

BOOTH AVE

PEEL CRES

PENTRE LA

NUNN'S LA

PH

WILLOW HAYES

SHAY LA

Brook Farm

WEST END

PO

Whitegate Farm

WHITEGATE LA

BAKER'S LA

PEEL HALL LA

KELSALL RD

DUCK LA

PENTRE CL

OLD HALL

IRONS LA

Hollowmoor Heath

Horton Hall

69

Old Hall Farm

Barrow Lane Farm

Baker Way

Salters Brook

ASHTON LA

Kelvin View

New Farm

Cheshire View Farm

3

Greenacres Farm

B5393

A54

Park Hall Farm

Picnic Area

Street Farm

Brook House Farm

Street Farm

68

BARROW LA

POOL LA

MILL LA

SANDY LA

Tarvin Sands Industries

KELSALL RD

Tarvin Sands

Pool Bank

SHAY LA

2

Tarvin Bridge

WOODWARD WLK

PH

BYE PASS RD

THE RIG

THE BRUEN

RYLANDS

PRYORS LA

ARDEN CL

Tarvin

Church Farm

Oscroft Hall

THE GREEN

Oscroft Farm

67

Grosvenor Farm

PARK CL

HIGH ST

PO

CHURCH ST

HOCKENHULL CRES

LANGFORD CT

Oscroft

Ash Farm

WILLINGTON RD

GROSVENOR RD

HOLM ST

A54

TOWNFIELD LA

FIELD LA

FIELD CL

ANDREW'S CL

HOCKENHULL AVE

HALL FIELDS RD

PITTS CL

TARPORLEY RD

CROSSFIELDS

DEANS WAY

MEADOW CL

PLATTS LA

SHEAF CL

CROS

HUNTER'S DR

TARPORLEY RD

Oscroft House

A51

DEANS CL

HEATH DR

HUNTER'S CRES

BATH LA

CROSS LANES

1

Golf Course

HEATH CL

BIRCH

BOOM CRES

Tarvin Cty Prim Sch

Brownheath Farm

Hockenhull Hall

HOCKENHULL LA

BROOMHEATH LA

A51

Moss Heyes

66

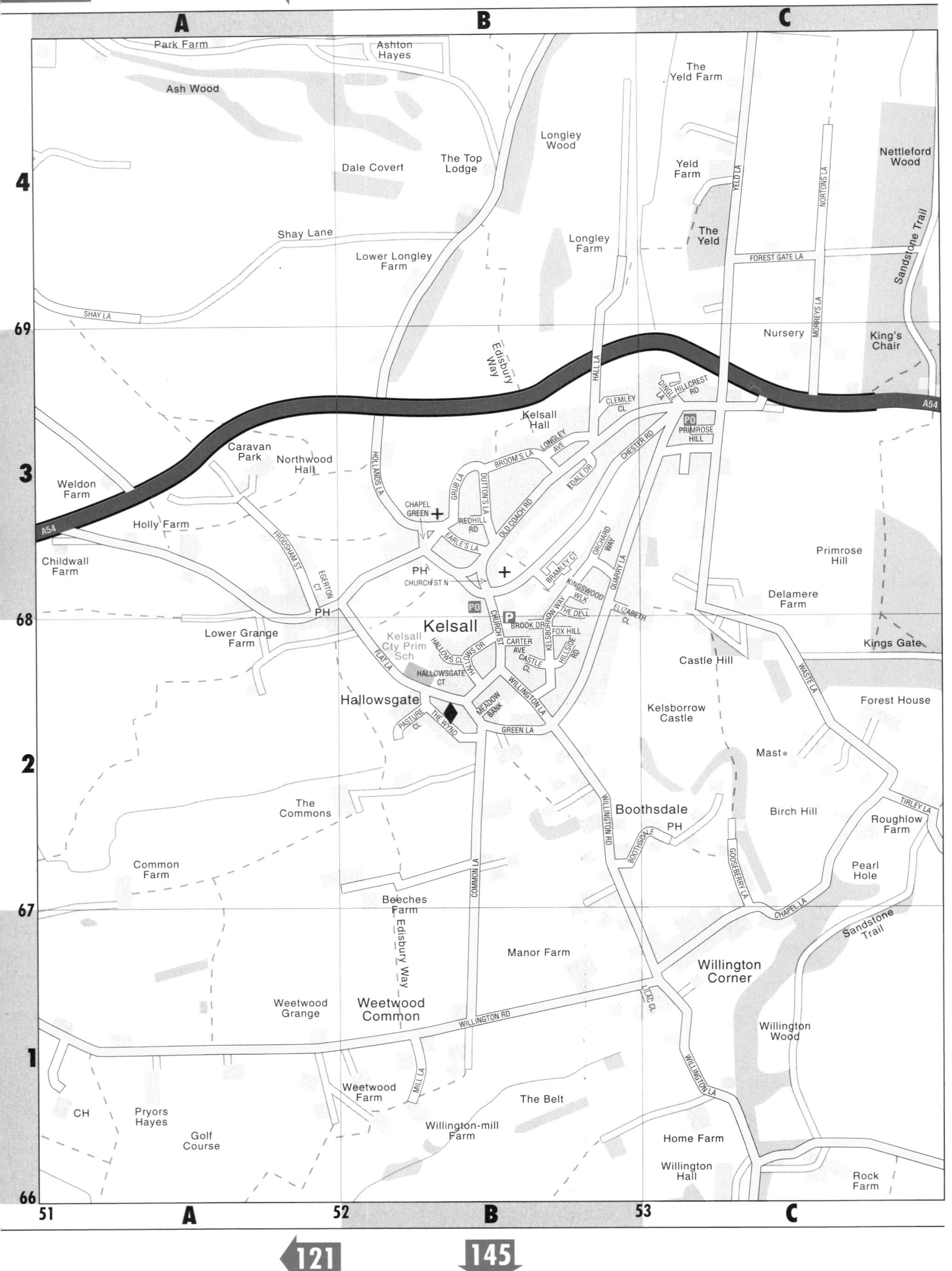

A   B   C

Park Farm

Ashton Hayes

Ash Wood

The Yeld Farm

Longley Wood

The Top Lodge

Dale Covert

Yeld Farm

Nettleford Wood

4

Shay Lane

Lower Longley Farm

Longley Farm

The Yeld

FOREST GATE LA

Sandstone Trail

SHAY LA

69

Edisbury Way

Nursery

King's Chair

NORTONS LA

MORREYS LA

YELD LA

HALL LA

A54

Caravan Park

Northwood Hall

Kelsall Hall

CLEMLEY CL

HILLCREST RD

PINGLE LA

3

Weldon Farm

Holly Farm

HOLLANDS LA

GRUB LA

BROOM'S LA

LONGLEY AVE

DUTTON'S LA

FOALE DR

CHESTER RD

PO PRIMROSE HILL

CHAPEL GREEN +

REDHILL RD

OLD COACH RD

ORCHARD WAY

Primrose Hill

A54

Childwall Farm

EARLE'S LA

PH

CHURCH ST N

+

BRAMLEY CT

KINGSWOOD WLK

QUARRY LA

Delamere Farm

68

PH

Lower Grange Farm

PO

Kelsall Cty Prim Sch

Kelsall

P

BROOK DR

THE DELL

CASTLE CL

ELIZABETH CL

Kings Gate

FLAT LA

HALLOWS CLOWS DR

CHURCH ST

KELSBORROW WAY

FOX HILL

CARTER AVE

HILLSIDE RD

Castle Hill

WASTE LA

HALLOWSGATE CT

Forest House

Hallowsgate

PASTURE CL

THE WYND

MEADOW BANK

WILLINGTON LA

GREEN LA

Kelsborrow Castle

Mast •

TIRLEY LA

2

The Commons

Boothsdale

Birch Hill

Roughlow Farm

Common Farm

COMMON LA

WILLINGTON RD

PH

BOOTHSDALE

GOOSEBERRY LA

Pearl Hole

67

Beeches Farm

Edisbury Way

Manor Farm

Willington Corner

CHAPEL LA

Sandstone Trail

Weetwood Grange

Weetwood Common

MILL LA

WILLINGTON RD

LTD CL

Willington Wood

1

CH

Pryors Hayes

Golf Course

Weetwood Farm

Willington-mill Farm

The Belt

WILLINGTON LA

Home Farm

Willington Hall

Rock Farm

66

51   A   52   B   53   C

100
124

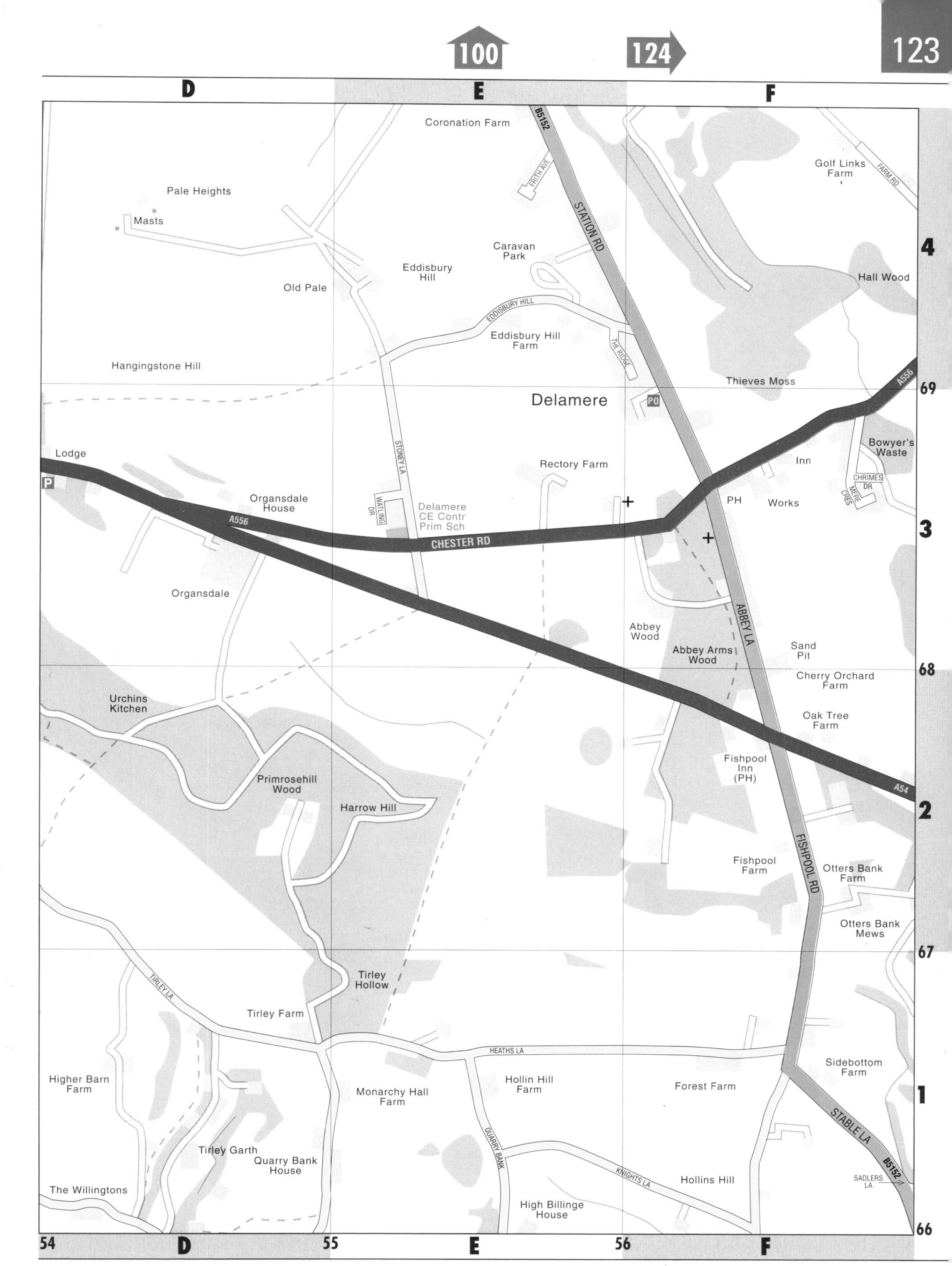
D
E
F
Coronation Farm
B5152
Golf Links Farm
FARM RD
FRITH AVE
Pale Heights
Masts
STATION RD
4
Caravan Park
Eddisbury Hill
Hall Wood
Old Pale
EDDISBURY HILL
Eddisbury Hill Farm
THE RIDGE
Hangingstone Hill
Thieves Moss
A556
69
Delamere
PO
Lodge
STONEY LA
Rectory Farm
Bowyer's Waste
Inn
P
CHRIMES DR
MERE CRES
Organsdale House
WATLING DR
Delamere CE Contr Prim Sch
PH
Works
A556
CHESTER RD
3
Organsdale
Abbey Wood
ABBEY LA
Abbey Arms Wood
Sand Pit
68
Cherry Orchard Farm
Urchins Kitchen
Oak Tree Farm
Fishpool Inn (PH)
Primrosehill Wood
A54
Harrow Hill
2
FISHPOOL RD
Fishpool Farm
Otters Bank Farm
Otters Bank Mews
67
Tirley Hollow
TIRLEY LA
Tirley Farm
HEATHS LA
Sidebottom Farm
Higher Barn Farm
Hollin Hill Farm
Forest Farm
Monarchy Hall Farm
1
STABLE LA
QUARRY BANK
Tirley Garth
Quarry Bank House
KNIGHTS LA
B5152
Hollins Hill
SADLERS LA
The Willingtons
High Billinge House
66
54
D
55
E
56
F

146
124

123
101

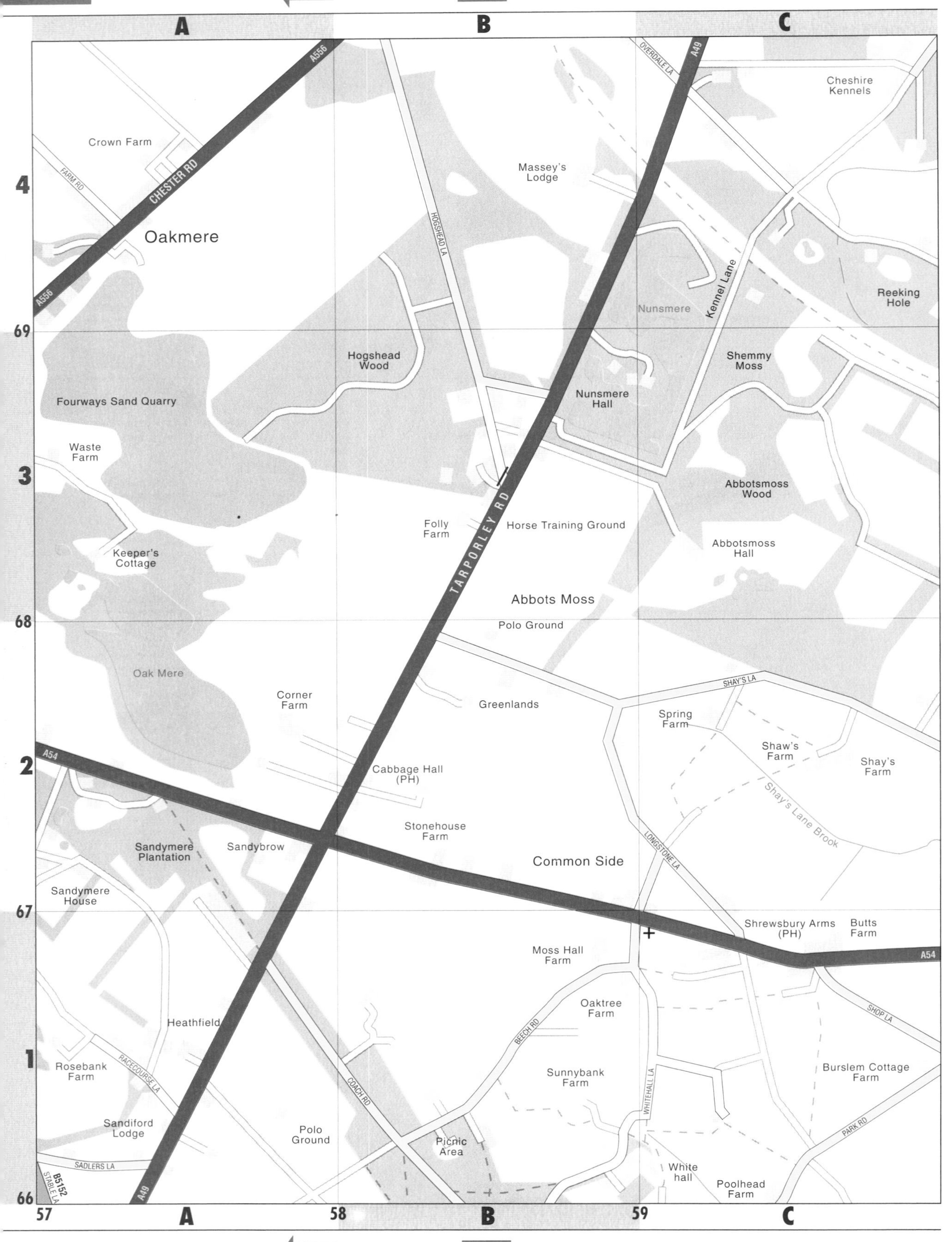
A
B
C
Crown Farm
CHESTER RD
A556
FARM RD
Oakmere
Massey's Lodge
HOGSHEAD LA
OVERDALE LA
A49
Cheshire Kennels
Reeking Hole
Kennel Lane
Nunsmere
Hogshead Wood
Shemmy Moss
Nunsmere Hall
Fourways Sand Quarry
Waste Farm
Abbotsmoss Wood
Folly Farm
Horse Training Ground
Keeper's Cottage
Abbotsmoss Hall
TARPORLEY RD
Abbots Moss
Polo Ground
Oak Mere
Corner Farm
Greenlands
SHAY'S LA
Spring Farm
Shaw's Farm
Shay's Farm
A54
Cabbage Hall (PH)
Shay's Lane Brook
Stonehouse Farm
Sandymere Plantation
Sandybrow
Common Side
LONGSTONE LA
Sandymere House
Shrewsbury Arms (PH)
Butts Farm
Moss Hall Farm
Oaktree Farm
SHOP LA
Heathfield
BEECH RD
Rosebank Farm
RACECOURSE LA
Sunnybank Farm
COACH RD
Burslem Cottage Farm
WHITEHALL LA
Sandiford Lodge
Polo Ground
Picnic Area
PARK RD
SADLERS LA
B5152
STABLE LA
White hall
Poolhead Farm
4
69
3
68
2
67
1
66
57
58
59

123
147

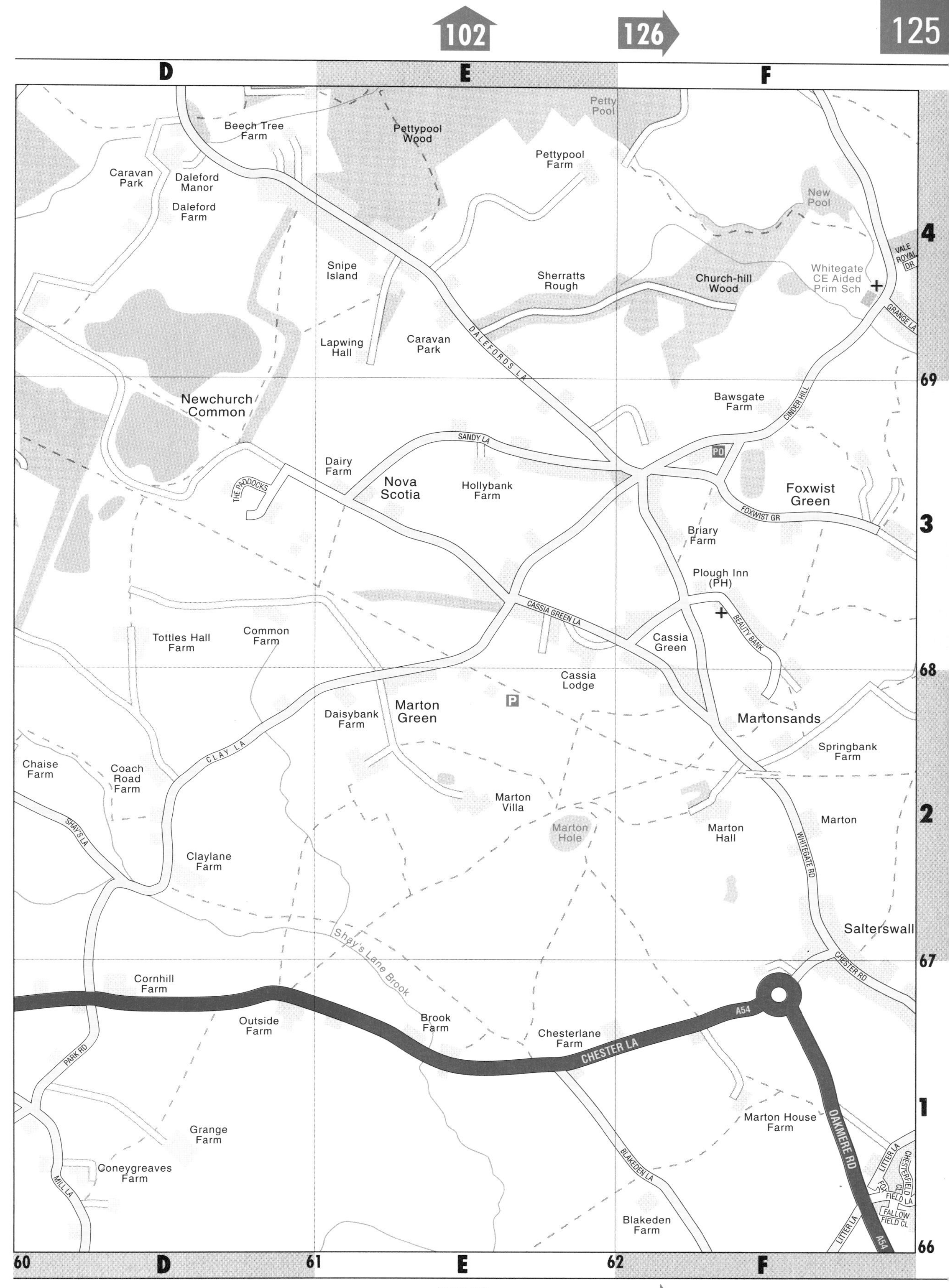

D

E

F

Beech Tree
Farm

Caravan
Park

Daleford
Manor

Daleford
Farm

Pettypool
Wood

Petty
Pool

Pettypool
Farm

New
Pool

4

Snipe
Island

Sherratts
Rough

Church-hill
Wood

Whitegate
CE Aided
Prim Sch

VALE
ROYAL
DR.

+

GRANGE LA

Lapwing
Hall

Caravan
Park

DALEFORDS LA

69

Newchurch
Common

SANDY LA

Bawsgate
Farm

CINDER HILL

PO

Foxwist
Green

Dairy
Farm

Nova
Scotia

Hollybank
Farm

FOXWIST GR

3

THE PADDOCKS

Briary
Farm

Plough Inn
(PH)

+

BEAUTY BANK

CASSIA GREEN LA

Tottles Hall
Farm

Common
Farm

Cassia
Green

68

Cassia
Lodge

Martonsands

Daisybank
Farm

Marton
Green

P

Springbank
Farm

Chaise
Farm

Coach
Road
Farm

CLAY LA

Marton
Villa

Marton
Hall

Marton

2

SHAY'S LA

Claylane
Farm

Marton
Hole

Salterswall

WHITEGATE RD

67

Cornhill
Farm

Shay's Lane Brook

CHESTER RD

PARK RD

Outside
Farm

Brook
Farm

Chesterlane
Farm

CHESTER LA

A54

Grange
Farm

Marton House
Farm

OAKMERE RD

1

MILL LA

Coneygreaves
Farm

BLAKEDEN LA

LITTER LA

CHESTERFIELD

FOX
FIELD LA

FALLOW
FIELD CL

Blakeden
Farm

LITTER LA

A54

66

60

D

61

E

62

F

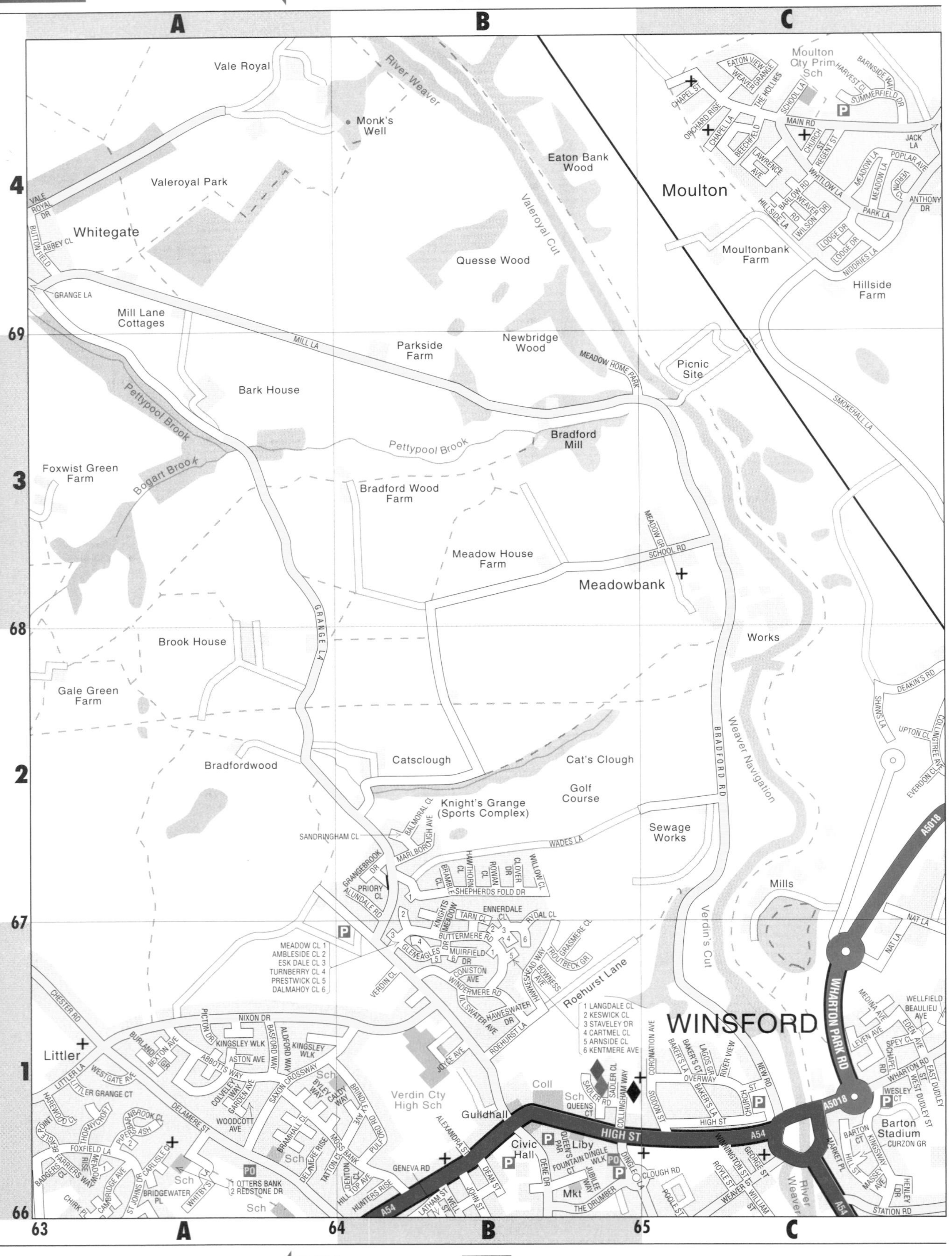

A   B   C

Vale Royal

Monk's Well

Eaton Bank Wood

Moulton City Prim Sch

Eaton View
Weavely Grange
The Hollies
Orchard Rise
Chapel St
Chapel La
Beechfield
Lawrence Ave
Hillside La
Barlow Rd
Weaver Dr
School La
Witlow La
Regent St
Main Rd
Church
Lodge Dr
Lodge Dr
Niddries La
Barnside Way
Harvest Ct
Summerfield Dr
Poplar Ave
Meadow La
Meadow La
Park La
Jack La
Anthony Dr

Moulton

4

Valeroyal Park

Whitegate

Valeroyal Cut

Quesse Wood

Moultonbank Farm

Hillside Farm

Grange La

Mill Lane Cottages

Newbridge Wood

Meadow Home Park

Picnic Site

Smokehall La

69

Pettypool Brook

Bark House

Parkside Farm

Pettypool Brook

Bradford Mill

Bogart Brook

Foxwist Green Farm

Bradford Wood Farm

Meadow Dr

School Rd

3

Meadow House Farm

Meadowbank

Brook House

Works

68

Gale Green Farm

Grange La

Bradford Rd

Weaver Navigation

Deakin's Rd

Upton Cl

Collimtree Ave

Everdon Cl

A5018

Bradfordwood

Catsclough

Cat's Clough

Golf Course

Knight's Grange (Sports Complex)

Sewage Works

2

Sandringham Cl

Balmoral Cl
Marlborough Ave
Grangebrook
Priory Cl
Alundale Rd
Brantle Cl
Hawthorn Rd
Clover Dr
Rowan Cl
Willow Cl
Shepherds Fold Dr

Wades La

Verdin's Cut

Mills

Shanks La

Nat La

Nat La

1 MEADOW CL 1
2 AMBLESIDE CL 2
3 ESK DALE CL 3
4 TURNBERRY CL 4
5 PRESTWICK CL 5
6 DALMAHOY CL 6

Knights Meadow
Gleneagles
Tarn Cl
Buttermere Rd
Muirfield
Dr
Ennerdale
Rydal Cl

Coniston Ave
Windermere Rd
Ullswater Ave
Haweswater Dr
Roehurst La

Grasmere Cl
Rydal Way
Borness
Thirlmere Ave
Patterdale Ave

Roehurst Lane

1 LANGDALE CL
2 KESWICK CL
3 STAVELEY DR
4 CARTMEL CL
5 ARNSIDE AVE
6 KENTMERE AVE

WINSFORD

67

Chester Rd

Littler

Littler La
Littler Grange Ct
Westgate Rye
Burland Ave
Bolton Gr
Picton La
Nixon Dr
Kingsley Wlk
Aldford Way
Bassford Way
Aston Ave
Abbott's Way
Kingsley Wlk
Crossway
Sch

Joyce Ave

Alexandra St

Coronation Ave

River View
Overway
New Rd
High St

Bakers Ct
Baker's La

Wharton Park Rd

Medina Ave
Leven Ave
Spey Ave
Chapel Ct
Wesley Ct

Beaulieu Ave
Wellfield

West Dudley
East Dudley
Wharton Rd

1

Hadwood Cl
Point Cl
Thornycroft
Rinbrook Rd
Delamere Cl
Columbine Way
Garden Ave
Woodcott Ave
Bramall Cl
Bramall
Tattnall Cl
Catby Way
Bindle La
Old Rd
Pulford

Verdin Cty High Sch

Guildhall

Coll

Sadler Rd
Sch
Queens St
Collingham Way

Sadler Cl

High St

Winnington Way

A5018

Barton Stadium
Curzon Gr

Badgers Cl
Carriers Cl
Foxfield La
Farmers Rise
Bridgewater Pl
St John's Dr
Carlisle Rd
Delamere Ct
Hill Top
Denton Cl
Bindle Bank
Purley Cl

Geneva Rd
Latham St
Well
John St
Dean St
Deneside

Civic Hall

Liby
Fountain Dingle
Jubilee Wlk

High St

George St
Winnington Way
Weaver St
William St
Massey Ave

Barton Ct
Kingsway
Market Pl
Curzon Gr

Henley Dr

Chirk Pl
Otters Bank
Redstone Dr

Sch

A54
Hunters Rise

Mkt
The Drumber
Pool La

Civic Hall

Clough Rd

River Weaver

A54

Station Rd

66

63   A   64   B   65   C

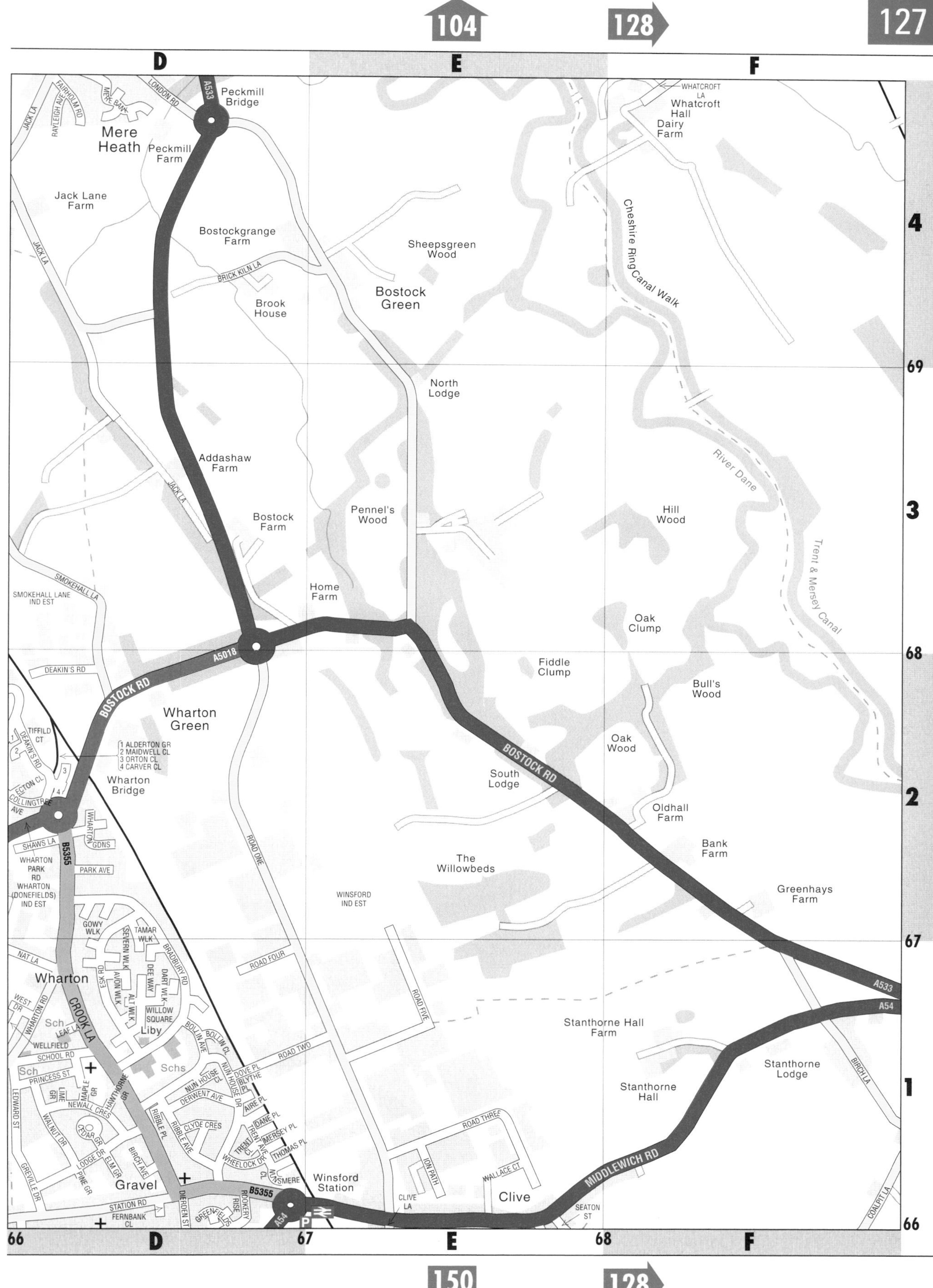

D   E   F

4

69

3

68

2

67

1

66

Peckmill
Bridge

Mere
Heath

Peckmill
Farm

LONDON RD

A533

Jack Lane
Farm

JACK LA

RAVELEIGH AV

MERE BANK

FAIRHOLM RD

JACK LA

Bostockgrange
Farm

BRICK KILN LA

Brook
House

Sheepsgreen
Wood

Bostock
Green

Whatcroft
Hall

WHATCROFT LA

Whatcroft
Dairy
Farm

Cheshire Ring Canal Walk

North
Lodge

Addashaw
Farm

JACK LA

Bostock
Farm

Pennel's
Wood

Hill
Wood

River Dane

SMOKEHALL LA

SMOKEHALL LANE
IND EST

Home
Farm

Oak
Clump

Fiddle
Clump

Trent & Mersey Canal

DEAKIN'S RD

A5018

BOSTOCK RD

Wharton
Green

Bull's
Wood

Oak
Wood

TIFFIELD
CT

DEAKIN'S RD

EGTON CL

1 ALDERTON GR
2 MAIDWELL CL
3 ORTON CL
4 CARVER CL

Wharton
Bridge

BOSTOCK RD

South
Lodge

Oldhall
Farm

Bank
Farm

Greenhays
Farm

COLLINGTREE
AVE

WHARTON
GDNS

SHAWS LA

B5355

WHARTON PARK
RD WHARTON
(DONEFIELDS)
IND EST

PARK AVE

WINSFORD
IND EST

The
Willowbeds

A533

GOWY
WLK

TAMAR
WLK

SEVERN WLK

BRADBURY RD

ROAD ONE

ROAD FOUR

A54

NAT LA

WEST
DR

WHARTON RD

Wharton

CROOK LA

DEE WAY

AVON WLK

ALT WLK

DART WLK

WILLOW
SQUARE

ROAD FIVE

Stanthorne Hall
Farm

Stanthorne
Lodge

BIRCH LA

Sch

Liby

Sch

WELLFIELD

SCHOOL RD

PRINCESS ST

Schs

NUN HOUSE CL

DOVE PL

BLYTHE

DERWENT AVE

BOLLIN CL

BOLLIN AVE

ROAD TWO

Stanthorne
Hall

LEDWARD ST

CEDAR GR

LODGE DR

ELM GR

LIME GR

NEWALL CRES

HAWTHORNE
GR

JEWELL PL

BIRCH LA

RIBBLE PL

DANE PL

AIRE PL

MERSEY PL

THOMAS PL

WHEELOCK DR

CLWYD CRES

TRENT CT

ROAD THREE

TOW PATH

WALLACE CT

MIDDLEWICH RD

SEATON
ST

COPELEY LA

Gravel

PINE GR

GREVILE DR

WALNUT DR

STATION RD

FERNBANK
CL

DIERDEN ST

B5355

A54

GREENFIELD

ROOKERY

RISE

P

Winsford
Station

CLIVE
LA

CLIVE
ST

Clive

66   67   68

D   E   F

127
105

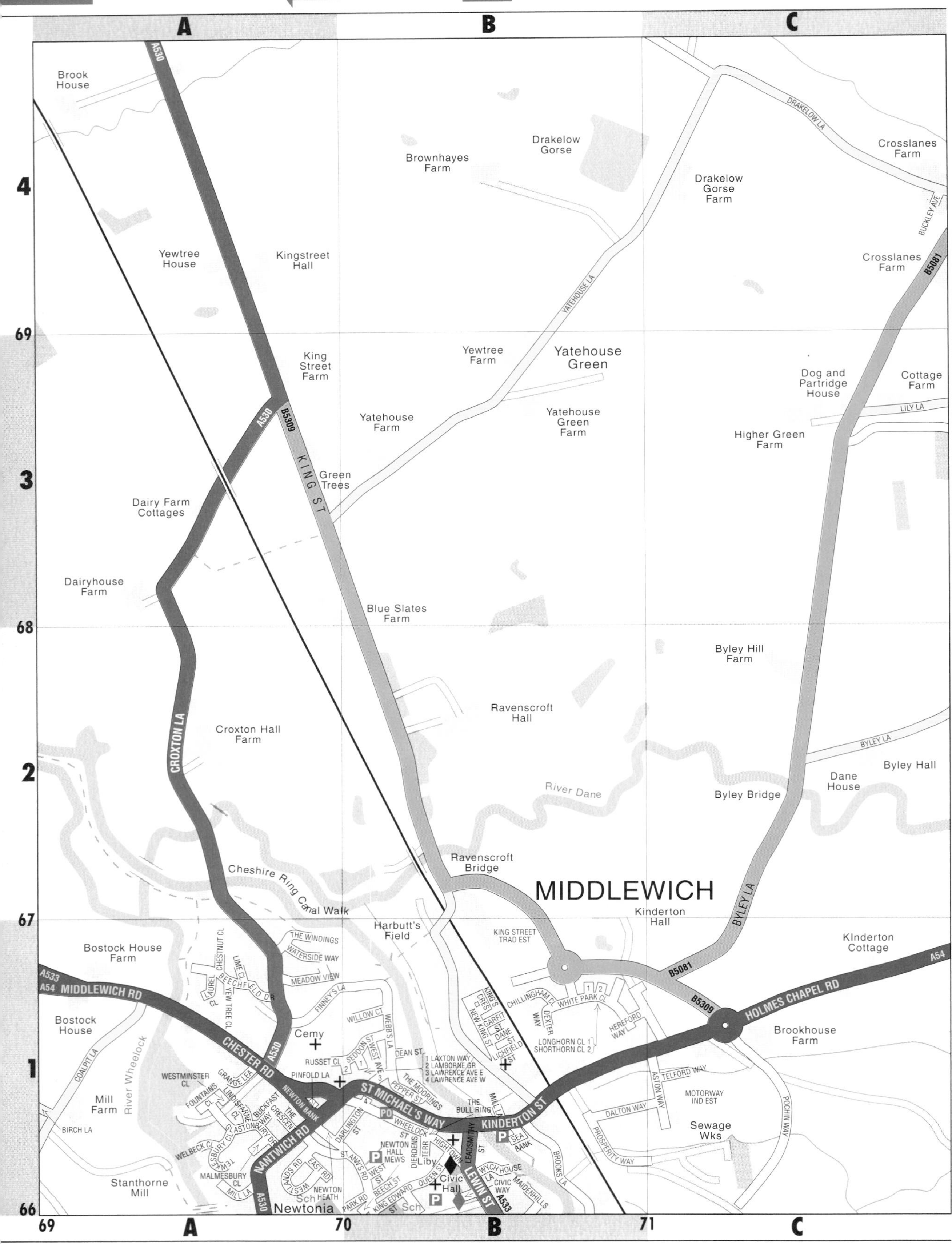
A
B
C
Brook House
Brownhayes Farm
Drakelow Gorse
Drakelow Gorse Farm
DRAKELOW LA
Crosslanes Farm
BUCKLEY AVE
Crosslanes Farm
B5081
Yewtree House
Kingstreet Hall
YATEHOUSE LA
King Street Farm
Yewtree Farm
Yatehouse Green
Dog and Partridge House
Cottage Farm
LILY LA
Yatehouse Farm
Yatehouse Green Farm
Higher Green Farm
A530
B5309
KING ST
Green Trees
Dairy Farm Cottages
Dairyhouse Farm
Blue Slates Farm
Byley Hill Farm
Ravenscroft Hall
Croxton Hall Farm
CROXTON LA
BYLEY LA
Byley Hall
Dane House
River Dane
Byley Bridge
Ravenscroft Bridge
Cheshire Ring Canal Walk
MIDDLEWICH
Kinderton Hall
Harbutt's Field
KING STREET TRAD EST
Kinderton Cottage
Bostock House Farm
A533
A54 MIDDLEWICH RD
A54
HOLMES CHAPEL RD
Brookhouse Farm
Bostock House
Cemy
CHESTER RD
Mill Farm
River Wheelock
COALPIT LA
BIRCH LA
ST MICHAEL'S WAY
KINDERTON ST
Sewage Wks
MOTORWAY IND EST
TELFORD WAY
DALTON WAY
ASTON WAY
PROSPERITY WAY
POCHIN WAY
NANTWICH RD
LEWIN ST
Stanthorne Mill
Newtonia
Civic Hall
Liby
Sch
1 LAXTON WAY
2 LAMBORNE GR
3 LAWRENCE AVE E
4 LAWRENCE AVE W
69
70
71
4
3
2
1
68
67
66

127
151

106

130

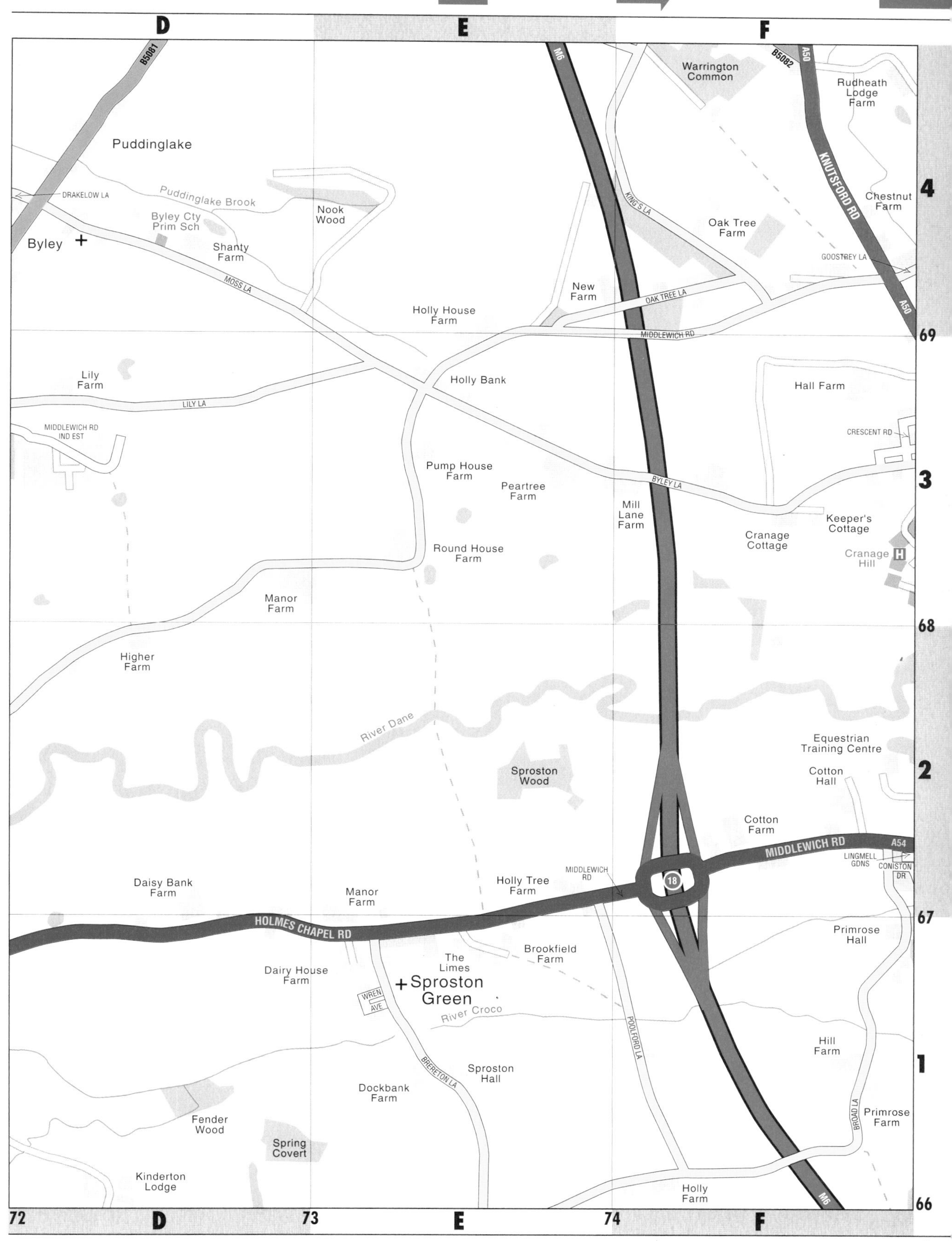

D
E
F
B5081
Puddinglake
DRAKELOW LA
Puddinglake Brook
Byley Cty
Prim Sch
Byley
Shanty
Farm
Nook
Wood
MOSS LA
Holly House
Farm
M6
Warrington
Common
B5082
A50
Rudheath
Lodge
Farm
KNUTSFORD RD
Chestnut
Farm
KING'S LA
Oak Tree
Farm
GOOSTREY LA
New
Farm
OAK TREE LA
MIDDLEWICH RD
A50
Lily
Farm
LILY LA
Holly Bank
Hall Farm
MIDDLEWICH RD
IND EST
CRESCENT RD
Pump House
Farm
Peartree
Farm
BYLEY LA
Mill
Lane
Farm
Keeper's
Cottage
Cranage
Cottage
Cranage
Hill
H
Round House
Farm
Manor
Farm
Higher
Farm
River Dane
Sproston
Wood
Equestrian
Training Centre
Cotton
Hall
Cotton
Farm
MIDDLEWICH RD
A54
LINGMELL
GDNS
CONISTON
DR
MIDDLEWICH
RD
18
Daisy Bank
Farm
Manor
Farm
Holly Tree
Farm
HOLMES CHAPEL RD
Primrose
Hall
Brookfield
Farm
The
Limes
Dairy House
Farm
Sproston
Green
WREN
AVE
River Croco
POOLFORD LA
Hill
Farm
BRERETON LA
Sproston
Hall
Dockbank
Farm
BROAD LA
Primrose
Farm
Fender
Wood
Spring
Covert
Kinderton
Lodge
Holly
Farm
M6
4
69
3
68
2
67
1
66
72
73
74

152
130

129
107

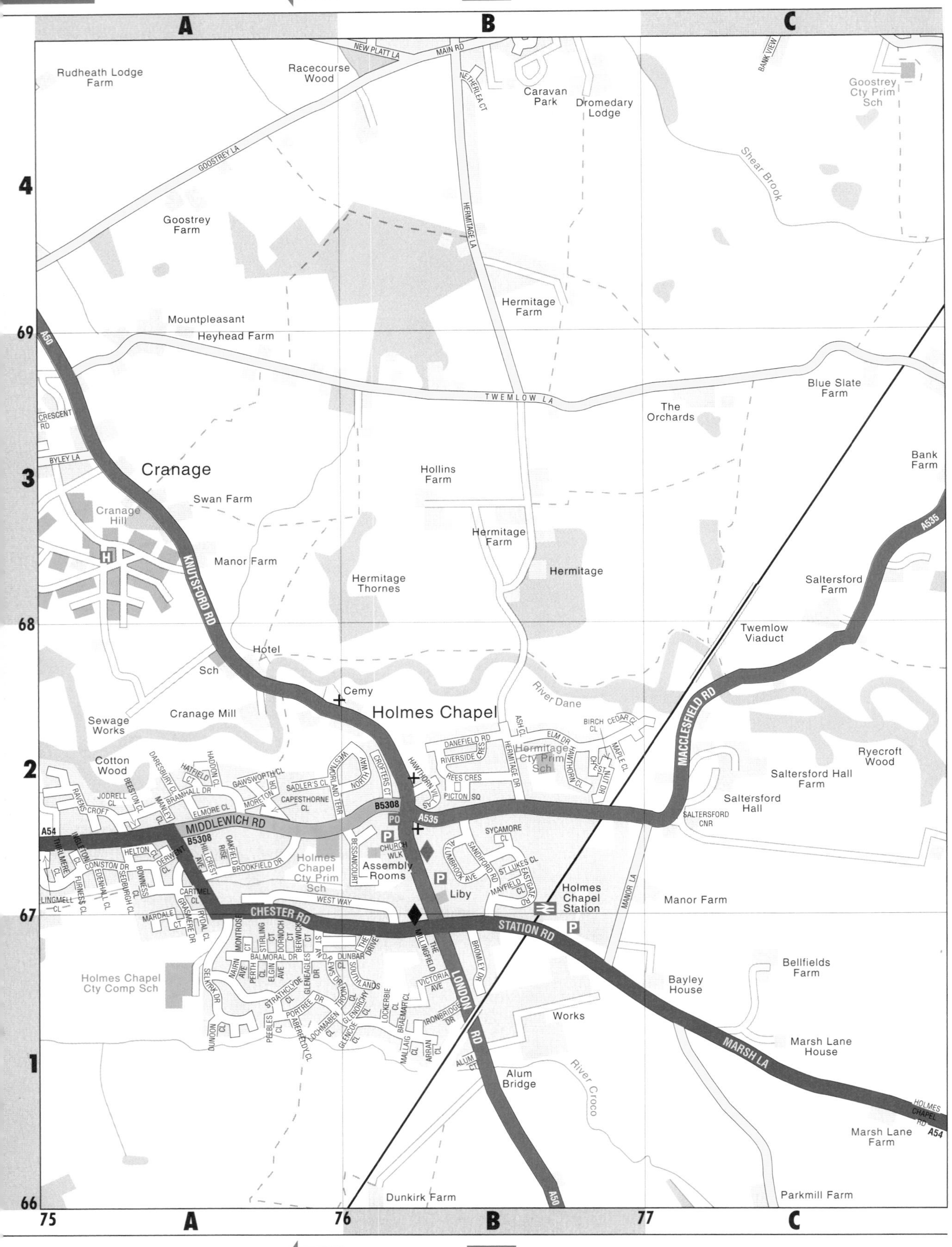
A
B
C
4
3
2
1
69
68
67
66
75
76
77
Rudheath Lodge Farm
Racecourse Wood
NEW PLATT LA
MAIN RD
NETHERLEA CT
Caravan Park
Dromedary Lodge
BANK VIEW
Goostrey Cty Prim Sch
GOOSTREY LA
Shear Brook
Goostrey Farm
HERMITAGE LA
Hermitage Farm
Mountpleasant
Heyhead Farm
A50
TWEMLOW LA
Blue Slate Farm
The Orchards
CRESCENT RD
BYLEY LA
Cranage
Hollins Farm
Bank Farm
Swan Farm
Cranage Hill
Hermitage Farm
A535
Manor Farm
KNUTSFORD RD
Hermitage Thornes
Hermitage
Saltersford Farm
Twemlow Viaduct
Hotel
Sch
Cemy
River Dane
Sewage Works
Cranage Mill
Holmes Chapel
MACCLESFIELD RD
ASH CL
BIRCH CL
CEDAR CL
DANEFIELD RD
ELM DR
Cotton Wood
HADDON CL
HATFIELD CT
GAWSWORTH CL
WESTMORLAND TERR
NORTH WAY
CROFTERS CT
HAWTHORN VIL
RIVERSIDE CRES
HERMITAGE DR
Hermitage Cty Prim Sch
HAWTHORN CL
MAPLE CL
NUT DR
Ryecroft Wood
DARESBURY CL
BRAMHALL DR
SADLER'S CL
REES CRES
Saltersford Hall Farm
RAVENSCROFT
JODRELL CL
BEESTON CL
MANLEY CL
ELMORE CL
MORETON DR
CAPESTHORNE CL
B5308
PICTON SQ
Saltersford Hall
MIDDLEWICH RD
PO
A535
SALTERSFORD CNR
A54
THIRLMERE CL
INGLETON CL
HELTON CL
DERWENT
B5308
HILLCREST AVE
OAKFIELD RISE
Holmes Chapel Cty Prim Sch
BESSANCOURT
P
CHURCH WLK
Assembly Rooms
ALUMBROOK AVE
SANDIFORD RD
SYCAMORE CL
ST LUKES CL
EASTGATE RD
MAYFIELD CL
CONISTON DR
EDENHALL CL
FURNESS CL
SEDBURGH CL
BOWNESS CL
BROOKFIELD DR
Liby
Holmes Chapel Station
MANOR LA
Manor Farm
LINGMELL CL
CARTMEL CL
MARDALE CT
GRASMERE DR
RYDAL CL
WEST WAY
CHESTER RD
STATION RD
MONTROSE CT
STIRLING CL
DORNOCH CT
BERWICK CT
ST ANDREWS DR
THE DRIVE
THE MILLINGFIELD
BROMLEY DR
Holmes Chapel Cty Comp Sch
BALMORAL DR
DUNBAR CL
SOUTHLANDS
NAIRN AVE
PERTH CL
ELGIN AVE
SELKIRK DR
STRATHCLYDE CL
GLENEAGLES DR
TROON CL
VICTORIA AVE
LONDON RD
Bellfields Farm
Bayley House
Works
Marsh Lane House
DUNOON CL
PEEBLES CL
PORTREE DR
ABERFELDY CL
LOCHMAREN CL
GLENCOE CL
GLENORCHY CL
LOCKERBIE CL
BRAEMAR CL
MALLAIG CL
ARRAN CL
IRONBRIDGE DR
MARSH LA
ALUM CT
Alum Bridge
River Croco
HOLMES CHAPEL RD
A54
Marsh Lane Farm
Dunkirk Farm
Parkmill Farm
A50

129
153

108
132

D
E
F
The Grange
Fairholme
A535
Beechwood Farm
Station Rd
Blackden Manor
Shinglar Wood
Goostrey Station
Redlion Brook
4
Broadway Farm
The Fields Farm
New Farm
Blackden Manor Farm
69
Goostrey La
Manor Farm
Blackyard Farm
Beechwood Farm
Twemlow La
Bank Farm
Grange Farm
Forty Acre La
Rowley House
3
A535
Twemlow Green
Kermincham House
Twemlow Hall
The Acres Farm
Kermincham Heath
Rowley Hall
Old Hall Farm
Bowshot Wood
Pigeon House Clough
68
Crosslane Farm
Cross La
Kermincham Hall
Ashtree Farm
Brook Farm
Chestnut Farm
2
Swettenham Brook
Greenhey Wood
Ford
Sandy La
West Farm
River Dane
Swettenham Rd
Swettenham Arms (PH)
Swettenham
Home Farm
Woodhouse Farm
Pinfold Rough
The Quinta
67
Stockery Park Farm
Swettenham Hall
Engine Wood
1
North Wood
Holmes Chapel Rd
Court House Farm
Davenport Hall Farm
Sandlow Green
A54
66
78
D
79
E
80
F

154
132

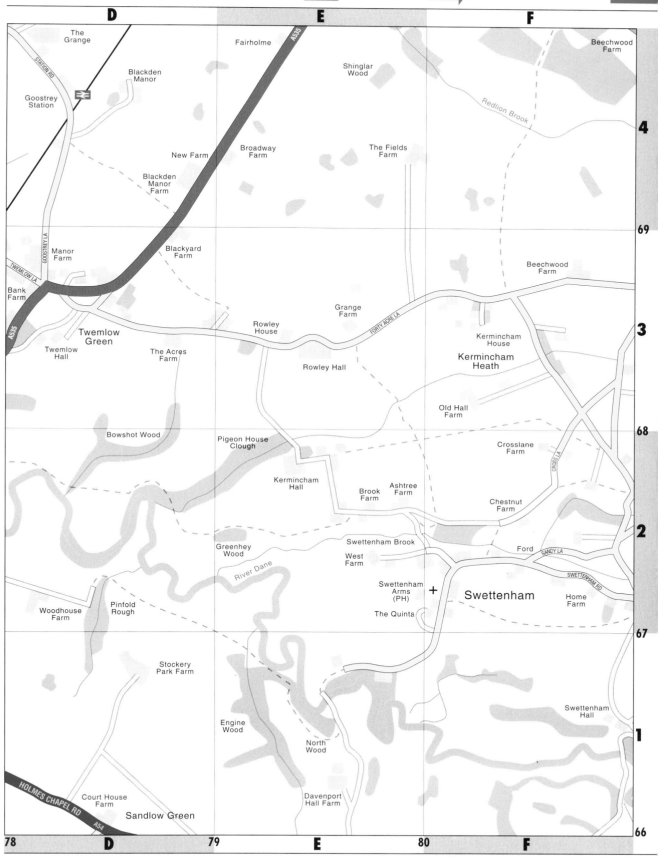

131
109

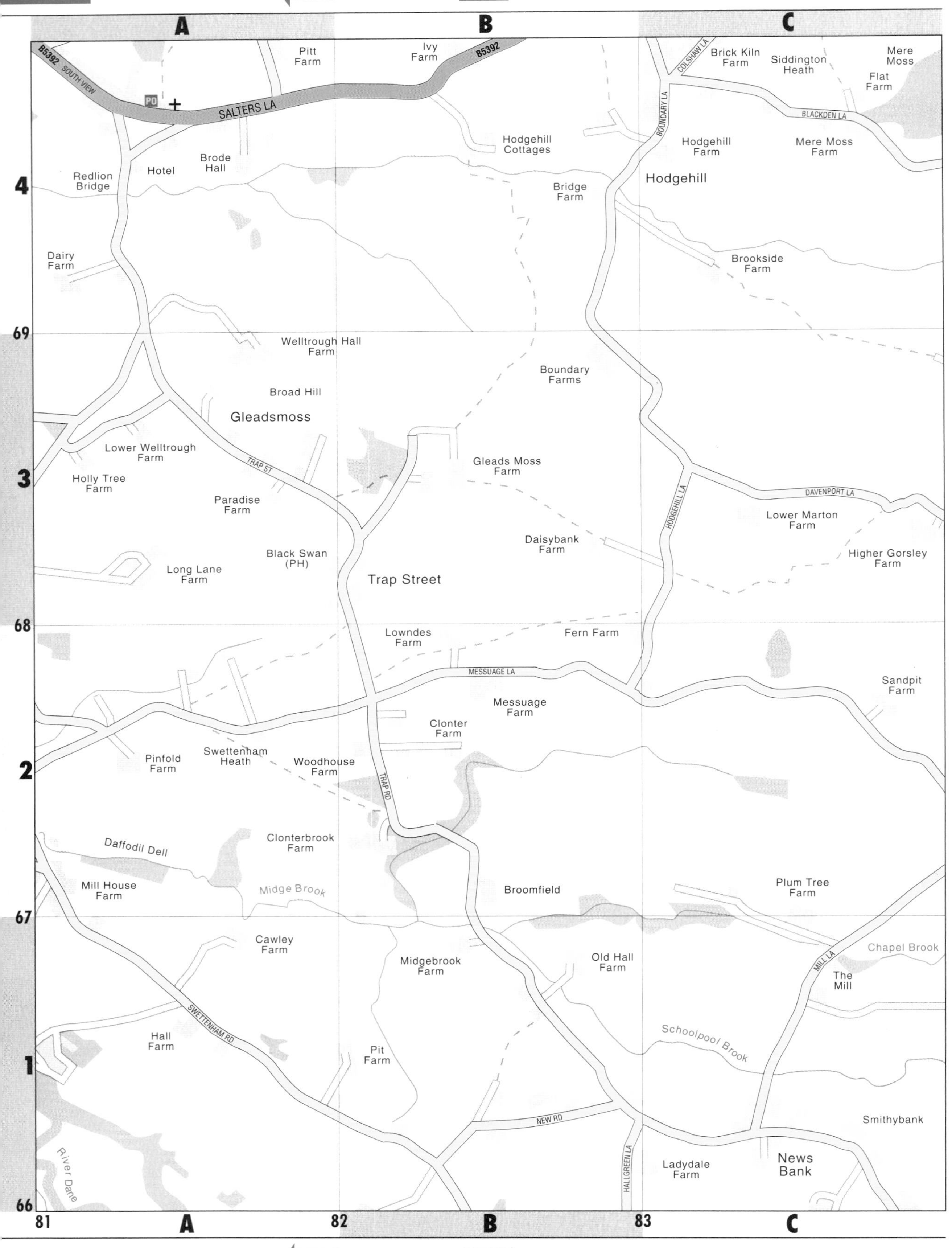
A
B
C
B5392 SOUTH VIEW
PO
SALTERS LA
B5392
Pitt Farm
Ivy Farm
COLSHAW LA
Brick Kiln Farm
Siddington Heath
Mere Moss
Flat Farm
BLACKDEN LA
BOUNDARY LA
Redlion Bridge
Hotel
Brode Hall
Hodgehill Cottages
Hodgehill Farm
Mere Moss Farm
4
Bridge Farm
Hodgehill
Dairy Farm
Brookside Farm
69
Welltrough Hall Farm
Boundary Farms
Broad Hill
Gleadsmoss
Lower Welltrough Farm
TRAP ST
Gleads Moss Farm
3
Holly Tree Farm
HODGEHILL LA
DAVENPORT LA
Paradise Farm
Lower Marton Farm
Daisybank Farm
Black Swan (PH)
Higher Gorsley Farm
Long Lane Farm
Trap Street
68
Lowndes Farm
Fern Farm
MESSUAGE LA
Sandpit Farm
Messuage Farm
Clonter Farm
Swettenham Heath
Pinfold Farm
Woodhouse Farm
2
TRAP RD
Daffodil Dell
Clonterbrook Farm
Mill House Farm
Midge Brook
Broomfield
Plum Tree Farm
67
Cawley Farm
Chapel Brook
Midgebrook Farm
Old Hall Farm
MILL LA
The Mill
SWETTENHAM RD
Schoolpool Brook
Hall Farm
Pit Farm
1
NEW RD
Smithybank
River Dane
HALLGREEN LA
Ladydale Farm
News Bank
66
81
A
82
B
83
C

131
155

110
134

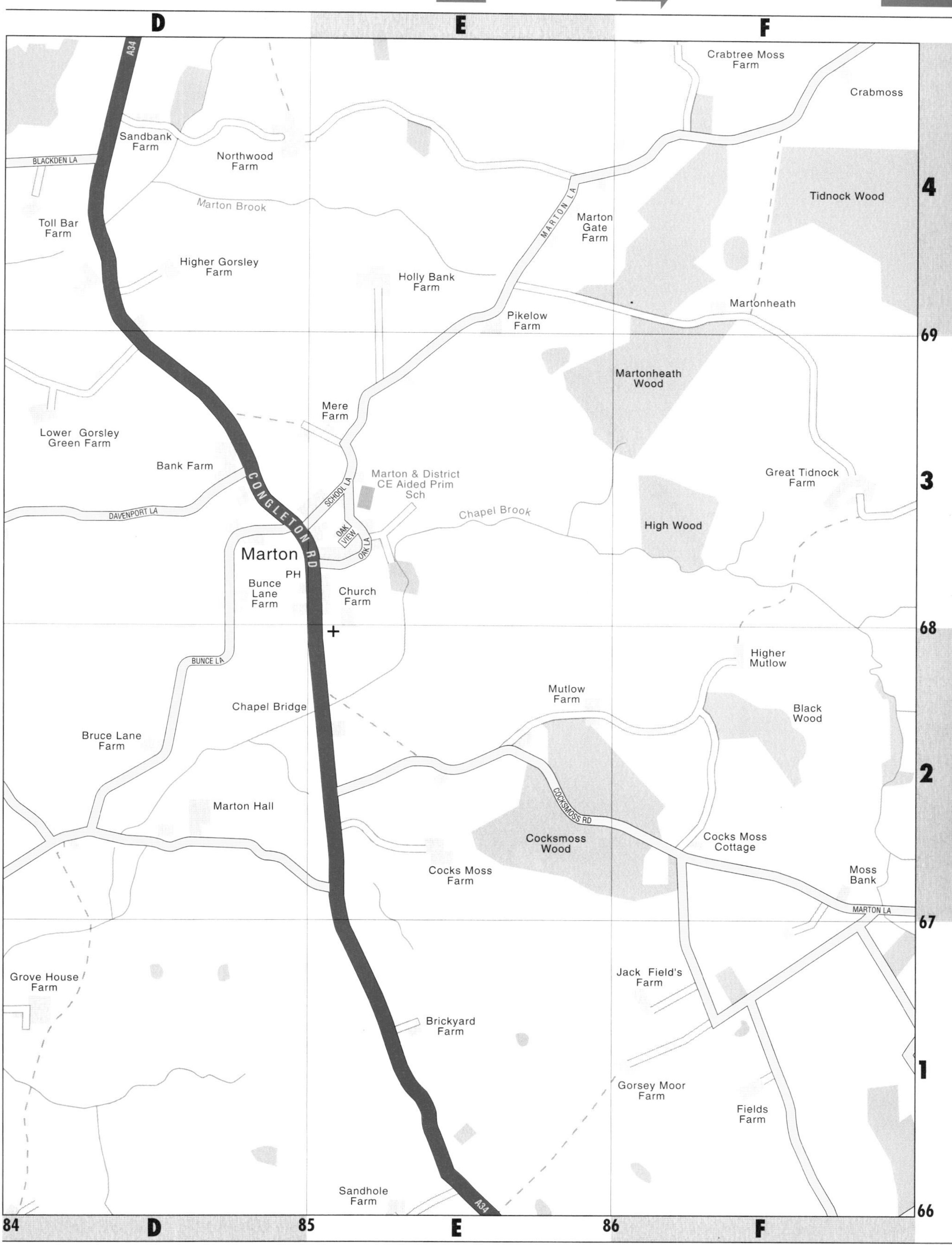
D
E
F
A34
Sandbank Farm
Northwood Farm
BLACKDEN LA
Marton Brook
Toll Bar Farm
Higher Gorsley Farm
Holly Bank Farm
Crabtree Moss Farm
Crabmoss
Tidnock Wood
MARTON LA
Marton Gate Farm
Martonheath
Pikelow Farm
Martonheath Wood
Mere Farm
Lower Gorsley Green Farm
Bank Farm
CONGLETON RD
SCHOOL LA
Marton & District CE Aided Prim Sch
Chapel Brook
Great Tidnock Farm
High Wood
DAVENPORT LA
OAK VIEW
OAK LA
Marton
PH
Bunce Lane Farm
Church Farm
BUNCE LA
Higher Mutlow
Mutlow Farm
Black Wood
Chapel Bridge
Bruce Lane Farm
Marton Hall
COCKSMOSS RD
Cocksmoss Wood
Cocks Moss Cottage
Cocks Moss Farm
Moss Bank
MARTON LA
Grove House Farm
Jack Field's Farm
Brickyard Farm
Gorsey Moor Farm
Fields Farm
Sandhole Farm
A34
4
69
3
68
2
67
1
66
84
85
86

156
134

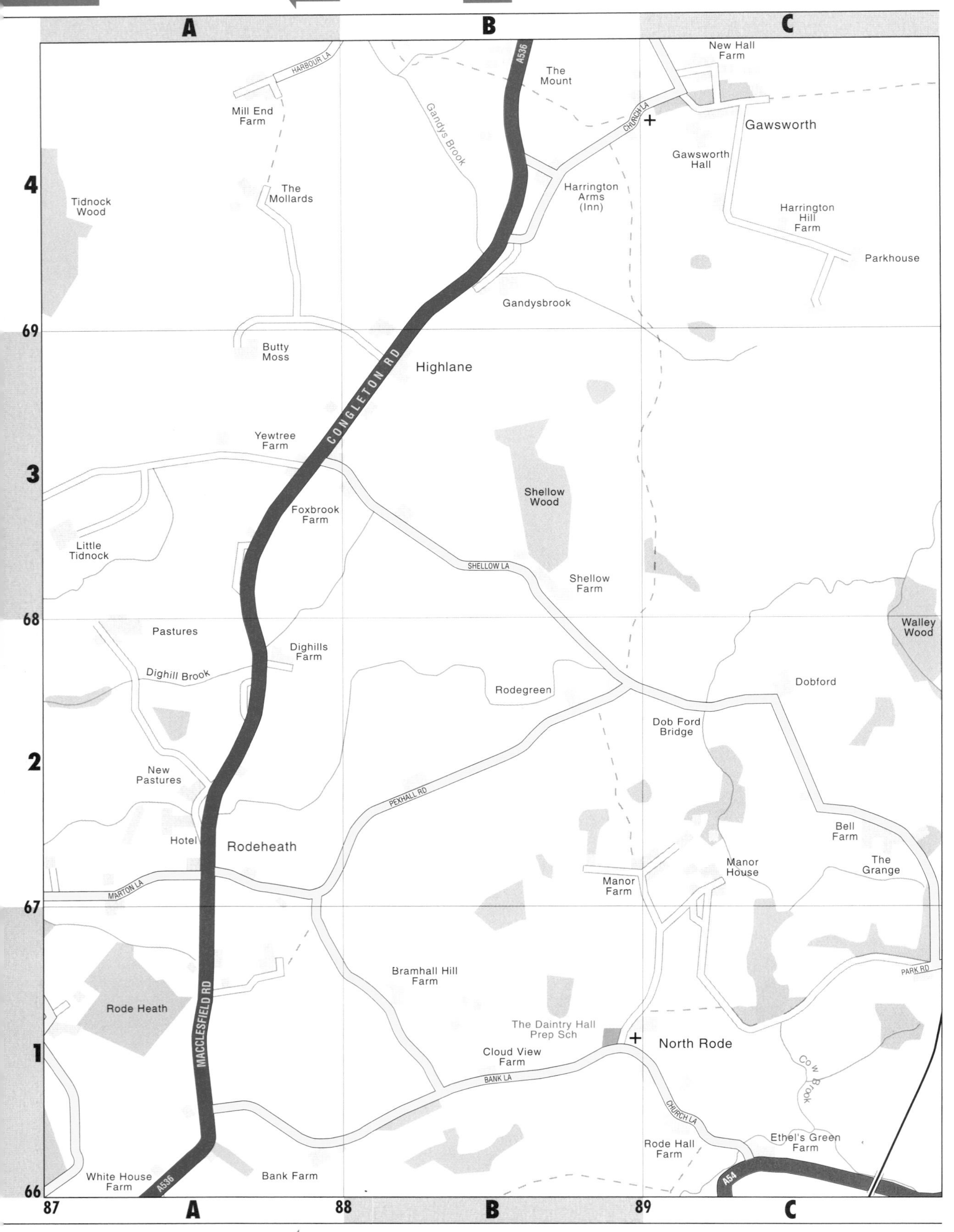

← 133
↑ 111

A   B   C

New Hall
Farm

HARBOUR LA

Mill End
Farm

Gandys Brook

The
Mount

CHURCH LA

Gawsworth

4

Tidnock
Wood

The
Mollards

Harrington
Arms
(Inn)

Gawsworth
Hall

Harrington
Hill
Farm

Parkhouse

69

Butty
Moss

CONGLETON RD

Highlane

Gandysbrook

3

Yewtree
Farm

Shellow
Wood

Little
Tidnock

Foxbrook
Farm

SHELLOW LA

Shellow
Farm

Walley
Wood

68

Pastures

Dighills
Farm

Rodegreen

Dobford

Dighill Brook

Dob Ford
Bridge

2

New
Pastures

PEXHALL RD

Bell
Farm

Hotel

Rodeheath

Manor
House

The
Grange

MARTON LA

Manor
Farm

67

PARK RD

Bramhall Hill
Farm

MACCLESFIELD RD

1

Rode Heath

The Daintry Hall
Prep Sch

North Rode

Cloud View
Farm

BANK LA

Cow Brook

White House
Farm

A536

Bank Farm

CHURCH LA

Rode Hall
Farm

Ethel's Green
Farm

A54

66

87   A   88   B   89   C

← 133
↓ 157

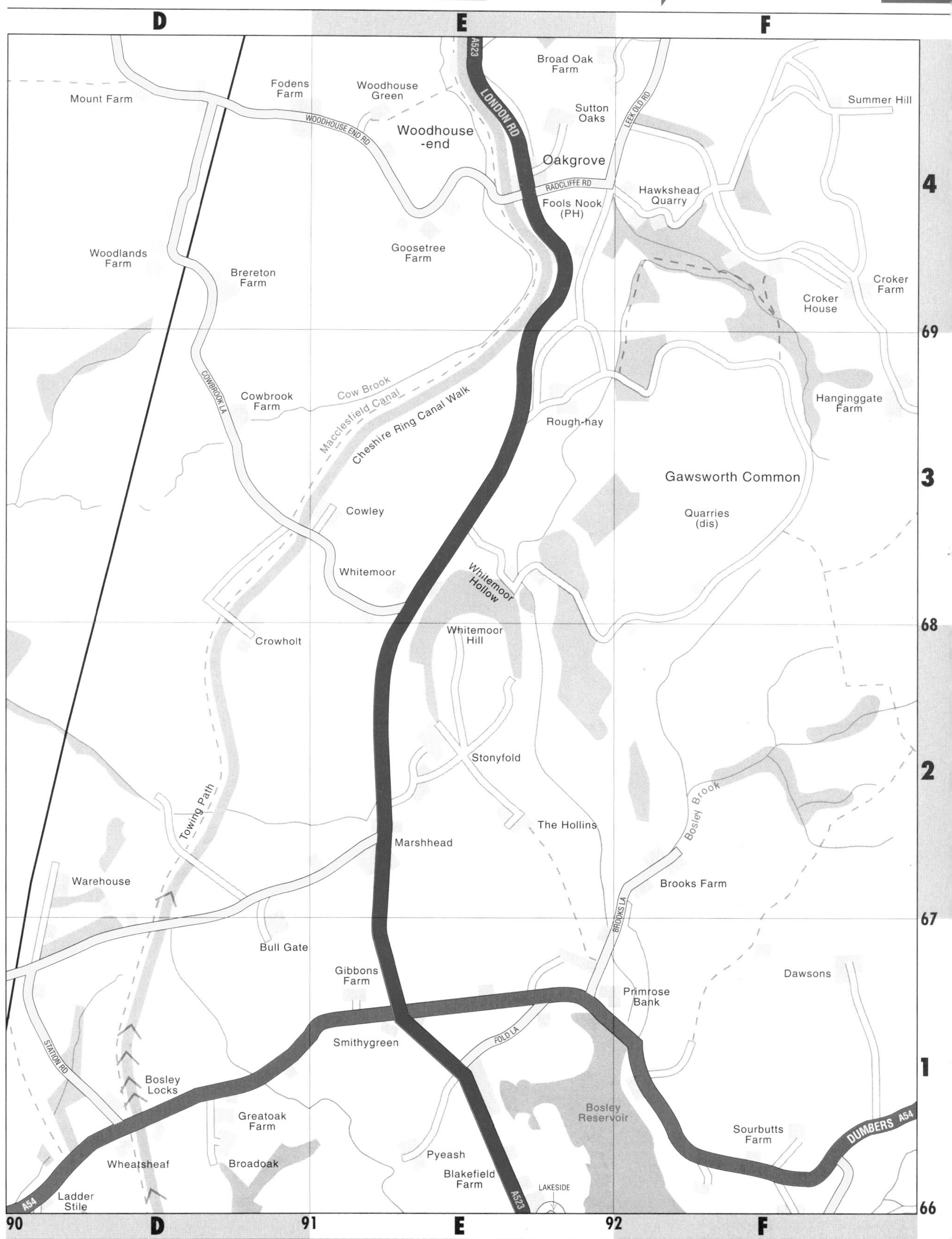

112
136
158
136

D E F

Mount Farm

Fodens Farm

Woodhouse Green

WOODHOUSE END RD

Woodhouse-end

Broad Oak Farm

Sutton Oaks

LEEK OLD RD

Summer Hill

LONDON RD

A523

Oakgrove

RADCLIFFE RD

Fools Nook (PH)

Hawkshead Quarry

4

Woodlands Farm

Brereton Farm

Goosetree Farm

Croker House

Croker Farm

69

COWBROOK LA

Cowbrook Farm

Cow Brook

Macclesfield Canal

Cheshire Ring Canal Walk

Rough-hay

Hanginggate Farm

Cowley

Gawsworth Common

3

Whitemoor

Whitemoor Hollow

Quarries (dis)

Crowholt

Whitemoor Hill

68

Towing Path

Stonyfold

Bosley Brook

2

The Hollins

Warehouse

Marshhead

Brooks Farm

BROOKS LA

67

Bull Gate

Gibbons Farm

Primrose Bank

Dawsons

STATION RD

Smithygreen

FOLD LA

Bosley Locks

Greatoak Farm

Bosley Reservoir

Sourbutts Farm

DUMBERS A54

1

Broadoak

Pyeash

A523

Wheatsheaf

Blakefield Farm

LAKESIDE

A54

Ladder Stile

66

90 D 91 E 92 F

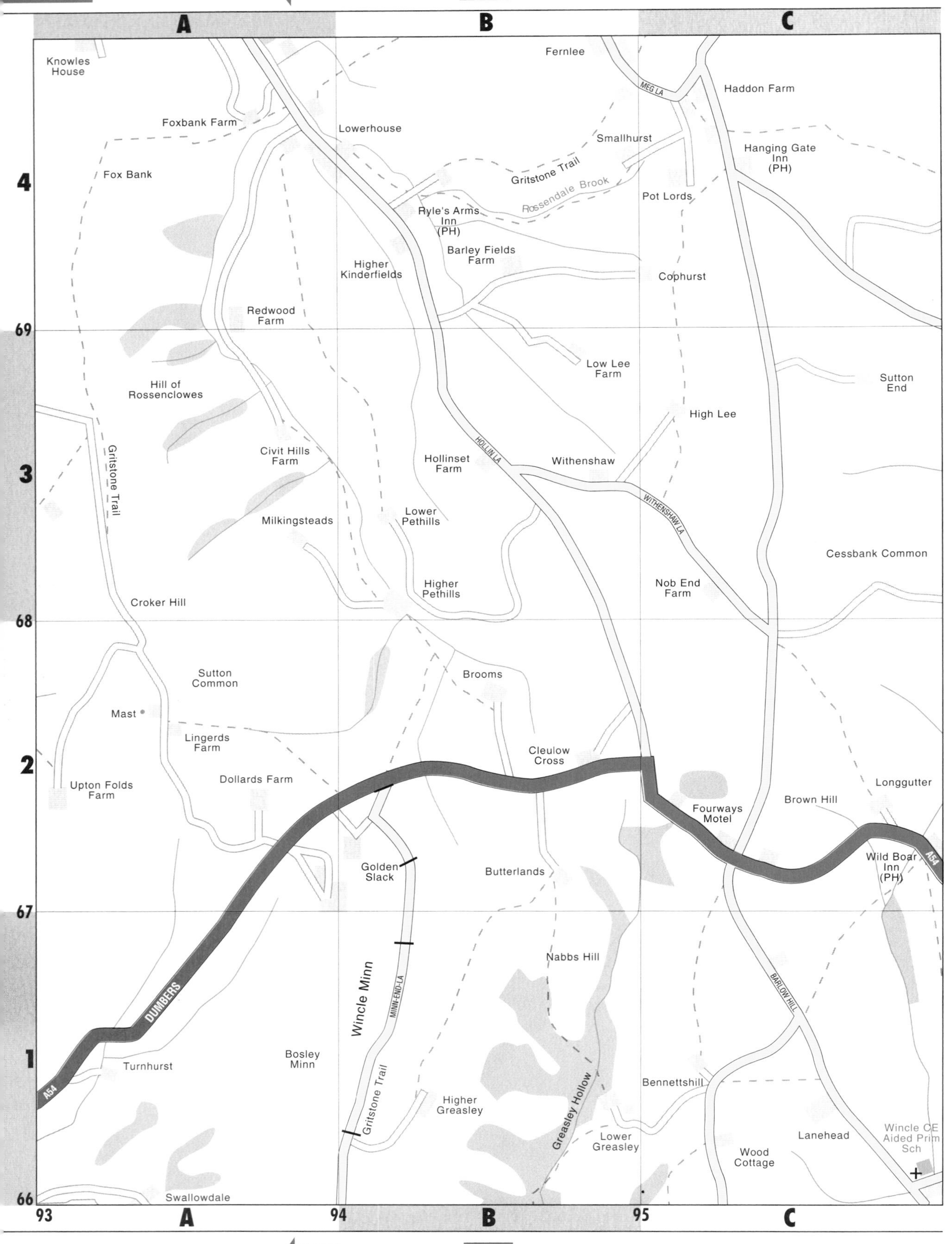

A B C

Knowles House
Foxbank Farm
Lowerhouse
Fernlee
MEG LA
Haddon Farm
Smallhurst
Fox Bank
Gritstone Trail
Hanging Gate Inn (PH)
Rossendale Brook
4
Ryle's Arms Inn (PH)
Pot Lords
Higher Kinderfields
Barley Fields Farm
Cophurst
Redwood Farm
69
Low Lee Farm
Sutton End
Hill of Rossenclowes
High Lee
Civit Hills Farm
HOLLIN LA
Hollinset Farm
Withenshaw
3
Gritstone Trail
Milkingsteads
Lower Pethills
WITHENSHAW LA
Cessbank Common
Croker Hill
Higher Pethills
Nob End Farm
68
Sutton Common
Brooms
Mast
Lingerds Farm
Cleulow Cross
2
Upton Folds Farm
Dollards Farm
Fourways Motel
Brown Hill
Longgutter
DUMBERS
Golden Slack
Butterlands
Wild Boar Inn (PH)
A54
67
MINN-END-LA
Nabbs Hill
BARLOW HILL
Wincle Minn
1
Turnhurst
Bosley Minn
Gritstone Trail
Higher Greasley
Greasley Hollow
Bennettshill
Lanehead
Wincle CE Aided Prim Sch
Lower Greasley
Wood Cottage
66
Swallowdale

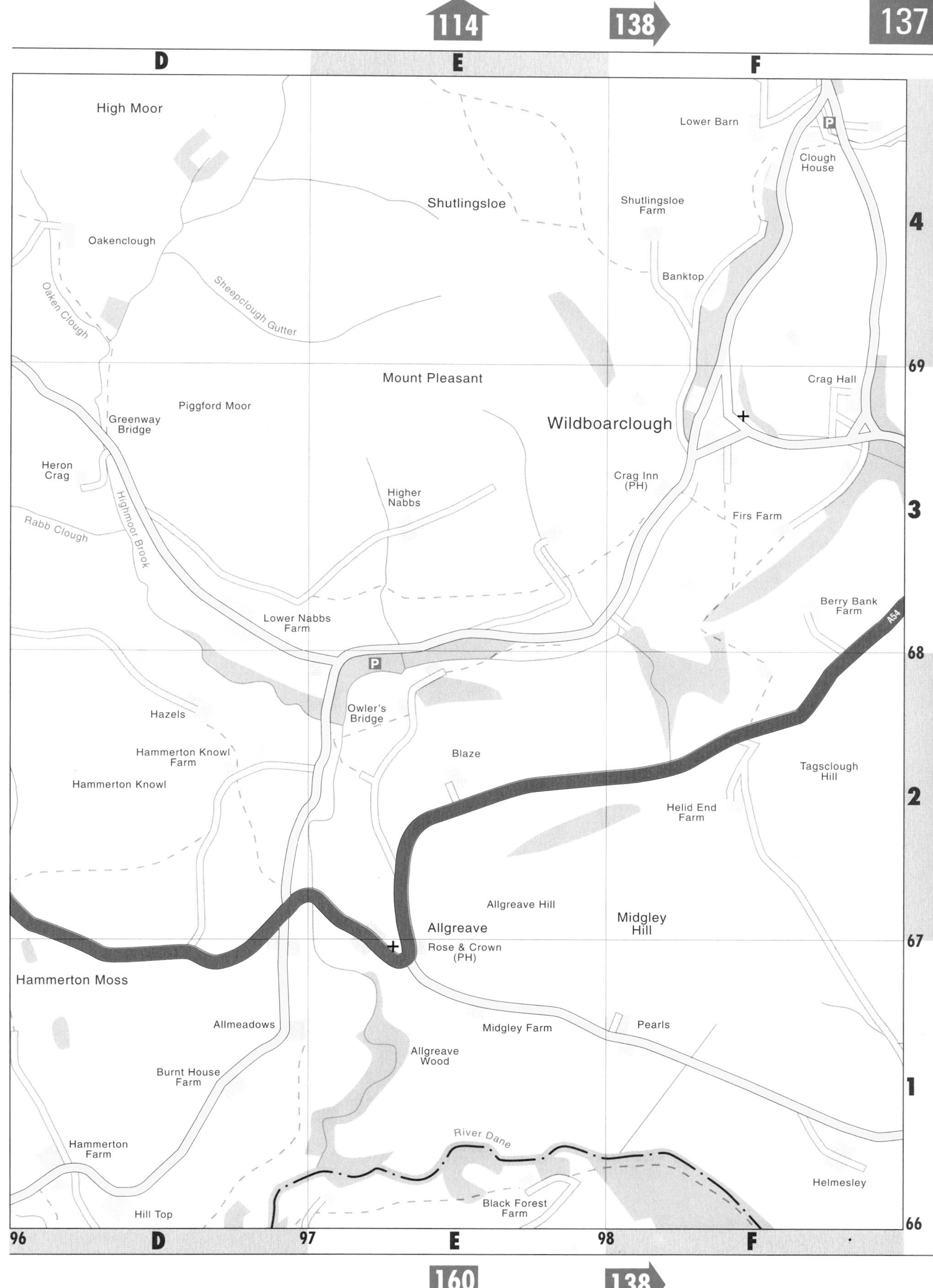

High Moor

Shutlingsloe

Lower Barn

Clough House

Shutlingsloe Farm

4

Oakenclough

Banktop

Oaken Clough

Sheepclough Gutter

69

Mount Pleasant

Crag Hall

Piggford Moor

Greenway Bridge

Wildboarclough

Heron Crag

Higher Nabbs

Crag Inn (PH)

Firs Farm

3

Rabb Clough

Highmoor Brook

Lower Nabbs Farm

Berry Bank Farm

A54

68

Hazels

P

Owler's Bridge

Hammerton Knowl Farm

Blaze

Tagsclough Hill

Hammerton Knowl

Helid End Farm

2

Allgreave Hill

Midgley Hill

Allgreave

67

Hammerton Moss

Rose & Crown (PH)

Allmeadows

Midgley Farm

Pearls

Burnt House Farm

Allgreave Wood

1

Hammerton Farm

River Dane

Helmesley

Hill Top

Black Forest Farm

66

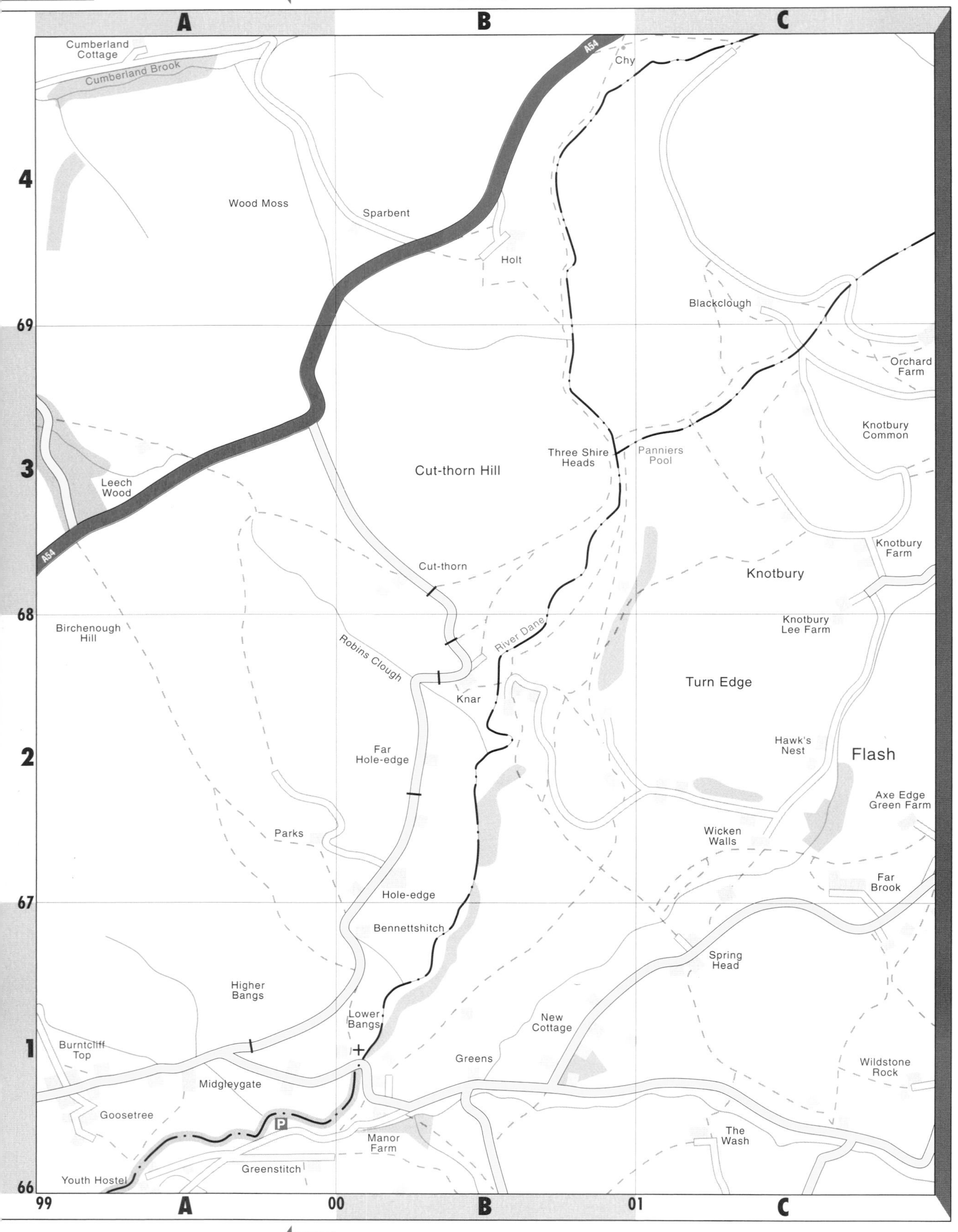

4

69

3

68

2

67

1

66

99

00

01

A

B

C

Cumberland
Cottage

Cumberland Brook

Wood Moss

Sparbent

Holt

A54

Chy

Blackclough

Leech
Wood

A54

Cut-thorn Hill

Three Shire
Heads

Panniers
Pool

Orchard
Farm

Knotbury
Common

Knotbury
Farm

Knotbury

Cut-thorn

Birchenough
Hill

Robins Clough

River Dane

Knar

Knotbury
Lee Farm

Turn Edge

Hawk's
Nest

Flash

Far
Hole-edge

Axe Edge
Green Farm

Parks

Wicken
Walls

Far
Brook

Hole-edge

Bennettshitch

Spring
Head

Higher
Bangs

Lower
Bangs

New
Cottage

Burntcliff
Top

Midgleygate

Greens

Wildstone
Rock

Goosetree

P

Manor
Farm

The
Wash

Greenstitch

Youth Hostel

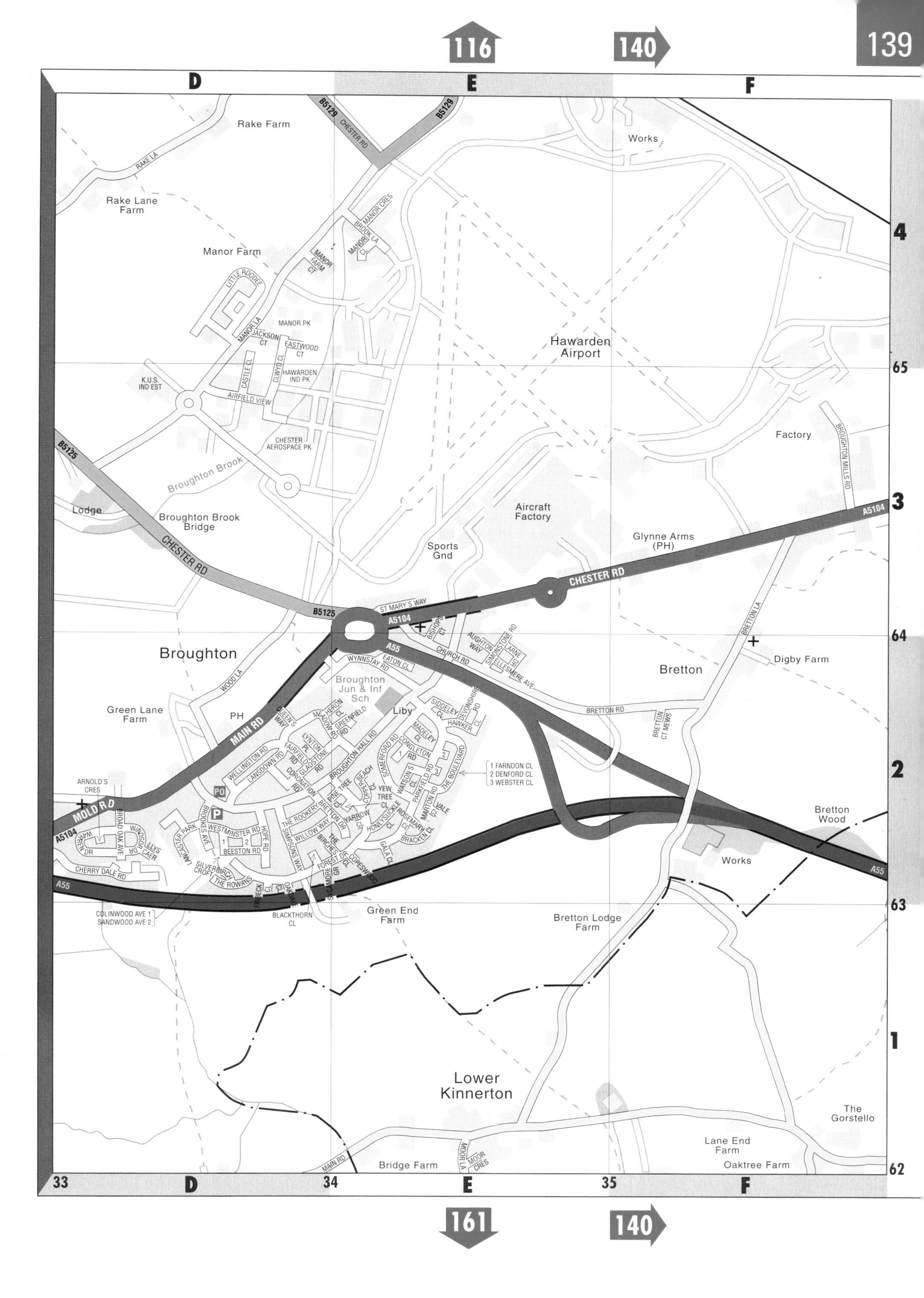

D
E
F

Rake Farm

B5128 CHESTER RD
B5129

Works

Rake La

Rake Lane
Farm

MANOR CRES

4

Manor Farm

MANOR LA
MANOR FARM CT
BROOK LA

LITTLE ROODIE
MANOR LA
JACKSON CT
MANOR PK
EASTWOOD CT

Hawarden
Airport

CASTLE CL
CLWYD CL
AIRFIELD VIEW
HAWARDEN IND PK

Factory

BROUGHTON MILLS RD

K.U.S.
IND EST

65

B5125

CHESTER AEROSPACE PK

A5104

3

Lodge

Broughton Brook

Broughton Brook
Bridge

CHESTER RD

Aircraft
Factory

Sports
Gnd

Glynne Arms
(PH)

CHESTER RD

B5125

ST MARY'S WAY
A5104

Broughton

WOOD LA

A55

EATON CL
WYNNSTAY RD

BISHOPS CT
CHURCH RD
AUGHTON WAY
LIMEKILNE RD
LARNE CL
ELLESMERE AVE

Bretton

64

Digby Farm

Broughton
Jun & Inf
Sch

Liby

SIDDELEY CL
RENSHAW CL
HAWKER

BRETTON RD

BRETTON LA

BRETTON CT MEWS

Green Lane
Farm

PH

MAIN RD

GREEN'S WAY
MC HEGON
AVON RD
GREENFIELD
LINTON RD
FAIRFIELD
BROUGHTON HALL RD
SOMERFORD RD
MADELEY CL
CONGLETON RD
THE BOULEVARD

WELLINGTON RD
LANSDOWN RD
GLADSTONE
CORONATION RD
PINE TREE
BRETTON DR
BEACH
YEW TREE
WATSON'S CL
PARKFIELD
MARTON RD
VALE

2

ARNOLD'S
CRES

PO

1 FARNDON CL
2 DENFORD CL
3 WEBSTER CL

A5104
MOLD RD

BROAD OAK AVE
WINDSOR DR
LLYS CAER

P

WESTMINSTER RD
HOPE RD
BEESTON RD
SIMPSONS WAY
WILLOW WAY
THE
BIRCHES DR
FOREST DR
HONEYSUCKLE CL
YARROW
ROSEMARY CL
BRACKEN CL
GALA CL

Bretton
Wood

63

A55

CHERRY DALE RD
SILVERBIRCH
CROFT THE ROWANS
FIRBECK CL
LANCASTER

SYCAMORE RD
COPSEWOOD CL

Works

A55

COLINWOOD AVE 1
SANDWOOD AVE 2
BLACKTHORN CL

Green End
Farm

Bretton Lodge
Farm

1

Lower
Kinnerton

The
Gorstello

Lane End
Farm

MAIN RD
MOOR LA
MOOR CRES

Bridge Farm

Oaktree Farm

62

33
D
34
E
35
F

139
117

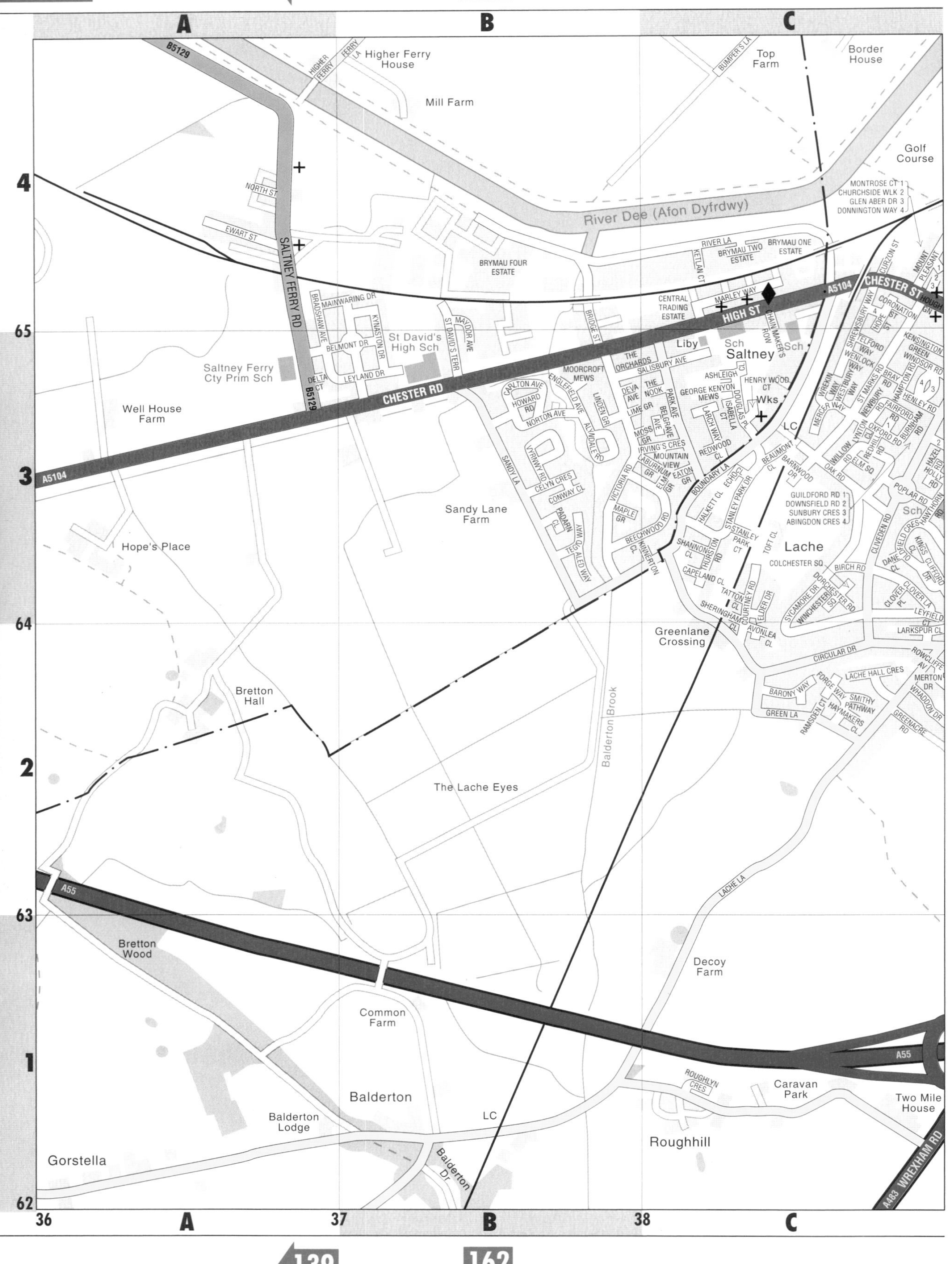
A
B
C
4
65
3
64
2
63
1
62
36
37
38
Higher Ferry House
HIGHER FERRY
FERRY LA
Mill Farm
BUMPER'S LA
Top Farm
Border House
Golf Course
MONTROSE CT 1
CHURCHSIDE WLK 2
GLEN ABER DR 3
DONNINGTON WAY 4
B5129
NORTH ST
EWART ST
SALTNEY FERRY RD
River Dee (Afon Dyfrdwy)
RIVER LA
KETLAN CT
BRYMAU TWO ESTATE
BRYMAU ONE ESTATE
BRYMAU FOUR ESTATE
CENTRAL TRADING ESTATE
MARLEY WAY
HIGH ST
A5104
CHESTER ST
CURZON ST
MOUNT PLEASANT
CORONATION
HOPE ST
HOUGHTON
CHAIN MAKERS ROW
BRADSHAW AVE
MAINWARING DR
KYNASTON DR
BELMONT DR
St David's High Sch
MAYDOR AVE
ST DAVID'S TERR
BRIDGE ST
Liby
Sch
Saltney
Sch
Saltney Ferry Cty Prim Sch
DELTA CT
LEYLAND DR
CHESTER RD
THE ORCHARDS
SALISBURY AVE
MOORCROFT MEWS
CARLTON AVE
HOWARD RD
NORTON AVE
ENGLEFIELD AVE
ALYNDALE RD
LINDEN GR
DEVA AVE
THE NOOK
LIME GR
MOSS GR
BELGRAVE AVE
PARK AVE
IRVING'S CRES
MOUNTAIN VIEW
LABURNUM GR
ELM GR
EATON GR
GEORGE KENYON MEWS
ASHLEIGH
LARCH WAY
ISABELLA CT
DOUGLAS PL
HENRY WOOD CT
Wks
REDWOOD CL
LC
BEAUMONT CL
BARNWOOD DR
SHREWSBURY WAY
TELFORD WAY
WESTBURY WAY
WENLOCK WAY
WREKIN WAY
MERCIA WAY
ST MARKS RD
NEWBURY RD
KENSINGTON GREEN
WINDSOR RD
BRAY RD
HAMPTON RD
HENLEY RD
FAIRFORD RD
OXFORD RD
BURNHAM RD
REDHILL RD
WILLOW RD
VINTON CL
ELM SQ
OAK RD
HAZEL RD
HOLLY RD
POPLAR RD
HAWTHORN RD
Well House Farm
A5104
SANDY LA
VYRNWY RD
CELYN CRES
CONWAY CL
PADARN CL
TEGID WAY
ALED WAY
VICTORIA RD
MAPLE GR
BEECHWOOD RD
KINNERTON
BOUNDARY LA
ECHO CL
HALKETT CL
STANLEY PARK DR
STANLEY PARK CT
TOFT CL
SHANNON CL
THURSTON RD
GUILDFORD RD 1
DOWNSFIELD RD 2
SUNBURY CRES 3
ABINGDON CRES 4
Sch
Lache
COLCHESTER SQ
BIRCH RD
CLIVEDEN RD
DANEFIELD CRES
KINGS CL
CLIFFORD DR
Sandy Lane Farm
Hope's Place
CAPELAND CL
TATTON CL
COURTNEY RD
ELDER DR
SHERINGHAM CL
AVONLEA CL
SYCAMORE DR
DORCHESTER RD
WINCHESTER SQ
CLOVER PL
CLOVER LA
LEYFIELD CT
LARKSPUR CL
Greenlane Crossing
CIRCULAR DR
ROWCLIFFE AV
MERTON DR
WHADDON DR
LACHE HALL CRES
BARONY WAY
FORGE WAY
SMITHY PATHWAY
HAYMAKERS CL
RAMSDEN CT
GREEN LA
GREENACRE RD
Bretton Hall
Balderton Brook
The Lache Eyes
A55
Bretton Wood
LACHE LA
Decoy Farm
Common Farm
A55
ROUGHLYN CRES
Caravan Park
Two Mile House
Balderton
Balderton Lodge
LC
Roughhill
Gorstella
Balderton Dr
A483 WREXHAM RD

A
B
C
36
37
38

139
162

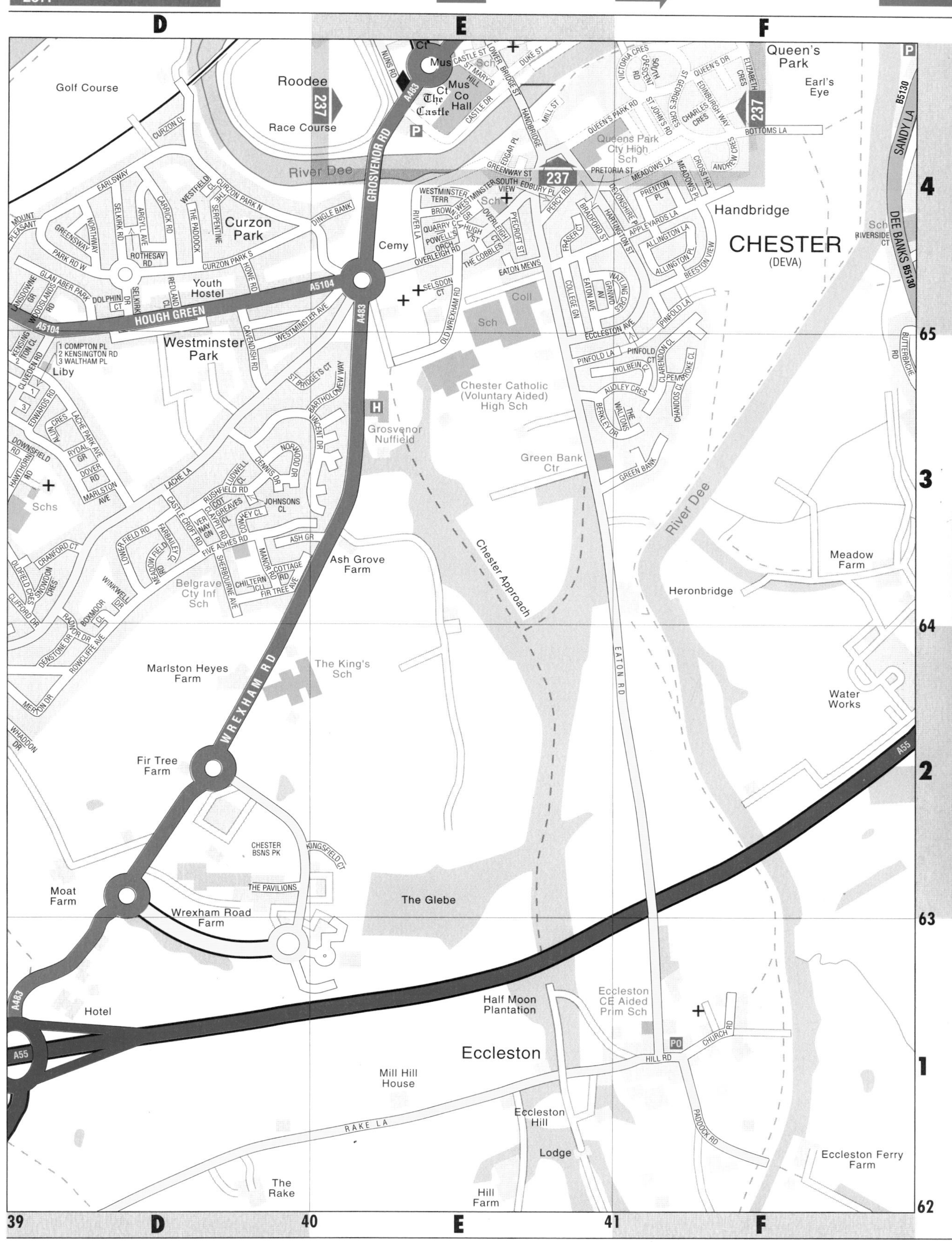

For full street detail of the highlighted area see page 237.

118

142

141

Golf Course

Roodee

237

Race Course

River Dee

Mus
Ct
The Castle
Mus Co Hall

P

EARLSWAY
CURZON CL
Curzon Park N
WESTFIELD
CARRICK RD
CURZON RD
ARGYLL AVE
THE PADDOCK
NORTHWAY
GREENSWAY
SERPENTINE
DINGLE BANK
GROSVENOR RD
Castle Dr
Mill St
Handbridge
Lower Bridge St
St Mary's Hill
Duke St
Castle St

Curzon Park

Cemy

Greenway St
Westminster South View
237

Westminster Terr
Brown St
Westminster Sch
River La
Quarry C
Powells
Orch
Hugh St
The Cobbles
Edbury Pl
Percy Rd
Pyecroft St

Queen's
Park
Earl's Eye
237

Bottoms La

P

B5130
SANDY LA

Queen's Park City High Sch

Victoria Cres
South Crescent
George's Cres
St John's Rd
Queen's Dr
Queen's Park Rd
Elizabeth Cres
Edinburgh Way
Charles Cres
Andr
Cross He
CHARLES ST
Meadows La
Pretoria St
Prenton Pl
Appleyards La
Allington La
Beeston View

CHESTER
(DEVA)

Sch
Riverside Ct
Dee Banks
B5130

Mount Pleasant
PARK RD W
GLAN ABER PARK
KINGSWINNE GR
WOODLANDS DR
DOLPHIN CT
ROTHESAY RD
SELKIRK RD
REDLAND DR
HOWE RD
Curzon Park S

Youth Hostel

HOUGH GREEN
A5104
A5104

A483

Westminster
Park

WESTMINSTER AVE
CAVENDISH RD
BARTHOLOMEW WAY
VINCENT DR
NORWOOD DR
OLD WREXHAM RD

Old Wrexham Rd
Selsdon Ct
College Gn
Sch
Coll
Sch

Chester Catholic
(Voluntary Aided)
High Sch

Fraser
Eaton Ave
Granby's
Hastings La
Clarendon Cl
Pinfold La
Pinfold
Watling St
Eccleston Ave
Pinfold La
Holbein
Audley Cres
Chandos Cl
Pembroke Ct
Berkeley Ct
The Waltings

Green Bank
Ctr

Green Bank

River Dee

Liby
1 Compton Pl
2 Kensington Rd
3 Waltham Pl
KENSINGTON CL
CLIFFORD RD
ALLIN CRES
LACHE PARK AVE
EDWARDS RD
RYDAL GR
DOVER RD
MARLSTON AVE

Schs

Downsfield Rd
Hawthorne Dr
Cranford Ct
Swindon Cres
Oldfield Dr
Clifford Ct
Deanstone Cl
Rowcliffe Ave
Roxmoor Cl
Meadow Dr
Whaddon Dr

Grosvenor
Nuffield
H

Lache La
Castlecroft Rd
Rushfield Rd
Dennis Dr
Ludwell Cl
Verdin St
May Dr
Ashey Cl
Johnsons Cl
Five Ashes Rd
Ash Gr
Shererwoine Ave
Chiltern Cl
Fir Tree Dr
Cottage Rd
Mandi Rd

Belgrave
Cty Inf
Sch

Ash Grove
Farm

Chester Approach

Marlston Heyes
Farm

The King's
Sch

Eaton Rd

WREXHAM RD

Meadow
Farm

Heronbridge

Water
Works

Fir Tree
Farm

A55

Moat
Farm

A483

Chester
Bsns Pk
Kingsfield Ct
The Pavilions

Wrexham Road
Farm

The Glebe

Half Moon
Plantation

Eccleston
CE Aided
Prim Sch

Church Rd
Paddock Rd
Hill Rd
PO

Hotel

A55

Eccleston

Mill Hill
House

Rake La

Eccleston
Hill

Lodge

Eccleston Ferry
Farm

The
Rake

Hill
Farm

4

65

3

64

2

63

1

62

141
119

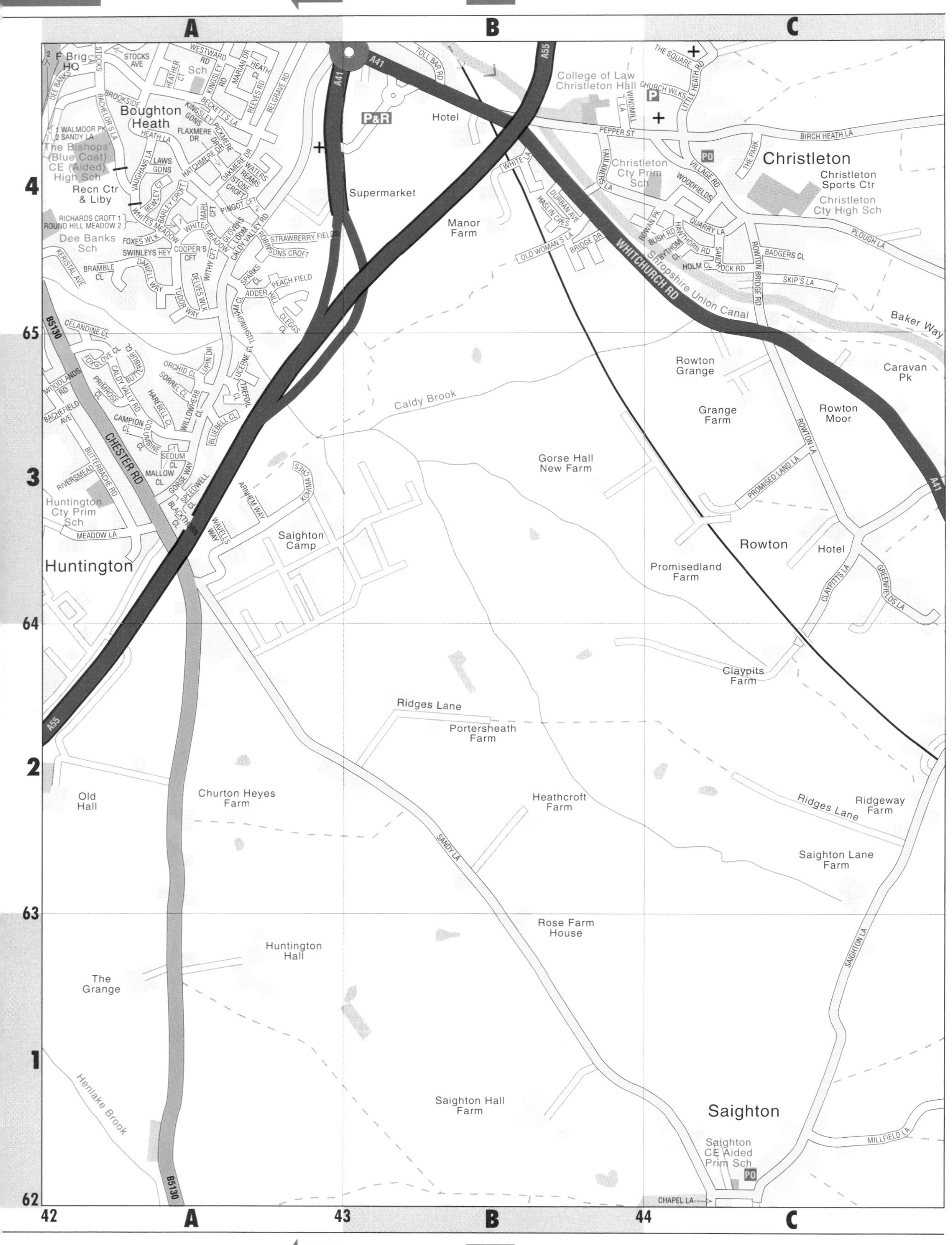
A
B
C
Boughton Heath
Sch
The Bishops' (Blue Coat) CE (Aided) High Sch
Recn Ctr & Liby
Dee Banks Sch
F Brig HQ
STOCKS AVE
WESTWARD RD
HEATHER CT
KINGSLEY RD
MARIAN DR
HEATH CL
REEVES RD
BELGRAVE RD
BROOKSIDE
BECKETT'S LA
KINGSLEY GDNS
FLAXMERE DR
PICKMERE DR
HEATH LA
1 WALMOOR PK
2 SANDY LA
VAUGHANS LA
LAWS GDNS
HATCHMERE DR
OAKMERE DR
WATERS REACH
STONE CROFT
PINGOT CFT
BEWLEY CT
BARLEY CROFT
WHITES MEADOW
WHITES WLK
RICHARDS CROFT 1
ROUND HILL MEADOW 2
FOXES WLK
SWINLEYS HEY
COOPER'S CFT
GLOVERS LOOM
CALDY VALLEY RD
ROBINSONS CROFT
STRAWBERRY FIELDS
BRAMBLE CL
DANIELL WAY
TUDOR WAY
DELVES WLK
WITHY CFT
SPARKS CL
ADDER HILL
PEACH FIELD
CLEGGS LA
KERISTAL AVE
DEE BANKS
CELANDINE CL
FOXGLOVE CL
BUTTERBUR CL
CALDY VALLEY RD
ORCHID CL
SORREL CL
LUPIN DR
LUCERNE CL
TREFOIL CL
BLUEBELL CL
WILLOWHERB CL
HAREBELL CL
PRIMROSE CL
CAMPION CL
COLUMBINE CL
SEDUM CL
MALLOW CL
GORSE WAY
SPEEDWELL CL
BLACKTHORN CL
WOODLANDS RD
BACHEFIELD AVE
BUTTERBACHE RD
RIVERSMEAD
CHESTER RD
B5130
Huntington Cty Prim Sch
MEADOW LA
Huntington
A55
A41
TOLL BAR RD
P&R
Hotel
Supermarket
Manor Farm
College of Law Christleton Hall
THE SQUARE
CHURCH WLKS
LITTLE HEATH RD
WINDMILL LA
PEPPER ST
BIRCH HEATH LA
THE PARK
PO
Christleton
Christleton Sports Ctr
Christleton Cty High Sch
Christleton Cty Prim Sch
FAULKNERS LA
VILLAGE RD
WOODFIELDS
WHITE LA
DURBAN AVE
HASLIN CRES
QUARRY LA
PLOUGH LA
OLD WOMAN'S LA
BRIDGE DR
WHITCHURCH RD
ROWAN PK
BUSH RD
HAWTHORN RD
HOLM CL
SANDROCK RD
ROWTON BRIDGE RD
BADGERS CL
SKIP'S LA
Shropshire Union Canal
Baker Way
Rowton Grange
Caravan Pk
Grange Farm
Rowton Moor
Caldy Brook
Gorse Hall New Farm
ROWTON LA
PROMISED LAND LA
ARNHEM WAY
KOHIMA CRES
WAVELLS WAY
Saighton Camp
Rowton
Hotel
Promisedland Farm
CLAYPITS LA
GREENFIELDS LA
Claypits Farm
Ridges Lane
Portersheath Farm
Old Hall
Churton Heyes Farm
Heathcroft Farm
Ridges Lane
Ridgeway Farm
SANDY LA
Saighton Lane Farm
Rose Farm House
Huntington Hall
The Grange
SAIGHTON LA
Henlake Brook
Saighton Hall Farm
Saighton
MILLFIELD LA
Saighton CE Aided Prim Sch
PO
CHAPEL LA
4
65
3
64
2
63
1
62
42
43
44

141
164

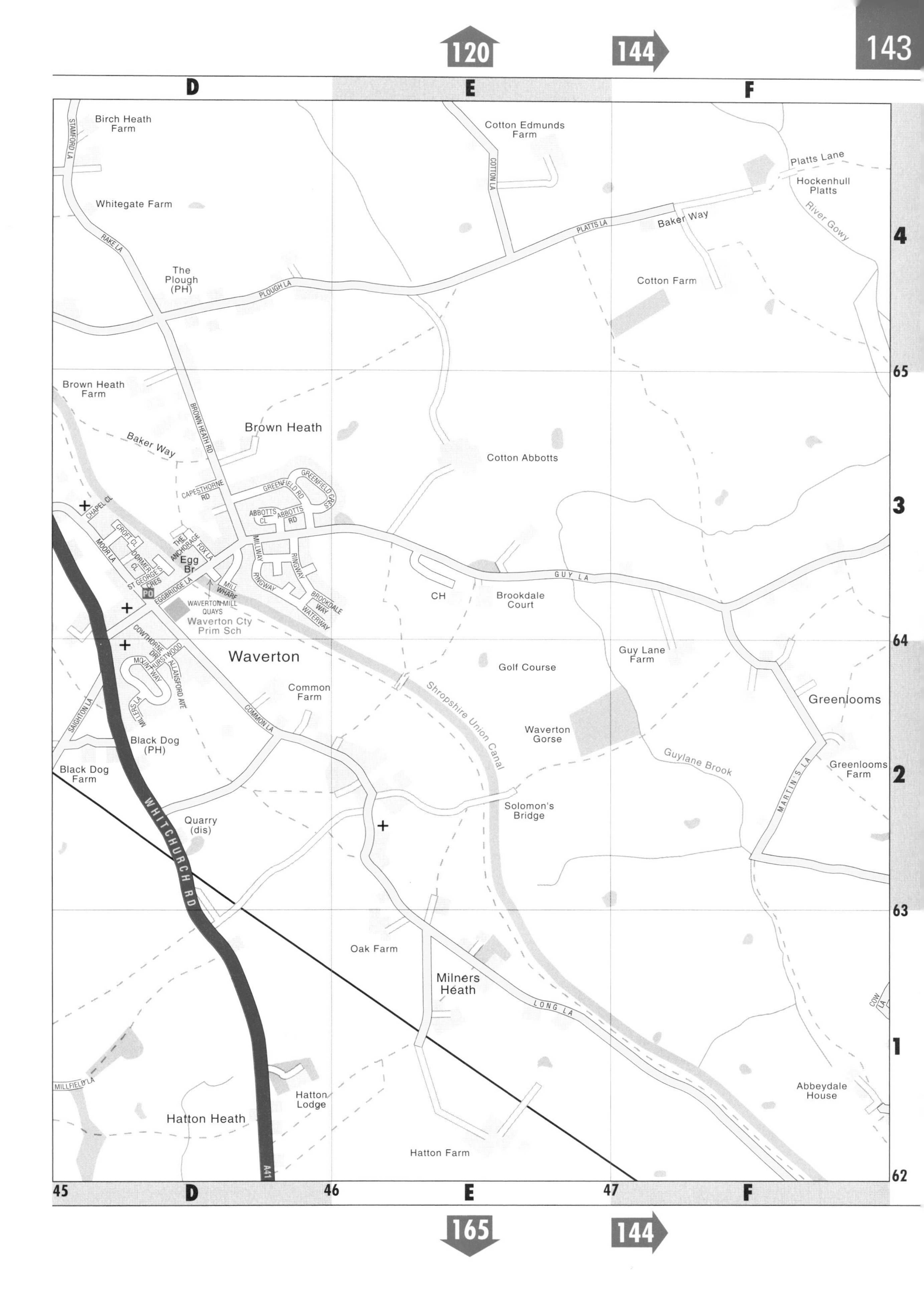
D
E
F
Birch Heath Farm
STAMFORD LA
Cotton Edmunds Farm
COTTON LA
Platts Lane
Hockenhull Platts
River Gowy
Whitegate Farm
Baker Way
PLATTS LA
RAKE LA
The Plough (PH)
PLOUGH LA
Cotton Farm
4
65
Brown Heath Farm
BROWN HEATH RD
Brown Heath
Baker Way
Cotton Abbotts
CAPESTHORNE RD
GREENFIELD RD
GREENFIELD CRES
ABBOTTS CL
ABBOTTS RD
CHAPEL CL
CROFT CL
MOOR LA
DORMER CL
THE ANCHORAGE
FOX LA
Egg Br
MILLWAY
RINGWAY
ST GEORGE'S CRES
EGGBRIDGE LA
MILL WHARF
WAVERTON MILL QUAYS
BROOKDALE WAY
WATERWAY
PO
Waverton Cty Prim Sch
CH
Brookdale Court
GUY LA
3
Guy Lane Farm
64
COWTHORNE DR
HURSTWOOD
MOUNTWAY
ALLANSFORD AVE
MILLERS LA
Waverton
Common Farm
Golf Course
Greenlooms
SAIGHTON LA
COMMON LA
Shropshire Union Canal
Waverton Gorse
Black Dog (PH)
Black Dog Farm
Guylane Brook
MARTIN'S LA
Greenlooms Farm
2
WHITCHURCH RD
Quarry (dis)
Solomon's Bridge
63
Oak Farm
Milners Heath
LONG LA
COW LA
1
MILLFIELD LA
Hatton Lodge
Abbeydale House
Hatton Heath
Hatton Farm
A41
62
45
46
47

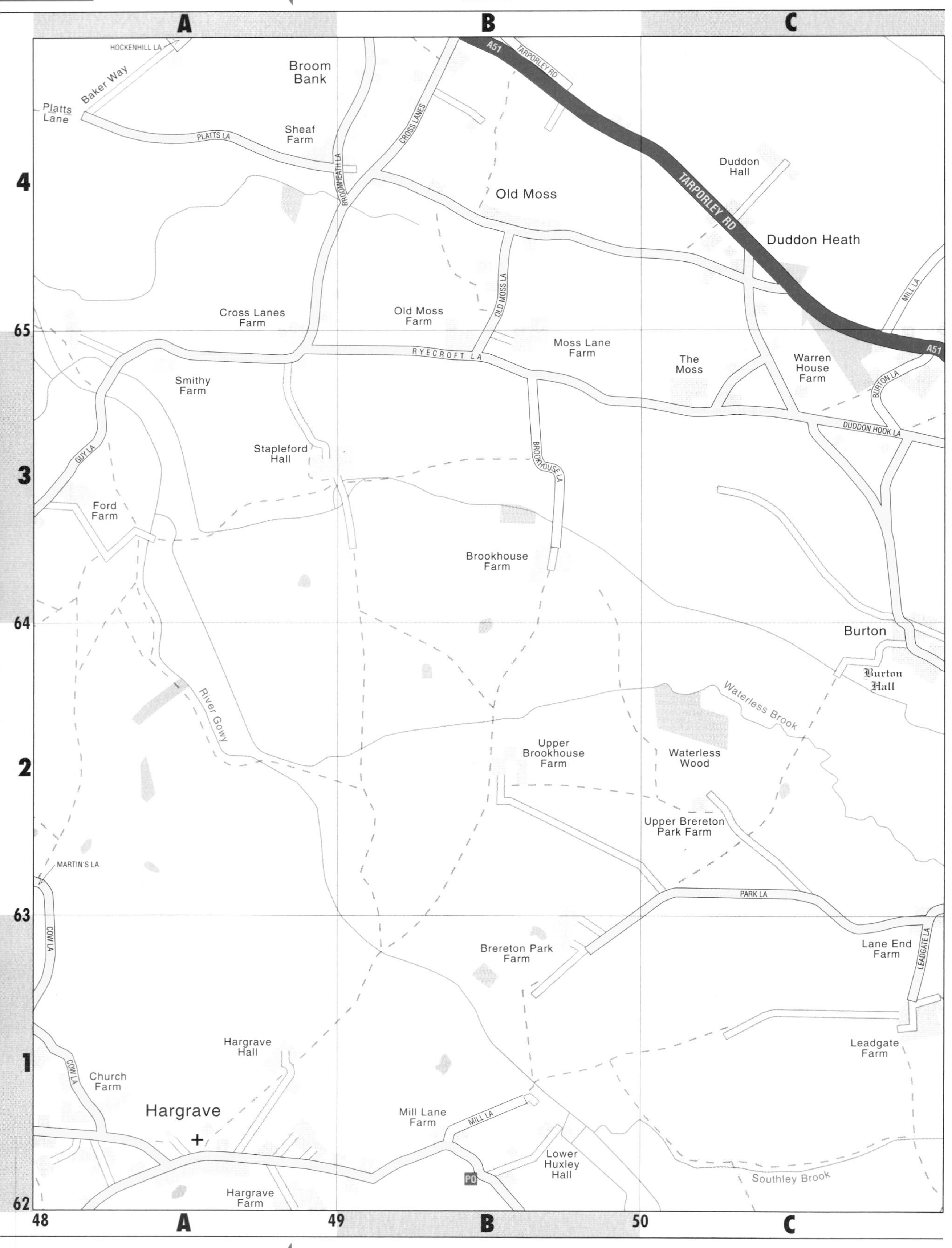

HOCKENHILL LA

Broom
Bank

Baker Way

Platts
Lane

PLATTS LA

Sheaf
Farm

CROSS LANES

A51

TARPORLEY RD

Old Moss

Duddon
Hall

TARPORLEY RD

Duddon Heath

4

BROOMHEATH LA

Cross Lanes
Farm

Old Moss
Farm

OLD MOSS LA

Moss Lane
Farm

The
Moss

Warren
House
Farm

A51

MILL LA

BURTON LA

65

RYECROFT LA

DUDDON HOOK LA

Smithy
Farm

GUY LA

Stapleford
Hall

BROOKHOUSE LA

3

Ford
Farm

Brookhouse
Farm

Burton

64

Burton
Hall

River Gowy

Waterless Brook

Upper
Brookhouse
Farm

Waterless
Wood

2

Upper Brereton
Park Farm

MARTIN'S LA

PARK LA

63

COW LA

Brereton Park
Farm

Lane End
Farm

LEADGATE LA

Hargrave
Hall

Leadgate
Farm

1

Church
Farm

COW LA

Hargrave

Mill Lane
Farm

MILL LA

Lower
Huxley
Hall

PO

Southley Brook

62

Hargrave
Farm

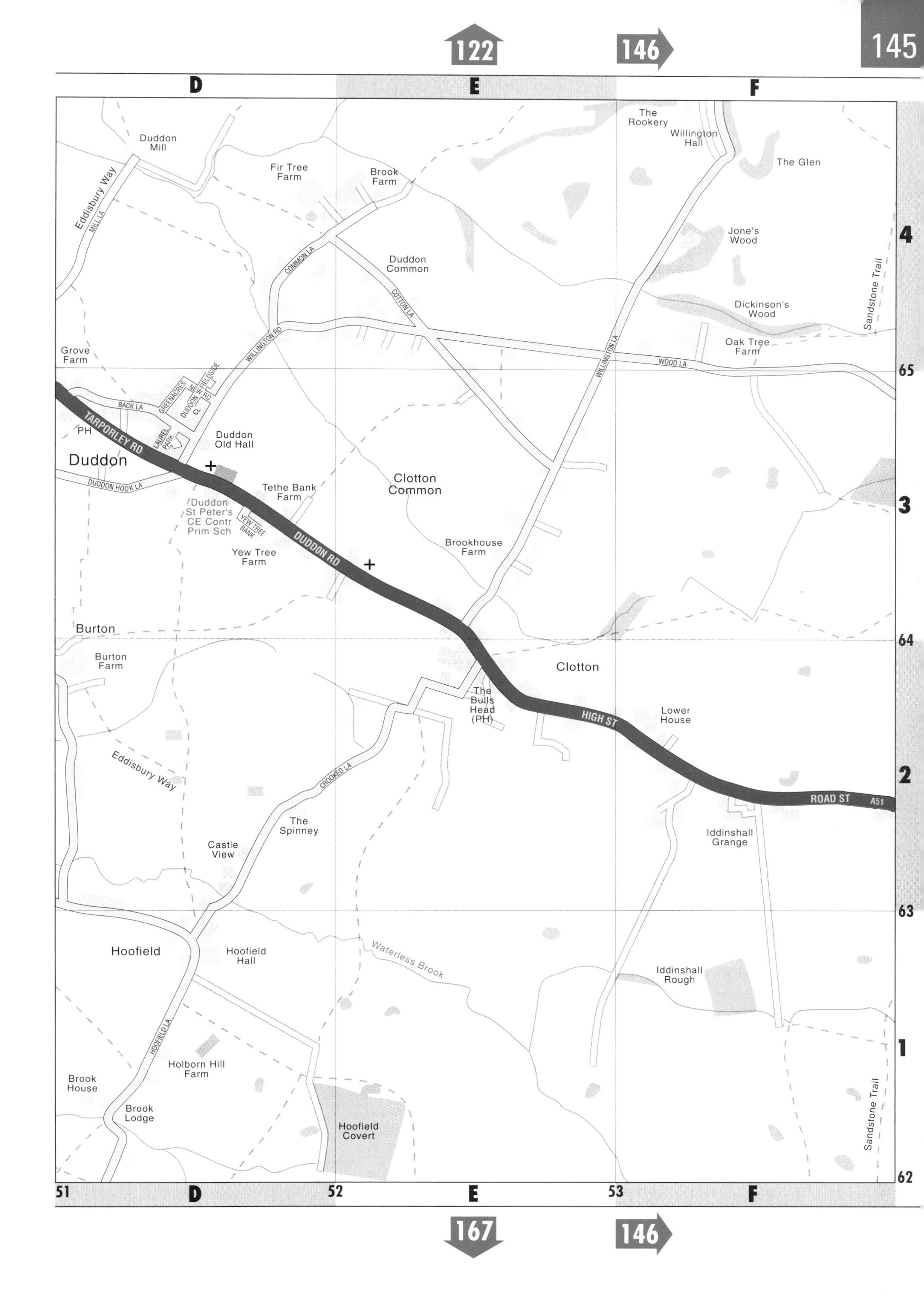

D E F

The Rookery
Willington Hall
The Glen

Duddon Mill
Fir Tree Farm
Brook Farm
Jone's Wood

Eddisbury Way
MILL LA
COMMON LA
Duddon Common
COTTON LA
Dickinson's Wood

4

Sandstone Trail

WILLINGTON RD
WILLINGTON LA
WOOD LA
Oak Tree Farm

Grove Farm
65

TARPORLEY RD
BACK LA
GREENACRES
DUDDON
NEW RD
CL
FIELDSIDE

PH
LAUREL PARK
Duddon Old Hall
Clotton Common

Duddon

DUDDON HOOK LA
+
Tethe Bank Farm
YEW TREE BANK
Duddon St Peter's CE Contr Prim Sch
DUDDON RD
+
Brookhouse Farm

3

Yew Tree Farm

Burton
64

Burton Farm
Clotton

Eddisbury Way
The Bulls Head (PH)
Lower House

CROOKED LA
HIGH ST

2

The Spinney
Castle View
Iddinshall Grange
ROAD ST   A51

63

Hoofield
Hoofield Hall
Waterless Brook
Iddinshall Rough

HOOFIELD LA
Holborn Hill Farm

1

Brook House
Brook Lodge
Hoofield Covert
Sandstone Trail

62

51   D   52   E   53   F

145
123

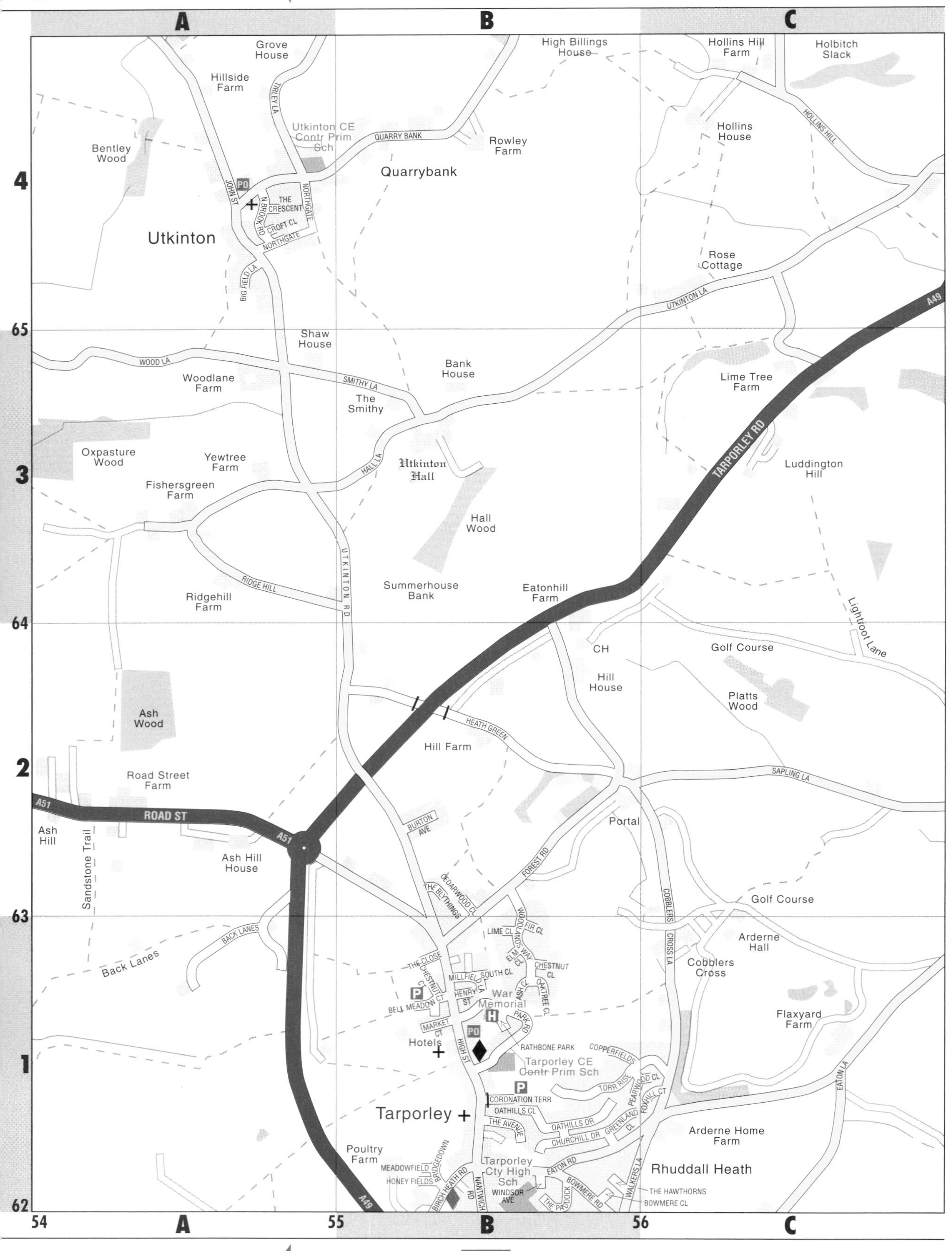
A
B
C
Grove House
Hillside Farm
High Billings House
Hollins Hill Farm
Holbitch Slack
Bentley Wood
Utkinton CE Contr Prim Sch
QUARRY BANK
Rowley Farm
Hollins House
HOLLINS HILL
Quarrybank
Utkinton
JOHN ST
PO
THE CRESCENT
N BROOK RD
CROFT CL
NORTHGATE
TIRLEY LA
BIG FIELD LA
Rose Cottage
UTKINTON LA
A49
Shaw House
WOOD LA
Woodlane Farm
SMITHY LA
The Smithy
Bank House
Lime Tree Farm
Oxpasture Wood
Yewtree Farm
HALL LA
Utkinton Hall
Fishersgreen Farm
TARPORLEY RD
Luddington Hill
Hall Wood
Summerhouse Bank
Eatonhill Farm
RIDGE HILL
Ridgehill Farm
UTKINTON RD
Lightfoot Lane
CH
Golf Course
Hill House
Platts Wood
Ash Wood
HEATH GREEN
Hill Farm
SAPLING LA
Road Street Farm
A51
ROAD ST
Ash Hill
Sandstone Trail
Ash Hill House
BURTON AVE
Portal
FOREST RD
CEDARWOOD CL
THE BLYTHINGS
COBBLERS CROSS LA
Golf Course
Arderne Hall
BACK LANES
Back Lanes
LIME CL
FIR CL
WOODLANDS WAY
ELM CL
THE CLOSE
CHESTNUT CT
MILLFIELD LA
SOUTH CL
CHESTNUT CL
Cobblers Cross
HENRY ST
ASH CL
OAKTREE CL
War Memorial
BELL MEADOW
MARKET CT
PARK RD
Flaxyard Farm
Hotels
HIGH ST
RATHBONE PARK
COPPERFIELDS
Tarporley CE Contr Prim Sch
TORR RISE
PEARWOOD CL
FOXHILL CT
CORONATION TERR
OATHILLS CL
Tarporley
THE AVENUE
OATHILLS DR
GREENLAND CL
CHURCHILL DR
Arderne Home Farm
EATON LA
Poultry Farm
BRIDGEDOWN
Tarporley Cty High Sch
EATON RD
Rhuddall Heath
MEADOWFIELD
HONEY FIELDS
BIRCH HEATH RD
NANTWICH RD
WINDSOR AVE
THE PADDOCK
BOWMERE RD
WALKERS LA
THE HAWTHORNS
BOWMERE CL
4
65
3
64
2
63
1
62
54
55
56

145
168

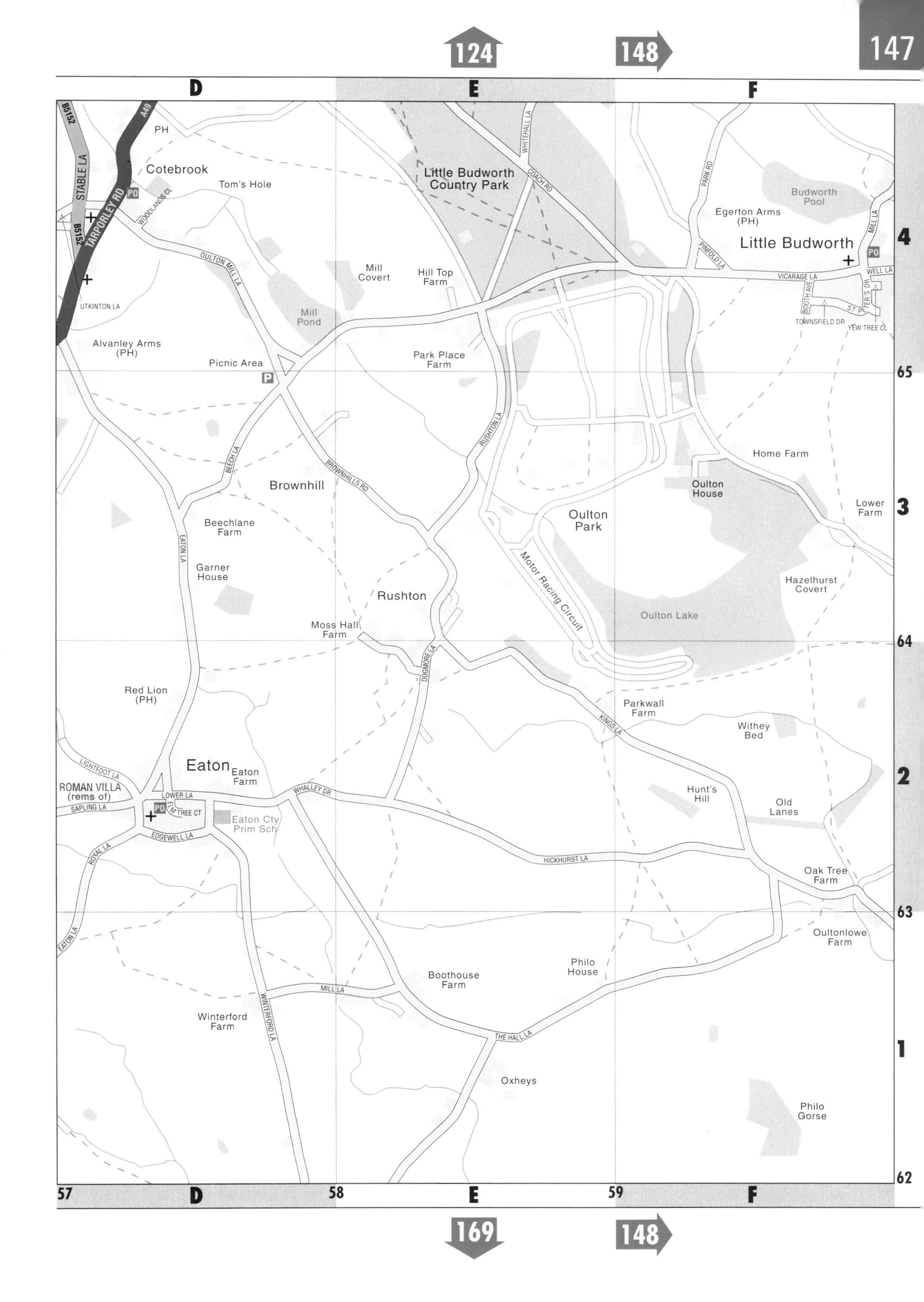

D   E   F

PH

Cotebrook

Tom's Hole

Little Budworth
Country Park

WHITEHALL LA

COACH RD

PARK RD

Budworth
Pool

PINFOLD LA

Egerton Arms
(PH)

MILL LA

STABLE LA

B5152

A49

TARPORLEY RD

B5152

WOODLANDS CL

OULTON MILL LA

UTKINTON LA

Little Budworth

4

VICARAGE LA

WELL LA

BOOTH AVE

ST PETER'S DR

Mill
Covert

Hill Top
Farm

TOWNSFIELD DR

YEW TREE CL

Alvanley Arms
(PH)

Picnic Area

Mill
Pond

Park Place
Farm

RUSHTON LA

65

Home Farm

Lower
Farm

3

BEECH LA

Brownhill

BROWNHILLS RD

Oulton
House

Oulton
Park

EATON LA

Beechlane
Farm

Garner
House

Rushton

Moss Hall
Farm

DOGMORE LA

Motor Racing Circuit

Hazelhurst
Covert

Oulton Lake

64

Red Lion
(PH)

Parkwall
Farm

KINGS LA

Withey
Bed

2

LIGHTFOOT LA

Eaton

Eaton
Farm

WHALLEY DR

Hunt's
Hill

Old
Lanes

ROMAN VILLA
(rems of)

LOWER LA

ELM TREE CT

PO

SAPLING LA

EDGEWELL LA

Eaton Cty
Prim Sch

HICKHURST LA

Oak Tree
Farm

ROYAL LA

EATON LA

63

Oultonlowe
Farm

Philo
House

Boothouse
Farm

WINTERFORD LA

MILL LA

Winterford
Farm

THE HALL LA

1

Oxheys

Philo
Gorse

62

57   D   58   E   59   F

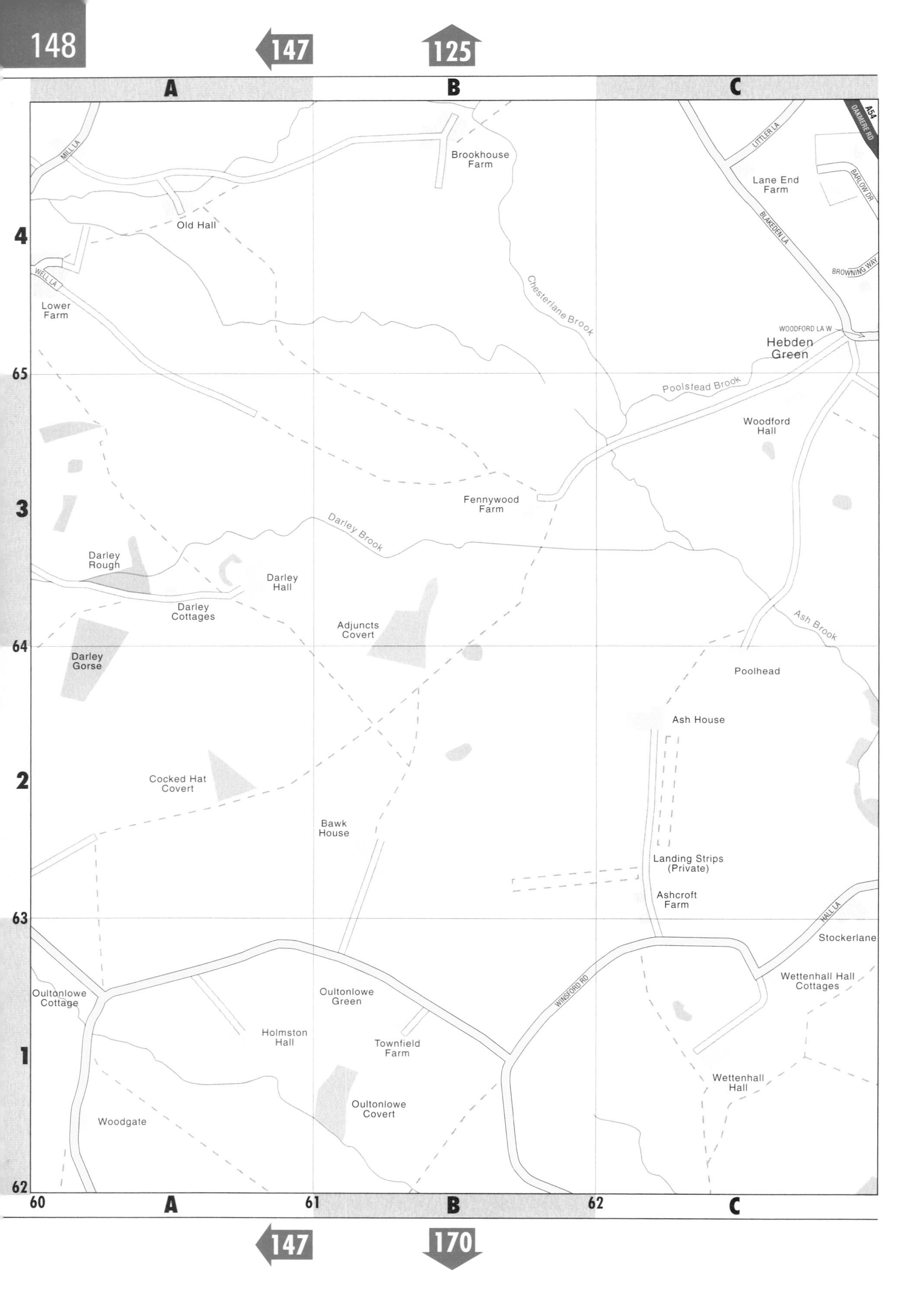
147
125
A
B
C
MILL LA
Brookhouse Farm
LITTLER LA
A54
OAKMERE RD
Lane End Farm
BARLOW DR
Old Hall
BLAKEDEN LA
4
WELL LA
BROWNING WAY
Lower Farm
Chesterlane Brook
WOODFORD LA W
Hebden Green
65
Poolstead Brook
Woodford Hall
3
Fennywood Farm
Darley Brook
Darley Rough
Darley Hall
Darley Cottages
Adjuncts Covert
Ash Brook
64
Darley Gorse
Poolhead
Ash House
2
Cocked Hat Covert
Bawk House
Landing Strips (Private)
Ashcroft Farm
63
HALL LA
Stockerlane
Oultonlowe Cottage
Oultonlowe Green
WINSFORD RD
Wettenhall Hall Cottages
1
Holmston Hall
Townfield Farm
Wettenhall Hall
Oultonlowe Covert
Woodgate
62
60
61
62
147
170

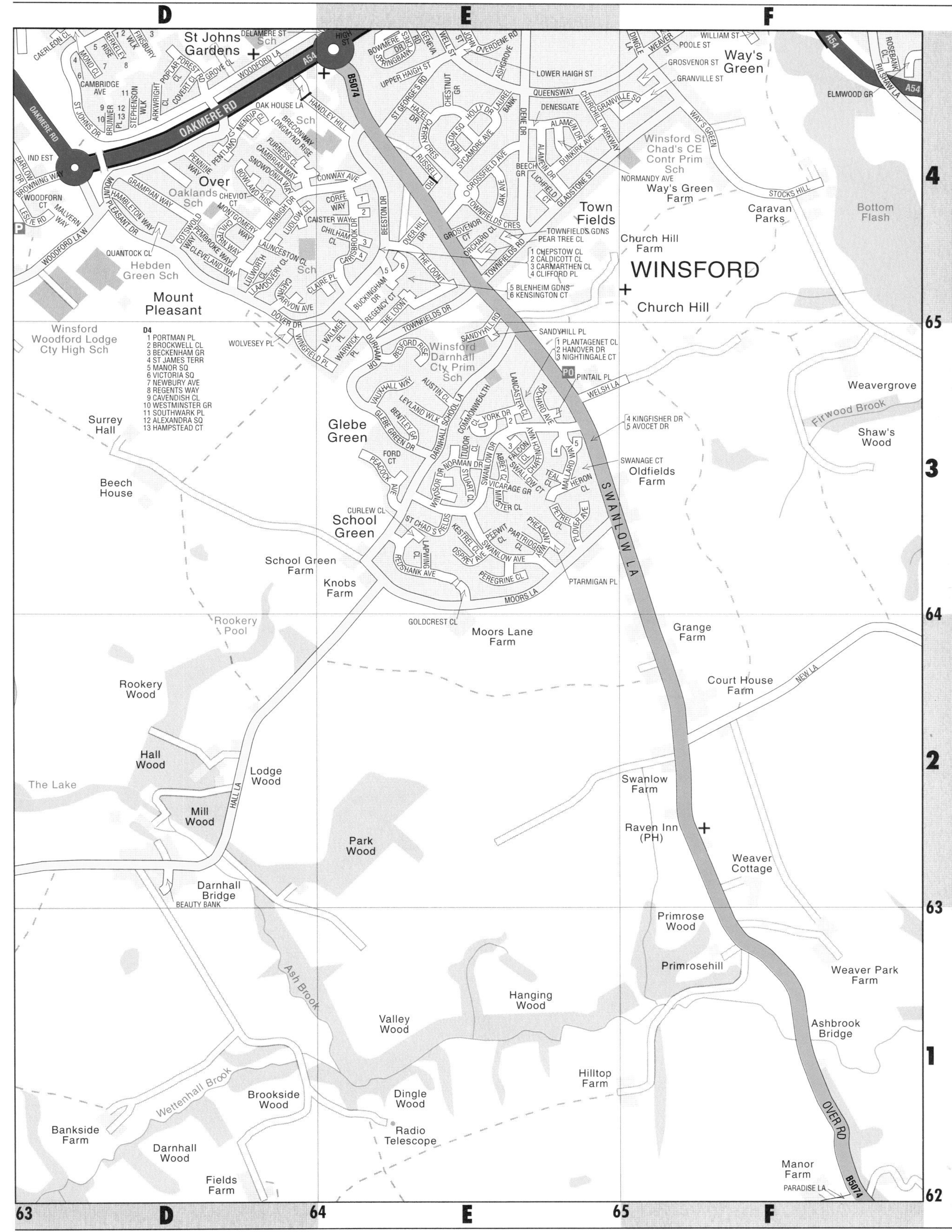

St Johns Gardens

OAKMERE RD

IND EST

Over

Oaklands Sch

Mount Pleasant

Winsford Woodford Lodge Cty High Sch

D4
1 PORTMAN PL
2 BROCKWELL CL
3 BECKENHAM GR
4 ST JAMES TERR
5 MANOR SQ
6 VICTORIA SQ
7 NEWBURY AVE
8 REGENTS WAY
9 CAVENDISH CL
10 WESTMINSTER GR
11 SOUTHWARK PL
12 ALEXANDRA SQ
13 HAMPSTEAD CT

Hebden Green Sch

Surrey Hall

Beech House

Glebe Green

School Green

School Green Farm

Knobs Farm

Town Fields

1 CHEPSTOW CL
2 CALDICOTT CL
3 CARMARTHEN CT
4 CLIFFORD PL
5 BLENHEIM GDNS
6 KENSINGTON CT

Winsford Darnhall Cty Prim Sch

1 PLANTAGENET CL
2 HANOVER DR
3 NIGHTINGALE CT

4 KINGFISHER DR
5 AVOCET DR

WINSFORD

Church Hill

Way's Green

Winsford St Chad's CE Contr Prim Sch

Way's Green Farm

Caravan Parks

Bottom Flash

Weavergrove

Shaw's Wood

Oldfields Farm

Moors Lane Farm

Rookery Pool

Rookery Wood

Hall Wood

Lodge Wood

The Lake

Mill Wood

Park Wood

Darnhall Bridge
BEAUTY BANK

Bankside Farm

Darnhall Wood

Brookside Wood

Fields Farm

Dingle Wood

Radio Telescope

Valley Wood

Hanging Wood

Hilltop Farm

Grange Farm

Court House Farm

Swanlow Farm

Raven Inn (PH)

Weaver Cottage

Primrose Wood

Primrosehill

Weaver Park Farm

Ashbrook Bridge

Manor Farm
PARADISE LA

SWANLOW LA

OVER RD

Firwood Brook

149
127

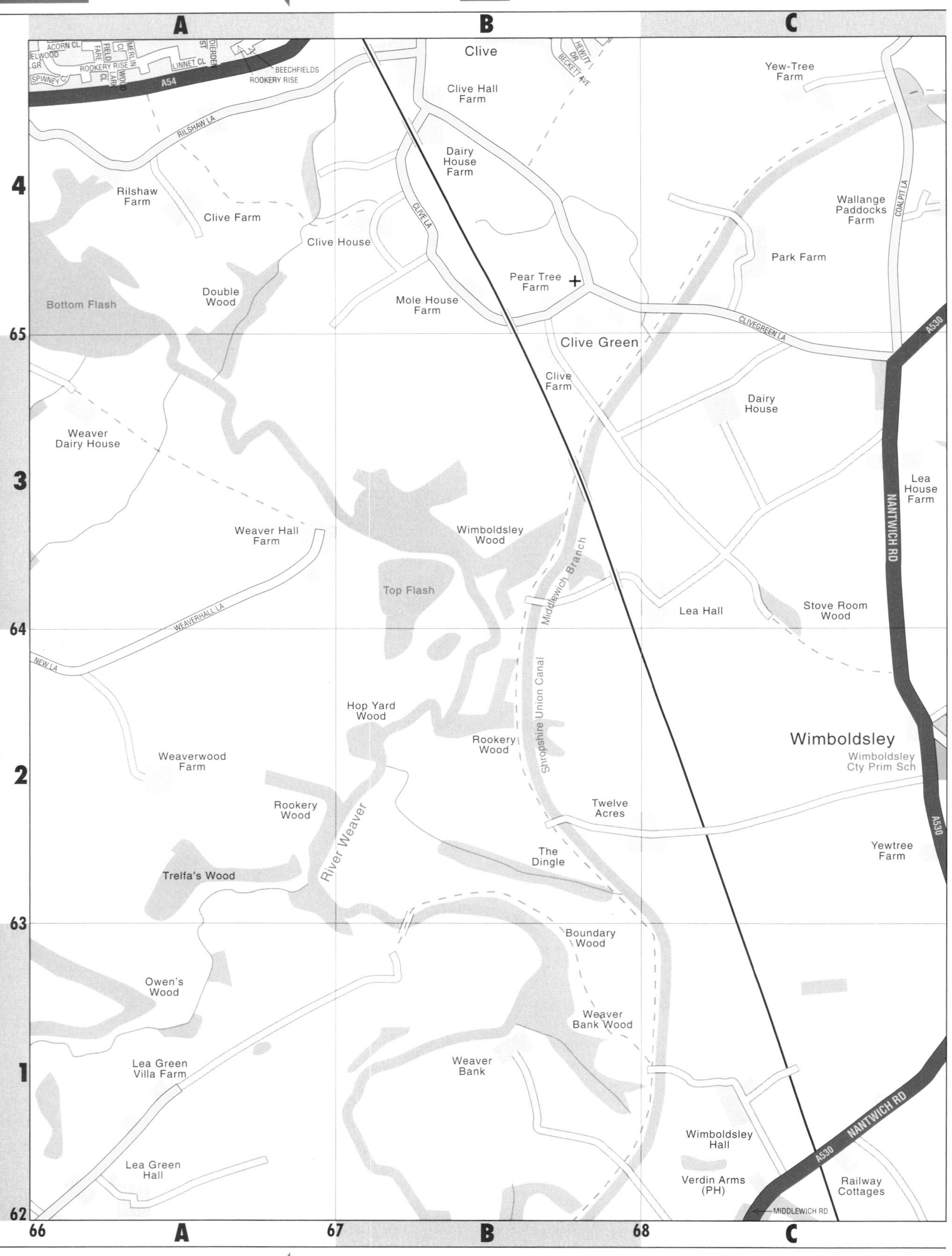

Clive

A54

ACORN CL
ELWOOD GR
MERLIN CL
ROOKERY RISE
FIELD FARE GL
LARK
SPINNEY CL
LINNET CL
DIE RDEN ST
BEECHFIELDS
ROOKERY RISE

RILSHAW LA

Rilshaw Farm

Clive Farm

Clive House

Bottom Flash

Double Wood

Clive Hall Farm

Dairy House Farm

CLIVE LA

HEWITT DR
BECKETT AVE

Mole House Farm

Pear Tree Farm

Clive Green

Clive Farm

Yew-Tree Farm

Wallange Paddocks Farm

Park Farm

CLIVEGREEN LA

Dairy House

COLPITT LA

A530 NANTWICH RD

Lea House Farm

Weaver Dairy House

Weaver Hall Farm

WEAVERHALL LA

Wimboldsley Wood

Top Flash

Middlewich Branch

Lea Hall

Stove Room Wood

NEW LA

Weaverwood Farm

Hop Yard Wood

Rookery Wood

Shropshire Union Canal

Rookery Wood

River Weaver

Twelve Acres

Wimboldsley
Wimboldsley Cty Prim Sch

A530

Trelfa's Wood

The Dingle

Yewtree Farm

Owen's Wood

Boundary Wood

Weaver Bank Wood

Lea Green Villa Farm

Weaver Bank

Wimboldsley Hall

A530 NANTWICH RD

Lea Green Hall

Verdin Arms (PH)

Railway Cottages

MIDDLEWICH RD

65
4
3
64
2
63
1
62

66   A   67   B   68   C

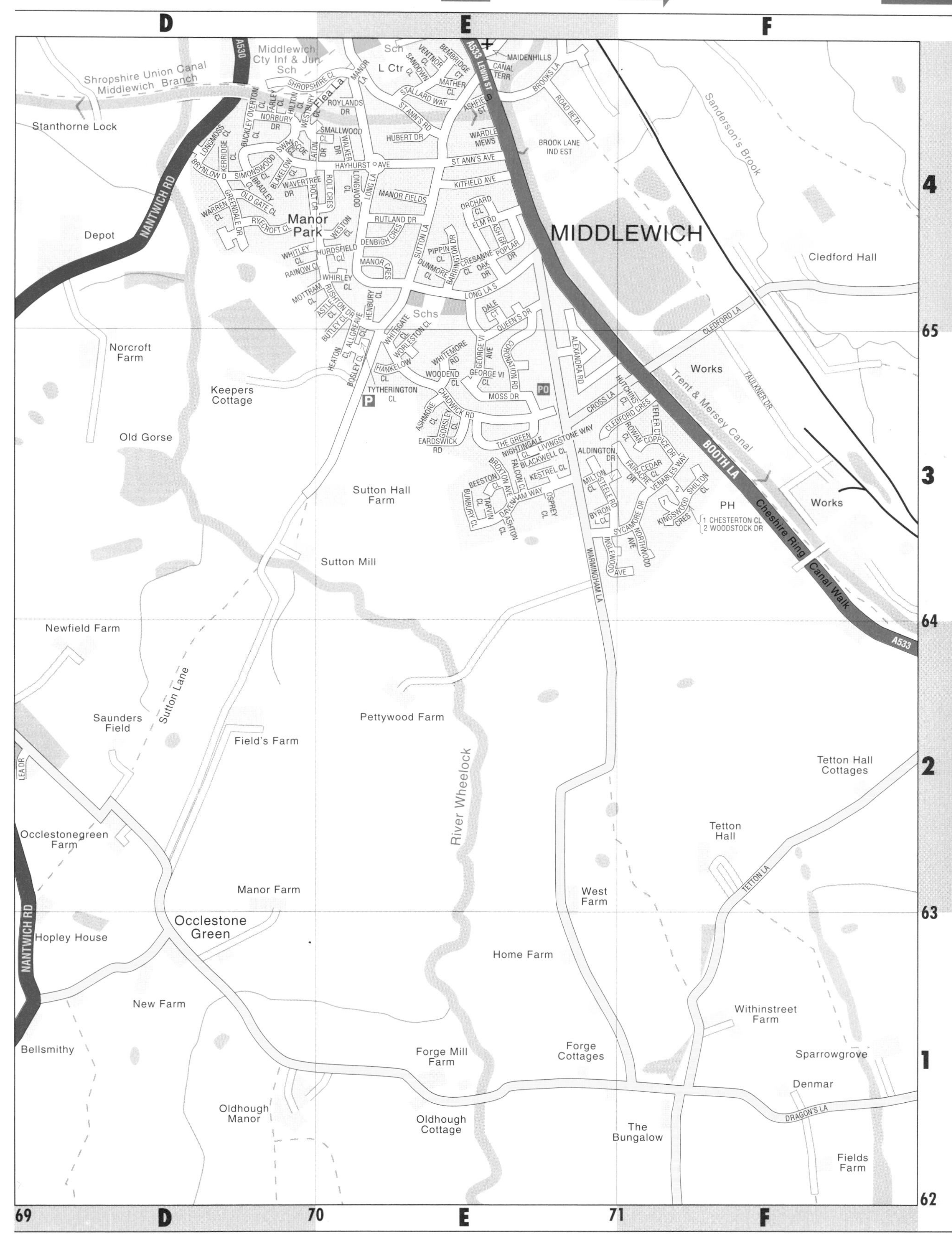

D
E
F

Shropshire Union Canal
Middlewich Branch

Middlewich
Cty Inf & Jun
Sch

Sch

Maidenhills

L Ctr

CANAL
TERR

BROOKS LA

Stanthorne Lock

NANTWICH RD

A530

SHROPSHIRE CL

FLEA LA

ROYLANDS DR

BUCKLEY OVERTON CL

FARLEY CL

MILTON CL

WESTON

NORBURY DR

LONGMOSS

KERRIDGE CL

BRYNLOW D

SIMONSWOOD

BRADLEY

BLAKELOW

SWANAGE

WAVERTREE DR

ROFT CRES

OLD GATE CL

WARREN CL

GREENDALE DR

RYCROFT CL

LONGWOOD CL

WESTON

MANOR PARK

SMALLWOOD CL

WALKER

HAYHURST AVE

HUBERT DR

ST ANN'S RD

ST ANN'S AVE

MATHER CL

ASHFIELD ST

A533 LEWIN ST

VENTNOR CT

SANDOW CL

BEMBRIDGE CT

GALLARD WAY

WARDLE MEWS

BROOK LANE IND EST

Depot

Norcroft
Farm

Keepers
Cottage

Old Gorse

WHITLEY CL

HURDSFIELD CL

RAINOW CL

WHIRLEY

MOTTRAM CL

RUSHTON DR

ASTLE CL

BUTLEY CL

HEATON CL

BOSLEY CL

ALLGREAVE

HENBURY CL

WORLESTON CL

WITTGATE CL

HANKELOW CL

WESTON

MANOR CRES

SUTTON LA

PIPPIN CL

DENBIGH CRES

DUNMORE CL

BARRINGTON DR

MANOR FIELDS

KITFIELD AVE

RUTLAND DR

ORCHARD CL

ELM RD

CRESANNE CL

OAK DR

POPLAR DR

FIRST GR RD

LONG LA

MIDDLEWICH

WHITEMORE CL

WOODEND CL

THE GREEN

GEORGE VI AVE

GEORGE CL

DALE CT

QUEEN'S DR

MOSS DR

LONG LA S

CORONATION DR

ALEXANDRA RD

CLEDFORD LA

Works

65

Cledford Hall

Sanderson's Brook

4

Tytherington
CL

P

Sutton Hall
Farm

Sutton Mill

ASHMORE CL

GOURSLEY CL

EARDSWICK RD

NIGHTINGALE

FALCON CL

BLACKWELL CL

BEESTON CL

MARVIN CL

BUNBURY CL

KESTREL CL

DAVENHAM WAY

DASHTON

OSPREY

LIVINGSTONE WAY

ALDINGTON DR

MILTON STEELE

BYRON CL

CLEDFORD CRES

ROWAN DR

COPPICE DR

CEDAR

TEFLER CL

SYCAMORE DR

NORTHWOOD AVE

INGLEWOOD

WARMINGHAM LA

VENMILL WAY

KINGSWOOD SHILTON CRES

1 CHESTERTON CL
2 WOODSTOCK DR

PH

Cheshire Ring

Canal Walk

BOOTH LA

Trent & Mersey Canal

FAULKNER DR

Works

3

64

A533

Newfield Farm

Saunders
Field

Sutton Lane

Field's Farm

LEA DR

Pettywood Farm

River Wheelock

Tetton Hall
Cottages

2

Occlestonegreen
Farm

Manor Farm

Tetton
Hall

TETTON LA

Occlestone
Green

NANTWICH RD

Hopley House

West
Farm

63

New Farm

Home Farm

Withinstreet
Farm

Bellsmithy

Forge Mill
Farm

Forge
Cottages

Sparrowgrove

Denmar

1

Oldhough
Manor

Oldhough
Cottage

The
Bungalow

DRAGON'S LA

Fields
Farm

62

151
129

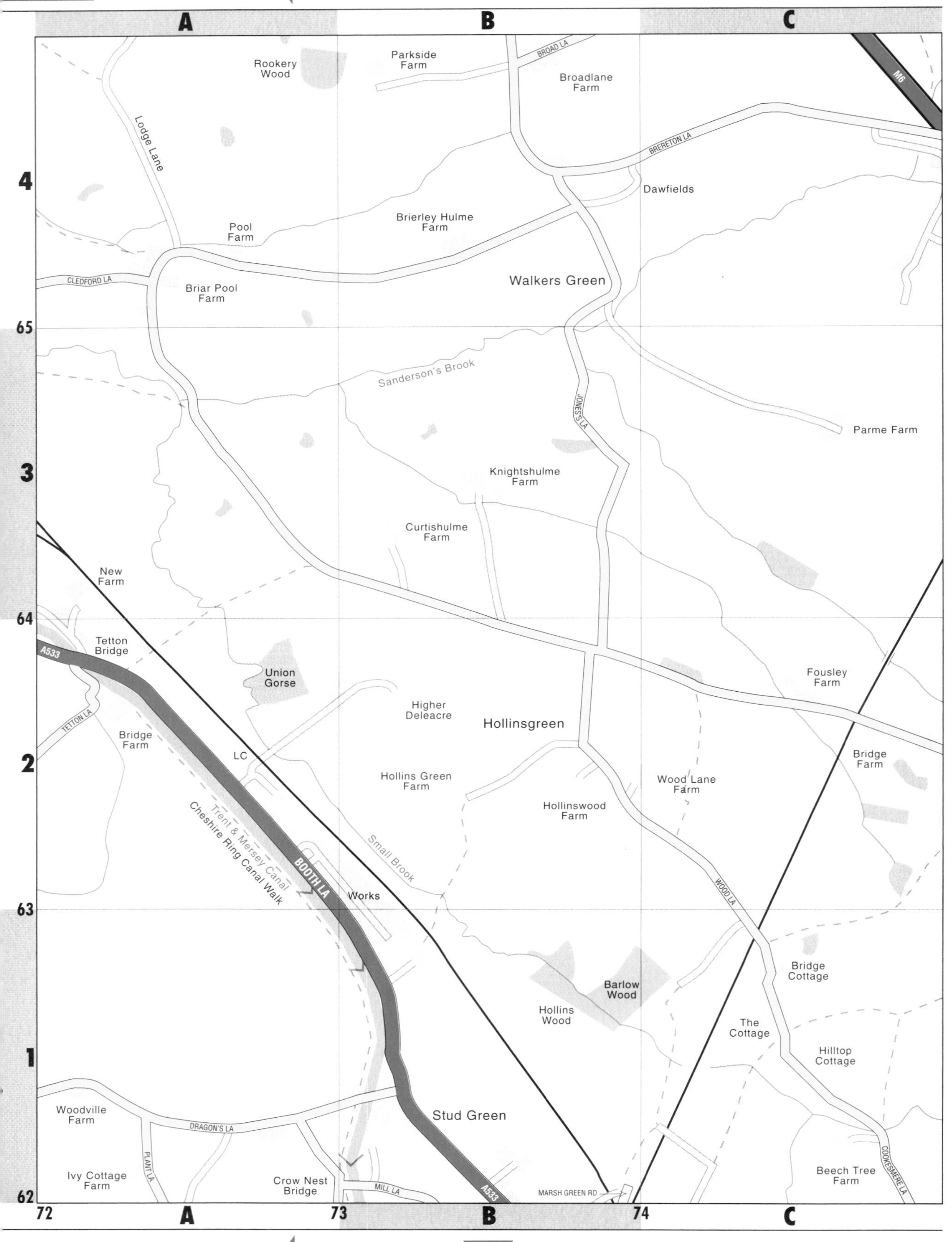
A
B
C
Rookery Wood
Parkside Farm
BROAD LA
Broadlane Farm
M6
Lodge Lane
BRERETON LA
Dawfields
Pool Farm
Brierley Hulme Farm
CLEDFORD LA
Briar Pool Farm
Walkers Green
Sanderson's Brook
JONES'S LA
Parme Farm
Knightshulme Farm
Curtishulme Farm
New Farm
Tetton Bridge
A533
Union Gorse
Fousley Farm
Higher Deleacre
TETTON LA
Bridge Farm
Hollinsgreen
LC
Bridge Farm
Hollins Green Farm
Wood Lane Farm
Hollinswood Farm
Trent & Mersey Canal
Cheshire Ring Canal Walk
Small Brook
BOOTH LA
Works
WOOD LA
Bridge Cottage
Barlow Wood
Hollins Wood
The Cottage
Hilltop Cottage
Woodville Farm
DRAGON'S LA
Stud Green
PLANT LA
Ivy Cottage Farm
Crow Nest Bridge
MILL LA
A533
MARSH GREEN RD
Beech Tree Farm
COOKESMERE LA
4
65
3
64
2
63
1
62
72
73
74

151
174

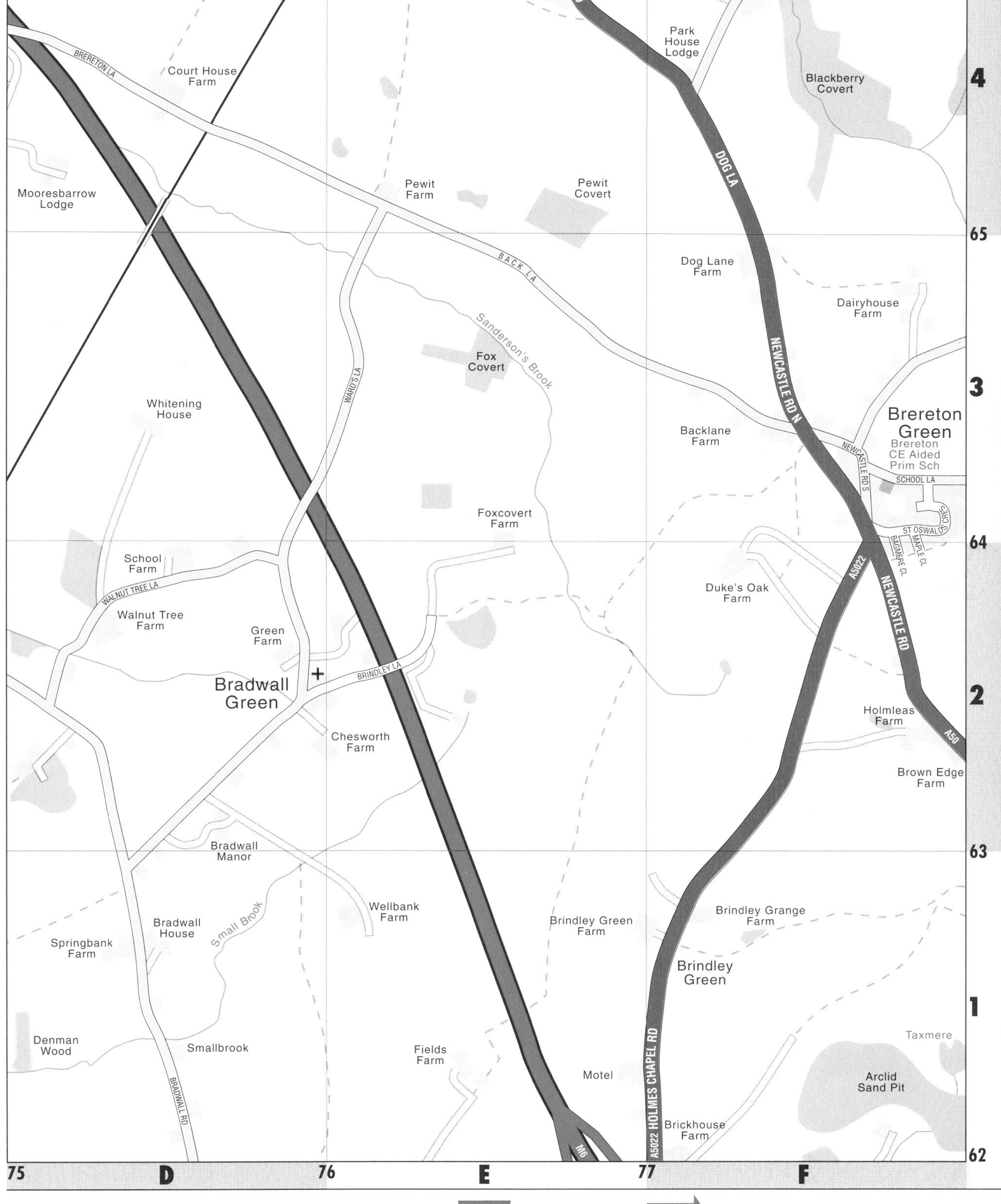

D

Allan Brook
Farm

A50 LONDON RD

MILL LA

Brereton
Pool

Court House
Farm

BRERETON LA

Park
House
Lodge

DOG LA

Blackberry
Covert

4

Mooresbarrow
Lodge

Pewit
Farm

Pewit
Covert

BACK LA

65

Dog Lane
Farm

Dairyhouse
Farm

Sanderson's Brook

Fox
Covert

WARD'S LA

NEWCASTLE RD N

Brereton
Green

Whitening
House

Foxcovert
Farm

Backlane
Farm

3

Brereton
CE Aided
Prim Sch

NEWCASTLE RD S

SCHOOL LA

School
Farm

WALNUT TREE LA

ST OSWALD'S

MAPLE CL.

ORCHS.

Walnut Tree
Farm

Green
Farm

BRINDLEY LA

Duke's Oak
Farm

A5022

BACKMERE CL.

64

Bradwall
Green

+

Chesworth
Farm

NEWCASTLE RD

Holmleas
Farm

2

A50

Brown Edge
Farm

Bradwall
Manor

63

Springbank
Farm

Bradwall
House

Small Brook

Wellbank
Farm

Brindley Green
Farm

Brindley Grange
Farm

Denman
Wood

Smallbrook

BRADWALL RD

Fields
Farm

Brindley
Green

A5022 HOLMES CHAPEL RD

Taxmere

1

Motel

M6

Brickhouse
Farm

Arclid
Sand Pit

62

153
131

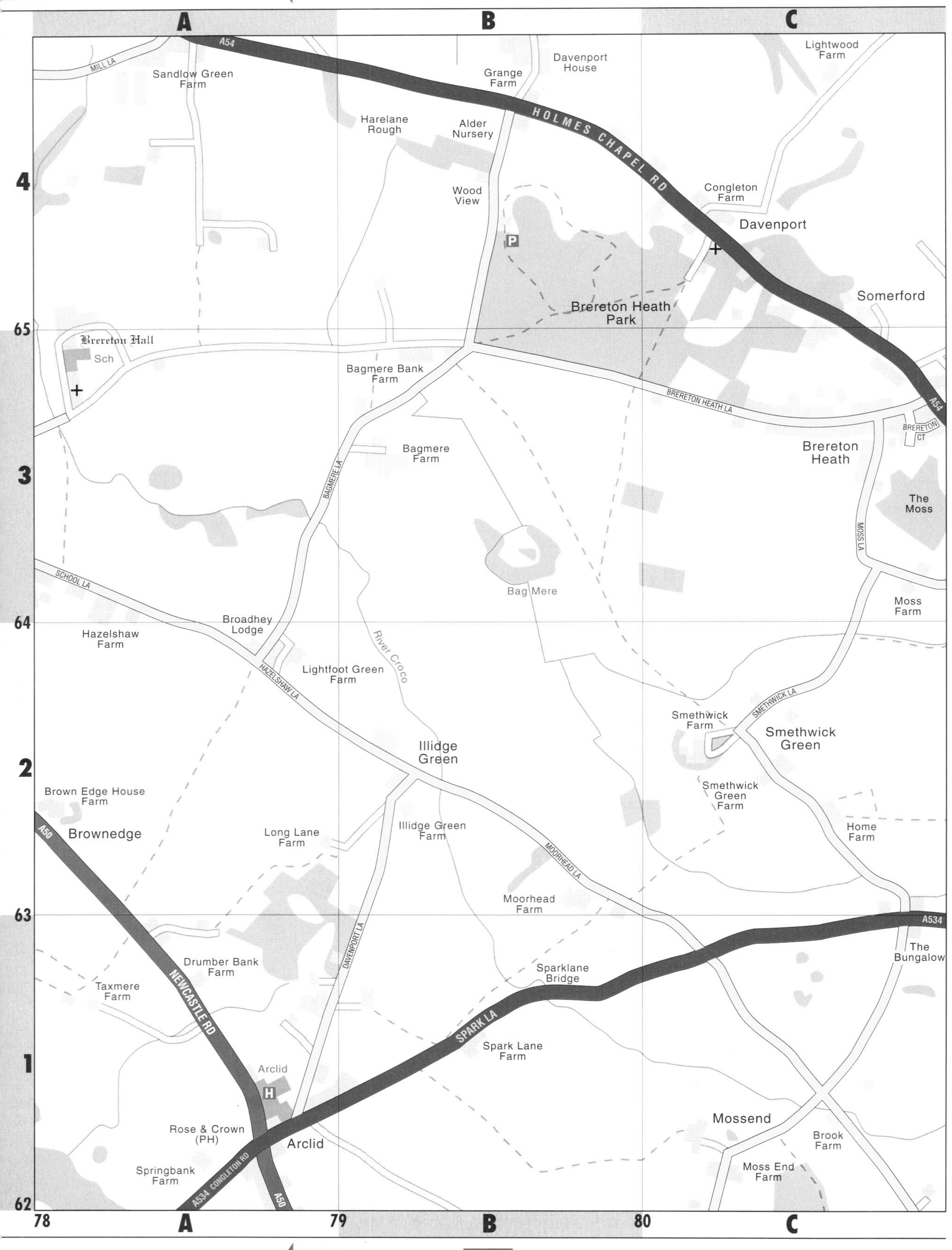
A
B
C
A54
MILL LA
Sandlow Green Farm
Grange Farm
Davenport House
Lightwood Farm
HOLMES CHAPEL RD
Harelane Rough
Alder Nursery
Wood View
Congleton Farm
Davenport
Brereton Heath Park
Somerford
Brereton Hall
Sch
Bagmere Bank Farm
BRERETON HEATH LA
A54
BRERETON CT
Brereton Heath
Bagmere Farm
BAGMERE LA
The Moss
MOSS LA
SCHOOL LA
Bag Mere
Moss Farm
Broadhey Lodge
Hazelshaw Farm
River Croco
Lightfoot Green Farm
HAZELSHAW LA
SMETHWICK LA
Smethwick Farm
Smethwick Green
Illidge Green
Brown Edge House Farm
Smethwick Green Farm
A50
Brownedge
Long Lane Farm
Illidge Green Farm
Home Farm
MOORHEAD LA
Moorhead Farm
A534
DAVENPORT LA
The Bungalow
Drumber Bank Farm
Sparklane Bridge
Taxmere Farm
NEWCASTLE RD
SPARK LA
Spark Lane Farm
Arclid
H
Mossend
Brook Farm
Rose & Crown (PH)
Arclid
CONGLETON RD
A534
Springbank Farm
Moss End Farm
A50
4
65
3
64
2
63
1
62
78
79
80

153
176

132
156

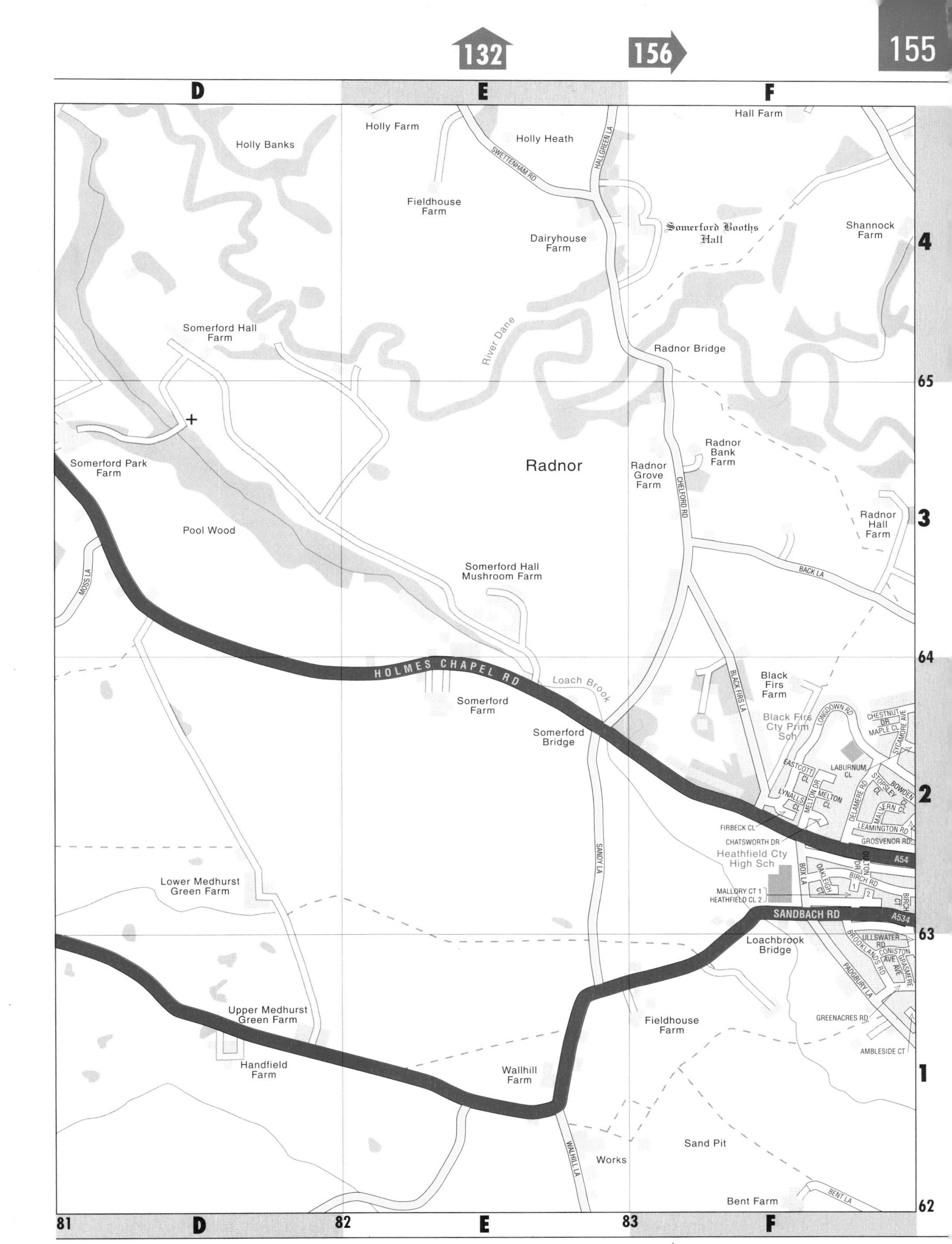
D
E
F
Holly Farm
Holly Banks
Holly Heath
Hall Farm
SWETTENHAM RD
HALLGREEN LA
Fieldhouse Farm
Somerford Booths Hall
Shannock Farm
Dairyhouse Farm
4
River Dane
Somerford Hall Farm
Radnor Bridge
65
Somerford Park Farm
Radnor
Radnor Bank Farm
Radnor Grove Farm
CHELFORD RD
Radnor Hall Farm
3
Pool Wood
MOSS LA
Somerford Hall Mushroom Farm
BACK LA
HOLMES CHAPEL RD
Loach Brook
64
Somerford Farm
BLACK FIRS LA
Black Firs Farm
Black Firs Cty Prim Sch
LONGDOWN RD
CHESTNUT DR
MAPLE CL
SYCAMORE AVE
Somerford Bridge
EASTCOTT CL
LABURNUM CL
LYNALLS CL
MELTON DR
MELTON CL
DELAMERE RD
STOPSLEY CL
BOWDEN CL
MALVERN CL
2
FIRBECK CL
LEAMINGTON RD
CHATSWORTH DR
GROSVENOR RD
Heathfield Cty High Sch
SANDY LA
A54
Lower Medhurst Green Farm
BOX LA
OAKLEIGH CT
BIRCH RD
MALLORY CT 1
HEATHFIELD CL 2
SANDBACH RD
A534
63
Loachbrook Bridge
ULLSWATER RD
BROOKLANDS RD
CONISTON AVE
GRASMERE AVE
PADGBURY LA
GREENACRES RD
Upper Medhurst Green Farm
Fieldhouse Farm
AMBLESIDE CT
Handfield Farm
Wallhill Farm
1
Sand Pit
WALHILL LA
Works
BENT LA
Bent Farm
62
81
D
82
E
83
F

177
156

155
133

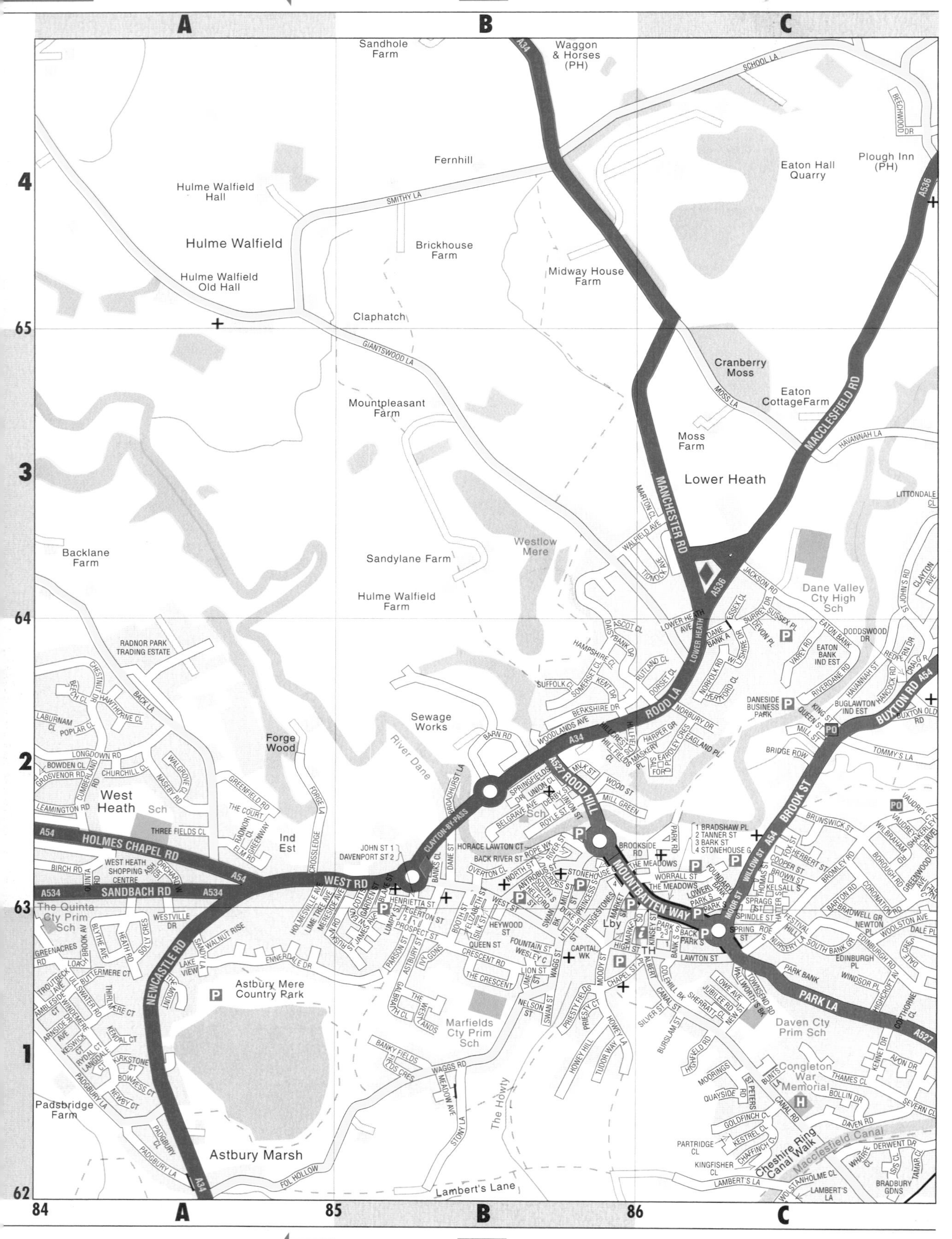
A
B
C
4
3
2
1
65
64
63
62
84
85
86
Sandhole Farm
Waggon & Horses (PH)
SCHOOL LA
BEECHWOOD DR
Fernhill
Plough Inn (PH)
Eaton Hall Quarry
Hulme Walfield Hall
SMITHY LA
A536
A34
Hulme Walfield
Brickhouse Farm
Midway House Farm
Hulme Walfield Old Hall
Claphatch
GIANTSWOOD LA
Cranberry Moss
Eaton Cottage Farm
MACCLESFIELD RD
MOSS LA
Mountpleasant Farm
Moss Farm
HAVANNAH LA
Lower Heath
MANCHESTER RD
LITTONDALE CL
Backlane Farm
Westlow Mere
Sandylane Farm
Hulme Walfield Farm
Dane Valley Cty High Sch
RADNOR PARK TRADING ESTATE
EATON BANK IND EST
DANESIDE BUSINESS PARK
BUGLAWTON IND EST
BUXTON RD
Sewage Works
ROOD LA
Forge Wood
River Dane
BRIDGE ROW
TOMMY'S LA
West Heath
Sch
ROOD HILL
A527
A54
HOLMES CHAPEL RD
Ind Est
BROOK ST
WEST RD
CLAYTON-BY-PASS
A534
SANDBACH RD
MOUNTBATTEN WAY
The Quinta Cty Prim Sch
Lby
TH
NEWCASTLE RD
PARK LA
Astbury Mere Country Park
Marfields Cty Prim Sch
Daven Cty Prim Sch
Congleton War Memorial
Padsbridge Farm
The Howty
Astbury Marsh
Cheshire Ring Canal Walk
Macclesfield Canal
Lambert's Lane
FOL HOLLOW
LAMBERT'S LA

155
178

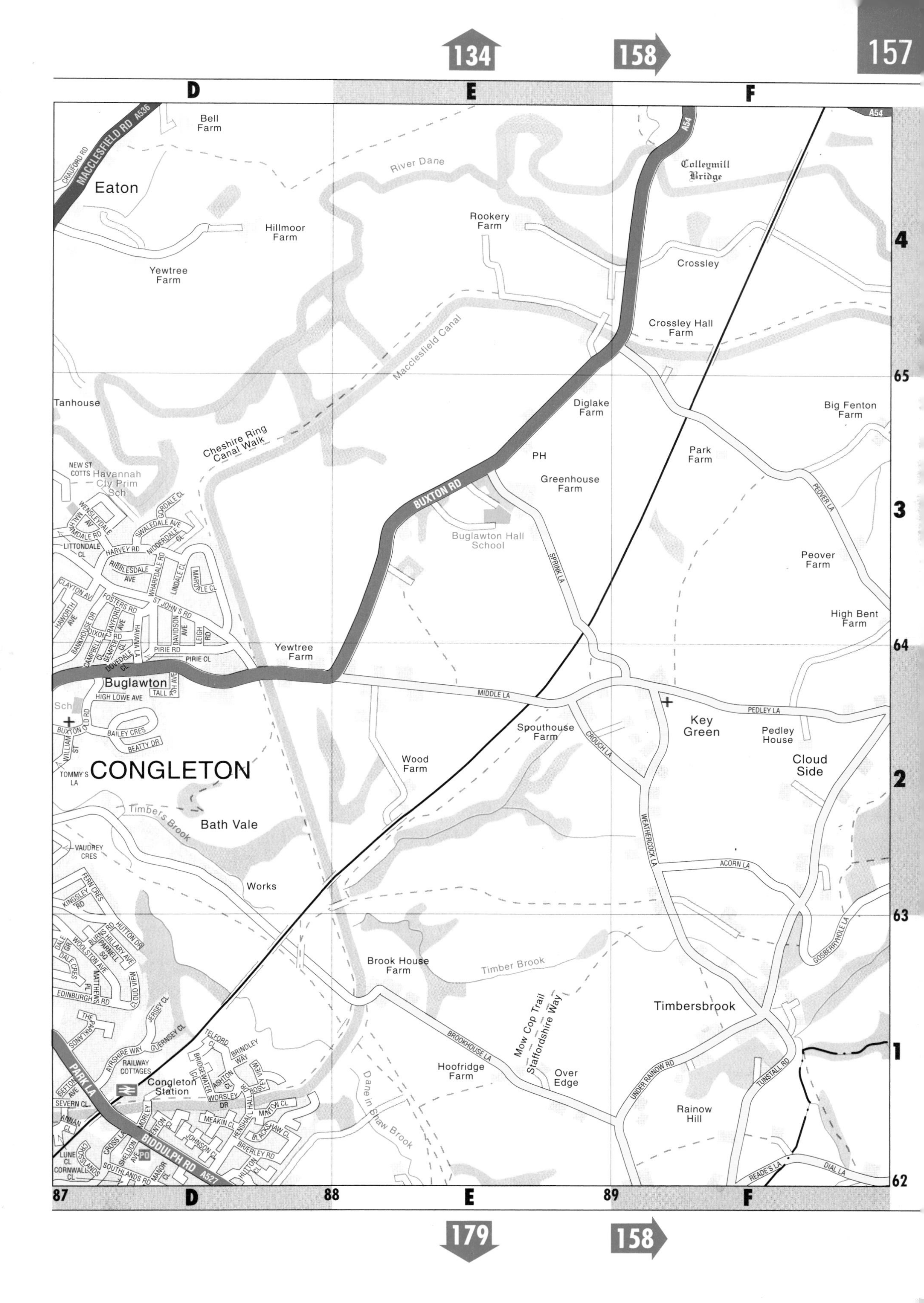
134
158
D
E
F
Bell Farm
MACCLESFIELD RD A536
CRAUFORD RD
Eaton
River Dane
A54
Colleymill Bridge
Hillmoor Farm
Rookery Farm
Yewtree Farm
Crossley
4
Macclesfield Canal
Crossley Hall Farm
65
Tanhouse
Diglake Farm
Big Fenton Farm
Cheshire Ring Canal Walk
PH
Park Farm
NEW ST COTTS
Havannah City Prim Sch
Greenhouse Farm
BUXTON RD
PEOVER LA
3
Buglawton Hall School
SPRINK LA
Peover Farm
High Bent Farm
Yewtree Farm
64
Buglawton
MIDDLE LA
PEDLEY LA
Spouthouse Farm
Key Green
Pedley House
CROUCH LA
Wood Farm
Cloud Side
CONGLETON
2
Timbers Brook
Bath Vale
WEATHERCOCK LA
VAUDREY CRES
ACORN LA
Works
63
GOSBERRYHOLE LA
Brook House Farm
Timber Brook
Mow Cop Trail
Staffordshire Way
Timbersbrook
BROOKHOUSE LA
1
Hoofridge Farm
Over Edge
UNDER RAINOW RD
TUNSTALL RD
Congleton Station
PARK LA
Dane in Shaw Brook
Rainow Hill
BIDDULPH RD A527
PO
READE'S LA
DIAL LA
62
87
88
89
179
158

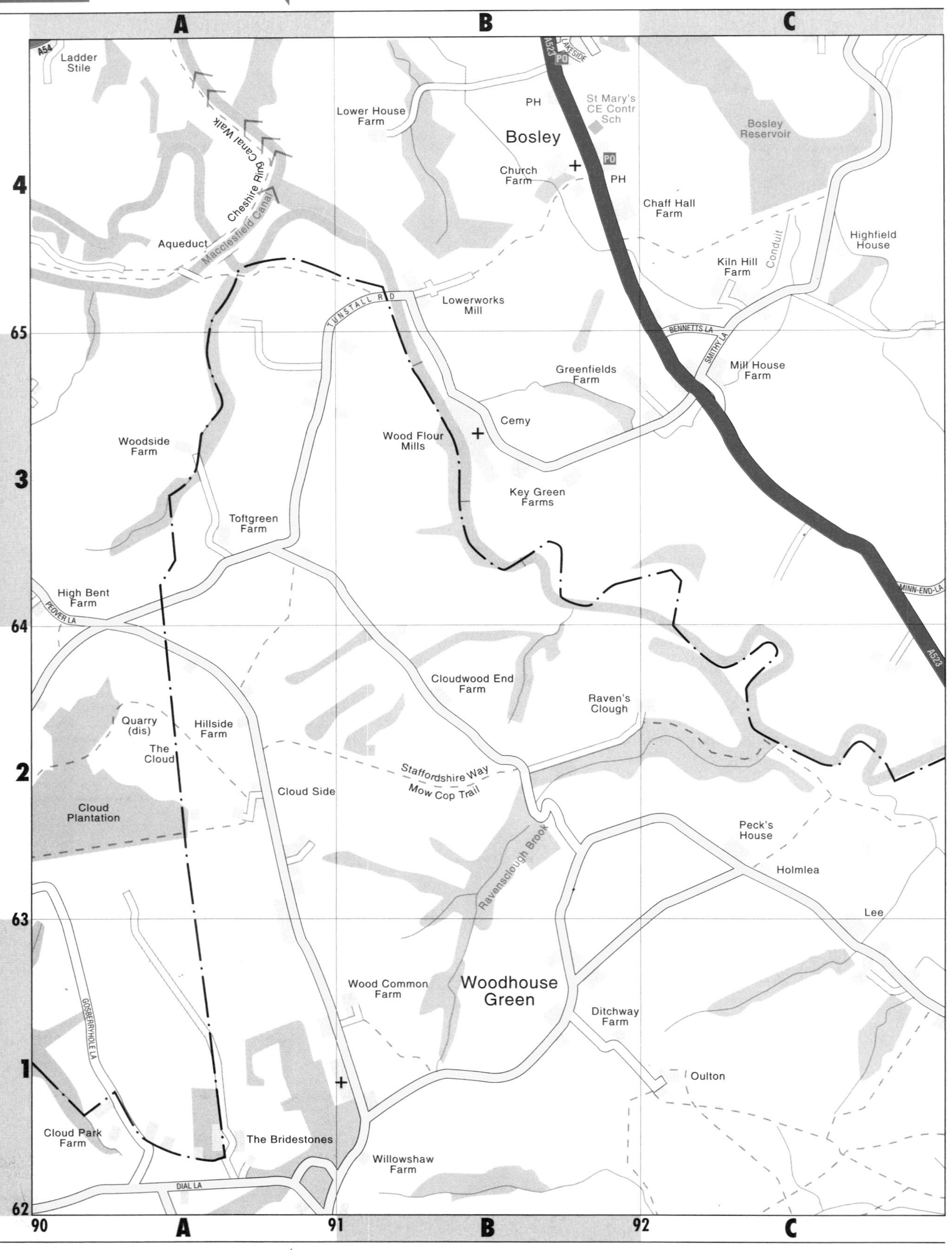

A54   Ladder Stile

Lower House Farm

PH

St Mary's CE Contr Sch

Bosley

Bosley Reservoir

Church Farm

PO

PH

Chaff Hall Farm

Cheshire Ring Canal Walk

Highfield House

Aqueduct

Kiln Hill Farm

Conduit

Macclesfield Canal

BENNETTS LA

SMITHY LA

Lowerworks Mill

TUNSTALL RD

Greenfields Farm

Mill House Farm

Woodside Farm

Wood Flour Mills

Cemy

Toftgreen Farm

Key Green Farms

MINN-END-LA

High Bent Farm

PEDLEY LA

A523

Cloudwood End Farm

Raven's Clough

Quarry (dis)

Hillside Farm

The Cloud

Cloud Side

Staffordshire Way

Mow Cop Trail

Peck's House

Cloud Plantation

Ravensclough Brook

Holmlea

Lee

Wood Common Farm

Woodhouse Green

Ditchway Farm

GOOSEBERRYHOLE LA

Oulton

Cloud Park Farm

The Bridestones

Willowshaw Farm

DIAL LA

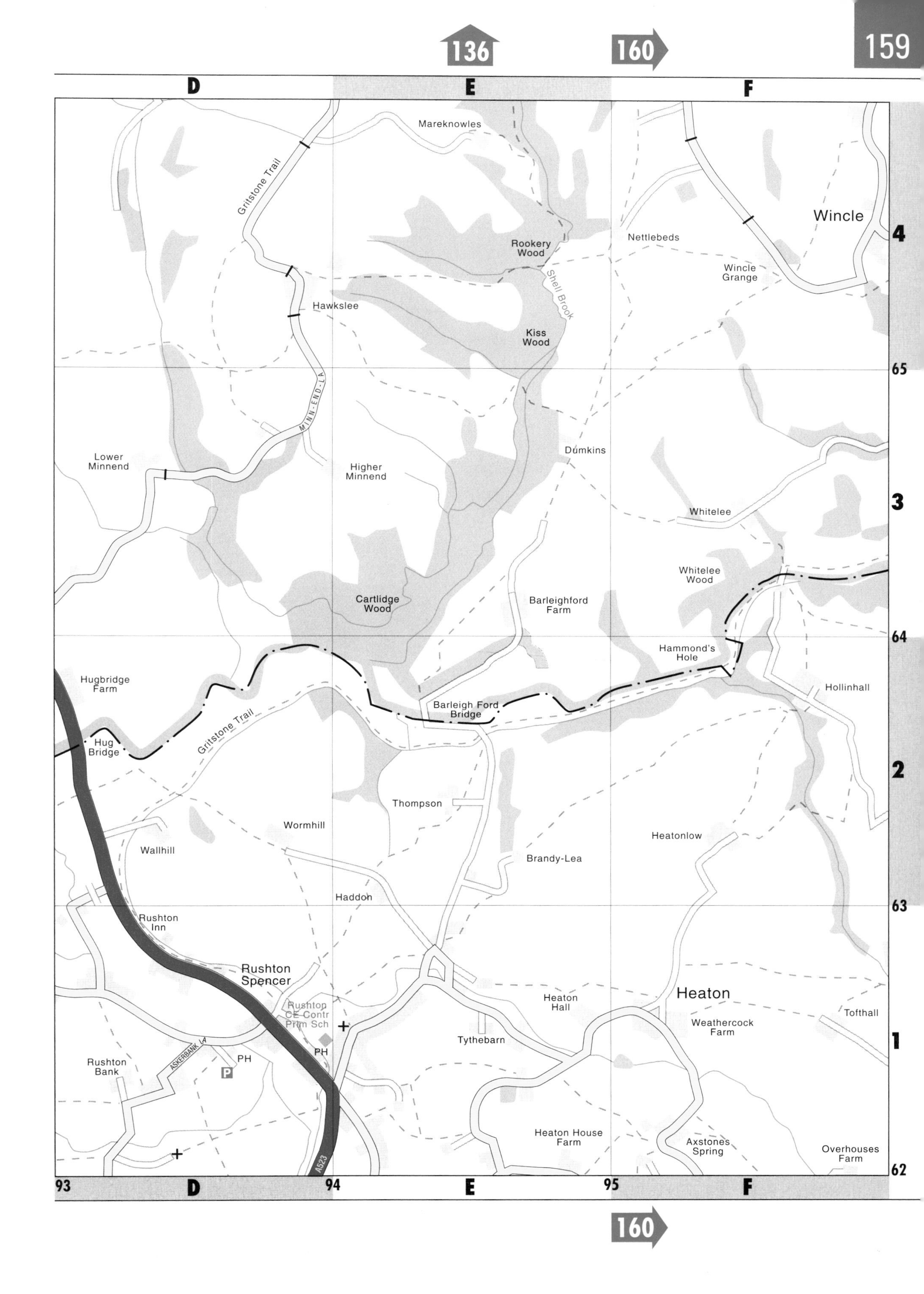

136
160

D E F

4
65
3
64
2
63
1
62

93 D 94 E 95 F

Mareknowles

Gritstone Trail

Rookery Wood

Nettlebeds

Wincle

Wincle Grange

Shell Brook

Hawkslee

Kiss Wood

Lower Minnend

MINN END LN

Higher Minnend

Dumkins

Whitelee

Whitelee Wood

Cartlidge Wood

Barleighford Farm

Hammond's Hole

Hollinhall

Gritstone Trail

Barleigh Ford Bridge

Hugbridge Farm

Hug Bridge

Thompson

Wormhill

Heatonlow

Wallhill

Brandy-Lea

Haddon

Rushton Inn

Rushton Spencer

Rushton CE Contr Prim Sch

Heaton Hall

Heaton

Weathercock Farm

Tofthall

PH

P

Tythebarn

Rushton Bank

PH

Heaton House Farm

Axstones Spring

Overhouses Farm

ASKERBANK LA

A523

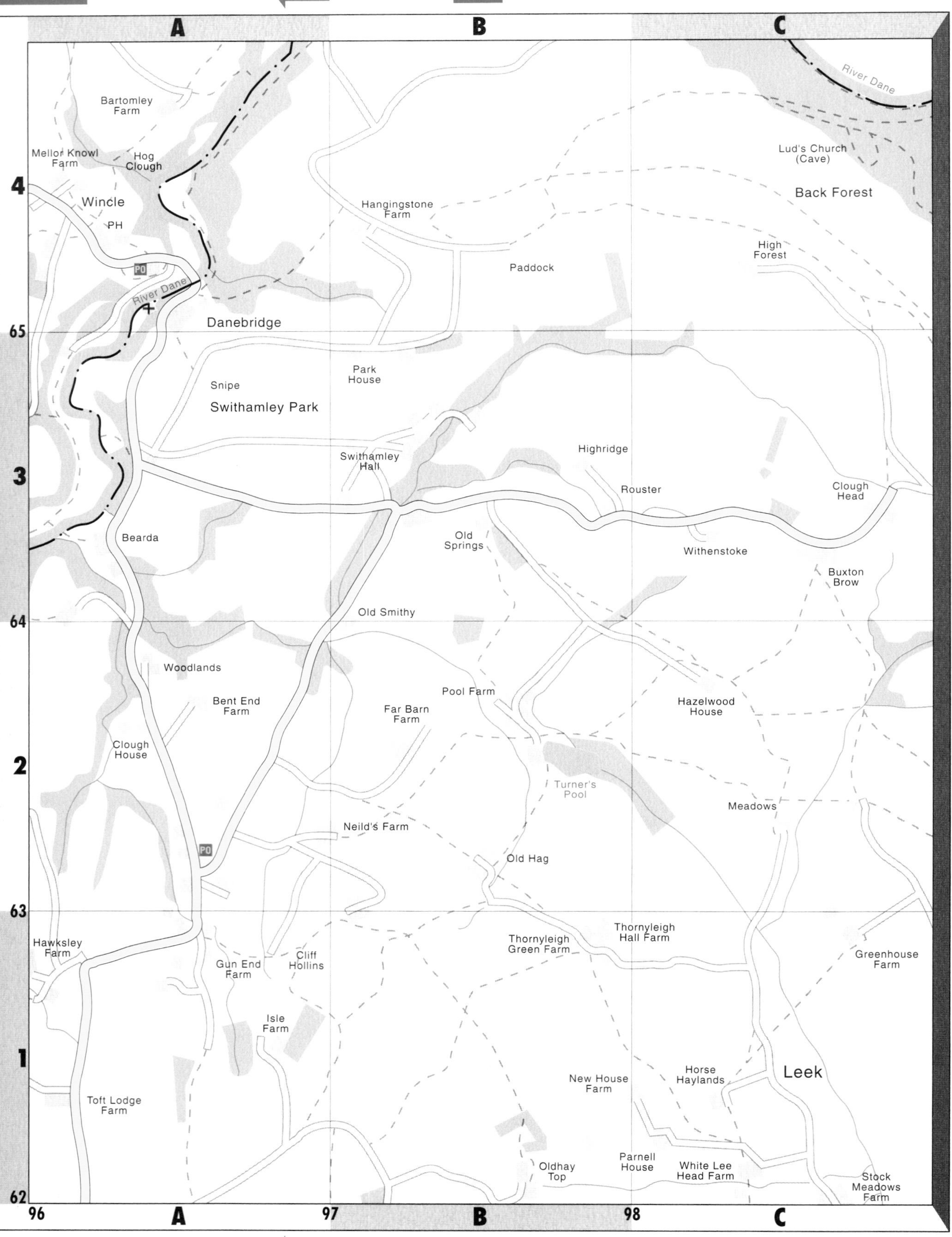

A B C

4

Bartomley
Farm

Mellor Knowl
Farm

Hog
Clough

Wincle

PH

PO

River Dane

Danebridge

65

Snipe

Swithamley Park

Park
House

Swithamley
Hall

Hangingstone
Farm

Paddock

Highridge

Rouster

River Dane

Lud's Church
(Cave)

Back Forest

High
Forest

Clough
Head

3

Bearda

Old Smithy

Old
Springs

Withenstoke

Buxton
Brow

64

Woodlands

Bent End
Farm

Far Barn
Farm

Pool Farm

Hazelwood
House

2

Clough
House

Turner's
Pool

Meadows

Neild's Farm

PO

Old Hag

63

Hawksley
Farm

Gun End
Farm

Cliff
Hollins

Thornyleigh
Green Farm

Thornyleigh
Hall Farm

Greenhouse
Farm

Isle
Farm

1

Toft Lodge
Farm

New House
Farm

Horse
Haylands

Leek

Oldhay
Top

Parnell
House

White Lee
Head Farm

Stock
Meadows
Farm

62

96

A

97

B

98

C

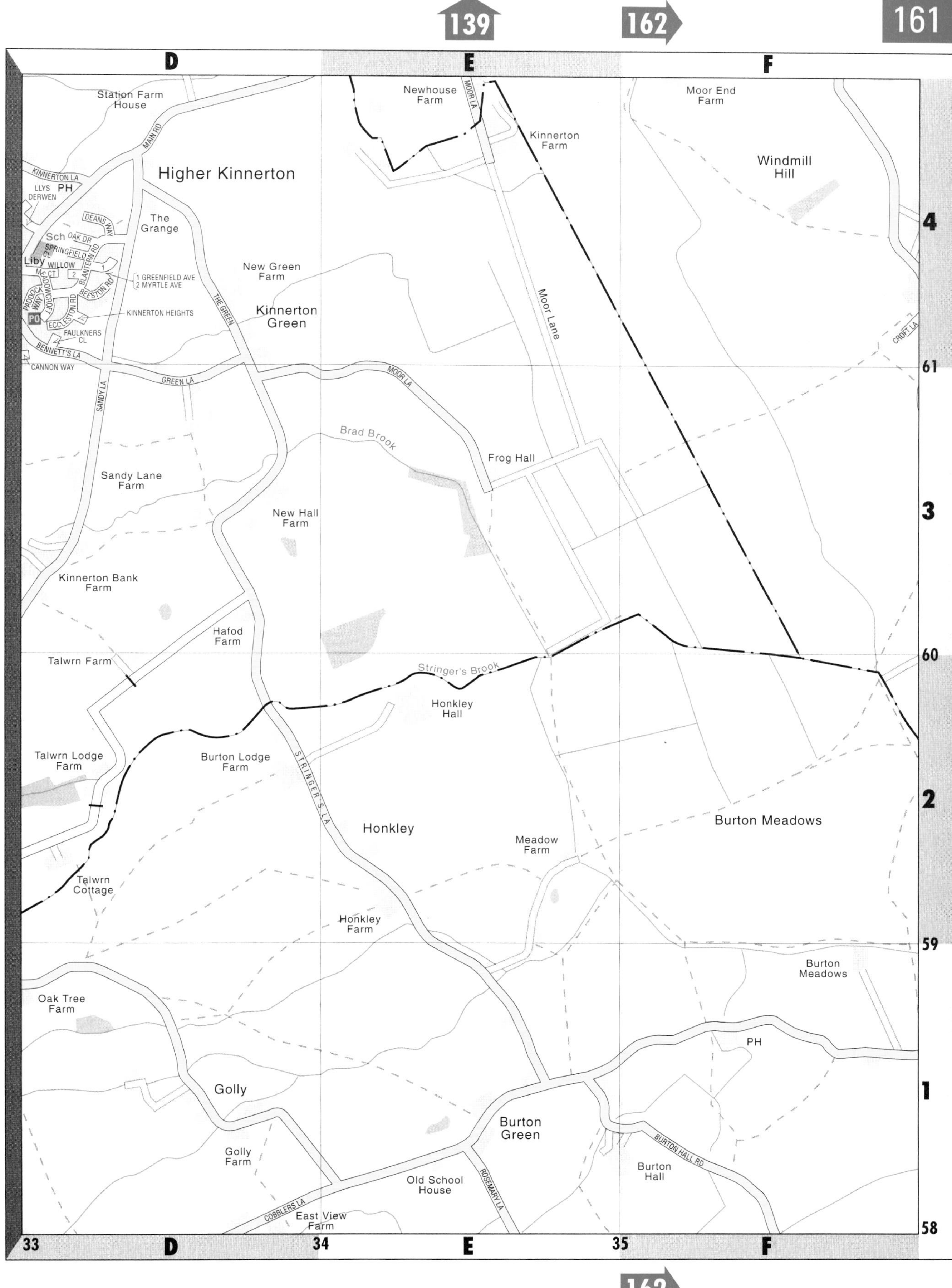

D   **E**   **F**

Station Farm House

Newhouse Farm

Moor End Farm

MAIN RD

KINNERTON LA

LLYS
DERWEN
PH

Higher Kinnerton

Kinnerton Farm

Windmill Hill

4

DEANS WAY

The Grange

Sch

OAK DR

Moor Lane

SPRINGFIELD CL

WILLOW

Liby

New Green Farm

MEADOWCROFT

BLANTERN RD

BEESTON RD

PADDOCK WAY

1 GREENFIELD AVE
2 MYRTLE AVE

CROFT LA

PO

ECCLESTON RD

FAULKNERS CL

Kinnerton Green

THE GREEN

KINNERTON HEIGHTS

BENNETT'S LA

61

CANNON WAY

GREEN LA

SANDY LA

MOOR LA

Brad Brook

Frog Hall

Sandy Lane Farm

New Hall Farm

3

Kinnerton Bank Farm

Hafod Farm

Stringer's Brook

60

Talwrn Farm

Honkley Hall

Talwrn Lodge Farm

Burton Lodge Farm

STRINGER'S LA

Honkley

Meadow Farm

Burton Meadows

2

Talwrn Cottage

Honkley Farm

59

Oak Tree Farm

Burton Meadows

PH

Golly

Burton Green

1

Golly Farm

BURTON HALL RD

Old School House

Burton Hall

ROSEMARY LA

COBBLERS LA

East View Farm

58

33   **D**   **34**   **E**   **35**   **F**

161
140

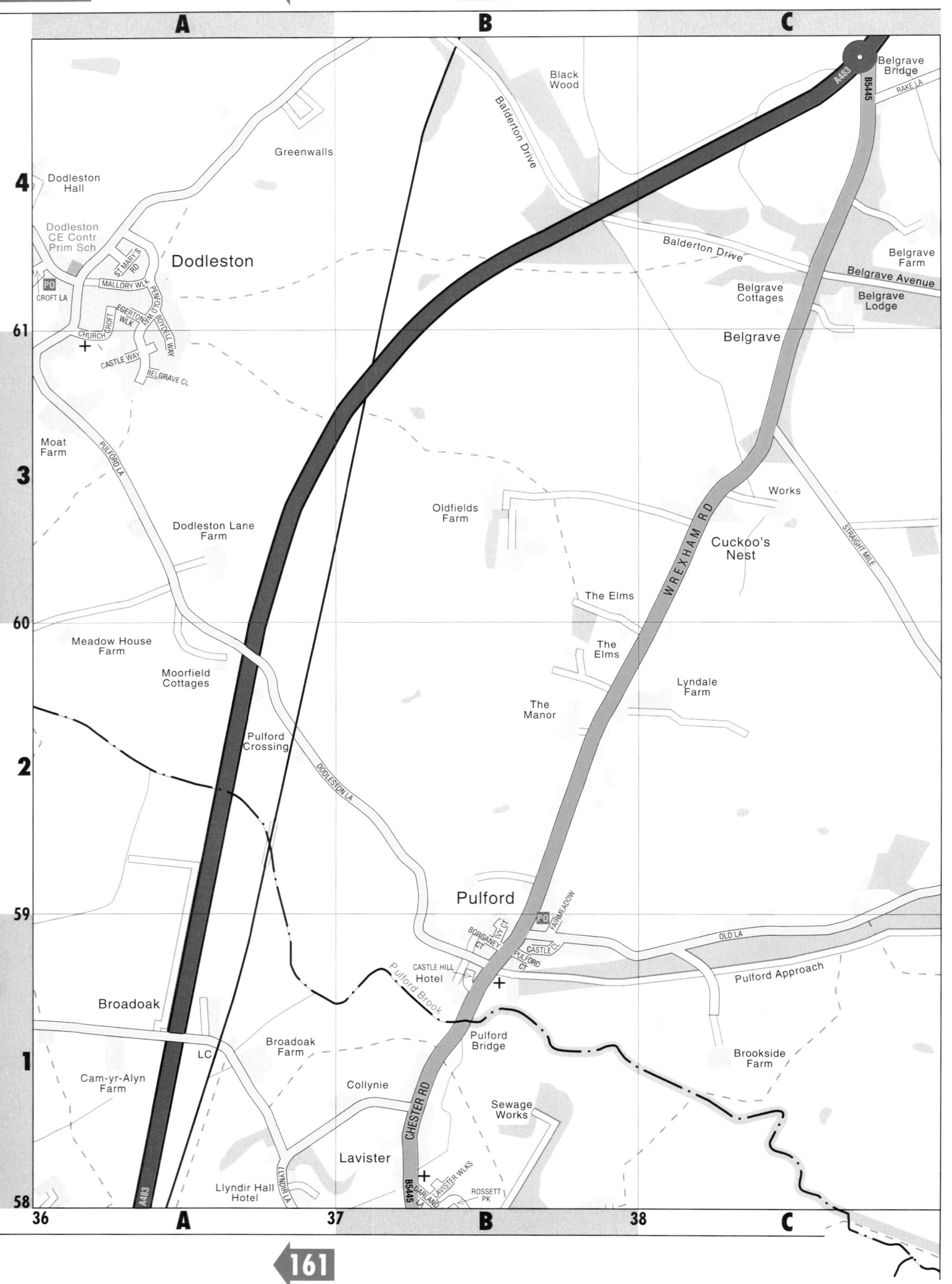

A
B
C
4
61
3
60
2
59
1
58
36
37
38
Dodleston Hall
Dodleston CE Contr Prim Sch
Dodleston
PO
CROFT LA
ST MARY'S RD
MALLORY WLK
EGERTON WLK
CROFT
CHURCH
PENFOLD WAY
BOYDELL WAY
CASTLE WAY
BELGRAVE CL
Greenwalls
Black Wood
Balderton Drive
Belgrave Bridge
A483
B5445
RAKE LA
Belgrave Farm
Belgrave Avenue
Belgrave Cottages
Belgrave Lodge
Belgrave
Moat Farm
PULFORD LA
Oldfields Farm
Works
WREXHAM RD
Cuckoo's Nest
STRAIGHT MILE
Dodleston Lane Farm
The Elms
The Elms
Meadow House Farm
Moorfield Cottages
Lyndale Farm
The Manor
Pulford Crossing
DODLESTON LA
Pulford
FAIRMEADOW
IVY CT
BORGANEY CT
CASTLE CL
PULFORD CT
OLD LA
CASTLE HILL
Hotel
Pulford Brook
Pulford Approach
Broadoak
Broadoak Farm
Pulford Bridge
Brookside Farm
LC
Cam-yr-Alyn Farm
Collynie
CHESTER RD
Sewage Works
Lavister
Llyndir Hall Hotel
LLYNDIR LA
DARLAND LA
LAVISTER WLKS
ROSSETT PK

161

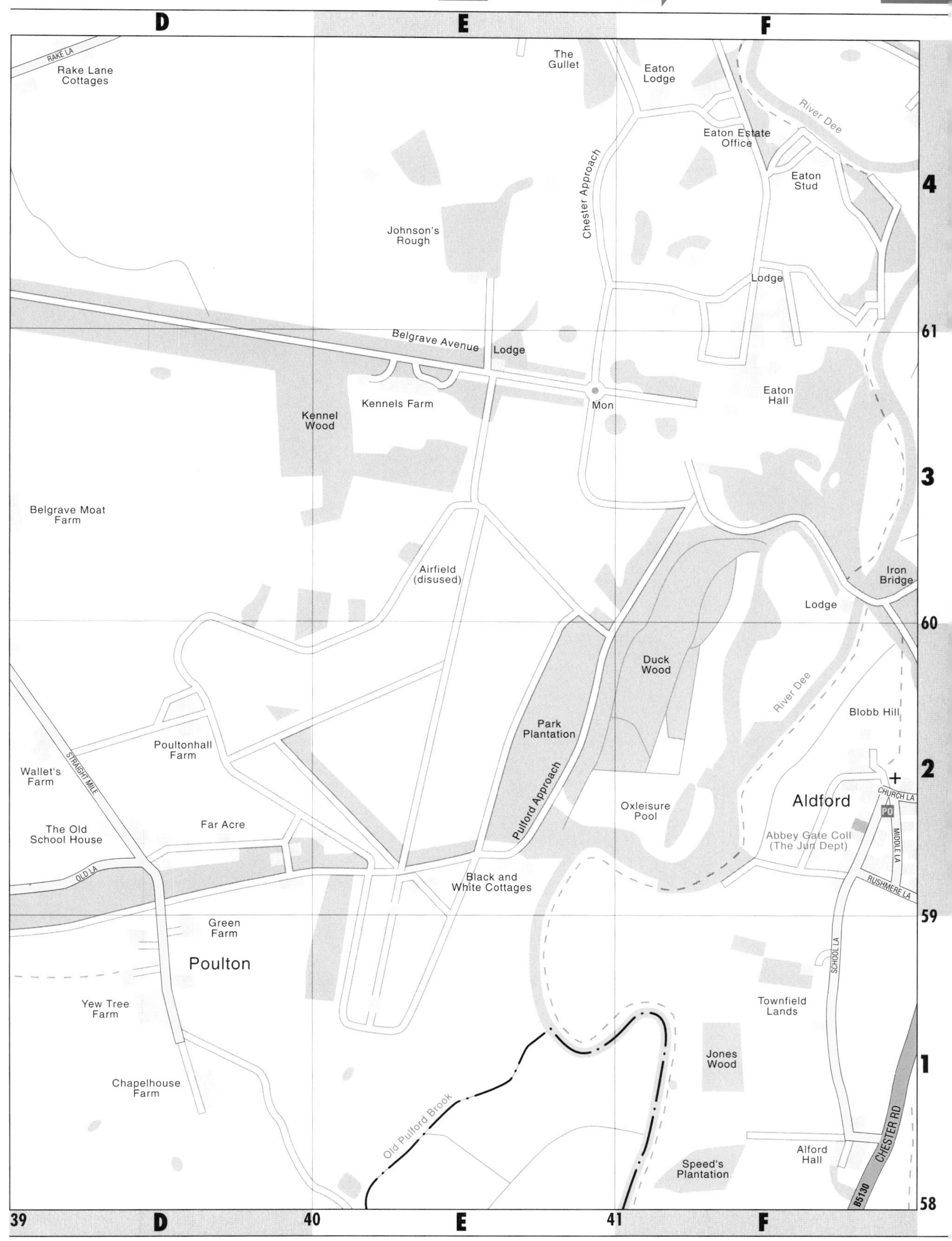

RAKE LA
Rake Lane
Cottages

The
Gullet

Eaton
Lodge

River Dee

Eaton Estate
Office

Eaton
Stud

4

Chester Approach

Lodge

Johnson's
Rough

Belgrave Avenue   Lodge

61

Kennels Farm

Mon

Eaton
Hall

Kennel
Wood

3

Belgrave Moat
Farm

Airfield
(disused)

Iron
Bridge

Lodge

60

Duck
Wood

River Dee

Blobb Hill

Park
Plantation

Pulford Approach

Wallet's
Farm

STRAIGHT MILE

Poultonhall
Farm

Oxleisure
Pool

Aldford

CHURCH LA

2

Abbey Gate Coll
(The Jun Dept)

MIDDLE LA

The Old
School House

OLD LA

Far Acre

Black and
White Cottages

RUSHMERE LA

59

Green
Farm

Poulton

Townfield
Lands

SCHOOL LA

Yew Tree
Farm

Jones
Wood

1

Chapelhouse
Farm

Old Pulford Brook

Speed's
Plantation

Alford
Hall

CHESTER RD

B5130

58

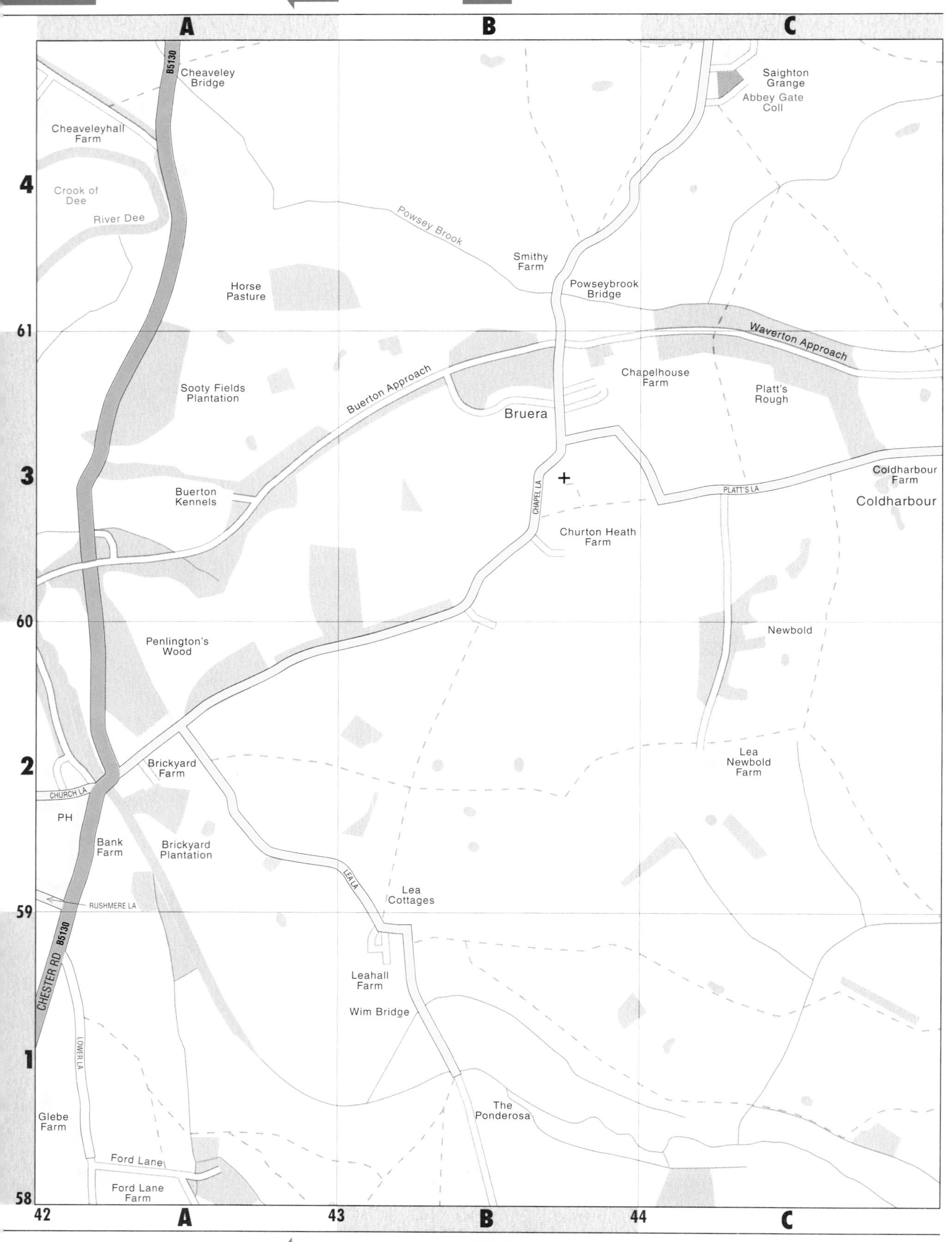

B5130

Cheaveley Bridge

Cheaveleyhall Farm

Crook of Dee

River Dee

4

Horse Pasture

Powsey Brook

Smithy Farm

Powseybrook Bridge

Saighton Grange
Abbey Gate Coll

Waverton Approach

61

Sooty Fields Plantation

Buerton Approach

Bruera

Chapelhouse Farm

Platt's Rough

3

Buerton Kennels

CHAPEL LA

Churton Heath Farm

PLATT'S LA

Coldharbour Farm

Coldharbour

60

Penlington's Wood

Newbold

2

Brickyard Farm

CHURCH LA

PH

Bank Farm

Brickyard Plantation

LEA LA

Lea Cottages

Lea Newbold Farm

59

RUSHMERE LA

CHESTER RD B5130

Leahall Farm

Wim Bridge

1

LOWER LA

Glebe Farm

Ford Lane

The Ponderosa

Ford Lane Farm

58

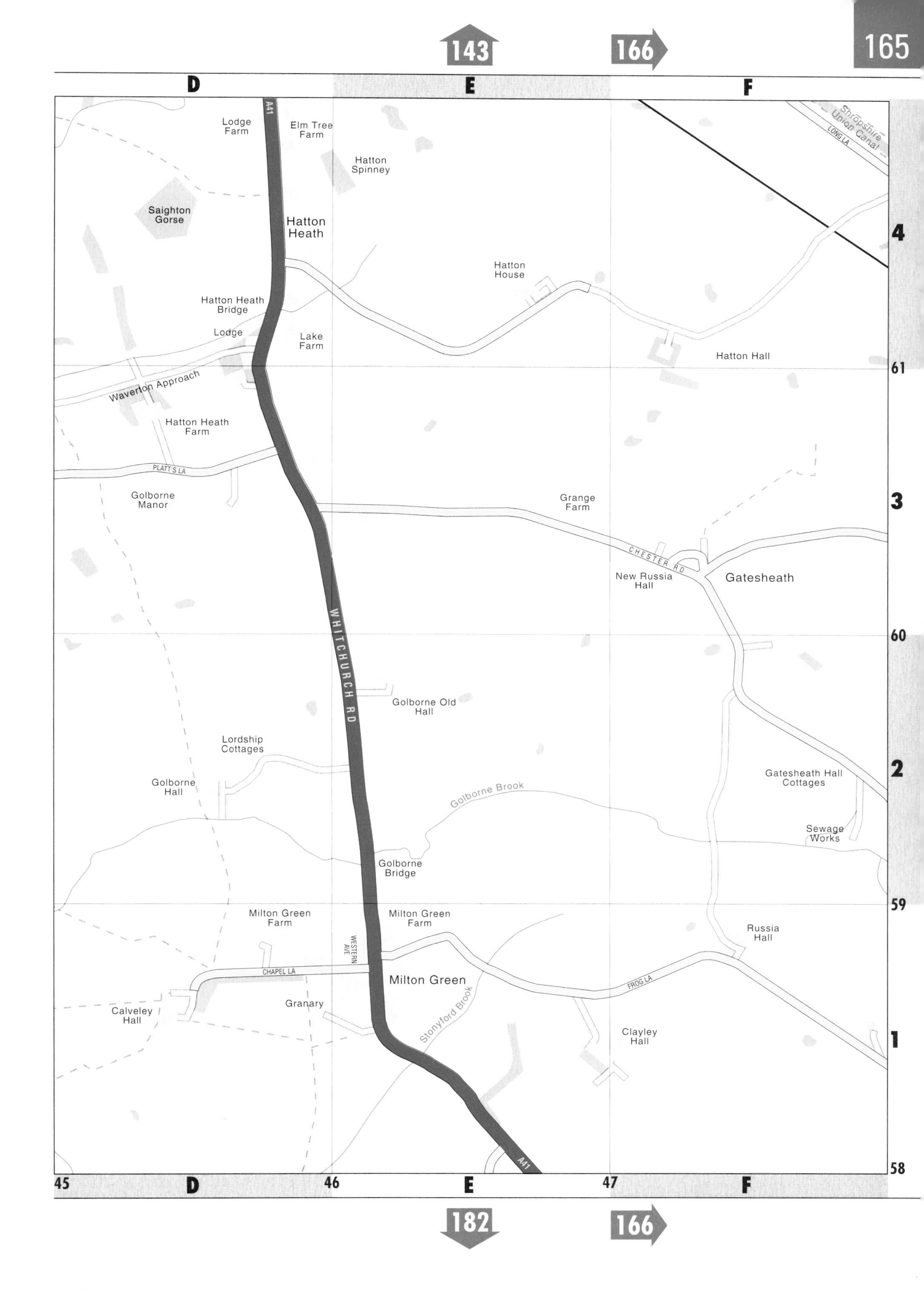
143
166
D
E
F
A41
Lodge Farm
Elm Tree Farm
Hatton Spinney
Shropshire Union Canal
LONG LA
Saighton Gorse
Hatton Heath
Hatton House
Hatton Heath Bridge
Lodge
Lake Farm
Hatton Hall
Waverton Approach
Hatton Heath Farm
PLATT'S LA
Golborne Manor
Grange Farm
CHESTER RD
New Russia Hall
Gatesheath
WHITCHURCH RD
Golborne Old Hall
Lordship Cottages
Golborne Hall
Golborne Brook
Gatesheath Hall Cottages
Sewage Works
Golborne Bridge
Milton Green Farm
Milton Green Farm
WESTERN AVE
Russia Hall
CHAPEL LA
Milton Green
FROG LA
Calveley Hall
Granary
Stonyford Brook
Clayley Hall
A41
4
61
3
60
2
59
1
58
45
46
47
182
166

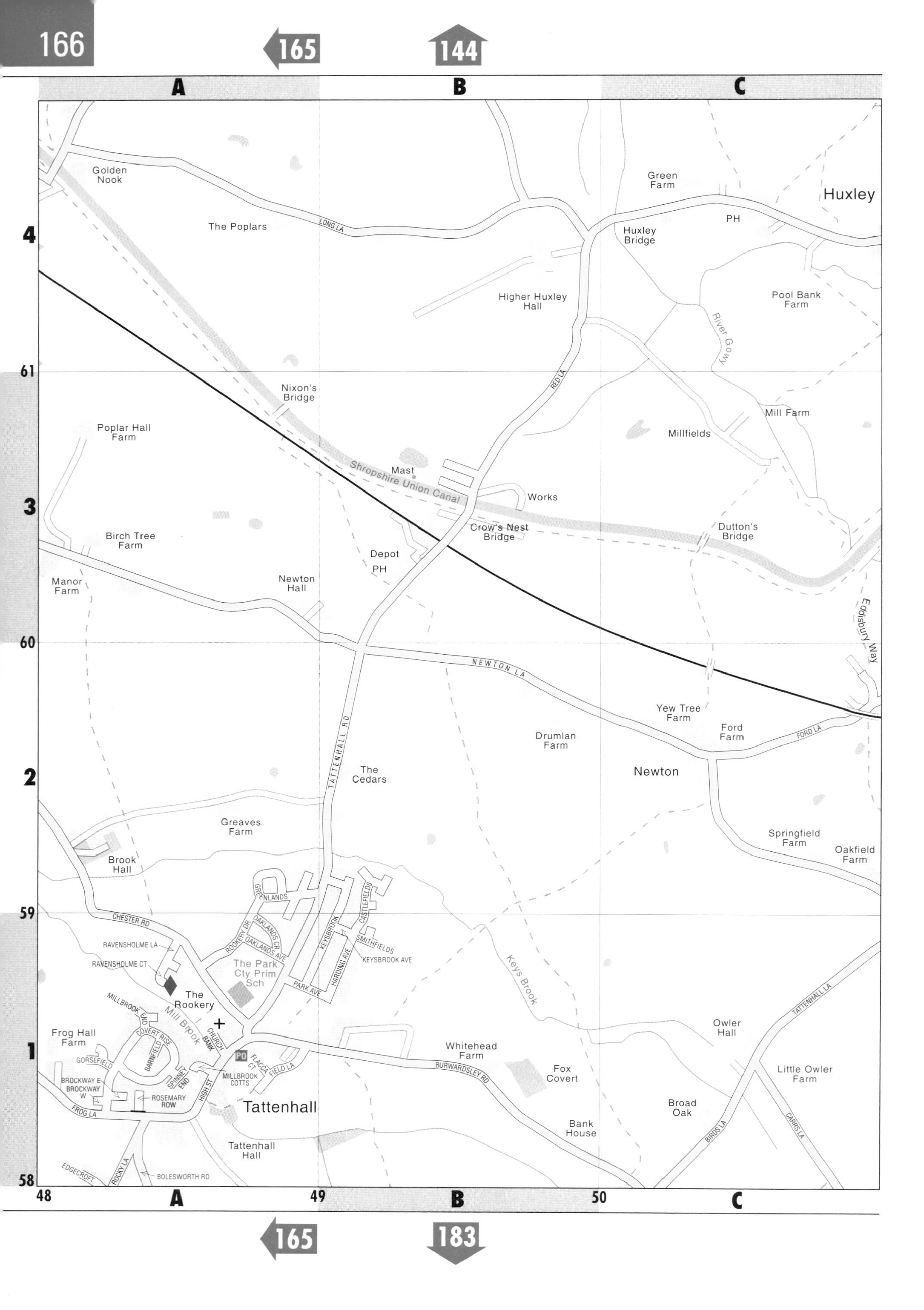

Golden Nook

The Poplars

LONG LA

Green Farm

PH

Huxley

Huxley Bridge

Higher Huxley Hall

Pool Bank Farm

River Gowy

Nixon's Bridge

RED LA

Mill Farm

Millfields

Poplar Hall Farm

Shropshire Union Canal

Mast

Works

Crow's Nest Bridge

Dutton's Bridge

Birch Tree Farm

Depot PH

Manor Farm

Newton Hall

Edisbury Way

NEWTON LA

Yew Tree Farm

Ford Farm

FORD LA

TATTENHALL RD

The Cedars

Drumlan Farm

Newton

Greaves Farm

Springfield Farm

Oakfield Farm

Brook Hall

CHESTER RD

GREENLANDS

Keys Brook

RAVENSHOLME LA

OAKLANDS DR

OAKLANDS AVE

KEYSBROOK

CASTLEFIELDS

RAVENSHOLME CT

The Park Cty Prim Sch

HARDING AVE

SMITHFIELDS

KEYSBROOK AVE

ROOKERY DR

PARK AVE

The Rookery

MILLBROOK RD

Mill Brook

Owler Hall

TATTENHALL LA

Frog Hall Farm

COVERT RISE

BARNFIELD RD

CHURCH BANK

PO

Whitehead Farm

BURWARDSLEY RD

Fox Covert

Little Owler Farm

GORSEFIELD

FLACCA CT

FIELD LA

BROCKWAY E
BROCKWAY W

SPINNEY END

HIGH ST

MILLBROOK COTTS

ROSEMARY ROW

Broad Oak

FROG LA

Tattenhall

Bank House

BIRDS LA

CARRS LA

EDGECROFT

ROCKY LA

Tattenhall Hall

BOLESWORTH RD

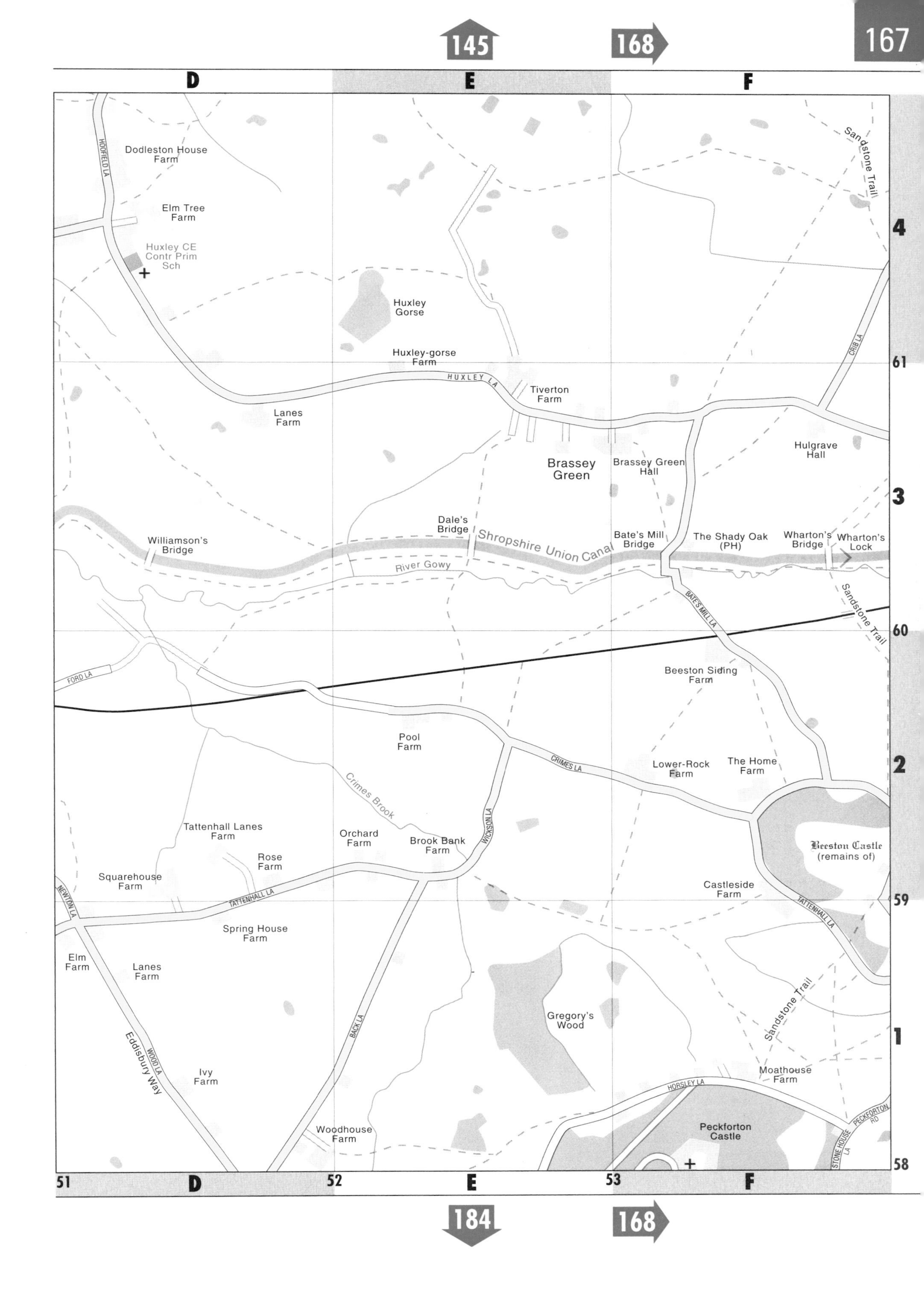

D   E   F

HOOFIELD LA

Dodleston House Farm

Elm Tree Farm

Huxley CE Contr Prim Sch

4

Huxley Gorse

Huxley-gorse Farm

61

HUXLEY LA

Tiverton Farm

Lanes Farm

Brassey Green

Brassey Green Hall

Hulgrave Hall

Sandstone Trail

CRIB LA

3

Dale's Bridge

Shropshire Union Canal

Williamson's Bridge

River Gowy

Bate's Mill Bridge

The Shady Oak (PH)

Wharton's Bridge

Wharton's Lock

BATE'S MILL LA

Sandstone Trail

60

FORD LA

Beeston Siding Farm

Pool Farm

CRIMES LA

Lower-Rock Farm

The Home Farm

2

Crimes Brook

WICKSON LA

Tattenhall Lanes Farm

Rose Farm

Orchard Farm

Brook Bank Farm

Beeston Castle (remains of)

Squarehouse Farm

NEWTON LA

TATTENHALL LA

Castleside Farm

TATTENHALL LA

59

Spring House Farm

Elm Farm

Lanes Farm

WOOD LA

BACK LA

Eddisbury Way

Gregory's Wood

Sandstone Trail

1

Ivy Farm

Moathouse Farm

HORSLEY LA

Woodhouse Farm

Peckforton Castle

STONE HOUSE LA

PECKFORTON RD

58

51   D   52   E   53   F

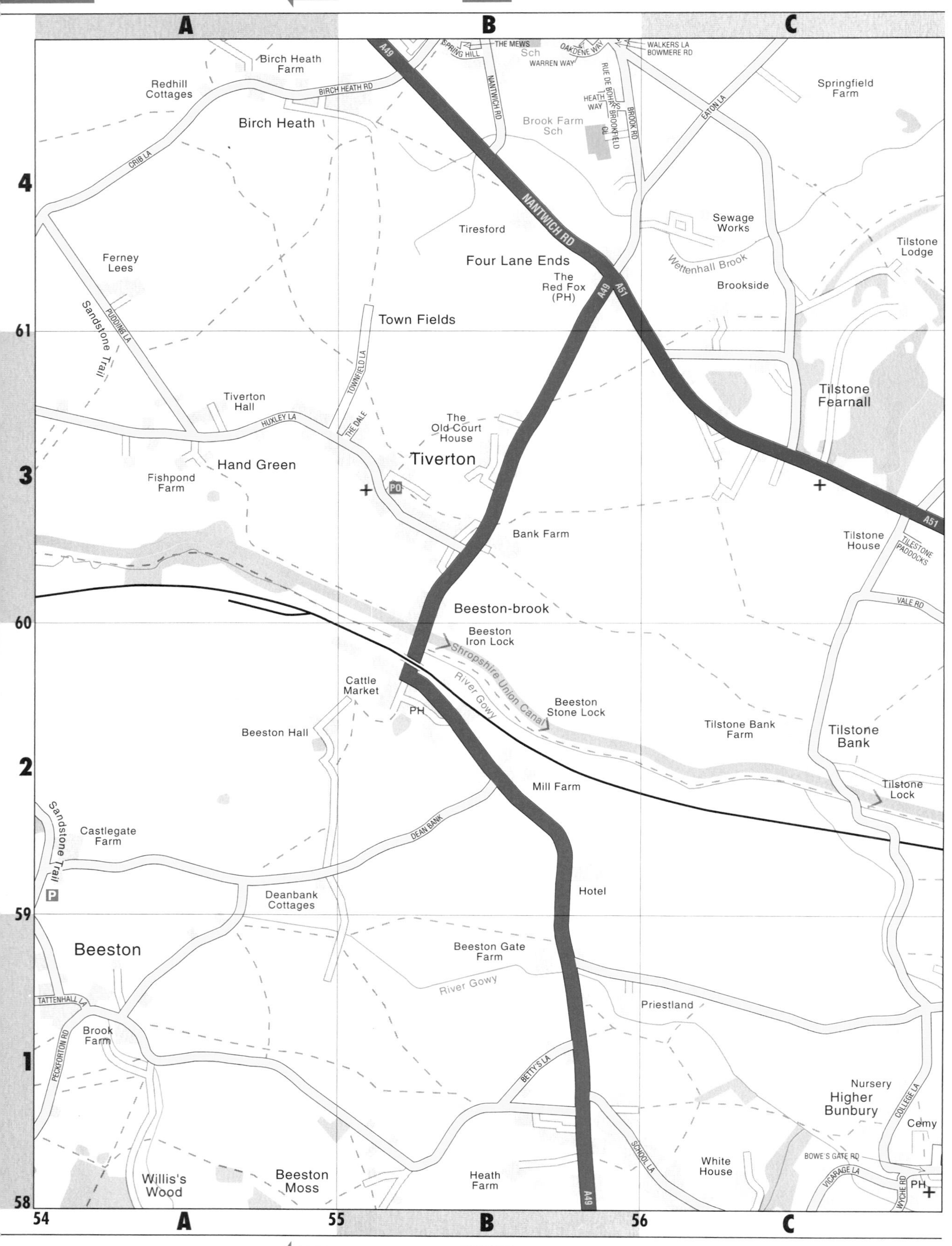

Birch Heath Farm
Redhill Cottages
Birch Heath
BIRCH HEATH RD
Ferney Lees
CRIB LA
SANDSTONE TRAIL
PUDDING LA
Tiverton Hall
Hand Green
HUXLEY LA
Fishpond Farm
THE DALE
TOWNFIELD LA
Town Fields
Tiresford
Four Lane Ends
The Red Fox (PH)
The Old Court House
Tiverton
P.O.
Bank Farm
Beeston-brook
Beeston Iron Lock
Shropshire Union Canal
River Gowy
Beeston Stone Lock
Cattle Market
PH
Beeston Hall
Mill Farm
DEAN BANK
Castlegate Farm
SANDSTONE TRAIL
P
Deanbank Cottages
Beeston
TATTENHALL LA
PECKFORTON RD
Brook Farm
Beeston Gate Farm
River Gowy
Hotel
BETTY'S LA
Willis's Wood
Beeston Moss
Heath Farm
SCHOOL LA
Priestland
White House
Higher Bunbury
Nursery
Cemy
COLLEGE LA
BOWE'S GATE RD
VICARAGE LA
WYCHE RD
PH
A49
NANTWICH RD
SPRING HILL
THE MEWS
Sch
WARREN WAY
OAKDENE WAY
WALKERS LA
BOWMERE RD
HEATH WAY
RUE DE BOHARS
BROOKFIELD DR
BROOK RD
Brook Farm Sch
Springfield Farm
EATON LA
Sewage Works
Wettenhall Brook
Brookside
A49
A51
Tilstone Lodge
Tilstone Fearnall
A51
Tilstone House
TILSTONE PADDOCKS
VALE RD
Tilstone Bank Farm
Tilstone Bank
Tilstone Lock

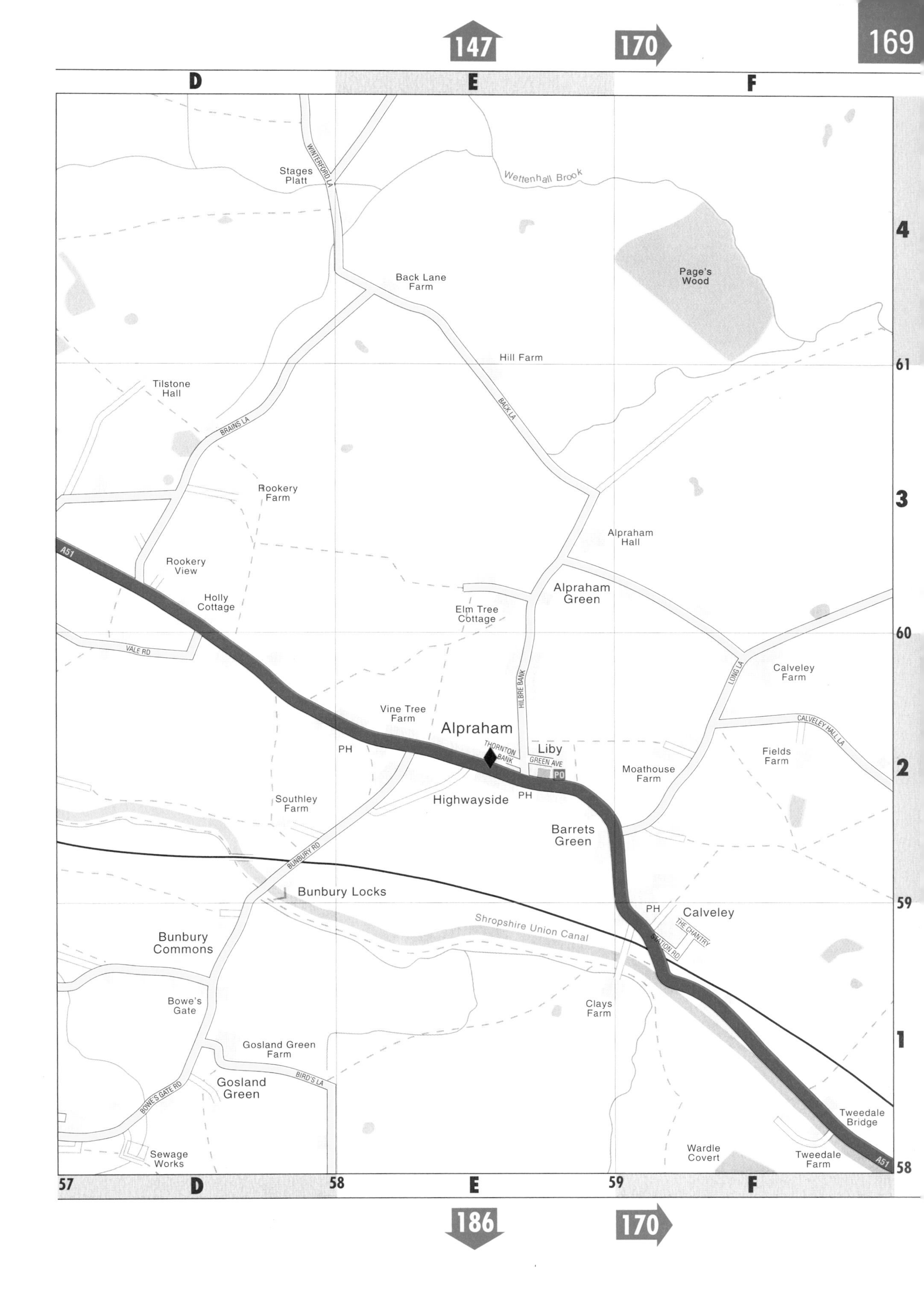
147
170
D
E
F
4
3
2
1
61
60
59
58
57
58
59
Stages Platt
WINTERFORD LA
Wettenhall Brook
Page's Wood
Back Lane Farm
Hill Farm
Tilstone Hall
BRAINS LA
BACK LA
Rookery Farm
Alpraham Hall
A51
Rookery View
Holly Cottage
Alpraham Green
Elm Tree Cottage
VALE RD
LONG LA
Calveley Farm
HILBRE BANK
Vine Tree Farm
Alpraham
CALVELEY HALL LA
PH
THORNTON BANK
Liby
GREEN AVE
PO
Fields Farm
Moathouse Farm
Southley Farm
Highwayside
PH
Barrets Green
BUNBURY RD
Bunbury Locks
PH
Calveley
THE CHANTRY
STATION RD
Shropshire Union Canal
Bunbury Commons
Bowe's Gate
Clays Farm
Gosland Green Farm
BIRD'S LA
Gosland Green
BOWE'S GATE RD
Tweedale Bridge
Sewage Works
Wardle Covert
Tweedale Farm
A51
186
170

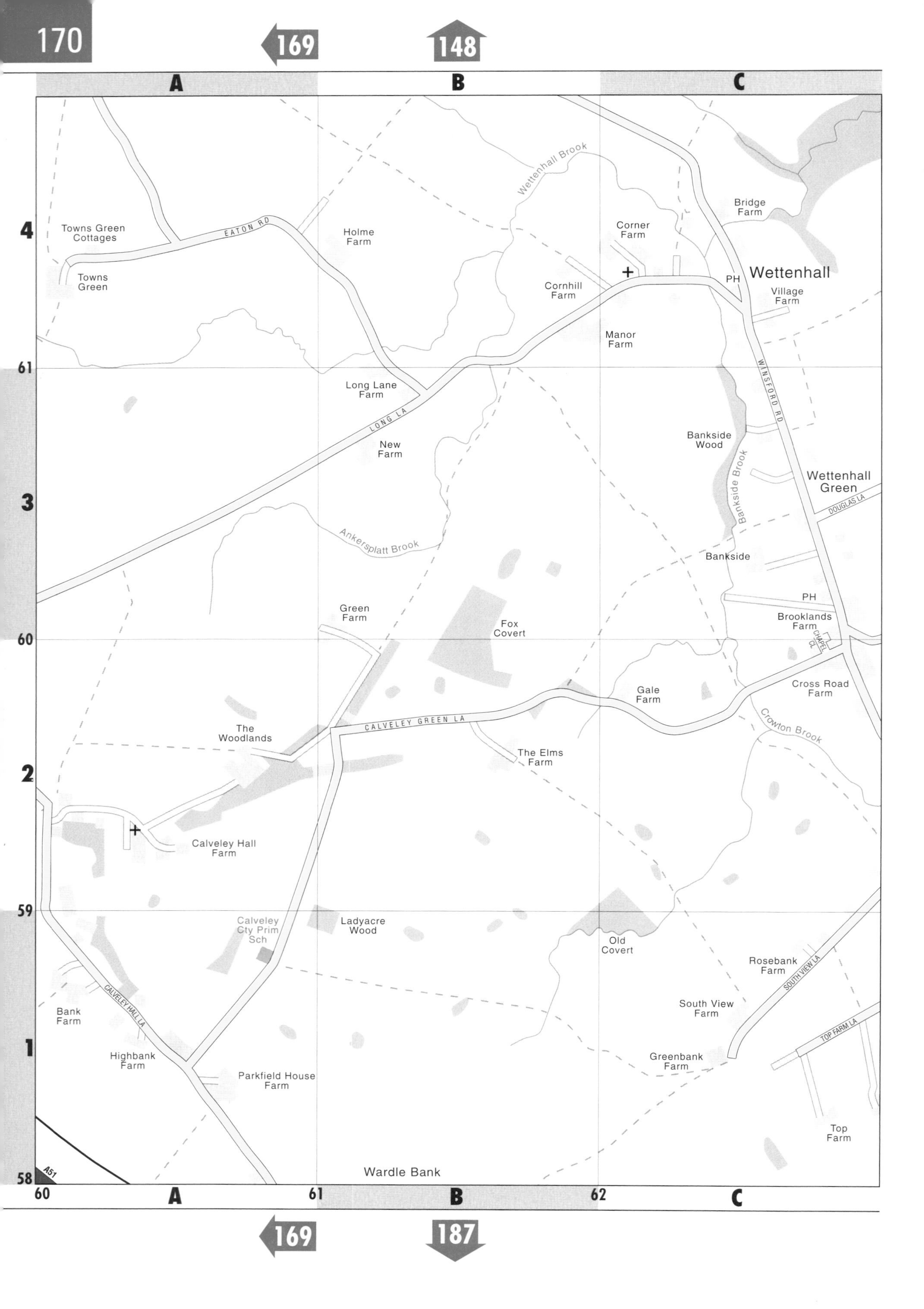
170
169
148
A
B
C
4
3
2
1
61
60
59
58
62
Towns Green Cottages
Towns Green
EATON RD
Holme Farm
Wettenhall Brook
Corner Farm
Bridge Farm
Wettenhall
PH
Village Farm
Cornhill Farm
Manor Farm
Long Lane Farm
LONG LA
New Farm
WINSFORD RD
Bankside Wood
Bankside Brook
Wettenhall Green
DOUGLAS LA
Ankersplatt Brook
Bankside
PH
Green Farm
Fox Covert
Brooklands Farm
CHAPEL CL
Gale Farm
Cross Road Farm
CALVELEY GREEN LA
Crowton Brook
The Woodlands
The Elms Farm
Calveley Hall Farm
Calveley Cty Prim Sch
Ladyacre Wood
Old Covert
Rosebank Farm
SOUTH VIEW LA
South View Farm
Bank Farm
CALVELEY HALL LA
Highbank Farm
TOP FARM LA
Greenbank Farm
Parkfield House Farm
Top Farm
A51
Wardle Bank
169
187

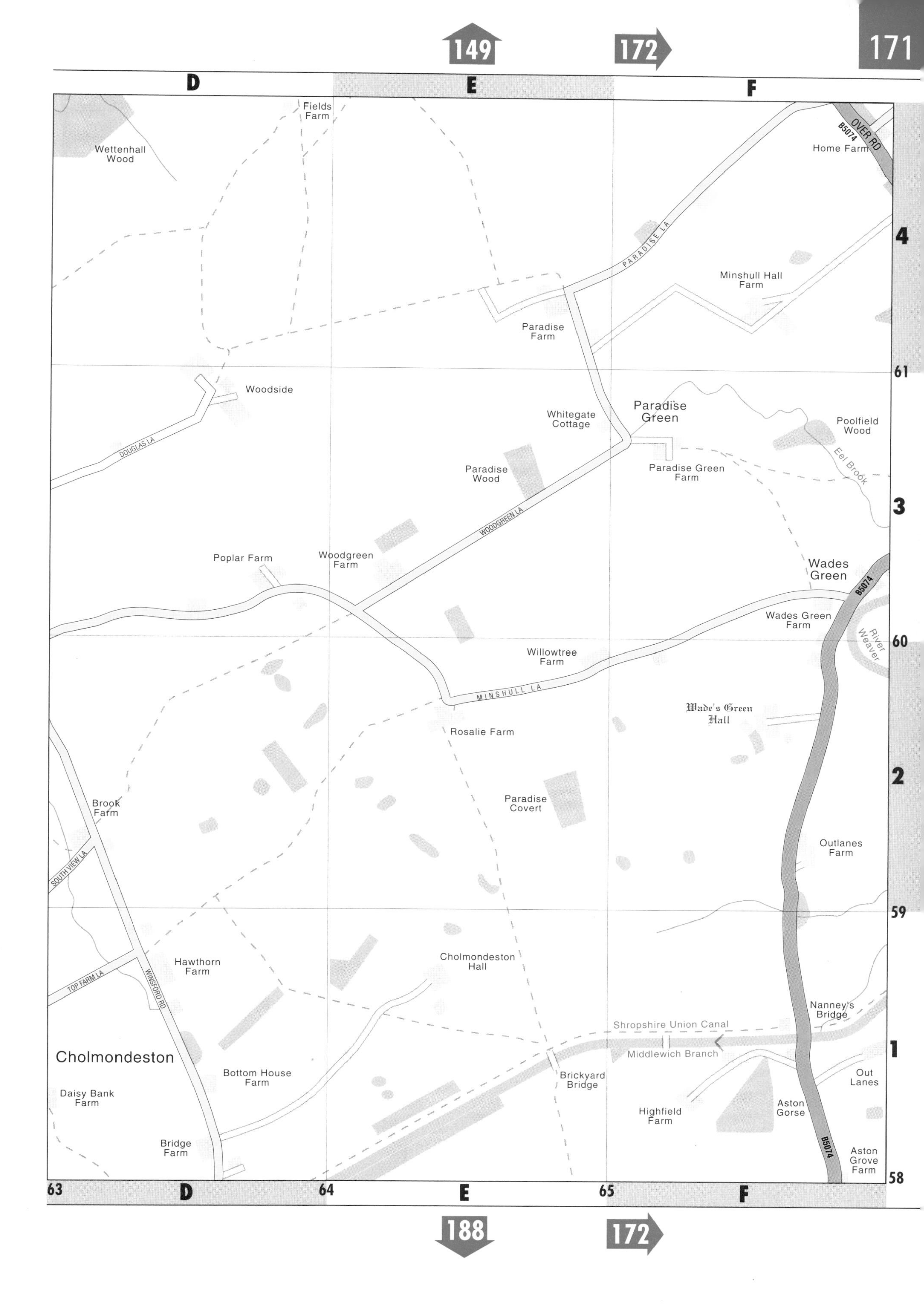

D E F

Fields
Farm

Wettenhall
Wood

OVER RD
B5074
Home Farm

PARADISE LA
4
Minshull Hall
Farm

Paradise
Farm

61

Woodside

DOUGLAS LA

Whitegate
Cottage

Paradise
Green

Poolfield
Wood

Eel Brook

Paradise
Wood

Paradise Green
Farm

3

WOODGREEN LA

Poplar Farm

Woodgreen
Farm

Wades
Green

B5074

Wades Green
Farm

River Weaver

60

Willowtree
Farm

MINSHULL LA

Wade's Green
Hall

Rosalie Farm

2

Brook
Farm

Paradise
Covert

Outlanes
Farm

SOUTH VIEW LA

59

Hawthorn
Farm

Cholmondeston
Hall

Nanney's
Bridge

TOP FARM LA

WINSFORD RD

Cholmondeston

Shropshire Union Canal

Middlewich Branch

1

Daisy Bank
Farm

Bottom House
Farm

Brickyard
Bridge

Highfield
Farm

Aston
Gorse

Out
Lanes

Bridge
Farm

B5074

Aston
Grove
Farm

58

171
150

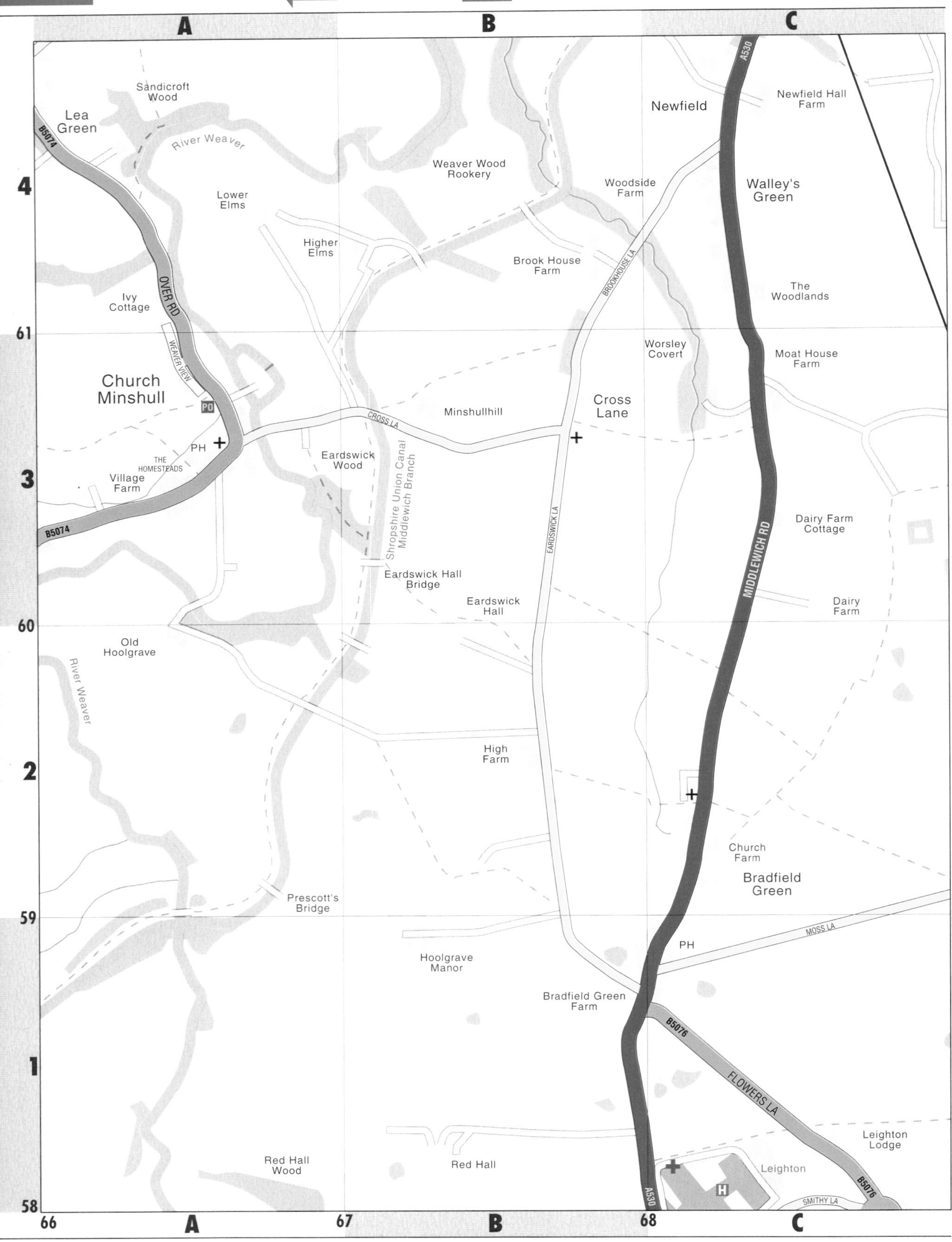
A
B
C
Sandicroft Wood
Lea Green
B5074
River Weaver
Weaver Wood Rookery
Newfield
Newfield Hall Farm
Lower Elms
Woodside Farm
Walley's Green
Higher Elms
Brook House Farm
BROOKHOUSE LA
A530
Ivy Cottage
OVER RD
The Woodlands
WEAVER VIEW
Worsley Covert
Moat House Farm
Church Minshull
PO
Cross Lane
Minshullhill
CROSS LA
PH
THE HOMESTEADS
Village Farm
Eardswick Wood
Shropshire Union Canal Middlewich Branch
EARDSWICK LA
MIDDLEWICH RD
Dairy Farm Cottage
Eardswick Hall Bridge
Eardswick Hall
Dairy Farm
Old Hoolgrave
River Weaver
High Farm
Church Farm
Bradfield Green
Prescott's Bridge
MOSS LA
Hoolgrave Manor
Bradfield Green Farm
B5076
FLOWERS LA
Leighton Lodge
Red Hall Wood
Red Hall
Leighton
H
SMITHY LA
4
61
3
60
2
59
1
58
66
67
68

171
189

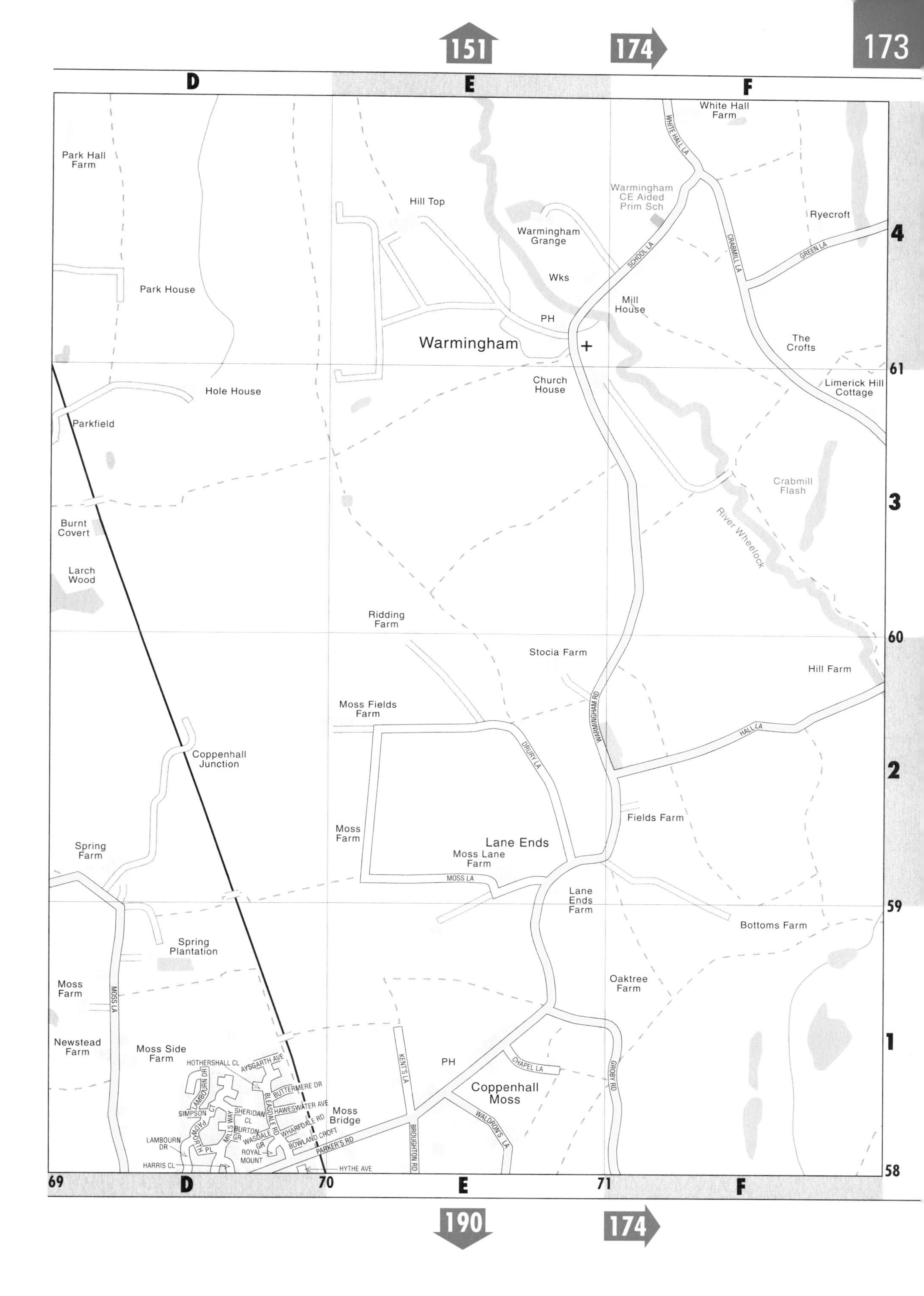

D
E
F

Park Hall
Farm

Park House

Hill Top

Warmingham
Grange

Wks

PH

Warmingham

White Hall
Farm

WHITE HALL LA

Warmingham
CE Aided
Prim Sch

SCHOOL LA

CRABMILL LA

GREEN LA

Ryecroft

4

Mill
House

Church
House

+

The
Crofts

61

Hole House

Parkfield

Limerick Hill
Cottage

Burnt
Covert

Larch
Wood

Ridding
Farm

Stocia Farm

River Wheelock

Crabmill
Flash

3

60

Moss Fields
Farm

Coppenhall
Junction

Spring
Farm

Moss
Farm

Spring
Plantation

Moss
Farm

Newstead
Farm

Moss Side
Farm

HOTHERSHALL CL

LAMBOURN DR

SIMPSON

HARRIS CL

AYSGARTH AVE

SHERIDAN CL

BURTON
GR

FRITH WY

MILLS GR

WASDALE
GR

BLEASDALE RD

BUTTERMERE DR

HAWESWATER AVE

WHARFDALE RD

ROYAL
MOUNT

BOWLAND CROFT

Moss
Bridge

PARKER'S RD

HYTHE AVE

KENT'S LA

BROUGHTON RD

PH

Coppenhall
Moss

CHAPEL LA

WALDRON'S LA

Lane Ends

Moss Lane
Farm

MOSS LA

Lane
Ends
Farm

DRURY LA

WARMINGHAM RD

HALL LA

Hill Farm

Fields Farm

2

Bottoms Farm

59

Oaktree
Farm

GROBY RD

1

58

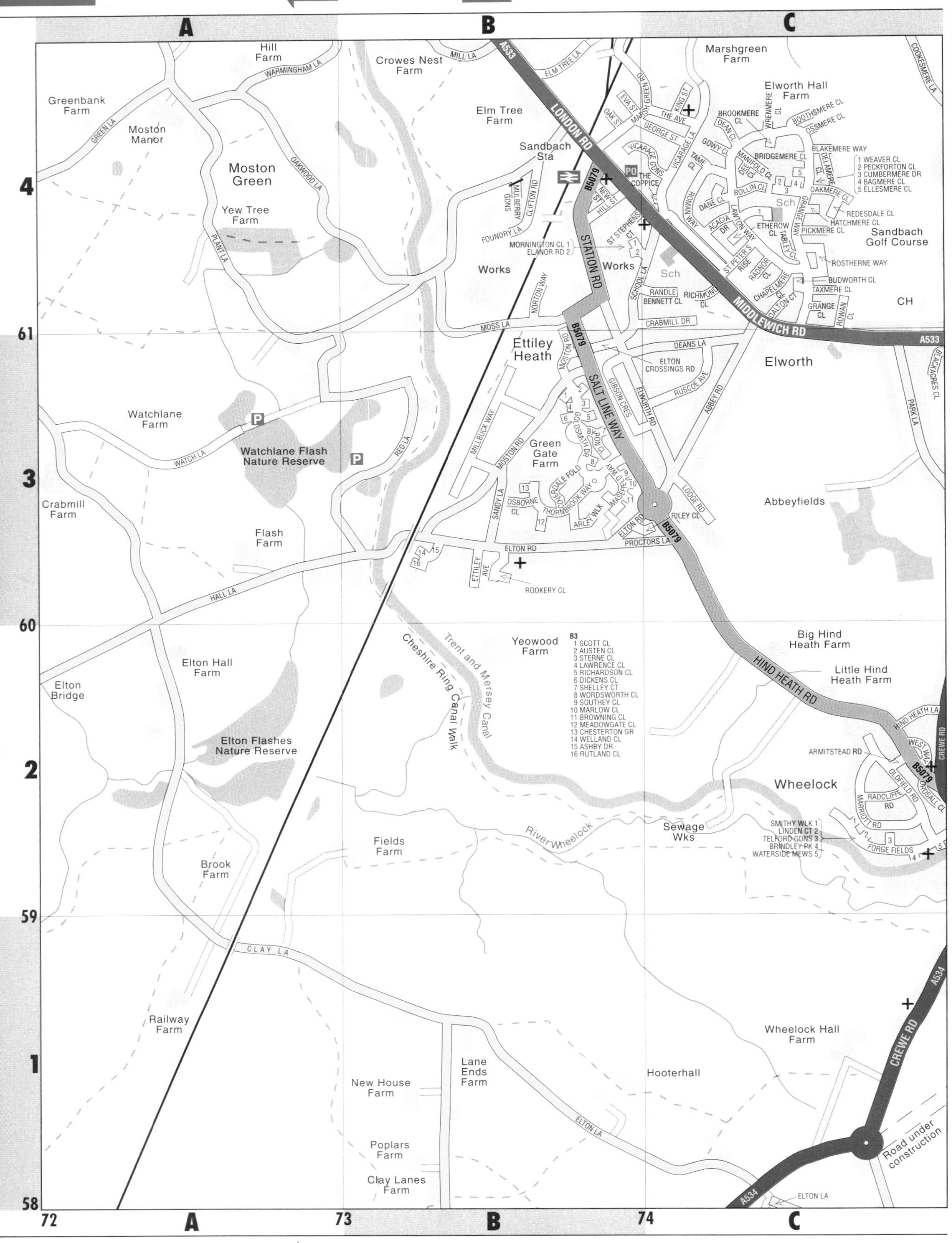

A B C

Hill Farm
Crowes Nest Farm
Marshgreen Farm
WARMINGHAM LA
MILL LA
ELM TREE LA
Elworth Hall Farm
Greenbank Farm
GREENBANK
EVA ST
KING ST
OAK ST
MAJOR ST
GEORGE ST
THE AVE
BROOKMERE CL
WRENMERE CL
BOOTHSMERE CL
OSSMERE CL
DEAN CL
Moston Manor
GREEN LA
A533
LONDON RD
Elm Tree Farm
VICARAGE GDNS
GOWY CL
BRIDGEMERE CL
BLAKEMERE WAY
1 WEAVER CL
2 PECKFORTON CL
3 CUMBERMERE DR
4 BAGMERE CL
5 ELLESMERE CL
Moston Green
Sandbach Sta
B5079
VICARAGE ST
MANIFOLD CL
OAKWOOD LA
CLIFTON RD
TAME CL
DANE CL
4
Yew Tree Farm
FOUNDRY LA
THE COPPICE
PO
NEWS
HILL ST
ST STEPHENS
BOLLIN CL
ACACIA DR
LAWTON WAY
ROMAN WAY
OAKMERE CL
ETHEROW CL
GRANGE WAY
ABLEY CL
PICKMERE CL
HATCHMERE CL
REDESDALE CL
Sch
Sandbach Golf Course
PLANT LA
MILLBERRY GDNS
SCHOOL LA
MORNINGTON CL 1
ELANOR RD 2
ST PETER'S RISE
CHAPELMERE CL
DALTON CT
ROWAN CL
ROSTHERNE WAY
BUDWORTH CL
TAXMERE CL
GRANGE CL
Works
Works
STATION RD
RANDLE
BENNETT CL
RICHMOND CL
CH
61
MOSS LA
NORTON WAY
CRABMILL DR
DEANS LA
MIDDLEWICH RD
A533
BLACKACRES CL
Ettiley Heath
B5079
ELTON CROSSINGS RD
RUSCOE AVE
ABBEY RD
Elworth
PARK LA
SALT LINE WAY
GIBSON CRES
ELWORTH RD
Watchlane Farm
P
MILLBUCK WAY
GOSTREY FOLD
GOSMAY CL
BOW CL
Abbeyfields
3
Watchlane Flash Nature Reserve
P
RED LA
WATCH LA
Green Gate Farm
MOSTON RD
SANDY LA
THORNBROOK WAY
AXLE WLK
MASS
ELTON RD
LODGE RD
RILEY CRES
B5079
Crabmill Farm
Flash Farm
OSBORNE CL
13
12
ARLE WLK
ELTON RD
ELTON RD
PROCTORS LA
HALL LA
ETTILEY AVE
15
16
ROOKERY CL
60
Yeowood Farm
B3
1 SCOTT CL
2 AUSTEN CL
3 STERNE CL
4 LAWRENCE CL
5 RICHARDSON CL
6 DICKENS CL
7 SHELLEY CT
8 WORDSWORTH CL
9 SOUTHEY CL
10 MARLOW CL
11 BROWNING CL
12 MEADOWGATE CL
13 CHESTERTON GR
14 WELLAND CL
15 ASHBY DR
16 RUTLAND CL
Big Hind Heath Farm
Little Hind Heath Farm
Elton Bridge
Elton Hall Farm
Cheshire Ring Canal Walk
Trent and Mersey Canal
HIND HEATH RD
HIND HEATH LA
CREWE RD
2
Elton Flashes Nature Reserve
ARMITSTEAD RD
WEST WAY
B5079
DRISSALL CL
Wheelock
RADCLIFFE RD
OLDFIELD RD
MARRIOTT RD
River Wheelock
Sewage Wks
SMITHY WLK 1
LINDEN CT 2
TELFORD GDNS 3
BRINDLEY PK 4
WATERSIDE MEWS 5
FORGE FIELDS
Brook Farm
Fields Farm
59
CLAY LA
Wheelock Hall Farm
CREWE RD
A534
Railway Farm
1
Lane Ends Farm
New House Farm
Hooterhall
Road under construction
ELTON LA
Poplars Farm
ELTON LA
Clay Lanes Farm
A534
ELTON LA
58

72 A 73 B 74 C

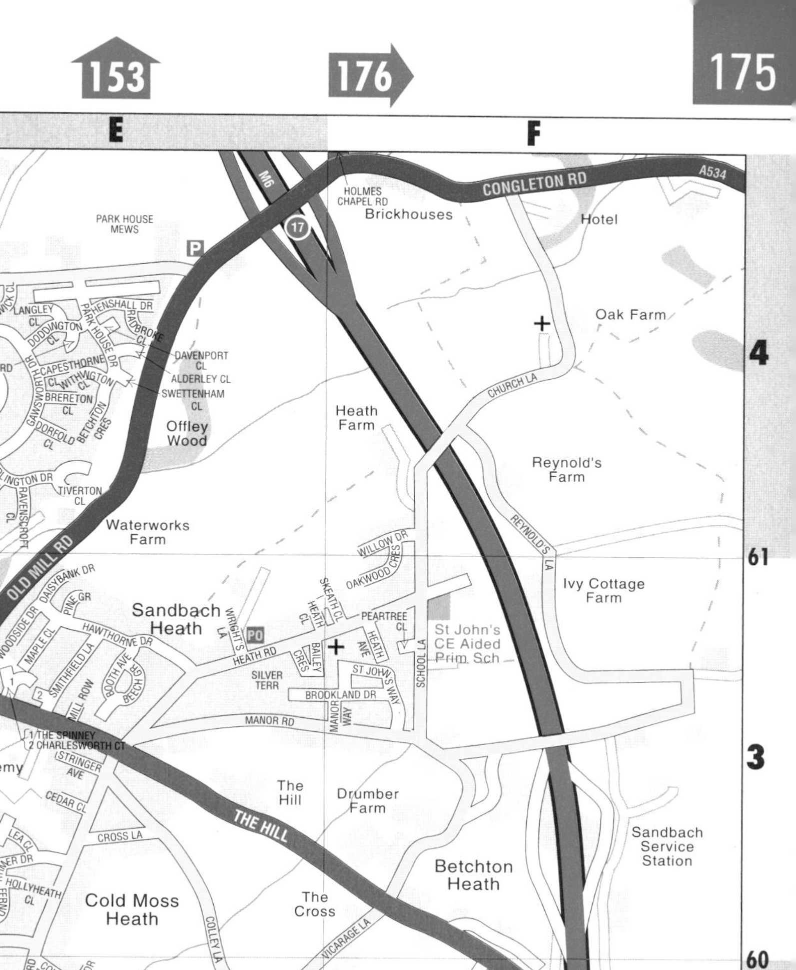

D **E** **F**

A534 CONGLETON RD

M6

HOLMES CHAPEL RD
Brickhouses
Hotel

17

Oakley Farm
PARK HOUSE MEWS
Oak Farm

Three Ways Farm
Offley Cty Inf & Jun Sch
P
Langley

DOVE CL
SWAN CL
ROBIN CL
COOKSMERE LA
BARLOW WAY
SYCAMORE GR
RAVEN CL
FINCH CL
DUKE'S CRES
QUEEN'S DR
PRINCESS DR

Heath Farm

CONGLETON RD
Pickwick CL
RIDLEY CL
DODDINGTON CL
RHENSHALL DR
PARK HOUSE DR
BROME
CROWBERRY
Bramall CL
Somerford CL
CAPESTHORNE CL
WITHINGTON DR
DAVENPORT CL
ALDERLEY CL
SWETTENHAM CL

Reynold's Farm

CHURCH LA

OFFLEY RD
Birtles CL
TATTON DR
MORETON DR
HAVENSCROFT AVE
BUNTINGTON DR
HARTFORD CL
BRERETON CL
SNELSON CL
FARNDON CL
BECKTON CRES

Offley Wood

REYNOLD'S LA

LIME CL AVE
BELMONT AVE
VICTORIA RD
SHELBERSON
CHURCH
SWETTOOTH LA
PLANT LA
ELWORTH ST
GREENACRES

FURNIVAL ST
SHELLY AVE
NEWFIELD ST
Sandbach Park
TIVERTON CL

Waterworks Farm

Ivy Cottage Farm

WILLOW DR

4

L Ctr
Sandbach Cty High Sch
P
COOPERS OPENING
COMMONS MILL
WELLS ST
Libv
DUNHAM CL
EATON CL
OLD MILL RD
DAYBANK DR
DAISYBANK DR
Sandbach Heath

OAKWOOD CRES

St John's CE Aided Prim Sch

61

BLACKACRES CL
MIDDLEWICH RD A533
CHAPEL ST
WESLEY AVE
BOLD ST
GREEN ST
HIGHTOWN
THE COMMONS
PANDA WAY
HOPE ST
PINE GR
HAWTHORNE DR
WRIGHT'S LA
HEATH RD
SHEATH LA
HEATH AVE
PEARTREE
BAILEY CRES
SCHOOL LA
PO

Court Works
CECIL RIGBY CL
CROWN BANK
THE GARDENS
MKT SQ
HIGH ST
MAPLE CL
SMITHFIELD ST
MILL ROW
BOOTH AVE
BEECH
SILVER TERR
ST JOHN'S WAY
BROOKLAND DR

A534
BELLE VUE TERR
UNION ST
BROOK RD
GEORGE'S WLK
1 THE SPINNEY
2 CHARLESWORTH CT
MANOR RD
MANOR WAY
STANHERST

Sandbach Sch - (Ind) (Boys)

Sandbach Cty Prim Sch
NEWHALL AVE
CONDLIFFE
ORMEROD
PALMERSTON
BINDA GDNS
STRINGER AVE
CEDAR CL
The Hill
Drumber Farm
Sandbach Service Station

3

FIELDS RD
PARK LA
FAIRFIELD AVE
DROVERS WAY
FIRST AVE
PRICE AVE
SECOND AVE
THIRD AVE
CORONATION CRES
TOWNFIELDS
LATHAM RD
SANDBACH
LAUREL
MARINER DR
HOLLYHEATH CL
LEA CL
Cemy
CROSS LA
Cold Moss Heath
The Cross
Betchton Heath

CREWE RD
CHARTWELL PARK
Wheelock Cty Prim Sch
MILL HILL LA
ROUNDINGS LA
HASSALL RD
COLDMOSS DR
COLLEY LA
VICARAGE LA
Boults Green Farm
Pear Tree Farm

60

Sandbach Mill
Road under construction
Oldhouse Farm
Vicarage Farm
STANNERHOUSE LA
NEWCASTLE RD A533
Dean Hill

2

ZAN DR
ZAN IND PK
Tall Chimneys
Malkin's Bank
Malkins Bank Farm
Woody Fields Farm

GAME ST
PO
CHAPEL ST
COTTON LA
Canal-side Farm
BOULTON LA
BETCHTON RD

BROOK TERR
GREENBANK PK
Wheelock Court
M/LL LA
Mill-house Farm
Trent and Mersey Canal
Club House
Cross Bank Farm

59

Wheelock
South Cheshire Way
Golf Course
JUBILEE VILLAS
Cheshire Ring Canal Walk

THE PADDOCK
CHARLES DR

1

Bank Farm
Hassall House Farm
P
M6
PO
PH

Hassall Moss
Butchers Bank Farm

58

75 **D** **76** **E** **77** **F**

175
154

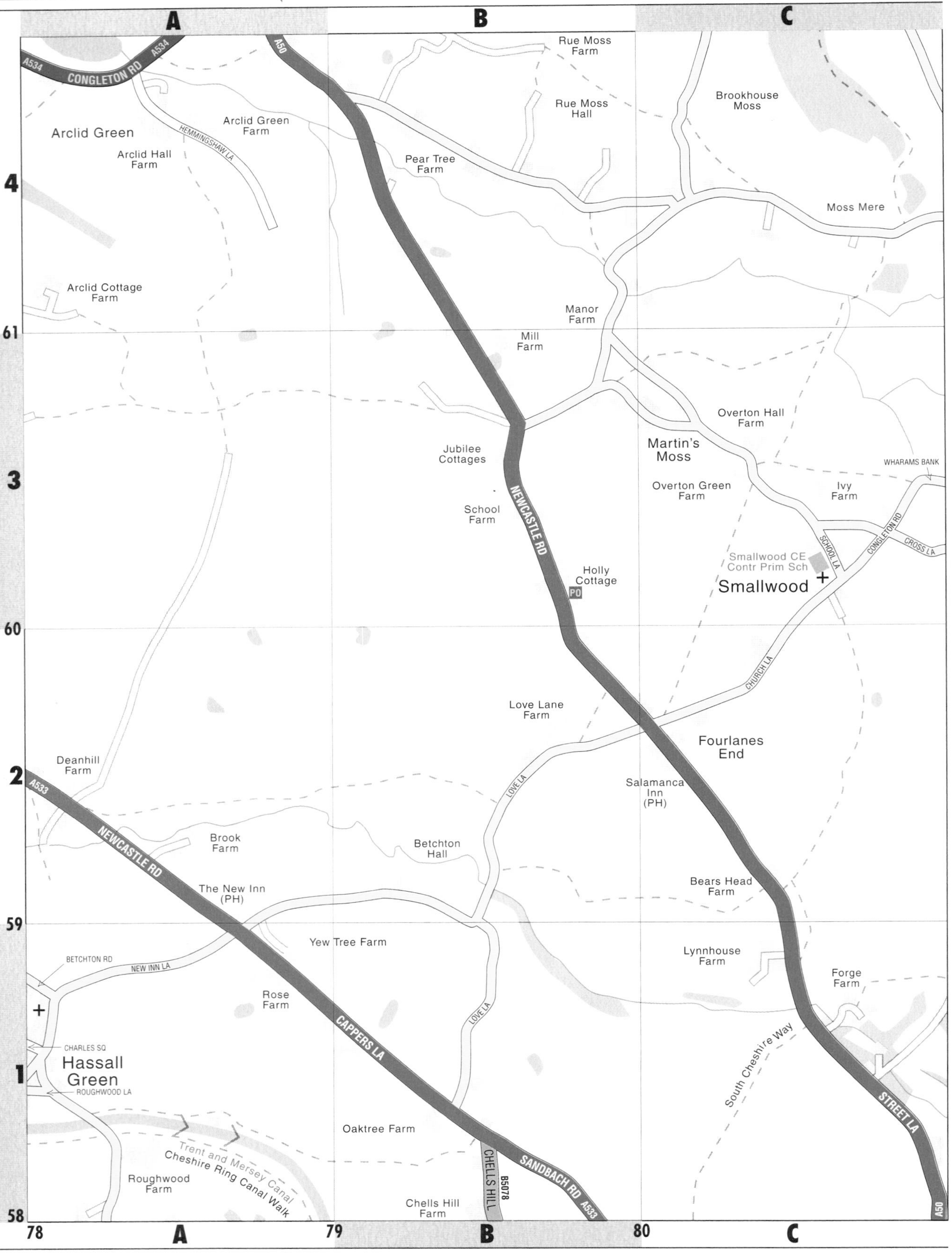

A   **B**   **C**

A534 CONGLETON RD A534

A50

Rue Moss Farm

Arclid Green

Arclid Green Farm

Rue Moss Hall

Brookhouse Moss

HEMMINGSHAW LA

Arclid Hall Farm

Pear Tree Farm

4

Moss Mere

Arclid Cottage Farm

Manor Farm

61

Mill Farm

Overton Hall Farm

Martin's Moss

WHARAMS BANK

Jubilee Cottages

Overton Green Farm

Ivy Farm

NEWCASTLE RD

3

School Farm

CONGLETON RD

CROSS LA

SCHOOL LA

Smallwood CE Contr Prim Sch

Holly Cottage

PO

Smallwood +

60

Love Lane Farm

CHURCH LA

Deanhill Farm

Fourlanes End

2 A533

Salamanca Inn (PH)

NEWCASTLE RD

Brook Farm

LOVE LA

Betchton Hall

Bears Head Farm

The New Inn (PH)

59

Lynnhouse Farm

BETCHTON RD

NEW INN LA

Yew Tree Farm

Forge Farm

+

Rose Farm

LOVE LA

CHARLES SQ

CAPPERS LA

South Cheshire Way

1 Hassall Green

ROUGHWOOD LA

STREET LA

Oaktree Farm

Trent and Mersey Canal
Cheshire Ring Canal Walk

CHELLS HILL

B5078

SANDBACH RD A533

Roughwood Farm

Chells Hill Farm

A50

58

78   **A**   **79**   **B**   **80**   **C**

175
193

155
178

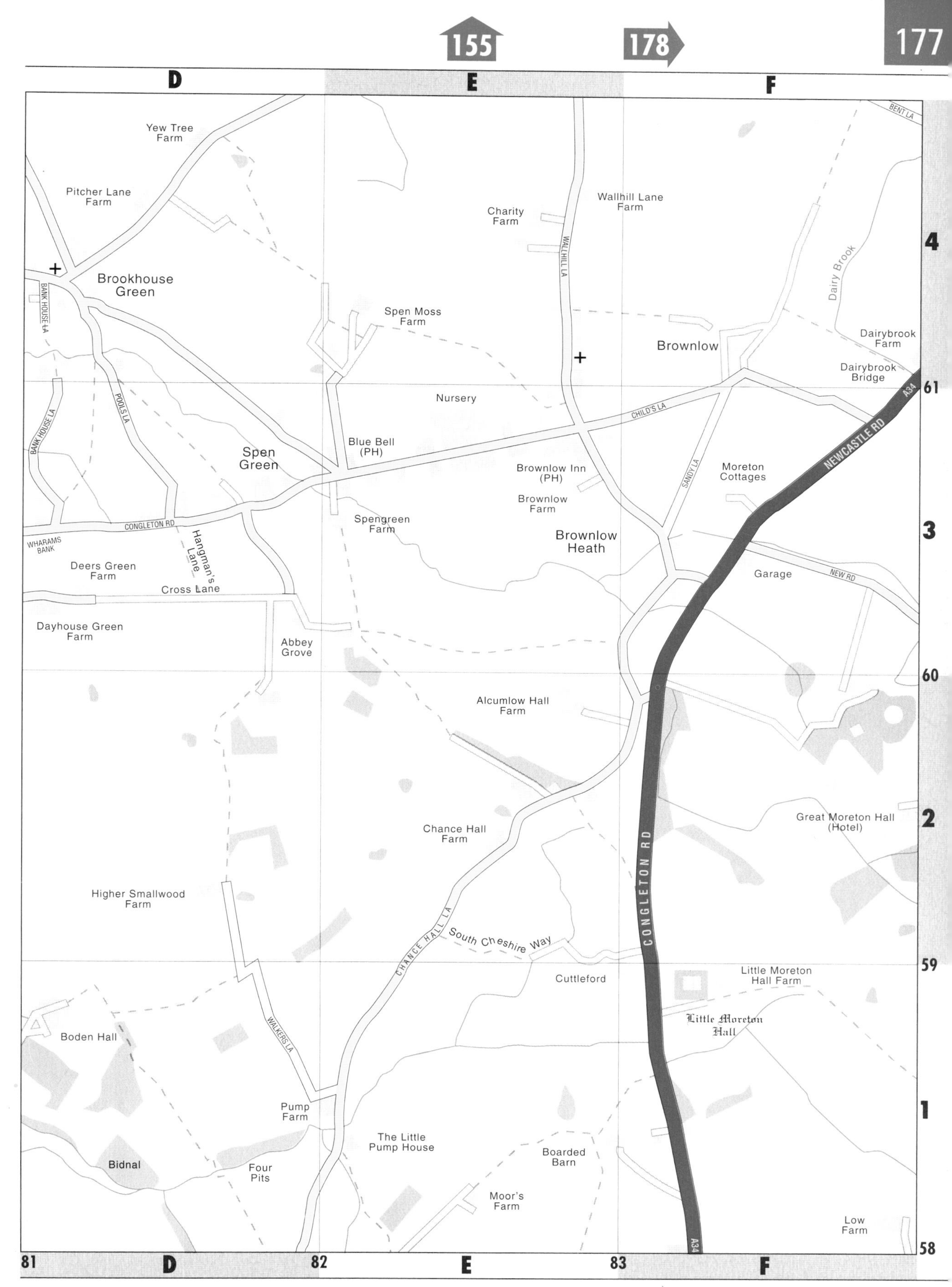
D
E
F
Yew Tree Farm
Pitcher Lane Farm
Brookhouse Green
BANK HOUSE LA
Charity Farm
Wallhill Lane Farm
WALLHILL LA
Spen Moss Farm
Brownlow
Dairy Brook
Dairybrook Farm
Dairybrook Bridge
BENT LA
Nursery
POOLS LA
BANK HOUSE LA
CHILD'S LA
A34
NEWCASTLE RD
Blue Bell (PH)
Spen Green
Brownlow Inn (PH)
Brownlow Farm
SANDY LA
Moreton Cottages
Spengreen Farm
CONGLETON RD
WHARAMS BANK
Hangman's Lane
Brownlow Heath
Deers Green Farm
Cross Lane
Garage
NEW RD
Dayhouse Green Farm
Abbey Grove
Alcumlow Hall Farm
Chance Hall Farm
Great Moreton Hall (Hotel)
Higher Smallwood Farm
CONGLETON RD
CHANCE HALL LA
South Cheshire Way
Cuttleford
Little Moreton Hall Farm
Little Moreton Hall
Boden Hall
WALKERS LA
Pump Farm
The Little Pump House
Boarded Barn
Bidnal
Four Pits
Moor's Farm
Low Farm
A34
4
61
3
60
2
59
1
58
81
D
82
E
83
F

194
178

177
156

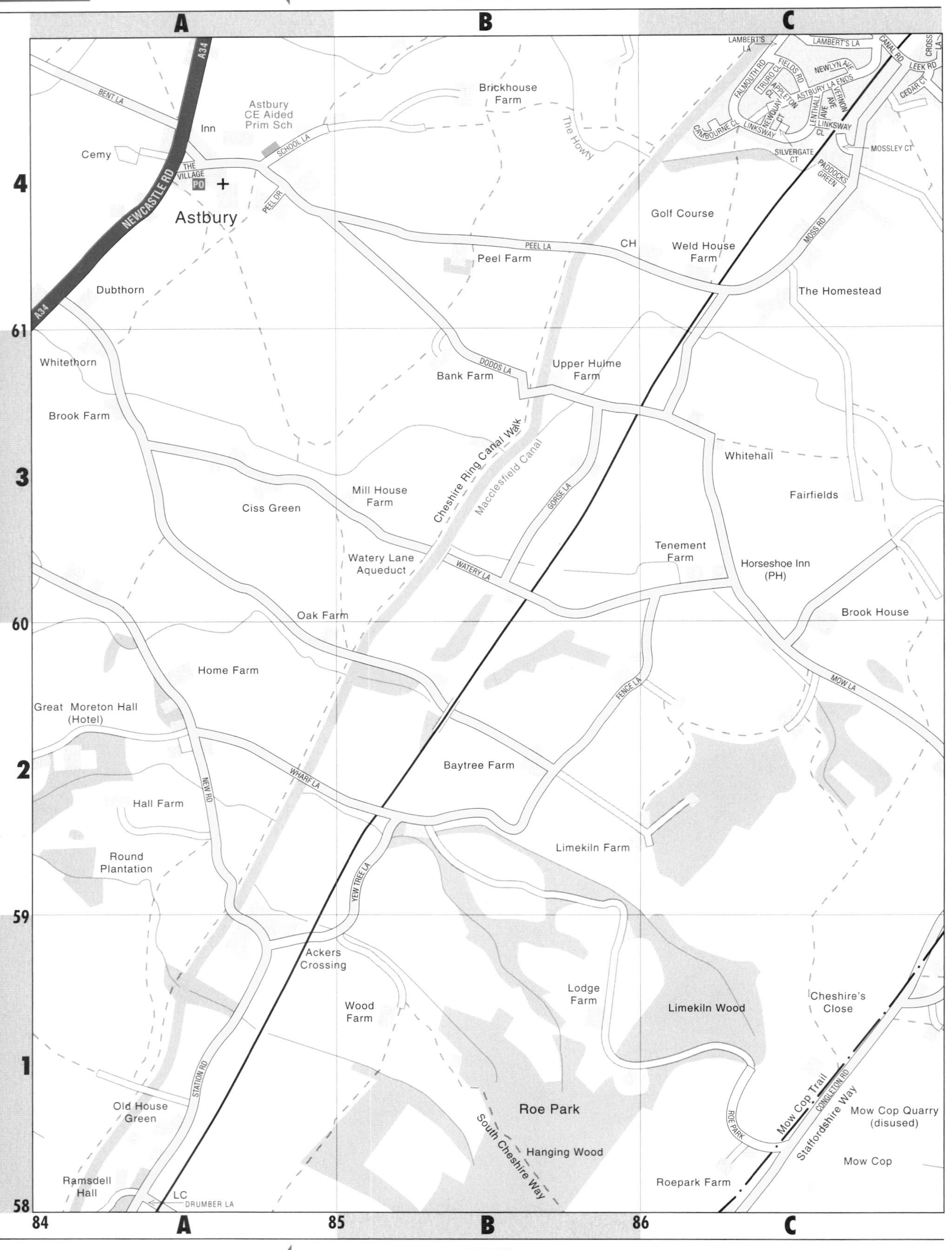
A
B
C
4
3
2
1
61
60
59
58
84
85
86
A34
NEWCASTLE RD
BENT LA
Cemy
Inn
THE VILLAGE
PO
Astbury
Astbury CE Aided Prim Sch
SCHOOL LA
PEEL DR
Brickhouse Farm
The Howty
LAMBERT'S LA
CANAL RD
CROSS LA
LEEK RD
CEDAR CT
FALMOUTH RD
TRURO CL
FIELDS RD
NEWLYN AVE
APPLETON CL
ASTBURY LA ENDS
VERNON AVE
LENTHALL AVE
NEWQUAY CT
CAMBOURNE CL
LINKSWAY
LINKSWAY CL
SILVERGATE CT
MOSSLEY CT
PADDOCKS GREEN
MOSS RD
Golf Course
CH
PEEL LA
Peel Farm
Weld House Farm
The Homestead
Dubthorn
Whitethorn
DODDS LA
Bank Farm
Upper Hulme Farm
Brook Farm
Whitehall
Cheshire Ring Canal Walk
Macclesfield Canal
GORSE LA
Mill House Farm
Ciss Green
Fairfields
Tenement Farm
Watery Lane Aqueduct
WATERY LA
Horseshoe Inn (PH)
Oak Farm
Brook House
Home Farm
MOW LA
FENCE LA
Great Moreton Hall (Hotel)
Baytree Farm
WHARF LA
NEW RD
Hall Farm
Limekiln Farm
Round Plantation
YEW TREE LA
Ackers Crossing
Wood Farm
Lodge Farm
Limekiln Wood
Cheshire's Close
STATION RD
Roe Park
Mow Cop Trail
CONGLETON RD
Staffordshire Way
Mow Cop Quarry (disused)
Old House Green
South Cheshire Way
Hanging Wood
ROE PARK
Mow Cop
Ramsdell Hall
LC
DRUMBER LA
Roepark Farm

177
195

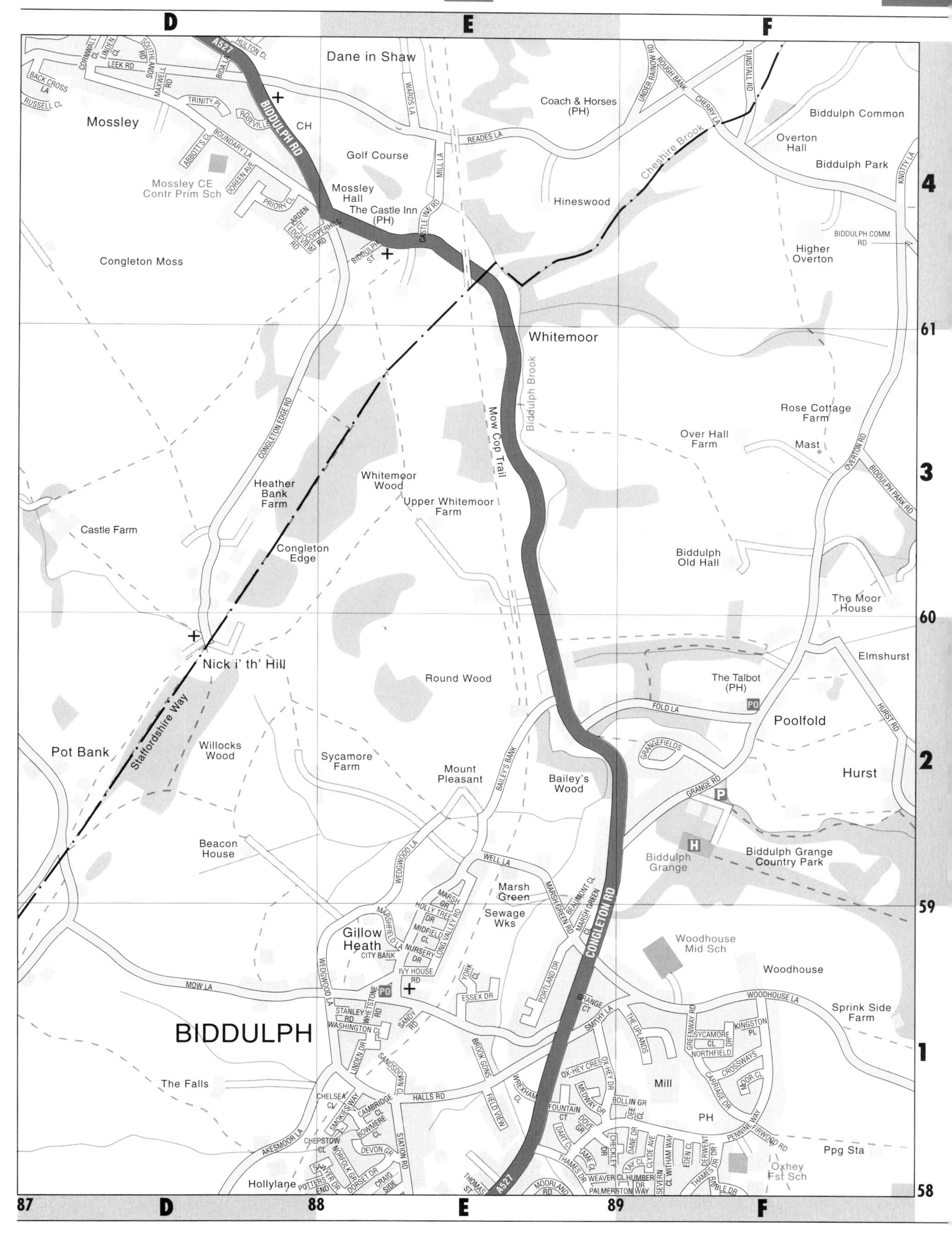

D **E** **F**

BACK CROSS LA
RUSSELL CL
CORNWALL CL
LINDEN CL
SOUTHALL RD
MAXWELL RD
LEEK RD
TRINITY PL
HULTON CL
BIDAL
A527
ROSEVILLE
BIDDULPH RD
CH
Dane in Shaw
WARDS LA
MILL LA
READES LA
Coach & Horses (PH)
UNDER RAINOW RD
ROUGH BANK
CHERRY LA
TUNSTALL RD
Biddulph Common
Mossley
ABBOTT'S CL
BOUNDARY LA
DOREEN AVE
Golf Course
Cheshire Brook
Overton Hall
Biddulph Park
KNOTTY LA
4
Mossley CE Contr Prim Sch
ARDEN CT
PRIORY CL
EDGE CROFT
COPPERHALL
BIDDULPH ST
Mossley Hall
The Castle Inn (PH)
CASTLE WAY RD
Hineswood
BIDDULPH COMM RD
Higher Overton
Congleton Moss
Whitemoor
61
CONGLETON EDGE RD
Mow Cop Trail
Biddulph Brook
Rose Cottage Farm
Over Hall Farm
Mast
OVERTON RD
BIDDULPH PARK RD
3
Heather Bank Farm
Whitemoor Wood
Upper Whitemoor Farm
Biddulph Old Hall
Castle Farm
Congleton Edge
The Moor House
60
Staffordshire Way
Nick i' th' Hill
Round Wood
The Talbot (PH)
PO
Elmshurst
HURST RD
Pot Bank
Willocks Wood
Sycamore Farm
BAILEY'S BANK
Bailey's Wood
FOLD LA
GRANGEFIELDS
GRANGE RD
P
Poolfold
Hurst
2
Beacon House
Mount Pleasant
WEDGWOOD LA
WELL LA
MARSH GREEN CL
BEAUMONT CL
MARSH GREEN RD
H
Biddulph Grange
Biddulph Grange Country Park
59
MOW LA
Gillow Heath
CITY BANK
WEDGWOOD LA
MASSEY'S LA
WHITESTONE RD
HOLLY TREE DR
MARSH GR CT
MIDFIELDS
NURSERY DR
LONG VALLEY RD
YORK CL
IVY HOUSE RD
PO
ESSEX DR
CONGLETON RD
GRANGE CT
SMITHY LA
THE PLAINS
Woodhouse Mid Sch
WOODHOUSE LA
Woodhouse
Sprink Side Farm
GREENWAY RD
SYCAMORE CL
KINGSTON PL
NORTHFIELD
MOOR CL
CROSSWAYS
BIDDULPH
STANLEY RD
WASHINGTON CL
SANDY RD
LINDEN DR
SANDS RD
BROOK GDNS
FIELD VIEW
OX-HEY FARM CL
OXHEY DR
MEDWAY DR
BOLLIN GR
DEE CL
Mill
PH
CARRIAGE DR
PENNINE FIRWOOD RD
1
The Falls
CHELSEA CL
SMOKIES WAY
CAMBRIDGE CT
BOWMERE
HALLS RD
FOUNTAIN CT
DIXIE CL
DANE DR
CLYDE AVE
WITHAM WAY
EDEN CL
DERWENT CL
Ppg Sta
AKESMOOR LA
CHEPSTOW CL
NORFOLK CL
DEVON CL
STANTON RD
WREXHAM CL
DART CL
DANE CL
CHECKLEY
TAME CL
SEVERN CL
HUMBER DR
RIBBLE DR
Oxhey Fst Sch
Hollylane
POTTERS END
DORSET DR
CRAIG SIDE
THOMAS ST
A527
MOORLAND RD
THAMES CL
WEAVER CL
PALMERSTON WAY
Sewage Wks
Marsh Green
58

87 **D** **88** **E** **89** **F**

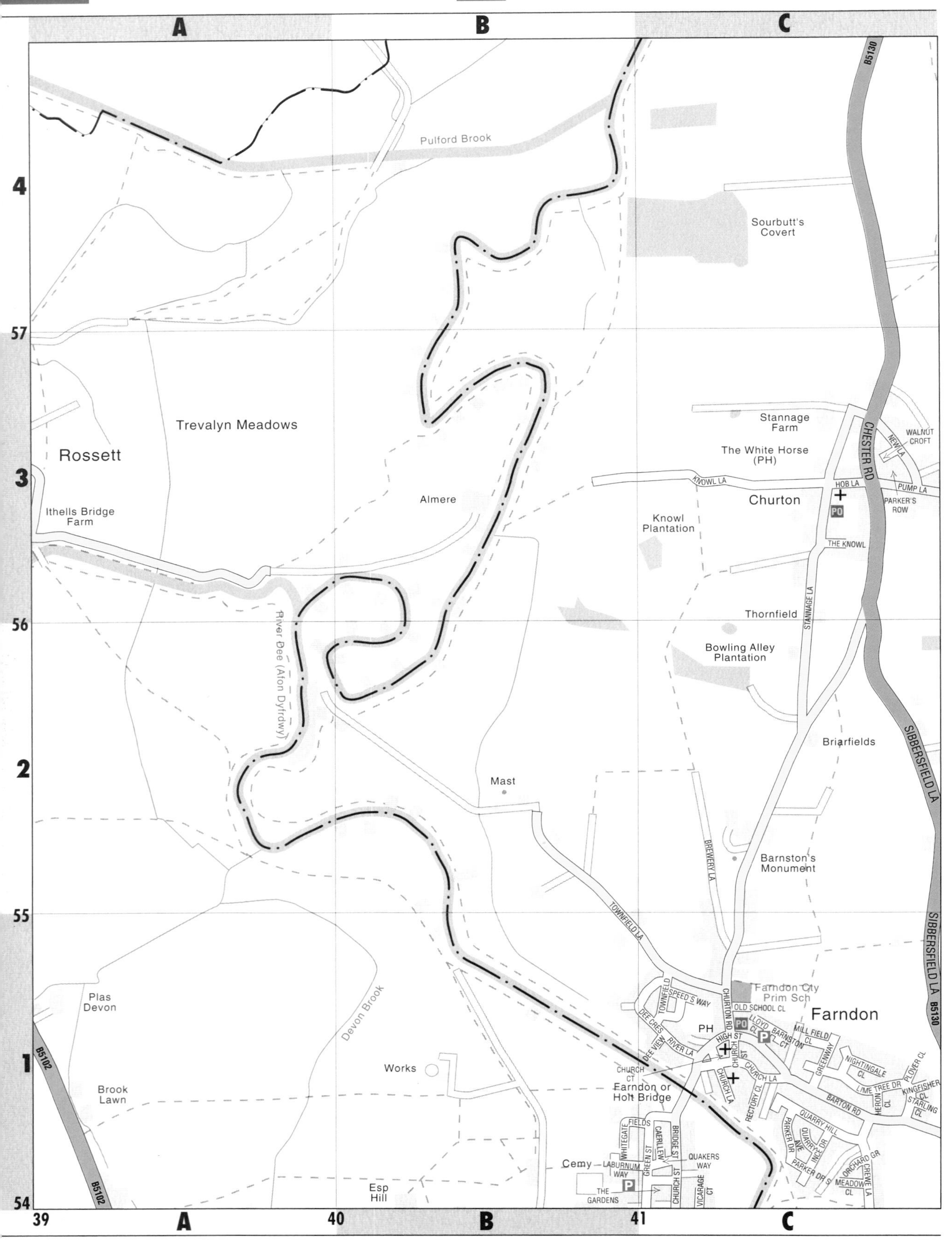

A B C

4

57

Pulford Brook

Sourbutt's
Covert

B5130

Trevalyn Meadows

Stannage
Farm

The White Horse
(PH)

Rossett

3

Almere

Churton

Ithells Bridge
Farm

KNOWL LA

CHESTER RD

NEW LA

WALNUT
CROFT

HOB LA

PO

PUMP LA

PARKER'S
ROW

Knowl
Plantation

THE KNOWL

56

River Dee (Afon Dyfrdwy)

Thornfield

Bowling Alley
Plantation

STANNAGE LA

2

Mast

Briarfields

Barnston's
Monument

BREWERY LA

SIBBERSFIELD LA

55

TOWNFIELD LA

B5130

Devon Brook

Plas
Devon

Farndon C of E
Prim Sch

Farndon

1

Works

B5102

Brook
Lawn

OLD SPEED'S WAY

OLD SCHOOL CL

TOWNFIELD

DEE CRES

CHURTON RD

RIVER LA

DEE VIEW

PH

HIGH ST

CHURCH
CT

CHURCH LA

PO

P

LLOYD
CL

BARNSTON
CT

MILL FIELD

GREENWAY

NIGHTINGALE
CL

LIME TREE DR

KINGFISHER
CL

STARLING
CL

Earndon or
Holt Bridge

RECTORY CT

CHURCH LA

BARTON RD

QUARRY HILL

PARKER DR

QUARRY LANE DR

ORCHARD GR

MEADOW
CL

Cemy

WHITEGATE
FIELDS

GREEN ST

CHURCH ST

BRIDGE ST

CAER LLEW

LABURNUM
WAY

QUAKERS
WAY

VICARAGE
CT

P

Esp
Hill

THE
GARDENS

B5102

54

39 A 40 B 41 C

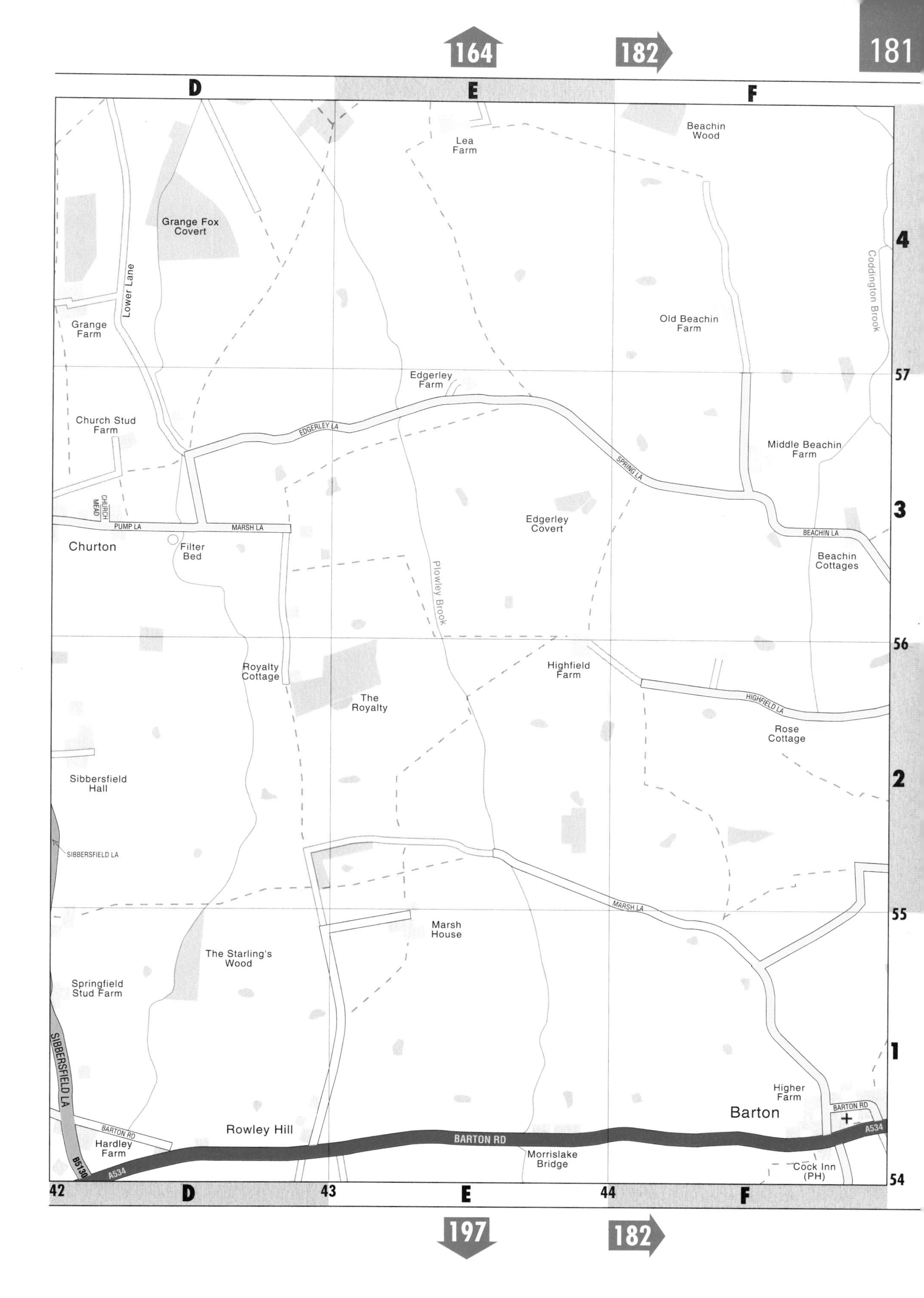

Beachin Wood

Lea Farm

Grange Fox Covert

Lower Lane

Grange Farm

Church Stud Farm

CHURCH MEAD

PUMP LA

Churton

MARSH LA

Filter Bed

Edgerley Farm

EDGERLEY LA

Old Beachin Farm

SPRING LA

Edgerley Covert

Middle Beachin Farm

BEACHIN LA

Beachin Cottages

Royalty Cottage

The Royalty

Plowley Brook

Highfield Farm

HIGHFIELD LA

Rose Cottage

Sibbersfield Hall

SIBBERSFIELD LA

Marsh House

MARSH LA

The Starling's Wood

Springfield Stud Farm

SIBBERSFIELD LA

BARTON RD

Hardley Farm

B5130

A534

Rowley Hill

BARTON RD

Morrislake Bridge

Higher Farm

Barton

BARTON RD

Cock Inn (PH)

A534

Coddington Brook

4

57

3

56

2

55

1

181
165

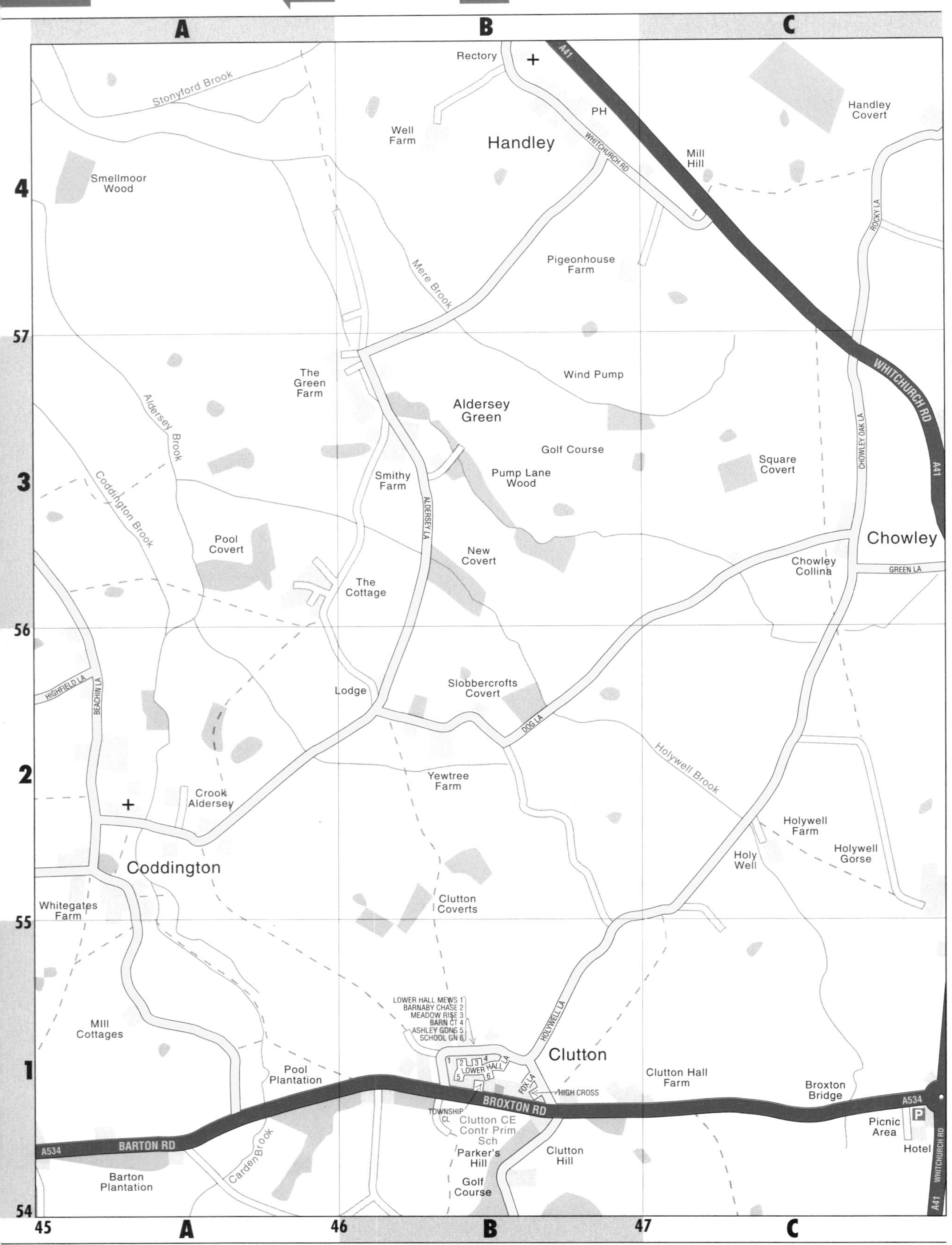
A
B
C
Rectory
Stonyford Brook
Well Farm
Handley
PH
WHITCHURCH RD
A41
Handley Covert
Mill Hill
Smellmoor Wood
4
ROCKY LA
Pigeonhouse Farm
Mere Brook
57
The Green Farm
Wind Pump
WHITCHURCH RD
Aldersey Brook
Aldersey Green
Golf Course
Square Covert
CHOWLEY OAK LA
A41
Coddington Brook
Smithy Farm
Pump Lane Wood
3
ALDERSEY LA
Chowley
Pool Covert
New Covert
Chowley Collina
GREEN LA
The Cottage
56
HIGHFIELD LA
BEACHIN LA
Lodge
Slobbercrofts Covert
DOG LA
Holywell Brook
2
Yewtree Farm
Crook Aldersey
Holywell Farm
Holywell Gorse
Holy Well
Coddington
Whitegates Farm
Clutton Coverts
55
LOWER HALL MEWS 1
BARNABY CHASE 2
MEADOW RISE 3
BARN CT 4
ASHLEY GDNS 5
SCHOOL GN 6
Mill Cottages
HOLYWELL LA
Clutton
1
LOWER HALL LA
FOX LA
HIGH CROSS
Pool Plantation
Clutton Hall Farm
Broxton Bridge
BROXTON RD
A534
TOWNSHIP CL
Clutton CE Contr Prim Sch
Picnic Area
P
A534
BARTON RD
Carden Brook
Parker's Hill
Clutton Hill
Hotel
WHITCHURCH RD
Barton Plantation
Golf Course
A41
54
45
A
46
B
47
C

181
198

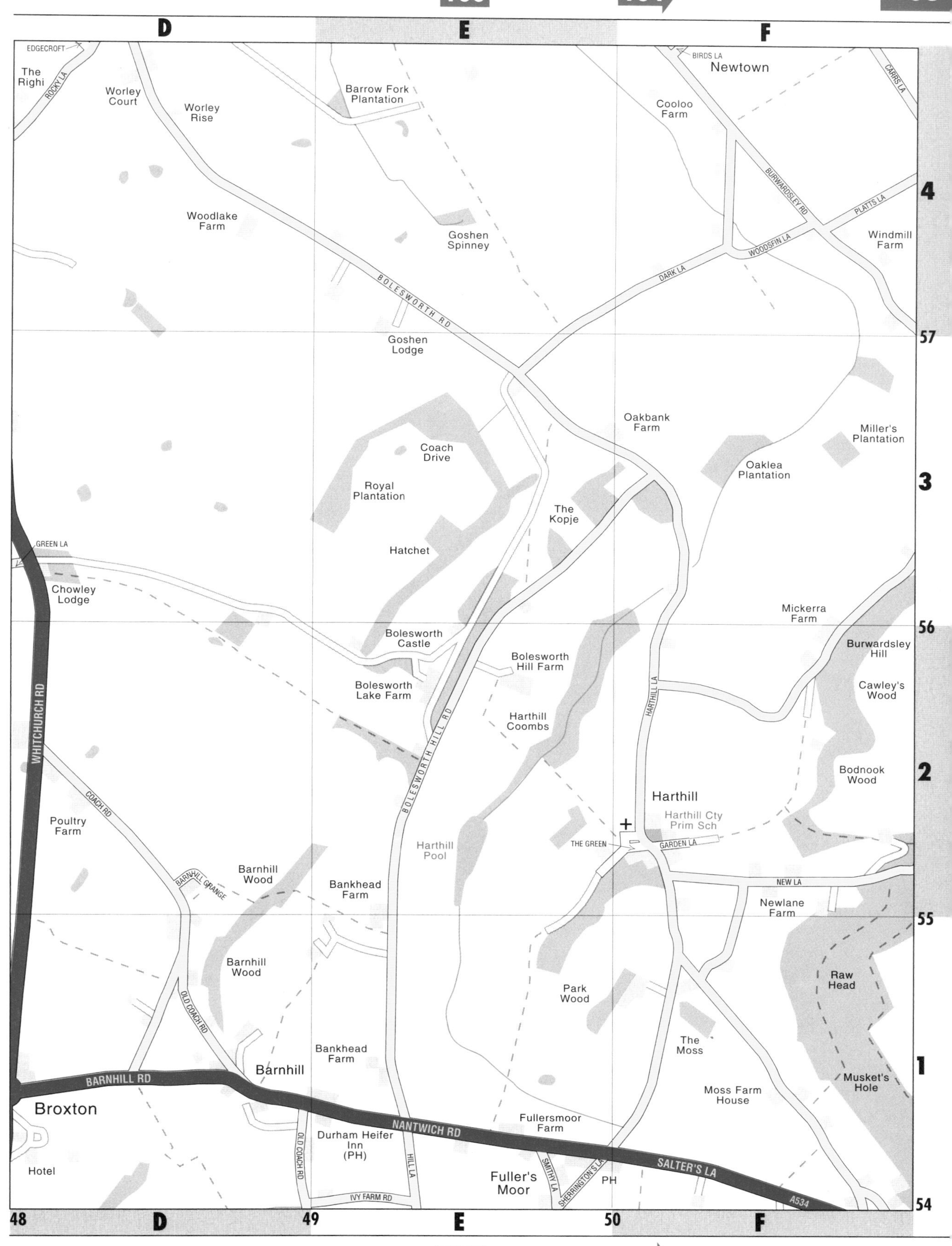

D
E
F
EDGECROFT
The Righi
ROCKY LA
Worley Court
Worley Rise
Barrow Fork Plantation
BIRDS LA
Newtown
Cooloo Farm
CARRS LA
Woodlake Farm
Goshen Spinney
BURWARDSLEY RD
PLATTS LA
Windmill Farm
WOODSFIN LA
DARK LA
BOLESWORTH RD
4
57
Goshen Lodge
Oakbank Farm
Miller's Plantation
Coach Drive
Oaklea Plantation
Royal Plantation
3
The Kopje
Hatchet
GREEN LA
Chowley Lodge
Mickerra Farm
56
Bolesworth Castle
Burwardsley Hill
Bolesworth Hill Farm
Bolesworth Lake Farm
Cawley's Wood
HARTHILL LA
WHITCHURCH RD
Harthill Coombs
BOLESWORTH HILL RD
Bodnook Wood
2
Harthill
Harthill Cty Prim Sch
Poultry Farm
COACH RD
Harthill Pool
THE GREEN
GARDEN LA
Barnhill Wood
BARNHILL GRANGE
Bankhead Farm
NEW LA
Newlane Farm
55
Barnhill Wood
Raw Head
Park Wood
OLD COACH RD
The Moss
Bankhead Farm
1
Barnhill
Musket's Hole
BARNHILL RD
Moss Farm House
Broxton
NANTWICH RD
Fullersmoor Farm
Durham Heifer Inn (PH)
SALTER'S LA
OLD COACH RD
HILL LA
Hotel
Fuller's Moor
SMITHY LA
SHERRINGTON'S LA
PH
A534
IVY FARM RD
54
48
D
49
E
50
F

183
167

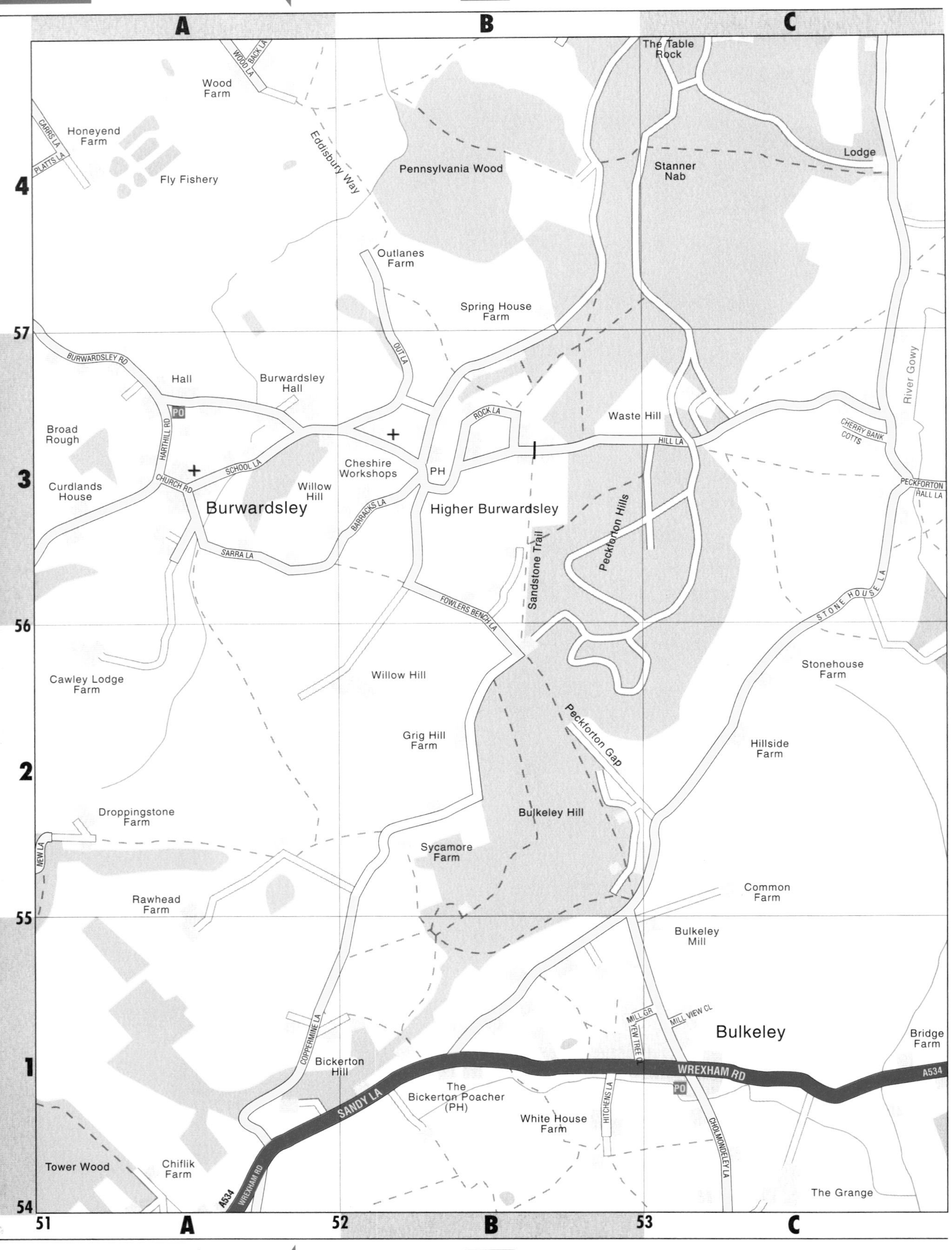
A
B
C
The Table Rock
Wood Farm
WOOD LA
WOOD BACK LA
Honeyend Farm
CARRS LA
PLATTS LA
Fly Fishery
Eddisbury Way
Pennsylvania Wood
Lodge
Stanner Nab
4
Outlanes Farm
Spring House Farm
57
BURWARDSLEY RD
Hall
Burwardsley Hall
OUT LA
PO
ROCK LA
Waste Hill
River Gowy
Broad Rough
HARTHILL RD
HILL LA
CHERRY BANK COTTS
Cheshire Workshops
PH
SCHOOL LA
Curdlands House
CHURCH RD
Willow Hill
3
Burwardsley
BARRACKS LA
Higher Burwardsley
PECKFORTON HALL LA
Peckforton Hills
Sandstone Trail
SARRA LA
STONE HOUSE LA
FOWLERS BENCH LA
56
Willow Hill
Cawley Lodge Farm
Stonehouse Farm
Peckforton Gap
Grig Hill Farm
Hillside Farm
2
Droppingstone Farm
Bulkeley Hill
NEW LA
Sycamore Farm
Rawhead Farm
Common Farm
55
Bulkeley Mill
MILL GR
MILL VIEW CL
COPPERMINE LA
YEW TREE CL
Bulkeley
Bridge Farm
1
Bickerton Hill
WREXHAM RD
A534
PO
The Bickerton Poacher (PH)
SANDY LA
HITCHENS LA
White House Farm
CHOLMONDELEY LA
Tower Wood
Chiflik Farm
A534
WREXHAM RD
The Grange
54
51
A
52
B
53
C

183
200

168
186

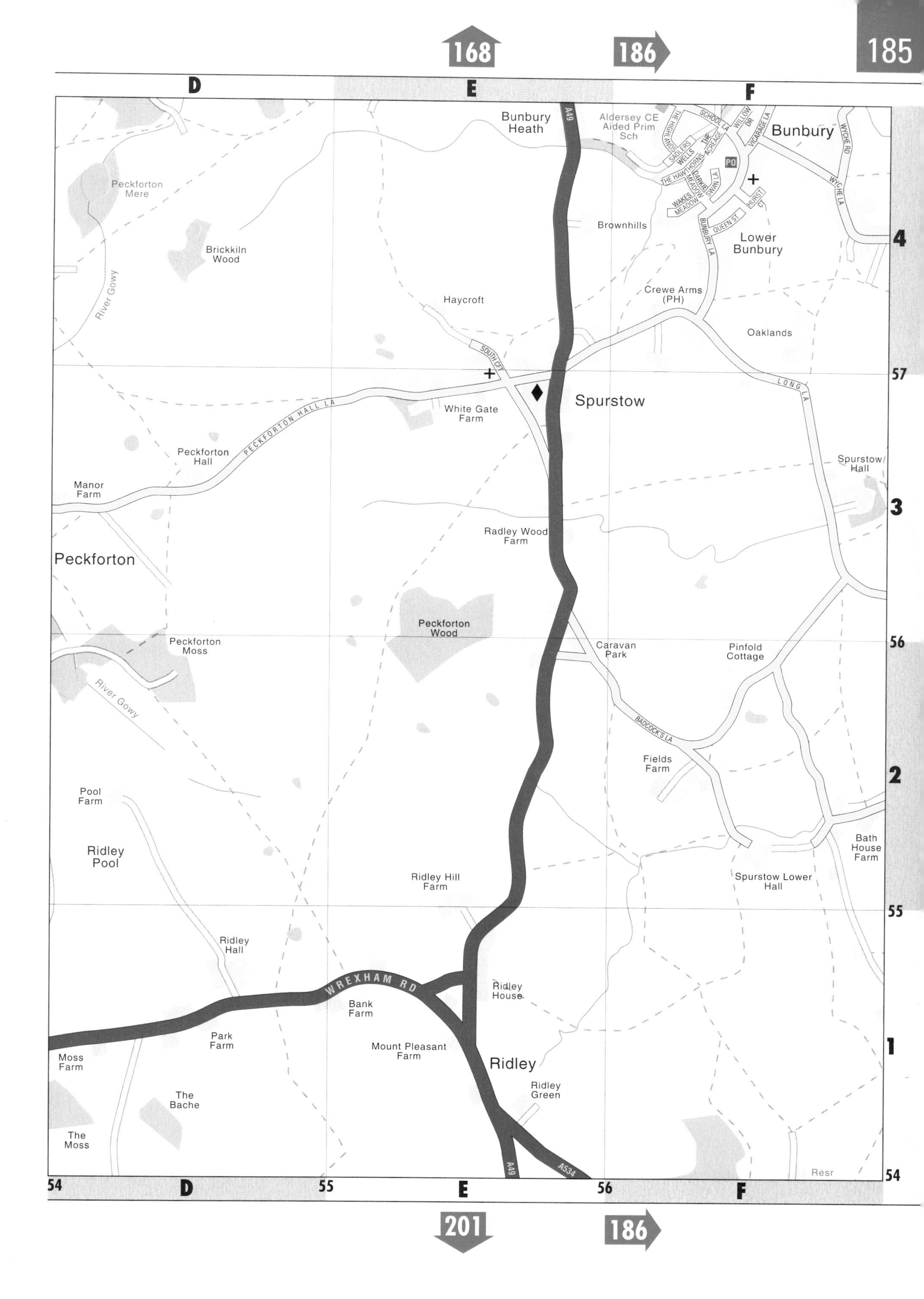
D
E
F
Bunbury Heath
Aldersey CE Aided Prim Sch
Bunbury
A49
SCHOOL LA
WILLOW DR
VICARAGE LA
THE HIGHLANDS
SADLERS WELLS
THE ACREAGE
THE HAWTHORNS
DARKIE MEADOW
SWAN LA
WAKES MEADOW
PO
HURST CT
QUEEN ST
BUNBURY LA
WYCHE RD
WYCHE LA
Peckforton Mere
Brickkiln Wood
Brownhills
Lower Bunbury
River Gowy
Haycroft
Crewe Arms (PH)
Oaklands
SOUTH CFT
LONG LA
Spurstow
White Gate Farm
PECKFORTON HALL LA
Peckforton Hall
Manor Farm
Spurstow Hall
Radley Wood Farm
Peckforton
Peckforton Wood
Peckforton Moss
Caravan Park
Pinfold Cottage
River Gowy
BADCOCK'S LA
Fields Farm
Pool Farm
Ridley Pool
Bath House Farm
Ridley Hill Farm
Spurstow Lower Hall
Ridley Hall
WREXHAM RD
Ridley House
Bank Farm
Park Farm
Mount Pleasant Farm
Moss Farm
Ridley
Ridley Green
The Bache
The Moss
A49
A534
Resr
4
57
3
56
2
55
1
54
54
55
56

201
186

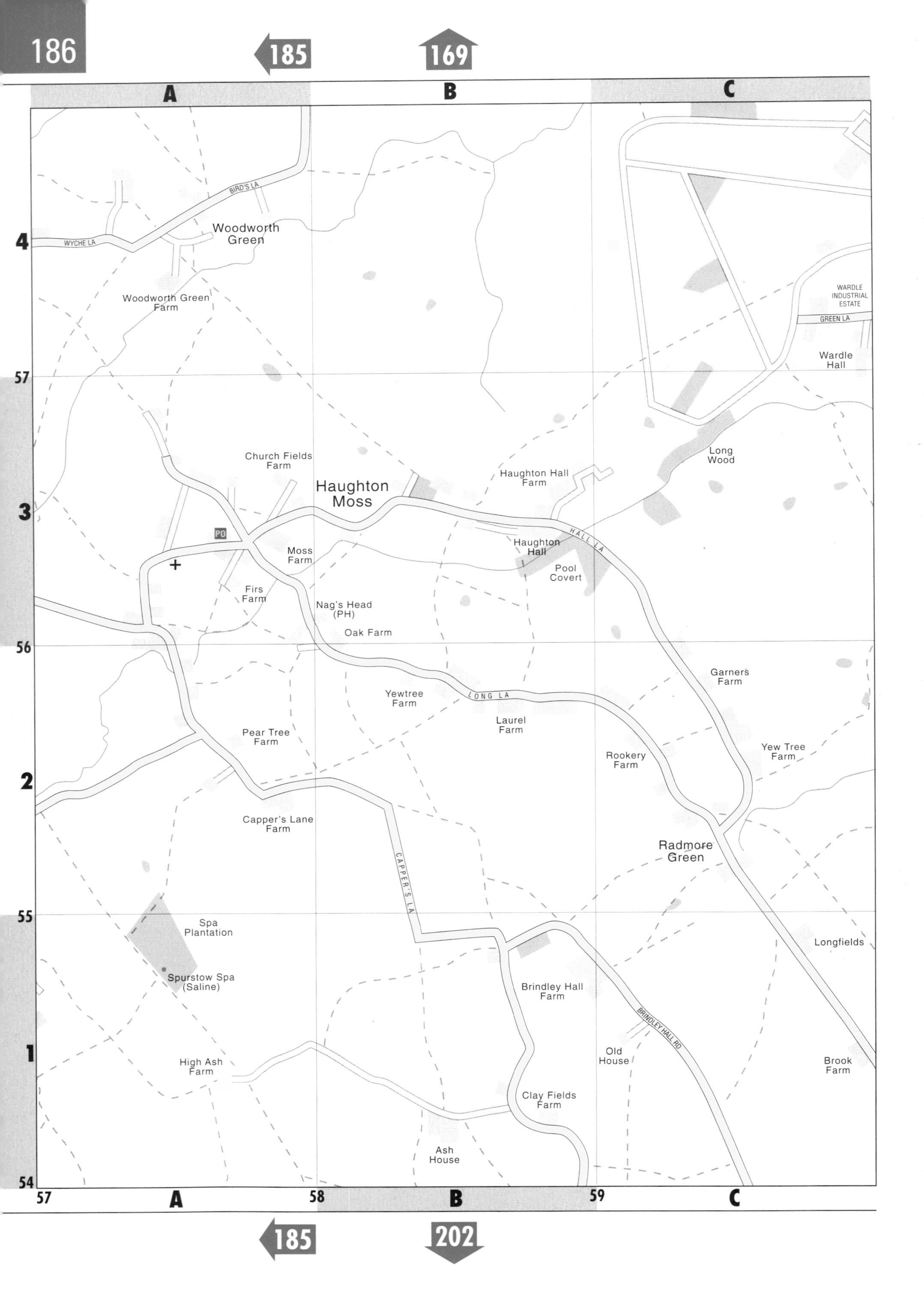

A B C

4

WYCHE LA
BIRD'S LA
Woodworth
Green

Woodworth Green
Farm

WARDLE
INDUSTRIAL
ESTATE
GREEN LA
Wardle
Hall

57

Long
Wood

Church Fields
Farm

Haughton Hall
Farm

Haughton
Moss

PO

Moss
Farm

Haughton
Hall

HALL LA

3

+

Firs
Farm

Pool
Covert

Nag's Head
(PH)

Oak Farm

56

Garner's
Farm

Yewtree
Farm

LONG LA

Laurel
Farm

Pear Tree
Farm

Yew Tree
Farm

Rookery
Farm

2

Capper's Lane
Farm

CAPPER'S LA

Radmore
Green

55

Spa
Plantation

Longfields

Spurstow Spa
(Saline)

Brindley Hall
Farm

BRINDLEY HALL RD

1

High Ash
Farm

Old
House

Brook
Farm

Clay Fields
Farm

54

Ash
House

57 A 58 B 59 C

D E F

A51
Wardle Hall Bridge
NANTWICH RD
Humble Bee Bank Cottages
Hill's Gorse
CALVELEY HALL LA
Wardle Bridge Farm
Radio Telescope
WARDLE INDUSTRIAL ESTATE
Green-lane Farm
Wardle
Rutters Bridge
Sandhole Bridge
Benyon's Bridge
Shropshire Union Canal
GREEN LA
WARDLE AVE
Wardle Old Hall
Middlewich Branch
Crossbanks Farm

4

Barbridge Junction
57
The Poplars Farm
Bar Bridge
Stoke Hall Farm
Jolly Tar (PH)
The Barbridge Inn
STOKEHALL LA
Works
PO
OLD CHESTER RD
Barbridge
BANKSIDE CL.
Bremilow's Bridge
Stoke Hall
The Rookery

3

Bullsgreen Farm
MILL POOL LA
CHESTER RD
CHAPEL ROW
Stoke Bank
Stokehall Bridge
Shropshire Union Canal
Clatterdishes Farm

56
Vicker's Bridge
Verona
Stoke Manor
Yew Tree Farm

Little Bachehouse Covert
Hurleston Reservoir
Hurleston Junction

2

Little Bache House
Works
Radmore Covert
Bachehouse Covert
Hurleston Bridge

55
Bache House
Corners Bridge
Bachehouse Bridge
Bachehouse Pool
Park Farm
New Farm
Martin's Bridge

1
LONG LA
Lee's Bridge
A51

54

187
171

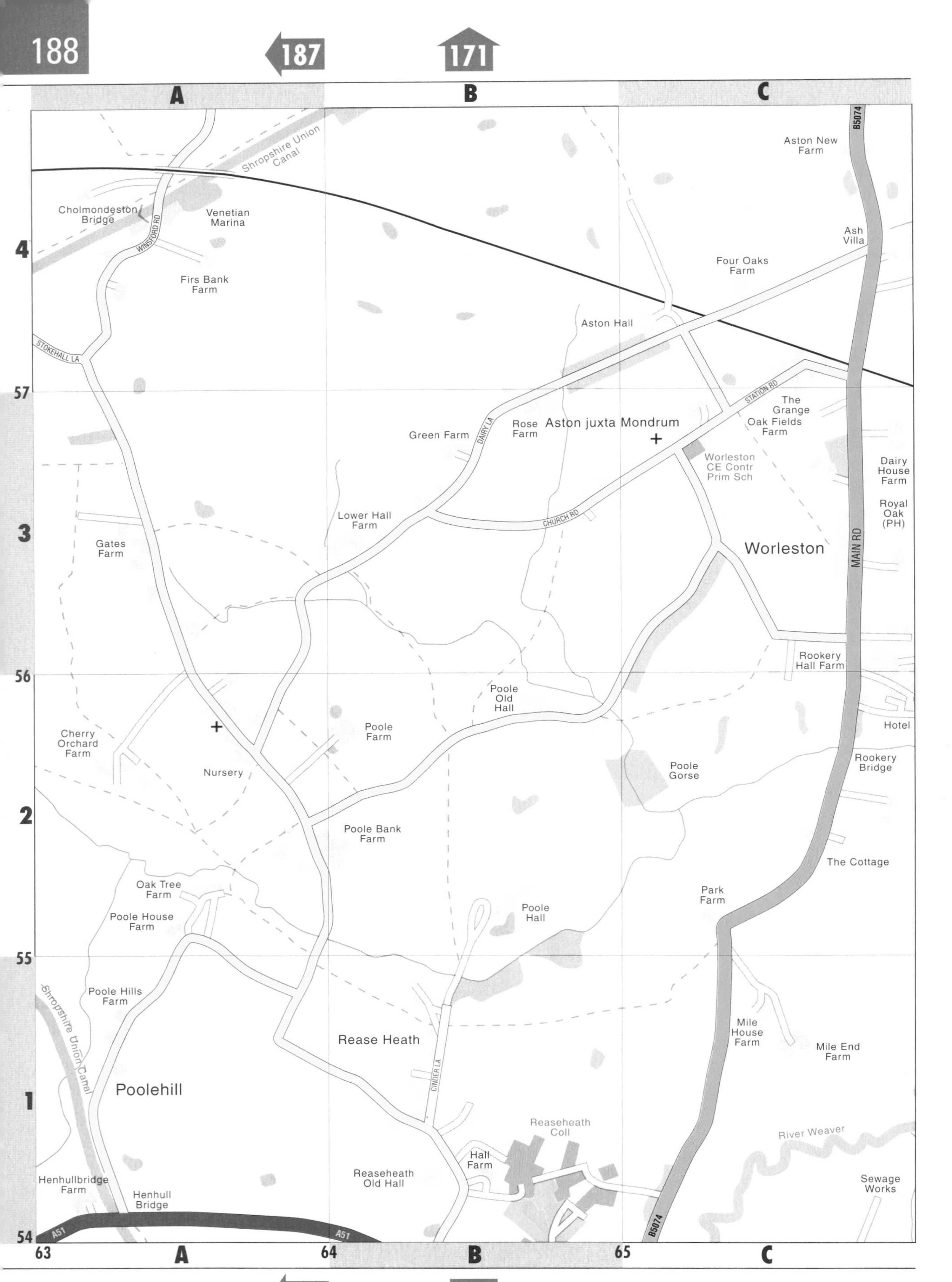
A
B
C
Shropshire Union Canal
Cholmondeston Bridge
Venetian Marina
WINSFORD RD
Firs Bank Farm
STOKEHALL LA
Aston New Farm
B5074
Ash Villa
Four Oaks Farm
Aston Hall
STATION RD
The Grange
Oak Fields Farm
Aston juxta Mondrum
Rose Farm
Green Farm
DAIRY LA
Worleston CE Contr Prim Sch
Dairy House Farm
Royal Oak (PH)
Lower Hall Farm
CHURCH RD
Gates Farm
Worleston
MAIN RD
Rookery Hall Farm
Poole Old Hall
Hotel
Cherry Orchard Farm
Poole Farm
Nursery
Poole Gorse
Rookery Bridge
Poole Bank Farm
The Cottage
Oak Tree Farm
Poole House Farm
Park Farm
Poole Hall
Poole Hills Farm
Shropshire Union Canal
Mile House Farm
Mile End Farm
Rease Heath
Poolehill
CINDER LA
Reaseheath Coll
River Weaver
Hall Farm
Henhullbridge Farm
Henhull Bridge
Reaseheath Old Hall
Sewage Works
A51
B5074
4
57
3
56
2
55
1
54
63
64
65

187
204

D E F

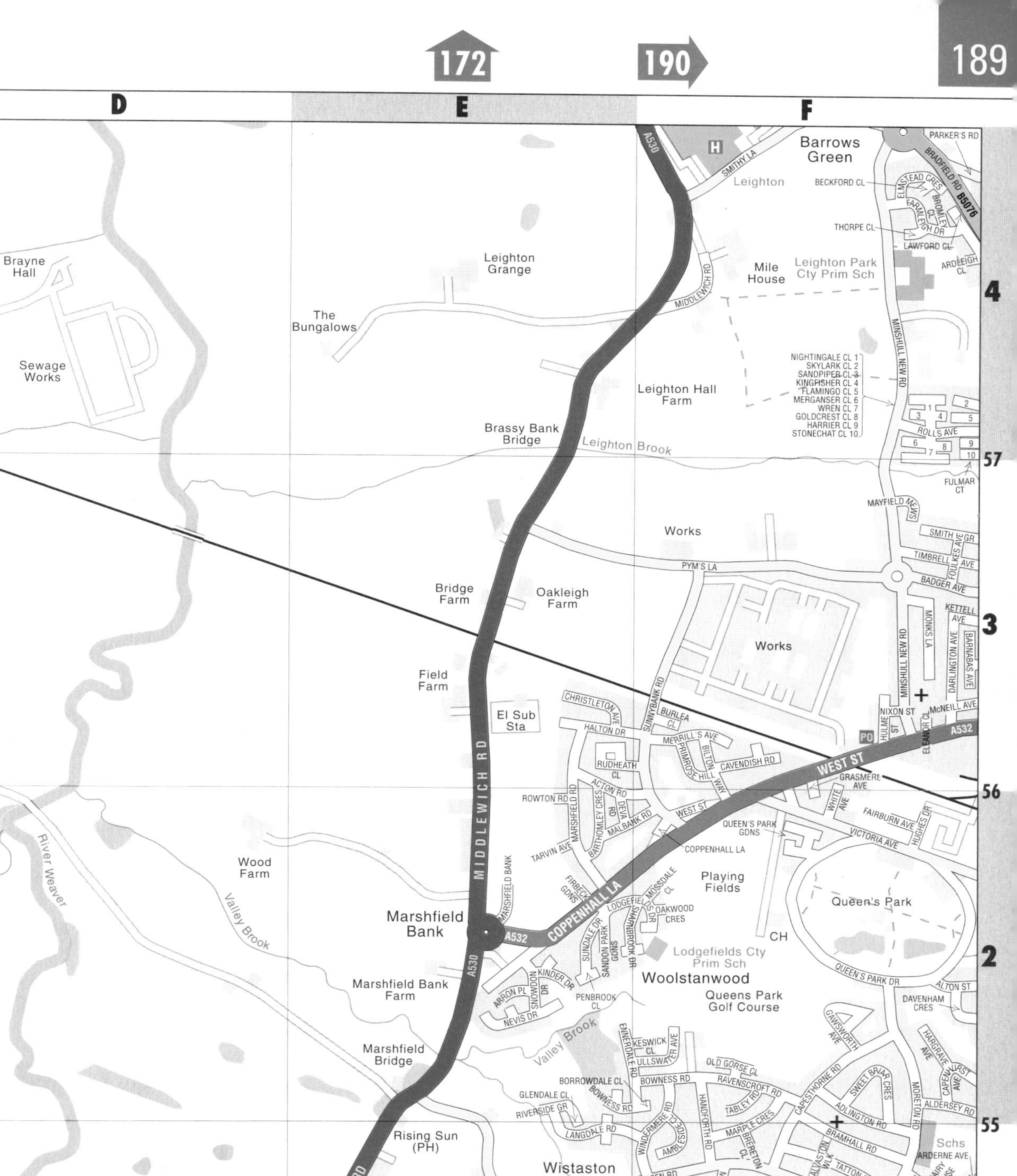
Barrows Green
Leighton
SMITHY LA
PARKER'S RD
BRADFIELD RD
B5076
BECKFORD CL
ELMSTEAD CRES
FARMLEIGH DR
BROMLEY CL
THORPE CL
LAWFORD CL
ARDLEIGH CL
Brayne Hall
Leighton Grange
Mile House
Leighton Park Cty Prim Sch
MIDDLEWICH RD
The Bungalows
Sewage Works
Leighton Hall Farm
MINSHULL NEW RD
NIGHTINGALE CL 1
SKYLARK CL 2
SANDPIPER CL 3
KINGFISHER CL 4
FLAMINGO CL 5
MERGANSER CL 6
WREN CL 7
GOLDCREST CL 8
HARRIER CL 9
STONECHAT CL 10
ROLLS AVE
Brassy Bank Bridge
Leighton Brook
FULMAR CT
MAYFIELD MEWS
Works
SMITH GR
FOULKES AVE
TIMBRELL AVE
PYM'S LA
BADGER AVE
Bridge Farm
Oakleigh Farm
KETTELL AVE
MONKS LA
DARLINGTON AVE
BARNABAS AVE
Works
Field Farm
El Sub Sta
CHRISTLETON AVE
HALTON DR
SUNNYBANK RD
BURLEA CL
NIXON ST
McNEILL AVE
HULME ST
ELEANOR CL
A532
PO
MERRILL'S AVE
PRIMROSE HILL
BILTON WAY
CAVENDISH RD
WEST ST
RUDHEATH CL
GRASMERE AVE
ACTON RD
ROWTON RD
MARSHFIELD RD
BARTHOMLEY CRES
DEVA RD
MALBANK RD
WHITE AVE
FAIRBURN AVE
HUGHES DR
QUEEN'S PARK GDNS
VICTORIA AVE
TARVIN AVE
COPPENHALL LA
MIDDLEWICH RD
MARSHFIELD BANK
Wood Farm
River Weaver
Valley Brook
FIRBECK GDNS
MOSSDALE CL
LODGEFIELDS DR
OAKWOOD CRES
Playing Fields
Queen's Park
Marshfield Bank
A530
A532
SUNDALE DR
SANDON PARK GDNS
SHARNBROOK DR
CH
Lodgefields Cty Prim Sch
Woolstanwood
KINDER DR
SNOWDON DR
ARRON PL
NEVIS DR
PENBROOK CL
QUEEN'S PARK DR
ALTON ST
DAVENHAM CRES
Queens Park Golf Course
Marshfield Bank Farm
GAWSWORTH AVE
HARGRAVE AVE
Valley Brook
KESWICK CL
ENNERDALE RD
ULLSWATER AVE
Marshfield Bridge
OLD GORSE CL
BORROWDALE CL
BOWNESS RD
RAVENSCROFT RD
CAPESTHORNE RD
SWEET BRIAR CRES
MORETON DR
CAPENHURST AVE
GLENDALE CL
ALDERSEY RD
RIVERSIDE GR
TABLEY RD
ADLINGTON RD
LANGDALE RD
WINDERMERE RD
CRICKET CL
HANDFORTH RD
MARPLE CRES
BRAMHALL RD
Rising Sun (PH)
AMBLESIDE CL
BRERETON CL
ALVASTON WLK
TATTON RD
Schs
ARDERNE AVE
Wistaston Green
DAIRY HOUSE WAY
WISTASTON GREEN RD
MULBERRY RD
LARCH RD
READESDALE AVE
WISTASTON GREEN CL
WOODFORD CL
NANTWICH RD
FIELD LA
ELM CL
WISTASTON AVE
BEECH DR
LAUREL DR
Alvaston Hall Hotel
FAIRBROOK
LABURNUM AVE
HAWTHORN LA
THIRLMERE RD
West End
PO
WOODSIDE AVE
VALLEY RD
FIELD AVE
WILLOW CRES
Wistaston Brook
WOODSIDE LA
WALDRON GDNS
MIDDLEWICH RD
Wistaston Bridge
WORDSWORTH CL 1
BYRON WAY 2
BROUGHTON LA
WISTASTON PARK
CLARE DR
BLAKE CL
SHELLEY DR
PRIOR CL
Robinson's Corner
CHURCH LA
PARK DR
CHESTERTON DR
LEAR DR
MILNER DR
A530
4
57
3
56
2
55
1
54

66 D 67 E 68 F

189
173

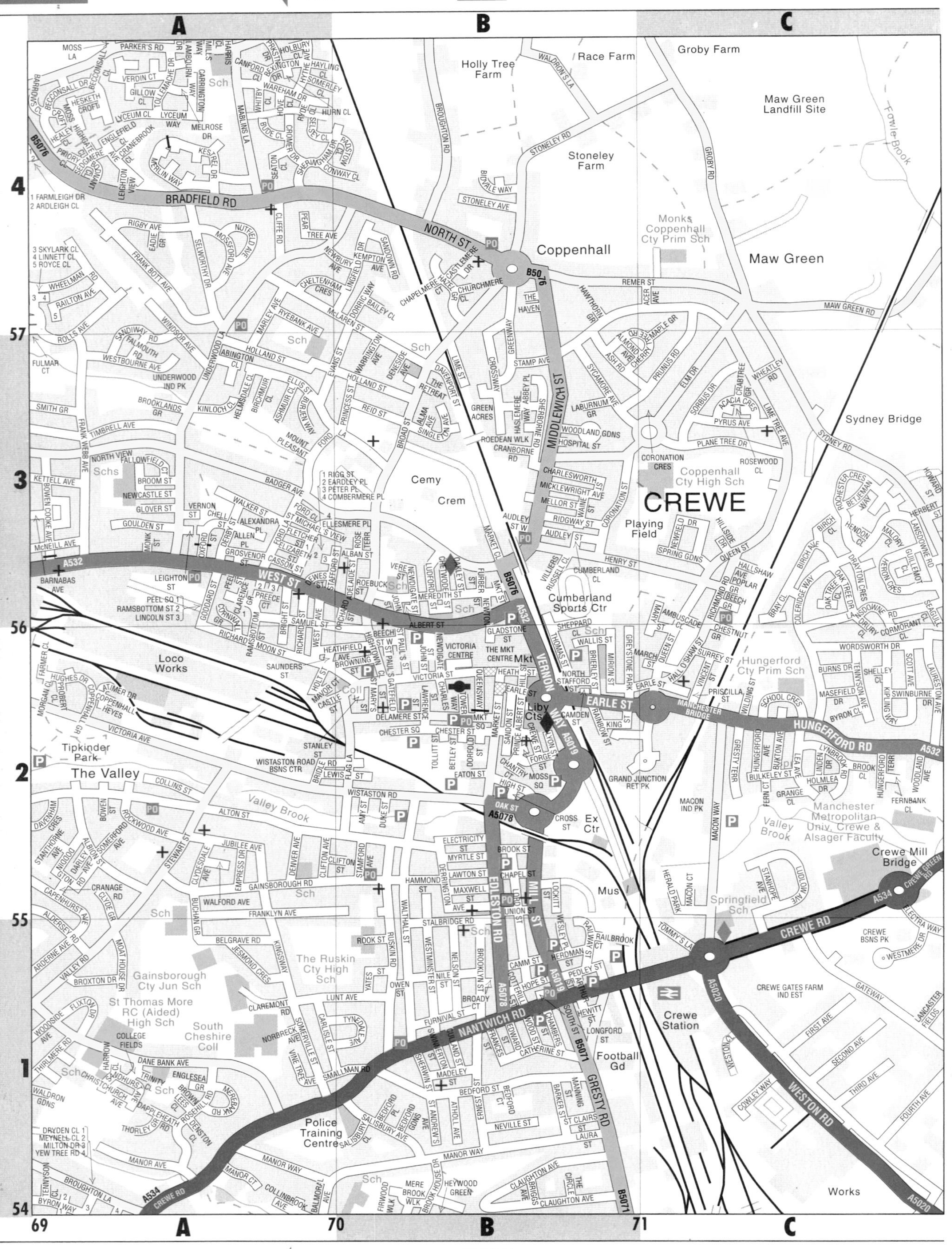
A
B
C
4
57
3
56
2
55
1
54
69
70
71
CREWE
Holly Tree Farm
Race Farm
Groby Farm
Maw Green Landfill Site
Fowle Brook
Stoneley Farm
Coppenhall
Monks Coppenhall Cty Prim Sch
Maw Green
Sydney Bridge
Cemy
Crem
Coppenhall Cty High Sch
Playing Field
Cumberland Sports Ctr
Hungerford Cty Prim Sch
Loco Works
Tipkinder Park
The Valley
Valley Brook
Mkt
Liby
Cts
Ex Ctr
Mus
Springfield Sch
Manchester Metropolitan Univ, Crewe & Alsager Faculty
Crewe Mill Bridge
CREWE BSNS PK
CREWE GATES FARM IND EST
Crewe Station
Football Gd
The Ruskin Cty High Sch
Gainsborough Cty Jun Sch
St Thomas More RC (Aided) High Sch
South Cheshire Coll
COLLEGE FIELDS
Police Training Centre
Works
UNDERWOOD IND PK
VICTORIA CENTRE
THE MKT CENTRE
WISTASTON ROAD BSNS CTR
GRAND JUNCTION RET PK
MACON IND PK
Valley Brook
BRADFIELD RD
NORTH ST
WEST ST
MIDDLEWICH ST
VERNON WAY
EARLE ST
HUNGERFORD RD
MANCHESTER BRIDGE
CREWE RD
WESTON RD
NANTWICH RD
EDLESTON RD
MILL ST
GRESTY RD
REMER ST
MAW GREEN RD
GROBY RD
STONELEY RD
BROUGHTON RD
SYDNEY RD
HENRY ST
WISTASTON RD
VICTORIA AVE
COLLINS ST
ALTON ST
MANOR WAY
A532
A534
A5019
A5020
A5078
B5071
B5076
1 FARMLEIGH DR
2 ARDLEIGH CL
3 SKYLARK CL
4 LINNETT CL
5 ROYCE CL
1 RIGG ST
2 EARDLEY PL
3 PETER PL
4 COMBERMERE PL
PEEL SQ 1
RAMSBOTTOM ST 2
LINCOLN ST 3
DRYDEN CL 1
MEYNELL CL 2
MILTON DR 3
YEW TREE RD 4

189
206

174
192

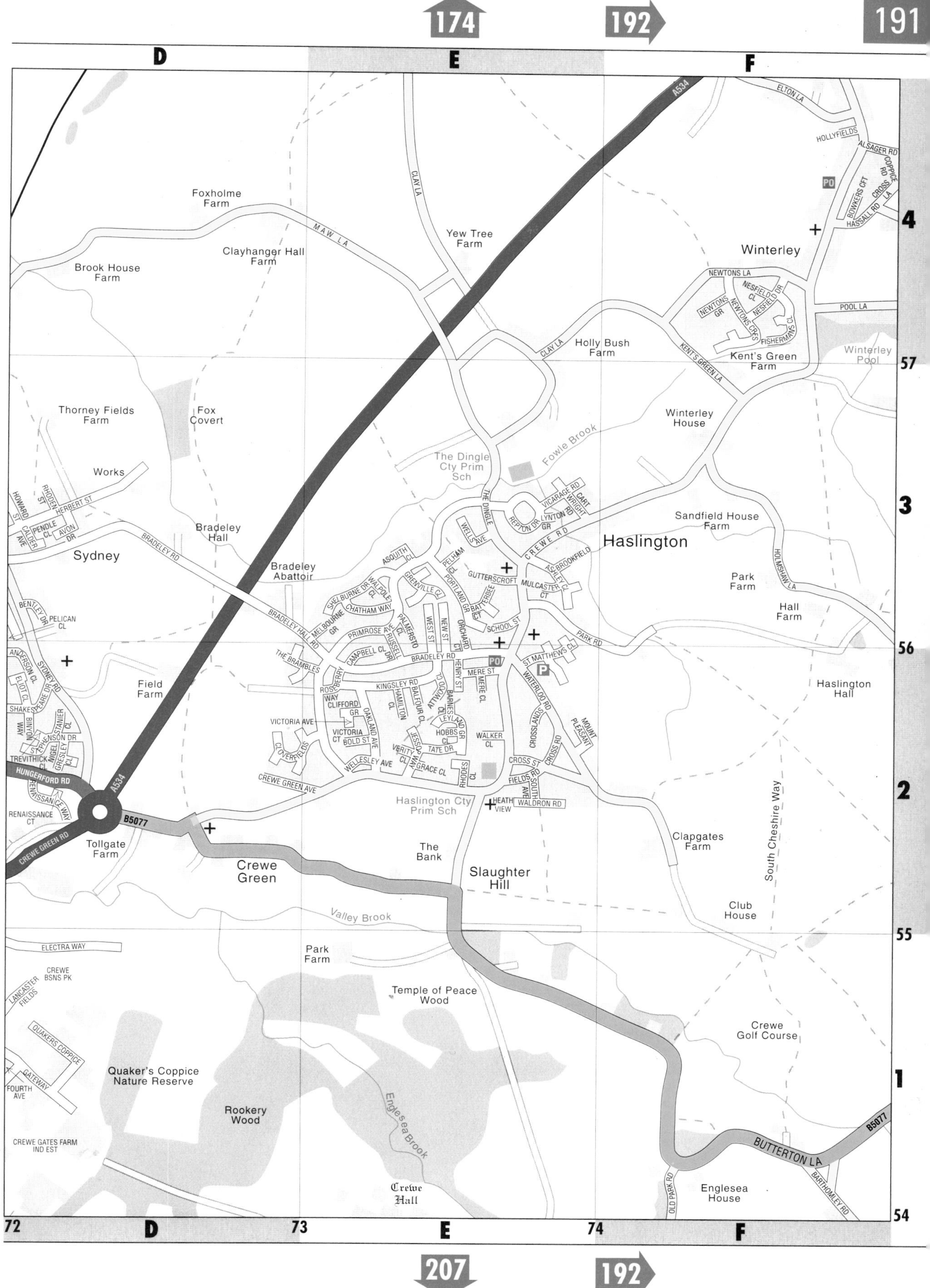
D
E
F
A534
ELTON LA
HOLLYFIELDS
ALSAGER RD
COPPICE RD
CROSS LA
BOWKERS CFT
HASSALL RD
PO
CLAY LA
Foxholme Farm
MAW LA
Yew Tree Farm
Clayhanger Hall Farm
Brook House Farm
Winterley
NEWTONS LA
NESFIELD CL
NESFIELD DR
NEWTONS GR
NEWTONS CRES
FISHERMANS CL
POOL LA
Holly Bush Farm
Kent's Green Farm
KENT'S GREEN LA
Winterley Pool
Thorney Fields Farm
Fox Covert
Winterley House
Fowle Brook
The Dingle Cty Prim Sch
Works
HOWARD ST
RHODEN ST
HERBERT ST
PENDLE CL
AVON DR
CALDER AVE
THE DINGLE
VICARAGE RD
CARTWRIGHT
REPTON DR
LYNTON GR
CREWE RD
Sandfield House Farm
Bradeley Hall
Sydney
BRADELEY RD
Haslington
ASQUITH CL
WELLS AVE
PELHAM CL
BROOKFIELD
Bradeley Abattoir
GRENVILLE CL
WALPOLE CL
SHELBURNE DR
MELBOURNE GR
CHATHAM WAY
PORTLAND GR
GUTTERSCROFT
BATTERBEE CT
MULCASTER CT
ASHLEY CL
HOLMSHAW LA
Park Farm
Hall Farm
BENTLEY DR
PELICAN CL
BRADELEY HALL RD
PRIMROSE AVE
PALMERSTON CL
WEST ST
NEW ST
ORCHARD CT
SCHOOL ST
PARK RD
RUSSELL CL
CAMPBELL CL
BRADELEY RD
PO
ST MATTHEWS CL
HENRY ST
MERE ST
MERE CL
P
WATERLOO RD
THE BRAMBLES
ANDERSON CL
ELIOT CL
SYDNEY RD
SHAKESPEARE DR
BINYON WAY
STANIER CL
STEPHENSON DR
NIGEL GR
GRESLEY CL
TREVITHICK CL
Field Farm
ROSEBERRY WAY
KINGSLEY RD
CLIFFORD GR
HAMILTON CL
BALFOUR CL
ATTWOOD CL
BARNES CL
LEYLAND GR
HOBBS CL
JESSOP WAY
TATE DR
VERITY CL
GRACE CL
RHODES CL
WALKER CL
CROSSLANDS
MOUNT PLEASANT
CROSS RD
CROSS ST
FIELDS RD
SOUTH AVE
WALDRON RD
VICTORIA AVE
VICTORIA CT
BOLD ST
OAKLAND AVE
CLOVERFIELDS
WELLESLEY AVE
Haslington Hall
HUNGERFORD RD
RENAISSANCE WAY
RENAISSANCE CT
CREWE GREEN AVE
CREWE GREEN RD
Haslington Cty Prim Sch
HEATH VIEW
B5077
Tollgate Farm
Crewe Green
The Bank
Slaughter Hill
Clapgates Farm
South Cheshire Way
Club House
Valley Brook
ELECTRA WAY
CREWE BSNS PK
LANCASTER FIELDS
Park Farm
Temple of Peace Wood
QUAKERS COPPICE
GATEWAY
FOURTH AVE
Quaker's Coppice Nature Reserve
Crewe Golf Course
Rookery Wood
Englesea Brook
CREWE GATES FARM IND EST
BUTTERTON LA
B5077
OLD PARK RD
Englesea House
BARTHOMLEY RD
Crewe Hall
4
57
3
56
2
55
1
54
72
73
74
D
E
F

207
192

191

175

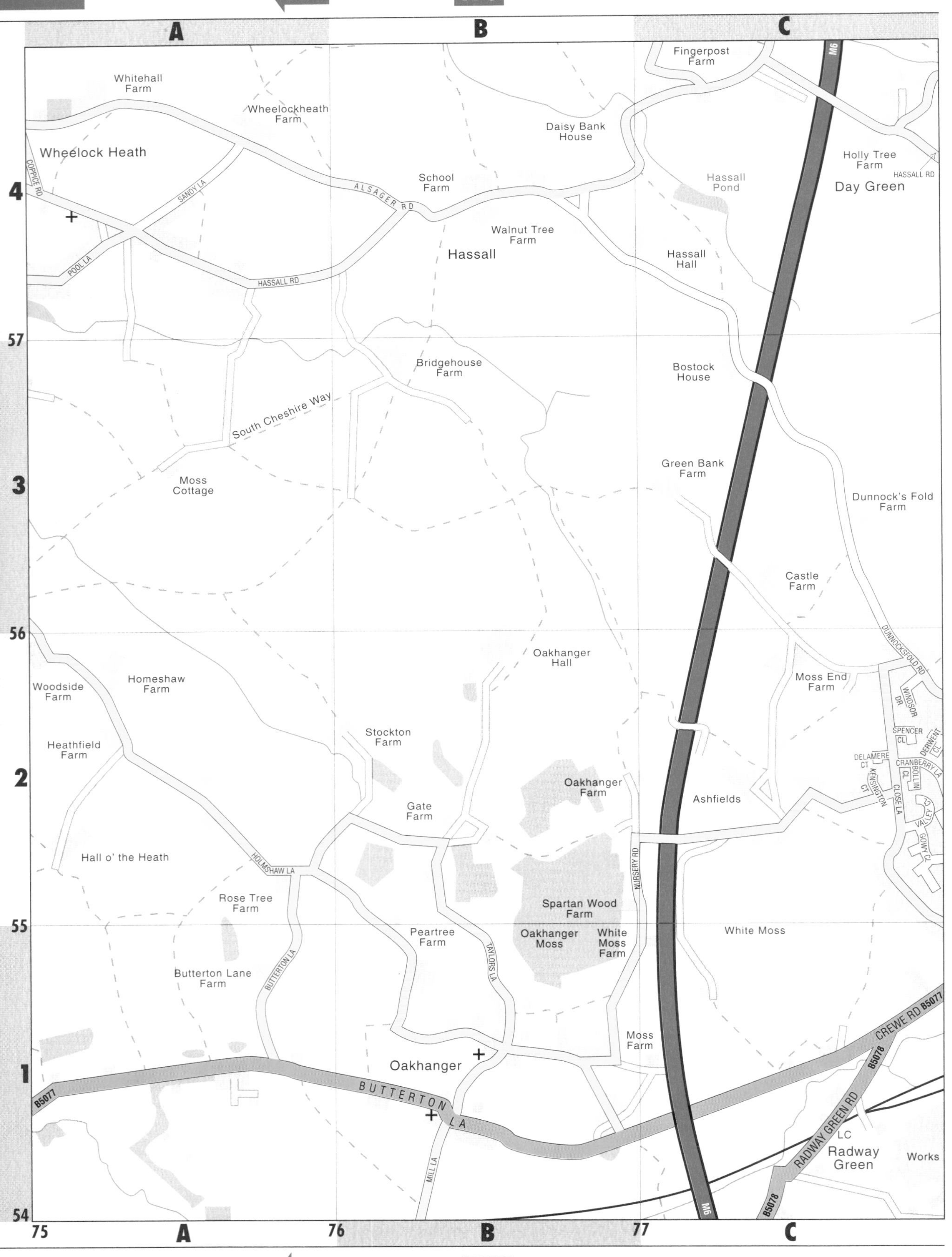

A
B
C
Fingerpost Farm
Whitehall Farm
Wheelockheath Farm
Daisy Bank House
Wheelock Heath
Holly Tree Farm
HASSALL RD
Day Green
COPPICE RD
SANDY LA
ALSAGER RD
School Farm
Hassall Pond
Walnut Tree Farm
Hassall
Hassall Hall
POOL LA
HASSALL RD
Bridgehouse Farm
Bostock House
South Cheshire Way
Moss Cottage
Green Bank Farm
Dunnock's Fold Farm
Castle Farm
DUNNOCKSFOLD RD
Oakhanger Hall
Moss End Farm
Woodside Farm
Homeshaw Farm
WINDSOR DR
Stockton Farm
Heathfield Farm
SPENCER CL
DERWENT CL
DELAMERE CT
CRANBERRY LA
KENSINGTON CT
BOLLIN CL
CLOSE LA
Oakhanger Farm
Ashfields
Gate Farm
VALLEY CL
GOWY CL
Hall o' the Heath
HOLMSHAW LA
NURSERY RD
Rose Tree Farm
Spartan Wood Farm
Peartree Farm
Oakhanger Moss
White Moss Farm
White Moss
TAYLORS LA
BUTTERTON LA
Butterton Lane Farm
CREWE RD B5077
B5078
Moss Farm
Oakhanger
B5077
BUTTERTON LA
RADWAY GREEN RD
LC
Radway Green
Works
MILL LA
M6
B5078
4
57
3
56
2
55
1
54
75
76
77

191

208

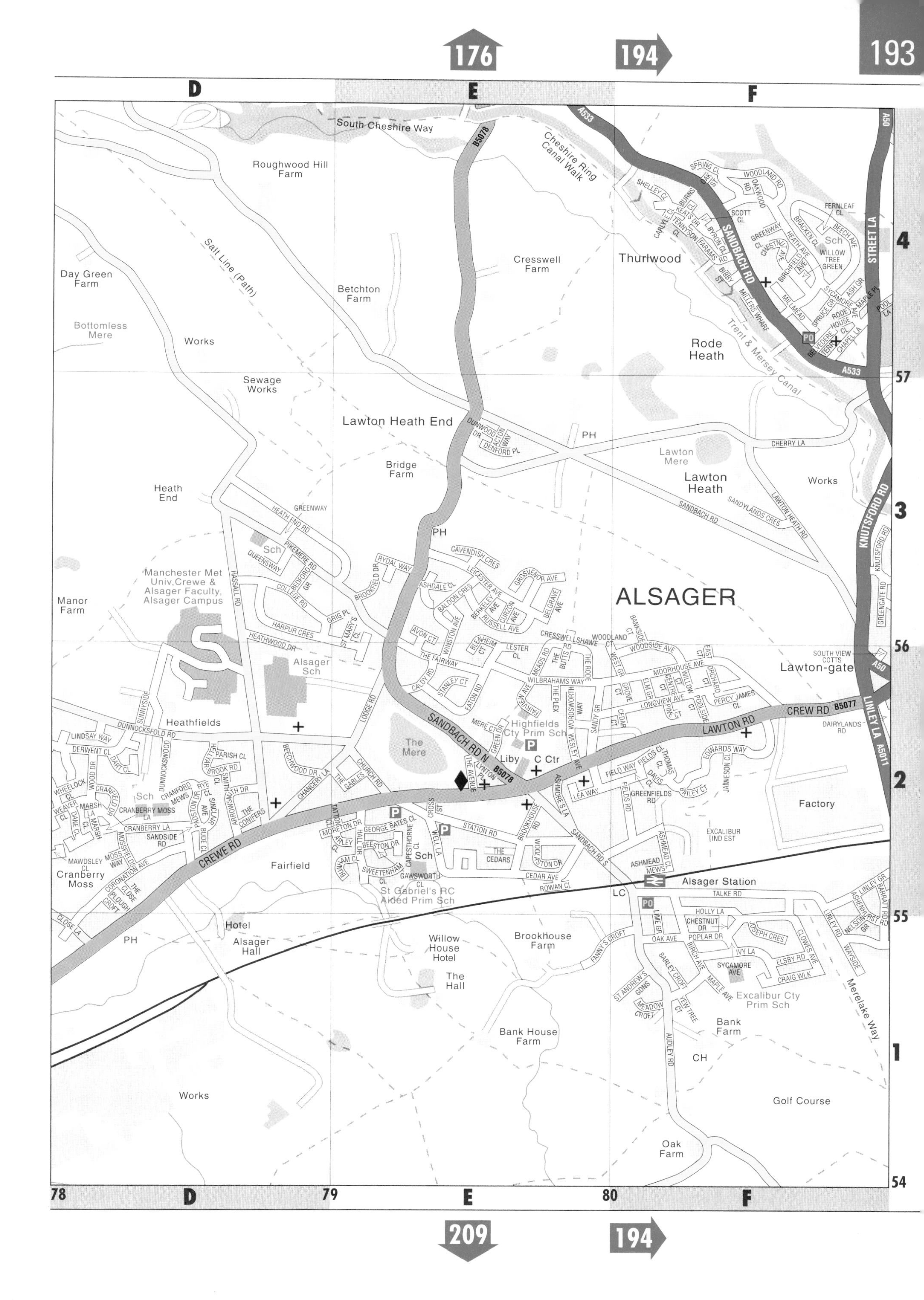
176
194
D
E
F
South Cheshire Way
Roughwood Hill Farm
Cheshire Ring Canal Walk
Day Green Farm
Salt Line (Path)
Betchton Farm
Cresswell Farm
Thurlwood
Bottomless Mere
Works
Rode Heath
Trent & Mersey Canal
Sewage Works
Lawton Heath End
PH
Lawton Mere
Lawton Heath
Bridge Farm
Heath End
Works
Manchester Met Univ,Crewe & Alsager Faculty, Alsager Campus
Manor Farm
ALSAGER
Alsager Sch
Lawton-gate
Heathfields
The Mere
Highfields Cty Prim Sch
Liby
C Ctr
Factory
Cranberry Moss
Fairfield
Sch
St Gabriel's RC Aided Prim Sch
Alsager Station
Hotel
Alsager Hall
Willow House Hotel
Brookhouse Farm
The Hall
Excalibur Cty Prim Sch
Bank House Farm
Bank Farm
Merelake Way
CH
Works
Golf Course
Oak Farm
SANDBACH RD N
CREWE RD
LAWTON RD
CREW RD
KNUTSFORD RD
STREET LA
LINLEY LA
SANDBACH RD
A533
A50
B5078
B5077
A5011
78
79
80
54
55
56
57
1
2
3
4
209
194

193

177

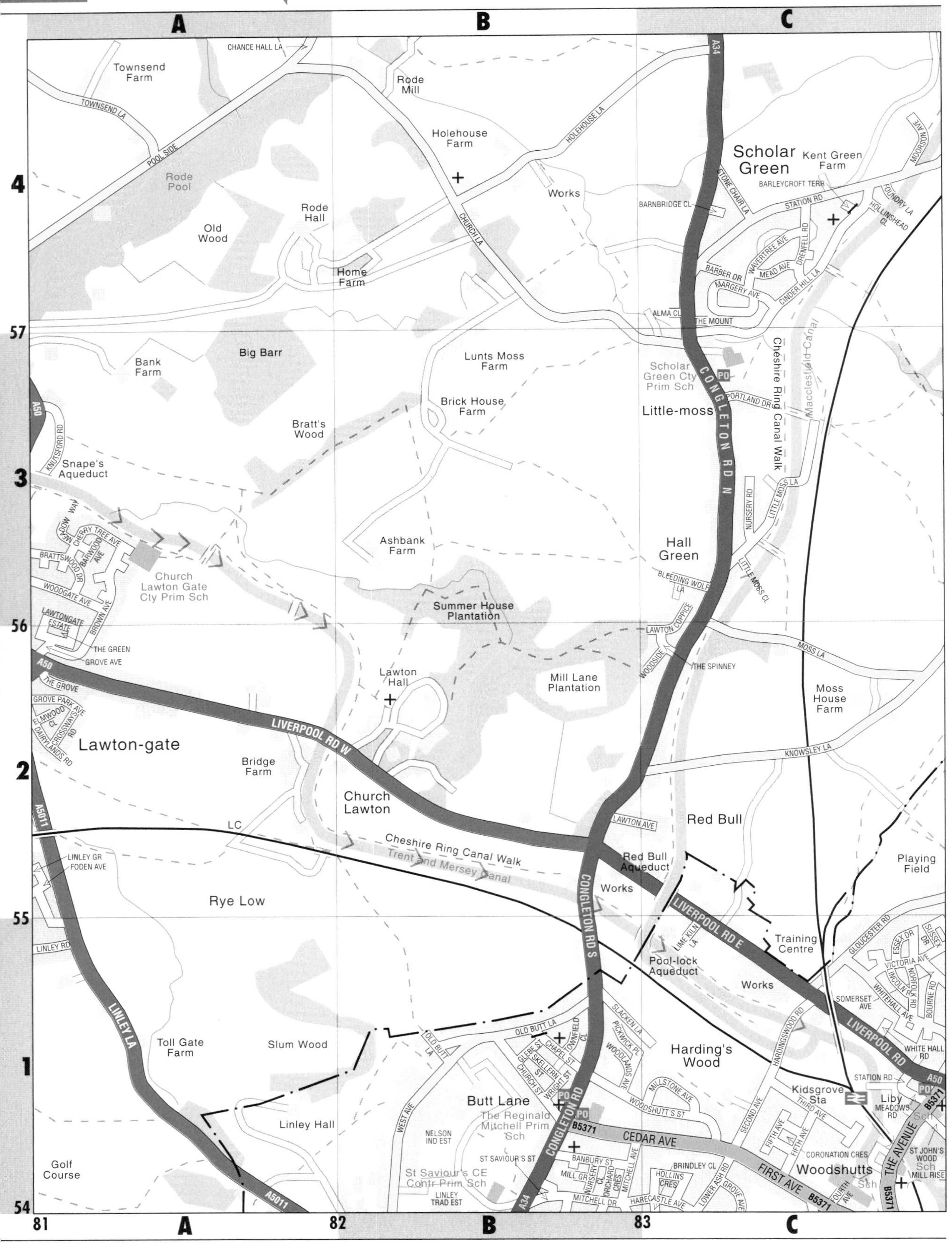

A
B
C
4
57
3
56
2
55
1
54
81
82
83
CHANCE HALL LA
Townsend Farm
TOWNSEND LA
POOL SIDE
Rode Pool
Rode Mill
Holehouse Farm
HOLEHOUSE LA
A34
Scholar Green
Kent Green Farm
MOORSON AVE
BARLEYCROFT TERR
STONE CHAIR LA
Works
BARNBRIDGE CL
STATION RD
FOUNDRY LA
HOLLINSHEAD CL
Old Wood
Rode Hall
CHURCH LA
Home Farm
WAVERTREE AVE
GRENFELL RD
BARBER DR
MEAD AVE
MARGERY AVE
CINDER HILL LA
ALMA CL
THE MOUNT
Bank Farm
Big Barr
Lunts Moss Farm
Scholar Green Cty Prim Sch
PO
CONGLETON RD N
Cheshire Ring Canal Walk
Macclesfield Canal
PORTLAND DR
Brick House Farm
Little-moss
A50
KNUTSFORD RD
Bratt's Wood
Snape's Aqueduct
NURSERY RD
LITTLE MOSS LA
MEADOW WAY
CHERRY TREE AVE
BARWOOD AVE
BRATTSWOOD DR
Ashbank Farm
Hall Green
Church Lawton Gate Cty Prim Sch
WOODGATE AVE
BLEEDING WOLF LA
LITTLE MOSS CL
LAWTONGATE ESTATE
BROWN AVE
Summer House Plantation
LAWTON COPPICE
MOSS LA
THE GREEN
GROVE AVE
WOODSIDE
THE SPINNEY
THE GROVE
Lawton Hall
Mill Lane Plantation
Moss House Farm
GROVE PARK AVE
ELMWOOD CL
CROSSWAY
DAIRYLANDS RD
LIVERPOOL RD W
Lawton-gate
KNOWSLEY LA
Bridge Farm
A5011
Church Lawton
LC
LAWTON AVE
Red Bull
Cheshire Ring Canal Walk
Trent and Mersey Canal
Red Bull Aqueduct
Playing Field
LINLEY GR
FODEN AVE
Rye Low
CONGLETON RD S
Works
LIVERPOOL RD E
LIME KILN LA
Training Centre
GLOUCESTER RD
ESSEX DR
SUSSEX DR
LINLEY RD
Pool-lock Aqueduct
VICTORIA AVE
NORFOLK RD
LINCOLN RD
Works
WHITEHALL AVE
SOMERSET AVE
BOURNE RD
LINLEY LA
Toll Gate Farm
Slum Wood
OLD BUTT LA
TOWNFIELD CL
SLACKEN LA
PICKWICK PL
WOODLANDS AVE
Harding's Wood
HARDINGSWOOD RD
LIVERPOOL RD
WHITE HALL RD
GLEBE ST
CHAPEL ST
SKELLERN ST
WRIGHT ST
CHURCH ST
MILLSTONE AVE
STATION RD
A50
Butt Lane
WOODSHUTT'S ST
Kidsgrove Sta
THIRD AVE
Liby
MEADOWS RD
B5371
Linley Hall
WEST AVE
NELSON IND EST
The Reginald Mitchell Prim Sch
CEDAR AVE
SECOND AVE
FIFTH AVE
THE AVENUE
St John's Wood Sch
ST SAVIOUR'S ST
BANBURY ST
MITCHELL AVE
BRINDLEY CL
CORONATION CRES
MILL RISE
Golf Course
St Saviour's CE Contr Prim Sch
MILL GR
NURSERY CL
ORCHARD CRES
HOLLINS CRES
LOWER ASH RD
GROVE AVE
FIRST AVE
Woodshutts
Sch
FOURTH AVE
LINLEY TRAD EST
MITCHELL DR
HARECASTLE AVE

193

210

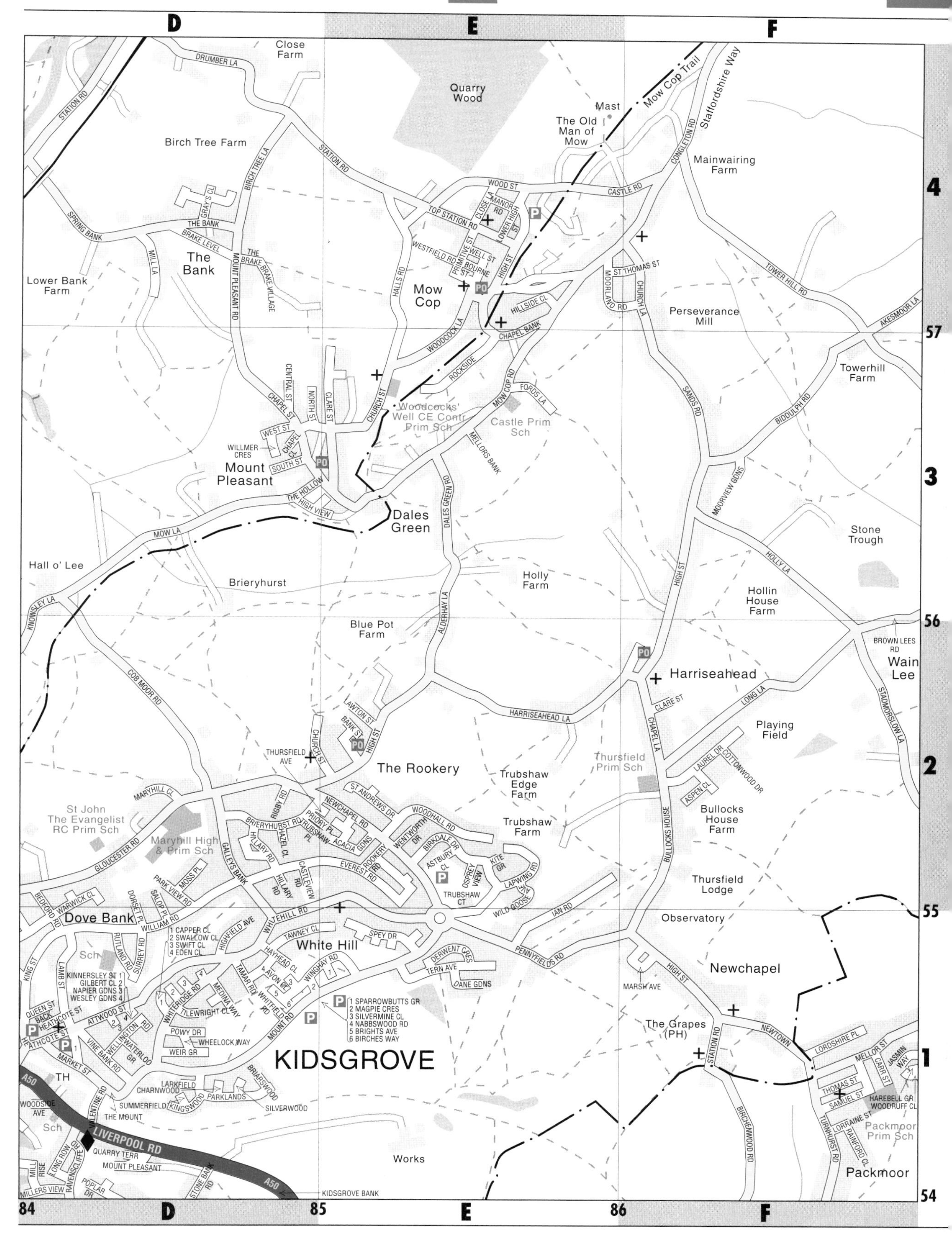
D
E
F
Close Farm
Quarry Wood
Mast
The Old Man of Mow
Mow Cop Trail
Staffordshire Way
Birch Tree Farm
Mainwairing Farm
The Bank
Lower Bank Farm
Mow Cop
Perseverance Mill
Towerhill Farm
Woodcocks' Well CE Contr Prim Sch
Castle Prim Sch
Mount Pleasant
Dales Green
Stone Trough
Hall o' Lee
Brieryhurst
Holly Farm
Hollin House Farm
Blue Pot Farm
Harriseahead
Wain Lee
Playing Field
The Rookery
Trubshaw Edge Farm
Thursfield Prim Sch
St John The Evangelist RC Prim Sch
Maryhill High & Prim Sch
Trubshaw Farm
Bullocks House Farm
Thursfield Lodge
Dove Bank
Observatory
White Hill
Newchapel
Sch
The Grapes (PH)
KIDSGROVE
TH
Sch
Works
Packmoor Prim Sch
Packmoor
LIVERPOOL RD
A50
KIDSGROVE BANK
1 CAPPER CL
2 SWALLOW CL
3 SWIFT CL
4 EDEN CL
KINNERSLEY ST 1
GILBERT CL 2
NAPIER GDNS 3
WESLEY GDNS 4
1 SPARROWBUTTS GR
2 MAGPIE CRES
3 SILVERMINE CL
4 NABBSWOOD RD
5 BRIGHTS AVE
6 BIRCHES WAY
4
57
3
56
2
55
1
54
84
85
86

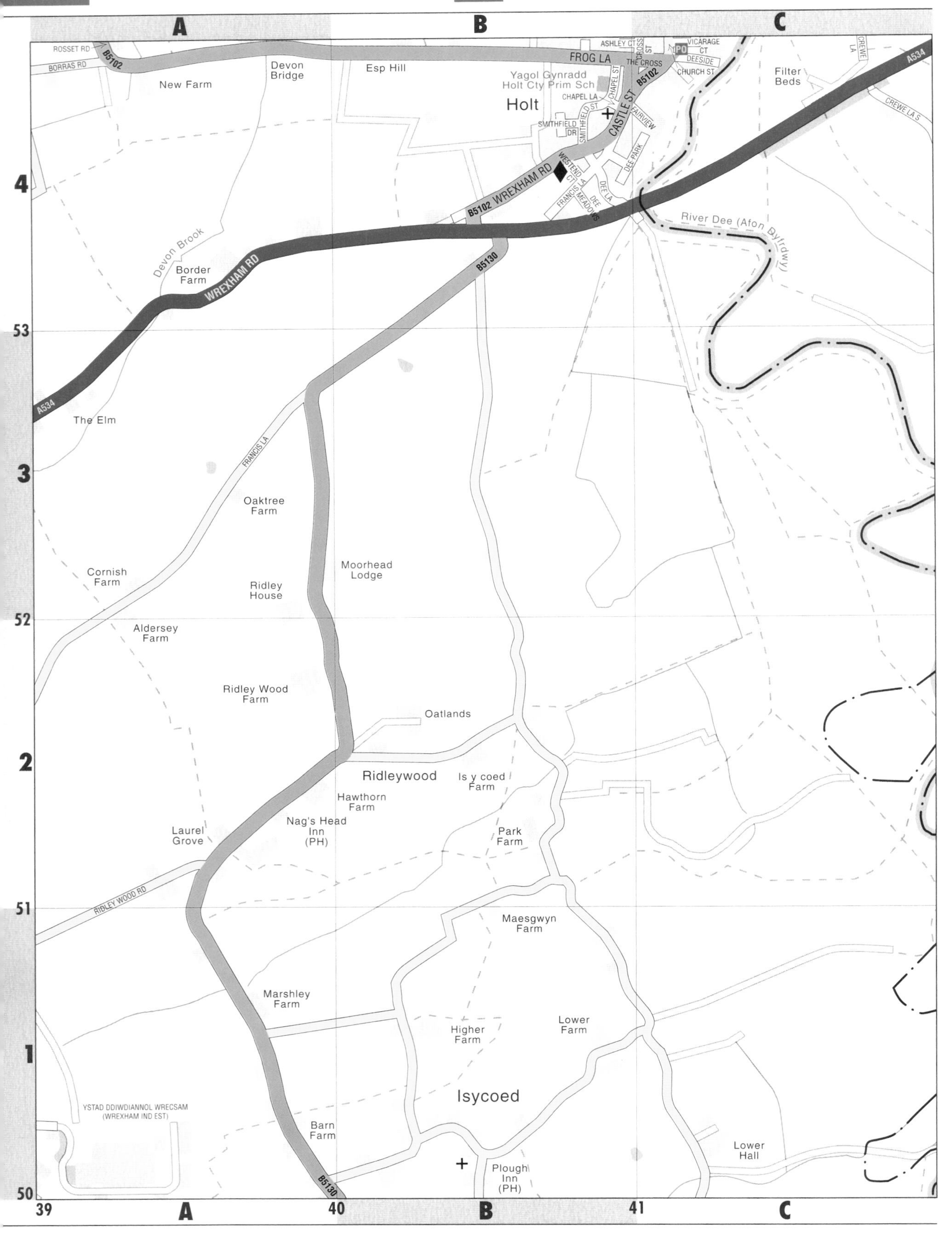

A B C

4

3

53

2

52

51

1

50

39 A 40 B 41 C

ROSSET RD
BORRAS RD
B5102
New Farm
Devon Bridge
Esp Hill
FROG LA
ASHLEY CT
THE CROSS
CROSS ST
PO
VICARAGE CT
DEESIDE
CHURCH ST
CREWE LA
A534
Yagol Gynradd
Holt Cty Prim Sch
Holt
CHAPEL LA
CHAPEL ST
CASTLE ST
FAIRVIEW
Filter Beds
CREWE LA S
SMITHFIELD DR
WESTEND CT
FRANCIS MEADOW S
DEE PARK
DEE LA
B5102 WREXHAM RD
B5102
River Dee (Afon Dyfrdwy)
B5130
WREXHAM RD
Devon Brook
Border Farm
A534
The Elm
FRANCIS LA
Oaktree Farm
Moorhead Lodge
Cornish Farm
Ridley House
Aldersey Farm
Ridley Wood Farm
Oatlands
Ridleywood
Is y coed Farm
Hawthorn Farm
Nag's Head Inn (PH)
Park Farm
Laurel Grove
RIDLEY WOOD RD
Maesgwyn Farm
Marshley Farm
Higher Farm
Lower Farm
Isycoed
YSTAD DDIWDIANNOL WRECSAM
(WREXHAM IND EST)
Barn Farm
B5130
Plough Inn (PH)
Lower Hall

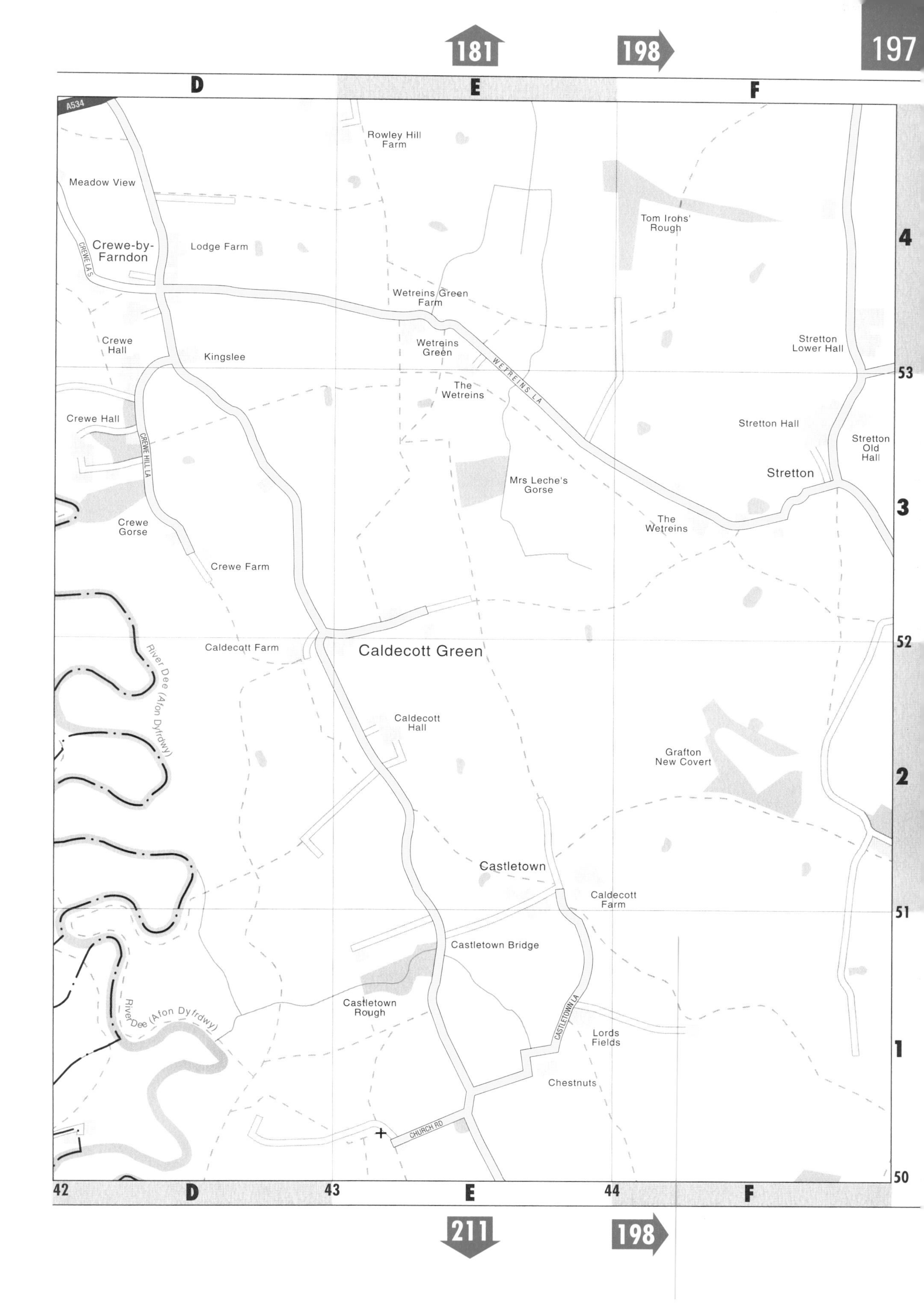
181
198
D
E
F
A534
Rowley Hill Farm
Meadow View
Tom Irons' Rough
Crewe-by-Farndon
CREWE LA S
Lodge Farm
4
Wetreins Green Farm
Crewe Hall
Wetreins Green
Stretton Lower Hall
Kingslee
WETREINS LA
53
The Wetreins
Crewe Hall
Stretton Hall
Stretton Old Hall
CREWE HILL LA
Mrs Leche's Gorse
Stretton
3
Crewe Gorse
The Wetreins
Crewe Farm
52
Caldecott Farm
Caldecott Green
River Dee (Afon Dyfrdwy)
Caldecott Hall
Grafton New Covert
2
Castletown
Caldecott Farm
51
Castletown Bridge
Castletown Rough
CASTLETOWN LA
River Dee (Afon Dyfrdwy)
Lords Fields
1
Chestnuts
CHURCH RD
50
42
D
43
E
44
F
211
198

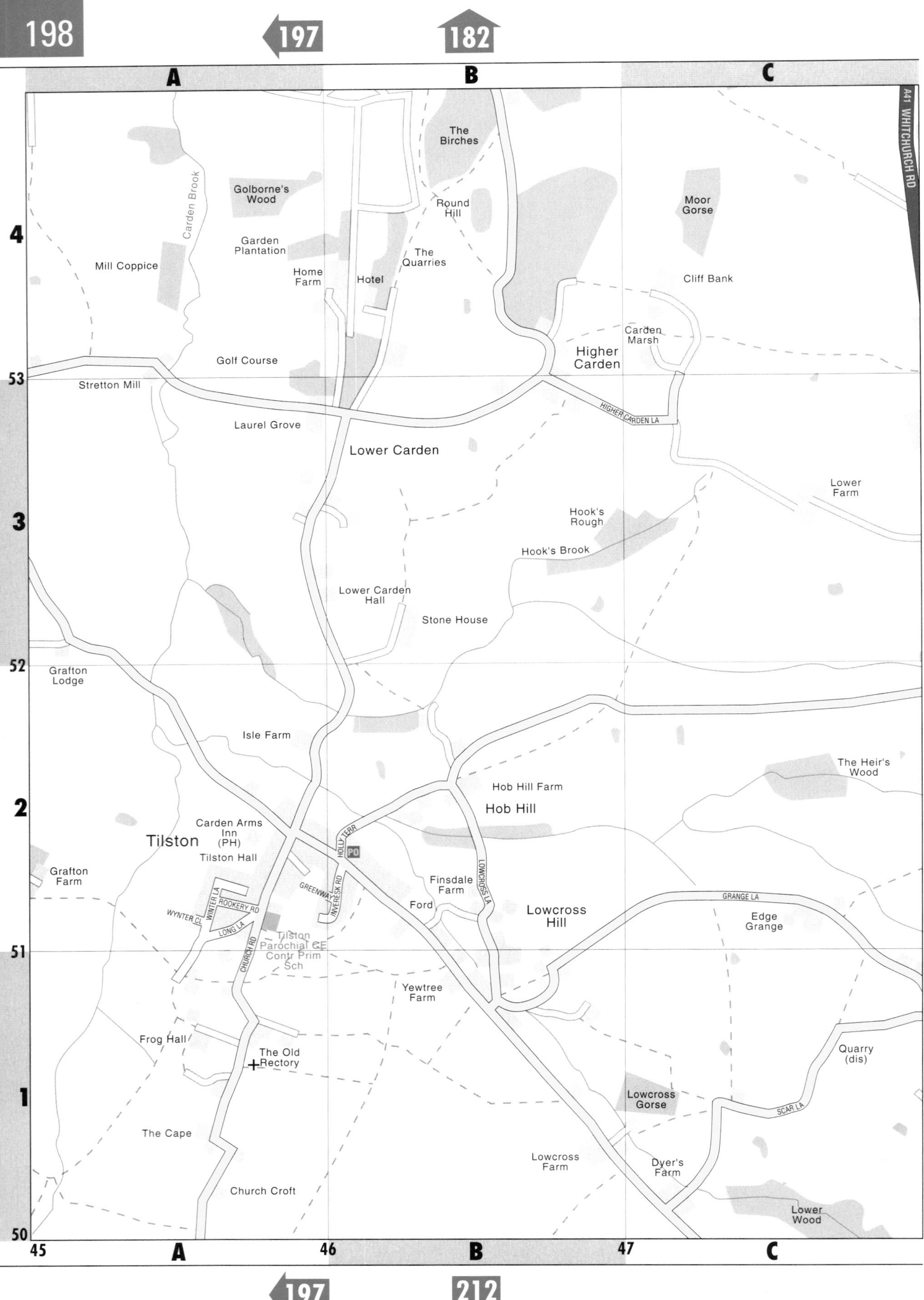

A41 WHITCHURCH RD

A   B   C

4

The Birches

Golborne's
Wood

Round
Hill

Moor
Gorse

Garden
Plantation

The
Quarries

Cliff Bank

Mill Coppice

Home
Farm

Hotel

Carden
Marsh

Carden Brook

Higher
Carden

53 Golf Course

Stretton Mill

HIGHER CARDEN LA

Lower
Farm

Laurel Grove

Lower Carden

Hook's
Rough

3

Hook's Brook

Lower Carden
Hall

Stone House

52 Grafton
Lodge

Isle Farm

The Heir's
Wood

Hob Hill Farm

2

Hob Hill

Carden Arms
Inn
(PH)

Tilston

Tilston Hall

HOLLY TERR

PO

Grafton
Farm

GREENWAY RD

INVERESK RD

Finsdale
Farm

LOWCROSS LA

GRANGE LA

Edge
Grange

WYNTER CL

WINTER LA

ROOKERY RD

Ford

Lowcross
Hill

LONG LA

CHURCH RD

Tilston
Parochial CE
Contr Prim
Sch

51

Yewtree
Farm

Quarry
(dis)

Frog Hall

The Old
Rectory

Lowcross
Gorse

SCAR LA

1

The Cape

Lowcross
Farm

Dyer's
Farm

Church Croft

Lower
Wood

50
45   A   46   B   47   C

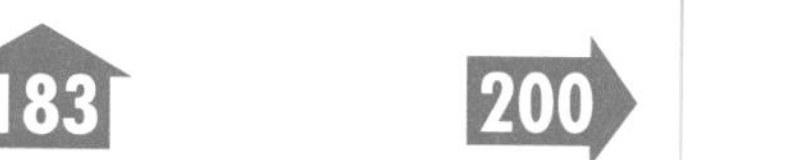

183
200

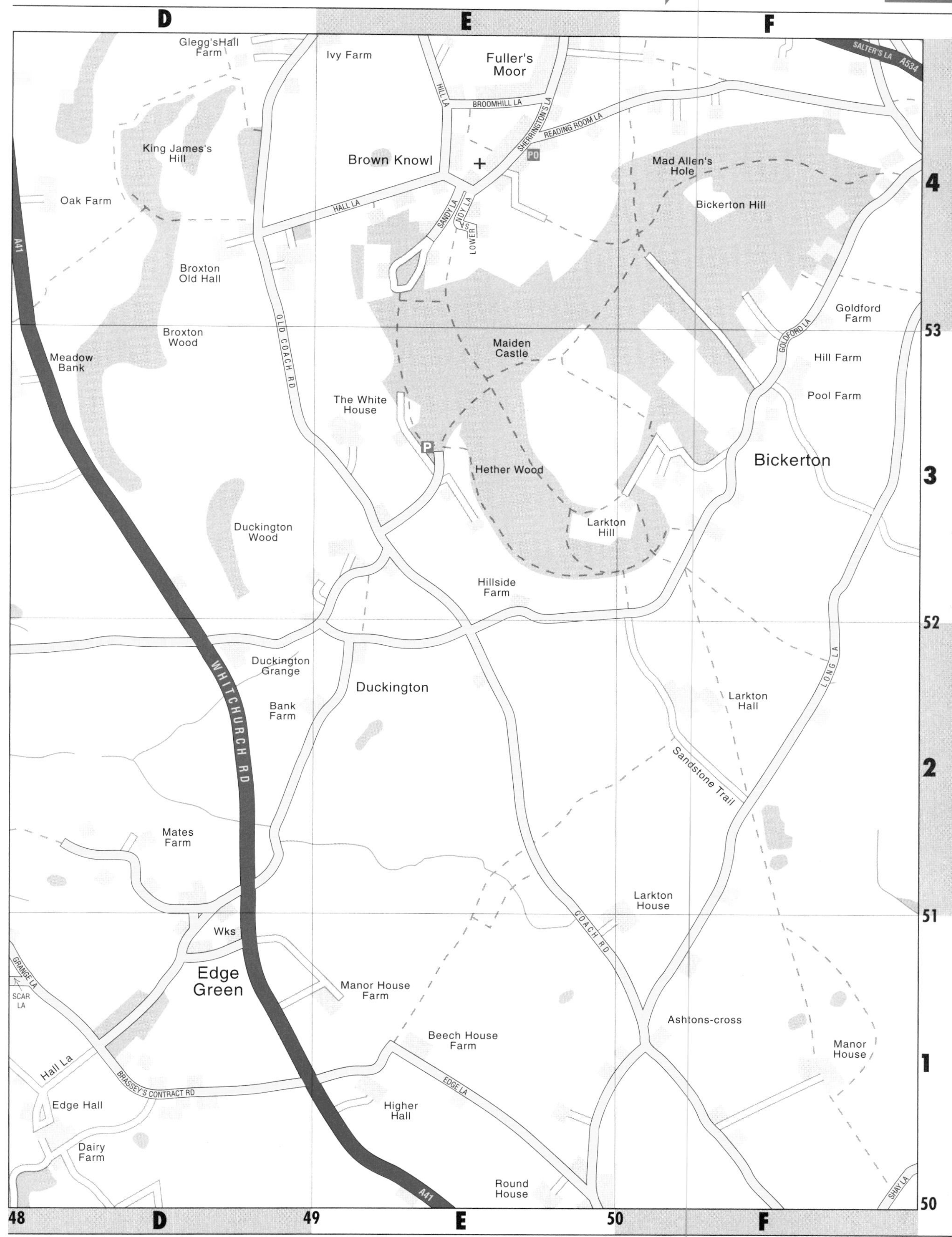

D
E
F
Glegg'sHall Farm
Ivy Farm
Fuller's Moor
HILL LA
BROOMHILL LA
SHERRINGTON'S LA
READING ROOM LA
SALTER'S LA
A534
King James's Hill
Brown Knowl
PO
Mad Allen's Hole
Oak Farm
HALL LA
SANDY LA
LOWER
Bickerton Hill
A41
Broxton Old Hall
Goldford Farm
Broxton Wood
OLD COACH RD
Maiden Castle
GOLDFORD LA
Meadow Bank
Hill Farm
The White House
Pool Farm
P
Bickerton
Hether Wood
Duckington Wood
Larkton Hill
Hillside Farm
Duckington Grange
WHITCHURCH RD
Duckington
LONG LA
Bank Farm
Larkton Hall
Sandstone Trail
Mates Farm
Larkton House
COACH RD
Wks
GRANGE LA
SCAR LA
Edge Green
Manor House Farm
Ashtons-cross
Beech House Farm
Manor House
Hall La
BRASSEY'S CONTRACT RD
EDGE LA
Edge Hall
Higher Hall
Dairy Farm
Round House
SHAY LA
A41
4
53
3
52
2
51
1
50
48
49
50

A   B   C

A534

WREXHAM RD

A534

Gallantry
Bank

LONG LA

Bickerton
Farm

Gallantry-bank
Farm

Bulkeley
Hall

Walnut -Tree
Farm

Manor
Farm

CHOLMONDELEY LA

4

Bulkeleyhay

Yewtree
Farm

Bickerton CE
Contr Prim Sch

Townsend
Farm

53

Bickerton
Hall

Fields
Farm

Gate House
Farm

Manor
Farm

3

Egerton
Green

Bankhouse
Farm

Green
Farm

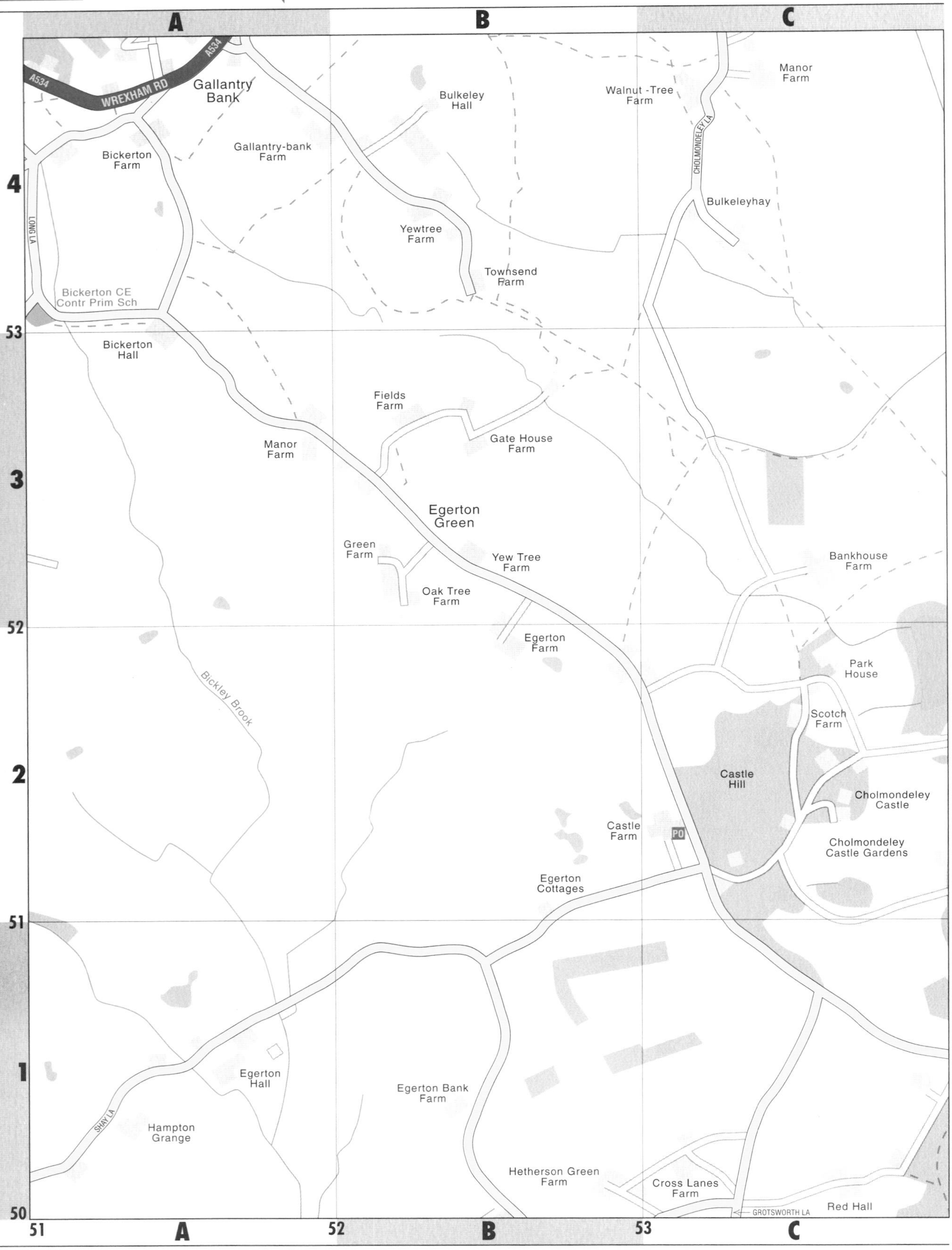

Yew Tree
Farm

Oak Tree
Farm

Bickley Brook

Egerton
Farm

52

Park
House

Scotch
Farm

2

Castle
Hill

Cholmondeley
Castle

Castle
Farm

PO

Cholmondeley
Castle Gardens

Egerton
Cottages

51

SHAY LA

Egerton
Hall

Egerton Bank
Farm

Hampton
Grange

1

Hetherson Green
Farm

Cross Lanes
Farm

Red Hall

50

GROTSWORTH LA

51   A   52   B   53   C

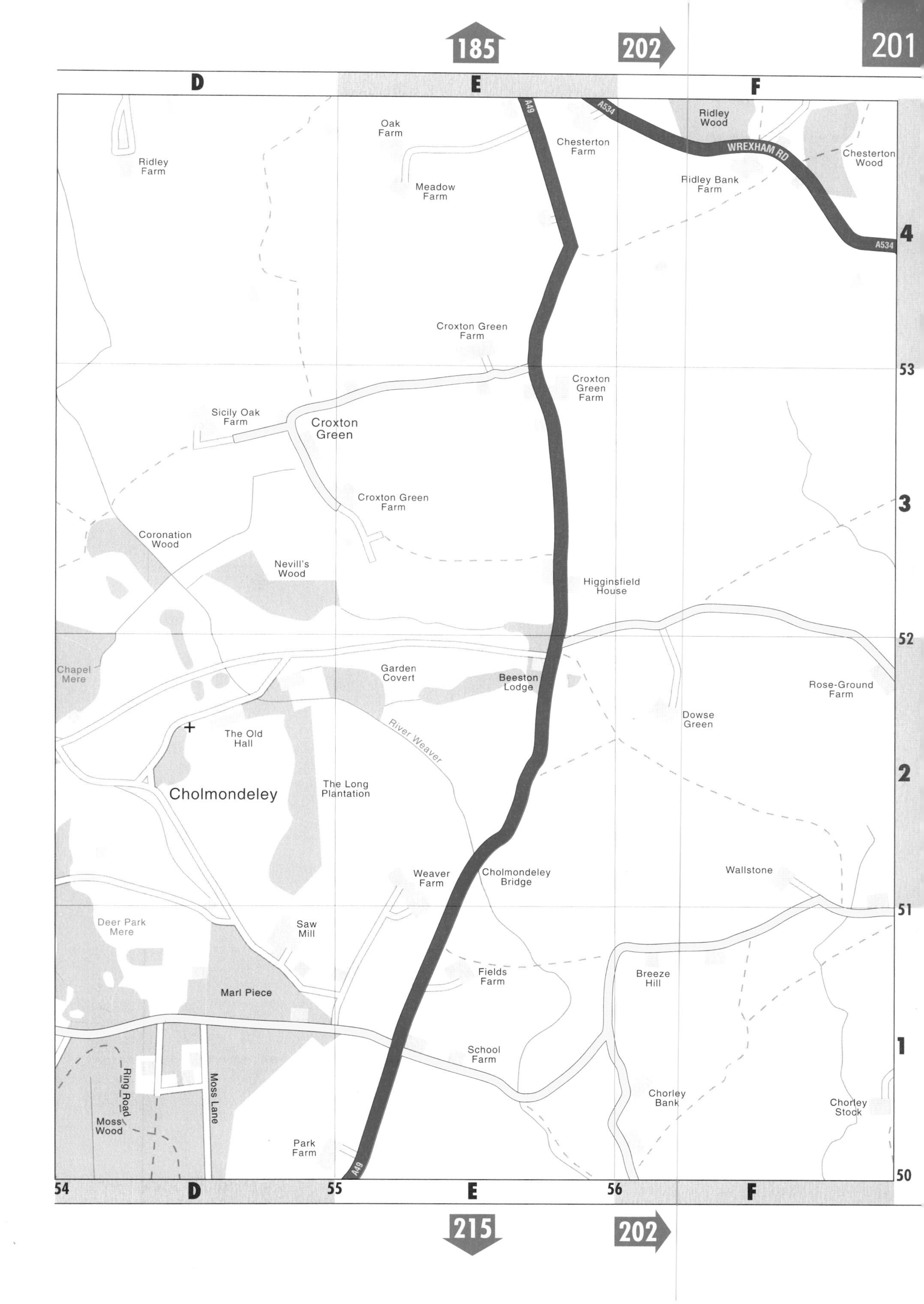

D   E   F

Ridley
Farm

Oak
Farm

Chesterton
Farm

Ridley
Wood

WREXHAM RD

Chesterton
Wood

A49

A534

Meadow
Farm

Ridley Bank
Farm

4

A534

Croxton Green
Farm

53

Croxton
Green
Farm

Sicily Oak
Farm

Croxton
Green

Croxton Green
Farm

3

Coronation
Wood

Nevill's
Wood

Higginsfield
House

52

Chapel
Mere

Garden
Covert

Beeston
Lodge

Rose-Ground
Farm

The Old
Hall

River Weaver

Dowse
Green

2

Cholmondeley

The Long
Plantation

Weaver
Farm

Cholmondeley
Bridge

Wallstone

Deer Park
Mere

Saw
Mill

51

Marl Piece

Fields
Farm

Breeze
Hill

School
Farm

1

Ring Road

Chorley
Bank

Chorley
Stock

Moss
Wood

Moss Lane

Park
Farm

A49

50

54   D   55   E   56   F

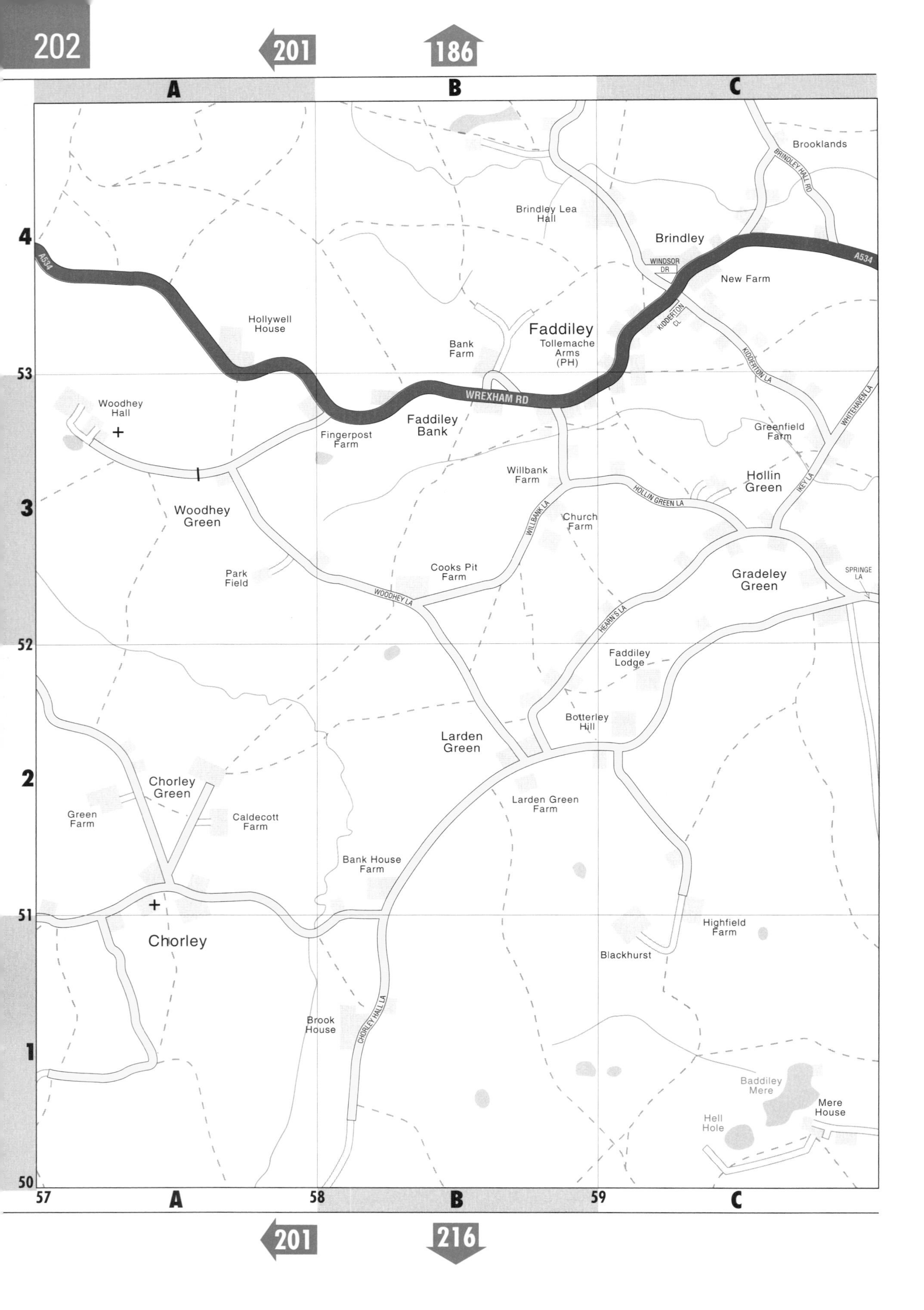

A

B

C

4

Brooklands

Brindley Lea
Hall

Brindley

BRINDLEY HALL RD

WINDSOR
DR

New Farm

A534

Hollywell
House

Bank
Farm

Faddiley

Tollemache
Arms
(PH)

KIDDERTON CL

KIDDERTON LA

53

WREXHAM RD

Woodhey
Hall

Faddiley
Bank

Greenfield
Farm

WHITEHAVEN LA

Fingerpost
Farm

Willbank
Farm

Hollin Green LA

Hollin
Green

HKY LA

3

Woodhey
Green

WILLBANK LA

Church
Farm

SPRINGE
LA

Park
Field

Cooks Pit
Farm

WOODHEY LA

Gradeley
Green

HEARN'S LA

52

Faddiley
Lodge

Botterley
Hill

Larden
Green

2

Chorley
Green

Green
Farm

Caldecott
Farm

Larden Green
Farm

Bank House
Farm

Highfield
Farm

51

Chorley

Blackhurst

CHORLEY HALL LA

Brook
House

1

Baddiley
Mere

Mere
House

Hell
Hole

50

57

A

58

B

59

C

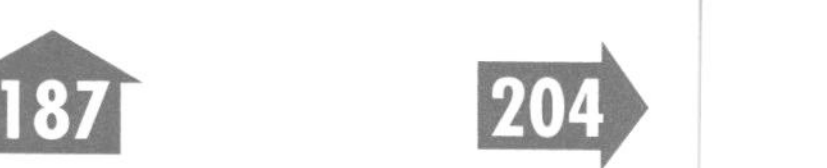

187
204

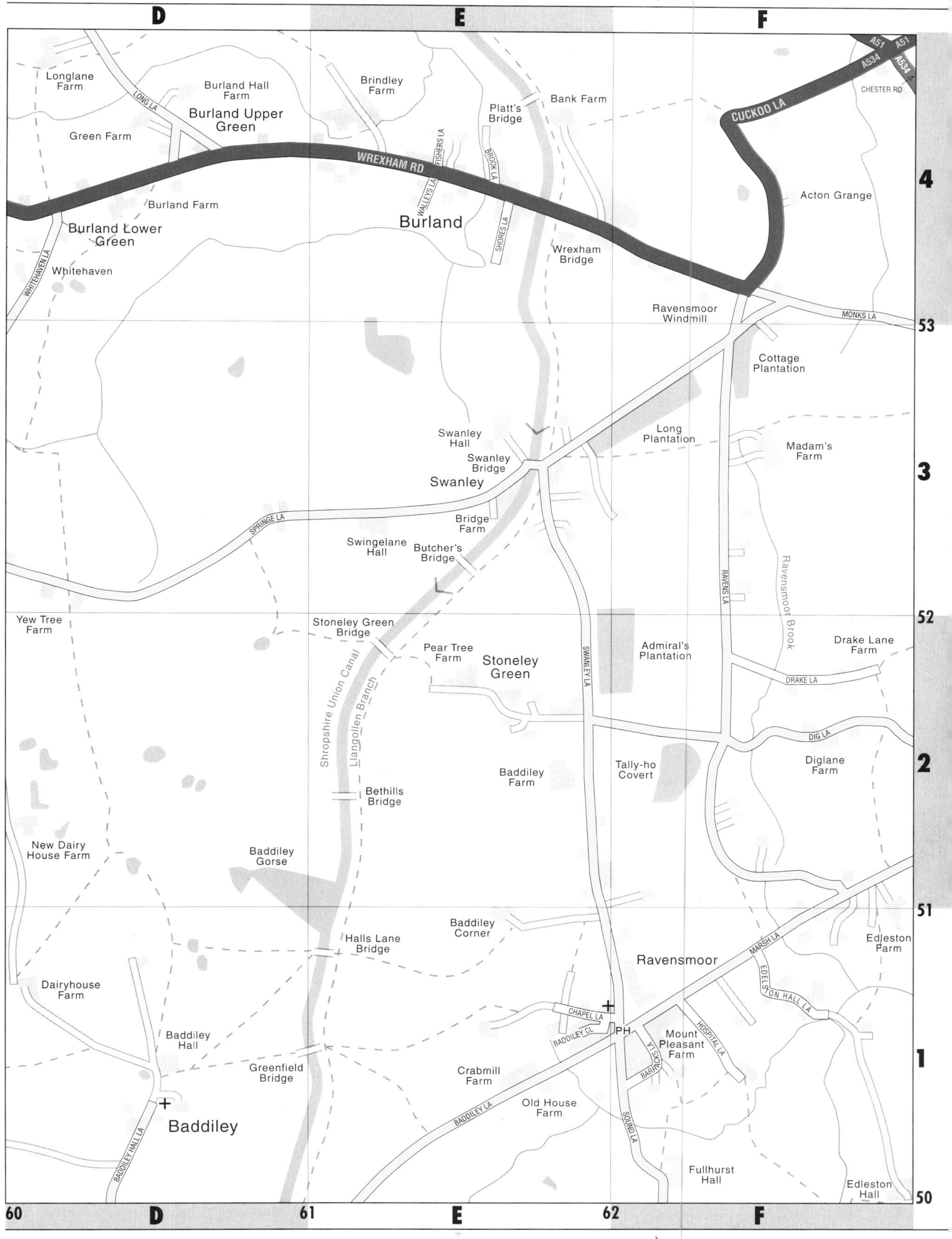

D
E
F
Longlane Farm
Burland Hall Farm
Brindley Farm
Platt's Bridge
Bank Farm
Burland Upper Green
Green Farm
LONG LA
WREXHAM RD
FISHERS LA
BROOK LA
WALLEYS LA
CUCKOO LA
A51
A534
CHESTER RD
Acton Grange
Burland Farm
Burland Lower Green
Burland
SHORES LA
Wrexham Bridge
WHITEHAVEN LA
Whitehaven
Ravensmoor Windmill
MONKS LA
Cottage Plantation
Long Plantation
Swanley Hall
Swanley Bridge
Madam's Farm
Swanley
SPRINGE LA
Bridge Farm
Swingelane Hall
Butcher's Bridge
RAVENS LA
Ravensmoor Brook
Yew Tree Farm
Stoneley Green Bridge
Pear Tree Farm
Stoneley Green
SWANLEY LA
Admiral's Plantation
Drake Lane Farm
DRAKE LA
Shropshire Union Canal
Llangollen Branch
DIG LA
Baddiley Farm
Tally-ho Covert
Diglane Farm
Bethills Bridge
New Dairy House Farm
Baddiley Gorse
Baddiley Corner
Halls Lane Bridge
Edleston Farm
Ravensmoor
MARSH LA
EDLESTON HALL LA
Dairyhouse Farm
CHAPEL LA
Baddiley Hall
BADDILEY CL
PH
Mount Pleasant Farm
HOSPITAL LA
BARRACKS LA
Greenfield Bridge
Crabmill Farm
Old House Farm
BADDILEY LA
SOUND LA
Baddiley
BADDILEY HALL LA
Fullhurst Hall
Edleston Hall
4
53
3
52
2
51
1
50
60
61
62

203
188

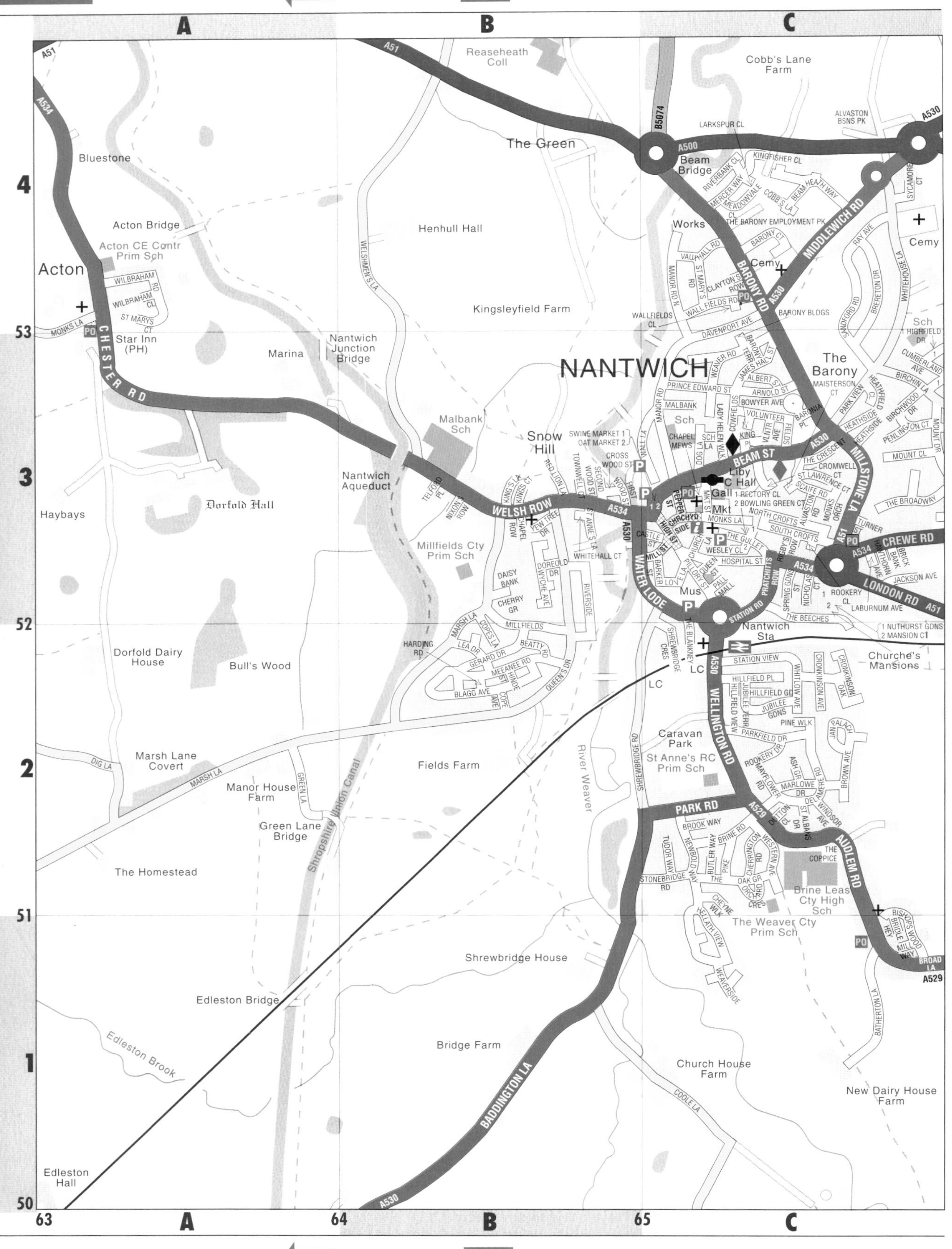
NANTWICH
Acton
Bluestone
Acton Bridge
Acton CE Contr Prim Sch
Star Inn (PH)
Reaseheath Coll
The Green
Henhull Hall
Kingsleyfield Farm
Marina
Nantwich Junction Bridge
Malbank Sch
Snow Hill
Nantwich Aqueduct
Dorfold Hall
Haybays
Millfields Cty Prim Sch
Dorfold Dairy House
Bull's Wood
Marsh Lane Covert
Manor House Farm
Green Lane Bridge
The Homestead
Fields Farm
Shropshire Union Canal
River Weaver
Caravan Park
St Anne's RC Prim Sch
Shrewbridge House
Edleston Bridge
Edleston Brook
Bridge Farm
Edleston Hall
Church House Farm
New Dairy House Farm
Brine Leas Cty High Sch
The Weaver Cty Prim Sch
Cobb's Lane Farm
Beam Bridge
Works
Cemy
The Barony
Nantwich Sta
Churche's Mansions
Mus
Liby
C Hall
Gall
Mkt
WELSH ROW
CHESTER RD
BEAM ST
WATER LODE
WELLINGTON RD
PARK RD
BADDINGTON LA
AUDLEM RD
BARONY RD
MIDDLEWICH RD
MILLSTONE LA
CREWE RD
LONDON RD
A51
A534
A530
A500
A529
B5074

203
218

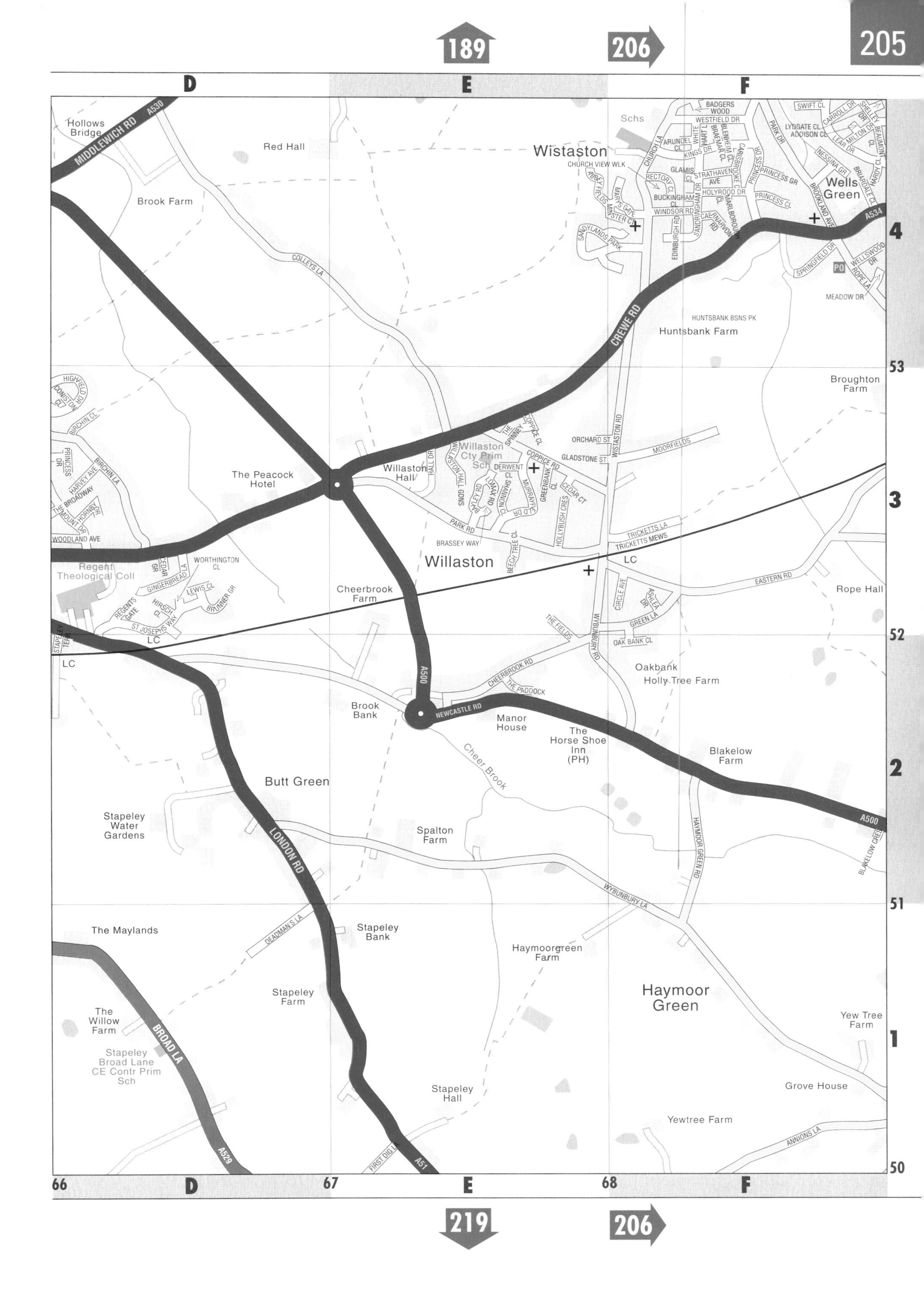

D
E
F

MIDDLEWICH RD
A530

Hollows
Bridge

Red Hall

Wistaston

Schs

BADGERS
WOOD
SWIFT CL
WESTFIELD DR
WHITE HART LA
ARUNDEL CL
WESTFIELD CL
BLENHEIM CL
BRAEMAR CL
KINGS DR
CHURCH LA
CHURCH VIEW WLK
CARROLL DR
LYBGATE CL
ADDISON CL
MILTON DR
EAR DR
SHELLEY RD
READMAN DR

Brook Farm

COLLEYS LA

ABBEY FIELDS
MINSTER CL
MARY GATE
RECTORY CL
GLAMIS CL
BUCKINGHAM CL
HOLYROOD DR
STRATHAVEN CL
CHRISBROOKE
CHRISTLETON CL
PRINCESS GR
PARK DR
BRUNDALE CL
ARDWYN
MESSINA GR
Wells
Green
A534

SANDYLANDS PARK
EDINBURGH RD
WINDSOR CL
SANDRINGHAM RD
MARLBOROUGH
CAERNARVON RD
PRINCESS CL
SPRINGFIELD DR
WELLSWOOD DR
ROPE LA
PO
MEADOW DR

4

CREWE RD

HUNTSBANK BSNS PK
Huntsbank Farm

53

Broughton
Farm

HIGHFIELD DR
CONISTON CL
BIRCHIN CL
BIRCHIN LA
PRINCESS DR
HARVEY AVE
HORNBY CL
BROADWAY
THE MOUNT
WOODLAND AVE

The Peacock
Hotel

THE SPINNEY
Willaston
Cty Prim
Sch
HALL DR
Willaston
Hall
DERWENT
WILLASTON HALL GDNS
COPPICE RD
COPPICE CL
MCKINLEY WY
OLD CL
ORCHARD ST
GLADSTONE ST
MURRAYFIELD
GREENBANK
CEDAR CT
WISTASTON RD
MOORFIELDS

3

Regent
Theological Coll
CEDAR GR
GINGERBREAD
LEWIS CL
BRUNNER GR
REGENTS GATE
HIRSCH CL
ST JOSEPHS WAY
ST JOSEPHS WAY
LC

Cheerbrook
Farm

Willaston

PARK RD
BRASSEY WAY
BEECH TREE CL
HOLLYBUSH CRES
TRICKETTS LA
TRICKETTS MEWS
LC

CIRCLE AVE
ASHLEA DR
GREEN LA
EASTERN RD
Rope Hall

STAPELEY TER
LC
LC

THE FIELDS
WITHYMOOR WAY
OAK BANK CL
52

A500

Brook
Bank
NEWCASTLE RD
Cheerbrook Rd
THE PADDOCK
Manor
House
Oakbank
Holly Tree Farm

The
Horse Shoe
Inn
(PH)

Butt Green

Cheer Brook

Spalton
Farm

Blakelow
Farm
HAYMOOR GREEN RD
A500
BLAKELOW CRES

2

Stapeley
Water
Gardens

LONDON RD

WYBUNBURY LA

51

The Maylands

DEADMAN'S LA

Stapeley
Bank

Haymoorgreen
Farm

Stapeley
Farm

Haymoor
Green

Yew Tree
Farm

The
Willow
Farm
BROAD LA
A529

Stapeley
Broad Lane
CE Contr Prim
Sch

1

Grove House

Stapeley
Hall
Yewtree Farm
ANNIONS LA

FIRST DIG LA
A51

50

66
D
67
E
68
F

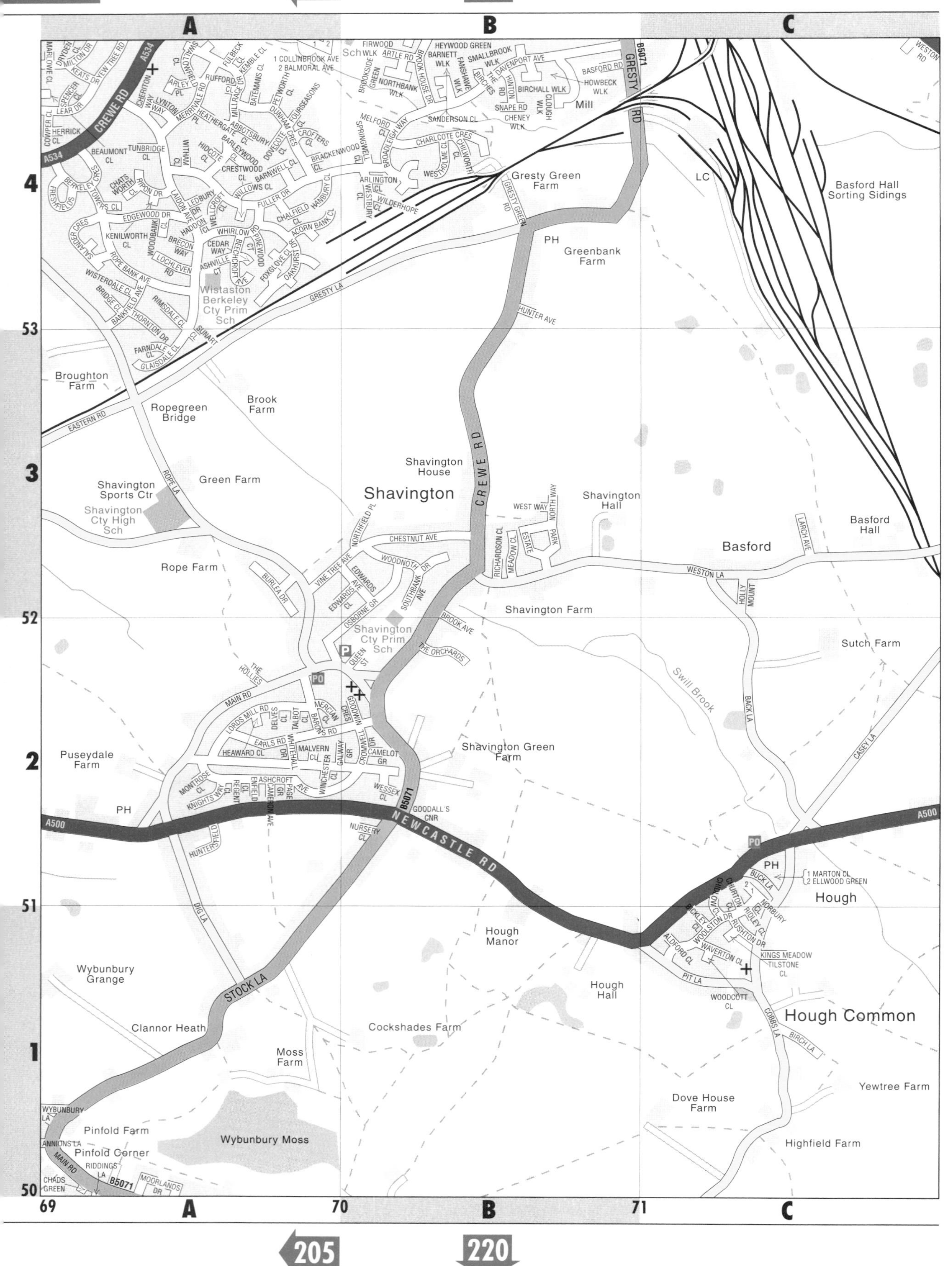

205
190

A
B
C

+ Cherition Cl
A534
CREWE RD
1 COLLINBROOK AVE
2 BALMORAL AVE
FIRWOOD
Sch WLK
HEYWOOD GREEN
ARTLE RD
BARNETT WLK
SMALLBROOK
WLK
B5071
GRESTY
WESTON RD
MARLOWE CL
MILTON CL
KEATS DR
CREW TREE RD
SPENCER
LEAR DR
BIRCH
HOUSE DR
NORTHBANK
WLK
BASFORD RD
HOWBECK
WLK
COWPER CL
HERRICK CL
ARLEY PL
LYNTON WAY
MERIVALE PL
HEATHERGATE
ABBOTSBURY
CL
RUFFORD
FULBECK
WILLOW CL
KEMBLE CL
BATEMANS CL
DELYTHORN
DUNHAM CRES
CROFTERS
FANSHAWE
WLK
SNAPE RD
CHENEY
WLK
THE DAVENPORT AVE
BIRCHALL WLK
Mill
BEAUMONT
CL
TUNBRIDGE
CL
WITHAM
CL
HIDCOTE
PL
BARLEYWOOD
FOURSEASONS
SANDERSON CL
4
A534
BERKELEY CL
CRESSWELL
CHATSWORTH CL
IRON DR
LEDBURY
CL
CRESTWOOD
CL
BARNWELL CL
WARBURY CL
ARLINGTON
WESTBURY
CHARLCOTE CRES
CHWORTH
Gresty Green
Farm
LC
Basford Hall
Sorting Sidings
EDGEWOOD DR
PINEWOOD
WILLOWS CL
WEST
HOLME CL
WESTERN
WILDEROPE
PH
Greenbank
Farm
KENILWORTH CL
HADDON
BRECON WAY
LOCHLEVEN
CEDAR WAY
REECHWOOD
ACORN BANK CL
FOVER
CHALFIELD
53
ROPE BANK AVE
ASHVILLE CT
OAK RISE
GRESTY LA
Wistaston
Berkeley
Cty Prim
Sch
HUNTER AVE
WISTERDALE CL
BRIDGE CL
BIRCHFIELD RD
RIMSDALE CL
THORNTON DR
SUNART
FARNDALE CL
GLAISDALE
Broughton
Farm
EASTERN RD
Ropegreen
Bridge
Brook
Farm
CREWE RD
3
Shavington
Sports Ctr
ROPE LA
Green Farm
Shavington
House
Shavington
West Way
North Way
Shavington
Hall
Basford
Hall
Shavington
Cty High
Sch
Rope Farm
NORTHFIELD CL
CHESTNUT AVE
RICHARDSON CL
MEADOW CL
PARK ESTATES
Basford
LARCH AVE
BURLEA DR
VINE TREE AVE
EDWARDS AVE
WOODNOTH DR
WESTON LA
MOUNT
2
Puseydale
Farm
ROPE LA
EDWARDS CL
OSBORNE GR
SOUTHBANK
AVE
Shavington
Farm
Sutch Farm
THE FOLLIES
Shavington
Cty Prim
Sch
P
QUEEN ST
BROOK AVE
THE ORCHARDS
Swill Brook
BACK LA
52
PO
MAIN RD
LORDS MILL RD
MERCIAN
BARONS RD
GOODWIN CRES
TWINNOW
CAMELOT GR
Shavington Green
Farm
CASEY LA
PH
DEVIES
TALBOT
GALWAY GR
CROMFORD GR
HEAWARD CL
WHITEHALL
MALVERN CL
PH
MONTROSE CL
KNIGHTS WAY
REGENT
EARLS RD
ASHCROFT
PAGE AVE
WINCHESTER
ENFIELD
CAMERON AVE
WESSEX CL
A500
A500
HUNTERS
NEWCASTLE RD
GOODALL'S
CNR
PO
PH
1 MARTON CL
2 ELLWOOD GREEN
NURSERY CL
B5071
CHURCH LA
BUCK LA
NORBURY
Hough
2
DIG LA
RIDLEY CL
BUCKLEY CL
WOOLSTON DR
RUSHTON CL
51
STOCK LA
Wybunbury
Grange
Hough
Manor
Hough
Hall
ALDFORD CL
WAVERTON CL
WOODCOTT
CL
KINGS MEADOW
TILSTONE
CL
+
Clannor Heath
Cockshades Farm
PIT LA
COBBS LA
BIRCH LA
Hough Common
1
Moss
Farm
Dove House
Farm
Yewtree Farm
WYBUNBURY
LA
Pinfold Farm
ANNIONS LA
MAIN RD
RIDDINGS
Wybunbury Moss
Highfield Farm
CHADS
GREEN
B5071
MOORLANDS
DR
Pinfold Corner
50
69
A
70
B
71
C

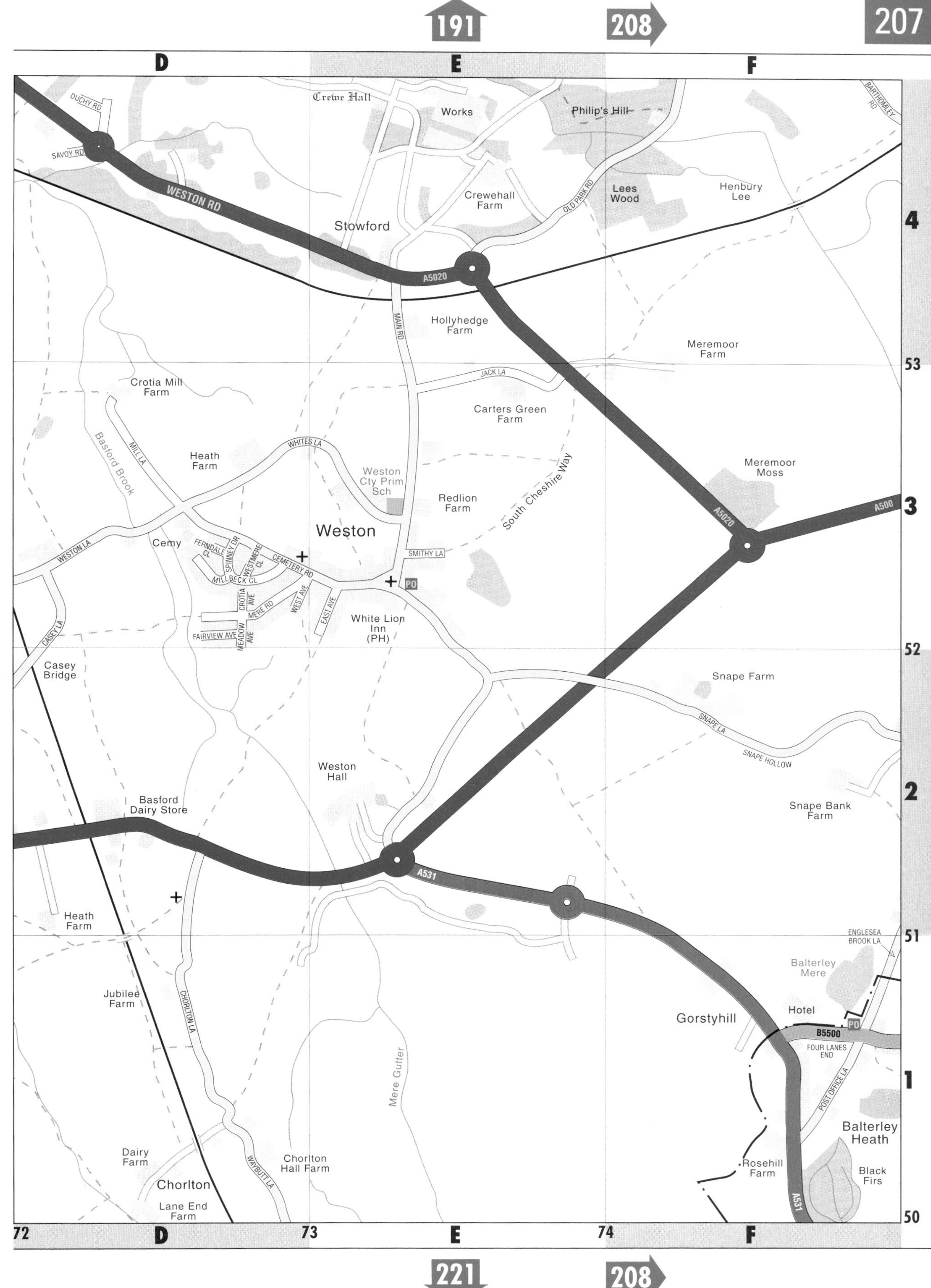
D
E
F
Crewe Hall
Works
Philip's Hill
DUCHY RD
SAVOY RD
BARTHOMLEY RD
WESTON RD
Crewehall Farm
OLD PARK RD
Lees Wood
Henbury Lee
Stowford
A5020
MAIN RD
Hollyhedge Farm
Meremoor Farm
Crotia Mill Farm
JACK LA
Carters Green Farm
Basford Brook
MILL LA
Heath Farm
WHITES LA
Weston Cty Prim Sch
Meremoor Moss
Redlion Farm
South Cheshire Way
A5020
A500
Weston
Cemy
WESTON LA
FERNDALE CL
SPINNEY DR
WESTMERE CL
CEMETERY RD
MILLBECK CL
SMITHY LA
PO
CROTIA AVE
MERE RD
WEST AVE
EAST AVE
White Lion Inn (PH)
FAIRVIEW AVE
MEADOW AVE
CASEY LA
Casey Bridge
Snape Farm
SNAPE LA
SNAPE HOLLOW
Weston Hall
Basford Dairy Store
Snape Bank Farm
A531
Heath Farm
ENGLESEA BROOK LA
Balterley Mere
Jubilee Farm
CHORLTON LA
Hotel
Gorstyhill
PO
B5500
FOUR LANES END
POST OFFICE LA
Mere Gutter
Balterley Heath
Dairy Farm
Chorlton Hall Farm
WAYBUTT LA
Rosehill Farm
Black Firs
Chorlton
Lane End Farm
A531
4
53
3
52
2
51
1
50
72
73
74

207
192

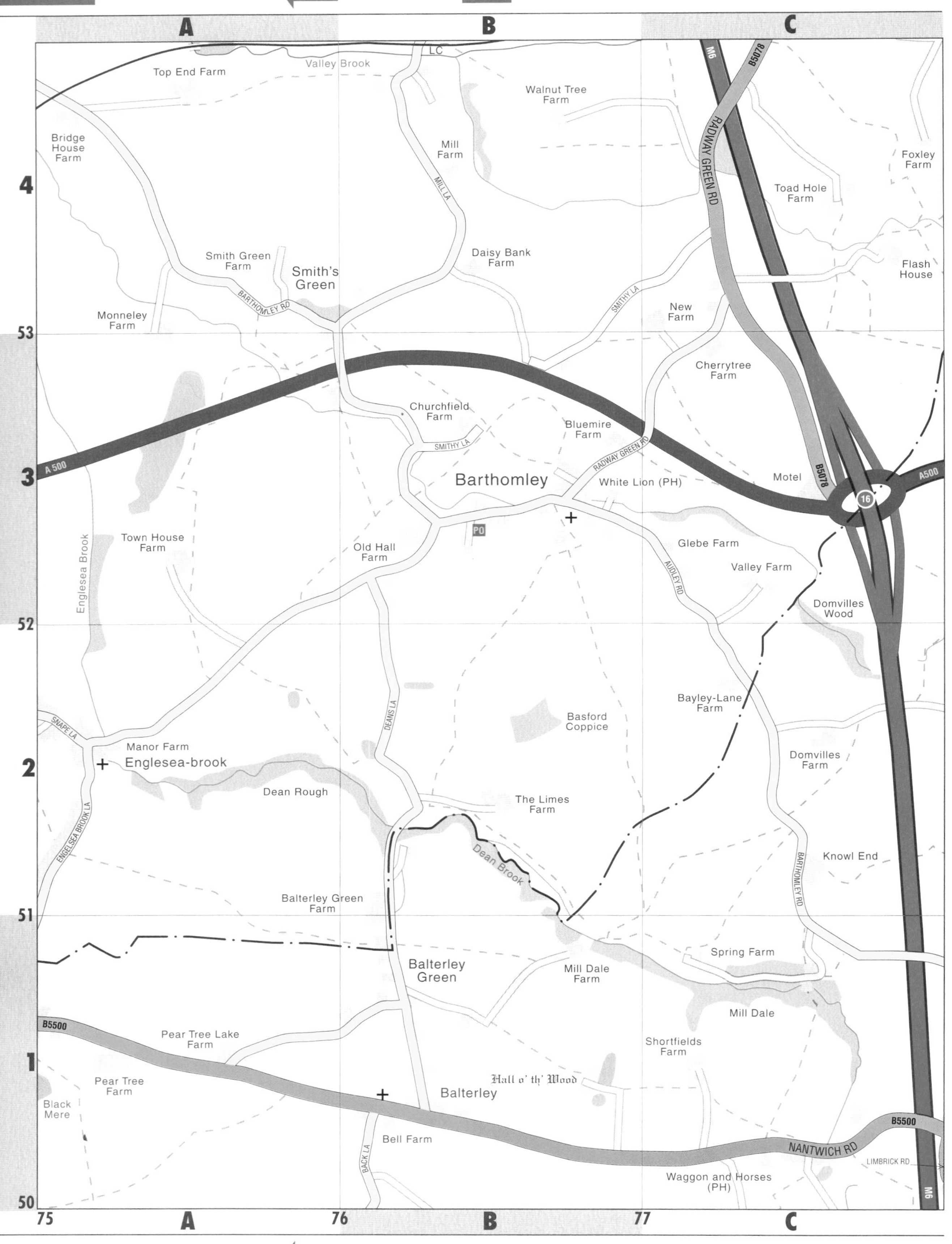

Top End Farm
Valley Brook
LC
Walnut Tree Farm
Foxley Farm
Bridge House Farm
Mill Farm
MILL LA
RADWAY GREEN RD
B5078
M6
Toad Hole Farm
Flash House
4
Smith Green Farm
Daisy Bank Farm
Smith's Green
New Farm
SMITHY LA
Monneley Farm
BARTHOMLEY RD
53
Cherrytree Farm
A 500
Churchfield Farm
SMITHY LA
Bluemire Farm
RADWAY GREEN RD
Motel
B5078
A500
3
Barthomley
White Lion (PH)
16
Town House Farm
Englesea Brook
PO
Old Hall Farm
Glebe Farm
Valley Farm
AUDLEY RD
Domvilles Wood
52
SNAPE LA
Manor Farm
Englesea-brook
DEANS LA
Basford Coppice
Bayley-Lane Farm
Domvilles Farm
2
ENGLESEA BROOK LA
Dean Rough
The Limes Farm
BARTHOMLEY RD
Knowl End
Dean Brook
Balterley Green Farm
51
Spring Farm
Balterley Green
Mill Dale Farm
B5500
Mill Dale
Pear Tree Lake Farm
Shortfields Farm
1
Pear Tree Farm
Hall o' th' Wood
Balterley
Black Mere
BACK LA
Bell Farm
B5500
NANTWICH RD
LIMBRICK RD
Waggon and Horses (PH)
M6
50

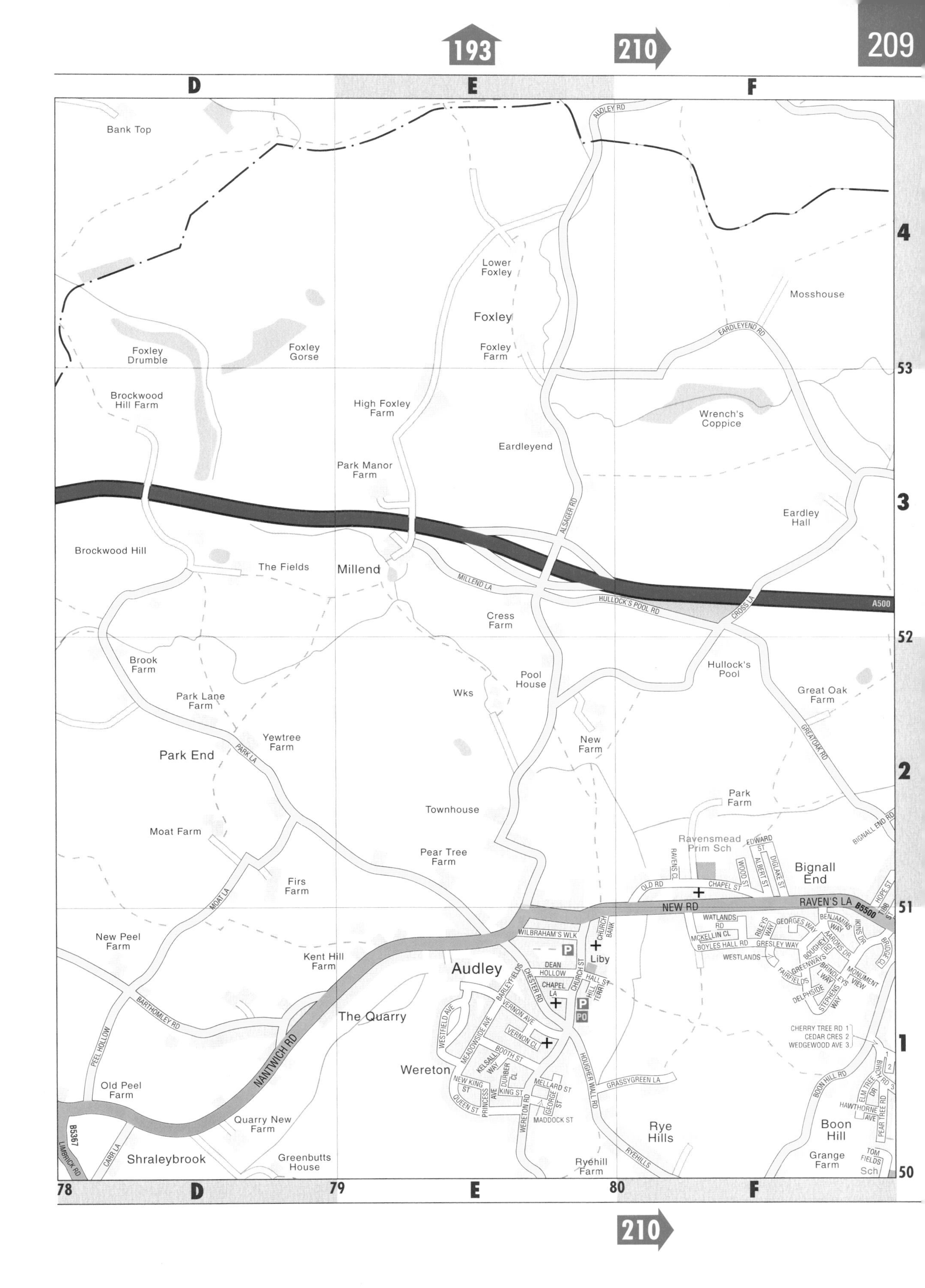
193
210
D
E
F
Bank Top
AUDLEY RD
Lower Foxley
Foxley
Mosshouse
EARDLEYEND RD
Foxley Drumble
Foxley Gorse
Foxley Farm
53
Brockwood Hill Farm
High Foxley Farm
Wrench's Coppice
Eardleyend
Park Manor Farm
ALSAGER RD
3
Eardley Hall
Brockwood Hill
The Fields
Millend
MILLEND LA
HULLOCK'S POOL RD
CROSS LA
A500
Cress Farm
52
Brook Farm
Pool House
Hullock's Pool
Wks
Great Oak Farm
Park Lane Farm
Yewtree Farm
GREATOAK RD
Park End
PARK LA
New Farm
2
Townhouse
Park Farm
Moat Farm
Ravensmead Prim Sch
BIGNALL END RD
Pear Tree Farm
EDWARD ST
RAVENS CL
WOOD ST
ALBERT ST
DIGLAKE ST
Bignall End
Firs Farm
MOAT LA
OLD RD
CHAPEL ST
HOPE ST
NEW RD
RAVEN'S LA
B5500
51
New Peel Farm
WILBRAHAM'S WLK
CHURCH BANK
WATLANDS RD
MCKELLIN CL
BOYLES HALL RD
RILEYS WAY
GEORGES WAY
BENJAMINS WAY
AARONS DR
BRIDGE CL
GRESLEY WAY
WESTLANDS
Kent Hill Farm
Audley
Liby
DEAN HOLLOW
BARLEYFIELDS
CHESTER RD
CHURCH ST
HALL ST
HILL TERR
CHAPEL LA
BOUGHEY RD
GREENWAYS
FAIRFIELDS
BRINDLEYS WAY
MONUMENT VIEW
DELPHSIDE
STEPHENS WAY
The Quarry
VERNON AVE
VERNON CL
PO
BARTHOMLEY RD
WESTFIELD AVE
MEADOWSIDE AVE
CHERRY TREE RD 1
CEDAR CRES 2
WEDGEWOOD AVE 3
1
PEEL HOLLOW
NANTWICH RD
BOOTH ST
KELSALL WAY
DURBER CL
HOUGHER WALL RD
Wereton
Old Peel Farm
NEW KING ST
KING ST
MELLARD ST
GRASSYGREEN LA
BOON HILL RD
ELM TREE DR
BIRCH DR
PRINCESS AVE
QUEEN ST
WERETON RD
GEORGE ST
HAWTHORNE AVE
PEAR TREE RD
Quarry New Farm
MADDOCK ST
Rye Hills
Boon Hill
B5367
LIMBRICK RD
CARR LA
Shraleybrook
Greenbutts House
RYEHILLS
Ryehill Farm
Grange Farm
TOM FIELDS
Sch
50
78
79
80

210

209
194

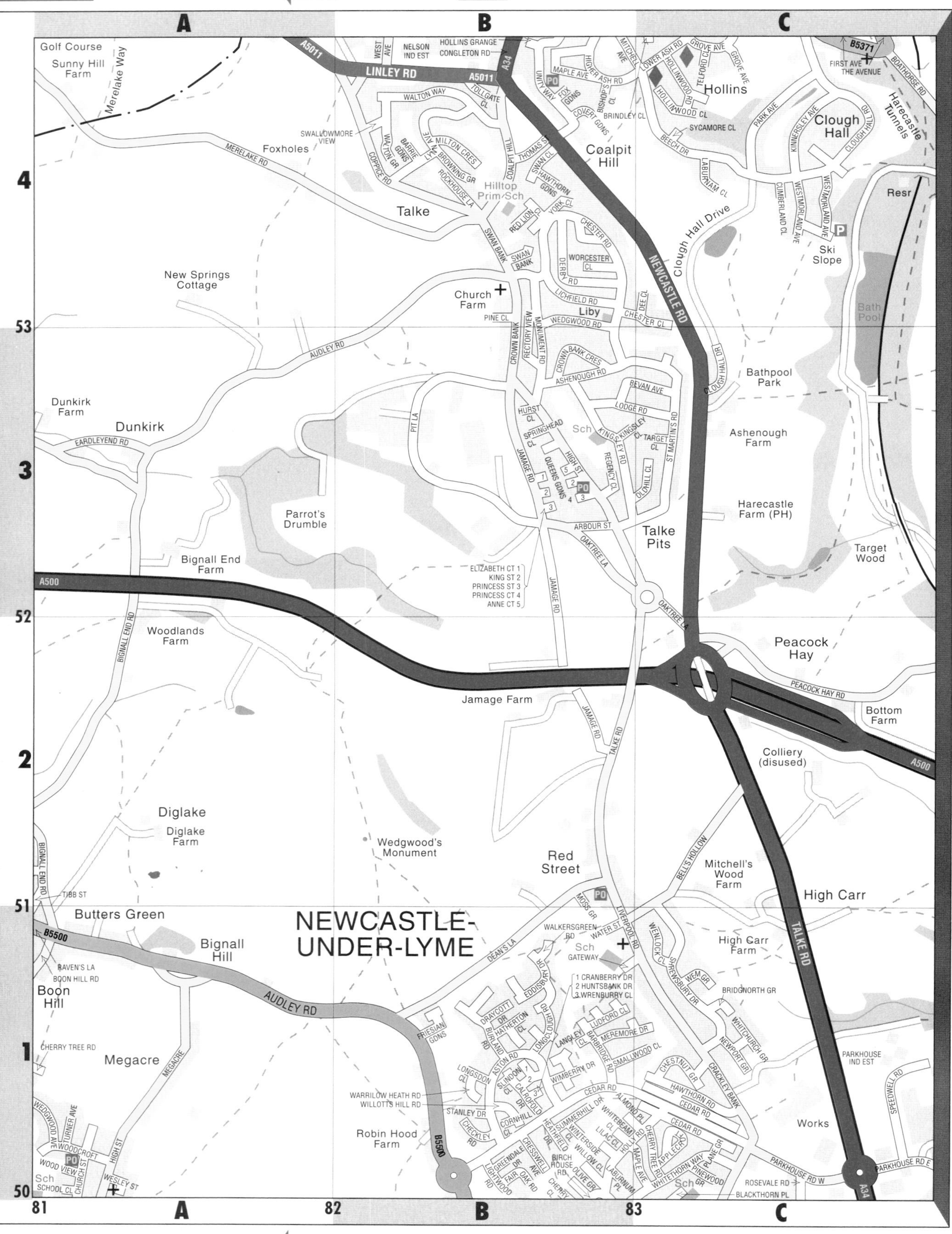
NEWCASTLE-UNDER-LYME
Talke
Talke Pits
Coalpit Hill
Hollins
Clough Hall
Harecastle Tunnels
Liby
Dunkirk
Dunkirk Farm
Foxholes
New Springs Cottage
Church Farm
Parrot's Drumble
Bignall End Farm
Woodlands Farm
Jamage Farm
Peacock Hay
Bottom Farm
Colliery (disused)
Bathpool Park
Ashenough Farm
Harecastle Farm (PH)
Target Wood
Ski Slope
Bath Pool
Resr
Diglake
Diglake Farm
Wedgwood's Monument
Red Street
Mitchell's Wood Farm
High Carr
High Carr Farm
Butters Green
Bignall Hill
Boon Hill
Megacre
Robin Hood Farm
Works
Golf Course
Sunny Hill Farm
Hilltop Prim Sch
NEWCASTLE RD
TALKE RD
LINLEY RD
AUDLEY RD
Clough Hall Drive
A500
A34
A5011
B5500
B5371
ELIZABETH CT 1
KING ST 2
PRINCESS ST 3
PRINCESS CT 4
ANNE CT 5
1 CRANBERRY DR
2 HUNTSBANK DR
3 WRENBURRY CL
PARKHOUSE IND EST
81
82
83
A
B
C
1
2
3
4
50
51
52
53

209

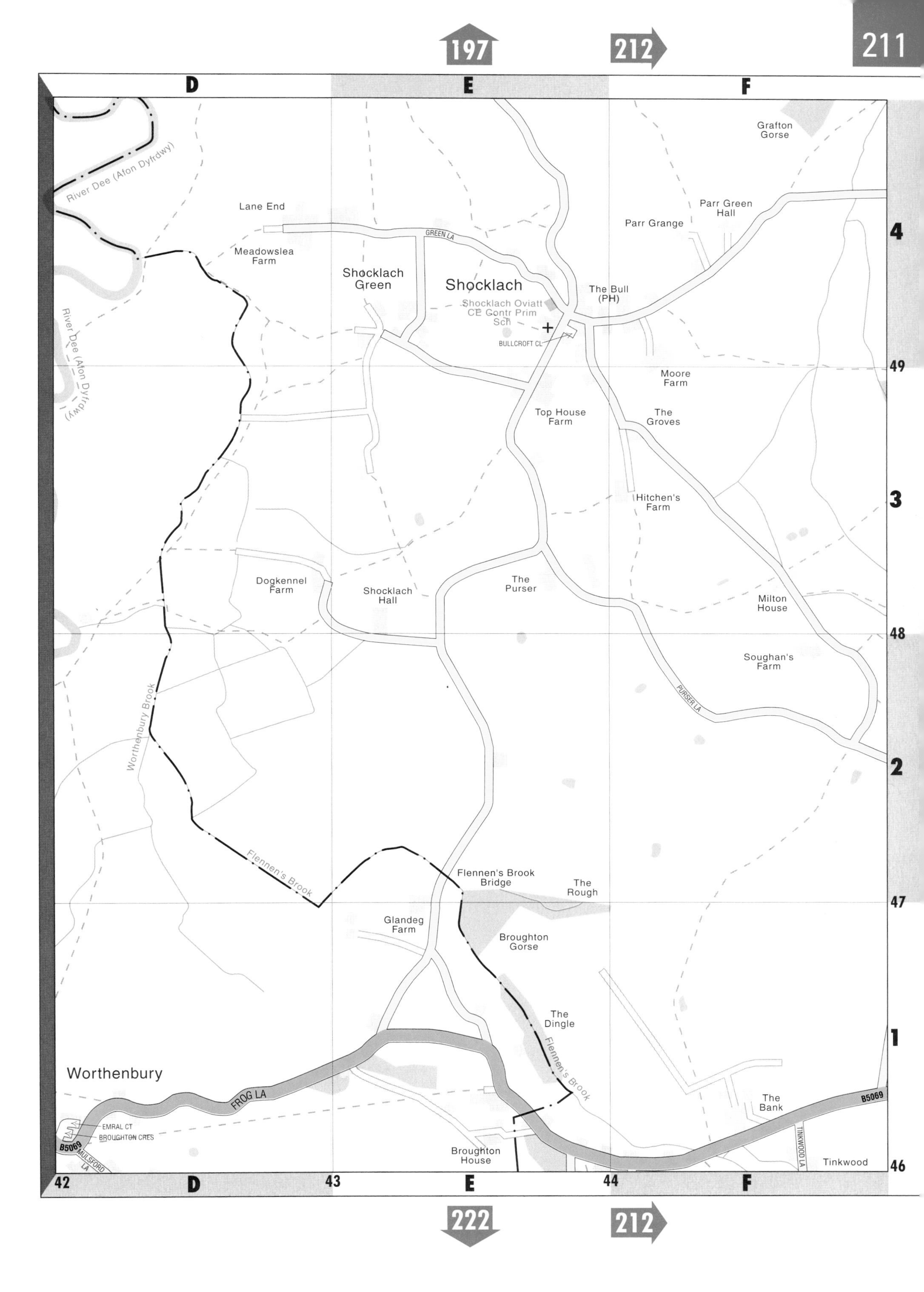

197
212

D E F

4

49

3

48

2

47

1

46

River Dee (Afon Dyfrdwy)

River Dee (Afon Dyfrdwy)

Lane End

Meadowslea Farm

GREEN LA

Shocklach Green

Shocklach

Shocklach Oviatt CE Contr Prim Sch

The Bull (PH)

BULLCROFT CL

Grafton Gorse

Parr Green Hall

Parr Grange

Moore Farm

Top House Farm

The Groves

Hitchen's Farm

Dogkennel Farm

Shocklach Hall

The Purser

Milton House

Soughan's Farm

PURSER LA

Worthenbury Brook

Flennen's Brook

Flennen's Brook Bridge

The Rough

Glandeg Farm

Broughton Gorse

The Dingle

Flennen's Brook

Worthenbury

FROG LA

EMRAL CT
BROUGHTON CRES

B5069

MULSFORD LA

Broughton House

The Bank

B5069

TINKWOOD LA

Tinkwood

42 D 43 E 44 F

222
212

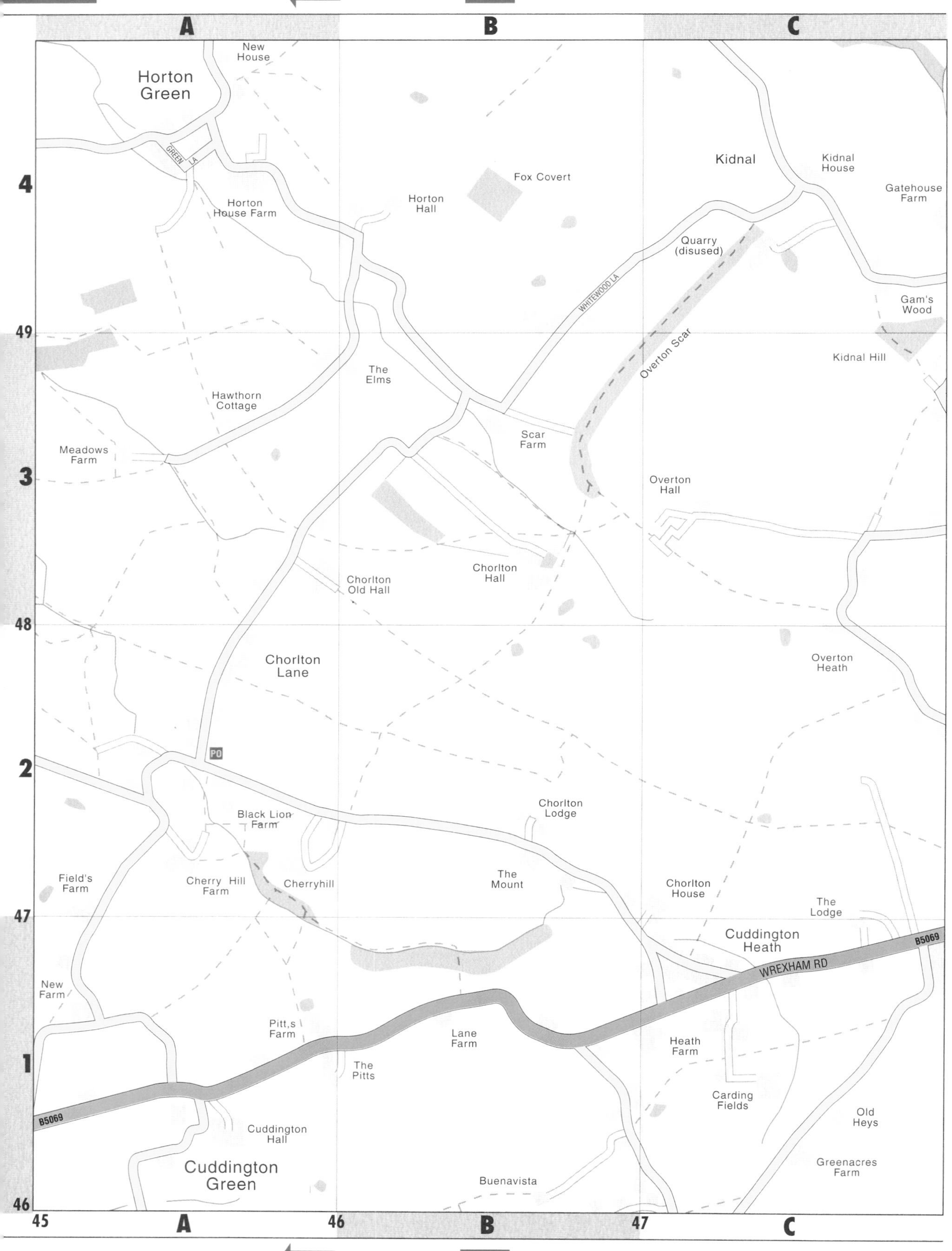

A   B   C

4   Horton
     Green
     New
     House
                    Fox Covert   Kidnal   Kidnal
                                                    House   Gatehouse
     Horton   Farm
     House Farm   Horton
                         Hall   Quarry
                                       (disused)   Gam's
                                                               Wood
49   Kidnal Hill
     Hawthorn   The   Overton Scar
     Cottage   Elms
                                                    Overton
     Meadows   Scar   Hall
3   Farm   Farm

                                                   Overton
                                                   Heath
48   Chorlton   Chorlton
              Old Hall   Hall

     Chorlton
     Lane

                                    Chorlton
                                    Lodge
2   PO

     Black Lion   Chorlton
     Farm   The   House   The
     Field's   Cherry Hill Mount   Lodge
     Farm   Farm   Cherryhill
47   Cuddington   B5069
     New   Heath
     Farm   WREXHAM RD
              Pitt,s   Lane
              Farm   Farm   Heath
              The   Farm
1   Pitts
     B5069   Carding   Old
                                          Fields   Heys
     Cuddington
     Hall   Greenacres
     Cuddington   Farm
46   Green   Buenavista
45   A   46   B   47   C

199
214

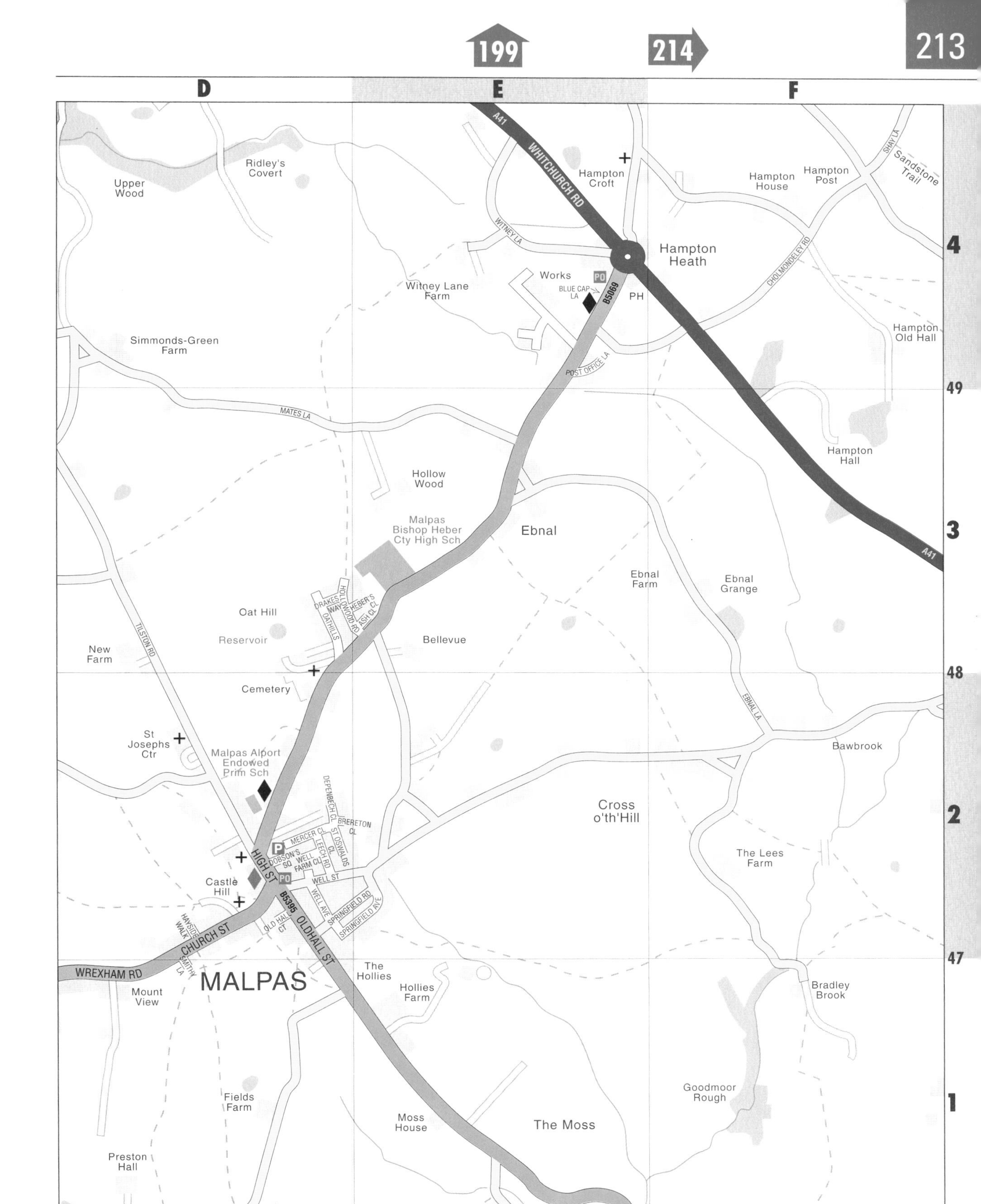
D
E
F
Upper Wood
Ridley's Covert
A41
WHITCHURCH RD
Hampton Croft
Hampton House
Hampton Post
SHAY LA
Sandstone Trail
4
WITNEY LA
Hampton Heath
Works
PO
BLUE CAP LA
B5069
PH
CHOLMONDELEY RD
Witney Lane Farm
Simmonds-Green Farm
Hampton Old Hall
POST OFFICE LA
49
MATES LA
Hampton Hall
Hollow Wood
Malpas Bishop Heber Cty High Sch
Ebnal
3
Ebnal Farm
Ebnal Grange
DRAKES WAY
HOLLOWOOD RD
HEBER'S
ASH CL
OATHILLS
Oat Hill
Reservoir
Bellevue
New Farm
TILSTON RD
48
Cemetery
EBNAL LA
St Josephs Ctr
Malpas Alport Endowed Prim Sch
Bawbrook
DEPENBECH CL
BRERETON CL
Cross o'th'Hill
2
MERCER CL
ST OSWALDS
P
DOBSON'S SQ
WELL FARM CL
LEECH RD
HIGH ST
The Lees Farm
PO
WELL ST
Castle Hill
B5395
OLDHALL ST
WELL AVE
SPRINGFIELD RD
SPRINGFIELD AVE
OLD HALL CT
HAYSIDE WALK
CHURCH ST
SMITHY LA
47
WREXHAM RD
MALPAS
The Hollies
Hollies Farm
Bradley Brook
Mount View
Goodmoor Rough
Fields Farm
1
Moss House
The Moss
Preston Hall
B5395
The Hough
Bradley Hall
46
48
49
50

224
214

213

200

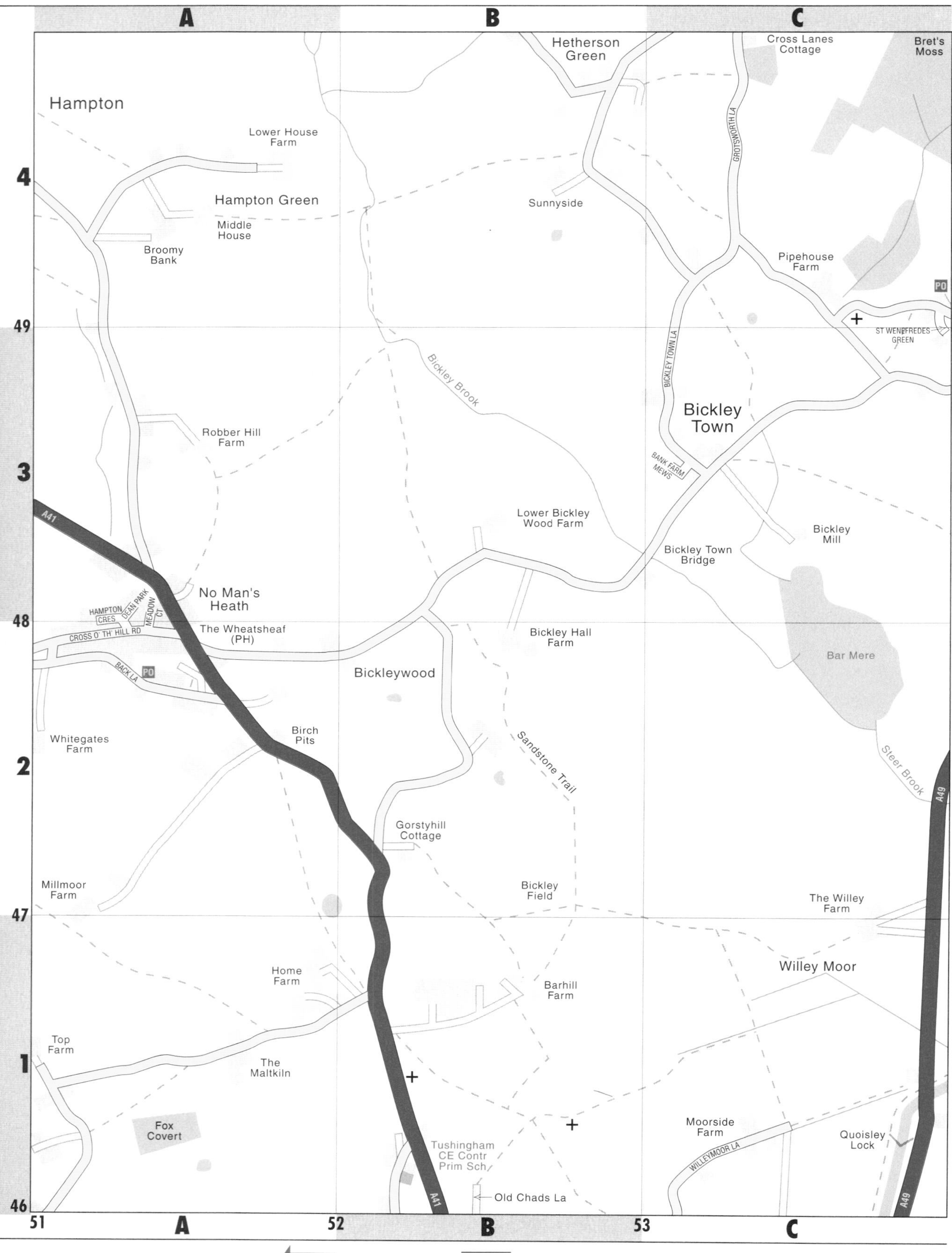

A   B   C

Hetherson Green

Cross Lanes Cottage

Bret's Moss

Hampton

Lower House Farm

4

Hampton Green

Sunnyside

Pipehouse Farm

Middle House

Broomy Bank

PO

St Wenefredes Green

49

GROTSWORTH LA

Bickley Brook

Bickley Town

Robber Hill Farm

BICKLEY TOWN LA

3

A41

BANK FARM MEWS

Lower Bickley Wood Farm

Bickley Town Bridge

Bickley Mill

No Man's Heath

HAMPTON CRES

DEER PARK

MEADOW CT

Bickley Hall Farm

48

CROSS O' TH' HILL RD

The Wheatsheaf (PH)

Bar Mere

BACK LA

PO

Bickleywood

Whitegates Farm

Birch Pits

Sandstone Trail

2

Gorstyhill Cottage

Steer Brook

A49

Millmoor Farm

Bickley Field

The Willey Farm

47

Willey Moor

Home Farm

Barhill Farm

Top Farm

1

The Maltkiln

+

Moorside Farm

Quoisley Lock

Fox Covert

Tushingham CE Contr Prim Sch

+

WILLEYMOOR LA

A41

Old Chads La

A49

46

51   A   52   B   53   C

213

225

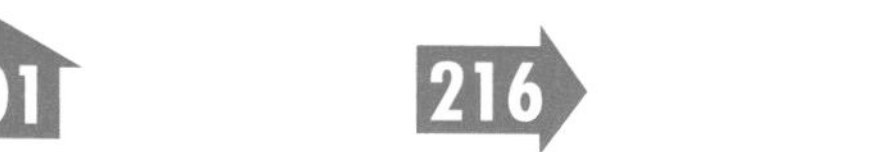
201
216

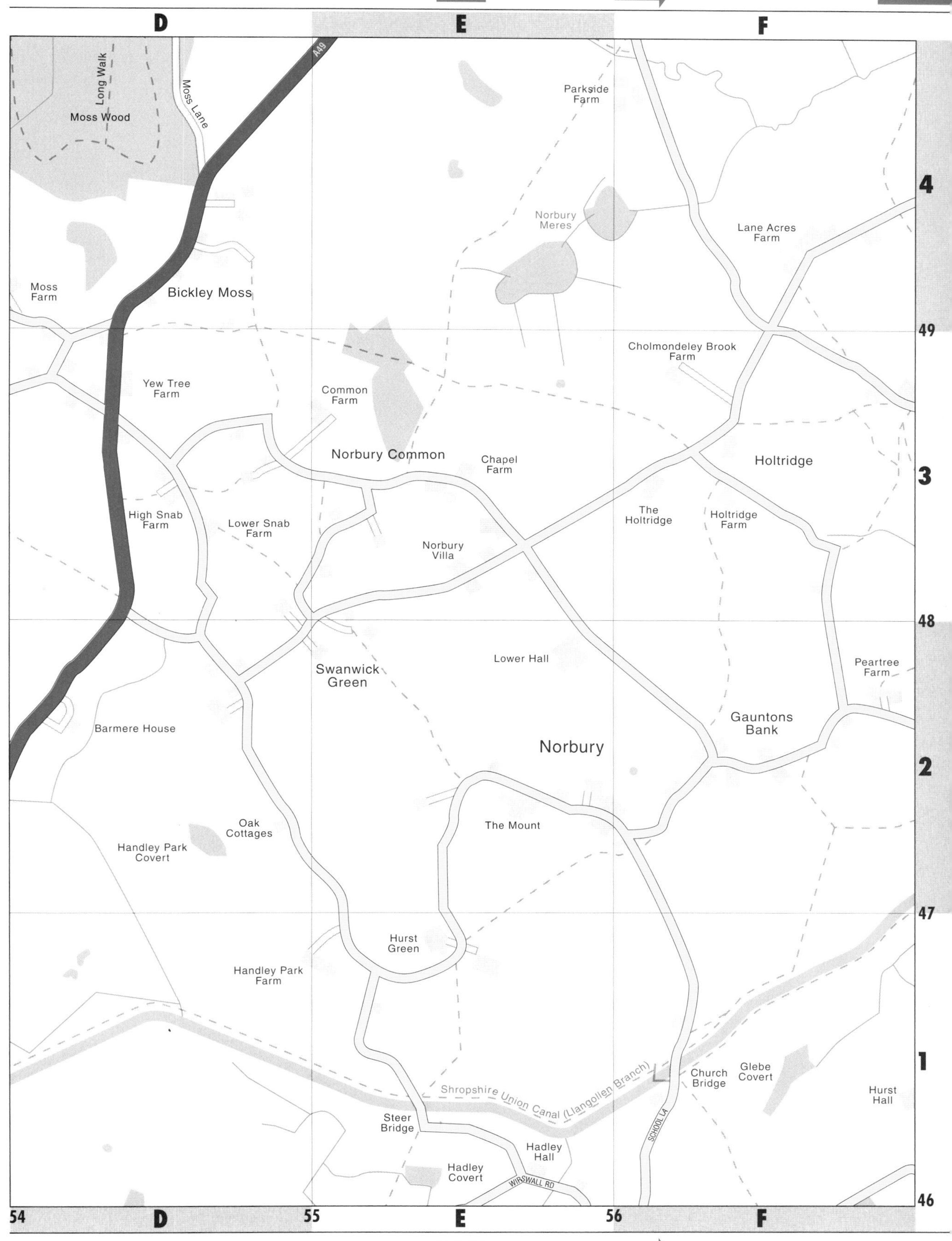
D
E
F
A49
Long Walk
Moss Wood
Moss Lane
Parkside Farm
Norbury Meres
Lane Acres Farm
Moss Farm
Bickley Moss
Cholmondeley Brook Farm
Yew Tree Farm
Common Farm
Norbury Common
Chapel Farm
Holtridge
The Holtridge
Holtridge Farm
High Snab Farm
Lower Snab Farm
Norbury Villa
Lower Hall
Peartree Farm
Swanwick Green
Barmere House
Gauntons Bank
Norbury
Oak Cottages
Handley Park Covert
The Mount
Hurst Green
Handley Park Farm
Shropshire Union Canal (Llangollen Branch)
Church Bridge
Glebe Covert
Hurst Hall
School La
Steer Bridge
Hadley Hall
Hadley Covert
Wirswall Rd
4
49
3
48
2
47
1
46
54
55
56
226
216

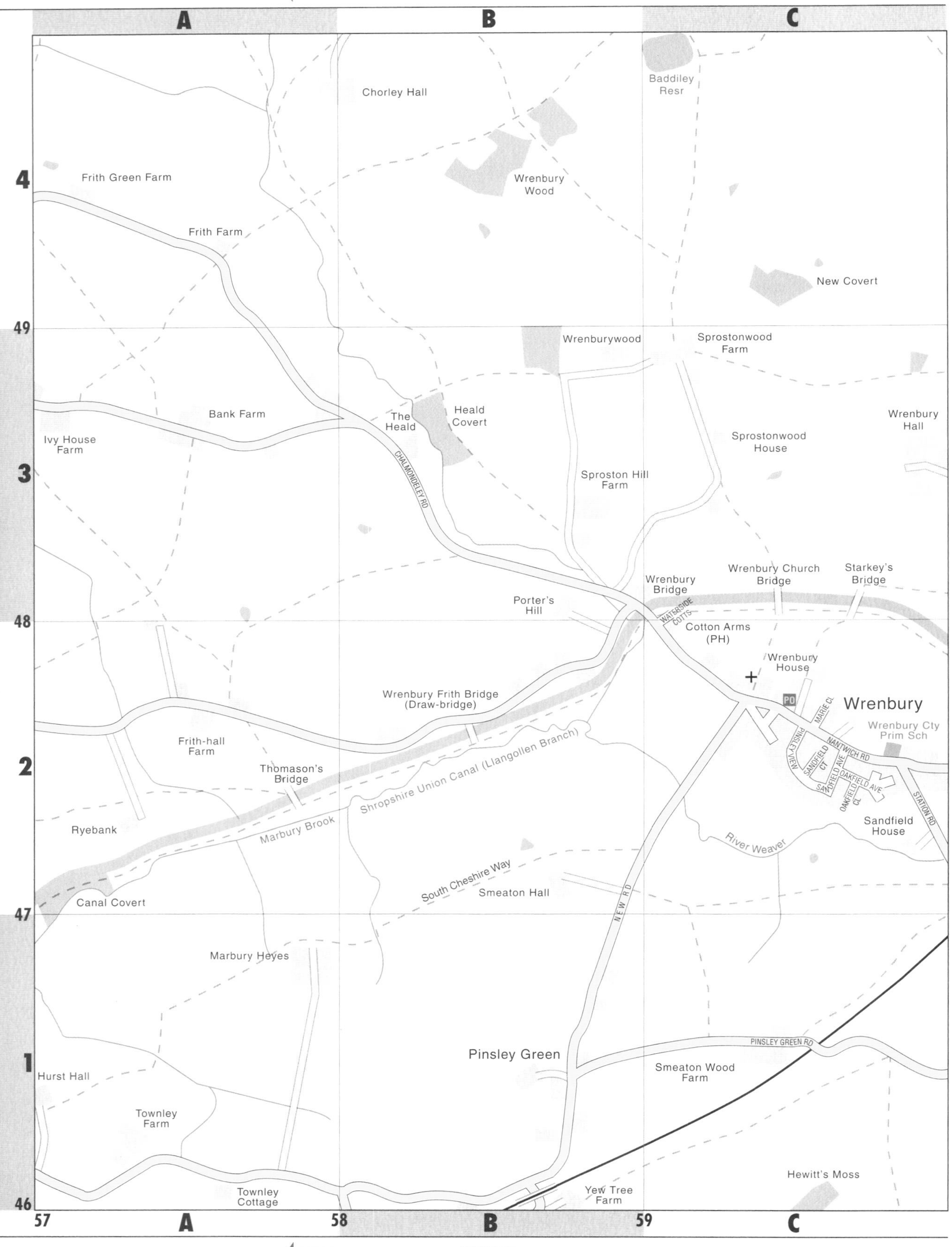

Chorley Hall

Baddiley Resr

Frith Green Farm

Wrenbury Wood

New Covert

Frith Farm

Wrenburywood

Sprostonwood Farm

Bank Farm

The Heald

Heald Covert

Sprostonwood House

Wrenbury Hall

Ivy House Farm

Sproston Hill Farm

CHOLMONDELEY RD

Wrenbury Bridge

Wrenbury Church Bridge

Starkey's Bridge

Porter's Hill

Cotton Arms (PH)

WATERSIDE COTTS

Wrenbury House

Wrenbury Frith Bridge (Draw-bridge)

PO

Wrenbury

Wrenbury Cty Prim Sch

Frith-hall Farm

Thomason's Bridge

Shropshire Union Canal (Llangollen Branch)

MARIE CL

NANTWICH RD

PINSLEY AVE

SANDFIELD CT

OAKFIELD AVE

SANDFIELD CT

OAKFIELD CL

STATION RD

Ryebank

Marbury Brook

Sandfield House

River Weaver

Canal Covert

South Cheshire Way

Smeaton Hall

NEW RD

Marbury Heyes

Pinsley Green

PINSLEY GREEN RD

Hurst Hall

Smeaton Wood Farm

Townley Farm

Hewitt's Moss

Townley Cottage

Yew Tree Farm

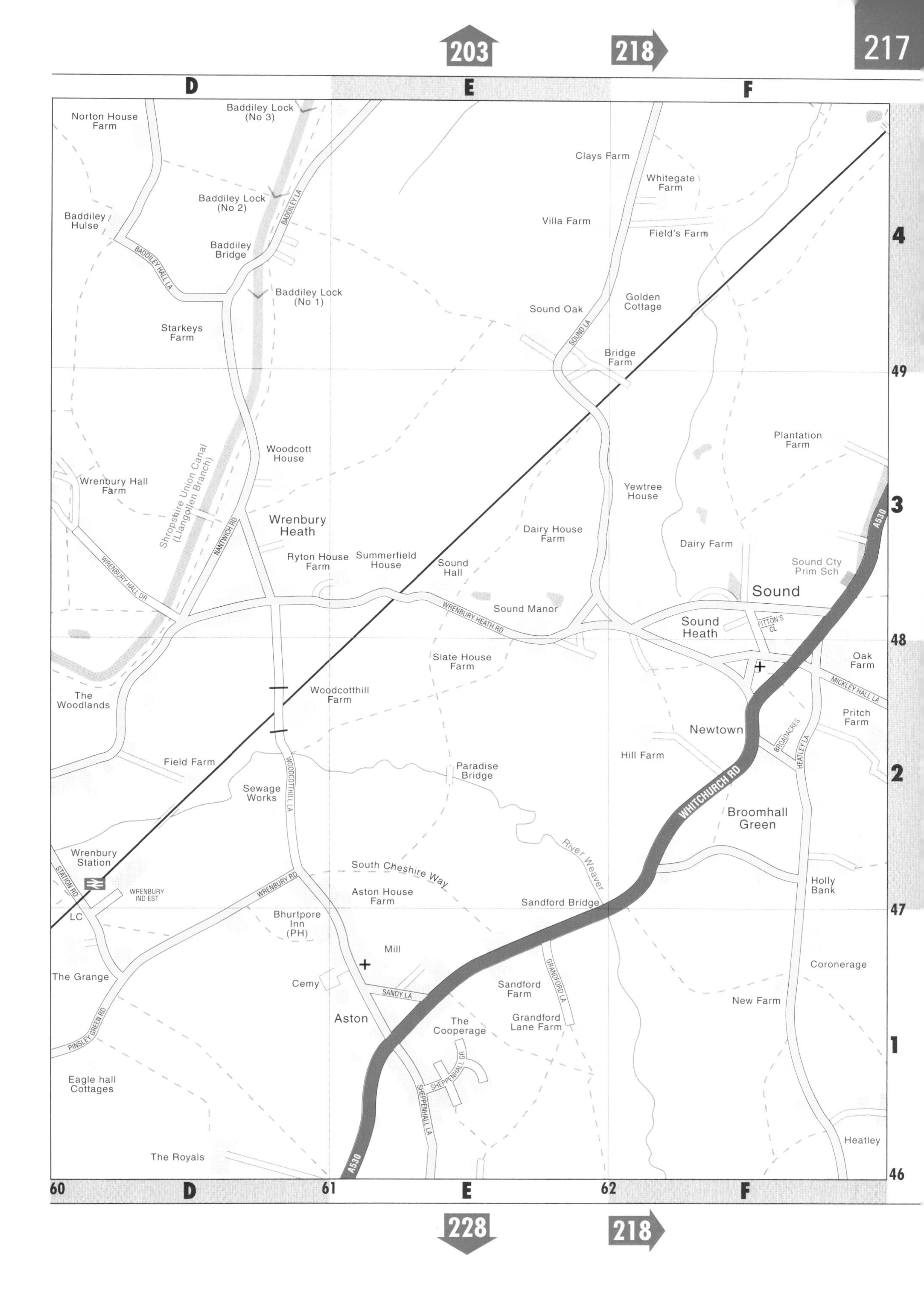

D

Norton House Farm

Baddiley Lock (No 3)

Baddiley Lock (No 2)

BADDILEY LA

Baddiley Hulse

Baddiley Bridge

BADDILEY HALL LA

Baddiley Lock (No 1)

Starkeys Farm

Clays Farm

Whitegate Farm

Villa Farm

Field's Farm

4

Golden Cottage

Sound Oak

SOUND LA

Bridge Farm

49

Shropshire Union Canal (Llangollen Branch)

Woodcott House

Wrenbury Hall Farm

WRENBURY HALL DR

NANTWICH RD

Wrenbury Heath

Ryton House Farm

Summerfield House

Sound Hall

Plantation Farm

Yewtree House

Dairy House Farm

Dairy Farm

Sound Cty Prim Sch

Sound

3

A530

WRENBURY HEATH RD

Sound Manor

Sound Heath

FITTON'S CL

48

The Woodlands

Woodcotthill Farm

Slate House Farm

Oak Farm

MICKLEY HALL LA

Newtown

BROADACRES

HEATLEY LA

Pritch Farm

Field Farm

WOODCOTTHILL LA

Sewage Works

Paradise Bridge

Hill Farm

Broomhall Green

2

WHITCHURCH RD

Wrenbury Station

STATION RD

WRENBURY RD

South Cheshire Way

River Weaver

Holly Bank

47

WRENBURY IND EST

LC

Aston House Farm

Sandford Bridge

Coronerage

Bhurtpore Inn (PH)

Mill

New Farm

The Grange

Cemy

SANDY LA

GRANDFORD LA

Sandford Farm

Grandford Lane Farm

PINSLEY GREEN RD

Aston

The Cooperage

1

Eagle hall Cottages

SHEPPENHALL GR

SHEPPENHALL LA

Heatley

The Royals

A530

46

60

D

61

E

62

F

217
204

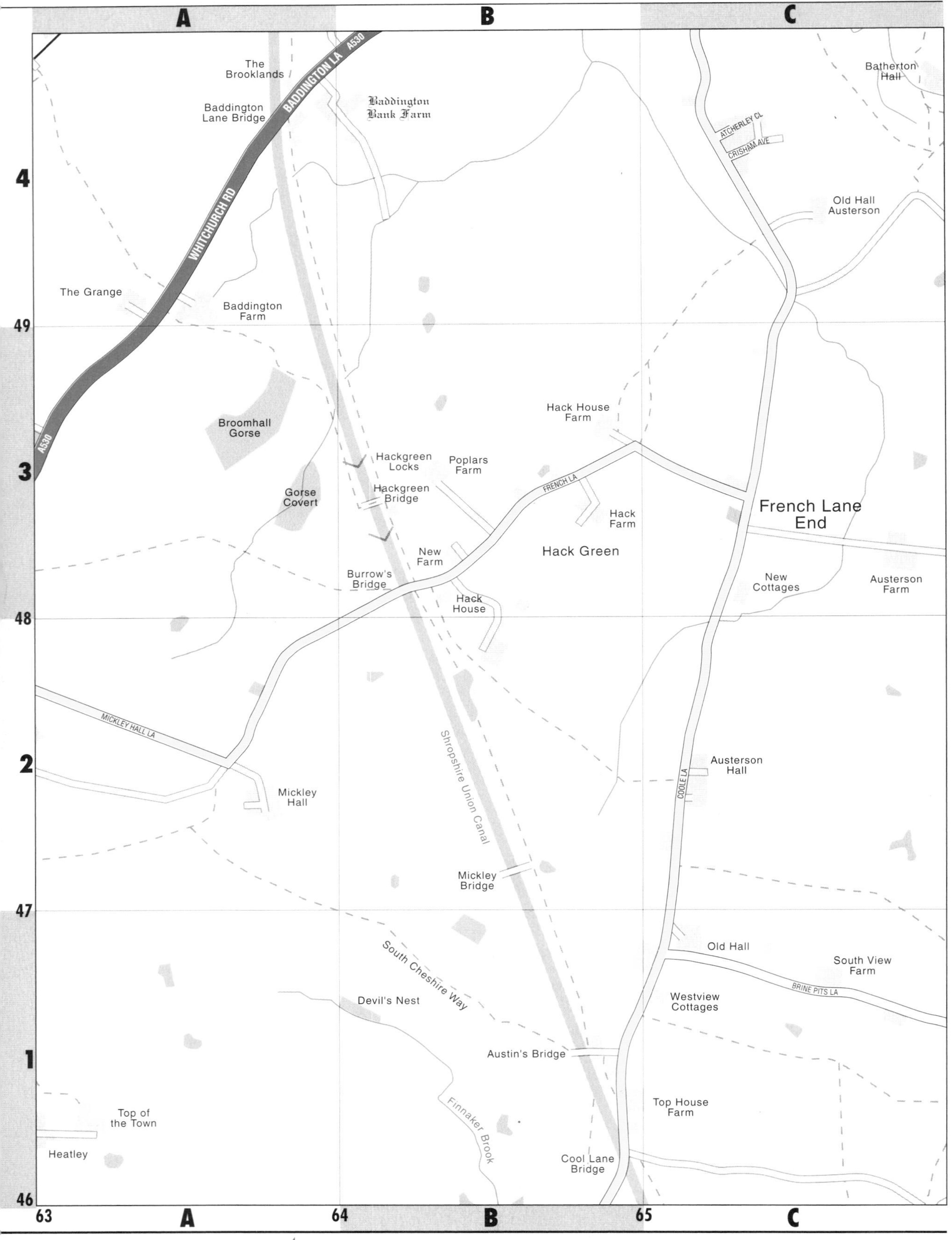

A   B   C

The Brooklands
Baddington Lane Bridge
BADDINGTON LA A530
Baddington Bank Farm
Batherton Hall
ATCHERLEY CL
CRISHAM AVE

4

WHITCHURCH RD

Old Hall Austerson

The Grange
Baddington Farm

49

Broomhall Gorse

Hack House Farm

Hackgreen Locks
Poplars Farm
French Lane End

3

Gorse Covert
Hackgreen Bridge
FRENCH LA
Hack Farm

A530

New Farm
Hack Green
New Cottages
Austerson Farm

Burrow's Bridge
Hack House

48

Mickley Hall La

Austerson Hall
COOLE LA

2

Mickley Hall

Shropshire Union Canal

47

Mickley Bridge

Old Hall
South View Farm
BRINE PITS LA

South Cheshire Way

Westview Cottages

Devil's Nest

1

Austin's Bridge

Top of the Town

Top House Farm

Heatley
Finnaker Brook
Cool Lane Bridge

46

63   A   64   B   65   C

217
229

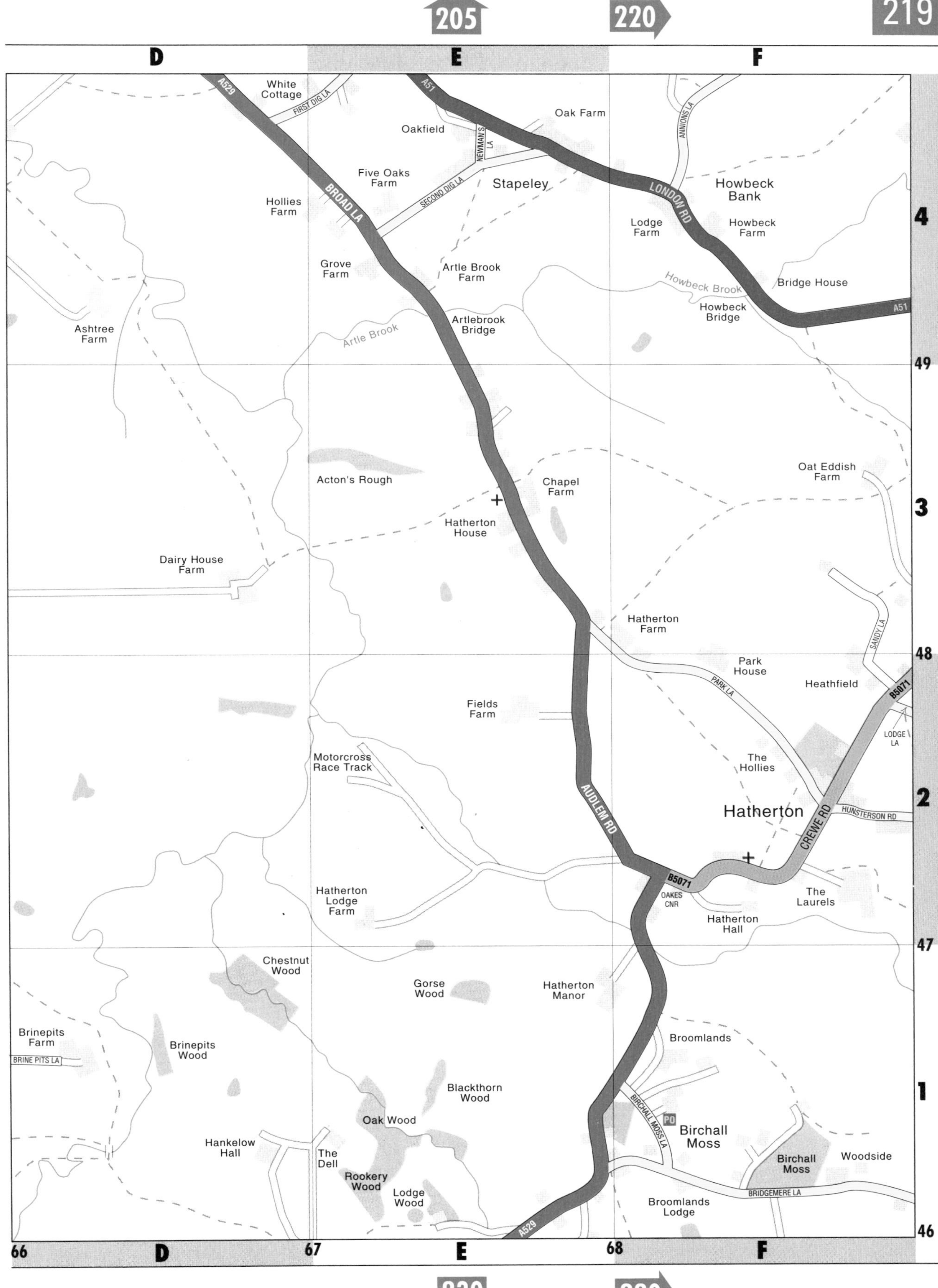

D
E
F

White Cottage

A529

FIRST DIG LA

A51

Oakfield

Oak Farm

NEWMAN'S LA

Five Oaks Farm

Stapeley

BROAD LA

SECOND DIG LA

ANNIONS LA

Howbeck Bank

LONDON RD

Hollies Farm

4

Lodge Farm

Howbeck Farm

Grove Farm

Artle Brook Farm

Howbeck Brook

Bridge House

Artlebrook Bridge

Howbeck Bridge

A51

Artle Brook

49

Ashtree Farm

Oat Eddish Farm

Acton's Rough

Chapel Farm

3

+

Hatherton House

Dairy House Farm

Hatherton Farm

Park House

SANDY LA

Heathfield

48

B5071

Park Lane

Fields Farm

PARK LA

LODGE LA

Motorcross Race Track

The Hollies

B5071

2

AUDLEM RD

Hatherton

CREWE RD

HUNSTERSON RD

Hatherton Lodge Farm

+

B5071

The Laurels

OAKES CNR

Hatherton Hall

47

Chestnut Wood

Gorse Wood

Hatherton Manor

Brinepits Farm

BRINE PITS LA

Brinepits Wood

Broomlands

1

Blackthorn Wood

BIRCHALL MOSS LA

Hankelow Hall

Oak Wood

PO

Birchall Moss

Birchall Moss

Woodside

The Dell

Rookery Wood

Lodge Wood

A529

Broomlands Lodge

BRIDGEMERE LA

46

66
D
67
E
68
F

219
206

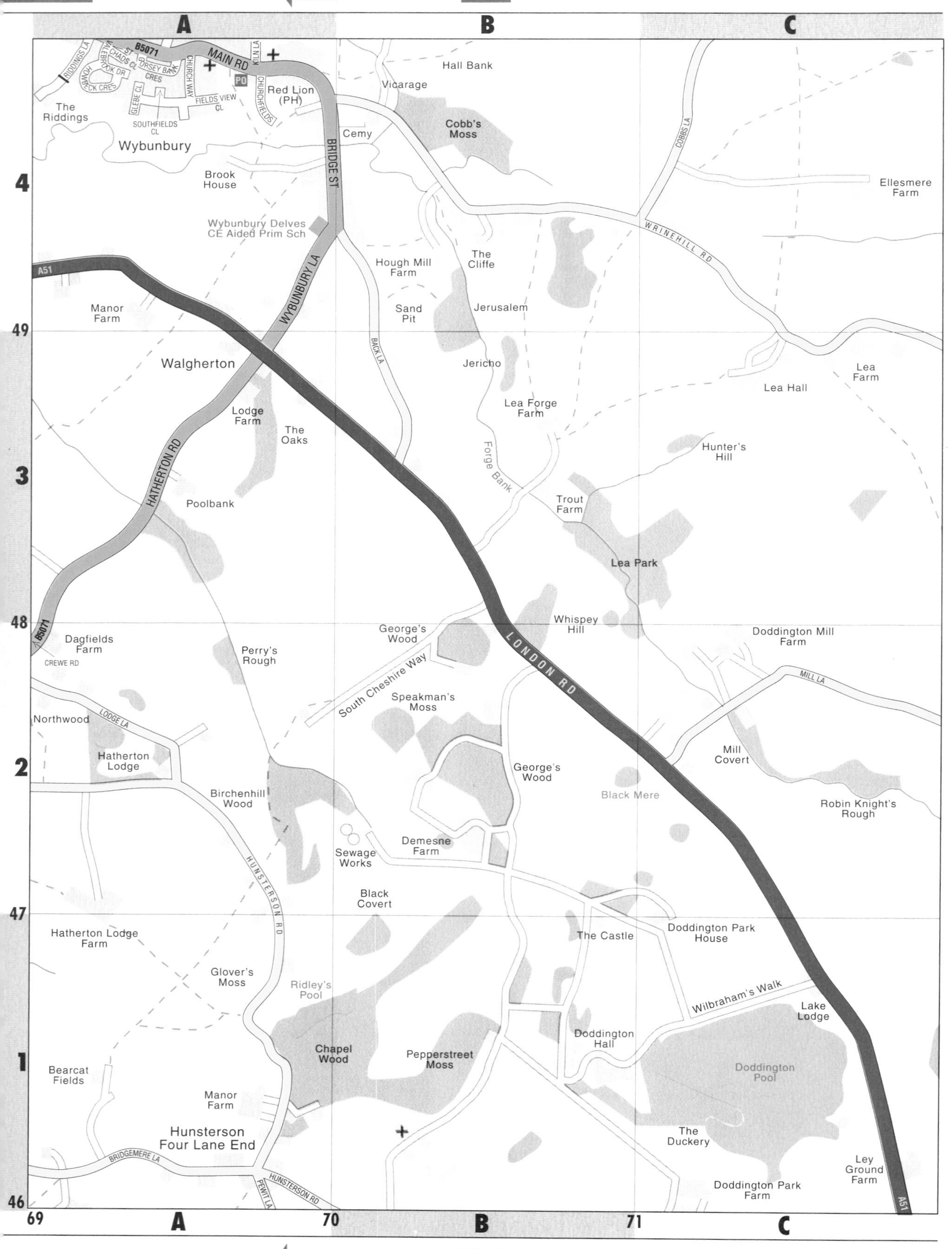
A
B
C
4
49
3
48
2
47
1
46
69
70
71
B5071
MAIN RD
KILN LA
RIDDINGS LA
ST CHADS CL
GORSEY BANK
CRES
CHURCH WAY
PO
Red Lion
(PH)
CHURCHFIELDS
FIELDS VIEW
CL
GLEBE CL
SOUTHFIELDS
CL
The
Riddings
Wybunbury
Cemy
BRIDGE ST
Brook
House
Wybunbury Delves
CE Aided Prim Sch
Hall Bank
Vicarage
Cobb's
Moss
COBBS LA
Ellesmere
Farm
WRINEHILL RD
A51
Manor
Farm
WYBUNBURY LA
Hough Mill
Farm
The
Cliffe
Sand
Pit
Jerusalem
BACK LA
Jericho
Walgherton
Lodge
Farm
The
Oaks
Lea Forge
Farm
Lea
Farm
Lea Hall
Hunter's
Hill
Forge
Bank
HATHERTON RD
Poolbank
Trout
Farm
Lea Park
Whispey
Hill
Doddington Mill
Farm
B5071
Dagfields
Farm
CREWE RD
Perry's
Rough
George's
Wood
South Cheshire Way
LONDON RD
MILL LA
Speakman's
Moss
Northwood
LODGE LA
Hatherton
Lodge
Mill
Covert
George's
Wood
Birchenhill
Wood
Black Mere
Robin Knight's
Rough
Sewage
Works
Demesne
Farm
HUNSTERSON RD
Black
Covert
Hatherton Lodge
Farm
The Castle
Doddington Park
House
Glover's
Moss
Ridley's
Pool
Wilbraham's Walk
Lake
Lodge
Chapel
Wood
Pepperstreet
Moss
Doddington
Hall
Doddington
Pool
Bearcat
Fields
Manor
Farm
Hunsterson
Four Lane End
The
Duckery
BRIDGEMERE LA
Ley
Ground
Farm
PEWIT LA
HUNSTERSON RD
Doddington Park
Farm
A51

219
231

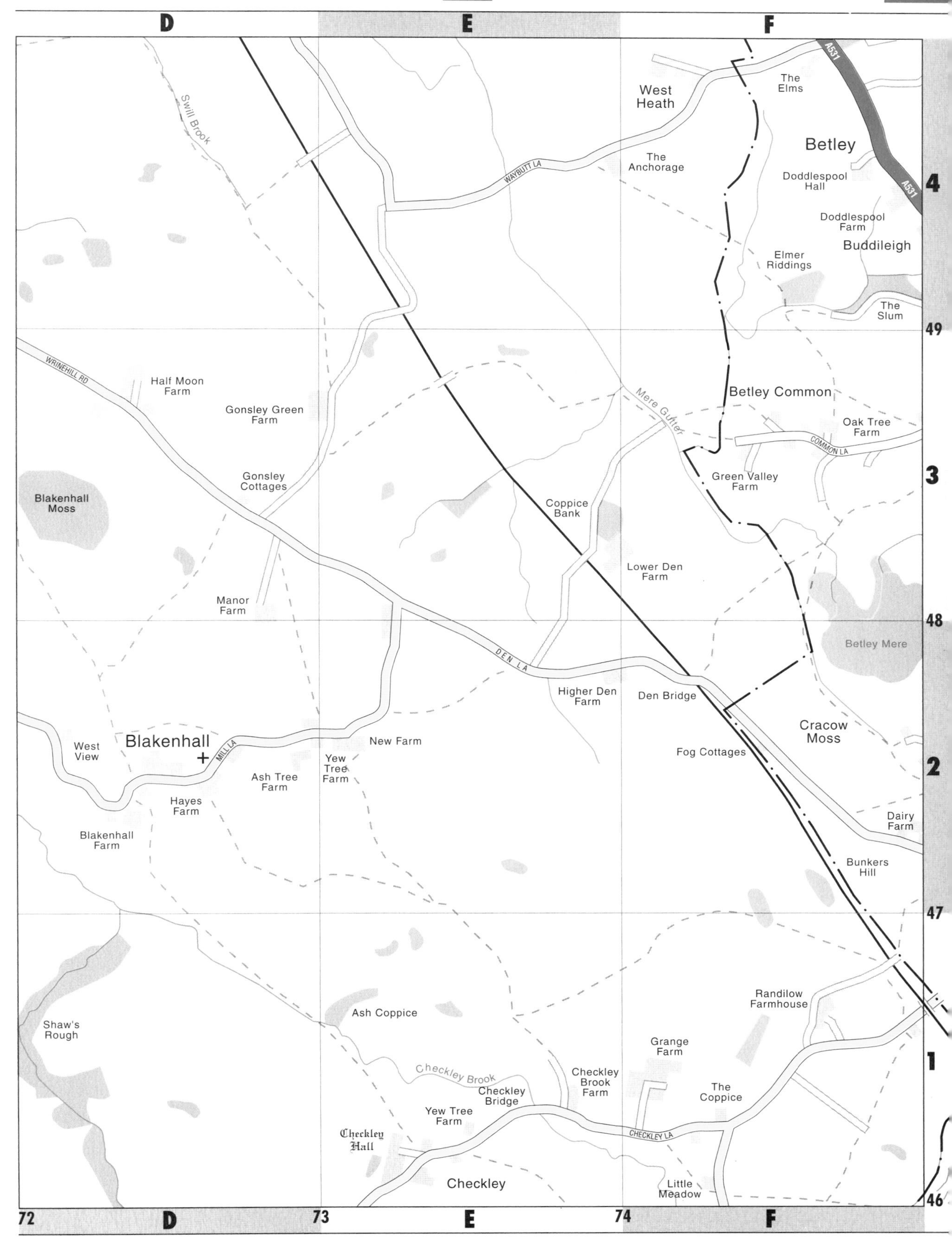

West Heath

The Elms

A531

Betley

Doddlespool Hall

Doddlespool Farm

Buddileigh

Elmer Riddings

The Slum

The Anchorage

WAYBUTT LA

Swill Brook

4

49

WRINEHILL RD

Half Moon Farm

Gonsley Green Farm

Gonsley Cottages

Blakenhall Moss

Manor Farm

Coppice Bank

Lower Den Farm

DEN LA

Mere Gutter

Betley Common

Oak Tree Farm

COMMON LA

Green Valley Farm

3

48

Betley Mere

Higher Den Farm

Den Bridge

Cracow Moss

West View

Blakenhall

MILL LA

Ash Tree Farm

New Farm

Yew Tree Farm

Fog Cottages

Dairy Farm

Bunkers Hill

2

Hayes Farm

Blakenhall Farm

Shaw's Rough

Ash Coppice

Checkley Brook

Checkley Bridge

Yew Tree Farm

Checkley Brook Farm

Grange Farm

Randilow Farmhouse

The Coppice

CHECKLEY LA

47

1

Checkley Hall

Checkley

Little Meadow

46

211

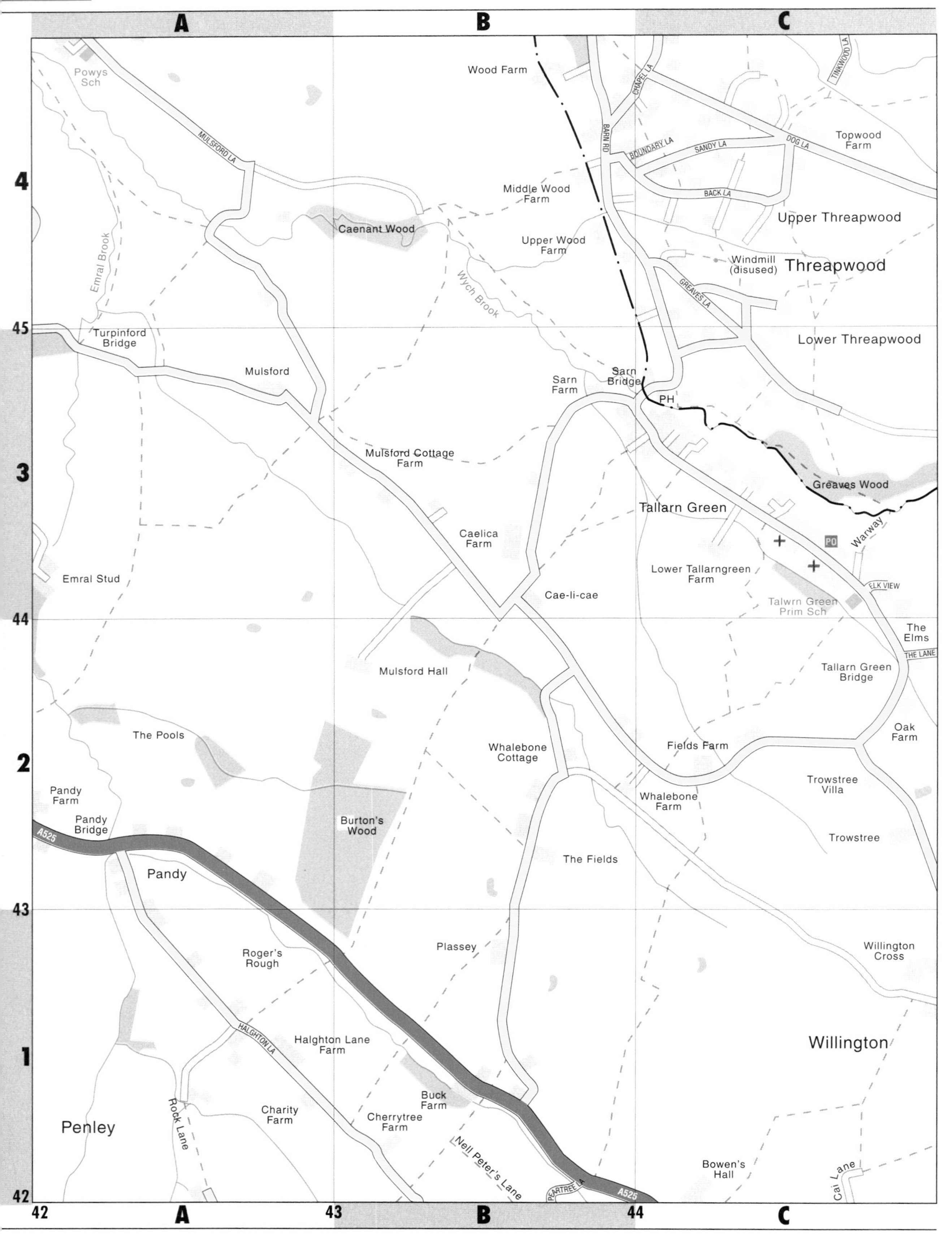

A
B
C
4
45
3
44
2
43
1
42
42
43
44
Powys Sch
Wood Farm
MULSFORD LA
CHAPEL LA
TINKWOOD LA
BARN RD
BOUNDARY LA
SANDY LA
DOG LA
Topwood Farm
BACK LA
Middle Wood Farm
Caenant Wood
Upper Wood Farm
Upper Threapwood
Emral Brook
Wych Brook
Windmill (disused)
Threapwood
GREAVES LA
Turpinford Bridge
Lower Threapwood
Mulsford
Sarn Farm
Sarn Bridge
PH
Mulsford Cottage Farm
Greaves Wood
Tallarn Green
Caelica Farm
Warway
PO
Emral Stud
Lower Tallarngreen Farm
ELK VIEW
Cae-li-cae
Talwrn Green Prim Sch
The Elms
THE LANE
Mulsford Hall
Tallarn Green Bridge
The Pools
Oak Farm
Whalebone Cottage
Fields Farm
Pandy Farm
Trowstree Villa
Whalebone Farm
Pandy Bridge
Burton's Wood
A525
Trowstree
Pandy
The Fields
Plassey
Willington Cross
Roger's Rough
HALGHTON LA
Halghton Lane Farm
Willington
Buck Farm
Charity Farm
Cherrytree Farm
Rock Lane
Penley
Nell Peter's Lane
Bowen's Hall
Cai Lane
PEARTREE LA

Crabtree
Farm

Newton Hall

✛ Oldcastle
Heath

Doglane
Farm

DOG LA

Oldcastle
Farm

Stockton Hall
Farm

The
Greaves

Oldcastle
Mill

Well
Rough

Woodhouse
Farm

Castle Hill

Kidruffin
Wood

Doley Wood

Wych Brook

Dymock's
Mill
(dis)

Dymock's Mill
Cottage

The
Gelli

Higher
Barns

Lane
Farm

The
Woodlands

Gelli
Farm

Black
Wood

Caeparbet
Wood

Lower
Barnes
Farm

The
Brook

THE LANE

Lees
Farm

Strift
House

Tybroughton
Hall

Brunett

Drury
Lane

Drury Farm

The
Lodge

SMOKEY LA

Ty Canol

Yew Tree
Farm

Bron Haul
Farm

Ash Tree
Farm

Old Hall
Holdings

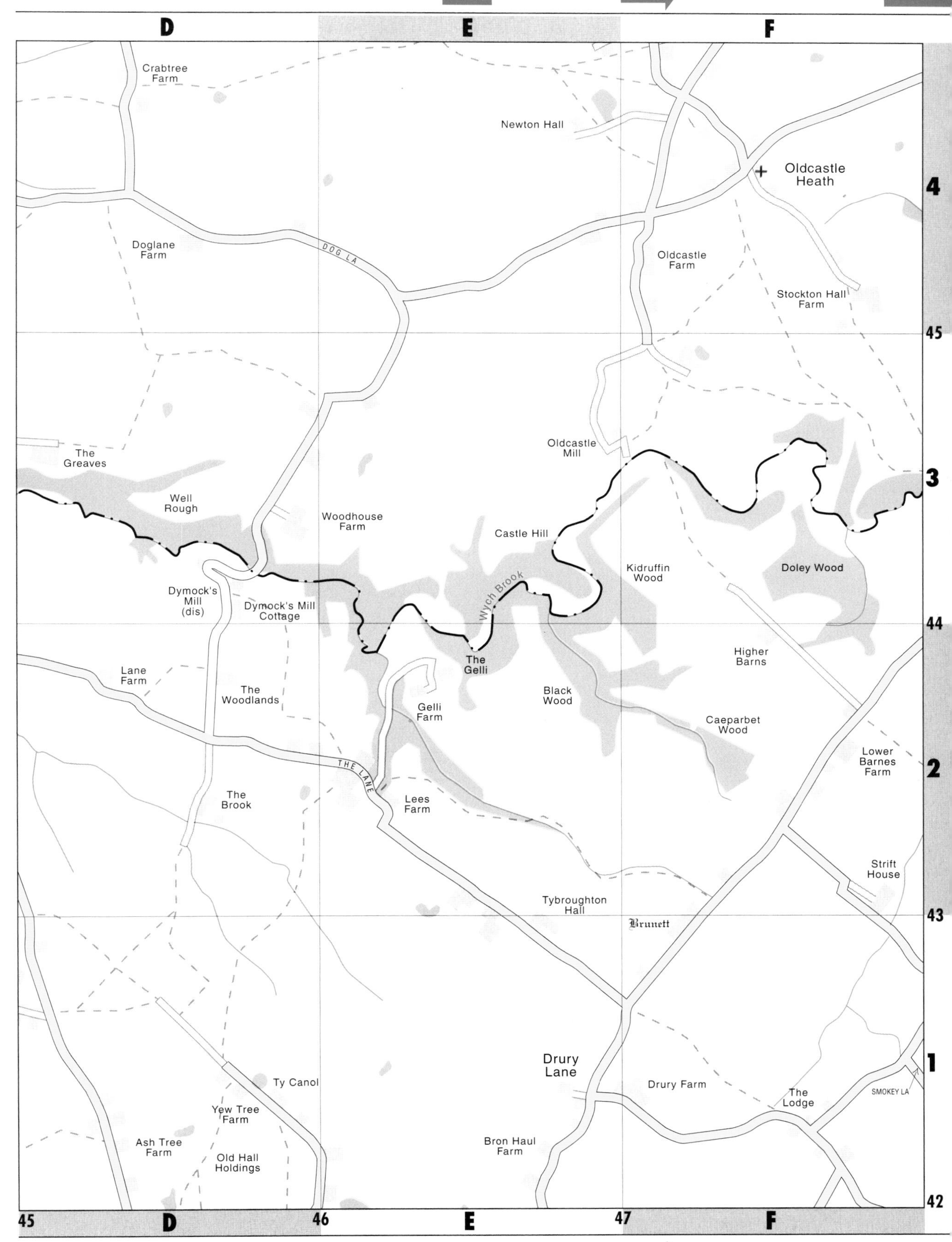

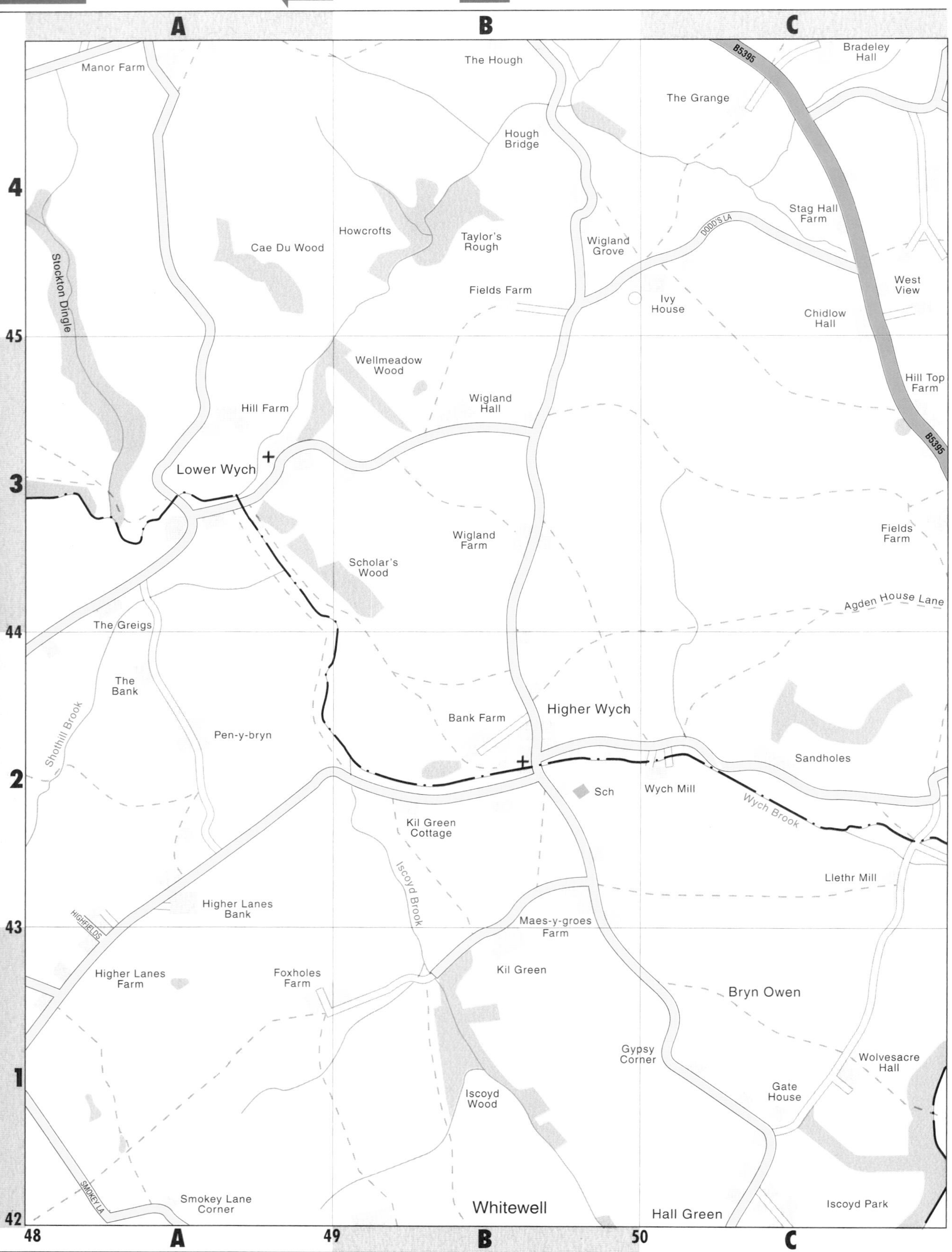

A **B** **C**

Manor Farm

The Hough

The Grange

B5395

Bradeley Hall

Hough Bridge

4

Cae Du Wood

Howcrofts

Taylor's Rough

Wigland Grove

DODD'S LA

Stag Hall Farm

West View

Fields Farm

Ivy House

Chidlow Hall

45

Stockton Dingle

Wellmeadow Wood

Hill Top Farm

Hill Farm

Wigland Hall

3

Lower Wych

Scholar's Wood

Wigland Farm

Fields Farm

Agden House Lane

44

The Greigs

The Bank

Bank Farm

Higher Wych

Sandholes

Shothill Brook

Pen-y-bryn

Sch

Wych Mill

Wych Brook

2

Kil Green Cottage

Iscoyd Brook

Llethr Mill

Higher Lanes Bank

Maes-y-groes Farm

43

HIGHFIELDS

Higher Lanes Farm

Foxholes Farm

Kil Green

Bryn Owen

Gypsy Corner

Wolvesacre Hall

1

Gate House

Iscoyd Wood

Smokey Lane Corner

SMOKEY LA

Whitewell

Hall Green

Iscoyd Park

42

48 **A** **49** **B** **50** **C**

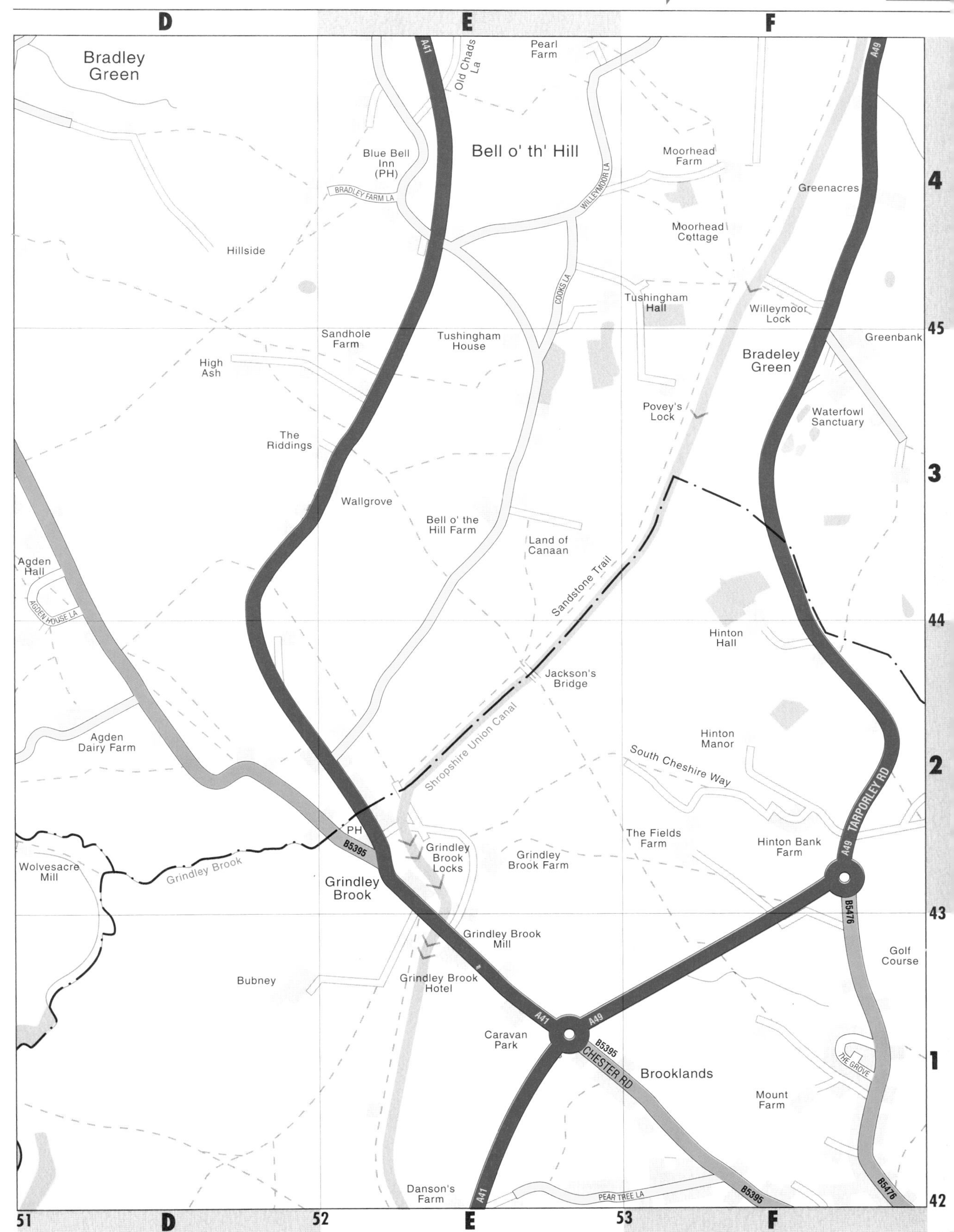

D
E
F
Bradley Green
A41
Old Chads La
Pearl Farm
A49
Blue Bell Inn (PH)
Bell o' th' Hill
Moorhead Farm
BRADLEY FARM LA
WILLEYMOOR LA
Greenacres
4
Moorhead Cottage
Hillside
COOKS LA
Tushingham Hall
Willeymoor Lock
Sandhole Farm
Tushingham House
45
Greenbank
High Ash
Bradeley Green
Povey's Lock
Waterfowl Sanctuary
The Riddings
3
Wallgrove
Bell o' the Hill Farm
Land of Canaan
Sandstone Trail
Agden Hall
AGDEN HOUSE LA
44
Hinton Hall
Jackson's Bridge
Agden Dairy Farm
Hinton Manor
Shropshire Union Canal
South Cheshire Way
2
TARPORLEY RD
PH
The Fields Farm
Hinton Bank Farm
B5395
Grindley Brook Locks
Grindley Brook Farm
Wolvesacre Mill
Grindley Brook
Grindley Brook
43
B5476
Grindley Brook Mill
Golf Course
Bubney
Grindley Brook Hotel
Caravan Park
B5395
CHESTER RD
Brooklands
1
THE GROVE
Mount Farm
Danson's Farm
PEAR TREE LA
42
51
52
53

225
215

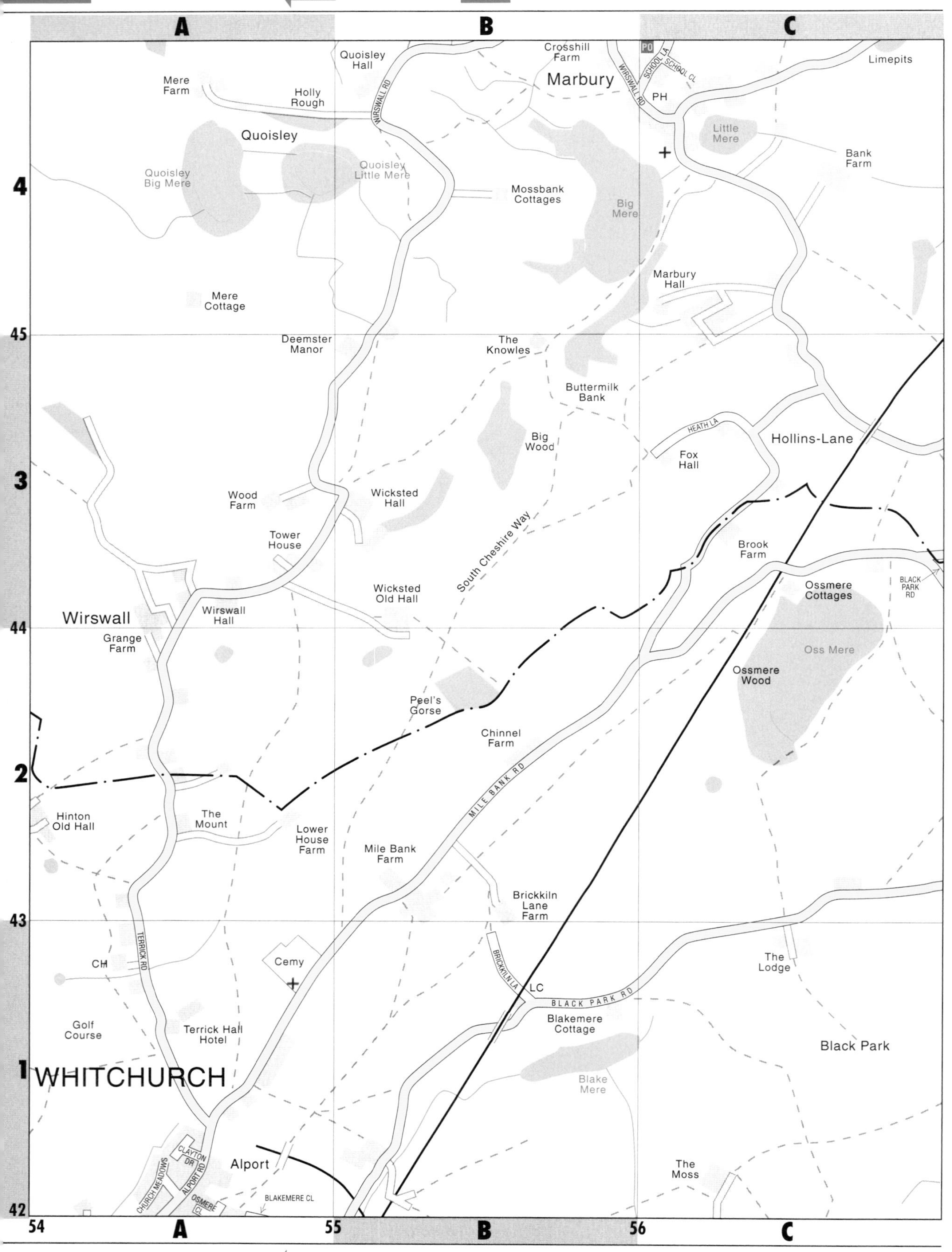
A
B
C
4
45
3
44
2
43
1
42
54
55
56
Quoisley Hall
Crosshill Farm
Marbury
Limepits
Mere Farm
Holly Rough
WIRSWALL RD
SCHOOL LA
SCHOOL CL
PO
PH
Quoisley
Little Mere
Bank Farm
Quoisley Big Mere
Quoisley Little Mere
Mossbank Cottages
Big Mere
Marbury Hall
Mere Cottage
Deemster Manor
The Knowles
Buttermilk Bank
HEATH LA
Big Wood
Hollins-Lane
Fox Hall
Wood Farm
Wicksted Hall
South Cheshire Way
Tower House
Brook Farm
Wicksted Old Hall
Ossmere Cottages
BLACK PARK RD
Wirswall
Wirswall Hall
Grange Farm
Oss Mere
Ossmere Wood
Peel's Gorse
Chinnel Farm
MILE BANK RD
Hinton Old Hall
The Mount
Lower House Farm
Mile Bank Farm
Brickkiln Lane Farm
TERRICK RD
Cemy
BRICKKILN LA
The Lodge
CH
LC
BLACK PARK RD
Blakemere Cottage
Golf Course
Terrick Hall Hotel
Black Park
WHITCHURCH
Blake Mere
CLAYTON DR
Alport
The Moss
CHURCH MEADOWS
ALPORT RD
OSMERE CL
BLAKEMERE CL

225

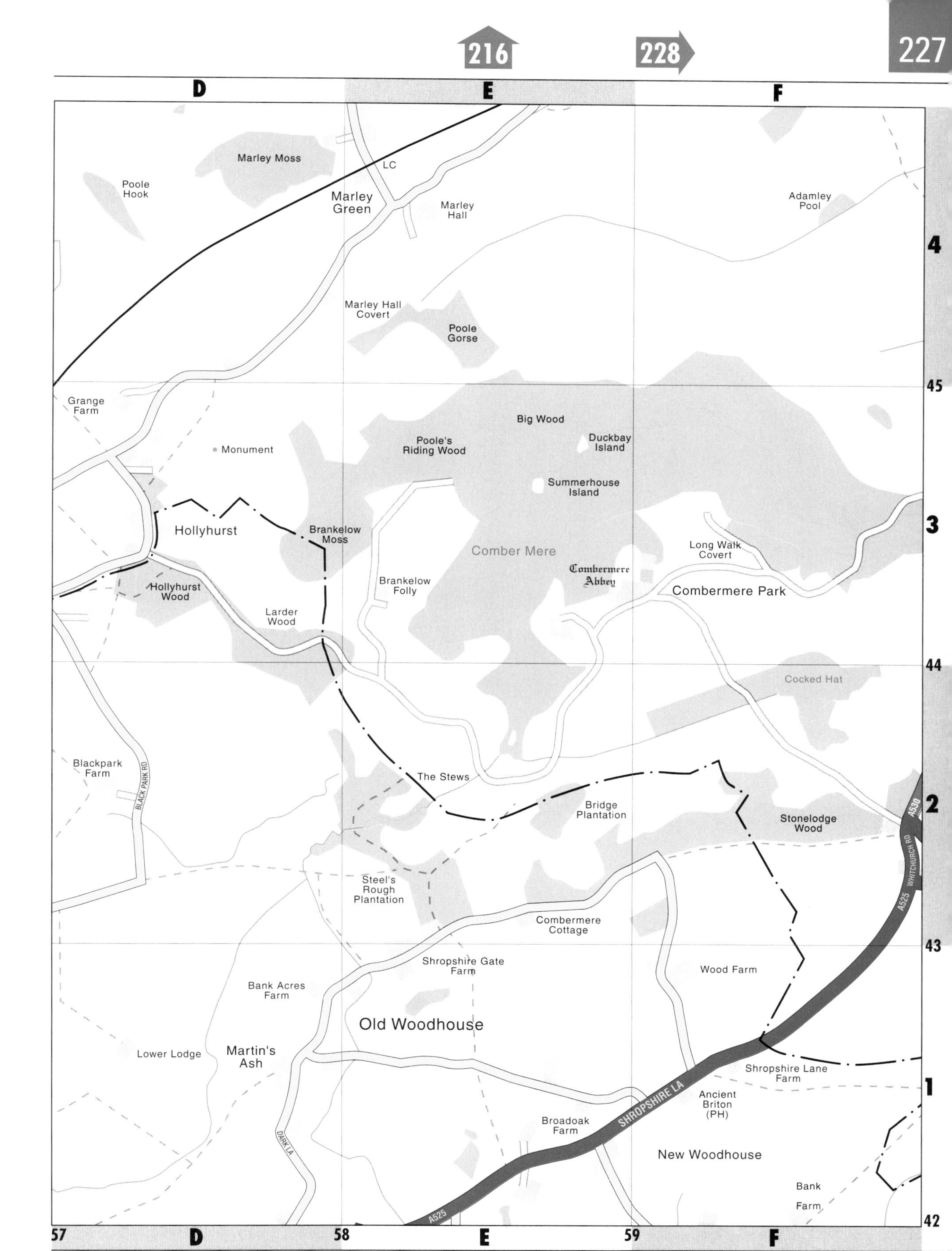

D
E
F

4

45

Marley Moss

Poole
Hook

Marley
Green

LC

Marley
Hall

Adamley
Pool

Marley Hall
Covert

Poole
Gorse

Grange
Farm

Monument

Big Wood

Poole's
Riding Wood

Duckbay
Island

Summerhouse
Island

Hollyhurst

Brankelow
Moss

Comber Mere

Long Walk
Covert

3

Hollyhurst
Wood

Larder
Wood

Brankelow
Folly

Combermere
Abbey

Combermere Park

44

Cocked Hat

Blackpark
Farm

BLACK PARK RD

The Stews

Bridge
Plantation

Stonelodge
Wood

A530 WHITCHURCH RD

2

A525

Steel's
Rough
Plantation

Combermere
Cottage

43

Shropshire Gate
Farm

Wood Farm

Bank Acres
Farm

Old Woodhouse

Lower Lodge

Martin's
Ash

Shropshire Lane
Farm

1

DARK LA

Broadoak
Farm

SHROPSHIRE LA

Ancient
Briton
(PH)

New Woodhouse

Bank
Farm

42

57
D
58
E
59
F

227

217

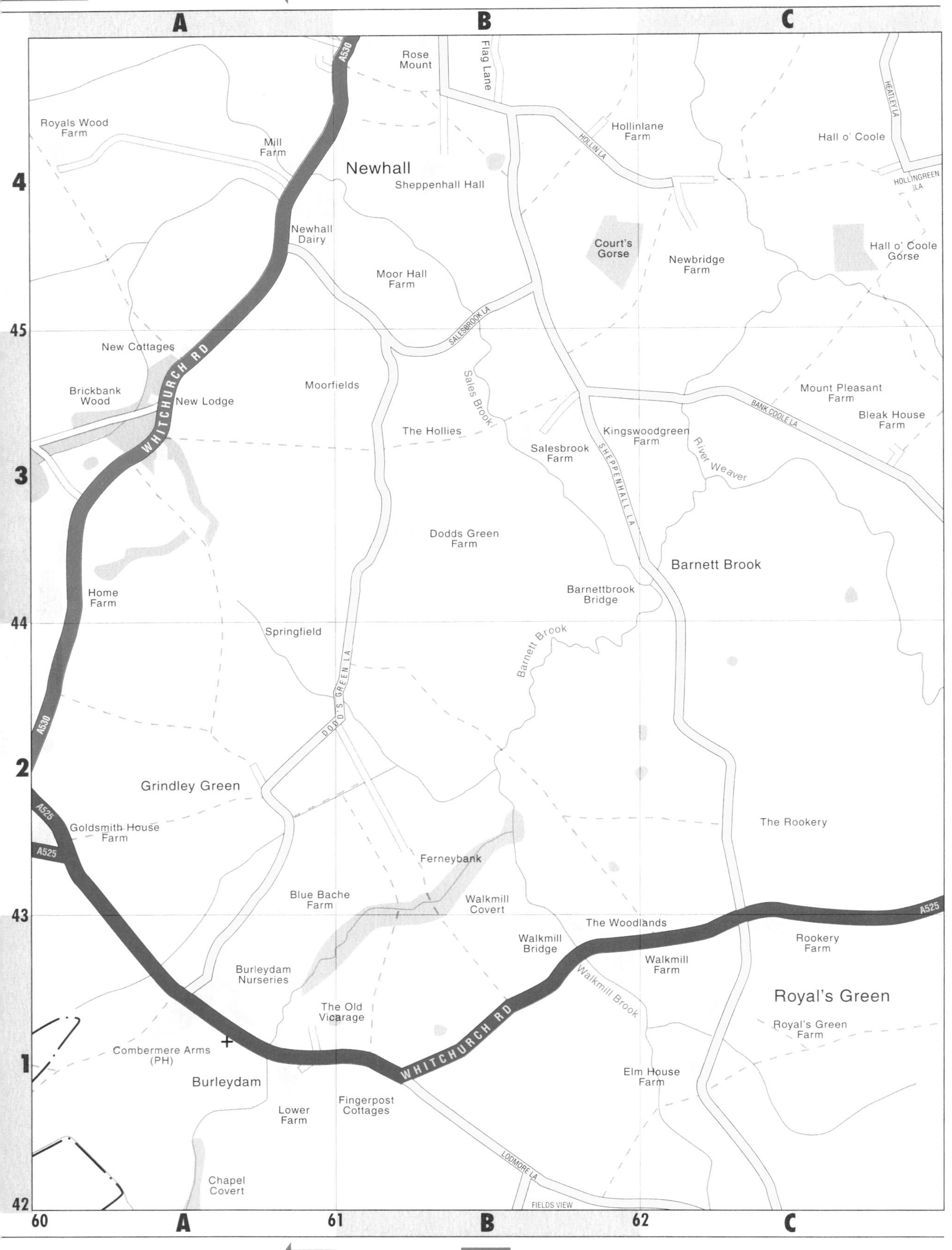

A
B
C
Rose Mount
Flag Lane
A530
Royals Wood Farm
Mill Farm
Newhall
Sheppenhall Hall
Hollinlane Farm
HOLLIN LA
HEATLEY LA
Hall o' Coole
HOLLINGREEN LA
Newhall Dairy
Court's Gorse
Newbridge Farm
Hall o' Coole Gorse
Moor Hall Farm
SALESBROOK LA
New Cottages
WHITCHURCH RD
Brickbank Wood
New Lodge
Moorfields
Sales Brook
Mount Pleasant Farm
BANK COOLE LA
Bleak House Farm
The Hollies
Kingswoodgreen Farm
Salesbrook Farm
SHEPPENHALL LA
River Weaver
Dodds Green Farm
Barnett Brook
Barnettbrook Bridge
Home Farm
Springfield
Barnett Brook
DODD'S GREEN LA
Grindley Green
A525
Goldsmith House Farm
The Rookery
Ferneybank
Blue Bache Farm
Walkmill Covert
The Woodlands
Walkmill Bridge
Rookery Farm
Burleydam Nurseries
Walkmill Farm
Walkmill Brook
Royal's Green
The Old Vicarage
Royal's Green Farm
Combermere Arms (PH)
Burleydam
Elm House Farm
Lower Farm
Fingerpost Cottages
LODMORE LA
Chapel Covert
FIELDS VIEW
4
45
3
44
2
43
1
42
60
61
62

227

233

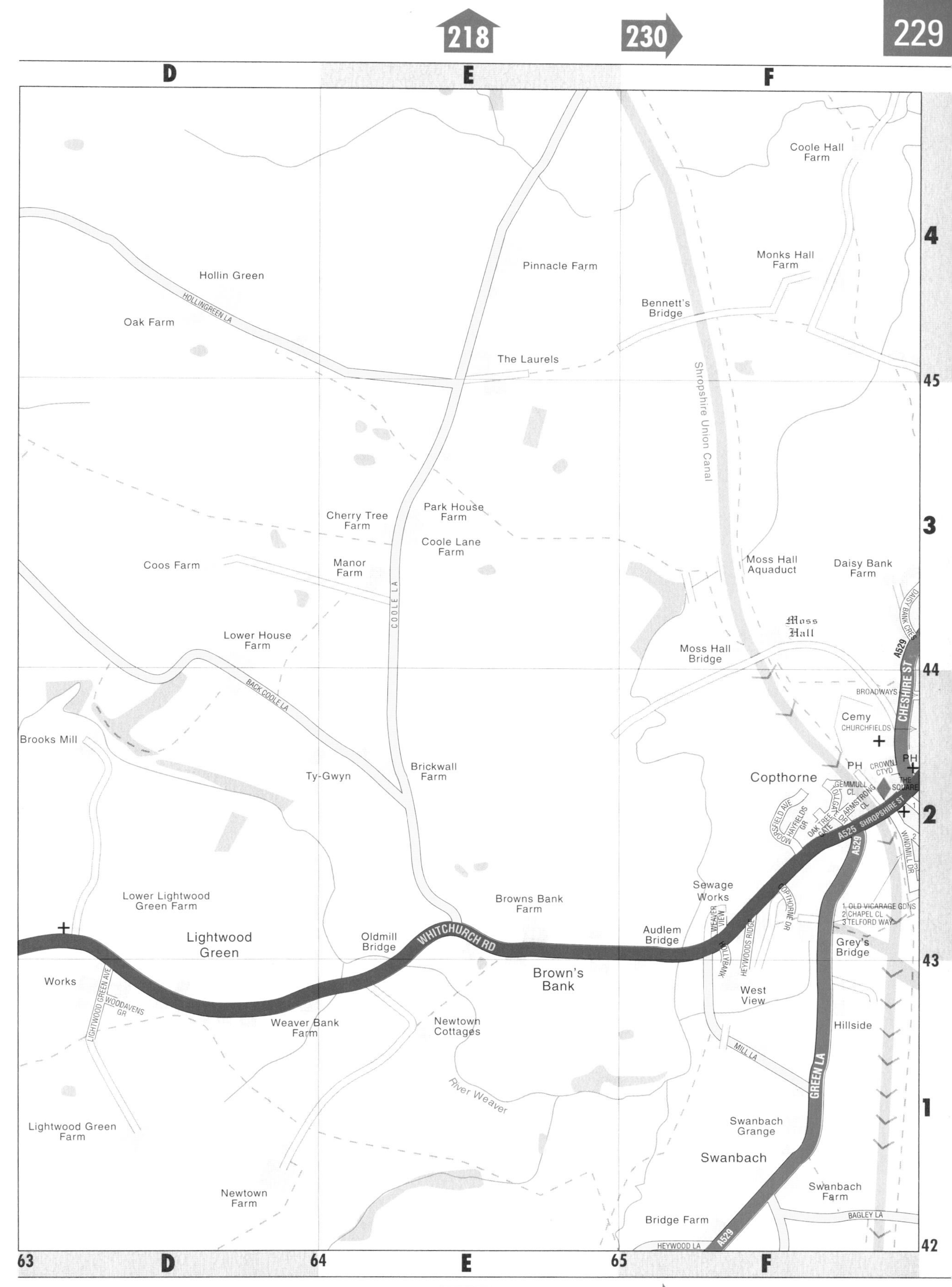

D   E   F

4

Coole Hall
Farm

Hollin Green

HOLLINGREEN LA

Oak Farm

Pinnacle Farm

Monks Hall
Farm

Bennett's
Bridge

The Laurels

45

Shropshire Union Canal

Cherry Tree
Farm

Park House
Farm

Coole Lane
Farm

3

Coos Farm

Manor
Farm

COOLE LA

Moss Hall
Aquaduct

Daisy Bank
Farm

Lower House
Farm

Moss
Hall

DAISY BANK CRES

A529

BACK COOLE LA

Moss Hall
Bridge

44

Brooks Mill

Ty-Gwyn

Brickwall
Farm

BROADWAYS

Cemy
CHURCHFIELDS

PH

CROWN
CTYD

PH

THE
SQUARE

CHESHIRE ST

Copthorne

GEMMULL
CL

ARMSTRONG
CL

A529

SHROPSHIRE ST

2

MOSS
FIELD AVE

HATFIELDS
GR

OAK TREE
DR

COPLEY WAY

A525

WINDMILL DR

Lower Lightwood
Green Farm

Lightwood
Green

Oldmill
Bridge

WHITCHURCH RD

Browns Bank
Farm

Sewage
Works

Audlem
Bridge

COPTHORNE DR

WEAVER
VIEW

HEYWOODS RIDGE

1 OLD VICARAGE GDNS
2 CHAPEL CL
3 TELFORD WAY

Grey's
Bridge

43

Works

LIGHTWOOD GREEN AVE

WOODAVENS
GR

Weaver Bank
Farm

Brown's
Bank

Newtown
Cottages

NEWBATTLE

West
View

MILL LA

GREEN LA

Hillside

Lightwood Green
Farm

River Weaver

Swanbach
Grange

Swanbach

Swanbach
Farm

1

Newtown
Farm

Bridge Farm

HEYWOOD LA

A529

BAGLEY LA

42

229
219

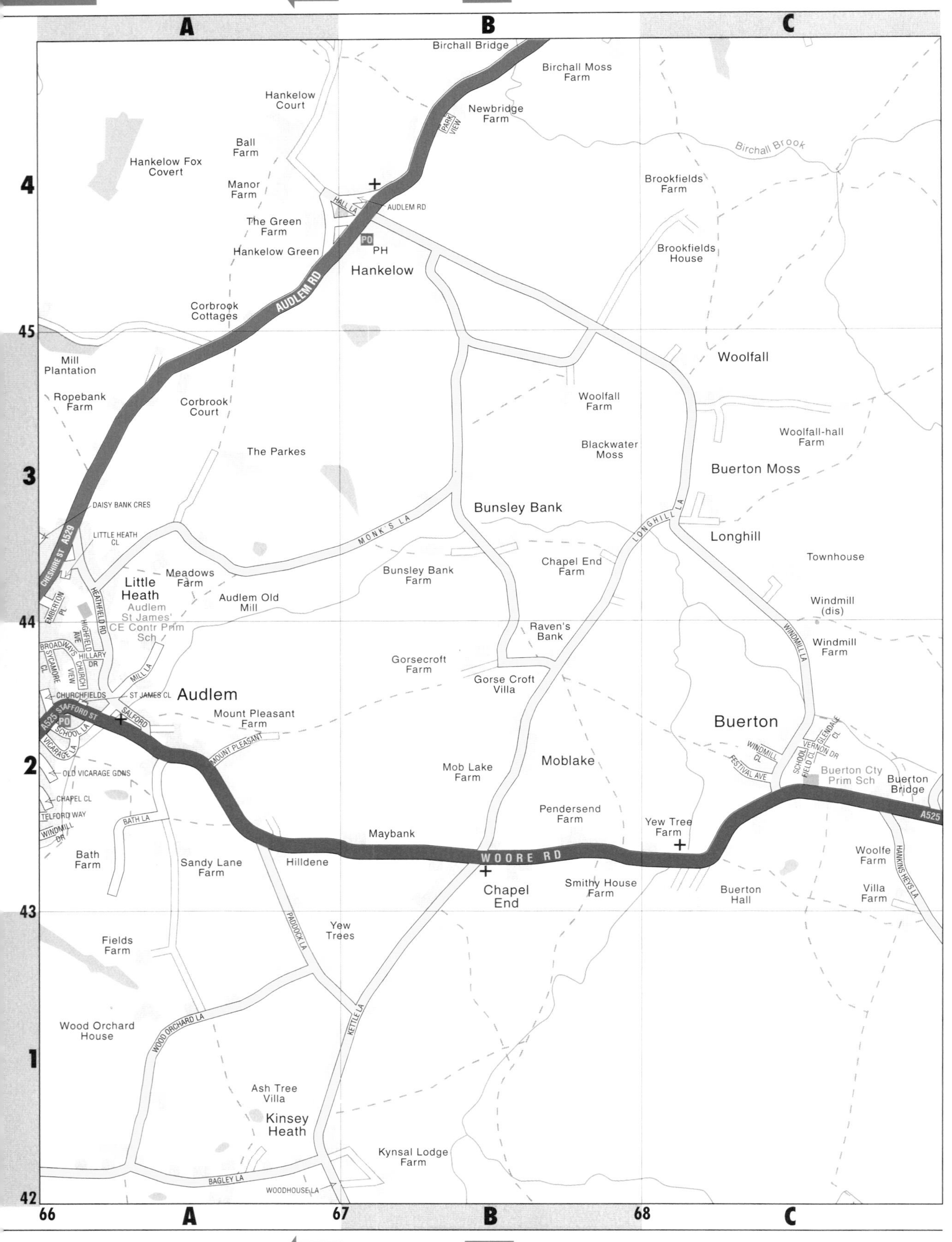
A
B
C
Birchall Bridge
Birchall Moss Farm
Hankelow Court
Newbridge Farm
PARK VIEW
Ball Farm
Hankelow Fox Covert
Birchall Brook
Manor Farm
HALL LA
AUDLEM RD
Brookfields Farm
The Green Farm
PO
PH
Hankelow Green
Hankelow
Brookfields House
AUDLEM RD
Corbrook Cottages
Woolfall
Mill Plantation
Woolfall Farm
Ropebank Farm
Corbrook Court
Woolfall-hall Farm
Blackwater Moss
The Parkes
Buerton Moss
DAISY BANK CRES
Bunsley Bank
LITTLE HEATH CL
MONK'S LA
LONGHILL LA
Longhill
CHESHIRE ST A529
Townhouse
Chapel End Farm
Meadows Farm
Bunsley Bank Farm
Little Heath
Audlem Old Mill
Windmill (dis)
EMBERTON PL
HEATHFIELD RD
Audlem St James' CE Contr Prim Sch
Raven's Bank
BROADWAYS
HIGHFIELD AVE
HILLARY DR
WINDMILL LA
Windmill Farm
SYCAMORE CL
CHURCH VIEW
MILL LA
Gorsecroft Farm
Gorse Croft Villa
CHURCHFIELDS
ST JAMES CL
Audlem
A525 STAFFORD ST
PO
SALFORD
Mount Pleasant Farm
Buerton
GLENDALE CL
SCHOOL LA
VICARAGE LA
MOUNT PLEASANT
WINDMILL CL
VERNON DR
SCHOOL FIELD CL
Moblake
FESTIVAL AVE
Buerton Cty Prim Sch
OLD VICARAGE GDNS
Mob Lake Farm
Buerton Bridge
CHAPEL CL
Pendersend Farm
A525
TELFORD WAY
BATH LA
Yew Tree Farm
WINDMILL DR
Maybank
Woolfe Farm
HANKINS HEYS LA
Bath Farm
WOORE RD
Sandy Lane Farm
Hilldene
Chapel End
Smithy House Farm
Buerton Hall
Villa Farm
Yew Trees
PADDOCK LA
Fields Farm
KETTLE LA
WOOD ORCHARD LA
Wood Orchard House
Ash Tree Villa
Kinsey Heath
Kynsal Lodge Farm
BAGLEY LA
WOODHOUSE LA
4
45
3
44
2
43
1
42
66
67
68

229
235

220

232

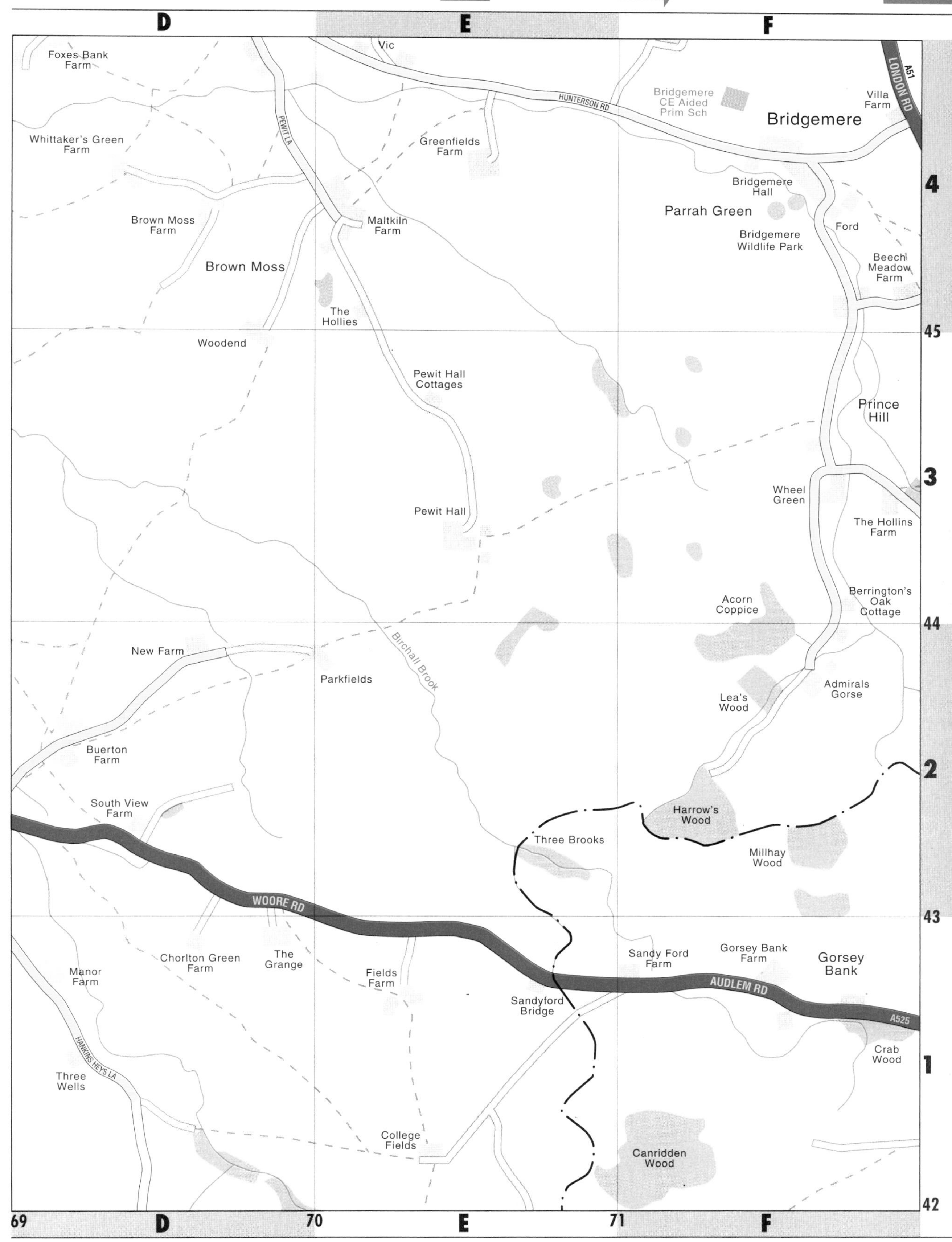

D
E
F
Foxes Bank Farm
Vic
HUNTERSON RD
Bridgemere CE Aided Prim Sch
Villa Farm
LONDON RD
A51
Bridgemere
Whittaker's Green Farm
PEWIT LA
Greenfields Farm
Bridgemere Hall
4
Parrah Green
Brown Moss Farm
Maltkiln Farm
Ford
Bridgemere Wildlife Park
Beech Meadow Farm
Brown Moss
The Hollies
Woodend
45
Pewit Hall Cottages
Prince Hill
3
Wheel Green
Pewit Hall
The Hollins Farm
Berrington's Oak Cottage
Acorn Coppice
44
New Farm
Birchall Brook
Parkfields
Admirals Gorse
Lea's Wood
Buerton Farm
2
South View Farm
Harrow's Wood
Three Brooks
Millhay Wood
WOORE RD
43
Manor Farm
Chorlton Green Farm
The Grange
Fields Farm
Sandy Ford Farm
Gorsey Bank Farm
Gorsey Bank
AUDLEM RD
Sandyford Bridge
A525
Crab Wood
1
HANKINS HEYS LA
Three Wells
College Fields
Canridden Wood
42
69
70
71

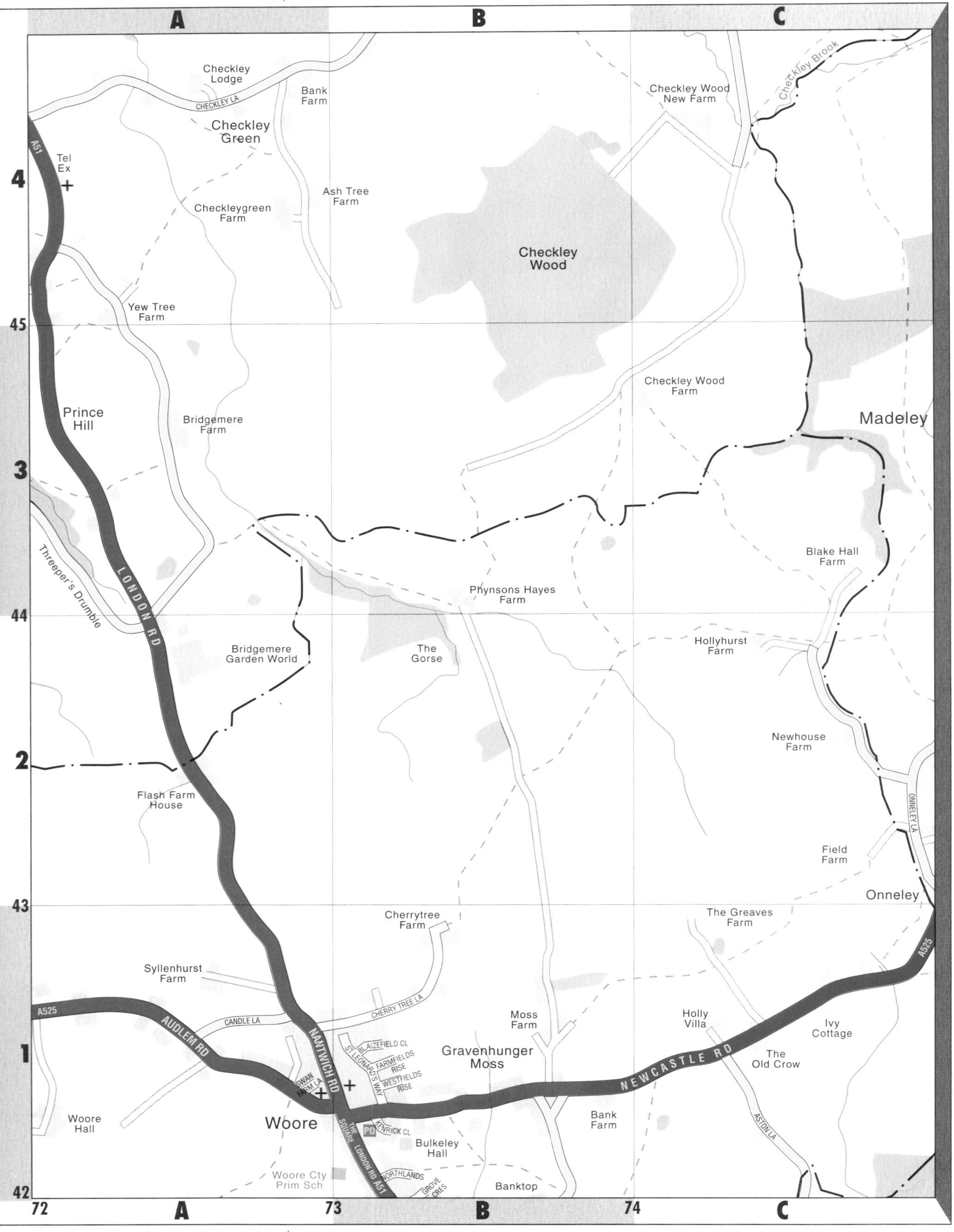

Checkley
Lodge

Bank
Farm

CHECKLEY LA

Checkley
Green

Checkley Wood
New Farm

Checkley Brook

Tel
Ex
+

4

Checkleygreen
Farm

Ash Tree
Farm

Checkley
Wood

A51

45

Yew Tree
Farm

Checkley Wood
Farm

Madeley

Prince
Hill

Bridgemere
Farm

LONDON RD

Blake Hall
Farm

Threeper's Drumble

3

Phynsons Hayes
Farm

44

Bridgemere
Garden World

The
Gorse

Hollyhurst
Farm

Newhouse
Farm

2

Flash Farm
House

ONNELEY LA

Field
Farm

Onneley

43

Cherrytree
Farm

The Greaves
Farm

A525

Syllenhurst
Farm

CANDLE LA

CHERRY TREE LA

Moss
Farm

Holly
Villa

Ivy
Cottage

A525

AUDLEM RD

NANTWICH RD

BLAIZEFIELD CL
FARMFIELDS
RISE
ST LEONARD'S WAY
WESTFIELDS
RISE

Gravenhunger
Moss

NEWCASTLE RD

The
Old Crow

ASTON LA

1

Woore
Hall

SWAN
FARM LA
+
+

Woore

PO

KENRICK CL

Bank
Farm

THE SQUARE

LONDON RD A51

Bulkeley
Hall

NORTHLANDS

GROVE CRES

Woore Cty
Prim Sch

Banktop

42

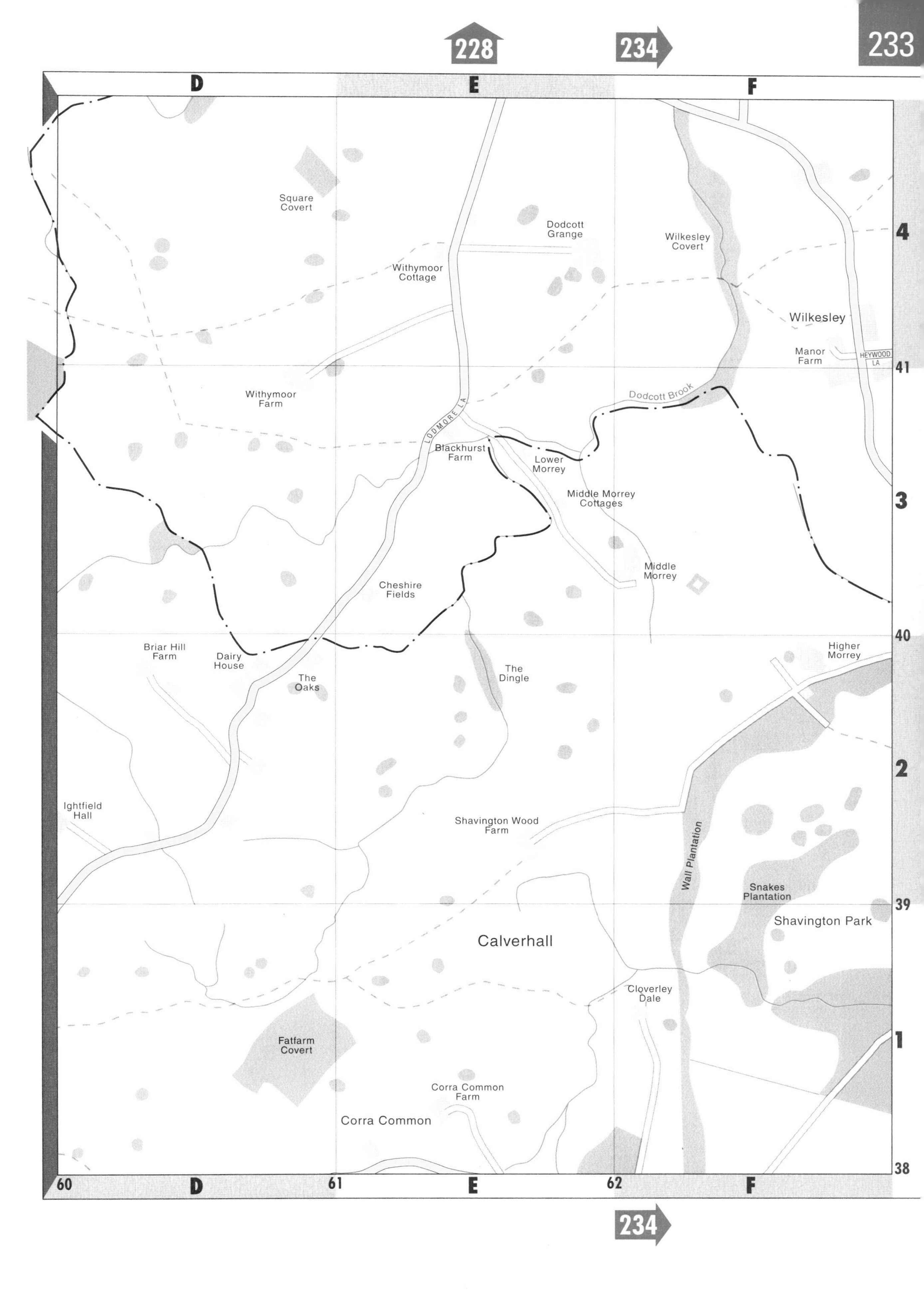

D E F

4

Square
Covert

Dodcott
Grange

Wilkesley
Covert

Withymoor
Cottage

Wilkesley

Manor
Farm

HEYWOOD
LA

41

Withymoor
Farm

Dodcott Brook

Blackhurst
Farm

Lower
Morrey

LODMORE LA

Middle Morrey
Cottages

3

Cheshire
Fields

Middle
Morrey

40

Briar Hill
Farm

Dairy
House

Higher
Morrey

The
Oaks

The
Dingle

2

Ightfield
Hall

Shavington Wood
Farm

Wall Plantation

Snakes
Plantation

Shavington Park

39

Calverhall

Cloverley
Dale

1

Fatfarm
Covert

Corra Common
Farm

Corra Common

38

233
229

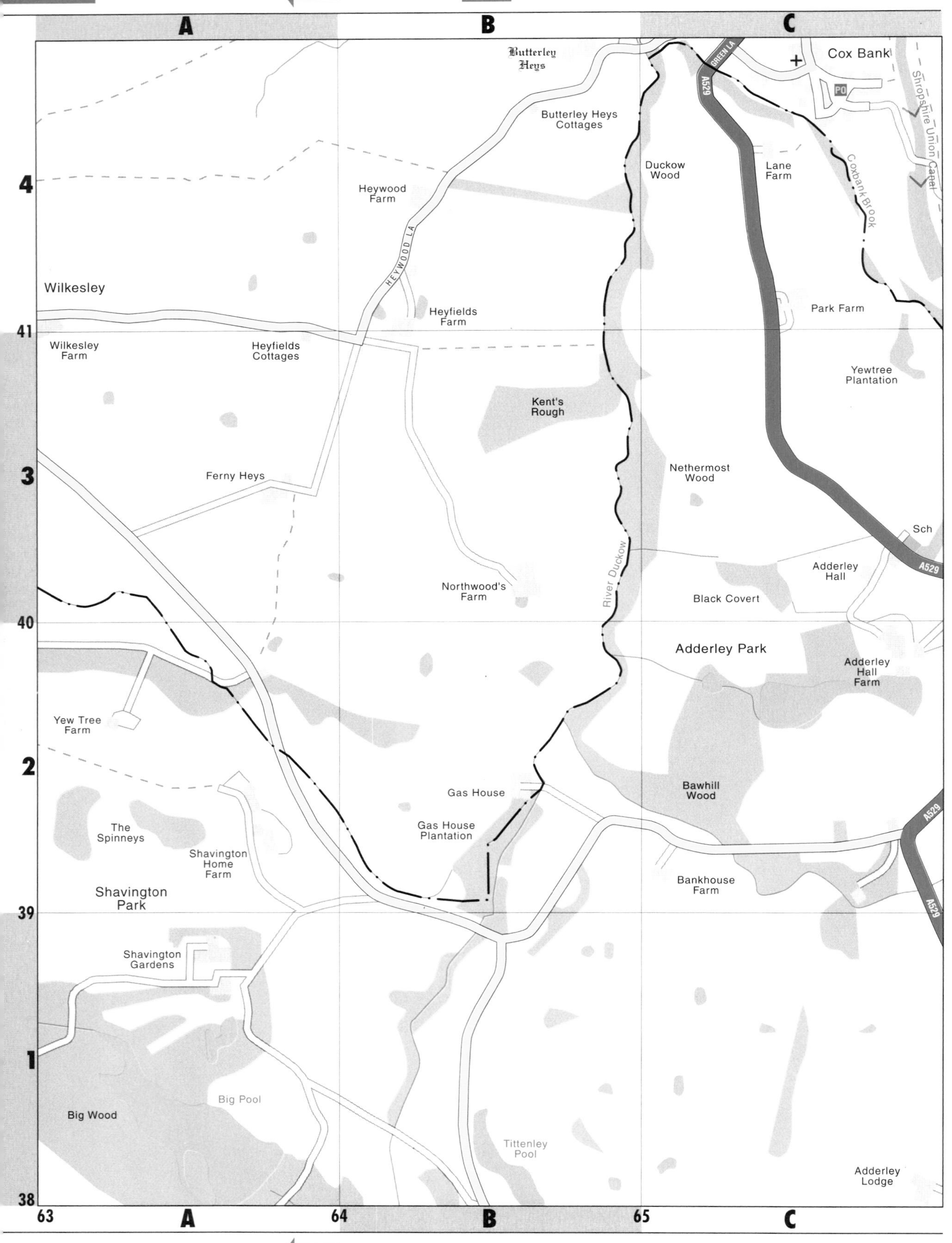

Butterley Heys

Butterley Heys Cottages

Cox Bank

GREEN LA

A529

PO

Shropshire Union Canal

Duckow Wood

Lane Farm

Coxbank Brook

Heywood Farm

HEYWOOD LA

Wilkesley

Heyfields Farm

Park Farm

Wilkesley Farm

Heyfields Cottages

Yewtree Plantation

Kent's Rough

Ferny Heys

Nethermost Wood

River Duckow

Sch

Northwood's Farm

Black Covert

Adderley Hall

A529

Adderley Park

Adderley Hall Farm

Yew Tree Farm

Gas House

Bawhill Wood

The Spinneys

Gas House Plantation

Shavington Home Farm

Bankhouse Farm

A529

Shavington Park

Shavington Gardens

Big Pool

Big Wood

Tittenley Pool

Adderley Lodge

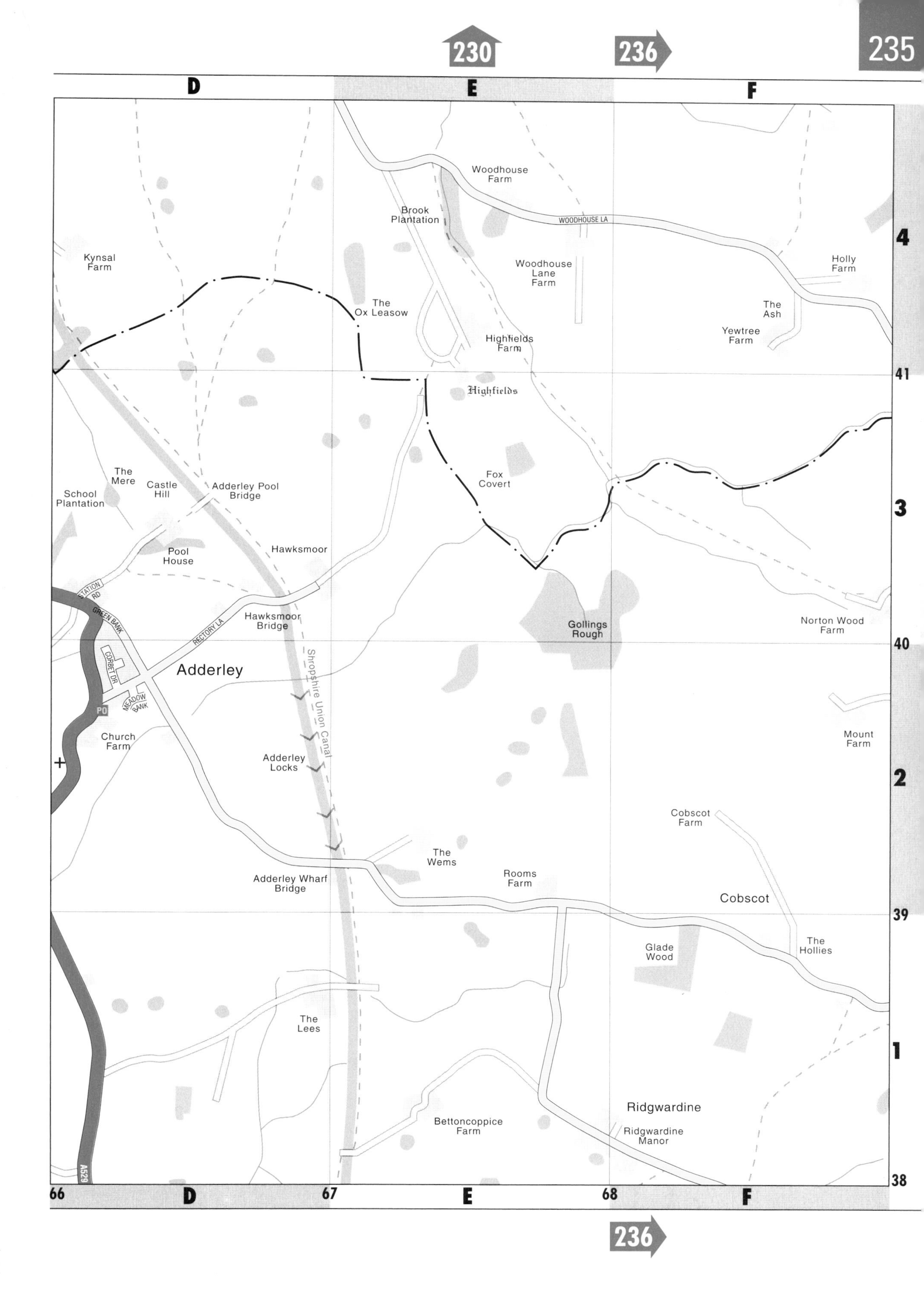

D
E
F

4

Woodhouse
Farm

Brook
Plantation

WOODHOUSE LA

Kynsal
Farm

Woodhouse
Lane
Farm

Holly
Farm

The
Ox Leasow

The
Ash

Yewtree
Farm

Highfields
Farm

41

Highfields

The
Mere

Castle
Hill

Adderley Pool
Bridge

Fox
Covert

3

School
Plantation

Norton Wood
Farm

Hawksmoor

Pool
House

STATION RD

GREEN BANK

Hawksmoor
Bridge

Gollings
Rough

40

RECTORY LA

Shropshire Union Canal

Adderley

CORBET DR

MEADOW BANK

Mount
Farm

PO

Church
Farm

Adderley
Locks

Cobscot
Farm

2

Cobscot

The
Wems

Rooms
Farm

Adderley Wharf
Bridge

39

Glade
Wood

The
Hollies

The
Lees

1

Ridgwardine

A529

Bettoncoppice
Farm

Ridgwardine
Manor

38

66
D
67
E
68
F

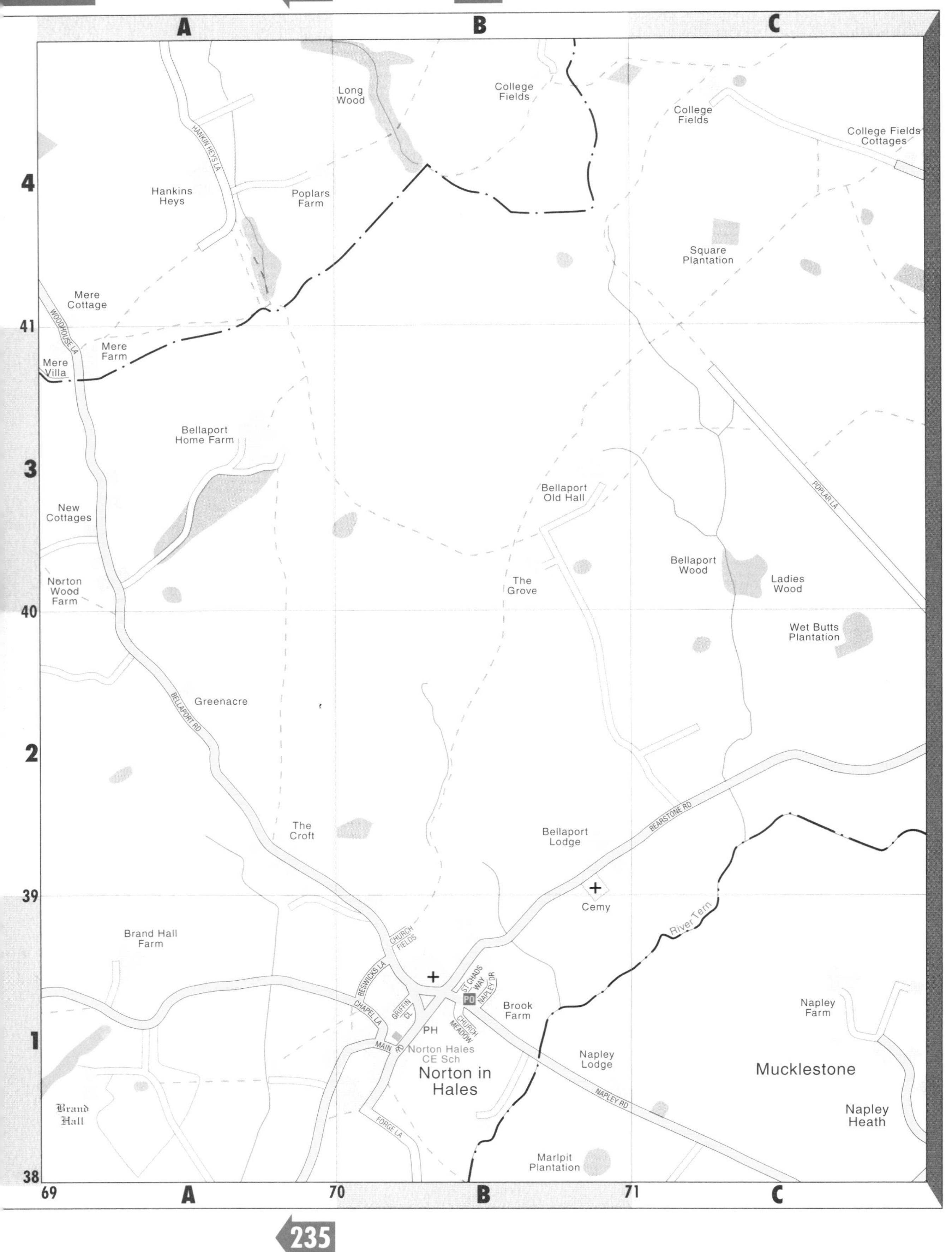

A   B   C

4

41

3

40

2

39

1

38

69   A   70   B   71   C

Long
Wood

College
Fields

College
Fields

College Fields
Cottages

Hankins
Heys

Poplars
Farm

Square
Plantation

Mere
Cottage

Mere
Farm

Mere
Villa

Bellaport
Home Farm

New
Cottages

Bellaport
Old Hall

Bellaport
Wood

Ladies
Wood

POPLAR LA

Norton
Wood
Farm

The
Grove

Wet Butts
Plantation

Greenacre

BELLAPORT RD

WOODHOUSE LA

HANKIN HEYS LA

The
Croft

Bellaport
Lodge

BEARSTONE RD

River Tern

Cemy

Brand Hall
Farm

CHURCH
FIELDS

BESWICKS LA

CHAPEL LA

GRIFFIN CL

MAIN RD

ST CHADS
WAY

NAPLEY DR

PO

CHURCH
MEADOW

Brook
Farm

Napley
Farm

PH

Norton Hales
CE Sch

Napley
Lodge

Mucklestone

Norton in
Hales

FORGE LA

Brand
Hall

NAPLEY RD

Napley
Heath

Marlpit
Plantation

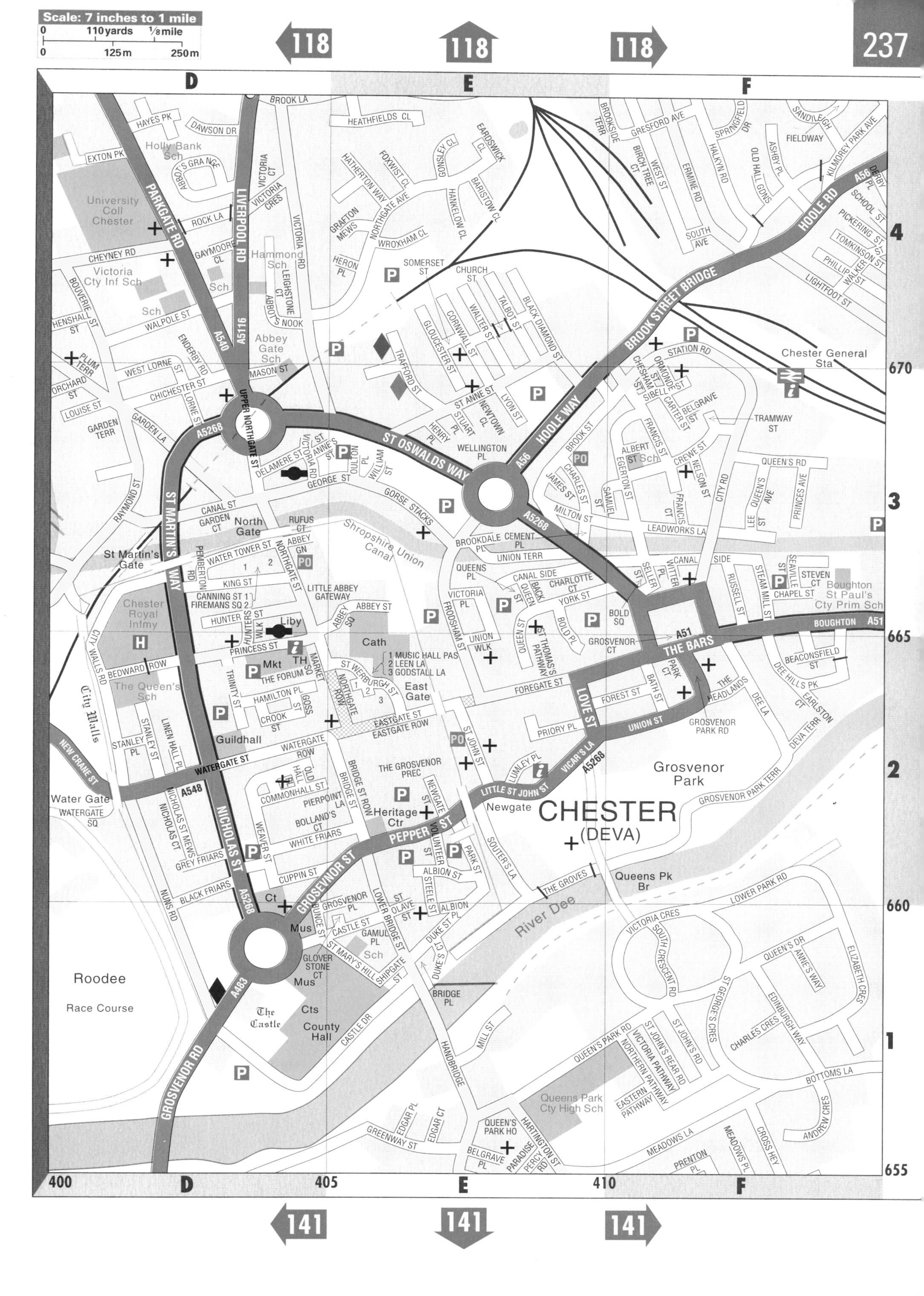
Scale: 7 inches to 1 mile
0 110 yards 1/8 mile
0 125 m 250 m
118
118
118
D
E
F
CHESTER
(DEVA)
Grosvenor Park
Roodee
Race Course
River Dee
Shropshire Union Canal
Chester General Sta
University Coll Chester
Chester Royal Infmy
The Castle
County Hall
Queens Pk Br
Queens Park Cty High Sch
Boughton St Paul's Cty Prim Sch
Cath
East Gate
North Gate
Water Gate
St Martin's Gate
Newgate
Heritage Ctr
Guildhall
ST OSWALDS WAY
BROOK STREET BRIDGE
HOOLE WAY
HOOLE RD
PARKGATE RD
LIVERPOOL RD
ST MARTIN'S WAY
NICHOLAS ST
GROSVENOR RD
GROSVENOR ST
PEPPER ST
LITTLE ST JOHN ST
VICAR'S LA
LOVE ST
UNION ST
FOREGATE ST
THE BARS
BOUGHTON
WATERGATE ST
EASTGATE ST
UPPER NORTHGATE ST
A540
A5116
A5268
A56
A51
A548
A483
670
665
660
655
4
3
2
1
400
405
410
141
141
141

Altrincham

Grid columns: A B C D E F
Grid rows: 8 89 7 6 5 88 4 87 3 2 87 1 86

Broadheath Prim Sch
South Trafford Coll of F Ed
Dairyhouse Farm
Higher House
Broadheath
Oldfield Brow
Brentwood Sch
Forest Sch
The New Wellington Sch
Altrincham Golf Course
Altrincham CE (VA) Prim Sch
Altrincham General
Altrincham Sta
Blessed Thomas Holford RC High Sch
Timperley Brook
Timperley Sta
St High's RC Prim Sch
Dunham Rd
The Devisdale
Altrincham Gram Sch for Girls
Altrincham Gram Sch for Boys
St Anne's
Bowdon
Rosehill
Altrincham Prep Sch
Bollin Prim Sch
Bowdon CE Prim Sch
Bowgreen
Hale Sta
Hale Rd
Stockport Rd

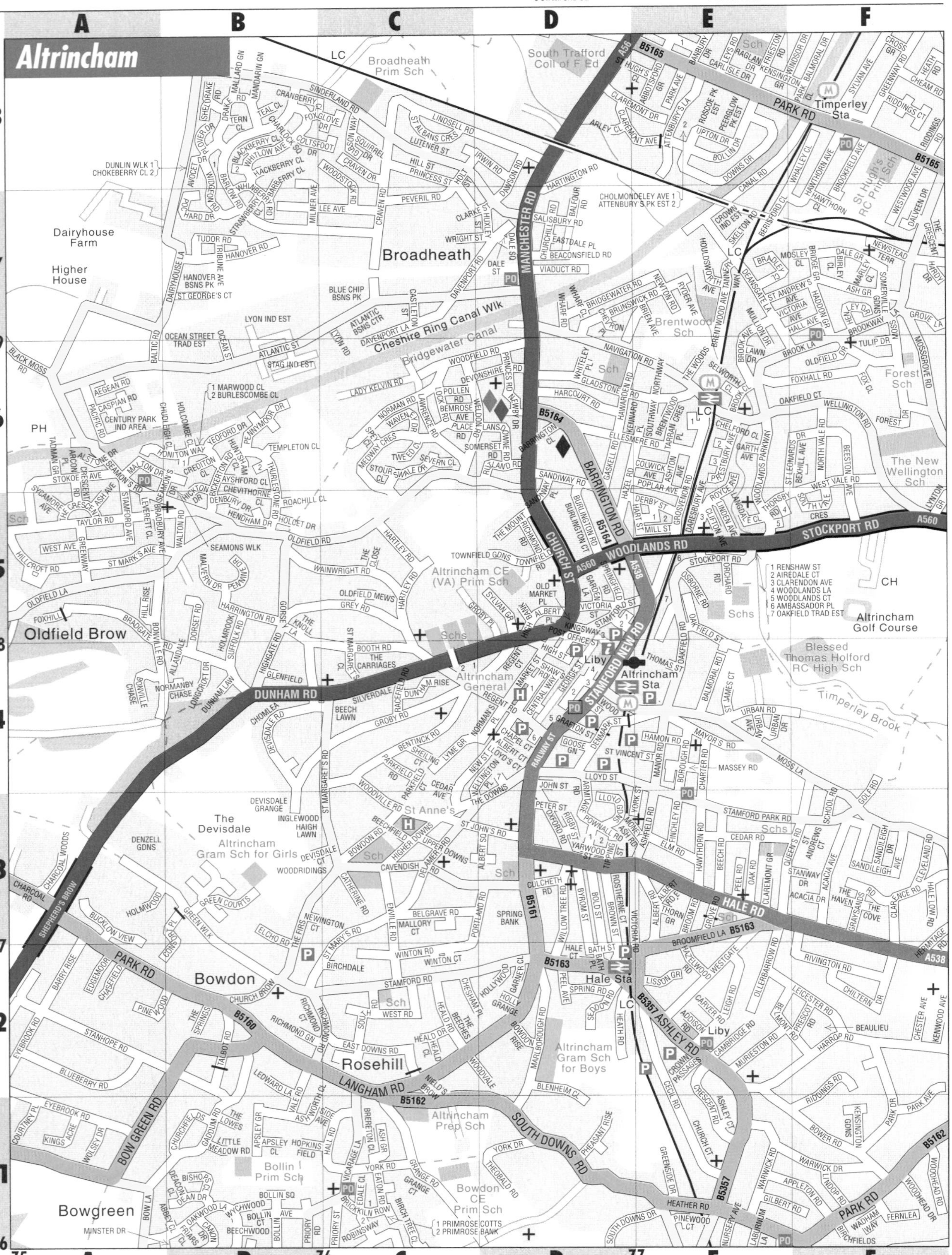

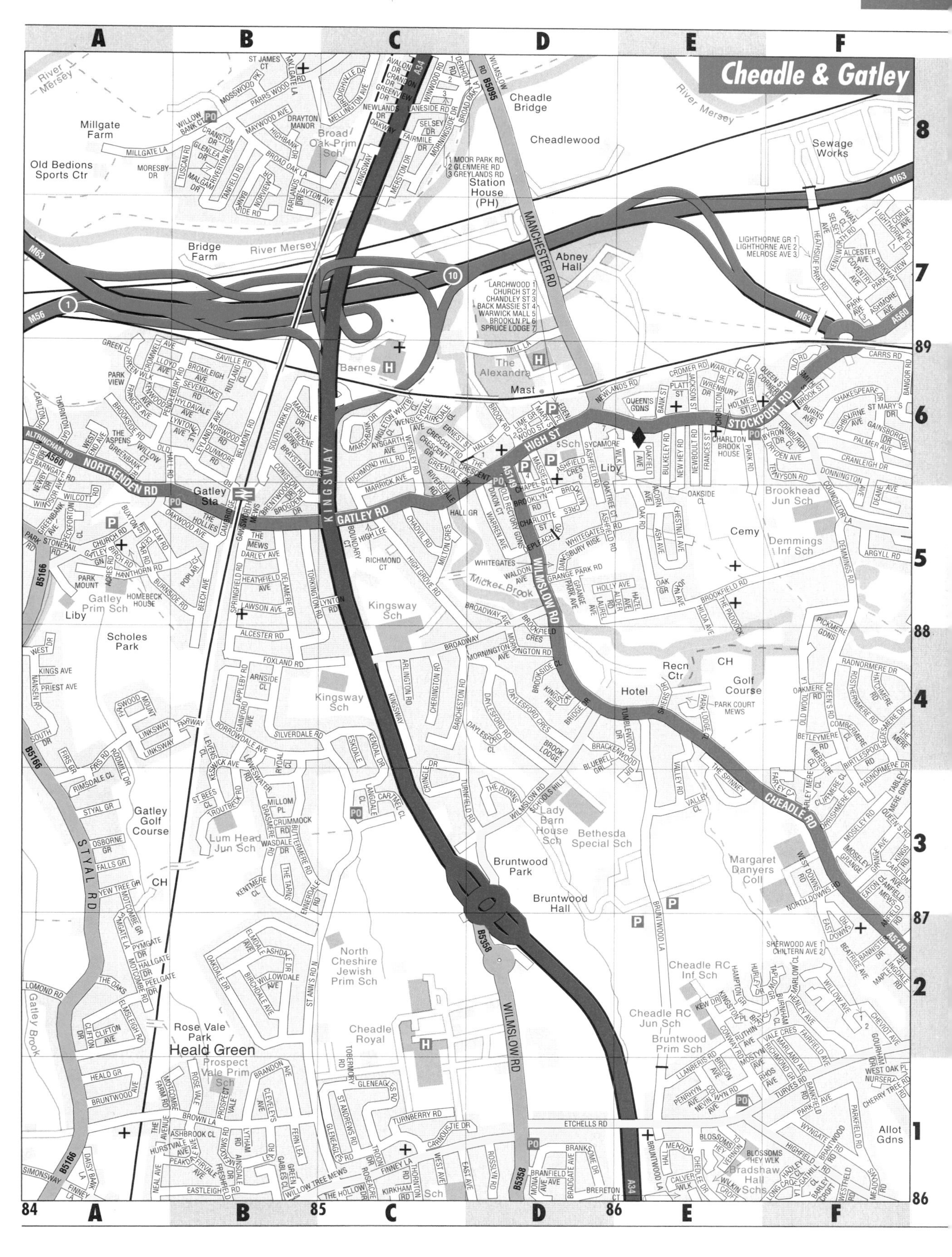
Cheadle & Gatley
A
B
C
D
E
F
8
7
89
6
5
88
4
3
87
2
1
86
84
85
River Mersey
Millgate Farm
Old Bedions Sports Ctr
Broad Oak Prim Sch
Cheadle Bridge
Cheadlewood
Sewage Works
Station House (PH)
Bridge Farm
Abney Hall
MANCHESTER RD
M63
M56
A560
Barnes
The Alexandra
Mast
HIGH ST
STOCKPORT RD
NORTHENDEN RD
GATLEY RD
KINGSWAY
Gatley Sta
Liby
Brookhead Jun Sch
Cemy
Demmings Inf Sch
Kingsway Sch
Micker Brook
WILMSLOW RD
Gatley Prim Sch
Scholes Park
Recn Ctr
Hotel
Golf Course
CHEADLE RD
Gatley Golf Course
Lum Head Jun Sch
Lady Barn House Sch
Bethesda Special Sch
Bruntwood Park
Bruntwood Hall
Margaret Danyers Coll
STYAL RD
North Cheshire Jewish Prim Sch
Cheadle RC Inf Sch
Cheadle RC Jun Sch
Bruntwood Prim Sch
Cheadle Royal
Rose Vale Park
Heald Green
Prospect Vale Prim Sch
Bradshaw Hall
Allot Gdns
Gatley Brook
B5166
B5358
A5149
A34
B5095

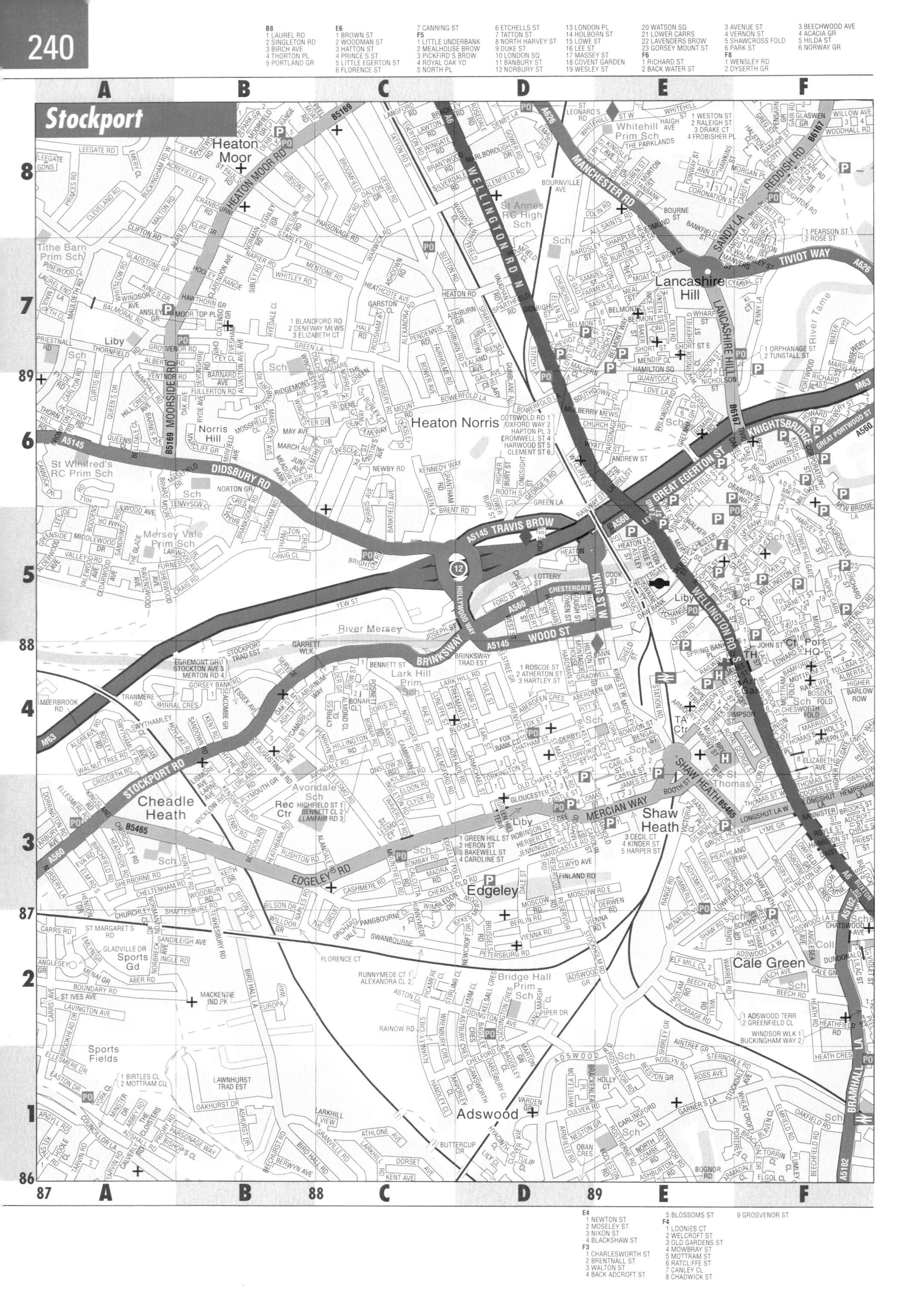

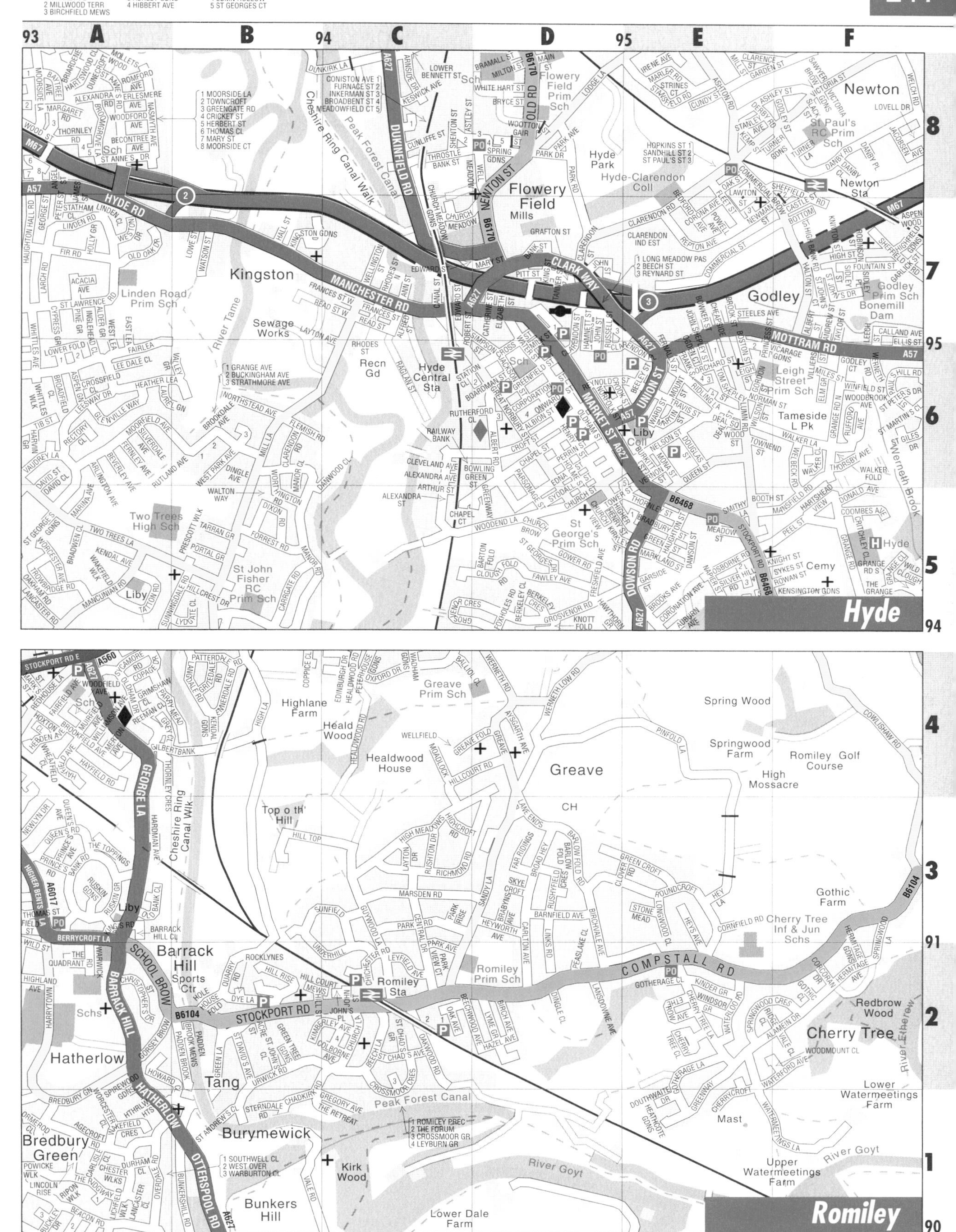

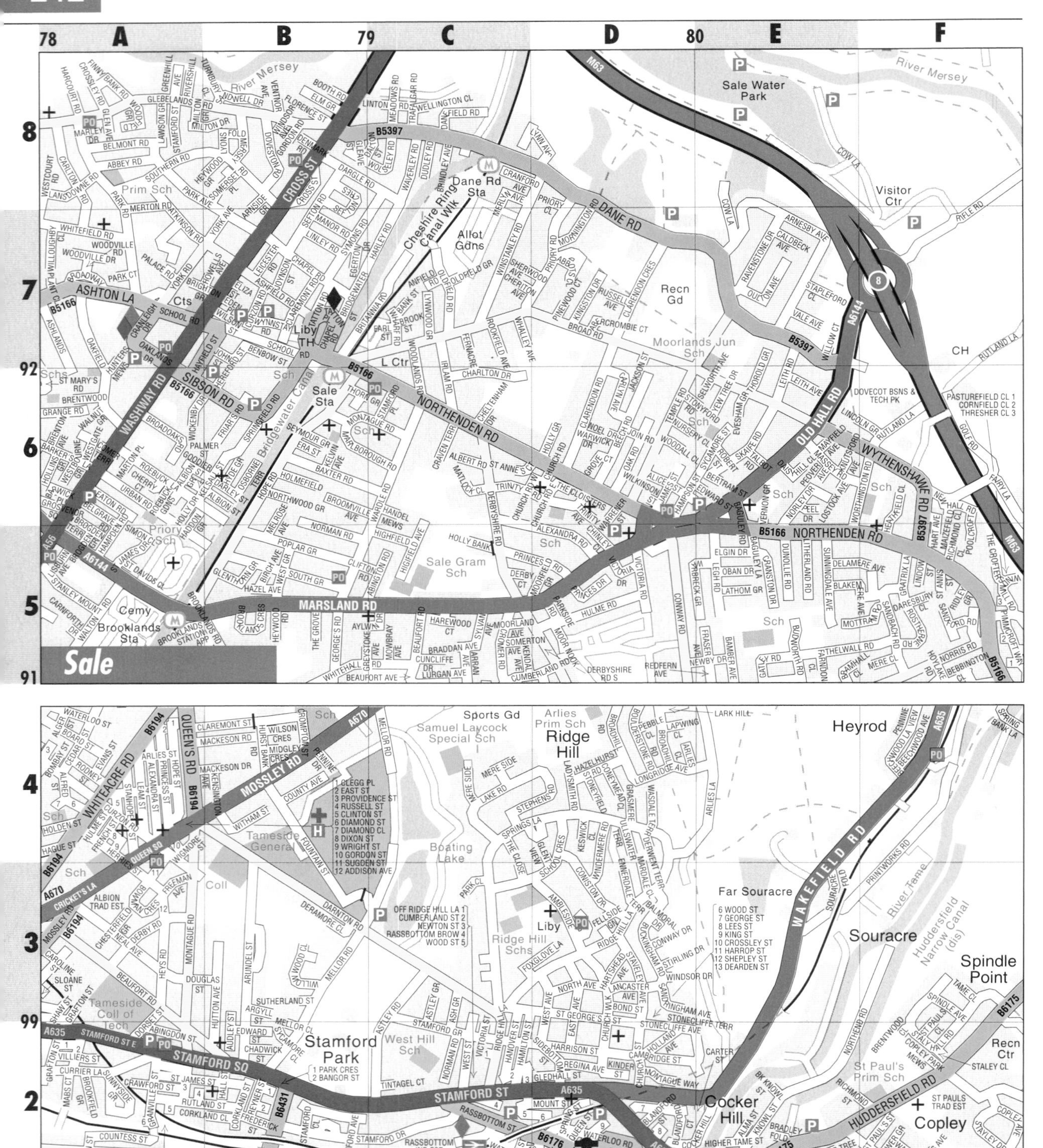
Sale
River Mersey
Sale Water Park
Visitor Ctr
CROSS ST
WASHWAY RD
ASHTON LA
SIBSON RD
NORTHENDEN RD
DANE RD
Dane Rd Sta
Cheshire Ring Canal Wlk
Allot Gdns
Recn Gd
Moorlands Jun Sch
OLD HALL RD
WYTHENSHAWE RD
MARSLAND RD
Sale Sta
Bridgewater Canal
Brooklands Sta
Cemy
Sale Gram Sch
Prim Sch
Priory Sch
Liby
TH
L Ctr
DOVECOT BSNS & TECH PK
Stalybridge
MOSSLEY RD
QUEEN'S RD
WHITEACRE RD
Tameside General
Coll
Tameside Coll of Tech
Samuel Laycock Special Sch
Sports Gd
Arlies Prim Sch
Ridge Hill
Boating Lake
Ridge Hill Schs
Heyrod
WAKEFIELD RD
Far Souracre
Souracre
Huddersfield Narrow Canal (dis)
Spindle Point
Stamford Park
West Hill Sch
STAMFORD SQ
STAMFORD ST
Cocker Hill
HUDDERSFIELD RD
Copley
St Paul's Prim Sch
Recn Ctr
Stalybridge Sta
Cockbrook
Ind Est
Works
River Tame
Hydes
HIGH ST
Sports Ctr
Mkt
Liby
Trinity Sch
Castle Hall
Fern Bank
MOTTRAM RD
Cemy
A B C D E F
A B C D E F

Street names are listed alphabetically and show the locality, the Postcode District, the page number and a reference to the square in which the name falls on the map page

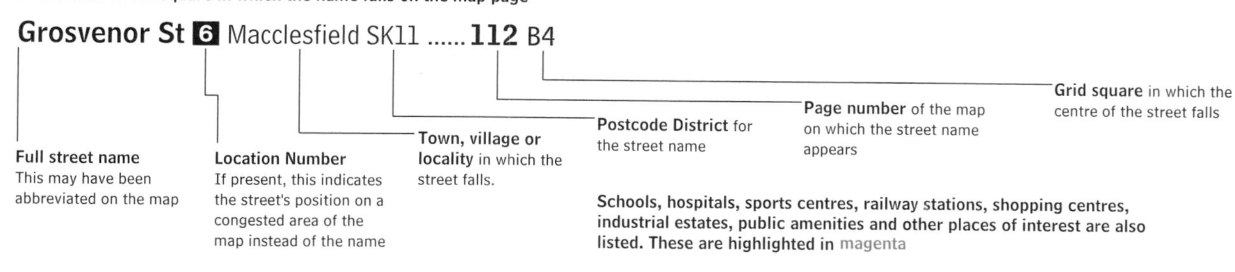

Grosvenor St **6** Macclesfield SK11 ...... **112** B4

Grid square in which the centre of the street falls

Full street name
This may have been abbreviated on the map

Location Number
If present, this indicates the street's position on a congested area of the map instead of the name

Town, village or locality in which the street falls.

Postcode District for the street name

Page number of the map on which the street name appears

Schools, hospitals, sports centres, railway stations, shopping centres, industrial estates, public amenities and other places of interest are also listed. These are highlighted in magenta

Abbreviations used in the index

App	Approach	Cl	Close	Ent	Enterprise	La	Lane	Rdbt	Roundabout
Arc	Arcade	Comm	Common	Espl	Esplanade	N	North	S	South
Ave	Avenue	Cnr	Corner	Est	Estate	Orch	Orchard	Sq	Square
Bvd	Boulevard	Cotts	Cottages	Gdns	Gardens	Par	Parade	Strs	Stairs
Bldgs	Buildings	Ct	Court	Gn	Green	Pk	Park	Stps	Steps
Bsns Pk	Business Park	Ctyd	Courtyard	Gr	Grove	Pas	Passage	St	Street, Saint
Bsns Ctr	Business Centre	Cres	Crescent	Hts	Heights	Pl	Place	Terr	Terrace
Bglws	Bungalows	Dr	Drive	Ho	House	Prec	Precinct	Trad Est	Trading Estate
Cswy	Causeway	Dro	Drove	Ind Est	Industrial Estate	Prom	Promenade	Wlk	Walk
Ctr	Centre	E	East	Intc	Interchange	Ret Pk	Retail Park	W	West
Cir	Circus	Emb	Embankment	Junc	Junction	Rd	Road	Yd	Yard

Town and village index

Acton	204 A4	Capenhurst	94 A4
Acton Bridge	76 C2	Cheadle	34 B4
Adderley	235 D2	Cheadle	239
Adlington	62 B3	Cheadle Hulme	35 D4
Alderley Edge	60 B1	Chelford	84 A1
Aldford	163 F2	Chester	118 C1
Allostock	106 C2	Cholmondeston	171 D1
Alpraham	169 E2	Chowley	182 C3
Alsager	193 F3	Christleton	142 C4
Altrincham	31 E4	Church Minshull	172 A3
Altrincham	238	Clutton	182 B1
Alvanley	73 E1	Coddington	182 A2
Antrobus	53 E2	Comberbach	78 B4
Appleton	27 D3	Congleton	157 D2
Ashley	31 F3	Connah's Quay	91 D1
Ashton	121 F4	Cranage	130 A3
Astbury	178 A4	Crewe	190 C3
Aston	217 E1	Croft	9 D4
Audlem	230 A2	Cronton	12 B3
Audley	209 E1	Crowton	76 B1
Backford	95 D2	Cuddington	101 F2
Barbridge	187 E3	Culcheth	5 D2
Barnton	78 B2	Daresbury	25 D1
Barthomley	208 B3	Davenham	104 A1
Barton	181 F1	Delamere	123 E3
Bate Heath	54 C2	Disley	38 B3
Bebington	43 F3	Dodleston	162 A4
Beeston	168 A1	Duddon	145 D3
Bell o' th' Hill	225 E4	Dunham Town	20 C2
Betley	221 F3	Dunham-on-the-Hill	97 F3
Bickerton	199 F3	Dutton	51 E1
Bickley Town	214 C3	Eaton	147 D2
Biddulph	179 D1	Eccleston	141 E1
Blacon	117 F2	Edge Green	199 D1
Blakenhall	221 D2	Ellesmere Port	70 A4
Bold Heath	13 F4	Elton	72 B2
Bollington	88 A4	Faddiley	202 B3
Bosley	158 B4	Farndon	180 C1
Bradwall Green	153 D2	Frodsham	74 B4
Bramhall	35 F4	Gatley	239
Brereton Green	153 F3	Glazebury	5 E3
Bridgemere	231 F4	Goldborne	3 E3
Broughton	139 D2	Goostrey	107 E1
Brown Knowl	199 E4	Great Barrow	120 C3
Broxton	183 D1	Great Budworth	79 D4
Buerton	230 C2	Great Sankey	15 D3
Bulkeley	184 C1	Guilden Sutton	119 F3
Bunbury	185 F4	Hale	21 E1
Burland	203 E4	Hale (G Manchester)	32 B4
Burton	67 E1	Halewood	21 D4
Burtonwood	6 C3	Hampton	214 A4
Burwardsley	184 A3	Handley	182 B4
Buxton	115 F4	Hargrave	144 A1

Hartford	103 E3	Mobberley	58 A3
Harthill	183 F2	Mollington	94 C1
Haslington	191 F3	Moore	25 D3
Hassall Green	176 A1	Mottram St Andrew	61 D1
Hatherton	219 F2	Mouldsworth	98 C1
Hatton	26 A1	Moulton	126 C4
Hawarden	116 A1	Mow Cop	195 E4
Haydock	1 B3	Nantwich	204 C3
Hazel Grove	36 B4	Neston	66 B4
Helsby	73 E2	Nether Alderley	85 D3
Henbury	111 D4	New Mills	39 E4
Heswall	40 C3	Newcastle-under-Lyme	210 B1
High Lane	37 F4	Newhall	228 B4
High Legh	29 D3	Newton-le-Willows	2 B2
Higher Kinnerton	161 D4	Norley	100 C3
Higher Walton	25 F4	Northwich	103 E4
Higher Wincham	79 F2	Norton in Hales	236 B1
Hollins Green	11 D1	Oakmere	124 A4
Holmes Chapel	130 B2	Ollerton	82 C3
Holt	196 B4	Packmoor	195 F1
Hough Common	206 C1	Partington	11 F1
Huntington	142 A3	Peckforton	185 D3
Huxley	166 C4	Penketh	14 C2
Hyde	241	Pickmere	80 A4
Irlam	11 E4	Picton	96 B2
Isycoed	196 B1	Plumley	81 D2
Kelsall	122 B2	Pott Shrigley	63 E2
Kettleshulme	64 C2	Poulton	163 D1
Kidsgrove	195 D1	Poynton	36 C2
Kingsley	75 E1	Prestbury	87 D4
Knutsford	57 D2	Preston on the Hill	51 D3
Lach Dennis	105 E3	Puddington	92 C4
Lawton-gate	194 A2	Pulford	162 B2
Ledsham	68 C1	Rainow	88 B3
Leigh	5 E4	Ravensmoor	203 F1
Lindow End	59 D1	Ridley	185 E1
Little Bollington	20 B1	Rode Heath	193 F4
Little Budworth	147 F4	Romiley	241
Little Leigh	77 E2	Rostherne	30 C2
Lostock	80 B1	Royal's Green	228 C1
Lower Peover	81 f1	Runcorn	49 E4
Lymm	18 C2	Saighton	142 C1
Macclesfield	112 A4	Sale	242
Macclesfield Forest	114 B3	Sandbach	175 D3
Malpas	213 D1	Saughall	94 A1
Manley	99 D2	Scholar Green	194 C4
Marbury	226 B4	Sealand	116 C3
Marston	79 D2	Shavington	206 B3
Marton	133 D3	Shocklach	211 E4
Mere	56 A4	Shotwick	93 D2
Mickle Trafford	119 F4	Siddington	110 A2
Middlewich	128 B1	Smallwood	176 C3
Milton Green	165 E1	Sound	217 F3

Sproston Green	129 E1
Spurstow	185 E3
St Helens	1 A1
Stalybridge	242
Stanlow	71 D3
Stapeley	219 E4
Stoak	96 A4
Stockport	240
Stretton	26 C1
Styal	33 F2
Sutton	50 A1
Sutton Lane Ends	112 C1
Swettenham	131 F2
Tabley	55 F2
Tarporley	146 B1
Tarvin	121 E2
Tattenhall	166 A1
Thornton Hough	42 A4
Thornton-le-Moors	71 F1
Threapwood	222 C4
Tilston	198 A2
Tiverton	168 B3
Trafford	96 C3
Utkinton	146 A4
Warmingham	173 E4
Warren	111 E1
Warrington	16 C3
Waverton	143 D2
Weaverham	102 B4
Weston	207 E3
Wettenhall	170 C4
Whaley Bridge	65 E4
Whitchurch	226 A1
Whitegate	126 A4
Whitewell	224 B1
Whitley	52 B2
Widnes	22 C4
Willaston	68 A4
Willaston (nr Nantwich)	205 E3
Wilmslow	60 A3
Wimboldsley	150 C2
Wincle	160 A4
Winsford	126 C1
Winwick	8 A3
Wistaston	205 E4
Withington	109 D1
Woodford	35 E1
Woore	232 A1
Worleston	188 C3
Worthenbury	211 D1
Wrenbury	216 C2
Wybunbury	220 A4
Wythenshawe	33 E4

108 Steps 29 SK11 .... 112 B4
Aarons Dr ST7 .... 209 F1
Abbey Cl Altrincham WA14 .. 238 B1
  Croft WA3 .... 9 D4
  Whitegate CW8 .... 126 A4
  Widnes WA8 .... 22 B4
  Winsford CW7 .... 149 D4
Abbey Fields CW2 .... 205 E4
Abbey Gate Coll CH3 .... 164 C4
Abbey Gate Coll
  (The Jun Dept) CH3 .. 163 F2
Abbey Gate Sch CH2 .... 237 D4
Abbey Gn CH1 .... 237 D3
Abbey Hey WA7 .... 50 B4
Abbey La Delamere CW8 .... 123 F3
  Hartford CW8 .... 103 D2
Abbey Pl CW1 .... 190 B3
Abbey Rd Cheadle SK8 .... 240 A1
  Goldborne WA3 .... 4 A1
  Haydock WA11 .... 1 C4
  Macclesfield SK10 .... 87 D1
  Sale M33 .... 242 A8
  Sandbach CW11 .... 174 C3
  Widnes WA8 .... 22 B4
Abbey Sq CH1 .... 237 E3
Abbey St CH1 .... 237 E3
Abbey Way CW8 .... 103 D2
Abbeyway N WA11 .... 2 A4
Abbeyway S WA12 .... 2 A4
Abbot's Dr CH2 .... 118 B2
Abbot's Grange CH2 .... 237 D4
Abbot's Nook CH2 .... 237 D4
Abbots Cl Macclesfield SK10 .. 87 D1
  Sale M33 .... 242 D7
Abbots Keep CH2 .... 118 B2
Abbots Mews L65 .... 70 A3
Abbots Pk CH2 .... 118 B2
Abbots Way CW8 .... 103 D2
Abbotsbury Cl Poynton SK12 36 B3
  Shavington CW2 .... 206 A4
Abbotsfield Cl WA4 .... 26 C3
Abbotsford Gr WA14 .... 238 E8
Abbott's Cl CW12 .... 179 D4
Abbott's Rd CH3 .... 143 D3
Abbotts Way CW7 .... 126 A1
Aber Rd SK8 .... 240 A2
Abercrombie Ct M33 .... 242 D7
Aberdare Cl WA5 .... 7 F1
Aberdaron Dr CH1 .... 117 F2
Aberdeen Cres SK3 .... 240 D4
Aberdeen Gr SK3 .... 240 D4
Aberfeldy Cl WA4 .... 130 A1
Abingdon Ave WA1 .... 17 F4
Abingdon St SK11 .... 111 F4
Abingdon Cres CH4 .... 140 C3
Abingdon St OL6 .... 242 A2
Abington Cl CW1 .... 190 A3
Abington Rd M33 .... 242 C5
Abington Wlk WA7 .... 50 B3
Abstone Cl WA1 .... 17 E4
Acacia Ave Altrincham WA15 238 F3
  Denton M34 .... 241 A7
  Knutsford WA16 .... 56 C1
  Warrington WA1 .... 17 E4
  Widnes WA8 .... 13 D2
  Wilmslow SK9 .... 59 F3
Acacia Cl CH2 .... 72 B2
Acacia Cres CW1 .... 190 C3
Acacia Dr Altrincham WA15 . 238 F3
  Ellesmere Port L66 .... 69 F1
  Sandbach CW11 .... 174 C4
Acacia Gdns ST7 .... 195 E2
Acacia Gr 4 Reddish SK5 .. 240 F8
  Runcorn WA7 .... 49 E4
Acacia St WA12 .... 1 C2
Academy St WA1 .... 16 A3
Academy Way WA1 .... 16 A3
Acer Ave CW1 .... 190 C4
Achilles Ave WA2 .... 8 A1
Ack La E SK7 .... 35 E3
Ack La W SK7 .... 35 E4
Ackerley Cl WA2 .... 8 C2
Ackers La WA4 .... 16 C1
Ackers Rd WA4 .... 16 C1
Ackersley Ct SK8 .... 35 D4
Acorn Ave SK8 .... 239 E5
Acorn Bank Cl CW2 .... 206 A4
Acorn Bsns Ctr SK4 .... 240 D5
Acorn Cl Cuddington CW8 .. 101 F1
  Winsford CW7 .... 150 A4
Acorn Dr L65 .... 70 A1
Acorn La CW12 .... 157 F2
Acorn St WA12 .... 2 B2
Acorn Terr SK22 .... 39 D3
Acre La Bebington L62 .... 43 E4
  Cheadle Hulme SK7 .... 35 E3
  Heswall L60 .... 41 E4
Acre Rd L66 .... 69 E3
Acre St SK6 .... 241 B2
Acreage The Bunbury CW6 .. 185 F4
  Goostrey CW4 .... 107 F1
Acrefield Ave SK4 .... 240 B8
Acrefield Rd WA4 .... 12 A1
Acres Cres WA6 .... 75 D1
Acres La Chester CH2 .... 118 B4
  Stalybridge SK15 .... 242 E1
Acres Rd SK8 .... 239 A5
Acreville Gr WA3 .... 5 E4
Acton Ave WA4 .... 26 B2
Acton Bridge Sta CW8 .... 76 C1
Acton CE Contr Prim Sch
  CW5 .... 204 A4
Acton Cl WA11 .... 1 B3

Acton La CW8 .... 76 C2
Acton Pl SK11 .... 111 F4
Acton Rd Burtonwood WA5 .... 6 C3
  Crewe CW2 .... 189 E3
Acton Way ST7 .... 193 E3
Adam Ave L66 .... 69 E2
Adam Cl L66 .... 69 E2
Adam St WA2 .... 16 A2
Adams Cl Newton-le-W WA12 .. 2 B1
  Poynton SK12 .... 36 C1
Adams Hill WA16 .... 57 D1
Adamson Ct WA4 .... 17 D1
Adamson St WA4 .... 16 A2
Adaston Ave L62 .... 43 F2
Adcroft St SK1 .... 240 F3
Adder Hill CH3 .... 142 A4
Adderly Cl WA7 .... 23 E1
Addingham Ave WA8 .... 22 B4
Addingham Cl WA8 .... 22 B4
Addison Cl CW2 .... 205 F4
Addison Rd WA15 .... 238 E2
Addison Sq WA8 .... 13 D1
Adela Rd WA7 .... 22 C1
Adelaide Rd Blacon CH1 ...... 117 E2
  Bramhall SK7 .... 35 F3
  Stockport SK3 .... 240 D4
Adelaide St CW1 .... 190 B3
Adey Rd WA13 .... 19 D3
Adfalent La L64 .... 68 A4
Adlington Cl SK12 .... 36 C1
Adlington Ct WA3 .... 9 F3
Adlington Cty Prim Sch
  SK10 .... 62 C3
Adlington Dr
  Northwich CW9 .... 104 A3
  Sandbach CW11 .... 175 E4
Adlington Pk SK10 .... 36 B1
Adlington Rd Bollington SK10 63 D1
  Crewe CW2 .... 189 F2
  Runcorn WA7 .... 24 B1
  Wilmslow SK9 .... 60 C4
Adlington St SK11 .... 112 B4
Adlington Wlk SK1 .... 240 E5
Admirals Rd WA3 .... 9 F2
Adshall Rd SK8 .... 240 A1
Adswood Gr SK3 .... 240 E2
Adswood La E SK3 .... 240 F2
Adswood La W SK2 & SK3 .. 240 F2
Adswood Prim Sch SK3 .. 240 E1
Adswood Rd SK3 & SK8 .. 240 D1
Adswood Terr SK3 .... 240 E2
Adwell Cl WA3 .... 4 A4
Aegean Rd WA14 .... 238 A6
Afton WA8 .... 12 A1
Agden Brow WA13 .... 19 F1
Agden Brow Pk WA13 .... 29 E4
Agden House La SY13 .... 225 D3
Agden La
  Little Bollington WA13, WA14 . 29 F4
  Lymm WA13 .... 19 F1
Agden Park La WA13 .... 29 E4
Agecroft Rd Northwich CW9 104 B4
  Romiley SK6 .... 241 A1
Ainley Cl WA7 .... 50 A3
Ainscough Rd WA3 .... 9 F2
Ainsdale Cl Bebington L63 .. 43 E3
  Bramhall SK7 .... 36 A4
  Penketh WA5 .... 14 C2
Ainsdale Dr SK8 .... 239 B1
Ainsworth La CW8 .... 76 A2
Ainsworth Rd CW8 .... 77 F1
Aintree Gr Ellesmere Port L66 69 E2
  Stockport SK3 .... 240 E1
Airdrie Cl L62 .... 43 E2
Aire WA8 .... 12 A1
Aire Cl L65 .... 70 A4
Aire Pl CW7 .... 127 D1
Airedale Cl Cheadle SK8 .... 239 C6
  Great Sankey WA5 .... 14 C4
Airedale Ct WA14 .... 238 E5
Airfield View CH4 .... 139 D3
Aitchison Rd CW9 .... 80 A1
Ajax Ave WA3 .... 9 F2
Akesmoor La Biddulph ST6 . 179 D1
  Kidsgrove ST7 .... 195 F4
Alamein Cres WA2 .... 16 B4
Alamein Dr Romiley SK6 .... 241 F2
  Winsford CW7 .... 149 E4
Alamein Rd Barnton CW8 .... 78 A2
  Chester CH2 .... 95 D1
Alan Dr WA15 .... 32 A4
Alan Rd SK4 .... 240 B8
Alan St CW9 .... 104 A4
Alandale Rd SK3 .... 240 C3
Alban St CW1 .... 190 B3
Albany Cres WA13 .... 18 B2
Albany Gdns L66 .... 69 E4
Albany Gr WA13 .... 18 B2
Albany Rd Bramhall SK7 ...... 35 F2
  Lymm WA13 .... 18 B2
  Wilmslow SK9 .... 59 F3
Albany Terr WA7 .... 23 D1
Albert Dr Neston L64 .... 66 B4
Albert Pl Altrincham WA14 .. 238 D5
  Penketh WA5 .... 14 B3
Albert Rd Altrincham WA15 .. 238 E1
  Bollington SK10 .... 87 F4
  Hyde SK14 .... 241 D6
  Manchester SK4 .... 240 A7
  Sale M33 .... 242 C6
  Warrington WA4 .... 17 D1
  Widnes WA8 .... 13 D1
  Wilmslow SK9 .... 60 A1

Albert Rd E WA15 .... 238 E3
Albert Row WA6 .... 49 D1
Albert Sq Altrincham WA14 . 238 D3
  Stalybridge SK15 .... 242 C1
  1 Widnes WA8 .... 23 D4
Albert St Audley ST7 .... 209 F2
  Chester CH2 .... 237 F3
  Crewe CW1 .... 190 B3
  Hyde SK14 .... 241 F7
  Irlam M44 .... 11 F3
  Knutsford WA16 .... 56 C1
  Macclesfield SK11 .... 112 B4
  Nantwich CW5 .... 204 C3
  Stockport SK3 .... 240 D5
Alberta St SK1 .... 240 F4
Albion Cl SK4 .... 240 E7
Albion Gdns SK15 .... 242 E1
Albion Pl M33 .... 242 A6
Albion Pl CH4 .... 237 E1
Albion Rd New Mills SK22 .... 39 D3
  Northwich CW9 .... 79 D1
Albion St Chester CH1 .... 237 E2
  Crewe CW2 .... 190 A2
  Hyde SK14 .... 241 D6
  Sale M33 .... 242 B6
  Stalybridge SK15 .... 242 E2
Albion Trad Est OL6 .... 242 A3
Albion Wlk CW9 .... 79 D1
Albury Cl WA11 .... 1 B4
Alcester Ave SK3 .... 239 F7
Alcester Rd SK8 .... 239 B4
Alcock St WA7 .... 23 D2
Aldcliffe WA3 .... 3 F4
Alder Ave Poynton SK12 ...... 36 C2
  Widnes WA8 .... 13 D2
Alder Cres WA2 .... 16 B4
Alder Dr L66 .... 69 F1
Alder Gr Chester CH2 .... 119 D2
  Denton M34 .... 241 A6
  Stockport SK3 .... 240 C4
Alder La Burtonwood WA12 .... 7 E4
  Cronton WA8 .... 12 A3
  Frodsham WA6 .... 48 B2
  Warrington WA2 .... 16 A4
  Winwick WA2 .... 7 E4
Alder Rd Cheadle SK8 .... 239 E5
  Goldborne WA3 .... 3 F4
  Warrington WA1 .... 17 E4
  Weaverham CW8 .... 102 B4
Alder Rise SK23 .... 65 E4
Alder Root La WA2 .... 7 E4
Alder St L12 .... 2 B2
Alder Wood Ave L24 .... 21 D2
Alderbank Rd WA5 .... 15 D3
Alderdale Dr SK9 .... 59 F3
Alderfield Dr L24 .... 21 D2
Aldergate Ave WA7 .... 50 B4
Alderhay La ST7 .... 195 E3
Alderley Ave WA3 .... 3 E4
Alderley Cl Hazel Grove SK7 .. 36 C4
  Poynton SK12 .... 36 C1
  Sandbach CW11 .... 175 E4
Alderley Edge
  Cty Prim Sch SK9 .... 60 A1
Alderley Edge Golf Course
  SK9 .... 59 F2
Alderley Edge Sta SK9 .... 60 A1
Alderley Lodge SK9 .... 60 A3
Alderley Rd Chelford SK10 .. 84 B2
  Mottram St Andrew SK10 .. 60 C1
  Northwich CW8 .... 103 F4
  Prestbury SK10 .... 86 C2
  Warrington WA4 .... 17 E2
  Wilmslow SK9 .... 60 A3
Alderley Wlk 22 SK11 .... 112 C4
Alderly Pl CH1 .... 117 F3
Alderney Cl
  Ellesmere Port L65 .... 70 B1
  Macclesfield SK11 .... 111 F4
Alders Rd SK6 .... 38 A4
Alders Way SK10 .... 86 C3
Aldersey CE Aided
  Prim Sch CW6 .... 185 F4
Aldersey Cl Runcorn WA7 .... 24 B1
  Saughall CH1 .... 94 A1
Aldersey La
  Coddington CH3 .... 182 B3
  Handley CH3 .... 182 B3
Aldersey Rd CW2 .... 190 A1
Aldersgate SK22 .... 39 D4
Aldersgate Dr L26 .... 21 D3
Aldersgate Rd SK7 .... 35 E3
Aldersgreen Ave SK6 .... 37 F4
Alderton Gr WA7 .... 127 D2
Alderwood Ave SK4 .... 240 A5
Aldewood Cl WA3 .... 10 A3
Aldford Cl Bebington L63 .... 43 D3
  Hough Common CW2 .... 206 C1
Aldford Pl SK9 .... 59 F1
Aldford Rd CH2 .... 118 C3
Aldford Way CW7 .... 126 A1
Aldgate L65 .... 70 A3
Aldington Dr CW10 .... 151 E3
Aldridge Dr WA5 .... 6 C4
Aled Way CH4 .... 140 B3
Alexander Dr WA8 .... 22 B4
Alexander Gr WA7 .... 23 E1
Alexandra Ave SK14 .... 241 C6
Alexandra Cl SK3 .... 240 C2
Alexandra Gr M44 .... 11 F4
Alexandra Hospl The SK8 239 D6
Alexandra Ind Est SK8 .... 22 C4
Alexandra Mews SK9 .... 49 D1
Alexandra Park Inf Sch
  SK3 .... 240 C3
Alexandra Pl CW1 .... 190 A3

Alexandra Rd
  Dukinfield M34 .... 241 A8
  Manchester SK4 .... 240 C7
  Middlewich CW10 .... 151 E3
  Sale M33 .... 242 D5
  Warrington WA4 .... 16 C1
  Warrington, Stockton Heath
  WA4 .... 16 B1
Alexandra Sq 12 CW7 .... 149 D4
Alexandra St
  Ashton-u-L OL6 .... 242 A4
  Ellesmere Port L65 .... 70 B4
  Hyde SK14 .... 241 C5
  Warrington WA1 .... 16 C4
  Widnes WA8 .... 23 D4
  Winsford CW7 .... 126 B1
Alforde St Widnes WA8 .... 23 D3
  Widnes WA8 .... 23 D4
Alfred Cl 12 WA8 .... 23 D4
Alfred Rd Goldborne WA3 .... 4 A4
  Haydock WA11 .... 1 C4
Alfred St Ashton-u-L OL6 .... 242 A4
  Denton SK14 .... 241 C7
  Irlam M44 .... 11 F3
  Newton-le-W WA12 .... 2 C2
  Northwich CW8 .... 103 F3
  Widnes WA8 .... 23 D4
Alger St OL6 .... 242 A4
Algernon St Warrington WA1 16 B3
  Warrington, Stockton Heath
  WA4 .... 16 B1
Algreave Rd SK3 .... 240 A4
Alice Cl WA8 .... 23 D2
Alice St M33 .... 242 D6
Alison Cl SK4 .... 240 B4
Alison Dr SK10 .... 87 F1
Alistair Dr L63 .... 43 E3
All Hallows
  (Special Agreement)
  Cath High Sch SK11 .... 112 A4
All Saints CE Prim Sch
  SK4 .... 240 D7
All Saints Dr WA4 .... 17 F2
All Saints Parish Church
  Sch
  WA7 .... 23 D2
All Saints' Rd SK4 .... 240 E8
All Saints Upton CE Contr
  Prim Sch WA8 .... 12 A2
Allandale WA14 .... 238 B4
Allans Cl L64 .... 66 C3
Allans Meadow L64 .... 66 C4
Allansford Ave CH3 .... 143 D2
Allcard St WA5 .... 15 F4
Allen Ave WA3 .... 3 E4
Allen Dr CW9 .... 103 F1
Allen Pl CW1 .... 190 A3
Allen Rd WA7 .... 48 B4
Allen St Bollington SK10 .... 88 A4
  Macclesfield SK11 .... 112 C4
  Warrington WA2 .... 16 A3
Allenby Rd M44 .... 11 E2
Allendale WA7 .... 50 A3
Allerby Way WA3 .... 3 F4
Allerton Rd WA8 .... 13 D1
Allgreave Cl CW10 .... 151 E3
Allington La CH4 .... 141 F4
Allington Pl CH4 .... 141 F4
Allotment Rd M44 .... 11 E3
Allport La L62 .... 43 E4
Allport Rd L62 .... 43 E4
Allports The L62 .... 43 E4
Allumbrook Ave CW4 .... 130 B2
Allysum Ct WA7 .... 49 F2
Alma Ave CW1 .... 190 B3
Alma Cl Macclesfield SK11 .. 112 A4
  Scholar Green ST7 .... 194 C4
Alma La SK9 .... 60 A4
Alma Rd SK7 .... 37 D4
Alma St Chester CH2 .... 118 C1
  Newton-le-W WA12 .... 2 A2
  Stalybridge SK15 .... 242 E2
Almeda Rd L24 .... 21 D1
Almer Dr WA5 .... 15 E3
Almond Ave Crewe CW1 .... 190 C3
  Runcorn WA7 .... 49 E4
Almond Cl SK3 .... 240 C4
Almond Dr WA5 .... 6 C3
Almond Gr Warrington WA1 .. 17 D4
  Widnes WA8 .... 22 B4
Almond Pl ST5 .... 210 C1
Almond Tree Cl L24 .... 21 F1
Almond Wlk M31 .... 11 E1
Alnwick Dr L65 .... 70 B1
Alpass Ave WA2 .... 16 A4
Alpine St WA12 .... 2 A2
Alport Rd SY13 .... 226 A1
Alpraham Cres CH2 .... 118 C3
Alric Wlk M22 .... 33 F4
Alsager Rd Audley ST7 .... 209 E3
  Haslington CW11 .... 192 B4
  Hassall Green CW11 .... 192 B4
Alsager Sch ST7 .... 193 D2
Alsager Sta ST7 .... 193 F2
Alsfeld Way SK22 .... 39 D4
Alstone Dr WA14 .... 238 A6
Alt WA8 .... 12 A1
Alt Wlk CW7 .... 127 D1
Alton Dr SK10 .... 87 F1
Alton Rd SK9 .... 59 F4
Alton St CW2 .... 190 A2
Altrincham CE (VA)
  Prim Sch
  WA14 .... 238 D5
Altrincham General Hospl
  WA14 .... 238 D4
Altrincham Golf Course
  WA15 .... 238 F5

Altrincham Gram Sch
  for Boys WA14 .... 238 D2
Altrincham Gram Sch
  for Girls Altrincham WA14 . 238 B3
  Altrincham WA14 .... 238 C3
Altrincham Prep Sch
  WA14 .... 238 C1
Altrincham Priory Hospl
  WA15 .... 32 A4
Altrincham Sta Styal SK9 .... 33 E2
  Wilmslow SK9 .... 33 E1
Altrincham Sta WA15 .... 238 E4
Alum Ct CW4 .... 130 B1
Alun Cres CH4 .... 141 D3
Alundale Rd CW7 .... 126 B2
Alvanley Cres SK3 .... 240 C2
Alvanley Cty Prim Sch WA6 73 E1
Alvanley Dr WA6 .... 73 E1
Alvanley Rd
  Ellesmere Port L66 .... 69 F2
  Helsby WA6 .... 73 E1
Alvanley Rise CW9 .... 104 A3
Alvanley Terr WA6 .... 74 A4
Alvanley View CH2 .... 72 A2
Alvanley Way L66 .... 69 F2
Alvaston Ave SK4 .... 240 B6
Alvaston Bsns Pk CW5 .... 204 C4
Alvaston Rd CW5 .... 204 C3
Alvaston Wlk CW2 .... 189 F1
Alverton Cl WA8 .... 22 B4
Alverton Rd SK10 .... 86 C1
Alveston Dr SK9 .... 34 B1
Alvis Rd CH5 .... 116 A2
Alwyn Gdns CH2 .... 118 B4
Alyn Rd CH2 .... 96 C1
Alyndale Rd CH4 .... 140 B3
Ambassador Pl WA15 .... 238 E5
Amberleigh Cl WA4 .... 27 D2
Amberley Dr WA15 .... 32 A4
Amberley Rd SK11 .... 112 A3
Ambleside Chester CH2 .... 119 D3
  Stalybridge SK15 .... 242 D3
Ambleside Cl Bebington L62 .. 43 F4
  Macclesfield SK11 .... 111 F3
  Runcorn WA7 .... 49 F3
  Winsford CW7 .... 126 B2
  Wistaston CW2 .... 189 F1
Ambleside Cres WA2 .... 8 B2
Ambleside Ct CW12 .... 155 F1
Ambleside Rd L65 .... 70 B1
Ambuscade Cl CW1 .... 190 C3
Amelia Cl WA8 .... 13 D2
Amelia St 3 Hyde SK14 .... 241 E6
  Warrington WA2 .... 16 B4
Amersham Cl SK10 .... 87 E2
Amis Gr WA3 .... 3 F4
Amy St CW2 .... 190 B2
Anchor Cl WA7 .... 50 B3
Anchorage The Neston L64 .. 66 B4
  Waverton CH3 .... 143 D3
Ancoats Rd SK9, WA16 .... 83 F4
Anderson Cl Crewe CW1 .... 191 D2
  Warrington WA2 .... 9 D1
Anderson Ct L62 .... 43 E3
Anderson St 10 SK11 .... 112 B4
Anderton Way 12 SK9 .... 34 B2
Andertons SK10 .... 86 A1
Andover Cl WA2 .... 8 C1
Andover Rd WA11 .... 1 C4
Andrew Cl WA8 .... 22 B4
Andrew Cres CH4 .... 237 F1
Andrew Gr SK10 .... 113 D4
Andrew La SK6 .... 37 F4
Andrew St Hyde SK14 .... 241 F7
  Stockport SK4 .... 240 D6
Andrew's Cl CH3 .... 121 D1
Andrew's Wlk L60 .... 41 D4
Anfield Mews SK8 .... 239 F3
Anfield Rd Cheadle SK8 .... 239 F3
  Sale M33 .... 242 C7
Angel St M34 .... 241 A8
Anglesea Ave SK2 .... 240 F7
Anglesey Cl L65 .... 70 B1
Anglesey Dr SK12 .... 36 C3
Anglesey Gr SK8 .... 240 A2
Anglesey Water SK12 .... 36 C3
Angus Rd L63 .... 43 E3
Angus Wlk SK10 .... 86 C1
Ankers Knowl La
  SK11, SK10 .... 114 B4
Ankers La SK11 .... 114 B4
Ann Cl L66 .... 69 E4
Ann St Denton SK14 .... 241 C7
  Northwich CW9 .... 79 E1
  Reddish SK5 .... 240 E8
  Runcorn WA7 .... 23 D2
Ann St W WA8 .... 23 D4
Annable Rd M44 .... 11 F4
Annan Cl CW12 .... 157 D1
Anne St ST7 .... 210 B2
Anne's Way CH4 .... 237 F1
Annette Ave WA12 .... 2 A3
Annie St WA2 .... 16 B3
Annions La CW5 .... 205 F1
Annis Cl SK9 .... 60 A1
Annis Rd SK9 .... 60 A1
Ansdell Rd WA8 .... 13 E1
Ansley Gr SK4 .... 240 B7
Anson Cl Bramhall SK7 .... 35 F3
  Warrington WA2 .... 8 C1
Anson Rd Poynton SK12 .... 37 D2
  Wilmslow SK9 .... 34 C1
Anthony Dr CW9 .... 126 C4
Anthony's Way L60 .... 41 D4
Antons Rd L26 .... 21 D3
Antony Rd WA4 .... 16 A1
Antrim Cl WA11 .... 1 B3
Antrim Dr L66 .... 69 F1

Antrim Rd WA2 8 A1
Antrobus St CW12 156 B2
Antrobus St Mark's Sch CW9 53 E2
Anvil Cl CH1 94 A1
Apple Market St CW9 103 F4
Apple Tree Cl L24 21 F1
Apple Tree Gr CH1 94 C4
Appleby Cl
Macclesfield SK11 111 F3
Stockport SK3 240 D1
Widnes WA8 22 B4
Appleby Rd Gatley SK8 239 B4
Warrington WA2 8 B2
Applecroft ST5 210 C1
Applecross Cl WA3 10 A3
Appledale Dr CH1 95 D4
Applefield CW8 103 E4
Appleford Cl WA4 26 C4
Appleton Cl CW12 178 C4
Appleton Dr L65 69 F2
Appleton Hall Gdns WA4 26 C3
Appleton Mews WA13 18 B2
Appleton Rd
Altrincham WA15 238 F1
Chester CH2 118 C3
Widnes WA8 13 D1
Appleton St Northwich CW8 78 B1
Widnes WA8 23 D4
Appleton Thorn Cty Prim Sch WA4 27 E2
Appleton Thorn Trad Est WA4 27 E3
Appleton Village WA8 13 D1
Appleton Wlk 15 SK9 34 B1
Appletree Gr WA2 8 C1
Appleyards La CH4 141 F4
Apprentice La SK9 33 F2
April Rise SK10 87 D1
Apron Rd M90 33 E3
Apsley Cl WA14 238 B1
Apsley Gr WA14 238 B1
Apsley St SK1 240 F5
Aragon Ct WA7 24 B2
Aragon Gn CH1 117 F3
Aran Cl L24 21 E1
Arbour Cl Macclesfield SK10 87 E2
Northwich CW9 104 B4
Arbour Cres SK10 87 E2
Arbour Mews SK10 87 E2
Arbour St ST7 210 B3
Arbourhay St SK10 87 F1
Arbury Ave SK3 240 A3
Arbury La WA2 8 B3
Arcade The
Ellesmere Port L65 70 A3
Northwich CW9 103 F4
Archer Ave WA4 16 C1
Archer Cl SK10 87 F4
Archers Way Blacon CH1 118 A2
Ellesmere Port L66 69 F1
Arclid Cl 12 SK9 34 C1
Arclid Hospl CW11 154 A1
Arcon Pl WA14 238 A6
Arden WA8 12 A1
Arden Cl Cheadle SK8 34 B4
Tarvin CH3 121 E2
Warrington WA3 10 A3
Arden Ct CW12 179 D4
Arden Dr L64 66 C3
Arden St SK22 39 E4
Arden Wlk SK1 240 E5
Ardenbrook Rise SK10 86 C3
Ardern Gr SK1 240 F4
Ardern Lea WA6 73 E1
Arderne Ave CW2 190 A1
Ardleigh Cl CW1 189 F4
Argosy Dr WA15 32 C4
Argyll Ave Bebington L62 43 E2
Chester CH4 141 D4
Argyll Cl SK10 87 D1
Argyll Rd SK8 239 F5
Argyll St OL6 242 B3
Arkenshaw Rd WA3 9 D4
Arkenstone Cl WA8 12 B1
Arkle Ave SK9 34 C2
Arklow Dr L24 21 E1
Arkwright Cl CW7 149 D4
Arkwright Ct WA7 23 F2
Arkwright Rd WA7 23 F2
Arley Ave WA4 26 B4
Arley Cl Alsager ST7 193 E2
Altrincham WA14 238 D8
Chester CH2 118 C3
Macclesfield SK11 112 A4
Arley Cty Prim Sch CW9 54 C3
Arley Dr WA8 12 A1
Arley End WA16 29 E2
Arley Hall CW9 54 B3
Arley Mere Cl SK8 239 F3
Arley Mossend La CW9 54 B1
Arley Pl CW2 206 A4
Arley Rd Antrobus CW9 54 A4
Appleton CW9 27 E1
Northwich CW9 104 B4
Arlies Cl SK15 242 D4
Arlies La SK15 242 E4
Arlies Prim Sch SK15 242 D4
Arlies St OL6 242 A4
Arlington Ave M34 241 A6
Arlington Cl CW2 206 B4
Arlington Cr SK9 59 F3
Arlington Dr Goldborne WA3 4 B4
Macclesfield SK11 112 A4
Penketh WA5 14 C2
Poynton SK12 36 B2
Arlington Rd SK8 239 C4
Arlington Way SK9 59 F3
Armadale Cl SK3 240 F1
Armett St SK11 112 B4
Armitage Rd WA14 238 D3
Armitstead Rd CW11 174 C2
Armour Ave WA2 8 A1
Armoury St SK3 240 E4
Armstrong Cl Audlem CW3 229 F2
Warrington WA3 9 E2
Armthorpe Dr L66 69 E3
Arncliffe Dr WA5 6 C3
Arndale WA7 49 F3
Arnesby Ave M33 242 E7
Arnfield Rd SK3 240 D1
Arnhem Cres WA2 16 B4
Arnhem Way CH3 142 A3
Arnold Pl WA8 22 B4
Arnold St Nantwich CW5 204 C3
Stockport SK3 240 E3
Arnold's Cres CH4 139 D2
Arnside Ave
Congleton CW12 156 A1
Haydock WA11 1 A3
Arnside Cl Gatley SK8 239 B4
High Lane SK6 37 F4
Winsford CW7 126 B1
Arnside Dr SK14 241 C8
Arnside Gr Sale M33 242 B8
Warrington WA4 16 A1
Arpley Rd WA1 16 A2
Arpley St WA1 16 A2
Arradon Ct CH2 118 C3
Arran Ave
Ellesmere Port L65 70 B1
Sale M33 242 C5
Arran Cl
Holmes Chapel CW4 130 B1
Warrington WA2 9 D1
Arran Dr WA6 74 B3
Arrivals Way M90 33 D4
Arron Pl CW2 189 E2
Arrowcroft Rd CH3 119 F3
Arrowsmith Dr ST7 193 D2
Arrowsmith Rd WA11 1 C4
Arthill La WA14 20 A1
Arthog Dr WA15 31 F4
Arthog Rd WA15 31 F4
Arthur Ave L65 70 B3
Arthur St Blacon CH1 118 A1
Crewe CW2 190 B1
Hyde SK14 241 C5
Lostock CW9 80 A1
Runcorn WA7 23 D1
Warrington WA2 16 A3
Artists La SK10 85 E4
Artle Rd CW2 206 B4
Arundel Ave SK7 36 B4
Arundel Cl Knutsford WA16 82 A4
Macclesfield SK10 87 F1
Wistaston CW2 205 F4
Arundel Ct L65 70 C2
Arundel Rd SK8 35 D3
Arundel St OL6 242 B3
Arundell Cl WA5 6 C3
Ascol Dr CW9 80 B2
Ascot Ave WA7 49 D3
Ascot Cl Congleton CW12 156 B2
Macclesfield SK10 87 E2
Warrington, Grappenhall WA4 17 E1
Warrington, Martinscroft WA1 17 F4
Ascot Dr L66 69 F2
Ash Ave Altrincham WA14 238 A5
Cheadle SK8 239 E5
Irlam M44 11 E3
Newton-le-W WA12 2 B1
Ash Cl Ellesmere Port L66 69 F1
Holmes Chapel CW4 130 B2
Malpas SY14 213 E3
Tarporley CW6 146 B1
Ash Gr Altrincham WA15 238 F7
Altrincham, Rosehill WA14 238 C1
Cheadle SK8 34 A4
Chester CH4 141 D3
Congleton CW12 156 A2
Ellesmere Port L66 69 E3
Goldborne WA3 3 D4
Knutsford WA16 57 E1
Macclesfield SK11 112 B2
Middlewich CW10 151 E4
Nantwich CW5 204 C2
Rode Heath ST7 193 F4
Runcorn WA7 49 E4
Stalybridge SK15 242 C3
Warrington WA4 16 B2
Weaverham CW8 102 C4
Widnes WA8 22 B4
Wilmslow SK9 34 B2
Ash Grove Cty Prim Sch SK11 112 B2
Ash Hay La CH2 96 B1
Ash House La CW8 77 E4
Ash La Appleton WA4 26 C4
Widnes L26, WA8 22 A4
Ash Lawn Ct CH2 118 B2
Ash Priors WA8 12 B2
Ash Rd Crewe CW1 190 B3
Cuddington CW8 101 F1
Elton CH2 72 B2
Haydock WA11 1 C4
Hollins Green WA3 11 D1
Lymm WA13 18 B2
Partington M31 11 E2
Penketh WA5 14 C2
Poynton SK12 36 C2
Winwick WA2 8 A3
Ash St Northwich CW9 79 D1
Stockport SK3 240 B4
Ash Terr SK11 112 B2
Ash Way L60 41 D3
Ashbank CW9 104 B4
Ashberry Cl SK9 60 B4
Ashberry Dr WA4 27 D3
Ashbourne Ave
Cheadle SK8 239 F6
Runcorn WA7 49 D3
Ashbourne Cl CH1 94 C4
Ashbourne Dr SK6 37 F3
Ashbourne Mews SK11 111 F4
Ashbourne Rd
Great Sankey WA5 15 D3
Hazel Grove SK7 36 C4
Ashbrook Ave WA7 49 F2
Ashbrook Cl SK8 239 B1
Ashbrook Cres WA2 16 B4
Ashbrook Dr SK10 87 D3
Ashbrook Rd Bollington SK10 87 F4
Nether Alderley SK10 85 F3
Ashburn Gr SK4 240 D7
Ashburn Rd SK4 240 D7
Ashburton Rd SK3 240 E1
Ashbury Cl WA7 24 B1
Ashbury Dr WA11 1 B4
Ashby Dr 15 CW11 174 B3
Ashby Pl CH2 237 F4
Ashcroft SK9 59 F3
Ashcroft Ave CW2 206 A2
Ashcroft Rd WA13 19 D2
Ashdale Cl ST7 193 E3
Ashdale Dr SK8 239 B2
Ashdend Cty Prim Sch SK9 59 F3
Ashdene Rd SK9 59 F3
Ashdown La WA3 10 A3
Ashdown Rd
Manchester SK4 240 C7
Ollerton WA16 82 C3
Ashenhurst Rd ST7 193 F2
Ashenough Rd ST7 210 B3
Ashfield Cl WA13 19 D2
Ashfield Cres Bebington L62 43 E4
Blacon CH1 117 E3
Cheadle SK8 239 D6
Ashfield Dr SK10 87 D1
Ashfield Gr M44 11 F3
Ashfield Rd
Altrincham WA15 238 E3
Bebington L62 43 E4
Cheadle SK8 239 D5
Cheadle SK8 239 D6
Ellesmere Port L65 70 B3
Sale M33 242 B7
Ashfield Rd N L65 70 B3
Ashford Cl SK9 34 B2
Ashford Rd SK9 60 A2
Ashford Way WA8 13 E1
Ashgate La CW9 79 F3
Ashgrove CW7 149 E4
Ashlands Frodsham WA6 74 B4
Sale M33 242 A7
Ashlea Dr CW5 205 F3
Ashleigh Cl CH4 140 C3
Ashley CE Contr Prim Sch WA15 31 F3
Ashley Cl Haslington CW1 191 E3
Warrington WA4 17 E2
Ashley Ct Altrincham WA15 238 E1
Holt LL13 196 B4
Ashley Dr
Cheadle Hulme SK7 35 E3
Hartford CW8 103 D3
Ashley Gdns Clutton CH3 182 B1
High Lane SK6 37 E4
3 Hyde SK14 241 E5
Ashley Grange CW9 103 F2
Ashley Mews 2 SK14 241 E5
Ashley Mill La WA14 31 E4
Ashley Mill Rd N WA14 31 F4
Ashley Rd Altrincham WA15 238 E2
Ashley WA15 31 F4
Mere WA16 56 B4
Rostherne WA14 31 E2
Runcorn WA7 23 E1
Wilmslow SK9 34 A1
Ashley Ret Pk WA8 23 D4
Ashley Sch WA8 12 B1
Ashley St SK14 241 E8
Ashley Sta WA15 31 F3
Ashley Way WA8 23 D4
Ashley Way W WA8 22 C4
Ashleys The SK4 240 B7
Ashmead Cl ST7 193 F2
Ashmead Mews ST7 193 F2
Ashmore Ave SK3 239 F7
Ashmore Cl
Middlewich CW10 151 E3
Warrington WA3 10 A2
Ashmore's La ST7 193 E2
Ashmuir Cl Blacon CH1 117 F2
Crewe CW1 190 A3
Ashness Dr SK7 35 F4
Ashridge St WA7 22 C2
Ashton Ave
Altrincham WA14 238 E6
Macclesfield SK10 86 B1
Ashton Cl Bebington L62 43 F2
Congleton CW12 157 D1
Frodsham WA6 49 E1
Middlewich CW10 151 E3
Runcorn WA7 48 C3
Ashton Dr WA6 49 E1
Ashton Hayes Cty Prim Sch CH3 121 F4
Ashton La Ashton CH3 121 F3
Sale M33 242 A7
Ashton Rd Hyde SK14 241 E8
Manley WA6 99 F2
Newton-le-W WA12 2 B3
Norley WA6 100 A2
Ashton St WA2 16 A3
Ashton's Green Sch WA9 1 A2
Ashton-under-Lyne Sixth Form Coll OL6 242 B3
Ashtree Cl Neston L64 67 D4
Prestbury SK10 87 E4
Ashtree Croft L64 68 A4
Ashtree Dr L64 67 D4
Ashtree Farm Ct L64 68 A4
Ashurst Dr SK3 & SK8 240 B1
Ashville Ct CW2 206 A4
Ashville Ind Est WA7 49 F2
Ashville Rd WA7 49 F2
Ashwood WA14 31 D4
Ashwood Ave Goldborne WA3 3 E4
Warrington WA1 16 C4
Ashwood Cl Barnton CW8 78 A2
Ellesmere Port L66 69 E1
Ashwood Cres CW8 78 A2
Ashwood Ct CH2 119 D2
Ashwood La CH2 96 A3
Ashwood Rd SK12 38 B3
Ashworth Cl WA14 238 B1
Ashworth Pk WA16 81 F4
Askerbank La SK11 159 D1
Askett Cl WA11 1 B4
Askrigg Ave L66 69 D3
Aspen Cl Ellesmere Port L66 69 F1
Heswall L60 41 E4
Kidsgrove ST7 195 F2
Stockport SK4 240 A5
Aspen Gn M34 241 A6
Aspen Gr Saughall CH1 117 D4
Warrington WA1 17 D4
Aspen Way Chester CH2 119 D2
High Lane SK6 38 A4
Aspen Wood SK14 241 F7
Aspens The
Cuddington CW8 101 E3
Gatley SK8 239 A6
Aspinall Cl WA2 9 D2
Aspull Cl WA3 9 E2
Asquith Cl CW1 191 E3
Assheton Wlk L24 21 F1
Astbury CE Aided Prim Sch CW12 178 A4
Astbury Cl
2 Altrincham WA15 238 E6
Goldborne WA3 4 A4
Kidsgrove ST7 195 E2
Astbury Cres SK3 240 D2
Astbury Dr CW8 78 A2
Astbury Lane Ends CW12 178 C4
Astbury St CW12 156 B1
Aster Cres WA7 49 F3
Aster Rd WA11 1 C4
Aster Wlk M31 11 F1
Astle Ct SK11 84 A2
Astley Cl Warrington WA4 16 A2
Widnes WA8 12 B2
Astley Ct M44 11 F4
Astley Gr SK15 242 C3
Astley Rd Irlam M44 11 F4
Stalybridge SK15 242 C2
Astley St Hyde SK14 241 C8
Stockport SK3 & SK4 240 E5
Astmoor Bridge La WA7 23 F1
Astmoor Cty Prim Sch WA7 23 F1
Astmoor East Interchange WA7 24 A2
Astmoor Ind Est WA7 23 F2
Astmoor La WA7 23 F1
Aston Ave CW7 126 A1
Aston Cl SK3 240 C2
Aston Ct WA1 9 E1
Aston Cty Prim Sch WA7 50 B1
Aston Fields Rd WA7 50 C2
Aston Gn WA7 50 C3
Aston La
Aston (nr Runcorn) WA7 50 C1
Runcorn WA7 50 C3
Sutton WA7 50 B1
Woore CW3 232 C1
Aston La N WA7 50 C2
Aston La S WA7 50 C2
Aston Rd ST5 210 B1
Aston Way
Middlewich CW10 128 C1
11 Wilmslow SK9 34 B3
Astule Dr SK11 112 A4
Atcherley Cl CW5 218 C4
Atherton Cty Inf Sch L65 69 F3
Atherton La M44 11 F3
Atherton Rd L65 69 F3
Atherton St SK3 240 D4
Athey St SK11 112 B4
Athlone Ave SK8 240 C1
Athlone Rd WA2 8 A1
Athol Cl L62 43 F3
Athol Dr L62 43 F3
Athol Rd SK7 35 E3
Athol St SK4 240 D7
Atholl Ave CW2 190 B1
Atholl Cl SK10 87 D1
Athy Cl WA12 1 C2
Atkinson Rd M33 242 A7
Atlanta Ave M90 33 D4
Atlantic Bsns Ctr WA14 238 C7
Atlantic St WA14 238 B6
Attenbury's La WA14 238 E8
Attenbury's Pk Est WA14 238 E8
Atterbury Cl WA8 12 B1
Attlee Ave WA3 5 D2
Attwood Cl CW1 191 E2
Attwood St ST7 195 D1
Aubourn Cl WA8 12 B2
Auburn Ave SK14 241 E5
Auckery Ave L66 69 E2
Auckland Rd CH1 117 E2
Audie Murphy Rd WA5 15 D3
Audlem Cl WA7 49 F2
Audlem Dr CW9 104 A3
Audlem Rd Audlem CW3 230 A4
Hatherton CW5 219 E2
Nantwich CW5 204 C2
Woore CW3 232 A1
Audlem St James' CE Contr Prim Sch CW3 230 A3
Audley Cres CH4 141 F3
Audley Rd Alsager ST7 193 F1
Audley ST7 210 A1
Barthomley CW2 208 C3
Kidsgrove ST7 210 A3
Newcastle-u-L ST7 210 A1
Audley St
Ashton-u-L OL6 242 B2
Crewe CW1 190 B3
Audley St W CW1 190 B3
Audre Cl WA5 14 B3
Aughton Way CH4 139 E2
Augusta Dr SK10 87 D2
Austell Rd M22 33 E4
Austen Cl 2 CW11 174 B3
Austin Cl CW7 149 E3
Austin St CW9 79 E1
Austral Ave WA1 17 E4
Australia La WA4 17 E1
Autumn Ave WA16 57 E1
Avalon Dr M20 239 C8
Avebury Cl Goldborne WA3 3 F4
Widnes WA8 13 F2
Avens Rd M31 11 F2
Avenue St 3 SK1 240 F6
Avenue The
Alderley Edge SK9 60 A1
Alsager ST7 193 E2
Altrincham WA15 31 F4
Bebington L62 43 E4
Comberbach CW9 78 B4
Gatley SK8 239 A1
Great Barrow CH3 120 C4
High Legh WA16 29 E3
Kidsgrove ST7 194 C1
Lymm WA13 18 B1
Marston CW9 79 D2
Newton-le-W WA12 2 B2
Sandbach CW11 174 C4
Tarporley CW6 146 B1
Avery Cl WA2 8 C1
Avery Cres WA11 1 B4
Avery Rd WA11 1 B4
Avery Sq WA11 1 B4
Aviemore Dr WA2 9 D2
Avocet Cl Newton-le-W WA12 2 B2
Warrington WA2 8 B2
Avocet Dr Altrincham WA14 238 B8
Winsford CW7 149 E3
Avon WA8 12 A1
Avon Ave WA5 14 C2
Avon Cl Kidsgrove ST7 195 D1
Macclesfield SK10 87 D1
Neston L64 66 C3
Avon Ct ST7 193 E3
Avon Dr Congleton CW12 156 C1
Crewe CW1 191 D3
Avon Rd Altrincham WA15 31 F4
Cheadle SK8 34 B4
Culcheth WA3 5 D1
Avon St SK3 240 E3
Avon Wlk CW7 127 D1
Avondale L65 70 A1
Avondale Ave L62 43 F3
Avondale Dr WA8 12 A1
Avondale Rd Haydock WA11 1 B4
Stockport SK3 240 C4
Avondale Sch SK3 240 B3
Avonlea Cl CH4 140 C3
Avonside Way SK11 112 B3
Avro Way WA15 32 C4
Axminster Wlk SK7 35 F4
Aycliffe Wlk 5 WA8 22 B4
Aylesbury Cl
Ellesmere Port L66 69 E2
Macclesfield SK10 87 E2
Aylesby Cl WA16 57 D1
Aylsham Cl WA8 12 B2
Aylwin Dr M33 242 C5
Ayrshire Way CW12 157 D1
Aysgarth Av CW1 173 D1
Aysgarth Ave Cheadle SK8 239 C6
Romiley SK6 241 D4
Ayshford Cl WA14 238 B6
Azalea Gr WA7 49 F2

Babage Rd CH5 116 A2
Babbacombe Rd WA5 14 C2
Bache Ave CH2 118 B3
Bache Dr CH2 118 B3
Bache Hall Ct CH2 118 B3
Bache Hall Est CH2 118 B3
Bache Sta CH2 118 B3
Bachefield Ave CH3 142 A3
Bachelor's La CH3 142 A4
Back Adcroft St 4 SK1 240 F3
Back Booth St WA12 2 A2
Back Bridge St WA12 2 A2
Back Brook Pl WA4 16 C2
Back Crosland Terr WA6 73 D1
Back Cross La CW12 179 D4
Back Eastford Rd WA4 16 A1
Back Eddisbury Rd
Macclesfield SK10 113 E4
Rainow SK10 113 E4

Back Forshaw St WA2 16 B4
Back Heathcote St ST7 195 D1
Back High St WA7 23 D1
Back Jodrell St SK22 39 D4
Back La Alpraham CW6 169 E3
Alvanley WA6 73 E1
Antrobus CW9 54 B4
Ashley WA15 32 A2
Bate Heath CW9 54 B4
Beeston CH3 167 E1
Betley CW2 208 B1
Brereton Green CW11 153 E3
Burtonwood WA5 6 B4
Congleton CW12 156 A2
Duddon CW6 145 D3
Dunham Town WA14 20 B3
High Legh WA14 29 F3
No Man's Heath SY14 214 A2
Penketh WA8 14 A2
Peover WA16 106 A4
Plumley WA16 81 D1
Radnor CW12 155 F3
Shavington CW2 206 C2
Threapwood SY14 222 C4
Whitley WA4 52 C2
Wybunbury CW5 220 B3
Back Lanes CW6 146 A1
Back Lawrence St WA12 2 A2
Back Legh St WA12 2 A2
Back Market St WA12 2 A2
Back Massie St SK8 239 D6
Back Paradise St 17 SK11 112 B4
Back Park St CW12 156 C1
Back Queen St CH1 237 E3
Back River St CW12 156 B2
Back Union Rd SK22 39 E4
Back Wallgate 27 SK11 112 B4
Back Water St 2 SK1 240 F6
Backford Cl WA7 50 B3
Backford Gdns CH1 94 C4
Badbury Cl WA11 1 B4
Badcock's La CW6 185 F2
Baddeley Cl SK3 240 D1
Baddiley Cl CW5 203 E1
Baddiley Hall La CW5 217 D4
Baddiley La CW5 203 E1
Baddington La CW5 204 B1
Badger Ave CW1 190 A3
Badger Bait L64 66 C3
Badger Cl WA7 50 A3
Badger Rd Macclesfield SK10 87 E1
Prestbury SK10 87 D4
Badgers Cl Christleton CH3 142 C4
Ellesmere Port CH1 94 C4
Winsford CW7 126 A1
Badgers Pk L64 66 C3
Badgers Set CW8 101 E3
Badgers Wlk CH2 95 F1
Badgers Wood CW2 205 F4
Badgersrake La
Ellesmere Port L66 68 C3
Ledsham L66 68 B2
Puddington L66 68 B2
Bag La Crowton CW8 101 F4
Cuddington CW8 101 F4
Norley WA6 101 D3
Bagley La CW3 230 A1
Bagmere Cl
Brereton Green CW11 153 F2
Sandbach CW11 174 C4
Bagmere La CW11 154 A3
Bagnall Cl WA5 15 E3
Bagot Ave WA5 15 F4
Bagstock Ave SK12 36 C1
Baguley Ave WA8 22 A3
Baguley Cres SK3 240 D2
Baguley La M33 242 E5
Baguley Rd M33 242 E6
Bahama Cl WA11 1 B4
Bahama Rd WA11 1 B4
Bailey Ave L65 69 F3
Bailey Cl CW1 190 B4
Bailey Cres
Congleton CW12 157 D2
Sandbach CW11 175 E3
Bailey Ct ST7 193 F2
Bailey La M31 11 F2
Bailey Wlk WA14 31 E4
Bailey's Bank ST6 179 E2
Bailey's La L24 21 D1
Baileys Cl WA8 13 D3
Baileys La L26 21 D4
Bainbridge Ave WA3 3 F4
Baines Ave M44 11 F4
Baker Dr L66 69 F2
Baker Rd WA7 48 B4
Baker St Macclesfield SK11 112 B4
Stalybridge SK15 242 E1
Stockport SK4 240 E7
Baker's Ct CW7 126 C1
Baker's La CW7 126 C1
Bakers Pl WA2 16 A4
Bakestondale Rd SK10 63 F2
Bakestonedale Rd SK10 64 A2
Bakewell Cl CH1 94 C4
Bakewell Rd
Burtonwood WA5 7 D4
Hazel Grove SK7 36 C4
Bakewell St SK3 240 D3
Bala Cl WA5 7 F1
Baldock Cl WA4 17 E2
Baldon Cres ST7 193 E3
Balfour Cl CW1 191 E2
Balfour Rd WA14 238 D7
Balham Cl WA8 13 D2
Balharry Ave WA11 1 C4
Ball La Bollington SK10 87 E3
Crowton WA6 75 F2
Kingsley WA6 75 F2
Ballater Cres CH3 119 D1
Ballater Dr WA2 8 C2
Balliol Cl Romiley SK6 241 C4
Sutton Lane Ends SK11 112 C2
Balmoral Ave Crewe CW2 190 A1
Northwich CW9 104 A3
Balmoral Cl Knutsford WA16 57 D1
Winsford CW7 126 B2
Balmoral Cres SK10 87 F1
Balmoral Dr
Altrincham WA14 238 F8
Helsby WA6 73 D2
High Lane SK6 37 F4
Holmes Chapel CW4 130 A1
Poynton SK12 36 B2
Stalybridge SK15 242 D3
Balmoral Gdns L65 70 B2
Balmoral Pk CH1 118 A2
Balmoral Rd
Altrincham WA15 238 E4
Manchester SK4 240 A7
Warrington WA4 16 C1
Widnes WA8 12 C2
Balmoral Way SK9 60 A3
Baltic Rd WA14 238 A6
Bamber Ave M33 242 E5
Bamburgh Ct L65 70 C2
Bamford Cl Cheadle SK8 34 B4
Runcorn WA7 49 E4
Bamford St
Macclesfield SK10 87 F1
Stockport SK1 240 F4
Banastre Dr WA12 2 C2
Banbury Cl SK10 87 F1
Banbury Dr
Altrincham WA14 238 E8
Great Sankey WA5 15 E3
Banbury St Kidsgrove ST7 194 B1
11 Stockport SK1 240 F5
Bancroft CW8 76 C2
Bancroft Rd WA8 13 E1
Bandon Cl L24 21 E1
Banff Ave L63 43 E3
Bangor Cl CH1 94 C4
Bangor Rd SK8 239 F6
Bangor St
Ashton-u-L OL6 & SK15 242 B2
Reddish SK5 240 F8
Bank Cl Chester CH2 118 C3
Macclesfield SK11 112 C4
Neston L64 67 D3
Bank Coole La CW5 228 C3
Bank Farm Mews SY14 214 C3
Bank Gdns WA5 14 C2
Bank House La Helsby WA6 73 E2
Smallwood CW11 177 D3
Smallwood CW11 177 D4
Bank La Eaton CW12 134 B1
Rainow SK10 89 E3
Bank Mews WA6 73 E2
Bank Rd Connah's Quay CH5 91 E1
Romiley SK6 241 A3
Bank Side CW8 77 E1
Bank Sq SK9 60 A4
Bank St Cheadle SK8 239 E6
Congleton CW12 156 C1
Goldborne WA3 3 D4
Hollins Green WA3 11 D3
Hyde SK14 241 D7
Kidsgrove ST7 195 E2
Newton-le-W WA12 1 C2
Sale M33 242 C7
Warrington WA1 16 A3
Widnes WA8 23 D2
Bank The ST7 195 D4
Bankes' La WA7 48 C3
Bankfield Ave Irlam M44 11 E3
Stockport SK4 240 C5
Wistaston CW2 206 A4
Bankfield Rd Cheadle SK8 239 F1
Widnes WA8 12 B1
Bankfield Sch The WA8 12 B1
Bankfield St SK5 240 E8
Bankfield Trad Est SK5 240 E8
Bankfields Dr L62 44 A3
Bankhall La WA15 31 F4
Bankhall Rd SK4 240 A6
Bankhey L64 66 C3
Bankhouse Dr CW12 157 D3
Banklands Cl M44 11 E3
Banks Cl CW12 156 B2
Banks Cres WA4 16 C2
Banks Rd L60 40 B4
Banks View CW4 107 F1
Bankside Altrincham WA15 32 B3
Runcorn WA7 50 C4
Bankside Cl Barbridge CW5 187 E3
Wilmslow SK9 34 B1
Bankside Ct Alsager ST7 193 F3
Manchester SK4 240 A6
Bankside Rd M20 239 B7
Banky Fields CW12 156 B1
Bann St SK3 240 E4
Bannister Dr SK8 239 F2
Bannister St SK1 240 F3
Barbauld St WA1 16 A3
Barber Dr ST7 194 C4
Barber St SK11 112 C3
Barber's La Antrobus CW9 53 E3
Northwich CW8 103 F4
Barberry Cl WA14 238 B7
Barberry Wlk M31 11 F1
Barbondale Cl WA5 14 C4
Barbridge Rd ST5 210 B1
Barcheston Rd SK8 239 C4
Barclay Rd SK12 36 C1
Bardell Cl SK12 36 B1
Bardsey Cl L65 70 B1
Bardsley Ave WA5 7 F1
Bardsley St SK4 240 D7
Barford Cl WA5 7 D1
Barford Dr Goldborne WA3 4 A4
Wilmslow SK9 34 B1
Barford Grange L66 68 B4
Barham Ct WA3 9 E2
Barington Dr WA7 50 C4
Baristow Cl CH2 237 E4
Bark St CW12 156 C1
Barker St Crewe CW2 190 B1
Nantwich CW5 204 C3
Barker's Hollow Rd WA4 51 D3
Barker's La M33 242 A6
Barkhill Rd CH2 119 D4
Barley Castle Cl WA4 27 D2
Barley Croft Alsager ST7 193 F1
Cheadle SK8 239 F1
Chester CH3 142 A4
Barley Dr SK7 35 F4
Barley Mow Cl L66 69 E1
Barley Rd WA4 17 E2
Barleycastle La WA4, CW9 27 E2
Barleycastle Trad Est WA4 27 E2
Barleycroft Terr ST7 194 C4
Barleyfields ST7 209 E1
Barleywood Cl CW2 206 A4
Barlow Dr CW7 148 C4
Barlow Fold SK6 241 D3
Barlow Fold Rd SK6 241 D3
Barlow Gr WA9 1 A1
Barlow Hill SK11 136 C1
Barlow Rd Altrincham WA14 238 B7
Moulton CW9 126 C4
Wilmslow SK9 34 A1
Barlow Way CW11 175 D4
Barmouth Cl WA5 7 F1
Barn Croft WA6 73 E2
Barn Croft Rd L26 21 D4
Barn Ct CH3 182 B1
Barn La WA3 2 C4
Barn Meadow CW8 78 C1
Barn Rd Congleton CW12 156 B2
Threapwood SY14 222 B4
Barn St WA8 23 D3
Barn Way WA12 2 A2
Barnabas Ave CW1 189 F3
Barnaby Chase CH3 182 B1
Barnaby Rd SK12 36 B1
Barnack Cl WA1 17 D4
Barnacre Dr L64 41 D1
Barnard Ave SK4 240 B6
Barnard Cl SK11 111 F3
Barnard St WA5 15 E2
Barnbridge Cl ST7 194 C4
Barnbrook Cl CW7 126 A1
Barncroft WA7 50 B4
Barncroft Cl SK11 84 A2
Barnes Ave Manchester SK4 240 A6
Warrington WA2 9 D1
Barnes Cl Blacon CH1 117 F3
Great Sankey WA5 15 D3
Haslington CW1 191 E2
Widnes WA8 13 E1
Barnes Hospl SK8 239 C6
Barnes Rd WA8 13 E1
Barneston Rd WA8 13 F2
Barnett Ave WA12 1 C2
Barnett St SK11 112 A4
Barnett Wlk CW2 206 B4
Barnfield CH3 166 A1
Barnfield Ave Romiley SK6 241 D3
Runcorn WA7 50 B3
Barnfield Cl L66 69 E1
Barnfield Rd Bollington SK10 87 F3
Warrington WA1 17 E4
Barngate Rd M22 239 A6
Barnham Cl WA3 3 D4
Barnhill Farm Cotts SY14 214 B1
Barnhill Grange CH3 183 D2
Barnhill Rd CH3 183 D1
Barnhouse La CH3 98 A2
Barns La WA13 20 A3
Barns Pl WA15 32 B4
Barnside Way
Macclesfield SK10 87 E2
Moulton CW9 126 C4
Barnstaple Way WA5 14 C2
Barnston Ct CH3 180 C1
Barnston Prim Sch L60 41 E4
Barnston Rd L60 41 D4
Barnston Towers Cl L60 41 E4
Barnswood Cl WA4 17 E1
Barnton Cl WA3 3 E4
Barnton Cty Inf Sch CW8 78 A1
Barnton Cty Jun Sch CW8 78 A2
Barnwell Ave WA3 4 B2
Barnwell Cl CW2 206 A4
Barnwood Dr CH4 140 C3
Baron Cl WA1 17 E4
Baron's Cl WA8 22 B4
Baronet Rd WA4 16 A1
Baronia Pl CW5 204 C3
Barons Cl WA7 23 F1
Barons Quay Rd CW9 78 C1
Barons Rd CW2 206 A2
Barony Bldgs CW5 204 C3
Barony Ct CW5 204 C4
Barony Employment Pk The CW5 204 C4
Barony Rd CW5 204 C4
Barony Terr CW5 204 C3
Barony Way CH4 140 C3
Barrack Hill SK6 241 A2
Barrack Hill Cl SK6 241 A3
Barrack Hill Prim Sch SK6 241 A2
Barracks La
Burwardsley CH3 184 B3
Macclesfield SK10 112 C4
Ravensmoor CW5 203 F1
Barracks Sq SK11 112 A3
Barrastitch La CW8 101 F3
Barratt Rd ST7 193 F2
Barrel Well Hill CH2 118 C1
Barrie Gdns ST7 210 B4
Barrington Cl WA14 238 D6
Barrington Rd WA14 238 D5
Barrow Ave WA2 8 B1
Barrow CE Contr Prim Sch CH3 120 B3
Barrow Gn SK8 34 B4
Barrow Hall Cty Prim Sch WA5 14 C4
Barrow Hall Farm CH3 120 C3
Barrow Hall La WA5 14 C4
Barrow La Altrincham WA15 32 A4
Great Barrow CH3 120 B3
Newton-le-W WA3 3 E1
Tarvin CH3 121 E2
Barrow Meadow SK8 34 C4
Barrow's Brow WA16 81 F1
Barrow's Green La WA8 13 F2
Barrow's Row WA8 13 D2
Barrowdale Rd WA3 3 D4
Barrows Cl CW1 190 A4
Barrule Cl WA4 26 B4
Barry Rise WA14 238 A2
Barry St WA4 16 B2
Barrymore Ave WA4 16 C2
Barrymore Cres CW9 78 B4
Barrymore Ct WA4 17 D1
Barrymore Rd Runcorn WA7 49 D4
Warrington WA4 17 D1
Weaverham CW8 77 F1
Barrymore Way L63 43 D3
Bars The CH2 237 F2
Barsbank Cl WA13 18 B2
Barsbank La WA13 18 B2
Barshaw Gdns WA4 26 C2
Barston Ave L65 69 F3
Bartegate WA7 50 A3
Bartholomew Way CH4 141 E3
Bartholomews Ct CH5 116 C3
Barthomley Cres CW2 189 E2
Barthomley Rd
Audley ST7 209 D1
Barthomley CW2 208 A4
Betley ST7 208 C2
Barton Ave WA4 17 D1
Barton Cl Runcorn WA7 50 B4
Wilmslow SK9 34 B1
Barton Ct CW7 126 C1
Barton Fold SK14 241 D5
Barton Rd Barton SY14 181 E1
Congleton CW12 156 C2
Farndon CH3 180 C1
Barton St Goldborne WA3 3 D4
Macclesfield SK11 112 B3
Barton Stad CW7 126 C1
Bartons Pl CW9 79 D1
Barwick Pl M33 242 A6
Barwood Ave ST7 194 A3
Basford Rd CW2 206 B4
Basford Way CW7 126 A1
Basil St SK4 240 E7
Baskervyle Cl L60 41 D3
Baskervyle Rd L60 41 D3
Baslow Dr SK8 34 B4
Bate's Mill La
Beeston CW6 167 F3
Tiverton CW6 167 F3
Bateman Rd CW9 80 A1
Batemans Cl CW2 206 A4
Batemill Cl SK10 86 C1
Batemill La
Peover WA16, SK11 108 B3
Withington WA16, SK11 108 B3
Bates La WA6 73 E2
Bath Cres SK8 35 D3
Bath La CW3 230 A2
Bath Pl WA14 238 D2
Bath St Altrincham WA14 238 D2
Chester CH1 237 F2
Sandbach CW11 175 E3
Warrington WA1 16 A3
Batherton Cl WA8 23 D4
Batherton La CW5 204 C1
Bathwood Dr L64 66 C3
Batterbee Ct CW1 191 E3
Battersby La WA2 16 B3
Battery La WA1 17 F4
Bawtry Ct WA2 8 C1
Baxter Cl WA7 50 B4
Baxter Rd M33 242 B6
Baxter St WA5 15 F3
Baycliffe WA13 18 B1
Baycliffe Cl WA7 49 E3
Bayley Rd CW5 205 E3
Bayley St SK15 242 C1
Bayswater Cl WA7 24 C2
Baytree Ave M34 241 A8
Baytree Cl L66 69 F1
Bayvil Cl WA7 50 C4
Beach Gr CW8 103 E3
Beach House La WA16 32 A1
Beach Rd Hartford CW8 103 D3
Northwich CW8 103 D3
Beachin La CH3 182 A2
Beacon Hill View WA7 48 B4
Beacon La L60 41 D4
Beacon Rd SK6 241 A1
Beaconsfield Cres WA8 13 D2
Beaconsfield Gr WA8 13 D2
Beaconsfield Rd
Altrincham WA14 238 D7
Runcorn WA7 22 C1
Widnes WA8 13 D2
Beaconsfield St CH2 237 F2
Beadnell Dr WA5 14 C2
Beaford Dr M22 33 F4
Beagle Point CW7 126 A1
Beagle Wlk M22 33 F4
Beam Heath Way CW5 204 C4
Beam St CW5 204 C3
Beamont Cty Schs WA2 16 B4
Beamont St WA8 23 D2
Beard Cres SK22 39 E4
Beardsmore Dr WA3 3 F4
Bearhurst La SK11 111 D2
Bearstone Rd
Norton in Hales TF9 236 C2
Woore TF9 236 C2
Beasley Cl L66 69 E2
Beatrice Ave SK8 239 F2
Beatrice St WA4 16 B2
Beatty Ave WA2 8 B1
Beatty Dr CW12 157 D2
Beatty Rd CW5 204 B2
Beaufort Ave M33 242 C5
Beaufort Chase SK9 34 C1
Beaufort Cl
Alderley Edge SK9 60 A1
Great Sankey WA5 15 D3
Runcorn WA7 49 D4
Widnes L26 22 A4
Beaufort Rd
Ashton-u-L OL6 242 A3
Sale M33 242 C5
Beaufort St WA5 15 F2
Beaulieu WA15 238 F2
Beaulieu Ave CW7 126 C1
Beaumaris Cres SK7 36 B4
Beaumaris Dr L65 70 B1
Beaumont Cl Biddulph ST6 179 E2
Chester CH4 140 C3
Prestbury SK10 86 C3
Wistaston CW2 205 F4
Beauty Bank
Foxwist Green CW7 125 F3
Winsford CW7 149 D2
Beaver Ctr The CW9 103 F4
Beaverbrook Ave WA3 5 D2
Beavers Cl WA16 79 F4
Bebbington Cl M33 242 F5
Bebington Rd L66 69 E2
Becconsall Cl CW1 190 A4
Becconsall Dr CW1 190 A4
Bechers WA8 12 A2
Beck La SK10 86 C1
Beckenham Gr 3 CW7 149 D4
Beckett Ave CW7 150 B4
Beckett Dr WA13 19 D4
Beckett's La CH3 142 A4
Beckford Cl CW1 189 F4
Becontree Ave M34 241 A8
Bedells La SK9 60 A3
Bedford Ave
Ellesmere Port L65 70 A1
Hyde SK14 241 E7
Bedford Ave E L65 70 A1
Bedford Ct CW2 190 B1
Bedford Gdns CW2 190 B1
Bedford Gr Alsager ST7 193 D3
Irlam WA3 11 D3
Bedford Pl CW2 190 B1
Bedford Rd Kidsgrove ST7 195 D2
Macclesfield SK11 112 A4
Bedford Rise CW7 149 E3
Bedford St Crewe CW2 190 B1
Warrington WA4 26 B4
Bedward Row CH1 237 D2
Beech Ave Culcheth WA3 5 D2
Frodsham WA6 74 B4
Gatley SK8 239 B5
Goldborne WA3 3 F4
Haydock WA11 1 C4
Mobberley WA16 57 F3
Penketh WA5 14 B2
Rode Heath ST7 193 F4
Stockport SK2 & SK3 240 F2
Warrington WA4 17 E2
Beech Cl Alderley Edge SK9 60 A2
Congleton CW12 156 A2
Cuddington CW8 101 F1
Newton-le-W WA12 2 B1
Ollerton WA16 82 C3
Partington M31 11 F1
Beech Cotts SK9 85 D4
Beech Cres SK12 36 C2
Beech Ct WA3 4 C1
Beech Dr Kidsgrove ST7 210 C4
Knutsford WA16 57 E1
Wistaston CW2 189 F1
Beech Farm Dr SK10 87 E1
Beech Gr Chester CH2 119 D2
Crewe CW1 190 C3
Ellesmere Port CH1 95 D4
Lymm WA13 18 A1
Macclesfield SK11 112 C3
Sandbach CW11 175 E3
Warrington, Latchford WA4 16 B2
Warrington, Paddington WA1 17 D4
Weaverham CW8 102 B4
Wilmslow SK9 60 A3
Winsford CW7 149 E4
Beech Hall Dr SK10 87 E1
Beech Hall Sch SK10 87 E1
Beech Hey La L64 43 D1
Beech Heyes Cl CW8 102 C4
Beech Heyes Dr CW8 102 C4

Beech La Barnton CW8 78 A2
Eaton CW6 147 D3
Macclesfield SK10 87 E1
Norley WA6 75 F1
Romiley SK6 241 C2
Wilmslow SK9 60 A3
Beech Lawn WA14 238 C4
Beech Rd Alderley Edge SK9 .. 60 A2
Altrincham WA15 238 E3
Common Side CW6 124 B1
Heswall L60 41 E4
High Lane SK6 37 F4
Runcorn WA7 49 E4
Sale M33 242 D6
Stockport SK2 & SK3 240 F2
Sutton WA7 50 A2
Warrington WA4 26 B4
Whaley Bridge SK23 65 F4
Beech Rise Crowton CW8 76 A1
Crowton CW8 76 B1
Whaley Bridge SK23 65 E3
Beech St Hyde SK14 241 D7
Middlewich CW10 128 B1
Beech St W CW1 190 B2
Beech Tree Cl CW5 205 E3
Beech View Rd WA6 75 E1
Beechcroft Ave CW2 206 A4
Beechcroft Dr L65 70 A1
Beeches The
Altrincham WA14 238 C2
Chester CH2 119 D3
Helsby WA6 73 E2
Nantwich CW5 204 C3
Beechfield
Altrincham WA14 238 C3
Moulton CW9 126 C4
Beechfield Ave SK9 59 F3
Beechfield Cl L60 41 D4
Beechfield Dr CW10 128 A1
Beechfield Gdns CW8 103 D3
Beechfield Rd
Alderley Edge SK9 85 D4
Cheadle Hulme SK8 35 D4
Ellesmere Port L65 70 A3
Stockport SK3 240 F1
Warrington WA4 17 D1
Beechfields CW7 150 A4
Beechlands Ave CH3 119 D1
Beechmill Dr WA3 4 C2
Beechmoore WA4 25 D3
Beechmuir CH1 117 F2
Beechtree Farm Cl WA16 29 E4
Beechtree La WA13 29 D4
Beechurst Rd SK8 240 B1
Beechway Bollington SK10 88 A4
Chester CH2 118 B3
High Lane SK6 37 F4
Wilmslow SK9 60 A3
Beechways WA4 26 B3
Beechways Dr L64 66 B4
Beechwood
Altrincham WA14 238 B1
Knutsford WA16 57 E1
Beechwood Ave
Great Sankey WA5 14 C3
Hartford CW8 103 D3
Newton-le-W WA12 2 B2
3 Reddish SK5 240 F8
Romiley SK6 241 D2
Runcorn WA7 49 F3
Stalybridge SK15 242 F4
Warrington WA1 16 C4
Beechwood Cty Prim Sch
Crewe CW1 190 B3
Runcorn WA7 49 F3
Beechwood Dr Alsager ST7 193 D2
Eaton (nr Congleton) CW12 156 C4
Ellesmere Port L66 69 E1
Higher Wincham CW9 79 F3
Wilmslow SK9 60 C4
Beechwood Gr SK8 35 D4
Beechwood La
Culcheth WA3 4 B2
Stalybridge SK15 242 F4
Beechwood Mews SK10 87 E1
Beechwood Rd
Bebington L62 43 E4
Broughton CH4 140 C3
Beecroft Cl WA5 7 E1
Beeley St SK14 241 E6
Beeston Ave WA15 238 F6
Beeston Brow SK10 88 A4
Beeston Castle CW6 167 F2
Beeston Cl Bollington SK10 63 E1
Holmes Chapel CW4 130 A2
Middlewich CW10 151 E3
Warrington WA3 9 E2
Beeston Ct WA7 24 B2
Beeston Dr Alsager ST7 193 E2
Knutsford WA16 82 A4
Winsford CW7 149 E4
Beeston Gn L66 69 F3
Beeston Gr SK3 240 E1
Beeston Mount SK10 63 E1
Beeston Rd Broughton CH4 139 D2
Higher Kinnerton CH4 161 D4
Wilmslow SK9 34 B3
Beeston St CW8 103 F4
Beeston Terr SK11 111 F3
Beeston View CH4 141 F4
Beggarman's La WA16 82 A4
Beilby Rd WA11 1 C4
Belfry Cl SK9 60 B4
Belfry Dr SK10 87 E2
Belgrave Ave Alsager ST7 193 E3
Broughton CH4 140 C3
Congleton CW12 156 B2
Warrington WA1 16 C4
Belgrave Cl Dodleston CH4 162 A3
Goldborne WN7 4 B4
Widnes WA8 13 F2
Belgrave Cty Inf Sch CH4 141 D3
Belgrave Dr L65 69 F3
Belgrave Pl CH4 237 E1
Belgrave Rd
Altrincham WA14 238 C3
Chester CH3 142 A4
Crewe CW2 190 A1
Irlam M44 11 E3
Macclesfield SK11 112 B2
Northwich CW9 104 A2
Sale M33 242 A6
Belgrave St CH2 237 F3
Belgravia Gdns WA15 31 F4
Bell Ave SK11 112 C2
Bell House Rd WA8 13 E1
Bell La WA4 17 F2
Bell Meadow Ct CW6 146 B1
Bellaport Rd TF9 236 A2
Bellard Dr CH2 119 D2
Belldale Cl SK4 240 A6
Belle Vue Terr CW11 175 D3
Bellemonte Rd WA6 74 B3
Belleville Ave M22 33 F4
Bellhouse La
Higher Walton WA4 25 E4
Warrington WA4 17 E1
Bellingham Dr WA7 49 D4
Bellsfield Cl WA13 18 C1
Bellvue La CH3 119 F2
Belmont Ave
Macclesfield SK10 86 B1
Sandbach CW11 175 D4
Warrington WA4 16 C2
Belmont Cl SK4 240 E7
Belmont Cres WA5 15 D3
Belmont Hall
(Boarding Sch) CW9 53 F1
Belmont Rd
Altrincham WA15 238 E2
Bramhall SK7 35 F3
Gatley SK8 239 B6
Great Budworth CW9 53 F1
Northwich CW9 104 B4
Sale M33 242 A8
Widnes WA8 13 E1
Belmont Sh Ctr SK4 240 E7
Belmont St SK4 240 E7
Belmont Way SK4 240 E7
Belvedere Cl WA6 49 E1
Belvedere Dr CH1 117 F2
Belvedere Rd WA12 2 A3
Belvedere Terr ST7 193 F4
Belvoir Rd Warrington WA4 26 A4
Widnes WA8 13 D1
Bembridge Cl
Great Sankey WA5 14 B4
Widnes WA8 12 C2
Bembridge Ct CW10 151 E4
Bemrose Ave WA14 238 C6
Ben Nevis Dr L66 68 C3
Benbow St M33 242 B7
Benbrook Gr 12 SK9 34 B1
Benbrook Way SK11 111 F1
Bendee Ave L64 67 D4
Bendee Rd L64 67 D4
Bengal St SK3 240 E4
Benja Fold SK7 35 F3
Benjamins Way ST7 209 F1
Bennet Cl L64 68 A4
Bennet Rd CW9 104 B3
Bennett Ave WA1 16 C3
Bennett Cl 4 SK3 240 C4
Bennett St Stalybridge SK15 242 D1
3 Stockport SK3 240 C4
Warrington WA1 16 A3
Bennett's La
Higher Kinnerton CH4 161 D4
Widnes WA8 13 F1
Bennetts La SK11 158 C3
Benson Rd WA3 9 E2
Benson Wlk 6 SK9 34 B1
Bent La Astbury CW12 178 A4
Crowton CW8 101 E4
Culcheth WA3 5 D1
Partington WA13 19 E4
Bentham Ave WA2 8 B2
Bentham Rd WA3 5 D1
Bentinck Rd WA14 238 C4
Bentinck St WA7 22 C2
Bentley Dr CW1 191 D3
Bentley Gr CW7 149 E3
Bentley's Farm La WA4 52 C3
Bentleys The SK5 240 F7
Benton Dr CH2 118 B2
Bentside Rd SK12 38 B3
Benty Heath La
Thornton Hough L64 42 C2
Willaston L64 43 D2
Beresford St WA1 16 C4
Berisford Cl WA15 238 E7
Berkeley Ave ST7 193 E3
Berkeley Cl Goldborne WA3 4 B4
Hyde SK14 241 D5
Berkeley Cres Hyde SK14 241 D5
Wistaston CW2 206 A4
Berkeley Ct WA7 24 B2
Berkeley Rise CW7 149 D4
Berkley Dr CH4 141 E3
Berkshire Cl SK10 86 C1
Berkshire Dr
Congleton CW12 156 B2
Irlam M44 11 E3
Warrington WA1 17 F4
Berlin Rd SK3 240 D2
Bernard Ave WA4 26 B4
Bernisdale Rd WA16 57 F2
Bernsdale Cl CH5 116 A2
Berristal Rd SK10 88 C2
Berry Cl Ellesmere Port L66 69 E2
Wilmslow SK9 60 A3
Berry Dr L66 69 E2
Berry Rd WA8 12 B1
Berrycroft La SK6 241 A3
Berrystead CW8 103 D2
Bertram St
Newton-le-W WA12 2 A2
Sale M33 242 E6
Berwick Ave L62 43 F2
Berwick Cl Macclesfield SK10 86 C1
Warrington WA1 17 F3
Berwick Ct CW4 130 A1
Berwick Gdns L66 69 D3
Berwick Gr L66 69 D3
Berwick Rd L66 69 D3
Berwyn Ave SK8 240 B1
Berwyn Cl L66 69 D3
Berwyn Gr WA9 1 A2
Bessancourt CW4 130 B2
Bessemer Rd M44 11 F3
Beswick St SK11 112 A4
Beswicks La Lindow End SK9 59 E2
Norton in Hales TF9 236 B1
Beswicks Rd CW8 78 C1
Betchton Cres CW11 175 E4
Betchton Rd CW11 175 F1
Betchworth Cres WA7 49 E3
Betchworth Way SK10 87 E2
Bethesda Spec Sch SK8 239 D3
Betjeman Cl WA4 16 C2
Betjeman Way CW1 190 C3
Betley Cl CW9 104 A3
Betley St CW1 190 B2
Betleymere Rd SK8 239 F4
Betsyfield Dr WA3 9 D4
Bettisfield Ave L62 43 E3
Betty's La CW6 168 B1
Bevan Ave ST7 210 C3
Bevan Cl WA5 15 E3
Beverley Ave Appleton WA4 26 B4
Denton M34 241 A6
Beverley Dr L60 41 D3
Beverley Rd WA5 15 E3
Beverley Way
Ellesmere Port L66 69 D4
Macclesfield SK10 87 E2
Bevin Ave WA3 5 D2
Bevyl Rd L64 41 D1
Bewley Ct CH3 142 A4
Bewsey Farm Cl WA5 15 E4
Bewsey Ind Est WA2 16 A4
Bewsey Rd WA5 15 F3
Bewsey St WA2 16 A3
Bexhill Ave
Altrincham WA15 238 F6
Warrington WA2 8 A2
Bexington Dr CW1 190 A4
Bexton Ave CW7 126 A1
Bexton Cty Prim Sch WA16 81 F4
Bexton La WA16 82 A4
Bexton Rd WA16 56 C1
Bibby Ave WA1 16 C3
Bibby St ST7 193 F4
Bickerton Ave WA6 74 B4
Bickerton CE Contr
Prim Sch SY14 200 A4
Bickerton Cl WA3 9 E2
Bickerton Rd WA14 238 B6
Bickerton Way CW9 103 F2
Bickley Cl
Hough Common CW2 206 C1
Runcorn WA7 23 E1
Warrington WA2 8 C2
Bickley Town La SY14 214 C3
Bicknell Cl WA5 15 D4
Bida La CW12 179 D4
Biddulph Common Rd
CW12 179 F4
Biddulph Grange Ctry Pk
ST8 179 F2
Biddulph Grange Hospl
ST8 179 F2
Biddulph Park Rd ST6 179 F3
Biddulph Rd Biddulph ST7 195 F3
Congleton CW12 179 D4
Kidsgrove ST7 195 F3
Biddulph St CW12 179 E4
Biddy's La SK10 88 A1
Bideford Rd WA5 14 C2
Bidston Cl CH2 118 B3
Bidston Dr SK9 34 C1
Bidston Gn L66 69 E2
Bidvale Way CW1 190 B4
Big Field La CW6 146 A4
Biggin Ct WA2 8 C1
Bignall End Rd ST7 210 A2
Billington Ave WA12 2 B3
Billington Cl WA5 14 C4
Billington Rd WA8 12 A2
Bilson Dr SK3 240 B3
Bilton Cl WA8 13 F1
Bilton Way CW1 189 F3
Bings Rd SK23 65 F4
Bingswood Ave SK23 65 F4
Bingswood Ind Est SK23 65 F4
Bingswood Rd SK23 65 F4
Binney Rd CW9 104 A4
Binns St SK15 242 B1
Binyon Way CW1 191 D2
Birch Ave Alsager ST7 193 F1
Crewe CW1 190 C3
Irlam M44 11 E3
Macclesfield SK10 87 D1
3 Manchester SK4 240 B8
Birch Ave continued
Romiley SK6 241 D2
Sale M33 242 B5
Warrington WA2 8 A2
Wilmslow SK9 59 F3
Winsford CW7 127 D1
Birch Brook Rd WA13 19 D3
Birch Cl Crewe CW1 190 C3
Holmes Chapel CW4 130 B2
Birch Cres WA12 1 C2
Birch Ct CW12 155 F2
Birch Fold CW4 107 D1
Birch Gdns CW11 175 E3
Birch Gr Ellesmere Port L66 70 A1
Higher Wincham CW9 79 F3
Knutsford WA16 57 E1
Lostock CW9 105 D4
Warrington, Bruche WA1 16 C4
Warrington, Latchford WA4 16 B2
Birch Heath La CH3 142 C4
Birch Heath Rd CW6 168 B4
Birch House Rd ST5 210 B1
Birch La
Hough Common CW2 206 C1
Winsford CW10 127 F1
Birch Rd Audley ST7 209 F1
Chester CH4 140 C3
Congleton CW12 155 F2
Gatley SK8 239 A5
Haydock WA11 1 C4
Partington M31 11 E2
Poynton SK12 36 C1
Runcorn WA7 49 E4
Widnes WA8 13 D2
Birch Rise CH2 118 B3
Birch Tree Ave SK7 37 D4
Birch Tree Cl WA14 238 C1
Birch Tree Ct CH2 237 F4
Birch Tree La Antrobus WA4 53 D3
Goostrey CW4 107 E1
The Bank ST7 195 D4
Birch Tree Rd WA3 3 F4
Birch Way SK10 86 C3
Birchall Ave WA3 4 C2
Birchall Moss La CW5 219 F1
Birchall St WA3 9 D4
Birchall Wlk CW2 206 B4
Birchdale WA14 238 C2
Birchdale Ave SK8 239 B2
Birchdale Cres WA4 26 B4
Birchdale Rd Appleton WA4 26 B4
Warrington WA1 17 D4
Birchen Rd L26 21 D4
Birchenwood Rd ST7 195 F1
Birches Cl L60 41 D4
Birches Croft Dr SK10 86 C1
Birches La Lach Dennis CW9 105 D4
Lostock CW9 105 D4
Birches The Broughton CH4 139 D2
Crewe CW2 206 B4
Neston L64 41 F1
Birches Way ST7 195 D1
Birchfield Ave
Rode Heath ST7 193 F4
Widnes WA8 13 D1
Birchfield Mews 3 SK14 241 D6
Birchfield Rd Cheadle SK3 240 A3
Great Sankey WA5 15 D3
Lymm WA13 19 D2
Widnes WA8 13 D2
Birchfields WA15 238 F1
Birchgate Cl SK10 86 C1
Birchin Cl CW5 205 D3
Birchin La CW5 205 D3
Birchinall Cl SK11 112 A4
Birchmuir CH1 117 F2
Birchmuir Cl CW1 190 A3
Birchvale Ave SK6 241 D3
Birchway Bollington SK10 88 A4
Cheadle Hulme SK7 35 E4
Heswall L60 41 E3
High Lane SK6 37 F4
Birchways WA4 26 C3
Birchwood Bvd WA3 9 E1
Birchwood CE Aided
Prim Sch WA3 9 F2
Birchwood Cl
Ellesmere Port L66 69 E1
Elton CH2 72 B2
Stockport SK4 240 A5
Birchwood
Comm High Sch WA3 9 E2
Birchwood Dr
Nantwich CW5 204 C3
Peover WA16 106 B4
Wilmslow SK9 60 B4
Birchwood Park Ave WA3 9 E3
Birchwood Sta WA3 9 F1
Bird Hall La SK3 & SK8 240 B2
Bird Hall Rd SK8 240 C1
Bird's La CW6 186 A4
Birds La CH3 166 C1
Birdwell Dr WA5 15 D3
Birkdale Ave L63 43 E3
Birkdale Cl Bramhall SK7 35 F4
Macclesfield SK10 87 E2
Birkdale Ct CW9 104 A4
Birkdale Dr ST7 195 E2
Birkdale Rd Penketh WA5 14 C2
Widnes WA8 13 D3
Birkenhead Rd L64 42 C1
Birkenhead St CW9 104 B4
Birkett Ave L65 70 B1
Birkin Cl WA16 57 E2
Birkinheath La WA14 31 D2
Birley Cl WA15 238 F7
Birley St WA12 2 B2
Birstall Ct WA7 49 E4
Birtles Cl Cheadle SK8 240 A1
Sandbach CW11 175 E4
Birtles La SK10 85 F1
Birtles Rd SK10 86 B1
Birtles Way 6 SK9 34 B3
Birtlespool Rd SK8 239 F4
Birtley Ct WA8 12 A1
Birtwistle Rd CW9 104 B3
Bishop Rd SK10 88 A4
Bishop Reeves Rd WA11 1 C4
Bishop St CH2 118 C2
Bishop's Cl Cheadle SK8 240 A1
Kidsgrove ST7 210 B4
Bishopdale Cl WA5 14 C4
Bishopgates Dr CW9 103 F2
Bishops' (Blue Coat)
CE (Aided) High Sch The
CH3 142 A4
Bishops Cl WA14 238 B1
Bishops Ct Broughton CH4 139 E2
Warrington WA2 7 F2
Bishops Gdns L65 70 A3
Bishops Way WA8 13 E2
Bishops Wood CW5 204 C1
Bishopsfield Ct CH2 118 C2
Bishopton Dr SK11 111 F4
Bispham Rd WA5 15 D2
Bittern Cl Poynton SK12 36 A2
Runcorn WA7 50 B4
Warrington WA2 8 B2
Bittern Gr SK10 87 D1
Bk Adcroft St SK1 240 F3
Bk Grosvenor St SK15 242 D1
Bk Knowl St SK15 242 E2
Bk Melbourne St SK15 242 D1
Black Denton's Pl WA8 13 E1
Black Diamond St CH2 237 E4
Black Firs Cty Prim Sch
CW12 155 F2
Black Firs La CW12 155 F2
Black Friars CH1 237 D2
Black La SK10 87 F1
Black Lion La L66 69 E3
Black Moss Rd WA14 20 C4
Black Park Rd SY13 226 B1
Black Rd SK11 112 C4
Blackacres Cl CW11 174 C3
Blackberry Cl WA14 238 B8
Blackboards La L66 69 D4
Blackbrook Cl WA8 12 B2
Blackbrooke Ave WA2 8 C1
Blackburn Cl WA3 3 F4
Blackburne Ave WA8 22 A3
Blackburne Cl WA2 9 E1
Blackcroft Ave CW8 78 A1
Blackden La Goostrey CW4 108 A2
Siddington SK11 132 C4
Blackden Wlk 9 SK9 34 B1
Blackdown Cl L66 69 D3
Blackeys La L64 66 C4
Blackhill La WA16 81 F4
Blackhurst Brow SK10 61 D1
Blackhurst St WA1 16 A3
Blackledge Cl WA2 9 D2
Blackshaw Cl CW12 157 D1
Blackshaw Dr WA5 7 D1
Blackshaw La SK9 59 F1
Blackshaw St
20 Macclesfield SK11 112 B4
4 Stockport SK3 240 E4
Blackthorn Cl
Broughton CH4 139 D2
Huntington CH3 142 A3
Blackthorn Pl ST5 210 C1
Blackthorn Wlk M31 11 E1
Blackthorne Ave CH1 95 D4
Blackwell Cl CW10 151 E3
Blacon Ave CH1 118 A3
Blacon Cty High Sch CH1 117 E2
Blacon Cty Inf Sch CH1 117 F3
Blacon Hall Cty Jun Sch
CH1 117 F3
Blacon Hall Rd CH1 117 F3
Blacon Point Rd CH1 117 F2
Blagg Ave CW5 204 B2
Blair Cl SK7 36 B4
Blair Dr WA8 12 A2
Blairgowrie Dr SK10 87 D2
Blaizefield Cl CW3 232 B1
Blake Cl Blacon CH1 117 F3
Wistaston CW2 189 F1
Blake La CW8 102 A1
Blake St CW12 156 B2
Blakeacre Rd L26 21 D3
Blakeden La CW7 148 C4
Blakeley Brow L63 43 D3
Blakeley Ct L63 43 D4
Blakeley Dene L63 43 D4
Blakeley Rd L63 43 D3
Blakelow Bank SK11 112 C3
Blakelow Cl CW10 151 D4
Blakelow Cres CW5 205 F2
Blakelow Rd SK11 112 C3
Blakely La WA16 58 C4
Blakemere Ave M33 242 E5
Blakemere Cl SY13 226 A1
Blakemere Ct L65 70 B4
Blakemere La WA6 100 B2
Blakemere Way CW11 174 C4
Blandford Ct SK15 242 D2
Blandford Dr SK11 111 F4
Blandford Rd
Great Sankey WA5 15 D3
Stockport SK4 240 C6
Blandford St SK15 242 D2

Blankney The CW5 204 C2
Blantern Rd CH4 161 D4
Blantyre St WA7 22 C2
Blaven Cl SK3 240 F1
Blaze Hill SK10 88 C4
Bleasdale Rd CW1 173 D1
Bleeding Wolf La ST7 194 C3
Blenheim Cl
Altrincham WA14 238 D2
Davenham CW9 103 F2
Macclesfield SK10 87 D1
Poynton SK12 36 C2
Warrington WA2 8 C1
Wilmslow SK9 60 B4
Wistaston CW2 205 F4
Blenheim Ct ST7 193 E3
Blenheim Gdns CW7 149 E4
Blessed Thomas Holford RC High Sch WA15 238 E4
Bloom St SK3 240 D4
Bloomsbury Way WA8 12 B2
Blossom Hts CW8 103 E4
Blossom Rd M31 11 F1
Blossoms Hey SK8 239 E1
Blossoms Hey Wlk SK8 239 E1
Blossoms La
Cheadle Hulme SK7 35 D1
Wilmslow SK7 35 D1
Blossoms St 5 SK2 240 F3
Blue Cap La SY14 213 E4
Blue Chip Bsns Pk WA14 238 C7
Blue Hatch WA6 74 B4
Bluebell Ave WA11 1 C4
Bluebell Cl Huntington CH3 142 A3
Macclesfield SK10 87 E2
Northwich CW8 78 C1
Bluebell Ct WA7 49 F2
Bluebell Gr SK8 239 D4
Bluebell La SK10 87 E2
Bluebell Mews SK10 87 E2
Blueberry Rd WA14 238 A2
Bluecoat St WA2 16 A4
Blundell Rd WA8 22 B4
Blyth Cl Macclesfield SK10 86 C1
Runcorn WA7 50 B3
Blyth Rd L63 43 E4
Blythe Ave
Cheadle Hulme SK7 35 E3
Congleton CW12 156 A1
Widnes WA8 13 D3
Blythe Pl CW7 127 D1
Blythings The CW6 146 B2
Board St OL6 242 A4
Boardman St SK14 241 D6
Boat Stage WA13 18 C2
Boathorse Rd ST7 210 C4
Boathouse La L64 41 E2
Bob's La M44 11 E2
Boddens Hill Rd SK4 240 A5
Boden St SK11 112 B4
Bodiam Ct L65 70 C1
Bodmin Ave SK10 86 C1
Bodmin Cl WA7 50 A3
Bodmin Dr SK7 35 F4
Bodnant Cl CW1 190 A4
Bold Cross WA8 13 F4
Bold Ind Est WA8 13 E3
Bold La Bold Heath WA5 6 B4
Burtonwood WA5 6 B4
Bold Pl CH1 237 E3
Bold Sq CH2 237 F3
Bold St Altrincham WA14 238 D3
Haslington CW1 191 E2
Runcorn WA7 23 D2
Sandbach CW11 175 D3
Warrington WA1 16 A3
Widnes WA8 23 D4
Bolesworth Hill Rd CH3 183 E2
Bolesworth Rd Broxton CH3 183 E4
Chester CH2 118 C3
Tattenhall CH3 183 E4
Boleyn Cl CH1 117 F3
Boleyn Ct WA7 24 B2
Boleynwood Ct SK9 34 A1
Bolland's Ct CH1 237 D2
Bollin Ave Altrincham WA14 238 B1
Winsford CW7 127 D1
Bollin Cl Alsager ST7 192 C2
Culcheth WA3 5 D1
Lymm WA13 19 D2
Sandbach CW11 174 C4
Winsford CW7 127 D1
Bollin Cross Sch SK9 34 A1
Bollin Ct Altrincham WA14 238 B1
Wilmslow SK9 60 B4
Bollin Dr Altrincham WA14 238 E8
Congleton CW12 156 C1
Lymm WA13 19 D2
Bollin Gr ST6 179 F1
Bollin Hill SK9 60 A4
Bollin Mews SK10 86 C4
Bollin Prim Sch WA14 238 B1
Bollin Sq WA14 238 B1
Bollin Way SK10 87 D3
Bollin Wlk SK9 60 A4
Bollinbarn SK10 87 D1
Bollinbarn Dr SK10 87 D1
Bollinbrook CE Aided Prim Sch SK10 87 D1
Bollinbrook Rd SK10 87 D1
Bollington Ave CW9 104 A3
Bollington Cross CE Contr Prim Sch SK10 87 F4
Bollington La SK10 84 C1
Bollington Rd SK10 87 F3
Bollinway WA15 32 A4
Bollinwood Chase SK9 60 B4
Bolshaw Cty Prim Sch SK8 34 A4
Bolshaw Farm La SK9 34 B3
Bolshaw Rd SK9 34 B3
Bolton Ave
Cheadle Hulme SK8 35 D3
Warrington WA4 16 C2
Bolton Cl Goldborne WA3 4 A4
Poynton SK12 36 B2
Bolton Jun Sch WA4 16 C2
Bombay Rd SK3 240 C3
Bombay St OL6 242 A4
Bomish La CW4, SK11 108 B2
Bonar Cl SK3 240 C4
Bonar Rd 5 SK3 240 C4
Bond Cl WA5 15 E2
Bond St Macclesfield SK11 112 B4
Northwich CW8 78 B1
Stalybridge SK15 242 D3
Bonis All La SK10 61 F2
Bonville Chase WA14 238 A4
Bonville Rd WA14 238 A4
Boon Hill Rd ST7 209 F1
Booth Ave Ashton CH3 121 F4
Little Budworth CW6 147 F4
Sandbach CW11 175 E3
Booth Bed La
Allostock WA16 107 D2
Goostrey WA16 107 D2
Booth Cl SK15 242 C1
Booth La Middlewich CW10 151 F3
Sandbach CW10 151 F3
Booth Rd Altrincham WA14 238 C4
Hartford CW8 103 D2
Sale M33 242 B8
Wilmslow SK9 34 A1
Booth St Audley ST7 209 E1
Congleton CW12 156 B1
Hyde SK14 241 E5
Newton-le-W WA12 2 A2
Stockport SK3 240 E3
Warrington WA5 15 F2
Booth's Hill Cl WA13 18 B2
Booth's Hill Rd WA13 18 B2
Booth's La WA13 18 A1
Boothbank La WA14 30 A3
Boothby St 8 SK11 112 B4
Boothfields WA16 57 E1
Booths La WA4 52 C3
Boothsdale CW6 122 B2
Boothsmere Cl CW11 174 C4
Border Rd L60 41 D4
Border Way CH3 119 E1
Bordon Rd SK3 240 B3
Borganey Ct CH4 162 B1
Borough Rd
Altrincham WA15 238 E4
Congleton CW12 156 C2
Borough St SK15 242 D1
Borras Rd LL13 196 A4
Borron Rd WA12 2 A3
Borrowdale Ave Gatley SK8 239 B4
Warrington WA2 8 B2
Borrowdale Cl Crewe CW2 189 F2
Frodsham WA6 74 B4
Borrowdale Rd WA8 22 B4
Borrowmore Est CH3 120 C4
Bosden Cl SK9 34 B3
Bosden Fold SK1 240 F4
Bosley Cl Middlewich CW10 151 E3
Wilmslow SK9 34 B1
Bosley Dr SK12 37 D2
Bosley Rd SK3 240 A4
Bosley View CW12 157 D1
Bostock Gn L65 69 F3
Bostock Rd
Macclesfield SK11 111 F4
Moulton CW10 127 E2
Winsford CW7 127 D2
Bostock St WA5 15 F3
Boston Ave WA7 23 E1
Boston Cl Cheadle Hulme SK7 35 E4
Culcheth WA3 4 C2
Boston St SK14 241 E6
Boswell Ave WA4 16 A1
Boteler Ave WA5 15 F4
Bottom St SK14 241 F7
Bottoms La CH4 237 F1
Boughey Rd ST7 209 F1
Boughton CH2 118 C1
Boughton Heath Cty Prim Sch CH3 142 A4
Boughton Hill Ave CH3 119 D1
Boughton Hill Dr CH3 119 D1
Boughton St Paul's Cty Inf Sch CH2 237 F3
Boulderstone Rd SK15 242 D4
Boulevard The
Broughton CH4 139 E2
Ellesmere Port L65 69 F2
Boulton Cl CW11 175 E2
Boundary Ct SK8 239 C5
Boundary La Chester CH4 140 C3
Congleton CW12 179 D4
Heswall L60 41 D4
Peover WA16 108 B4
Siddington SK11 132 C4
Threapwood SY14 222 C4
Boundary La N CW8 101 F1
Boundary La S CW8 101 F1
Boundary Pk L64 66 B4
Boundary Rd SK8 240 A2
Boundary St Northwich CW9 79 F1
Warrington WA1 16 C4
Boundary Terr SK9 33 F3
Bourne Ave WA3 3 E4
Bourne Rd ST7 194 C1
Bourne St Mow Cop ST7 195 E4
Reddish SK4 240 E8
Wilmslow SK9 59 F3
Bournemouth Cl WA7 50 B3
Bournville Ave SK4 240 E8
Bouverie St CH2 237 D4
Boverton Cl WA5 7 F1
Bow Green Rd WA14 238 A1
Bow La WA14 31 D4
Bow St SK3 240 C4
Bowden Cl Congleton CW12 156 A2
Culcheth WA3 4 C2
Warrington WA1 16 C4
Bowden Cres SK22 39 E4
Bowden Dr CW9 104 B4
Bowden View La WA16 29 F1
Bowdon CE Aided Prim Sch WA14 238 C1
Bowdon Prep Sch WA14 238 C2
Bowdon Rd WA14 238 C3
Bowdon Rise WA14 238 D2
Bowdon St SK3 240 E4
Bowe's Gate Rd CW6 169 D1
Bowen Cl Bramhall SK7 35 F3
Widnes WA8 12 B2
Bowen Cooke Ave CW1 190 A3
Bowen St CW2 190 A2
Bower Ave SK4 240 C6
Bower Cres WA4 26 B1
Bower Gr SK15 242 F2
Bower Rd Altrincham WA15 238 F1
Heswall L60 41 E4
Bower St WA8 13 E1
Bowerfield Ave SK7 36 B4
Bowerfield Cres SK7 36 C4
Bowerfold La SK4 240 D6
Bowers Bsns Pk WA8 23 D4
Bowery Ave SK8 34 C3
Bowfell Cl L63 43 E2
Bowfell Dr SK6 37 F4
Bowker St SK14 241 E7
Bowkers Cft CW11 191 F4
Bowland Cl Runcorn WA7 49 F3
Warrington WA3 10 A3
Bowland Croft CW1 173 D1
Bowland Rise CW7 149 D4
Bowling Green Ct
Nantwich CW5 204 C3
Northwich CW8 78 C1
Bowling Green St SK14 241 D6
Bowman Ave WA4 17 D3
Bowman Cres OL6 242 A3
Bowmere Cl Biddulph ST6 179 E1
Tarporley CW6 146 B1
Bowmere Dr CW7 149 E4
Bowmere Rd CW6 146 B1
Bowness Ave Bebington L63 43 E3
Irlam M44 11 E2
Warrington WA2 8 B1
Winsford CW7 126 B1
Bowness Cl CW4 130 A2
Bowness Ct CW12 156 A1
Bowness Rd CW2 189 E2
Bowood Ct WA2 8 A2
Bowring Dr L64 41 D1
Bowyer Ave CW5 204 C3
Box La CW12 155 F2
Box Tree Mews SK11 112 A4
Box Wlk M31 11 E1
Boxgrove Cl WA8 13 D2
Boxmoor Cl CH4 141 D3
Boydell Ave
Warrington, Grappenhall WA4 17 D1
Warrington, Westy WA4 16 C2
Boydell Way CH4 162 A3
Boyle Ave WA2 8 C1
Boyles Hall Rd ST7 209 F1
Brabyns Ave SK6 241 D3
Bracadale Dr SK3 240 F1
Bracepeth Ct L65 70 B2
Bracken Cl Broughton CH4 139 E2
Macclesfield SK10 86 C1
Rode Heath ST7 193 F4
Warrington WA3 9 E3
Bracken Rd L66 69 F2
Bracken Way Barnton CW8 78 A2
Comberbach CW9 78 B4
Frodsham WA6 74 B3
Higher Wincham CW9 79 E2
Knutsford WA16 82 A4
Brackendale Elton CH2 72 A2
Runcorn WA7 49 E4
Brackenlea Pl SK3 240 D1
Brackenwood Cl CW2 206 A4
Brackenwood Dr SK8 239 E4
Brackenwood Mews
Warrington WA4 17 E1
Wilmslow SK9 60 C4
Brackley Ave M44 11 E3
Brackley St Runcorn WA7 22 C2
Warrington WA4 16 B1
Bradburn Rd M44 11 F4
Bradburns La CW8 103 D3
Bradbury Ave WA14 238 A5
Bradbury Gdns CW12 156 C1
Bradbury Rd CW7 127 D1
Bradbury St SK14 241 E5
Braddan Ave M33 242 C5
Braddon Cl CW9 103 F2
Bradeley Hall Rd CW1 191 E3
Bradeley Rd Haslington CW1 191 E2
Haslington, Sydney CW1 191 D3
Bradfield Rd CW1 190 A4
Bradford La SK10 85 E2
Bradford Rd CW7 126 C2
Bradford St CH4 141 E4
Bradgate Ave SK8 239 D1
Bradgate Rd WA14 238 A5
Brading Wlk M22 33 F4
Bradlegh Rd WA12 2 A1
Bradley Bvd WA5 15 D3
Bradley Cl Altrincham WA15 238 E7
Middlewich CW10 151 D4
Bradley Farm La SY13 225 E4
Bradley Fold SK15 242 E2
Bradley La Burtonwood WA5 2 A1
Frodsham WA6 74 B3
Newton-le-W WA5, WA12 1 C1
Bradley St SK11 112 C3
Bradley Way WA8 13 E1
Bradshaw Ave CH4 140 A4
Bradshaw Hall Inf Sch SK8 239 E1
Bradshaw Hall Jun Sch SK8 239 E1
Bradshaw Hall La SK8 34 C4
Bradshaw La Lymm WA13 19 E2
Warrington WA4 17 D2
Bradshaw Lane Cty Prim Sch WA4 17 D1
Bradshaw Pl CW12 156 C1
Bradshaw St WA8 13 D1
Bradwall Rd CW11 175 D4
Bradwall St CW11 175 D4
Bradwell Cl L65 70 A2
Bradwell Dr SK8 34 B4
Bradwell Gr CW12 156 C2
Bradwell Rd Goldborne WA3 3 F4
Hazel Grove SK7 36 C4
Bradwen Cl M34 241 A5
Braemar Ave CW9 104 B4
Braemar Cl
Holmes Chapel CW4 130 B1
Warrington WA2 9 D2
Wistaston CW2 205 F4
Braemar Ct L65 70 C2
Braeside Cl
Ellesmere Port L66 69 E3
Macclesfield SK11 112 C3
Braham Cres M44 11 E2
Braidwood Ave WA16 57 E2
Brains La CW6 169 D3
Braintree Rd M22 33 F4
Brairwood SK9 60 B4
Braithwaite Cl WA7 49 E3
Brake Level ST7 195 D4
Brake The ST7 195 D4
Brake Village ST7 195 D4
Brakeley Rd CW8 77 E2
Bramall Cl CW11 175 E4
Bramall St SK14 241 D8
Bramble Cl Chester CH3 142 A4
Macclesfield SK10 87 D1
Penketh WA5 14 C2
Winsford CW7 126 B2
Bramble Way WA7 49 F2
Brambles The CW1 191 D2
Brambling Cl WA7 49 F3
Bramhall Cl Sale M33 242 E5
Winsford CW7 126 A1
Bramhall Ctr The SK7 35 F3
Bramhall Dr Bebington L62 43 F2
Holmes Chapel CW4 130 A2
Bramhall High Sch SK7 35 F4
Bramhall La SK2 & SK3 240 F1
Bramhall La S SK7 35 F4
Bramhall Park Golf Course SK7 35 E4
Bramhall Rd CW2 189 F1
Bramhall St WA5 15 F3
Bramhall Sta SK7 35 F3
Bramley Cl Bramhall SK7 35 F3
Ellesmere Port CH1 94 C4
Wilmslow SK9 59 E2
Bramley Cres SK4 240 B5
Bramley Ct CW6 122 B3
Bramley Dr SK7 35 F3
Bramley Rd SK7 35 F3
Bramley Wlk WA6 73 D1
Brampton Ave SK10 87 D1
Brampton Ct WA9 1 A2
Bramway Cheadle Hulme SK7 35 E4
High Lane SK6 37 F4
Branch Way WA11 1 B3
Brancote Gdns L62 43 E4
Branden Dr WA16 57 D1
Brandon WA8 12 A1
Brandon Ave SK8 239 B1
Brandon Cl SK9 34 B1
Brandwood Ave WA2 8 A1
Branfield Ave SK8 239 D1
Branksome Dr SK8 239 D1
Branksome Rd SK4 240 B5
Bransdale Cl WA5 14 C4
Bransdale Way SK11 111 F4
Brantfield Ct WA2 8 C1
Brantwood Rd Cheadle SK8 239 F1
Manchester SK4 240 C8
Brassey St CH3 118 C1
Brassey Way CW5 205 E3
Brassey's Contract Rd SY14 199 D1
Brathay Cl WA2 8 A2
Brathwaite Rd WA3 3 E4
Brattswood Dr ST7 194 A3
Bray Cl Cheadle SK8 239 E2
Crewe CW1 190 C3
Runcorn WA7 49 E3
Bray Rd CH4 140 C3
Braystan Gdns SK8 239 B6
Bread St SK11 112 B4
Breamar Cl CH3 119 E2
Breck Rd WA8 13 D1
Breck The L66 69 F4
Brecon Ave SK8 239 E1
Brecon Dr L66 69 F1
Brecon Way CW2 206 A4
Breconway CW7 149 D4
Bredbury Gn SK6 241 A1
Bredon Cl L66 69 D3
Breezehill Cl L64 66 C4
Breezehill Pk L64 66 C4
Breezehill Rd L64 66 C4
Brendon Ave WA2 8 A2
Brendon Gr WA9 1 A2
Brent Cl SK12 36 A2
Brent Rd SK4 240 C5
Brentfield WA8 12 B1
Brentnall Cl WA5 15 E3
Brentnall St 2 SK1 240 F3
Brenton Ave M33 242 A6
Brenton Ct SK8 34 C4
Brentwood M33 242 A6
Brentwood Ave
Altrincham WA14 238 E7
Irlam M44 11 E3
Brentwood Cl SK15 242 F2
Brentwood Cres WA14 238 E6
Brentwood Dr SK8 239 B5
Brentwood Rd CH1 117 F3
Brentwood Sch WA14 238 E7
Brereton CE Aided Prim Sch CW11 153 F3
Brereton Cl
Altrincham WA14 238 C1
Crewe CW2 189 F1
Malpas SY14 213 D2
Runcorn WA7 50 A4
Sandbach CW11 175 E4
Brereton Ct
Brereton Green CW12 154 C3
Cheadle SK8 239 E1
Brereton Dr CW5 204 C4
Brereton Gr M44 11 F3
Brereton Hall Sch CW11 154 A3
Brereton Heath La CW12 154 C3
Brereton Heath Pk CW12 154 B4
Brereton La
Brereton Green CW11 153 D4
Sproston Green CW10 152 C4
Brereton Rd Hartford CW8 103 D2
Wilmslow SK9 34 C2
Breton Cl CH2 118 C3
Bretton Ct Mews CH4 139 F2
Bretton Dr CH4 139 D2
Bretton La CH4 139 F3
Bretton Rd CH4 139 F2
Bretton Wlk M22 33 E4
Brewery La CH3 180 C2
Brewery St
4 Altrincham WA14 238 D4
Stockport SK1 240 F7
Brian Ave Warrington WA2 16 B4
Warrington, Stockton Heath WA4 16 C1
Briar Ave WA3 11 D1
Briar Cl WA16 57 D2
Briar Dr L60 41 D4
Briar La CW8 102 C4
Briar Rd WA3 3 D4
Briardale Cl CW2 205 F4
Briardale Gdns L66 69 E3
Briardale Rd
Ellesmere Port L66 69 E3
Willaston L64 43 D1
Briardene M34 241 A8
Briarfield Ave WA8 12 A1
Briarfield Rd
Ellesmere Port L65 70 A3
Heswall L60 41 D4
Briarlands Cl SK7 35 E3
Briars Mount SK4 240 A6
Briarstead Cl SK7 35 E4
Briarswood ST7 195 D1
Briarwood Ave
Macclesfield SK11 112 B3
Warrington WA1 16 C4
Brick Bank CW5 204 C3
Brick Bank La WA16 107 D1
Brick Kiln La CW10 127 D4
Brick St Newton-le-W WA12 1 C2
Warrington WA1 16 B3
Brickfield Bsns Ctr CW9 79 E1
Brickfield La CH3 119 F1
Brickhill La WA15 32 A2
Brickhurst Way WA1 17 D4
Brickkiln La
Dunham Town WA14 20 B2
Whitchurch SY13 226 B1
Brickkiln Row WA14 238 C1
Bridal Ct SK7 35 F1
Bridge Ave Altrincham WA15 32 B3
Warrington WA4 16 C2
Bridge Ave E WA4 16 C3
Bridge Cl Audley ST7 209 F1
Cuddington CW8 102 A2
Lymm WA13 19 D2
Wistaston CW2 206 A4
Bridge Ct Chester CH2 119 D1
Neston L64 66 C4
Bridge Dr Cheadle SK8 239 D4
Christleton CH3 142 B4
Wilmslow SK9 34 B2
Bridge End Dr SK10 87 D4
Bridge End La SK10 87 D4
Bridge Foot WA1 16 A2
Bridge Gn SK10 87 D4
Bridge Gr WA15 238 F7
Bridge Hall Prim Sch SK3 240 D2
Bridge La Appleton WA4 26 C4
Cuddington CW8 101 F2
Frodsham WA6 49 E1
Warrington WA1 17 E4
Bridge Meadow L66 69 F1
Bridge Pl CH4 237 E1

Bridge Rd WA1 17 E4
Bridge Row CW12 156 C2
Bridge St Broughton CH4 140 B4
Chester CH1 237 E2
Goldborne WA3 3 D4
Holt LL13 180 C1
Macclesfield SK11 112 B4
Neston L64 66 C4
Newton-le-W WA12 2 A2
Northwich CW9 79 F1
Runcorn WA7 23 D2
Stalybridge SK15 242 C1
Stockport SK1 240 F6
Warrington WA1 16 A3
Whaley Bridge SK23 65 F4
Wybunbury CW5 220 B4
Bridge St Row CH1 237 E2
Bridge Terr CH3 119 D1
Bridge View Cl WA8 23 D2
Bridgedown CW6 146 B1
Bridgefield Ave SK9 34 B1
Bridgefield St SK1 240 E6
Bridgeman Rd CH1 117 F2
Bridgeman St WA5 15 E2
Bridgemere CE Aided Prim Sch CW5 231 F4
Bridgemere Cl CW11 174 C4
Bridgemere Garden World CW5 232 A2
Bridgemere La CW5 219 F1
Bridgemere Way CW9 103 F2
Bridgend CH2 97 D1
Bridgend Cl WA8 12 B2
Bridges Rd L65 70 C3
Bridgeside Dr WA6 73 D2
Bridgestones CW12 156 B1
Bridgewater Ave WA4 16 C2
Bridgewater Cl Cheadle SK8 34 B4
Congleton CW12 157 D1
Bridgewater Cty High Sch (Lower Sch) WA4 26 B3
Bridgewater Cty High Sch Upper Sch & Sixth Form Coll WA4 26 B4
Bridgewater Dr CH3 119 E1
Bridgewater Mews WA4 26 B4
Bridgewater Pl CW7 126 A1
Bridgewater Rd WA14 238 D7
Bridgewater St Lymm WA13 18 C2
Runcorn WA7 23 D1
Sale M33 242 B7
Bridgeway East WA7 24 B1
Bridgeway West WA7 24 B1
Bridgewood Dr L66 69 E1
Bridgfield Cl SK6 37 F4
Bridgnorth Gr ST5 210 C1
Bridle Cl L62 43 F4
Bridle Hey CW5 204 C1
Bridle Pk L62 43 F4
Bridle Rd Bebington L62 43 F3
Crewe CW2 190 A2
Woodford SK7 35 F1
Bridle Way Ellesmere Port L66 69 E2
Woodford SK7 35 F1
Bridlemere Ct WA1 16 C4
Briedden Way L66 69 D3
Brien Ave WA14 238 E7
Brierley Cty Prim Sch CW1 190 B2
Brierley Rd CW12 157 D1
Brierley St Crewe CW1 190 B2
Stalybridge SK16 242 A1
Briers Cl WA2 8 C2
Brieryhurst Rd ST7 195 D2
Briggs Ave CW2 190 B1
Bright St Ashton-u-L OL6 242 A2
Crewe CW1 190 A3
Brighton Cres SK11 113 D2
Brighton Gr 1 Hyde SK14 241 E5
Sale M33 242 B7
Brighton Rd SK4 240 C5
Brighton Road Ind Est SK4 240 C5
Brighton St WA5 15 F3
Brights Ave ST7 195 D1
Brightwell Cl WA5 14 C3
Brimelow Cres WA5 14 C2
Brimstage Cl L60 41 E4
Brimstage Gn L60 41 E4
Brimstage Rd L60 41 E4
Brindley Ave Sale M33 242 C8
Warrington WA4 16 C2
Winsford CW7 126 B1
Brindley Cl ST7 194 C1
Brindley Gr 13 SK9 34 C1
Brindley Hall Rd
Burland CW5 202 C4
Faddiley CW5 186 C1
Brindley La CW11 153 E2
Brindley Pk 4 CW11 174 C2
Brindley Rd WA7 23 F2
Brindley St WA7 22 C2
Brindley Way
Congleton CW12 157 D1
Macclesfield SK11 112 B2
Brindleys Way ST7 209 F1
Brine Leas Cty High Sch CW5 204 C2
Brine Pits La CW5 218 C1
Brine Rd CW5 204 C2
Brinell Dr M44 11 F3
Brinksway SK3 240 C4
Brinksway Trad Est 1 SK3 240 C4
Brinley Cl L62 43 E3
Brinton Cl WA8 22 C4
Brisbane Cl SK7 35 F3
Brisbane Rd CH1 117 E2
Bristol Ave WA7 50 C3
Bristol Cl Blacon CH1 117 F3
Cheadle SK8 34 A4
Bristol Dr L66 69 F1
Bristow Cl WA5 15 D4
Britannia Rd M33 242 C7
Brittania Dr CW9 104 C4
Brittania Gdns WA6 73 D1
Brittania Rd WA6 73 D1
Brixham Ave SK8 34 C4
Brixham Wlk SK7 35 F4
Broad Hey SK6 241 D3
Broad La Altrincham WA15 32 A4
Appleton WA4 27 E4
Burtonwood WA5 1 B1
Heswall L60 40 B4
Holmes Chapel CW4 129 F1
Sproston Green CW4 129 F1
Stapeley CW5 205 D1
Broad Oak Ave
Broughton CH4 139 D2
Haydock WA11 1 A3
Penketh WA5 14 C2
Broad Oak La
Manchester M20 239 B8
Manchester M20 239 C8
Broad Oak Prim Sch M20 239 C8
Broad Rd M33 242 D7
Broad St CW1 190 B3
Broad Street Cty Inf Sch CW1 190 B3
Broad Wlk SK9 59 F4
Broadacre CW9 78 B3
Broadacres CW5 217 F2
Broadbent Ave WA4 16 C2
Broadbent St SK14 241 D8
Broadcar Rd SK11 113 E3
Broadfield Cl M34 241 A6
Broadfields WA7 50 B4
Broadheath Prim Sch WA14 238 C8
Broadheys La WA16 28 B3
Broadhurst Ave
Culcheth WA3 4 C1
Warrington WA5 15 E2
Broadhurst La CW12 156 B2
Broadhurst St SK3 240 F3
Broadlake L64 67 F4
Broadland Gdns L66 69 F1
Broadland Rd L66 69 F1
Broadleigh Way CW2 206 B4
Broadley Ave WA3 3 E4
Broadmead Chester CH3 119 E1
Heswall L60 41 E4
Broadoak Comp Sch M31 11 F1
Broadoak La High Legh WA16 29 E3
Mobberley WA16 57 F3
Broadoaks Rd M33 242 A6
Broadwalk SK10 87 D3
Broadway Altrincham WA15 32 A4
Barnton CW8 78 A2
Cheadle SK8 239 C4
Sale M33 242 A7
Widnes WA8 12 A1
Wilmslow SK9 60 A3
Broadway Ave SK8 239 D5
Broadway E CH2 118 C3
Broadway The CW5 204 C3
Broadway W CH2 118 B3
Broadways CW3 230 A2
Broadwood Cl SK6 37 F4
Broady Ct CW2 190 B1
Brock Gdns L24 21 F1
Brock Rd WA3 9 E2
Brockhurst St CW9 104 A4
Brockhurst Way CW9 104 A3
Brocklehurst Ave SK10 87 F1
Brocklehurst Ct SK10 87 E2
Brocklehurst Dr SK10 87 D4
Brocklehurst Way SK10 87 E2
Brockway E CH3 166 A1
Brockway W CH3 166 A1
Brockwell Cl 2 CW7 149 D4
Brodie Cl CH2 95 E1
Brogden Ave WA3 4 C2
Brogden Dr SK8 239 B5
Brogden Gr M33 242 A5
Brogden Terr M33 242 A5
Broken Banks 21 SK11 112 B4
Broken Cross SK11 111 F4
Broken Cross Cty Prim Sch SK11 111 F4
Brokencross Pl CW9 104 C4
Bromborough Golf Course L63 43 D3
Bromborough Rake Sta L62 43 E4
Bromborough Sta L63 43 E3
Bromborough Village Rd L62 43 F4
Bromleigh Ave SK8 239 B6
Bromley Ave WA3 3 E4
Bromley Cl Crewe CW1 189 F4
Heswall L60 40 C4
Warrington WA2 8 C2
Bromley Dr CW4 130 B1
Bromley Rd
Congleton CW12 156 C2
Macclesfield SK10 111 F4
Brompton Gdns WA5 15 F4
Brompton Rd SK4 240 A6
Brompton Way L66 69 F1
Bronington Ave L62 43 E3
Brook Acre Cty Prim Sch WA2 8 C1
Brook Ave Altrincham WA15 238 E6
Shavington CW2 206 B3
Warrington, Stockton Heath WA4 16 C1
Warrington, Westy WA4 16 C3
Wilmslow SK9 34 B2
Brook Bottom Rd SK22 39 D4
Brook Cl Altrincham WA15 238 E6
Crewe CW1 190 C2
Cronton WA8 12 B3
Brook Ct CW11 175 D3
Brook Dr Cheadle Hulme SK8 35 D4
Great Sankey WA5 15 D3
Kelsall CW6 122 B2
Brook End WA9 1 A1
Brook Farm Sch CW6 168 B4
Brook Furlong WA6 48 C1
Brook Gdns ST6 179 E1
Brook Hey L64 41 D1
Brook House Dr CW2 206 B4
Brook La Altrincham WA15 238 F6
Broughton CH5 139 E4
Burland CW5 203 E4
Chester CH2 118 C2
Knutsford WA16 57 D1
Northwich CW9 104 B4
Warrington WA3 18 A4
Wilmslow SK9 59 F2
Brook Lane Ind Est CW10 151 E4
Brook Lodge SK8 239 D4
Brook Pl WA4 16 C2
Brook Rd Cheadle SK8 239 D6
Ellesmere Port L66 69 E3
Lymm WA13 18 B2
Tarporley CW6 168 B4
Brook Side CW8 102 B4
Brook St Cheadle SK8 239 F6
Chester CH2 237 E3
Congleton CW12 156 C2
Crewe CW2 190 B2
Goldborne WA3 3 D4
Hyde SK14 241 E7
Knutsford WA16 57 D1
Macclesfield SK10 87 E1
Macclesfield SK11 112 B4
Macclesfield SK11 112 C4
Neston L64 66 C4
Northwich CW9 79 D1
Northwich CW9 79 F1
Runcorn WA7 23 D1
Sale M33 242 C7
Widnes WA8 13 D1
Brook Street Bridge CH2 237 F4
Brook Terr CW11 175 D2
Brook Way Great Sankey WA5 15 D3
Nantwich CW5 204 C2
Brook Well L64 66 C3
Brookdale WA8 12 A2
Brookdale Ave Denton M34 241 B6
Knutsford WA16 57 E1
Brookdale Pl CH1 237 E3
Brookdale Way CH3 143 D3
Brooke Ave CH2 118 B4
Brooke Dr SK9 34 B2
Brooke Way 11 SK9 34 B2
Brookes Ave CH4 139 D2
Brookfield CW1 191 E3
Brookfield Ave
Altrincham WA15 238 F8
Poynton SK12 36 B2
Romiley SK6 241 A4
Runcorn WA7 23 F1
Brookfield Cl Lymm WA13 18 B2
Tarporley CW6 168 B4
Brookfield Cres
Cheadle SK8 239 D4
Goostrey CW4 107 F1
Brookfield Dr Alsager ST7 193 E3
Chester CH2 118 C2
Holmes Chapel CW4 130 A2
Brookfield Gr OL6 242 A2
Brookfield La SK11 112 C4
Brookfield Park WA4 17 D1
Brookfield Rd Cheadle SK8 239 E5
Comberbach CW9 78 B4
Culcheth WA3 4 B2
Lymm WA13 18 B2
Brookfield St WA12 2 A2
Brookfields Sch WA8 13 E1
Brookhead Dr SK8 240 A2
Brookhead Jun Sch SK8 239 F5
Brookhouse Cl SK10 86 C1
Brookhouse La
Church Minshull CW10 172 B4
Congleton CW12 157 E1
Duddon CH3 144 B3
Whitley WA4 52 A1
Brookhouse Rd Alsager ST7 193 E2
Sandbach CW11 175 D3
Brookhurst Ave L63 43 E3
Brookhurst Cl L63 43 E3
Brookhurst Prim Sch L62 43 E3
Brookhurst Rd L63 43 E3
Brookkash Rd M22 34 A4
Brookland Ave CW2 205 F4
Brookland Dr CW11 175 F3
Brookland La WA9 1 A1
Brookland St WA1 16 C4
Brooklands Ave SK11 112 A4
Brooklands Cres M33 242 B5
Brooklands Dr
Goostrey CW4 107 F1
Northwich CW9 104 A2
Brooklands Gr CW1 190 A3
Brooklands Mews SK11 112 A4
Brooklands Rd
Congleton CW12 155 F1
Neston L64 41 E1
Sale M33 242 B5
Brooklands Sta M33 242 A5
Brooklands Station App M33 242 A5
Brookledge La SK10 62 C3
Brookln Pl SK8 239 D6
Brooklyn Cres SK8 239 D5
Brooklyn Dr
Ellesmere Port L65 69 F3
Lymm WA13 18 C2
Brooklyn Rd SK8 239 D5
Brooklyn St CW2 190 B1
Brookmere Cl CW11 174 C4
Brooks Ave SK14 241 E5
Brooks Dr WA15 32 B4
Brooks La Bosley SK11 135 F1
Middlewich CW10 128 B1
Brooks St SK1 240 F3
Brookside Ashton CH3 121 F4
Chester CH3 142 A4
Cuddington CW8 101 F2
Kingsley WA6 75 E1
Brookside Ave
Great Sankey WA5 15 D2
Lymm WA13 18 B2
Poynton SK12 36 C2
Sutton Lane Ends SK11 112 C1
Warrington WA4 16 B1
Brookside Cl Cheadle SK8 239 D4
Haydock WA11 1 A4
Brookside Ct SK10 87 D1
Brookside Cty Inf Sch L66 69 E2
Brookside Gn CW2 206 B4
Brookside La SK6 37 F4
Brookside Prim Sch SK6 37 F3
Brookside Rd
Congleton CW12 156 B2
Gatley SK8 239 A6
Brookside Terr CH2 237 F4
Brookside View WA11 1 A4
Brookside Way WA11 1 A4
Brookvale Ave N WA7 50 A3
Brookvale Ave S WA7 50 A3
Brookvale Cl WA5 6 C3
Brookvale Cty Comp Sch WA7 50 B3
Brookvale Cty Inf Sch WA7 50 A3
Brookvale Cty Jun Sch WA7 50 A3
Brookway WA15 238 F7
Brookway La WA9 1 A1
Brookwood Cl WA4 26 A4
Broom Ave WA4 26 C3
Broom Cres CH3 121 D1
Broom Field Cl SK9 60 C4
Broom La WA16 81 F1
Broom Rd Altrincham WA15 238 E3
Partington M31 11 F1
Broom St CW1 190 A3
Broom's La CW6 122 B3
Broome Ct WA7 50 A3
Broomehouse Ave M44 11 F4
Broomfield Cl SK11 84 A2
Broomfield La WA15 238 E3
Broomfield Rd SK4 240 C8
Broomfields Cty Jun Sch WA4 26 C4
Broomfields Rd WA4 26 B4
Broomfields Recn Ctr WA4 26 B4
Broomgrove La M34 241 A8
Broomheath La
Duddon CH3 144 B4
Tarvin CH3 121 E1
Tarvin, Broom Bank CH3 144 B4
Broomhill La
Brown Knowl CH3 199 E4
Great Barrow CH3 120 C4
Broomlands L60 40 C4
Broomsfield La CW8 78 A2
Broomville Ave M33 242 B6
Broseley Ave WA3 4 B2
Broseley La WA3 4 B3
Brotherton Cl L62 43 E4
Brough St W SK11 112 B4
Brougham St SK15 242 C1
Broughton Ave WA3 3 E4
Broughton Cres SY14 211 D1
Broughton Hall Rd CH4 139 E2
Broughton Jun & Inf Sch CH4 139 E2
Broughton La CW2 189 F1
Broughton Mills Rd CH4 139 F3
Broughton Rd Adlington SK10 62 B3
Crewe CW1 190 B4
Reddish SK5 240 F8
Broughville Dr M20 239 C8
Brow Cty Prim Sch The WA7 23 F1
Brow La Antrobus CW9 53 E3
Heswall L60 40 C4
Brow The WA6 75 E1
Browmere Dr WA3 9 D4
Brown Ave
Lawton-gate ST7 194 A3
Nantwich CW5 204 C2
Brown Heath Rd
Christleton CH3 143 D3
Waverton CH3 143 D3
Brown La SK8 239 B1
Brown Lees Cl CW2 190 A1
Brown Lees Rd ST7 195 F2
Brown St Alderley Edge SK9 60 A1
Altrincham WA14 238 D3
Congleton CW12 156 C2
Macclesfield SK11 112 B4
1 Stockport SK1 240 E6
Widnes WA8 23 E4
Brown's La Chester CH4 141 E4
Wilmslow SK9 60 C4
Brownhill Dr WA1 16 C4
Brownhills Rd CW6 147 E3
Browning Ave WA8 22 C4
Browning Cl Blacon CH1 117 F3
11 Sandbach CW11 174 B3
Browning Dr L65 69 F2
Browning Gn L65 69 F2
Browning Gr ST7 210 B4
Browning St CW1 190 B2
Browning Way CW7 149 D4
Brownlow Cl SK12 36 C1
Broxton Ave CW10 151 E3
Broxton Cl WA8 12 B2
Broxton Dr CW2 190 A1
Broxton Rd Broxton CH3 182 B1
Clutton CH3 182 B1
Ellesmere Port L66 69 F3
Bruce Ave WA2 8 B1
Bruce Cres L63 43 E3
Bruce Dr L66 69 E2
Bruche Ave WA1 16 C4
Bruche Cty Inf Sch WA1 17 D4
Bruche Cty Jun Sch WA1 17 D4
Bruche Dr WA1 16 C4
Bruche Heath Gdns WA1 17 D4
Bruen The CH3 121 E2
Bruera Rd L65 69 F2
Brunel Rd SK11 112 B2
Brunner Bsns Ctr CW8 78 B1
Brunner Gr CW5 205 D3
Brunner Pl CW7 149 D4
Brunner Rd WA8 23 D4
Brunswick Cres L66 69 F2
Brunswick Hill SK11 112 B4
Brunswick Rd
Altrincham WA14 238 D7
Newton-le-W WA12 1 C2
Brunswick St
35 Macclesfield SK11 112 B4
St Helens WA9 1 A2
Brunswick Terr SK11 112 B4
Bruntleigh Ave WA4 17 D2
Bruntwood Ave SK8 239 A1
Bruntwood La Cheadle SK8 239 E1
Cheadle SK8 239 E2
Bruntwood Prim Sch SK8 239 E2
Brussels Rd SK3 240 D2
Bryant Ave WA4 16 C3
Bryce St SK14 241 D8
Brymau Four Est CH4 140 B4
Brymau One Est CH4 140 C4
Brymau Three Est CH4 140 B4
Brymau Two Est CH4 140 C4
Brynlow Dr CW10 151 D4
Brynmore Dr SK11 112 C4
Brynn St WA8 23 D4
Brynton Cl SK10 87 E1
Brynton Rd SK10 87 E1
Buchan Cl WA5 15 D4
Buchan Gr CW2 190 A2
Buck La CW2 206 C2
Buckbean Way CW4 107 F1
Buckden Way SK11 112 B4
Buckfast Ave WA11 2 A4
Buckfast Cl
Cheadle Hulme SK8 35 D3
Macclesfield SK10 87 E1
Penketh WA5 14 C2
Poynton SK12 36 B3
Buckfast Ct WA7 24 C2
Buckfast Way CW10 128 A1
Buckingham Ave
Chester CH3 119 D1
Denton M34 241 B6
Widnes WA8 13 D2
Buckingham Cl CW2 205 F4
Buckingham Dr
Davenham CW9 103 F2
Great Sankey WA5 15 E2
Knutsford WA16 57 D1
Winsford CW7 149 E4
Buckingham Rd
Ellesmere Port L65 70 B1
Irlam M44 11 E3
Poynton SK12 36 B2
Stalybridge SK15 242 D3
Wilmslow SK9 59 F3
Buckingham Rd W SK4 240 A8
Buckingham Way SK2 240 F2
Buckland Cl WA8 22 B4
Buckley Ave CW10 128 C4
Buckley Cl CW10 151 D4
Buckley Dr SK6 241 A1
Buckley St
Macclesfield SK11 112 B4
Warrington WA2 16 A3
Bucklow Ave
Mobberley WA16 58 A2
Partington M31 11 F2
Bucklow Gdns WA13 19 D2
Bucklow View WA14 238 A3
Bucklow Wlk 19 SK11 112 C4
Bucklowhill La WA16 30 A2
Buckton St WA1 16 B4
Bude Cl Alsager ST7 193 D2
Bramhall SK7 35 F4
Crewe CW1 190 A4
Bude Rd WA8 12 C1
Budworth Ave
Warrington WA4 16 C2
Widnes WA8 12 B1
Budworth Cl Runcorn WA7 49 E4
Sandbach CW11 174 C4
Budworth Heath La CW9 54 B1
Budworth La
Comberbach CW9 78 C4
Great Budworth CW9 78 C4
Budworth Rd
Bate Heath CW9 54 C1
Ellesmere Port L66 69 F1
Sale M33 242 E5
Tabley WA16 55 E1

Budworth Wlk SK9 34 C1
Buerton Cty Prim Sch CW3 230 C2
Buffs La L60 41 D4
Buggen La L64 66 B4
Buglawton Cty Prim Sch CW12 157 D2
Buglawton Hall Sch CW12 157 E3
Buglawton Ind Est CW12 156 C2
Builowas Rd L64 41 F1
Bulkeley Rd Cheadle SK8 239 E6
Poynton SK12 36 C2
Wilmslow SK9 34 B2
Bulkeley St Chester CH3 119 D1
Stockport SK3 240 D4
Bull Hill L64 66 C3
Bull Hill La SK10 88 B1
Bull Ring CW9 103 F4
Bull Ring The CW10 128 B1
Bullcroft Cl SY14 211 E4
Bullock St SK2 240 F3
Bullocks House Rd ST7 195 F2
Bullocks La
Macclesfield SK11 112 C2
Sutton Lane Ends SK11 112 C2
Bumper's La CH1 117 F1
Bunbury Cl
Middlewich CW10 151 E3
Northwich CW9 104 A3
Stoak CH2 96 A4
Bunbury Dr WA7 49 E3
Bunbury Gn L65 70 B1
Bunbury La CW6 185 F4
Bunbury Rd CW6 169 E2
Bunce La SK11 133 D2
Bunce St CH4 237 D1
Bungalow Rd WA12 2 C1
Bunham Cl ST7 193 E2
Bunkershill Rd SK6 241 B1
Buntingford Rd WA4 17 E2
Bunts La CW12 156 C1
Burdett Rd L66 69 F1
Burfield Dr WA4 26 B4
Burford Ave SK7 35 E3
Burford Cl SK9 59 F3
Burford Cres SK9 59 F3
Burford La WA13 19 E1
Burgamot La CW9 78 B4
Burges St CH2 118 C2
Burgess Ave WA4 16 A1
Burgess Dr CH1 117 D3
Burgess Pl CW8 103 F4
Burgess St SK10 112 C4
Burjen Way CW1 190 A3
Burkhardt Dr WA12 2 C2
Burkitt St SK14 241 E6
Burland Cl WA7 22 C1
Burland Gr CW7 126 A1
Burland Rd ST5 210 B1
Burlea Cl CW2 189 F3
Burlea Dr CW2 206 A3
Burlescombe Cl WA14 238 B6
Burley Ct SK4 240 C6
Burley La WA4 27 E2
Burleyhurst La WA16 58 C3
Burlington Ct WA14 238 D5
Burlington Rd WA14 238 D5
Burnell Rd L65 70 C2
Burnet Cl WA2 9 E1
Burnfell WA3 3 F4
Burnham Cl Cheadle SK8 239 F2
Culcheth WA3 4 C2
Penketh WA5 14 C3
Widnes WA8 12 B2
Burnham Rd CH4 140 C3
Burns Ave SK8 239 F6
Burns Cl Ellesmere Port L66 69 F2
Rode Heath ST7 193 F4
Burns Cres WA8 22 C4
Burns Dr CW1 190 C2
Burns Gr WA2 8 B1
Burns Rd CW12 157 D1
Burns Way CH1 117 F3
Burnsall Ave WA3 3 F4
Burnsall Dr WA8 12 B2
Burnside WA15 32 B4
Burnside Ave WA4 16 B1
Burnside Cl SK9 60 B3
Burnside Rd SK8 239 B5
Burnt Acre SK11 84 A2
Burran Rd M22 33 E4
Burrough Cl WA3 9 F2
Burrows Hill CW8 103 D4
Burrows St WA11 1 A3
Burrows The CW8 101 E3
Burscough Way WA8 22 A3
Burslam St CW12 156 C1
Burton Ave CW6 146 B2
Burton Bishop Wilson CE Aided Prim Sch L64 67 E1
Burton Cl Culcheth WA3 4 C2
Widnes WA8 12 C2
Burton Dr SK12 36 B2
Burton Gn L66 69 E2
Burton Gr CW1 173 D1
Burton Hall Rd LL12 161 F1
Burton La CW6 144 C3
Burton Manor Coll L64 67 E1
Burton Rd Blacon CH1 117 F3
Neston L64 66 C3
Warrington WA2 8 B1
Burton St SK4 240 E7
Burton Wlk SK4 240 E7
Burtonwood Cty Prim Sch WA5 6 C4
Burtonwood Rd
Burtonwood WA5 7 D1
Great Sankey WA5 15 D4
Burtonwood Service Area WA5 7 D2
Burwardsley Rd CH3 166 B1
Bury St SK5 240 F7
Bush Rd Christleton CH3 142 C4
Widnes WA8 22 C3
Bushell Cl L64 66 C4
Bushell Rd L64 66 C4
Bushway L60 40 B4
Butler Way CW5 204 C2
Butley Cl Macclesfield SK10 87 E2
Middlewich CW10 151 E4
Butley Lanes SK10 61 F1
Butley Sch SK10 61 F3
Butter Ave WA5 7 F1
Butterbache Rd CH3 142 A3
Butterbur Cl CH3 142 A3
Buttercup Dr SK3 240 D1
Buttermarket St WA1 16 A3
Buttermere Ave
Ellesmere Port L65 70 B2
Warrington WA2 8 B2
Buttermere Cl WA6 74 B4
Buttermere Ct CW12 156 A1
Buttermere Dr
Altrincham WA15 32 B3
Crewe CW1 173 D1
Buttermere Gr WA7 49 E3
Buttermere Rd Gatley SK8 239 B3
Partington M31 11 F2
Winsford CW7 126 B1
Butterton La Crewe CW1 192 B1
Haslington CW1 192 B1
Button Field CW8 126 A4
Butts The Alsager ST7 193 E2
Runcorn WA7 23 F1
Buxton Ave CW1 190 C2
Buxton Cl WA5 15 D4
Buxton New Rd
Macclesfield Forest SK11 114 B4
Rainow SK10 88 B1
Buxton Old Rd
Congleton CW12 157 D2
Disley SK12 38 C2
Macclesfield SK10 113 E4
Rainow SK10 113 E4
Buxton Rd
Congleton CW12 157 E3
Disley SK12 38 C3
Hazel Grove SK7 37 E4
High Lane SK6 37 E4
Macclesfield SK10 112 C4
New Mills SK23 39 E2
Whaley Bridge SK23 39 E2
Buxton Rd W SK12 38 A3
Buxton St SK8 239 A5
Bye Pass Rd CH3 121 D2
Bye Pass The CH3 119 F1
Byland Ave SK8 35 D3
Bylands Cl SK12 36 B2
Byley Cty Prim Sch CW10 129 D4
Byley La Cranage CW10 129 E3
Middlewich CW10 128 C2
Sproston Green CW10 128 C2
Byley Way CW7 126 A1
Byng Ave M44 11 E2
Byrom St WA14 238 D3
Byron Cl Blacon CH1 117 F3
Crewe CW1 190 C2
Middlewich CW10 151 E3
Rode Heath ST7 193 F4
Byron Ct WA2 8 B1
Byron Dr SK8 239 F6
Byron St WA7 23 D1
Byron Way CW2 190 A1
Byron's La SK11 112 C3
Byrons St SK11 112 B3
Bythom Cl CH3 142 C4

Cabot Cl WA5 7 E1
Cabot Pl SK5 240 F8
Cabul Cl WA2 16 B4
Cadishead Inf Sch M44 11 E3
Cadishead Jun Sch M44 11 F3
Cadnant Cl CH1 117 E2
Cadshaw Cl WA3 9 E3
Caerleon Cl CW7 149 D4
Caerllew LL13 180 C1
Caernarvon Ave CW7 149 D4
Caernarvon Cl WA7 23 F1
Caernarvon Ct L65 70 B1
Caernarvon Rd CW2 205 F4
Caesars Cl WA7 23 F1
Cairns Cres CH1 117 E2
Cairo St WA1 16 A3
Caister Way CW7 149 E4
Caithness Ct WA7 23 D1
Calamine St SK11 112 C3
Calcutta Rd SK3 240 C3
Calday Gr WA11 1 A4
Caldbeck Ave Sale M33 242 E7
Warrington WA2 8 B1
Caldene Terr SK23 65 F4
Calder Ave CW1 191 D3
Calder Cl Bollington SK10 87 F4
Poynton SK12 36 B1
Widnes WA8 13 F2
Calder Way L66 69 E3
Calderfield Cl WA4 26 A4
Caldicott Ave L62 43 E4
Caldicott Cl CW7 149 E4
Caldwell Rd WA8 23 D4
Caldwell's Gate La CW9 54 A4
Caldy Cl CH2 118 B3
Caldy Dr L66 69 E2
Caldy Rd Alsager ST7 193 E2
Wilmslow SK9 34 B2
Caldy Valley Rd
Chester CH3 142 A4
Huntington CH3 142 A4
Caldy Way CW7 126 A1
Cale Gn SK2 240 F2
Cale Green Prim Sch SK3 240 F2
Cale St SK2 240 F2
Calland Ave SK14 241 F7
Callands Cty Prim Sch WA5 7 F1
Callands Rd WA5 7 E1
Calmington La WA7 24 C2
Calrofold Dr ST5 210 B1
Calrofold La SK10 88 B1
Calstock Cl WA5 14 C2
Calveley Ave L62 43 F2
Calveley Cty Prim Sch CW6 170 A1
Calveley Green La
Alpraham CW6, CW7 170 B2
Wettenhall CW6, CW7 170 B2
Calveley Hall La CW6 170 A1
Calver Rd WA2 8 A2
Calver Wlk SK8 239 E1
Calverley Cl SK9 60 B4
Calverly Cl WA7 50 B3
Calverly Rd SK8 240 A1
Calvers WA7 23 F1
Camamile Wlk M31 11 F1
Camberley Cl SK7 36 A4
Camborne Ave SK10 111 F4
Camborne Cl WA7 50 B3
Cambourne Cl CW12 178 C4
Cambourne Rd WA5 6 C3
Cambrai Ave WA4 16 B1
Cambrian Ave CH3 119 D1
Cambrian Cl L66 69 D3
Cambrian Rd SK3 240 C4
Cambrian Way CW7 149 D4
Cambridge Ave
Macclesfield SK11 112 A4
Wilmslow SK9 59 F4
Winsford CW7 126 A1
Cambridge Cl Biddulph ST6 179 E1
Warrington WA4 26 A4
Cambridge Gdns
Appleton WA4 26 B3
Helsby WA6 73 E2
Cambridge Rd
Altrincham WA15 238 E2
Bebington L62 43 F4
Chester CH2 118 C3
Ellesmere Port L65 70 B3
Gatley SK8 239 B5
Macclesfield SK11 112 A4
Cambridge Road Cty Prim Sch L65 70 B3
Cambridge St Runcorn WA7 23 E1
Stalybridge SK15 242 D2
Widnes WA8 23 D4
Camden Ct WA7 24 B1
Camden Rd L65 70 A3
Camden St CW1 190 B2
Camelot Cl WA12 1 C2
Camelot Gr CW2 206 B2
Camelot Way WA7 50 A4
Cameron Ave Runcorn WA7 48 C4
Shavington CW2 206 A2
Cameron Ct WA2 8 A2
Cameron Rd WA8 23 D4
Camm St CW2 190 B1
Campbell Ave WA7 49 D4
Campbell Cl
Congleton CW12 157 D2
Haslington CW1 191 E2
Macclesfield SK10 87 D1
Campbell Cres WA5 14 C3
Campden Way SK9 34 B2
Campion Cl Huntington CH3 142 A3
Warrington WA3 9 E3
Campsey Ash WA8 12 C2
Camrose Cl WA7 49 E3
Camsley La WA13 18 A2
Canaan WA3 4 B4
Canada Cl WA2 9 D1
Canadian Ave CH2 119 D2
Canal Bridge Ent Pk L65 70 B3
Canal Ct Trad Est L65 70 B4
Canal Rd Altrincham WA14 238 E8
Congleton CW12 156 C1
Canal Reach WA7 24 B1
Canal Side Appleton WA4 17 E1
Barnton CW8 78 A1
Chester CH2 118 C1
Chester CH2 237 F3
Macclesfield SK11 112 C4
Moore WA4 25 E3
Preston on the Hill WA4 50 C3
Runcorn WA7 48 B4
Canal St Chester CH1 237 D3
Congleton CW12 156 C1
Hyde SK14 241 C7
Macclesfield SK11 112 C4
Newton-le-W WA12 1 C2
Runcorn WA7 23 D1
Stalybridge SK15 242 D1
Stockport SK1 240 F4
Whaley Bridge SK23 65 F4
Canal Terr CW10 151 E4
Canalside L65 70 B3
Canberra Ave WA2 8 B2
Canberra Rd SK7 35 F3
Canberra Sq WA2 8 B1
Canberra Way CH1 117 E2
Candelan Way WA16 29 E2
Candle La CW3 232 A1
Candleston Cl WA5 7 F1
Canford Cl Crewe CW1 190 A4
Great Sankey WA5 15 E3
Canley Cl 7 SK1 240 F4
Cann La Appleton WA4 26 C2
Bate Heath CW9 55 D3
Cannel Ct WA7 50 A3
Cannell St WA5 15 E2
Canning St Chester CH1 237 D3
7 Stockport SK4 240 E6
Canniswood Rd WA11 1 A3
Cannock Cl CH1 94 C4
Cannock Dr SK4 240 A6
Cannon St L65 70 A3
Cannon Way CH4 161 D4
Canon Dr WA14 238 B1
Canon St WA7 23 D2
Canon Wilson Cl WA11 1 B3
Canons Rd WA5 15 E3
Canterbury Cl CH1 94 C4
Canterbury Ct 5 SK10 112 C4
Canterbury Rd Blacon CH1 117 F3
Widnes WA8 22 B4
Canterbury St WA4 16 B2
Cantley Cl WA7 49 E3
Canton Pl CW8 103 E4
Canton St SK11 112 B3
Canton Wlks SK11 112 B3
Canute Pl WA16 57 D1
Capeland Cl CH4 140 C3
Capenhurst Ave
Crewe CW2 190 A2
Warrington WA2 9 D1
Capenhurst CE Contr Prim Sch CH1 94 A4
Capenhurst Gdns L66 69 E1
Capenhurst Grange Sch L66 69 F1
Capenhurst La
Capenhurst CH1 94 A4
Ellesmere Port L65 70 A2
Capenhurst Sta CH1 69 E1
Capesthorne Cl Alsager ST7 193 E2
Davenham CW9 103 F2
Hazel Grove SK7 36 C4
Holmes Chapel CW4 130 A2
Sandbach CW11 175 E4
Capesthorne Hall SK11 110 A3
Capesthorne Rd
Crewe CW2 189 F2
Hazel Grove SK7 36 C4
High Lane SK6 37 F4
Warrington WA2 8 C1
Waverton CH3 143 D3
Wilmslow SK9 59 F3
Capethorne Way 24 SK11 112 C4
Capitol Wlk CW12 156 B1
Capper Cl ST7 195 D1
Capper's La Faddiley CW6 186 B2
Spurstow CW6 186 B2
Cappers La CW11 176 B1
Carden Cl WA3 9 E2
Cardenbrook Gr 5 SK9 34 B1
Carderston Cl WA7 49 F2
Cardiff Cl CH1 94 C4
Cardigan Cl
Macclesfield SK11 112 A4
Warrington WA5 7 E1
Carey St WA8 13 D1
Carisbrook Ave SK10 87 F1
Carisbrook Dr CW7 149 E4
Carisbrooke Cl CW2 205 F4
Carleton Rd SK12 37 E2
Carlett Bvd L62 43 F3
Carlett Park Coll of Tech L62 44 A4
Carlile St SK3 240 E4
Carlingford Cl SK3 240 E1
Carlingford Rd WA4 26 A4
Carlisle Cl Macclesfield SK11 111 F3
Mobberley WA16 58 A2
Romiley SK6 241 A1
Winsford CW7 126 A1
Carlisle Dr WA14 238 E8
Carlisle Rd CH1 117 F3
Carlisle St Alderley Edge SK9 60 A1
Crewe CW2 190 A1
Warrington WA4 26 B4
Carlow Cl L24 21 E1
Carlton Ave Broughton CH4 140 B3
Cheadle SK8 239 F3
Cheadle Hulme SK7 35 E3
Romiley SK6 241 D2
Runcorn WA7 23 E1
Wilmslow SK9 34 B1
Carlton Cl
Mickle Trafford CH2 119 F4
Neston L64 41 E1
Carlton Cres L66 69 F4
Carlton Dr M22 & SK8 239 A6
Carlton Pl CH2 119 D2
Carlton Rd Lymm WA13 19 D3
Manchester SK4 240 A6
Northwich CW9 104 A4
Sale M33 242 A8
Carlton St Warrington WA4 26 B4
Widnes WA8 23 D4
Carlton Way WA3 11 E3
Carlyle Cl ST7 193 F4
Carlyle Cres L66 69 F2
Carlyn Ave M33 242 D6
Carmarthen Cl
Warrington WA5 7 E1
Winsford CW7 149 E4
Carmel Cl CH1 117 E2
Carmel Ct WA8 13 D2
Carmel Mews SK9 34 A1
Carmenna Dr SK7 35 F4
Carmichael Cl M31 11 F2
Carmichael St SK3 240 D4
Carnegie Cl SK10 87 D1
Carnforth Dr M33 242 A5
Carnoustie Cl SK9 60 B4
Carnoustie Dr Gatley SK8 239 C1
Macclesfield SK10 87 E3
Carnoustie Gr WA11 1 A3
Carol Dr L60 41 E4
Carol St WA4 16 B2
Caroline St
Ashton-u-L OL6 242 A3
Irlam M44 11 F4
Stalybridge SK15 242 D1
Stockport SK3 240 D3
Widnes WA8 23 D4
Carpenter Gr WA2 9 D1
Carr Brow SK6 38 A4
Carr La Audley ST7 209 D1
Goldborne WA3 4 A4
Hale WA8, L24 21 F2
Lindow End SK9 59 E1
Widnes WA8, L24 21 F2
Carr St ST7 195 F1
Carr Wood Ave SK7 35 F4
Carrgate Rd M34 241 B5
Carrgreen La WA13 19 F3
Carriage Dr Biddulph ST6 179 F1
Frodsham WA6 74 A3
Carriages The WA14 238 C4
Carrick Dr L65 70 A1
Carrick Rd CH4 141 D4
Carrington Cl WA3 9 E2
Carrington Way CW1 190 A4
Carroll Dr CW2 205 F4
Carrs Ave SK3 & SK8 240 A2
Carrs Ct SK9 60 A4
Carrs La CH3 166 C1
Carrs Rd SK8 239 F6
Carrwood Altrincham WA15 32 A4
Knutsford WA16 57 E1
Carrwood Rd SK9 59 F4
Carsdale Rd M22 33 F4
Carter Ave CW6 122 B2
Carter La SK11 84 A2
Carter St Chester CH2 237 F3
Stalybridge SK15 242 E2
Cartier Cl WA5 15 E4
Cartledge Cl CW8 102 A2
Cartmel Ave WA2 8 B2
Cartmel Cl Gatley SK8 239 C3
Holmes Chapel CW4 130 A2
Macclesfield SK10 87 D1
Warrington WA5 7 F1
Winsford CW7 126 B1
Cartmel Dr L66 69 F1
Cartmell Cl WA7 49 D3
Cartridge La WA4 27 F3
Cartwright Rd CW1 191 E3
Cartwright St Runcorn WA7 23 E1
Warrington WA5 15 F3
Carver Cl CW7 127 D2
Carver Rd WA15 238 E2
Case Rd WA11 1 B3
Casey La CW2 206 C2
Cashmere Rd SK3 240 C3
Caspian Rd WA14 238 A6
Cassia Green La CW7 125 E3
Cassley Rd L24 21 D2
Casson St CW1 190 A3
Castle Bank CW8 103 F4
Castle Cl Broughton CH4 139 D3
Kelsall CW6 122 B2
Pulford CH4 162 B1
Castle Croft Rd CH4 141 D3
Castle Ct CW8 103 F4
Castle Dr Chester CH4 237 E1
Ellesmere Port L65 70 A2
Heswall L60 40 C4
Castle Gn WA5 7 D1
Castle Hall Cl SK15 242 E1
Castle Hall Ct SK15 242 D1
Castle Hall View SK15 242 D1
Castle Hill Newton-le-W WA12 2 C2
Prestbury SK10 86 C3
Pulford CH4 162 B1
Castle Hill Ct SK10 86 C4
Castle Inn Rd CW12 179 E4
Castle Mill La WA15 32 A3
Castle Prim Sch ST7 195 E3
Castle Rd Kidsgrove ST7 195 E4
Runcorn WA7 49 F4
Castle Rise Prestbury SK10 86 C3
Runcorn WA7 23 E1
Castle St Chester CH4 237 E1
Crewe CW1 190 B2
Holt LL13 196 B4
Hyde SK14 241 F7
Macclesfield SK11 112 B4
Nantwich CW5 204 C3
Northwich CW8 103 F4
Stalybridge SK15 242 D1
Stockport SK3 240 D3
Stockport SK3 240 E4
Widnes WA8 13 E1
Castle St Mall 32 SK11 112 B4
Castle View Cty Prim Sch WA7 49 E4
Castle Way Altrincham WA15 32 B4
Dodleston CH4 162 A3
Castle Yard SK1 240 F6
Castlefields CH3 166 B2
Castlefields Ave E WA7 24 A1
Castlefields Ave N WA7 23 F1
Castlefields Ave S WA7 24 A1
Castleford Dr SK10 86 C3
Castlegate SK10 86 C3
Castlegate Mews SK10 86 C3
Castlemead Wlk CW9 103 F2
Castlemere Dr CW1 190 B4

Castleton Dr SK6 .... 37 F3
Castleton St WA14 .... 238 C7
Castletown Cl SK10 .... 87 E2
Castletown La CH3 .... 197 E1
Castleview Rd ST7 .... 195 D2
Catchpenny La SK11 .... 108 C2
Cateford Cl WA8 .... 12 B1
Catford Gn L24 .... 21 D2
Catfoss Cl WA2 .... 8 C1
Cathcart Gn CH3 .... 119 F3
Cathedral Church of Christ & the Blessed Virgin Mary CH1 .... 237 E2
Catherine Rd WA14 .... 238 C3
Catherine St Chester CH1 .... 118 A1
Crewe CW2 .... 190 B1
Hyde SK14 .... 241 D7
Macclesfield SK11 .... 112 B4
Warrington WA5 .... 15 F4
Warrington WA2 .... 16 A4
Widnes WA8 .... 23 D4
Catherine Way WA12 .... 2 A1
Catterall Ave WA2 .... 8 B1
Caughall Rd CH2 .... 95 F1
Caunce Ave Goldborne WA3 .... 3 D4
Haydock WA11 .... 1 A3
Causeway Ave WA4 .... 16 B2
Causeway The 2 WA14 .... 238 D4
Cavalier Dr CH1 .... 117 F3
Cavan Cl SK3 .... 239 F7
Cavell Dr L65 .... 70 A2
Cavendish Cl
Great Sankey WA5 .... 15 E4
Macclesfield SK10 .... 87 E2
9 Winsford CW7 .... 149 D4
Cavendish Cres ST7 .... 193 E3
Cavendish Farm Rd WA7 .... 49 D3
Cavendish Gdns L65 .... 70 A2
Cavendish Mews SK9 .... 60 A3
Cavendish Rd
Altrincham WA14 .... 238 C3
Chester CH4 .... 141 D3
Crewe CW2 .... 189 F3
Hazel Grove SK7 .... 36 C4
Cavendish Sch WA7 .... 49 E3
Cavendish St 4 WA7 .... 22 C1
Caversham Cl WA4 .... 26 C3
Cawdor Dr CH3 .... 119 D1
Cawdor St Runcorn WA7 .... 22 C2
Warrington WA4 .... 26 B4
Cawfield Ave WA8 .... 12 B1
Cawley Ave WA3 .... 4 C2
Cawley St
17 Macclesfield SK11 .... 112 C4
Runcorn WA7 .... 23 D1
Cawood Cl L66 .... 69 D3
Cawthorne Ave WA4 .... 17 D1
Caxton Cl Ellesmere Port L66 .... 69 F2
Widnes WA8 .... 12 B2
Cecil Rd WA15 .... 238 E2
Cecil Rigby Cl CW11 .... 175 D3
Cecil St Chester CH3 .... 119 D1
Stalybridge SK15 .... 242 E1
Cedab Rd L65 .... 70 B3
Cedar Ave Alsager ST7 .... 193 E2
Altrincham WA14 .... 238 C4
Connah's Quay CH5 .... 91 E1
Deeside Ind Est CH5 .... 116 A4
Ellesmere Port L66 .... 69 E3
Goldborne WA3 .... 3 F4
Kidsgrove ST7 .... 194 B1
Runcorn WA7 .... 49 E4
Sutton WA7 .... 50 A2
Widnes WA8 .... 13 D1
Cedar Cl Holmes Chapel CW4 .... 130 B2
Lostock CW9 .... 80 A2
Middlewich CW10 .... 151 F3
Poynton SK12 .... 36 C2
Sandbach CW11 .... 175 E3
Cedar Cres Audley ST7 .... 209 F1
Newton-le-W WA12 .... 2 B1
Cedar Ct Alsager ST7 .... 193 F2
Congleton CW12 .... 178 C4
Croft WA3 .... 4 C1
Willaston (nr Nantwich) CW5 .... 205 E3
Cedar Dr Barnton CW8 .... 78 A2
Chester CH2 .... 119 D2
Cedar Gr Chester CH2 .... 119 D2
Haydock WA11 .... 1 C4
Macclesfield SK11 .... 112 B3
Nantwich CW5 .... 205 D3
Neston L64 .... 66 C4
Warrington, Latchford WA4 .... 16 B2
Warrington, Paddington WA1 .... 17 D4
Winsford CW7 .... 127 D1
Cedar Mews CH1 .... 117 F2
Cedar Pk CH3 .... 119 E1
Cedar Rd Altrincham WA15 .... 238 E3
Gatley SK8 .... 239 A5
Great Sankey WA5 .... 14 B4
Newcastle-u-L ST5 .... 210 B1
Partington M31 .... 11 F2
Weaverham CW8 .... 102 B4
Cedar St OL6 .... 242 A4
Cedar Way CW2 .... 206 A4
Cedardale Dr CH1 .... 94 C4
Cedardale Pk WA8 .... 13 F2
Cedarfield Rd WA13 .... 19 D2
Cedars The ST7 .... 193 E2
Cedarway Heswall L60 .... 41 D3
Wilmslow SK9 .... 59 F3
Cedarways WA4 .... 26 B3
Cedarwood CW8 .... 101 E3
Cedarwood Ave SK4 .... 240 A5
Cedarwood Cl CW6 .... 146 B2
Celandine Cl CH3 .... 142 A4
Celyn Cres CH4 .... 140 B3
Cement Pl CH2 .... 237 E3
Cemetery Rd CW2 .... 207 D3
Cemlyn Cl CH1 .... 117 F2
Central Ave
Ellesmere Port L65 .... 70 B2
Warrington WA2 .... 16 B4
Warrington, Latchford WA4 .... 16 A2
Central Dr Barnton CW8 .... 78 A2
Cheadle SK8 .... 34 B4
Haydock WA11 .... 1 A3
Romiley SK6 .... 241 C3
Central Expressway WA7 .... 49 F4
Central Gr CW9 .... 104 B4
Central Rd Northwich CW9 .... 104 B4
Partington M31 .... 11 F2
Central St ST7 .... 195 D3
Central Trad Est CH4 .... 140 C4
Central Way
Altrincham WA14 .... 238 D4
Newton-le-W WA12 .... 2 C1
Centre Ct ST7 .... 193 F2
Centre Park Sq WA1 .... 16 A2
Centurion Cl WA3 .... 9 E2
Centurion Row WA7 .... 23 F1
Century Park Ind Area WA14 .... 238 A6
Chadkirk Rd SK6 .... 241 B1
Chads Gn CW5 .... 206 A1
Chadvil Rd SK8 .... 239 C5
Chadwick Ave Croft WA3 .... 9 D4
Warrington WA4 .... 16 C1
Chadwick Cl SK9 .... 34 B1
Chadwick Rd
Middlewich CW10 .... 151 E3
Runcorn WA7 .... 23 F2
Chadwick St
Ashton-u-L OL6 .... 242 B2
8 Stockport SK1 .... 240 F4
Chadwick Terr SK10 .... 87 F1
Chaffinch Cl
Congleton CW12 .... 156 C1
Warrington WA3 .... 9 F2
Chaffinch Way CW7 .... 149 E3
Chaigley Sch WA4 .... 17 F2
Chain Maker's Row CH4 .... 140 C4
Chalfield Ave L66 .... 69 E3
Chalfield Cl
Ellesmere Port L66 .... 69 E3
Wistaston CW2 .... 206 A4
Chalfont Cl WA4 .... 26 C3
Chalgrave Cl WA8 .... 13 F2
Chalkwell Dr L60 .... 41 E4
Challinor St CH3 .... 119 D1
Chalmondeley Rd CW5 .... 216 A3
Chamber Brook La WA6 .... 75 E1
Chambers St CW2 .... 190 B1
Chance Hall La
Astbury CW12 .... 177 E2
Scholar Green CW12 .... 177 E2
Chancel La SK9 .... 60 A4
Chancery La Alsager ST7 .... 193 D2
Bollington SK10 .... 88 A4
Chandley St SK8 .... 239 D6
Chandos Cl CH4 .... 141 F3
Change La L64 .... 68 A4
Channel The CH1 .... 95 D2
Chantler Ave WA4 .... 16 C2
Chantry Ave CW8 .... 103 D2
Chantry Cl SK12 .... 38 C3
Chantry Ct Blacon CH1 .... 117 F1
Crewe CW1 .... 190 B2
Macclesfield SK11 .... 112 B3
Chantry Fold SK12 .... 38 C3
Chantry Rd SK12 .... 38 B3
Chantry The CW6 .... 169 F1
Chantry Wlk L60 .... 41 D3
Chapel Ave WA6 .... 75 E1
Chapel Bank ST7 .... 195 E3
Chapel Cl Audlem CW3 .... 229 F2
Cholmondeston CW7 .... 170 C2
Comberbach CW9 .... 78 B4
Ellesmere Port L65 .... 70 B4
Mount Pleasant ST7 .... 195 D3
Saughall CH1 .... 94 A1
Waverton CH3 .... 143 D3
Chapel Cross Rd WA2 .... 9 D1
Chapel Ct Altrincham WA14 .... 238 D4
Chelford SK11 .... 84 A2
Hyde SK14 .... 241 C5
Northwich CW9 .... 103 F4
Chapel Dr WA15 .... 32 B4
Chapel Gn CW6 .... 122 B3
Chapel House La L64 .... 93 D4
Chapel La Acton Bridge CW8 .... 76 C2
Alldford CH3 .... 164 B3
Allostock WA16 .... 106 C2
Altrincham WA15 .... 32 B4
Appleton WA4 .... 27 D2
Audley ST7 .... 209 E1
Burtonwood WA5 .... 6 C3
Chester CH3 .... 119 D1
Crewe CW1 .... 173 E1
Cronton WA8 .... 12 B2
Delamere CW6 .... 122 C1
Dutton WA4 .... 77 D4
Hollins Green WA3 .... 10 C1
Holt LL13 .... 196 B4
Kidsgrove ST7 .... 195 F2
Kingsley WA6 .... 75 E1
Manley WA6 .... 98 C2
Mere WA16 .... 30 A2
Milton Green CH3 .... 165 D1
Moulton CW9 .... 126 C4
Norton in Hales TF9 .... 236 B1
Partington M31 .... 11 F1
Rainow SK10 .... 88 C3
Ravensmoor CW5 .... 203 E1
Rode Heath ST7 .... 193 F4
Chapel La continued
Threapwood SY14 .... 222 C4
Warrington WA4 .... 26 B4
Wilmslow SK9 .... 60 A3
Withington SK11 .... 109 E1
Chapel Mews
Ellesmere Port L65 .... 70 A2
Nantwich CW5 .... 204 C3
Chapel Rd Alderley Edge SK9 .... 60 A1
Ollerton WA16 .... 82 C3
Penketh WA5 .... 14 C2
Saighton CH3 .... 164 B3
Sale M33 .... 242 B7
Whaley Bridge SK23 .... 65 F3
Winsford CW7 .... 126 C1
Chapel Row Barbridge CW5 .... 187 E3
Nantwich CW5 .... 204 B3
Chapel St Alderley Edge SK9 .... 60 A1
Audley ST7 .... 209 F2
Bollington SK10 .... 88 A4
Cheadle SK8 .... 239 D5
Chester CH2 .... 237 F3
Congleton CW12 .... 156 B1
Crewe CW2 .... 190 B2
Haydock WA11 .... 1 C3
Higher Wincham CW9 .... 79 E2
Holt LL13 .... 196 B4
Hyde SK14 .... 241 D6
Kidsgrove ST7 .... 194 B1
Macclesfield SK11 .... 112 B3
Moulton CW9 .... 126 C4
Mount Pleasant ST7 .... 195 D3
New Mills SK22 .... 39 D3
Newton-le-W WA12 .... 2 A2
Northwich CW8, CW9 .... 103 F4
Sandbach CW11 .... 175 D3
Sandbach, Wheelock CW11 .... 175 D2
Stalybridge SK15 .... 242 D2
Weaverham CW8 .... 77 E1
Whaley Bridge SK23 .... 65 F4
Widnes WA8 .... 23 D4
Chapel Wlk WA3 .... 4 A4
Chapel Wlks
Cheadle Hulme SK8 .... 35 D3
Lymm WA13 .... 19 E1
Chapel Yd WA2 .... 16 A3
Chapelfields WA6 .... 74 A4
Chapelmere Cl CW11 .... 174 C4
Chapelmere Ct CW1 .... 190 B4
Chapman Cl WA8 .... 12 B2
Charcoal Rd WA14 .... 20 C2
Charcoal Woods WA14 .... 238 A3
Charity La SK11 .... 114 A3
Charlcote Cres CW2 .... 206 B4
Charlecote Rd SK12 .... 36 C2
Charles Ave Davenham CW9 .... 103 F1
Great Sankey WA5 .... 14 B4
Charles Cres CH4 .... 237 F1
Charles Price Gdns L65 .... 70 B3
Charles Rd CH2 .... 95 E1
Charles Sq CW11 .... 175 F1
Charles St Chester CH2 .... 237 E3
Chester, Hoole Pk CH2 .... 118 C2
Crewe CW1 .... 190 B2
Goldborne WA3 .... 3 D4
Irlam M44 .... 11 F3
Widnes WA8 .... 23 D4
Charlesworth Cres SK23 .... 39 E2
Charlesworth Ct 2 CW11 .... 175 E3
Charlesworth Rd SK23 .... 39 E2
Charlesworth St
Crewe CW1 .... 190 B3
1 Stockport SK1 .... 240 F3
Charlock Sq WA14 .... 238 B8
Charlook Wlk M31 .... 11 F1
Charlotte Ct CH1 .... 237 E3
Charlotte St Cheadle SK8 .... 239 D5
Chester CH1 .... 118 A1
Macclesfield SK11 .... 112 B4
Charlotte St W 14 SK11 .... 112 B4
Charlotte Wlk 16 WA8 .... 23 D4
Charlton Cl WA7 .... 50 A4
Charlton Dr M33 .... 242 C6
Charlton St
Macclesfield SK11 .... 112 B4
Warrington WA4 .... 16 C2
Charminster Cl WA5 .... 15 D3
Charnock Ave WA12 .... 1 C2
Charnock Rd WA3 .... 4 C2
Charnwood ST7 .... 195 D1
Charnwood Cl
Macclesfield SK10 .... 87 D1
Warrington WA3 .... 10 A3
Charnwood Cres SK7 .... 36 B4
Charter Ave WA2 .... 16 A4
Charter Cres L66 .... 69 F2
Charter Rd
Altrincham WA15 .... 238 E4
Bollington SK10 .... 88 A4
Charter Way SK10 .... 87 F2
Charterhall Dr CH2 .... 118 C1
Chartwell Pk CW11 .... 175 D2
Chase Dr L66 .... 69 F1
Chase The L63 .... 43 E3
Chase Way L66 .... 69 F1
Chasefield WA14 .... 238 A2
Chaser Ct CH1 .... 117 F2
Chasewater Cl WA7 .... 24 C2
Chatburn Ct WA3 .... 4 C1
Chatfield Dr WA3 .... 9 F2
Chatham St
15 Macclesfield SK11 .... 112 B4
Stockport SK3 .... 240 D4
Chatham Way CW1 .... 191 E3
Chatswood Ave SK2 .... 240 F2
Chatsworth Ave
Culcheth WA3 .... 4 C2
Macclesfield SK11 .... 111 F3
Chatsworth Cl
Ellesmere Port L66 .... 69 E3
Wistaston CW2 .... 206 A4
Chatsworth Dr Chester CH2 .... 119 D3
Congleton CW12 .... 155 F2
Widnes WA8 .... 12 B2
Chatsworth Rd
Hazel Grove SK7 .... 36 C4
High Lane SK6 .... 37 F3
Wilmslow SK9 .... 59 F2
Chatteris Pk WA7 .... 24 B1
Chatterton Dr WA7 .... 50 C4
Chatwell Gdns WA4 .... 26 C3
Chaucer Cl CH1 .... 117 F3
Chaucer Pl WA4 .... 16 C2
Chaucer St WA7 .... 23 D1
Cheadle Etchells Prim Sch SK8 .... 34 B4
Cheadle Heath Jun & Inf Sch SK3 .... 240 A3
Cheadle Hulme High Sch SK8 .... 35 D4
Cheadle Hulme Sch SK8 .... 35 D4
Cheadle La Peover WA16 .... 106 A4
Plumley WA16 .... 81 D1
Cheadle Old Rd SK3 .... 240 C3
Cheadle Prep Sch SK8 .... 34 B4
Cheadle Prim Sch SK8 .... 239 D6
Cheadle RC Inf Sch SK8 .... 239 E2
Cheadle RC Jun Sch SK8 .... 239 E2
Cheadle Rd SK8 .... 239 F3
Cheadle Royal Hospl SK8 .... 239 C2
Cheam Rd WA15 .... 238 F8
Cheapside SK14 .... 241 E7
Checkley Dr ST6 .... 179 E1
Checkley La CW3 .... 221 F1
Checkley Rd ST5 .... 210 B1
Chedlee Dr SK8 .... 34 C4
Chedworth Dr WA8 .... 12 B2
Cheerbrook Rd CW5 .... 205 E2
Cheese Hill La CW8 .... 101 D2
Chelford Ave WA3 .... 3 E4
Chelford Cl
Altrincham WA15 .... 238 E6
Blacon CH1 .... 117 F1
Chelford Ct 2 SK8 .... 34 C3
Chelford Gr SK3 .... 240 D1
Chelford La WA16 .... 83 E1
Chelford Rd
Chelford SK10, SK11 .... 84 B1
Chelford, Marthall WA16 .... 83 E2
Henbury SK10 .... 110 C4
Macclesfield SK11 .... 111 E4
Nether Alderley SK9 .... 84 B4
Nether Alderley, Monks Heath SK10 .... 85 D1
Prestbury SK10 .... 86 B3
Radnor CW12 .... 155 F3
Wilmslow SK9 .... 34 B3
Chelford Sta SK11 .... 84 A1
Chell St CW1 .... 190 A3
Chells Hill CW11 .... 176 B1
Chelmsford Rd SK3 .... 240 C4
Chelsea Cl ST6 .... 179 E1
Chelston Dr SK9 .... 34 B3
Cheltenham Cl WA5 .... 15 D4
Cheltenham Cres
Crewe CW1 .... 190 A4
Runcorn WA7 .... 49 D3
Cheltenham Dr M33 .... 242 C6
Cheltenham Rd
Cheadle SK3 .... 240 A3
Ellesmere Port L65 .... 70 B2
Chemical St WA12 .... 2 A2
Cheney Wlk CW2 .... 206 B4
Chepstow Cl Biddulph ST6 .... 179 E1
Winsford CW7 .... 149 E4
Cherington Cl SK9 .... 34 C2
Cherington Cres SK11 .... 112 A4
Cherington Rd SK8 .... 239 C4
Cheriton Ave M33 .... 242 C7
Cheriton Way CW2 .... 206 A4
Cherrington Rd CW5 .... 204 C2
Cherry Bank Cotts CW6 .... 184 C3
Cherry Blossom Rd WA7 .... 49 F2
Cherry Cl Newcastle-u-L ST5 .... 210 B1
Newton-le-W WA12 .... 1 C2
Willaston L64 .... 67 E4
Cherry Cnr WA13 .... 28 A4
Cherry Cres CW7 .... 149 E4
Cherry Ct M33 .... 242 A6
Cherry Dale Rd CH4 .... 139 D2
Cherry Gr
Ellesmere Port L66 .... 70 A1
Nantwich CW5 .... 204 B3
Cherry Grove Cty Prim Sch CH3 .... 119 D1
Cherry Grove Rd CH3 .... 119 D1
Cherry La Congleton CW12 .... 179 F4
Cuddington CW8 .... 101 F1
Lawton Heath ST7 .... 193 F3
Lymm WA13 .... 28 A4
Weaverham CW8 .... 102 B4
Cherry Rd CH3 .... 119 D1
Cherry Tree Ave
Barnton CW8 .... 78 A2
Lawton-gate ST7 .... 194 A3
Lymm WA13 .... 18 B1
Penketh WA5 .... 14 C2
Poynton SK12 .... 36 C2
Runcorn WA7 .... 49 E4
Cherry Tree Cl Hale L24 .... 21 F1
Haydock WA11 .... 1 A3
Romiley SK6 .... 241 E2
Wilmslow SK9 .... 60 C4
Cherry Tree Dr
Hazel Grove SK7 .... 37 D4
St Helens WA9 .... 1 A1
Cherry Tree Inf Sch SK6 .... 241 E3
Cherry Tree Jun Sch SK6 .... 241 E2
Cherry Tree La
Romiley SK6 .... 241 E2
Woore CW3 .... 232 B1
Cherry Tree Rd Audley ST7 .... 209 F1
Crewe CW1 .... 190 C3
Goldborne WA3 .... 3 F4
Newcastle-u-L ST5 .... 210 C1
Cherry Wlk
Cheadle Hulme SK7 .... 35 E4
Partington M31 .... 11 E1
Peover WA16 .... 106 B4
Cherrycroft SK6 .... 241 E1
Cherryfields Rd SK11 .... 111 F4
Cherrysutton WA8 .... 12 A2
Cherrywood Cres CW8 .... 78 A2
Cherwell Cl
Cheadle Hulme SK8 .... 35 D4
Warrington WA2 .... 8 B1
Cheryl Ct CW8 .... 102 A2
Cheryl Dr WA8 .... 13 E1
Chesford Grange WA1 .... 17 F4
Chesham Cl SK9 .... 59 F2
Chesham Pl WA14 .... 238 C2
Chesham Rd SK9 .... 59 F2
Chesham St CH2 .... 237 F3
Cheshire Cl WA12 .... 2 C2
Cheshire Oaks Outlet Village L65 .... 70 C1
Cheshire St CW3 .... 229 F2
Cheshire View SK10 .... 88 A3
Cheshire Workshops CH3 .... 184 B3
Cheshyre Dr WA7 .... 23 F1
Cheshyre's La WA7 .... 48 C4
Chessington Cl WA4 .... 26 C3
Chest Nut Cl CW6 .... 146 B1
Chester Aerospace Pk CH4 .... 139 D3
Chester Ave
Altrincham WA15 .... 238 F2
Goldborne WA3 .... 3 E4
Chester Bsns Pk CH4 .... 141 D2
Chester Catholic (Voluntary Aided) High Sch CH4 .... 141 E3
Chester Cl Irlam M44 .... 11 E3
Kidsgrove ST7 .... 210 C4
Runcorn WA7 .... 24 A1
14 Wilmslow SK9 .... 34 C1
Chester Gates CH1 .... 94 B3
Chester General Sta CH2 .... 237 F3
Chester High Rd L64 .... 67 E4
Chester La CW7 .... 125 E1
Chester New Rd WA4 .... 25 F4
Chester Rd Acton CW5 .... 204 A3
Audley ST7 .... 209 E1
Barbridge CW5 .... 187 E3
Broughton CH4 .... 139 E3
Churton CH3 .... 180 C3
Daresbury WA4 .... 25 D1
Delamere CW6, CW8 .... 123 E3
Ellesmere Port L65 .... 70 A1
Ellesmere Port, Great Sutton L66 .... 69 E2
Flint CH6 .... 91 D2
Frodsham WA6 .... 74 A4
Gatesheath CH3 .... 165 F3
Hartford CW8 .... 102 C2
Hartford, Greenbank CW8 .... 103 E3
Hawarden CH5 .... 116 A1
Hazel Grove SK7 .... 36 B4
Heswall L60 .... 41 E3
Higher Walton WA4 .... 25 E3
Holmes Chapel CW4 .... 130 A1
Huntington CH3 .... 142 A3
Kelsall CW6 .... 122 B3
Kidsgrove ST7 .... 210 B4
Knutsford WA16 .... 56 A3
Lavister LL12 .... 162 B1
Macclesfield SK11 .... 112 A4
Mere WA16 .... 56 A3
Middlewich CW10 .... 128 A1
Neston L64 .... 66 C4
Northwich CW8 .... 103 E3
Oakmere CW8 .... 124 A4
Plumley WA16 .... 80 C3
Poynton SK12 .... 36 B2
Rostherne WA14 .... 30 B3
Runcorn WA7 .... 50 C3
Sutton WA7 .... 50 A2
Tabley WA16 .... 56 A1
Tattenhall CH3 .... 166 A1
Warrington WA4 .... 17 D1
Weaverham CW8 .... 102 B2
Whitchurch SY13 .... 225 E1
Winsford CW7 .... 125 F1
Woodford SK12 .... 36 B2
Chester Retail Pk CH1 .... 118 A2
Chester Row WA12 .... 7 E4
Chester Royal Infmy CH1 .... 237 D3
Chester Sq CW1 .... 190 B2
Chester St Chester CH4 .... 140 C4
Crewe CW1 .... 190 B2
Stockport SK3 .... 240 D5
Warrington WA1 .... 16 A3
Widnes WA8 .... 13 D1
Chester Way CW8, CW9 .... 104 A4
Chester West Employment Pk CH1 .... 117 F1
Chester Wlks SK6 .... 241 A1
Chester Zoological Gdns CH2 .... 95 F1
Chesterfield Cl CW7 .... 125 F1
Chesterfield Gr OL6 .... 242 A3
Chesterfield Rd L62 .... 43 E2

Chestergate
Macclesfield SK11 112 B4
Stockport SK3 240 E5
Chestergate Mall 34 SK11 112 B4
Chesterton Cl CW10 151 F3
Chesterton Dr CW2 189 F1
Chesterton Gr 13 CW11 174 B3
Chestnut Ave Cheadle SK8 239 E5
Ellesmere Port L66 69 F1
Great Sankey WA5 14 B4
Irlam M44 11 E3
Macclesfield SK10 87 F1
Rode Heath ST7 193 F4
Shavington CW2 206 B3
Widnes WA8 13 D1
Chestnut Cl Chester CH2 119 D2
Cuddington CW8 101 F1
Middlewich CW10 128 A1
Tarporley CW6 146 B1
Wilmslow SK9 60 C4
Chestnut Ct CW6 146 B1
Chestnut Dr
Congleton CW12 156 A2
Holmes Chapel CW4 130 B2
Poynton SK12 36 C2
Chestnut Gr Barnton CW8 78 A2
Bebington L62 43 E4
Crewe CW1 190 C3
Goldborne WA3 3 F4
Newcastle-u-L ST5 210 C1
Winsford CW7 149 E4
Chestnut La WA6 73 F2
Chestnut Lodge Sch WA8 12 C1
Chestnut Villas SK4 240 C6
Chestnut Wlk M31 11 E1
Chesworth Fold SK1 240 F4
Chetham Ct WA2 8 A2
Chetton Dr WA7 50 C4
Chetwode Mews WA4 52 B1
Chetwode St CW1 190 B3
Chetwood Dr WA8 12 C2
Cheveley Cl SK10 87 E1
Chevin Gdns SK7 36 A4
Cheviot Ave Cheadle SK8 239 F2
Warrington WA2 8 A2
Cheviot Cl
Ellesmere Port L66 69 D3
Stockport SK4 240 D7
Cheviot Ct CW7 149 D4
Chevithorne Cl WA14 238 B5
Chevron Cl CH1 117 F2
Chevron Hey CH1 117 F2
Chevron Pl WA14 238 D7
Cheyne Wlk CW5 204 C2
Cheyney Rd Blacon CH1 118 A2
Chester CH1 118 A2
Chicago Ave M90 33 D4
Chichester Cl WA7 50 B3
Chichester Rd SK6 241 C2
Chichester St CH1 237 D3
Chidlow Cl
Hough Common CW2 206 C2
Widnes WA8 23 D3
Child's La CW12 177 F3
Childer Cres L66 69 D4
Childer Gdns L66 69 D4
Childer Thornton Cty Prim
Sch L66 69 D4
Childwall Ct L66 69 F4
Childwall Gdns L66 69 F4
Childwall Rd L66 69 F4
Chilham Cl CW7 149 E4
Chilham Pl SK11 111 F3
Chilington Ave WA8 22 B4
Chillingham Cl CW10 128 B1
Chiltern Ave Cheadle SK8 239 F2
Macclesfield SK11 112 A4
Warrington WA2 8 A2
Chiltern Cl Chester CH4 141 D3
Cuddington CW8 102 A1
Chiltern Cres WA2 8 A2
Chiltern Dr WA15 238 F2
Chiltern Pl WA2 8 A2
Chiltern Rd Culcheth WA3 4 C2
St Helens WA9 1 A2
Warrington WA2 8 A2
Chiltern Way CW7 149 D4
Chilton Dr L66 69 F1
Chilworth Cl CW2 206 B4
China La WA4 16 B1
Chines The CW8 101 E3
Chinley Cl Manchester SK4 240 B7
Sale M33 242 D5
Chippingdall Cl WA5 15 E3
Chipstead Cl CW8 103 D2
Chirk Cl CH2 118 C3
Chirk Pl CW7 126 A1
Chirton Cl WA11 1 B4
Chisledon Cl WA11 1 B4
Chiswick Cl WA7 50 B4
Chiswick Gdns WA4 26 C3
Chokeberry Cl WA14 238 B8
Chollerton Cl WA16 29 E2
Cholmondeley Ave WA14 238 E8
Cholmondeley Castle
Gdns SY14 200 C2
Cholmondeley La SY14 200 C4
Cholmondeley Rd
Ellesmere Port L65 69 F2
Hampton SY14 213 F4
Runcorn WA7 49 E2
Cholmondeley St WA8 23 D2
Cholmondely St SK11 112 B3
Chomlea WA14 238 B4
Chorley Hall Cl SK9 59 F1
Chorley Hall La
Alderley Edge SK9 60 A1
Chorley CW5 202 B1
Chorley St WA2 16 A3
Chorley's La WA8 13 F2
Chorlton Cl WA7 24 B1
Chorlton Dr SK8 239 E6
Chorlton La CW2 207 D1
Chowley Oak La CH3 182 C3
Chrimes Dr CW8 123 F3
Christ Church CE Aided
Prim Sch L65 70 A1
Christ The King RC Prim
Sch L62 43 F4
Christchurch Ave CW2 190 A1
Christie Cl L66 44 A1
Christie St WA8 13 E1
Christleton Ave CW2 189 E3
Christleton Ct WA7 24 B2
Christleton Cty High Sch
CH3 142 C4
Christleton Cty Prim Sch
CH3 142 C4
Christleton Dr L66 69 F3
Christleton Rd CH3 119 D1
Christleton Sports Ctr
CH3 142 C4
Christleton Way 15 SK9 34 B3
Christopher Dr L62 44 A3
Chudleigh Cl WA14 238 B6
Church Ave SK9 34 A1
Church Bank Audley ST7 209 E1
Tattenhall CH3 166 A1
Church Bk SK23 65 E4
Church Brow
Altrincham WA14 238 B2
Hyde SK14 241 D5
Church Cl CW8 77 E1
Church College Cl CH1 118 A2
Church Coppenhall Cty
Jun Sch CW1 190 A3
Church Croft CH4 162 A3
Church Ct Altrincham WA15 238 E1
Ashton CH3 121 F4
Farndon CH3 180 C1
Church Dr WA2 9 D1
Church End L24 21 E1
Church Farm Ct Heswall L60 40 C4
Willaston L64 67 F4
Church Fields TF9 236 B1
Church Gn WA13 19 D4
Church Hall Cl CH1 117 F2
Church Hill WA16 57 D1
Church La Aldford CH3 163 F2
Appleton WA4 17 D1
Backford CH1 95 D2
Bebington L62 44 A2
Chester CH2 118 B4
Culcheth WA3 4 C2
Eaton CW12 134 C1
Ellesmere Port L66 69 E2
Elton WA6 72 B1
Farndon CH3 180 C1
Goldborne WA3 3 E4
Guilden Sutton CH3 119 F3
Henbury SK11 111 E4
Kidsgrove ST7 195 F4
Mobberley WA16 58 B3
Nantwich CW5 204 C3
Neston L64 66 C4
New Mills SK22 39 E4
Rainow SK10 88 C3
Romiley SK6 241 C2
Sandbach CW11 175 F4
Scholar Green ST7 194 B4
Smallwood CW11 176 C2
Stoak CH2 96 A4
Sutton Lane Ends SK11 112 C2
Warren SK11 134 B4
Weaverham CW8 77 E1
Wistaston CW2 205 F4
Woodford SK7 35 E1
Church Lawton Gate Cty
Prim Sch ST7 194 A3
Church Manor SK4 240 B8
Church Mead CH3 181 D3
Church Meadow
Hyde SK14 241 C7
Norton in Hales TF9 236 B1
Church Meadow Gdns
SK14 241 C7
Church Meadow La L60 40 C4
Church Meadows
Little Leigh CW8 77 E3
Whitchurch SY13 226 A1
Church Mews
Bollington SK10 88 A4
Knutsford WA16 57 D1
Church Par L65 70 B3
Church Rd Alsager ST7 193 E2
Ashton CH3 121 F4
Barnton CW8 78 A1
Broughton CH4 139 E2
Burwardsley CH3 184 A3
Cheadle Hulme SK8 35 D4
Eccleston CH4 141 F1
Frodsham WA6 74 B4
Gatley M22 & SK8 239 A5
Hale L24 47 F4
Halewood L26 21 D4
Haydock WA11 1 C4
Little Leigh CW8 77 E2
Lymm WA13 18 C1
New Mills SK22 39 E4
Northwich CW8, CW9 104 A4
Sale M33 242 D6
Saughall CH1 94 A1
Shocklach CH3 197 E1
Church Rd continued
Stockport SK4 240 E6
Thornton Hough L63 42 A3
Tilston SY14 198 A2
Wilmslow, Davenport Green
SK9 59 F2
Wilmslow, Handforth SK9 34 B2
Worleston CW5 188 B3
Church Rd E M33 242 D6
Church Rd W M33 242 D6
Church St Altrincham WA14 238 D5
Audley ST7 210 A1
Bollington SK10 88 A4
Cheadle SK8 239 D6
Chester CH2 237 E4
Connah's Quay CH5 91 E1
Davenham CW9 104 A2
Ellesmere Port L65 70 B3
Farndon CH3 180 C1
Frodsham WA6 74 A4
Great Budworth CW9 79 D4
Higher Wincham CW9 79 F3
Holt LL13 180 C1
Hyde SK14 241 D5
Kelsall CW6 122 B2
Kidsgrove, Butt Lane ST7 194 B1
Kidsgrove, The Rookery ST7 195 D2
Macclesfield SK11 112 B4
Malpas SY14 213 D2
Moulton CW9 126 C4
Mount Pleasant ST7 195 E3
Newton-le-W WA12 2 C2
Runcorn WA7 23 D2
Sandbach CW11 175 E3
Stalybridge SK15 242 D2
Stockport SK4 240 E7
Tarvin CH3 121 E1
Warrington WA1 16 B3
Weaverham CW8 77 E1
Widnes WA8 23 D3
Wilmslow SK9 60 A4
Winsford CW7 126 C1
Church St N CW6 122 B3
Church St W SK11 112 B4
Church Terr 10 SK9 34 B2
Church View Audlem CW3 230 A2
Hyde SK14 241 D5
Kingsley WA6 75 D1
Knutsford WA16 57 D1
Lymm WA13 19 D2
Wilmslow SK9 34 A1
Church View Terr SK11 112 C2
Church View Wlk CW2 205 F4
Church Way Blacon CH1 117 F3
Wybunbury CW5 220 A4
Church Wk WA2 8 A3
Church Wlk
Holmes Chapel CW4 130 B2
Knutsford WA16 57 D1
Lower Peover WA16 81 F1
Northwich CW9 104 A4
Stalybridge SK15 242 D3
Wilmslow SK9 59 F3
Church Wlks CH3 142 C4
Church Wood View WA13 18 C2
Churche's Mansions CW5 204 C2
Churchfield Rd WA6 74 B4
Churchfields
Altrincham WA14 238 B1
Audlem CW3 230 A2
Barnton CW8 78 A2
Croft WA3 9 D4
Cuddington CW8 102 A1
Helsby WA6 73 E2
Knutsford WA16 57 E1
Widnes WA8 13 D3
Wybunbury CW5 220 A4
Churchgate SK1 240 F5
Churchill Ave WA3 5 D2
Churchill Cl CW12 156 A2
Churchill Dr CW6 146 B1
Churchill Parkway CW7 149 E4
Churchill Rd WA14 238 D7
Churchill St SK4 240 D7
Churchill Way
Macclesfield SK11 112 B4
Neston L64 66 C4
Churchley Cl SK3 240 A2
Churchley Rd SK3 240 A3
Churchmere Cl CW1 190 B4
Churchside SK11 112 B4
Churchside Wlk CH4 140 C4
Churchward Cl CH2 118 B2
Churchway Alvanley WA6 73 E1
Macclesfield SK10 86 C1
Churchway Rd L24 21 D1
Churchyard Side CW5 204 C3
Churton Cl Davenham CW9 103 F2
Hough Common CW2 206 C2
Churton Rd Chester CH3 119 D1
Farndon CH3 180 C1
Churton St CH3 119 D1
Cicely Mill La WA16 30 B2
Cinder Cl CH3 119 F3
Cinder Hill CW7 125 F3
Cinder Hill La ST7 194 C4
Cinder La Appleton WA4 17 F1
Chelford SK11 83 F1
Guilden Sutton CH3 119 F3
Lostock CW9 105 D4
Peover WA16 108 B4
Worleston CW5 188 B1
Cinnamon Brow WA2 8 C2
Cinnamon Brow CE Aided
Prim Sch WA2 8 C2
Cinnamon La WA2 8 C1
Cinnamon La N WA2 8 C2
Circle Ave CW5 205 F3
Circle The Crewe CW2 190 B1
Mere WA16 30 B1
Circuit The
Alderley Edge SK9 60 A2
Cheadle Hulme SK8 35 D4
Stockport SK3 240 C2
Wilmslow SK9 59 E3
Circular Dr CH4 140 C2
City Bank ST6 179 E1
City Rd CH2 237 F3
City Walls Rd CH1 237 D2
Civic Way Ellesmere Port L65 70 A2
Middlewich CW10 128 B1
Clair Ave CH5 116 A2
Claire Pl CW7 149 E4
Clamhunger La WA16 56 B4
Clamley Ct L24 21 D2
Clanfield Ave WA8 12 B2
Clap Gate Cres WA8 22 A3
Clap Gates Cres WA5 15 F4
Clap Gates Rd WA5 15 F4
Clare Ave Chester CH2 119 D2
Wilmslow SK9 34 B2
Clare Dr Ellesmere Port L65 70 A1
Macclesfield SK10 87 E2
Wistaston CW2 189 F1
Clare Rd SK5 240 F8
Clare St Kidsgrove ST7 195 F2
Mount Pleasant ST7 195 E3
Claremont Ave
Altrincham WA14 238 E8
Widnes WA8 13 E2
Claremont Cl CW9 103 F2
Claremont Dr
Altrincham WA14 238 E8
Widnes WA8 13 D2
Claremont Gr WA15 238 E3
Claremont Rd
Cheadle Hulme SK8 35 D4
Crewe CW2 190 A1
Culcheth WA3 4 B2
Runcorn WA7 23 D1
Sale M33 242 B7
Claremont St OL6 242 B4
Clarence Ave Chester CH3 119 D1
Widnes WA8 13 D2
Clarence Ct SK9 60 A3
Clarence Gr CW1 190 A3
Clarence Rd
Altrincham WA15 238 F3
Bollington SK10 63 D1
Warrington WA4 17 D1
Clarence St Hyde SK14 241 E8
Newton-le-We WA12 1 C2
Runcorn WA7 22 C2
Stalybridge
OL6 & SK15 & SK16 242 B1
Warrington WA1 16 C4
Clarence Terr
Bollington SK10 63 D1
Runcorn WA7 23 D2
Clarendon Ave
Altrincham WA15 238 E5
Manchester SK4 240 B7
Clarendon Cl Chester CH4 141 F3
Runcorn WA7 50 B4
Clarendon Cres M33 242 D7
Clarendon Ct WA2 7 F2
Clarendon Dr SK10 88 A1
Clarendon Ind Est SK14 241 E7
Clarendon Pl SK14 241 E6
Clarendon Rd Denton M34 241 B6
Hyde SK14 241 E7
Irlam M44 11 F4
Sale M33 242 D6
Clarendon St Hyde SK14 241 D7
Reddish SK5 240 F7
Clares Farm Cl WA1 17 F4
Clark Way SK14 241 D7
Clarke Ave Culcheth WA3 5 D2
Warrington WA4 16 B1
Clarke Gdns 17 WA8 23 D4
Clarke La Bollington SK10 87 F3
Langley SK11 113 E2
Clarke St WA14 238 D7
Clarke Terr SK11 112 B3
Clarkethorn Terr SK4 240 E7
Clarks Terr WA7 48 B4
Clary Meadow CW8 78 C1
Clatterbridge Hospl L63 42 B4
Clatterbridge Rd L63 42 B4
Claude St WA1 16 B3
Claughton Ave CW2 190 B1
Claverton Cl WA7 49 D3
Clay Heys SK11 84 A2
Clay La Burtonwood WA5 6 C3
Haslington CW11 174 A1
Marton Green CW7 125 D2
Peover WA16 108 A4
Sandbach CW11 174 A1
Wilmslow, Handforth SK9 34 B3
Wilmslow, Lindow SK9 59 E3
Claydon Gdns WA3 10 C1
Clayhill Gn L66 69 E4
Clayhill Light Ind Pk L64 41 F1
Claypit Rd CH4 141 D3
Claypitts La CH3 142 C3
Clayton Av CW12 157 D3
Clayton Ave WA3 3 F4
Clayton Cres Runcorn WA7 22 C1
Widnes WA8 12 C1
Clayton Dr SY13 226 A1
Clayton Rd WA3 9 F3
Clayton's Row CW5 204 C4
Clayton-by-pass CW12 156 B2
Cleave Rd CW8 77 E1
Cleaver Rd CH1 117 F2
Cledford Cres CW10 151 F3
Cledford Cty Inf & Jun
Sch CW10 151 E4
Cledford La CW10 151 F4
Cleethorpes Rd WA7 50 B4
Cleeve Way SK8 35 D3
Cleeves Cl WA1 16 B3
Clegg Pl OL6 242 A4
Clegg St SK11 112 C4
Clegge St WA2 16 A4
Cleggs Cl CH3 142 A4
Clelland St WA4 16 B2
Clement St SK4 240 E7
Clemley Cl CW6 122 B3
Clerewood Ave SK8 34 A4
Clevedon Cl SK11 112 A4
Cleveland Ave SK14 241 C6
Cleveland Dr
Ellesmere Port L66 69 D3
Goldborne WA3 3 E4
Cleveland Rd
Altrincham WA15 238 F3
Manchester SK4 240 A8
Warrington WA2 8 A2
Cleveland Way CW7 149 D4
Cleveleys Ave Gatley SK8 239 B1
Widnes WA8 13 E1
Cleveleys Rd WA5 15 D2
Cleves Cl CH1 117 E3
Cliff Gr SK4 240 B8
Cliff La Acton Bridge CW8 76 B2
Appleton WA4 17 E1
Lymm WA16 28 A3
Macclesfield SK10 88 A1
Rainow SK10 88 A1
Cliff Rd Acton Bridge CW8 76 C2
Wilmslow SK9 60 A4
Cliff Side SK9 60 A4
Cliff View WA6 74 A4
Cliffbrook Gr 8 SK9 34 B1
Cliffe Rd Appleton WA4 26 B4
Crewe CW1 190 A4
Neston L64 66 C3
Cliffe St Warrington WA1 16 A3
Widnes WA8 13 E1
Cliffmere Cl SK8 239 F3
Clifford Dr CH4 140 C3
Clifford Gr CW1 191 E2
Clifford Pl CW7 149 E4
Clifford Rd
Macclesfield SK11 112 A4
Penketh WA5 15 D2
Poynton SK12 36 B2
Wilmslow SK9 59 F3
Clifton Ave
Altrincham WA15 238 E5
Bebington L62 43 F2
Crewe CW2 190 A2
Culcheth WA3 4 B2
Gatley SK8 239 A2
Clifton Cl WA1 17 E4
Clifton Cres WA6 49 E1
Clifton Dr Blacon CH1 117 F2
Gatley M22 239 A6
Gatley, Heald Green SK8 239 A2
Northwich CW9 104 A3
Wilmslow SK9 59 F2
Clifton Gdns L65 70 B2
Clifton La WA7 49 F2
Clifton Park Ave CH5 91 E1
Clifton Rd Manchester SK4 240 A8
Runcorn WA7 49 F2
Runcorn, Heath WA7 49 D3
Sale M33 242 B5
Sandbach CW11 174 B4
Clifton St Alderley Edge SK9 60 A1
Crewe CW2 190 A2
Warrington WA4 16 B2
Cliftonville Rd WA1 17 E3
Clincton Cl L26 22 A4
Clincton View WA8 22 A4
Clinton St OL6 242 A4
Clipsley Cres WA11 1 A4
Clipsley La WA11 1 A3
Clitheroe Rd CW8 77 F1
Clive Ave WA2 8 B1
Clive La CW7 150 B4
Cliveden Rd CH4 140 C3
Clivegreen La CW10 150 C4
Clock Face Rd WA8 13 F4
Cloisters The Cheadle SK8 240 A1
Sale M33 242 D6
Clomley Gdns L24 21 F1
Close La Alsager ST7 192 C2
Mow Cop ST7 195 E4
Close The Alsager ST7 193 D2
Altrincham WA14 238 C5
Blacon CH1 117 E2
Northwich CW8 103 E3
Saughall CH1 94 A1
Stalybridge SK15 242 C4
Tarporley CW6 146 B1
Closeburn Ave L60 40 C3
Cloud The CW12 158 A2
Cloud View CW12 157 D1
Cloudberry Wlk M31 11 F1
Clough Ave Warrington WA2 8 A1
Wilmslow SK9 34 A1
Clough Bank SK10 87 F4
Clough Fold Rd SK14 241 D5
Clough Hall Dr ST7 210 C3
Clough Hall Rd ST7 210 C4
Clough Hall Sch The ST7 194 C1
Clough La CW8 103 E3
Clough Rd CW7 126 C1
Clough The WA7 23 F1
Clough Wlk CW2 206 B4
Cloughside SK12 38 C3
Cloughwood Sch CW8 103 E3

Clovelly Ave WA5 14 C4
Clovelly Gr WA7 50 B3
Clover Ave Frodsham WA6 74 B4
Stockport SK3 240 D1
Clover Ct WA7 50 A3
Clover Dr CW7 126 B2
Clover La CH4 140 C3
Clover Pl CH4 140 C3
Clover Rd SK6 241 E3
Cloverdale CW8 103 E4
Cloverdale Rd SK11 112 A3
Cloverfield WA7 50 B4
Cloverfield Gdns L66 69 E4
Cloverfields CW1 191 E2
Clowes Ave ST7 193 F1
Clowes St SK11 112 A4
Clumber Cl SK12 36 C2
Clumber Rd SK12 36 C2
Clutton CE Contr Prim Sch CH3 182 B1
Clwyd Ave SK3 240 D3
Clwyd Cl CH4 139 D3
Clwyd Way L66 69 D3
Clyde Ave ST6 179 F1
Clyde Cres CW7 127 D1
Clyde Gr CW2 190 A2
Clyde Rd SK3 240 C3
Clydesdale L65 70 A2
Clydesdale Ave CW2 190 A2
Clydesdale Rd WA4 26 B4
Coach Rd Bickerton SY14 199 E1
Chowley CH3 183 D2
Edge Green SY14 199 E1
Hampton SY14 199 E1
Little Budworth CW6 147 E4
Coachway SK10 86 C4
Coalbrookdale Rd L64 41 F1
Coalpit Hill ST7 210 B4
Coalpit La Langley SK11 113 E3
Mollington CH1 94 B2
Winsford CW10 127 F1
Coare St SK10 87 E1
Coastguard La L64 41 D1
Cob Hall La WA6 98 B3
Cob Moor Rd
Kidsgrove ST7 195 D2
Lawton-gate ST7 195 D2
Cobal Ct WA6 74 A4
Cobb's La CW5 204 C4
Cobbett's Way SK9 59 F2
Cobblers Cross La CW6 146 C1
Cobblers La LL12 161 D1
Cobbles The Chester CH4 141 E4
Cuddington CW8 101 E2
Lower Peover WA16 81 F1
Cobbs Cty Inf Sch The WA4 26 C4
Cobbs La Appleton WA4 26 C4
Hough Common CW2 206 C1
Cobden St
Ashton-u-L OL6 242 A2
Newton-le-W WA12 2 B2
Warrington WA2 16 A3
Cock Hall La SK11 113 E2
Cock La CW9 78 C4
Cocker Hill SK15 242 E2
Cockhedge Ctr WA1 16 A3
Cockhedge La WA1 16 B3
Cockhedge Way WA1 16 A3
Cockington Cl CW9 104 A2
Cocklade La L24 21 E1
Cockpit La CW8 102 A1
Cocksheadhey Rd SK10 63 E1
Cocksmoss Rd SK11 133 E2
Coe La WA14 30 B4
Coerdon Dr WA4 17 E1
Cogshall La Comberbach CW9 78 A4
Little Leigh CW9 77 F4
Northwich CW9 78 B3
Colborne Ave SK6 241 C2
Colborne St WA12 2 C2
Colchester Pl SK4 240 C7
Colchester Sq CH4 140 C3
Coldmoss Dr CW11 175 E2
Coldstream Cl WA2 8 C2
Cole Ave WA12 2 B2
Colebrook Cl WA3 10 A2
Coleclough Pl WA3 4 C2
Colehill Bank CW12 156 C1
Colehill Pl CH5 91 E1
Colenso Gr SK4 240 B7
Coleridge Cl CH1 118 A3
Coleridge Way CW1 190 C3
Colin Rd SK4 240 E8
Colinwood Ave CH4 139 D2
Collar House Dr SK10 86 C3
College Cl Warrington WA1 16 B3
Wilmslow SK9 59 F4
College Fields CW2 190 A1
College Gn CH4 141 E4
College La CW6 168 C1
College of Law Christleton Hall CH3 142 B4
College Rd ST7 193 D3
College View CH5 91 E1
Colley La
Hassall Green CW11 175 E3
Sandbach CW11 175 E3
Colleys La Nantwich CW2 205 E4
Willaston (nr Nantwich) CW2 205 E4
Collier St WA7 22 C2
Collier's Row WA7 48 C4
Colliers La CW9 54 C1
Colliery Green Cl L64 66 C3
Colliery Green Ct L64 66 C3
Colliery Green Dr L64 66 C3
Collin St WA5 15 F3
Collinbrook Ave CW2 190 A1
Collingham Gn L66 69 D3
Collingham Way CW7 126 B1
Collingtree Ave CW7 127 D2
Collingwood Cl
Macclesfield SK10 87 D1
Poynton SK12 37 D2
Collingwood Rd WA12 2 A2
Collins Green Rd WA5 1 C1
Collins St CW2 190 A2
Collinson Ct WA6 74 A4
Colmere Ct L65 70 B4
Colne Rd WA5 6 C3
Colshaw Cty Prim Sch SK9 34 B1
Colshaw Dr SK9 34 B1
Colshaw La SK11 109 F1
Colshaw Wlk SK9 34 B1
Coltsfoot Dr WA14 238 B8
Columbine Cl
Huntington CH3 142 A3
Widnes WA8 12 A2
Columbine Wlk M31 11 F1
Colveley Way CW7 126 A1
Colville Ct WA2 8 A2
Colville Rd SK11 111 F4
Colwick Ave WA14 238 E6
Colwyn Cl WA5 7 F1
Colwyn Rd Bramhall SK7 35 F4
Cheadle SK8 239 E1
Comber Way WA16 82 A4
Comberbach Cty Prim Sch CW9 78 B4
Combermere Cl SK8 239 F4
Combermere Pl CW1 190 A3
Comboy Dr CW9 104 B3
Combs Cl SK22 39 D4
Comer Terr M33 242 A6
Commercial Ave SK8 34 C3
Commercial Brow SK14 241 E8
Commercial Rd SK10 112 C4
Commercial St SK14 241 E7
Common Farm La SK11 83 F1
Common La Betley CW3 221 F3
Chelford SK11 83 F1
Culcheth WA3 4 C2
Duddon CW6 145 D4
Kelsall CW6 122 B2
Lach Dennis CW9 105 F3
Stretton WA4 52 C4
Tarvin CW6 122 B2
Warrington WA4 16 C1
Waverton CH3 143 D2
Common Rd WA12 1 C2
Common St WA12 1 C2
Common The WA7 49 F4
Commonhall St CH1 237 D2
Commons Mill CW11 175 D4
Commons The CW11 175 D3
Commonside WA6 73 F1
Commonwealth Cl CW7 149 E3
Company's Cl WA7 48 C3
Compass Cl WA7 50 B3
Compstall Rd SK6 241 E2
Compton Cl WA11 1 B4
Compton Pl Chester CH4 141 D3
Ellesmere Port L65 70 A3
Compton St SK15 242 E1
Concord Pl WA2 8 B1
Condliffe Cl CW11 175 E3
Conery Cl WA6 73 E2
Coney Gr WA7 50 A3
Coneymead SK15 242 D4
Congleton Cl SK9 85 D4
Congleton Edge Rd CW12 179 D3
Congleton La
Siddington SK11 109 E3
Withington SK11 109 E3
Congleton Rd
Alderley Edge SK10 85 D3
Astbury CW12 177 F2
Biddulph ST6 179 E1
Biddulph, Mow Cop CW12 178 C1
Broughton CH4 139 E2
Kidsgrove ST7 194 B1
Macclesfield SK11 112 A3
Marton SK11 133 D3
Nether Alderley SK10 85 D3
Sandbach CW11 175 D4
Scholar Green CW12 177 F2
Siddington SK11 110 A3
Smallwood CW11 177 D3
Smallwood, Arclid Green CW11 176 A4
Warren SK11 111 F1
Congleton Rd N
Lawton-gate ST7 194 C3
Scholar Green ST7 194 C3
Congleton Rd S ST7 194 B2
Congleton Sta CW12 157 D1
Congleton War Memorial Hospl CW12 156 C1
Conifer Cl CH1 95 D4
Conifer Gr WA5 14 C4
Conifer Wlk M31 11 E1
Conifers The ST7 193 D2
Coniston Ave
Bebington L63 43 E2
Congleton CW12 155 F1
Dukinfield SK14 241 C8
Penketh WA5 14 B2
Winsford CW7 126 B1
Coniston Cl Hooton L66 44 A1
Nantwich CW5 205 D3
Runcorn WA7 49 E3
Coniston Dr Frodsham WA6 74 B4
Holmes Chapel CW4 130 A2
Stalybridge SK15 242 D3
Wilmslow SK9 34 B2
Coniston Rd Chester CH2 118 C3
Gatley SK8 239 B5
High Lane SK6 37 E4
Neston L64 66 C3
Partington M31 11 F2
Coniston Way SK11 111 F3
Connah's Quay High Sch CH5 91 E1
Connaught Ave WA1 16 C4
Connaught Cl SK9 60 B4
Connaught Dr WA12 2 B1
Conroy Way WA12 7 E4
Consort Pl WA14 238 B3
Constable Dr SK9 60 C4
Constables Cl WA7 24 A1
Constance Rd M31 11 F2
Constance Way WA8 23 D3
Convamore Rd SK7 35 E4
Conway Ave Irlam M44 11 F4
Warrington WA5 7 F1
Winsford CW7 149 E4
Conway Cl Broughton CH4 140 B3
Crewe CW1 190 B4
Great Sankey WA5 14 C3
Knutsford WA16 82 A4
Conway Cres SK10 87 F1
Conway Ct L65 70 B2
Conway Dr Newton-le-W WA12 2 C2
Stalybridge SK15 242 D3
Conway Rd Cheadle SK8 239 E2
Sale M33 242 D5
Conway St SK5 240 E8
Coogee Ave WA5 14 C4
Cook Ave WA11 1 C4
Cook St Ellesmere Port L65 70 B3
Stockport SK3 240 E5
Cooke's La CW9 104 C3
Cooks La SY13 225 E4
Cooksmere La CW11 175 D4
Coole La
French Lane End CW5 218 C2
Newhall CW3 229 E3
Coombe Dr WA7 49 D4
Coombe Park L66 69 E3
Coombes Ave SK14 241 F5
Coope Rd SK10 87 F3
Cooper Ave
Newton-le-W WA12 1 C2
Warrington WA2 8 A1
Cooper La WA11 1 B3
Cooper St Congleton CW12 156 C2
Runcorn WA7 23 D2
Stockport SK1 240 F3
Widnes WA8 13 D1
Cooper's Cft CH3 142 A4
Cooper's La CH5 91 E1
Coopers Opening CW11 175 D4
Cop Meadow SK11 112 C1
Copage Dr SK6 241 A4
Cope Ave CW5 204 B2
Copeland Gr WA7 49 F3
Copeland Rd WA4 16 A1
Copes La CW5 204 B2
Copeswood Cl CH4 139 E2
Copgrove Wlk M22 33 F4
Copley Ave SK15 242 F2
Copley Park Mews SK15 242 F2
Coppenhall Cty High Sch CW1 190 C3
Coppenhall Gr CW2 190 A2
Coppenhall Heyes CW2 190 A2
Coppenhall La CW2 189 E2
Copper Beach Cl CH4 139 E2
Copper St SK11 112 C3
Copper Wood CW8 101 F3
Copperfield Cl WA3 9 E3
Copperfield Rd
Cheadle Hulme SK8 35 D3
Poynton SK12 36 B1
Copperfields Tarporley CW6 146 B1
Wilmslow SK9 60 B4
Copperhill Rd CW12 179 D4
Coppermine La SY14 184 A1
Coppice CW8 101 E3
Coppice Cl Disley SK12 38 A3
Romiley SK6 241 B4
Runcorn WA7 24 A1
Willaston (nr Nantwich) CW5 205 E3
Coppice Dr Disley SK12 38 A3
Middlewich CW10 151 F3
Coppice Gn WA5 7 D1
Coppice Gr WA16 57 D2
Coppice La SK12 38 A3
Coppice Rd
Haslington CW11 192 A4
Kidsgrove ST7 210 B4
Poynton SK12 37 D2
Willaston (nr Nantwich) CW5 205 E3
Coppice Rise SK11 112 B3
Coppice The
Altrincham WA15 32 A4
Nantwich CW5 204 C2
Sandbach CW11 174 C4
Whaley Bridge SK23 65 F3
Coppice Way SK9 34 C2
Coppins Cl Chester CH3 119 D1
Helsby WA6 73 D2
Coppins The Warrington WA2 8 B1
Wilmslow SK9 59 F2
Copse The Altrincham WA15 32 B4
Newton-le-W WA12 2 A2
Runcorn WA7 50 A3
Copthorne Cl CW12 156 C1
Copthorne Dr CW3 229 F2
Corbet Ave WA2 16 A4
Corbet Dr TF9 235 D2
Corbet St WA2 16 A4
Corcoran Dr SK6 241 F2
Cordale Cl WA5 14 C4
Corfe Way CW7 149 E4
Coridor Rd L65 71 D3
Corkland Cl OL6 242 B2
Corkland St OL6 242 B2
Corks La SK12 38 C3
Corley Ave SK3 239 F7
Cormorant Cl CW1 190 C2
Cormorant Dr WA7 22 C1
Cornbrook Rd SK11 112 B2
Corner Croft SK9 60 A2
Corner Ct SK8 239 F6
Cornerhouse La WA8 12 B2
Corners The CW8 102 C4
Cornfield Cl
Ellesmere Port L66 69 F1
Macclesfield SK10 87 E2
Sale M33 242 F5
Cornfield Rd SK6 241 E3
Cornforth Way WA8 12 C2
Cornhill Cl ST5 210 B1
Cornish Cl M22 33 E4
Cornishway M22 33 E4
Cornishway Ind Est M22 33 E4
Cornubia Rd WA8 23 E4
Cornwall Ave WA7 23 D1
Cornwall Cl
Congleton CW12 157 D1
High Lane SK6 37 F4
Macclesfield SK10 86 C1
Runcorn WA7 23 F1
Cornwall Gr CW1 190 A3
Cornwall Rd Cheadle SK8 34 A4
Chester CH2 118 B4
Irlam M44 11 E3
Widnes WA8 13 D2
Cornwall St Chester CH2 237 E4
Warrington WA1 16 C4
Cornwell Cl SK9 60 B4
Corona Ave SK14 241 E7
Coronation Ave
Alsager ST7 193 D2
Glazebury WA3 5 E4
Hyde SK14 241 E5
Warrington WA4 17 E1
Winsford CW7 126 C1
Coronation Bldgs SK10 88 A4
Coronation Cres
Crewe CW1 190 C3
Kidsgrove ST7 194 C1
Sandbach CW11 175 D3
Coronation Dr
Frodsham WA6 49 E1
Haydock WA11 2 A4
Newton-le-W WA12 2 C1
Penketh WA5 14 C2
Widnes WA8 22 A4
Coronation Gr CW8 78 A2
Coronation Rd
Broughton CH4 139 D2
Congleton CW12 156 C2
Ellesmere Port L65 70 B2
Middlewich CW10 151 E3
Runcorn, Higher Runcorn WA7 23 D1
Runcorn, Preston Brook WA7 50 C3
Coronation St Chester CH4 140 C4
Crewe CW1 190 B3
Macclesfield SK11 112 B3
Reddish SK5 240 E8
Coronation Terr CW6 146 B1
Coroner's La WA8 13 D2
Coronet Ave CW9 103 F2
Coronet Way WA8 22 A4
Corporation St Hyde SK14 241 D6
Stalybridge SK15 242 D1
Stockport SK1 240 F6
Correction Brow SK12 37 E3
Corstons La L64 67 D3
Corwen Cl WA5 7 F1
Cossack Ave WA2 8 A1
Cotebrook Dr CH2 118 B4
Cotebrook Rd CW9 104 B4
Cotes Pl CH1 117 F2
Cotesmore Dr L60 41 E4
Cotgreaves Cl CH4 141 D3
Cotswold Ave WA3 3 E3
Cotswold Cl Chester CH2 118 C3
Cuddington CW8 102 A1
Macclesfield SK10 86 C1
Cotswold Gr WA9 1 A2
Cotswold Rd Stockport SK4 240 D7
Warrington WA2 8 A2
Cotswold Way CW7 149 D4
Cottage Cl Bebington L63 43 E3
Neston L64 66 C4
Cottage Dr East L60 40 C3
Cottage Dr West L60 40 C3
Cottage La Heswall L60 40 C3
Macclesfield SK10 112 C4
Cottage Rd CH4 141 D3
Cottage St SK11 112 A4
Cottam Dr WA2 9 D2
Cotterdale Cl WA5 14 C4
Cotterill WA7 49 E4
Cotterill Dr WA1 17 E4
Cotterill St CW2 190 B1
Cottesmore Gdns WA15 32 B4
Cotton La Duddon CW6 145 E4
Runcorn WA7 49 E4
Sandbach CW11 175 D2
Cotton Tree St SK3 & SK4 240 E5
Cottonwood Dr ST7 195 F2
Cottrell Rd WA15 32 B4
Coulton Rd WA8 13 F2
Counce Ave WA12 2 B1
Countess Ave SK8 34 C3
Countess Cl SK11 111 F4
Countess of Chester Hospl CH2 118 A3
Countess Rd SK11 112 A4
Countess St OL6 242 A2
Countess Way CH2 118 B2
Counting House Rd SK12 38 C3
County Ave OL6 242 B4
Courier Row SK10 87 F4
Court La CW8 77 D1
Court The CW12 156 A2
Courtney Gn SK9 34 B1
Courtney Pl WA14 238 A1
Courtney Rd CH4 140 C2
Cousens Way CH1 118 A2
Cove The WA15 238 F3
Covent Garden 18 SK1 240 F5
Coventry Ave Cheadle SK3 239 F7
Ellesmere Port CH1 94 C4
Coverdale Cl WA5 14 B4
Covert Cl CW7 149 D4
Covert Gdns ST7 210 B4
Covert Rise CH3 166 A1
Covington Pl SK9 60 A3
Cow La Ashley WA15 31 F3
Bollington SK10 88 A4
Hargrave CH3 144 A1
Macclesfield SK11 112 B3
Norley WA6 101 D3
Rainow SK10 88 B2
Sale M33 242 E7
Cowanway WA8 12 C3
Cowbrook La SK11 135 D3
Cowdell St WA2 16 A4
Cowfields CW5 204 C3
Cowhey Cl CH4 141 D3
Cowley Way CW1 190 C1
Cowlishaw Rd SK14 & SK6 241 F4
Cowper Cl CW2 206 A4
Cowthorne Dr CH3 143 D2
Coyt Rd SK23 65 F3
Crab La WA2 9 D2
Crabmill Dr CW11 174 C4
Crabmill La Norley WA6 100 C3
Warmingham CW11 173 F4
Crabtree Ave
Altrincham WA15 32 B4
Disley SK12 38 C3
Crabtree Fold WA7 50 B4
Crabtree Gr CW1 190 C3
Crabtree La WA16 29 D3
Crabwall Pl CH1 117 F3
Crackley Bank Prim Sch ST5 210 C1
Cradley WA8 12 B1
Cragside Way SK9 60 B3
Craig Cl Macclesfield SK11 112 A3
Stockport SK4 240 B5
Craig Dr SK23 65 F3
Craig Gdns L66 69 F4
Craig Rd Congleton CW12 156 C2
Macclesfield SK11 112 A3
Stockport SK4 240 B5
Craig Wlk ST7 193 F1
Craigleigh Gr L62 43 F2
Craigside ST6 179 E1
Craithe Rd CH3 119 D1
Crampton Dr WA15 32 B4
Cranage Cl WA7 49 E4
Cranage Hill Hospl CW4 130 A3
Cranage Rd CW2 190 A2
Cranage Way 12 SK9 34 B3
Cranberry Cl WA14 238 B8
Cranberry Cty Inf & Jun Sch ST7 193 D2
Cranberry Dr ST5 210 B1
Cranberry La ST7 193 D2
Cranberry Moss La ST7 193 D2
Cranberry Rd M31 11 F2
Cranborne Rd Crewe CW1 190 B3
Warrington WA4 16 A1
Cranbourne Ct SK4 240 B8
Cranbourne Rd SK4 240 B8
Crandon Dr M20 239 C8
Cranebrook Cl CW1 190 A4
Cranfield Dr ST7 193 D2
Cranford Ave
Knutsford WA16 56 C1
Macclesfield SK11 112 C4
Sale M33 242 C8
Cranford Cl L62 43 F2
Cranford Ct Chester CH4 141 D3
Warrington WA1 17 F4
Cranford Mews ST7 193 D2
Cranford Rd SK9 34 A1
Cranham Ave WA3 3 F4
Cranleigh Cl WA4 26 A4
Cranleigh Cres CH1 118 A2
Cranleigh Dr Cheadle SK8 239 F6
Hazel Grove SK7 37 D4
Sale M33 242 A7
Cranmere Cl CW9 104 A2
Cranshaw La WA8 13 D3
Cranston Dr
Manchester M20 239 B8
Sale M33 242 E5
Cranswick Gn L66 69 E3
Crantock Dr SK8 34 B4
Cranwell Ave WA3 4 C2
Cranworth St SK15 242 E1
Crauford Rd CW12 157 D4
Craven Ave WA3 3 F4
Craven Ct WA2 7 F2
Craven Dr WA14 238 C8

Craven Rd WA14 .... 238 C7
Craven Terr M33 .... 242 C6
Crawford Ave WA8 .... 12 A1
Crawford Pl WA7 .... 49 D3
Crawford St OL6 .... 242 A2
Crawford's Wlk CH2 .... 118 C2
Crawley Ave WA2 .... 8 A2
Crayford Ave CW12 .... 157 D3
Crediton Cl WA14 .... 238 B6
Cresanne Cl CW10 .... 151 E4
Crescent Dr Helsby WA6 .... 73 D2
Whaley Bridge SK23 .... 39 E1
Crescent Gr SK8 .... 239 C6
Crescent Pk SK4 .... 240 C6
Crescent Rd
Alderley Edge SK9 .... 60 A1
Altrincham WA15 .... 238 E1
Altrincham, Oldfield Brow WA14 .... 238 A6
Cheadle SK8 .... 239 C6
Congleton CW12 .... 156 B1
Cranage CW4 .... 129 F3
Ellesmere Port L65 .... 70 B3
Rostherne WA16 .... 30 A2
Crescent The
Altrincham WA15 .... 238 F7
Altrincham, Oldfield Brow WA14 .... 238 A5
Cheadle SK8 .... 239 D6
Chester CH2 .... 118 B2
Congleton CW12 .... 156 B1
Ellesmere Port L65 .... 69 F3
Hartford CW8 .... 103 D3
Lymm WA13 .... 18 C1
Macclesfield SK10 .... 87 F1
Middlewich CW10 .... 128 A1
Mottram St Andrew SK10 .... 61 D1
Nantwich CW5 .... 204 C3
New Mills SK22 .... 39 D4
Northwich CW8, CW9 .... 103 F3
Rostherne WA16 .... 30 A2
Utkinton CW6 .... 146 A4
Weaverham CW8 .... 77 F1
Cressbrook Rd WA4 .... 16 B1
Cressington Gdns L65 .... 70 B3
Cresswell Ave
New Mills SK22 .... 39 E4
Newcastle-u-L ST5 .... 210 B1
Cresswell Cl WA5 .... 7 E1
Cresswell St SK22 .... 39 E4
Cresta Dr WA7 .... 48 C3
Crestwood Cl CW2 .... 206 A4
Crew Ave SK10 .... 87 F1
Crew Rd ST7 .... 193 F2
Crewe Bsns Pk CW1 .... 190 C1
Crewe Gates Farm Ind Est CW1 .... 190 C1
Crewe Golf Course CW1 .... 191 F1
Crewe Green Ave CW1 .... 191 E2
Crewe Green Rd CW1 .... 191 D2
Crewe Hill La CH3 .... 197 D3
Crewe La CH3 .... 180 C1
Crewe La S CH3 .... 197 D4
Crewe Rd Alsager ST7 .... 193 D2
Crewe CW1 .... 190 C1
Haslington CW1 .... 191 E3
Hatherton CW5 .... 219 F2
Nantwich CW5 .... 205 E3
Sandbach CW11 .... 175 D2
Shavington CW2 .... 206 B3
Willaston (nr Nantwich) CW5 .... 205 E3
Wistaston CW5 .... 205 E3
Crewe St Chester CH2 .... 237 F3
Crewe CW1 .... 190 B2
Crewe Sta CW1 .... 190 C1
Crewood Common Rd CW8 .... 76 A2
Crib La CW6 .... 168 A4
Criccieth Ct L65 .... 70 B1
Criccieth Rd SK3 .... 240 A3
Cricket St M34 .... 241 A8
Cricket's La OL6 .... 242 A3
Criftin Cl L66 .... 69 E1
Crimes La CH3, CW6 .... 167 E2
Cringle Dr SK8 .... 239 C3
Crisham Ave CW5 .... 218 C4
Critchley Cl SK14 .... 241 F5
Critchley Rd L24 .... 21 D2
Croasdale Dr WA7 .... 49 F3
Crocus St CW8 .... 78 A2
Croesmere Dr L66 .... 69 E1
Croft Cl Altrincham WA15 .... 32 B3
Utkinton CW6 .... 146 A4
Waverton CH3 .... 143 D3
Croft Ct L65 .... 70 C2
Croft Cty Prim Sch WA3 .... 9 D4
Croft Heath Gdns WA3 .... 9 D4
Croft La Dodleston CH4 .... 162 A4
Knutsford WA16 .... 82 A4
Croft Rd SK9 .... 59 F2
Croft St Goldborne WA3 .... 3 D4
Hyde SK14 .... 241 D6
Stalybridge SK15 .... 242 E2
Widnes WA8 .... 23 D3
Croft The Chester CH2 .... 118 B3
Runcorn WA7 .... 23 F1
Croften Dr L64 .... 66 C3
Crofters Cl
Ellesmere Port L66 .... 69 F1
Wistaston CW2 .... 206 A4
Crofters Ct CW4 .... 130 B2
Crofters Gn SK9 .... 59 F3
Crofters Heath L66 .... 69 F1
Crofters Lea CW8 .... 103 E4
Crofters Pk CH5 .... 116 A2
Crofters The M33 .... 242 F5
Crofters Way CH1 .... 116 C4
Crofton Cl WA4 .... 27 E3
Crofton Gdns WA3 .... 4 C2
Crofton Rd WA7 .... 22 C1
Croftside WA1 .... 17 F4
Croftside Way SK9 .... 60 B3
Croftsway L60 .... 40 B4
Cromer Dr CW1 .... 190 A4
Cromer Rd Cheadle SK8 .... 239 E6
Sale M33 .... 242 C5
Cromford Ct SK23 .... 65 F3
Cromford Mews SK23 .... 65 F3
Cromley Rd SK6 .... 37 F3
Crompton Rd SK11 .... 112 B4
Crompton St OL6 .... 242 B4
Cromwell Ave Gatley SK8 .... 239 A6
Great Sankey WA5 .... 15 D4
Warrington WA5 .... 7 E2
Cromwell Ave S WA5 .... 15 E2
Cromwell Ct Irlam M44 .... 11 F4
Nantwich CW5 .... 204 C3
Cromwell Dr CW2 .... 206 B2
Cromwell Rd
Cheadle Hulme SK7 .... 35 E3
Ellesmere Port L65 .... 70 B3
Irlam M44 .... 11 F4
Northwich CW8 .... 103 F4
Cromwell St
Stockport SK4 .... 240 D7
Widnes WA8 .... 23 D3
Cronkinson Ave CW5 .... 204 C2
Cronkinson Oak CW5 .... 204 C2
Cronton CE Sch WA8 .... 12 B3
Cronton La WA8 .... 12 C3
Cronton Park Ave WA8 .... 12 B3
Cronton Park Cl WA8 .... 12 B3
Cronton Rd WA8 .... 12 B3
Cronulla Dr WA5 .... 14 B4
Crook La CW7 .... 127 D1
Crook St Chester CH1 .... 237 D2
Hyde SK14 .... 241 E6
Crooked La CH3 .... 145 E2
Crookedyard Rd SK11 .... 113 F4
Crookenden Cl CH2 .... 95 E1
Crookenden Rd CH2 .... 95 E1
Croppers Rd WA2 .... 8 C2
Crosby Ave WA2 .... 16 A4
Crosby Gr L64 .... 68 A4
Crosby St SK2 .... 240 F3
Crosfield St WA1 .... 16 A3
Cross Gn CH2 .... 118 C3
Cross Gr WA15 .... 238 F8
Cross Hey CH4 .... 237 F1
Cross La Audley ST7 .... 209 F3
Church Minshull CW1 .... 172 B3
Congleton CW12 .... 157 D1
Croft WA3 .... 9 E4
Frodsham WA6 .... 73 D4
Haslington CW11 .... 191 F4
Middlewich CW10 .... 151 E3
Neston L64 .... 66 C3
Newton-le-W WA12 .... 2 A2
Sandbach CW11 .... 175 E3
Smallwood CW11 .... 176 C3
Swettenham CW12 .... 131 F2
Warrington WA4 .... 17 D2
Wilmslow SK9 .... 60 C4
Cross La E M31 .... 11 F2
Cross La W M31 .... 11 F1
Cross Lanes
Tarvin, Old Moss CH3 .... 144 B4
Tarvin, Oscroft CH3 .... 121 E1
Cross O' Th' Hill Rd SY14 .... 214 A2
Cross Rd Cheadle SK8 .... 34 A4
Haslington CW1 .... 191 E2
Cross St Alsager ST7 .... 193 E2
3 Altrincham WA14 .... 238 D4
Barnton CW8 .... 78 A2
Chester CH2 .... 118 C1
Congleton CW12 .... 156 B2
Crewe CW1 .... 190 B2
Goldborne WA3 .... 3 D4
Haslington CW1 .... 191 E2
Holt LL13 .... 196 C4
Hyde SK14 .... 241 D6
Macclesfield SK11 .... 112 C3
Marston CW9 .... 79 E2
Neston L64 .... 66 C4
New Mills SK22 .... 39 E4
Runcorn WA7 .... 23 D2
Sale M32 & M33 .... 242 B8
Warrington WA2 .... 16 A4
Widnes WA8 .... 13 E1
Cross The Holt LL13 .... 196 C4
Lymm WA13 .... 18 C2
Cross Wood St CW5 .... 204 B3
Crossall St SK11 .... 112 B4
Crossdale Rd L62 .... 43 E3
Crossfield Ave WA3 .... 4 C1
Crossfield Cl Denton M34 .... 241 A6
Stalybridge SK15 .... 242 D1
Crossfield Rd
Bollington SK10 .... 87 F3
Wilmslow SK9 .... 34 B2
Crossfields CH3 .... 121 D1
Crossings The WA12 .... 2 B2
Crossland Terr WA6 .... 73 D1
Crosslands
Congleton CW12 .... 157 D1
Haslington CW1 .... 191 E2
Crossledge CW12 .... 156 A2
Crossley Ave L66 .... 69 F3
Crossley Cres CH2 .... 119 D3
Crossley Dr L60 .... 40 B4
Crossley East Hospl WA6 .... 99 E4
Crossley Rd M33 .... 242 A8
Crossley St
Stalybridge SK15 .... 242 C2
Warrington WA1 .... 16 B3
Crossmoor Cres SK6 .... 241 C1
Crossmoor Gr SK6 .... 241 C2
Crossway Bramhall SK7 .... 35 F3
Crewe CW1 .... 190 B3
Widnes WA8 .... 22 B4
Crossway The L63 .... 42 B2
Crossways ST6 .... 179 F1
Crossways Rd ST7 .... 194 A2
Crosthwaite Ave L62 .... 43 F2
Croston Cl
Alderley Edge SK9 .... 60 B1
Widnes WA8 .... 12 B2
Crotia Ave CW2 .... 207 D3
Crouch La CW12 .... 157 E2
Crouchley Hall Mews WA13 .... 18 C1
Crouchley La WA13 .... 18 C1
Croughton Ct L66 .... 69 F4
Croughton Rd
Ellesmere Port L66 .... 69 F4
Stoak CH2 .... 96 A4
Stoak, Croughton CH2 .... 95 F3
Crow Gdns WA12 .... 2 A2
Crow La E WA12 .... 2 B2
Crow La W WA12 .... 2 A2
Crow Wood Pl WA8 .... 13 E2
Crowbrook Gr SK9 .... 34 B1
Crowder's La CW9 .... 105 D2
Crowland Gdns SK8 .... 35 D3
Crowley La CW9 .... 28 A2
Crown Ave WA8 .... 22 A4
Crown Bank CW11 .... 175 D3
Crown Bank Cres ST7 .... 210 B3
Crown Ctyd CW3 .... 229 F2
Crown Fields Cl WA12 .... 2 A3
Crown Gate WA7 .... 49 F4
Crown Gn WA13 .... 19 D2
Crown Ind Est WA14 .... 238 E7
Crown La WA16 .... 106 B4
Crown Park Dr WA12 .... 2 A3
Crown Passages WA15 .... 238 E2
Crown St Newton-le-W WA12 .... 2 A2
Northwich CW8 .... 103 F4
Warrington WA1 .... 16 A3
Crown St W SK11 .... 112 B4
Crownest La CW9 .... 78 C4
Crowton Christ Church CE Aided Prim Sch CW8 .... 76 A1
Crowton View WA6 .... 101 D3
Croxton La CW10 .... 128 A2
Croxton Way CW8 .... 103 D2
Croyde Cl M22 .... 33 F4
Croyde Rd L24 .... 21 D2
Crum Hill CW9 .... 104 A4
Crummock Rd SK8 .... 239 B3
Cryers La Elton CH2 .... 72 A1
Thornton-le-M CH2 .... 96 C4
Cty High Sch Leftwich The CW9 .... 104 A2
Cuckoo La Acton CW5 .... 203 F4
Neston L64 .... 67 E4
Cuckstoolpit Hill 11 SK11 .... 112 C4
Cuddington Cres SK3 .... 240 D2
Cuddington Cty Prim Sch CW8 .... 101 F1
Cuddington La CW8 .... 101 E2
Cuddington Sta CW8 .... 102 A2
Cuddington Way 3 SK9 .... 34 B3
Cuerdley Gn WA5 .... 14 A1
Cuerdley Rd WA5 .... 14 B2
Culbin Cl WA3 .... 10 A3
Culcheth Cty Prim Sch WA3 .... 5 D2
Culcheth Hall Prep Sch WA14 .... 238 D3
Culcheth High Sch WA3 .... 5 D2
Culcheth Hill Dr WA3 .... 4 C2
Culcheth Rd WA14 .... 238 D3
Culford Cl WA7 .... 24 B1
Culland St CW2 .... 190 B1
Cullen Cl L63 .... 43 E2
Cullen Rd WA7 .... 48 B4
Culver Rd SK3 .... 240 D1
Cumber Cl SK9 .... 59 E2
Cumber Dr SK9 .... 59 E3
Cumber La SK9 .... 59 F2
Cumberland Ave Irlam M44 .... 11 E3
Nantwich CW5 .... 204 C3
Cumberland Cl Crewe CW1 .... 190 B3
Kidsgrove ST7 .... 210 C4
Cumberland Cres WA11 .... 1 A3
Cumberland Dr
Altrincham WA14 .... 31 D4
Bollington SK10 .... 88 A4
Cumberland Gr L66 .... 69 E2
Cumberland Rd
Congleton CW12 .... 156 A2
Partington M31 .... 11 F1
Sale M33 .... 242 D5
Cumberland Sports Ctr CW1 .... 190 B3
Cumberland St
37 Macclesfield SK11 .... 112 B4
Stalybridge SK15 .... 242 C2
Warrington WA4 .... 16 B2
Cumbermere Dr CW11 .... 174 C4
Cumbers Dr L64 .... 67 D3
Cumbers La L64 .... 67 D3
Cumbrae Dr L65 .... 70 B1
Cuncliffe Cl WA7 .... 50 A4
Cuncliffe Dr M33 .... 242 C5
Cundiff Cl SK11 .... 112 C3
Cundy St SK14 .... 241 E8
Cunliffe Ave WA12 .... 2 A3
Cunliffe St Dukinfield SK14 .... 241 C8
Stockport SK3 .... 240 C4
Cunningham Cl WA5 .... 14 B4
Cunningham Dr
Bebington L63 .... 43 E4
Runcorn WA7 .... 22 C1
Wythenshawe M22 .... 34 A4
Cunningham Rd WA8 .... 22 B4
Cuppin St CH1 .... 237 D2
Curlender Way L24 .... 21 F1
Curlew Cl Goldborne WA3 .... 3 E4
Winsford CW7 .... 149 E3
Curlew Gr WA3 .... 9 F2
Currans Rd WA2 .... 8 A1
Currier La OL6 .... 242 A2
Curtis Rd SK4 .... 240 A6
Curzon Ave ST7 .... 193 E3
Curzon Cl CH4 .... 141 D4
Curzon Gr CW7 .... 126 C1
Curzon Mews SK9 .... 60 A3
Curzon Pk N CH4 .... 141 D4
Curzon Pk S CH4 .... 141 D4
Curzon Rd
Ashton-u-L OL6 .... 242 A4
Cheadle SK8 .... 34 A4
Poynton SK12 .... 36 C1
Sale M33 .... 242 B7
Curzon St Chester CH4 .... 140 C4
6 Runcorn WA7 .... 22 C1
Cuthbert Rd SK8 .... 239 E6
Cygnet Cl L66 .... 69 E2
Cyman Cl CH1 .... 117 E2
Cymbal Ct SK5 .... 240 F7
Cynthia Ave WA1 .... 17 D4
Cynthia Rd WA7 .... 22 C1
Cypress Ave
Ellesmere Port L66 .... 69 F1
Widnes WA8 .... 13 D1
Cypress Cl Stockport SK3 .... 240 C4
Warrington WA1 .... 17 F4
Cypress Gr Denton M34 .... 241 A7
Runcorn WA7 .... 49 E4
Cyprus Way SK6 .... 38 A4
Cyril Bell Cl WA13 .... 18 C2
Cyril St WA2 .... 16 A4

Daffodil Cl WA8 .... 13 F2
Dagnall Ave WA5 .... 7 F1
Daintry Hall Prep Sch The CW12 .... 134 B1
Daintry St SK11 .... 112 C4
Daintry Terr 12 SK11 .... 112 C4
Dairy Farm Cl WA13 .... 18 C2
Dairy House La
Cheadle Hulme SK7 .... 35 D2
Wilmslow SK7 .... 35 D2
Dairy House Rd SK8 .... 35 D3
Dairy House Way CW2 .... 189 F1
Dairy La CW5 .... 188 B3
Dairybrook Gr 14 SK9 .... 34 B1
Dairyground Rd SK7 .... 35 F4
Dairyhouse La WA14 .... 238 B7
Dairylands Rd ST7 .... 193 F2
Daisy Ave WA12 .... 2 B1
Daisy Bank CW5 .... 204 B3
Daisy Bank Cres CW3 .... 229 F3
Daisy Bank La Anderton CW8 .... 78 B2
Gatley SK8 .... 239 A1
Daisy Bank Mill Cl WA3 .... 4 C2
Daisy Bank Rd Lymm WA13 .... 18 B2
Penketh WA5 .... 14 C2
Daisy St SK1 & SK2 .... 240 F3
Daisy Way SK6 .... 37 F4
Daisybank Dr
Congleton CW12 .... 156 B2
Sandbach CW11 .... 175 E3
Daisyhill Cl M33 .... 242 E6
Dalby Ct WA3 .... 10 A3
Dalby Ct CW9 .... 104 C3
Dale Ave Bebington L62 .... 43 E4
Bramhall SK7 .... 35 F4
Ellesmere Port L66 .... 69 E3
Dale Cl Warrington WA5 .... 15 F2
Widnes L26 .... 22 A4
Dale Cres CW12 .... 156 C1
Dale Ct CW10 .... 151 E4
Dale Dr Chester CH2 .... 118 B4
Ellesmere Port L65 .... 69 F3
Dale Gdns L65 .... 70 A2
Dale Gr Altrincham WA15 .... 238 F7
Congleton CW12 .... 157 D1
Irlam M44 .... 11 F3
Dale Head Rd SK10 .... 86 C2
Dale Hey L66 .... 43 F1
Dale House Fold SK12 .... 37 D2
Dale La WA4 .... 26 C4
Dale Rd Bebington L62 .... 43 E3
Goldborne WA3 .... 3 D4
New Mills SK22 .... 39 E4
Dale Sq WA14 .... 238 D7
Dale St Altrincham WA14 .... 238 D7
Chester CH3 .... 119 D1
Macclesfield SK11 .... 112 C4
Runcorn WA7 .... 23 D1
Stalybridge SK15 .... 242 C1
Stockport SK3 .... 240 D3
Dale The Great Sankey WA5 .... 14 C3
Neston L64 .... 66 C3
Tiverton CW6 .... 168 B3
Dale View WA12 .... 2 C2
Dale's Sq CW9 .... 103 F3
Dalebrook Ct SK4 .... 240 C5
Dalecroft WA6 .... 72 C1
Dalefords La
Cuddington CW8 .... 102 A1
Nova Scotia CW8 .... 125 E4
Dales Green Rd ST7 .... 195 E3
Dalesford Cl WA3 .... 4 B4
Dalesford Cres SK11 .... 111 F4
Daleside CH2 .... 118 B4
Dalesway L60 .... 40 C4
Dalewood Cres CH2 .... 72 A2
Dalham La WA2 .... 16 A3
Dallam Cty Prim Sch WA5 .... 7 F1
Dalmahoy Cl CW7 .... 126 B1
Dalston Dr SK7 .... 35 E3
Dalton Bank WA1 .... 16 B3
Dalton Cl CH1 .... 117 F2
Dalton Ct Runcorn WA7 .... 23 F2
Sandbach CW11 .... 174 C4
Dalton Gr SK4 .... 240 C8
Dalton St Runcorn WA7 .... 23 E1
Sale M33 .... 242 C8
Dalton Way CW10 .... 128 B1
Dalveen Dr WA15 .... 238 F7
Dalwood Cl WA7 .... 50 C4
Dam Head La WA3 .... 11 D3
Dam La Croft WA3 .... 8 C4
Hollins Green WA3 .... 11 D2
Mobberley WA16 .... 58 B2
Warrington WA1 .... 17 E4
Dame Hollow SK8 .... 34 B4
Damery Ct SK7 .... 35 F4
Damery Rd SK7 .... 35 F4
Damhead La L64 .... 67 F4
Damian Dr WA12 .... 2 A3
Dams La WA16 .... 106 B3
Damson La WA16 .... 58 A2
Damson Wlk M31 .... 11 E1
Danby Cl Hyde SK14 .... 241 F8
Runcorn WA7 .... 49 E3
Warrington WA5 .... 15 F4
Danby Pl SK14 .... 241 F8
Danby Rd SK14 .... 241 F8
Dane Ave Cheadle SK3 .... 240 A4
Partington M31 .... 11 F2
Dane Bank Ave
Congleton CW12 .... 156 C2
Crewe CW2 .... 190 A1
Dane Bank Dr SK12 .... 38 B3
Dane Bank Rd CW9 .... 104 A4
Dane Cl Alsager ST7 .... 193 D2
Sandbach CW11 .... 174 C4
Dane Dr Biddulph ST6 .... 179 F1
Wilmslow SK9 .... 60 B3
Dane Gdns ST7 .... 195 E1
Dane Gr CH2 .... 119 F4
Dane Hill Cl SK12 .... 38 B3
Dane Pl CW7 .... 127 D1
Dane Rd M33 .... 242 D7
Dane Road Sta M33 .... 242 C8
Dane St Congleton CW12 .... 156 B2
Middlewich CW10 .... 128 B1
Northwich CW9 .... 103 F4
Dane Valley Cty High Sch CW12 .... 156 C3
Danebank Rd WA13 .... 18 B2
Danebank Rd E WA13 .... 18 B2
Danefield Ct SK8 .... 34 B4
Danefield Rd
Holmes Chapel CW4 .... 130 B2
Northwich CW9 .... 104 A4
Sale M33 .... 242 C8
Danes Sq SK11 .... 112 B3
Danesbury Rise SK8 .... 239 D5
Danescroft WA8 .... 12 A2
Daneside Bsns Pk CW12 .... 156 C2
Daneswell Rd L24 .... 21 D1
Daniel Adamson Ave M31 .... 11 E2
Daniel Cl WA3 .... 10 A2
Daniel's La SK1 .... 240 E6
Daniell Way CH3 .... 142 A4
Dans Rd WA8 .... 13 F1
Danwood Cl M34 .... 241 B5
Dappleheath Rd CW2 .... 190 A1
Darent Rd WA11 .... 1 A4
Daresbury Ave WA15 .... 238 E5
Daresbury Cl
Holmes Chapel CW4 .... 130 A2
Sale M33 .... 242 F5
Stockport SK3 .... 240 D1
Daresbury Cty Prim Sch WA4 .... 25 D1
Daresbury Expressway
Daresbury WA4 .... 25 D2
Runcorn WA7 .... 24 B2
Daresbury La WA4 .... 25 E1
Dargle Rd M33 .... 242 B8
Darian Ave M22 .... 33 E4
Dark Ash La
Ashton CH3, WA6 .... 99 D2
Manley CH3, WA6 .... 99 D2
Dark La Henbury SK11 .... 111 D4
Kingsley WA6 .... 75 D1
Marston CW9 .... 79 E3
Old Woodhouse SY13 .... 227 D1
Tattenhall CH3 .... 183 F4
Warren SK11 .... 111 E2
Warren SK11 .... 111 E2
Whitley WA4 .... 52 B3
Darkie Meadow CW6 .... 185 F4
Darland La CH4 .... 162 B1
Darley Ave Crewe CW2 .... 190 A2
Gatley SK8 .... 239 B5
Warrington WA2 .... 8 C2
Darley Cl WA8 .... 12 A2
Darley Rd SK7 .... 36 C4
Darley St M33 .... 242 B6
Darleydale Dr L62 .... 43 F3
Darlington Ave CW1 .... 189 F3
Darlington Cres CH1 .... 94 A1
Darlington St CW10 .... 128 B1
Darnaway Cl WA3 .... 10 A3
Darnhall School La CW7 .... 149 E3
Darnton Rd OL6 & SK15 .... 242 B3
Dart Cl Alsager ST7 .... 193 D2
Biddulph ST6 .... 179 E1
Dart Wlk CW7 .... 127 D1
Dartnall Cl SK12 .... 38 A3

Darwin Gr SK7 35 F3
Darwin Rd CH1 117 E2
Darwin St CW8 103 F4
Darwin Street Cty Prim Sch CW8 103 F4
Daryl Rd L60 41 D4
Daten Ave WA3 9 F3
Dauncey Cl CH2 95 E1
Davehall Ave SK9 60 A4
Daven Cty Prim Sch CW12 156 C1
Daven Rd CW12 156 C1
Davenham Ave WA1 16 C4
Davenham Cres CW2 190 A2
Davenham Ct CW9 104 A2
Davenham Rd
Davenham CW9 104 C2
Lach Dennis CW9 104 C2
8 Wilmslow SK9 34 B2
Davenham Way CW10 151 E3
Davenport Ave Crewe CW2 206 B4
Nantwich CW5 204 C4
Warrington WA1 16 C3
Wilmslow SK9 59 F2
Davenport Cl CW11 175 E4
Davenport La
Altrincham WA14 238 C7
Brereton Green CW11 154 B1
Marton SK11 132 C3
Mobberley WA16 58 B3
Davenport Rd
Altrincham WA14 238 C7
Heswall L60 40 C4
Davenport Row WA7 49 E4
Davenport St
Congleton CW12 156 B1
Crewe CW1 190 B3
Macclesfield SK11 112 C4
Davenport Sta SK3 240 F1
Davey La SK9 60 A1
Daveylands SK9 60 B4
David Cl M34 241 A5
David Lewis Manchester Epiletic Colony The SK9 84 A3
David Rd WA13 18 B2
David St Denton M34 241 A6
Northwich CW8 103 F4
David's Ave WA5 15 D3
Davidson Ave CW12 157 D3
Davies Ave Cheadle SK9 34 A3
Newton-le-W WA12 2 B2
Warrington WA4 16 C2
Davies Cl WA8 23 D2
Davies Way WA13 18 B2
Davis Cl ST7 193 F2
Davy Rd WA7 23 F2
Daw Bank SK3 240 E5
Dawlish Ave SK8 34 C4
Dawlish Cl Bramhall SK7 35 F4
Hollins Green WA3 11 D2
Dawn Cl L64 67 D3
Dawn Gdns L65 70 A2
Dawpool Cl CH2 118 B3
Dawpool Dr L62 43 E4
Dawson Dr CH2 237 D4
Dawson Rd
Altrincham WA14 238 D8
Bollington SK10 88 A4
Cheadle SK8 34 B4
Macclesfield SK11 111 F4
Dawson St SK14 241 E5
Dawstone Rd L60 41 D4
Daylesford Cl SK8 239 D4
Daylesford Cres SK8 239 D4
Daylesford Rd SK8 239 D4
De Lacy Row WA7 24 A1
Deacon Cl Altrincham WA14 238 B1
Croft WA3 9 D4
Deacon Rd WA8 13 D1
Deacon Trad Est WA12 2 A1
Deadman's La CW5 205 D1
Deakin's Rd CW7 127 D2
Deal Sq SK14 241 E6
Deal St SK14 241 E6
Dean Bank CW6 168 B2
Dean Cl Bollington SK10 88 A4
Partington M31 11 F2
Sandbach CW11 174 C4
7 Widnes WA8 23 D4
Wilmslow SK9 34 B1
Dean Cres WA2 8 A1
Dean Ct SK10 88 A4
Dean Dr Altrincham WA14 238 B1
Wilmslow SK9 34 B1
Dean Hollow ST7 209 E1
Dean La SK7 36 C4
Dean Meadow WA12 2 B2
Dean Pk SY14 214 A3
Dean Rd Goldborne WA3 3 D4
Irlam M44 11 F3
Wilmslow SK9 34 C2
Dean Row Cty Jun Sch SK9 34 C1
Dean Row Rd SK9 34 B1
Dean St Middlewich CW10 128 B1
Northwich CW9 104 B4
Stalybridge SK15 242 D1
Widnes WA8 23 D4
Winsford CW7 126 B1
Dean Valley Cty Prim Sch SK10 87 F4
Dean's La ST5 210 B1
Deane Ave SK8 239 F5
Deanery Cl CH2 118 B2
Deanery Way SK1 240 F6
Deans Cl Chester CH2 118 B3
Tarvin CH3 121 D1
Deans La Barthomley CW2 208 B2
Sandbach CW11 174 C3
Warrington WA4 17 F2
Deans Rd L65 70 C2
Deans Way
Higher Kinnerton CH4 161 D4
Tarvin CH3 121 D1
Deansgate L65 70 A3
Deansgate La
WA14 & WA15 238 E7
Deansway WA8 22 B4
Deanwater Cl WA3 9 E2
Deanwater Ct SK8 34 B4
Deanway SK9 34 B1
Dearden St SK15 242 D2
Dearnford Ave L62 43 E3
Dearnford Cl L62 43 E3
Debra Cl L66 69 E2
Debra Rd L66 69 E2
Dee Banks CH4 141 F4
Dee Banks Sch CH3 142 A4
Dee Cl Biddulph ST6 179 F1
Kidsgrove ST7 210 C4
Sandbach CW11 174 C4
Dee Cres CH3 180 C1
Dee Fords Ave CH3 119 D1
Dee Hills Pk CH2 237 F2
Dee La Chester CH2 237 F2
Holt LL13 196 B4
Dee Meadows LL13 196 B4
Dee Park Cl L60 41 D3
Dee Park Rd L60 41 D3
Dee Pk LL13 196 B4
Dee Point Cty Prim Sch CH1 117 E2
Dee Side L60 40 B4
Dee View CH3 180 C1
Dee View Rd
Connah's Quay CH5 91 E1
Heswall L60 40 C4
Dee Way CW7 127 D1
Deepdale WA8 12 B2
Deer Park Ct WA7 49 F3
Deerwood Cl
Ellesmere Port L66 69 E4
Macclesfield SK10 86 C1
Deerwood Cres L66 69 E4
Deeside Ellesmere Port L65 70 A2
Holt LL13 196 C4
Deeside Cl L65 70 A1
Deeside Coll of F Ed (Coleg Glannau Dyfrdwy) CH5 91 E1
Deeside Cres CH1 116 C3
Deeside Ind Est (Parc Ddiwydiannol Glannau Dyfrdwy) CH5 93 D1
Deeside La CH1 116 C2
Deirdre Ave WA8 13 D1
Delafield Cl WA2 8 C2
Delamer Rd WA14 238 C3
Delamere Ave Bebington L62 43 F2
Ellesmere Port L66 69 F3
Goldborne WA3 3 F3
Sale M33 242 E5
Widnes WA8 12 B1
Delamere CE Contr Prim Sch CW6 123 E3
Delamere Cl Bebington L62 43 F2
Sandbach CW11 174 C4
Delamere Ct Alsager ST7 192 C2
Bebington L62 43 F2
Delamere Dr
Ellesmere Port L66 69 F3
Macclesfield SK10 87 F1
Delamere Forest Sch WA6 100 B2
Delamere Gn L66 69 F2
Delamere Park Way E CW8 101 E3
Delamere Park Way W
CW8 101 E3
Delamere Rd Ashton CH3 99 D1
Congleton CW12 155 F2
Gatley SK8 239 B5
Nantwich CW5 204 C2
Norley WA6 100 A3
Wilmslow SK9 34 C2
Delamere Rise CW7 126 A1
Delamere St Chester CH1 237 D3
Crewe CW1 190 B2
Warrington WA5 15 F3
Winsford CW7 126 A1
Delamere Sta CW8 100 B1
Delamore's Acre L64 68 A4
Delavor Cl L60 40 C4
Delavor Rd L60 40 C4
Delenty Dr WA3 9 F2
Delery Dr WA1 16 C4
Delford Rd WA16 82 B4
Delfur Rd SK7 35 F4
Delhi Rd M44 11 F4
Dell Cl L63 43 D3
Dell Dr WA2 9 D1
Dell La L60 41 D4
Dell The Cuddington CW8 101 E3
Guilden Sutton CH3 119 F3
Kelsall CW6 122 B2
Delmar Rd WA16 57 E1
Delph La Daresbury WA4 25 D1
Warrington WA2 8 C3
Winwick WA2 7 F3
Winwick WA2 8 C3
Delphfield WA7 50 B4
Delphfields Rd WA4 26 B4
Delphside ST7 209 F1
Delta Ct CH4 140 A3
Delves Ave WA5 15 F4
Delves Cl CW2 206 A2
Delves Wlk CH3 142 A4
Delvine Dr CH2 118 B3
Demage Dr L66 69 E2
Demage La Backford CH1 94 C2
Chester CH2 118 B4
Demage La S CH2 118 B4
Demesne Cl SK15 242 F1
Demesne Cres SK15 242 F1
Demesne Dr SK15 242 F1
Demmings Inf Sch SK8 239 F5
Demmings Rd SK8 239 F5
Den La CW3 221 E2
Denbigh Cl Hazel Grove SK7 36 B4
Helsby WA6 73 D1
Denbigh Cres CW10 151 E4
Denbigh Ct L65 70 B2
Denbigh Dr CW7 149 D4
Denbigh Gdns L65 70 B2
Denbigh St Chester CH1 118 A2
Stockport SK4 240 D7
Denbury Ave WA4 16 C1
Denbury Dr WA14 238 B5
Denby La SK4 240 D8
Dene Ave WA12 1 C2
Dene Ct SK4 240 C6
Dene Dr CW7 149 E4
Denehurst Cl WA5 14 C2
Denehurst Park Way CW8 101 E3
Denesgate CW7 149 E4
Deneside Ave CW1 190 B3
Deneway Cheadle Hulme SK7 35 E4
High Lane SK6 37 F4
Stockport SK4 240 C6
Deneway Cl SK4 240 C6
Deneway Mews SK4 240 C6
Denewood Ct SK9 60 A3
Denford Cl CH4 139 E2
Denford Pl ST7 193 E3
Denhall Cl CH2 118 C3
Denhall La L64 67 D1
Denham Ave WA5 15 D3
Denham Dr SK7 35 E4
Denholm Rd M20 239 C8
Denise Ave WA5 14 C3
Denison Rd SK7 36 C4
Denmark Rd M33 242 B8
Denmark St WA14 238 D4
Dennett Cl WA1 17 F3
Dennis Dr CH4 141 D3
Dennis Rd WA8 23 E4
Dennison Rd SK8 35 D4
Densham Ave WA2 8 A1
Denston Cl CW2 190 A1
Denstone Dr CH4 141 D2
Dentdale Wlk M22 33 E4
Dentith Dr CH1 117 F3
Denton Cl CW7 126 B1
Denton Dr CW9 79 E1
Denton Drive Ind Est CW9 79 E1
Denton St WA8 13 E1
Denver Ave CW2 190 A2
Denzell Gdns WA14 238 A3
Depenbech Cl SY14 213 D2
Depleach Rd SK8 239 D5
Depmore La WA6 75 D1
Deramore Cl OL6 242 B3
Derby Cl Irlam M44 11 E3
Neston L64 66 C2
Newton-le-W WA12 2 A2
Derby Ct M33 242 C5
Derby Dr WA1 16 C4
Derby Pl CH2 118 C2
Derby Range SK4 240 B8
Derby Rd Ashton-u-L OL6 242 A3
Goldborne WA3 3 E4
Hyde SK14 241 E8
Kidsgrove ST7 210 B4
Manchester SK4 240 C8
Warrington WA4 16 B1
Widnes WA8 13 E2
Derby Row WA12 7 E4
Derby St Altrincham WA14 238 E5
Congleton CW12 156 B2
Crewe CW1 190 A3
Newton-le-W WA12 2 A2
Stockport SK3 240 D4
Derbyshire Hill Cty Prim Sch WA9 1 A1
Derbyshire Hill Rd WA9 1 A1
Derbyshire Rd
Partington M31 11 E1
Poynton SK12 37 E3
Sale M33 242 C6
Derbyshire Rd S M33 242 D5
Derek Ave WA2 8 C1
Derrington Ave CW2 190 B2
Derwen Rd SK3 240 E3
Derwen Sch CH4 161 D4
Derwent Ave CW7 127 D1
Derwent Cl Alsager ST7 193 D2
Culcheth WA3 5 D1
Holmes Chapel CW4 130 A2
Macclesfield SK11 112 A3
Partington M31 11 F2
Willaston (nr Nantwich)
CW5 205 E3
Derwent Cres ST7 195 E1
Derwent Dr Biddulph ST6 179 F1
Cheadle Hulme SK7 35 E3
Congleton CW12 156 C1
Hooton L66 44 A1
Wilmslow SK9 34 B3
Derwent Rd Chester CH2 118 C3
High Lane SK6 37 F4
Warrington WA4 16 A1
Widnes WA8 12 B1
Derwent Terr SK15 242 D4
Derwent Way L64 66 C4
Desoto Rd WA8 22 C3
Desoto Rd E WA8 22 C3
Desoto Rd W WA8 22 C3
Deva Ave CH4 140 B3
Deva Bsns Pk CH5 116 A4
Deva Cl SK12 36 A2
Deva Ct CH2 118 C1
Deva La CH2 118 B3
Deva Link CH1 118 A2
Deva Rd CW2 189 E2
Deva Stad (Chester City FC) CH1 117 F1
Deva Terr CH2 237 F2
Devisdale Grange WA14 238 B3
Devisdale Rd WA14 238 B4
Devon Cl SK10 86 C1
Devon Gr ST6 179 E1
Devon Pl Congleton CW12 156 C2
Widnes WA8 13 D2
Devon Rd Chester CH2 118 C3
Irlam M44 11 E3
Partington M31 11 F1
Devonshire Dr SK9 60 A1
Devonshire Gdns WA12 2 B1
Devonshire Pl Chester CH4 141 F4
Runcorn WA7 23 D1
Devonshire Rd
Altrincham WA14 238 D6
Broughton CH4 139 E2
Hazel Grove SK7 36 C4
Manchester SK4 240 B7
Warrington WA1 16 C4
Dewar Ct WA7 23 F2
Dewes St CW1 190 A3
Dewhurst Rd WA3 9 E1
Dexter Way CW10 128 B1
Dial La CW12 158 A1
Dial Rd WA15 32 B4
Dial St WA1 16 B3
Diamond Cl OL6 242 A4
Diamond St OL6 242 A4
Dibbins Gn L63 43 D4
Dibbinsdale Rd L63 43 D4
Dickens Cl
Cheadle Hulme SK8 35 D3
6 Sandbach CW11 174 B3
Dickens La SK12 36 C1
Dickenson St WA2 16 B4
Dickinson Cl WA11 1 A3
Dickson Cl WA8 23 D4
Dickson St 2 WA8 23 D4
Dicksons Dr CH2 118 B2
Didsbury Rd SK4 240 B6
Dierden St CW7 127 D1
Dierdens Terr CW10 128 B1
Dig La Acton CW5 203 F2
Frodsham WA6 74 A4
Ravensmoor CW5 203 F2
Shavington CW2 206 A2
Diglake St ST7 209 F2
Diglee Rd SK23 39 E2
Dinas Cl CH1 117 E2
Dingle Ave Denton M34 241 B6
Lindow End SK9 59 E2
Newton-le-W WA12 1 C1
Dingle Bank CH4 141 E4
Dingle Bank Cl WA13 18 C2
Dingle Cl Macclesfield SK10 87 D2
Romiley SK6 241 D2
Dingle Cty Prim Sch The CW1 191 E3
Dingle La Appleton WA4 26 C3
Kelsall CW6 122 C3
Sandbach CW11 175 E3
Winsford CW7 126 B1
Dingle The Barnton CW8 78 A2
Haslington CW1 191 E3
Lymm WA13 18 C2
Dingle Way CW8 101 F3
Dingle Wlk CW7 126 B1
Dinglebrook Gr 2 SK9 34 C1
Dingleway WA4 26 B4
Dinmor Rd M22 33 E4
Dirty La WA14 30 C3
Disley Cty Prim Sch SK12 38 B3
Disley Sta SK12 38 B3
Ditchfield La WA16 29 E2
Ditchfield Pl WA8 22 A4
Ditchfield Rd Penketh WA5 14 C2
Widnes WA8 22 A4
Ditton CE Contr Prim Sch WA8 12 A1
Ditton CE Prim Sch WA8 12 B1
Ditton Rd Widnes WA8 23 D3
Widnes, Ditton Marsh WA8 22 B3
Dixon Ave WA12 2 B3
Dixon Cl WA11 2 A4
Dixon Ct SK8 239 D5
Dixon Dr SK11 84 A2
Dixon Rd Congleton CW12 157 D3
Denton M34 241 B5
Dixon St Ashton-u-L OL6 242 A4
Irlam M44 11 F4
Warrington WA1 16 A3
Dobb Hedge Cl WA15 32 B3
Dobell's Rd CW9 103 F3
Dobers La Frodsham WA6 74 B2
Kingsley WA6 74 B2
Dobson's Sq SY14 213 D2
Dock Rd Northwich CW9 103 F4
Widnes WA8 23 D3
Widnes, Ditton Marsh WA8 22 C3
Dock St Ellesmere Port L65 70 B4
Widnes WA8 23 D3
Dock Yard Rd L65 70 C3
Dodd's Green La SY13 228 A2
Dodd's La Appleton WA4 27 D3
Bradley Green SY14 224 C4
Doddington Cl CW11 175 E4
Doddington Rd CW2 190 A2
Dodds La CW12 178 B3
Doddswood Dr CW12 156 C2
Dodge Hill SK1 & SK4 240 E6
Dodgsley Dr WA6 75 E1
Dodleston CE Contr Prim Sch CH4 162 A4
Dodleston La
Dodleston CH4 162 B2
Pulford CH4 162 B2
Doe's Meadow Rd L63 43 D4
Doeford Cl WA3 4 C3
Dog La Brereton Green CW11 153 F4
Chowley CH3 182 B2
Coddington CH3 182 B2
Nantwich CW5 204 C3
Threapwood SY14 223 E4
Dogmore La CW6 147 E2
Dolly La SK23 39 F2
Dolphin Cres L66 69 F1
Dolphin Ct CH4 141 D4
Dombey Rd SK12 36 B1
Domestic App M90 33 E4
Domville Cl WA13 18 C2
Don Wlk L65 70 A4
Donagh Cl SK10 86 C1
Donald Ave SK14 241 F5
Donkey La SK9 60 A3
Donne Pl CH1 117 F3
Donnington Ave SK8 239 F6
Donnington Way CH4 140 C4
Dooley's Grig SK11 108 C1
Dooley's La SK9 33 E1
Dorac Ave SK8 34 B4
Dorchester Cl SK9 60 B4
Dorchester Pk WA7 24 C2
Dorchester Rd Chester CH4 140 C3
Great Sankey WA5 15 E3
Dorchester Way
Burtonwood WA5 6 C3
Macclesfield SK10 87 E2
Doreen Ave CW12 179 D4
Doreold Dr CW5 204 B3
Dorfold St CW1 190 B2
Dorfold Way CH2 118 A4
Doric Ave WA6 74 B4
Dorin Park Sch CH2 118 B3
Doris Rd SK3 240 C4
Dormer Cl CH3 143 D3
Dorney Cl WA4 26 C3
Dornoch Ct CW4 130 A1
Dorothea St WA2 16 B4
Dorric Way CW1 190 B4
Dorrington Cl WA7 50 B4
Dorrington Rd SK3 240 A3
Dorrit Cl SK12 36 C1
Dorset Ave SK8 240 C1
Dorset Cl CW12 156 C2
Dorset Ct WA7 50 A3
Dorset Dr ST6 179 E1
Dorset Pl Chester CH2 119 D3
Kidsgrove ST7 195 D1
Dorset Rd Altrincham WA14 238 B5
Chester CH2 118 B4
Irlam M44 11 E3
Dorset St OL6 242 A2
Dorset Way WA1 17 D4
Dorset Wlk SK10 86 C1
Douglas Ave WA9 6 A3
Douglas Cl Hartford CW8 103 E3
Widnes WA8 13 F2
Douglas La CW7 171 D3
Douglas Pl CH4 140 C3
Douglas St
Ashton-u-L OL6 242 A3
Hyde SK14 241 E6
Doune Ct L65 70 B2
Dounrey Cl WA2 9 D2
Douthwaite Dr SK6 241 E1
Dove Bank Prim Sch ST7 195 D1
Dove Cl Ellesmere Port L65 70 A4
Helsby WA6 73 E3
Sandbach CW11 175 D4
Warrington WA3 9 F2
Dove Cote Gn WA5 7 D1
Dove Gr ST6 179 E1
Dove Pl CW7 127 D1
Dovecot Bsns & Tech Pk M33 242 F6
Dovecote Cl CW2 206 A4
Dovedale Cl Bebington L62 43 F3
Congleton CW12 157 D2
High Lane SK6 37 F4
Warrington WA2 8 C2
Dovedale Ct WA8 12 A2
Dover Cl WA7 50 C3
Dover Ct L65 70 B1
Dover Dr Ellesmere Port L65 70 B1
Winsford CW7 149 D4
Dover Rd Chester CH4 141 D3
Macclesfield SK10 87 F1
Warrington WA4 17 D2
Dovesmead Rd L60 41 E4
Doveston Rd M33 242 B8
Doward St WA8 13 E1
Downes Cl SK10 87 D1
Downesway SK9 59 F1
Downham Ave WA3 4 C1
Downham Dr L60 41 D4
Downham Pl CH1 117 F2
Downham Rd S L60 41 D4
Downing Cl SK11 112 C2
Downs Dr WA14 238 E8
Downs End WA16 57 E1
Downs Rd WA7 23 D1
Downs The
Altrincham WA14 238 D3
Cheadle SK8 239 D3
Cuddington CW8 101 E3

Downsfield Rd CH4 141 D3
Downside WA8 12 A2
Downswood Ct CH2 118 B2
Downswood Dr CH2 118 B2
Downway La WA9 1 A1
Dowson Rd SK14 241 E5
Dragon Yd WA8 13 D2
Dragon's La CW11 152 A1
Drake Ave M44 11 F3
Drake Cl WA5 7 E1
Drake Ct SK5 240 E8
Drake La Acton CW5 203 F2
Ravensmoor CW5 203 F2
Drake Rd Altrincham WA14 .. 238 B8
Neston L64 41 F1
Drakelow La
Lach Dennis CW10 128 C4
Middlewich CW10 128 C4
Drakes Way SY14 213 D3
Draxford Ct SK9 60 A3
Draycott Dr ST5 210 B1
Drayton Ave SK8 34 A4
Drayton Cl Runcorn WA7 22 C1
Wilmslow SK9 34 B1
Drayton Cres CW1 190 C3
Drayton Manor M20 239 B8
Drenfell Rd ST7 194 C4
Drill Field Rd CW9 103 F4
Drive A CH5 93 D1
Drive B CH5 93 D1
Drive C CH5 93 D1
Drive The Altrincham WA15 ... 32 B4
Holmes Chapel CW4 130 B1
Lymm WA13 19 E1
Drome Rd CH5 93 D1
Drovers Way CW11 175 D3
Drumber La ST7 195 D4
Drumber The CW7 126 B1
Drumble Field SK11 84 A2
Drummond Ave L66 69 E2
Drummond Ct WA8 13 E1
Drummond Way SK10 86 C1
Druridge Dr WA5 14 C2
Drury Cl CW1 190 C3
Drury La Knutsford WA16 57 D1
Warmingham CW1 173 E2
Dryden Ave SK8 239 F6
Dryden Cl CW2 190 A1
Dryden Pl WA2 8 B1
Dryhurst Dr SK12 38 B3
Dryhurst La SK12 38 B3
Dublin Croft L66 69 F1
Duchy Rd CW1 207 D4
Duchy St SK3 240 D3
Duck La CH3 121 F4
Duckworth Gr WA2 9 D1
Duddon Cl Davenham CW9 .. 103 F2
Duddon CW6 145 D3
Duddon Hook La CW6 144 C3
Duddon Rd CW6 145 D3
Duddon St Peter's CE Contr Prim Sch CW6 145 D3
Dudleston Rd L66 69 D3
Dudley Ave WA7 23 E1
Dudley Cres L62 44 A2
Dudley Rd Ellesmere Port L65 70 A3
Irlam M44 11 E2
Sale M33 242 C8
Dudley St WA2 16 A4
Dudley Wlk SK11 111 F4
Dudlow Green Rd WA4 32 C3
Dufton Wlk M22 33 F4
Duke Ave Cheadle Hulme SK8 34 C3
Glazebury WA3 5 E4
Duke St Alderley Edge SK9 60 A1
Chester CH4 237 E1
Congleton CW12 156 B1
Crewe CW2 190 B2
Macclesfield SK11 112 B4
Newton-le-W WA12 2 A2
Stalybridge SK15 242 C1
9 Stockport SK1 240 F5
Duke's Cres CW11 175 D4
Duke's Ct CH4 237 E1
Dukes Way CW9 103 F2
Dukesway CH2 118 C4
Dukinfield Rd SK14 241 C8
Dulas Ct CH2 118 B4
Dulverton Ave CH3 119 E1
Dumbah La SK10 87 E3
Dumbers SK11 136 A1
Dunbar Cl
Connah's Quay CH5 91 E1
Ellesmere Port L66 69 E3
Holmes Chapel CW4 130 B1
Dunblane Ave SK4 240 D6
Duncan Ave
Newton-le-W WA12 2 B3
Runcorn WA7 23 E1
Duncan St WA2 16 B4
Duncansby Cres WA5 14 C3
Duncansby Dr L63 43 E2
Dundalk La WA8 22 B4
Dundalk Rd WA8 22 C4
Dundee Cl WA2 8 C2
Dundee Ct L65 70 C2
Dundonald Ave WA4 16 B1
Dundonald Rd SK8 35 D4
Dundonald St SK2 240 F2
Dundrennan Cl SK12 36 B3
Dunecroft M34 241 A8
Dunham Cl Bebington L62 43 F2
Sandbach CW11 175 E3
Dunham Cres CW2 206 A4
Dunham Ct WA6 97 F3
Dunham Forest Golf Course WA14 20 C2
Dunham Lawn WA14 238 B4
Dunham Massey Hall WA14 20 B2
Dunham Pk WA14 20 C2
Dunham Rd
Altrincham WA14 238 B4
Northwich CW9 104 A2
Partington WA13 19 F4
Wilmslow SK9 34 B3
Dunham Rise WA14 238 C4
Dunham Way CH2 118 C3
Dunham-on-Hill Cty Prim Sch WA6 97 F3
Dunkirk Ave CW7 149 E4
Dunkirk Dr L65 70 A1
Dunkirk La Capenhurst CH1 ... 94 B4
Dukinfield SK14 241 B8
Ellesmere Port L65 70 A1
Dunley Cl WA3 10 A3
Dunlin Ave WA12 2 B2
Dunlin Cl Poynton SK12 36 A2
Runcorn WA7 49 F3
Warrington WA2 8 C2
Dunlin Wlk WA14 238 B8
Dunlop St WA4 16 A2
Dunmore Cl CW10 151 E4
Dunmore Cres L66 69 D3
Dunmore Rd
Ellesmere Port L66 69 D3
Gatley SK8 239 B6
Dunmow Rd WA4 17 E2
Dunn's La CH3 121 F4
Dunnock Cl WA2 8 C2
Dunnock Gr WA3 9 F2
Dunnocksfold Rd ST7 193 D2
Dunnockswood ST7 193 D2
Dunollie Rd M33 242 E5
Dunoon Cl CW4 130 A1
Dunraven Rd L64 67 D4
Dunscar Cl WA3 9 E3
Dunsford WA8 12 B2
Dunsmore Cl WA11 1 B4
Dunstan La L64 67 F2
Dunster Cl CW9 104 A2
Dunster Gr L60 41 D4
Dunster Rd SK10 87 F1
Dunwood Dr ST7 193 E3
Durban Ave CH3 142 B4
Durber Cl ST7 209 E1
Durham Cl
Macclesfield SK10 86 C1
Romiley SK6 241 A1
Warrington WA1 17 F4
Durham Ct L65 70 C2
Durham Dr CW7 149 E3
Durham Gr M44 11 E3
Durham Rd Blacon CH1 117 F3
Widnes WA8 13 D2
Durlston Cl WA8 12 B1
Durrell Way WA3 3 F4
Dutton Cl CW5 204 C2
Dutton Gn L65 70 C2
Dutton La CW8 101 E3
Duxford Ct WA2 8 C1
Dyar Terr CW8 78 B1
Dyberth Rd CH1 117 E2
Dye House La SK22 39 E4
Dye La SK6 241 B2
Dyer St WA3 2 C4
Dyers Cl WA13 19 D2
Dyers La WA13 19 D2
Dykin Cl WA8 13 F2
Dykin Rd WA8 13 F2
Dysart St OL6 242 A2
Dyserth Gr 2 SK5 240 F8
Dystelegh Rd SK12 38 B3
Eadie Gr CW1 190 A4
Eaglaisway SK10 86 C1
Eagland Pl CW12 156 C2
Eagle Brow WA13 18 B2
Eagle La L66 69 E4
Eagles Way WA7 49 F3
Eaglesfield CW8 103 E2
Ealing Rd WA5 15 D3
Eanlewood La WA7 50 B4
Eardley Cres CW12 156 C2
Eardley Pl CW1 190 A3
Eardleyend Rd ST7 209 F4
Eardswick Cl CH2 237 E4
Eardswick La CW1 172 B3
Eardswick Rd CW10 151 E3
Earl Rd Cheadle Hulme SK8 34 C3
Manchester SK4 240 C8
Wilmslow SK8 34 C3
Earl St Sale M33 242 C7
Stockport SK3 240 D4
Warrington WA2 16 A4
Earle Cl WA12 1 C2
Earle Cres L64 41 E1
Earle Dr L64 41 E1
Earle Rd WA8 23 E4
Earle St Crewe CW1 190 B2
Newton-le-W WA12 2 A2
Earle's La CW6 122 B3
Earles La
Higher Wincham CW9 79 F3
Marston CW9 79 F3
Earlestown District CE Jun & Inf Sch WA12 2 A2
Earlestown Sta WA12 2 A2
Earls Gdns L65 70 A3
Earls Oak CH2 118 B4
Earls Rd CW2 206 A2
Earls Way Davenham CW9 103 F2
Runcorn WA7 49 F3
Earlston Ct CH2 237 F2
Earlsway Chester CH4 141 D4
Macclesfield SK11 111 F4
Earndale WA8 13 D3
Easby Cl Cheadle Hulme SK8 .. 35 D3
Poynton SK12 36 B2
Easenhall Cl WA8 13 E3
Easingwold 2 WA14 238 C4
East Ave Bollington SK10 87 F4
Cheadle SK8 34 B4
Great Sankey WA5 15 D2
Northwich CW9 104 B3
Stalybridge SK15 242 D3
Warrington WA2 16 B4
Warrington, Stockton Heath WA4 16 B1
Weston CW2 207 E3
East Ct ST7 193 F2
East Dam Wood Rd L24 21 D1
East Downs Rd
Altrincham WA14 238 C2
Cheadle SK8 239 F2
East Dudley St CW7 126 C1
East Gn CH5 116 A3
East La Cuddington CW8 102 A2
Runcorn WA7 49 F4
East Lancashire Rd
Goldborne WA3 3 E3
Haydock WA11 1 B4
East Lea M34 241 A6
East Mains L24 21 D2
East Millwood Rd L24 21 D2
East Park Rd SK11 112 A3
East Rd Halewood L24 21 D3
Middlewich CW10 128 A1
Wythenshawe M90 33 E4
East St Ashton-u-L OL6 242 A4
Widnes WA8 13 E1
East View WA4 17 E1
Eastbury Cl WA8 13 E3
Eastcott Cl CW12 155 F2
Eastdale Pl WA14 238 D7
Eastdale Rd WA1 17 D4
Easter Ct WA5 7 D1
Eastern Pathway CH4 237 F1
Eastern Rd Shavington CW5 . 205 F3
Willaston (nr Nantwich) CW5 205 F3
Eastfields Gr CH1 117 D4
Eastford Rd WA4 16 A1
Eastgate Rd CW4 130 B2
Eastgate Row CH1 237 E2
Eastgate St CH1 237 E2
Eastham Ctry Pk L62 44 A4
Eastham Glenburn Cty Inf Sch L62 43 F3
Eastham Rake Bebington L62 43 F2
Willaston L62 43 F2
Eastham Rake Sta L62 43 E2
Eastham Village Rd L62 44 A2
Eastham Way 9 SK9 34 B3
Eastleigh Rd SK8 239 B1
Easton Dr SK8 240 A1
Eastward Ave SK9 59 F3
Eastway Ellesmere Port L66 ... 69 E4
Widnes WA8 13 D1
Eastwood WA7 24 B1
Eastwood Ave WA12 2 C2
Eastwood Ct CH4 139 D3
Eastwood Rd WA5 6 C4
Eaton Ave CH4 141 E4
Eaton Bank CW12 156 C2
Eaton Bank Ind Est CW12 156 C2
Eaton Cl Broughton CH4 139 E2
Cheadle SK8 239 F3
Poynton SK12 37 D2
Sandbach CW11 175 E4
Eaton Cres CW9 103 F1
Eaton Cty Prim Sch CW6 .. 147 D2
Eaton Dr Alderley Edge SK9 59 F1
Middlewich CW10 151 D4
Eaton Gr CH4 140 C3
Eaton La Davenham CW9 103 F1
Eaton CW6 146 C1
Goostrey CW4 107 E1
Macclesfield SK11 112 B3
Tarporley CW6 168 C4
Eaton Mews CH4 141 E4
Eaton Rd Alsager ST7 193 E2
Altrincham WA14 238 C1
Chester CH4 141 F2
Eccleston CH4 141 F2
Sale M33 242 A6
Tarporley CW6 146 B1
Wettenhall CW7 170 B4
Eaton St Crewe CW2 190 B2
Runcorn WA7 23 D1
Eaton View CW9 126 C4
Eaves Brow Rd WA3 9 D4
Eaves Knoll Rd SK22 39 D4
Ebnal La SY14 213 F2
Eccles Cl SK23 65 E4
Eccles Rd SK23 65 F3
Eccleston Ave Bebington L62 43 E4
Chester CH4 141 E3
Ellesmere Port L66 69 F3
Eccleston CE Aided Prim Sch CH4 141 F1
Eccleston Cl WA3 9 E3
Eccleston Dr WA7 23 E1
Eccleston Rd CH4 161 D4
Eccleston Way 2 SK9 34 B2
Eccups La SK9 59 E4
Echo Cl CH4 140 C3
Ecton Ave SK10 113 D4
Ecton Cl CW7 127 D2
Edale Cl Altrincham WA14 ... 238 C1
Bebington L62 43 F3
Cheadle SK8 34 B4
Edale Dr CW6 122 B3
Edbury Pl CH4 141 E4
Eddisbury Cl SK11 112 C4
Eddisbury Dr ST5 210 B1
Eddisbury Hill CW8 123 E4
Eddisbury Rd L66 69 F1
Eddisbury Sq WA6 74 A4
Eddisbury Terr SK11 112 C4
Eddisford Dr WA3 4 B2
Edelsten St WA5 15 F3
Edelston Hall La CW5 203 F1
Eden Ave
Fowley Common WA3 5 E2
High Lane SK6 37 F4
Winsford CW7 126 C1
Eden Cl Biddulph ST6 179 F1
Ellesmere Port L66 69 E3
Kidsgrove ST7 195 D1
Wilmslow SK9 59 F3
Eden Dr SK10 87 F1
Eden Pl Cheadle SK8 239 D6
Sale M33 242 B7
Edenbridge Gdns WA4 26 C2
Edendale WA8 12 A1
Edenfield Cl WA16 58 A2
Edenfield Rd WA16 58 A2
Edenhall Cl CW4 130 A2
Edgar Ct CH4 237 E1
Edgar Pl CH4 237 E1
Edgars Dr WA2 9 D1
Edge Gr CH2 118 C1
Edge La SY14 199 E1
Edge View La WA16 59 D1
Edgecroft CH3 166 A1
Edgehill Chase SK9 60 C4
Edgeley Fold SK3 240 C3
Edgeley Park (Stockport County FC) SK3 240 E3
Edgeley Rd SK3 240 B3
Edgemoor WA14 238 A2
Edgerley La CH3 181 D3
Edgerton Rd WA3 3 F4
Edgeview Rd CW12 179 D4
Edgeway Henbury SK11 111 E4
Wilmslow SK9 60 A3
Edgewell La CW6 147 D2
Edgewood Dr Bebington L62 . 43 E3
Wistaston CW2 206 A4
Edgworth St WA2 16 A3
Edinburgh Cl SK8 239 F6
Edinburgh Ct L65 70 B2
Edinburgh Dr
Macclesfield SK10 87 D1
Romiley SK6 241 C4
Edinburgh Pl CW12 156 C1
Edinburgh Rd
Congleton CW12 156 C1
Widnes WA8 22 A4
Wistaston CW2 205 F4
Edinburgh Way CH4 237 F1
Edison Rd WA7 23 E2
Edith St WA7 22 C2
Edleston Cty Prim Sch CW2 190 B2
Edleston Rd CW2 190 B2
Edlestone Gr 9 SK9 34 C1
Edmund Cl SK4 240 E8
Edna St Chester CH2 118 C2
Hyde SK14 241 D6
Edward Gdns WA1 17 F3
Edward Rd WA5 14 B3
Edward St
Ashton-u-L OL6 242 B2
Audley ST7 209 F2
Crewe CW2 190 B1
Ellesmere Port L65 70 B4
Haydock WA11 1 A3
Hyde SK14 241 C7
Macclesfield SK11 112 A4
Northwich CW9 104 B4
Sale M33 242 E6
Stockport SK1 240 F4
Widnes WA8 13 E1
Edwards Ave CW2 206 B3
Edwards Cl CW2 206 B3
Edwards Rd CH4 141 D3
Edwards Way Alsager ST7 ... 193 F2
Widnes WA8 22 B4
Edwin St WA8 13 E1
Egdon Cl WA8 13 F1
Egerton WA16 29 E3
Egerton Ave Hartford CW8 . 103 D2
Partington WA13 19 E4
Warrington WA1 16 C4
Egerton Ct CW6 122 A3
Egerton Cty Prim Sch WA16 56 C1
Egerton Dr Chester CH2 118 B3
Sale M33 242 B7
Egerton Moss WA15 31 F3
Egerton Rd Blacon CH1 117 E3
Lymm WA13 18 B1
Wilmslow SK9 34 A1
Egerton Rd S SK4 240 C8
Egerton Sq WA16 57 D1
Egerton St Chester CH2 237 F3
Congleton CW12 156 B1
Ellesmere Port L65 70 B3
Runcorn WA7 23 D2
Warrington, Howley WA1 16 B3
Warrington, Stockton Heath WA4 16 B1
Egerton Street Sch CH2 237 F3
Egerton Wlk CH4 162 A4
Eggbridge La CH3 143 D3
Egremont Gr 2 SK3 240 B4
Egypt St Warrington WA1 16 A3
Widnes WA8 22 C4
Eisenhower Cl WA5 15 D3
Elaine Cl Ellesmere Port L66 .. 69 E2
Widnes WA8 13 E1
Elaine St WA1 16 B4
Elanor Rd 2 CW11 174 B4
Elcho Rd WA14 238 B3
Elcombe Ave WA3 3 F4
Elder Dr CH4 140 C3
Elderberry Way SK9 60 C4
Elderberry Wlk M31 11 E1
Eldon Rd Macclesfield SK11 . 111 F4
Stockport SK3 240 C3
Eldon St WA1 16 B3
Eldon Terr L64 66 C4
Eleanor Cl CW1 189 F3
Eleanor St
Ellesmere Port L65 70 B3
Widnes WA8 23 D4
Electra Way CW1 191 D1
Electricity St CW2 190 B2
Elf Mill Cl SK3 240 E2
Elgar Ave L62 43 F3
Elgar Cl L65 69 F2
Elgin Ave
Holmes Chapel CW4 130 A1
Macclesfield SK10 87 D1
Warrington WA4 16 A1
Elgin Cl CH3 119 D2
Elgin Dr M33 242 E5
Elgin St SK15 242 E1
Elgol Cl SK3 240 F1
Eliot Cl CW1 191 D2
Eliza St M33 242 B7
Elizabeth Ave Disley SK12 ..... 38 B3
Stockport SK1 240 F4
Elizabeth Cl CW6 122 B3
Elizabeth Cres CH4 237 F1
Elizabeth Ct Kidsgrove ST7 .. 210 B3
Stockport SK4 240 C6
Widnes WA8 23 D4
Elizabeth Dr WA1 17 D4
Elizabeth Rd Haydock WA11 ... 1 C4
Partington M31 11 F2
Elizabeth St
Congleton CW12 156 B1
Crewe CW1 190 A3
Hyde SK14 241 D7
Macclesfield SK11 112 B4
Elizabethan Way CW9 104 C3
Elk View SY14 222 C3
Elkan Cl WA8 13 F1
Elkan Rd WA8 13 F1
Ella Gr WA16 57 D1
Elland Dr L66 69 E3
Ellen Brook Rd M22 33 E4
Ellen St Stockport SK4 240 D7
Warrington WA5 15 F4
Ellerby Cl WA7 50 C4
Ellerton Ave L66 69 E3
Ellerton Cl WA8 12 B2
Ellesmere Ave
Broughton CH4 139 E2
Chester CH2 118 B3
Ellesmere Cl CW11 174 C4
Ellesmere Dr SK8 240 A1
Ellesmere Pl CW1 190 A3
Ellesmere Port Cath (Aided) High Sch L65 70 A2
Ellesmere Port Hospl L65 ... 70 A1
Ellesmere Port Sta L65 70 B3
Ellesmere Port Stadium The L65 70 C2
Ellesmere Rd
Altrincham WA14 238 E6
Cheadle SK3 240 A3
Culcheth WA3 4 C2
Northwich CW9 104 A2
Warrington WA4 16 A1
Ellesmere St Runcorn WA7 ... 23 D1
Warrington WA1 16 B3
Ellesworth Cl WA5 15 E4
Elliot St 9 WA8 23 D4
Ellis La WA6 49 E1
Ellis St Crewe CW1 190 A3
Hyde SK14 241 F6
Widnes WA8 22 C4
Ellison St
Warrington, Howley WA1 16 B3
Warrington, Stockton Heath WA4 16 B1
Elloway Rd L24 21 D2
Ellwood Gn CW2 206 C2
Elm Ave Newton-le-W WA12 2 B1
Widnes WA8 13 D1
Elm Beds Rd SK12 37 E1
Elm Cl Partington M31 11 F1
Poynton SK12 36 C2
Tarporley CW6 146 B1
Wistaston CW2 189 F1
Elm Cres SK9 60 A2
Elm Dr Crewe CW1 190 C3
Holmes Chapel CW4 130 B2
Macclesfield SK10 87 F1
Elm Gn L64 67 F4
Elm Gr Alderley Edge SK9 60 A1
Alsager ST7 193 F2
Broughton CH4 140 C3
Ellesmere Port L66 70 A1
Hyde SK14 241 F6
Sale M33 242 B8
Warrington WA1 16 C4
Wilmslow SK9 34 B2
Winsford CW7 127 D1
Elm Rd Altrincham WA15 238 E3
Congleton CW12 156 A2
Gatley SK8 239 A5
Haydock WA11 1 C4
High Lane SK6 37 F4

Elm – Fis 257

Elm Rd continued
Hollins Green WA3 11 D1
Middlewich CW10 151 E4
Penketh WA5 14 C2
Runcorn WA7 49 E4
Warrington WA2 8 A2
Weaverham CW8 102 B4
Willaston L64 67 F4
Elm Rd S SK3 240 A3
Elm Ridge Dr WA15 32 B4
Elm Rise Frodsham WA6 74 B4
Prestbury SK10 86 C3
Elm Sq CH4 140 C3
Elm St Ellesmere Port L65 70 B4
Northwich CW9 79 D1
Elm Tree Ave Lymm WA13 18 B1
Warrington WA1 16 C4
Elm Tree Ct CW6 147 D2
Elm Tree Dr ST7 209 F1
Elm Tree La CW11 174 B4
Elm Tree Rd Goldborne WA3 3 F4
Lymm WA13 18 B1
Elmbridge Prim Sch WA15 32 B4
Elmdale Ave SK8 239 B2
Elmfield Cl SK9 60 A1
Elmfield Rd
Alderley Edge SK9 60 A2
Stockport SK3 240 F1
Elmir CH1 117 F2
Elmore Cl
Holmes Chapel CW4 130 A2
Runcorn WA7 24 B1
Elms The Goldborne WA3 3 F4
Runcorn WA7 22 C1
Elmsleigh Rd SK8 239 A2
Elmstead Cres CW1 189 F4
Elmstead Rd SK11 84 A2
Elmsway Altrincham WA15 32 A4
Bollington SK10 88 A4
Cheadle Hulme SK7 35 E4
High Lane SK6 37 F3
Elmtree Dr SK4 240 C6
Elmwood WA7 24 B1
Elmwood Ave Chester CH2 118 C2
Warrington WA1 16 C4
Elmwood Cl ST7 194 A2
Elmwood Gr CW7 149 F4
Elmwood Rd CW8 78 A2
Elnor Ave SK23 65 F3
Elnor La SK23 65 F2
Elsby Rd ST7 193 F1
Elston Ave WA12 2 B3
Elstree Ave CH3 119 D2
Elstree Gr SK3 240 D4
Elswick Ave SK7 35 F4
Eltham Cl WA8 13 F2
Eltham Wlk WA8 13 F2
Elton Cl Bebington L62 43 F2
Goldborne WA3 3 F4
Warrington WA3 9 E2
Elton Crossings Rd CW11 174 B3
Elton Cty Prim Sch CH2 72 A2
Elton Dr SK7 36 B4
Elton La Elton WA6 72 C2
Haslington CW11 174 B1
Elton Lordship La WA6 73 D4
Elton Rd CW11 174 B3
Elvington Cl WA7 49 F2
Elworth Ave WA8 13 D3
Elworth CE Contr Prim Sch CW11 174 C4
Elworth Hall Cty Prim Sch CW11 174 C4
Elworth Rd CW11 174 C3
Elworth St CW11 175 D4
Elworth Way 6 SK9 34 B2
Elwyn Dr L26 21 D4
Ely Cl CH1 94 C4
Ely Ct 6 SK10 112 C4
Embassy Cl CH1 117 E2
Emberton Pl CW3 230 A3
Embleton Ct WA7 49 E3
Embridge Cswy SK10, SK17 90 A3
Emerald Rd M22 33 F4
Emery Cl SK4 240 A8
Emily St 14 WA8 23 D4
Emlyn Gr SK8 240 A2
Emmerdale Ave WA2 8 A2
Emmett St CW8 78 A2
Empress Dr Crewe CW2 190 A2
Reddish SK4 240 D8
Emral Ct SY14 211 D1
Emslie Ct L64 66 B4
Enderby Rd CH1 237 D3
Endon Av SK10 88 A4
Endsleigh Cl CH2 118 B4
Endsleigh Gdns CH2 118 B4
Enfield Cl CW2 206 A2
Enfield Park Rd WA2 9 D2
Enfield Rd L65 70 A3
Engelsea Brook La CW2 208 A2
Englefield Ave CH4 140 B3
Englefield Cl CW1 190 A4
Englesea Gr CW2 190 A1
English Martyrs RC Sch WA11 1 C4
Ennerdale Chester CH2 118 C3
Macclesfield SK11 111 F3
Ennerdale Ave L62 43 F2
Ennerdale Cl CW7 126 B2
Ennerdale Dr
Congleton CW12 156 A1
Frodsham WA6 74 B4
Ennerdale Rd Crewe CW2 189 E2
Gatley SK8 239 B3
Partington M31 11 F2
Romiley SK6 241 B4
Ennerdale Terr SK15 242 D3
Ennis Cl L24 21 E1
Enticott Rd M44 11 E3
Enville Rd WA14 238 C3
Enville St WA4 16 B2
Epping Dr WA1 17 E4
Epsom Ave SK9 34 C2
Epsom Gdns WA4 26 C4
Epworth Cl WA5 6 C4
Era St M33 242 B6
Eric Ave WA1 16 C4
Eric St WA8 13 E1
Erlesmere Ave M34 241 A8
Ermine Rd CH2 237 F4
Ernest St Cheadle SK8 239 C6
Crewe CW2 190 B1
Errington Ave L65 70 B3
Errwood Cl L24 21 F1
Erskine Rd M31 11 F1
Erwood St WA2 16 A3
Esk Dale Cl CW7 126 B1
Esk Rd CW7 127 D1
Eskdale Ellesmere Port L65 70 A2
Gatley SK8 239 C4
Eskdale Ave
Cheadle Hulme SK7 35 E3
Warrington WA2 8 B2
Eskdale Cl Bebington L62 43 F3
Runcorn WA7 49 E3
Essex Ave SK3 240 B4
Essex Cl CW12 156 C3
Essex Dr Biddulph ST6 179 E1
Kidsgrove ST7 194 C1
Essex Gdns M44 11 E2
Essex Rd CH2 119 D3
Essex Wlk SK10 86 C1
Esther St WA8 13 D1
Esthers La CW8 102 B4
Etchells Prim Sch SK8 239 C1
Etchells Rd SK8 239 D1
Etchells St 6 SK1 240 F5
Ethelda Dr CH2 119 D3
Etherow Ave SK6 241 E2
Etherow Cl CW11 174 C4
Eton Dr L63 41 F3
Eton Rd L65 70 B2
Etterick Pk CH3 119 D1
Ettiley Ave CW11 174 B3
Euclid Ave WA4 17 D1
Europa Bvd WA5 7 E2
Europa Way Cheadle SK3 240 B2
Ellesmere Port L65 70 B3
Eustace St WA2 16 A3
Eva Rd SK3 240 A3
Eva St CW11 174 B4
Evans Cl WA11 1 C4
Evans Pl WA4 16 B2
Evans St Ashton-u-L OL6 242 A4
Crewe CW1 190 B3
Evansleigh Dr CH5 116 A2
Evelyn St WA5 15 E2
Evelyn Street Cty Prim Sch WA5 15 F2
Everdon Cl CW7 126 C2
Everest Cl L66 69 F2
Everest Rd ST7 195 E2
Everglade Cl SK11 112 A3
Everite Rd WA8 22 A4
Eversley WA8 12 A1
Eversley Cl Appleton WA4 26 C3
Frodsham WA6 74 B3
Eversley Ct CH2 118 B2
Eversley Pk CH2 118 B2
Evesham Ave SK4 240 B7
Evesham Cl
Macclesfield SK10 87 F2
Warrington WA4 26 B4
Evesham Gr M33 242 E6
Ewart St CH4 140 A4
Ewloe Ct L65 70 B1
Ewrin La SK10 89 E3
Excalibur Cty Prim Sch ST7 193 F1
Excalibur Ind Est ST7 193 F2
Excalibur Way M44 11 F4
Exchange Cl 25 SK11 112 B4
Exchange St
Macclesfield SK11 112 B4
Stockport SK3 240 E5
Exeter Cl SK8 34 C4
Exeter Pl CH1 117 F3
Exeter Rd L65 70 B3
Exeter Wlk SK7 35 F4
Exit Rd W M90 33 D4
Exmouth Cres WA7 50 C3
Exmouth Way WA5 6 C3
Exton Pk CH2 237 D4
Eyam Rd SK7 36 C4
Eyebrook Rd WA14 238 A2

Factory La Disley SK12 38 C4
Widnes WA8 13 D2
Factory Rd CH5 116 A2
Fair Haven's Ct WA8 23 D4
Fair Mead WA16 82 A4
Fair Oak Rd ST5 210 B1
Fair View Cl CW8 77 F2
Fairacre Dr CW10 151 F3
Fairacres Rd SK6 37 F4
Fairbourne Ave
Alderley Edge SK9 60 A2
Wilmslow SK9 59 F2
Fairbourne Cl
Warrington WA5 7 F2
Wilmslow SK9 59 F2
Fairbourne Dr SK9 59 F2
Fairbrook CW2 189 F1
Fairbrother Cres WA2 8 B1
Fairburn Ave CW2 189 F2
Fairburn Cl WA8 13 F2
Fairclough Ave WA1 16 B2
Fairclough Cres WA11 1 A3
Fairclough St
Burtonwood WA5 6 C3
Newton-le-W WA12 2 A2
Fairfax Dr Runcorn WA7 23 E1
Wilmslow SK9 59 F2
Fairfield Ave Cheadle SK8 239 F2
Ellesmere Port L65 70 A1
Romiley SK6 241 A4
Sandbach CW11 175 D3
Fairfield CE Aided Prim Sch WA1 16 B3
Fairfield Cty High Sch WA8 13 D2
Fairfield Cty Inf Sch WA8 13 D1
Fairfield Cty Jun Sch WA8 13 D1
Fairfield Gdns WA4 16 C1
Fairfield Rd Broughton CH4 139 D2
Chester CH2 119 D2
Irlam M44 11 E3
Lymm WA13 18 C2
Northwich CW9 104 A2
Warrington WA4 16 C1
Widnes WA8 13 D1
Fairfield St WA1 16 B3
Fairfields ST7 209 F1
Fairford Rd CH4 140 C3
Fairford Way SK9 60 B4
Fairhaven Cl Bramhall SK7 35 F4
Great Sankey WA5 15 D2
Fairhaven Dr L63 43 E3
Fairhaven Rd WA8 13 E1
Fairhills Rd M44 11 F4
Fairholm Rd CW9 127 D4
Fairholme Ave L64 41 E1
Fairholme Cl CH1 94 A1
Fairholme Rd SK4 240 C7
Fairlawn SK4 240 D7
Fairlawn Cl L63 43 D3
Fairlea M34 241 A6
Fairmeadow CH4 162 B1
Fairmile Dr M20 239 C8
Fairoak Ct WA7 50 C2
Fairoak La WA7 50 C2
Fairview LL13 196 C4
Fairview Ave Alsager ST7 193 E2
Weston CW2 207 D3
Fairview Rd
Ellesmere Port L65 70 A1
Macclesfield SK11 112 A3
Fairway Cheadle Hulme SK7 35 E3
Gatley SK8 239 B4
Hawarden CH5 116 A1
Fairway The ST7 193 E2
Fairways Appleton WA4 26 B3
Frodsham WA6 74 B4
Fairways Dr L66 69 E4
Fairy La M33 242 F6
Fairywell Cl SK9 34 B1
Falcon Cl Middlewich CW10 151 E3
New Mills SK22 39 E4
Winsford CW7 149 E3
Falcon Dr CW1 190 A4
Falcon Rd L66 69 F2
Falcondale Rd WA2 8 A3
Falconers Gn WA5 7 D1
Falcons Way WA7 49 F3
Fallibroome Cl SK11 111 F4
Fallibroome High Sch SK10 86 C1
Fallibroome Rd SK11 111 F4
Fallowfield WA7 23 E1
Fallowfield Cl CW7 125 F1
Fallowfield Ct CW1 190 A3
Fallowfield Gr WA2 9 D1
Falls Gr SK8 239 A3
Falmouth Cl SK10 111 F4
Falmouth Dr WA5 14 C2
Falmouth Pl WA7 50 C3
Falmouth Rd
Congleton CW12 178 C4
Crewe CW1 190 A3
Falstone Cl WA3 10 A3
Falstone Dr WA7 50 C4
Fanner's La WA16 28 B3
Fanny's Croft ST7 193 E1
Fanshawe La SK11 110 C3
Fanshawe Wlk CW2 206 B4
Far Ridings SK6 241 D3
Faraday Rd
Ellesmere Port L65 70 A2
Runcorn WA7 23 E2
Faraday St WA3 9 F2
Farams Rd ST7 193 F4
Farbailey Cl CH4 141 D3
Farfields Cl SK11 111 F1
Faringdon Rd WA2 8 A3
Farlands Dr M20 239 B7
Farley Cl CW10 151 D4
Farley Ct SK8 239 F3
Farm Cl CW8 77 E1
Farm Dr CH5 91 E1
Farm La Appleton WA4 26 C4
Disley SK12 38 A3
Withington SK11 108 C1
Farm Rd Northwich CW9 104 C4
Oakmere CW8 124 A4
Weaverham CW8 77 E1
Farm Way WA12 2 C1
Farmdale Dr CH2 72 A2
Farmer Cl CW2 190 A2
Farmer St SK4 240 E7
Farmer's La WA5 7 D3
Farmers Heath L66 69 E1
Farmfield Dr SK10 87 E2
Farmfields Rise CW3 232 B1
Farmleigh Dr CW1 189 F4
Farmleigh Gdns WA5 15 E3
Farmstead Way L66 69 F1
Farndale Cl CW2 206 A3
Farndon Cl Broughton CH4 139 E2
Cuddington CW8 102 A2
Sale M33 242 E5
Farndon Cty Prim Sch CH3 180 C1
Farndon Rd L66 69 F3
Farne Cl CH2 95 E4
Farnham Ave SK11 112 A3
Farnham Cl Appleton WA4 26 C4
Cheadle Hulme SK8 35 D4
Farnhill Cl WA7 50 B4
Farnley Cl WA7 24 B1
Farnworth CE Contr Prim Sch WA8 13 D2
Farnworth Cl WA8 13 D2
Farnworth Rd WA5 14 B2
Farnworth St WA8 13 D2
Farr Hill Dr L60 40 C4
Farr Hill Rd L60 40 C4
Farr St SK3 240 D4
Farrant St WA8 23 D4
Farrell Rd WA4 26 B4
Farrell St WA1 16 B3
Farriers Way CW7 126 A1
Farthing La CW9 79 D4
Farwood Cl SK10 86 C1
Faulkner Dr CW10 151 F3
Faulkner St CH2 118 C2
Faulkner's La
Lindow End WA16 58 C1
Mobberley WA16 58 C1
Faulkners Cl CH4 161 D4
Faulkners La CH3 142 B4
Fawley Ave SK14 241 D5
Fawns Keep SK9 60 B4
Fawns Leap CW8 101 F3
Fearndown Way SK10 87 E2
Fearnhead La WA2 9 D1
Fearnley Way WA12 2 B1
Feather La L60 40 C4
Feilden Ct CH1 94 C1
Felix Rd CW8 103 F4
Fellside Gn SK15 242 D3
Felskirk Rd M22 33 E4
Fence Ave SK10 112 C4
Fence Ave Ind Est SK10 112 C4
Fence La CW12 178 B2
Fenham Dr WA5 14 C2
Fennel St WA1 16 B3
Fenton Cl Congleton CW12 157 D1
Widnes WA8 12 B2
Fenwick La WA7 49 E3
Fenwick Rd L66 69 F1
Ferguson Ave L66 69 F3
Ferguson Dr WA2 8 B1
Ferma La CH3 120 B3
Fern Ave WA12 2 B1
Fern Bank SK15 242 F1
Fern Cl WA3 9 E2
Fern Cres Congleton CW12 157 D2
Stalybridge SK15 242 F1
Fern Ct CW1 190 C2
Fern Lea SK8 239 B1
Fern Lea Dr SK11 112 A4
Fern Rd L65 70 A1
Fern Way CW8 77 E1
Fernacre M33 242 C7
Fernally St SK14 241 E6
Fernbank Cl Crewe CW1 190 C2
Winsford CW7 127 D1
Fernbank Rise SK10 88 A4
Fernbankcl WA3 9 F2
Ferndale Ave CH2 72 A2
Ferndale Cl Bold Heath WA8 13 F4
Sandbach CW11 175 E3
Warrington WA1 17 E4
Weston CW2 207 D3
Ferndale Cres SK11 111 F4
Fernhill Rd CH1 117 F3
Fernhurst WA7 49 E4
Fernilee Cty Inf Sch SK23 65 F2
Fernlea WA15 238 F1
Fernlea Rd Heswall L60 41 D4
Marston CW9 79 D3
Fernleaf Cl ST7 193 F4
Fernleigh CW8 103 E4
Fernley Ave M34 241 A6
Fernwood Gr SK9 60 B4
Ferry Cl CH5 116 A3
Ferry La Sealand CH1 117 E1
Warrington WA4 17 F2
Ferry Rd L62 44 A3
Ferryview Wlk WA7 23 F1
Festival Ave Buerton CW3 230 C2
Warrington WA2 8 B1
Festival Cres WA2 8 B1
Festival Dr SK10 85 F3
Festival Hill CW12 156 C1
Festival Rd L65 69 F3
Festival Way WA7 49 E4
Fiddler's Ferry Rd WA8 13 E1
Fiddlers La CH1 94 B1
Field Ave CW2 189 F1
Field Cl Bollington SK10 87 F4
Cheadle Hulme SK7 35 E2
Northwich CW8 103 E4
Tarvin CH3 121 D1
Field Hey La L64 43 D1
Field La Appleton WA4 26 B3
Tarvin CH3 121 D1
Tattenhall CH3 166 A1
Wistaston CW2 189 F1
Field Side Cl WA16 58 A2
Field St SK6 241 A3
Field View ST6 179 E1
Field View Cl SK11 112 C3
Field Way ST7 193 F2
Field Wlk M31 11 E1
Fieldbank SK11 112 A4
Fieldbank Rd SK11 112 A4
Fieldfare CW7 150 A4
Fieldfare Cl WA3 9 F2
Fieldgate WA8 22 A4
Fieldhead Mews SK9 60 C4
Fieldhead Rd SK9 60 C4
Fieldhouse Row WA7 49 E4
Fielding Ave SK12 36 C1
Fields Cl ST7 193 F2
Fields Cres CW12 156 B1
Fields Dr CW11 175 D3
Fields Rd Alsager ST7 193 F2
Congleton CW12 178 C4
Haslington CW1 191 E2
Fields The CW5 205 E3
Fields View SY13 228 B1
Fields View Cl CW5 220 A4
Fieldsend Dr WN7 4 B4
Fieldside CW6 145 D3
Fieldsway WA7 49 D3
Fieldview Dr WA2 8 B1
Fieldway Chester CH2 118 C2
Ellesmere Port L66 69 D4
Frodsham WA6 74 B4
Saughall CH1 94 A1
Weaverham CW8 77 E1
Widnes WA8 13 E1
Fife Rd WA1 16 C4
Fifth Ave Kidsgrove ST7 194 C1
Runcorn WA7 49 F4
Fiji St WA5 15 F3
Filkin's La CH3 119 D1
Finch La L26 21 D4
Finchdale Gdns WA3 4 A4
Finchett Dr CH1 118 A2
Finchley Rd WA15 238 E3
Findlay Cl WA12 2 A1
Finlan Rd WA8 23 D4
Finland Rd SK3 240 D3
Finlay Ave WA5 14 C2
Finlow Hill La SK10 85 F3
Finney Cl SK9 34 B1
Finney Dr SK9 34 B1
Finney Gr WA11 1 C3
Finney La Cheadle SK8 34 A4
Gatley SK8 239 C1
Wythenshawe SK8 34 A4
Finney's La CW10 128 A1
Finningley Ct WA2 8 C1
Finny Bank Rd M33 242 A8
Finsbury Park WA8 13 E3
Finsbury Wlk CW7 149 D4
Fir Ave Bramhall SK7 35 F4
Halewood L26 21 D4
Fir Cl Halewood L26 21 D4
Poynton SK12 36 C2
Tarporley CW6 146 B1
Fir Ct SK10 86 C1
Fir Gr Macclesfield SK11 112 B3
Warrington WA1 16 C4
Weaverham CW8 102 C4
Fir La CW8 102 A1
Fir Rd Bramhall SK7 35 F4
Denton M34 241 A7
Fir St Irlam M44 11 E3
Stockport SK4 240 E6
Widnes WA8 13 E1
Fir Tree Ave Chester CH4 141 D3
Goldborne WA3 3 F4
Knutsford WA16 82 B4
Fir Tree Cl WA4 26 B1
Fir Tree La Burtonwood WA5 7 D4
Chester CH3 119 F1
Fir Way L60 41 D3
Firbank CH2 72 B2
Firbank Cl WA7 24 B1
Firbeck Cl Broughton CH4 139 D2
Congleton CW12 155 F2
Firbeck Gdns CW2 189 E2
Firdale Rd CW8 103 E4
Firemans Sq CH1 237 D3
Firman Cl WA5 15 D4
Firs Gr SK8 239 A4
Firs La WA4 26 A3
Firs Rd SK8 239 A4
Firs Sch The CH2 118 C3
Firs The WA14 238 B3
First Ave Adlington SK10 36 B1
Crewe CW1 190 C1
Deeside Ind Est CH5 93 D1
Kidsgrove ST7 194 C1
Sandbach CW11 175 D3
First Dig La CW5 219 E4
First Wood St CW5 204 B3
Firswood Mount SK8 239 A4
Firthfields Cl CW9 103 F1
Firths Fields CW9 103 F1
Firtree Ave WA1 17 D4
Firtree Cl CW8 78 A2
Firtree Gr CH1 95 D4
Firvale Ave SK8 239 B1
Firwood Rd ST6 179 F1
Firwood Wlk CW2 190 B1
Fisher Rd CH1 117 F2
Fisher St WA7 23 D2
Fisherfield Dr WA3 10 A3
Fishermans Cl CW11 191 F4
Fishers La CW5 203 E4
Fishpool Rd CW8 123 F2
Fistral Ave SK8 34 B4

Fitton St CW9 80 A1
Fitton's Cl CW5 217 F3
Fitz Cl SK10 87 E2
Fitz Cres SK10 87 E2
Fitz Walter Rd WA1 17 E4
Fitzherbert St WA2 16 B4
Fitzwilliam Ave SK11 112 C2
Fitzwilliam Wlk WA7 24 A1
Five Ashes Rd CH4 141 D3
Fiveways Par SK7 36 C4
Flacca Ct CH3 166 A1
Flag La Crewe CW1, CW2 190 B2
Neston L64 66 C4
Flag La N CH2 118 C4
Flag La S CH2 118 B4
Flamingo Cl CW1 189 F4
Flander Cl WA8 12 B1
Flash La Antrobus CW9 53 F3
Bollington SK10 87 E4
Flashes La L64 67 D3
Flat La Kelsall CW6 122 B2
Sandbach CW11 175 D3
Flatt La L65 70 A3
Flatts La SK23 64 C2
Flaxley Cl WA3 10 A3
Flaxmere Dr CH3 142 A4
Fleet La WA9 1 A1
Fleet St Ellesmere Port L65 70 A3
Hyde SK14 241 E7
Fleetwood Cl WA5 15 D2
Fleetwood Wlk WA7 50 B3
Fleming St L65 70 B3
Flemish Rd M34 241 B6
Flers Ave WA4 16 B2
Fletcher Dr SK6 37 F3
Fletcher Gr CW9 104 B3
Fletcher St Crewe CW1 190 A3
Stockport SK1 240 F5
Warrington WA4 16 A2
Fletchers La WA13 18 C2
Fletsand Rd SK9 60 B3
Flint Cl L64 66 C3
Flint Ct L65 70 B1
Flint Dr L64 66 C3
Flint Gr M44 11 E3
Flint Meadow L64 66 C4
Flint St Macclesfield SK11 112 C4
Stockport SK3 240 E3
Flittogate La WA16 80 C4
Flixton Dr CW2 190 A1
Florence Ct SK3 240 B2
Florence St Sale M33 242 B8
6 Stockport SK4 240 E6
Warrington WA4 16 B2
Florist St SK3 240 E3
Flower St CW8 103 F4
Flowers La CW1 172 C1
Flowery Field Prim Sch SK14 241 D8
Fluin La WA6 74 B4
Foden Ave ST7 194 A2
Foden La Lindow End SK9 59 E1
Woodford SK7 35 E2
Foden St SK10 87 E1
Foden Wlk 11 SK9 34 B1
Fogg's La CW9, WA4 53 D3
Fol Hollow CW12 156 A1
Fold La Biddulph ST6 179 F2
Bosley SK11 135 E1
Fold The SK10 87 D4
Folden Cl L66 69 D3
Folds The L63 42 A3
Foley Wlk M22 33 F4
Folkestone Cl SK10 87 D1
Folkstone Way WA7 50 B4
Folly La WA5 15 F4
Forbes Cl WA3 9 F2
Forbes Pk SK7 35 E4
Ford Cl CW1 190 A3
Ford Ct CW7 149 E3
Ford La Crewe CW1 190 A3
Tattenhall CH3 166 C2
Ford St Stockport SK3 240 D5
Warrington WA1 16 B3
Ford's La SK7 35 E3
Fordington Rd WA5 15 D3
Fords La ST7 195 E3
Fordton L Ctr WA2 8 A2
Foregate St CH1 237 E2
Foreland Cl WA5 14 B4
Forest Ave CW4 107 E1
Forest Cl Cuddington CW8 101 F2
Rainow SK10 88 C3
Forest Dr Altrincham WA15 238 F6
Broughton CH4 139 D2
Forest Gate La CW6 122 C4
Forest Gdns M31 11 E2
Forest La WA6 100 B3
Forest Park Sch M33 242 A6
Forest Pl CW9 79 D1
Forest Rd Cuddington CW8 101 F2
Ellesmere Port L66 69 F4
Heswall L60 41 D4
Macclesfield SK11 113 F3
Tarporley CW6 146 B2
Winsford CW7 149 D4
Forest Sch WA15 238 F6
Forest St Chester CH1 237 F2
Weaverham CW8 102 B4
Forester Ave WA16 57 E1
Forester Dr SK15 242 D1
Foresters Cl WA6 101 D3
Forge Cl Cronton WA8 12 B3
Warren SK11 111 E1
Forge Fields CW11 174 C2
Forge La Congleton CW12 156 A2
Norton in Hales TF9 236 B1
Forge Rd Ellesmere Port L66 69 E3
Great Sankey WA5 14 C3
Whaley Bridge SK23 65 F4
Forge Sh Ctr The WA4 16 B1
Forge St CW1 190 B2
Forge Way CH4 140 C2
Formby Cl WA5 14 C2
Formby Dr SK8 34 A4
Forrest Dr SK11 113 E2
Forrest Rd M34 241 B5
Forshaw St WA2 16 B4
Forshaw's La WA5 6 C4
Forster Ave CW8 102 C4
Forster St WA2 16 A4
Forsythia Wlk M31 11 E1
Forty Acre La
Cranage CW4 131 E3
Swettenham CW4 131 E3
Forum The Chester CH1 237 D2
Romiley SK6 241 C2
Forwood Rd L62 43 E4
Foster St WA8 13 D1
Fosters Rd CW12 157 D3
Fothergill St WA1 16 B4
Fotheringay Ct L65 70 B1
Foulkes Ave CW1 189 F3
Foundary Bank CW12 156 C2
Foundry Ct 13 SK11 112 B4
Foundry La Sandbach CW11 174 B4
Scholar Green ST7 194 C4
Widnes WA8 22 B3
Foundry St Bollington SK10 88 A4
Newton-le-W WA12 2 A2
Warrington WA2 16 A3
Fountain Cl SK12 36 B2
Fountain Ct Biddulph ST6 179 E1
Winsford CW7 126 B1
Fountain La Davenham CW9 103 F1
Frodsham WA6 74 A4
Fountain Sq SK12 38 B3
Fountain St
Ashton-u-L OL6 242 B4
Congleton CW12 156 B1
Hyde SK14 241 F7
Macclesfield SK11 112 C4
Fountains Ave WA11 1 C4
Fountains Cl
Middlewich CW10 128 A1
Runcorn WA7 50 B3
Fountains Rd SK7 35 E3
Fountains Wlk WA3 4 A4
Four Lanes End CW2 207 F1
Fourseasons Cl CW2 206 A4
Fourth Ave Crewe CW1 190 C1
Deeside Ind Est CH5 92 C1
Kidsgrove ST7 194 C1
Runcorn WA7 49 F4
Fowey Cl SK10 86 B1
Fowler Rd CH1 117 E2
Fowler St SK10 87 E1
Fowlers Bench La CH3 184 B3
Fowley Common La WA3 5 E3
Fox Bank Ct SK3 240 D4
Fox Bench Cl SK7 35 E3
Fox Cl WA15 238 F6
Fox Cover CH3 119 F3
Fox Covert WA7 50 B4
Fox Covert La Picton CH2 96 A1
Stoak CH2 96 A1
Fox Gdns Kidsgrove ST7 210 B4
Lymm WA13 18 B2
Fox Gr WA16 57 E1
Fox Hill CW6 122 B2
Fox La Clutton CH3 182 B1
Waverton CH3 143 D3
Fox Lea CH1 117 D4
Fox St Congleton CW12 156 C2
Runcorn WA7 23 D1
Stockport SK3 240 D4
Warrington WA5 15 F3
Fox's Dr CH5 116 A3
Foxall Way L66 69 E1
Foxcote WA8 12 A1
Foxcover Rd L60 41 E4
Foxcovert La WA16 106 C4
Foxdale Ct WA4 26 B4
Foxes Fold CW8 78 C1
Foxes Hey CW8 101 E3
Foxes Wlk CH3 142 A4
Foxfield Cl WA2 8 C2
Foxfield La CW7 126 A1
Foxglove Cl Bollington SK10 88 B4
Huntington CH3 142 A3
Wistaston CW2 206 A4
Foxglove Ct WA6 74 B4
Foxglove Dr WA14 238 C8
Foxglove La SK15 242 D3
Foxglove Way L64 66 C3
Foxglove Wlk M31 11 F1
Foxhall Rd WA15 238 F6
Foxhill WA14 238 A5
Foxhill Ct CW6 146 C1
Foxhill Gr WA6 73 E2
Foxhills Cl WA4 26 B2
Foxholes Rd SK14 241 D5
Foxhunter Cl CH3 121 F4
Foxland Rd SK8 239 B4
Foxlea CW9 78 B4
Foxley Cl WA13 19 D1
Foxley Heath WA8 22 C4
Foxwist Cl CH2 237 E4
Foxwist Gr CW7 125 F3
Foxwood Dr WA16 108 A4
Frances Ave SK8 239 A6
Frances St Cheadle SK8 239 E6
Crewe CW2 190 B1
Frances St continued
Denton SK14 241 C7
Irlam M44 11 F3
Macclesfield SK11 112 A4
8 Stockport SK1 & SK3 240 E4
Frances St W SK14 241 C7
Francis Cl WA8 22 B4
Francis Ct CH2 237 F3
Francis La LL13 196 A3
Francis Rd Frodsham WA6 49 E1
Irlam M44 11 F4
Warrington WA4 16 B1
Francis St CH2 237 F3
Frank Bott Ave CW1 190 A4
Frank Perkins Way M44 11 F4
Frank St Hyde SK14 241 E6
Widnes WA8 13 E1
Frank Webb Ave CW1 190 A3
Franklin Cl WA5 15 E4
Fraser Ave M33 242 E5
Fraser Ct CH4 141 E4
Fraser Rd WA5 14 B3
Frawley Ave WA12 2 B3
Freckleton Cl WA5 15 D2
Frederick St
Ashton-u-L OL6 & SK15 242 B2
Warrington WA4 16 C2
Widnes WA8 23 D4
Fredric Pl WA7 23 D2
Free Green La WA16 107 D4
Freeman Ave OL6 242 A3
Freemantle St SK3 240 D4
French Ave SK15 242 F1
French La
French Lane End CW5 218 B3
Sound CW5 218 B3
French St
Ashton-u-L OL6 242 A4
Stalybridge SK15 242 F1
Widnes WA8 13 E1
Freshfield SK8 34 A4
Freshfield Ave SK14 241 D5
Freshfield Dr SK10 87 E2
Freshfields
Comberbach CW9 78 B4
Wistaston CW2 206 A4
Freshfields Dr WA2 9 E1
Freshmeadow La WA6 73 D1
Freshwater Cl WA5 14 B4
Friar's Cl SK9 59 F4
Friar's Rd M33 242 B6
Friars Cl Altrincham WA14 238 B1
Rainow SK10 88 B3
Friars Gate WA1 16 A2
Friars La WA1 16 A2
Friars Way SK10 86 C1
Frida Cres CW8 103 F3
Friends La WA5 14 B3
Friesian Gdns ST5 210 B1
Frieston Rd WA14 238 E8
Frith Ave CW8 123 E4
Frith Terr SK11 112 B2
Frobisher Pl SK5 240 E8
Frobisher Rd L64 66 C4
Froda Ave WA6 74 A4
Frodsham Ave SK4 240 C7
Frodsham CE Contr Prim Sch WA6 74 A4
Frodsham Cty High Sch WA6 74 A4
Frodsham Manor House Cty Jun Sch WA6 49 E1
Frodsham Rd WA6 73 E1
Frodsham St Chester CH1 237 E3
Kelsall CW6 122 A3
Frodsham St Luke's RC Aided Prim Sch WA6 74 A4
Frodsham Sta WA6 74 A4
Frodsham Way 5 SK9 34 C2
Frog La Handley CH3 165 F1
Holt LL13 196 A4
Milton Green CH3 165 F1
Pickmere WA16 55 D1
Tattenhall CH3 166 A1
Worthenbury SY14 211 D1
Froghall La
High Legh WA16 29 E4
Warrington WA2 16 A3
Frome Ct L65 70 A4
Front St CW11 175 E3
Frosts Mews L65 70 A3
Fryer Rd CW9 80 A2
Fuchsia Cl L66 69 F1
Fulbeck WA8 12 B1
Fulbeck Cl CW2 206 A4
Fulbrook Dr SK8 35 D3
Fuller Dr CW2 206 A4
Fullerton Rd Hartford CW8 103 D2
Manchester SK4 240 B6
Fulmar Cl SK12 36 A2
Fulmar Ct CW1 189 F4
Fulmards Cl SK9 60 B4
Fulshaw Ave SK9 60 A3
Fulshaw CE Contr Prim Sch SK9 59 F3
Fulshaw Cross SK9 60 A3
Fulshaw Ct SK9 60 A2
Fulshaw Park S SK9 60 A2
Fulshaw Pk SK9 60 A3
Fulton Gr CW9 103 F1
Fulwood Gdns L66 69 E3
Fulwood Mews L66 69 E3
Fulwood Rd
Ellesmere Port L66 69 E3
Goldborne WA3 3 F4
Furber St CW1 190 B3
Furnace St SK14 241 C8
Furne Rd CH1 117 F2
Furness Cl
Holmes Chapel CW4 130 A2
Poynton SK12 36 B2
Winsford CW7 149 D4
Furness Ct WA7 24 C2
Furness Gr SK4 240 A5
Furness Lodge Cl SK23 39 E2
Furness Rd SK7 35 E3
Furness Row SK23 39 E2
Furness Vale Sta SK23 39 E2
Furnival St Crewe CW2 190 B1
Sandbach CW11 175 D4
Furrocks Cl L64 66 C3
Furrocks La L64 66 C3
Furrocks Way L64 66 C3
Furrows The CH1 94 C4
Fylde Ave SK8 34 B4
Fylde Rd SK4 240 A6
Fytton Cl SK11 111 E1

Gable Wlk SK9 60 A4
Gables Cl WA2 8 C2
Gables The ST7 193 E2
Gabriel Bank CW8 76 A1
Gadbrook Bsns Ctr CW9 104 B3
Gadbrook Pk CW9 104 B3
Gadbrook Rd CW9 104 B3
Gaddum Rd WA14 238 B1
Gail Ave SK4 240 D6
Gail Cl SK9 60 A1
Gainford Ave SK8 239 B4
Gainford Cl WA8 12 B2
Gainsborough Cl SK9 60 C4
Gainsborough Ct WA8 12 A1
Gainsborough Cty Inf Sch CW2 190 A2
Gainsborough Cty Jun Sch CW2 190 A1
Gainsborough Dr SK8 239 F6
Gainsborough Rd
Crewe CW2 190 A2
Warrington WA4 16 A1
Gair Rd SK5 240 F8
Gair St SK14 241 D8
Gairloch Cl WA2 8 C2
Gaisgill Ct WA8 12 B1
Gala Cl CH4 139 E2
Galbraith Cl CW12 156 B1
Gale Rd SK22 39 E4
Galion Way WA8 12 C2
Galleys Bank ST7 195 D2
Gallowsclough La
Norley WA6 100 C2
Oakmere WA6 100 C2
Galway Gr CW2 206 A3
Game St CW11 175 D2
Gamul Pl CH4 237 E1
Ganton Cl WA8 13 D2
Garden Ave CW7 126 A1
Garden Ct CH1 237 D3
Garden La Altrincham WA14 238 D5
Chester CH1 237 D3
Harthill CH3 183 F2
Garden Rd WA16 56 C2
Garden St Bollington SK10 87 F4
Congleton CW12 156 B2
Hyde SK14 241 E8
Macclesfield SK10 87 F1
Garden Terr Chester CH1 237 D3
Chester, Hoole Park CH2 118 C1
Garden Wlk M31 11 E1
Gardens The Holt LL13 180 C1
Sandbach CW11 175 D3
Gardner Ave WA11 1 B3
Garfit St CW10 128 B1
Garigill Cl WA8 13 E3
Garlick St SK14 241 F7
Garner Cl WA14 238 D2
Garner St WA2 16 B4
Garner's La SK3 240 E1
Garnets La WA8 22 A2
Garnett Ave WA4 17 D2
Garnett St SK1 240 F5
Garrett Field WA3 9 E3
Garrett Wlk SK3 240 C4
Garsdale Cl WA5 15 D4
Garside Ave WA3 3 E4
Garside St SK14 241 E5
Garston Cl SK4 240 C7
Garth Ave WA15 238 E6
Garth Dr CH2 118 B3
Garth Hts SK9 60 B4
Garth Rd L65 71 D3
Garton Dr WA3 3 F4
Garven Pl WA1 16 A3
Garwood Cl WA5 15 E4
Gas Rd SK11 112 B4
Gas St SK4 240 E5
Gaskell Ave Knutsford WA16 56 C1
Warrington WA4 17 D2
Gaskell Rd WA14 238 D6
Gaskell St WA4 16 B1
Gatcombe Mews SK9 60 A3
Gate Warth St WA5 15 E2
Gateacre Ct L66 69 F4
Gatefield St CW1 190 B2
Gatesheath Dr CH2 118 B4
Gatesheath La CH3 165 F3
Gateway CW1 190 C1
Gathill Cl SK8 239 F1
Gatley Gn SK8 239 A5
Gatley Golf Course SK8 239 A3
Gatley Prim Sch SK8 239 A5
Gatley Rd Cheadle SK8 239 C5
Sale M33 242 E5
Gatley Sta SK8 239 B5
Gaunts Way WA7 49 F3
Gavin Rd WA8 22 A4
Gawend La SK11 112 B1
Gawer Pk CH2 118 B2
Gawesworth Way 3 SK9 34 C2
Gawsworth Ave CW2 189 F2
Gawsworth Cl Alsager ST7 193 E2
Bramhall SK7 35 F3
Holmes Chapel CW4 130 A2
Northwich CW9 104 A2
Poynton SK12 36 C1
Stockport SK3 240 D1
Gawsworth Cty Prim Sch SK11 111 E1
Gawsworth Dr CW11 175 E4
Gawsworth Hall SK11 134 C4
Gawsworth Mews SK8 239 B5
Gawsworth Rd
Ellesmere Port L66 69 F3
Macclesfield SK11 111 E3
Warren SK11 111 E3
Gayhurst Ave WA2 8 C1
Gaymoore Cl CH2 237 D4
Gaynor Ave WA11 1 C4
Gayton Cl CH2 118 C3
Gayton Farm Rd L60 41 D3
Gayton La L60 41 D3
Gayton Parkway L60 41 E3
Gayton Prim Sch L60 41 D3
Gayton Rd L60 41 D3
Gee St SK3 240 D3
Gemini Bsns Pk WA5 7 F2
Gemmull Cl CW3 229 F2
General St WA1 16 B3
Geneva Rd CW7 126 B1
George Bates Cl ST7 193 E2
George Kenyon Mews CH4 140 C3
George La SK6 241 A4
George Rd WA5 15 E2
George St Alderley Edge SK9 60 A1
Altrincham WA14 238 D4
Audley ST7 209 E1
Barnton CW8 78 A2
Chester CH1 237 D3
Denton M34 241 A7
Ellesmere Port L65 70 B4
Knutsford WA16 57 D1
Macclesfield SK11 112 B4
Newton-le-W WA12 2 A2
Sandbach CW11 174 C4
Stalybridge SK15 242 D2
Whaley Bridge SK23 65 F4
Winsford CW7 126 C1
George St W SK11 112 B4
George VI Ave CW10 151 E3
George VI Cl CW10 151 E3
George's Cl SK12 36 C2
George's La CW9 54 B1
George's Rd Sale M33 242 B5
Stockport SK4 240 D6
George's Rd E SK12 36 C2
George's Rd W SK12 36 C2
George's Wlk CW11 175 D3
Georges Cres WA4 17 D1
Georges Way ST7 209 F1
Gerard Dr CW5 204 B2
Gerosa Ave WA2 8 A4
Gerrard Ave
Ellesmere Port L66 69 E2
Warrington WA5 15 F4
Gerrard Dr CW8 77 E1
Gerrard Rd WA3 9 D4
Gerrard St
Stalybridge SK15 242 E1
Widnes WA8 23 D4
Gerrards Ave CH3 119 D1
Giantswood La CW12 156 B3
Gibb Hill CW9 53 E1
Gibbon Dr CW9 80 A2
Gibson Cres CW11 174 B3
Gibson St
Warrington, Howley WA1 16 B3
Warrington, Stockton Heath WA4 16 B1
Gibson Way WA14 238 C8
Gibsons Rd SK4 240 B8
Gig La WA1 17 F4
Gigg La WA4 25 D3
Gilbert Cl ST7 195 D1
Gilbert Rd WA15 238 E1
Gilbertbank SK6 241 B4
Gilchrist Ave SK11 111 F4
Gilchrist Rd M44 11 F3
Gilderdale Cl WA3 10 A3
Gill Bent Rd SK8 35 D4
Gillan Cl WA7 50 B3
Gillow Cl CW1 190 A4
Gilmore St SK3 240 E3
Giltbrook Cl WA8 12 C2
Gilwell Cl WA4 17 E1
Gingerbread La CW5 205 D3
Girton Cl L65 70 B2
Girton Rd L65 70 B2
Girvin Dr L64 66 C3
Glade The SK4 240 A5
Gladewood Cl SK9 60 B4
Gladstone Ave CH1 118 A1
Gladstone Ct SK4 240 B7
Gladstone Gr SK4 240 A7
Gladstone Mews SK4 240 E7
Gladstone Rd
Altrincham WA14 238 D6
Broughton CH4 139 D2
Chester CH1 118 A2
Neston L64 66 C4
Gladstone St Crewe CW1 190 B2
Northwich CW8 103 F4
Warrington WA2 16 A3
8 Widnes WA8 23 D4

Gladstone St continued
Willaston (nr Nantwich) CW5 ... 205 E3
Winsford CW7 ... 149 E4
Gladville Dr SK8 ... 240 A2
Glaisdale Cl CW2 ... 206 A3
Glamis Cl Chester CH3 ... 119 D1
Wistaston CW2 ... 205 F4
Glan Aber Pk CH4 ... 141 D4
Glandon Dr SK7 ... 35 E4
Glanvor Rd SK3 ... 240 C4
Glastonbury Ave
Cheadle Hulme SK7 ... 35 E3
Chester CH2 ... 118 B4
Goldborne WA3 ... 4 B4
Glastonbury Cl WA7 ... 24 C2
Glastonbury Dr
Middlewich CW10 ... 128 A1
Poynton SK12 ... 36 B3
Glaswen Gr SK5 ... 240 F8
Glazebrook La WA3 ... 11 D3
Glazebrook St WA1 ... 16 B3
Glazebrook Sta WA3 ... 11 D3
Glazebury CE (VA) Prim Sch WA3 ... 5 E4
Glaziers La WA3 ... 4 B1
Gleadmere WA8 ... 12 B1
Gleave Av SK10 ... 88 A4
Gleave Rd WA5 ... 6 C3
Gleave St M33 ... 242 B8
Glebe Ave WA4 ... 17 E1
Glebe Cl CW5 ... 220 A4
Glebe Green Dr CW7 ... 149 E3
Glebe La WA8 ... 13 D3
Glebe Meadows CH2 ... 96 C1
Glebe Rd CW8 ... 102 A2
Glebe St ST7 ... 194 B1
Glebe The WA7 ... 23 F1
Glebecroft Av CH2 ... 72 A2
Glebeland WA3 ... 4 C2
Glebelands Rd
Knutsford WA16 ... 57 D1
Sale M33 ... 242 A8
Glebeway Rd L65 ... 70 C3
Gledhall St SK15 ... 242 D2
Glen Aber Dr CH4 ... 140 C4
Glen Ave M33 ... 242 A8
Glen Cl WA3 ... 11 D1
Glen Rd L66 ... 69 E2
Glen The Blacon CH1 ... 117 F3
Runcorn WA7 ... 49 F3
Glenathol Rd L66 ... 69 E2
Glenbourne Pk SK7 ... 35 E3
Glenburn Ave L62 ... 43 F2
Glencoe Cl CW4 ... 130 B1
Glencoe Rd L66 ... 69 E2
Glencourse Rd WA8 ... 13 D3
Glendale Av CH2 ... 72 A2
Glendale Ave CH5 ... 116 A2
Glendale Cl Buerton CW3 ... 230 C2
Wistaston CW2 ... 189 E2
Glendene Ave SK7 ... 35 E3
Glendyke Rd L66 ... 69 E2
Gleneagles Cl Bramhall SK7 .. 36 A4
Chester CH3 ... 119 D2
Wilmslow SK9 ... 60 B4
Gleneagles Dr
Haydock WA11 ... 1 A3
Holmes Chapel CW4 ... 130 A1
Macclesfield SK10 ... 87 E2
Widnes WA8 ... 13 D3
Winsford CW7 ... 126 B1
Gleneagles Rd
Ellesmere Port L66 ... 69 E2
Gatley SK8 ... 239 C1
Glenesk Rd L66 ... 69 E2
Glenfield WA14 ... 238 B4
Glenfield Dr SK12 ... 36 B2
Glenfield Rd SK4 ... 240 D8
Glenholme Rd SK7 ... 35 E4
Glenlea Dr M20 ... 239 B8
Glenmaye Rd L66 ... 69 E2
Glenmere Rd M20 ... 239 C8
Glenn Pl WA8 ... 12 C1
Glenorchy Cl CW4 ... 130 B1
Glenside Cl CH1 ... 117 E3
Glenside Dr SK9 ... 60 B3
Glent View SK15 ... 242 D4
Glenthorn Gr M33 ... 242 B5
Glenton Pk L64 ... 66 C3
Glenville Cl WA7 ... 49 D3
Glenville Way M34 ... 241 A6
Glenwood Cl L66 ... 69 E3
Glenwood Gdns L66 ... 69 E3
Glenwood Rd L66 ... 69 E3
Gleyve WA16 ... 29 E3
Gloucester Ave WA3 ... 3 D4
Gloucester Cl
Ellesmere Port CH1 ... 94 C4
Macclesfield SK10 ... 87 F2
Warrington WA1 ... 17 E4
Gloucester Rd Cheadle SK8 .. 34 B4
Kidsgrove ST7 ... 194 C1
Knutsford WA16 ... 81 F4
Poynton SK12 ... 36 B2
Widnes WA8 ... 13 D2
Gloucester St Chester CH2 .. 237 E4
Stockport SK3 ... 240 D3
Glover Rd WA3 ... 9 E2
Glover St Crewe CW1 ... 190 A3
Newton-le-W WA12 ... 2 B2
Glovers Loom CH3 ... 142 A4
Gloverstone Ct CH4 ... 237 E1
Glyn Ave L62 ... 43 F4
Goathland Way SK11 ... 112 B3
Goddard Rd WA7 ... 23 F2
Goddard St CW1 ... 190 A3
Godfrey St WA2 ... 16 B4
Godley Ct SK14 ... 241 F6
Godley Prim Sch SK14 ... 241 F7
Godley St SK14 ... 241 F8
Godscroft La WA6 ... 73 F3
Godshill Cl WA5 ... 14 B4
Godstall La CH1 ... 237 E2
Godstow WA7 ... 24 C2
Godward Rd SK22 ... 39 D4
Golborne Dale Rd WA3 ... 3 D2
Golborne Rd Goldborne WA3 ... 3 E4
Winwick WA2 ... 8 A4
Golborne St WA1 ... 16 A3
Gold Triangle Complex WA8 ... 22 A3
Goldborne All Saints RC Sch WA3 ... 3 D4
Goldborne Cty Prim Sch WA3 ... 3 D4
Goldborne La WA16 ... 28 C1
Goldcliffe Cl WA5 ... 7 E2
Goldcrest Cl Crewe CW1 ... 189 F4
Runcorn WA7 ... 49 F3
Winsford CW7 ... 149 E3
Golden Sq WA1 ... 16 A3
Goldfinch Cl CW12 ... 156 C1
Goldfinch La WA3 ... 9 F2
Goldford La SY14 ... 199 F3
Goldsmith Dr CW11 ... 174 B3
Golf Rd Altrincham WA15 ... 238 F3
Sale M33 ... 242 F6
Golftyn Dr CH5 ... 91 E1
Golftyn La CH5 ... 91 E1
Gongar La CH3 ... 98 C1
Gonsley Cl CH2 ... 237 E4
Gonville Ave SK11 ... 112 C2
Gooch Dr WA12 ... 2 B1
Goodall St SK11 ... 112 C4
Goodall's Cnr CW2 ... 206 B2
Goodier St M33 ... 242 A6
Goodrington Rd SK9 ... 34 C2
Goodwood Cl Barnton CW8 ... 78 A2
Chester CH1 ... 118 A1
Goodwood Gr L66 ... 69 F2
Goose Gn WA14 ... 238 D4
Goose La WA4 ... 26 A1
Gooseberry La Kelsall CW6 122 C2
Runcorn WA7 ... 24 B1
Goosebrook Cl CW9 ... 78 B4
Goosebrook La WA4, CW9 ... 52 C1
Goosetrey Cl 10 SK9 ... 34 C1
Goostrey Cty Prim Sch CW4 ... 130 C4
Goostrey Cty Prim Sch (The Annexe) CW4 ... 107 F1
Goostrey La Cranage CW4 .. 130 A4
Goostrey CW4 ... 130 A4
Goostrey Sta CW4 ... 131 D4
Gordale Cl CW12 ... 157 D3
Gordon Ave Bebington L62 ... 43 F4
Haydock WA11 ... 1 C4
Warrington WA1 ... 17 D4
Gordon La CH1 ... 95 D3
Gordon Rd M33 ... 242 B8
Gordon St
Ashton-u-L OL6 ... 242 A4
Hyde SK14 ... 241 E6
Stalybridge SK15 ... 242 E1
Stockport SK4 & SK5 ... 240 E7
Gore La SK9 ... 59 E1
Gorse Bank Rd WA15 ... 32 B4
Gorse Cl WA6 ... 101 D3
Gorse Covert Cty Prim Sch WA3 ... 10 A3
Gorse Covert Rd WA3 ... 10 A3
Gorse Hall Cty Prim Sch SK15 ... 242 D1
Gorse Hall Dr SK15 ... 242 C1
Gorse La CW12 ... 178 B3
Gorse Sq M31 ... 11 E2
Gorse Stacks CH1 ... 237 E3
Gorse The WA14 ... 31 D4
Gorse Way CH3 ... 142 A3
Gorsefield CH3 ... 166 A1
Gorsefield Ave L62 ... 43 E3
Gorsefield Cl L62 ... 43 E3
Gorsefield Hey SK9 ... 60 C4
Gorselands SK8 ... 35 D3
Gorsewood Rd WA7 ... 50 B3
Gorsey Bank Cres CW5 ... 220 A4
Gorsey Bank Cty Prim Sch SK9 ... 59 F4
Gorsey Bank Rd SK3 ... 240 B4
Gorsey Brow SK6 ... 241 A2
Gorsey La Altrincham WA14 . 238 B5
Bold Heath WA9 ... 6 B3
Partington WA13 ... 20 A4
Warrington WA2 ... 16 B4
Widnes WA8 ... 13 F1
Gorsey Mount St 23 SK1 ... 240 F5
Gorsey Rd SK9 ... 59 F4
Gorseywell La WA7 ... 50 C3
Gorsley Cl CW10 ... 151 E3
Gorstage La CW8 ... 102 B4
Gorsthills Cty Prim Sch L66 ... 69 E2
Gorston Wlk M22 ... 33 E4
Gosberryhole La CW12 ... 158 A1
Gosforth Ct WA7 ... 49 F4
Gosforth Pl CH2 ... 118 C2
Gosling Cl WA4 ... 26 A1
Gosling Rd WA3 ... 9 D4
Gosport Dr WA2 ... 8 C1
Goss St CH1 ... 237 D2
Gotherage Cl SK6 ... 241 E2
Gotherage La SK6 ... 241 E2
Gothic Cl SK6 ... 241 F2
Gothurst Ct WA8 ... 22 B4
Gough Ave WA2 ... 8 A1
Gough St SK3 ... 240 D5
Gough's La WA16 ... 82 B4
Goulden St Crewe CW1 ... 190 A3
Warrington WA5 ... 15 F3
Goulders Ct WA7 ... 50 A3
Gourham Dr SK8 ... 239 F2
Gower Rd Hyde SK14 ... 241 D5
Reddish SK4 ... 240 D8
Gowy Cl Alsager ST7 ... 192 C2
Sandbach CW11 ... 174 C4
Wilmslow SK9 ... 34 C1
Gowy Cres CH3 ... 121 D1
Gowy Ct L66 ... 69 F4
Gowy Rd CH2 ... 96 C1
Gowy Wlk CW7 ... 127 D2
Goyt Pl SK23 ... 65 F4
Goyt Rd Disley SK12 ... 38 B3
New Mills SK22 ... 39 E3
Goyt Valley Ind Est SK23 ... 39 E2
Goyt View SK22 ... 39 D3
Goyt's La SK17 ... 90 C1
Grace Ave WA2 ... 16 A4
Grace Cl CW1 ... 191 E2
Gradwell St SK3 ... 240 D4
Grafton Mall 5 WA14 ... 238 D4
Grafton Mews CH2 ... 237 E4
Grafton Rd L65 ... 70 B4
Grafton St Altrincham WA14 238 D4
Ashton-u-L OL6 ... 242 A2
Hyde SK14 ... 241 D7
Newton-le-W WA12 ... 2 A2
Reddish SK4 ... 240 E7
Warrington WA5 ... 15 F3
Graham Ave L66 ... 69 E3
Graham Cl WA8 ... 12 B1
Graham Dr Disley SK12 ... 38 B3
Halewood L26 ... 21 D4
Graham Rd Blacon CH1 ... 117 F2
Widnes WA8 ... 22 B4
Grainger's Rd CW9 ... 103 F3
Grammar School Rd
Lymm WA13 ... 18 C1
Warrington WA4 ... 16 C2
Grampian Way Bebington L62 43 F3
Neston L64 ... 66 C3
Winsford CW7 ... 149 D4
Granby Cl WA7 ... 50 B3
Granby Rd
Cheadle Hulme SK8 ... 35 D4
Warrington WA4 ... 26 A4
Grand Junction Ret Pk CW1 ... 190 B2
Grandford La CW5 ... 217 E1
Grange Ave Barnton CW8 ... 78 A2
Cheadle SK8 & M19 ... 239 F3
Denton M34 ... 241 B6
Warrington WA4 ... 16 C2
Grange Cl Crewe CW1 ... 190 C2
Goldborne WA3 ... 3 E3
Hyde SK14 ... 241 F5
Sandbach CW11 ... 174 C4
Grange Cres L66 ... 44 A1
Grange Ct Altrincham WA14 238 C1
Biddulph ST6 ... 179 E1
Grange Ctr L65 ... 70 A3
Grange Cty Comp Sch The WA7 ... 23 E1
Grange Cty Inf Sch The WA7 ... 23 E1
Grange Cty Jun Sch The WA7 ... 23 E1
Grange Dr Hartford CW8 ... 103 D3
Penketh WA5 ... 15 D2
Thornton Hough L63 ... 42 A4
Widnes WA8 ... 12 B1
Grange Jun Sch The CW8 ... 103 D3
Grange La Edge Green SY14 ... 198 C2
Tilston SY14 ... 198 C2
Weaverham CW8 ... 102 A4
Winsford CW7 ... 126 A2
Grange Lea CW10 ... 128 A1
Grange Park Ave
Cheadle SK8 ... 239 D5
Runcorn WA7 ... 23 E1
Wilmslow SK9 ... 60 A4
Grange Park Rd SK8 ... 239 D5
Grange Rd Altrincham WA14 238 C1
Ashton CH3 ... 99 D1
Barnton CW8 ... 78 A2
Biddulph ST6 ... 179 F2
Chester CH3 ... 119 E1
Chester, Bache CH2 ... 118 B2
Cuddington CW8 ... 101 F1
Ellesmere Port L65 ... 70 B2
Haydock WA11 ... 1 B3
Hyde SK14 ... 241 F5
Macclesfield SK11 ... 112 B3
Northwich, Rudheath CW9 ... 104 B3
Runcorn WA7 ... 23 E1
Sale M33 ... 242 A6
Grange Rd N SK14 ... 241 F6
Grange Rd S SK14 ... 241 F5
Grange Rd W CH3 ... 119 E1
Grange Sch The CW8 ... 103 D3
Grange The Hartford CW8 .. 103 D3
Hyde SK14 ... 241 F5
Grange Valley WA11 ... 1 B3
Grange Valley Prim Sch WA11 ... 1 B3
Grange Way CW11 ... 174 C4
Grangebrook Dr CW7 ... 126 B2
Grangefields ST6 ... 179 F2
Grangeland Dr WA16 ... 83 F2
Grangelands SK10 ... 86 C1
Grangemoor WA7 ... 49 E4
Grangeside CH2 ... 118 B4
Grangeway Runcorn WA7 ... 49 E4
Wilmslow SK9 ... 34 B2
Grangeway Ct WA7 ... 49 E4
Granston Cl WA5 ... 7 F1
Grant Cl WA5 ... 7 E1
Grant Rd WA5 ... 15 D3
Grant St WA12 ... 2 A2
Grantham Ave
Warrington WA1 ... 16 C4
Warrington, Lower Walton WA4 ... 26 A4
Grantham Cl CW9 ... 104 B4
Grantham Rd SK4 ... 240 C6
Granville Dr L66 ... 69 D4
Granville Rd
Cheadle SK3 & SK8 ... 240 C1
Chester CH1 ... 118 A2
Northwich CW9 ... 104 A3
Wilmslow SK9 ... 59 F3
Granville Sq CW7 ... 149 F4
Granville St
Ashton-u-L OL6 ... 242 A2
Runcorn WA7 ... 23 D2
Warrington WA1 ... 16 B3
Winsford CW7 ... 149 F4
Grapes St SK11 ... 112 B4
Grappenhall CE Aided Prim Sch WA4 ... 17 D1
Grappenhall Hall Sch WA4 . 17 D1
Grappenhall La WA4 ... 27 F3
Grappenhall Rd
Ellesmere Port L65 ... 69 F2
Warrington WA4 ... 16 B1
Grasmere SK11 ... 111 F3
Grasmere Ave
Congleton CW12 ... 155 F1
Crewe CW2 ... 189 F3
Warrington WA2 ... 8 C2
Grasmere Cl
Stalybridge SK15 ... 242 D4
Winsford CW7 ... 126 B1
Grasmere Cres SK7 ... 35 F4
Grasmere Dr
Holmes Chapel CW4 ... 130 A2
Runcorn WA7 ... 49 E3
Grasmere Rd
Alderley Edge SK9 ... 60 A1
Chester CH2 ... 118 C3
Ellesmere Port L65 ... 70 B1
Frodsham WA6 ... 74 B4
Gatley SK8 ... 239 B3
Lymm WA13 ... 18 C2
Neston L64 ... 66 C3
Partington M31 ... 11 F2
Grason Ave SK9 ... 34 B1
Grasscroft Rd SK15 ... 242 D1
Grassfield Way WA16 ... 82 A4
Grassmere Cres SK6 ... 37 F4
Grassmoor Cl L62 ... 43 F4
Grassygreen La ST7 ... 209 F1
Gratrix La M33 ... 242 F5
Gratrix Rd L62 ... 43 E4
Gravel La SK9 ... 59 F3
Graveyard La WA16 ... 58 C3
Gray Ave WA11 ... 1 B3
Gray's Cl ST7 ... 195 D4
Graylag Cl WA7 ... 49 F3
Graysands Rd WA15 ... 238 F3
Greasby Dr L66 ... 69 F2
Great Ashfield WA8 ... 12 B2
Great Budworth CE Contr Prim Sch CW9 ... 79 D4
Great Delph WA11 ... 1 B4
Great Egerton St
SK1 & SK4 ... 240 E6
Great King St SK11 ... 112 B4
Great Norbury St SK14 ... 241 D6
Great Portwood St SK1 ... 240 F6
Great Queen St SK11 ... 112 B4
Great Riding WA7 ... 50 B4
Great Sankey Cty High Sch WA5 ... 14 C4
Great Sankey Cty Prim Sch WA5 ... 15 D3
Great Sankey L Ctr WA5 ... 14 C4
Great Underbank SK1 ... 240 F5
Greatoak Rd ST7 ... 209 F2
Greave SK6 ... 241 D4
Greave Fold SK6 ... 241 D4
Greave Prim Sch SK6 ... 241 D4
Greaves La SY14 ... 222 C4
Greaves Rd SK9 ... 59 F4
Grebe Cl Knutsford WA16 ... 57 D2
Poynton SK12 ... 36 A2
Greeba Ave WA4 ... 16 A2
Greek St Runcorn WA7 ... 22 C2
Stockport SK1 & SK3 ... 240 E4
Green Acre Cl WA16 ... 82 A4
Green Ave Alpraham CW6 ... 169 E2
Barnton CW8 ... 78 A2
Davenham CW9 ... 103 F2
Green Bank Adderley TF9 ... 235 D3
Chester CH4 ... 141 F3
Green Bank Ctr CH4 ... 141 E3
Green Bridge Cl WA7 ... 24 A1
Green Cl SK8 ... 239 A6
Green Coppice WA7 ... 50 B4
Green Courts WA14 ... 238 B3
Green Croft SK6 ... 241 E3
Green Dr Alsager ST7 ... 193 E2
Wilmslow SK9 ... 34 B1
Green Gables Cl SK8 ... 239 B1
Green Hall Mews SK9 ... 60 A3
Green Hill St SK3 ... 240 D3
Green Hill Terr SK3 ... 240 D3
Green Jones Brow WA5 ... 6 C3
Green La Acton CW5 ... 204 A2
Alderley Edge SK9 ... 59 F1
Appleton WA4 ... 27 D3
Audlem CW3 ... 229 F1
Green La continued
Barbridge CW5 ... 187 D4
Bollington SK10 ... 63 D1
Burtonwood WA5 ... 6 C4
Chester CH3, CH4 ... 119 D2
Chester, Lache CH4 ... 140 C2
Chowley CH3 ... 182 C3
Davenham CW9 ... 103 F2
Disley SK12 ... 38 B2
Ellesmere Port L65 ... 70 B2
Ellesmere Port, Sutton Green L66 ... 69 E2
Higher Kinnerton CH4 ... 161 D3
Higher Wincham CW9 ... 79 F2
Horton Green SY14 ... 212 A4
Irlam M44 ... 11 F3
Kelsall CW6 ... 122 B2
Knutsford WA16 ... 56 B2
Lindow End SK9 ... 84 C4
Manchester SK4 ... 240 B7
Peover WA16 ... 83 E1
Picton CH2 ... 96 B2
Plumley WA16 ... 80 C3
Poynton SK12 ... 37 E2
Romiley SK6 ... 241 B2
Sandbach CW11 ... 173 F4
Saughall CH1 ... 117 E4
Shocklach SY14 ... 211 E4
Stockport SK4 ... 240 D6
Stockport, Heaton Norris SK4 ... 240 C6
Warrington WA1 ... 17 D4
Widnes WA8 ... 12 C1
Willaston (nr Nantwich) CW5 ... 205 F3
Wilmslow SK9 ... 60 A4
Winwick WA2 ... 8 A4
Green La Cl WA2 ... 8 A4
Green La E CH5 ... 116 B4
Green La W CH5 ... 93 D2
Green Lane Ind Est SK4 ... 240 D6
Green Lane Sch WA1 ... 17 D4
Green Lawns Dr CH1 ... 94 C4
Green Mdws SK11 ... 111 F3
Green Meadows WA3 ... 3 F3
Green Oaks Path WA8 ... 23 E4
Green Oaks Way WA8 ... 23 E4
Green Pk CW8 ... 102 C4
Green Rd M31 ... 11 F2
Green St Alderley Edge SK9 ... 60 A1
Holt LL13 ... 180 C1
Hyde SK14 ... 241 E5
Knutsford WA16 ... 57 D1
Macclesfield SK11 ... 112 C4
Sandbach CW11 ... 175 D4
Stockport SK3 ... 240 F2
Warrington WA5 ... 15 F3
Green The Cheadle SK8 ... 34 C4
Ellesmere Port L65 ... 70 A1
Hartford CW8 ... 103 D3
Harthill CH3 ... 183 F2
Higher Kinnerton CH4 ... 161 D4
Lawton-gate ST7 ... 194 A2
Middlewich CW10 ... 151 E3
Neston L64 ... 66 B4
Neston L64 ... 66 C3
Stockport SK4 ... 240 C6
Tarvin CH3 ... 121 F1
Thornton Hough L63 ... 42 B2
Wilmslow SK9 ... 34 C2
Green Tree Gdns SK6 ... 241 B2
Green View WA13 ... 19 D3
Green Villa Pk SK9 ... 59 F2
Green Way CH1 ... 94 A1
Green Wlk
Altrincham WA14 ... 238 B3
Cuddington CW8 ... 102 A2
Gatley SK8 ... 239 A6
Partington M31 ... 11 E1
Greenacre Dr L63 ... 43 E4
Greenacre Rd CH4 ... 140 C2
Greenacres Crewe CW1 ... 190 B3
Duddon CW6 ... 145 D3
Frodsham WA6 ... 74 B3
Lymm WA13 ... 19 D2
Sandbach CW11 ... 175 D4
Greenacres Cl WA3 ... 4 A4
Greenacres Rd CW12 ... 155 F1
Greenall Ave WA5 ... 14 B2
Greenall Rd CW9 ... 104 A4
Greenalls Ave WA4 ... 16 B1
Greenbank Ave
Ellesmere Port L66 ... 69 E4
Gatley M22 ... 239 A5
Greenbank Cl CW5 ... 205 E3
Greenbank Dr SK10 ... 88 A4
Greenbank Gdns WA4 ... 16 C1
Greenbank La CW8 ... 103 E3
Greenbank Pk CW11 ... 175 D1
Greenbank Rd
Chester CH2 ... 119 D2
Gatley SK8 ... 239 A6
Warrington WA4 ... 16 C1
Greenbank Residential Sch CW8 ... 103 E3
Greenbank St WA4 ... 16 B1
Greenbank Sta CW8 ... 103 E3
Greenbridge Rd WA7 ... 24 A1
Greencourts Bsns Pk M22 ... 34 A4
Greendale Dr
Middlewich CW10 ... 151 D4
Newcastle-u-L ST5 ... 210 B1
Greendale La SK10 ... 86 A4
Greenfield Ave CH4 ... 161 D4

Greenfield Cl
New Mills SK22 39 D4
Stockport SK3 240 E2
Greenfield Cres CH3 143 D3
Greenfield Gdns CH2 72 A2
Greenfield La
Chester CH2 119 D3
Frodsham WA6 49 D1
Greenfield Prim Sch
SK14 241 D6
Greenfield Rd
Bollington SK10 88 A4
Broughton CH4 139 E2
Congleton CW12 156 A2
Ellesmere Port L66 69 D4
Waverton CH3 143 D3
Greenfield St SK14 241 D6
Greenfield Way CW8 102 A2
Greenfields Chester CH2 95 F1
Winsford CW7 127 D1
Greenfields Ave
Appleton WA4 26 B4
Bebington L62 43 E4
Shavington CW2 206 A2
Greenfields Cl Neston L64 66 C3
Newton-le-W WA12 2 B2
Warrington WA1 17 E4
Greenfields Cres L62 43 E4
Greenfields Croft L64 66 C3
Greenfields Dr L64 66 C3
Greenfields Rd ST7 193 F2
Greengate Rd
Dukinfield M34 241 A8
Lawton-gate ST7 193 F3
Greengates Cres L64 66 C3
Greenhalgh St SK4 240 E6
Greenhill Ave M33 242 A8
Greenhill La WA4 52 A3
Greenhill Wlk SK12 38 B3
Greenhills Cl SK11 112 C4
Greenhouse Farm Rd
WA7 50 A4
Greenhythe Rd SK9 34 B3
Greenland Cl CW6 146 B1
Greenlands CH3 166 A2
Greenlaw Cl CW9 104 A3
Greenlea Cl L65 70 A1
Greenore Dr L24 21 E1
Greensbridge La L26 21 D4
Greenshall La SK12 38 C3
Greenshank Cl WA12 2 B2
Greenside SK4 240 A5
Greenside Ave WA6 74 B4
Greenside Ct CW9 105 E3
Greenside Dr
Altrincham WA14 238 E1
Lostock CW9 105 D4
Greensway CH4 141 D4
Greenvale Dr SK8 239 C6
Greenview Dr M20 239 C8
Greenway Alsager ST7 193 D3
Altrincham WA14 238 A5
Appleton WA4 26 B4
Cheadle Hulme SK7 35 E3
Congleton CW12 156 A2
Crewe CW1 190 B4
Farndon CH3 180 C1
Great Sankey WA5 14 C4
Hyde SK14 241 D5
Romiley SK6 241 E1
Tilston SY14 198 B2
Warrington WA1 16 C4
Wilmslow SK9 60 A3
Greenway Cl Helsby WA6 73 D2
Rode Heath ST7 193 F4
Greenway Dr CW9 104 B4
Greenway Rd
Altrincham WA15 238 F8
Biddulph ST6 179 F1
Cheadle SK9 34 B3
Runcorn WA7 23 D1
Speke L24 21 D2
Widnes WA8 13 D1
Greenway St CH4 237 E1
Greenway Wlk CW9 104 B4
Greenways ST7 209 F1
Greenwell Rd WA11 1 B3
Greenwood Ave
Chester CH4 141 E4
Congleton CW12 156 C2
Greenwood Cl Croft WA3 4 C1
Weaverham CW8 77 E1
Greenwood Cres WA2 8 C1
Greenwood Dr
Newton-le-W WA12 2 B1
Wilmslow SK9 60 B4
Greenwood Rd WA13 18 C1
Greenwood St [1] WA14 238 D4
Greg Ave SK10 87 F4
Greg Mews SK9 34 A1
Gregory Ave SK6 241 C1
Gregory Cl WA5 15 E4
Gregson Rd WA8 13 E1
Grenfell Cl L64 41 E1
Grenfell Pk L64 41 E1
Grenfell St [11] WA8 23 D4
Grenville Cl CW1 191 E3
Grenville Cres L63 43 E4
Grenville Rd L64 41 F1
Grenville St SK3 240 D4
Gresford Ave CH2 237 F4
Gresford Cl WA5 7 F1
Gresham Wlk SK4 240 E7
Gresley Way ST7 209 F1
Gresty Green Rd CW2 206 B4
Gresty La CW2 206 A4
Gresty Rd CW2 190 B1
Gresty Road Football Gd (Crewe Alexandra FC)
CW2 190 B1
Gresty Terr CW1 190 C2
Greta Ave SK9 34 B3
Greville Dr CW7 127 D1
Grey Cl SK6 241 A4
Grey Friars CH1 237 D2
Grey Rd WA14 238 C5
Grey St Stalybridge SK15 242 F1
Warrington WA1 16 B3
Greyhound Park Rd
CH1 117 F2
Greyhound Pk CH1 118 A1
Greyhound Rd SK10 86 A3
Greylands Rd M20 239 C8
Greymarsh Dr SK12 36 C1
Greymist Ave WA1 17 E4
Greys Ct WA1 9 E1
Greystoke Ave M33 242 B5
Greystoke Dr SK9 60 A1
Greystoke Rd SK10 87 F1
Greystone Heath Sch
WA5 14 C3
Greystone Pk CW1 190 B2
Greystone Rd WA5 14 C2
Greystones L66 69 E2
Greystones Rd CH3 119 E1
Grice St WA4 16 B1
Griffin Cl Blacon CH1 117 F3
Burtonwood WA5 6 C3
New Mills SK22 39 E3
Norton in Hales TF9 236 B1
Griffin Mews WA8 13 D2
Griffiths Dr CW9 104 B3
Griffiths Rd Lostock CW9 79 F1
Northwich CW9 104 C4
Griffiths St WA4 16 C2
Grig Pl ST7 193 E3
Grimsditch La
Daresbury WA4 52 A3
Whitley WA4 52 A3
Grimshaw Ave SK10 88 A4
Grimshaw Cl SK6 241 A4
Grimshaw La SK10 88 A4
Grindley Bank CH2 119 F4
Grindley Gdns L65 70 B1
Grisedale Ave WA2 8 A2
Grisedale Cl WA7 49 F3
Grisedale Rd L62 43 F4
Grisedale Way SK11 112 A3
Grizedale WA8 12 C2
Grizedale Rd SK6 241 B4
Groarke Dr WA5 14 B3
Groby Pl WA14 238 D5
Groby Rd Altrincham WA14 238 C4
Crewe CW1 190 C4
Groby St SK15 242 F1
Grosvenor Ave
Alsager ST7 193 E3
Goldborne WA3 3 E4
Hartford CW8 103 D2
Warrington WA1 16 C4
Grosvenor Cl
Great Sankey WA5 15 E3
Wilmslow SK9 60 A2
Grosvenor Cres SK14 241 C5
Grosvenor Ct Chester CH1 237 F2
Winsford CW7 149 E4
Grosvenor Dr SK12 36 B2
Grosvenor Gdns WA12 2 B1
Grosvenor Nuffield Hospl
CH4 141 E3
Grosvenor Pk Rd CH2 237 F2
Grosvenor Pk Terr CH2 237 F2
Grosvenor Pl CH4 237 E1
Grosvenor Prec The CH1 237 E2
Grosvenor Rd
Altrincham WA14 238 E5
Chester CH4 141 E4
Congleton CW12 156 A2
Haydock WA11 1 A4
Hyde SK14 241 D5
Manchester SK4 240 B7
Tarvin CH3 121 D1
Widnes WA8 13 D2
Grosvenor Sq M33 242 A6
Grosvenor St Chester CH1 237 D2
Crewe CW1 190 A3
[6] Macclesfield SK11 112 B4
Runcorn WA7 23 D2
Stalybridge SK15 242 D1
[9] Stockport SK1 240 F4
Winsford CW7 149 F4
Grotsworth La SY14 214 C4
Grotto La WA16 108 A4
Grounds St WA2 16 A4
Grove Arc SK9 60 A4
Grove Ave Chester CH3 119 D2
Kidsgrove ST7 194 C1
Lawton-gate ST7 194 A2
Lostock CW9 80 A2
Lymm WA13 18 B2
Wilmslow SK9 60 A4
Grove Cl CW7 149 D4
Grove Cres CW3 232 B1
Grove Ct Alsager ST7 193 F2
Sale M33 242 D6
Grove Gdns CH3 119 F1
Grove La SK8 35 D3
Grove Park Ave ST7 194 A2
Grove Pk WA16 57 D1
Grove Prim Sch The SK8 35 D4
Grove Rd Altrincham WA15 238 E3
Backford CH1 94 C2
Grove Rise WA13 18 C2
Grove St New Mills SK22 39 D4
Runcorn WA7 22 C2
Stalybridge SK16 242 A1
Warrington WA4 16 B2
Wilmslow SK9 60 A4
Grove The
Cheadle Hulme SK8 35 D3
Knutsford WA16 57 E2
Lawton-gate ST7 194 A2
Penketh WA5 14 C2
Sale M33 242 B5
Stockport SK3 240 E3
Grovemount CW9 103 F1
Groves The Chester CH1 237 E2
Ellesmere Port CH1 95 D4
GroveThe SY13 225 F1
Grovewood Mews SK11 112 B3
Grub La CW6 122 B3
Grundy Cl WA8 12 C2
Grundy St WA3 3 D4
Guardian St WA5 15 F3
Guernsey Cl Appleton WA4 26 B4
Congleton CW12 157 D1
Guernsey Dr L65 70 B1
Guernsey Rd WA8 13 F2
Guest St WA8 23 D4
Guests Slack WA6 100 A4
Guilden Gn CH3 119 F2
Guilden Sutton CE Contr
Prim Sch CH2 119 F3
Guilden Sutton La CH2 119 E3
Guildford Ave SK8 35 D3
Guildford Cl WA2 9 D1
Guildford Rd CH4 140 C3
Guillemot Cl CW1 190 C3
Gull Cl SK12 36 A2
Gullane Cl SK10 87 D2
Gullet The CW5 204 C3
Gullivers World Theme Pk
WA5 7 E1
Gulls Way L60 40 C4
Gunco La
Macclesfield SK11 112 C3
Prestbury SK10 87 E4
Gunn Gr L64 66 C4
Gutterscroft CW1 191 E3
Gutticar Rd WA8 12 A1
Guy La Hargrave CH3 143 E3
Waverton CH3 143 E3
Guywood La SK6 241 C3

Hackberry Cl WA14 238 B8
Hacked Way La SK11 113 F3
Haddon Cl
Alderley Edge SK9 59 F1
High Lane SK6 37 F3
Holmes Chapel CW4 130 A2
Macclesfield SK11 112 A3
Wistaston CW2 206 A4
Haddon Dr WA8 12 B2
Haddon Gr
Altrincham WA15 238 F7
Sale M33 242 A6
Haddon La L64 67 E2
Haddon Rd Burton L64 67 E1
Cheadle SK8 34 B4
Hadfield Cl WA8 13 F1
Hadfield St CW9 79 D1
Hadleigh Cl WA5 14 C3
Hadley Ave L62 43 E4
Hadley Cl SK8 239 F1
Hadlow La L64 67 F4
Hadlow Rd L64 67 F3
Hadrian Dr CH1 117 F3
Hadrian Way CW8 102 A1
Hafod Cl Blacon CH1 117 E2
Connah's Quay CH5 91 E1
Hag Bank La SK12 38 B4
Hague Bar Prim Sch SK22 38 C4
Hague Bar Rd SK22 39 D4
Hague Fold SK22 38 C4
Hague St OL6 242 A4
Haig Ave Great Sankey WA5 15 D3
Irlam M44 11 E2
Haig Ct WA16 57 E2
Haig Rd Knutsford WA16 57 E2
Widnes WA8 13 D1
Haigh Lawn WA14 238 B3
Hale Ave SK12 36 B1
Hale Bank Rd WA8 21 F3
Hale CE Contr Sch L24 21 E1
Hale Ct WA14 238 D2
Hale Gate Rd Hale L24 21 F1
Widnes WA8 22 A2
Hale Golf Course WA15 32 A4
Hale Gr WA5 15 D3
Hale Low Rd WA15 238 F3
Hale Prep Sch WA15 238 E3
Hale Rd Altrincham WA15 32 B4
Hale L24 21 D1
Manchester SK4 240 C7
Widnes WA8 22 B4
Hale Road Ind Est WA8 22 B3
Hale St WA2 16 A4
Hale Sta WA14 238 D2
Hale View WA7 48 C4
Hale View Rd WA6 73 E2
Halebank CE Contr Prim
Sch WA8 22 A3
Halewood La Ends L26 21 D4
Haley Rd N WA5 6 C3
Haley Rd S WA5 6 C3
Half St SK11 112 B3
Halfacre La WA4 17 F1
Halghton La SY13 222 A1
Halifax Cl WA2 8 B1
Halkett Cl CH4 140 C3
Halkyn Rd CH2 237 F4
Hall Ave
Altrincham WA15 238 F7
Widnes WA8 12 A1
Hall Cl SK10 87 E2
Hall Dr Alsager ST7 193 E2
Appleton WA4 26 B3
Marston CW9 79 D3
Willaston (nr Nantwich)
CW5 205 E3
Hall Gr Cheadle SK8 239 C6
Macclesfield SK10 87 E2
Hall Hill SK10 87 F4
Hall La Antrobus CW9 53 D1
Appleton WA4 27 D4
Audlem CW3 230 B4
Bold Heath WA9 6 A2
Brown Knowl CH3 199 E4
Cronton WA8 12 B4
Daresbury WA4 25 E1
Haughton Moss CW6 186 B3
Higher Wincham CW9 79 F2
Kelsall CW6 122 B3
Little Leigh CW9 77 F4
Lostock CW9 79 F2
Mobberley WA16 58 B2
Partington M31 11 F2
Pickmere WA16 55 D1
Sandbach CW11 174 A3
Stretton WA4 52 C4
Sutton Lane Ends SK11 112 C2
Utkinton CW6 146 B3
Warmingham CW11 173 F2
Winsford CW7 149 D2
Hall La The CW6 147 E1
Hall Meadow SK8 239 E1
Hall Moss La SK7 35 E2
Hall Nook WA5 14 C2
Hall O'shaw St CW1 190 C2
Hall Rd Altrincham WA14 238 C1
Haydock WA11 1 C4
Warrington WA1 17 E4
Wilmslow SK9 60 A4
Wilmslow, Handforth SK9 34 C2
Hall St Ashton-u-L OL6 242 B2
Audley ST7 209 E1
Cheadle SK8 239 D6
Denton SK14 241 B7
Macclesfield SK11 112 B4
New Mills SK22 39 D4
Warrington WA1 16 B3
Hall Terr WA5 14 C4
Hall Wood Ave WA11 1 C4
Hall Wood Rd SK9 34 C1
Halla Way WA4 16 C2
Hallastone Rd WA6 73 E2
Hallcroft M31 11 F2
Hallcroft Pl WA4 17 D1
Hallefield Cres SK11 112 C4
Hallefield Dr [14] SK11 112 C4
Hallefield Rd [15] SK11 112 C4
Hallfield Dr CH2 72 A2
Hallfield Park L66 69 E2
Hallfields Rd Tarvin CH3 121 E1
Warrington WA2 16 B4
Hallgate Dr SK8 239 A2
Hallgreen La CW12 155 E4
Halliday Cl WA3 9 F2
Halliwell's Brow WA16 29 D2
Hallows Ave WA2 16 B4
Hallows Cl CW6 122 B2
Hallows Dr CW6 122 B2
Hallowsgate Ct CW6 122 B2
Halls Rd Biddulph ST6 179 E1
Mow Cop ST7 195 E4
Hallsgreen La CH2 96 C4
Hallshaw Ave CW1 190 C3
Hallwood Cl WA7 49 D3
Hallwood Dr L66 68 B2
Hallwood Link Rd WA7 49 F3
Hallwood Park Ave WA7 49 F3
Hallwood Park Cty Prim
Sch WA7 49 F3
Halsall Ave WA2 16 B4
Halsall Cl WA7 50 B3
Halston Cl SK5 240 F8
Halstone Ave SK9 59 F2
Halton Brook Ave WA7 23 E1
Halton Coll of F Ed WA8 23 D4
Halton Coll of F Ed
(Annexe) Runcorn WA7 23 F2
Widnes WA8 23 D4
Halton Cres L66 69 F1
Halton Ct WA7 23 E1
Halton Dr CW2 189 E3
Halton General Hospl
WA7 49 F3
Halton Link Rd WA7 49 F4
Halton Lodge Ave WA7 49 E4
Halton Lodge Cty Prim Sch
WA7 49 E4
Halton Rd Chester CH2 118 C3
Ellesmere Port L66 69 F1
Great Sankey WA5 14 B4
Runcorn WA7 23 E1
Halton St Haydock WA11 1 C3
Hyde SK14 241 F7
Halton St Mary's CE Aided
Prim Sch WA7 50 A4
Halton Station Rd WA7 49 F2
Halton View Rd WA8 13 E1
Halton Way L66 69 F1
Hamble Dr WA5 15 D2
Hamble Way SK10 86 C1
Hambledon Cl L66 69 D3
Hambleton Cl WA8 12 B2
Hambleton Rd SK8 34 B4
Hambleton Way CW7 149 D4
Hambletts Hollow WA6 100 C3
Hamilton Ave
Hawarden CH5 116 A2
Irlam M44 11 E2
Hamilton Cl
Haslington CW1 191 E2
Macclesfield SK10 113 D4
Neston L64 41 D1
Hamilton Cres SK4 240 B5
Hamilton Pl CH1 237 D2
Hamilton Rd
Connah's Quay CH5 91 E1
Lymm WA13 18 B2
Hamilton Sq SK4 240 E7
Hamilton St Chester CH2 118 C2
Stalybridge SK15 242 C2
Hammond Sch
Chester CH2 237 D4
Chester, Hoole Bank CH2 119 D4
Hammond St CW2 190 B2
Hamnet Ct WA3 9 F2
Hamnett St SK14 241 D7
Hamon Rd WA15 238 E4
Hampden Rd M33 242 A5
Hampshire Cl CW12 156 B2
Hampshire Rd M31 11 E1
Hampshire Wlk SK10 86 C1
Hampson Ave WA3 4 C2
Hampson Cres SK9 34 B2
Hampson St M33 242 D6
Hampstead Ct [13] CW7 149 D4
Hampton Cl Neston L64 66 C3
Widnes WA8 13 F2
Hampton Cres Neston L64 66 C3
No Man's Heath SY14 214 A2
Hampton Ct WA7 24 B2
Hampton Dr Cronton WA8 12 B3
Great Sankey WA5 15 E2
Hampton Gdns L65 70 A3
Hampton Gr SK8 239 E2
Hampton Rd Chester CH4 140 C3
Irlam M44 11 E2
Hamsterley Cl WA3 10 A3
Hanbury Cl CW2 206 A4
Hancock Rd CW12 156 C2
Hand St SK11 112 A4
Handbridge CH4 237 E1
Handel Mews M33 242 C6
Handford Ave L62 43 F3
Handford Rd CH2 118 C3
Handforth Cl WA4 17 E2
Handforth Hall Cty Prim
Sch SK9 34 B2
Handforth La WA7 49 E3
Handforth Rd Crewe CW2 189 F2
Wilmslow SK9 34 C1
Handforth Sta SK9 34 B2
Handley Cl SK3 240 C1
Handley Hill CW7 149 E4
Handley St WA7 22 C2
Hangman's La CW9 105 E4
Hankelow Cl Chester CH2 237 E4
Middlewich CW10 151 E3
Hankey St WA7 22 C1
Hankins Heys La CW3 231 D1
Hankinson Cl M31 11 F1
Hanley Cl Disley SK12 38 B3
Widnes WA8 12 B1
Hanley Rd WA8 12 B1
Hanns Hall Rd L64 67 E4
Hanover Bsns Pk WA14 238 B7
Hanover Dr CW7 149 E3
Hanover Rd WA14 238 B7
Hanover St
Stalybridge SK15 242 C2
Warrington WA1 16 A2
Hapsford Cl WA3 9 E2
Hapsford La
Dunham-on-t-H WA6 97 F4
Elton CH2 72 B2
Elton, Hapsford WA6 72 C1
Hapton Pl SK4 240 E7
Harbord St WA1 16 B2
Harbour Cl WA7 50 B3
Harbour La SK11 111 E1
Harburn Wlk M22 33 F4
Harcourt Cl WA3 9 F2
Harcourt Rd
Altrincham WA14 238 D6
Sale M33 242 A8
Hardcastle Rd SK3 240 D3
Harden Pk SK9 60 A2
Harding Ave
Tattenhall CH3 166 B1
Warrington WA2 8 C1
Harding Rd Chester CH2 118 A4
Nantwich CW5 204 B2
Hardingswood Rd ST7 194 C1
Hardknott Rd L62 43 F4
Hardman Ave SK6 241 A3
Hardman St SK3 240 D4
Hardwick Cl SK6 37 F3
Hardwick Dr SK11 112 A3
Hardwick Grange WA1 17 F4
Hardwick Rd WA7 23 E2
Hardwicke Rd SK12 36 C2
Hardy Cl Ellesmere Port L66 69 F2
Wistaston CW2 205 F4
Hardy Dr Altrincham WA15 238 F7
Cheadle Hulme SK7 35 E4
Hardy Rd WA13 18 B1
Hardy St Warrington WA2 16 A3
Warrington WA2 16 A4
Hare La CH3 119 E2
Hare's La WA6 73 F4
Harebell Cl CH3 142 A3
Harebell Gr ST7 195 F1
Harecastle Ave ST7 194 C1
Harefield Dr SK9 60 A3

Harefield Rd SK9 34 C2
Harehill Gdn SK10 86 A3
Harewood Ave L66 69 E2
Harewood Cl CW7 126 A1
Harewood Ct M33 242 C5
Harewood Way SK11 112 A3
Harfield Gdns L66 69 E3
Hargrave Ave CW2 189 F2
Hargrave Dr L66 69 F3
Hargrave La L63 42 C3
Hargreaves Ct WA8 13 E1
Hargreaves Rd CW9 104 B4
Harington Cl CH2 95 E1
Harington Rd CH2 118 B4
Harlech Cl WA5 7 F1
Harlech Ct L65 70 B2
Harlech Way L65 70 B2
Harley Rd M33 242 C7
Harlow Cl WA4 17 E2
Harlyn Ave SK7 35 F4
Harlyn Gdns WA5 14 B2
Harn The L66 69 E2
Harold Rd WA11 1 C4
Harper Cl
Ellesmere Port L66 69 E2
Macclesfield SK11 112 B3
Harper Gr CW12 156 C2
Harper St SK3 240 E3
Harpers Rd WA2 9 D1
Harpur Cres ST7 193 D3
Harraps Pl SK11 112 A3
Harrier Cl CW1 189 F4
Harriet St M44 11 F3
Harrington Dr SK11 111 E1
Harrington Rd WA14 238 B5
Harris Cl CW1 173 D1
Harris Rd CW9 80 A1
Harris St WA8 13 E1
Harriseahead La ST7 195 E2
Harrison Dr Allostock CW4 107 D1
Haydock WA11 1 A3
Harrison Gr CH5 116 A2
Harrison Sq WA5 7 F1
Harrison St
Stalybridge SK15 242 D2
Stockport SK1 & SK2 240 F3
Widnes WA8 22 A3
Harrison Way WA12 2 B2
Harrisons Pl CW8 103 F4
Harrogate Cl Bebington L62 43 E2
Warrington WA5 7 D1
Harrogate Rd L62 43 E2
Harrop Rd Altrincham WA15 238 F2
Bollington SK10 88 B4
Runcorn WA7 23 D1
Harrop St SK15 242 D2
Harrow Cl Appleton WA4 26 C3
Crewe CW2 190 A1
Harrow Dr WA7 23 F1
Harrow Gr L62 43 F4
Harrow Rd L65 70 B2
Harrowgate Cl WA5 15 D4
Harrytown SK6 241 A2
Harrytown RC High Sch SK6 241 A2
Hart Ave M33 242 F5
Hart St WA14 238 E5
Hartford Ave SK9 59 F3
Hartford Bsns Ctr CW8 102 C2
Hartford Cl CW11 175 E4
Hartford Cty High Sch CW8 103 E3
Hartford Cty Prim Sch CW8 103 D2
Hartford Dr L65 69 F2
Hartford Manor Cty Prim Sch CW8 103 E3
Hartford Rd CW9 103 F1
Hartford Sta CW8 103 D2
Hartford Way CH1 118 A1
Harthill Cty Prim Sch CH3 183 F2
Harthill La CH3 183 D2
Harthill Rd Blacon CH1 117 F3
Burwardsley CH3 184 A3
Hartington Dr SK7 36 C4
Hartington Rd
Altrincham WA14 238 D8
Bramhall SK7 35 F3
Cheadle SK8 34 B4
High Lane SK6 37 F4
Hartington St CH4 141 F4
Hartland Cl Poynton SK12 36 B3
Widnes WA8 13 D3
Hartley Cl WA13 18 C2
Hartley Gr SK10 87 F4
Hartley Rd WA14 238 C5
Hartley St SK3 240 D4
Hartshead Ave SK15 242 D3
Hartshead View SK14 241 F5
Hartswood Cl
Appleton WA4 26 C2
Dukinfield M34 241 A8
Harty Rd WA11 1 A3
Harvard Cl WA7 24 B1
Harvard Ct WA2 8 A2
Harvest Cl CW9 126 C4
Harvest Rd SK10 87 E2
Harvey Ave Nantwich CW5 205 D3
Newton-le-W WA12 1 C2
Harvey La WA3 3 D4
Harvey Rd CW12 157 D3
Harvey St SK1 240 F5
Harvin Gr M34 241 A6
Harwood Gdns WA4 17 D1
Harwood St SK4 240 E7
Haryngton Ave WA5 15 F4
Haseley Cl SK12 36 C3
Haslam Rd SK3 240 E2
Haslemere Ave WA15 32 B3
Haslemere Dr WA5 14 B2
Haslemere Way CW1 190 B3
Haslin Cres CH3 142 B4
Haslington Cty Prim Sch CW1 191 E2
Hassall Rd Alsager ST7 193 D3
Haslington CW11 192 A4
Hassall Green CW11 192 A4
Sandbach CW11 175 E2
Hassall St SK15 242 E1
Hassall Way [6] SK8 34 C3
Hastings Ave WA2 8 A2
Hasty La Altrincham M90 32 C4
Wythenshawe WA15 32 C4
Hatch Mere WA6 100 B3
Hatchery Cl WA4 27 D2
Hatchings The WA13 18 C1
Hatchmere Cl
Sandbach CW11 174 C4
Warrington WA5 15 F3
Hatchmere Dr CH3 142 A4
Hatchmere Rd SK8 239 F4
Hatfield Ct CW4 130 A2
Hatfield Gdns WA4 26 C2
Hathaway Cl SK8 34 A4
Hathaway Dr SK11 112 B3
Hatherlow SK6 241 A1
Hatherlow Hts SK6 241 A1
Hatherton Cl
Davenham CW9 103 F2
Newcastle-u-L ST5 210 B1
Hatherton Rd CW5 220 A3
Hatherton Way CH2 237 E4
Hatley La WA6 73 F4
Hatter St CW12 156 C2
Hatton Ave L62 43 F2
Hatton La Appleton WA4 26 A1
Hatton WA4 26 A1
Northwich CW8 103 E3
Stretton WA4 26 A1
Hatton Rd CH1 117 F3
Hatton St Macclesfield SK11 112 B4
[3] Stockport SK1 240 E6
Haughton Hall Rd M34 241 A7
Haughton St SK14 241 E5
Havana La CW12 157 D3
Havannah Cty Prim Sch CW12 157 D3
Havannah La
Congleton CW12 156 C3
St Helens WA9 1 A2
Havannah St CW12 156 C2
Haven The Altrincham WA15 238 F3
Crewe CW1 190 B4
Havergal St [5] WA7 22 C1
Havisham Cl WA3 9 E3
Hawarden Gdns L65 70 B1
Hawarden Ind Pk CH4 139 D3
Hawarden Rd WA14 238 D6
Haweswater Av CW1 173 D1
Haweswater Ave WA11 1 A3
Haweswater Cl WA7 50 A3
Haweswater Dr CW7 126 B1
Hawick Cl L66 69 D3
Hawk Rd SK22 39 F4
Hawk St CW11 175 D3
Hawke St SK15 242 F1
Hawker Cl CH4 139 E2
Hawkeshead Way CW7 126 B1
Hawkins La SK10 88 B2
Hawkins Rd L64 41 F1
Hawkins St SK5 240 E8
Hawkins View CH3 120 C3
Hawks Ct WA7 49 F3
Hawks Way L60 40 C4
Hawkshaw Cl WA3 9 E2
Hawkshead Rd WA5 6 C3
Hawkstone Gr WA6 73 E2
Hawley Dr WA15 32 A4
Hawley La WA15 32 A4
Hawley's Cl WA5 7 F1
Hawley's La WA2 8 A1
Haworth Ave CW12 157 D3
Haworth Cl SK11 112 A3
Hawthorn Ave
Altrincham WA15 238 F8
Nantwich CW5 204 C3
Newton-le-W WA12 2 B2
Runcorn WA7 23 D1
Widnes WA8 13 D1
Wilmslow SK9 60 A4
Hawthorn Bank SK22 39 D3
Hawthorn Bsns Pk WA2 16 A4
Hawthorn Cl
Altrincham WA15 238 F7
Holmes Chapel CW4 130 B2
Winsford CW7 126 B2
Hawthorn Dr M44 11 E3
Hawthorn Gdns ST7 210 B4
Hawthorn Gr
Cheadle Hulme SK7 35 E3
Crewe CW1 190 B4
Hyde SK14 241 D5
Manchester SK4 240 B7
Warrington WA4 16 B2
Wilmslow SK9 60 A4
Hawthorn La Bebington L62 43 E4
Wilmslow SK9 60 A4
Wistaston CW2 189 F1
Hawthorn Pk SK9 60 A4
Hawthorn Rd
Altrincham WA15 238 E3
Bollington SK10 87 F4
Chester CH4 140 C3
Christleton CH3 142 C4
Ellesmere Port L66 69 E3
Gatley SK8 239 A5
Hawthorn Rd continued
Neston L64 41 E1
Newcastle-u-L ST5 210 C1
Plumley WA16 80 C2
Weaverham CW8 102 B4
Hawthorn Rise SK10 86 C3
Hawthorn St SK9 60 A3
Hawthorn Terr
Manchester SK4 240 B7
Wilmslow SK9 60 A3
Hawthorn View
Deeside Ind Est CH5 116 A4
Wilmslow SK9 60 A4
Hawthorn Villas CW4 130 B2
Hawthorn Way SK10 87 F1
Hawthorn Wlk
Higher Wincham CW9 79 E2
Partington M31 11 E1
Wilmslow SK9 60 A4
Hawthorne Ave Audley ST7 209 F1
Fowley Common WA3 5 E2
Great Sankey WA5 15 D3
Warrington WA1 17 D4
Hawthorne Cl
Congleton CW12 156 A2
Haydock WA11 1 A3
Hawthorne Dr
Sandbach CW11 175 E3
Willaston L64 43 D1
Hawthorne Gr Barnton CW8 77 F2
Poynton SK12 37 E2
Warrington WA4 16 B1
Warrington WA1 16 C4
Winsford CW7 127 D1
Hawthorne Rd WA4 26 B4
Hawthorne St WA2 16 A4
Hawthorns The
Bunbury CW6 185 F4
Ellesmere Port L66 69 F4
Northwich CW8 103 E4
Tarporley CW6 146 B1
Hay Croft SK8 34 C4
Haycastle Cl WA5 7 F1
Haycroft Cl L66 69 E1
Haydock Cl CH1 118 A1
Haydock High Sch WA11 1 B3
Haydock La WA11 1 B4
Haydock Lane Ind Est WA11 1 C4
Haydock Park Golf Course WA12 2 C3
Haydock St
Newton-le-W WA12 2 A2
Warrington WA2 16 A3
Haye's Rd M44 11 F3
Hayes Cres WA6 49 E1
Hayes Dr CW8 78 B2
Hayes Pk CH2 237 D4
Hayfield Ave SK6 241 A4
Hayfield Cl SK10 87 D2
Hayfield Rd New Mills SK22 39 E4
Romiley SK6 241 A4
Warrington WA1 17 E4
Hayfield St M33 242 B7
Hayfields WA16 57 E2
Hayfields Gr CW3 229 F2
Hayhead Cl ST7 195 D1
Hayhurst Ave CW10 151 E4
Hayhurst Cl CW8 103 F4
Hayle Cl SK10 86 B1
Hayling Cl CW1 190 A4
Haymakers Cl CH4 140 C2
Haymakers Way CH1 117 D4
Haymoor Green Rd CW5 205 F2
Hayside Wlk SY14 213 D2
Hayton St WA16 56 C1
Haywood Cres WA7 24 B1
Hazel Ave Cheadle SK8 239 E5
Macclesfield SK11 112 A3
Romiley SK6 241 D2
Runcorn WA7 48 C4
Sale M33 242 B5
Hazel Cl Ellesmere Port L66 69 F1
Kidsgrove ST7 195 D2
Hazel Dr Lymm WA13 18 C1
Poynton SK12 36 C2
Weaverham CW8 102 B4
Winsford CW7 149 E4
Wythenshawe M22 34 A4
Hazel Gr Alsager ST7 194 A2
Crewe CW1 190 B4
Goldborne WA3 3 D4
Warrington WA1 17 D4
Hazel Grove High Sch SK7 36 B4
Hazel Rd Altrincham WA14 238 D6
Chester CH4 140 C3
Hazel St WA1 16 B4
Hazel Wlk M31 11 E1
Hazelbadge Cl SK12 36 B2
Hazelbadge Rd SK12 36 B2
Hazelborough Cl WA3 10 A3
Hazelcroft SK9 85 D4
Hazelehurst Rd WA6 74 B3
Hazelhurst Dr SK10 88 A4
Hazelhurst Rd SK15 242 D4
Hazelmere Cl CW8 103 E3
Hazelshaw La CW11 154 A2
Hazelwood Mews WA4 17 E1
Hazelwood Rd
Altrincham WA15 238 E2
Barnton CW8 78 A2
Wilmslow SK9 60 B4
Hazlemere Ave SK11 112 A3
Headland Cl WA3 3 F3
Headlands The CH2 237 F2
Heald Cl WA14 238 C2
Heald Dr WA14 238 C2
Heald Gr SK8 239 A1
Heald Green Sta M22 34 A4
Heald Rd WA14 238 C2
Heald St WA12 1 C2
Healdwood Rd SK6 241 C4
Healey Cl CW1 190 A4
Hearn's La Burland CW5 202 C3
Faddiley CW5 202 C3
Heary St SK11 112 C3
Heath Ave
Ellesmere Port L65 70 A1
Rode Heath ST7 193 F4
Sandbach CW11 175 F3
Heath Bank CH2 119 E3
Heath Cl Chester CH3 142 A4
Sandbach CW11 175 E3
Tarvin CH3 121 D1
Heath Cres SK2 & SK3 240 F1
Heath Ct L66 69 D3
Heath Cty Comp Sch The WA7 49 D4
Heath Dr Runcorn WA7 49 D4
Tarvin CH3 121 D1
Heath End Rd ST7 193 D3
Heath Gn CW6 146 B2
Heath Gr L66 69 D4
Heath La Allostock WA16 106 C3
Chester CH3 142 A4
Croft WA3 4 A1
Ellesmere Port L66 68 B4
Goldborne WA3 3 E3
Great Barrow CH3 120 C3
Great Budworth CW9 54 A1
High Legh WA16 28 B3
Little Leigh WA4 77 D4
Marbury SY13 226 C3
Peover WA16 106 C3
Stoak CH2 95 F4
Willaston L66 68 B4
Heath Rd
Altrincham, Hale WA14 238 D2
Altrincham, Timperley WA15 238 F8
Bollington SK10 87 F3
Chester CH2 118 B4
Congleton CW12 156 A1
Penketh WA5 14 C3
Runcorn WA7 23 D1
Sandbach CW11 175 E3
Stockport SK2 & SK3 240 F2
Weaverham CW8 77 F1
Widnes WA8 12 C1
Heath Rd S WA7 48 C3
Heath St Crewe CW1 190 B2
Goldborne WA3 3 D4
Warrington WA4 26 B4
Heath Terr CH2 118 B4
Heath Way CW6 168 B4
Heathbank Rd Cheadle SK8 34 C4
Stockport SK3 240 B3
Heathbrook CW9 104 C4
Heathcote Ave SK4 240 C7
Heathcote Cl CH2 118 B2
Heathcote Gdns
Northwich CW9 104 B4
Romiley SK6 241 E1
Heathcote St ST7 195 D1
Heather Ave M44 11 E3
Heather Brae WA12 2 A2
Heather Cl
Ellesmere Port L66 69 F2
Macclesfield SK11 112 B2
Runcorn WA7 49 F2
Warrington WA3 9 E3
Heather Ct CH3 142 A4
Heather Lea M34 241 A6
Heather Rd WA14 238 E1
Heather Wlk M31 11 E1
Heatherfield Ct SK9 60 C4
Heathergate Pl CW2 206 A4
Heathfield SK9 60 A3
Heathfield Ave Crewe CW1 190 B2
Gatley SK8 239 B5
Heathfield Cl
Congleton CW12 155 F2
Nantwich CW5 204 C3
Sale M33 242 F6
Heathfield Cty High Sch CW12 155 F2
Heathfield Dr ST5 210 B1
Heathfield Park WA4 17 D1
Heathfield Pk WA8 12 B2
Heathfield Rd Audlem CW3 230 A3
Ellesmere Port L65 70 A3
Stockport SK2 & SK3 240 F2
Heathfield Sq WA16 56 C1
Heathfields Cl CH2 237 E4
Heathgate Ave L24 21 D1
Heathland Terr SK3 240 E3
Heathlands Rd L66 69 D4
Heathmoor Ave WA3 3 E3
Heaths La CW6 123 E1
Heathside CW5 204 C3
Heathside Park Rd SK3 239 F7
Heathside Rd SK3 240 A3
Heathview CW1 191 E2
Heathview Cl WA8 22 A3
Heathview Rd WA8 22 A3
Heathway L60 41 D4
Heathwood Dr ST7 193 D3
Heathwood Gr WA1 17 D4
Heatley Cl WA13 19 D2
Heatley La CW5 217 F2
Heatley Way SK9 34 B2
Heaton Cl CW10 151 E3
Heaton Ct Manchester SK4 240 B8
Warrington WA3 9 F3
Heaton La SK4 240 E5
Heaton Moor Rd SK4 240 B8
Heaton Rd SK4 240 C7
Heaton Sq CW7 149 E4
Heaward Cl CW2 206 A2
Hebden Ave
Fowley Common WA3 5 D2
Romiley SK6 241 A4
Hebden Green Sch CW7 149 D4
Heber's Cl SY14 213 E3
Hedge Hey WA7 24 A1
Hedge Row SK10 63 E1
Hedgerow Dr CW9 79 E2
Hefferston Rise CW8 102 A4
Heights The WA6 73 E2
Helena Cl WA16 57 E1
Helford St CW12 156 B2
Hellath View CW5 204 C1
Hellyar-Brook Rd ST7 193 D2
Helmsdale Cl CW1 190 A3
Helmsdale La WA5 15 E3
Helmsley Cl WA5 15 F4
Helsby Ave L62 43 F2
Helsby Cty High Sch WA6 73 E3
Helsby Horns Mill Cty Prim Sch WA6 73 D1
Helsby Rd WA6 73 E1
Helsby St WA1 16 B3
Helsby Sta WA6 73 D2
Helsby Way SK9 34 B2
Helston Cl Bramhall SK7 35 F4
Penketh WA5 14 C3
Runcorn WA7 50 A3
Helston Gr SK8 34 B4
Helton Cl CW4 130 A2
Hemlegh Vale WA6 73 D1
Hemming St CW8 78 B1
Hemmingshaw La CW11 176 A4
Hemsworth Ave L66 69 E3
Henbury Cl CW10 151 E4
Henbury High Sch SK10 111 F4
Henbury La SK8 34 C3
Henbury Pl WA7 49 D3
Henbury Rd SK9 34 B2
Henbury Rise SK11 111 E4
Henderson Cl WA5 14 B3
Henderson Rd WA8 22 C4
Henderson St SK11 112 B4
Hendham Dr WA14 238 B5
Hendon Cl CW1 190 C3
Hendon Dr SK3 240 A3
Henley Ave Cheadle SK8 239 F2
Irlam M44 11 F3
Henley Cl Appleton WA4 26 C3
Neston L64 66 C3
Henley Ct WA7 23 E1
Henley Dr Altrincham WA15 238 F7
Winsford CW7 126 C1
Henley Rd Chester CH4 140 C3
Neston L64 66 C3
Henrietta St CW12 156 B2
Henry Pl CH2 237 E3
Henry St Crewe CW1 190 B3
Haslington CW1 191 E2
Hyde SK14 241 D6
Lymm WA13 18 C2
Tarporley CW6 146 B1
Warrington WA1 16 A3
Widnes WA8 13 E1
Henry Wood Ct CH4 140 C3
Henshall Ave WA4 16 C2
Henshall Dr CW11 175 E4
Henshall Hall Dr CW12 157 D1
Henshall La WA14 20 B3
Henshall Rd SK10 87 F4
Henshall St CH2 237 D4
Henshaw La SK11 110 C1
Hepherd St WA5 15 E2
Hepley Rd SK12 37 D2
Herald Pk CW1 190 C2
Heralds Cl WA8 22 A4
Heralds Gn WA5 7 D1
Herbert St Burtonwood WA5 6 C3
Congleton CW12 156 C2
Crewe CW1 191 D3
Dukinfield M34 241 A8
Lostock CW9 80 A1
Stockport SK3 240 D3
Herberts La L60 40 C4
Herdman St CW2 190 B1
Hereford Ave
Ellesmere Port CH1 94 C4
Goldborne WA3 3 D4
Hereford Cl
Macclesfield SK10 86 C1
Warrington WA1 17 E4
Hereford Dr SK9 34 C2
Hereford Pl CH1 118 A3
Hereford St M33 242 B6
Hereford Way CW10 128 B1
Hereward Rd CH3 119 D1
Hermitage Ave SK6 241 F2
Hermitage Ct CH1 117 D4
Hermitage Cty Prim Sch CW4 130 B2
Hermitage Dr CW4 130 B2
Hermitage Gdns SK6 241 F2
Hermitage Green La WA3 3 D1
Hermitage La
Cranage CW4 130 B4
Goostrey CW4 130 B4
Hermitage Rd CH1 117 D4
Hermitage The L60 40 C4
Heron Cl Broughton CH4 139 D2
Farndon CH3 180 C1
Knutsford WA16 57 D2
Winsford CW7 149 E3
Heron Cres CW1 190 C3

Heron Ct Neston L64 66 B4
Northwich CW9 79 E1
Heron Dr SK12 36 A2
Heron Pl CH2 237 E4
Heron St SK3 240 D3
Herons Way WA7 24 C2
Herrick Cl CW2 206 A4
Herries St OL6 242 A4
Hertford Cl
Congleton CW12 156 C2
Warrington WA1 17 F4
Hertford Gr M44 11 E3
Hesketh Cl WA5 14 C2
Hesketh Croft CW1 190 A4
Hesketh Dr CW9 80 A2
Hesketh Meadow La WA3 3 F4
Hesketh Rd L24 21 F1
Hesketh St SK4 240 E7
Hesketh St N WA5 15 E2
Hesnall Cl WA3 5 E4
Hessle Dr L60 40 C4
Heswall Ave WA3 4 C2
Heswall Rd L66 69 E2
Heswall Sta L60 41 E4
Hewitt Dr CW7 150 B4
Hewitt Gr CW9 79 F3
Hewitt St Chester CH2 118 C2
Crewe CW2 190 B1
Northwich CW9 79 E1
Warrington WA4 16 B2
Hewood Cl WA12 7 E4
Hey Lock Cl WA12 7 E4
Hey Shoot La WA3 5 E3
Heybridge La SK10 87 D3
Heyes Ave WA11 1 B3
Heyes Dr WA13 18 B1
Heyes Farm Rd SK11 111 F4
Heyes La Alderley Edge SK9 60 B2
Appleton WA4 26 C4
Heyes Pk CW8 102 C2
Heyes Rd WA8 22 B4
Heyeswood La CW8 103 D2
Heyfield Park Rd L66 69 D4
Heygarth Prim Sch L62 43 F3
Heys Ave Bebington L62 43 E4
Romiley SK6 241 E3
Heys La SK6 241 E3
Heys Prim Sch The OL6 242 A3
Heys Rd OL6 242 A3
Heys The WA7 23 F1
Heysbank Rd SK12 38 B3
Heyscroft Rd SK4 240 A6
Heysham Cl WA7 50 B3
Heysoms Ave CW8 103 E4
Heysoms Cl CW8 103 E4
Heythrop Dr L60 41 E4
Heywood Cl SK9 60 A1
Heywood Gn CW2 206 B4
Heywood Gr M33 242 B8
Heywood La CW3 234 B4
Heywood Rd
Alderley Edge SK9 60 A1
Ellesmere Port L66 69 E3
Sale M33 242 B5
Heywood St CW12 156 B1
Heywoods Ridge CW3 229 F2
Heywoods The CH2 118 B2
Heyworth Ave SK6 241 D3
Hibbert Ave 4 SK14 241 E5
Hibbert St New Mills SK22 39 D3
6 Widnes WA8 23 D4
Hibel Rd SK10 87 E1
Hickhurst La CW6 147 E2
Hickmore Heys CH3 119 F3
Hickory Cl WA1 17 F4
Hickson St CW8 78 A2
Hickton Dr WA14 238 B6
Hidcote Cl CW2 206 A4
Hield Gr CW9 79 E4
Hield La CW9 79 E4
Higginbotham Gn SK11 112 C3
High Bank WA14 238 D5
High Bank Cl M44 11 E3
High Bank Rd SK14 241 F7
High Bank Side SK1 240 F5
High Bent Ave SK8 35 D3
High Cross CH3 182 B1
High Ct SK10 88 A4
High Elm Dr WA15 32 B4
High Elm Rd WA15 32 B4
High Elms SK8 35 D3
High Field WA14 20 A1
High Gates Cl WA5 15 F4
High Grove Rd SK8 239 C5
High Hill Rd SK22 39 E4
High La SK6 241 B4
High Lane Prim Sch SK6 37 F4
High Lea Rd SK22 39 D4
High Lee SK8 239 C5
High Legh Cty Prim Sch
WA16 29 E3
High Legh Rd WA13, WA16 29 E4
High Lowe Ave CW12 157 D2
High Meadow SK8 34 C4
High Meadows SK6 241 C3
High St Altrincham WA14 238 D4
Audley ST7 210 A1
Bollington SK10 88 A4
Broughton CH4 140 C4
Cheadle SK8 239 D6
Congleton CW12 156 B1
Crewe CW2 190 B2
Duddon CW6 145 E2
Farndon CH3 180 C1
Frodsham WA6 49 D1
High St continued
Goldborne WA3 3 D4
Great Budworth CW9 79 D4
Hale L24 21 E1
Hyde SK14 241 F7
Kidsgrove, Harriseahead ST7 195 F3
Kidsgrove, Newchapel ST7 195 F1
Kidsgrove, Talke ST7 210 B3
Kidsgrove, The Rookery
ST7 195 E2
Macclesfield SK11 112 B3
Malpas SY14 213 D2
Mow Cop ST7 195 E4
Nantwich CW5 204 C3
Neston L64 66 C4
New Mills SK22 39 E4
Newton-le-W WA12 2 B2
Norley WA6 100 C3
Northwich CW8, CW9 103 F4
Runcorn WA7 23 D1
Sandbach CW11 175 D3
Stalybridge, Castle Hall
SK15 242 D1
Stalybridge, Hydes
SK15 & SK16 242 C1
Stockport SK1 240 F5
Tarporley CW6 146 B1
Tarvin CH3 121 E1
Tattenhall CH3 166 A1
Warrington WA1 16 B3
Weaverham CW8 77 E1
Winsford CW7 126 B1
High View Helsby WA6 73 E2
Mount Pleasant ST7 195 D3
Higham Ave WA5 7 F1
Highbank Cl CW8 78 A2
Highbank Dr M20 239 B8
Highbank Rd
Kingsley WA6 75 E1
Northwich CW8 103 E4
Highcliffe Ave CH1 118 A2
Highcroft Ave CW12 156 C1
Highcroft Rd SK6 241 C3
Higher Ash Rd ST7 210 B4
Higher Ashton WA8 12 C2
Higher Barlow Row SK1 240 F4
Higher Bents La SK6 241 A3
Higher Bury St SK4 240 D6
Higher Carden La SY14 198 B3
Higher Downs
Altrincham WA14 238 C3
Knutsford WA16 57 E1
Higher Fence Rd SK10 87 F1
Higher Ferry CH1 140 A4
Higher Henry St SK14 241 D5
Higher Heyes Dr WA6 75 E1
Higher Hillgate SK1 & SK2 240 F4
Higher La Bollington SK10 88 A3
Dutton WA4 51 E2
Kettleshulme SK23 64 C3
Lymm WA13 19 D1
Higher Rd Halewood L24 21 D3
Widnes WA8 21 E3
Higher Tame St SK15 242 E2
Highfield Elton CH2 72 A2
Prestbury SK10 87 D3
Sale M33 242 C5
Highfield Ave
Appleton WA4 26 B2
Audlem CW3 230 A2
Goldborne WA3 2 C4
Great Sankey WA5 15 D3
Kidsgrove ST7 195 D1
Lostock CW9 80 A2
Highfield Cl L64 66 C4
Highfield Cres
Widnes WA8 13 D1
Wilmslow SK9 34 B1
Highfield Cty Prim Sch
CH1 117 F2
Highfield Dr Lymm WA13 18 B1
Macclesfield SK10 87 D1
Nantwich CW5 205 D3
Highfield Est SK9 34 B1
Highfield Gdns SK14 241 F7
Highfield La
Coddington CH3 181 F2
Winwick WA2 8 B4
Highfield Parkway SK7 35 E2
Highfield Pl CW8 103 F4
Highfield Rd Blacon CH1 117 E3
Bollington SK10 88 A4
Cheadle SK8 239 F1
Congleton CW12 156 C1
Ellesmere Port L65 70 B3
Ellesmere Port, Little Sutton
L66 69 D3
Lymm WA13 18 B1
Macclesfield SK11 112 B4
Neston L64 66 C4
Northwich CW8 103 F4
Poynton SK12 36 A2
Widnes WA8 13 D1
Highfield Rd N L65 70 B3
Highfield Sch L26 21 D4
Highfield St 2 SK3 240 C4
Highfield Terr SK22 39 E4
Highfields SY13 224 A1
Highfields Cty Prim Sch
Alsager ST7 193 E2
Nantwich CW5 204 C3
Highgate Cl CW1 190 A4
Highgate Rd WA14 238 B4
Highgrove Mews SK9 60 A3
Highland Ave SK6 241 A2
Highland Way WA16 82 A4
Highlands Rd WA7 48 C4
Highlands The CW6 185 F4
Hightown Crewe CW1 190 B2
Middlewich CW10 128 B1
Sandbach CW11 175 D3
Hightree Dr SK11 111 E4
Highwood Rd WA4 26 B4
Higifield Ave M33 242 C5
Hignett Ave WA9 1 A1
Hilary Ave SK8 34 B4
Hilary Cl Chester CH3 119 D1
Great Sankey WA5 14 B3
Stockport SK4 240 D6
Widnes WA8 13 F2
Hilary Rd Bebington L62 43 F3
Wythenshawe M22 33 E4
Hilbre Bank CW6 169 E2
Hilbre Dr L65 70 B1
Hilda Ave SK8 239 E5
Hilda Gr SK5 240 F8
Hilda St 5 SK5 240 F8
Hilden Rd WA2 8 C1
Hill Cl L64 67 D3
Hill Cliffe Rd WA4 26 A4
Hill Court Mews SK6 241 B2
Hill Crest Ave SK4 240 A6
Hill Ct L64 67 D3
Hill Dr SK9 34 C2
Hill Farm Cl WA2 8 C2
Hill Fields Cl CW12 156 B2
Hill La Brown Knowl CH3 199 E4
Burwardsley CW6 184 C3
Peckforton CW6 184 C3
Hill Rd CH4 141 F1
Hill Rd N WA6 73 E2
Hill Rd S WA6 73 E2
Hill Rise
Altrincham WA14 238 A5
Romiley SK6 241 B2
Hill St Altrincham WA14 238 C8
Crewe CW1 190 B2
Macclesfield SK11 112 B3
Romiley SK6 241 B2
Runcorn WA7 23 D1
Sandbach CW11 174 B4
Winsford CW7 126 C1
Hill Terr ST7 209 E1
Hill The
Hassall Green CW11 175 E3
Sandbach CW11 175 E3
Hill Top Altrincham WA15 32 A4
Barnton CW8 78 A1
Romiley SK6 241 B3
Hill Top Ave
Cheadle Hulme SK8 35 D4
Wilmslow SK9 60 A4
Winsford CW7 126 B1
Hill Top La Heswall L60 41 D4
Neston L64 67 D3
Hill Top Rd
Acton Bridge CW8 76 C1
Dutton WA4 51 E1
Warrington WA4 16 C1
Warrington, Woolston WA1 17 E4
Hill Top Rise SK23 65 E4
Hill View Bollington SK10 87 F4
Whaley Bridge SK23 65 E4
Widnes WA8 12 C3
Hill View Ave WA6 73 D1
Hill View Cty Prim Sch
WA7 49 F2
Hillary Ave CW12 157 D1
Hillary Dr CW3 230 A2
Hillary Rd ST7 195 D2
Hillberry Cres WA4 16 A2
Hillbre Ave L60 40 C3
Hillbre Way SK9 34 B2
Hillbrook Rd SK7 35 E3
Hillcourt Rd High Lane SK6 37 F4
Romiley SK6 241 C4
Hillcrest CW12 156 B2
Hillcrest Ave CW4 130 A2
Hillcrest Dr Denton M34 241 B5
Ellesmere Port L66 69 D3
Hillcrest Gram Sch SK3 240 F2
Hillcrest Rd
Bollington SK10 87 F4
Ellesmere Port L66 69 D3
Kelsall CW6 122 C3
Warren SK11 112 A2
Hillcroft Rd WA14 238 A5
Hillfield Frodsham WA6 74 A4
Runcorn WA7 50 B4
Hillfield Gdns CW5 204 C2
Hillfield Pl CW5 204 C2
Hillfield Rd L66 69 E4
Hillfield View CW5 204 C2
Hillfields CW12 156 B2
Hillfoot Cres WA4 26 A4
Hillfoot La WA6 74 C2
Hillingden Ave L26 21 D4
Hillington Rd SK3 240 C4
Hillock La WA1 17 E4
Hillsboro Ave WA6 74 B4
Hillsdown Way L66 69 E1
Hillside Lymm WA13 19 F1
Northwich CW8 103 E4
Hillside Ave
Newton-le-W WA12 1 C1
Runcorn WA7 48 C4
Hillside Cl Bramhall SK7 36 A4
Disley SK12 38 B3
Kidsgrove ST7 195 E4
Hillside Ct SK10 88 A1
Hillside Dr Crewe CW1 190 C3
Ellesmere Port L66 69 F4
Macclesfield SK10 88 A1
Hillside Gr WA5 14 C2
Hillside La CW9 126 C4
Hillside Pk WA16 57 E1
Hillside Rd Appleton WA4 26 B2
Blacon CH1 117 F2
Frodsham WA6 74 B4
Heswall L60 41 D4
Kelsall CW6 122 B2
Knutsford WA16 57 D1
Hillside View SK22 39 D4
Hilltop WA7 50 B4
Hilltop Prim Sch ST7 210 B4
Hilltop Rd
Guilden Sutton CH3 119 F3
Lymm WA13 18 B1
Hillview Rise CW8 78 C1
Hilton Ave WA5 15 D3
Hilton Cl Macclesfield SK11 111 F4
Middlewich CW10 151 D4
Hilton Dr M44 11 E3
Hilton Rd New Mills SK6 38 A4
Poynton SK12 37 E3
Hilton St SK3 240 D4
Hinchley Cl CW8 103 D2
Hind Heath La CW11 174 C2
Hind Heath Rd CW11 174 C2
Hinde St CW5 204 B2
Hinderton Dr L60 40 C3
Hinderton La L64 67 D4
Hinderton Rd L64 66 C4
Hinderton Sch L65 69 F2
Hindle Ave WA5 7 F1
Hindley Cres CW8 78 A2
Hindley St SK1 240 F4
Hinton Cres WA4 26 C4
Hinton Rd Crewe CW2 206 B4
Runcorn WA7 23 D1
Hitch Lowes SK11 84 A2
Hitchen's Cl WA7 50 B4
Hitchens La SY14 184 B1
Hob Hey La WA3 4 B2
Hob La Churton CH3 180 C3
Dunham-on-t-H WA6 97 E3
Trafford WA6 97 E3
Hobart Cl SK7 35 F2
Hobart Way CH1 117 E2
Hobb La WA4 25 E3
Hobbs Cl CW1 191 E2
Hobbs Hill La WA16 28 C1
Hobby Ct WA7 49 F3
Hobcroft La WA16 58 A4
Hobson St SK11 112 B3
Hockenhull Ave CH3 121 D1
Hockenhull Cres CH3 121 E1
Hockenhull La CH3 121 D1
Hocker La SK10 85 E2
Hockerley Ave SK23 65 E4
Hockerley Cl SK23 65 E4
Hockerley La SK23 65 E4
Hockley Cl SK12 37 D2
Hockley Rd SK12 37 D2
Hodge La Hartford CW8 103 D3
Weaverham CW8 102 B3
Hodgehill La SK11 132 C3
Hodgkingson Ave WA5 7 F1
Hoghton Rd L24 21 F1
Hogshead La CW8 124 B4
Holbein Cl CH4 141 F3
Holborn St 14 SK1 240 F5
Holbrook Cl WA5 14 C3
Holbury Cl CW1 190 A4
Holcet Dr WA14 238 B5
Holcombe Ave WA3 3 E4
Holcombe Cl WA14 238 B6
Holcombe Dr SK10 87 D2
Holcroft La WA3 5 E1
Holden Pl WA2 16 C4
Holden St OL6 242 A4
Hole House Fold SK6 241 B2
Hole House La CW8 77 F2
Holehouse La
Adlington SK10 62 B1
Langley SK11 113 E2
Scholar Green ST7 194 B4
Holes La WA1 17 D4
Holford Ave Lostock CW9 80 A2
Warrington WA5 15 F4
Holford Cres WA16 57 D1
Holford Way WA12 2 C2
Holgrave Cl WA16 29 E2
Holker Cl SK12 36 C2
Holkham Cl WA8 12 C1
Holland Ave SK15 242 D2
Holland Cl CW11 175 E3
Holland Rd SK7 35 F4
Holland St Crewe CW1 190 A3
18 Macclesfield SK11 112 B4
Hollands La CW6 122 B3
Hollands Pl SK11 112 C4
Hollands Rd CW9 103 F4
Hollies La SK9 60 C4
Hollies Rd L26 21 D4
Hollies The Gatley SK8 239 B5
Manchester SK4 240 B7
Moulton CW9 126 C4
Runcorn WA7 49 E4
Shavington CW2 206 A2
Hollin Green La
Burland CW5 202 C3
Faddiley CW5 202 C3
Hollin La Newhall CW5 228 B4
Styal SK9 33 F3
Sutton Lane Ends SK11 136 B3
Hollin Rd SK10 88 A4
Hollingford Pl WA16 82 A4
Hollingreen La CW5 229 D4
Hollinhey Cty Prim Sch
SK11 112 C2
Hollins Cres ST7 194 C1
Hollins Dr WA2 8 A3
Hollins Gr M33 242 A6
Hollins Grange ST7 210 B4
Hollins Hill CW6 146 C4
Hollins La Antrobus CW9 53 F2
Winwick WA2 7 F3
Hollins Rd SK11 112 C3
Hollins Terr SK11 112 C3
Hollins Way WA8 22 A3
Hollinshead Cl ST7 194 C4
Hollinwood Cl ST7 210 C4
Hollinwood Rd Disley SK12 38 B3
Kidsgrove ST7 210 C4
Hollow Dr WA4 16 C1
Hollow La Kingsley WA6 75 D2
Knutsford WA16 57 D1
Hollow Oak La CW8 101 E2
Hollow The Gatley SK8 239 C1
Mount Pleasant ST7 195 D3
Holloway WA7 22 C1
Hollowood Rd SY14 213 D3
Holly Ave Cheadle SK8 239 D5
Newton-le-W WA12 2 B2
Holly Bank M33 242 C5
Holly Bank Rd SK9 34 A1
Holly Bank Sch CH2 237 D4
Holly Bush La WA3 10 B1
Holly Cl Connah's Quay CH5 91 E1
Hale L24 21 E1
Mickle Trafford CH2 119 F4
Holly Ct Helsby WA6 73 E3
Stockport SK3 240 E1
Holly Dr Sale M33 242 A6
Winsford CW7 149 E4
Holly Gr Denton M34 241 A7
Sale M33 242 D6
Tabley WA16 56 A2
Warrington WA1 17 D4
Holly Grange WA14 238 D2
Holly Hedge La WA4 25 E3
Holly La Alsager ST7 193 F2
Kidsgrove ST7 195 F3
Styal SK9 33 F3
Holly Mount CW2 206 C3
Holly Rd Cheadle Hulme SK7 35 F3
Chester CH4 140 C3
Ellesmere Port L65 70 B3
Goldborne WA3 3 E4
Haydock WA11 1 A3
High Lane SK6 37 F4
Lymm WA13 19 D3
Macclesfield SK11 112 A4
Newcastle-u-L ST5 210 C1
Penketh WA5 14 C3
Poynton SK12 36 C2
Weaverham CW8 102 B4
Holly Rd N SK9 60 A3
Holly Rd S SK9 60 A3
Holly Terr Penketh WA5 14 C3
Tilston SY14 198 B2
Holly Tree Dr Biddulph ST6 179 E1
Peover WA16 106 B4
Holly Wlk Northwich CW8 103 E4
Partington M31 11 E1
Hollybank Audlem CW3 229 F2
Moore WA4 25 D3
Hollybank Rd WA7 49 F4
Hollybush Cres CW5 205 E3
Hollyfield Rd L65 70 A3
Hollyfields CW11 191 F4
Hollyheath Cl CW11 175 E3
Hollythorn Ave SK7 35 E4
Hollytree Rd WA16 80 C2
Hollywood WA14 238 D2
Hollywood Way
SK3 & SK4 240 D5
Holm Cl CH3 142 C4
Holm Dr CH2 72 B2
Holm Oak Way CH1 94 C4
Holme St Hyde SK14 241 D6
Tarvin CH3 120 C1
Holmefield M33 242 B6
Holmes Chapel Cty Comp
Sch CW4 130 A1
Holmes Chapel Cty Prim
Sch CW4 130 A2
Holmes Chapel Rd
Allostock WA16 106 A2
Brereton Green CW12 154 B4
Congleton CW12 155 E2
Lach Dennis CW9 105 F2
Middlewich CW10 128 C1
Ollerton WA16 82 B2
Peover WA16 82 B2
Sandbach CW11 153 F1
Sproston Green CW4 129 E1
Withington SK11 109 D4
Holmes Chapel Sta CW4 130 B2
Holmes Ct WA3 9 E2
Holmes St Cheadle SK8 239 E6
Stockport SK2 & SK3 240 E3
Holmesville Ave CW12 156 A2
Holmeswood Cl SK9 60 B4
Holmfield Ave WA7 23 E1
Holmfield Cl SK4 240 D7
Holmfield Dr
Cheadle Hulme SK8 35 D4
Ellesmere Port L66 69 E2
Holmlea Dr CW1 190 C2
Holmlea Way SK10 86 B3
Holmrook WA14 238 B5
Holmsfield Rd WA1 16 B3
Holmshaw La CW1 192 A2
Holmwood WA14 238 A3
Holmwood Dr L65 70 A1
Holt Hey L64 67 D3
Holt La WA7 49 F4
Holt St Altrincham WA14 238 C8
Crewe CW1 190 A2
Stockport SK1 240 F4

Holt's La SK9 33 F2
Holy Family RC Jun & Inf Sch WA8 12 B3
Holy Family RC Prim Sch M33 242 E6
Holy Spirit RC Prim Sch The WA7 49 E4
Holyhead Cl WA5 7 E2
Holyrood Ave WA8 13 D2
Holyrood Dr CW2 205 F4
Holyrood Way CH3 119 D1
Holywell Cl L64 41 D1
Holywell La CH3 182 B1
Home Farm Ave SK10 86 C1
Home Pk CH1 94 C1
Homecrofts L64 66 C3
Homestead Ave WA11 1 C3
Homestead Rd SK12 38 B3
Homesteads The CW5 172 A3
Homeway WA6 73 D1
Homewood Cres CW8 103 D3
Honey Fields CW6 146 B1
Honey Suckle Cl CH1 94 C4
Honeysuckle Cl
Broughton CH4 139 E2
Widnes WA8 13 D2
Honeysuckle Dr SK15 242 F2
Hong Kong Ave M90 33 D4
Honister Ave WA2 8 B1
Honiton Way
Altrincham WA14 238 B6
Penketh WA5 14 C2
Hood La WA5 15 E2
Hood La N WA5 15 E3
Hood Manor Cty Prim Sch WA5 15 E3
Hood Rd WA8 12 C1
Hoofield La Duddon CH3 145 D1
Huxley CH3 167 D4
Hoogreen La
High Legh WA16 29 F1
Mere WA16 29 F1
Hooker St CW8 103 F4
Hookstone Dr L66 69 E3
Hoole All Saints' CE Contr Inf Sch CH2 119 D2
Hoole Cl SK8 240 A1
Hoole Gdns CH2 119 D2
Hoole La CH2 119 D2
Hoole Rd CH2 119 D2
Hoole Way CH2 237 E3
Hooley Range SK4 240 B7
Hooleyhey La
Macclesfield Forest SK10 89 E2
Rainow SK10 89 E2
Hoolpool La WA6 72 C3
Hooper St SK1 & SK3 240 E5
Hooton Gn L66 44 A1
Hooton La L66 44 A1
Hooton Rd Hooton L66 43 E1
Willaston L66 43 E1
Hooton Sta L66 43 E1
Hooton Way Hooton L66 44 A1
13 Wilmslow SK9 34 B3
Hope Ave SK9 34 B2
Hope Croft L66 69 F1
Hope Farm Prec L66 69 F1
Hope Farm Rd L66 69 F1
Hope Green Way SK12 36 B1
Hope La Adlington SK12 36 C1
Adlington, Hope Green SK10 36 B1
Hope Rd Broughton CH4 139 D2
Sale M33 242 B6
Hope St Ashton-u-L OL6 242 A4
Audley ST7 209 F2
Chester CH4 140 C4
Crewe CW2 190 B1
Macclesfield SK11 112 C4
Newton-le-W WA12 2 A2
Northwich CW8 103 F4
Sandbach CW11 175 D3
Stockport SK4 240 D5
Hope St W SK11 112 B4
Hope Terr SK3 240 E4
Hopefield Rd WA13 19 D2
Hopes Carr SK1 240 F5
Hopkins Field WA14 238 B1
Hopkins St SK14 241 E8
Hopwood St WA1 16 B3
Horace Black Gdns L65 70 B3
Horace Gr SK4 240 E8
Horace Lawton Ct CW12 156 B2
Horbury Gdns L66 69 E3
Hornbeam Ave L66 69 F1
Hornbeam Cl WA7 24 B1
Hornbeam Rd L26 21 D4
Hornby Dr CW5 205 D3
Hornby La WA2 8 A3
Horncastle Cl WA3 3 F4
Horridge Ave WA12 2 B3
Horrocks La WA1 16 A3
Horrocks Rd CH2 118 C3
Horsemarket St WA1 16 A3
Horseshoe Cl WA6 75 D1
Horseshoe Cres WA2 8 C2
Horseshoe La SK9 60 A1
Horsley La CW6 167 F1
Horstone Cres L66 69 F1
Horstone Gdns L65 70 A1
Horstone Rd L66 69 F1
Hospital La CW5 203 F1
Hospital St Crewe CW1 190 B3
Nantwich CW5 204 C3
Hospital Way WA7 49 F4
Hotel Rd M90 33 E4
Hotel St WA12 2 A2
Hothershall Cl CW1 173 D1
Hough Cl SK10 88 B3
Hough Gn Ashley WA15 31 F3
Chester CH4 141 D4
Hough Green Rd WA8 12 B2
Hough Green Sta WA8 12 A1
Hough Hill Rd SK15 242 D1
Hough La Alderley Edge SK9 60 B2
Barnton CW8 78 A2
Barnton CW8 78 A2
Norley WA6 100 C3
Wilmslow SK9 60 B2
Hough's La WA4 26 A3
Hougher Wall Rd ST7 209 E1
Houghley Cl SK10 87 E1
Houghton Cft WA8 12 B3
Houghton Cl Chester CH2 118 C2
Newton-le-W WA12 2 A2
Houghton St
Newton-le-W WA12 2 A2
Warrington WA2 16 A3
Widnes WA8 13 E1
Houldsworth Ave WA14 238 E7
Houndings La CW11 175 D3
Housesteads Dr CH2 118 C2
Housman Cl CH1 118 A3
Hove Cl CW1 190 A4
Hove The WA7 50 B3
Hover Prec WA12 2 A1
Howard Ave Bebington L62 43 E4
Lymm WA13 19 D2
Howard Cl SK6 241 A2
Howard Ct Neston L64 41 F1
Runcorn WA7 24 B2
Howard Rd Broughton CH4 140 B3
Culcheth WA3 5 D1
Howard St Crewe CW1 191 D3
Stockport SK1 240 F6
Howards Way L64 67 D3
Howarth Ct WA7 23 D1
Howbeck Cres CW5 220 A4
Howbeck Wlk CW2 206 B4
Howe Rd CH4 141 D4
Howe St SK10 87 F1
Howells Ave
Ellesmere Port L66 69 E2
Sale M33 242 B7
Howey Hill CW12 156 B1
Howey La Congleton CW12 156 B1
Frodsham WA6 74 A4
Howey Rise WA6 74 A4
Howgill Cl L66 68 C3
Howley La WA1 16 C3
Howson Rd WA2 8 B2
Howty Cl SK9 34 B1
Hoxton Cl SK6 241 A4
Hoylake Cl WA7 50 B3
Hoylake Rd Sale M33 242 F5
Stockport SK3 240 B4
Hoyle St WA5 15 F4
Hubert Dr CW10 151 E4
Huddersfield Rd SK15 242 F2
Hudson Cl WA5 15 E4
Hudson Gr WA3 3 F4
Hugh St CH4 141 E4
Hughes Ave WA2 8 B1
Hughes Dr Crewe CW2 189 F2
Crewe, The Valley CW2 190 A2
Hughes Pl WA2 8 B1
Hughes St WA4 16 B2
Hulley Pl SK10 87 F1
Hulley Rd SK10 87 F1
Hullock's Pool Rd ST7 209 F3
Hully St SK15 242 C2
Hulme Hall Ave SK8 35 D4
Hulme Hall Cres SK8 35 D4
Hulme Hall Jun Sch SK8 35 D4
Hulme Hall La WA16 106 A2
Hulme Hall Rd SK8 35 D4
Hulme Hall Sch SK8 35 D4
Hulme La Allostock WA16 106 B4
Peover WA16 106 B4
Hulme Rd M33 242 D5
Hulme Sq SK11 112 B3
Hulme St Ashton-u-L OL6 242 A4
Crewe CW1 189 F3
Hulse La CW9 105 E3
Hulseheath La WA16 30 A2
Humber Cl WA8 13 F2
Humber Dr ST6 179 F1
Humber Rd
Ellesmere Port L66 69 F1
Warrington WA2 8 C1
Hume St WA1 16 B3
Humphrey's Cl WA7 50 B4
Hungerford Ave CW1 190 C2
Hungerford Cty Prim Sch CW1 190 C2
Hungerford Pl CW11 175 D3
Hungerford Rd CW1 190 C2
Hungerford Terr CW1 190 C2
Hunsterson Rd
Bridgemere CW5 231 E4
Hatherton CW5 220 A2
Hunt Cl WA5 15 D4
Hunt Rd WA11 1 C3
Hunter Ave
Shavington CW2 206 B4
Warrington WA2 8 A2
Hunter St CH1 237 D3
Hunter's Cres CH3 121 E1
Hunter's Dr CH3 121 E1
Hunters Cl SK9 34 C1
Hunters Ct Helsby WA6 73 E2
Runcorn WA7 49 F3
Hunters Field CW8 103 E4
Hunters Hill Kingsley WA6 75 E1
Weaverham CW8 77 E1
Hunters Mews Sale M33 242 A7
Wilmslow SK9 60 B4
Hunters Rise CW7 126 B1
Hunters Way L64 66 B4
Hunters Wlk CH1 237 D3
Huntersfield CW2 206 A2
Huntington Cty Prim Sch CH3 142 A3
Huntley Rd SK3 240 B3
Huntley St WA5 15 E2
Huntly Chase SK9 60 B4
Hunts Cl CH3 119 D1
Hunts La WA4 16 C1
Huntsbank Bsns Pk CW2 205 F4
Huntsbank Dr ST5 210 B1
Huntsham Cl WA14 238 B6
Huntsman Dr M44 11 F4
Hurdsfield Cl CW10 151 E4
Hurdsfield Cty Prim Sch SK10 87 F1
Hurdsfield Gn SK10 87 F1
Hurdsfield Ho SK10 87 F1
Hurdsfield Ind Est SK10 87 F2
Hurdsfield Rd SK10 88 A1
Hurford Ave L65 69 F2
Hurlbote Cl SK9 34 B3
Hurlestone Cl CH2 96 C1
Hurley Cl WA5 15 E3
Hurley Dr SK8 239 E2
Hurn Cl CW1 190 A4
Hurst Ave SK7 35 E3
Hurst Bank Rd OL6 242 B4
Hurst Cl ST7 210 B3
Hurst Ct CW6 185 F4
Hurst La Bollington SK10 88 A4
Glazebury WA3 5 D4
Hurst Lea Rd SK22 39 E4
Hurst Mews WA6 75 E1
Hurst Mill La WA3 5 E4
Hurst Rd ST6 179 F2
Hurst St WA8 23 D2
Hurst The WA6 75 E1
Hursthead Cty Jun Sch SK7 35 E4
Hursthead Inf Sch SK7 35 E3
Hursthead Rd SK8 35 D4
Hurstvale Ave SK8 239 B1
Hurstwood CH3 143 D2
Hutchins' Cl CW10 151 F3
Hutchinson St WA8 23 D3
Huttfield Rd L24 21 D2
Hutton Ave OL6 242 B3
Hutton Cl Congleton CW12 157 D1
Culcheth WA3 4 C3
Hutton Dr CW12 157 D1
Huxley CE Contr Prim Sch CH3 167 D4
Huxley Cl Bramhall SK7 35 F4
Macclesfield SK10 87 D1
Huxley Ct L66 69 F4
Huxley Dr SK7 35 F4
Huxley La Huxley CH3 167 E3
Tiverton CH3, CW6 167 E3
Huxley St Altrincham WA14 238 D7
Northwich CW8 103 F4
Hyacinth Cl Haydock WA11 1 C3
Stockport SK3 240 D1
Hyde Bank Rd SK22 39 E4
Hyde Central Sta SK14 241 C6
Hyde Cl Ellesmere Port L65 69 F2
Runcorn WA7 49 E3
Hyde Gr M33 242 B6
Hyde Hospl SK14 241 F5
Hyde Rd M34 & SK14 241 A7
Hyde St Paul's RC Prim Sch SK14 241 F8
Hyde Tech Sch SK14 241 D8
Hyde-Clarendon Coll SK14 241 E8
Hyldavale Ave SK8 239 B6
Hylton Ct L65 70 C1
Hylton Dr SK7 35 E4
Hythe Ave CW1 190 A4
Hythe Rd SK3 240 B4

Ian Rd ST7 195 E1
Ikey La CW5 202 C3
Ikins Dr ST7 209 F1
Ilex Ave WA2 8 A4
Ilford Gdns WA4 26 B2
Illingworth Ave SK15 242 F2
Imperial Ave CH1 117 E2
Imperial Mews L65 70 A3
Ince Ave L62 43 F2
Ince Cl SK4 240 E7
Ince Dr CH3 180 C1
Ince & Elton Sta CH2 72 A2
Ince La Elton CH2 72 A2
Trafford CH2 96 C3
Ince Orch CH2 72 A2
Ince St SK4 240 E7
Ingersley Rd SK10 88 B4
Ingham Ave WA12 2 B1
Ingham Cl CH3 119 D1
Ingham Rd WA8 12 C2
Ingle Rd SK8 240 A2
Inglegreen L60 41 D4
Inglehead Cl M34 241 A6
Inglenook Rd WA5 14 C2
Ingleton Cl Cheadle SK8 239 C6
Holmes Chapel CW4 130 A2
Ingleton Gr WA7 49 E3
Ingleton Rd SK3 240 C3
Inglewood WA14 238 B3
Inglewood Ave CW10 151 E3
Inglewood Cl WA3 10 A3
Inkerman St SK14 241 D8
Inman Ave WA9 1 A1
Innisfree Cl L66 69 E3
Insall Rd WA2 8 C1
Intack La CW9 28 A2
Intake Cl L64 68 A4
International App M22 33 E4
Inveresk Rd SY14 198 B2
Inward Way L65 70 A4
Ion Path CW7 127 E1
Irby Cl L66 69 F2
Ireland Rd Hale L24 21 F1
Haydock WA11 1 B3
Ireland St Warrington WA2 16 A4
Widnes WA8 13 E1
Irene Ave SK14 241 E8
Iris Cl WA8 12 B1
Iris Wlk M31 11 F1
Irlam & Cadishead Comm High Sch M44 11 F4
Irlam Rd M33 242 C6
Irlam Sta M44 11 F4
Ironbridge Dr CW4 130 B1
Irons La CH3 120 C4
Irvine Dr M22 34 A4
Irving's Cres CH4 140 C3
Irwell Gr WA4 16 A1
Irwell La WA7 23 D2
Irwell Rise SK10 87 F4
Irwell St WA8 23 D2
Irwin Dr SK9 34 B3
Irwin Rd WA14 238 D8
Isabella Ct CH4 140 C3
Isherwood Cl WA2 8 C2
Isis Cl CW12 156 C1
Islay Cl L65 70 B1
Iveagh Cl WA7 50 A4
Iver Cl Chester CH2 118 C4
Cronton WA8 12 B3
Iver Rd CH2 118 B4
Ivy Bank Cty Prim Sch SK11 112 A3
Ivy Ct CH4 162 B1
Ivy Dr CW8 102 A1
Ivy Farm Dr L64 66 C3
Ivy Farm Gdns WA3 4 B2
Ivy Farm Rd CH3 183 E1
Ivy Gdns CW12 156 B1
Ivy House Rd ST6 179 E1
Ivy La Alsager ST7 193 F1
Macclesfield SK11 112 A3
Ivy Meade Cl SK11 111 F4
Ivy Meade Rd SK11 111 F3
Ivy Mews CH2 119 D3
Ivy Rd Goldborne WA3 3 D4
Macclesfield SK11 112 A4
Poynton SK12 36 C2
Warrington WA1 17 F4
Ivy St WA7 23 D1
Ivy Wlk M31 11 E1
Ivychurch Mews WA7 23 E1

Jack La Moulton CW9 127 D3
Weston CW2 207 E3
Jackson Ave Culcheth WA3 4 C2
Nantwich CW5 204 C3
Warrington WA1 16 C3
Jackson Ct CH4 139 D3
Jackson La SK10 88 A4
Jackson Rd CW12 156 C3
Jackson St Burtonwood WA5 6 C3
Cheadle SK8 239 E6
Haydock WA11 1 A4
Hyde SK14 241 D6
Macclesfield SK11 112 B3
Sale M33 242 D7
Jackson's La SK7 36 B4
Jacksons Edge Rd SK12 38 A3
Jacobsen Ave SK14 241 F8
Jamage Rd ST7 210 B3
James Ave L66 69 E2
James Cl WA8 23 D2
James Hall St CW5 204 C3
James Leech St SK1 & SK3 240 E4
James Pl CH2 118 C1
James Rd WA11 1 C4
James St Chester CH2 237 E3
Dukinfield M34 241 A8
Macclesfield SK11 112 B3
Northwich CW9 104 B4
Sale M33 242 D6
Stockport SK3 240 E3
Warrington WA1 16 A3
Jamieson Cl Alsager ST7 193 F2
Chester CH3 119 D1
Jan Palach CW5 204 C2
Jarman SK11 112 C2
Jasmin Way ST7 195 F1
Jasmine Gr WA8 22 B4
Jasmine Wlk M31 11 F1
Jay Cl WA3 10 A2
Jays Cl WA7 50 C4
Jayton Ave M20 239 B8
Jedburgh Ave L66 69 D3
Jellicoe Ave M44 11 F3
Jennet's La WA3 5 E4
Jennings St SK3 240 D3
Jenny La SK7 35 F2
Jensen Ct WA7 23 E2
Jersey Ave L65 70 B1
Jersey Cl CW12 157 D1
Jersey Rd SK5 240 F8
Jervis Cl WA2 9 D2
Jesmond Cres CW2 190 A1
Jesmond Gr SK8 35 D4
Jesmond Rd CH1 118 A1
Jessop Way CW1 191 E2
JH Godwin Cty Prim Sch CH1 117 E2
Jockey St WA2 16 A4
Jodrell Bank Science Ctr SK11 108 B2
Jodrell Cl
Holmes Chapel CW4 130 A2
Macclesfield SK11 112 C4
Jodrell Meadow SK23 65 F4
Jodrell Rd SK23 65 E4
Jodrell St
Macclesfield SK11 112 C4
New Mills SK22 39 D4
John Ave SK8 239 E5
John Brunner Cres CW8 103 F3
John Fryer Ave CW9 80 A3
John Lloyd Ct M44 11 F4
John May Ct SK10 87 E1
John Middleton Cl L24 21 F1
John Nicholas Cres L65 70 B3
John Rd WA13 18 B2
John Shepley St SK14 241 E6
John St Altrincham WA14 238 D4
Bollington SK10 88 A4
Congleton CW12 156 B1
Crewe CW1 190 B2
Crewe CW1 190 B3
Ellesmere Port L65 70 A3
Goldborne WA3 3 D4
Hyde SK14 241 D7
Irlam M44 11 F3
Macclesfield SK11 112 B3
Romiley SK6 241 C2
Sale M33 242 B7
Stockport SK1 240 F5
Utkinton CW6 146 A4
Warrington WA2 16 A3
Winsford CW7 126 B1
John Street Cty Prim Sch L65 70 A3
John's Pl SK6 241 C2
Johns Ave WA11 1 C4
Johns Cl SK10 88 B3
Johnson Ave WA12 2 A3
Johnson Cl CW12 157 D1
Johnson St SK23 65 F4
Johnson's La WA8 23 F4
Johnsons Cl CH4 141 D3
Join Rd M33 242 D6
Jonathan's Way CH1 117 F3
Jones Sq SK1 240 F3
Jones's La CW10 152 B3
Jonson Rd L64 66 C4
Jordangate 36 SK11 112 B4
Joseph Cres ST7 193 F1
Joseph St WA8 13 E1
Joules Ct SK1 240 F5
Jowett St SK5 240 F8
Joy La WA5 6 C2
Joyce Ave CW7 126 B1
Joynson St M33 242 B7
Jubilee Ave Crewe CW2 190 A2
Penketh WA5 14 C2
Stalybridge SK16 242 B1
Warrington WA1 16 C4
Jubilee Cres WA11 1 C4
Jubilee Gdns
Nantwich CW5 204 C2
New Mills SK22 39 E4
Jubilee Gr WA13 18 B2
Jubilee Rd CW12 156 C1
Jubilee St SK22 39 E4
Jubilee Terr CW5 204 C2
Jubilee Villas CW11 175 E1
Jubilee Way Widnes WA8 12 C1
Winsford CW7 126 B1
Jubits La WA8 13 D4
Juddfield St WA11 1 A4
Judy La SK11 113 D2
Julian Way WA8 12 C2
Jumper La SK10 88 C4
Junction Eight Bsns Ctr L65 70 A4
Junction La WA12 2 A2
Junction Rd SK1 & SK2 240 F3
June Ave Bebington L62 43 F4
Stockport SK4 240 B6
Juniper Dr L66 69 F1
Juniper Gr L66 69 F1
Juniper La WA3 18 A4
Juniper Rise SK10 86 C1
Jupiter Dr CH1 117 F1
Justice St SK10 87 E1

K Edward Rd WA16 57 D1
K.U.S. Ind Est CH5 139 D3
Karen Cl WA5 7 D3
Karen Way L66 69 E2
Kay La WA13 29 D4
Kay St SK15 242 D1
Kaye Ave WA3 4 C2
Keats Cl CH1 94 C4
Keats Dr Macclesfield SK10 86 C1
Rode Heath ST7 193 F4
Wistaston CW2 206 A4
Keats Gr WA2 8 B1
Keats La CW9 80 A3
Keats Terr CH1 118 A3
Keble St WA8 13 D1
Keckwick La Daresbury WA4 25 D2
Runcorn WA7 24 C2
Keele Cres SK11 112 A3
Keeper's La CW8 102 C4
Keepers Cl WA16 57 E2
Keepers La CW9 53 E2
Keepers Wlk WA7 23 F1
Keith Ave WA5 14 C3
Keith Dr Bebington L63 43 E3
Cheadle SK3 240 B3
Kelburn Ct WA3 9 F3

Kelsall Ave L62 43 F2
Kelsall Cl Bebington L62 43 F2
Warrington WA3 9 E2
Widnes WA8 12 B1
Kelsall Cres SK3 240 D2
Kelsall Cty Prim Sch CW6 122 B2
Kelsall Rd Ashton CH3 121 F4
Cheadle SK8 240 A1
Tarvin CH3 121 E2
Kelsall St Congleton CW12 156 C2
Sale M33 242 B6
Kelsall Way Audley ST7 209 E1
2 Wilmslow SK9 34 B3
Kelsborrow Way CW6 122 B2
Kelsterton Ct CH5 91 E1
Kelsterton La CH6 91 D1
Kelsterton Rd CH6, CH5 91 D1
Kelvin Ave M33 242 B6
Kelvin Cl WA3 9 E3
Kelvin Gr CH2 118 C2
Kemberton Dr WA8 13 D3
Kemble Cl CW2 206 A4
Kemmel Ave WA4 16 B2
Kemp St SK14 241 E8
Kempsell Way L26 21 D4
Kempton Ave CW1 190 B4
Kempton Cl Chester CH1 118 A1
Newton-le-W WA12 2 B3
Runcorn WA7 49 E3
Kempton Way SK10 87 E2
Kendal Ave Denton M34 241 A5
Sale M33 242 C5
Warrington WA2 8 B1
Kendal Cl Chester CH2 119 D3
Ellesmere Port L66 69 E1
Macclesfield SK11 111 F3
Kendal Ct CW12 156 A1
Kendal Dr
Cheadle Hulme SK7 35 E3
Ellesmere Port L66 69 F1
Gatley SK8 239 C4
Kendal Gdns SK6 241 B4
Kendal Rd
Macclesfield SK11 111 F3
Widnes WA8 12 B1
Kendal Rise WA7 49 E3
Kendrick St WA1 16 A3
Kenilworth Ave
Knutsford WA16 57 E1
Runcorn WA7 49 D4
Wilmslow SK9 34 B2
Kenilworth Cl
Macclesfield SK11 111 F3
Wistaston CW2 206 A4
Kenilworth Ct L65 70 C1
Kenilworth Dr
Hazel Grove SK7 36 B4
Warrington WA1 16 C4
Kenilworth Gdns WA12 2 B1
Kenilworth Gn SK11 111 F3
Kenilworth Rd Cheadle SK3 239 F7
Goldborne WA3 3 F4
Macclesfield SK11 111 F3
Neston L64 66 C3
Kenley Ave WA8 12 B3
Kenmare Bank CW9 104 A3
Kenmore Gr M44 11 E3
Kennard Pl WA14 238 E6
Kennedy Ave SK10 86 C1
Kennedy Cl CH2 119 D3
Kennedy Way SK4 240 C6
Kennel La CW8 102 A1
Kennelwood Rd CW9 78 B4
Kennerley's La SK9 60 A4
Kennet Dr CW12 156 C1
Kennet Rd WA11 1 B3
Kennet Way SK11 111 F4
Kenneth Rd WA8 22 B4
Kenrick Cl CW3 232 B1
Kensington Ave
Ashton-u-L OL6 242 B4
Warrington WA4 17 E1
Kensington Cl CH4 141 D3
Kensington Ct Alsager ST7 192 C2
Wilmslow SK9 60 A3
Winsford CW7 149 E4
Kensington Gdns
Altrincham WA15 238 F1
Hyde SK14 241 F5
Kensington Gn CH4 140 C3
Kensington Gr
Altrincham WA14 238 E8
Stalybridge SK15 242 D1
Kensington Rd Chester CH4 141 D3
Ellesmere Port L65 70 A3
Stockport SK3 240 B3
Kensington St SK14 241 E5
Kensington Way CW9 103 F2
Kent Ave Bollington SK10 87 F3
Cheadle SK8 240 C1
Kent Cl L63 43 D4
Kent Dr CW12 156 B2
Kent Gdn CH2 118 C3
Kent Gr WA7 23 D1
Kent Rd Chester CH2 118 C3
Great Sankey WA5 15 E2
Irlam M44 11 E3
Partington M31 11 F1
Stockport SK3 240 B4
Kent St Warrington WA4 16 B2
Widnes WA8 13 D1
Kent Wlk Macclesfield SK10 86 C1
Newton-le-W WA12 2 B1
Kent's Green La CW11 191 F4
Kent's La CW1 173 E1
Kentmere Ave CW7 126 B1
Kentmere Cl SK8 239 B3
Kenton Rd L26 21 D4
Kentridge Dr L66 69 E2
Kentwell Dr SK10 87 E2
Kenview Cl WA8 22 A2
Kenwick Cl L66 69 E2
Kenwood Ave
Altrincham WA15 238 F2
Cheadle Hulme SK7 35 E3
Gatley SK8 239 A6
Kenworthy St SK15 242 D1
Kenyon Ave WA5 14 C3
Kenyon La WA3 3 F2
Kenyon's La WA11 1 C4
Kenyon's La N WA11 1 C4
Kerfoot Bsns Pk WA2 16 A4
Kerfoot St WA2 16 A4
Keristal Ave CH3 142 A4
Kerridge Cl CW10 151 D4
Kerridge Rd SK10 88 A2
Kerry Cft L66 69 F1
Kershaw Gr SK11 112 A4
Kershaw St WA8 12 B1
Kestrel Ave WA16 57 D2
Kestrel Cl Congleton CW12 156 C1
Middlewich CW10 151 E3
Winsford CW7 149 E3
Kestrel Dr CW1 190 A4
Kestrel La WA3 9 F2
Kestrel Rd Heswall L60 41 E4
Northwich CW8 103 E4
Kestrels Way WA7 49 F3
Keswick Ave Bebington L63 43 E2
Dukinfield SK14 241 C8
Gatley SK8 239 B4
Macclesfield SK11 111 F3
Warrington WA2 8 B1
Keswick Cl Chester CH2 119 D3
Crewe CW2 189 F2
Irlam M44 11 E2
Macclesfield SK11 111 F3
Stalybridge SK15 242 D4
Widnes WA8 12 B1
Winsford CW7 126 B1
Keswick Cres WA2 8 B1
Keswick Ct CW12 156 A1
Keswick Dr
Cheadle Hulme SK7 35 E3
Frodsham WA6 74 B4
Keswick Rd SK6 37 F4
Ketlan Ct CH4 140 C4
Kettell Ave CW1 190 A3
Kettle La CW3 230 B1
Kettleshulme St James Sch SK23 64 C2
Kettleshulme Way SK12 37 D2
Kettleshulme Wlk 7 SK9 34 C1
Kew Dr SK8 239 E2
Keyes Cl WA3 9 F2
Keyes Gdns WA3 9 F2
Keysbrook CH3 166 B1
Keysbrook Ave CH3 166 B1
Kidderton Cl CW5 202 C4
Kidderton La Burland CW5 202 C4
Faddiley CW5 202 C4
Kidsgrove Bank ST7 195 D1
Kidsgrove Sta ST7 194 C1
Kilbuck La WA11 2 A4
Kilburn Ave L62 43 F3
Kilburn Cl SK8 34 A4
Kilburn Rd SK3 240 C3
Kildare Cl L24 21 E1
Kildonnan Rd WA4 17 D1
Kilford Cl WA5 7 F1
Killingworth La WA3 10 A3
Kilmorey Park Rd CH2 118 C2
Kilmorey Pk CH2 118 C2
Kilmorey Pk Ave CH2 237 F4
Kiln Croft La SK9 34 C2
Kiln La CW5 220 A4
Kilncroft WA7 50 A3
Kilsby Dr WA8 13 F1
Kilshaw Rd WA5 6 C3
Kilsyth Cl WA2 8 C2
Kimberley Ave SK6 241 C2
Kimberley Dr WA4 16 B1
Kimberley St Stockport SK3 240 E3
Warrington WA5 15 F3
Kimberley Terr CH2 118 C1
Kinder Dr CW2 189 E2
Kinder Gr SK6 241 E2
Kinder St Stalybridge SK15 242 D2
Stockport SK3 240 E3
Kinder View SK22 39 E4
Kinderton Cl WA16 29 E2
Kinderton St CW10 128 B1
King Arthur's Wlk WA7 24 A1
King Edward Rd 2 SK11 112 B4
King Edward St
Macclesfield SK11 112 B4
Middlewich CW10 128 B1
Warrington WA1 16 C4
King George Ave CW9 104 A4
King George Cres WA1 16 C4
King George Rd WA11 2 A4
King James Ct WA7 49 F3
King Pl CW5 204 C3
King St Audley ST7 209 E1
Chester CH1 237 D3
Congleton CW12 156 C2
Crewe CW1 190 B2
Ellesmere Port L65 70 B3
Hartford CW8 103 D3
Hyde SK14 241 D7
Kidsgrove ST7 195 D1
Kidsgrove, Talke ST7 210 B3
Knutsford WA16 57 D1
King St continued
Lach Dennis CW9 104 C3
Macclesfield SK10 112 C4
Middlewich CW10 128 A3
Newton-le-W WA12 2 A2
Northwich CW9 104 C3
Runcorn WA7 23 D2
Sandbach CW11 174 C4
Stalybridge SK15 242 D2
King St E SK1 240 F6
King Street Trad Est CW10 128 B1
King's Ave WA3 3 F4
King's Cres CW10 128 B1
King's Cres E CH3 119 D1
King's Cres W CH3 119 D1
King's Dr SK4 240 A7
King's La Cranage CW10 106 B1
Lach Dennis CW10 106 B1
Nantwich CW5 204 B3
King's Rd Romiley SK6 241 A3
Wilmslow SK9 59 F4
King's Sch in Macclesfield The SK10 87 E1
King's Sch The
Chester CH4 141 D2
Macclesfield SK10 112 C4
Kingfisher Cl
Congleton CW12 156 C1
Crewe CW1 189 F4
Farndon CH3 180 C1
Nantwich CW5 204 C4
Runcorn WA7 49 F3
Warrington WA3 9 F2
Kingfisher Ct CW9 79 E1
Kingfisher Dr CW7 149 E3
Kingfisher Gr CW9 79 F3
Kingham Cl WA8 13 E1
Kings Acre WA14 238 A1
Kings Ave SK8 239 A4
Kings Cl Chester CH4 140 C3
Wilmslow SK9 60 A3
Kings Ct Nantwich CW5 204 B3
Runcorn WA7 24 B2
Stockport SK5 240 F7
Kings Dr Helsby WA6 73 D2
Wistaston CW2 205 F4
Kings Gate CW8 102 A1
Kings Grove Cty High Sch CW2 190 A2
Kings La CW6 147 E2
Kings Meadow Runcorn WA7 50 B4
Shavington CW2 206 C1
Kings Mews L66 69 E4
Kings Rd Connah's Quay CH5 91 E1
Ellesmere Port L66 69 E4
Goldborne WA3 3 D4
Irlam M44 11 F3
Warrington WA2 9 D1
Kingsbury Cl WA4 26 B2
Kingsdale Rd WA5 14 C4
Kingsfield Ct CH4 141 E2
Kingshead Cl WA7 24 A1
Kingsland Rd SK3 240 A3
Kingsley Ave Bebington L62 43 F2
Reddish SK4 240 E8
Wilmslow SK9 34 B1
Kingsley Cl Hartford CW8 103 E3
Kidsgrove ST7 210 B3
Kingsley Cres WA7 23 D1
Kingsley Dr Appleton WA4 26 B4
Northwich CW9 104 A3
Kingsley Gdns CH3 142 A4
Kingsley Gn WA6 74 C3
Kingsley & Newton Cty Prim Sch WA6 74 C1
Kingsley Rd Chester CH3 142 A4
Congleton CW12 157 D2
Crowton CW8 76 A1
Ellesmere Port L65 70 B3
Frodsham WA6 74 C2
Haslington CW1 191 E2
Kidsgrove ST7 210 B3
Kingsley WA6 74 C2
Runcorn WA7 23 D1
Kingsley St John's CE Aided Prim Sch WA6 75 E1
Kingsley Wlk CW7 126 A1
Kingsmead Chester CH2 118 B4
Davenham CW9 103 F2
Kingsmead Ct WA3 9 D4
Kingston Ave
Great Sankey WA5 14 C3
Macclesfield SK11 112 C4
Kingston Cl WA7 23 F1
Kingston Dr M33 242 D7
Kingston Gdns SK14 241 B7
Kingston Hill SK8 239 D4
Kingston Pl Biddulph ST6 179 F1
Cheadle SK8 239 E2
Kingston Rd SK9 34 B3
Kingston St SK3 240 D5
Kingsway Altrincham WA14 238 D5
Bollington SK10 87 F4
Cheadle M20 & SK8 239 C6
Chester CH2 118 C3
Crewe CW2 190 A1
Frodsham WA6 74 A4
Heswall L60 41 E3
Newton-le-W WA12 2 B1
Northwich CW9 104 A4
Widnes WA8 13 D1
Winsford CW7 126 C1
Kingsway Cty High Sch CH2 118 C3
Kingsway N WA1 16 C3
Kingsway S WA4 16 C2
Kingsway Sch SK8 239 C4
Kingsway W CH2 118 C2
Kingswood Kidsgrove ST7 195 D1
Poynton SK12 36 C2
Kingswood Ave CH1 94 B1
Kingswood Cres CW10 151 F3
Kingswood La CH1 94 B1
Kingswood Rd WA5 7 D1
Kingswood Wlk CW6 122 B3
Kinloch Cl Crewe CW1 190 A3
Halewood L26 21 D4
Kinnerley Rd L65 70 A2
Kinnersley Ave ST7 210 C4
Kinnersley St ST7 195 D1
Kinnerton Cl CH4 140 C3
Kinnerton Hts CH4 161 D4
Kinnerton La CH4 161 D4
Kinnington Way CH1 94 C4
Kinnock Parr WA5 6 C3
Kinross Cl WA2 8 C2
Kinsale Dr WA3 9 E2
Kinsey Rd L65 70 B1
Kinsey St CW12 156 C1
Kinsey's La CH2 71 F3
Kintore Cl L63 43 E2
Kintore Dr WA5 14 B3
Kipling Ave WA2 8 B1
Kipling Cres WA8 22 C4
Kipling Rd CH1 117 F3
Kipling Way CW1 190 C2
Kirby Cl CH2 118 B3
Kircaldy Ave WA5 14 B3
Kirkacre Ave WA12 7 E4
Kirkby Rd WA3 4 C2
Kirkfell Dr SK6 37 F4
Kirkham Ave WA3 3 F3
Kirkham Cl WA5 15 D2
Kirkham Rd Cheadle SK8 34 B4
Widnes WA8 13 E1
Kirkley St SK14 241 E5
Kirkstall Cl SK10 87 D1
Kirkstall Dr SK12 36 B2
Kirkstead Rd SK7 35 E3
Kirkstone Ave WA2 8 B1
Kirkstone Cres WA7 50 A2
Kirkstone Ct CW12 156 A1
Kirkwall Dr WA5 15 D2
Kirkwood Cl CH3 119 D1
Kishfield La SK23 65 D3
Kitchen St CH1 118 A1
Kitchener Ave M44 11 E2
Kite Gr ST7 195 E2
Kitfield Ave CW10 151 E4
Kitt's Moss La SK7 35 E3
Knap The L60 41 D3
Knight Rd WA5 6 C3
Knight St Hyde SK14 241 E5
Macclesfield SK11 112 C4
Knight's Cl SK11 112 C4
Knight's Grange (Sports Complex) CW7 126 B2
Knights La CW6 123 F1
Knights Meadow CW7 126 B2
Knights Way CW2 206 A2
Knightsbridge SK1 240 F6
Knightsbridge Ave
Davenham CW9 103 F2
Warrington WA4 17 E1
Knightwake Rd SK22 39 D4
Knivton St SK14 241 F7
Knole Ave SK12 36 C2
Knoll St SK22 39 D4
Knoll The Altrincham WA14 238 B5
Runcorn WA7 49 F4
Knott Fold SK14 241 D5
Knottingley Dr L66 69 E3
Knotty La CW12 179 F4
Knowe The L64 68 A4
Knowl Hey Rd L26 21 D3
Knowl La CH3 180 C3
Knowl St SK15 242 E2
Knowl The CH3 180 C3
Knowle Cl L66 69 F2
Knowle Gn SK9 34 B2
Knowle Pk SK9 34 B2
Knowles Ind Est SK23 39 E2
Knowles St WA8 13 E1
Knowsley Ave WA3 3 E4
Knowsley La ST7 194 C2
Knowsley Rd Chester CH2 118 C2
Hazel Grove SK7 36 C4
Macclesfield SK11 112 B3
Knutsford Ave M33 242 E6
Knutsford Cty High Sch WA16 56 C1
Knutsford Cty High Sch (Lower Sch) WA16 56 C1
Knutsford Cty High Sch (Upper Sch) WA16 56 C1
Knutsford L Ctr WA16 56 C1
Knutsford Rd Antrobus CW9 53 E2
Appleton WA4 27 F4
Chelford SK11 84 A1
Cranage CW4 130 A3
Great Budworth CW9 54 A1
Holmes Chapel CW4 130 A3
Lawton-gate ST7 193 F3
Lindow End SK9, WA16 59 F2
Mobberley WA16 57 F2
MobberleyKnolls Green WA16 58 C2
Warrington WA4 16 B2
Wilmslow SK9, WA16 59 F2
Knutsford Road Wlk 20 SK11 112 C4
Knutsford Service Area WA16 56 B1
Knutsford Sta WA16 57 D1
Knutsford View WA15 32 B4
Knutsford Way CH1 117 F1
Kohima Cres CH3 142 A3
Kronsbec Ave L66 69 E3
Kynaston Dr CH4 140 A4

Labelia Wlk M31 11 E1
Labernum Farm Cl L64 67 D3
Laburnam Cl
Congleton CW12 156 A2
Kidsgrove ST7 210 C4
Laburnum Ave
Nantwich CW5 204 C3
Warrington WA1 17 E4
Wistaston CW2 189 F1
Laburnum Cres CW8 78 A2
Laburnum Gr
Broughton CH4 140 C3
Crewe CW1 190 B3
Ellesmere Port CH1 95 D4
Runcorn WA7 49 E4
Weaverham CW8 102 B4
Laburnum La
Altrincham WA15 31 F4
Penketh WA5 14 B3
Laburnum Pl ST5 210 B1
Laburnum Rd
Davenham CW9 103 F2
Goldborne WA3 3 F4
Irlam M44 11 E3
Macclesfield SK11 112 C3
Northwich CW9 104 B3
Laburnum Way Holt LL13 180 B1
Stockport SK3 240 B4
Lacey Ave SK9 34 A1
Lacey Ct Widnes WA8 23 D4
Wilmslow SK9 34 A1
Lacey Gn SK9 34 A1
Lacey Gr SK9 34 B1
Lacey Green Cty Prim Sch SK9 34 A1
Lacey St WA8 23 D4
Lache Cty Inf & Jun Sch CH4 141 D3
Lache Hall Cres CH4 140 C2
Lache La Chester CH4 141 D3
Dodleston CH4 140 C2
Lache Park Ave CH4 141 D3
Lacy St SK1 240 F4
Ladies Mile WA16 56 C1
Ladies Wlk L64 66 C4
Lady Barn House Sch SK8 239 D3
Lady Helen Wlk CW5 204 C3
Lady Kelvin Rd WA14 238 C6
Lady La Croft WA3 9 E4
Mobberley WA16 58 B4
Ladybarn Ave WA3 2 C4
Ladybarn Cr SK7 35 F3
Ladybrook Gr 10 SK9 34 B1
Ladybrook Prim Sch SK7 35 F4
Ladycroft Cl WA1 17 F4
Ladyfield St SK9 60 A4
Ladyfield Terr SK9 60 A4
Ladypit Rd SK23 39 F2
Ladypool L24 21 E1
Ladys Cl SK12 36 C2
Ladysmith Rd SK15 242 D4
Ladysmith St SK3 240 E3
Ladythorn Cres SK7 35 F3
Ladythorn Gr SK7 35 F4
Ladythorn Rd SK7 35 F3
Ladywood Rd WA5 7 E1
Lagos Gr CW7 126 C1
Laira St WA2 16 B4
Lake House Cl CW8 77 E1
Lake La WA4 52 C3
Lake Rd SK15 242 C4
Lake View CW12 156 A1
Lakelands Cl SK10 112 C4
Lakeside SK11 158 B4
Lakeside Cl WA8 22 A4
Lakeside Dr Poynton SK12 36 C3
Warrington WA1 16 A2
Lakeside Rd WA13 18 B1
Laleston Cl WA8 22 C4
Lamb La WA14 31 E3
Lamb St ST7 195 D1
Lambert Ct WA8 23 D4
Lambert Way CW8 103 D2
Lambert's La CW12 156 C1
Lamborne Gr CW10 128 B1
Lambourn Ave WA8 12 B3
Lambourn Cl SK12 36 B2
Lambourn Dr CW1 173 D1
Lambourne Cl
Ellesmere Port CH1 94 C4
Wythenshawe M22 33 E4
Lambourne Gr WA9 1 A2
Lambs La WA1 17 D4
Lambsickle Cl WA7 48 C3
Lambsickle La WA7 49 D3
Lampeter Cl WA5 7 F1
Lampits La CH3 120 C3
Lamport Cl WA8 13 F2
Lanark Wlk SK10 86 C1
Lancashire Hill
SK1 & SK4 & SK5 240 E7
Lancashire Rd M31 11 F1
Lancaster Ave Goldborne WA3 3 E4
Runcorn WA7 48 C4
Stalybridge SK15 242 D3
Widnes L35 12 A1
Lancaster Cl Hazel Grove SK7 36 B4
Newton-le-W WA12 1 C2
Romiley SK6 241 A1
Winsford CW7 149 E3
Lancaster Ct 9 SK10 112 C4
Lancaster Dr CH3 119 D1
Lancaster Fields CW1 191 D1
Lancaster Gdns L65 70 B2

Lancaster Pk CH4 .... 139 D2
Lancaster Rd Denton M34 .. 241 A5
  Irlam M44 .... 11 E3
  Widnes WA8 .... 13 D2
  Wilmslow SK9 .... 34 C1
Lancaster St WA5 .... 15 F3
Lancelyn Dr SK9 .... 60 B4
Lancer Ct WA7 .... 23 F2
Lancers Cft L66 .... 69 F1
Lancing Ave WA2 .... 8 A2
Lancing Rd L65 .... 70 B2
Land Cut La WA3 .... 9 E2
Land La SK9 .... 60 B3
Lander Cl WA5 .... 15 E4
Landor Cl WA3 .... 3 F4
Landscape Dean WA6 .... 73 E2
Landsdowne St SK10 .... 87 F1
Landseer Ave Neston L64 .... 66 C4
  Warrington WA4 .... 16 A1
Landseer Dr SK11 .... 111 F4
Landswood Pk CW8 .... 103 D2
Lane Ends SK6 .... 241 D3
Lane Head Ave WA3 .... 3 F4
Lane Head Rd SK23 .... 65 E3
Lane The Whitewell SY14 .... 223 E2
  Willington SY14 .... 223 E2
Laneside Rd
  Manchester M20 .... 239 C8
  New Mills SK22 .... 39 F4
Langcliffe Cl WA3 .... 4 C2
Langdale Ave WA13 .... 18 C2
Langdale Cl
  Altrincham WA15 .... 238 E5
  Gatley SK8 .... 239 C3
  High Lane SK6 .... 37 F4
  Macclesfield SK11 .... 111 F3
  Warrington WA2 .... 8 C1
  Widnes WA8 .... 22 B4
  Winsford CW7 .... 126 B1
Langdale Ct CW12 .... 156 A1
Langdale Rd
  Cheadle Hulme SK7 .... 35 E3
  Partington M31 .... 11 F2
  Romiley SK6 .... 241 B4
  Runcorn WA7 .... 23 D1
  Wistaston CW2 .... 189 E1
Langdale Way WA6 .... 49 E1
Langden Cl WA3 .... 4 B2
Langfield WA3 .... 3 F4
Langfield Gr L62 .... 43 E3
Langford Ct CH3 .... 121 E1
Langford Rd Lostock CW9 .. 80 A2
  Manchester M20 .... 240 C8
Langford St 11 SK11 .... 112 B4
Langham Rd
  Altrincham WA14 .... 238 C2
  Stockport SK4 .... 240 B5
Langland Cl WA5 .... 7 F1
Langley Ave WA12 .... 2 B1
Langley Cl Goldborne WA3 .... 3 E4
  Newcastle-u-L ST5 .... 210 B1
  Sandbach CW11 .... 175 E4
Langley Ct L65 .... 70 C2
Langley Dr SK9 .... 34 C2
Langley Hall Cl SK11 .... 113 D2
Langley Rd Northwich CW9 .. 104 A3
  Sutton Lane Ends SK11 .... 113 D2
Langport Dr CH3 .... 119 E1
Langton Cl WA8 .... 12 A2
Langton Gn WA1 .... 17 E4
Langwell Cl WA3 .... 10 A3
Lanreath Cl SK10 .... 86 B1
Lansdown Cl SK7 .... 35 E4
Lansdown Rd CH4 .... 139 D2
Lansdowne Culcheth WA3 .... 4 C2
  Frodsham WA6 .... 74 B3
Lansdowne Ave SK6 .... 241 D2
Lansdowne Gr CH4 .... 141 D4
Lansdowne Rd
  Altrincham WA14 .... 238 D6
  Connah's Quay CH5 .... 91 E1
  Crewe CW1 .... 190 C3
  Great Barrow CH3 .... 120 B2
  Sale M33 .... 242 A8
Lapwing Cl
  Newton-le-W WA12 .... 2 B1
  Stalybridge SK15 .... 242 D4
  Winsford CW7 .... 149 E3
Lapwing Gr WA7 .... 50 A3
Lapwing La Penketh WA4 .... 25 C1
  Withington SK11 .... 109 E3
Lapwing Rd ST7 .... 195 E2
Larch Ave
  Macclesfield SK11 .... 112 A3
  Newton-le-W WA12 .... 2 B1
  Penketh WA5 .... 14 C3
  Shavington CW2 .... 206 C3
  Widnes WA8 .... 13 D1
Larch Cl Goldborne WA3 .... 3 F3
  Poynton SK12 .... 36 C2
  Runcorn WA7 .... 49 E4
  Weaverham CW8 .... 102 B4
Larch Rd Denton M34 .... 241 A7
  Haydock WA11 .... 1 C4
  Partington M31 .... 11 F2
  Runcorn WA7 .... 49 E4
  Wistaston CW2 .... 189 F1
Larch Rise SK10 .... 86 B3
Larch Way CH4 .... 140 C3
Larchdale Cl CH1 .... 94 C4
Larchfields CH1 .... 117 D4
Larchtree Cl WA8 .... 78 A2
Larchway Cheadle Hulme SK7 .. 35 E4
  High Lane SK6 .... 37 F4
Larchways WA4 .... 26 B3
Larchwood SK8 .... 239 D6
Larchwood Dr SK9 .... 60 C4

Lark Hall Cl SK10 .... 113 D4
Lark Hall Cres SK10 .... 113 D4
Lark Hall Rd SK10 .... 113 D4
Lark Hill SK15 .... 242 D4
Lark Hill Prim Sch SK3 .... 240 C4
Lark Hill Rd SK3 .... 240 C4
Larkfield Ave WA1 .... 17 D3
Larkfield Rd SK8 .... 240 C1
Larkhill View SK3 & SK8 .... 240 C1
Larkspur Cl Chester CH4 .... 140 C2
  Nantwich CW5 .... 204 C4
  Runcorn WA7 .... 49 F2
Larkstoke Cl WA4 .... 26 C3
Larksway L60 .... 41 A4
Larne Ave SK3 .... 240 B3
Larwood Ave SK4 .... 240 B5
Lasky La WA4 .... 17 F2
Latchford Rd L60 .... 41 D3
Latchford St WA4 .... 17 D2
Latham Ave Helsby WA6 .... 73 D1
  Newton-le-W WA12 .... 2 B2
  Runcorn WA7 .... 23 E1
  Warrington WA2 .... 16 A4
Latham Rd CW11 .... 175 D3
Latham St CW7 .... 126 B1
Lathom Gr M33 .... 242 E5
Lathom Rd M44 .... 11 F4
Lathom Way SK10 .... 87 E1
Latimer Dr CW2 .... 190 A2
Launceston Cl Runcorn WA7 .. 50 B3
  Winsford CW7 .... 149 D4
Launceston Dr Bramhall SK7 .. 35 F4
  Penketh WA5 .... 14 C2
Laura St CW2 .... 190 B1
Laurel Ave Cheadle SK8 .... 239 D5
  Newton-le-W WA12 .... 2 B2
  Warrington WA1 .... 17 E4
Laurel Bank Warrington WA4 .. 17 F1
  Widnes WA8 .... 13 D2
  Winsford CW7 .... 149 E4
Laurel Cl Barnton CW8 .... 78 A2
  Middlewich CW10 .... 128 A1
  Sandbach CW11 .... 175 D3
Laurel Dr Ellesmere Port L65 .. 70 A1
  Goldborne WA3 .... 3 E4
  Kidsgrove ST7 .... 195 F2
  Willaston L64 .... 43 D1
  Wistaston CW2 .... 189 F1
Laurel End La SK4 .... 240 A7
Laurel Gn M34 .... 241 A6
Laurel Gr CH2 .... 119 D2
Laurel St 1 SK4 .... 240 B8
Laurel St SK4 .... 240 E6
Laurel Way SK7 .... 35 E4
Laurel Wlk M31 .... 11 F1
Laurelwood Dr L66 .... 69 F1
Laureston Ave CW1 .... 190 C2
Lavender Cl WA7 .... 23 E1
Lavender Dr CW9 .... 104 C4
Lavender Wlk M31 .... 11 E1
Lavenders Brow 22 SK1 .... 240 F5
Lavenham Cl
  Hazel Grove SK10 .... 36 C4
  Macclesfield SK10 .... 87 E1
Lavington Ave SK8 .... 240 A2
Lavister Cl CW9 .... 103 F2
Lavister Wlks CH4 .... 162 B1
Law St CH2 .... 118 C2
Lawford Cl CW1 .... 189 F4
Lawford Dr L41 .... 41 E4
Lawn Ave WA1 .... 16 C4
Lawn Dr Altrincham WA15 .... 238 E6
  Chester CH2 .... 118 B4
Lawnhurst Trad Est
  SK3 & SK8 .... 240 B1
Lawns Ave L63 .... 43 D3
Lawnsdale Cl M44 .... 101 E3
Lawnswood Gr CH2 .... 72 A2
Lawrence Ave E CW10 .... 128 B1
Lawrence Ave W CW10 .... 128 B1
Lawrence Cl 4 CW11 .... 174 B3
Lawrence Pl SK12 .... 36 B1
Lawrence Rd WA14 .... 238 C6
Lawrence St Crewe CW1 .... 190 B2
  Hawarden CH5 .... 116 A2
  Newton-le-W WA12 .... 2 A2
  Stockport SK1 .... 240 E5
Laws Gdns CH3 .... 142 A4
Lawson Ave SK8 .... 239 B5
Lawson Cl WA1 .... 17 F4
Lawson Gr M33 .... 242 A8
Lawton Ave Bramhall SK7 .... 35 F4
  Lawton-gate ST7 .... 194 B2
Lawton Cl WA3 .... 4 C2
Lawton Coppice ST7 .... 194 C2
Lawton Heath Rd ST7 .... 193 F3
Lawton Rd Alsager ST7 .... 193 F2
  Manchester SK4 .... 240 A8
Lawton St Congleton CW12 .. 156 C1
  Crewe CW2 .... 190 B2
  Hyde SK14 .... 241 E7
  Kidsgrove ST7 .... 195 E2
  Stalybridge SK15 .... 242 E1
Lawton Way CW11 .... 174 C4
Lawtongate Est ST7 .... 194 A2
Laxey Ave WA1 .... 17 E3
Laxton Cl CH1 .... 94 C4
Laxton Way CW10 .... 128 B1
Layland Ave WA3 .... 4 C2
Layton Ave SK14 .... 241 C6
Layton Cl WA3 .... 9 F2
Layton Dr SK6 .... 241 C3
Lea Ave Crewe CW1 .... 190 C2
  Goostrey CW4 .... 107 E1
Lea Bank Cl SK11 .... 112 A4

Lea Cl CW11 .... 175 E3
Lea Cross Gr WA8 .... 12 B2
Lea Ct SK4 .... 240 B8
Lea Dr Nantwich CW5 .... 204 B2
  Wimboldsley CW10 .... 151 D2
Lea La CH3 .... 164 B2
Lea Rd Gatley SK8 .... 239 B1
  Manchester SK4 .... 240 C8
Lea St SK22 .... 39 D4
Lea Way ST7 .... 193 E2
Leacroft Rd WA3 .... 10 A3
Leadbeaters Cl SK11 .... 112 C4
Leadbeaters Rd SK11 .... 112 C4
Leadgate La CH1 .... 144 C1
Leadsmithy St CW10 .... 128 B1
Leadworks La CH2 .... 237 F3
Leaf La CW7 .... 127 D1
Leafield Dr SK8 .... 34 C3
Leafield Rd SK12 .... 38 B3
Leafy Way CW8 .... 102 B4
Leahurst Ct 18 CH2 .... 118 C2
Leahurst University of
  Liverpool Veterinary
  Field Sta L64 .... 67 E4
Leam St OL6 .... 242 A4
Leamington Ave WA12 .... 2 B1
Leamington Cl
  Great Sankey WA5 .... 14 C3
  Neston L64 .... 66 C3
Leamington Rd
  Congleton CW12 .... 155 F2
  Macclesfield SK10 .... 86 C1
Lear Dr CW2 .... 205 F3
Leas Cl L66 .... 69 E3
Leaside WA7 .... 23 E1
Leaside Rd CH1 .... 117 F3
Leaside Way SK9 .... 60 B3
Leatham Cl WA3 .... 9 F2
Leathers La L26 .... 21 D4
Leawood Cl CW8 .... 103 D3
Ledbury Dr WA2 .... 206 A4
Ledge Ley SK8 .... 34 C4
Ledger Rd WA11 .... 1 A3
Ledley St SK10 .... 87 F4
Ledsham Cl WA3 .... 9 E2
Ledsham Hall La L66 .... 68 C2
Ledsham La L66 .... 68 C2
Ledsham Park Dr L66 .... 69 D3
Ledsham Rd L66 .... 69 D3
Ledston Cl WA7 .... 24 B1
Ledward La WA14 .... 238 B2
Ledward St CW7 .... 127 D1
Ledyard Cl WA5 .... 15 E4
Lee Ave WA14 .... 238 C7
Lee Cl WA16 .... 56 C1
Lee Dale Cl M34 .... 241 A6
Lee Dr CW8 .... 103 F4
Lee Rd WA5 .... 15 D3
Lee St Chester CH2 .... 237 F3
  16 Stockport SK1 .... 240 F5
Leech Rd SY14 .... 213 D2
Leech St Hyde SK14 .... 241 F6
  Stalybridge SK15 .... 242 D1
Leegate Gdns SK4 .... 240 A8
Leegate Rd SK4 .... 240 A8
Leek Old Rd SK11 .... 112 C1
Leek Rd CW12 .... 179 D4
Leen La CH1 .... 237 D2
Lees La Ellesmere Port L65 .. 70 C2
  Mottram St Andrew SK10 .. 61 D4
  Neston L64 .... 67 D4
  Stanlow L65 .... 70 C2
Lees Rd SK7 .... 35 E3
Lees St SK15 .... 242 D2
Leeside SK4 .... 240 A5
Leesway Dr M34 .... 241 A6
Leftwich Cty Prim Sch
  CW9 .... 104 A2
Legh Gdns WA16 .... 57 D1
Legh Rd Adlington SK10 .. 62 B3
  Haydock WA11 .... 1 A3
  Knutsford WA16 .... 82 A4
  Prestbury SK10 .... 87 D4
  Sale M33 .... 242 E5
Legh St Goldborne WA3 .... 3 D4
  Lymm WA13 .... 18 C2
  Newton-le-W WA12 .... 2 A2
  Warrington WA1 .... 16 A3
Legh Vale Cty Prim Sch
  WA11 .... 1 A3
Leicester Ave ST7 .... 193 E3
Leicester Rd
  Altrincham WA15 .... 238 F2
  Sale M33 .... 242 B7
Leicester St Northwich CW9 .. 79 D1
  Warrington WA5 .... 15 F3
Leigh Ave Knutsford WA16 .. 57 D2
  Widnes WA8 .... 13 D1
Leigh Golf Course WA3 .... 4 B3
Leigh Green Cl 4 WA8 .. 22 B4
Leigh La CW8 .... 77 E3
Leigh Rd Altrincham WA15 .. 238 E2
  Congleton CW12 .... 157 D3
  Disley SK12 .... 38 A3
  Wilmslow SK9 .... 59 E3
Leigh St Hyde SK14 .... 241 E6
  Macclesfield SK11 .... 112 C4
Leigh Street Prim Sch
  SK14 .... 241 E6
Leigh Way CW8 .... 77 E1
Leigh's Brow CW8 .... 77 F2
Leighstone Ct CH2 .... 237 D4
Leighton Chase L64 .... 41 E1
Leighton Ct L64 .... 66 B4
Leighton Dr WA3 .... 4 A4
Leighton Hospl CW1 .... 172 C1
Leighton Park Cty Prim
  Sch CW1 .... 189 F4

Leighton Pk L64 .... 66 B2
Leighton Rd L64 .... 41 E1
Leighton St CW1 .... 190 A3
Leighton View CW1 .... 190 A4
Leightons The L64 .... 66 B4
Leinster Gdns WA7 .... 22 C2
Leinster St WA7 .... 22 C2
Leith Ave M33 .... 242 E6
Leith Rd M33 .... 242 E6
Lenfield Dr WA11 .... 1 A3
Lenham Wlk M22 .... 33 E4
Lenthall Ave CW12 .... 178 C4
Leon Cl WA5 .... 14 B4
Leonard St Blacon CH1 .. 118 A2
  Runcorn WA7 .... 48 B3
  Warrington WA2 .... 16 B4
  Warrington, Stockton Heath
  WA4 .... 16 B1
Leslie Rd CW7 .... 149 D4
Lessingham Rd WA8 .... 12 C4
Lester Cl ST7 .... 193 E2
Leven Ave CW7 .... 126 C1
Leven Wlk L65 .... 70 A4
Levens Cl SK8 .... 239 B1
Levens Way 3 WA8 .... 22 B4
Leveret Rd L24 .... 21 D2
Leverett Cl WA14 .... 238 A5
Levisham Gdns WA5 .... 15 F4
Lewin St CW10 .... 128 B1
Lewis Ave WA5 .... 7 F1
Lewis Cl CW5 .... 205 D3
Lewis Cres WA8 .... 23 D4
Lewis Gr WA8 .... 12 B1
Lewis St CW1 .... 190 B2
Lexden St WA5 .... 15 F3
Leycester Cl WA16 .... 82 B4
Leycester Rd
  Knutsford WA16 .... 82 A4
  Mobberley WA16 .... 57 F4
Leyfield Ave SK6 .... 241 C2
Leyfield Ct CH4 .... 140 C3
Leygate View SK22 .... 39 D4
Leyland Ave SK8 .... 239 B6
Leyland Dr CH4 .... 140 B3
Leyland Gr
  Haslington CW1 .... 191 E2
  Haydock WA11 .... 1 A3
Leyland St SK1 & SK4 .... 240 E5
Leyland Wlk CW7 .... 149 E3
Leys Rd WA14 .... 238 E8
Leyton Cl WA7 .... 49 D3
Libson Cl WA2 .... 9 D2
Lichfield Ave WA3 .... 3 E4
Lichfield Cl WA16 .... 57 E1
Lichfield Ct
  3 Macclesfield SK10 .. 112 C4
  Winsford CW7 .... 149 E4
Lichfield Dr CH1 .... 94 C4
Lichfield Rd Blacon CH1 .. 117 F3
  Kidsgrove ST7 .... 210 B4
Lichfield St CW10 .... 128 B1
Lichfield Wlk SK6 .... 241 A1
Lidgetts La SK10 .... 88 B2
Liebig St WA8 .... 23 D4
Light Alders La SK12 .... 38 A3
Light Oaks Rd WA3 .... 5 E3
Lightburn St 7 WA7 .... 22 C1
Lightfoot Cl L60 .... 41 D4
Lightfoot La Eaton CW6 .. 147 D2
  Heswall L60 .... 41 D4
Lightfoot St CH2 .... 118 C1
Lighthorne Ave SK3 .... 239 F7
Lighthorne Gr SK3 .... 239 F7
Lighthorne Rd SK3 .... 239 F7
Lighthouse Rd L24 .... 47 F4
Lightley Cl WA11 .... 175 D2
Lightwood Green Ave
  CW3 .... 229 D1
Lightwood Rd ST5 .... 210 D1
Lilac Ave Great Sankey WA5 .. 15 D3
  Knutsford WA16 .... 56 C1
  Widnes WA8 .... 13 D1
Lilac Cl Newcastle-u-L ST5 .. 210 B1
  Tarvin CW6 .... 122 C1
Lilac Cres WA7 .... 49 E4
Lilac Dr CW8 .... 103 E3
Lilac Gr Ellesmere Port CH1 .. 95 D4
  Warrington WA4 .... 16 C1
Lilac St SK3 .... 240 F2
Lilac Wlk M31 .... 11 E1
Lilford Ave WA5 .... 15 F4
Lilford Dr WA5 .... 14 C3
Lilford St WA5 .... 15 F4
Lillyfield L60 .... 40 C3
Lily Ave WA12 .... 2 B1
Lily St SK3 .... 240 D1
Lily La Cranage CW10 .... 129 D3
  Middlewich CW10 .... 129 D3
Lime Ave Frodsham WA6 .. 74 B4
  Northwich CW8, CW9 .. 103 F3
  Weaverham CW8 .... 102 B4
Lime Cl Hollins Green WA3 .... 11 B1
  Middlewich CW10 .... 128 A1
  Sandbach CW11 .... 175 D4
  Tarporley CW6 .... 146 B1
Lime Ct CW9 .... 103 F3
Lime Gr Alsager ST7 .... 193 F1
  Broughton CH4 .... 140 B3
  Cheadle SK8 .... 239 D6
  Chester CH2, CH4 .... 119 D2
  Elton CH2 .... 72 A2
  Goldborne WA3 .... 3 F3
  Macclesfield SK10 .... 112 C4
  Runcorn WA7 .... 49 E4
  Winsford CW7 .... 127 D1
Lime Kiln La ST7 .... 194 C1

Lime St Congleton CW12 .. 156 B1
  Crewe CW1 .... 190 B3
  Ellesmere Port L65 .... 70 B4
Lime Tree Ave
  Congleton CW12 .... 156 A2
  Crewe CW1 .... 190 C3
Lime Tree Cl CH1 .... 95 D4
Lime Tree Dr CH3 .... 180 C1
Lime Tree Gr L60 .... 41 E4
Lime Tree La WA16 .... 29 E3
Lime Trees Prim Sch
  M33 .... 242 E5
Lime View SK11 .... 112 B1
Lime Wlk Partington M31 .. 11 E1
  Wilmslow SK9 .... 34 B1
Limefield Ave WA13 .... 18 C1
Limehurst Gr L62 .... 43 E3
Limekiln La WA5 .... 6 C2
Limekiln Row WA7 .... 50 A4
Limes La WA4 .... 52 B3
Limes The WA4 .... 4 C2
Limetree Ave
  Warrington, Paddington WA1 .. 17 D4
  Warrington, Stockton Heath
  WA4 .... 16 A1
Limeways WA4 .... 26 C3
Limewood Cres WA8 .... 78 A2
Limewood Gr CW8 .... 78 A2
Lincoln Ave Cheadle SK8 .. 34 A4
  Irlam M44 .... 11 E2
Lincoln Cl Goldborne WA3 .. 4 B4
  Macclesfield SK10 .... 86 C1
  Rainow SK10 .... 88 C3
  Runcorn WA7 .... 49 E3
  Warrington WA1 .... 17 F3
Lincoln Dr CH2 .... 119 D3
Lincoln Gr M33 .... 242 F6
Lincoln Pl SK10 .... 86 C1
Lincoln Rd Blacon CH1 .. 117 F3
  Ellesmere Port L66 .... 69 E2
  Kidsgrove ST7 .... 194 C1
  Wilmslow SK9 .... 34 C1
Lincoln Rise SK6 .... 241 A1
Lincoln Sq WA8 .... 13 D1
Lincoln St CW1 .... 190 A3
Lincoln Wlk SK10 .... 86 C1
Lincombe Hey SK10 .... 87 E4
Lincombe Rd M22 .... 33 E4
Lindale Cl CW12 .... 157 D3
Linden Ave WA15 .... 238 E5
Linden Cl
  Congleton CW12 .... 179 D4
  Denton M34 .... 241 A7
  Ellesmere Port CH1 .... 94 C4
  Warrington WA1 .... 17 E4
Linden Ct 2 Sandbach CW11 .. 174 C2
  Widnes WA8 .... 12 C2
Linden Dr Biddulph ST6 .. 179 E1
  Crewe CW1 .... 190 C2
  Helsby WA6 .... 73 D1
  Mickle Trafford CH2 .... 96 C1
Linden Gr Broughton CH4 .. 140 B3
  Cheadle Hulme SK7 .... 35 E2
  Chester CH2 .... 119 D2
Linden Rd M34 .... 241 A7
Linden Road Prim Sch
  M34 .... 241 A7
Linden Way High Lane SK6 .. 38 A4
  Widnes WA8 .... 12 C2
Lindfield Cl WA4 .... 25 D3
Lindfield Est N SK9 .... 60 A3
Lindfield Est S SK9 .... 60 A3
Lindi Ave WA4 .... 17 E1
Lindisfarne Ave
  Ellesmere Port L65 .... 70 B1
  Goldborne WA3 .... 4 B4
Lindisfarne Cl CW10 .... 128 A1
Lindisfarne Dr SK12 .... 36 B2
Lindley Ave WA4 .... 16 C2
Lindop Cl WA16 .... 57 E1
Lindop Rd WA15 .... 238 F1
Lindow Cty Prim Sch
  SK9 .... 59 E2
Lindow Fold Dr SK9 .... 59 E3
Lindow La SK9 .... 59 F4
Lindow Par SK9 .... 59 F3
Lindow St M33 .... 242 F5
Lindrick Cl SK10 .... 87 E2
Lindrum Ave SK11 .... 112 B3
Linds Worth Cl WA5 .... 15 E3
Lindsay St SK15 .... 242 E1
Lindsay Way ST7 .... 193 D2
Lindsay Wlk CW8 .... 102 A2
Lindsell Rd WA14 .... 238 C8
Linear View WA1 .... 2 B1
Linen Hall Pl CH1 .... 237 D2
Lines Rd M44 .... 11 F4
Lingdale Rd SK8 .... 239 F2
Lingdale Wlk SK11 .... 112 B3
Lingfield Cl SK10 .... 87 E2
Lingfield Dr CW1 .... 190 B4
Lingfield Rd WA7 .... 22 C1
Lingley Green Ave WA5 .. 14 B4
Lingley Rd WA5 .... 14 B3
Linglongs Ave SK23 .... 65 E3
Linglongs Rd SK23 .... 65 E3
Lingmell Gdns CW4 .... 129 F2
Lingwell Rd WA8 .... 12 B1
Lingwood Rd WA5 .... 14 C3
Link The SK9 .... 34 B2
Links Ave L66 .... 69 E4
Links Cl L63 .... 43 D3
Links Rd Romiley SK6 .. 241 D2
  Wilmslow SK9 .... 59 F2

Linkside Ave WA2 ... 8 A3
Linkside Way CH1 ... 94 C4
Linksway Chester CH2 ... 118 B4
Congleton CW12 ... 178 C4
Gatley SK8 ... 239 A4
Linksway Cl CW12 ... 178 C4
Linkway WA7 ... 49 E4
Linley Gr Alsager ST7 ... 193 F2
Stockport SK3 ... 240 D1
Linley La ST7 ... 194 A1
Linley Rd Alsager ST7 ... 193 F1
Cheadle Hulme SK8 ... 35 D4
Kidsgrove ST7 ... 210 B4
Sale M33 ... 242 B7
Linley Trad Est ST7 ... 194 B1
Linnards La
Higher Wincham CW9, WA16 . 80 A3
Plumley CW9, WA16 ... 80 A3
Linnet Cl Newton-le-W WA12 ... 2 B2
Warrington WA2 ... 8 B2
Winsford CW7 ... 150 A4
Linnet Gr Macclesfield SK10 ... 87 D1
Warrington WA3 ... 9 F2
Linnets Way L60 ... 40 C4
Linton Cl CW1 ... 190 A4
Linton Cl WA16 ... 57 E1
Linton Gdns WA4 ... 26 B2
Linton Rd M33 ... 242 C8
Linwood Ave WA4 ... 26 B4
Linwood Cl WA7 ... 50 B3
Lion St CW12 ... 156 B1
Lisburn Ave M33 ... 242 A5
Liskeard Cl WA7 ... 50 A3
Liskeard Dr SK7 ... 35 F4
Lismore Ave SK3 ... 240 B4
Lismore Wlk M22 ... 33 F4
Lisson Gr WA15 ... 238 E2
Lister Rd WA7 ... 23 E2
Litherland Rd M33 ... 242 E5
Litter La CW7 ... 125 F1
Little Abbey Gateway CH1 237 D3
Little Aston Cl SK10 ... 87 E2
Little Bollington CE Contr Prim Sch WA14 ... 20 A1
Little Budworth Ctry Pk CW6 ... 147 E4
Little Delph WA11 ... 1 B4
Little Egerton St 5 SK1 ... 240 E6
Little Gn L66 ... 69 E2
Little Heath Cl CW3 ... 230 A3
Little Heath La WA14 ... 20 B3
Little Heath Rd
Chester CH3 ... 119 F1
Christleton CH3 ... 142 C4
Little La L64 ... 41 D1
Little Leigh Cty Prim Sch CW8 ... 77 E3
Little Meadow Cl SK10 ... 87 D4
Little Meadow Rd WA14 ... 238 B1
Little Moreton Hall CW12 .. 177 F1
Little Moss Cl ST7 ... 194 C3
Little Moss La ST7 ... 194 C3
Little Roodee CH5 ... 139 D4
Little St Congleton CW12 ... 156 B1
3 Macclesfield SK11 ... 112 B4
Little St John St CH1 ... 237 E2
Little Stanney La CH2 ... 95 F4
Little Sutton CE Contr Prim Sch L66 ... 69 D3
Little Sutton Sta L66 ... 69 E3
Little Underbank 1 SK1 ... 240 F5
Little Wissage L66 ... 69 F1
Littlebourne WA7 ... 50 C4
Littlecote Ave WA4 ... 26 B2
Littledale Rd WA5 ... 14 B4
Littledales La CW8 ... 102 C2
Littlegate WA7 ... 49 F4
Littler Grange Ct CW7 ... 126 A1
Littler Rd WA11 ... 1 A3
Littlestone Cl WA8 ... 13 D2
Littleton Cl Davenham CW9 . 103 F2
Great Sankey WA5 ... 15 E2
Littleton La CH3 ... 119 F1
Littondale Cl CW12 ... 157 D3
Liverpool Pl WA8 ... 12 B1
Liverpool Rd Backford CH1 ... 95 D2
Chester CH2 ... 118 B3
Great Sankey WA5 ... 15 E2
Haydock WA11 ... 1 A4
Irlam M44 ... 11 F3
Kidsgrove ST7 ... 195 D1
Neston L64 ... 41 F1
Newcastle-u-L ST5 ... 210 B1
Warrington WA5 ... 15 E2
Widnes WA8 ... 12 B1
Willaston L64 ... 41 F2
Liverpool Rd E
Kidsgrove ST7 ... 194 C1
Lawton-gate ST7 ... 194 C1
Liverpool Rd W ST7 ... 194 A2
Liverpool Row WA12 ... 7 E4
Liverpool St CW9 ... 104 B4
Livingstone Cl
Great Sankey WA5 ... 15 E4
Macclesfield SK11 ... 111 F4
Livingstone Rd L65 ... 70 B4
Livingstone Way CW10 ... 151 E3
Llanberis Rd SK8 ... 239 E1
Llandaff Cl L66 ... 69 F1
Llandovery Cl CW7 ... 149 D4
Llanfair Rd 7 SK3 ... 240 C4
Lloyd Ave SK8 ... 239 A6
Lloyd Cl CH3 ... 180 C1
Lloyd Cres WA12 ... 1 C2
Lloyd Dr L65 ... 70 B1
Lloyd Gdns WA14 ... 238 D3
Lloyd Pl CH1 ... 117 F2
Lloyd Sq 6 WA14 ... 238 D4
Lloyd St
Altrincham WA14 & WA15 ... 238 D4
Stockport SK4 ... 240 D7
Lloyd's Ct WA14 ... 238 D4
Llyndir La LL12 ... 162 A1
Llys Caer CH4 ... 139 D2
Llys Derwen CH4 ... 161 D4
Loachbrook Ave CW12 ... 156 A1
Lobelia Gr WA7 ... 49 F3
Loch St WA7 ... 23 D2
Lochinvar Ave L66 ... 68 C3
Lochleven Rd CW2 ... 206 A4
Lochmaben Cl CW4 ... 130 A1
Lock La M31 ... 11 F2
Lock Rd Altrincham WA14 ... 238 C6
Bebington L62 ... 44 A4
Warrington WA1 ... 16 C3
Locker Ave WA2 ... 8 A1
Lockerbie Cl WA2 ... 8 C2
Lockett Rd WA8 ... 13 D2
Lockett St WA4 ... 16 B2
Lockgate East WA7 ... 24 B1
Lockgate West WA7 ... 24 A1
Locking Stumps Cty Prim Sch WA3 ... 9 E2
Locking Stumps La WA3 ... 9 D2
Lockitt St CW2 ... 190 B2
Locksley Cl SK4 ... 240 C6
Lockton La WA5 ... 15 F4
Lodge Brow SK10 ... 63 D1
Lodge Cl WA13 ... 19 D2
Lodge Dr Moulton CW9 ... 126 C4
Winsford CW7 ... 127 D1
Lodge Hollow WA6 ... 73 D2
Lodge La Antrobus CW9 ... 54 A3
Cronton WA8 ... 12 A2
Dutton WA4 ... 76 B4
Hartford CW8 ... 103 D2
Hatherton CW5 ... 220 A2
Hyde SK14 ... 241 D8
Lostock CW9 ... 80 A1
Newton-le-W WA11 ... 2 A4
Runcorn WA7 ... 49 F4
Saughall CH1 ... 94 A1
Warrington WA5 ... 15 F4
Lodge Rd Alsager ST7 ... 193 E2
Kidsgrove ST7 ... 210 B3
Knutsford WA16 ... 57 E2
Sandbach CW11 ... 174 C3
Widnes WA8 ... 22 A4
Lodgefields Cty Prim Sch CW2 ... 189 F2
Lodgefields Dr CW2 ... 189 F2
Lodmore La SY13 ... 233 E3
Lofthouse Gate WA8 ... 12 C2
Lomas Sq SK11 ... 112 B3
Lomas St SK3 ... 240 D3
Lomax Rd CW5 ... 205 E3
Lomond Gr L65 ... 69 F2
London Pl 13 SK1 ... 240 F5
London Rd Adlington SK10 ... 62 B3
Alderley Edge SK9 ... 60 A1
Allostock WA16 ... 107 D3
Appleton WA4 ... 26 B3
Blakenhall CW5 ... 220 B2
Brereton Green CW4 ... 130 B1
Bridgemere CW5 ... 232 A3
Davenham CW9 ... 104 A1
Davenham CW9 ... 104 A1
Frodsham WA6 ... 74 A4
Hatherton CW5 ... 220 B2
Holmes Chapel CW4 ... 130 B1
Macclesfield SK11 ... 112 B2
Nantwich CW5 ... 204 C3
Northwich CW9 ... 103 F4
Prestbury SK10 ... 62 A1
Sandbach CW11 ... 174 B4
Stapeley CW5 ... 205 D2
Sutton Lane Ends SK11 ... 112 B2
Warrington WA4 ... 26 B3
Woore CW5 ... 232 A3
London Rd S SK12 ... 36 B2
London Rd Terr SK11 ... 112 B3
London Row WA12 ... 7 E4
London Sq 10 SK1 ... 240 F5
Loney St SK11 ... 112 B4
Long Acre CW8 ... 77 E1
Long Acres Rd L64 ... 41 F1
Long Barn La WA1 ... 17 E4
Long Croft La SK8 ... 34 C4
Long Hill SK23 ... 65 F1
Long La Alpraham CW6 ... 169 F2
Bickerton SY14 ... 199 F2
Bollington SK10 ... 63 D1
Burland CW5 ... 203 D4
Chester CH2 ... 119 D3
Faddiley CW6 ... 186 B2
Hargrave CH3 ... 143 E1
Haughton Moss CW6 ... 186 B2
Huxley CH3 ... 166 B4
Kidsgrove ST7 ... 195 F2
Middlewich CW10 ... 151 E4
Peover WA16 ... 107 E4
Saughall CH1 ... 94 A1
Spurstow CW6 ... 186 B2
Tilston SY14 ... 198 A2
Warrington WA2 ... 8 A1
Waverton CH3 ... 143 E1
Wettenhall CW7 ... 170 B3
Whaley Bridge SK23 ... 65 F2
Long La S CW10 ... 151 E4
Long Lane Cty Prim Sch WA2 ... 8 A1
Long Looms CH3 ... 120 C3
Long Marl Dr SK9 ... 34 C2
Long Meadow L60 ... 40 C3
Long Meadow Pas SK14 ... 241 D7
Long Row ST7 ... 195 D1
Long Shoot Rd SK11 ... 108 C1
Long Spinney WA7 ... 50 B4
Long Valley Rd ST6 ... 179 E1
Long Wlk M31 ... 11 E1
Longacre St SK11 ... 112 B4
Longacres Rd WA15 ... 32 B4
Longbarn Bvd WA2 ... 9 E1
Longbarn Cty Prim Sch WA3 ... 9 D1
Longbenton Way WA7 ... 24 A2
Longburgh Cl CH2 ... 118 C2
Longbutt La WA13 ... 18 C1
Longbutts La SK11 ... 111 F1
Longclough Rd ST5 ... 210 B1
Longcroft Dr WA14 ... 238 B4
Longdale Dr CH1 ... 117 E3
Longden Ct SK7 ... 35 F3
Longden La SK11 ... 113 D3
Longden St SK11 ... 112 C4
Longdin St WA4 ... 16 C2
Longdown Rd CW12 ... 155 F2
Longfield Ave Cheadle SK8 ... 34 B4
Chester CH2 ... 118 B4
Longfield Gdns M44 ... 11 E2
Longford St Crewe CW2 ... 190 B1
Warrington WA2 ... 16 A4
Longhill La CW3 ... 230 C3
Longhorn Cl CW10 ... 128 B1
Longlands Dr SK22 ... 39 D4
Longlands Rd SK22 ... 39 D4
Longley Ave CW6 ... 122 B3
Longlooms Rd L65 ... 70 B1
Longmeade Gdns SK9 ... 60 B3
Longmeadow
Cheadle Hulme SK7 ... 35 E4
Weaverham CW8 ... 102 B4
Longmoss Cl CW10 ... 151 D4
Longmynd Rise CW7 ... 149 D4
Longnor Rd Cheadle SK8 ... 34 B4
Hazel Grove SK7 ... 36 C4
Longridge WA16 ... 57 E2
Longridge Ave SK15 ... 242 D4
Longridge Trad Est WA16 ... 57 E2
Longsdon Cl ST5 ... 210 B1
Longshaw St WA5 ... 7 F1
Longshut La SK1 & SK2 ... 240 F3
Longshut La W SK2 ... 240 F3
Longsides Rd WA15 ... 32 B4
Longsight La SK8 ... 34 C3
Longsight St SK4 ... 240 D6
Longsons The SK5 ... 240 F7
Longston Ave WA3 ... 3 E4
Longstone La CW6 ... 124 C2
Longview Ave ST7 ... 193 F2
Longwood Cl
Middlewich CW10 ... 151 E4
Romiley SK6 ... 241 E3
Longwood Rd Appleton WA4 26 C3
Stretton WA4 ... 26 C3
Lonsdale Cl WA8 ... 22 B4
Looe Cl WA8 ... 12 C1
Looms The L64 ... 41 D1
Loonies Ct 1 SK1 ... 240 F4
Loont The CW7 ... 149 E4
Lord Nelson St WA1 ... 16 B3
Lord St Bollington SK10 ... 88 A4
Chester CH3 ... 118 C1
Crewe CW2 ... 190 B2
Croft WA3 ... 9 D4
Macclesfield SK11 ... 112 B4
Newton-le-W WA12 ... 2 A2
Runcorn WA7 ... 22 C2
Stockport SK1 ... 240 F5
Warrington WA4 ... 16 A2
Lord's St M44 ... 11 E3
Lords La WA3 ... 9 E2
Lords Mill Rd CW2 ... 206 A2
Lordship La WA6 ... 73 D4
Lordshire Pl ST7 ... 195 F1
Loreto Convent Gram Sch WA14 ... 238 C5
Loreto Convent Prep Sch WA14 ... 238 C5
Lorland Rd SK3 ... 240 B3
Lorne Gr SK3 ... 240 E2
Lorne St CH1 ... 237 D3
Lorraine St ST7 ... 195 F1
Lostock Ave Sale M33 ... 242 E6
Warrington WA5 ... 15 F4
Lostock Gralam CE Contr Prim Sch CW9 ... 80 A1
Lostock Gralam Sta CW9 ... 80 A1
Lostock Hall Cty Prim Sch SK12 ... 36 A2
Lostock Hall Rd SK12 ... 36 A2
Lostock Hollow CW9 ... 80 A1
Lostock Rd SK12 ... 36 B1
Lostock Way SK9 ... 34 B2
Lottery St SK3 ... 240 D5
Louise St CH1 ... 237 D3
Loushers La WA4 ... 16 B1
Loushers Lane Day Sch WA4 ... 16 B1
Lovage Cl WA2 ... 9 E1
Lovat Dr WA16 ... 82 A4
Love La Hassall Green CW11 176 B2
Nantwich CW5 ... 204 C3
Stockport SK4 ... 240 E6
Love St CH1 ... 237 E2
Lovel Terr WA8 ... 22 A3
Lovell Dr SK14 ... 241 F8
Lovely La WA5 ... 15 F3
Low Hill WA6 ... 97 E3
Low Leighton Rd SK22 ... 39 E4
Low Meadow SK23 ... 65 E4
Lowcross La SY14 ... 198 B2
Lowe Ave Congleton CW12 .. 156 C1
Warrington WA4 ... 16 C2
Lowe Cres CW9 ... 53 E2
Lowe Dr WA16 ... 57 D1
Lowe St Denton M34 ... 241 B7
Goldborne WA3 ... 3 D4
Macclesfield SK11 ... 112 B4
15 Stockport SK1 ... 240 F5
Lower Ash Rd ST7 ... 194 C1
Lower Bank St 18 SK11 ... 112 C4
Lower Beech Cotts SK10 ... 87 E1
Lower Bennett St SK14 ... 241 C8
Lower Bridge St CH4 ... 237 E1
Lower Brook St CH5 ... 91 E1
Lower Bury St SK4 ... 240 D6
Lower Carrs 21 SK1 ... 240 F5
Lower Church St WA8 ... 23 D3
Lower Cl L26 ... 21 D4
Lower Darwin St CW8 ... 103 F3
Lower Exchange St SK11 ... 112 B4
Lower Field Rd CH4 ... 141 D3
Lower Fold M34 ... 241 A6
Lower Greenshall La SK12 .. 38 C3
Lower Hague SK22 ... 38 C4
Lower Haigh St CW7 ... 149 E4
Lower Hall La CH3 ... 182 B1
Lower Hall Mews CH3 ... 182 B1
Lower Heath CW12 ... 156 C2
Lower Heath Ave CW12 ... 156 C2
Lower High St ST7 ... 195 E4
Lower Hillgate SK1 ... 240 F5
Lower House La WA8 ... 22 C4
Lower La CW6 ... 147 D2
Lower Macclesfield Rd SK23 65 F3
Lower Meadow Rd SK9 ... 34 C2
Lower Mersey St L65 ... 70 B4
Lower Moat Cl SK4 ... 240 E7
Lower Park Cres SK12 ... 36 B3
Lower Park Cty Prim Sch SK12 ... 36 B2
Lower Park Rd Chester CH4 237 F2
Poynton SK12 ... 36 A3
Lower Park St CW12 ... 156 C2
Lower Peover CE Aided Prim Sch WA16 ... 81 F1
Lower Rake La WA6 ... 73 D2
Lower Rd Halewood L26 ... 21 E4
Widnes WA8 ... 21 E3
Lower Robin Hood La WA6 73 D2
Lower Sandy La CH3 ... 199 E4
Lower Wash La WA4 ... 16 C2
Lowerfield Rd SK10 ... 87 F1
Lowerhouse SK10 ... 87 F4
Lowerlea SK12 ... 38 B3
Lowes La SK11 ... 111 F1
Lowes The WA14 ... 238 B1
Loweswater Cl WA2 ... 8 A2
Loweswater Cres WA11 ... 1 A3
Loweswater Rd SK8 ... 239 B3
Lowfield Gdns WA3 ... 5 E4
Lowfield Gr SK2 ... 240 F3
Lowfield Rd SK2 & SK3 ... 240 E3
Lowfields Ave L62 ... 43 F2
Lowfields Cl L62 ... 43 F2
Lowland Way WA16 ... 82 A4
Lowlands Rd 3 WA7 ... 22 C1
Lowry Cl WA5 ... 15 E3
Lowther Ave WA3 ... 4 C2
Lowther St SK10 ... 88 B4
Lowton Gdns WA3 ... 3 D3
Lowton Jun & Inf Sch WA3 .. 4 A4
Lowton Rd WA3 ... 3 E4
Lowton Sch WA3 ... 4 A4
Lowton West Cty Prim Sch WA3 ... 3 E4
Loxdale Dr L65 ... 69 F2
Loxley Cl Great Sankey WA5 .. 15 D4
Macclesfield SK11 ... 112 A4
Loyola Hey L35 ... 12 C4
Lucerne Cl CH3 ... 142 A3
Lucy St SK3 ... 240 E4
Ludford Cl ST5 ... 210 B1
Ludford St CW1 ... 190 B3
Ludlow Ave CW1 ... 190 C2
Ludlow Cl
Macclesfield SK10 ... 87 F1
Winsford CW7 ... 149 D4
Ludlow Cres WA7 ... 49 D4
Ludlow Dr L65 ... 70 C2
Ludlow Rd CH1 ... 118 A3
Ludwell Cl CH4 ... 141 D3
Lugsdale Rd WA8 ... 23 D4
Luke's Ave WA3 ... 3 E4
Lulworth Cl CW7 ... 149 D4
Lum Head Jun Sch SK8 ... 239 B3
Lumb Brook Rd WA4 ... 26 C4
Lumb Cl SK7 ... 35 F3
Lumb La SK7 ... 35 F3
Lumber La WA5 ... 6 C4
Lumley Pl CH1 ... 237 E2
Lumley Rd Chester CH2 ... 118 B2
Macclesfield SK11 ... 111 F4
Lumley Wlk L24 ... 21 F1
Lumn Hollow 4 SK14 ... 241 E6
Lumn Rd SK14 ... 241 E6
Lumpy St CW12 ... 156 B2
Lundy Dr CH2 ... 95 E4
Lune Cl CW12 ... 157 D1
Lune Way WA8 ... 12 B1
Lunehurst WA3 ... 3 F4
Lunt Ave CW2 ... 190 B1
Lunt's Heath Rd WA8 ... 13 D3
Lunts Heath Cty Prim Sch WA8 ... 13 D3
Lupin Dr Haydock WA11 ... 1 C3
Huntington CH3 ... 142 A3
Lupus Way L66 ... 69 F2
Lurgan Ave M33 ... 242 C5
Luscombe Cl L26 ... 21 D4
Lutener St WA14 ... 238 C8
Luther Gr WA9 ... 1 A1
Luton Rd L65 ... 70 A3
Luton St WA8 ... 23 D4
Lutyens Cl SK11 ... 111 F4
Lyceum Cl CW1 ... 190 A4
Lyceum Way CW1 ... 190 A4
Lychgate WA4 ... 25 F4
Lycroft Cl WA7 ... 49 D3
Lydbury Cl WA5 ... 7 E1
Lydden Rd L65 ... 70 A4
Lydgate Cl Denton M34 ... 241 B5
Wistaston CW2 ... 205 F4
Lydiat La SK9 ... 60 A1
Lydiate La Runcorn WA7 ... 48 B4
Willaston L64 ... 42 C1
Lydiate The L60 ... 40 C4
Lydney Ave SK8 ... 34 B4
Lydstep Ct WA5 ... 7 F1
Lydyett La CW8 ... 78 A2
Lymcote Dr CW8 ... 103 D2
Lyme Ave Macclesfield SK11 112 B3
Wilmslow SK9 ... 34 A1
Lyme Comm Inf Sch WA12 ... 1 C2
Lyme Gr Altrincham WA14 ... 238 C4
Lymm WA13 ... 18 B1
Romiley SK6 ... 241 D2
Stockport SK2 & SK3 ... 240 F3
Lyme Green Bsns Pk SK11 112 B2
Lyme Green Settlement SK11 ... 112 B1
Lyme Hall SK12 ... 38 A1
Lyme Park Ctry Pk SK12 ... 38 A1
Lyme Rd Disley SK12 ... 38 A3
Poynton SK12 ... 37 E2
Lyme St Haydock WA11 ... 1 C3
Newton-le-W WA12 ... 1 C2
Lymewood Dr Disley SK12 ... 38 B3
Wilmslow SK9 ... 60 C4
Lymm Cherry Tree Cty Prim Sch WA13 ... 18 B1
Lymm Cl SK3 ... 240 D2
Lymm High (VC) Sch WA13 19 D2
Lymm Rd
Little Bollington WA14 ... 20 A1
Warrington WA4 ... 17 F2
Lymm Statham Cty Prim Sch WA13 ... 18 B2
Lymmhay La WA13 ... 18 C2
Lymmington Ave WA13 ... 18 B2
Lynalls Cl CW12 ... 155 F2
Lynbrook Rd CW1 ... 190 C2
Lyncastle Rd WA4 ... 27 E2
Lyncastle Way WA4 ... 27 E2
Lyncombe Cl SK8 ... 35 D3
Lyndale Ave Bebington L62 ... 43 F2
Warrington WA2 ... 16 B4
Lyndene Gdns SK8 ... 239 B6
Lyndhurst Cl SK9 ... 59 E3
Lyndon Gr WA7 ... 49 D4
Lyngard Cl SK9 ... 34 C1
Lyngarth Ho 1 WA14 ... 238 E6
Lynham Ave WA5 ... 15 D3
Lynn Ave Kidsgrove ST7 ... 210 B4
Sale M33 ... 242 D8
Lynn Cl WA7 ... 49 E4
Lynn Gr SK11 ... 112 B3
Lynndene L66 ... 69 E4
Lynneal Ave L66 ... 69 E1
Lynside Wlk M22 ... 33 F4
Lynthorpe Ave M44 ... 11 E3
Lynton Ave M44 ... 11 F3
Lynton Cl Heswall L60 ... 41 D3
Penketh WA5 ... 14 C2
Lynton Cres WA8 ... 12 C1
Lynton Gr
Altrincham WA15 ... 238 F5
Haslington CW1 ... 191 E3
Lynton La SK9 ... 60 A1
Lynton Park Rd SK8 ... 34 C4
Lynton Pl Alsager ST7 ... 193 E2
Broughton CH4 ... 139 D2
Lynton Rd SK8 ... 239 C5
Lynton Way CW2 ... 206 A4
Lyntonvale Ave SK8 ... 239 B6
Lynwood WA15 ... 32 A4
Lynwood Ave WA3 ... 3 F3
Lynwood Gr M33 ... 242 C7
Lynwood Rd CH1 ... 117 F3
Lyon Ind Est WA14 ... 238 B7
Lyon Rd WA14 ... 238 C7
Lyon St Chester CH2 ... 237 E3
Crewe CW1 ... 190 B2
Macclesfield SK11 ... 112 B4
Warrington WA4 ... 16 C2
Lyon's La WA4 ... 26 C3
Lyons Fold M33 ... 242 B8
Lyons Rd WA5 ... 15 D2
Lyster Cl WA3 ... 9 F2
Lytham Dr SK7 ... 36 A4
Lytham Rd SK8 ... 239 B1
Lytham St SK3 ... 240 F2
Lytherton Ave M44 ... 11 E2
Lythgoes La WA2 ... 16 A3

Mableden Cl SK8 ... 34 B4
Mablins La CW1 ... 190 A4
Mablins Lane Cty Prim Sch CW1 ... 190 A4
Mabs Ct OL6 ... 242 A2
Macarthur Dr WA5 ... 15 E3
Macclesfield Coll
Macclesfield SK11 ... 112 A3
Macclesfield SK11 ... 112 B4
Macclesfield District General Hospl SK11 ... 112 A4

Macclesfield Rd
Alderley Edge SK9 .... 85 E4
Congleton CW12 .... 156 C3
Eaton CW12 .... 134 A1
Hazel Grove SK7 .... 36 C4
Holmes Chapel CW4 .... 130 C2
Kettleshulme SK23, SK10 .... 64 B2
Nether Alderley SK9 .... 85 E4
Prestbury SK10 .... 86 C2
Rainow SK10 .... 89 D4
Whaley Bridge SK23 .... 65 E3
Wilmslow SK9 .... 60 B3
Macclesfield Sta SK11 .... 112 B4
Macdermott Rd WA8 .... 22 C3
Macdonald Rd M44 .... 11 F4
Mackenzie Ind Pk SK3 & SK8 .... 240 B2
Mackeson Dr OL6 .... 242 B4
Mackeson Rd OL6 .... 242 B4
Macon Ct CW1 .... 190 C2
Macon Ind Pk CW1 .... 190 C2
Macon Way CW1 .... 190 C2
Maddock St ST7 .... 209 E1
Maddocks Hill CW8 .... 100 C3
Madeley Cl Altrincham WA14 .... 31 F4
Broughton CW2 .... 139 E2
Madeley St CW2 .... 190 B1
Madeline McKenna Ct WA8 .... 12 B2
Madras Rd SK3 .... 240 C3
Madron Ave SK10 .... 86 B1
Maelor Cl L63 .... 43 E3
Mag La WA16 .... 28 C3
Magdala Pl CW9 .... 104 B4
Maggoty La SK11 .... 111 E1
Magnolia Cl
Ellesmere Port L66 .... 69 F1
Partington M31 .... 11 F1
Warrington WA1 .... 17 F4
Magnolia Dr WA7 .... 49 F2
Magnolia Rise SK10 .... 86 C3
Magpie Cres ST7 .... 195 D1
Mahood St SK3 .... 240 D3
Maidenhills CW10 .... 128 B1
Maidstone Cl SK10 .... 87 D1
Maidwell Cl CW7 .... 127 D2
Main Cl WA11 .... 1 A3
Main La WA3 .... 3 F2
Main Rd Broughton CH4 .... 139 D2
Goostrey CW4 .... 107 F1
Higher Kinnerton CH4 .... 161 D4
Langley SK11 .... 113 E2
Moulton CW9 .... 126 C4
Norton in Hales TF9 .... 236 B1
Shavington CW2 .... 206 A2
Weston CW2 .... 207 E3
Worleston CW5 .... 188 C3
Wybunbury CW5 .... 220 A4
Main St Frodsham WA6 .... 74 A4
Great Barrow CH3 .... 120 C3
Hyde SK14 .... 241 D8
Runcorn WA7 .... 49 F4
Maintree Cres L24 .... 21 D2
Mainwaring Dr
Broughton CH4 .... 140 B4
Wilmslow SK9 .... 60 B4
Mainwaring Rd WA16 .... 108 A4
Mairesfield Ave WA4 .... 17 D1
Maisterson Ct CW5 .... 204 C3
Maitland Way CH1 .... 117 E2
Maitland Wood Cl CW9 .... 104 B4
Maizefield Cl M33 .... 242 F6
Major Cross St 15 WA8 .... 23 D4
Makepeace Cl CH3 .... 119 E2
Malaga Ave M90 .... 33 D4
Malakoff St SK15 .... 242 B1
Malam Dr CW9 .... 104 B3
Malbank CW5 .... 204 C3
Malbank Rd CW2 .... 189 F2
Malbank Sch CW5 .... 204 B3
Malcolm Ave WA2 .... 8 B1
Malcolm Cres L63 .... 43 E3
Malcolm St WA7 .... 23 D1
Malgam Dr M20 .... 239 B8
Malhamdale Rd CW12 .... 157 D3
Malin Cl L24 .... 21 E1
Maliston Rd WA5 .... 15 D3
Mallaig Cl CW4 .... 130 B1
Mallard Cl Knutsford WA16 .... 57 D1
Runcorn WA7 .... 49 F3
Warrington WA2 .... 8 B2
Mallard Cres SK12 .... 36 A2
Mallard Gn WA14 .... 238 B8
Mallard La WA3 .... 9 F2
Mallard Way CW7 .... 149 E3
Mallory Ct Altrincham WA14 238 C1
Congleton CW12 .... 155 D2
Mallory Rd L65 .... 70 A2
Mallory Wlk CH4 .... 162 A4
Mallow Cl CH3 .... 142 A3
Mallow Wlk M31 .... 11 F1
Mallowdale Cl CW4 .... 43 F3
Malmesbury Ave SK8 .... 35 D3
Malmesbury Cl
Middlewich CW10 .... 128 A1
Poynton SK12 .... 36 B2
Malmesbury Pk WA7 .... 24 B1
Malory Cl CW1 .... 190 C3
Malpas Alport Endowed Prim Sch SY14 .... 213 D2
Malpas Bishop Heber Cty High Sch SY14 .... 213 E3
Malpas Cl Northwich CW9 .... 104 B4
Wilmslow SK9 .... 34 C1
Malpas Dr WA5 .... 15 E2
Malpas Rd Ellesmere Port L65 69 F2
Northwich CW9 .... 104 B4
Runcorn WA7 .... 49 E4

Malpas Way WA5 .... 15 E2
Malt Kiln Rd WA16 .... 80 C2
Malt St WA16 .... 57 D1
Malta Rd CH2 .... 95 D1
Maltmans Rd WA13 .... 18 B2
Malton Ave WA3 .... 3 F4
Malton Cl WA8 .... 12 B3
Malton Dr Altrincham WA14 238 A6
Hazel Grove SK7 .... 36 B4
Malton Rd SK4 .... 240 A8
Malvern Ave L65 .... 70 B2
Malvern Cl
Congleton CW12 .... 155 F2
Great Sankey WA5 .... 15 D4
Shavington CW2 .... 206 A2
Stockport SK4 .... 240 D7
Malvern Dr
Altrincham WA14 .... 238 B5
Macclesfield SK10 .... 87 F2
Malvern Rd Blacon CH1 .... 118 A3
Knutsford WA16 .... 81 F4
St Helens WA9 .... 1 A1
Malvern Way CW7 .... 149 D4
Manchester Airport M90 .... 33 D3
Manchester Airport Sta M90 .... 33 D4
Manchester Bridge CW1 .. 190 C2
Manchester Met Univ, Crewe & Alsager Faculty CW1 .... 190 C2
Manchester Met Univ, Crewe & Alsager Faculty, Alsager Campus ST7 .... 193 D3
Manchester New Rd M31 .... 11 F2
Manchester Rd
Altrincham WA14 .... 238 D7
Cheadle M20, SK8 .... 239 D7
Congleton CW12 .... 156 C3
Denton SK14 .... 241 C2
Hollins Green WA3 .... 11 D1
Knutsford WA16 .... 56 C2
Lostock CW9 .... 79 E1
Macclesfield SK10 .... 87 E2
Northwich CW9 .... 79 E1
Partington M31 .... 11 F2
Reddish SK4 .... 240 E8
Warrington WA3 .... 18 A4
Warrington, Bruche WA1 .... 16 C4
Warrington, Woolston WA1 ... 17 E4
Wilmslow SK9 .... 34 B1
Manchester Row WA12 .... 7 E4
Mancroft Cl WA1 .... 17 F4
Mancunian Rd M34 .... 241 A5
Mandarin Gn WA14 .... 238 B8
Manifold Cl CW11 .... 174 C4
Manifold Dr SK6 .... 37 F3
Manley Cl Antrobus CW9 .... 53 E2
Holmes Chapel CW4 .... 130 A2
Northwich CW9 .... 104 A3
Manley Cty Prim Sch WA6 .. 99 D3
Manley Gdns WA5 .... 15 F3
Manley Gr SK3 .... 35 F3
Manley La
Dunham-on-t-H WA6 .... 97 F3
Manley WA6 .... 98 B2
Manley Rd Alvanley WA6 .... 98 C4
Frodsham WA6 .... 74 A2
Manley WA6 .... 99 D3
Warren SK11 .... 112 A3
Manley View CH2 .... 72 B2
Manna Dr CH2 .... 72 B2
Manners La L60 .... 40 C3
Manning La S CH2 .... 119 D3
Manning St CW2 .... 190 B1
Mannings La CH2 .... 119 D3
Manor Ave Crewe CW2 .... 190 A1
Goldborne WA3 .... 3 E4
Goostrey CW4 .... 107 F1
Marston CW9 .... 79 D3
Newton-le-W WA12 .... 1 C2
Manor Cl Bramhall SK7 .... 35 E4
Broughton CH5 .... 139 E4
Congleton CW12 .... 157 D1
Denton SK14 .... 241 B6
Great Barrow CH3 .... 120 C3
Neston L64 .... 66 B4
Warrington WA1 .... 17 E4
Wilmslow SK9 .... 59 F4
Manor Cres Broughton CH4 .. 139 E4
Knutsford WA16 .... 57 D1
Macclesfield SK10 .... 87 E2
Middlewich CW10 .... 151 E4
Manor Ct Crewe CW2 .... 190 A1
Goldborne WA3 .... 3 E4
Manor Dr Barnton CW8 .... 78 A1
Chester CH3 .... 119 E1
Northwich, Rudheath CW9 .. 104 B4
Manor Farm Cl CW2 .... 119 F4
Manor Farm Cres CH1 .... 94 A4
Manor Farm Ct CW5 .... 139 D4
Manor Farm Rd WA7 .... 24 B2
Manor Fell WA7 .... 50 A4
Manor Fields CW10 .... 151 E4
Manor Gdns SK9 .... 60 B4
Manor Gr CW8 .... 103 E3
Manor La Broughton CH5 .... 139 D4
Davenham CW9 .... 104 B1
Ellesmere Port L66 .... 69 E2
Holmes Chapel CW4 .... 130 B2
Middlewich CW10 .... 151 E4
Ollerton WA16 .... 82 C3
Manor Park Ave WA7 .... 24 B2
Manor Park Cty Prim Sch WA16 .... 57 E1
Manor Pk Great Barrow CH3 120 C3
Hawarden CH4 .... 139 D4
Manor Pk N WA16 .... 57 E1
Manor Pk S WA16 .... 57 E1

Manor Pl WA8 .... 12 A1
Manor Rd Altrincham WA15 . 238 E4
Bebington L62 .... 43 F3
Chester CH4 .... 141 D3
Cuddington CW8 .... 101 F1
Denton M34 .... 241 B5
Frodsham WA6 .... 49 E1
Haydock WA11 .... 1 C4
Lymm WA13 .... 18 C1
Mow Cop ST7 .... 195 E4
Nantwich CW5 .... 204 C3
Runcorn WA7 .... 23 E1
Sale M33 .... 242 B7
Sandbach CW11 .... 175 D3
Sealand CH5 .... 116 A3
Thornton Hough L63 .... 42 A4
Whaley Bridge SK23 .... 65 F3
Widnes WA8 .... 12 A1
Wilmslow SK9 .... 59 F4
Manor Rd N WA5 .... 204 C4
Manor Sq 5 CW7 .... 149 D4
Manor St CW8 .... 103 E3
Manor Way Crewe CW2 .... 190 B1
Sandbach CW11 .... 175 F3
Manora Rd CW9 .... 104 A4
Manorfield Cl CH1 .... 69 D1
Manorial Rd S L64 .... 66 B4
Manse Field Rd WA6 .... 75 D1
Manse Gdns WA12 .... 2 B2
Mansell Cl WA8 .... 13 E3
Mansfield Cl WA3 .... 10 A2
Mansfield Cty Prim Sch L65 .... 69 F2
Mansfield Rd
Ellesmere Port L65 .... 70 A1
Hyde SK14 .... 241 F5
Mansion Cl CW5 .... 204 C3
Mansion Dr WA16 .... 57 D1
Manston Rd WA5 .... 14 C2
Manuel Perez Rd WA5 .... 15 D3
Manvers St SK5 .... 240 E7
Manx St WA2 .... 16 A2
Maori Dr WA6 .... 74 A4
Maple Ave Alsager ST7 .... 193 F1
Cheadle SK8 .... 239 F2
Disley SK12 .... 39 D3
Ellesmere Port L66 .... 69 E3
Goldborne WA3 .... 3 F4
Haydock WA11 .... 1 A4
Kidsgrove ST7 .... 210 B4
Macclesfield SK11 .... 112 B3
Newcastle-u-L ST5 .... 210 C1
Newton-le-W WA12 .... 2 A2
Poynton SK12 .... 36 C2
Runcorn WA7 .... 49 E4
Sutton WA7 .... 50 A2
Widnes WA8 .... 13 D1
Maple Cl
Brereton Green CW11 .... 153 F2
Congleton CW12 .... 155 F2
Holmes Chapel CW4 .... 130 B2
Sandbach CW11 .... 175 E3
Maple Cres WA5 .... 14 C2
Maple Gr Barnton CW8 .... 78 A2
Bebington L62 .... 43 E4
Broughton CH4 .... 140 B3
Chester CH2 .... 119 D2
Crewe CW1 .... 190 C4
Ellesmere Port CH1 .... 95 D4
Northwich, Greenbank CW8 .... 103 E4
Warrington WA4 .... 16 B2
Winsford CW7 .... 127 D1
Maple La CW8 .... 101 F1
Maple Rd Alderley Edge SK9 60 A2
Bramhall SK7 .... 35 F3
Partington M31 .... 11 F2
Warrington WA1 .... 17 F4
Winwick WA2 .... 8 A3
Mapleton Dr WA7 .... 49 F2
Maplewood Gr CH1 .... 117 D4
Maplewood Rd SK9 .... 60 C4
Mapplewell Cres WA5 .... 15 D3
Marble Arch WA16 .... 57 D1
Marbury Ctry Pk CW9 .... 78 C3
Marbury Gdns L65 .... 69 F3
Marbury La CW9 .... 78 C3
Marbury Rd Chester CH3 .... 119 E1
Comberbach CW9 .... 78 B3
Marston CW9 .... 78 B3
Northwich CW9 .... 78 B3
Wilmslow SK9 .... 34 A1
Marbury St WA4 .... 16 B2
March Ave SK4 .... 240 B6
March St CW1 .... 190 C2
Marchbank Dr SK8 .... 239 C6
Marchwiel Rd L65 .... 70 B2
Marcien Way WA8 .... 12 C2
Marcliff Gr Knutsford WA16 .. 57 F1
Stockport SK4 .... 240 B6
Marcross Cl WA5 .... 7 F1
Mardale Ave WA2 .... 8 B2
Mardale Cl Congleton CW12 156 C1
Stalybridge SK15 .... 242 D3
Mardale Cres WA13 .... 18 C2
Mardale Ct WA4 .... 130 A1
Mardale Dr SK8 .... 239 B6
Mardon Cl WA16 .... 57 E2
Marfields Cty Prim Sch CW12 .... 156 B1
Marfords Ave L63 .... 43 E4
Margaret Ave WA1 .... 17 D4
Margaret Ct WA8 .... 23 D4
Margaret Danyers Coll SK8 .... 239 F3
Margaret Rd M34 .... 241 A8
Margaret's La L66 .... 69 D4

Margery Ave ST7 .... 194 C4
Marian Dr CH3 .... 142 A4
Marian Rd WA11 .... 1 C
Marie Cl CW5 .... 216 C2
Marigold Cl SK11 .... 111 F4
Marina Ave Denton M34 .... 241 A5
Great Sankey WA5 .... 15 E2
Marina Cl SK9 .... 34 B3
Marina Dr Chester CH2 .... 118 C4
Ellesmere Port L65 .... 70 A3
Warrington WA2 .... 8 B1
Marina Gr WA7 .... 23 D1
Marina La WA7 .... 50 C4
Marina Village WA7 .... 50 C4
Marina Ave M31 .... 11 E2
Marine Dr L60 .... 40 B4
Mariner Cl WA7 .... 50 B3
Marion Dr WA7 .... 48 C3
Maritime Cl WA12 .... 2 B3
Mark Ave L66 .... 69 E2
Mark Cl CH2 .... 118 C1
Mark Rake L62 .... 43 E4
Market Cl CW1 .... 190 B2
Market Ct CW6 .... 146 B1
Market Ctr The CW1 .... 190 B2
Market Gate WA1 .... 16 A3
Market Pl Bollington SK10 .. 88 A4
1 Hyde SK14 .... 241 D6
Macclesfield SK11 .... 112 B4
Stockport SK1 .... 240 F6
Winsford CW7 .... 126 C1
Market Sq Chester CH1 .... 237 D2
Congleton CW12 .... 156 C1
Crewe CW1 .... 190 B2
Sandbach CW11 .... 175 D3
Market St
Altrincham WA14 .... 238 D4
Congleton CW12 .... 156 B1
Crewe CW1 .... 190 B2
Crewe CW1 .... 190 B3
Disley SK12 .... 38 B3
Hyde SK14 .... 241 D6
Kidsgrove ST7 .... 195 D1
Nantwich CW5 .... 204 C3
New Mills SK22 .... 39 D4
Newton-le-W WA12 .... 2 A2
Northwich CW9 .... 103 F4
Stalybridge SK15 .... 242 D1
Whaley Bridge SK23 .... 65 F4
Widnes WA8 .... 23 D4
Market Way WA1 .... 16 A3
Markham Cl WA8 .... 13 D3
Markland St SK14 .... 241 E5
Marl Cft CH3 .... 142 A4
Marl Edge SK10 .... 87 D3
Marl Heys CH2 .... 118 C4
Marland Ave SK8 .... 239 F2
Marlborough Ave
Alderley Edge SK9 .... 60 A1
Winsford CW7 .... 126 B2
Marlborough Cl
Knutsford WA16 .... 57 E2
Macclesfield SK10 .... 87 E2
Wistaston CW2 .... 205 F4
Marlborough Cres
Warrington WA4 .... 16 C1
Widnes WA8 .... 13 D3
Marlborough Ct 20 SK11 .. 112 B4
Marlborough Cty Prim Sch The SK10 .... 87 E2
Marlborough Dr
Helsby WA6 .... 73 D1
Macclesfield SK10 .... 87 E2
Reddish SK4 .... 240 D8
Marlborough Rd
Altrincham WA14 .... 238 D2
Ellesmere Port L65 .... 70 B2
Sale M33 .... 242 B6
Marlborough Wlk L65 .... 70 B2
Marlcroft Ave SK4 .... 240 B6
Marler Rd SK14 .... 241 E8
Marley Ave CW1 .... 190 A4
Marley Cl WA15 .... 238 F7
Marley Dr M33 .... 242 A8
Marley Rd SK12 .... 36 C1
Marley Way CW4 .... 140 C4
Marlfield Rd
Altrincham WA15 .... 32 B4
Warrington WA4 .... 17 D1
Marline Ave L63 .... 43 E3
Marling Cl WA6 .... 74 B3
Marling Park WA8 .... 12 A1
Marlow Ave CH2 .... 118 B4
Marlow Cl Cheadle SK8 .... 239 F2
10 Sandbach CW11 .... 174 B3
Warrington WA3 .... 9 E3
Marlow Dr Altrincham WA14 . 20 C1
Wilmslow SK9 .... 34 B3
Marlowe Cl Blacon CH1 .... 118 A3
Widnes WA8 .... 12 C1
Marlowe Ct SK11 .... 112 B3
Marlowe Dr CW5 .... 204 C2
Marlowe Rd Neston L64 .... 66 C4
Northwich CW9 .... 104 B3
Marlston Ave CH4 .... 141 D3
Marlston Pl WA7 .... 49 D3
Marple Cres CW2 .... 189 F2
Marple Rd SK6 .... 104 B4
Marquis Dr SK8 .... 34 B4
Marrick Ave SK8 .... 239 C5
Marriott Rd CW11 .... 174 C3
Marriott St SK1 .... 240 F4
Marron Ave WA2 .... 8 A1
Marsden Ave WA4 .... 17 D2
Marsden Rd SK6 .... 241 C3
Marsden Terr 16 SK11 .... 112 B4
Marsh Ave ST7 .... 195 F1

Marsh Cl Alsager ST7 .... 193 D2
Stockport SK3 .... 240 D2
Marsh Gr ST6 .... 179 E2
Marsh Green Cl ST6 .... 179 E1
Marsh Green Rd
Biddulph ST6 .... 179 E1
Sandbach CW11 .... 174 C4
Marsh Hall Rd WA8 .... 13 D2
Marsh House La WA2 .... 16 B4
Marsh La Acton CW5 .... 204 A2
Alsager ST7 .... 193 D2
Churton CH3 .... 181 D3
Coddington CH3 .... 181 F2
Crowton CW8 .... 101 D4
Dutton WA4 .... 51 F2
Elton CH2 .... 72 A2
Frodsham WA6 .... 74 A4
Holmes Chapel CW4 .... 130 C1
Mere WA14 .... 30 C2
Nantwich CW5 .... 204 B3
New Mills SK22 .... 39 E3
Penketh WA5 .... 14 B1
Ravensmoor CW5 .... 203 F1
Runcorn WA7 .... 23 F2
Marsh Rd WA4 .... 27 D2
Marsh St Warrington WA1 .... 16 B4
Widnes WA8 .... 23 D3
Marshall Ave WA5 .... 7 F1
Marshall Ct OL6 .... 242 A2
Marshall La CW8 .... 103 E3
Marshall Rd WA1 .... 17 E4
Marshfield Bank CW2 .... 189 E2
Marshfield La ST6 .... 179 E1
Marshfield Rd CW2 .... 189 E2
Marshgate WA8 .... 22 A3
Marshgate Pl WA6 .... 49 E1
Marshlands Rd L64 .... 66 C3
Marsland Rd M33 .... 242 B5
Marsland St SK1 .... 240 F6
Marson St WA2 .... 16 A3
Marston Cl L62 .... 43 F2
Marston La CW9 .... 79 E3
Marten Ave L63 .... 43 E4
Martens Rd M44 .... 11 F3
Marthall La Chelford WA16 .. 83 D4
Ollerton WA16 .... 82 C3
Marthall Way SK8 .... 34 C3
Martham Cl WA4 .... 17 D2
Martin Ave
Newton-le-W WA12 .... 2 B3
Newton-le-W, Newton Common WA12 .... 1 C1
Warrington WA2 .... 8 C1
Martin Cl Chester CH2 .... 118 B4
Culcheth WA3 .... 4 C2
Runcorn WA7 .... 50 A4
Martin Rd Chester CH2 .... 118 B4
Frodsham WA6 .... 74 A4
Martin St SK14 .... 241 E6
Martin's La CH3 .... 143 F2
Martindale Gr WA7 .... 49 E3
Martland Ave WA3 .... 3 E4
Martlet Ave SK12 .... 38 B3
Marton Cl Congleton CW12 . 156 C3
Hough Common CW2 .... 206 C2
Marton & District CE Aided Prim Sch SK11 .... 133 E3
Marton Gn SK3 .... 240 D1
Marton La Eaton SK11 .... 134 D1
Marton SK11 .... 133 E4
Warren SK11 .... 111 D1
Marton Pl M33 .... 242 A6
Marton Rd CH4 .... 139 E2
Marton Way 4 SK8 .... 34 C3
Marwood Cl WA14 .... 238 B6
Mary Dendy Hospl SK9 .... 83 F4
Mary St Cheadle SK8 .... 239 D6
Crewe CW1 .... 190 C3
Denton M34 .... 241 A8
Hyde SK14 .... 241 D7
Widnes WA8 .... 23 E4
Maryhill Cl ST7 .... 195 D2
Maryhill High & Prim Sch ST7 .... 195 D2
Maryhill Rd WA7 .... 49 D4
Marys Gate CW2 .... 205 F4
Masefield Ave WA8 .... 22 C4
Masefield Dr Blacon CH1 .... 117 F3
Crewe CW1 .... 190 C2
Stockport SK4 .... 240 A6
Maskery Pl CW12 .... 156 C3
Mason Ave Warrington WA1 . 16 C4
Widnes WA8 .... 13 D2
Mason Cl L66 .... 69 E1
Mason St Chester CH2 .... 237 D3
Runcorn WA7 .... 23 E2
Warrington WA1 .... 16 B3
Masons La SK10 .... 87 F1
Massey Ave Hartford CW8 .. 103 D2
Lymm WA13 .... 18 A1
Warrington WA5 .... 7 F1
Winsford CW7 .... 126 C1
Massey Brook La WA13 .... 18 A1
Massey Rd
Altrincham WA15 .... 238 E4
Sale M33 .... 242 E6
Massey St
Alderley Edge SK9 .... 60 A1
17 Stockport SK1 .... 240 F5
Masseyfield Rd WA7 .... 50 A3
Massie St SK8 .... 239 D6
Mates La SY14 .... 213 D3
Mather Ave Goldborne WA3 .. 3 F3
Runcorn WA7 .... 48 B4
Mather Cl CW10 .... 151 E4

Mather Dr Comberbach CW9 78 B4
Northwich CW9 104 B4
Mathers Cl WA2 9 D2
Mathieson Rd WA8 22 C3
Matlock Cl
Great Sankey WA5 15 D4
Sale M33 242 C6
Warrington WA5 7 D1
Matlock Dr SK7 36 C4
Matlock Rd SK8 34 B4
Matterdale Cl WA6 74 B4
Matthew Cl CH2 118 C1
Matthews Pl CW12 157 D1
Matthews St WA1 16 B4
Matty's La WA6 74 A4
Mauldeth Cl SK4 240 A7
Mauldeth Rd SK4 & M19 240 A7
Mavor Ct CW1 190 A2
Maw Green Rd CW1 190 C4
Maw La CW1 191 E4
Mawdsley Ave WA1 17 F4
Mawdsley Cl ST7 193 D2
Mawson Cl WA5 15 E4
Maxfield Cl SK11 111 F4
Maxwell Cl L65 70 A1
Maxwell Rd CW12 179 D4
Maxwell St CW2 190 B2
May Ave Cheadle Hulme SK8 35 D3
Stockport SK4 240 C6
May Rd Cheadle Hulme SK8 35 D3
Heswall L60 41 D4
May Wlk M31 11 E1
Mayberry Gr WA2 9 D1
Maybrook Pl WA4 16 C2
Maydews Pas 22 SK11 112 B4
Maydor Ave CH4 140 B4
Mayfair Cl
Great Sankey WA5 14 B4
Poynton SK12 36 C2
Mayfair Dr CW9 103 F2
Mayfair Gr WA8 12 B1
Mayfield L66 69 F4
Mayfield Ave
Macclesfield SK11 112 B3
Sale M33 242 E6
Widnes WA8 12 A1
Mayfield Cl CW4 130 B2
Mayfield Dr Bebington L62 44 A3
Cuddington CW8 102 A2
Goldborne WA3 4 B4
Mayfield Gdns L64 41 F1
Mayfield Gr
Cuddington CW8 102 A2
Wilmslow SK9 59 F3
Mayfield Mews CW1 189 F4
Mayfield Rd Blacon CH1 117 E3
Bramhall SK7 35 F2
Mobberley WA16 57 F2
Northwich CW9 104 B4
Warrington WA4 17 D1
Mayfield Terr SK11 112 B3
Mayfield View WA13 18 C1
Mayflower Rd CW5 204 C2
Mayor's Rd WA15 238 E4
Maythorn Ave WA3 9 D4
Maytree Ave CH3 119 D1
Maywood Ave M20 239 B8
McCarthy Cl WA3 10 A2
McClellan Pl WA8 13 D1
McGarva Way L65 70 B2
Mckee Ave WA2 8 A1
Mckellin Cl ST7 209 F1
McLaren St CW1 190 B4
McMinnis Ave WA9 1 A1
McNeill Ave CW1 190 A3
Mead Ave ST7 194 C4
Mead Cl WA16 56 C1
Mead Rd WA1 17 D4
Meade The SK9 60 B4
Meadow Ave
Congleton CW12 156 B1
Goostrey CW4 107 E1
Warrington WA4 16 A1
Weston CW2 207 D3
Meadow Bank
Adderley TF9 235 D2
Kelsall CW6 122 B2
Stockport SK4 240 B6
Meadow Brow SK9 60 A1
Meadow Cl Cuddington CW8 102 A2
Farndon CH3 180 C1
Goostrey CW4 107 F1
Helsby WA6 73 D2
High Lane SK6 37 F4
Neston L64 66 C3
Newton-le-W WA12 1 C2
Shavington CW2 206 B3
Tarvin CH3 121 D1
Whaley Bridge SK23 65 E4
Widnes WA8 12 B2
Willaston L64 67 F4
Wilmslow SK9 59 F2
Winsford CW7 126 B2
Meadow Croft Alsager ST7 193 F1
Willaston L64 67 F4
Meadow Ct Mollington CH1 94 C1
No Man's Heath SY14 214 A2
Meadow Cty Prim Sch
L66 69 F1
Meadow Dr Barnton CW8 78 A2
Knutsford WA16 81 F4
Prestbury SK10 87 D4
Wistaston CW2 205 F4
Meadow Field Rd CH4 141 D3
Meadow Gate CW9 79 F3
Meadow Gr
Northwich CW9 104 A3
Winsford CW7 126 C3
Meadow Home Pk CW7 126 B3
Meadow Ind Est SK5 240 F7
Meadow La Disley SK12 38 B3
Ellesmere Port L65 70 B3
Huntington CH3 142 A3
Moulton CW9 126 C4
Warrington WA2 9 D1
Willaston L64 42 C1
Meadow Rd Broughton CH4 139 E2
Weaverham CW8 102 C4
Meadow Rise Clutton CH3 182 B1
Winsford CW7 126 A1
Meadow Row WA7 24 A1
Meadow St Hyde SK14 241 E5
New Mills SK22 39 E4
Northwich CW9 104 A4
Meadow View Elton CH2 72 A2
Middlewich CW10 128 A1
Sealand CH5 116 A3
Meadow View Dr WA6 74 A4
Meadow Way
Lawton-gate ST7 194 A3
Macclesfield SK10 87 F1
Wilmslow SK9 59 F2
Meadow Wlk M31 11 E1
Meadowbank Gdns WA3 5 E4
Meadowcroft
Higher Kinnerton CH4 161 D4
Saughall CH1 94 A1
Meadowfield
Tarporley CW6 146 B1
Whaley Bridge SK23 65 E4
Meadowfield Ct SK14 241 D8
Meadowgate Cl 12 CW11 174 B3
Meadows La Chester CH4 237 F1
Saughall CH1 117 D4
Meadows Pl CH4 141 F4
Meadows Rd Cheadle SK8 34 C4
Gatley SK8 239 B1
Kidsgrove ST7 194 C1
Sale M33 242 C8
Meadows The Ashton CH3 121 F4
Congleton CW12 156 C2
Irlam M44 11 F3
Neston L64 66 C3
Meadowside Adlington SK10 63 D4
Disley SK12 39 D3
Northwich CW9 103 E4
Whaley Bridge SK23 65 E4
Meadowside Ave ST7 209 E1
Meadowside Rd L62 43 E4
Meadowsway CH2 118 B4
Meadowsweet Rd WA16 57 F2
Meadowvale Cl CW5 204 C4
Meads Rd ST7 193 E2
Meadscroft Dr SK9 59 F1
Meadway Bramhall SK7 35 F3
Ellesmere Port L66 69 D4
Goldborne WA3 3 E4
Heswall L60 40 C3
High Lane SK6 37 F4
Poynton SK12 36 A2
Prestbury SK10 87 D3
Runcorn WA7 49 F4
Widnes WA8 12 A1
Meakin Cl CW12 157 D1
Meal St New Mills SK22 39 E4
Reddish SK4 240 E7
Mealhouse Brow 2 SK1 240 F5
Meddings Cl SK9 85 D4
Medina Ave CW7 126 C1
Medina Way ST7 195 D1
Medway Cl Goldborne WA3 4 B4
Warrington WA2 8 C1
Wilmslow SK9 34 B1
Medway Cres WA14 238 C6
Medway Dr ST6 179 E1
Medway Rd WA3 5 D1
Mee St SK11 112 C3
Meeanee Rd CW5 204 B2
Meerbrook Rd SK3 240 A4
Meeting La WA5 14 C3
Meg La Macclesfield SK11 111 F4
Sutton Lane Ends SK11 113 E1
Megacre ST7 210 A1
Melbourne Ave M90 33 D4
Melbourne Gr CW1 191 E3
Melbourne Rd Blacon CH1 117 E2
Bramhall SK7 35 F3
Melbourne St SK15 242 D1
Melbury Ct WA3 9 F3
Melbury Rd SK8 35 D3
Melchett Cres CW9 104 B4
Melford Cl CW2 206 B4
Melford Ct WA1 17 E4
Melford Dr
Macclesfield SK10 87 E1
Runcorn WA7 23 E1
Meliden Gr WA6 73 D1
Melkridge Cl CH2 119 D2
Melksham Cl SK11 112 A4
Mell La WA6 98 C2
Mellard St ST7 209 E1
Mellington Ave M20 239 C8
Mellock Cl L64 66 C3
Mellock La L64 66 C4
Mellor Cl Ashton-u-L OL6 242 B2
Runcorn WA7 24 B1
Mellor Cres WA16 56 C1
Mellor Rd
Ashton-u-L OL6 242 B3
Ashton-u-L OL6 242 C4
Mellor St Crewe CW1 190 B3
Packmoor ST7 195 F1
Mellors Bank ST7 195 E3
Melrose Ave Appleton WA4 26 B4
Burtonwood WA5 6 C4
Cheadle SK3 239 F7
Chester CH3 119 D1
Sale M33 242 B6
Melrose Cres SK12 37 E3
Melrose Dr Crewe CW1 190 A4
Ellesmere Port CH1 94 C4
Melton Ave WA4 26 A4
Melton Cl CW12 155 F2
Melton Dr CW12 155 F2
Melton Rd WA7 49 E4
Melton St SK5 240 F8
Melverly Dr CH1 117 E2
Melville Cl Warrington WA2 16 A4
Widnes WA8 13 E1
Melville Rd M44 11 E3
Menai Gr SK8 240 A2
Menai Rd SK3 240 E2
Mendell Cl L62 43 F4
Mendell Prim Sch L62 43 E4
Mendip Ave WA2 8 A2
Mendip Cl Cheadle SK8 34 A4
Ellesmere Port L66 69 F2
Stockport SK4 240 E7
Mendip Ct SK4 240 E7
Menin Ave WA4 16 B2
Menlow Cl WA4 17 E1
Mentmore Gdns WA4 26 C3
Mentone Rd SK4 240 C7
Meols Cl Ellesmere Port L66 69 F2
Hale L24 21 F1
Mercer Cl SY14 213 D2
Mercer Rd WA11 1 B3
Mercer St Burtonwood WA5 6 C3
Newton-le-W WA12 2 B2
Mercer Way Chester CH4 140 C3
Nantwich CW5 204 C4
Mercian Cl CW2 206 A2
Mercian Way SK3 240 E3
Mercury Ct CH1 117 F1
Mere Ave L63 43 D3
Mere Bank CW9 127 D4
Mere Brook Wlk CW2 190 B1
Mere Cl Ellesmere Port L66 69 E1
Haslington CW1 191 E2
Pickmere WA16 80 A4
Sale M33 242 F5
Mere Cres CW8 123 F3
Mere Ct ST7 193 E2
Mere La Cuddington CW8 102 A1
Pickmere WA16 79 F4
Mere Rd Marston CW9 79 D3
Newton-le-W WA12 2 C2
Warrington WA2 9 D1
Weston CW2 207 D3
Mere Side SK15 242 C4
Mere St CW1 191 E2
Merebank Rd CW2 190 A1
Merebrook Rd SK11 111 F4
Merecroft CH3 119 D1
Meredith Ave WA4 17 D1
Meredith St CW1 190 B3
Merehaven Cl WA16 80 A4
Mereheath La
Knutsford WA16 56 C3
Mere WA16 56 C3
Mereheath Pk WA16 56 C2
Merelake Rd Alsager ST7 210 A4
Kidsgrove ST7 210 A4
Meremore Dr ST5 210 B1
Mereside Ave CW12 156 A2
Mereside Cl Cheadle SK8 239 F4
Macclesfield SK10 87 D1
Mereside Rd WA16 30 B1
Merevale Cl WA7 49 F3
Merganser Cl CW1 189 F4
Meriton Rd SK9 34 B2
Merlin Ave WA16 57 D2
Merlin Cl Runcorn WA7 24 A1
Winsford CW7 150 A4
Merlin Way CW1 190 A4
Merlyn Ave M33 242 C8
Merrick Cl WA2 8 C1
Merridale The WA15 32 A4
Merriden Rd SK10 87 D1
Merrill's Ave CW12 189 F3
Merriman Ave WA16 57 E2
Merrivale Rd CW2 206 A4
Merrydale Cl SK10 86 C1
Merryman's La SK9 84 A4
Mersey Pl CW7 127 D1
Mersey Rd Runcorn WA7 23 D2
Sale M33 242 B8
Widnes WA8 23 D2
Mersey Sq SK1 & SK4 240 E5
Mersey St Runcorn WA7 23 D2
St Helens WA9 1 A2
Warrington WA1 16 A3
Mersey Vale Prim Sch SK4 240 A5
Mersey View WA7 48 B4
Mersey View Rd WA8 22 A2
Mersey Wlk WA4 16 C3
Merseyton Rd L65 70 B4
Merseyway SK1 240 F6
Merston Dr M20 239 C8
Merstone Cl L26 21 D4
Merton Ave Hazel Grove SK7 36 C4
Romiley SK6 241 A4
Merton Cl L64 66 C3
Merton Dr CH4 141 D2
Merton House Sch CH2 118 B2
Merton House Sch
(Downswood) CH2 237 D4
Merton Rd Bebington L62 44 A2
Ellesmere Port L66 69 F2
Sale M33 242 A8
5 Stockport SK3 240 B4
Mertoun Rd WA4 16 A1
Mervyn Rd CW8 77 F1
Merwood Ave SK8 34 B4
Messuage La CW12 132 B2
Meteor Cres WA2 8 B1
Mevagissey Rd WA7 50 B3
Mevril Rd SK23 65 F3
Mews The Barnton CW8 78 A1
Gatley SK8 239 B5
Styal SK9 33 E2
Tarporley CW6 168 B4
Meyer St SK2 & SK3 240 F2
Meynell Cl CW2 190 A1
Meynell Pl CH1 118 A3
Micawber Rd SK12 36 C1
Mickle Trafford Cty Prim
Sch CH2 119 F4
Micklegate WA7 50 B4
Micklewright Ave CW1 190 B3
Mickley Hall La CW5 218 A2
Mid Cheshire Coll
(London Road Studios)
CW9 103 F3
Mid Cheshire Coll
(Verdin Ctr) CW7 126 B1
Mid-Cheshire Coll CW8 103 E3
Middle Hillgate SK1 240 F4
Middle La Aldford CH3 163 F2
Congleton CW12 157 E2
Kingsley WA6 74 C1
Partington M31 11 E1
Middle Wlk Frodsham WA6 74 A4
Knutsford WA16 57 D1
Middlecroft CH3 119 F3
Middlehills SK11 113 D3
Middlehurst Ave CW8 102 C4
Middlehurst Rd WA4 17 D1
Middlewich Cty High Sch
CW10 151 E4
Middlewich Cty Inf & Jun
Sch CW10 151 D4
Middlewich Rd
Allostock WA16 106 B3
Church Minshull CW1 172 C3
Cranage CW4 129 F2
Cranage CW10 129 F3
Crewe CW2 189 E2
Holmes Chapel CW4 130 A2
Nantwich CW5 204 C4
Northwich CW9 104 B4
Ollerton WA16 82 A2
Peover WA16 106 B3
Peover, Smithy Green WA16 81 F1
Sandbach CW11 174 C4
Winsford CW10 127 F1
Worleston CW2 189 E2
Middlewich Rd Ind Est
CW10 129 D3
Middlewich St CW1 190 B3
Middlewood WA3 3 F4
Middlewood Dr SK4 240 A5
Middlewood Rd
High Lane SK6 37 E4
Poynton SK12 37 E3
Middlewood Sta (Lower)
SK6 37 E3
Middlewood View SK6 37 E4
Midfield Cl ST6 179 E1
Midgley Cres OL6 242 B4
Midhurst Cl SK8 34 C4
Midland St WA8 13 D1
Midland Terr SK22 39 E4
Midland Way WA1 16 A3
Midway SK8 35 D3
Milborne Cl CH2 118 C3
Mile Bank Rd SY13 226 B2
Miles Cl WA3 9 F2
Miles St SK14 241 F6
Milk St Congleton CW12 156 B2
Hyde SK14 241 D6
Mill Ave WA5 14 C4
Mill Bank L64 67 D3
Mill Brow WA8 13 E1
Mill Cl Chester CH2 118 B3
Knutsford WA16 57 E2
Warrington WA2 8 C2
Mill Cotts SK10 88 A4
Mill Field Cl CH3 180 C1
Mill Gn Congleton CW12 156 B2
Willaston L64 67 F4
Mill Gr Bulkeley SY14 184 C1
Kidsgrove ST7 194 B1
Mill Green La WA8 13 F3
Mill Green Sch WA12 2 C2
Mill Hill Ave SK7 36 B4
Mill Hill Dr CW11 175 D3
Mill Hill Hollow
Hazel Grove SK7 36 B4
Poynton SK12 36 B4
Mill Hill La CW11 175 D2
Mill La Adlington SK10 62 A3
Audlem, Little Heath CW3 230 A2
Audlem, Swanbach CW3 229 F1
Barthomley CW2 208 B4
Blakenhall CW5 221 D2
Bold Heath WA8 13 E3
Brereton Green CW4 153 F4
Burton L64 67 E1
Cheadle SK8 239 D6
Chester CH2 118 B3
Congleton CW12 179 E4
Cronton WA8 12 B3
Crowton WA6 75 F2
Cuddington CW8 101 F3
Denton M34 & SK14 241 B6
Duddon CW6 145 D4
Eaton CW6 147 E1
Ellesmere Port L66 69 F3
Mill La continued
Goostrey CW4 107 F1
Great Barrow CH3 120 C3
Hazel Grove SK7 36 C4
Heswall L60 41 D4
Higher Walton WA4 25 F4
Huxley CH3 144 B1
Kingsley WA6 75 F2
Lindow End SK9 84 A4
Little Budworth CW6 125 D1
Lymm WA13 19 E2
Macclesfield SK11 112 B4
Middlewich CW10 128 B1
Middlewich, Newtonia CW10 128 A1
Mobberley WA16 58 A2
Mottram St Andrew SK10 61 E3
Neston L64 67 E3
News Bank CW12 132 C1
Newton-le-W WA12 2 C2
Peover WA16 108 B4
Prestbury SK10 61 F3
Sandbach CW11 174 B4
Siddington SK11 109 F3
Smallwood CW11 175 D1
Sutton WA6 49 F1
Tarvin, Tarvin Sands CH3 121 E2
Tarvin, Westwood Common
CW6 122 B1
The Bank ST7 195 D4
Warrington WA2 8 C2
Warrington, Stockton Heath
WA4 16 C1
Weston CW2 207 D3
Whitegate CW7 126 A3
Willaston L64 42 C1
Winwick WA2 7 F3
Winwick WA2 7 F3
Wythenshawe WA15 32 C2
Mill Park Dr L62 43 F2
Mill Park Inf Sch L62 43 F2
Mill Park Jun Sch L62 43 F2
Mill Pool La CW5 187 E3
Mill Rd SK11 112 B3
Mill Rise ST7 195 D1
Mill Row CW11 175 E3
Mill St
Altrincham WA14 & WA15 238 E5
Chester CH4 237 E1
Congleton CW12 156 B2
Congleton CW12 156 C2
Crewe CW2 190 B2
Goldborne WA3 3 D4
Hyde SK14 241 E8
Macclesfield SK11 112 B4
Neston L64 66 B4
Stalybridge SK15 242 F1
Warrington WA1 16 A3
Wilmslow SK9 60 A4
Mill St Mall 31 SK11 112 B4
Mill Stream Cl CW4 107 F1
Mill View Cl SY14 184 C1
Mill Way CW5 204 C1
Mill Wharf CH3 143 D3
Millar Cres WA8 23 D4
Millbank WA13 18 C2
Millbank Cl SK11 84 A2
Millbank Dr SK10 86 C1
Millbank Jun Sch M31 11 F2
Millbeck Cl CW2 207 D3
Millbrook Cotts CH3 166 A1
Millbrook End CH3 166 A1
Millbrook Gr 3 SK9 34 B1
Millbrook St SK1 240 F4
Millbuck Way CW11 174 B3
Milldale Rd WA3 4 A4
Millend La ST7 209 E3
Miller St WA4 16 B2
Millers La Lymm WA13 19 D3
Waverton CH3 143 D2
Millers Meadow SK10 88 C3
Millers View ST7 195 D1
Millers Wharf ST7 193 F4
Millersdale Cl L62 43 F3
Millersdale Gr WA7 49 E3
Milley La WA16 80 B4
Millfield La Haydock WA11 1 C4
Saighton CH3 142 C1
Tarporley CW6 146 B1
Millfield Rd WA8 13 E1
Millfield Terr L66 69 E4
Millfields CW5 204 B2
Millfields Cty Prim Sch
CW5 204 B3
Millgate Cuddington CW8 101 F2
Stockport SK1 240 F6
Millhouse Ave WA4 16 B1
Millhouse La Croft WA3 9 D3
Warrington WA3 9 D3
Millingfield The CW4 130 B1
Millingford Ind Est WA3 3 D4
Millington Cl Runcorn WA7 49 F2
Widnes WA8 22 C4
Millington Hall La WA14 30 A3
Millington La
Rostherne WA14 30 A3
Weaverham CW8 102 A3
Millom Pl SK8 239 B3
Millrace Dr CW2 206 A4
Mills Way CW1 173 D1
Millstone Ave ST7 194 C1
Millstone Cl SK12 36 C3
Millstone La CW5 204 C3
Millstone Pas SK11 112 C3
Millway
Altrincham WA15 32 B4
Waverton CH3 143 D3
Millway Rd L24 21 D2
Millwood Ct L24 21 D2

Millwood Cty Prim Jun,
Mix Sch L24 .... 21 D2
Millwood Terr **2** SK14 ..... 241 D6
Milne Cl CW2 .... 189 F1
Milner Ave WA14 .... 238 B7
Milner Cop L60 .... 41 D4
Milner Rd Heswall L60 ...... 41 D4
Northwich CW8 .... 103 E3
Milner St WA5 .... 15 F3
Milnthorpe Rd WA5 .... 6 C3
Milton Ave Irlam M44 .... 11 F3
Newton-le-W WA12 .... 2 A2
Widnes WA8 .... 22 C4
Milton Cl
Higher Wincham CW9 ...... 80 A3
Middlewich CW10 .... 151 E3
Milton Cres Cheadle SK8 .. 239 C5
Kidsgrove ST7 .... 210 B4
Milton Dr Poynton SK12 .... 36 B2
Wistaston CW2 .... 206 A4
Milton Gr Helsby WA6 ...... 73 D1
Poynton SK12 .... 36 B2
Sale M33 .... 242 A8
Warrington WA4 .... 16 B2
Milton Rd Blacon CH1 ..... 117 F3
Bramhall SK7 .... 35 F4
Ellesmere Port L65 .... 70 B2
Goldborne WA3 .... 3 E4
Widnes WA8 .... 23 D4
Milton Rough CW8 .... 76 C1
Milton St Chester CH2 .... 237 E3
Hyde SK14 .... 241 D8
Widnes WA8 .... 23 D4
Milvain Dr WA2 .... 8 B1
Milverton Dr SK8 .... 35 D3
Mine Way WA11 .... 1 C4
Miners Way Speke L24 ...... 21 D2
Widnes WA8 .... 23 D4
Minerva Ave CH1 .... 117 F1
Minerva Cl WA4 .... 16 B1
Minn-End-La Bosley SK11 . 159 D3
Wincle SK11 .... 159 D3
Minor Ave SK11 .... 112 B2
Minor Cl WA13 .... 18 C1
Minshull La
Church Minshull CW5 ..... 171 E2
Wettenhall CW7 .... 171 E2
Minshull New Rd CW1 ..... 189 F4
Minshull St WA16 .... 57 D1
Minster Cl CW7 .... 149 D4
Minster Ct Runcorn WA7 .. 48 C4
Wistaston CW2 .... 205 F4
Minster Dr Altrincham WA14 . 31 D4
Cheadle SK8 .... 240 C1
Minton Cl CW12 .... 157 D1
Minton Way WA8 .... 13 D3
Mirfield Ave SK4 .... 240 B6
Mirfield Cl WA3 .... 3 E4
Mirion St CW1 .... 190 B2
Misty Cl WA8 .... 12 B1
Mitchell Ave
Burtonwood WA5 .... 6 C3
Kidsgrove ST7 .... 194 B1
Mitchell Dr ST7 .... 194 B1
Mitchell St Goldborne WA3 .. 3 D4
Warrington WA4 .... 26 B4
Mithril Cl WA8 .... 13 F2
Mitton Cl WA3 .... 4 C3
Moadlock SK6 .... 241 C4
Moat House Dr CW2 .... 190 A1
Moat La Audlem CW3 ...... 209 D2
Hollins Green WA3 .... 10 C1
Mobberley CE Contr Prim
Sch WA16 .... 58 B3
Mobberley Ave ST7 .... 17 E2
Mobberley Rd Ashley WA14 . 31 F2
Knutsford WA16 .... 57 E2
Wilmslow SK9 .... 33 E1
Mobberley Sta WA16 .... 57 F4
Moelfre Dr SK7 .... 35 E4
Mold Rd CH4 .... 139 D2
Mollets Wood M34 .... 241 A8
Mollington Ct CH1 .... 94 C1
Mollington Rd M22 .... 33 F4
Molly Pitcher Way WA5 .... 15 D3
Molly Potts Cl WA16 .... 82 A4
Molyneux Ave WA5 .... 15 F4
Mona Ave SK8 .... 239 D1
Mona St SK14 .... 241 E6
Monarch Cl M44 .... 11 F3
Mond Cl CW7 .... 149 D4
Mond Rd WA8 .... 23 D4
Mond St CW8 .... 78 A2
Money Ash Rd WA15 ...... 238 C3
Monica Dr WA5 .... 13 D3
Monk St CW1 .... 190 A3
Monk's La CW3 .... 230 B3
Monks Coppenhall Cty
Prim Sch CW1 .... 190 C4
Monks Gr L65 .... 70 A3
Monks La Acton CW5 ..... 203 F4
Crewe CW3 .... 189 F3
Nantwich CW5 .... 204 C3
Monks Orch CW5 .... 204 C3
Monks St WA5 .... 15 F3
Monks Way CW8 .... 103 D2
Monkswood Cl WA5 .... 7 F1
Monmouth Cl WA1 .... 17 F4
Monroe Cl WA1 .... 17 D4
Monsall Cl SK11 .... 112 C4
Monsall Dr SK11 .... 112 C4
Montague Rd
Ashton-u-L OL6 .... 242 A3
Sale M33 .... 242 B6
Montague Way SK15 ...... 242 D2
Montclare Cres WA4 .... 16 C1
Montcliffe Cl WA3 .... 9 E3

Montgomery Cl WA16 ...... 57 E2
Montgomery Rd WA8 ...... 22 B4
Montgomery Way CW7 ... 149 D4
Montmorency Rd WA16 .... 57 E2
Montpelier Ave WA7 .... 48 C3
Montrose Cl
Macclesfield SK10 .... 87 D1
Shavington CW2 .... 206 A2
Warrington WA2 .... 8 C2
Montrose Ct Chester CH4 . 140 C4
Holmes Chapel CW4 ...... 130 A1
Monument Rd ST7 .... 210 B3
Monument View ST7 ...... 209 F1
Mood Gdns SK9 .... 60 A1
Moody St CW12 .... 156 B1
Moon St WA8 .... 23 D4
Moor Cl ST6 .... 179 F1
Moor Cres CH4 .... 139 E1
Moor La Elton WA6 .... 72 C1
Frodsham WA6 .... 74 A4
Hawarden CH5 .... 116 A1
Heswall L60 .... 40 C4
Higher Kinnerton CH4 .... 161 E4
Higher Kinnerton, Kinnerton
Green CH4 .... 161 E3
Waverton CH3 .... 143 D3
Widnes WA8 .... 23 D4
Wilmslow SK9 .... 59 F3
Woodford SK7 .... 35 F2
Moor La S WA8 .... 22 C4
Moor Lodge SK4 .... 240 B8
Moor Nook M33 .... 242 D5
Moor Park Rd M20 .... 239 C8
Moor St CW12 .... 156 C1
Moor Top Pl SK4 .... 240 B7
Moorcroft WA16 .... 80 C2
Moorcroft Ave CH3 .... 119 D1
Moorcroft Cres CH3 ...... 119 E2
Moorcroft Mews CH4 .... 140 B3
Moordale Rd WA16 .... 57 D1
Moorditch La WA6 .... 48 B1
Moore Ave St Helens WA9 . 1 A2
Warrington WA4 .... 17 E2
Moore Cl WA8 .... 13 E1
Moore Cty Prim Sch WA4 . 25 D3
Moore Dr WA11 .... 1 C3
Moore Gr WA13 .... 19 D3
Moore La WA4 .... 25 E3
Moorfield Ave M34 .... 241 A6
Moorfield Cres WA3 .... 4 A4
Moorfield Cty Prim Sch
WA8 .... 13 E2
Moorfield Dr Neston L64 ... 41 E1
Wilmslow SK9 .... 59 F3
Moorfield Gr
Manchester SK4 .... 240 B8
Sale M33 .... 242 D5
Moorfield Rd WA8 .... 13 E2
Moorfields
Willaston (nr Nantwich)
CW5 .... 205 F3
Wistaston CW5 .... 205 F3
Moorhead La CW11 ...... 154 B2
Moorhill Rd SK11 .... 112 B2
Moorhouse Ave ST7 ...... 193 F2
Moorhouse Cl CH2 .... 118 B3
Mooring Cl WA7 .... 50 B3
Moorings CW12 .... 156 C1
Moorings Cl L64 .... 41 D1
Moorings The Disley SK12 . 38 C3
Heswall L60 .... 40 B4
Middlewich CW10 .... 128 B1
Moorland Ave M33 .... 242 C5
Moorland Cl L60 .... 41 D4
Moorland Dr Cheadle SK8 . 34 C4
Runcorn WA7 .... 50 C4
Moorland Pk L60 .... 41 D4
Moorland Rd Biddulph ST6 . 179 E1
Ellesmere Port L66 .... 69 F4
Kidsgrove ST7 .... 195 E4
Moorlands Ave CW8 ...... 102 A2
Moorlands Cl SK10 .... 87 E2
Moorlands Dr CW5 .... 206 A1
Moorlands Jun Sch M33 . 242 E7
Moorlands Pk CW8 ...... 102 A2
Moors La CW7 .... 149 E3
Moorsbrook Gr **4** SK9 ... 34 C1
Moorsfield Ave CW3 ...... 229 F2
Moorside WA16 .... 57 D1
Moorside Ave L64 .... 66 B4
Moorside Ct Denton M34 . 241 A8
Moorside La
Dukinfield M34 .... 241 A8
Neston L64 .... 66 B4
Pott Shrigley SK10 .... 63 F2
Moorside Rd SK4 .... 240 A6
Moorson Ave ST7 .... 194 C4
Moorview Gdns ST7 ..... 195 F3
Moorway L60 .... 41 D4
Moran Cl SK9 .... 34 C1
Moran Cres SK11 .... 112 A4
Moran Rd SK11 .... 112 A4
Morcott La L24 .... 21 E1
Moresby Cl WA7 .... 50 C4
Moresby Dr M20 .... 239 B8
Moreton Ave SK7 .... 35 F3
Moreton Dr Alsager ST7 .. 193 E2
Holmes Chapel CW4 ...... 130 A2
Sandbach CW11 .... 175 E4
Wilmslow SK9 .... 34 C2
Moreton Rd CW2 .... 189 F2
Moreton St CW8 .... 78 B1
Moreton Terr WA6 .... 74 A4
Morgan Ave WA2 .... 8 B1
Morgan Cl Blacon CH1 ... 117 F3
Crewe CW2 .... 190 A2
Morgan Pl SK5 .... 240 F8

Morland Ave Bebington L62 .. 43 E3
Neston L64 .... 66 C4
Morley Cl CH2 .... 119 F4
Morley Dr CW12 .... 157 D1
Morley Gn SK9 .... 33 E1
Morley Rd Runcorn WA7 .. 23 D1
Warrington WA4 .... 16 A1
Morley St WA1 .... 16 B3
Mornant Ave CW8 .... 103 D2
Morningside Dr M20 ..... 239 C8
Mornington Ave
Cheadle SK8 .... 239 D4
Ellesmere Port L65 .... 70 B2
Mornington Cl **1** CW11 ... 174 B4
Mornington Rd
Cheadle SK8 .... 239 D4
Sale M33 .... 242 D7
Morphany La WA4 .... 51 F3
Morreys La CW6 .... 122 C4
Morris Ave WA4 .... 16 C2
Morris Cl WA11 .... 1 A1
Morris Dr CW8 .... 77 E1
Morris Pk CW8 .... 103 D2
Morrison Cl WA5 .... 15 D3
Mort Ave WA4 .... 17 D2
Mortimer Ave WA2 .... 16 A4
Mortimer Dr CW11 .... 175 E3
Mortlake Cl WA8 .... 12 B2
Mortlake Cres CH3 ...... 119 D1
Morton Ave WA6 .... 73 D1
Morton Cl WA5 .... 15 E4
Morton Dr Poynton SK12 .. 36 C2
Sutton Lane Ends SK11 . 112 C2
Morton Rd Blacon CH1 ... 117 F2
Runcorn WA7 .... 50 B4
Morton St SK4 .... 240 E8
Morven Cl WA2 .... 8 C2
Moscow Rd SK3 .... 240 D3
Moscow Rd E SK3 .... 240 D3
Mosedale Gr WA7 .... 49 F3
Moseley Ave WA4 .... 17 D2
Moseley Grange SK8 .... 239 E3
Moseley Rd SK8 .... 239 E3
Moseley St **2** SK3 .... 240 E4
Mosley Av WA15 .... 238 F7
Moss Bank
Cheadle Hulme SK7 .... 35 E3
Chester CH2 .... 118 B2
Winsford CW7 .... 126 B1
Moss Bank Rd WA8 .... 23 E4
Moss Bower Rd SK11 .... 112 B2
Moss Brow SK10 .... 87 B4
Moss Brow La WA16 ...... 28 B2
Moss Cl Warrington WA4 .. 16 C1
Willaston L64 .... 68 A4
Moss Croft CW5 .... 190 A4
Moss Dr Manley WA6 ...... 98 C2
Middlewich CW10 .... 151 E3
Moss Farm Recn Ctr CW8 . 103 E4
Moss Gate WA3 .... 10 A3
Moss Gr Broughton CH4 .. 140 B3
Lymm WA13 .... 19 D2
Moss Green Way WA9 ..... 1 A1
Moss Hey Prim Sch SK7 .. 35 E3
Moss La Alderley Edge SK9 . 60 A1
Altrincham WA14 & WA15 . 238 E4
Altrincham, Timperley WA15 . 238 F7
Bollington SK10 .... 87 F4
Brereton Green CW12 ... 154 C3
Cheadle Hulme SK7 .... 35 E3
Church Minshull CW1 .... 172 C1
Congleton CW12 .... 156 C3
Cranage CW10 .... 129 D4
Crewe CW1 .... 173 D1
Cuddington CW8 .... 102 A2
Dunham Massey WA13 ... 20 A4
Fowley Common WA3 .... 5 F3
High Legh WA16 .... 29 F3
High Legh, Sink Moss WA16 . 28 B2
Hollins Green WA3 .... 10 C3
Irlam M44 .... 11 E3
Knutsford WA16 .... 56 B3
Lawton-gate ST7 .... 194 C2
Lostock CW9 .... 105 E4
Macclesfield SK11 .... 112 B2
Manley WA6 .... 99 D2
Middlewich CW10 .... 129 D4
Mobberley WA16 .... 58 C2
Moore WA4 .... 25 D3
Mottram St Andrew SK10 . 61 D1
Norley WA6 .... 101 D3
Northwich CW8 .... 103 E4
Ollerton WA16 .... 83 E2
Partington WA13 .... 11 F1
Partington M31 .... 11 F1
Sandbach CW11 .... 174 B4
Siddington SK11 .... 109 F1
St Helens WA9 .... 1 A1
Styal SK9 .... 33 F3
Warmingham CW1 .... 173 E2
Moss Pl ST7 .... 195 F3
Moss Rd Alderley Edge SK9 . 60 B1
Astbury CW12 .... 178 C4
Congleton CW12 .... 178 C4
Iriam M44 .... 11 E4
Northwich CW8 .... 103 E4
Warrington WA4 .... 17 D2
Moss Rose SK9 .... 33 F3
Moss Side La Antrobus CW9 . 53 E4
Hollins Green WA3 .... 10 C2
Penketh WA4 .... 24 C4
Moss Side Rd M44 .... 11 F3
Moss Sq Crewe CW1 ..... 190 B2
Macclesfield SK11 .... 112 B2
Moss St Weaverham CW8 . 77 E1
Widnes WA8 .... 23 E4
Moss Terr Northwich CW8 . 78 B1
Warren SK11 .... 112 A3

Moss The CW9 .... 78 B4
Moss View Rd SK11 ...... 112 A2
Moss Way ST7 .... 193 D2
Mossdale Cl Crewe CW2 . 189 F2
Great Sankey WA5 .... 15 D4
Mossfield Cl SK4 .... 240 B6
Mossfields ST7 .... 193 D2
Mossford Ave CW1 ...... 190 A4
Mossgrove Rd WA15 .... 238 F6
Mosshall La WA4 .... 26 C1
Mosslands Cl L66 .... 69 F1
Mossley Ave L62 .... 43 E4
Mossley CE Contr Prim
Sch CW12 .... 179 D4
Mossley Ct CW12 .... 178 C4
Mossley Rd OL6 .... 242 B4
Mossvale L66 .... 69 E4
Mosswood Pk M20 ...... 239 B8
Mosswood Rd SK9 .... 34 C1
Moston Gr WA13 .... 18 B2
Moston Rd Chester CH2 . 118 B4
Sandbach CW11 .... 174 B3
Moston Way L66 .... 69 F2
Mostyn Ave Cheadle SK8 . 239 E1
Heswall L60 .... 40 B4
Mostyn Gdns L64 .... 41 E1
Mostyn House Sch L64 ... 66 B4
Mostyn Pl CH1 .... 117 F3
Motcombe Farm Rd SK8 . 239 B1
Motcombe Gr SK8 .... 239 A3
Motcombe Rd SK8 ...... 239 A2
Motorway Ind Est CW10 . 128 C3
Motram Cl WA8 .... 17 D2
Mothershead Rd WA8 ... 23 D4
Mottram Cl Cheadle SK8 . 240 A1
Middlewich CW10 .... 151 D4
Mottram Fold SK1 .... 240 F4
Mottram Old Rd SK15 ... 242 F1
Mottram Rd
Alderley Edge SK9 .... 60 B1
Hyde SK14 .... 241 F6
Sale M33 .... 242 F5
Mottram St **5** SK1 ...... 240 F4
Mottram St Andrew GM
Prim Sch SK10 .... 61 D1
Moughland La WA7 .... 49 D4
Moulders La WA1 .... 16 A2
Mouldsworth Cl WA3 ... 103 F2
Mouldsworth Sta CH3 .... 99 D1
Moulton Av Davenham CW9 . 103 F2
Knutsford WA16 .... 57 C1
Runcorn WA7 .... 49 F2
Moulton City Prim Sch
CW9 .... 126 C4
Mount Ave L60 .... 40 C4
Mount Carmel Sch SK9 ... 60 A1
Mount Farm Way L66 ..... 69 F2
Mount Hall Mews L60 .... 40 C4
Mount Pl CH2 .... 118 C1
Mount Pleasant
Audlem CW3 .... 230 A2
Bollington SK10 .... 88 A4
Chester CH2 .... 140 C4
Crewe CW1 .... 190 A3
Elton CH2 .... 72 A2
Haslington CW1 .... 191 E2
Kidsgrove ST7 .... 195 D1
Widnes WA8 .... 13 D1
Wilmslow SK9 .... 60 A4
Mount Pleasant Ave WA9 .. 1 A2
Mount Pleasant Dr CW7 . 149 D4
Mount Pleasant Rd
Davenham CW9 .... 103 F1
The Bank ST7 .... 195 D4
Mount Rd Kidsgrove ST7 . 195 D1
Runcorn WA7 .... 49 F4
Stockport SK4 .... 240 C6
Mount St Hyde SK14 .... 241 E6
Stalybridge SK15 .... 242 D2
Widnes WA8 .... 13 D1
Mount Terr SK11 .... 112 C4
Mount The
Altrincham WA14 .... 238 D5
Altrincham, Halebarns WA15 . 32 E4
Chester CH3 .... 118 C1
Congleton CW12 .... 156 A1
Great Budworth CW9 ..... 79 D4
Heswall L60 .... 40 C4
Kidsgrove ST7 .... 195 D1
Scholar Green ST7 ...... 194 C4
Mount Way CH3 .... 143 D2
Mountain View
Broughton CH4 .... 140 C3
Helsby WA6 .... 73 D2
Mountbatten Way CW12 . 156 B2
Mountfield Rd Bramhall SK7 . 35 F3
Stockport SK3 .... 240 C3
Mourne Cl L66 .... 69 D3
Mow Cop Rd ST7 .... 195 E3
Mow La Biddulph ST6 ... 179 D1
Mount Pleasant ST7 ..... 195 D3
Mowbray Ave M33 ...... 242 C5
Mowbray **4** SK1 .... 240 F4
Mowcroft La WA8 .... 14 A2
Mowpen Brow WA16 ...... 29 D3
Moxon Ave WA4 .... 16 C3
Moyles Cl WA8 .... 12 B1
Mudhouse La L64 .... 67 F1
Mudhurst La SK12 .... 38 C1
Muir Rd CH1 .... 117 F2
Muirfield Ave SK6 .... 241 A4
Muirfield Cl Northwich CW9 . 104 A4
Warrington WA2 .... 9 D2
Wilmslow SK9 .... 60 B4
Muirfield Dr
Macclesfield SK10 .... 87 E2
Winsford CW7 .... 126 A1
Mulberry Ave WA3 .... 3 F4

Mulberry Cl Cheadle SK8 .. 34 B4
Elton CH2 .... 72 B2
Warrington WA1 .... 17 F3
Mulberry Gdns CW11 .... 174 B4
Mulberry Mews SK4 ..... 240 E6
Mulberry Mount St SK3 . 240 E4
Mulberry Rd CW2 .... 189 F1
Mulberry Rise CW8 ...... 103 E4
Mulcaster Ct CW1 .... 191 E3
Mull Cl L65 .... 70 B1
Mullen Cl WA5 .... 7 F1
Mullins Ave WA12 .... 2 B3
Mullion Dr WA15 .... 238 E6
Mullion Gr WA2 .... 9 D1
Mulsford La SY14 .... 222 A4
Murdishaw Ave WA7 ...... 50 B3
Murdishaw West Cty Prim
Sch WA7 .... 50 B3
Muriel Cl WA5 .... 14 B3
Murieston Rd WA15 ..... 238 E2
Murray Cl SK10 .... 87 D1
Murrayfield SK10 .... 87 D3
Murrayfield Dr CW5 ..... 205 E3
Museum St WA1 .... 16 A2
Music Hall Pass CH1 .... 237 E2
Myddleton La WA2 .... 8 B3
Myrica Gr CH2 .... 119 D2
Myrtle Ave Haydock WA11 . 1 A4
Higher Kinnerton CH4 .... 161 D4
Newton-le-W WA12 .... 2 B1
Myrtle Gr Chester CH2 ... 119 D2
Warrington WA4 .... 16 B2
Widnes WA8 .... 22 B4
Myrtle Rd M31 .... 11 F2
Myrtle St Ellesmere Port L65 . 70 B4
Stockport SK3 .... 240 B4
Mythholme Ave M44 ...... 11 E2

Nab Cl SK10 .... 63 E1
Nab La SK10 .... 63 E1
Nabbswood Rd ST7 ..... 195 D1
Nairn Ave CW4 .... 130 A1
Nairn Cl Bebington L63 ... 43 E2
Warrington WA2 .... 9 D2
Nancy View SK10 .... 88 A4
Nansen Rd SK8 .... 239 A4
Nansmoss La SK9 .... 33 E1
Nantwich Rd Audley ST7 . 209 D1
Barbridge CW5 .... 187 A4
Betley ST7 .... 208 C1
Broxton CH3 .... 183 E1
Crewe CW2 .... 190 B1
Ellesmere Port L66 .... 69 F2
Middlewich CW10 .... 151 D4
Tarporley CW6 .... 168 B4
Tiverton CW6 .... 168 B4
Wimboldsley CW10 ...... 150 C3
Winsford CW7 .... 126 A1
Woore CW3 .... 232 A1
Worleston CW7 .... 189 E1
Wrenbury CW5 .... 217 D3
Nantwich Sta CW5 ...... 204 C2
Nantwich Way **5** SK8 .... 34 C4
Naomi Cl CH1 .... 117 E3
Napier Gdns ST7 .... 195 D1
Napier Rd Chester CH2 . 118 B4
Manchester SK4 .... 240 B7
Napier St Hyde SK14 .... 241 E5
Warrington WA1 .... 16 B3
Naples Rd SK3 .... 240 B3
Napley Dr TF9 .... 236 B1
Napley Rd Mucklestone TF9 . 236 B1
Norton in Hales TF9 ..... 236 B1
Nares Cl WA5 .... 7 F1
Narrow La SK10 .... 37 D1
Naseby Rd CW12 .... 156 A2
Nasmyth Ave M34 .... 241 A8
Nat La CW7 .... 126 C1
Nathan Dr WA11 .... 1 C3
Naughton Lea WA8 .... 12 B2
Naughton Rd WA8 .... 23 D4
Navigation Cl WA7 .... 50 B3
Navigation Prim Sch
WA14 .... 238 D6
Navigation Rd
Altrincham WA14 & WA15 . 238 D6
Northwich CW8 .... 103 F4
Navigation Road Sta
WA14 .... 238 E6
Navigation St WA1 .... 16 B3
Naylor Ave WA3 .... 3 D4
Naylor Cres L66 .... 69 F4
Naylor Ct CW9 .... 103 F4
Naylor Rd WA8 .... 13 E1
Naylor St WA1 .... 16 A3
Neal Ave Ashton-u-L OL6 . 242 A3
Cheadle SK8 .... 34 A4
Gatley SK8 .... 239 A1
Neath Cl SK12 .... 36 B3
Needham Cl WA7 .... 23 E1
Needham Dr CW8 .... 103 E2
Needhams Wharf Cl SK10 . 88 A1
Neil St WA8 .... 13 D1
Neills Rd WA9 .... 6 A3
Nelson Ave Haydock WA11 . 1 A4
Crewe CW2 .... 190 B1
Hyde SK14 .... 241 E6
Macclesfield SK11 .... 112 B4
Nelson Cl SK12 .... 37 D2
Nelson Dr M44 .... 11 F3
Nelson Gr ST7 .... 193 F1
Nelson Ind Est ST7 ..... 194 B1
Nelson Rd L65 .... 70 B4
Nelson St Chester CH2 . 237 F3
Congleton CW12 .... 156 B1
Crewe CW2 .... 190 B1
Hyde SK14 .... 241 E6
Macclesfield SK11 .... 112 B4

Nelson St continued
Newton-le-W WA12 .... 2 A2
Runcorn WA7 .... 23 D2
Widnes WA7 .... 23 D1
Nemos Cl WA6 .... 73 E1
Neptune Cl WA7 .... 50 B4
Nesfield Cl SK11 .... 191 F4
Nesfield Dr CW11 .... 191 F4
Nessina Gr CW2 .... 205 F4
Neston Cty High Sch L64 .... 41 F1
Neston Cty Prim Sch L64 ... 66 C4
Neston Dr CH2 .... 118 C3
Neston Gn L66 .... 69 E2
Neston Gr SK3 .... 240 D1
Neston Rd Neston L64 .... 67 D2
Thornton Hough L63 .... 41 F3
Willaston L64 .... 67 F4
Neston St Mary's CE Contr
Prim Sch L64 .... 41 F1
Neston Sta L64 .... 66 C4
Neston Way [13] SK9 .... 34 B2
Nether Alderley Cty Prim
Sch SK10 .... 85 D3
Nether Alderley Old Mill
SK10 .... 85 D3
Nether Fold SK10 .... 87 D4
Netherfield WA8 .... 22 B4
Netherfields SK9 .... 85 D4
Netherlea CW4 .... 130 B4
Netherley Rd L35 .... 12 A1
Netherpool Rd L66 .... 69 F4
Netherton Dr WA6 .... 74 A4
Neumann St CW9 .... 104 A4
Neville Ave St Helens WA9 .... 1 A1
Warrington WA5 .... 8 B1
Neville Cres WA5 .... 15 D2
Neville Dr CH3 .... 119 D1
Neville Rd Bebington L62 .... 43 F4
Chester CH3 .... 119 D1
Neville St Crewe CW2 .... 190 B1
Newton-le-W WA12 .... 2 A2
Nevin Ave SK8 .... 239 E1
Nevin Cl SK7 .... 36 A4
Nevin Rd CH1 .... 117 C2
Nevis Dr CW2 .... 189 E2
New Bank Pl WA8 .... 12 A1
New Bank Rd WA8 .... 12 A1
New Barnet WA8 .... 12 C2
New Chester Rd L62 .... 43 F3
New Crane Bank CH1 .... 118 A1
New Crane St CH1 .... 118 A1
New Cut La WA1 .... 17 E4
New Farm Ct CH3 .... 120 C3
New Grosvenor Rd L65 .... 70 A4
New Hall Ave SK8 .... 34 A4
New Hall La Croft WA3 .... 4 C1
Culcheth WA3 .... 5 D1
New Hall Rd M33 .... 242 F6
New Hall St SK10 .... 87 C1
New Hey La L64 .... 68 A3
New Hey Rd SK8 .... 239 E6
New Horwich Rd SK23 .... 65 F4
New Inn La CW11 .... 176 A1
New King St Audley ST7 .... 209 E1
Middlewich CW10 .... 128 B1
New La Appleton WA4 .... 27 D3
Churton CH3 .... 180 C3
Croft WA3 .... 9 D4
Harthill CH3 .... 183 F2
Winsford CW7 .... 149 F2
New Manchester Rd
WA1 .... 17 D4
New Manor Rd WA4 .... 51 D3
New Mills Central Sta
SK22 .... 39 D4
New Mills Newtown Sta
SK22 .... 39 D3
New Mills Sch (Lower Sch)
The SK22 .... 39 D4
New Mills Sch The SK22 ... 39 E4
New Moss Rd M44 .... 11 E3
New Pale Rd WA6 .... 99 E3
New Platt La CW4 .... 130 B4
New Rd Anderton CW9 .... 78 B2
Antrobus CW9 .... 27 E1
Astbury CW12 .... 178 A4
Audley ST7 .... 209 F2
Duddon CW6 .... 145 D3
Ellesmere Port L66 .... 69 D4
Lymm WA13 .... 18 C2
Mere WA16 .... 30 C2
News Bank CW12 .... 132 B1
Prestbury SK10 .... 87 D4
Warrington WA4 .... 16 B2
Whaley Bridge SK23 .... 65 F3
Whaley Bridge, Bridgemont
SK23 .... 39 F1
Winsford CW7 .... 126 C1
Wrenbury CW5 .... 216 B2
New School La L66 .... 44 A1
New St
Altrincham WA14 .... 238 D4
Congleton CW12 .... 156 C1
Haslington CW1 .... 191 E3
Neston L64 .... 66 C3
New Mills SK22 .... 39 E4
Runcorn WA7 .... 23 D1
Sandbach CW11 .... 174 B4
Widnes WA8 .... 23 D1
Wilmslow SK9 .... 59 F3
New St Cotts CW12 .... 157 D3
New Warrington Rd
CW9 .... 79 D1
New Wellington Sch The
WA15 .... 238 F6

Newall Cres CW7 .... 127 D1
Newberry Gr SK3 .... 240 D1
Newbold Way CW5 .... 204 C2
Newboult Rd SK8 .... 239 E6
Newbridge Cl
Runcorn WA7 .... 50 B3
Warrington WA5 .... 7 E1
Newbridge Rd L65 .... 70 C2
Newburgh Cl WA7 .... 24 B1
Newbury Ave Crewe CW1 ... 190 B3
[7] Winsford CW7 .... 149 D4
Newbury Cl
Cheadle Hulme SK8 .... 35 D3
Widnes WA8 .... 13 F1
Newbury Rd Cheadle SK8 .... 34 B4
Chester CH4 .... 140 C3
Newby Ct CW12 .... 156 A1
Newby Dr
Altrincham WA14 .... 238 D6
Gatley M22 .... 239 A6
Sale M33 .... 242 E6
Newby Rd SK4 .... 240 C6
Newcastle Rd
Astbury CW12 .... 178 A4
Brereton Green CW11 .... 153 F2
Congleton CW12 .... 156 A1
Hassall Green CW11 .... 176 A2
Haymoor Green CW5 .... 205 E2
Hough Common CW2 .... 206 B2
Kidsgrove ST7 .... 210 C4
Shavington CW2 .... 206 B2
Smallwood CW11 .... 176 B3
Woore CW3 .... 232 C1
Newcastle Rd N CW11 ..... 153 F3
Newcastle Rd S CW11 ..... 153 F3
Newcastle St CW1 .... 190 A3
Newchapel Rd ST7 .... 195 E2
Newchurch Cty Prim Sch
WA3 .... 4 C2
Newchurch La WA3 .... 4 C1
Newcombe Ave WA2 .... 16 C4
Newcroft CH1 .... 94 A1
Newcroft Dr SK3 .... 240 D2
Newdigate Ct Crewe CW1 .. 190 B2
Crewe CW1 .... 190 B3
Newfield Ct WA13 .... 19 D3
Newfield Dr CW1 .... 190 C3
Newfield St CW11 .... 175 D4
Newgate
Macclesfield SK11 .... 112 B4
Wilmslow SK9 .... 59 E4
Newgate St CH1 .... 237 E2
Newhall Ave CW11 .... 175 D3
Newhall Cl CH2 .... 118 C3
Newhall Rd CH2 .... 118 C3
Newham Cl SK11 .... 112 C2
Newhaven Rd WA2 .... 8 A2
Newington Ct WA14 .... 238 B3
Newland Cl WA8 .... 12 B2
Newland Mews WA3 .... 4 C3
Newlands Ave Bramhall SK7 .. 35 F4
Cheadle Hulme SK8 .... 35 D4
Newlands Cl
Cheadle Hulme SK8 .... 35 D4
Frodsham WA6 .... 74 B3
Newlands Dr Goldborne WA3 ... 3 E4
Manchester M20 .... 239 C8
Wilmslow SK9 .... 59 F3
Newlands Rd Cheadle SK8 ... 239 D6
Macclesfield SK10 .... 111 F4
Warrington WA4 .... 16 C1
Newlyn Ave
Congleton CW12 .... 178 C4
Macclesfield SK10 .... 86 B1
Newlyn Cl WA7 .... 50 A3
Newlyn Dr SK6 .... 241 A3
Newlyn Gdns WA5 .... 14 B2
Newman St Hyde SK14 ...... 241 E7
Warrington WA4 .... 16 C2
Newman's La CW5 .... 219 E4
Newmoore La WA7 .... 24 C2
Newnham Dr L65 .... 70 B2
Newplatt La
Allostock CW4 .... 107 D1
Cranage CW4 .... 107 D1
Newport Gr ST5 .... 210 C1
Newquay Cl WA7 .... 50 A3
Newquay Ct CW12 .... 178 C4
Newquay Dr Bramhall SK7 ... 35 F4
Macclesfield SK10 .... 111 E4
Newry Ct CH2 .... 118 B2
Newry Pk CH2 .... 118 B2
Newry Pk E CH2 .... 118 B2
Newsham Cl WA4 .... 12 A4
Newsholme Cl WA3 .... 4 C2
Newstead Cl SK12 .... 36 B3
Newstead Terr WA15 .... 238 F7
Newton Bank CW10 .... 128 A1
Newton Bank Sch WA12 ...... 2 C2
Newton Comm Hospl
WA12 .... 2 A1
Newton Cty Prim Sch
CH2 .... 118 C2
Newton Gr WA2 .... 8 C2
Newton Hall Ct CH2 .... 118 C3
Newton Hall Dr CH2 .... 118 C3
Newton Hall La WA16 .... 58 C3
Newton Hall Mews
CW10 .... 128 B1
Newton Heath CW10 .... 128 A1
Newton Hollow WA6 .... 74 B1
Newton La Chester CH2 ..... 118 C2
Daresbury WA4 .... 51 F2
Newton-le-W WA12 .... 2 C3
Tattenhall CH3 .... 166 B2
Newton Park Dr WA12 .... 2 C2
Newton Park View CH2 ...... 118 B2
Newton Pl CW12 .... 156 C1

Newton Rd
Altrincham WA14 .... 238 E7
Ellesmere Port L65 .... 70 B3
Goldborne WA3 .... 3 E3
St Helens WA9 .... 1 A2
Warrington WA2 .... 8 A3
Wilmslow SK9 .... 34 A1
Winwick WA2 .... 8 A3
Newton St Crewe CW1 .... 190 B3
Hyde SK14 .... 241 D8
Macclesfield SK11 .... 112 B4
Stalybridge SK15 .... 242 C2
[1] Stockport SK3 .... 240 E4
Newton Sta SK14 .... 241 F8
Newton-le-Willows Cty
Prim Sch WA12 .... 2 B2
Newton-le-Willows High
Sch WA12 .... 2 B3
Newton-le-Willows Sta
WA12 .... 2 C2
Newtons Cres CW11 .... 191 F4
Newtons Gr CW11 .... 191 F4
Newtons La CW11 .... 191 F4
Newtown Kidsgrove ST7 ..... 195 F1
Neston L64 .... 66 C4
Newtown Cl CH2 .... 237 E3
Newtown Cty Prim Sch
SK22 .... 39 D3
Nicholas Ave CW9 .... 104 B3
Nicholas Cl CH1 .... 237 D2
Nicholas Rd
Weaverham CW8 .... 77 E1
Widnes WA8 .... 22 B4
Nicholas St CH1 .... 237 D2
Nicholas St Mews CH1 ...... 237 D2
Nicholls St WA4 .... 17 D1
Nicholson Ave SK10 .... 87 F1
Nicholson Cl SK10 .... 87 F1
Nicholson St
Stockport SK4 & SK5 .... 240 E6
Warrington WA5 .... 15 F3
Nickelby Rd SK12 .... 36 C2
Nickolson Cl CH2 .... 119 F4
Nicol Ave WA1 .... 17 F4
Nidderdale Cl CW12 .... 157 D3
Niddries La CW9 .... 126 C4
Nield Ct CH2 .... 118 B4
Nield's Brow WA14 .... 238 C2
Nigel Gresley Cl CW1 .... 191 D2
Nigel Rd L60 .... 41 E4
Nigel Wlk WA7 .... 24 A1
Nightgale Cl CW1 .... 189 F4
Nightingale Cl
Farndon CH3 .... 180 C1
Middlewich CW10 .... 151 E3
Runcorn WA7 .... 49 F3
Warrington WA3 .... 9 F2
Wilmslow SK9 .... 34 A1
Nightingale Ct CW7 .... 149 E3
Nile St CW2 .... 190 B1
Nitchingham Sk9 .... 60 B3
Nixon Dr CW7 .... 126 A1
Nixon Rd CW8 .... 101 F2
Nixon St Crewe CW1 .... 189 F3
Macclesfield SK11 .... 112 A4
[3] Stockport SK3 .... 240 E4
No 2 Passage SK3 .... 240 D5
Noahs Ark La WA16 .... 58 C1
Noble Cl WA3 .... 9 F2
Noel Dr M33 .... 242 D6
Nook La Antrobus CW9 .... 53 F3
Goldborne WA3 .... 3 D4
Warrington WA4 .... 17 D2
Warrington, Fearnhead WA2 .. 9 D1
Nook The Broughton CH4 ... 140 C3
Cheadle Hulme SK7 .... 35 E3
Chester CH2 .... 118 C2
Guilden Sutton CH3 .... 119 E2
Noon Ct WA12 .... 2 A1
Nora St WA1 .... 16 B3
Norbreck Ave Cheadle SK8 .. 239 D6
Crewe CW2 .... 190 A1
Norbreck Dr WA5 .... 15 D2
Norbury Ave [4] Hyde SK14 . 241 D6
Warrington WA2 .... 16 B4
Norbury Cl
Hough Common CW2 .... 206 C2
Knutsford WA16 .... 57 E2
Widnes WA8 .... 13 F1
Norbury Dr Congleton CW12 156 C2
Middlewich CW10 .... 151 D4
Norbury Hollow Rd SK7 ...... 37 D4
Norbury St
Macclesfield SK11 .... 112 B4
Northwich CW9 .... 104 A4
[12] Stockport SK1 .... 240 F5
Norbury Way [8] Sk9 .... 34 B3
Norcott Ave WA4 .... 16 C1
Norcott Dr WA5 .... 6 C3
Norden Cl WA3 .... 9 E3
Norfolk Cl M44 .... 11 E3
Norfolk Dr WA5 .... 14 C3
Norfolk Gr ST6 .... 179 E1
Norfolk Pl WA8 .... 22 B4
Norfolk Rd Chester CH2 ..... 118 C2
Congleton CW12 .... 156 C2
Ellesmere Port L65 .... 70 B3
Kidsgrove ST7 .... 194 C1
Norfolk St Hyde SK14 .... 241 D6
Runcorn WA7 .... 23 D2
Norfolk Wlk SK10 .... 86 C1
Norgrove Cl WA7 .... 50 B4
Norland St WA8 .... 13 E1
Norland's La Cronton L35 .... 12 C4
Widnes WA8 .... 12 C4
Norleane Cres WA7 .... 49 D4
Norley Ave Bebington L62 ... 43 F2
Ellesmere Port L65 .... 69 F3

Norley CE Contr Prim Sch
WA6 .... 100 C3
Norley Dr Chester CH3 ...... 119 E1
Sale M33 .... 242 E6
Norley La Crowton CW8 ...... 76 A1
Norley WA6 .... 101 D4
Norley Rd Cuddington CW8 . 101 F2
Kingsley WA6 .... 75 D1
Kingsley, Commonside WA6 100 A3
Norley WA6 .... 100 C2
Norman Ave Haydock WA11 .. 2 A4
Newton-le-W WA12 .... 2 C2
Norman Cl CH1 .... 94 C4
Norman Dr CW7 .... 149 E3
Norman Rd
Altrincham WA14 .... 238 C6
Manchester SK4 .... 240 B7
Runcorn WA7 .... 23 D1
Sale M33 .... 242 B5
Stalybridge SK15 .... 242 C2
Norman St Hyde SK14 .... 241 E6
Warrington WA2 .... 16 A3
Norman Way CW7 .... 117 C3
Norman's La WA4 .... 52 C3
Norman's Pl WA14 .... 238 D4
Normandy Chase WA14 .... 238 B4
Normandy Rd CW7 .... 149 E4
Normandy Rd CH2 .... 95 E1
Normanton Rd SK3 & SK8 .. 240 A2
Norreys Ave WA5 .... 15 F4
Norris Ave SK4 .... 240 C6
Norris Bank Prim Sch
SK4 .... 240 B7
Norris Bank Terr SK4 .... 240 C5
Norris Hill Dr SK4 .... 240 C6
Norris Rd Blacon CH1 .... 117 F3
Sale M33 .... 242 F5
Norris St WA2 .... 16 B4
North Ave Stalybridge SK15 242 D3
Warrington WA2 .... 16 A4
North Brook Rd CW6 .... 146 A4
North Cestrian Gram Sch
WA14 .... 238 C5
North Cheshire Jewish
Prim Sch SK8 .... 239 C2
North Crofts CW5 .... 204 C3
North Downs WA16 .... 57 E1
North Downs Rd SK8 .... 239 F3
North Dr Heswall L60 .... 41 D4
High Legh WA16 .... 29 E2
Northwich CW9 .... 104 C4
North Fields WA8 .... 57 E2
North Florida Rd WA11 .... 1 C4
North Gn CH5 .... 116 A3
North Harvey St [8] SK1 .... 240 F5
North Mead SK10 .... 87 D3
North Parade L64 .... 41 D1
North Park Brook Rd WA5 ... 7 F1
North Pl [5] SK1 .... 240 F5
North Rd Altrincham WA15 .. 32 A4
Ellesmere Port L65 .... 70 A4
Ellesmere Port, Hooton Park
L65 .... 44 C1
Halewood L24 .... 21 D3
North St Broughton CH4 .... 140 A4
Chester CH3 .... 119 D1
Congleton CW12 .... 156 B2
Crewe CW1 .... 190 B4
Hawarden CH5 .... 116 A2
Haydock WA11 .... 1 C3
Mount Pleasant ST7 .... 195 D3
North Stafford St CW1 ...... 190 B2
North Vale Rd WA15 .... 238 F6
North View Crewe CW1 ...... 190 A3
Great Sankey WA5 .... 14 C4
North Way
Holmes Chapel CW4 .... 130 B2
Shavington CW2 .... 206 B3
Northbank Ind Pk M44 ..... 11 F3
Northbank Wlk CW2 .... 206 B4
Northbury Rd L65 .... 69 F1
Northcombe Rd SK3 .... 240 E1
Northcote Rd SK7 .... 35 F4
Northdale Rd WA1 .... 17 D4
Northend Rd SK15 .... 242 E2
Northenden Rd
Gatley M22 & SK8 .... 239 A6
Sale M33 .... 242 C6
Sale M33 .... 242 E5
Northern La WA8 .... 12 A2
Northern Pathway CH4 ..... 237 F1
Northern Rise L66 .... 69 F2
Northfield Dr Biddulph ST6 . 179 F1
Wilmslow SK9 .... 60 B4
Northfield Pl CW2 .... 206 B3
Northgate CW6 .... 146 A4
Northgate Ave Chester CH2 237 E4
Macclesfield SK10 .... 87 C1
Northgate Rd SK3 .... 240 C4
Northgate Row CH1 .... 237 E2
Northgate St CH1 .... 237 D3
Northlands CW3 .... 232 B1
Northolt Ct WA8 .... 8 C1
Northstead Ave M34 .... 241 B6
Northumberland Rd M31 ... 11 F1
Northward Rd SK9 .... 59 F3
Northway Altrincham WA14 . 238 E6
Chester CH4 .... 141 D4
Lymm WA13 .... 18 B2
Northwich CW8 .... 78 B1
Runcorn WA7 .... 49 F4
Warrington WA8 .... 8 A1
Widnes WA8 .... 12 B1
Northwich Rd
Antrobus CW9, WA4 .... 53 D3
Cranage CW4, WA16 .... 106 C1
Dutton WA4 .... 51 D1
Great Budworth CW9 .... 78 C4
Ellesmere Port L65 .... 69 F3

Northwich Rd continued
Knutsford WA16 .... 56 B1
Runcorn WA7 .... 50 C2
Runcorn, Brookvale WA7 ...... 50 B4
Stretton WA4 .... 52 C4
Tabley WA16 .... 56 B1
Weaverham CW8 .... 102 C4
Whitley WA4 .... 52 C3
Northwich Sta CW9 .... 104 A4
Northwood Ave
Middlewich CW10 .... 151 F3
Newton-le-W WA12 .... 2 C2
Northwood Gr M33 .... 242 B6
Northwood La WA16 .... 28 C1
Northwood Rd WA7 .... 23 F1
Norton Ave Broughton CH4 140 B3
Penketh WA5 .... 14 C3
Norton Gate WA7 .... 50 B4
Norton Gr SK4 .... 240 B5
Norton Hales CE Sch
TF9 .... 236 B1
Norton Hill WA7 .... 24 B1
Norton La
Runcorn, Norton WA7 .... 24 B1
Runcorn, Town Park WA7 ..... 50 A4
Norton Priory Cty High Sch
WA7 .... 24 A1
Norton Rd CH3 .... 119 E1
Norton Station Rd WA7 ..... 50 B4
Norton View WA7 .... 50 A4
Norton Village WA7 .... 24 B1
Norton Way CW11 .... 174 B4
Norton's La
Great Barrow CH3 .... 98 A1
Mouldsworth CH3 .... 98 A1
Nortons La CW6 .... 122 C4
Nortonwood La WA7 .... 24 B1
Norview Dr M20 .... 239 B8
Norville L66 .... 69 E4
Norway Gr [6] SK5 .... 240 F8
Norwich Ave WA3 .... 3 E4
Norwich Ct [1] SK10 .... 112 C4
Norwich Dr CH1 .... 94 C4
Norwood Ave
Cheadle Hulme SK7 .... 35 E3
Goldborne WA3 .... 3 F4
High Lane SK6 .... 37 E4
Norwood Dr CH4 .... 141 D3
Norwood Rd SK8 .... 239 B6
Nottingham Cl WA1 .... 17 F3
Nun House Cl CW7 .... 127 D1
Nun House Dr CW7 .... 127 D1
Nuns Rd CH1 .... 237 D1
Nunsmere Cl CW7 .... 127 D1
Nursery Ave WA15 .... 31 F4
Nursery Cl Kidsgrove ST7 .. 194 B1
Sale M33 .... 242 D6
Shavington CW2 .... 206 B2
Widnes WA8 .... 13 E2
Nursery Dr Biddulph ST6 ... 179 E1
Poynton SK12 .... 36 B2
Nursery La Cheadle SK3 .... 240 A3
Congleton CW12 .... 156 C1
Nether Alderley SK10 .... 84 B3
Siddington SK11 .... 110 A2
Wilmslow SK9 .... 59 F3
Nursery Rd Barnton CW8 .... 78 A2
Haslington CW1 .... 192 C2
Scholar Green ST7 .... 194 C3
Stockport SK4 .... 240 C6
Nursery The CW8 .... 103 E3
Nutfield Ave CW1 .... 190 A4
Nuthurst Gdns CW5 .... 204 C3
Nuttall Ct WA3 .... 9 E2
Nuttall St M44 .... 11 F3

O'Connell Cl WA11 .... 1 B3
O'Leary St WA2 .... 16 B4
Oak Ave Alsager ST7 .... 193 F1
Disley SK12 .... 39 D3
Goldborne WA3 .... 3 D4
Haydock WA11 .... 1 C4
Irlam M44 .... 11 E3
Macclesfield SK11 .... 112 A3
Manchester SK4 .... 240 B6
Newton-le-W WA12 .... 2 B2
Romiley SK6 .... 241 C2
Wilmslow SK9 .... 59 F3
Winsford CW7 .... 149 E4
Oak Bank La SK10 .... 52 D3
Oak Bank Cl CW5 .... 205 F2
Oak Bank Dr SK10 .... 63 D1
Oak Bank La CH2 .... 119 E3
Oak Cl SK9 .... 59 F3
Oak Cotts SK9 .... 33 F2
Oak Dr Cheadle Hulme SK7 .. 35 E4
Higher Kinnerton CH4 .... 161 D4
Middlewich CW10 .... 151 E4
Runcorn WA7 .... 49 E4
Oak Gr Cheadle SK8 .... 239 E5
Ellesmere Port L65 .... 70 A2
Nantwich CW5 .... 204 C2
Poynton SK12 .... 36 B2
Oak House La CW7 .... 149 D4
Oak La Bollington SK10 .... 88 A3
Cuddington CW8 .... 101 F1
Marton SK11 .... 133 E3
Wilmslow SK9 .... 59 F3
Oak Lea Ave SK9 .... 60 A3
Oak Meadow CW8 .... 102 C4
Oak Mews SK9 .... 34 B1
Oak Rd Altrincham WA15 ... 238 E3
Cheadle SK8 .... 239 E5
Chelford SK11 .... 84 A2
Chester CH4 .... 140 C3
Hooton L66 .... 43 F1
Lymm WA13 .... 18 B2
Mottram St Andrew SK10 ..... 86 A4

Oak Rd continued
Partington M31 11 E1
Penketh WA5 14 C2
Sale M33 242 D6
Oak St Crewe CW2 190 B2
Croft WA3 9 D4
Ellesmere Port L65 70 B4
Hyde SK14 241 E8
Northwich CW9 79 D1
Rode Heath ST7 193 F4
Sandbach CW11 174 B4
Stockport SK3 240 B4
Oak Tree Cl CW1 190 C3
Oak Tree Dr CW1 190 C3
Oak Tree Gate CW3 229 F2
Oak Tree La CW4, CW10 129 F4
Oak View Knutsford WA16 57 E1
Marton SK11 133 E3
Speke L24 21 D2
Oak Wood Rd WA16 29 F1
Oakdale Ave WA4 16 B1
Oakdale Cl CH4 139 D2
Oakdale Dr SK8 239 B2
Oakdene Ave Cheadle SK8 34 A4
Ellesmere Port L66 69 E3
Warrington WA1 17 E4
Oakdene Cl L62 43 E3
Oakdene Way CW6 168 B4
Oakenclough Cl SK9 34 B1
Oakes Cnr CW5 219 F2
Oakfield M33 242 A7
Oakfield Ave Cheadle SK8 239 E6
Chester CH2 118 B4
Knutsford WA16 57 E2
Wrenbury CW5 216 C2
Oakfield Cl
Alderley Edge SK9 60 A2
Wrenbury CW5 216 C2
Oakfield Ct WA15 238 F6
Oakfield Cty Inf & Jun Sch
WA8 22 A4
Oakfield Dr Chester CH2 118 B4
Widnes WA8 22 A4
Oakfield Rd Alderley Edge SK9 60 A1
Altrincham WA15 238 E4
Bebington L62 43 E4
Blacon CH1 117 E2
Ellesmere Port L66 68 C4
Plumley WA16 80 C2
Poynton SK12 36 C2
Stockport SK3 240 F1
Oakfield Rise CW4 130 A2
Oakfield St WA15 238 E5
Oakfield Trad Est WA15 238 E5
Oakham Rd M34 241 A5
Oakhill Cl SK10 87 D2
Oakhurst Chase SK9 60 A1
Oakhurst Dr
Cheadle SK3 & SK8 240 B1
Wistaston CW2 206 A4
Oakland Ave CW1 191 E2
Oakland St
Warrington WA1 16 C4
Widnes WA8 23 D2
Oaklands CH3 119 F2
Oaklands Ave CH3 166 A1
Oaklands Cl SK9 34 C1
Oaklands Cres CH3 166 A1
Oaklands Cty Inf Sch SK9 34 C1
Oaklands Dr Lymm WA13 18 B1
Sale M33 242 A7
Oaklands Rd Goldborne WA3 3 F4
Ollerton WA16 82 C3
Oaklands Sch CW7 149 D4
Oaklea Ave CH2 118 C2
Oakleigh Knutsford WA16 82 B4
Manchester SK4 240 B7
Oakleigh Ct CW12 155 F2
Oakleigh Rise CW8 78 C1
Oakley Cl CW11 175 D4
Oakley St CW1 190 B3
Oakley Villas SK4 240 B7
Oakmere Cl CW11 174 C4
Oakmere Dr Chester CH3 142 A4
Ellesmere Port L66 69 F1
Penketh WA5 14 C2
Oakmere Rd Cheadle SK8 239 F4
Wilmslow SK9 34 B3
Winsford CW7 125 F1
Oakmere St WA7 23 D1
Oaks Dr The CH2 118 B4
Oaks Pl WA8 23 D4
Oaks The Bebington L62 43 E4
Gatley SK8 239 A2
Oaksdean Ct SK9 34 A1
Oakside Cl SK8 239 E6
Oaksway L60 41 E3
Oaktree Cl Barnton CW8 78 A2
Tarporley CW6 146 B1
Oaktree Ct Cheadle SK8 239 D5
Chester CH2 119 D2
Oakway M20 239 C8
Oakways WA4 26 B3
Oakwood Av SK9 59 F3
Oakwood Ave Gatley SK8 239 B5
Warrington WA1 16 C4
Oakwood Avenue Cty Prim
Schs WA1 16 B4
Oakwood Cl L66 69 E1
Oakwood Cres Crewe CW2 189 F2
Sandbach CW11 175 F3
Oakwood Ct WA14 31 D4
Oakwood Dr SK10 87 E3
Oakwood Gate WA3 9 E2
Oakwood La
Altrincham WA14 238 B1
Barnton CW8 78 A1
Sandbach CW11 174 A4
Oakwood Rd Disley SK12 38 B3
Rode Heath ST7 193 F4
Romiley SK6 241 C2
Oat Market CW5 204 C3
Oathills SY14 213 D3
Oathills Cl CW6 146 B1
Oathills Dr CW6 146 B1
Oatlands SK9 85 D4
Oban Dr Heswall L60 41 D4
Sale M33 242 E5
Oban Gr WA2 9 D2
Ocean St WA14 238 B6
Ocean Street Trad Est
WA14 238 B7
Off Ridge Hill La SK15 242 C2
Offley Ave CW11 175 D4
Offley Cty Inf & Jun Sch
CW11 175 D4
Offley Rd CW11 175 D4
Ogden Ct SK14 241 E6
Ogden Rd SK7 35 E3
Oglet La L24 46 C4
Oil Sites Rd L65 71 E3
Okell St WA7 23 D1
Old Bank Cl SK6 241 A3
Old Bedions Sports Ctr
M20 239 A8
Old Boston WA11 2 A4
Old Boston Trad Est WA11 2 A4
Old Brickworks Ind Est
SK10 63 F2
Old Butt La ST7 194 B1
Old Chapel St SK3 240 D3
Old Cherry La WA13 28 A4
Old Chester Rd
Barbridge CW5 187 E3
Ellesmere Port L66 69 E2
Helsby WA6 73 E2
Higher Walton WA4 25 F4
Old Church Cl L65 70 B4
Old Coach Rd
Broxton SY14 199 D3
Edge Green SY14 199 D3
Kelsall CW6 122 B3
Old Farm Cl L64 68 A4
Old Gardens St 3 SK1 240 F4
Old Gate Cl CW10 151 D4
Old Gorse Cl CW2 189 F2
Old Hall Ave SK23 65 F2
Old Hall Cl WA4 26 A4
Old Hall Cres SK9 34 C2
Old Hall Ct Ashton CH3 121 F4
Malpas SY14 213 D2
Old Hall Cty Prim Sch
WA5 15 E4
Old Hall Dr L65 70 A2
Old Hall Gdns CH2 237 F4
Old Hall La Elton CH2 72 A2
Knutsford WA16 56 A2
Tabley WA16 55 F2
Woodford SK7 61 E4
Old Hall Pk CH3 119 F3
Old Hall Pl CH1 237 D2
Old Hall Rd Gatley SK8 239 A6
Great Sankey WA5 15 E4
Northwich CW9 104 A3
Sale M33 242 E6
Old Hall St SK10 87 E1
Old Hey Wlk WA12 2 B1
Old Higher Rd WA8 21 E3
Old Hutte La L24 21 D3
Old La Acton Bridge CW8 76 C2
Antrobus CW9 53 E2
Davenham CW9 104 B1
Poulton CH4 162 C1
Pulford CH4 162 C1
Old Liverpool Rd WA5 15 F2
Old Man of Mow The
ST7 195 E4
Old Market Pl
Altrincham WA14 238 D5
Knutsford WA16 57 D1
Old Mill Cl L60 41 D4
Old Mill Ct CH2 118 B3
Old Mill La Hazel Grove SK7 37 D4
Macclesfield SK11 112 C3
Whitley WA4 52 C2
Old Mill Rd CW11 175 E3
Old Moss La Leigh WA3 5 F3
Tarvin CH3 144 B4
Old Oak Dr M34 241 A7
Old Orchard Antrobus CW9 53 E2
Wilmslow SK9 60 A4
Old Orchard The CW8 101 F2
Old Park Rd CW1 207 E4
Old Pearl La CH3 119 D1
Old Quay Cl L64 66 B4
Old Quay La L64 66 B4
Old Quay St WA7 23 D2
Old Rd Anderton CW9 78 B2
Audley ST7 209 F2
Cheadle SK8 239 F6
Hyde SK14 241 D8
Stockport SK4 240 E7
Warrington WA4 16 A2
Whaley Bridge SK23 65 F2
Whaley Bridge, Furness Vale
SK23 39 E2
Whaley Bridge, New Horwich
SK23 65 F3
Wilmslow SK9 60 A4
Wilmslow, Handforth SK9 34 B2
Old Rectory Gdns SK8 239 D5
Old School Cl CH3 180 C1
Old School House La
WA2 8 A4
Old Smithy La WA13 18 B1
Old St SK15 242 D2
Old Stack Yd CH3 120 C3
Old Upton La WA8 12 C2
Old Vicarage Gdns CW3 229 F2
Old Vicarage Rd L64 68 A4
Old Wargrave Rd WA12 2 B2
Old Warrington Rd CW9 79 D1
Old Whint Rd WA11 1 A3
Old Woman's La CH3 142 B4
Old Wool La SK8 239 F4
Old Wrexham Rd CH4 141 E4
Oldfield Brow Prim Sch
WA14 238 A5
Oldfield Cres CH4 140 C3
Oldfield Cty Prim Sch
CH3 119 E2
Oldfield Dr
Altrincham WA15 238 F6
Chester CH3 119 E1
Mobberley WA16 58 A2
Oldfield Gr M33 242 C7
Oldfield La WA14 20 C2
Oldfield Mews WA14 238 C5
Oldfield Rd
Altrincham WA14 238 B5
Ellesmere Port L65 70 A3
Lymm WA13 18 B2
Sale M33 242 C7
Sandbach CW11 174 C2
Oldgate WA8 22 B4
Oldhall St SY14 213 D2
Oldham Dr SK6 241 A4
Oldham St Bollington SK10 88 A4
Hyde SK14 241 D6
Warrington WA4 16 B2
Oldham's Rise SK10 87 E2
Oldhams Hill CW8 78 C1
Oldhill Cl ST7 210 C3
Olive Dr L64 66 C4
Olive Gr ST5 210 B1
Olive Rd L64 66 C4
Oliver Cl SK10 87 F4
Oliver La L66 69 E2
Oliver St
Stockport SK1 & SK3 240 F4
Warrington WA2 16 A3
Ollerbarrow Rd WA15 238 E2
Ollersett Ave SK22 39 E4
Ollersett View Hospl SK22 39 E4
Ollershaw La CW9 79 E2
Ollerton Cl WA4 17 D2
Ollerton Inf & Jun Sch
WA16 83 D2
Ollerton Rd 14 SK9 34 B3
Ollier St 18 WA8 23 D4
One Oak La SK9 60 C4
Onneley La CW3 232 C2
Onslow Rd Blacon CH1 117 E2
Stockport SK3 240 C4
Onston La CW8 101 F4
Onward St SK14 241 D6
Openshaw La M44 11 F3
Orange Gr WA2 8 C1
Orange La CW9 79 E1
Orchard Ave
Acton Bridge CW8 76 C2
Lymm WA13 18 C2
Partington M31 11 F2
Whaley Bridge SK23 65 E4
Orchard Brow WA3 11 D1
Orchard Cl Barnton CW8 78 A2
Cheadle Hulme SK7 35 E4
Chester CH2 118 B3
Ellesmere Port L66 69 F1
Frodsham WA6 74 A3
Goostrey CW4 107 F1
Higher Wincham CW9 80 A3
Macclesfield SK11 112 A3
Middlewich CW10 151 E4
Poynton SK12 36 C2
Weaverham CW8 77 E1
Wilmslow SK9 59 F3
Winsford CW7 149 E4
Orchard Cres
Kidsgrove ST7 194 B1
Nantwich CW5 204 C2
Nether Alderley SK10 84 C3
Orchard Croft CH3 119 F3
Orchard Ct Alsager ST7 193 F2
Chester CH3 119 D1
Haslington CW1 191 E2
Orchard Dene CW8 101 E3
Orchard Dr
Little Leigh CW8 77 E3
Neston L64 66 C3
Wilmslow SK9 34 C1
Orchard Gn SK9 60 A1
Orchard Gr CH3 180 C1
Orchard Haven L66 69 F1
Orchard La L66 69 D4
Orchard Park La CH2 72 B2
Orchard Pl WA6 73 E2
Orchard Rd
Altrincham WA15 238 E5
Ellesmere Port L65 70 A1
Lymm WA13 19 D3
Whaley Bridge SK23 65 E4
Orchard Rise CW9 126 C4
Orchard St Chester CH1 237 D3
Crewe CW1 190 B3
Hyde SK14 241 E6
Northwich CW9 104 A4
Stockport SK1 240 F5
Warrington WA1 16 B3
Warrington, Fearnhead WA2 9 D1
Warrington, Hillcliffe WA4 26 B4
Willaston (nr Nantwich)
CW5 205 E3
Orchard Vale SK3 240 C2
Orchard Way
Congleton CW12 156 A2
Kelsall CW6 122 B3
Widnes WA8 12 A2
Orchards The
Broughton CH4 140 B3
Pickmere WA16 79 F3
Shavington CW2 206 B2
Orchid Cl Huntington CH3 142 A3
Irlam M44 11 F4
Orchil Cl L66 69 D3
Ordnance Ave WA3 9 F2
Ordsall Cl CW11 174 C2
Orford Ave Disley SK12 38 B3
Warrington WA2 16 B4
Orford Cl Hale L24 21 E1
High Lane SK6 37 F4
Orford Gn WA2 8 B1
Orford La WA2 16 A4
Orford Rd WA2 16 C4
Orford St WA1 16 A3
Oriel Bank High Sch SK3 240 F1
Orkney Cl Ellesmere Port L65 70 B1
Widnes WA8 13 F2
Orme Cl Macclesfield SK10 87 E2
Prestbury SK10 87 D4
Orme Cres SK10 87 E2
Ormerod Cl Romiley SK6 241 A1
Sandbach CW11 175 E3
Ormesby Gr L63 43 D3
Ormond Cl WA8 12 B1
Ormonde Rd CH2 118 B2
Ormonde St CH2 237 F3
Ormston Ave WA12 2 A3
Orphanage St SK4 & SK5 240 E7
Orrell Cl WA5 15 D3
Orrishmere Rd SK8 239 F3
Orton Cl CW7 127 D2
Ortonbrook Prim Sch M31 11 F1
Orwell Cl SK9 34 B1
Osborne Ave WA2 8 B1
Osborne Gr Gatley SK8 239 A3
Shavington CW2 206 B3
Osborne Rd
Altrincham WA15 238 E5
Goldborne WA3 3 F4
Hyde SK14 241 E5
Stockport SK2 240 F3
Warrington WA4 16 A1
Osborne Terr M33 242 B6
Osbourne Pl 7 WA14 238 D4
Osier Cl CH2 72 B2
Osmere Cl SY13 226 A1
Osprey Ave CW7 149 E3
Osprey Cl
Middlewich CW10 151 E3
Runcorn WA7 49 F3
Warrington WA2 8 C2
Osprey Dr SK9 60 B4
Osprey View ST7 195 E2
Ossett Cl WA7 50 B4
Ossmere Cl CW11 174 C4
Ostler's La WA16 58 C4
Otters Bank CW7 126 A1
Otterspool Rd SK6 241 B1
Oughtrington Cres WA13 19 D2
Oughtrington Cty Prim Sch
WA13 19 D2
Oughtrington La WA13 19 D1
Oughtrington View WA13 19 D2
Oulton Ave Chester CH2 118 B4
Sale M33 242 E7
Oulton Dr CW12 155 F2
Oulton Mill La Eaton CW6 147 D4
Utkinton CW6 147 D4
Oulton Pl CH1 237 E3
Our Lady of Lourdes RC
Prim Sch M31 11 F2
Our Lady of Perpetual
Succour RC Aided Inf Sch
WA8 12 A1
Our Lady of Perpetual
Succour RC Aided Jun Sch
WA8 22 A4
Our Lady's RC Aided Prim
Sch Runcorn WA7 50 A3
Warrington WA4 16 C2
Our Lady's RC Inf & Jun
Sch L65 70 A2
Our Lady's RC Prim Sch
SK3 240 E4
Out La CH3 184 B3
Outwood Dr SK8 34 A4
Outwood La M90 33 D4
Outwood La W M90 33 D4
Outwood Prim Sch SK8 34 B4
Outwood Rd SK8 34 A4
Oval The Cheadle SK8 34 A4
Ellesmere Port L65 70 B2
Ovenhouse La SK10 87 F4
Over Hill Dr CW7 149 E4
Over Rd CW5 172 A4
Overdale La CW8 101 E1
Overdale Rd Disley SK12 38 C3
Romiley SK6 241 A1
Willaston L64 43 D1
Overdene Rd CW7 149 E4
Overfields WA16 57 E2
Overhill Dr SK9 60 C4
Overhill La SK9 60 C4
Overhill Rd SK9 60 B4
Overleigh Ct CH4 141 E4
Overleigh Rd CH4 141 E4
Overleigh St Mary's CE
Contr Prim Sch CH4 141 E4
Overpool Gdns L66 69 F2
Overpool Rd L65 69 F3
Overpool Sta L66 69 F3
Overton Cl
Congleton CW12 156 B2
Middlewich CW10 151 D4
Overton Dr WA6 74 B3
Overton Rd ST6 179 F3
Overton Way 4 SK9 34 B3
Overway CW7 126 C1
Overwood Ave CH1 94 C1
Overwood La Blacon CH1 117 E2
Mollington CH1 94 B1
Ovington Cl WA7 49 F2
Owen Cl CH1 117 F3
Owen St Crewe CW2 190 B1
Stockport SK3 240 D5
Warrington WA2 16 A4
Owley Wood Rd CW8 77 F1
Ox-Hey Cres ST6 179 E1
Ox-Hey Dr ST6 179 E1
Oxborough Cl WA8 12 C2
Oxenham Rd WA2 8 A2
Oxford Cl CH1 94 C4
Oxford Ct 4 SK10 112 C4
Oxford Dr Halewood L26 21 D4
Romiley SK6 241 C4
Thornton Hough L63 41 F3
Oxford Gr M44 11 E3
Oxford Rd Altrincham WA14 238 D3
Chester CH4 140 C3
Macclesfield SK11 112 A4
Runcorn WA7 49 D4
Oxford St Crewe CW1 190 A3
Newton-le-W WA12 2 A2
Stalybridge SK15 242 F1
Oxford St continued
Warrington WA4 16 B2
Widnes WA8 23 D4
Oxford Way SK4 240 D7
Oxhey Fst Sch ST8 179 F1
Oxheys WA7 50 B4
Oxmead Cl WA2 9 D1
Oxmoor Cl WA7 50 A3
Oxney Cl SK11 111 F4
Oxton Cl WA8 12 B2
Oxton Gn L66 69 E2

Pacific Rd WA14 238 A6
Packmoor Prim Sch ST7 195 F1
Packsaddle Pk SK10 86 C3
Padarn Cl CH4 140 B3
Padden Brook SK6 241 B2
Padden Brook Mews SK6 241 B2
Paddington Bank WA1 16 C3
Paddock Brow SK10 87 D3
Paddock Chase SK12 36 C3
Paddock Dr L64 41 E1
Paddock Hill WA16 59 D1
Paddock La Audlem CW3 230 A1
Dunham Town WA13 20 A3
Kettleshulme SK23 64 C2
Partington WA13 19 E4
Whaley Bridge SK23 65 F3
Paddock Rd CH4 141 F1
Paddock Rise WA7 49 F2
Paddock The Cheadle SK8 239 E5
Chester CH4 141 D4
Ellesmere Port L66 69 E2
Elton CH2 72 A2
Hartford CW8 103 E2
Hassall Green CW11 175 F1
Helsby WA6 73 E1
Heswall L60 41 E4
Lymm WA13 19 E2
Tarporley CW6 146 B1
Whaley Bridge SK23 65 F3
Willaston (nr Nantwich)
CW5 205 E2
Wilmslow SK9 34 B2
Paddock Way CH4 161 D4
Paddock Wlk CW8 101 E3
Paddockhill La WA16 59 D2
Paddocks Gn CW12 178 C4
Paddocks The
Nova Scotia CW8 125 D3
Prestbury SK10 87 D3
Padgate Bsns Ctr WA1 17 D4
Padgate Cty High Sch WA2 8 C1
Padgate La WA1 16 C4
Padgate Sta WA1 9 D1
Padgbury Cl CW12 156 A1
Padgbury La CW12 156 A1
Padston Dr ST7 193 D2
Padstow Cl Crewe CW1 190 B4
Macclesfield SK10 111 F4
Penketh WA5 14 C2
Padstow Dr SK7 35 F4
Padstow Sq WA7 50 A3
Padworth Pl CW1 173 D1
Page Gr CW2 206 A2
Page La WA8 13 E1
Paignton Cl WA5 14 C2
Painswick Rd L66 69 F1
Paisley Ave L62 43 F2
Palace Fields Ave WA7 50 A4
Palace Fields Local Ctr
WA7 50 A3
Palace Hey L64 67 D3
Palace Rd M33 242 A7
Palacefields Cty Prim Sch
WA7 50 A3
Palatine Cl CH1 117 E3
Palgrave Cl CH1 118 A3
Palin Dr WA5 14 B4
Pall Mall CW5 204 C3
Pallard Ave WA6 74 B4
Palliser Cl WA3 10 A2

Palm Gr L66 70 A1
Palmer Ave SK8 239 F6
Palmer Cres WA5 15 E4
Palmer Rd CW11 175 E3
Palmer St M33 242 A6
Palmerston Cl CW1 191 E3
Palmerston Rd SK11 112 A4
Palmerston St SK10 88 A4
Palmerston Way ST6 179 E1
Palmerstone Cl CH1 118 A2
Palmyra Sq N WA1 16 A3
Palmyra Sq S WA1 16 A3
Panda Way CW11 175 D3
Pangbourne Cl
Appleton WA4 26 C3
Stockport SK3 240 C2
Panton Pl CH2 118 C2
Panton Rd CH2 118 C2
Parade Rd M90 33 E4
Parade The Blacon CH1 117 F3
Neston L64 41 D1
Paradise CH4 237 E1
Paradise La CW5 171 F4
Paradise Mill (Mus) SK11 112 B4
Paradise St SK11 112 B4
Paragon Cl WA8 13 D3
Parbold Ct WA8 22 B4
Parchments The WA12 2 B2
Parish Cl ST7 193 D2
Park Ave Altrincham WA15 238 F1
Altrincham, Timperley WA14 238 E8
Broughton CH4 140 C3
Cheadle SK8 239 F1
Cheadle SK3 239 F7
Cheadle Hulme SK7 35 E3
Haydock WA11 1 A3
Hyde SK14 241 D8
Kidsgrove ST7 210 C4
Poynton SK12 36 C2
Romiley SK6 241 C2
Sale M33 242 A8
Saughall CH1 94 A1
Tattenhall CH3 166 A1
Warrington WA4 16 B2
Weaverham CW8 77 E1
Whaley Bridge SK23 39 E2
Widnes WA8 13 D1
Wilmslow SK9 60 B4
Winsford CW7 127 D2
Park Ave N WA12 2 B1
Park Ave S WA12 2 B1
Park Bank CW12 156 C1
Park Brook Rd SK11 112 A4
Park Bvd WA1 16 A2
Park Cl Altrincham WA14 238 F8
Stalybridge SK15 242 C3
Tarvin CH3 121 D1
Park Court Mews SK8 239 E4
Park Cres Appleton WA4 26 B3
Ashton-u-L OL6 242 B2
Cuddington CW8 101 F2
Whaley Bridge SK23 39 E2
Wilmslow SK9 34 A1
Park Ct Chester CH2 237 F2
Frodsham WA6 74 A4
Runcorn WA7 49 D4
Sale M33 242 A7
Park Cty Prim Sch The
Runcorn WA7 24 A1
Tattenhall CH3 166 A1
Park Dr Altrincham WA15 238 F1
Chester CH2 119 D2
Ellesmere Port L65 70 A2
Hyde SK14 241 D8
Stockport SK4 240 B6
Wistaston CW2 205 F4
Park Dr S CH2 119 D2
Park Est CW2 206 B3
Park Gn SK11 112 B4
Park Gr SK4 240 B8
Park House Dr
Prestbury SK10 87 D4
Sandbach CW11 175 E4
Park House La SK10 87 D4
Park House Mews CW11 175 E4
Park La Appleton WA4 26 A3
Audley ST7 209 D2
Bate Heath WA16 79 F4
Congleton CW12 156 C1
Frodsham WA6 74 A4
Hargrave CH3 144 C2
Hartford CW8 103 D2
Hatherton CW5 219 F2
Higher Walton WA4 25 F3
Little Bollington WA14 20 A1
Macclesfield SK11 112 B3
Moulton CW9 126 C4
Pickmere WA16 79 F4
Poynton SK12 36 C2
Sandbach CW11 174 C3
Park Lane Sch SK11 112 A3
Park Lodge Cl SK8 239 E4
Park Mount SK8 239 A5
Park Mount Cl SK11 112 A3
Park Mount Dr SK11 112 A3
Park Rd
Altrincham WA15 238 F1
Altrincham, Bowdon WA14 238 A2
Bebington L62 43 F3
Cheadle SK8 239 E6
Congleton CW12 156 C2
Disley SK12 38 A3
Eaton CW12 134 C1
Ellesmere Port L65 70 B2
Goldborne WA3 3 D4
Park Rd continued
Great Sankey WA5 14 B4
Haslington CW1 191 E3
Heswall L60 41 D4
High Lane SK6 37 F3
Hyde SK14 241 D8
Little Budworth CW6 124 C1
Lymm WA13 29 E4
Macclesfield SK11 112 B3
Middlewich CW10 128 B1
Nantwich CW5 204 C2
New Mills SK22 39 E4
Northwich CW8 78 B1
Partington WA13 19 E4
Romiley SK6 241 C3
Runcorn WA7 49 D4
Sale M33 242 A8
Stalybridge SK15 & SK16 242 A1
Tarporley CW6 146 B1
Thornton-le-M CH2 71 F1
Warrington WA2 8 B1
Whaley Bridge SK23 65 E3
Widnes WA8 13 D1
Willaston L64 68 A4
Willaston (nr Nantwich) CW5 205 E3
Wilmslow SK9 59 F4
Park Rd N WA12 2 C2
Park Rd S WA12 2 B1
Park Rd W CH4 141 D4
Park Rise SK6 241 C3
Park Road Cty Prim Sch WA5 14 C3
Park Road Prim Sch
Altrincham WA14 238 E8
Sale M33 242 A8
Park St Bollington SK10 88 A4
Chester CH1 237 E2
Congleton CW12 156 C1
Haydock WA11 1 A3
Macclesfield SK11 112 B4
Neston L64 66 C4
Northwich CW8 103 F4
Stalybridge SK15 242 E1
6 Stockport SK1 240 F6
Park The Christleton CH3 142 C4
Penketh WA5 14 B2
Park Vale Rd SK11 112 B3
Park View Audlem CW3 230 B4
Bebington L62 43 E4
Cheadle SK3 239 F7
Gatley SK8 239 A6
Little Bollington WA14 20 A1
Park View Ct SK6 241 C2
Park View Rd ST7 195 D2
Park W CH1 117 F1
Park Way CH1 94 A1
Park West L60 40 C4
Park Wlk CH2 118 C2
Parkdale Ind Est WA4 16 B2
Parkdale Rd WA1 17 D4
Parker Ave CW8 103 D3
Parker Dr CH3 180 C1
Parker Dr S CH3 180 C1
Parker St Macclesfield SK11 112 C4
Runcorn WA7 23 D2
Warrington WA1 16 A3
Parker's Rd CW1 190 A4
Parker's Row CH3 180 C3
Parkers Ct WA7 49 F3
Parkett Heyes Rd SK11 111 F4
Parkfield L65 70 A1
Parkfield Ave WA4 17 D2
Parkfield Ct WA14 238 C4
Parkfield Dr
Ellesmere Port L65 70 A2
Helsby WA6 73 D2
Nantwich CW5 204 C2
Parkfield Rd
Altrincham WA14 238 C4
Broughton CH4 139 E2
Cheadle SK8 239 F1
Knutsford WA16 82 A4
Northwich CW9 104 B4
Parkfields La WA2 8 C1
Parkgate WA16 57 E2
Parkgate Ave WA16 108 A4
Parkgate Ct CH1 118 A2
Parkgate Cty Prim Sch L64 41 E1
Parkgate La
Knutsford WA16 57 E2
Thornton Hough L63 41 F3
Parkgate Rd Chester CH1 118 A2
Macclesfield SK11 112 B2
Mollington CH1 117 F4
Neston L64 66 B4
Puddington L66 68 B1
Saughall CH1 94 B2
Shotwick CH1 93 F4
Warrington WA4 16 B1
Parkgate Trad Est WA16 57 E2
Parkgate Way Runcorn WA7 50 B4
9 Wilmslow SK9 34 B2
Parkhill Ct WA16 57 D1
Parkhouse Ind Est ST5 210 C1
Parkhouse Rd E ST5 210 C1
Parkhouse Rd W ST5 210 C1
Parkland Cl WA4 27 D2
Parkland Dr CH2 72 A2
Parklands Ellesmere Port L66 69 E3
Kidsgrove ST7 195 D1
Widnes WA8 12 B2
Parklands Cty Prim Sch L66 69 E3
Parklands Dr Elton CH2 72 B2
Heswall L60 41 E3
Parklands Gdns L66 69 E3
Parklands The
Congleton CW12 157 D1
Reddish SK4 240 E8
Parklands View L66 69 E3
Parklands Way SK12 36 C2
Parklea L66 69 E3
Parkroyal Cty Prim Sch SK11 112 B4
Parkside SK6 37 E4
Parkside Cl SK6 37 E4
Parkside Hospl SK10 112 A4
Parkside Rd
Newton-le-W WA3, WA12 3 D1
Sale M33 242 D5
Winwick WA3, WA12 3 D1
Parkstone Dr CW1 190 A4
Parksway WA1 17 E4
Parkview Pk WA13 29 E4
Parkway Cheadle SK3 239 F7
Deeside Ind Est CH5 92 C1
Wilmslow SK9 60 A3
Parkwood Cl Bebington L62 43 F4
Lymm WA13 18 B1
Parliament St CW8 103 F4
Parliament Way CH1 94 C4
Parlington Cl WA8 22 B4
Parnell Sq CW12 157 D1
Parr Flat Comm Jun Sch WA9 1 A2
Parr Gr WA11 1 A3
Parr St Macclesfield SK11 112 B4
Warrington WA1 16 B2
Widnes WA8 13 E1
Parrs Wood Rd M20 239 B8
Parry Dr WA4 17 F2
Parry Mead SK6 241 A4
Parson St CW12 156 B1
Parsonage Ct SK4 240 B8
Parsonage Gn SK9 60 A4
Parsonage Rd
Manchester SK4 240 C8
Widnes WA8 23 D2
Parsonage St Hyde SK14 241 D5
Macclesfield SK11 112 B4
Stockport SK4 240 E6
Parsonage Way
Cheadle SK8 240 B1
Great Sankey WA5 15 D3
Parsons La CH2 118 A4
Partington Prim Sch M31 11 F2
Partridge Cl
Congleton CW12 156 C1
Warrington WA3 9 F2
Winsford CW7 149 E3
Partridge Way CW9 79 F3
Parvey La SK11 112 C1
Pasture Cl Kelsall CW6 122 B2
Macclesfield SK10 87 E2
Pasture Dr WA3 9 D4
Pasture La WA2 9 D1
Pasturefield Cl M33 242 F5
Patch La SK7 35 E3
Patmos La WA16 105 F4
Patrivale Cl WA1 16 C3
Patten La WA1 16 A3
Patterdale Ave WA2 8 B1
Patterdale Rd
Partington M31 11 F2
Romiley SK6 241 B4
Patterson Cl WA3 9 F2
Patterson St WA12 2 A2
Paul Cl WA5 14 B3
Paul St WA2 16 A3
Paulden Rd CW9 80 A1
Pavement La WA16 57 F2
Pavilions The
Davenham CW9 103 F1
Eccleston CH4 141 D2
Paxford Pl SK9 60 A3
Payne Cl WA5 15 E3
Paythorne Cl WA3 4 C2
Peach Field CH3 142 A4
Peach Gr WA11 1 C4
Peach Tree Cl L24 21 F1
Peacock Ave Cheadle SK9 34 A3
Warrington WA1 16 C3
Winsford CW7 149 E3
Peacock Hay Rd ST7 210 C2
Peacock La WA16 29 F3
Peacock Way SK9 34 B3
Peak Rd SK22 39 E4
Peakdale Ave SK8 239 B1
Pear Tree Ave Crewe CW1 190 A4
Runcorn WA7 49 E4
Pear Tree Cl Frodsham WA6 49 E1
Hale L24 21 F1
Winsford CW7 149 E4
Pear Tree Dr
Higher Wincham CW9 80 A3
Stalybridge SK15 242 E2
Pear Tree Farm Cotts CW9 104 C2
Pear Tree La
Acton Bridge CW8 76 C2
Whitchurch SY13 225 E1
Pear Tree Rd ST7 209 F1
Pear Tree Way
Chester CH2 118 C3
Ellesmere Port L66 69 F1
Pearl La CH3 119 D1
Pearl St SK10 87 D4
Pearle St SK10 87 E1
Pearlings The CH3 119 D1
Pearson Ave WA4 16 B1
Pearson St
23 Macclesfield SK11 112 C4
Reddish SK5 240 F7
Peartree Cl CW11 175 F3
Peartree La SY13 222 B1
Peartree Pl WA4 16 B2
Pearwood Cl CW6 146 B1
Peaslake Cl SK6 241 D2
Peasley Cl WA2 9 D1
Pebble Brook Cty Prim Sch CW2 190 B1
Pebble Cl SK15 242 D4
Peck Mill La WA6 98 A4
Peckfield Cl WA7 50 A3
Peckforton Castle CW6 167 F1
Peckforton Cl Gatley M22 239 A5
Sandbach CW11 174 C4
Peckforton Dr
Ellesmere Port L66 69 F2
Runcorn WA7 49 F2
Peckforton Hall La
Peckforton CW6 185 D3
Spurstow CW6 185 D3
Peckforton Rd CW6 168 A1
Peckforton Way
Chester CH2 118 C3
Northwich CW8 103 F4
Peckmill Cl SK9 34 C1
Pedley Hill Adlington SK10 62 C4
Rainow SK10 88 C2
Pedley House La WA16 58 C1
Pedley La Chelford WA16 83 E4
Congleton CW12 157 F2
Pedley St CW2 190 B1
Peebles Cl
Ellesmere Port L66 68 C3
Holmes Chapel CW4 130 A1
Peel Ave WA14 238 D2
Peel Cres CH3 121 F4
Peel Dr Astbury CW12 178 A4
Sale M33 242 E6
Peel Hall La CH3 121 F4
Peel Hollow ST7 209 D1
Peel House La WA8 13 D1
Peel La CW12 178 B4
Peel Rd WA15 238 E3
Peel Sq CW1 190 A3
Peel St Crewe CW1 190 A3
Hyde SK14 241 F5
Macclesfield SK11 112 B3
Newton-le-W WA12 2 A2
Runcorn WA7 22 C1
Stalybridge SK15 242 C1
Stockport SK2 240 F2
Peelgate Dr SK8 239 A2
Peerglow Pk Est WA14 238 E8
Peerswood Ct L64 66 C3
Peewit Cl CW7 149 E3
Peggie's La SK10 62 B1
Pelham Cl CW1 191 E3
Pelham Rd WA4 17 E2
Pelican Cl CW1 191 D3
Pemberton Cl L64 68 A4
Pemberton Rd CH1 237 D3
Pembridge Ct L65 70 C2
Pembridge Gdns L65 70 C2
Pembroke Cl CH4 141 F3
Pembroke Ct WA7 24 B3
Pembroke Dr L65 70 A2
Pembroke Gdns WA4 26 B2
Pembroke Gr M44 11 E3
Pembroke Rd SK11 111 F4
Pembroke Way CW7 149 D4
Pemston Ct L66 69 F4
Penare WA7 50 B3
Penbrook Cl CW2 189 E2
Pendennis Rd SK4 240 C7
Pendine Cl WA5 7 E1
Pendle Cl CW1 191 D3
Pendle Gdns WA3 4 C1
Pendlebury Rd SK8 239 B6
Pendlebury St WA4 17 D2
Penfold Cl CH1 94 A4
Penfold Hey CH2 118 B4
Penfold Way CH4 162 A4
Penfolds WA7 23 E1
Penhale Mews SK7 35 F4
Penistone Dr L66 69 D3
Penkeith's La WA7 23 D2
Penketh Ave WA5 15 F4
Penketh Ct WA7 23 D1
Penketh Cty High Sch WA5 15 D3
Penketh Cty Prim Sch WA5 14 B2
Penketh Rd WA5 15 D2
Penkford La WA5 1 B1
Penkford Sch WA12 1 C2
Penkford St WA12 1 C2
Penkrth South Cty Prim Sch WA5 14 C2
Penlington Ct CW5 204 C3
Penmann Cres L26 21 D4
Penmark Cl WA5 7 E1
Penmon Cl CH1 117 E2
Penn Gdns L65 70 A3
Penn House Cl SK7 35 F4
Penn La WA7 22 C1
Pennant Cl WA3 10 A2
Pennine Ct SK10 87 F1
Pennine Dr
Altrincham WA14 238 B5
Ashton-u-L OL6 242 B4
Pennine Rd WA2 8 C1
Pennine View SK15 242 F4
Pennine Way Biddulph ST6 179 F1
Winsford CW7 149 D4
Pennine Wlk L66 69 D3
Pennington Cl WA6 49 E1
Pennington Flash Ctry Pk WA3 4 A4
Pennington Gn L66 69 E2
Pennington La WA5 1 B1
Penningtons La SK11 111 F3
Penny La Burtonwood WA5 1 B1
Cronton WA8 12 A3
Haydock WA11 2 A4
Rainow SK10 88 B2
Stockport SK5 240 F7
Penny's La
Lach Dennis CW9 105 D3
Northwich CW9 104 C4
Pennyfields Rd ST7 195 E1
Pennymoor Dr WA14 238 B6
Pennypleck La CW9 28 A1
Penrhyn Ave SK8 239 E1
Penrhyn Cres
Hazel Grove SK7 36 B4
Runcorn WA7 49 D4
Penrhyn Rd Northwich CW8 103 F4
Stockport SK3 240 C4
Penrith Ave
Macclesfield SK11 111 F3
Warrington WA2 8 B1
Penrith Cl Frodsham WA6 49 E1
Partington M31 11 F2
Penrose Gdns WA5 14 B2
Penry Ave M44 11 F3
Penryn Cl WA5 14 C2
Pensarn Gdns WA5 7 E1
Pensarn Gr SK5 240 F8
Pensby Ave CH2 118 B3
Pensby Dr L66 69 E2
Pensby Rd L60 40 C4
Penshaw Ct WA7 49 F4
Pentland Ave WA2 8 A2
Pentland Cl Chester CH3 119 D1
Winsford CW7 149 D4
Pentland Pl WA2 8 A2
Pentre Cl CH3 121 F4
Pentre La CH3 121 F4
Penzance Cl SK10 111 F4
Peover Ave M33 242 E6
Peover Hall WA16 107 F4
Peover La Chelford SK11 108 C4
Congleton CW12 157 F3
Peover Rd 3 SK8 34 C3
Peover Superior Endowed Contr Prim Sch WA16 108 A4
Pepper St Appleton WA4 27 D2
Chelford SK11 83 F1
Chester CH1 237 E2
Christleton CH3 142 B4
Hale L24 21 E1
Henbury SK11 111 D4
Lymm WA13 18 C2
Middlewich CW10 128 B1
Mobberley WA16 31 F1
Nantwich CW5 204 C3
Peppers The WA13 18 C2
Percival Cl CH2 118 B4
Percival La Ollerton WA16 83 D2
Runcorn WA7 22 C1
Percival Rd Chester CH2 118 B4
Ellesmere Port L65 70 A3
Percival St WA1 16 B3
Percy James Cl ST7 193 F2
Percy Rd CH4 141 E4
Percy St Northwich CW9 104 A4
Stalybridge SK15 242 E2
Stockport SK1 240 F6
Warrington WA5 15 F3
Peregrine Cl CW7 149 E3
Perimeter Rd CH2 72 B3
Perrey St WA7 23 D1
Perrin Ave WA7 48 C4
Perrin St SK14 241 D6
Perrins Rd WA5 6 C3
Perth Cl Bramhall SK7 35 F3
Holmes Chapel CW4 130 A1
Warrington WA2 8 C2
Peter House Rd SK11 112 C2
Peter Pl CW1 190 A3
Peter Salem Dr WA5 15 D3
Peter St Altrincham WA14 238 D3
Denton M34 241 A7
Goldborne WA3 3 D4
Macclesfield SK11 112 B4
Northwich CW9 79 D1
Peter St W SK11 112 B4
Peterborough Cl SK10 87 D1
Peterhouse Gdns SK6 241 C4
Peters Cl SK10 87 D4
Petersburg Rd SK3 240 D2
Petersfield Gdns WA3 4 C2
Petersgate WA7 50 B4
Petersham Dr WA4 26 C3
Peterstone Cl WA5 7 E1
Petrel Ave SK12 36 A2
Petrel Cl CW7 149 E3
Petunia Cl SK11 112 A3
Petworth Ave WA2 8 A2
Petworth Cl CW2 206 A4
Pevensey Dr WA16 82 A4
Peveril Cl WA4 26 B4
Peveril Dr SK7 36 C4
Peveril Gdns SK12 39 D3
Peveril Mews SK12 39 D3
Peveril Rd WA14 238 C7
Peveril Wlk SK11 111 F4
Pewit La CW5 231 D4
Pewithall Cty Jun Sch WA7 49 D4
Pewterspear La WA4 26 C2
Pexhall Rd CW12 134 B2
Pexhill Ct SK4 240 A6
Pexhill Dr SK10 111 F4
Pexhill Rd Henbury SK11 111 E3
Macclesfield SK11 111 E3
Siddington SK11 110 B2
Warren SK10, SK11 111 E3

Pheasant Cl WA3 .... 9 F2
Pheasant Dr CW9 .... 79 F3
Pheasant Field L24 .... 21 E1
Pheasant Rise WA14 .... 238 D1
Pheasant Way CW7 ...... 149 E3
Pheasant Wlk WA16 ...... 29 E2
Philip Rd WA5 .... 22 A4
Philip St CH5 .... 116 A1
Philips Dr WA5 .... 14 B4
Philips La L66 .... 69 E2
Phillip St CH2 .... 118 C2
Phillips Rd CH1 .... 117 E2
Phillips Way L60 .... 40 C4
Phipps' La WA5 .... 6 C4
Phoenix Ave WA5 .... 7 F1
Phoenix St CH5 .... 116 A2
Phythian Cres WA5 .... 14 C2
Piccadilly SK1 .... 240 F5
Pichael Nook WA4 .... 17 D2
Pickenham Cl SK11 ...... 111 F3
Pickering Cres WA4 .... 17 E2
Pickering Rd WA8 .... 22 A3
Pickering St CH2 .... 237 F4
Pickering's Pasture WA8 ... 22 A2
Pickerings Cl WA7 .... 49 E3
Pickford St SK11 .... 112 B4
Pickford's Brow 3 SK1 .... 240 F5
Pickmere Cl
  Sandbach CW11 .... 174 C4
  Stockport SK3 .... 240 C2
Pickmere Dr Bebington L62 ... 43 F2
  Chester CH3 .... 142 A4
  Runcorn WA7 .... 50 B3
Pickmere Gdns SK8 .... 239 F4
Pickmere La
  Higher Wincham CW9 ... 79 F3
  Pickmere WA16 .... 55 E1
  Tabley WA16 .... 55 E1
Pickmere Rd SK9 .... 34 B3
Pickmere St WA5 .... 15 F3
Pickwick Cl CW11 .... 175 E4
Pickwick Pl ST7 .... 194 E3
Pickwick Rd SK12 .... 36 B2
Picow St WA7 .... 23 D1
Picton Ave
  Ellesmere Port L65 ..... 70 B3
  Runcorn WA7 .... 23 D1
Picton Cl Bebington L62 .. 43 F2
  Davenham CW9 .... 103 F2
  Warrington WA3 .... 9 E2
Picton Dr Wilmslow SK9 .. 34 C1
  Winsford CW7 .... 126 A1
Picton Gorse La
  Chester CH2 .... 119 D4
  Picton CH2 .... 119 D4
Picton La Mickle Trafford CH2 96 B3
  Picton CH2 .... 96 B2
  Stoak CH2 .... 96 B2
Picton Sq CW4 .... 130 B2
Piele Rd WA11 .... 1 C4
Pierce St SK11 .... 112 B4
Pierpoint La CH1 .... 237 E2
Pierpoint St Goldborne WA3 .. 3 D4
  Warrington WA5 .... 15 F4
Pigot Pl WA4 .... 16 C3
Pike La WA6 .... 75 D2
Pike Rd SK10 .... 89 D3
Pike St WA4 .... 16 B1
Pike The CW5 .... 204 C3
Pikemere Rd ST7 .... 193 D3
Pikemore Cty Prim Sch
  ST7 .... 193 D3
Pikenall La CW8 .... 76 B2
Pilgrim Cl WA2 .... 8 A3
Pillmoss La WA4 .... 52 A4
Pillory St CW5 .... 204 C3
Pimblett Rd WA11 .... 1 C4
Pimblett St WA3 .... 3 D4
Pimmcroft Way M33 ...... 242 F5
Pincot Rd SK22 .... 39 E4
Pine Ave Newton-le-W WA12 .. 2 B1
  Widnes WA8 .... 13 D1
Pine Cl Haydock WA11 ..... 1 B3
  Macclesfield SK10 .... 87 F1
Pine Ct ST7 .... 193 F2
Pine Gdns CH2 .... 118 B3
Pine Gr Chester CH2 ..... 119 D2
  Denton M34 .... 241 A7
  Ellesmere Port L66 ..... 70 A1
  Goldborne WA3 .... 3 E4
  Sandbach CW11 .... 175 E3
  Warrington WA1 .... 17 D1
  Winsford CW7 .... 127 D1
Pine Rd Bramhall SK7 .... 35 F4
  Heswall L60 .... 41 E4
  Macclesfield SK10 .... 87 F1
  Poynton SK12 .... 36 C2
  Runcorn WA7 .... 49 E4
Pine St SK3 .... 240 D4
Pine Tree Cl CH4 .... 139 E2
Pine Trees WA16 .... 57 F4
Pine Wlk CW5 .... 204 C2
Pinedale Cl CH1 .... 95 D4
Pinehey L64 .... 41 E1
Pinehurst SK10 .... 86 C3
Pinellas WA7 .... 23 D2
Pinetree Cl CW8 .... 78 A2
Pineways WA4 .... 26 B3
Pinewood WA14 .... 238 A2
Pinewood Ave WA1 .... 16 C4
Pinewood Cl Elton CH2 ... 72 B2
  Manchester SK4 .... 240 A4
Pinewood Ct
  Altrincham WA14 & WA15 .. 238 E1
  Sale M33 .... 242 D7
  Wilmslow SK9 .... 34 C1

Pinewood Dr L60 .... 41 D4
Pinewood Gr ST5 .... 210 C1
Pinewood Rd
  Burtonwood WA5 .... 7 D4
  Wilmslow SK9 .... 60 C4
Pinfold Ct CH4 .... 141 F3
Pinfold La Chelford WA16 .. 83 E3
  Chester CH4 .... 141 F4
  Little Budworth CW6 ... 147 F4
  Middlewich CW10 .... 128 A1
  Plumley WA16 .... 81 D2
  Romiley SK6 .... 241 E4
  Wythenshawe M90 .... 32 C3
Pinfold St 12 SK11 ...... 112 B4
Pinfold Way CW8 .... 77 E1
Pingard's La CW8 .... 101 E3
Pingate Dr SK8 .... 35 D3
Pingate La SK8 .... 35 D3
Pingate La S SK8 .... 35 D3
Pingot Croft CH3 .... 142 A4
Pinmill Brow WA6 .... 74 A4
Pinmill Cl WA6 .... 74 B4
Pinners Brow WA2 .... 16 A3
Pinsley Green Rd CW5 ... 216 C1
Pinsley View CW5 .... 216 C2
Pintail Pl CW7 .... 149 E3
Pipe La WA9 .... 9 E1
Piper's Cl L60 .... 40 B4
Piper's End L60 .... 40 B4
Piper's La L60 .... 40 B4
Pipers Ash CW7 .... 126 A1
Pipers Ct CH2 .... 119 D2
Pipers La Chester CH2 ... 119 D2
  Puddington L64 .... 93 D4
Pipers The WA3 .... 3 F4
Pipit Ave WA12 .... 2 B2
Pipit La WA3 .... 9 F2
Pippin Cl CW10 .... 151 E4
Pippits Row WA7 .... 49 F2
Pirie Cl CW12 .... 157 D2
Pirie Rd CW12 .... 157 D2
Pit La
  Hough Common CW2 ... 206 C1
  Kidsgrove ST7 .... 210 B3
  Widnes WA8 .... 13 D2
Pitt St Hyde SK14 .... 241 D7
  Macclesfield SK11 ...... 112 B3
  Stockport SK3 .... 240 D4
  Warrington WA5 .... 15 F4
  Widnes WA8 .... 23 D3
Pitts Cl CH3 .... 121 E1
Pitts Heath La WA4 ...... 24 C2
Pitville Terr WA8 .... 22 B4
Pius XII RC Aided Prim Sch
  L66 .... 69 E3
Place Rd WA14 .... 238 C6
Plaistow Ct WA7 .... 49 F4
Plane Gr ST5 .... 210 C1
Plane Tree Dr CW1 ...... 190 C3
Plane Tree Gr WA11 .... 2 A4
Plane Tree Rd M31 .... 11 E2
Plant Cl M33 .... 242 A7
Plant La CW11 .... 174 A4
Plant St CW11 .... 175 D4
Plantagenet Cl CW7 .... 149 E3
Plantation Cl WA7 .... 24 A1
Plantation Dr L66 .... 69 F4
Plantation St OL6 & SK16 .. 242 A2
Plas Newton La CH2 .... 118 C3
Platt Ave CW11 .... 175 D4
Platt St SK8 .... 239 E6
Platt's La CH3 .... 164 C3
Platts La Christleton CH3 .. 143 E4
  Tarvin CH3 .... 121 D1
  Tarvin, Broom Bank CH3 .. 144 A4
  Tattenhall CH3 .... 183 F4
Platts St WA11 .... 1 A3
Play St SK1 .... 240 F4
Pleasance Way WA12 ...... 2 B2
Pleasant St
  Macclesfield SK10 .... 87 F1
  Northwich CW8 .... 103 F4
Pleasant Way SK7 .... 35 E3
Pleck Rd L65 .... 70 A1
Plemstall Cl CH2 .... 119 F4
Plemstall La CH2 .... 97 D1
Plemstall Way CH2 .... 96 C1
Plex The ST7 .... 193 E2
Plinston Ave WA4 .... 16 C2
Plough La CH3 .... 143 D4
Ploughmans Cl CH1 ..... 94 C4
Ploughmans Way
  Ellesmere Port CH1 ..... 94 C4
  Macclesfield SK10 .... 87 D2
Plover Ave CW7 .... 149 E3
Plover Cl Farndon CH3 .. 180 C1
  Newton-le-W WA12 .... 2 B2
Plover Dr
  Altrincham WA14 ...... 238 B8
  Runcorn WA7 .... 50 B4
Plovers La WA6 .... 73 E3
Plum Terr CH1 .... 237 D3
Plumbs Fold CW8 .... 78 A1
Plumley Cl Chester CH3 .. 119 E1
  Stockport SK3 .... 240 F1
Plumley Moor Rd WA16 .. 81 E1
Plumley Rd SK9 .... 34 B3
Plumley Sta WA16 .... 81 D2
Plumpstons La WA6 ...... 49 D1
Plumtre Ave WA5 .... 15 F4
Plymouth Cl WA7 .... 50 C3
Plymouth Dr SK7 .... 35 F4
Plymouth Gr SK3 .... 240 B3
Plymyard Ave L62 .... 43 E3
Plymyard Cl L62 .... 43 E3
Plymyard Copse L62 ..... 43 E3
Poachers La WA4 .... 16 C2
Pochard Ave CW7 .... 149 E3

Pochard Dr
  Altrincham WA14 ...... 238 B7
  Poynton SK12 .... 36 A2
Pochard Rise WA7 .... 50 B4
Pochin Way CW10 .... 128 C1
Pocket Nook La WA3 ...... 4 A4
Pocklington Ct WA2 .... 8 C1
Pole La CW9 .... 53 F1
Poleacre Dr WA8 .... 12 B1
Police St 1 WA14 .... 238 D5
Pollen Rd WA14 .... 238 C6
Polperro Cl
  Macclesfield SK10 .... 86 B1
  Penketh WA5 .... 14 C2
Pond St WA3 .... 4 A4
Pond View Cl L60 .... 41 E4
Pond Wlk WA9 .... 1 A1
Pool End Cl SK10 .... 87 E2
Pool End Rd SK10 .... 87 E2
Pool Ind Est L65 .... 70 A4
Pool House Rd SK12 ..... 37 E3
Pool La Elton CH2 .... 71 F2
  Haslington CW11 ...... 192 A4
  Lymm WA13 .... 18 A2
  Runcorn WA7 .... 23 D2
  Tarvin CH3 .... 121 E2
  Warrington WA4 .... 16 A1
Pool Rd WA3 .... 11 D2
Pool Side ST7 .... 194 A4
Pool St Macclesfield SK11 .. 112 C3
  Widnes WA8 .... 23 D4
Poolcroft M33 .... 242 F5
Poole Ave WA2 .... 8 A1
Poole Cres WA2 .... 8 A1
Poole Hall La L66 .... 69 F4
Poole Hall Rd L65 .... 69 F4
Poole La CH2 .... 71 F1
Poolford La CW4 .... 129 E1
Pools La CW11 .... 177 D3
Pools Platt La CW9 .... 53 F3
Poolside Cl ST7 .... 193 F2
Poolside Rd WA7 .... 23 D1
Pooltown Cty Jun Sch
  L65 .... 69 F3
Pooltown Rd L65 .... 69 F3
Poplar Ave
  Altrincham WA14 ...... 238 E6
  Culcheth WA3 .... 4 C1
  Moulton CW9 .... 126 C4
  Newton-le-W WA12 .... 2 B2
  Penketh WA5 .... 14 C2
  Runcorn WA7 .... 49 E4
  Wilmslow SK9 .... 59 F3
Poplar Dr Alsager ST7 .. 193 F1
  Kidsgrove ST7 .... 195 D1
  Middlewich CW10 .... 151 E4
Poplar Gr Bollington SK10 .. 88 A4
  Crewe CW1 .... 190 C3
  Elton CH2 .... 72 A2
  Haydock WA11 .... 1 B3
  Sale M33 .... 242 B5
Poplar La TF9 .... 236 C3
Poplar Rd Chester CH4 .. 140 C3
  Haydock WA11 .... 1 B3
  Macclesfield SK11 ...... 112 B3
  Weaverham CW8 .... 102 B4
Poplar Way SK6 .... 38 A4
Poplars Ave WA2 .... 8 B2
Poplars The WN7 .... 4 A4
Poplor Weint L64 .... 66 C4
Popular Gr M44 .... 11 E3
Popular Wlk M31 .... 11 E1
Porlock Cl Heswall L60 .. 41 D3
  Penketh WA5 .... 14 C2
Port St SK1 .... 240 E6
Portal Gr M34 .... 241 B5
Porter Ave WA12 .... 2 B3
Porter Dr CW9 .... 104 B3
Porter St WA7 .... 23 E1
Porter Way CW9 .... 104 B3
Porters Croft CH3 ...... 119 F3
Portford Cl SK10 .... 86 C1
Porthcawl Cl WA8 .... 12 B2
Portland Dr Biddulph ST6 .. 179 E1
  Scholar Green ST7 ...... 194 C1
Portland Gr Haslington CW1 191 E3
  5 Manchester SK4 ..... 240 B8
Portland Pl WA6 .... 73 E2
Portland Rd WA14 ...... 238 D3
Portland St
  Newton-le-W WA12 .... 1 C2
  Runcorn WA7 .... 22 C2
Portland Wlk SK11 ...... 111 F4
Portleven Rd WA7 .... 50 A3
Portloe Rd SK8 .... 34 A4
Portman Pl 1 CW7 ...... 149 D4
Portmarnock Cl SK10 .... 87 D2
Portola Cl WA4 .... 17 E1
Portrea Cl SK3 .... 240 F1
Portree Ave L63 .... 43 E3
Portree Dr CW4 .... 130 A1
Portrush Dr SK10 .... 87 E2
Portside WA7 .... 50 C4
Portsmouth Pl WA7 ...... 50 C3
Portwood Pl SK1 .... 240 F6
Posnett St SK3 .... 240 C4
Post Office La Betley CW2 .. 207 F1
  Hampton SY14 .... 213 A4
  Norley WA6 .... 100 C3
  Runcorn WA7 .... 48 B4
Post Office Pl CW9 ...... 79 D1
Post Office St WA14 .... 238 D5
Postles Pl CW9 .... 103 F3

Pott Shrigley Church Sch
  SK10 .... 63 E2
Potters End ST6 .... 179 E1
Potters Cl WA8 .... 21 F3
Poulton Cres WA1 .... 17 E4
Poulton Dr WA8 .... 22 B4
Poulton Hall Rd L63 ..... 43 D4
Poulton Rd L63 .... 43 D4
Pound Rd L66 .... 69 E4
Povey Rd WA2 .... 8 B1
Powell Ave Hyde SK14 .. 241 E7
  Warrington WA3 .... 9 F2
Powell St WA4 .... 16 C2
Powell's Orch CH4 ...... 141 F4
Powey La Mollington CH1 94 A3
  Saughall CH1 .... 94 A3
Powicke Wlk SK6 .... 241 A1
Pownall Ave SK7 .... 35 F4
Pownall Ct SK9 .... 59 F4
Pownall Green Cty Prim
  Sch SK7 .... 35 F4
Pownall Hall Sch SK9 .... 59 F4
Pownall Rd
  Altrincham WA14 ...... 238 D3
  Wilmslow SK9 .... 59 F4
Pownall Sq SK11 .... 112 B4
Pownall St SK10 .... 87 E1
Powy Dr ST7 .... 195 D1
Powys St WA5 .... 15 F3
Poynton Cl WA4 .... 17 D2
Poynton Cty High Sch
  SK12 .... 36 C1
Poynton St 9 SK11 ...... 112 B4
Poynton Sta SK12 .... 36 B2
Pratchitts Row CW5 .... 204 C3
Preece Cl WA8 .... 12 B2
Preece Ct CW1 .... 190 A3
Preesall Ave SK8 .... 34 A4
Prenton Pl CH4 .... 141 F4
Prescot Rd
  Altrincham WA15 ...... 238 F2
  Widnes WA8 .... 12 B1
Prescot St CH2 .... 118 C2
Prescott Rd SK9 .... 34 A1
Prescott St WA4 .... 16 C2
Prescott Wlk M34 ...... 241 B5
Prestbury Ave WA15 .... 238 E6
Prestbury CE Aided Prim
  Sch SK10 .... 86 C4
Prestbury Dr WA4 .... 17 E2
Prestbury La SK10 .... 87 D4
Prestbury Rd
  Macclesfield SK10 .... 87 D1
  Macclesfield SK11 ...... 112 B4
  Nether Alderley SK10 .... 86 A3
  Nether Alderley, Adder's Moss
    SK10 .... 85 F3
  Wilmslow SK9 .... 60 C3
Prestbury Sta SK10 ...... 87 D4
Preston Rd M44 .... 11 F3
Preston On The Hill WA4 .. 50 C3
Preston St W SK11 ..... 112 A3
Prestwich Ave WA3 .... 4 C2
Prestwick Cl
  Macclesfield SK10 .... 87 E3
  Winsford CW7 .... 126 B1
Prestwood Ct WA3 .... 10 A4
Pretoria St CW1 .... 190 A4
Price Ave CW11 .... 175 D3
Price Gr WA9 .... 1 A1
Priest Ave WA9 .... 239 A4
Priest La SK10 .... 61 D1
Priest St WA7 .... 23 E1
Priestfield Rd L65 .... 70 B3
Priestley Coll WA1 .... 16 B2
Priestley St WA5 .... 15 F3
Priestner Dr WA6 .... 73 D2
Priestway La L64 .... 67 F1
Priesty Ct CW12 .... 156 B1
Priesty Fields CW12 .... 156 B1
Primitive St ST7 .... 195 E4
Primrose Ave
  Haslington CW1 .... 191 E3
  Macclesfield SK11 ...... 112 A3
Primrose Bank WA14 ... 238 C1
Primrose Cl
  Huntington CH3 .... 142 A3
  Runcorn WA7 .... 50 A4
  Warrington WA2 .... 8 B1
  Widnes WA8 .... 12 C1
Primrose Cotts WA14 ... 238 C1
Primrose Gr WA11 .... 1 C4
Primrose Hill Crewe CW2 .. 189 F3
  Cuddington CW8 .... 101 F2
  Kelsall CH3 .... 122 C3
Primrose La WA6 .... 73 D1
Prince Albert St CW1 ... 190 B2
Prince Edward St CW5 .. 204 C3
Prince Henry Sq WA1 .... 16 A3
Prince Rd SK12 .... 37 E2
Prince William Ave CH5 .. 116 A4
Prince's Rd SK6 .... 241 A3
Prince's Rd SK6 .... 241 A3
Prince's St 4 Stockport SK1 240 E6
  Widnes WA8 .... 23 D4
Princes Ave Bebington L62 .. 43 F3
  Chester CH2 .... 237 F3
  Northwich CW9 .... 104 A4
Princes Cl WA7 .... 23 F1
Princes Dr M33 .... 242 D5
Princes Pk CW8 .... 78 A1
Princes Pl WA8 .... 12 C1
Princes Rd
  Altrincham WA14 ...... 238 D6
  Ellesmere Port L65 ..... 70 A3
  Manchester SK4 .... 240 A8
  Sale M33 .... 242 D5

Princes St WA12 .... 2 A2
Princes Way SK11 .... 111 F4
Princess Ave Audley ST7 209 E1
  Great Sankey WA5 ...... 14 C4
  Haydock WA11 .... 2 A4
  Warrington WA1 .... 16 C3
  Warrington, Paddington WA1 17 D4
Princess Cl CW2 .... 205 F4
Princess Cres
  Middlewich CW10 ...... 151 E3
  Warrington WA1 .... 16 C3
Princess Ct ST7 .... 210 B3
Princess Dr Bollington SK10 .. 87 F4
  Nantwich CW5 .... 205 E3
  Sandbach CW11 .... 175 D4
  Wistaston CW2 .... 205 F4
Princess Gr CW2 .... 205 F4
Princess Rd Lymm WA13 .. 18 B2
  Wilmslow SK9 .... 59 F3
Princess St
  Altrincham WA14 ...... 238 C8
  Ashton-u-L OL6 .... 242 A4
  Bollington SK10 .... 87 F4
  Chester CH1 .... 237 D2
  Congleton CW12 ...... 156 B2
  Crewe CW1 .... 190 B3
  Hyde SK14 .... 241 E6
  Kidsgrove ST7 .... 210 B3
  Knutsford WA16 .... 57 D1
  Northwich CW9 .... 79 F1
  Runcorn WA7 .... 23 D2
  Warrington WA5 .... 15 E2
  Winsford CW7 .... 127 D1
Princess Wlk SK7 .... 36 A4
Princeway WA6 .... 74 A4
Printworks Rd SK15 ... 242 F4
Prior Cl CW2 .... 189 F1
Priory Ave CW9 .... 103 F2
Priory Cl Chester CH2 .. 118 B2
  Congleton CW12 ...... 179 D4
  Crewe CW1 .... 190 A4
  Runcorn WA7 .... 24 A1
  Sale M33 .... 242 D7
  Winsford CW7 .... 126 B2
Priory Dr SK10 .... 86 C1
Priory La SK10 .... 86 C1
Priory Pl Chester CH1 .. 237 E2
  Kidsgrove ST7 .... 195 E2
Priory Rd Altrincham WA14 .. 51 F4
  Cheadle SK8 .... 240 A1
  Runcorn WA7 .... 24 B1
  Sale M33 .... 242 D7
  Wilmslow SK9 .... 59 F4
Priory Sch M33 .... 242 A6
Priory St Altrincham WA14 .. 238 C1
  Northwich CW9 .... 104 A4
  Warrington WA4 .... 16 A2
Priory The WA2 .... 8 A4
Priory Way CW8 .... 103 D2
Priscilla St CW1 .... 190 C2
Pritchard Dr CW9 ...... 103 F1
Probert Cl CW2 .... 190 A2
Proctors Cl WA8 .... 13 E1
Proctors Cl CW11 ...... 174 C3
Proffits La WA6 .... 73 F2
Promised Land La CH3 .. 142 C3
Prospect Ave M44 .... 11 F3
Prospect Dr
  Altrincham WA15 .... 32 B4
  Davenham CW9 .... 103 F1
Prospect La WA3 .... 10 B2
Prospect Rd M44 .... 11 F3
Prospect St CW12 ...... 156 B1
Prospect Vale SK8 ...... 239 B1
Prospect Vale Prim Sch
  SK8 .... 239 B1
Prosperity Way CW10 .. 128 B1
Prosser Rd CH2 .... 95 E1
Provan Way CH1 .... 117 E3
Providence St OL6 ..... 242 A4
Provident St WA9 .... 1 A2
Prunus Rd CW1 .... 190 C3
Pryors The CH3 .... 121 E2
Ptarmigan Pl CW7 ...... 149 E3
Public Hall St WA7 ...... 23 D2
Pudding La CW6 .... 168 A4
Puddington La Neston L64 .. 92 C4
  Puddington L64 .... 93 D4
Puffin Ave SK12 .... 36 A2
Pulford Cl Davenham CW9 .. 103 F2
  Runcorn WA7 .... 49 F3
Pulford Ct CH4 .... 162 B1
Pulford La CH4 .... 162 A3
Pulford Rd Blacon CH1 .. 117 F3
  Ellesmere Port L65 ..... 69 F2
  Winsford CW7 .... 126 B1
Pullman Cl L60 .... 41 E4
Pullman Dr CW9 .... 104 B4
Pump La Churton CH3 ... 181 D3
  Runcorn WA7 .... 49 F4
Pumptree Mews SK11 .. 111 F4
Purdy Cl WA5 .... 7 E1
Purley Dr M44 .... 11 E3
Purser La SY14 .... 211 F2
Puss Bank Cty Inf & Jun
  Sch SK10 .... 112 C4
Putney Ct WA7 .... 49 F4
Pye Cl WA11 .... 2 A4
Pye Rd L60 .... 41 D4
Pyecroft Cl WA5 .... 14 B3
Pyecroft Rd WA5 .... 14 B3
Pyecroft St CH4 .... 141 E4
Pym's La CW1 .... 189 F3
Pymgate Dr SK8 .... 239 A2
Pymgate La SK8 .... 239 A2

Pyrus Ave CW1 190 C3
Pyrus Gr WA6 73 E2
Pytcheley Hollow WA6 100 C3

Quad The CH1 117 F1
Quadrant Cl WA7 50 B3
Quadrant The Blacon CH1 117 F1
Romiley SK6 241 A2
Quail Cl WA2 8 B2
Quakers Coppice CW1 191 D1
Quakers Way LL13 180 C1
Quantock Cl
Ellesmere Port L66 69 D3
Stockport SK4 240 E6
Winsford CW7 149 D4
Quarry Ave CH3 180 C1
Quarry Bank CW6 146 B4
Quarry Bank Mill SK9 33 F1
Quarry Bank Rd SK9 33 F2
Quarry Cl Chester CH4 141 E4
Runcorn WA7 23 E1
Quarry Hill CH3 180 C1
Quarry La Appleton WA4 26 B3
Christleton CH3 142 C4
Kelsall CW6 122 B3
Quarry Rd New Mills SK22 39 E4
Romiley SK6 241 B2
Willaston L64 42 B1
Quarry St SK15 242 C1
Quarry Terr ST7 195 D1
Quay Fold WA5 15 F3
Quay Pl WA7 50 C4
Quay Side WA6 49 E1
Quay The WA6 49 E1
Quayle Cl WA11 1 B3
Quayside Congleton CW12 156 C1
Neston L64 66 C3
Quayside Mews WA13 18 C2
Quayside Way SK11 112 C4
Queasteybirch La WA4 26 A1
Quebec Rd WA2 16 B4
Queen Anne Ct SK9 60 B3
Queen Sq OL6 242 A4
Queen St Audley ST7 209 E1
Bollington SK10 88 A4
Bunbury CW6 185 F4
Cheadle SK8 239 F6
Chester CH1 237 E2
Congleton CW12 156 B1
Congleton CW12 156 C2
Crewe CW1 190 C3
Ellesmere Port L65 70 B4
Goldborne WA3 3 D4
Hyde SK14 241 E6
Kidsgrove ST7 195 D1
Knutsford WA16 56 C1
Macclesfield SK11 112 B4
Middlewich CW10 128 B1
Nantwich CW5 204 C3
Newton-le-W WA12 2 A2
Northwich CW9 103 F4
Shavington CW2 206 B2
Stalybridge SK15 242 D2
Queen Victoria St 26 SK11 112 B4
Queen's Ave Chester CH2 237 F3
Connah's Quay CH5 91 E1
Glazebury WA3 5 E4
Hawarden CH5 116 A2
Macclesfield SK10 87 F1
Romiley SK6 241 A3
Widnes WA8 22 A4
Queen's Cl Macclesfield SK10 87 F1
Runcorn WA7 22 C1
Queen's Dr Chester CH4 237 F1
Manchester SK4 240 A6
Middlewich CW10 151 E4
Nantwich CW5 204 B2
Sandbach CW11 175 D4
Queen's Gdns SK8 239 E6
Queen's Par CW7 126 B1
Queen's Park Gdns CW2 189 F2
Queen's Park Ho CH4 237 E1
Queen's Park Rd CH4 237 E1
Queen's Rd WA15 238 F3
Queen's Rd OL6 242 A4
Queen's Rd Cheadle SK8 239 F4
Chester CH2 237 F3
Romiley SK6 241 A3
Runcorn WA7 22 C1
Wilmslow SK9 60 A3
Queen's Sch (Jun Dept) The CH2 118 B2
Queen's Sch The CH1 237 D2
Queen's Way CH4 139 D2
Queens Ave
Ellesmere Port L65 70 A2
Warrington WA1 16 C4
Queens Cl Bollington SK10 87 F3
Manchester SK4 240 A6
Queens Cres Chester CH2 118 C4
Warrington WA1 17 D4
Queens Ct Manchester SK4 240 A7
Winsford CW7 126 B1
Queens Dr Goldborne WA3 3 E4
Helsby WA6 73 D2
Heswall L60 40 C4
Newton-le-W WA12 2 B3
Warrington WA4 17 D1
Queens Gdns
Ellesmere Port L65 70 A3
Kidsgrove ST7 210 B3
Queens Park Cty High Sch CH4 237 E1
Queens Park Golf Course CW2 189 F2
Queens Pl CH1 237 E3
Queens Rd
Chester CH1, CH3 119 D2
Ellesmere Port L66 69 E4
Haydock WA11 2 A4
Queensbury Way WA8 12 B2
Queensgate Bramhall SK7 35 F3
Northwich CW8 103 F4
Queensgate Prim Sch SK7 35 F2
Queensway Alsager ST7 193 D3
Cheadle SK8 34 B4
Chester CH2 118 C3
Crewe CW1 190 B2
Frodsham WA6 74 A4
Heswall L60 41 E3
Knutsford WA16 56 C2
Poynton SK12 36 B2
Runcorn WA7 22 C2
Widnes WA8 22 C3
Winsford CW7 149 E4
Quillet The L64 66 C4
Quinn St WA8 23 D4
Quinta Cty Prim Sch The CW12 156 A1
Quinta Rd CW12 156 A2

Raby Ave L63 43 D3
Raby Cl Bebington L63 43 D4
Heswall L60 40 C4
Widnes WA8 13 F1
Raby Ct L65 70 B2
Raby Dr L63 43 D3
Raby Gdns L64 66 C4
Raby Hall Rd Bebington L63 43 D3
Thornton Hough L63 42 C3
Raby Mere Rd Bebington L63 42 C4
Thornton Hough L63 42 B3
Raby Park Cl L64 66 C4
Raby Park Rd L64 41 F1
Raby Rd Neston L64 66 C4
Thornton Hough L63 42 A3
Race The SK9 34 B1
Racecourse La CW6 124 A1
Racecourse Pk SK9 59 F3
Racecourse Rd SK9 59 F3
Racefield Cl WA13 18 C2
Racefield Rd
Altrincham WA14 238 C4
Knutsford WA16 56 C1
Radcliffe Ave WA3 4 C2
Radcliffe Rd
Sandbach CW11 174 C2
Sutton Lane Ends SK11 135 E4
Raddel La WA4 52 B3
Raddle Wharf L65 70 B4
Radford Cl WA8 22 B4
Radlett Cl WA5 14 C2
Radley Dr L63 41 F3
Radley La WA2 8 C2
Radnor Cl Congleton CW12 156 A2
Sandbach CW11 174 C4
Radnor Dr Chester CH4 141 D2
Widnes WA8 12 B1
Radnor Park Trad Est CW12 156 A2
Radway Gn L66 69 F3
Radway Green Rd CW2 208 C4
Rae St SK3 240 C4
Raeburn Ave Bebington L62 43 F3
Neston L64 66 C4
Raeburn Prim Sch L62 43 E3
Raglan Ct WA3 9 F3
Raglan Dr WA14 238 E8
Raglan Rd Macclesfield SK10 87 F1
Sale M33 242 A5
Raglan St SK14 241 C6
Ragley Cl SK12 36 C2
Railbrook Ct CW2 190 B1
Railton Ave CW1 190 A4
Railway Age Ex Ctr The CW1 190 B2
Railway Bank SK14 241 C6
Railway Cotts CW12 157 D1
Railway Rd SK1 & SK3 240 E4
Railway St
Altrincham WA14 238 D4
Crewe CW2 190 B1
Newton-le-W WA12 2 A2
Stockport SK4 240 E6
Railway Terr CH5 116 A2
Railway View WA5 1 B1
Rainbow Cl WA8 12 B2
Rainbow St CW1 190 B2
Rainford Cl ST7 195 F1
Rainow Cl CW10 151 D4
Rainow Cty Prim Sch SK10 88 B2
Rainow Rd
Macclesfield SK10 88 A1
Rainow SK10 88 A1
Stockport SK3 240 C2
Rainow View SK10 63 E1
Rainow Way
17 Wilmslow SK9 34 B1
3 Wilmslow SK9 34 C1
Rake La Backford CH2 95 E3
Christleton CH3 143 D4
Dunham-on-t-H CH2 97 D4
Dunham-on-t-H WA6 97 F4
Eccleston CH4 141 E1
Frodsham WA6 72 C3
Hawarden CH5 139 D4
Helsby WA6 73 E2
Helsby, Helsby Marsh WA6 73 D3
Stoak CH2 95 E3
Rake The Bebington L62 43 E4
Burton L64 67 E1
Rake Way CH1 94 A1
Raleigh Cl WA5 7 E1
Raleigh Rd L64 41 F1
Raleigh St SK5 240 E8
Ramp Rd E M90 33 E4
Ramp Rd S M90 33 E4
Ramp Rd W M90 33 D4
Rampit Cl WA11 1 C4
Ramsbottom St CW1 190 A3
Ramsbrook La Hale L24 21 E2
Widnes L24 21 E2
Ramsdale Rd SK7 35 F4
Ramsden Ct CH4 140 C2
Ramsey Cl Warrington WA3 9 F2
Widnes WA8 13 F2
Ramsfield Rd L24 21 D2
Randle Bennett Cl CW11 174 C4
Randle Meadow L66 69 F1
Randolph Pl SK3 240 E3
Range Rd SK3 240 E3
Rangemoor Cl WA3 10 A3
Rannoch Cl L65 69 F2
Ranworth Rd WA5 14 C3
Rappax Rd WA15 32 A4
Rassbottom Brow SK15 242 C2
Rassbottom Ind Est SK15 242 C2
Rassbottom St SK15 242 C2
Ratcliffe St 6 SK1 240 F4
Rathbone Pk CW6 146 B1
Rathbone St WA12 2 A2
Rathlin Cl WA8 13 F2
Rathmell Cl WA3 4 C2
Raven Cl CW11 175 D4
Raven's La ST7 209 F2
Ravenbank Cty Prim Sch WA13 18 C2
Ravenfield Dr WA8 12 B2
Ravenho La SK10 88 B2
Ravenoak Park Rd SK8 35 D4
Ravenoak Rd SK8 35 D4
Ravens Cl ST7 209 F2
Ravens La Acton CW5 203 F3
Swanley CW5 203 F3
Ravenscliffe Rd ST7 195 D1
Ravenscroft CW4 130 A2
Ravenscroft Cl CW11 175 E4
Ravenscroft Rd CW2 189 F2
Ravensdale Cl WA2 8 B2
Ravensfield CW8 101 E2
Ravensholme Ct CH3 166 A1
Ravensholme La CH3 166 A1
Ravensmead Prim Sch ST7 209 F2
Ravenstone Dr M33 242 E7
Ravenswood CW8 103 D2
Ravenswood Ave SK4 240 A5
Ravenswood Dr SK8 35 D4
Ravenswood Rd SK9 59 F2
Ravenwood Dr WA15 32 B4
Rawcliffe Cl WA8 12 C2
Rawdon Cl WA7 50 A4
Rawlings Cl WA3 9 F2
Rawlinson Cres L26 21 D4
Rawson Rd CH1 117 F2
Ray Ave CW5 204 C4
Rayleigh Ave CW9 127 D4
Rayleigh Way SK10 86 C1
Raymond Ave WA4 16 B1
Raymond St CH1 237 D3
Raymond Way L64 67 D4
Rays Brow CW8 78 A1
Read St SK14 241 C7
Read St W SK14 241 C7
Reades La CW12 179 E4
Readesdale Ave CW2 189 F1
Reading Room La CH3 199 E4
Reaper Cl WA5 15 E3
Reaseheath Coll CW5 188 B1
Reay St WA8 13 E1
Record Bsns Pk WA2 16 A4
Rectory Ave WA3 3 E4
Rectory Cl Denton M34 241 A6
Farndon CH3 180 C1
Heswall L60 40 C4
Nantwich CW5 204 C3
Wistaston CW2 205 F4
Rectory La Adderley TF9 235 D3
Capenhurst CH1 94 A4
Heswall L60 40 C4
Ledsham L66 68 C1
Lymm WA13 18 C2
Rectory View ST7 210 B3
Red Bank Ave WA12 2 C1
Red Brow La
Preston on the Hill WA7, WA4 50 C4
Runcorn WA7, WA4 50 C4
Red Cow Yd WA16 57 D1
Red Ct L66 69 E4
Red House La WA14 20 B4
Red La Appleton WA4 26 B4
Disley SK12 38 B3
Frodsham WA6 74 B4
Huxley CH3 166 B3
Sandbach CW11 174 B3
Warrington WA4 26 B4
Whitley WA4 52 B1
Red Lion Cl ST7 210 B4
Red Lion La
Ellesmere Port L66 69 E4
Nantwich CW5 204 B3
Red Pike L66 69 E4
Red Stone Hill WA6 73 E2
Redacre SK12 36 C3
Redbourne Dr WA8 12 A2
Redbrook Cl L62 43 E3
Redbrook Gr 2 SK9 34 B1
Redbrook Rd M31 11 F1
Redbrook Way SK10 62 B3
Redcar Dr L62 43 E3
Reddish Ave SK23 65 E3
Reddish Cres WA13 18 C2
Reddish La Lymm WA13 19 D3
Whaley Bridge SK23 65 E3
Reddish Rd SK23 65 E3
Reddy La WA14 30 A4
Redesdale Cl
Sandbach CW11 174 C4
Warrington WA2 8 C1
Redesmere Cl CW9 104 A3
Redesmere Dr
Alderley Edge SK9 60 A1
Cheadle SK8 239 F4
Redesmere La SK11 110 A2
Redesmere Rd SK9 34 B3
Redfern Ave M33 242 E5
Redfern Dr CW12 156 C2
Redgate CW8 103 E4
Redhill Rd Chester CH4 140 C3
Kelsall CW6 122 B3
Redhills Mews L65 70 A3
Redhouse La Disley SK12 38 C3
Romiley SK6 241 A4
Redland Cl CH4 141 D4
Redmayne Cl WA12 2 A2
Redmere Dr L60 41 E4
Redmoor La Disley SK12 39 D2
New Mills SK22 39 D3
Redpoll La WA3 9 F2
Redruth Ave SK10 86 C1
Redruth Cl WA7 50 B3
Redshank Ave CW7 149 E3
Redshank Cl WA12 2 B2
Redshank La WA3 9 F2
Redstone Dr CW7 126 A1
Redvales Ct WA3 9 E2
Redvers Ave L66 44 A1
Redway La SK10 88 A4
Redwood Cl Barnton CW8 78 A2
Broughton CH4 140 C3
Warrington WA1 17 F4
Redwood Dr
Ellesmere Port L66 69 F1
Elton CH2 72 B2
Reece Cl CH2 119 F4
Reed La CW9 53 E3
Reedgate La CW9 27 F1
Reedsmere Cl WA4 16 C1
Reedsmere Wlk CW9 78 B4
Reel Cl WA1 17 E3
Reeman Cl SK6 241 A4
Reeman Ct SK9 34 A1
Rees Cres CW4 130 B2
Reeve St WA3 4 A4
Reeves Rd CH3 142 A4
Regal Cl L66 69 F2
Regal Cres WA8 22 A4
Regency Cl ST7 210 B3
Regency Ct CW7 149 E4
Regency Pk SK9 59 F3
Regency Prep Sch SK11 112 A4
Regency Way CW9 103 F2
Regent Ave Haydock WA11 1 A4
Macclesfield SK11 112 A3
Warrington WA1 17 D4
Regent Bk SK9 59 F3
Regent Cl Bramhall SK7 35 E2
Shavington CW2 206 A2
Wilmslow SK9 59 F3
Regent Ct WA14 238 D4
Regent Rd
Altrincham WA14 238 D4
Widnes WA8 13 D1
Regent St
Ellesmere Port L65 70 A3
Moulton CW9 126 C4
Newton-le-W WA12 2 A2
Runcorn WA7 23 D2
Warrington WA1 16 A3
Regent Theological Coll CW5 205 D3
Regents Cl CH3 119 D1
Regents Gate CW5 205 D3
Regents Way 8 CW7 149 D4
Regina Ave SK15 242 D2
Reginald Mitchell Prim Sch The ST7 194 B1
Reid Ave WA5 15 F4
Reid St CW1 190 B3
Remer St CW1 190 C4
Rena Cl SK4 240 D7
Rena Ct SK4 240 D7
Renaissance Ct CW1 191 D2
Renaissance Way CW1 191 D2
Rendel Cl WA12 2 B1
Rendlesham Cl WA3 10 A3
Renfrew Ave L62 43 F3
Renfrew Cl SK10 86 C1
Renown Cl WA3 9 E2
Renshaw Rd CW9 79 E1
Renshaw St WA14 238 E5
Rensherds Pl WA16 29 E3
Renton Ave WA7 23 E1
Repton Ave SK14 241 E7
Repton Cl WA16 29 E2
Repton Dr CW1 191 E3
Repton Rd L65 70 B2
Reservoir Rd
Stockport SK3 240 D3
Whaley Bridge SK23 65 E4
Reservoir Terr CH2 118 C1
Retreat The Crewe CW1 190 B3
Romiley SK6 241 C1
Reuben St SK4 240 E8
Revesby Cl WA8 12 B1
Rex Bldgs SK9 60 A3
Reynard St SK14 241 D7
Reyner St OL6 242 B2
Reynold St SK14 241 D6
Reynold's La CW11 175 F3
Reynolds Ave WA9 1 A1
Reynolds Mews SK9 60 C4
Reynolds St WA4 16 C2
Rhoden St CW1 191 D3
Rhodes Cl CW1 191 E2
Rhodes St Denton SK14 241 C7
Warrington WA2 16 B4
Rhodes St N SK14 241 C7
Rhodesway L60 41 D4
Rhona Cl L63 43 E2
Rhona Dr WA5 14 C3
Rhos Ave SK8 239 E1
Rhuddlan Ct L65 70 B1
Rhuddlan Rd CH1 117 E2
Rhum Cl L65 70 B1
Rhyl St WA8 22 C4
Ribble Ave CW7 127 D1
Ribble Cl Culcheth WA3 4 C1
Widnes WA8 13 F2
Ribble Dr ST6 179 F1
Ribble Pl CW7 127 D1
Ribblesdale L65 70 A2
Ribblesdale Ave CW12 157 D3
Ribblesdale Cl L62 43 F3
Ribchester Gdns WA3 5 D2
Richard Cl WA7 24 A1
Richard Evans Comm Prim Sch WA11 1 A3
Richard Moon St CW1 190 A2
Richard St Crewe CW1 190 A3
Northwich CW9 104 B4
1 Stockport SK1 240 F6
Richards Croft CH3 142 A4
Richardson Cl 5
Sandbach CW11 174 B3
Shavington CW2 206 B3
Richardson St WA2 16 B4
Richmond Ave Haydock WA11 1 A4
Runcorn WA7 23 F1
Warrington WA4 17 D2
Warrington, Thelwall WA4 17 E2
Wilmslow SK9 34 B2
Richmond Cl Culcheth WA3 4 B2
Lymm WA13 19 D2
Sale M33 242 F5
Sandbach CW11 174 C4
Stalybridge SK15 242 D1
Richmond Cres CH3 119 E1
Richmond Ct
Altrincham WA14 238 B2
Cheadle SK8 239 C5
Ellesmere Port L65 70 B2
Richmond Dr Lymm WA13 19 D2
Northwich CW9 104 A2
Richmond Gn WA14 238 B2
Richmond Gr SK8 239 F1
Richmond Hill
Knutsford WA16 57 D1
Macclesfield SK11 112 C3
Richmond Hill Rd SK8 239 C6
Richmond Pl SK11 112 C3
Richmond Rd
Altrincham WA14 238 D5
Altrincham, Rosehill WA14 238 C2
Crewe CW1 190 C3
Romiley SK6 241 C3
Richmond St 2 Hyde SK14 241 E6
Stalybridge SK15 242 F2
Warrington WA4 17 D2
Widnes WA8 13 E1
Rickaby Cl L63 43 E4
Ridding La WA7 50 A3
Riddings Ct WA15 238 F8
Riddings La Hartford CW8 103 D2
Wybunbury CW5 220 A4
Riddings Rd WA15 238 F2
Ridge Cl SK6 241 F2
Ridge Hill
Sutton Lane Ends SK11 113 D1
Utkinton CW6 146 A3
Ridge Hill La SK15 242 D3
Ridge Pk SK7 35 E3
Ridge The CW8 123 E4
Ridge View SK11 112 B3
Ridgeborne Cl WA5 7 E1
Ridgemont Ave SK4 240 B6
Ridgeway Alvanley WA6 74 A1
Goldborne WA3 3 F4
Wilmslow SK9 60 C4
Ridgeway Gdns WA13 18 B2
Ridgeway The Cronton WA8 12 B3
Disley SK12 38 B3
Heswall L60 41 D4
Runcorn WA7 50 B3
Tarvin CH3 121 E2
Ridgewell Ave WA3 3 E4
Ridgmont Rd SK7 35 F3
Ridgway St Crewe CW1 190 B3
Warrington WA2 16 B4
Ridgway The SK6 241 A1
Ridings Cty Inf Sch The CH1 94 A1
Ridings The CH1 117 D4
Ridley Cl CW2 206 C1
Ridley Dr WA5 15 E2
Ridley Gr M33 242 F5
Ridley Rd SK10 87 F4
Ridley Wood Rd LL13 196 A2
Ridling La SK14 241 E6
Ridsdale 2 WA8 22 B4
Rifle Rd M21 & M33 242 F7
Rigby Ave CW1 190 A4
Rigby Rd ST7 195 D2
Rigby St Altrincham WA14 238 D3
Goldborne WA3 3 D4
Rigby's Row CW5 204 C3
Rigg St CW1 190 A3

Riley Bank Mews WA6 .... 74 A1
Riley Cl CW11 .... 174 C3
Riley Dr WA7 .... 49 D4
Rileys Way ST7 .... 209 F1
Rilshaw La CW7 .... 150 A4
Rilston Ave WA3 .... 4 B2
Rimington Cl WA3 .... 4 C2
Rimsdale Cl Gatley SK8 .... 239 A3
Wistaston CW2 .... 206 A4
Ring Rd CH3 .... 119 E2
Ring-o-Bells La SK12 .... 38 B3
Ringsfield Rd L24 .... 21 D1
Ringstead Cl SK9 .... 34 B1
Ringstead Dr SK9 .... 34 B1
Ringstone Way SK23 .... 65 E4
Ringway Ellesmere Port L66 ... 69 F2
Neston L64 .... 41 F1
Waverton CH3 .... 143 D3
Ringway Golf Course
WA15 .... 32 B4
Ringway Rd Runcorn WA7 .... 23 E1
Wythenshawe M22, M90 .... 33 E4
Ringway Rd W M90 .... 33 E4
Ringwood Cl WA3 .... 10 A3
Ripley Ave SK8 .... 35 D3
Ripley Cl SK7 .... 36 C4
Ripley St WA5 .... 15 F3
Ripon Ave
Ellesmere Port L66 .... 69 E3
Goldborne WA3 .... 3 E4
Ripon Cl WA12 .... 2 B3
Ripon Dr CW2 .... 206 A4
Ripon Row WA7 .... 49 E3
Ripon Wlk SK6 .... 241 A1
Rise The SK23 .... 65 E3
Riseley St SK11 .... 112 B4
Riseley's Pas 33 SK11 .... 112 B4
Rising Sun Cl SK11 .... 112 A3
Rising Sun Rd SK11 .... 112 A2
Risley Moss Ctry Pk WA3 ... 10 A2
Risley Rd WA3 .... 9 F3
Rivacre Brow L66 .... 69 F4
Rivacre Rd Bebington L62 .... 44 A2
Ellesmere Port L65 .... 44 B1
Rivacre Valley Ctry Pk
L66 .... 69 E4
Rivacre Valley Cty Prim
Sch L66 .... 69 F4
River La Broughton CH4 .... 140 C4
Chester CH4 .... 141 E4
Farndon CH3 .... 180 C1
Partington M31 .... 11 F2
River Rd WA4 .... 16 A2
River St Congleton CW12 .... 156 B2
Macclesfield SK11 .... 112 C3
Wilmslow SK9 .... 60 A4
River View CW7 .... 126 C1
Riverbank Cl
Bollington SK10 .... 87 F4
Heswall L60 .... 40 C3
Nantwich CW5 .... 204 C4
Riverbank Rd L60 .... 40 C3
Riverdane Rd CW12 .... 156 C2
Rivermead Ave WA15 .... 32 B4
Riversdale Frodsham WA6 .... 49 E1
Warrington WA1 .... 17 F4
Riversdale Rd
Cheadle SK8 .... 239 C5
Runcorn WA7 .... 49 F4
Rivershill M33 .... 242 A8
Rivershill Gdns WA15 .... 32 B3
Riverside Nantwich CW5 .... 204 B3
Northwich CW9 .... 104 A3
Riverside Bsns Pk SK9 .... 60 A4
Riverside Cl WA1 .... 16 B2
Riverside Cres CW4 .... 130 B2
Riverside Ct Chester CH4 .... 141 F4
Langley SK11 .... 113 E2
Riverside Dr CW8 .... 103 F3
Riverside Gr CW2 .... 189 E2
Riverside Pk CH5 .... 116 A4
Riverside Ret Pk WA4 .... 16 B2
Riverside Wlk L64 .... 66 B3
Riversmead CH3 .... 142 A3
Riverton Rd M20 .... 239 B8
Riverview Rd L64 .... 66 C3
Rivington Ct WA1 .... 17 F4
Rivington Gr M44 .... 11 E3
Rivington Rd
Altrincham WA15 .... 238 F2
Ellesmere Port L65 .... 70 B3
Runcorn WA7 .... 50 C2
Rixton Ave WA5 .... 15 F4
Roaches The SK11 .... 112 A3
Roachill Cl WA14 .... 238 B5
Road Beta CW10 .... 151 E4
Road Five CW7 .... 127 E1
Road Four CW7 .... 127 D1
Road One CW7 .... 127 D2
Road St CW6 .... 146 A2
Road Three CW7 .... 127 E1
Road Two CW7 .... 127 D1
Roadside Ct WA3 .... 3 E4
Roan Ct SK11 .... 112 C4
Roan House Way SK11 .... 112 C4
Roan Mews SK11 .... 112 C4
Rob Rd WA12 .... 2 C3
Robert Moffat WA16 .... 29 E3
Robert St Hyde SK14 .... 241 C7
Northwich CW8 .... 103 F3
Runcorn WA7 .... 23 E1
Sale M33 .... 242 E6
Warrington WA5 .... 15 F3
Widnes WA8 .... 13 D1
Robert's Terr CH1 .... 118 A1
Roberts Ave WA11 .... 1 A3
Roberts Ct WA7 .... 49 F3
Roberts Dr CW9 .... 104 B3
Roberts Rd CW9 .... 80 A1
Robin Cl Rainow SK10 .... 88 C3
Runcorn WA7 .... 50 B4
Sandbach CW11 .... 175 D4
Robin Cres SK11 .... 112 B1
Robin Hood Ave SK11 .... 112 B3
Robin Hood La WA6 .... 73 D1
Robin La Chelford SK11 .... 84 A2
Sutton Lane Ends SK11 .... 112 B1
Robin's La Bramhall SK7 .... 35 F4
Cheadle Hulme SK7 .... 35 E4
Robins Cft L66 .... 69 F1
Robins Cl SK7 .... 35 F4
Robins La WA3 .... 4 B1
Robins Way SK10 .... 88 A4
Robinsbay Rd M22 .... 33 F4
Robinson St Hyde SK14 .... 241 F7
Stalybridge SK15 .... 242 C1
Stockport SK3 .... 240 D3
Robinsons Croft CH3 .... 142 A4
Robinsway WA14 .... 238 C1
Robson St WA1 .... 16 B3
Roby Gr WA5 .... 15 D3
Roche Gdns SK8 .... 35 D3
Rochester Cl Goldborne WA3 .. 3 D4
Great Sankey WA5 .... 15 E3
Rochester Cres CW1 .... 190 C3
Rochester Dr L65 .... 70 B2
Rochford Ave M22 .... 33 E4
Rock Bank SK23 .... 65 F3
Rock Dr WA6 .... 49 E1
Rock Farm Cl L64 .... 67 D3
Rock Farm Dr L64 .... 67 D3
Rock Farm Gr L64 .... 67 D3
Rock La Burwardsley CW6 .... 184 B3
Chester CH2 .... 237 D4
Widnes WA8 .... 12 C2
Rock Rd CH5 .... 91 F1
Rock St SK22 .... 39 E4
Rock The WA6 .... 73 E1
Rockfield Cl WA8 .... 12 B1
Rockfield Dr WA6 .... 73 E1
Rockford Lodge WA16 .... 57 E1
Rockhouse La ST7 .... 210 B4
Rockingham Cl WA3 .... 10 B3
Rocklands La L63 .... 42 B4
Rocklee Gdns L64 .... 67 D3
Rocklife La CH6 .... 91 D2
Rocklynes SK6 .... 241 B2
Rocksavage Expressway
WA7 .... 49 E3
Rockside ST7 .... 195 E3
Rockwood Ave CW2 .... 190 A2
Rocky La Heswall L60 .... 40 C4
Tattenhall CH3 .... 182 C4
Rocky La S L60 .... 41 D4
Roddy La WA6 .... 75 F1
Rode Hall ST7 .... 194 A4
Rode Heath Cty Prim Sch
ST7 .... 193 F4
Rode House Cl ST7 .... 193 F4
Rode The ST7 .... 193 E2
Rodeheath Cl SK9 .... 60 B4
Rodepool Cl SK9 .... 34 B1
Rodgers Cl WA6 .... 49 D1
Rodmill Dr SK8 .... 239 A4
Rodney St
Ashton-u-L OL6 .... 242 A4
Macclesfield SK11 .... 112 B4
Warrington WA2 .... 16 A3
Roe Pk CW12 .... 178 C1
Roe St Congleton CW12 .... 156 C1
Macclesfield SK11 .... 112 B4
Roebuck Gdns M33 .... 242 A6
Roebuck La M33 .... 242 A6
Roebuck St CW1 .... 190 B3
Roeburn Way WA5 .... 14 B2
Roedean Wlk CW1 .... 190 B3
Roehampton Dr WA7 .... 49 F4
Roehurst La CW7 .... 126 B1
Roemarsh Ct WA7 .... 49 F3
Roewood La
Macclesfield SK10 .... 88 A1
Macclesfield, Higherfence
SK10 .... 113 D4
Roften Ind Est L66 .... 43 E1
Rokeby Ct WA7 .... 24 B3
Rokeden WA12 .... 2 B2
Roland Ave WA7 .... 22 C1
Rolands Wlk WA7 .... 23 F1
Rolleston St WA2 .... 16 A3
Rolls Ave CW1 .... 190 A4
Rolt Cres CW10 .... 151 D4
Roman Cl WA7 .... 23 F1
Roman Ct L64 .... 66 C4
Roman Dr CH1 .... 117 E3
Roman Rd Stockport SK4 .... 240 E6
Warrington WA4 .... 16 B1
Widnes WA8 .... 22 C3
Roman Rise CW8 .... 78 A2
Roman Way CW11 .... 174 C4
Romanes St CW8 .... 103 F4
Romford Ave M34 .... 241 A8
Romiley Prec SK6 .... 241 C2
Romiley Prim Sch SK6 .... 241 C2
Romiley Rd L66 .... 69 F3
Romiley Sta SK6 .... 241 C2
Romney Cl L64 .... 66 C4
Romney Croft L64 .... 66 C4
Romney Way L64 .... 66 C4
Romsey Dr SK7 .... 35 E3
Ronald Dr WA2 .... 9 D1
Ronaldshay WA8 .... 13 F1
Ronaldsway Halewood L26 .... 21 D4
Heswall L60 .... 40 C3
Rood Hill CW12 .... 156 B2
Rood La CW12 .... 156 C2
Rook Rd WA4 .... 16 C2
Rook St CW2 .... 190 B1
Rookery Cl Nantwich CW5 .. 204 C3
Sandbach CW11 .... 174 B3
Rookery Dr Nantwich CW5 . 204 C2
Tattenhall CH3 .... 166 A1
Rookery Rd Kidsgrove ST7 ... 195 E2
Tilston SY14 .... 198 A2
Rookery Rise CW7 .... 127 D1
Rookery The Broughton CH4 139 D2
Newton-le-W WA12 .... 2 B2
Rookerypool Cl SK9 .... 34 B1
Rookfield Ave M33 .... 242 C7
Rooks Way L60 .... 40 C4
Roome St WA2 .... 16 B4
Rooth St SK4 .... 240 D6
Rope Bank Ave CW2 .... 206 A4
Rope La Shavington CW2 .... 206 A3
Wistaston CW2 .... 206 A3
Rope Wlk CW12 .... 156 B2
Ropewalk The L64 .... 66 B4
Rosam Ct WA7 .... 49 F3
Roscoe Ave
Newton-le-W WA12 .... 2 C2
Warrington WA2 .... 16 B4
Roscoe Cres WA7 .... 48 C4
Roscoe Pk Est WA14 .... 238 E8
Roscoe Rd M44 .... 11 F4
Roscoe St SK3 .... 240 D4
Roscote Cl L60 .... 40 C4
Roscote The L60 .... 40 C4
Rose Ave Haydock WA11 .... 1 C3
Irlam M44 .... 11 F4
Rose Bank WA13 .... 18 C2
Rose Cl WA7 .... 50 B3
Rose Cres WA8 .... 22 C4
Rose Gdns L64 .... 66 C3
Rose Lea Cl WA8 .... 13 D2
Rose St Reddish SK5 .... 240 F7
Widnes WA8 .... 22 C4
Rose Terr Crewe CW1 .... 190 B3
Stalybridge SK15 .... 242 D1
Rose Vale SK8 .... 239 B1
Rose View Ave WA8 .... 13 D1
Rose Wlk M31 .... 11 E1
Roseacre Dr Cheadle SK8 .... 34 B4
Gatley SK8 .... 239 C1
Rosebank Cl CW7 .... 149 F4
Rosebank Rd M44 .... 11 E2
Rosebank Sch CW8 .... 78 A2
Rosebank Wlk CW8 .... 78 A2
Roseberry Way CW1 .... 191 E2
Rosedale Ave Goldborne WA3 .. 3 E4
Warrington WA1 .... 17 E4
Rosedale Rd SK4 .... 240 D8
Rosefield Ave WA13 .... 18 C2
Roseheath Dr L26 .... 21 D3
Rosehill Ave WA9 .... 6 A3
Rosehill Rd CW2 .... 190 A1
Rosemary Ave Runcorn WA7 49 F2
Warrington WA4 .... 16 C1
Rosemary Cl
Broughton CH4 .... 139 E2
Great Sankey WA5 .... 15 E3
Rosemary Dr WA12 .... 2 C2
Rosemary La LL12 .... 161 E1
Rosemary Row CH3 .... 166 A1
Rosemary Wlk M31 .... 11 F1
Rosemere Dr CH1 .... 94 C4
Rosemoor Gdns WA4 .... 26 C3
Rosendale Dr WA3 .... 10 A3
Rosevale Rd ST5 .... 210 C1
Roseville Dr CW12 .... 179 D4
Rosewood Ave
Chester CH2 .... 118 B3
Frodsham WA6 .... 74 B4
Stockport SK4 .... 240 A5
Warrington WA1 .... 16 C4
Rosewood Cl CW1 .... 190 C3
Rosewood Gr CH1 .... 117 D4
Roslyn Rd SK3 .... 240 E1
Ross Ave SK3 .... 240 E1
Ross Cl WA5 .... 15 E4
Ross Dr L66 .... 69 E3
Ross Rd L65 .... 70 A3
Ross St WA8 .... 13 D1
Rossall Cl L24 .... 21 F1
Rossall Dr SK7 .... 35 F3
Rossall Gr L66 .... 69 E3
Rossall Rd Great Sankey WA5 15 D2
Widnes WA8 .... 13 E1
Rossbank Rd L65 .... 70 A4
Rosscliffe Rd L65 .... 70 A3
Rossenclough Rd SK9 .... 34 B1
Rossendale Rd SK8 .... 34 B4
Rossett Ave M22 .... 33 E4
Rossett Cl WA5 .... 7 F1
Rossett Pk CH4 .... 162 B1
Rossett Rd LL13 .... 180 A1
Rossfield Rd L65 .... 70 A3
Rossfield Rd N L65 .... 70 A4
Rosslyn Cl CH5 .... 116 A1
Rosslyn La CW8 .... 102 A2
Rosslyn Rd Chester CH3 .... 119 D2
Gatley SK8 .... 239 D1
Rossmill La WA15 .... 32 A4
Rossmore Bsns Pk L65 .... 70 A4
Rossmore Cty Prim Sch
L66 .... 69 E4
Rossmore Gdns L66 .... 69 E3
Rossmore Ind Est L65 .... 70 A3
Rossmore Rd E L65 .... 69 F4
Rossmore Rd W L66 .... 69 E4
Rossmount Rd L65 .... 70 A3
Rosswood Rd L65 .... 70 A3
Rostherne Ave
Ellesmere Port L66 .... 69 F2
Goldborne WA3 .... 3 E4
High Lane SK6 .... 37 F4
Rostherne Cl WA5 .... 15 E2
Rostherne Cres WA8 .... 12 B1
Rostherne Ct WA14 .... 238 D3
Rostherne Rd Sale M33 .... 242 F5
Stockport SK3 .... 240 E1
Wilmslow SK9 .... 59 F3
Rostherne St 1 WA14 .... 238 D3
Rostherne Way CW11 .... 174 C4
Rosthernmere Rd SK8 .... 239 F4
Rostrevor Rd SK3 .... 240 E1
Rothay Dr WA5 .... 14 B2
Rothbury Cl WA7 .... 49 E3
Rother Dr L65 .... 70 A4
Rothesay Cl WA7 .... 23 F1
Rothesay Dr L62 .... 43 F2
Rothesay Rd CH4 .... 141 D4
Rough Bank CW12 .... 179 F4
Rough Heys La SK11 .... 111 D4
Roughlea Ave WA3 .... 4 B2
Roughley Ave WA5 .... 15 E2
Roughlyn Cres CH4 .... 140 C1
Roughwood La CW11 .... 176 A1
Round Gdns SK10 .... 88 A4
Round Hill Meadow CH3 .. 142 A4
Round Meadow SK10 .... 88 C3
Round Thorn WA3 .... 9 D4
Round Way SK22 .... 39 E4
Roundabout The WA8 .... 12 B3
Roundcroft SK6 .... 241 E3
Roundhey SK8 .... 34 B4
Roundway SK7 .... 35 E3
Roundy La SK10 .... 62 C3
Routledge St WA8 .... 13 D1
Rowan Ave WA3 .... 3 F4
Rowan Cl Alsager ST7 .... 193 E2
Great Sankey WA5 .... 14 B4
Middlewich CW10 .... 151 F3
Newton-le-W WA12 .... 2 B1
Runcorn WA7 .... 49 E4
Sandbach CW11 .... 174 C4
Winsford CW7 .... 126 B2
Rowan Dr SK7 .... 35 E4
Rowan Gr CH5 .... 91 E1
Rowan Pk CH3 .... 142 C4
Rowan Pl CH2 .... 119 D2
Rowan Rd CW8 .... 102 B4
Rowan St SK14 .... 241 F5
Rowan Way SK10 .... 87 F1
Rowan Wlk M31 .... 11 E1
Rowans The CH4 .... 139 D2
Rowanside SK10 .... 86 C3
Rowanside Dr SK9 .... 60 C4
Rowcliffe Ave CH4 .... 141 D2
Rowe St WA1 .... 16 A3
Rowland Cl WA2 .... 9 D2
Rowley Bank La WA16 .... 29 D1
Rowley Rd SK7 .... 36 C4
Rowley Way WA16 .... 82 A4
Rowson Dr M44 .... 11 E3
Rowthorn Cl WA8 .... 22 C4
Rowton Brideg Rd CH3 .... 142 C4
Rowton Cl CW9 .... 103 F2
Rowton La CH3 .... 142 C3
Rowton Rd CW2 .... 189 E2
Roxbo Rough Cl WA5 .... 7 D3
Roxburgh Cl SK10 .... 87 D1
Roxburgh Rd L66 .... 68 C3
Roxby Way WA16 .... 82 A4
Roxholme Wlk M22 .... 33 E4
Royal Ave WA8 .... 12 B1
Royal Gdns
Altrincham WA14 .... 20 C1
Northwich CW9 .... 103 F2
Royal George St SK1 & SK3 240 F4
Royal La CW6 .... 147 D2
Royal Meadows SK10 .... 87 D1
Royal Mews CW9 .... 104 B3
Royal Mount CW1 .... 173 D1
Royal Oak Yd 4 SK1 .... 240 F5
Royal Pl WA8 .... 22 A4
Royal Rd SK12 .... 38 B3
Royal Sch for the Deaf The
SK8 .... 34 B3
Royce Ave WA15 .... 238 E5
Royce Cl CW1 .... 190 A4
Royden Ave Irlam M44 .... 11 F4
Runcorn WA7 .... 49 D4
Royds Cl CW8 .... 103 D2
Roylands Dr CW10 .... 151 E4
Royle St Congleton CW12 .... 156 B2
Northwich CW9 .... 104 A4
Stockport SK1 .... 240 F3
Winsford CW7 .... 126 C1
Royle's Pl CW8 .... 103 E3
Royleen Dr WA6 .... 74 B3
Royon Dr SK3 .... 240 B3
Royston Ave WA1 .... 17 D4
Royston Cl
Ellesmere Port L65 .... 69 F2
Goldborne WA3 .... 3 F4
Rozel Cres WA5 .... 15 D3
Rudd Ave WA9 .... 1 A1
Rudheath Cl CW2 .... 189 E3
Rudheath Cty High Sch
CW9 .... 104 B4
Rudheath Cty Prim Sch
CW9 .... 104 B3
Rudheath L Ctr CW9 .... 104 B4
Rudloe Ct WA2 .... 8 C1
Rudstone Cl L66 .... 69 D3
Rudyard Cl SK11 .... 112 A3
Rue De Bohars CW6 .... 168 B4
Rufford Ave SK14 .... 241 F6
Rufford Cl CW2 .... 206 A4
Rufford Ct WA1 .... 17 F4
Rufus Ct CH1 .... 237 D3
Rugby Cl SK10 .... 87 F2
Rugby Dr SK10 .... 87 F2
Rugby House SK10 .... 87 E2
Rugby Rd L65 .... 70 B2
Ruislip Ct WA2 .... 8 C1
Runcorn Docks Rd WA7 .... 22 C1
Runcorn East Sta WA7 .... 50 B4
Runcorn Rd Barnton CW8 .... 78 A1
Little Leigh CW8 .... 77 E3
Moore WA4 .... 25 E3
Runcorn Spur Rd WA7 .... 49 E4
Runcorn Sta WA7 .... 22 C1
Runger La WA15 .... 32 C4
Runnell The L64 .... 41 E2
Runnymede WA1 .... 17 E4
Runnymede Cl SK3 .... 240 C2
Runnymede Ct SK3 .... 240 C2
Runnymede Dr WA11 .... 1 A3
Ruscoe Ave CW11 .... 174 C3
Ruscolm Cl WA5 .... 14 B4
Rushey Cl WA15 .... 32 B4
Rushfield Cres WA7 .... 50 A3
Rushfield Rd
Cheadle Hulme SK8 .... 35 D3
Chester CH4 .... 141 D3
Rushgreen Rd WA13 .... 19 D2
Rushmere La CH3 .... 163 F2
Rushmore Gr WA1 .... 17 D4
Rusholme Cl L26 .... 21 D3
Rushside Rd SK8 .... 35 D3
Rushton Ave WA12 .... 2 A2
Rushton CE Contr Prim
Sch SK11 .... 159 D1
Rushton Cl Northwich CW9 .. 104 B4
Widnes WA8 .... 12 C2
Rushton Dr Chester CH2 .... 118 B4
Hough Common CW2 .... 206 C1
Middlewich CW10 .... 151 E4
Romiley SK6 .... 241 C3
Rushton Fold SK10 .... 61 D1
Rushton La Eaton CW6 .... 147 E3
Little Budworth CW6 .... 147 E3
Rushton Rd
Cheadle Hulme SK8 .... 35 D3
Stockport SK3 .... 240 B3
Rushy View WA12 .... 2 A2
Rushyfield Cres SK6 .... 241 D3
Ruskin Ave
Newton-le-W WA12 .... 2 B2
Warrington WA2 .... 8 B1
Ruskin Ct WA16 .... 57 D1
Ruskin Cty High Sch The
CW2 .... 190 B1
Ruskin Dr L65 .... 70 B2
Ruskin Gdns SK6 .... 241 A3
Ruskin Gr SK6 .... 241 A3
Ruskin Rd
Congleton CW12 .... 156 B1
Crewe CW2 .... 190 B1
Ruskin Way WA16 .... 57 D2
Russell Ave Alsager ST7 .... 193 E3
High Lane SK6 .... 37 F4
Sale M33 .... 242 D7
Russell Cl CW12 .... 179 D4
Russell Ct WA8 .... 13 D2
Russell Dr CW1 .... 191 E2
Russell Gdns SK4 .... 240 B5
Russell Rd Runcorn WA7 .... 48 C4
Winsford CW7 .... 149 E4
Russell St
Ashton-u-L OL6 .... 242 A4
Chester CH2 .... 237 F3
Hyde SK14 .... 241 D7
Russet Cl CW10 .... 128 A1
Russet Rd CW8 .... 102 B4
Russett Sch The CW8 .... 102 C4
Rutherford Cl SK14 .... 241 D6
Ruthin Ave SK8 .... 239 E2
Ruthin Ct L65 .... 70 B2
Ruthin Wlk WA6 .... 73 D1
Rutland Ave Denton M34 .... 241 B6
Goldborne WA3 .... 3 E4
Halewood L26 .... 21 D4
Warrington WA4 .... 26 A4
Rutland Cl
Ashton-u-L OL6 .... 242 A2
Congleton CW12 .... 156 C2
Gatley SK8 .... 239 B6
16 Sandbach CW11 .... 174 B3
Rutland Dr
Middlewich CW10 .... 151 E4
Weaverham CW8 .... 77 E1
Rutland La M33 .... 242 F6
Rutland Pl CH2 .... 119 D3
Rutland Rd
Altrincham WA14 .... 238 D6
Hazel Grove SK7 .... 36 C4
Irlam M44 .... 11 E3
Kidsgrove ST7 .... 195 D1
Macclesfield SK11 .... 112 B2
Partington M31 .... 11 F1
Rutland St
Ashton-u-L OL6 .... 242 A2
Runcorn WA7 .... 22 C1
Ryburn Rd SK11 .... 112 A3
Rydal Ave High Lane SK6 .... 37 F4
Warrington WA4 .... 16 A1
Rydal Cl Ellesmere Port L65 .... 70 B1
Gatley SK8 .... 239 B4
Holmes Chapel CW4 .... 130 A1
Neston L64 .... 66 C3
Winsford CW7 .... 126 B2
Rydal Ct CW12 .... 156 A1
Rydal Dr WA15 .... 32 B4
Rydal Gr Chester CH4 .... 141 D3
Helsby WA6 .... 73 D1
Runcorn WA7 .... 49 D4

Rydal Pl SK11 .... 112 A3
Rydal St WA12 .... 2 B2
Rydal Way Alsager ST7 .. 193 E3
Widnes WA8 .... 12 B1
Ryde Ave SK4 .... 240 B6
Ryde Cl CW1 .... 190 A4
Ryder Ave WA14 .... 238 E7
Ryder Rd Warrington WA1 .... 17 E4
Widnes WA8 .... 13 D3
Ryders St CW8 .... 103 F4
Rye Pl ST7 .... 193 D2
Ryebank Ave CW1 .... 190 A4
Ryebank Way SK10 .... 87 E2
Ryecroft CH2 .... 72 A2
Ryecroft Cl CW10 .... 151 D4
Ryecroft La Duddon CW6 .. 144 B3
Mobberley WA16 .... 57 F2
Ryecroft Rd L60 .... 41 E4
Ryedale Cl SK4 .... 240 B7
Ryehills ST7 .... 209 F1
Rylands St
  Warrington WA1 .... 16 A3
  5 Widnes WA8 .... 23 D4
Ryle St SK11 .... 112 B3
Ryle's Park Rd SK11 ...... 112 B3
Ryles Cl SK11 .... 112 B3
Ryles Cres SK11 .... 112 B3
Ryles Park Cty High Sch
  SK11 .... 112 A3
Ryleys La SK9 .... 59 F1
Ryleys Sch The SK9 .... 59 F1

Sabre Cl WA7 .... 50 B4
Sack La CW9 .... 54 C3
Sacred Heart RC Aided
  Prim Sch WA5 .... 15 F3
Saddleback Dr SK10 .... 86 C4
Saddlers Rise WA7 .... 50 B4
Sadler Cl CW7 .... 126 B1
Sadler Rd CW7 .... 126 B1
Sadler St WA8 .... 13 E1
Sadler's Cl CW4 .... 130 A2
Sadlers La CW6 .... 124 A1
Sadlers Wells CW6 .... 185 F4
Saffron Cl WA2 .... 9 D1
Saffron Wlk M31 .... 11 F1
Sagars Rd SK9 .... 34 B2
Sage Cl WA2 .... 9 E1
Saighton CE Aided Prim
  Sch CH3 .... 142 C1
Saighton La Saighton CH3 .. 142 C1
  Waverton CH3 .... 142 C1
SS Peter & Paul RC Aided
  High Sch WA8 .... 22 C4
SS Peter & Paul RC High
  Sch WA8 .... 12 C1
St Aelred's RC High Sch
  WA12 .... 2 B2
St Alban Rd WA5 .... 14 C3
St Alban's RC Aided Prim
  Sch SK10 .... 86 C1
St Alban's RC Aided Sch
  WA5 .... 15 F3
St Albans Cl WA11 .... 2 A4
St Albans Cres WA14 ...... 238 C8
St Albans Dr CW5 .... 204 C2
St Albans Pl SK22 .... 39 E4
St Albans St SK22 .... 39 E4
St Ambrose Coll WA15 ...... 32 A4
St Ambrose RC Jun Mix Inf
  Sch L24 .... 21 D1
St Ambrose RC Prim Sch
  SK3 .... 240 C1
St Ambrose Rd WA8 .... 13 E1
St Andrew's Ave WA15 ..... 238 F7
St Andrew's CE Prim Sch
  WA2 .... 8 B2
St Andrew's Cl SK6 .... 241 B1
St Andrew's Gdns ST7 ..... 193 F1
St Andrew's Rd
  Ellesmere Port L65 .... 70 C2
  Macclesfield SK11 .... 112 A4
St Andrews Cl
  Northwich CW9 .... 104 C4
  Warrington WA2 .... 9 D2
St Andrews Ct WA15 ...... 238 F3
St Andrews Dr
  Holmes Chapel CW4 ...... 130 A1
  Kidsgrove ST7 .... 195 E2
St Andrews Rd
  Gatley SK8 .... 239 C1
  Manchester SK4 .... 240 B8
St Andrews Sch (Special
  Needs) CH4 .... 141 E4
St Andrews Wlk
  Mickle Trafford CH2 .... 96 C1
  New Mills SK22 .... 39 E4
St Ann's Ave CW10 .... 151 E4
St Ann's CE Aided Prim
  Schs WA4 .... 16 B4
St Ann's Rd CW10 .... 151 E4
St Ann's Rd N SK8 .... 239 B2
St Ann's Rd S SK8 .... 34 B4
St Ann's Sq SK8 .... 34 B4
St Anne St CH2 .... 237 E3
St Anne's CE Prim Sch
  M33 .... 242 D6
St Anne's Ct M33 .... 242 C6
St Anne's Cty Prim Sch
  M34 .... 241 A8
St Anne's Dr M34 .... 241 A8
St Anne's Hospl WA14 .... 238 C3
St Anne's La CW5 .... 204 B3
St Anne's RC Prim Sch
  CW5 .... 204 C2

St Anne's Rd
  Dukinfield M34 .... 241 A8
  Widnes WA8 .... 13 D1
St Annes Ave WA4 .... 17 D1
St Annes Ave E WA4 .... 17 D1
St Annes RC High Sch
  SK4 .... 240 D8
St Anns St M33 .... 242 F5
St Anthony's Prim Sch
  CH4 .... 140 C3
St Asaph Dr WA5 .... 7 F2
St Asaph Rd CH1 .... 94 C4
St Augustine's Ave WA4 .... 16 C2
St Augustine's RC Aided
  Prim Sch WA7 .... 24 A1
St Augustine's RC Aided
  Sch WA4 .... 16 C2
St Augustine's Rd SK3 .... 240 B4
St Austel Cl WA5 .... 14 C2
St Austell Ave SK10 .... 86 C1
St Austell Cl
  Macclesfield SK10 .... 86 C1
  Runcorn WA7 .... 50 A3
St Austell Dr SK8 .... 34 A4
St Austins La WA1 .... 16 A2
St Barnabas CE Aided Prim
  Sch WA5 .... 15 F3
St Barnabas CE Contr Prim
  Sch SK11 .... 112 B3
St Barnabas Ct SK11 ...... 112 B3
St Barnabas Pl WA5 .... 15 F3
St Basil's RC Aided Prim
  Sch WA8 .... 12 A1
St Bede's Ave CW8 .... 77 E1
St Bede's RC Aided Inf &
  Jun Sch WA8 .... 13 D1
St Bede's RC Prim Sch
  CW8 .... 102 C4
St Bees Cl SK8 .... 239 B3
St Benedicts Cl WA2 .... 16 A4
St Benedicts RC Aided Prim
  Sch Warrington WA2 .... 16 B4
  Wilmslow SK9 .... 34 C2
St Bernard's RC Aided Prim
  Sch L65 .... 70 C4
St Berteline's CE Aided
  Prim Sch WA7 .... 50 B4
St Brannocks Rd SK8 .... 35 D4
St Brides Cl WA5 .... 14 C2
St Bridget's RC Aided Prim
  Sch WA2 .... 8 C2
St Bridgets Cl WA2 .... 8 C2
St Bridgets Ct CH4 .... 141 D3
St Catherine's RC Prim Sch
  WA3 .... 3 F4
St Catherines Dr CW8 .... 103 D2
St Chad's Ave SK6 .... 241 C2
St Chad's CE Prim Sch
  ST5 .... 210 B1
St Chad's Fields CW7 .... 149 E3
St Chad's Gr SK11 .... 241 C2
St Chad's RC Aided Comp
  Sch WA7 .... 49 E4
St Chad's Rd CH1 .... 117 F2
St Chads Cl CW5 .... 220 A4
St Chads Way TF9 .... 236 B1
St Christopher's Dr SK6 .. 241 A2
St Christopher's RC Prim
  Sch WA4 .... 241 A2
St Christophers Cl CH2 .. 118 B4
St Clairs St CW2 .... 190 B1
St Clare's RC Aided Prim
  Sch CH4 .... 141 D3
St Clement's RC Aided Sch
  WA7 .... 49 D4
St David Rd L62 .... 44 A3
St David's Ave SK6 .... 241 B2
St David's High Sch CH4 .. 140 B3
St David's Terr CH4 .... 140 B3
St Davids Cl M33 .... 242 A5
St Davids Dr
  Ellesmere Port CH1 .... 94 C4
  Warrington WA3 .... 7 F1
St Edward's RC Aided Prim
  Sch Macclesfield SK11 ... 112 B3
  Runcorn WA7 .... 23 D2
St Edwards Cl SK11 .... 112 B3
St Elmo Pk SK12 .... 37 E2
St Elphins Cl WA1 .... 16 B3
St Gabriel's RC Aided Prim
  Sch ST7 .... 193 E2
St George's CE Inf Sch
  SK2 .... 240 F2
St George's CE Jun Sch
  SK2 .... 240 F2
St George's CE (VA) Prim
  Sch SK14 .... 241 D5
St George's Cres
  Chester CH4 .... 237 F1
  Waverton CH3 .... 143 D3
St George's Ct
  Altrincham WA14 .... 238 B7
  Widnes WA8 .... 22 B4
St George's Gdns M34 .... 241 A5
St George's Pl SK11 ...... 112 B4
St George's Rd CW7 .... 149 E4
St George's St
  Macclesfield SK11 .... 112 B3
  Stalybridge SK15 .... 242 D3
St George's Way L63 .... 42 A3
St Georges Ave CH1 .... 94 C4
St Georges Cl WA4 .... 26 C2
St Georges Ct **5** SK14 .. 241 E6
St Georges Dr SK14 ...... 241 D5
St Georges Rd SK22 .... 39 E4
St Giles Dr SK14 .... 241 F6
St Gregory's RC Aided High

St Gregory's RC Aided Prim
  Sch SK10 .... 87 F4
St Helen's Coll Newton
  Campus WA12 .... 2 A2
St Helens CE Prim Sch
  WA3 .... 11 D1
St Helens Cl WA3 .... 11 D2
St Helens Rd
  Goldborne WA3, WN7 .... 4 A4
  Northwich CW9 .... 104 A4
St Hilary's Sch SK9 .... 85 D4
St Hilary's Sch for Girls
  SK9 .... 60 A1
St Hilda's Dr WA6 .... 49 E1
St Hugh's Cl WA14 .... 238 E8
St Hugh's RC Prim Sch
  WA15 .... 238 F8
St Ives Ave SK8 .... 240 A2
St Ives Cl SK10 .... 86 C1
St Ives Pk CH5 .... 116 A2
St James Ave Chester CH2 . 118 C4
  Congleton CW12 .... 156 B1
  Warren SK11 .... 111 F1
St James Cl Audlem CW3 .. 230 A2
  Frodsham WA6 .... 49 E1
St James Ct
  Altrincham WA14 .... 238 E4
  Manchester M20 .... 239 B8
St James' Dr M33 .... 242 A5
St James' Dr SK9 .... 60 A3
St James' RC High Sch
  SK8 .... 34 C3
St James' Sq SK22 .... 39 E4
St James St OL6 .... 242 A2
St James Terr **4** CW7 .. 149 D4
St James' Way SK8 .... 34 C3
St James Wlk CW8 .... 103 F4
St James's CE Contr Jun
  Sch WA4 .... 119 F3
St James's CE Contr Prim
  Sch WA4 .... 240 E6
St John Ave WA4 .... 16 A1
St John Fisher RC Aided
  Prim Sch WA8 .... 13 E1
St John Fisher RC Prim
  Sch M34 .... 241 B5
St John St Chester CH1 .. 237 E2
  Newton-le-W WA12 .... 2 A2
St John The Evangelist RC
  Prim Sch ST7 .... 195 D2
St John The Evangelist RC
  Prim Sch (Annexe) ST7 . 194 C1
St John Vianney Lower
  Sch SK4 .... 240 B6
St John's Ave
  Knutsford WA16 .... 56 C1
  Lostock CW9 .... 79 C2
St John's CE Aided Prim
  Sch Bollington SK10 .... 88 C3
  Macclesfield SK11 .... 112 A4
  Sandbach CW11 .... 175 F3
St John's Cl
  Northwich CW9 .... 104 C4
  Romiley SK6 .... 241 B1
St John's Ct SK14 .... 241 F7
St John's Dr SK14 .... 241 F7
St John's La SK9 .... 59 F2
St John's RC Sch WA4 ..... 16 C3
St John's Rd
  Altrincham WA14 .... 238 D3
  Bebington L62 .... 44 A3
  Chester CH4 .... 237 F1
  Congleton CW12 .... 156 C3
  Knutsford WA16 .... 57 D1
St John's Rear Rd CH4 ... 237 F1
  Wilmslow SK9 .... 59 F2
St John's the Evangelist
  RC Prim Sch ST7 .... 194 C1
St John's Way
  Cuddington CW8 .... 102 A1
  Sandbach CW11 .... 175 F3
St John's Wood ST7 ...... 194 C1
St John's Wood Cty Prim
  Sch WA16 .... 57 E1
St Johns Dr CW7 .... 149 D4
St Joseph's Cl WA5 .... 14 C3
St Joseph's RC Aided Prim
  Sch WA5 .... 14 C3
St Joseph's RC Prim Sch
  M33 .... 242 B6
St Joseph's RC Sch SK1 .. 240 F5
St Josephs Way CW5 ..... 205 D3
St Katherines Way WA1 ... 16 B3
St Lawrence Ct CW5 ...... 204 C3
St Lawrence Rd
  Denton M34 & M16 .... 241 A7
  Frodsham WA6 .... 74 A4
St Leonard's Way CW3 ... 232 B1
St Leonards Dr WA15 ..... 238 F6
St Lesmo Ct SK3 .... 240 C3
St Lesmo Rd SK3 .... 240 C3
St Lewis RC Prim Sch
  WA3 .... 4 A1
St Luke's CE Prim Sch
  WA3 .... 3 F4
St Luke's Cres WA8 .... 13 D2
St Luke's RC Aided Prim
  Sch WA6 .... 74 A4
St Luke's Way WA6 .... 49 D1
St Lukes Cl CW4 .... 130 B2
St Margaret's Ave WA2 ..... 8 B1
St Margaret's CE Aided Jun
  Sch WA2 .... 8 B1
St Margaret's CE Contr Inf
  Sch WA2 .... 8 B1
St Margaret's Cl WA14 ... 238 C4

St Margaret's Rd
  Altrincham WA14 .... 238 C4
  Cheadle SK8 .... 240 A2
St Mark's Ave WA14 ...... 238 A5
St Mark's CE Prim Sch
  SK6 .... 241 A4
St Mark's RC Church Sch
  L26 .... 21 D4
St Marks Cres CH1 .... 94 C4
St Marks Rd CH4 .... 140 C3
St Martin's Ave SK4 .... 240 C6
St Martin's Cl SK14 .... 241 F6
St Martin's Rd ST7 .... 210 C3
St Martin's Way CH1 ...... 237 D3
St Martins Dr L66 .... 69 E1
St Martins La WA7 .... 50 B4
St Martins RC Aided Prim
  Sch WA7 .... 50 B4
St Mary's Ave CW8 .... 77 E1
St Mary's CE Contr Sch
  SK11 .... 158 B4
St Mary's CE Prim Sch
  Bebington L62 .... 44 A3
  Goldborne WA3 .... 4 A4
  Irlam M44 .... 11 C3
  Sale M33 .... 242 A6
St Mary's Cl Alsager ST7 . 193 E3
  Appleton WA4 .... 26 B3
St Mary's Dr SK8 .... 239 F6
St Mary's Hill CH4 .... 237 E1
St Mary's Inf Sch CH1 ... 237 E1
St Mary's RC Aided Prim
  Sch Congleton CW12 ..... 156 B2
  Crewe CW2 .... 190 A1
St Mary's RC Inf Sch WA12 . 2 B2
St Mary's Rd
  Altrincham WA14 .... 238 C3
  Disley SK12 .... 38 B3
  Dodleston CH4 .... 162 A4
  Nantwich CW5 .... 204 C4
  Penketh WA5 .... 14 C3
  Runcorn WA7 .... 23 F1
St Mary's Rd M33 .... 242 A6
St Mary's Rd WA7 .... 23 D2
St Mary's St Crewe CW1 . 190 B2
  Warrington WA1 .... 16 B2
St Marys Cl L24 .... 21 F1
St Marys Ct CW5 .... 204 A4
St Matthew's CE Prim Sch
  SK3 .... 240 E4
St Matthew's Rd SK3 ..... 240 D4
St Matthew's Terr SK3 ... 240 D4
St Matthews CE Aided
  Prim Sch WA4 .... 26 C1
St Matthews Cl
  Appleton WA4 .... 26 B4
  Haslington CW1 .... 191 E2
St Mawes Cl WA8 .... 12 C1
St Mawgan Ct WA2 .... 8 C1
St Michael's Ave SK7 ...... 35 F4
St Michael's Cl
  Little Leigh CW8 .... 77 E3
  Widnes WA8 .... 22 B4
St Michael's Ind Est WA8 . 22 B4
St Michael's RC Prim Sch
  WA8 .... 22 B4
St Michael's Rd WA8 .... 22 B4
St Michael's View CW1 .. 190 A3
St Michael's Way CW10 .. 128 B1
St Monicas Cl WA4 .... 26 B4
St Nicholas Cl CW5 .... 204 C3
St Nicholas RC (Aided)
  High Sch CW8 .... 103 E3
St Nicholas Rd WA3 .... 4 A4
St Olave St CH4 .... 237 E1
St Oliver Plunkett RC
  Aided Prim Sch WA3 .... 9 F2
St Oswald's CE Aided Prim
  Sch CH1 .... 94 C1
St Oswald's Cres CW11 .. 153 F3
St Oswald's RC Prim Sch
  WA1 .... 16 C4
St Oswalds Cl
  Malpas SY14 .... 213 D2
  Winwick WA2 .... 8 A3
St Oswalds Way CH1 ...... 237 E3
St Paul of the Cross RC
  Aided Prim Sch WA3 .... 6 C3
St Paul's Cl CW1 .... 190 B2
St Paul's Hill Rd SK14 .... 241 F6
St Paul's Pl CW9 .... 79 D1
St Paul's Rd
  13 Macclesfield SK11 . 112 C4
  Manchester SK4 .... 240 B8
  Widnes WA8 .... 23 D4
St Paul's St
  Crewe CW1 .... 190 B2
  Hyde SK14 .... 241 E7
  Stalybridge SK15 .... 242 F2
St Pauls Cl SK15 .... 242 F2
St Pauls Gdns L66 .... 69 D4
St Pauls RC Aided Prim Sch
  SK12 .... 36 C1
St Pauls Trad Est SK15 .. 242 F2
St Peter's Ave WA16 .... 56 C1
St Peter's CE Prim Sch
  Heswall L60 .... 40 C4
  Newton-le-W WA12 .... 2 C2
St Peter's Cl Heswall L60 . 40 C4

St Peter's Dr Hyde SK14 . 241 F6
  Little Budworth CW6 ...... 147 F4
St Peter's RC Aided Prim
  Sch WA1 .... 17 E4
St Peter's Prim Sch
  SK15 .... 242 D1
St Peter's Rise CW11 ..... 174 C4
St Peter's Sq SK1 .... 240 F5
St Peter's Way WA11 .... 16 A3
St Peters Rd CW12 .... 156 C1
St Peters Way CH2 .... 119 F4
St Petersgate SK1 & SK3 240 F5
St Philips Church & Comm
  Prim Sch WA5 .... 7 E1
St Saviour's CE Contr Prim
  Sch ST7 .... 194 B1
St Saviour's RC Aided Inf
  & Jun Sch L66 .... 69 F2
St Saviour's St ST7 .... 194 B1
St Stephen Rd WA5 .... 14 C3
St Stephen's Ave WA2 ...... 8 A2
St Stephen's Prim Sch
  WA2 .... 8 A2
St Stephens Cl L60 .... 41 E3
St Stephens Ct CW11 .... 174 B4
St Teresa's RC Prim Sch
  CH1 .... 117 F3
St Theresa's RC Aided
  Prim Sch CH1 .... 117 F3
St Thomas' CE Prim Sch
  ST7 .... 195 D1
St Thomas' CE Prim Sch
  SK1 .... 240 F4
St Thomas Ct WA8 .... 12 C1
St Thomas Hospl SK3 .... 240 F4
St Thomas More RC
  (Aided) High Sch CW2 .. 190 A1
St Thomas of Canterbury
  CE Aided Jun Sch
  CH2 .... 237 D4
St Thomas St ST7 .... 195 F4
St Thomas's CE Aided Prim
  Sch WA4 .... 16 B1
St Thomas's Pathway CH1 237 E2
St Thomas's Pl SK1 .... 240 F4
St Vincent Dr CW8 .... 102 C2
St Vincent Rd WA5 .... 14 C3
St Vincent St WA15 .... 238 C4
St Vincent's RC Aided Prim
  Sch WA16 .... 57 C4
St Vincent's RC Inf Sch
  WA15 .... 238 E5
St Vincent's RC Jun Sch
  WA15 .... 238 E5
St Vincent's RC Prim Sch
  Penketh WA5 .... 14 C2
  St Helens WA9 .... 1 A2
St Wenefredes Gn SY14 . 214 C3
St Werburgh CE Aided
  Prim Sch WA4 .... 16 A1
St Werburgh St CH1 ...... 237 E2
St Werburgh's & St
  Columba's RC Aided
  Prim Sch CH2 .... 118 C1
St Wilfred's Dr WA4 .... 17 E1
St Wilfrid's RC Prim Sch
  CW8 .... 103 E3
St Winefride's RC Aided
  Prim Sch L64 .... 66 C4
St Winefride's RC Prim Sch
  L64 .... 66 C3
St Winifred's RC Prim Sch
  SK4 .... 240 A6
Salander Cres CW2 .... 206 A4
Sale Gram Sch M33 ...... 242 C5
Sale Sta M33 .... 242 B6
Sale Water Pk M33 .... 242 E8
Salerno Rd CH2 .... 95 D1
Salesbrook La CW5 .... 228 B3
Salford CW3 .... 230 A2
Salford Pl CW12 .... 156 C2
Salisbury Ave
  Broughton CH4 .... 140 C3
  Crewe CW2 .... 190 B1
Salisbury Cl Crewe CW2 . 190 B1
  Ellesmere Port CH1 .... 94 C4
Salisbury Ct **8** SK10 ... 112 C4
Salisbury Pl SK10 .... 87 F2
Salisbury Rd
  Altrincham WA14 .... 238 D7
  Haydock WA11 .... 1 C4
Salisbury St Blacon CH1 . 118 A2
  Goldborne WA3 .... 3 D2
  Runcorn WA7 .... 23 D1
  Warrington WA1 .... 16 B3
  4 Widnes WA8 .... 23 D4
Salkeld St CW9 .... 104 A4
Salop Pl ST7 .... 195 D2
Salop Wlk SK10 .... 86 C1
Salt Line Way CW11 ...... 174 B3
Salt Mus The CW8 .... 103 F4
Saltash Cl WA7 .... 50 A3
Salter's La Bickerton SY14 . 199 F4
  Fuller's Moor CH3 .... 183 F1
  Picton CH2 .... 119 E4
Salters La Siddington SK11 . 109 F1
  Withington SK11 .... 132 A4
Saltersbrook Gr **1** SK9 .... 34 C1
Saltersford Cnr CW4 ..... 130 C2
Saltersgate ST7 .... 195 E1
Saltings Cl WA6 .... 49 E1
Saltney Ferry Cty Prim Sch
  CH4 .... 140 A3
Saltney Ferry Rd CH4 .... 140 A4
Salton Gdns WA5 .... 15 F4
Saltwood Dr WA7 .... 50 B3
Samuel Laycock Spec Sch
  SK15 .... 242 C4

Samuel St Chester CH2 237 F3
Crewe CW1 190 A3
Macclesfield SK11 112 B4
Packmoor ST7 195 F1
Stockport SK4 240 D7
Warrington WA5 15 F2
Sanbec Gdns WA8 12 B3
Sand La SK10 84 C3
Sandalwood Cl WA2 8 B1
Sandbach Cty High Sch CW11 175 D4
Sandbach Cty Prim Sch CW11 175 D3
Sandbach Golf Course CW11 174 C4
Sandbach Rd
Congleton CW12 156 A2
Hassall Green CW11 176 B1
Lawton Heath ST7 193 F3
Rode Heath ST7 193 F4
Sale M33 242 F5
Sandbach Rd N ST7 193 E2
Sandbach Rd S ST7 193 E2
Sandbach Sch - (Ind) (Boys) CW11 175 D3
Sandbach Service Sta CW11 175 F3
Sandbach Sta CW11 174 B4
Sanderling Rd WA12 2 B2
Sanders Hey Cl WA7 50 A3
Sanders Sq SK11 112 B3
Sanderson Cl Crewe CW2 206 B4
Great Sankey WA5 14 B3
Sandfield Ave CW5 216 C2
Sandfield Cl WA3 3 F4
Sandfield Cres WA3 5 E4
Sandfield Ct Frodsham WA6 74 A4
Wrenbury CW5 216 C2
Sandfield La
Acton Bridge CW8 76 C1
Hartford CW8 103 E2
Sandfield Pk L60 40 B4
Sandfields WA6 74 A4
Sandford Rd Nantwich CW5 204 C4
Sale M33 242 F5
Sandgate Rd SK10 87 F1
Sandham Gr L60 41 E4
Sandham Rd L24 21 D2
Sandheys L64 41 E1
Sandhill St SK14 241 F8
Sandhole La Chelford WA16 83 E2
Crowton CW8 101 D4
Sandhurst Ave CW2 190 A1
Sandhurst Dr SK9 34 B1
Sandhurst Rd L24 21 D3
Sandhurst St WA4 16 C2
Sandicroft Cl WA3 9 E3
Sandiford Rd CW4 130 B2
Sandileigh CH2 118 C2
Sandileigh Ave
Altrincham WA15 238 F3
Cheadle SK8 240 A2
Knutsford WA16 56 C1
Sandileigh Dr WA15 238 F3
Sandiway Bebington L63 43 E3
Knutsford WA16 57 D1
Sandiway Ave WA8 12 A1
Sandiway Cl CW8 102 A1
Sandiway Cty Prim Sch CW8 102 A2
Sandiway Golf Course CW8 102 B1
Sandiway La CW9 53 D1
Sandiway Pk CW8 102 C2
Sandiway Pl WA14 238 D5
Sandiway Rd
Altrincham WA14 238 D6
Crewe CW1 190 A4
Wilmslow SK9 34 B3
Sandle Bridge La WA16 83 F3
Sandle Bridge Rise WA16 83 F3
Sandon Cres L64 66 C3
Sandon Park Gdns CW2 189 E2
Sandon Pl WA8 13 E1
Sandon Rd CH2 118 C2
Sandon St CW1 190 B2
Sandown Cl Culcheth WA3 4 C2
Middlewich CW10 151 E4
Runcorn WA7 49 E3
Wilmslow SK9 60 A4
Sandown Cres CW8 102 A2
Sandown Dr WA15 32 B3
Sandown Pl SK11 111 F4
Sandown Rd Crewe CW1 190 B4
Stockport SK3 240 B4
Sandpiper Cl Crewe CW1 189 F4
Newton-le-W WA12 2 B2
Sandpiper Dr SK3 240 D2
Sandra Dr WA12 2 B2
Sandringham Ave
Chester CH3 119 D1
Helsby WA6 73 D2
Stalybridge SK15 242 D3
Sandringham Cl
Altrincham WA14 20 C1
Davenham CW9 103 F2
Winsford CW7 126 B2
Sandringham Dr
Great Sankey WA5 15 E2
Poynton SK12 36 B2
Stockport SK4 240 A5
Wistaston CW2 205 F4
Sandringham Gdns L65 70 B1
Sandringham Rd WA8 13 D2
Sandrock Rd CH3 142 C4
Sands Rd ST7 195 F3
Sandsdown Cl ST6 179 E1
Sandside Rd ST7 193 D2
Sandstone Wlk L60 41 D4
Sandwell Dr M33 242 B8
Sandwich Dr SK10 87 E2
Sandwood Ave CH4 139 D2
Sandy Brow La WA3 3 F1
Sandy Cl SK10 87 F4
Sandy Gr ST7 193 E2
Sandy La Allostock WA16 106 C3
Astbury CW12 177 F3
Aston CW5 217 E1
Bold Heath WA8 14 A3
Broughton CH4 140 B3
Brown Knowl CH3 199 E4
Bulkeley SY14 184 B1
Chester CH3 119 D1
Congleton CW12 155 E2
Congleton, Astbury Marsh CW12 156 A1
Croft WA3 9 D4
Cronton WA8 12 B3
Goldborne WA3 2 C4
Goldborne, Wash End WA3 4 A4
Goostrey CW4 107 E1
Haslington CW11 192 A4
Hatherton CW5 219 F3
Higher Kinnerton CH4 161 D3
Huntington CH3 142 B2
Lymm WA13 19 D2
Macclesfield SK10 86 B1
Neston L64 67 D3
Nova Scotia CW8 125 E3
Penketh WA5 15 D2
Romiley SK6 241 D3
Runcorn, Preston Brook WA7 50 C3
Runcorn, Weston Point WA7 48 C4
Saighton CH3 142 B2
Sandbach CW11 174 B3
Stalybridge SK15 242 B1
Stockport SK4 & SK5 240 E7
Swettenham CW12 131 F2
Tarvin CH3 121 E2
Threapwood SY14 222 C4
Warrington WA2 8 B1
Warrington, Cobbs WA4 26 B4
Weaverham CW8 77 E1
Widnes WA8 12 B3
Wilmslow SK9 59 F4
Sandy La W WA2 8 A2
Sandy Moor La WA7 24 B2
Sandy Rd ST6 179 E1
Sandyhill Pl CW7 149 E3
Sandyhill Rd CW7 149 E3
Sandylands Cres ST7 193 F3
Sandylands Pk CW2 205 E4
Sankey St Goldborne WA3 3 D4
Newton-le-W WA12 2 A2
Warrington WA1 16 A3
Widnes WA8 23 D3
Sankey Sta WA5 14 C3
Sankey Valley Ind Est WA12 2 A1
Sankey Valley Park WA12 1 B2
Sankey Way
Great Sankey WA5 15 E3
Warrington WA5 15 E3
Sanky La WA4 25 F1
Santon Dr WA3 3 F4
Sapling La CW6 146 C2
Sarra La CH3 184 A3
Sarsfield Ave WA3 3 E4
Saughall Cl CW9 103 F2
Saughall Hey CH1 94 A1
Saughall Rd CH1 117 F3
Saunders St CW1 190 A2
Saundersfoot Cl WA5 7 F1
Saunderton Cl WA11 1 B4
Saville Ave WA5 15 F4
Saville Rd SK8 239 B6
Saville St SK11 112 C3
Savoy Rd CW1 207 D4
Sawley Cl Culcheth WA3 5 D1
Runcorn WA7 50 C4
Sawley Dr SK7 35 E3
Sawpit St WA13 20 A3
Sawyer Brow SK14 241 F8
Sawyer Dr ST6 179 E1
Saxon Crossway CW7 126 A1
Saxon Rd WA7 23 E1
Saxon Terr WA8 13 D1
Saxon Way Blacon CH1 117 F3
Ellesmere Port CH1 94 C4
Sandbach CW11 175 E3
Saxons La Northwich CW8 103 F3
Northwich, Greenbank CW8 103 E4
Sayce St WA8 13 D1
Scafell Ave WA2 8 B2
Scafell Cl Bebington L63 43 E2
High Lane SK6 37 F4
Scaife Rd CW5 204 C3
Scaliot Cl SK22 39 D4
Scar La SY14 198 C1
Sceptre Cl WA12 2 A2
Scholar Green Cty Prim Sch ST7 194 C3
Scholar's Ct L64 66 C4
Scholars' Green La WA13 18 C1
School Ave L64 66 C3
School Bank WA6 101 D3
School Brow Romiley SK6 241 A2
Warrington WA1 16 B3
School Cl Audley ST7 210 A1
Knutsford WA16 56 C1
Marbury SY13 226 C4
Poynton SK12 36 C2
School Cres Crewe CW1 190 C2
Stalybridge SK15 242 D4
School Ct SK3 240 F2
School Field Cl CW3 230 C2
School Gn CH3 182 B1
School Hill L60 40 C4
School La Aldford CH3 163 F1
Antrobus CW9 53 E2
Astbury CW12 178 A4
Audlem CW3 230 A2
Bold Heath WA8 13 F4
Brereton Green CW11 153 F3
Bunbury CW6 168 C1
Burwardsley CH3 184 A3
Cheadle Hulme SK8 35 D4
Cuddington CW8 102 A1
Dunham Town WA14 20 B3
Eaton (nr Congleton) CW12 156 C4
Ellesmere Port L66 69 D4
Elton CH2 72 A2
Frodsham WA6 74 B4
Great Budworth CW9 79 D4
Guilden Sutton CH3 119 F3
Hartford CW8 103 E2
Henbury SK11 111 D3
Hollins Green WA3 11 D1
Irlam M44 11 E3
Lostock CW9 80 A1
Marbury SY13 215 F1
Marton SK11 133 E3
Mickle Trafford CH2 119 F4
Moulton CW9 126 C4
Nantwich CW5 204 C3
Neston L64 66 C3
Neston, Parkgate L64 41 D1
Nether Alderley SK10 86 A3
Norley WA6 100 B3
Ollerton WA16 83 D2
Poynton SK12 36 C2
Runcorn WA7 49 F4
Sandbach, Betchton CW11 175 F3
Sandbach, Ettiley Heath CW11 174 B4
Smallwood CW11 176 C3
Warmingham CW11 173 F4
Warrington WA3 10 B3
Whitley WA4 52 C3
Willaston L64 42 A1
School Mews SK7 35 F4
School Rd Altrincham WA15 238 F3
Ellesmere Port L65 70 A3
Lach Dennis CW9 104 B3
Sale M33 242 A7
Sale M33 242 B7
Warrington WA2 8 B1
Wilmslow SK9 34 B2
Winsford CW7 127 D1
Winsford, Meadowbank CW7 126 C3
School Rd N CW9 104 C3
School Rd S CW9 104 C3
School St Chester CH2 118 C2
Goldborne WA3 3 D4
Haslington CW1 191 E3
Newton-le-W WA12 2 A2
Warrington WA4 16 A2
School Way Northwich CW9 104 A4
Widnes WA8 13 E2
Schools Hill SK8 239 D3
Schooner Cl WA7 50 B3
Scilly Cl L65 70 B1
Scotch Hall La CW9 53 D2
Scotland Rd WA1 16 A3
Scott Ave Crewe CW1 190 C2
Widnes WA8 22 C4
Scott Cl Macclesfield SK10 113 D4
Reddish SK5 240 F8
Rode Heath ST7 193 F4
1 Sandbach CW11 174 B3
Scott Rd SK10 87 D4
Scott St WA2 16 B3
Scott Wlk WA12 2 B1
Scotthorpe Cl SK11 111 F3
Scotton Ave L66 69 D3
Scretton Green Distribution Pk WA4 27 E2
Scroggins La M31 11 F2
Sea Bank CW10 128 B1
Sea La WA7 23 E1
Sea View L64 66 C2
Seabank Rd L60 40 C3
Seabury St WA4 17 D2
Seacombe Dr L66 69 F2
Seacombe Gr SK3 240 B4
Seafield Ave L60 40 C3
Seaford Cl WA7 24 B1
Seaford Pl WA2 8 A2
Seagull Cl CW1 190 C3
Seahill Rd CH1 116 C4
Seal Rd SK7 35 F4
Sealand Cl WA2 8 C1
Sealand Ind Est CH1 117 F1
Sealand Rd Blacon CH1 117 E2
Chester CH1 118 A1
Sealand CH5 116 B3
Sealand Way 1 SK9 34 B2
Seamon's Dr WA14 238 A6
Seamon's Rd WA14 238 A6
Seamons Wlk WA14 238 B5
Seathwaite Cl WA7 49 F3
Seaton Cl CW1 190 A4
Seaton Pk WA7 24 C2
Seaton St CW7 127 E1
Seaview Ave L62 44 A3
Seaville St CH2 237 F3
Secker Ave WA4 16 B1
Secker Cl WA4 16 B1
Second Ave Adlington SK10 36 B1
Crewe CW1 190 C1
Deeside Ind Est CH5 92 C2
Kidsgrove ST7 194 C1
Runcorn WA7 49 F4
Sandbach CW11 175 D3
Second Dig La CW5 219 E4
Second Wood St CW5 204 B3
Sedbergh Gr WA7 49 F3
Sedburgh Cl CW4 130 A2
Seddon Rd WA14 238 D2
Seddon St CW10 128 B1
Sedgefield Cl SK9 34 B1
Sedgefield Rd CH1 118 A1
Sedgewick Cres WA5 6 C3
Sedgmere Ave CW1 190 A4
Sedum Cl CH3 142 A3
Sefton Ave Congleton CW12 157 D1
Widnes WA8 13 D2
Sefton Cres M33 242 B8
Sefton Dr SK9 34 B1
Sefton Rd Chester CH2 119 D2
Sale M33 242 B7
Sefton St WA12 1 C2
Seftons The SK9 34 B1
Selby Cl Poynton SK12 36 B3
Runcorn WA7 24 C2
Selby Gdns SK7 35 E3
Selby Gn L66 69 D3
Selby St Reddish SK4 240 D8
Warrington WA5 15 F3
Selkirk Ave Bebington L62 43 F2
Warrington WA4 17 D2
Selkirk Cl Ellesmere Port L66 68 C3
Macclesfield SK10 86 C1
Selkirk Dr Chester CH4 141 D4
Holmes Chapel CW4 130 A1
Selkirk Rd CH4 141 D4
Seller St CH2 237 F3
Selsdon Ct CH4 141 E4
Selsey Ave SK3 239 F7
Selsey Cl CW1 190 A4
Selsey Dr M20 239 C8
Selworth Ave M33 242 E6
Selworth Cl WA15 238 E6
Selworthy Dr Crewe CW1 190 A4
Warrington WA4 17 E2
Selwyn Cl WA8 13 E2
Selwyn Dr
Cheadle Hulme SK7 35 E4
Sutton Lane Ends SK11 112 C2
Semper Cl CW12 157 D2
Seneschal Ct WA7 49 F3
Senna La Antrobus CW9 53 D1
Comberbach CW9 78 B4
Sennen Cl WA7 50 B3
Sephton Ave WA3 4 C2
Sergeant York Loop WA5 15 D3
Serin Cl WA12 2 B2
Serpentine The CH4 141 D4
Service St SK3 240 B4
Servite Cl L65 69 F3
Set St SK15 242 C1
Sett Cl SK22 39 D4
Seven Sisters La WA16 82 C3
Sevenoaks Cl SK10 87 D1
Sevenoaks Rd SK8 239 B6
Severn Cl Altrincham WA14 238 C6
Biddulph ST6 179 F1
Congleton CW12 156 C1
Macclesfield SK10 86 C1
Warrington WA2 8 C1
Widnes WA8 13 F2
Severn Dr SK7 35 E3
Severn Rd WA3 4 C1
Severn Wlk CW7 127 D1
Severnvale L65 70 A2
Sewell St WA7 23 D1
Sextant Cl WA7 50 B3
Sexton Ave WA9 1 A1
Seymour Chase WA16 82 A4
Seymour Ct WA7 24 B2
Seymour Dr
Ellesmere Port L66 69 F3
Warrington WA1 17 D4
Seymour Gr M33 242 B6
Seymour Rd SK8 35 D4
Shackleton Cl WA5 15 E4
Shadewood Cres WA4 17 D1
Shadewood Rd SK11 112 A3
Shadowmoss Rd M22 33 F4
Shady Brook La CW8 77 E1
Shaftesbury Ave
Chester CH3 119 E1
Penketh WA5 14 C1
Shaftesbury Rd SK3 240 B2
Shaftesbury Way WA5 6 C4
Shaftway Cl WA11 1 C4
Shakerley Ave CW12 156 C2
Shakespeare Cl CW9 104 B4
Shakespeare Dr
Cheadle SK8 239 F6
Crewe CW1 191 D2
Shakespeare Gr WA2 8 B1
Shakespeare Rd
Neston L64 41 F1
Widnes WA8 13 D1
Shalcombe Cl L26 21 D4
Shalford Dr M22 33 E4
Shall Acres L65 69 F3
Shallacres L66 69 F4
Shallcross Ave SK23 65 F2
Shallcross Cres SK23 65 F2
Shallcross Rd SK23 65 F2
Shanklin Cl WA5 14 B3
Shannon Cl Chester CH4 140 C3
Willaston (nr Nantwich) CW5 205 E3
Shargate Cl SK9 34 B1
Sharnbrook Dr CW2 189 E2
Sharon Park Cl WA4 17 E1
Sharp St Warrington WA1 16 B3
Widnes WA8 23 D4
Sharples St SK4 240 E7
Sharpley St SK11 112 B4
Sharston Cres WA16 57 D1
Shavington Ave CH2 118 C2
Shavington Cty High Sch CW2 206 A3
Shavington Cty Prim Sch CW2 206 B2
Shavington Sports Ctr CW2 206 A3
Shavington Way CW9 103 F2
Shaw Dr WA16 57 E2
Shaw Entry WA8 12 A4
Shaw Heath SK2 & SK3 240 E3
Shaw Moor Ave SK15 242 F1
Shaw Rd SK4 240 B8
Shaw Rd S SK3 240 E2
Shaw St Ashton-u-L OL6 242 A3
Culcheth WA3 5 D2
Haydock WA11 1 C3
Macclesfield SK11 112 B4
Runcorn WA7 22 C1
Warrington WA2 16 A3
Shaw's Ave WA2 16 B4
Shaw's Rd WA14 238 D4
Shawcross Fold 5 SK1 240 F6
Shawell Ct WA8 13 F1
Shaws Fold SK9 33 F2
Shaws La
Mottram St Andrew SK10 86 B4
Winsford CW7 126 C2
Winsford CW7 127 D2
Shay La Ashton CH3 122 A4
Hampton SY14 200 A1
Tarvin CH3 121 F2
Shay's La CW6 124 C2
Sheaf Cl CH3 121 E1
Shearbrook La CW4 107 F1
Sheardhall Ave SK12 38 C3
Sheath St CW9 104 A4
Shed La CH3 119 D1
Sheepfield Cl L66 69 E4
Sheerwater Cl WA1 16 C4
Sheffield Cl WA5 15 E3
Sheffield Rd SK14 241 F8
Sheffield Row WA12 7 E4
Sheffield St SK4 240 E7
Sheiling Ct WA14 238 C4
Sheilings The WA3 3 F4
Shelagh Ave WA8 13 D1
Shelbourne Mews SK11 111 F4
Shelburne Dr CW1 191 E3
Sheldon Ave Chester CH3 119 D1
Congleton CW12 157 D1
Sheldon Rd SK7 36 C4
Sheldrake Dr L64 66 C3
Sheldrake Rd WA14 238 B8
Shellbrook Gr 1 SK9 34 B1
Shelley Ave CW9 80 A3
Shelley Cl Crewe CW1 190 C2
Rode Heath ST7 193 F4
Shelley Ct 7 CW11 174 B3
Shelley Dr CW2 189 F1
Shelley Gr WA4 16 C2
Shelley Rd Blacon CH1 117 F3
Widnes WA8 13 D1
Shellow La SK11 134 B3
Shellway Rd L65 71 D2
Shelton Cl WA8 13 F2
Shenton St SK14 241 C8
Shepcroft La WA4 26 B2
Shepherd's Brow WA14 238 A3
Shepherd's La CH2 118 B3
Shepherds Fold Dr CW7 126 B2
Shepherds Row WA7 23 F1
Shepley Cl SK7 36 B4
Shepley St 1 Hyde SK14 241 E6
Stalybridge SK15 242 D2
Sheppard Cl CW1 190 B3
Sheppenhall Gr CW5 217 E1
Sheppenhall La
Newhall CW5 228 B3
Royal's Green CW5 228 B3
Shepperton Cl WA4 26 C3
Shepsides Cl L66 69 E2
Shepton Rd L66 69 F1
Sherborne Cl WA7 24 C2
Sherborne Rd
Cheadle SK3 240 A3
Crewe CW1 190 B3
Sherbourne Ave CH4 141 D3
Sherbourne Cl SK8 35 D3
Sherbourne Rd
Ellesmere Port L65 70 B2
Macclesfield SK11 111 F4
Sherbourne Way WA5 6 C3
Sherbrook Rise SK9 60 B3
Sherbrooke Rd SK12 38 B3
Sheri Dr WA12 2 B1
Sheridan Ave WA3 3 E4
Sheridan Cl CW1 173 D1
Sheringham Cl CH4 140 C3
Sheringham Dr CW1 190 A4
Sheringham Rd WA5 14 C3
Sherlock Ave WA11 1 C4
Sherratt Cl CW12 156 C1
Sherrington's La CH3 199 E4
Sherwin St CW2 190 B1
Sherwood Ave
Cheadle SK8 239 F2
Sale M33 242 D7
Stockport SK4 240 A5
Sherwood Cl WA8 12 B1
Sherwood Cres WA5 6 C3
Sherwood Gr WA6 73 D2
Sherwood Rd SK11 112 B3

Shetland Cl Warrington WA2 .. 8 C2
Widnes WA8 .... 13 F2
Shetland Dr Bebington L62 .. 43 F4
Ellesmere Port L65 .... 70 B1
Shevington Cl WA8 .... 13 F2
Shevington Wlk WA8 .... 13 F2
Shield St SK3 .... 240 E4
Shiers St SK8 .... 239 E4
Shiggins Cl WA5 .... 15 E3
Shillingford Cl WA4 .... 26 C3
Shilton Cl CW10 .... 151 F3
Ship St WA6 .... 49 E1
Shipbrook Rd Chester CH2 . 118 C3
Lach Dennis CW9 .... 104 A2
Northwich CW9 .... 104 B3
Shipgate St CH4 .... 237 E1
Shipton Cl
Great Sankey WA5 .... 15 D4
Widnes WA8 .... 12 B2
Shirley Ave SK8 .... 34 B3
Shirley Dr WA4 .... 17 D1
Shirley Gr SK10 .... 240 E2
Shirleys Dr SK10 .... 87 D3
Shirleys St SK10 .... 87 D3
Shocklach Oviatt CE Contr
Prim Sch SY14 .... 211 E4
Shocklach Rd CH2 .... 118 C3
Shones Croft L64 .... 67 D3
Shop La CW6 .... 124 C1
Shopping Precinct The
CH2 .... 72 A2
Shoreham Dr WA5 .... 15 D2
Shores Green Dr CW9 ..... 79 F3
Shores La CW5 .... 203 E4
Shorewell Cl WA5 .... 14 B4
Short Cl WA12 .... 1 C2
Short La Haydock WA11 .... 1 C3
28 Macclesfield SK11 .... 112 B4
Newton-le-W WA12 .... 1 C1
Stockport SK4 .... 240 E7
Widnes WA8 .... 23 D3
Short St E SK4 .... 240 E7
Shorthorn Cl CW10 .... 128 B1
Shotwick La CH1 .... 93 F3
Shotwick Rd CH1 .... 93 D2
Shrewbridge Cres CW5 .... 204 C2
Shrewbridge Rd CW5 ...... 204 B2
Shrewsbury Dr ST5 .... 210 C1
Shrewsbury Gdns SK7 ..... 35 E3
Shrewsbury Rd L65 .... 70 B3
Shrewsbury St WA4 .... 16 B2
Shrewsbury Way CH4 ...... 140 C3
Shrigley Cl SK9 .... 34 B1
Shrigley Rd Bollington SK10 .. 63 D3
Pott Shrigley SK10 .... 63 D3
Poynton SK12 .... 37 E2
Shrigley Rd N SK12 .... 37 E2
Shrigley Rise SK10 .... 63 E1
Shropshire Cl
Middlewich CW10 .... 151 D4
Warrington WA1 .... 17 F3
Shropshire La
Newhall SY13 .... 227 F1
Old Woodhouse SY13 ..... 227 F1
Shropshire Rd L65 .... 70 C2
Shropshire St CW3 .... 229 F2
Shurlach Rd CW9 .... 104 B3
Shutley La CW8 .... 77 E3
Sibbersfield La CH3 .... 180 C2
Sibell St CH2 .... 237 F3
Sibley Rd SK4 .... 240 B7
Sibson Rd M33 .... 242 B6
Siddall St CW9 .... 104 A4
Siddeley Cl CH4 .... 139 E2
Siddeley Dr WA12 .... 1 C2
Siddington Ave
Northwich CW9 .... 104 A2
Stockport SK3 .... 240 D2
Siddington Bank SK11 .... 109 F2
Siddington Rd Poynton SK12 36 C1
1 Wilmslow SK9 .... 34 B3
Siddon St CW7 .... 126 C1
Side Ave WA14 .... 238 C1
Side End La SK23 .... 64 C2
Sidebottom St SK15 ...... 242 D2
Sidlaw Cl L66 .... 69 D3
Sidley Pl SK14 .... 241 F7
Sidley St SK14 .... 241 F7
Sidmouth Cl WA5 .... 14 C2
Sidmouth Gr SK8 .... 34 C4
Sidney Rd L64 .... 41 F1
Siemens Rd M44 .... 11 F3
Silcock St WA3 .... 3 D4
Silk Hill SK23 .... 65 F4
Silk Mill St WA16 .... 57 D1
Silk Mus & Heritage Ctr
SK11 .... 112 B4
Silk Rd The Bollington SK10 .. 87 F2
Macclesfield SK10 .... 87 F2
Silk St CW12 .... 156 B1
Silsden Ave WA3 .... 4 A4
Silvan Ct SK10 .... 87 C1
Silver Ave WA11 .... 1 A3
Silver Hill Rd SK14 ...... 241 E5
Silver La Croft WA3 ...... 9 F4
Warrington WA2 .... 10 B3
Silver St Bollington SK10 .. 88 A4
Congleton CW12 .... 156 C1
Warrington WA2 .... 16 A3
Silver Terr CW11 .... 175 E3
Silverbirch Croft CH4 .... 139 D2
Silverbirch Way CH1 ..... 94 C4
Silverdale Altrincham WA14 238 C1
Northwich CW8 .... 103 E4

Silverdale Ave M34 .... 241 A6
High Lane SK6 .... 37 F4
Silverdale Cl Frodsham WA6 .. 74 B4
Silverdale Dr SK9 .... 60 A2
Silverdale Rd Gatley SK8 .. 239 B4
Manchester SK4 .... 240 D8
Newton-le-W WA12 .... 2 A2
Warrington WA4 .... 16 A1
Silvergate Ct CW12 ...... 178 C4
Silvermine Cl ST7 .... 195 D1
Silvermuir CH1 .... 117 F2
Silverne Dr L65 .... 70 A1
Silverthorne Cl SK15 .... 242 D1
Silverwood ST7 .... 195 D1
Simms Cross Cty Prim Sch
.... 23 D4
Simon Cl M33 .... 242 A5
Simons La WA6 .... 74 A3
Simonside WA8 .... 12 B1
Simonstone Rd CH4 ..... 139 E2
Simonswood Cl CW10 ... 151 D4
Simpkin Ave WA4 .... 16 C2
Simpson Cl CH2 .... 95 E1
Simpson Ct CW1 .... 173 D1
Simpson La SK10 .... 63 E4
Simpson Rd CH2 .... 95 E1
Simpson St Hyde SK14 .. 241 D6
7 Stockport SK3 .... 240 E4
Simpsons Way CW4 ..... 139 D2
Sinclair Ave Alsager ST7 . 193 D2
Warrington WA2 .... 8 A1
Widnes WA8 .... 23 D4
Sinderland La WA14 .... 20 C4
Sinderland Rd WA14 .... 238 C8
Singapore Ave M90 .... 33 D4
Singleton Ave CW1 .... 190 B3
Singleton Rd
Ellesmere Port L65 ..... 69 F2
2 Manchester SK4 ..... 240 D8
Sir John Deane's Sixth
Form Coll CW9 .... 103 F3
Sir Thomas Boteler Cty
High Sch The WA4 ..... 16 C2
Siskin Cl WA12 .... 2 B2
Six Acre Gdns WA4 .... 25 D3
Six Acre La WA4 ...... 25 D3
Sixpenny Wlk WA1 .... 16 B3
Sixth Ave CH5 .... 92 C1
Skaife Rd M33 .... 242 E6
Skeath Cl CW11 ...... 175 F3
Skellern St ST7 ...... 194 B1
Skelton Rd WA14 ..... 238 E7
Skiddaw Cl WA7 ..... 50 A2
Skip's La CH3 .... 142 C4
Skipton Cl SK7 .... 36 B4
Skipton Dr L66 .... 69 E3
Skye Cl Ellesmere Port L65 .. 70 B1
Widnes WA8 .... 13 F2
Skye Croft SK6 ...... 241 D3
Skylark Cl WA1 ..... 189 F4
Slack St Hyde SK14 .. 241 F8
Macclesfield SK11 .... 112 C3
Slacken La ST7 ...... 194 B1
Slade La Mobberley WA16 .. 58 A4
Nether Alderley SK10 .. 85 F3
Slade St CW9 .... 104 A4
Slag La Goldborne WA3 .. 3 E4
Haydock WA11 .... 1 B1
Slater St Macclesfield SK11 .. 112 B3
Warrington WA4 ...... 16 B2
Slindon Cl ST5 ...... 210 B1
Sloane St SK15 ..... 242 D1
Slutchers La WA1 ... 16 A2
Small Ave WA2 ..... 8 B1
Small Cres WA2 .... 8 B1
Small La WA16 ..... 58 A4
Smallbrook Wlk CW2 206 B4
Smallman Rd CW2 .. 190 B1
Smallwood CE Contr Prim
Sch CW11 .... 176 C3
Smallwood Cl
Middlewich CW10 .... 151 E4
Newcastle-u-L ST5 ... 210 B1
Smenhurst Cl SK9 ... 59 F2
Smethwick La
CW11, CW12 .... 154 C2
Smith Cl ST7 .... 193 D2
Smith Cres WA2 .... 16 B4
Smith Dr WA2 ...... 16 B4
Smith Gr CW1 ...... 190 A3
Smith La Mobberley WA16 .. 57 F3
Rainow SK10 .... 89 D3
Smith Rd WA8 ...... 22 C4
Smith St Cheadle SK8 .. 239 F6
Macclesfield SK11 .... 112 B3
Warrington WA1 ..... 16 A3
Smith's La CW8 .... 77 E1
Smithfield Dr LL13 .. 196 B4
Smithfield La CW11 . 175 E3
Smithfield St LL13 .. 196 B4
Smithfields CH3 .... 166 B1
Smithills Cl WA3 ... 9 E3
Smiths Lawn SK9 ... 60 A3
Smithy Brow Croft WA3 .. 8 C4
Rainow SK10 .... 88 B4
Smithy Cl Cronton WA8 .. 12 B3
Saughall CH1 .... 94 A1
Willaston L64 .... 67 D2
Smithy Gn SK8 ..... 35 D4
Smithy Hill L63 ..... 42 A3
Smithy La
Barthomley CW2 .... 208 B3
Barthomley CW2 .... 208 B4
Biddulph ST6 .... 179 E1
Bosley SK11 .... 158 C3
Congleton CW12 .... 156 B4
Crewe CW1 .... 189 F4
Croft WA3 .... 9 D4

Smithy La continued
Cronton WA8 .... 12 B3
Cuddington CW8 ..... 102 A3
Dunham Town WA14 . 20 B2
Ellesmere Port L66 ... 69 E3
Fuller's Moor CH3 .... 183 E1
Great Budworth CW9 . 79 D4
Helsby WA6 .... 73 E3
Hyde SK14 .... 241 E5
Kingsley WA6 .... 75 D1
Little Leigh CW8 .... 77 D3
Lostock CW9 .... 80 A1
Malpas SY14 .... 213 D2
Mottram St Andrew SK10 .. 61 E1
Mouldsworth CH3 ... 98 C1
Partington M31 ..... 11 F2
Utkinton CW6 ...... 146 B3
Weston CW2 .... 207 E3
Willaston L64 ...... 68 A4
Smithy Pathway CH4 .. 140 C2
Smithy The CH2 .... 118 B4
Smithy Vale SK10 .. 87 F4
Smithy Wlk 1 CW11 174 C2
Smokehall La CW7, CW9 126 C3
Smokehall Lane Ind Est
CW7 .... 127 D3
Smokey La SY13 .... 224 A1
Smokies Way ST6 .. 179 E1
Smyth Wlk M31 .... 11 E1
Snab La L64 .... 66 C2
Snabwood Cl L64 .. 66 C3
Snaefell Rise WA4 . 26 B4
Snape Hollow CW2 207 F2
Snape La CW2 ..... 207 F2
Snape Rd Crewe CW2 206 B4
Macclesfield SK10 .. 87 F1
Snapebrook Gr 6 SK9 34 C1
Snelson La
Chelford SK11 ..... 108 C4
Chelford, Marthall WA16 .. 83 E2
Snipe Cl SK12 ..... 36 A2
Snow Hill SK11 .... 112 C3
Snowberry Cl WA8 .. 13 F2
Snowberry Wlk M31 11 E1
Snowdon
Ellesmere Port L66 .. 69 D3
Great Sankey WA5 .. 14 B4
Snowdon Cres CH4 141 D3
Snowdon Dr CW2 . 189 E2
Snowdon St CW8 .. 77 F2
Snowdonia Way CW7 149 D4
Snowdrop Cl WA7 . 49 F2
Solly Cres CW12 .. 156 A1
Solway Cl Bebington L62 .. 8 C2
High Legh WA16 ... 29 E2
Neston L64 .... 66 C3
Solway Gr WA7 ... 49 E3
Solway Rd SK8 ... 78 B1
Somerford Ave CW2 190 A2
Somerford Cl CW11 175 E4
Somerford Rd CH4 139 E2
Somerford Wlk WA8 13 F2
Somerley Cl CW1 .. 190 A4
Somerset Ave ST7 194 C1
Somerset Cl
Congleton CW12 .. 156 B2
Irlam M44 .... 11 E3
Somerset Pl M33 . 242 B8
Somerset Rd
Altrincham WA14 .. 238 D6
Chester CH2 ...... 118 C3
Somerset St CH2 . 237 E4
Somerset Way WA1 17 D4
Somerton Ave M33 242 C5
Somerton Cl SK11 111 F4
Somerton Rd SK11 111 F4
Somerville Cl
Bebington L62 .... 43 D3
High Legh WA16 .. 29 E2
Neston L64 ...... 66 C3
Somerville Cres L65 70 B2
Somerville Gdns WA15 238 F7
Somerville Rd WA8 22 B4
Somerville St CW2 190 A1
Soot Hill CW9 .... 78 B2
Sorbus Cl CH2 ... 72 B2
Sorbus Dr CW1 .. 190 C3
Sorby Rd M44 ... 11 F4
Sorrel Cl Huntington CH3 142 A3
Warrington WA2 .. 9 E1
Soss Moss Hospl SK10 84 B3
Sossmoss La SK10 84 B3
Sound Cty Prim Sch CW5 .. 217 F3
Sound La Ravensmoor CW5 . 203 F1
Sound CW5 .... 217 E4
Souracre Fold SK15 242 E3
Souter's La CH1 .. 237 E2
South Acre Dr
Macclesfield SK11 . 113 D4
Wilmslow SK9 .... 34 B2
South Ave Chester CH2 237 F4
Haslington CW1 .. 191 E2
Warrington WA4 .. 16 A4
Warrington, Stockton Heath
WA4 .... 16 B1
South Bank CH2 . 118 B2
South Bank Gr CW1 156 C1
South Bank Terr WA7 22 C2
South Bank SK9 .. 60 A1
South Cft CW6 ... 185 E3
South Cheshire Coll CW2 .. 190 A1
South Cheshire Coll
(Annexe) CW1 ... 190 B2
South Cl Tarporley CW6 146 B1
Wilmslow SK9 .... 59 F3
South Crescent Rd CH4 .. 237 F1
South Crofts CW5 204 C3
South Dale WA5 .. 14 C3
South Downs WA16 57 E1
South Downs Dr WA14 238 D1

South Downs Rd WA14 238 D1
South Dr Gatley SK8 .. 239 A4
Heswall L60 .... 41 D4
Northwich CW9 ... 104 B3
Plumley WA16 .... 80 C2
South Gn CH5 .... 116 A3
South Gr Alderley Edge SK9 .. 60 A1
Sale M33 .... 242 B5
South La WA8 .... 13 F2
South Lane Entry WA8 13 F3
South Mead SK10 36 A3
South Meadway SK6 37 F4
South Oak La SK9 59 F3
South Par WA7 ... 48 B4
South Park Dr SK12 36 C3
South Park Rd Gatley SK8 239 B6
Macclesfield SK11 . 112 B4
South Pier Rd L65 70 B4
South Rd
Altrincham, Ashley Heath
WA14 .... 31 F4
Altrincham, Rosehill WA14 238 C2
Ellesmere Port L65 . 70 B2
Runcorn WA7 .... 48 B4
Speke L24 .... 21 D2
Stanlow L65 ..... 70 C2
South St Alderley Edge SK9 .. 60 A1
Chester CH3 ..... 119 D1
Congleton CW12 . 156 B2
Crewe CW2 ...... 190 B1
Mount Pleasant ST7 195 D3
3 Widnes WA8 .. 23 D4
South Trafford Coll of
F Ed WA14 ...... 238 D8
South Vale Cres WA15 238 F5
South View Ave WA8 111 E1
South View Rd CH1 118 A1
South View Chester CH4 .. 141 E4
New Mills SK22 .. 39 D4
Withington SK11 . 132 A4
South View Cotts ST7 193 F2
South View La CW7 170 C1
South Way CH1 .. 117 F2
South West Ave SK10 87 F3
South Wirral High Sch L62 .. 43 E2
Southampton Way WA7 50 C3
Southbank CW9 .. 79 D4
Southbank Ave CW2 206 B3
Southdale Rd WA1 17 D4
Southdown Cl
Macclesfield SK10 . 87 E2
Stockport SK4 ... 240 E6
Southdown Cres SK8 34 C4
Southern Rd M33 242 A8
Southern St WA4 16 B1
Southey Cl 9
Sandbach CW11 . 174 B3
Widnes WA8 .... 22 C4
Southfield SK10 . 87 D2
Southfield Cl SK9 34 B2
Southfield Rd L66 69 E3
Southfields WA16 57 E2
Southfields Ave WA5 14 C2
Southfields Cl CW5 220 A4
Southlands CW4 . 130 B1
Southlands Ave WA5 14 C2
Southlands Mews WA7 22 C1
Southlands Rd CW12 179 D4
Southlands View CW4 107 F1
Southpoint SK4 .. 240 A6
Southport St WA9 1 A2
Southward Rd WA11 2 A4
Southwark Pl 11 CW7 149 D4
Southway
Altrincham WA14 238 E6
Runcorn WA7 .... 49 F4
Widnes WA8 .... 22 B4
Southway Ave WA4 26 B4
Southwell Cl Goldborne WA3 .. 3 E4
Romiley SK6 ..... 241 A1
Southwood Ave WA7 24 B1
Southworth Ave WA5 15 F4
Southworth La
Croft WA3, WA2 .. 8 C4
Winwick WA3, WA2 8 C2
Southworth Rd WA12 2 C2
Sovereign Cl
Northwich CW9 .. 104 C3
Runcorn WA7 .... 50 B4
Sovereign Ct WA3 9 E2
Sovereign Way CH1 117 F1
Spark Hall Cl WA4 26 C1
Spark La Runcorn WA7 23 F1
Smallwood CW11 . 154 B1
Sparks Cl CH3 ... 142 A4
Sparrow La WA16 57 D1
Sparrowbutts Gr ST7 195 E1
Sparrowhawk Cl WA7 50 A4
Sparth Ct SK4 ... 240 D7
Sparth Hall SK4 . 240 D7
Sparth La SK4 .. 240 D7
Sparthfield Rd SK4 240 D7
Spath La SK8 ... 34 C3
Spath La E SK8 . 35 D3
Spath La W SK8 . 35 D3
Spathfield Ct SK4 240 D7
Spawell Cl WA3 . 3 F4
Speakman Ave WA12 2 B3
Speakman St WA7 22 C2
Speed's Way CH3 180 C1
Speedwell Cl Heswall L60 41 E4
Huntington CH3 . 142 A3
Speedwell Dr L60 41 E4
Speedwell Rd ST5 210 C1
Speke Bvd Halewood L24 21 D2
Speke L24 .... 21 D2
Speke Rd WA8 .. 22 B4
Spencer Brook SK10 86 C3

Spencer Cl Alsager ST7 .. 192 C2
Widnes WA8 ...... 12 C1
Wistaston CW2 ... 206 A4
Spencer Rd L64 .. 41 F1
Spencer St WA8 . 78 A4
Spenlow Cl SK12 . 36 C1
Spennymoor Ct WA14 .. 238 C6
Spey Cl Altrincham WA14 238 C6
Winsford CW7 ... 126 C1
Spey Dr ST7 ..... 195 E1
Spike Island WA8 23 B3
Spindle Ave SK15 242 F3
Spindle St CW12 . 156 C1
Spink La WA16 .. 80 A3
Spinnaker Cl WA7 50 B3
Spinner Cres CW9 78 B4
Spinney CW8 .... 101 E3
Spinney Ave Goostrey CW4 107 F1
Widnes WA8 .... 12 A3
Spinney Cl Wilmslow SK9 .. 34 B2
Winsford CW7 ... 150 A4
Spinney Dr Ellesmere Port L66 69 E1
Weston CW2 .... 207 D3
Spinney End CH3 166 A1
Spinney La WA16 56 C2
Spinney Mead SK10 87 F1
Spinney The Cheadle SK8 .. 239 E3
Heswall L60 ..... 41 E3
Lawton-gate ST7 . 194 C2
Neston L64 ..... 41 E1
Norley L64 ..... 100 C3
1 Sandbach CW11 175 E3
Willaston (nr Nantwich)
CW5 .... 205 E3
Spinney Wlk WA7 24 A1
Spirewood Gdns SK6 241 A2
Spital Wlk CH2 .. 118 C1
Spodegreen La WA14 30 B4
Spout La WA16 .. 58 A2
Spragg St CW12 . 156 C2
Spring Ave L66 .. 69 E3
Spring Bank
Altrincham WA14 238 D3
Stalybridge SK15 242 E1
The Bank ST7 ... 195 D4
Spring Bank La
Adlington SK10 .. 63 D3
Stalybridge SK15 242 F4
Spring Bank Rd SK22 39 E4
Spring Cl ST7 .... 193 F4
Spring Ct WA7 ... 23 D1
Spring Gdns Crewe CW1 190 C3
Ellesmere Port L66 69 E3
Hyde SK14 ...... 241 D8
Macclesfield SK10 87 E1
Spring Hill CW6 . 168 B4
Spring La Coddington CH3 .. 181 F3
Croft WA3 .... 9 D3
Lymm WA13 .... 19 F2
Spring Meadow CW8 78 A4
Spring Mount SK22 39 E4
Spring Rd Altrincham WA14 238 D3
Poynton SK12 ... 36 C1
Spring St Congleton CW12 .. 156 C1
Stalybridge SK15 242 E2
Widnes WA8 .... 23 D3
Wilmslow SK9 ... 60 A4
Springbank SK10 87 F4
Springbank Cl WA7 49 D3
Springbank Cres WA7 149 E4
Springbourne WA6 74 B3
Springcroft L64 . 41 E1
Springe La CW5 . 203 D3
Springfield Ave
Goldborne WA3 .. 2 C4
Helsby WA6 ..... 73 D2
Lymm WA13 .... 19 D3
Malpas SY14 .... 213 E2
Warrington WA4 . 17 D2
Warrington, Paddington WA1 17 D2
Springfield Cl CH4 161 D4
Springfield Cres CW8 77 F2
Springfield Dr Chester CH2 118 C4
Wilmslow SK9 ... 59 E3
Wistaston CW2 .. 205 F4
Springfield Park WA11 1 B4
Springfield Prim Sch M33 242 B6
Springfield Rd
Altrincham WA14 238 D5
Gatley SK8 ...... 239 B5
Macclesfield SK11 111 F4
Malpas SY14 .... 213 D2
Mobberley WA16 57 F2
Sale M33 .... 242 B6
Widnes WA8 .... 22 A4
Springfield Sch CW1 190 C2
Springfield St WA1 16 A3
Springfields
Cuddington CW8 . 101 E2
Knutsford WA16 . 57 E2
Mickle Trafford CH2 119 F4
Prestbury SK10 .. 87 D4
Springfields Dr CW12 156 B2
Springhead Prim Sch ST7 210 B3
Springhill SK10 .. 88 A1
Springhill Ave L62 43 E3
Springholm Dr WA4 26 B2
Springmount WA3 3 F4
Springs La SK15 . 242 C4
Springs The WA8 238 B2
Springwell Cl CW2 206 B4
Springwood Ave WA16 57 E2
Springwood Cl CH1 117 E2
Springwood Cres SK6 241 E2
Springwood La SK6 241 E3
Sprink La CW12 . 157 E3

Sproston Way CW9 103 F2
Spruce Ave CW8 102 A2
Spruce Cl Goldborne WA3 3 F4
Warrington WA1 17 F4
Spruce Gr ST7 193 F4
Spruce Lodge SK8 239 D6
Spuley La Pott Shrigley SK10 63 E1
Rainow SK10 63 E1
Spunhill Ave L66 69 E1
Spurlong Rd WA5 6 C3
Spurston Cl WA16 29 E2
Square St SK11 112 C3
Square The
Altrincham WA15 32 B4
Audlem CW3 229 F2
Christleton CH3 142 C4
Hyde SK14 241 D6
Ince CH2 71 F3
Manchester SK4 240 C7
Neston L64 41 D1
Woore CW3 232 B1
Squires Ave WA8 23 D4
Squires Cl WA11 1 A3
Squirrel Cl CW8 103 E4
Squirrel Dr WA14 238 C8
Squirrel's Jump SK9 60 B1
Squirrels Chase SK10 86 C3
Stable La CH3 99 D2
Stablings The SK9 60 A3
Stadium Ind Est CH1 118 A2
Stadium Way CH1 118 A2
Stadmorslow La ST7 195 F2
Stafford Cl SK10 86 C1
Stafford Gdns L65 70 A3
Stafford Rd WA4 16 B1
Stafford St Audlem CW3 230 A2
Crewe CW1 190 B3
Stafford Wlk SK10 86 C1
Stag Ind Est WA14 238 B6
Stage La WA13 19 E2
Staines Cl WA4 26 C3
Stainmore Cl WA3 10 A3
Staithes Rd M22 33 E4
Stalbridge Rd CW2 190 B1
Staley Cl SK15 242 F2
Stallard Way CW10 151 E4
Stalmine Ave SK8 34 A4
Staly Hall Rd SK15 242 F2
Stalybridge Ridge Hill Cty Inf Sch SK15 242 C3
Stalybridge Ridge Hill Jun Sch SK15 242 C3
Stalybridge Sta SK15 242 C2
Stamford Ave
Altrincham WA14 238 A5
Ashton-u-L SK15 242 B2
Crewe CW2 190 B2
Stamford Cl
Ashton- u-Lyne SK15 242 B2
Macclesfield SK11 112 B2
Stamford Ct Chester CH3 119 E1
Lymm WA13 18 C2
Macclesfield SK11 112 B3
Stamford Dr SK15 242 C2
Stamford Gr SK15 242 C2
Stamford Grange 1 WA14 238 C4
Stamford High Sch OL6 242 B4
Stamford La CH3 120 B1
Stamford New Rd WA14 238 D4
Stamford Park Inf Sch WA15 238 E3
Stamford Park Jun Sch WA15 238 E3
Stamford Park Rd WA15 238 E3
Stamford Pl M33 242 C6
Stamford Rd
Alderley Edge SK9 60 A1
Altrincham WA14 238 C2
Blacon CH1 117 F3
Little Bollington WA14 20 A1
Macclesfield SK11 112 B2
Wilmslow SK9 34 A1
Stamford Sq
3 Altrincham WA14 238 D5
Ashton-u-L OL6 242 A2
Stamford St
Altrincham WA14 238 D5
Ellesmere Port L65 70 A3
Sale M33 242 A8
Stalybridge OL6 & SK15 242 C2
Stamford St E OL6 242 A2
Stamford Way 2 WA14 238 D5
Stamore Rd WA7 23 E1
Stamp Ave CW1 190 B3
Stanbank St SK4 240 E8
Stanbridge Ct SK4 240 E6
Standford Dr CW9 104 A3
Stanhope Ave CW1 190 C2
Stanhope Cl SK9 60 B4
Stanhope Rd WA14 238 A2
Stanhope St OL6 242 A4
Stanier Cl CW1 191 D2
Stanlaw Rd L65 70 B2
Stanley Ave
Great Sankey WA5 14 B4
Hyde SK14 241 E8
Warrington WA4 16 C1
Stanley Bank Rd WA11 1 A4
Stanley Cl Hartford CW8 103 D2
Widnes WA8 13 E1
Stanley Ct ST7 193 E2
Stanley Dr ST5 210 B1
Stanley Gr Manchester SK4 240 B8
Northwich CW9 79 F1
Stanley Green Ind Est SK8 34 C3
Stanley Green Ret Pk SK8 34 C3
Stanley Hall La SK12 38 B3
Stanley La L62 43 F2
Stanley Mount M33 242 A5
Stanley Park Ct CH4 140 C3
Stanley Park Dr CH4 140 C3
Stanley Pl Chester CH1 237 D2
Warrington WA4 16 C1
Stanley Rd Biddulph ST6 179 E1
Cheadle SK8 34 C3
Cheadle Hulme SK8 34 C3
Ellesmere Port L65 70 B4
Knutsford WA16 56 C1
Manchester SK4 240 B7
Stanley Rd Ind Est WA16 57 D1
Stanley St Chester CH1 237 D2
Crewe CW1 190 B2
Newton-le-W WA12 2 A2
Northwich CW9 104 B4
Runcorn WA7 23 D2
Stalybridge SK15 242 C1
Warrington WA1 16 A2
Stanley Woods Ave CH2 95 E4
Stanlow Abbey Cty Prim Sch L65 70 C1
Stanlow & Thornton Sta L65 71 E3
Stannage La CH3 180 C3
Stanner Cl WA5 7 E1
Stannerhouse La CW11 175 F2
Stanney Cl Bebington L62 43 F2
Neston L64 66 C4
Stanney Cty High Sch L65 70 B1
Stanney Grange Cty Prim Sch L65 70 B2
Stanney Grange Sports Complex The L65 70 C2
Stanney La Ellesmere Port L65 70 B2
Stoak L65 70 C1
Stanney Mill La
Ellesmere Port L65 70 C1
Stanlow L65 70 C1
Stanney Mill Rd L65 70 C1
Stanney Ten Ind Est L65 70 C1
Stanney Woods Ave L65 70 B1
Stanney Woods Ctry Pk L66 70 A1
Stanneybrook Cl WA6 101 D3
Stanneylands Cl SK9 34 B1
Stanneylands Dr SK9 34 A1
Stanneylands Rd SK9 34 A2
Stansfield Ave WA1 16 C3
Stansfield Rd SK14 241 E8
Stanstead Ave WA5 14 C2
Stanthorne Ave CW2 190 A2
Stanton Cl WA11 1 B3
Stanton Ct L64 66 C4
Stanton Dr CH2 118 B3
Stanton Gdns SK4 240 B5
Stanton Rd WA4 17 E2
Stanway Dr WA15 238 F3
Stapeley Broad Lane CE Contr Prim Sch CW5 205 D1
Stapeley Terr CW5 205 D2
Stapeley Water Gdns CW5 205 D2
Stapleford Cl M33 242 E7
Stapleford Ct L66 69 F4
Stapleton Ave WA2 16 B4
Stapleton Rd SK10 87 D1
Stapleton Way WA8 22 A3
Stapley Cl WA7 22 C1
Star La Lymm WA13 18 B2
Macclesfield SK11 112 B2
Starbeck Dr L66 69 D3
Starkey Gr WA4 16 C2
Starling Cl Farndon CH3 180 C1
Runcorn WA7 50 B4
Start La SK23 65 D4
Statham Ave Lymm WA13 18 B2
Warrington WA2 8 B1
Statham Cl Denton M34 241 A7
Lymm WA13 18 B2
Statham Dr WA13 18 B2
Statham La WA13 18 A3
Statham St SK11 112 B4
Station Ave
Ellesmere Port L66 69 E4
Helsby WA6 73 D2
Station Cl Hyde SK14 241 D6
Neston L64 66 C4
Station Gn L66 69 E4
Station Hill CW8 76 C1
Station La CH3 119 F4
Station Rd Acton Bridge CW8 77 D1
Adderley TF9 235 D3
Alpraham CW6 169 F1
Alsager ST7 193 E2
Astbury ST7 178 A1
Backford CH1 95 D2
Biddulph ST6 179 E1
Chelford SK11 84 A1
Chester CH2 237 F4
Crowton CW8 76 B1
Delamere CW8 123 E4
Dunham Town WA14 20 A3
Eaton SK11 135 D1
Ellesmere Port L65 70 B3
Ellesmere Port, Little Sutton L66 69 E4
Elton CH2 72 A3
Goostrey CW4 131 D4
Great Sankey WA5 14 B4
Hawarden CH5 116 A1
Haydock WA11 1 B3
Heswall L60 40 C3
Holmes Chapel CW4 130 B1
Irlam M44 11 F4
Kidsgrove ST7 194 C1
Station Rd continued
Kidsgrove, Newchapel ST7 195 F1
Lostock CW9 80 A1
Mobberley WA16 57 F4
Mouldsworth CH3 99 D2
Mow Cop ST7 195 E4
Nantwich CW5 204 C3
Neston L64 66 B4
Neston L64 66 C4
Neston, Burton L64 67 D1
New Mills SK22 39 D4
Northwich CW9 79 D1
Runcorn WA7 22 C1
Sandbach CW11 174 B4
Scholar Green ST7 195 D4
Stockport SK3 240 E4
Styal SK9 34 A2
Sutton WA7 50 A2
Warrington WA4 16 C1
Warrington, Fearnhead WA2 9 D1
Weaverham CW8 77 D1
Whaley Bridge SK23 39 E2
Wilmslow SK9 60 A4
Wilmslow, Handforth SK9 34 B2
Winsford CW7 127 D1
Worleston CW5 188 C3
Station Rd N WA2 9 D1
Station Rd S WA2 9 D1
Station St SK10 87 E1
Station View Chester CH2 118 C1
Nantwich CW5 204 C2
Staveley Ave SK15 242 D3
Staveley Dr CW7 126 B1
Stayley Dr SK15 242 F2
Steam Mill St CH2 237 F3
Stearns Cl CH1 118 A3
Steel St WA1 16 C4
Steele Rd CW10 151 E3
Steele St CH1 237 E2
Steeles Ave SK14 241 E7
Steeple Ct L64 66 C4
Steeple St SK10 87 F1
Stein Ave WA3 3 F4
Stenhills Cres WA7 23 E1
Step Hill 10 SK11 112 B4
Stephen St WA1 16 B3
Stephen's Gr WA6 73 D1
Stephens Gdns L66 69 D3
Stephens Rd SK15 242 C4
Stephens Terr L66 69 D3
Stephens Way ST7 209 F1
Stephenson Dr CW1 191 D2
Stephenson Wlk CW7 149 D4
Sterndale Rd Romiley SK6 241 B1
Stockport SK3 240 E1
Sterne Cl 3 CW11 174 B3
Stetchworth Rd WA4 16 A1
Steven Ct CH2 237 F3
Stevenage Cl SK11 112 A4
Stevenage Dr SK11 112 A4
Stevens Rd L60 41 E4
Stevens St SK9 60 A1
Steventon WA7 24 C2
Steward's Ave WA8 22 C4
Stewart St CW2 190 A2
Stile End CH2 119 F4
Stiles The CW8 101 E3
Stiperstones Cl L66 68 C3
Stirling Cl Chester CH3 119 D1
Macclesfield SK10 86 C1
Stockport SK3 240 C2
Warrington WA1 17 F4
Stirling Ct Ellesmere Port L65 70 B2
Holmes Chapel CW4 130 A1
Stirling Dr SK15 242 D3
Stirrup Cl WA2 9 D2
Stitch La SK4 240 D7
Stock La
Hough Common CW5 206 A1
Shavington CW5 206 A1
Stockdale Ave SK3 240 F1
Stockham Cl WA7 50 A4
Stockham La WA7 50 A4
Stockholm Rd SK3 240 E2
Stockley Farm CW9 54 C4
Stockley La WA4 52 C4
Stockport Coll of F & H Ed
Stockport SK2 240 F2
Stockport SK1 240 F4
Stockport Infmy SK3 240 E4
Stockport Rd
Altrincham WA15 238 F5
Cheadle SK8 239 E6
Cheadle, Cheadle Heath SK3 240 A3
Romiley SK6 241 B2
Warrington WA4 17 F2
Stockport Rd E SK6 241 A4
Stockport Sta SK3 240 E4
Stockport Trad Est SK4 240 B5
Stocks Ave CH3 119 D1
Stocks Gdns SK15 242 F1
Stocks Hill CW7 149 F4
Stocks La Chester CH3 119 D1
Penketh WA5 14 B3
Peover WA16 82 C1
Stalybridge SK15 242 F1
Stockswell Rd L35 12 A2
Stockton Ave 4 SK3 240 B4
Stockton Heath Cty Prim Sch WA4 16 B1
Stockton La WA4 16 C1
Stockton Rd SK9 59 F2
Stoke Abbott Cl SK7 35 F4
Stoke Cl L62 43 F2
Stoke Gdns L65 70 B2
Stokehall La
Barbridge CW5 187 F3
Cholmondeston CW5 187 F3
Stokesay Ct L65 70 C2
Stokoe Ave WA14 238 A6
Stone Barn La WA7 50 A3
Stone Chair La ST7 194 C4
Stone Croft CH3 142 A4
Stone Cross La WA3 3 E4
Stone Heyes La CW8 77 F3
Stone House La CW6 184 C3
Stone Mead SK6 241 E3
Stone Mead Ave WA15 32 B4
Stone Pit La WA3 3 F1
Stone Pl CH2 118 C2
Stoneacre Gdns WA4 26 C2
Stonebank Dr L64 67 D3
Stonebridge Rd CW5 204 C2
Stonechat Cl Crewe CW1 189 F4
Runcorn WA7 49 F3
Stonecliffe Ave SK15 242 D2
Stonecliffe Terr SK15 242 D3
Stonecrop Cl Runcorn WA7 49 F2
Warrington WA3 9 E2
Stonehaven Dr WA2 9 D2
Stoneheads Rise SK23 65 E4
Stonehill Cl WA4 26 B2
Stonehills La WA7 23 E1
Stonehouse Gn CW12 156 B2
Stonelea WA7 24 A1
Stoneleigh Cl SK10 87 E1
Stoneleigh Gdns WA4 17 E1
Stoneley Ave CW1 190 B4
Stoneley Rd CW1 190 B4
Stonemill Terr SK5 240 F7
Stonepail Rd M22 & SK8 239 A5
Stones Manor La CW8 103 E3
Stoney Holt WA7 50 B4
Stoney La Delamere CW6 123 E3
Wilmslow SK9 59 F3
Stoneyfield SK15 242 D4
Stoneyfold La SK11 113 D3
Stoneyhurst Cres WA3 4 B3
Stoneyland Dr SK22 39 D4
Stony La CW12 156 B1
Stonyford Rd M33 242 D6
Stopford St SK3 240 D4
Stopsley Cl CW12 155 F2
Stour Cl WA14 238 C6
Stour Ct L65 70 A4
Straight Length WA6 73 F4
Straight Mile
Eccleston CH4 162 C3
Poulton CH4 163 D2
Straker Ave L65 69 F3
Stratford Rd Blacon CH1 117 F2
Neston L64 66 B3
Stratford Sq SK8 34 B4
Stratford Way SK11 112 B3
Strathaven Ave CW2 205 F4
Strathclyde Cl CW4 130 A1
Strathearn Rd L60 40 C4
Strathmore Ave M34 241 B6
Stratton Cl WA7 50 A3
Stratton Pk WA8 12 C3
Stratton Rd WA5 15 D3
Strawberry Cl
Altrincham WA14 238 B7
Warrington WA3 9 E2
Strawberry Dr CH1 95 D4
Strawberry Fields CH3 142 A4
Strawberry Gn CH1 95 D4
Strawberry La
Acton Bridge CW8 76 C2
Mollington CH1 94 B2
Wilmslow SK9 59 F3
Street Hey La L64 43 D1
Street La Adlington SK10 62 B4
Rode Heath ST7 176 C1
Whitley WA4 52 B2
Street The Buxton SK17 90 B3
Chester CH2 119 E4
Mickle Trafford CH2 119 E4
Stretton Ave WA3 3 E4
Stretton Cl L62 43 F2
Stretton Mill SY14 198 A3
Stretton Rd WA4 26 C1
Stretton Way 5 SK9 34 B3
Stretton Wlk CW9 103 F2
Strines Ct SK14 241 E8
Stringer Ave CW11 175 E3
Stringer Cres WA4 16 C2
Stringer's La LL12, CH4 161 D2
Strumness Cl WA2 9 D2
Stuart Cl Chester CH3 119 E2
Winsford CW7 149 E3
Stuart Ct SK10 87 D1
Stuart Dr WA4 16 C1
Stuart Pl CH2 237 E3
Stuart Rd WA7 24 B2
Stubbs La Lostock CW9 80 A1
Mobberley WA16 58 C2
Stubbs Pl CH1 117 F2
Stubbs Terr SK11 112 C4
Stubby La SK10 84 C1
Styal Cl CW9 103 F2
Styal Ctry Pk SK9 33 F2
Styal Cty Prim Sch SK9 33 F2
Styal Gr SK8 239 A3
Styal Rd
Gatley M22 & SK8 & M90 & SK9 239 A3
Wilmslow SK9 34 A1
Wythenshawe M22 33 F4
Styal Sta SK9 34 A2
Styal View SK9 34 A1
Sudbrook Cl WA3 3 F4
Sudbury Dr SK8 34 B4
Sudbury Rd SK7 36 C4
Sudlow La Knutsford WA16 56 B1
Plumley WA16 81 E4
Suez St Newton-le-W WA12 2 A2
Warrington WA1 16 A3
Suffolk Ave L65 69 F3
Suffolk Cl Congleton CW12 156 B2
Macclesfield SK10 86 C1
Warrington WA1 17 F3
Suffolk Dr SK9 34 B1
Suffolk Pl WA8 22 B4
Suffolk Rd WA14 238 B5
Suffolk St WA7 22 C2
Sugar La Adlington SK10 63 D1
Manley WA6 98 C3
Rainow SK10 88 B3
Sugar Pit La WA16 56 C2
Sugden St OL6 242 A3
Sulby Ave WA4 16 A2
Sulgrave Ave SK12 36 C2
Summer Cl WA7 23 F1
Summer La Daresbury WA4 51 E4
Runcorn WA7 23 F1
Summerfield ST7 195 D1
Summerfield Ave WA5 7 F1
Summerfield Dr CW9 126 C4
Summerfield Pl SK9 60 A3
Summerfield Rd
Guilden Sutton CH3 119 F3
Mobberley WA16 57 F2
Summerfields WA16 57 E2
Summerhill Dr ST5 210 B1
Summerhill Rd SK10 86 C2
Summerlea SK8 35 D4
Summers Ave SK15 242 F2
Summers Cl WA16 82 A4
Summers Way WA16 82 A4
Summertrees Rd L66 69 F2
Summerville Gdns WA4 16 C1
Summit Cl WA4 26 C1
Sumner Rd CH1 117 F2
Sumner St WA11 1 A3
Sumpter Pathway CH2 118 C2
Sunart Cl CW2 206 A3
Sunbank La WA15 32 C3
Sunbeam St WA12 2 B2
Sunbury Cl SK9 34 C1
Sunbury Cres CH4 140 C3
Sunbury Gdns WA4 26 C4
Suncroft Cl WA1 17 F4
Suncroft Rd L60 41 E4
Sundale Dr CW2 189 E2
Sunderland St SK11 112 B4
Sundown Cl SK22 39 D4
Sunfield SK6 241 C3
Sunfield Cl L66 69 E2
Sunningdale Ave Sale M33 242 E5
Widnes WA8 12 A1
Sunningdale Cl
Burtonwood WA5 6 C4
Northwich CW9 104 C4
Sunningdale Dr
Bebington L63 43 D3
Bramhall SK7 36 A4
Sunningdale Rd
Cheadle Hulme SK8 35 D4
Denton M34 241 B5
Macclesfield SK11 112 A3
Sunningdale Way L64 66 C2
Sunninghey Ct SK9 59 F2
Sunny Bank Wilmslow SK9 60 A3
Wilmslow, Lindow SK9 59 E2
Sunny Bank Cl SK11 112 B3
Sunny Bank Rd WA14 31 E4
Sunnybank Cl WA12 2 B2
Sunnybank Rd CW2 189 F3
Sunnyside Alsager ST7 193 D2
Great Sankey WA5 14 B4
Sunnyside Cres OL6 242 A2
Sunnyside Gr OL6 242 A2
Sunnyside La WA7 24 C2
Surrey Dr CW12 156 C3
Surrey Rd Chester CH2 119 D3
Kidsgrove ST7 195 D1
Warren SK11 112 A2
Surrey St Crewe CW1 190 C2
Runcorn WA7 23 D1
Warrington WA4 16 B2
Surridge WA16 29 E3
Susan Dr WA5 14 B3
Susan St WA8 13 E1
Sussex Ave SK11 112 A3
Sussex Dr ST7 194 C1
Sussex Pl CW12 156 C3
Sussex Rd Chester CH2 118 C2
Irlam M44 11 E3
Partington M31 11 F1
Stockport SK3 240 B4
Sussex St WA8 13 E1
Sussex Way CH2 118 C2
Sutherland Ct WA7 23 D1
Sutherland Dr Bebington L62 43 E2
Macclesfield SK10 87 D1
Sutherland St OL6 242 B3
Sutherland Way CH3 119 D2
Sutton Ave Culcheth WA3 4 C2
Neston L64 66 C3
Sutton Causeway WA6 49 F1
Sutton Cl Bebington L62 43 F2
Higher Wincham CW9 79 F3
Macclesfield SK11 112 B3
Mickle Trafford CH2 119 F4
Sutton Cty High Sch L66 69 F3
Sutton Dr CH2 118 C3
Sutton Green Cty Prim Sch L66 69 E3
Sutton Hall Dr L66 69 D3
Sutton Hall Gdns L66 69 D3

Sutton La CW10 .... **151** E4
Sutton Rd Alderley Edge SK9 . **59** F1
  Manchester SK4 .... **240** C7
  Poynton SK12 .... **37** D1
Sutton St Runcorn WA7 .... **23** D1
  Warrington WA1 .... **16** B2
Sutton Way
  Ellesmere Port L66 .... **69** F2
  1 Wilmslow SK8 .... **34** C3
Sutton Way Cty Jun Sch
  L66 .... **69** F2
Sutton's La WA8 .... **23** D4
Swaine St SK3 .... **240** E5
Swale Dr WA14 .... **238** C6
Swale Rd L65 .... **70** A4
Swaledale Ave CW12 .... **157** D3
Swaledale Cl Bebington L62 .. **43** F3
  Great Sankey WA5 .... **14** B4
Swallow Cl Kidsgrove ST7 ... **195** D1
  Macclesfield SK10 .... **113** D4
  Warrington WA3 .... **9** F2
Swallow Ct CW7 .... **149** E3
Swallow Dr CW11 .... **175** D4
Swallow St SK1 .... **240** F3
Swallowfield Cl CW2 .... **206** A4
Swallowfield Gdns WA4 ...... **26** C3
Swan Ave WA9 .... **1** A1
Swan Bank Congleton CW12 **156** B1
  Kidsgrove ST7 .... **210** B4
Swan Cl Ellesmere Port L66 ... **69** F2
  Kidsgrove ST7 .... **210** B4
  Poynton SK12 .... **36** A2
Swan Ct CW8 .... **101** F4
Swan Farm La CW3 .... **232** A1
Swan Gr WA16 .... **106** B4
Swan La Bunbury CW6 .... **185** F4
  Cheadle Hulme SK8 .... **35** D4
Swan Rd WA12 .... **1** C2
Swan St Congleton CW12 ...... **156** B1
  Wilmslow SK9 .... **60** A4
Swanage Cl WA4 .... **16** C1
Swanage Ct CW7 .... **149** E3
Swanbourne Gdns SK3 .... **240** C2
Swanley La CW5 .... **203** E2
Swanlow Ave CW7 .... **149** E3
Swanlow Dr CW7 .... **149** E3
Swanlow La CW7 .... **149** F3
Swansea Av SK10 .... **88** A4
Swanscoe Cl CW12 .... **151** D4
Swanscoe La SK10 .... **88** A2
Swanwick Cl CW4 .... **107** E1
Sweet Briar Cres CW2 .... **189** F2
Sweet Brier Cl CW8 .... **78** A2
Sweetenham Cl ST7 .... **193** E2
Sweetfield Gdns L66 .... **69** E4
Sweetfield Rd L66 .... **69** E4
Sweettooth La CW11 .... **175** D4
Swettenham Cl CW11 .... **175** E4
Swettenham Rd
  Swettenham CW12 .... **132** A1
  Wilmslow SK9 .... **34** B3
Swettenham St SK11 .... **112** C4
  Warrington WA4 .... **8** C2
  Wistaston CW2 .... **205** F4
Swift Cl Kidsgrove ST7 .... **195** D1
  Wistaston CW2 .... **205** F4
Swinburne Dr CW1 .... **190** C2
Swindale Ave WA2 .... **8** A2
Swinden Cl WA7 .... **24** B1
Swine Market CW5 .... **204** C3
Swineyard La WA16 .... **28** B2
Swinford Ave WA8 .... **13** F1
Swinley Chase SK9 .... **34** C1
Swinleys Hey CH3 .... **142** A4
Swinnerton St CW2 .... **190** B1
Swinton Sq WA16 .... **57** D1
Swireford Rd WA6 .... **73** D1
Swiss Cott SK10 .... **87** D1
Swiss Hill SK9 .... **60** A1
Swithin Rd M22 .... **33** F4
Swynnerton Way WA8 .... **13** D3
Swythamley Cl SK3 .... **240** A4
Swythamley Rd SK3 .... **240** A4
Sycamore Ave Alsager ST7 . **193** E2
  Altrincham WA14 .... **238** A5
  Congleton CW12 .... **155** F2
  Crewe CW1 .... **190** B3
  Haydock WA11 .... **1** A3
  Newton-le-W WA12 .... **2** B2
  Rode Heath ST7 .... **193** F4
  Widnes WA8 .... **13** D1
  Winsford CW7 .... **149** E4
Sycamore Cl
  Ashton-u-L OL6 .... **242** B2
  Audlem CW3 .... **230** A2
  Biddulph ST6 .... **179** F1
  Holmes Chapel CW4 .... **130** B2
  Kidsgrove ST7 .... **210** C4
  Wilmslow SK9 .... **34** A1
Sycamore Cres
  Barnton CW8 .... **78** A2
  Hollins Green WA3 .... **11** D1
  Macclesfield SK11 .... **112** A4
Sycamore Ct CW5 .... **204** C4
Sycamore Dr Chester CH4 ... **140** C3
  Ellesmere Port L66 .... **70** A4
  Lymm WA13 .... **18** B2
  Middlewich CW10 .... **151** F3
  Sutton WA7 .... **50** A2
Sycamore Farm Cl SK10 ...... **87** D1
Sycamore Gr
  Broughton CH4 .... **139** D2
  Sandbach CW11 .... **175** D4
Sycamore La WA5 .... **15** D3
Sycamore Lane Cty Prim
  Sch WA5 .... **15** D3

Sycamore Rd Partington M31 **11** F2
  Romiley SK6 .... **241** A4
  Runcorn WA7 .... **49** E4
Sycamore Rise SK11 .... **112** A3
Sycamore St Sale M33 .... **242** E6
  Stockport SK3 .... **240** B4
Sycamore Wlk SK8 .... **239** D6
Syddal Cr SK7 .... **35** E2
Syddal Gn SK7 .... **35** E3
Syddall Ave SK8 .... **34** B4
Syddall St SK14 .... **241** D6
Sydney Ave M90 .... **33** D4
Sydney Rd Blacon CH1 .... **118** A2
  Bramhall SK7 .... **35** F3
  Crewe CW1 .... **190** C3
Sydney St Northwich CW8 ... **103** E4
  Runcorn WA7 .... **48** B4
Sykes Meadow SK3 .... **240** D2
Sykes St SK14 .... **241** F5
Sylvan Ave Altrincham WA15 **238** F8
  Sale M33 .... **242** C5
  Wilmslow SK9 .... **59** F3
Sylvan Cl CW8 .... **103** E4
Sylvan Gr WA14 .... **238** D5
Symondley Rd SK11 .... **112** C1
Symons Rd M33 .... **242** B7
Synge St WA2 .... **16** B4
Sytch Croft L64 .... **66** C4

Tabley Ave WA8 .... **12** B1
Tabley Cl Knutsford WA16 ..... **56** C2
  Sandbach CW11 .... **174** C4
Tabley Gr WA16 .... **56** C1
Tabley Hill La
  Knutsford WA16 .... **56** A1
  Tabley WA16 .... **56** A1
Tabley Mere Gdns SK8 .... **239** F3
Tabley Rd Crewe CW2 .... **189** F2
  Knutsford WA16 .... **56** C2
  Wilmslow SK9 .... **34** B3
Tabley St CW9 .... **79** D1
Tabor St SK4 .... **112** C3
Tadgers La WA6 .... **73** E4
Tadman Gr WA14 .... **238** A6
Talbot Ave L64 .... **66** C3
Talbot Cl Neston L64 .... **66** C3
  Shavington CW2 .... **206** A4
  Warrington WA3 .... **9** F2
Talbot Gdns L64 .... **66** C3
Talbot Rd
  Alderley Edge SK9 .... **60** A1
  Altrincham WA14 .... **238** B2
  Dunham-on-t-H WA6 .... **97** F4
  Ellesmere Port L66 .... **69** F2
  Sale M33 .... **242** E6
Talbot St Chester CH2 .... **237** E4
  Goldborne WA3 .... **3** D4
  Stockport SK1 & SK3 .... **240** E5
Talfryn Cl CH5 .... **91** E1
Talisman Cl WA7 .... **50** B4
Talke Rd Alsager ST7 .... **193** F2
  Audley ST5 .... **210** C1
Tall Ash Ave CW12 .... **157** D2
Tall Trees Cl CW8 .... **103** E3
Talwrn Green Prim Sch
  SY14 .... **222** D1
Tamar Cl Congleton CW12 ... **156** C1
  Macclesfield SK10 .... **86** C1
Tamar Rd Haydock WA11 .... **1** B3
  Kidsgrove ST7 .... **195** D1
Tamar Wlk CW7 .... **127** D1
Tame Cl Biddulph ST6 .... **179** E1
  Sandbach CW11 .... **174** C4
  Stalybridge SK15 .... **242** F3
Tame St SK15 .... **242** B1
Tame Wlk **13** SK9 .... **34** B1
Tameside Coll of Tech
  Ashton-u-L OL6 .... **242** A3
  Hyde SK14 .... **241** E6
Tameside General Hospl
  OL6 .... **242** B4
Tameside L Pk SK14 .... **241** F6
Tamworth Cl SK7 .... **36** B4
Tamworth St WA12 .... **2** A2
Tan House La
  Burtonwood WA5 .... **7** D3
  Widnes WA8 .... **23** E4
Tanfield Rd M20 .... **239** B8
Tanhouse Ind Est WA8 .... **23** E4
Tankersley Gr WA5 .... **15** D3
Tanner St
  Congleton CW12 .... **156** C1
  Hyde SK14 .... **241** D7
Tanner's La WA3 .... **3** D4
Tanners La WA2 .... **16** A3
Tannery La Neston L64 .... **66** C4
  Penketh WA5 .... **14** B2
Tannery Way WA14 .... **238** E7
Tanyard Dr WA15 .... **32** B4
Tanyard La WA15 .... **32** A3
Tapley Ave SK12 .... **36** C1
Taplow Cl WA4 .... **26** C3
Taplow Gr SK8 .... **239** F2
Target Cl ST7 .... **210** C3
Target Rd L60 .... **40** B4
Tarn Cl CW7 .... **126** B1
Tarn Ct WA1 .... **17** F4
Tarn Mount SK11 .... **112** A3
Tarnbeck WA7 .... **50** B4
Tarns The SK8 .... **239** B3
Tarnway WA3 .... **3** F4
Tarparley Wlk **11** SK9 .... **34** C1
Tarporley CE Contr Prim
  Sch CW6 .... **146** B1
Tarporley Cl SK3 .... **240** D1
Tarporley Cty High Sch
  CW6 .... **146** B1

Tarporley Rd
  Common Side CW6, CW8 ..... **124** B3
  Duddon SK4 .... **145** D3
  Ellesmere Port L66 .... **69** F2
  Little Leigh WA4 .... **52** A1
  Stretton WA4 .... **52** B4
  Tarvin CW6 .... **121** C1
  Utkinton CW6 .... **146** C3
  Whitchurch SY13 .... **225** F2
  Whitley WA4 .... **52** B2
Tarran Gr M34 .... **241** B5
Tarran Pl WA14 .... **238** E6
Tarrant Ct CH1 .... **94** C1
Tarvin Ave CW2 .... **189** E2
Tarvin Cl Ellesmere Port L65 .. **70** B2
  Goldborne WA3 .... **3** F4
  Macclesfield SK11 .... **112** C3
  Middlewich CW10 .... **151** E3
  Runcorn WA7 .... **49** E3
Tarvin Cty Prim Sch CH3 ... **121** D1
Tarvin Rd Alvanley WA6 .... **73** F2
  Bebington L62 .... **43** F2
  Chester, Boughton CH3 .... **119** D1
  Chester, Vicarscross CH3 ..... **119** F1
  Christleton CH3 .... **120** B2
  Frodsham WA6 .... **73** F2
  Manley WA6 .... **99** D2
  Tarvin CH3 .... **120** C2
Tarvin Sands Industries
  CH3 .... **121** D2
Tarvin Way SK9 .... **34** B3
Tasman Cl WA5 .... **15** E4
Tate Cl WA8 .... **12** B1
Tate Dr CW1 .... **191** E2
Tattenhall La Beeston CH3 .. **167** E1
  Beeston CH3 .... **167** F1
  Tattenhall CH3 .... **167** D1
Tattenhall Rd CH3 .... **166** B2
Tatton Cl Alsager ST7 .... **193** E2
  Chester CH4 .... **140** C3
  Davenham CW9 .... **103** F2
  Winsford CW7 .... **126** B1
Tatton Ct SK4 .... **240** C8
Tatton Dr CW11 .... **175** E4
Tatton Hall WA16 .... **56** C4
Tatton Lodge WA16 .... **57** E1
Tatton Park WA16 .... **57** D4
Tatton Pl M33 .... **242** B7
Tatton Rd Crewe CW2 .... **189** F1
  Denton M34 .... **241** A5
  Sale M33 .... **242** B7
  Wythenshawe SK8 .... **34** C3
Tatton Rd S SK4 .... **240** C8
Tatton St Knutsford WA16 ..... **57** D1
  Stalybridge SK15 .... **242** E1
  7 Stockport SK3 .... **240** F5
Tatton Stile WA16 .... **58** A2
Tavener Cl L63 .... **43** E3
Tavistock Rd WA5 .... **14** C2
Tavlin Ave WA5 .... **7** F1
Tawney Cl ST7 .... **195** D1
Taxal & Fernilee CE Contr
  Prim Sch SK23 .... **65** E3
Taxal Lodge Sch SK23 .... **65** E3
Taxal Moor Rd SK23 .... **65** E2
Taxi Rd M90 .... **33** D4
Taxmere Cl CW11 .... **174** C4
Tay Cl ST6 .... **179** F1
Taylor Ind Est WA3 .... **4** C1
Taylor Rd Altrincham WA14 . **238** A5
  Haydock WA11 .... **1** C4
Taylor St Hyde SK14 .... **241** F7
  Stalybridge SK15 .... **242** E1
  Warrington WA4 .... **16** A1
  Widnes WA8 .... **13** E1
Taylor's La WA5 .... **14** A1
Taylors La CW1 .... **192** B1
Taylors Row WA7 .... **23** E1
Teal Ave WA16 .... **57** D1
Teal Cl Altrincham WA14 ...... **238** B8
  Warrington WA2 .... **8** C2
  Warrington, Oakwood WA3 ...... **9** F2
  Winsford CW7 .... **149** E3
Teals Way L60 .... **40** C4
Tebay Rd L62 .... **43** F4
Tedder Dr M22 .... **33** F4
Tedder Sq WA8 .... **22** B4
Teddington Cl WA4 .... **26** C3
Tees Ct L65 .... **70** A4
Teesdale Cl WA5 .... **14** C4
Teesdale Rd WA11 .... **1** B4
Tefler Ct CW10 .... **151** F3
Tegg's Nose Ctry Pk SK11 . **113** C3
Teggsnose La SK11 .... **113** B3
Tegid Way CH4 .... **140** B3
Tegsnose Mt SK11 .... **113** E2
Telegraph Rd L60 .... **41** D4
Telford Cl Congleton CW12 .. **157** D1
  Kidsgrove ST7 .... **210** C4
  Macclesfield SK10 .... **88** A1
  Widnes WA8 .... **12** B2
Telford Gdns **3** CW11 .... **174** C2
Telford Pl CW5 .... **204** B3
Telford Rd L65 .... **70** C2
Telford Way Audlem CW3 ..... **229** F2
  Chester CH4 .... **140** C3
  Middlewich CW10 .... **128** C1
Telford's Quay L65 .... **70** B4
Tempest Rd SK9 .... **60** B1
Temple Moor Inf Sch
  M33 .... **242** E6
Temple Rd M33 .... **242** D6
Templeton Cl WA14 .... **238** B6
Tenby Cl WA5 .... **7** F1
Tenby Dr WA7 .... **23** E1
Tenby Rd Macclesfield SK11 . **111** F3
  Stockport SK3 .... **240** B3
Tennyson Ave CW1 .... **190** C2

Tennyson Cl
  Macclesfield SK11 .... **111** F3
  Rode Heath ST7 .... **193** F4
  Stockport SK4 .... **240** B6
  Warrington WA2 .... **190** A1
Tennyson Dr WA2 .... **8** B1
Tennyson Rd Cheadle SK8 ... **239** F6
  Ellesmere Port L65 .... **70** A2
  Widnes WA8 .... **13** D1
Tennyson Wlk CH1 .... **118** A3
Tern Ave SK11 .... **15** D4
Tern Cl Altrincham WA14 ..... **238** B8
  Widnes WA8 .... **13** D2
Tern Dr SK12 .... **36** A2
Terence Ave WA1 .... **16** C3
Terminal Rd E M90 .... **33** D4
Terminal Rd N M90 .... **33** C4
Terminal Rd S M90 .... **33** D4
Tern Ave ST7 .... **195** E1
Terra Nova Sch CW4 .... **108** B1
Terrace Rd WA8 .... **23** D3
Terrick Rd SY13 .... **226** A1
Tetchill Cl Ellesmere Port L66 **69** E1
  Runcorn WA7 .... **50** B4
Tetton La CW10 .... **151** F2
Tewkesbury Cl
  Cheadle Hulme SK8 .... **35** D3
  Chester CH2 .... **118** B4
  Ellesmere Port CH1 .... **94** C4
  Middlewich CW10 .... **128** A1
  Poynton SK12 .... **36** B2
Tewkesbury Dr SK10 .... **87** F2
Tewkesbury Rd
  Cheadle SK8 .... **240** B2
  Goldborne WA3 .... **3** D4
Thackeray Dr CH3 .... **119** E2
Thames Cl Congleton CW12 . **156** C1
  Warrington WA2 .... **8** B1
Thames Dr ST6 .... **179** E1
Thames Gdns L65 .... **70** A2
Thames Rd WA3 .... **4** C1
Thames Side L65 .... **70** A2
Thamesdale L65 .... **70** A2
Thaxted Wlk M22 .... **33** E4
Theatre Ct CW9 .... **103** F4
Thelwall Cl **3** WA15 .... **238** E6
Thelwall Cty Inf Sch WA4 ... **17** E2
Thelwall Cty Jun Sch WA4 .. **17** E2
Thelwall Ind Est WA4 .... **17** D2
Thelwall La WA4 .... **17** D2
Thelwall Massey Hall Sch
  WA4 .... **17** F1
Thelwall New Rd WA4 .... **17** E2
Thelwall Rd
  Ellesmere Port L66 .... **69** F2
  Sale M33 .... **242** E5
Theobald Rd WA14 .... **238** D1
Thetford Cl SK10 .... **87** E2
Thetford Rd WA5 .... **14** C3
Thewlis St WA5 .... **15** F3
Third Ave Adlington SK10 .... **36** B1
  Crewe CW1 .... **190** C1
  Deeside Ind Est CH5 .... **92** C1
  Kidsgrove ST7 .... **194** C1
  Runcorn WA7 .... **49** F4
  Sandbach CW11 .... **175** D3
Thirlmere Ave WA2 .... **8** B2
Thirlmere Cl
  Alderley Edge SK9 .... **59** F1
  Frodsham WA6 .... **49** E1
  Holmes Chapel CW4 .... **130** A2
Thirlmere Ct CW12 .... **156** A1
Thirlmere Dr SK11 .... **18** C2
Thirlmere Rd Chester CH2 ... **119** D3
  Ellesmere Port L65 .... **70** A1
  Neston L64 .... **66** C3
  Partington M31 .... **11** F2
  Wistaston CW2 .... **190** A1
Thirlmere Way **1** WA8 .... **22** B4
Thirsk Cl WA7 .... **49** E3
Thistle Sq M31 .... **11** F1
Thistle Wlk M31 .... **11** F1
Thistleton Cl SK11 .... **112** B3
Thistlewood Dr SK9 .... **60** B4
Thomas Cl Alsager ST7 .... **193** E2
  Blacon CH1 .... **117** F3
  Denton M34 .... **241** A8
  Ellesmere Port L65 .... **70** A1
  Mickle Trafford CH2 .... **119** F4
Thomas Pl CW7 .... **127** D1
Thomas St
  Altrincham WA15 .... **238** E4
  Biddulph ST6 .... **179** E1
  Congleton CW12 .... **156** C2
  Crewe CW1 .... **190** B2
  Goldborne WA3 .... **3** D4
  Kidsgrove ST7 .... **210** B4
  Packmoor ST7 .... **195** F1
  Romiley SK6 .... **241** A3
  Runcorn WA7 .... **23** D2
  Stockport SK1 .... **240** F3
  18 Widnes WA8 .... **23** D4
Thomas Trad Ctr M44 .... **11** F4
Thomas Wedge CE Contr
  Jun Sch The CH1 .... **94** A1
Thomasons Bridge La
  WA4 .... **25** F3
Thompson Ave WA3 .... **4** C2
Thompson Cl WA12 .... **2** B1
Thompson St WA3 .... **9** F2
Thomson St SK3 .... **240** D4
Thoresway Rd SK9 .... **59** F3
Thoriby Rd WA3 .... **4** C2
Thorley Gr CW2 .... **190** A1
Thorley La M90 .... **33** D4
Thorley Mews SK7 .... **35** F4

Thorn Cl Penketh WA5 .... **14** C2
  Runcorn WA7 .... **49** E4
Thorn Dr SK8 .... **34** A4
Thorn Gr Altrincham WA15 .. **238** E3
  Cheadle Hulme SK8 .... **35** D4
  Sale M33 .... **242** B6
Thorn La CW8 .... **103** E3
Thorn Rd Cheadle Hulme SK7 . **35** F4
  Runcorn WA7 .... **49** E4
  Warrington WA1 .... **17** D4
Thorn Tree Cl L24 .... **21** F1
Thorn Wlk M31 .... **11** E1
Thornberry Cl CH1 .... **117** D4
Thornbury Ave WA3 .... **3** F4
Thornbush Cl WA3 .... **3** F4
Thorne Cl SK10 .... **87** D3
Thorne Dr L66 .... **69** D2
Thorney Dr SK7 .... **35** E3
Thorneyholme Dr WA16 .... **57** D1
Thornfield Cl WA3 .... **3** E4
Thornfield Hey SK9 .... **60** C4
Thornfield Rd WA3 .... **240** A7
Thornfield Sch SK4 .... **240** A7
Thorngrove Dr SK9 .... **60** B3
Thorngrove Hill SK9 .... **60** B3
Thorngrove Rd SK9 .... **60** B3
Thornhills WA8 .... **12** A2
Thornleigh Ave L62 .... **43** F2
Thornleigh Dr L66 .... **69** F3
Thornley Cres SK6 .... **241** A4
Thornley Rd Dukinfield M34 **241** A8
  Lymm WA13 .... **18** B2
Thornley St SK14 .... **241** E5
Thornsgreen Rd M22 .... **33** E4
Thornton Ave WA8 .... **22** C4
Thornton Ave SK11 .... **112** A3
Thornton Bank CW6 .... **169** E2
Thornton Common Rd
  Bebington L63 .... **43** D4
  Thornton Hough L63 .... **42** B4
Thornton Cres L60 .... **41** D3
Thornton Dr Chester CH2 .... **118** B3
  Wilmslow SK9 .... **34** B2
  Wistaston CW2 .... **206** A4
Thornton Gate M22 & SK8 .. **239** A6
Thornton Green La CH2 .... **96** C4
Thornton Hough Cty Prim
  Sch L63 .... **42** A4
Thornton Mews L66 .... **69** D4
Thornton Pl **4** SK4 .... **240** B8
Thornton Rd Cheadle SK8 ...... **34** B4
  Ellesmere Port L65 .... **70** C2
  Great Sankey WA5 .... **15** D2
Thornton Sq SK11 .... **112** A3
Thorntondale Dr WA5 .... **14** C4
Thorntree Gn WA4 .... **27** D3
Thornway Bollington SK10 ..... **88** A4
  Cheadle Hulme SK7 .... **35** E4
  High Lane SK6 .... **37** F4
Thornwythe Gr L66 .... **69** F2
Thornycroft CW7 .... **126** A1
Thornycroft Cl SK11 .... **111** F1
Thornycroft St **16** SK11 .... **112** C4
Thorold Gr M33 .... **242** E6
Thorp St SK10 .... **112** B4
Thorpe Cl CW1 .... **189** F4
Thorsby Ave SK14 .... **241** F6
Thorsby Rd WA15 .... **238** E5
Thowler La WA4 .... **30** A3
Threaphurst La SK7 .... **37** E4
Three Fields Cl CW12 .... **156** A2
Threeways CW8 .... **101** E2
Thresher Cl M33 .... **242** F5
Throstle Bank St SK14 .... **241** C8
Thurlestone Rd WA14 .... **238** B6
Thurlow WA3 .... **3** F4
Thursfield Ave ST7 .... **195** D2
Thursfield Prim Sch ST7 ... **195** F2
Thurstaston Rd L60 .... **40** C4
Thurston Cl WA5 .... **15** E3
Thurston Gn SK9 .... **60** A1
Thurston Rd CH4 .... **140** C3
Thynne St WA1 .... **16** A2
Tib St SK14 .... **241** A6
Tibb St ST7 .... **209** F1
Tibbs Cross La WA8 .... **13** E4
Tidal La WA1 .... **16** C4
Tideswell Cl SK8 .... **34** B4
Tideswell Rd SK7 .... **36** C4
Tidnock Ave CW12 .... **156** C3
Tiffild Ct CW7 .... **127** D2
Tilbury Pl WA7 .... **50** C3
Tildsley Cres WA7 .... **48** C3
Tile La WA8 .... **12** A3
Tilestone Paddocks CW6 .... **168** C3
Tilewright Cl ST7 .... **195** D1
Tillard Ave SK3 .... **240** B4
Tilley St WA1 .... **16** B3
Tilman Cl WA5 .... **15** D4
Tilston Ave WA4 .... **17** D2
Tilston Parochial CE Contr
  Prim Sch SY14 .... **198** A2
Tilston Rd Edge Green SY14 **213** D3
  Malpas SY14 .... **213** D3
Tilston Wlk **5** SK9 .... **34** C1
Tilstone Cl
  Hough Common CW2 .... **206** C1
  Northwich CW9 .... **104** A3
Timber La CW9 .... **103** F4
Timber St SK10 .... **87** F1
Timberfields Rd CH1 .... **117** D4
Timberley Ave WA4 .... **17** D2
Timbersbrook Gr **4** SK9 .... **34** B1
Timberscombe Gdns WA1 .... **17** F3
Timbrell Ave CW1 .... **190** A3
Timmis Cl WA2 .... **9** D2
Timmis Cres WA8 .... **13** D1
Timperley St WA8 .... **23** D4

Timperley Sta WA15 238 F8
Tinkwood La SY14 211 F1
Tinsley St WA4 16 C2
Tintagel Cl
Macclesfield SK10 111 F4
Runcorn WA7 50 A3
Tintagel Ct SK15 242 C2
Tintern Ave CH2 118 C3
Tintern Cl WA5 7 F1
Tintern Rd SK8 35 D3
Tipping St WA14 238 D3
Tirley La CW6 123 D1
Tithe Barn Prim Sch SK4 240 A7
Tithebarn Cl L60 40 C4
Tithebarn Dr L64 41 D1
Tithebarn Rd WA15 32 B4
Tithings The WA7 23 F1
Tiverton Cl Chester CH2 118 C3
Sandbach CW11 175 E4
Widnes WA8 12 B2
Tiverton Sq WA5 14 C2
Tiviot Dale SK1 240 F6
Tiviot Way SK1 & SK4 & SK5 240 F7
Tobermory Cl WA11 1 A3
Tobermory Rd SK8 239 C1
Todbrook Cl SK23 65 E3
Toft Cl Chester CH4 140 C3
Widnes WA8 12 C1
Toft Rd WA16 82 A4
Toft Way SK9 34 C2
Toll Bar Ave SK11 112 C4
Toll Bar Rd Christleton CH3 142 B4
Macclesfield SK11 111 F4
Warrington WA2 8 A2
Tolland La WA15 31 F4
Tollard Cl SK8 35 D3
Tollbar St SK1 240 F4
Tollemache Dr CW1 190 A4
Tollemache Terr CH2 118 C1
Tollgate Cl ST7 210 B4
Tollgate Dr CW3 229 F2
Tollitt St CW1 190 B2
Tom Fields ST7 209 F1
Tom La WA14 30 C3
Tom Shepley St SK14 241 E6
Tomkinson St CH2 237 F4
Tomlins Terr CH1 117 F3
Tomlinson Ave WA2 16 B4
Tommy's La
Congleton CW12 156 C2
Crewe CW1 190 C1
Tonbridge Cl SK10 87 D1
Toogood Cl CH2 119 F4
Top Farm La CW7 170 C1
Top Rd Frodsham WA6 74 B3
Kingsley WA6 75 D1
Top Station Rd ST7 195 E4
Topgate Cl L60 41 D4
Topping Ct WA3 9 D2
Toppings The SK6 241 A3
Torbrook Gr 7 SK9 34 B1
Torkington Rd Gatley SK8 239 B5
Wilmslow SK9 60 B3
Torkington St SK3 240 D4
Toronto Ave M90 33 D4
Torr Rd SK11 112 B2
Torr Rise CW6 146 B1
Torr Top St SK22 39 E4
Torridon Gr L65 69 F2
Torrin Cl SK3 240 F1
Torrvale Rd SK22 39 D4
Totland Gr CH2 118 C2
Totton Ct WA1 9 E1
Tourney Gn WA5 7 D1
Tower Hill SK10 88 B2
Tower Hill Rd ST7 195 F4
Tower La Runcorn WA7 50 B4
Weaverham CW8 77 D1
Tower Rd CH1 118 A1
Tower St Hyde SK14 241 D5
Stalybridge SK16 242 A1
Tower Way CW1 190 B2
Towers Cl Poynton SK12 36 C3
Wistaston CW2 206 A4
Towers Ct WA5 15 F4
Towers La WA6 98 B4
Towers Rd SK12 36 C3
Towfield La WA13 19 D4
Town Farm La WA6 100 C4
Town Hill WA1 16 A3
Town La Hale L24 21 E1
Mobberley WA16 58 A2
Neston L64 66 C3
Town Sq CW9 103 F4
Town Well WA6 75 E1
Town's View SK15 242 E1
Towncroft M34 241 A8
Towneley Ct WA8 13 D1
Townend St SK14 241 E6
Townfield Ave CH3 180 C1
Townfield Cl ST7 194 B1
Townfield Ct CW8 78 A2
Townfield Gdns WA14 238 D5
Townfield La
Allostock WA16 106 C3
Barnton CW8 78 A2
Farndon CH3 180 B1
Frodsham WA6 74 B4
Mollington CH1 94 B1
Tarvin CH3 121 D1
Tiverton CW6 168 B3
Townfield Rd
Altrincham WA14 238 D5
Mobberley WA16 58 A2
Townfield View WA7 24 B1
Townfields Knutsford WA16 57 E1
Sandbach CW11 175 D3
Townfields Cres CW7 149 E4
Townfields Dr CW7 149 E4
Townfields Gdns CW7 149 E4
Townfields Rd CW7 149 E4
Townley Pl 23 SK11 112 B4
Townley St SK11 112 B4
Townsend La ST7 194 A4
Townsend Rd CW12 156 C1
Townsfield Dr CW6 147 F4
Townshend Rd CW9 80 A2
Township Cl CH3 182 B1
Townwell Ct CW5 204 B3
Tracy Dr WA12 2 C2
Trafalgar Ave SK12 37 D2
Trafalgar Cl SK12 37 D2
Trafalgar Ct WA8 23 D3
Trafalgar Rd M33 242 C8
Trafford Ave WA5 15 F4
Trafford Cres WA7 49 E3
Trafford Rd
Alderley Edge SK9 60 A1
Wilmslow SK9 34 A1
Trafford St CH2 237 E3
Tragan Dr WA5 14 B2
Tramway Rd M44 11 F4
Tramway St CH2 237 F3
Tranmere Dr SK9 34 C1
Tranmere Rd 1 SK3 240 B4
Trap Rd CW12 132 B2
Trap St SK11 132 A3
Traver's Entry WA9 6 A4
Travis Brow SK4 240 D5
Travis St Hyde SK14 241 E6
10 Widnes WA8 23 D4
Treborth Rd CH1 117 E2
Tree Bank Cl WA7 49 D4
Tree Tops L64 66 C2
Tree Way WA16 82 A4
Treen Cl SK10 86 B1
Treetops Cl WA1 16 C4
Trefoil Cl Huntington CH3 142 A3
Warrington WA3 9 E3
Tregele Cl CH1 117 E2
Trenance Cl WA7 50 B3
Trenchard Dr M22 33 F4
Trent Ave CW7 127 D1
Trent Cl Cheadle Hulme SK7 35 E3
Widnes WA8 13 D2
Winsford CW7 127 D1
Trent Way L60 41 D3
Trentdale L65 70 A2
Trentham Cl WA8 13 D2
Trentham St WA7 22 C2
Trevithick Cl CW1 191 D2
Trevone Cl WA16 57 D1
Tribune Ave WA14 238 B7
Tricketts La CW5 205 F3
Tricketts Mews CW5 205 F3
Trinity Ave M33 242 D6
Trinity Cl CW2 190 A1
Trinity Ct WA3 9 F3
Trinity La SK11 112 C2
Trinity Pl Congleton CW12 179 D4
13 Widnes WA8 23 D4
Trinity Rd M33 242 D6
Trinity Sch SK15 242 C1
Trinity Sq SK10 87 F1
Trinity St Chester CH1 237 D2
Runcorn WA7 23 D2
Stalybridge SK15 242 D1
Trinity Terr CW8 103 F4
Troon Cl Bebington L63 43 E3
Bramhall SK7 36 A4
Haydock WA11 1 A3
Holmes Chapel CW4 130 B1
Troon Dr SK8 239 C1
Trossach Cl WA2 8 C1
Troutbeck Ave
Congleton CW12 156 A1
Newton-le-W WA12 1 C2
Warrington WA5 15 F4
Troutbeck Gr CW7 126 B1
Troutbeck Rd SK8 239 B3
Trouthall La WA16 81 D1
Trowbridge Rd M34 241 A5
Trubshaw Ct ST7 195 E2
Trubshaw Pl ST7 195 D2
Trumans La L66 69 E4
Truro Cl Bramhall SK7 35 F4
Congleton CW12 178 C4
Macclesfield SK10 86 C1
Runcorn WA7 50 B3
Warrington WA1 17 D4
Tudor Cl
Ellesmere Port CH1 94 C4
Northwich CW9 104 C3
Warrington WA4 17 D1
Winsford CW7 149 E3
Tudor Gn Blacon CH1 117 F3
Wilmslow SK9 34 C1
Tudor Rd Altrincham WA14 238 B7
Runcorn WA7 24 B2
Wilmslow SK9 34 C1
Tudor Way Chester CH3 142 A4
Congleton CW12 156 B1
Nantwich CW5 204 C2
Tudorway L60 41 D4
Tulip Cl SK3 240 D1
Tulip Dr WA15 238 F6
Tulip Rd Haydock WA11 1 C3
Partington M31 11 F1
Tully Ave WA12 1 C2
Tumblewood Dr SK8 239 E4
Tunbridge Cl
Great Sankey WA5 15 D4
Wistaston CW2 206 A4
Tunnel Rd CW8 78 A1
Tunnicliffe Rd SK11 112 C2
Tunnicliffe St 1 SK11 112 B4
Tunstall Rd Bosley SK11 158 B4
Congleton CW12 157 F1
Woodhouse Green
SK11, CW12 158 B4
Tunstall St SK4 240 E6
Turf La SK11 112 B2
Turnall Rd WA8 22 A4
Turnberry Cl Lymm WA13 18 B2
Macclesfield SK10 87 E2
Northwich CW9 104 C4
Winsford CW7 126 B1
Turnberry Dr SK9 60 B4
Turnberry Rd SK8 239 C1
Turnbury Cl M33 242 B8
Turner Ave ST7 210 A1
Turner Cl WA8 12 B2
Turner Gdns SK14 241 E8
Turner La SK14 241 F8
Turner St Bollington SK10 88 A4
Nantwich CW5 204 C3
Warrington WA2 16 A3
Turnfield Rd SK8 239 D3
Turnhurst Rd ST7 195 F1
Turnock St SK11 112 C4
Turnstone Ave WA12 2 B2
Turret Hall Dr WA3 3 F4
Turriff Dr L63 43 E2
Turrocks Cl L64 66 C3
Turrocks Croft L64 66 C3
Turton Cl Hale L24 21 F1
Warrington WA3 9 E3
Turton St WA3 3 D4
Turves Rd SK8 239 F1
Tuscan Cl WA8 13 D3
Tuscan Rd M20 239 B8
Tushingham CE Contr Prim Sch SY13 214 B1
Tushingham Cl CH3 142 A4
Tuson Dr WA8 12 C3
Tutor Bank Dr WA12 2 B2
Tweed Cl WA14 238 C6
Tweedsmuir Cl WA2 9 D2
Twemlow Ave CW11 175 D4
Twemlow La CW4 130 B3
Twenty Acre Rd WA5 15 E4
Twinnies Ct SK9 34 A1
Twinnies Rd SK9 34 A1
Twiss Green Dr WA3 4 C2
Twiss Green La WA3 4 C2
Twiss Green Sch WA3 4 C2
Twist Ave WA3 3 E4
Two Acre Gr L66 69 F1
Two Trees High Sch M34 241 A5
Two Trees La M34 241 A5
Twyford Cl WA8 13 D3
Twyford La WA8 13 E3
Tyler St SK9 60 A1
Tyne Cl WA2 8 C1
Tynedale Ave CW2 190 B1
Tynemouth Rd WA7 50 B3
Tynesdale L65 70 A2
Tynwald Cres WA8 12 C3
Tynwald Dr WA4 26 B4
Tyrer Rd WA12 7 E4
Tytherington Bsns Pk SK10 87 E3
Tytherington Cty High Sch SK10 87 E1
Tytherington Dr SK10 87 F2
Tytherington La SK10 87 E3
Tytherington Park Rd SK10 87 E2
Tytherington Sh Ctr SK10 87 E2

Ullapool Cl L66 68 C3
Ullswater SK11 111 F3
Ullswater Ave Crewe CW2 189 F2
Warrington WA2 8 B2
Winsford CW7 126 B1
Ullswater Cres CH2 119 D3
Ullswater Gr WA7 49 E3
Ullswater Rd
Congleton CW12 156 A1
Ellesmere Port L65 70 B1
Wilmslow SK9 34 B2
Ullswater Terr SK15 242 D4
Ulverston Ave WA2 8 A2
Ulverston Cl WA11 1 A3
Ulviet Gate WA16 29 E2
Under Rainow Rd CW12 157 F1
Underbridge La WA4 25 E3
Underhill SK6 241 C2
Underway The WA7 49 F4
Underwood Cl SK10 86 C1
Underwood Ind Pk CW1 190 A3
Underwood La CW1 190 A3
Underwood Rd SK9 60 B1
Underwood West Cty Inf & Jun Sch CW1 190 A3
Unicorn Gateway SK11 112 B4
Union Cl CW12 156 B2
Union Rd Macclesfield SK11 112 C4
New Mills SK22 39 E4
Union St Chester CH1 237 F2
Congleton CW12 156 B2
Crewe CW2 190 B2
Hyde SK14 241 E6
Macclesfield SK11 112 B4
Runcorn WA7 23 D1
Sandbach CW11 175 D3
Stockport SK1 240 F4
Warrington WA1 16 A3
Union Terr CH1 237 E3
Union Wlk CH1 237 E2
Univ of Liverpool Botanic Gdns The L64 67 D2
University Coll Chester CH2 237 D4
Upcast La SK9 59 F2
Uplands CW8 101 E2
Uplands Rd CW9 78 C2
Uplands The Biddulph ST6 179 F1
Runcorn WA7 50 A4
Upper Cambrian Rd CH1 118 A1
Upper Downs WA14 238 C3
Upper Haigh St CW7 149 E4
Upper Mersey Rd WA8 23 D3
Upper Mersey St L65 70 B4
Upper Northgate St CH1 237 D3
Upper Raby Rd L64 42 A1
Upton Acresfield Cty Prim Sch CH2 118 C4
Upton Ave SK8 35 D4
Upton Bridle Path WA8 12 C2
Upton Cl Goldborne WA3 3 E4
Winsford CW7 126 C2
Upton Dr Altrincham WA14 238 E8
Chester CH2 118 B3
Penketh WA5 14 C3
Upton Grange WA8 12 B2
Upton La CH2 118 B4
Upton Manor Cty Jun Sch CH2 118 C4
Upton Mill View Cty Prim Sch CH2 118 C3
Upton Priory Cty Inf & Jun Sch SK10 86 C1
Upton Rd L66 69 E2
Upton St Mary's Inf Sch CH2 118 C4
Upton Way 10 SK9 34 B3
Upton Westlea Cty Prim Sch CH2 118 C4
Upton-by-Chester Cty High Sch CH2 118 C3
Upwood Rd WA3 3 E4
Urban Ave WA15 238 E4
Urban Dr WA15 238 E4
Urban Rd Altrincham WA15 238 E4
Sale M33 242 A6
Ure Ct L65 70 A4
Urwick Rd SK6 241 B2
Utkinton CE Contr Prim Sch CW6 146 A4
Utkinton La CW6 146 C4
Utkinton Rd Tarporley CW6 146 B3
Utkinton CW6 146 B3

Vahler Terr WA7 23 E1
Vale Ave Sale M33 242 E7
Warrington WA2 16 A4
Vale Cl Broughton CH4 139 E2
Romiley SK6 241 F2
Vale Cres SK8 239 F2
Vale Ct WA4 51 D2
Vale Gdns
Ellesmere Port L65 70 A2
Helsby WA6 73 D2
Vale Head SK9 34 B1
Vale Owen Rd WA2 8 B1
Vale Rd Alpraham CW6 169 D2
Altrincham WA14 238 B1
Ellesmere Port L65 70 A2
Hartford CW8 103 E2
Marston CW9 79 D3
Romiley SK6 241 B1
Tiverton CW6 168 C3
Wilmslow SK9 59 F4
Vale Royal Dr CW8 126 A4
Vale View CW9 79 E1
Valebrook Dr CW5 220 A4
Valentine Rd
Kidsgrove ST7 195 D1
Newton-le-W WA12 1 C2
Valewood Ave SK4 240 A5
Valiant Cl WA2 8 C1
Valley Cl Alsager ST7 192 C2
Cheadle SK8 239 E3
Knutsford WA16 82 A4
Valley Ct WA2 8 C1
Valley Dr Chester CH2 118 B3
Ellesmere Port L66 69 E3
Wilmslow SK9 34 B2
Valley Gr M34 241 B6
Valley La CW8 101 F2
Valley Rd Bebington L62 43 E4
Bramhall SK7 35 F4
Cheadle SK8 239 E3
Crewe CW2 190 A1
Macclesfield SK11 112 A3
Stockport SK4 240 A5
Weaverham CW8 77 E1
Wistaston CW2 189 F1
Valley Sch SK7 35 E3
Valley View
Ellesmere Port L66 69 E3
Newton-le-W WA12 2 A1
Northwich CW9 104 B4
Valley Way Knutsford WA16 82 A4
Stalybridge SK15 242 F1
Vanguard Ct WA3 9 E2
Varden Gr SK3 240 D1
Vardon Dr SK9 60 B3
Varey Rd CW12 156 C2
Vaudrey Cres CW12 156 C2
Vaudrey Dr WA1 17 E4
Vaudrey La M34 241 A6
Vaudrey St SK15 242 D1
Vaughan Rd
Stockport SK4 240 D7
Whaley Bridge SK23 65 F3
Vaughans La CH3 142 A4
Vauxhall Cl WA5 14 C2
Vauxhall Rd CW5 204 C4
Vauxhall Way CW7 149 E3
Vearows Pl CW8 103 F4
Venable's Rd CH1 117 F2
Venables Rd CW9 79 D1
Venables Way
High Legh WA16 29 E2
Middlewich CW10 151 F3
Venns Rd WA2 16 B4
Ventnor Ave M33 242 B8
Ventnor Cl
Great Sankey WA5 14 B4
Middlewich CW10 151 E4
Ventnor Rd SK4 240 A6
Verbena Cl M31 11 F2
Verbina Cl WA7 49 F2
Verdin Ave CW8 78 C1
Verdin Cl Moulton CW9 126 C4
Winsford CW7 126 B1
Verdin Ct CW1 190 A4
Verdin Cty High Sch CW7 126 B1
Verdin St CW9 104 B4
Vere St CW1 190 B3
Verity Cl CW1 191 E2
Vernay Gn CH4 141 D3
Vernon Ave Audley ST7 209 E1
Congleton CW12 178 C4
Hooton L66 44 A1
Vernon Cl Audley ST7 209 E1
Cheadle SK8 239 E1
Poynton SK12 36 B1
Saughall CH1 117 D4
Vernon Cty Inf Sch The SK12 36 C2
Vernon Cty Jun Sch The SK12 36 C2
Vernon Dr CW3 230 C2
Vernon Gr M33 242 E5
Vernon Rd Chester CH1 118 A1
Poynton SK12 36 C1
Vernon St Crewe CW1 190 A3
Hyde SK14 241 E6
Macclesfield SK10 112 C4
4 Stockport SK1 240 F6
Warrington WA1 16 A2
Vernon Way CW1 190 B2
Vernon Wlk SK1 240 E5
Veronica Way L66 69 E4
Vetch Cl WA3 11 D3
Vetches The CH3 119 F3
Viaduct Rd WA14 238 D7
Viaduct St
Newton-le-W WA12 2 A2
Stockport SK3 240 E5
Vicar's La CH1 237 E2
Vicarage Ave SK8 35 D4
Vicarage Cl
Guilden Sutton CH3 119 F3
Hale L24 21 F1
Vicarage Ct LL13 196 C4
Vicarage Dr WA11 1 A4
Vicarage Gdns Hyde SK14 241 F6
Sandbach CW11 174 C4
Vicarage Gr CW7 149 E3
Vicarage Hill WA6 73 E2
Vicarage La
Altrincham WA14 238 C1
Audlem CW3 230 A2
Bunbury CW6 168 C1
Burton L64 67 E1
Frodsham WA6 74 B4
Hassall Green CW11 175 F3
Helsby WA6 73 E2
Little Budworth CW6 147 F4
Poynton SK12 36 C3
Sandbach CW11 174 C4
Vicarage Rd Chester CH2 118 C2
Haslington CW1 191 E3
Haydock WA11 1 A4
Northwich CW9 104 A4
Stockport SK3 240 E2
Widnes WA8 23 D4
Vicarage Row L62 44 A3
Vicarage Wlk CW9 104 A4
Vicars Cross Rd CH3 119 E1
Vicker's Cl CH3 121 F4
Vickers Rd WA8 22 C2
Vickers Way CW9 104 A4
Victoria Ave
Altrincham WA15 238 F7
Crewe CW1, CW2, CW4 190 A2
Great Sankey WA5 14 B3
Haslington CW1 191 E2
Heswall L60 41 D3
Holmes Chapel CW4 130 B1
Kidsgrove ST7 194 C1
Warrington WA4 17 D1
Widnes WA8 13 D2
Victoria Cl
Cheadle Hulme SK7 35 E3
Stockport SK3 240 E3
Victoria Com Cty High Sch CW1 190 B3
Victoria Cres Chester CH2 237 D4
Chester, Handbridge CH4 237 F1
Victoria Ct Chester CH2 237 D4
Haslington CW1 191 E2
Victoria Ctr CW1 190 B2
Victoria Cty Inf Sch CH2 237 D4
Victoria Dr M33 242 D5
Victoria Gall CW5 204 C3
Victoria Gdns SK14 241 F8
Victoria Gr WA8 13 D2
Victoria Mkt SK15 242 D1
Victoria Pathway CH4 237 F1
Victoria Pk CW8 78 C1
Victoria Pl Chester CH1 237 E3
Warrington WA4 16 B1

Victoria Rd
Altrincham WA15 .... 238 D3
Broughton CH4 .... 140 B3
Chester CH1 .... 237 D3
Chester CH2 .... 237 D4
Ellesmere Port L65 .... 70 B3
Great Sankey WA5 .... 15 D2
Macclesfield SK10 .... 87 D1
Neston L64 .... 67 D3
Newton-le-W WA12 .... 2 B2
Northwich CW9 .... 104 A4
Penketh WA5 .... 14 B2
Runcorn WA7 .... 23 D1
Sale M33 .... 242 D5
Warrington WA4 .... 16 C1
Warrington, Stockton Heath
  WA4 .... 16 B1
Widnes WA8 .... 23 D3
Wilmslow SK9 .... 60 A3
Victoria Road Cty Prim
Sch Northwich CW9 .... 104 A4
  Runcorn CW9 .... 23 D1
Victoria Sq
Warrington WA4 .... 16 B1
6 Winsford CW7 .... 149 D4
Victoria St
Altrincham WA14 .... 238 D5
Crewe CW1 .... 190 B2
Hyde SK14 .... 241 F8
Knutsford WA16 .... 56 C1
New Mills SK22 .... 39 D3
Northwich CW9 .... 79 F1
Sandbach CW11 .... 175 D4
Stalybridge SK15 .... 242 C2
Warrington WA1 .... 16 B3
Widnes WA8 .... 23 D4
Victoria Way SK7 .... 35 E4
Victoria Wlk 2 SK10 ...... 112 C4
Victory Rd M44 .... 11 E2
Vienna Rd SK3 .... 240 D2
Vienna Rd E SK3 .... 240 E2
Viewlands Dr SK9 .... 34 B1
Villa Rd CH5 .... 116 A4
Villagate La WA4 .... 27 E3
Village Cl Lostock CW9 .... 105 D4
  Runcorn WA4 .... 50 A4
  Warrington WA4 .... 17 F2
Village Ct SK9 .... 34 B1
Village La WA4 .... 52 B2
Village Rd Christleton CH3 . 142 C4
  Great Barrow CH3 .... 120 C3
  Heswall L60 .... 40 C4
Village The Astbury CW12 . 178 A4
  Burton L64 .... 67 E1
  Prestbury SK10 .... 86 C3
Village Way SK9 .... 34 B1
Villars St WA1 .... 16 B3
Villiers Russell Cl CW1 .. 190 B3
Villiers St
Ashton-u-L OL6 .... 242 A2
Hyde SK14 .... 241 F6
Vincent Cl WA5 .... 15 E4
Vincent Dr CH4 .... 141 E3
Vincent St Crewe CW1 .... 190 C2
  Macclesfield SK11 .... 112 B4
Vine Bank Rd ST7 .... 195 D1
Vine Cl SK11 .... 112 A3
Vine Cres WA5 .... 14 B4
Vine Rd L66 .... 69 F1
Vine St Bollington SK10 ... 88 A4
  Runcorn WA7 .... 23 D1
  Widnes WA8 .... 23 D4
Vine Tree Ave Crewe CW2 . 190 A1
  Shavington CW2 .... 206 A3
Vine Tree Cty Prim Sch
  CW2 .... 190 A1
Violet Cl WA3 .... 9 E3
Violet St Stockport SK2 ... 240 F2
  Widnes WA8 .... 23 D4
Virginia Chase SK8 .... 34 C4
Virginia Dr CH1 .... 117 E2
Viscount Dr Cheadle SK8 .. 34 B4
  Wythenshawe WA15 .... 32 C4
Vista Ave WA12 .... 2 A2
Vista Rd Haydock WA12 ... 2 A3
  Newton-le-W WA12 .... 2 A3
  Runcorn WA7 .... 49 D4
Vista The M44 .... 11 E2
Vista Way WA12 .... 2 A2
Volunteer Ave CW5 .... 204 C3
Volunteer Fields CW5 ..... 204 C3
Volunteer St Chester CH1 . 237 E2
  Frodsham WA6 .... 49 E1
Vose Cl WA5 .... 15 E3
Vulcan Cl Newton-le-W WA12 . 2 B1
  Warrington WA2 .... 8 C1
Vyrnwy Rd CH4 .... 140 B3

Waddington Cl
Goldborne WA3 .... 3 F4
  Warrington WA2 .... 8 C1
Wade Cres CW8 .... 78 A2
Wade Deacon Cty High Sch
  WA8 .... 13 D1
Wade St CW9 .... 79 D1
Wadebrook Gr 16 SK9 .... 34 B1
Wades La CW7 .... 126 B2
Wadeson Way WA3 .... 9 D4
Wadham Gdns SK6 .... 241 C4
Wadham Way WA15 .... 238 F1
Wadsworth Cl SK9 .... 34 C2
Wagg St CW12 .... 156 B1
Waggs Rd CW12 .... 156 B1
Wagon La WA11 .... 1 A3
Waine St CW1 .... 190 B3

Wainwright Rd WA14 ...... 238 C5
Wainwright St SK16 .... 242 A1
Waitney Croft SK10 .... 113 D4
Wakefield Cres SK6 .... 241 A1
Wakefield Rd
Ellesmere Port L66 .... 69 F1
Stalybridge SK15 .... 242 E3
Wakefield St WA5 .... 3 D4
Wakeham St SK11 .... 111 F4
Wakes Meadow CW6 .... 185 F4
Walden Cl WA4 .... 17 E2
Walden Dr CH1 .... 93 E4
Waldon Ave SK8 .... 239 D5
Waldon Rd SK11 .... 112 A3
Waldron Gdns CW2 .... 189 F1
Waldron Rd CW1 .... 191 E2
Waldron's La CW1 .... 173 E1
Walfield Ave CW12 .... 156 B3
Walford Ave CW2 .... 190 A2
Walgrove Cl CW12 .... 156 A2
Walker Ave SK15 .... 242 F2
Walker Cl Haslington CW1 . 191 E2
  Hyde SK14 .... 241 F6
Walker Dr CW10 .... 151 E4
Walker Fold SK14 .... 241 F6
Walker La Hyde SK14 .... 241 F6
  Sutton Lane Ends SK11 .... 112 C1
Walker St Chester CH2 ..... 237 E4
  Crewe CW1 .... 190 A3
  Stockport SK1 .... 240 E5
  Warrington WA2 .... 16 A3
Walkers La
Ellesmere Port L66 .... 69 E3
Penketh WA5 .... 14 C2
Scholar Green ST7 .... 177 D1
Tarporley CW6 .... 146 B1
Walkersgreen Rd ST5 ...... 210 B1
Wall Fields Rd CW5 .... 204 C4
Wall Hill Way CW8 .... 76 C2
Wall La CW5 .... 204 C3
Wallace Ct CW7 .... 127 E1
Wallace St Northwich CW8 . 103 F4
  Widnes WA8 .... 23 D4
Wallcroft L64 .... 68 A4
Waller St SK11 .... 112 C3
Wallerscote Cty Prim Sch
  CW8 .... 102 C4
Wallerscote Rd CW8 .... 102 C4
Walleys La CW5 .... 203 E4
Wallfields Cl CW5 .... 204 C4
Wallhill La CW11 .... 177 E4
Wallingford Rd SK9 .... 34 B3
Wallis St Crewe CW1 .... 190 B2
  Warrington WA4 .... 16 A2
Wallrake L60 .... 40 C4
Walls Ave CH1 .... 118 A1
Wallsend Ct WA8 .... 12 C2
Wallworth's Bank CW12 .. 156 C1
Walmer Pl CW7 .... 149 E3
Walmoor Pk CH3 .... 119 D1
Walmsley Dr
Newton-le-W WA12 .... 2 B2
  Reddish SK5 .... 240 F7
  Widnes WA8 .... 23 E4
Walnut Ave CW8 .... 102 B4
Walnut Cl Chester CH2 ..... 118 B4
  Warrington WA1 .... 17 F4
  Wilmslow SK9 .... 60 C4
Walnut Croft CH3 .... 180 C3
Walnut Dr CW7 .... 127 D1
Walnut Gr
Ellesmere Port L66 .... 70 A1
  Sale M33 .... 242 A6
Walnut La CW8 .... 103 D3
Walnut Rd M31 .... 11 E2
Walnut Rise CW12 .... 156 A1
Walnut Tree La CW11 ...... 153 D2
Walnut Tree Rd SK3 .... 240 A4
Walpole Cl CW1 .... 191 E3
Walpole Gr WA2 .... 8 B1
Walpole Rd WA7 .... 49 E3
Walpole St CH2 .... 237 D4
Walsh Cl WA2 .... 2 B3
Walsingham Dr WA7 .... 24 B1
Walsingham Rd WA5 .... 14 C3
Walter St Chester CH2 ...... 237 E4
  Warrington WA1 .... 16 C4
  Widnes WA8 .... 13 E1
Walthall St CW2 .... 190 B1
Waltham Ave WA3 .... 5 E4
Waltham Ct WA7 .... 24 C2
Waltham Dr SK8 .... 35 D3
Waltham Pl CH4 .... 141 D3
Walton Ave WA5 .... 14 C3
Walton Gr ST7 .... 210 B4
Walton Hall WA4 .... 25 F3
Walton Heath Dr SK10 .... 87 E2
Walton Heath Rd WA4 ..... 16 A1
Walton Lea Rd
Higher Walton WA4 .... 25 F4
  Warrington WA4 .... 26 A4
Walton New Rd WA4 .... 26 A4
Walton Pl CH1 .... 117 F2
Walton Rd
Altrincham WA14 .... 238 B5
  Culcheth WA3 .... 4 C2
  Warrington WA4 .... 26 B4
Walton St Runcorn WA7 ... 23 D1
  3 Stockport SK1 .... 240 F3
Walton St Denton M34 ..... 241 B5
  Kidsgrove ST7 .... 210 B4
Waltons The CH4 .... 141 F3
Wansfell Pl WA2 .... 8 A2
War Memorial Hospl CW6 . 146 B1
Warbreck Gr M33 .... 242 D5
Warburton Bridge Rd WA3 . 11 D1

Warburton Cl
Altrincham WA15 .... 32 B3
  Lymm WA13 .... 19 D2
  Romiley SK6 .... 241 A1
Warburton Dr WA5 .... 32 B3
Warburton La M31, WA13 . 11 F1
Warburton Rd 7 SK9 ...... 34 B2
Warburton St WA4 .... 16 B1
Warburton View WA3 ...... 11 D1
Ward Ave SK10 .... 88 A4
Ward Cl WA5 .... 7 D1
Ward La SK12 .... 38 C2
Ward St SK14 .... 241 E6
Ward's La CW11 .... 153 E3
Ward's Terr CH2 .... 118 C2
Wardle Ave CW5 .... 187 E4
Wardle Cres SK11 .... 111 F1
Wardle Ind Est CW5 .... 187 D4
Wardle Mews CW10 .... 151 E4
Wardle Rd M33 .... 242 C6
Wardley Rd WA4 .... 16 A1
Wardour Cl SK11 .... 111 F4
Wardour St WA5 .... 15 F3
Wards La CW12 .... 179 E4
Wareham Cl WA1 .... 17 E4
Wareham Dr CW1 .... 190 A4
Warford Ave SK12 .... 37 D1
Warford Cres SK9 .... 84 A4
Warford Hall (Mary Dendy
Hospl) SK9 .... 84 A3
Warford La WA16 .... 59 D1
Wargrave CE Prim Sch
  WA12 .... 2 B1
Wargrave House Sch
  WA12 .... 2 B1
Wargrave Mews WA12 .... 2 B1
Wargrave Rd
Newton-le-W WA12 .... 2 B1
  Newton-le-W, Wargrave WA12 . 2 B2
Warham St SK9 .... 60 A4
Waring Ave St Helens WA9 . 1 A1
  Warrington WA4 .... 16 C3
Warkworth Cl WA8 .... 12 B2
Warkworth Ct L65 .... 70 C2
Warley Cl SK8 .... 239 E6
Warmingham CE Aided
Prim Sch CW11 .... 173 F4
Warmingham La
Middlewich CW10 .... 151 E3
  Sandbach CW11 .... 174 A4
Warmingham Rd
Crewe CW1 .... 173 E2
  Sandbach CW1 .... 173 E2
Warnley Cl WA4 .... 12 B2
Warren Ave Cheadle SK8 .. 239 D5
  Heswall L60 .... 40 B4
  Knutsford WA16 .... 56 C1
  Lostock CW9 .... 80 A2
Warren Cl Warrington WA16 . 56 C1
  Middlewich CW10 .... 151 D4
  Poynton SK12 .... 36 A2
Warren Croft WA7 .... 50 B4
Warren Ct Ellesmere Port L66 . 69 E2
  Frodsham WA6 .... 74 B3
Warren Dr Altrincham WA15 . 32 B4
  Appleton WA4 .... 26 B4
  Broughton CH4 .... 139 D2
  Ellesmere Port L66 .... 69 F4
  Newton-le-W WA12 .... 2 C2
  Warren SK11 .... 111 E1
Warren Gr SK11 .... 111 E1
Warren La Hartford CW8 ... 103 D2
  Warrington WA1 .... 17 E4
Warren Lea SK12 .... 36 C3
Warren Rd Appleton WA4 .. 26 B4
  Stockport SK3 .... 240 E2
  Warrington WA2 .... 8 B1
Warren St SK1 .... 240 F6
Warren Way Tarporley CW6 . 168 B4
  Wilmslow SK9 .... 60 C4
Warrener St M33 .... 242 D6
Warrilow Heath Rd ST5 ... 210 B1
Warrington Ave
Crewe CW1 .... 190 B3
  Ellesmere Port L65 .... 70 A1
Warrington Bank Quay Sta
  WA5 .... 15 F2
Warrington Bsns Pk WA2 .. 8 B1
Warrington Central Sta
  WA2 .... 16 A3
Warrington Collegiate Inst
Padgate Campus WA2 ...... 9 D2
Warrington District General
Hospl WA5 .... 15 F3
Warrington La WA13 .... 19 F2
Warrington Rd
Bold Heath WA8 .... 13 E4
  Comberbach CW9 .... 78 B4
  Croft WA3 .... 9 F4
  Cronton L35 .... 12 C4
  Cuddington CW8 .... 102 A3
  Dunham-on-t-H WA6 .... 97 E3
  Glazebury WA3 .... 5 A4
  Goldborne WA12 .... 3 D3
  Hatton WA4 .... 25 F2
  Little Leigh CW8 .... 77 D3
  Lymm WA13 .... 18 A2
  Mere WA16 .... 56 B4
  Mickle Trafford CH2 .... 119 F4
  Penketh WA5 .... 14 C2
  Runcorn, Castlefields WA7 ... 23 F1
  Runcorn, Manor Park WA7 ... 24 A2
  Warrington WA3 .... 9 F4
  Warrington, Locking Stumps
  WA3 .... 9 E2
  Widnes WA8 .... 13 E1
  Widnes, Moss Bank WA8 ...... 23 E4

Warrington Road Cty Prim
Sch WA8 .... 13 E1
Warrington St SK15 .... 242 E1
Warrington Tech Coll
North Campus
  WA2 .... 8 A1
Warton Cl Bramhall SK7 ... 36 A4
  Penketh WA5 .... 15 D2
Warwick Ave
Great Sankey WA5 .... 14 B4
  Newton-le-W WA12 .... 2 B1
  Warrington WA5 .... 15 F4
Warwick Cl Kidsgrove ST7 . 195 D2
  Knutsford WA16 .... 57 E1
  Macclesfield SK11 .... 111 F3
  Manchester SK4 .... 240 D8
  Neston L64 .... 66 C3
Warwick Ct
Ellesmere Port L65 .... 70 C1
  Manchester SK4 .... 240 C7
Warwick Cty Prim Sch
  SK11 .... 111 F3
Warwick Dr
Altrincham WA15 .... 238 E1
  Hazel Grove SK7 .... 36 B4
  Sale M33 .... 242 D6
Warwick Mall SK8 .... 239 D6
Warwick Pl CW7 .... 149 E3
Warwick Rd
Altrincham WA15 .... 238 E1
  Blacon CH1 .... 117 F3
  Irlam M44 .... 11 E3
  Macclesfield SK11 .... 111 F3
  Manchester SK4 .... 240 C7
  Romiley SK6 .... 241 E2
Warwick Wlk SK11 .... 111 F3
Wasdale Dr SK8 .... 239 B3
Wasdale Gr CW1 .... 173 D1
Wasdale Terr SK15 .... 242 D4
Wash La Allostock WA16 ... 106 C2
  Kelsall CW6 .... 122 C2
  Warrington WA4 .... 16 C2
Washington Cl ST6 .... 179 E1
Washington Dr WA5 .... 15 D3
Washway Rd M33 .... 242 A6
Wasley Cl WA2 .... 8 C2
Waste La Cuddington CW8 . 101 F2
  Kelsall CW6 .... 122 C2
Watch La CW11 .... 174 A3
Water La SK9 .... 60 A4
Water Lode CW5 .... 204 C3
Water Rd SK15 .... 242 C2
Water St Bollington SK10 .. 88 A4
  Hyde SK14 .... 241 D6
  Macclesfield SK11 .... 112 B4
Water St continued
Newcastle-u-L ST5 .... 210 B1
  Newton-le-W WA12 .... 2 B2
  Northwich CW9 .... 104 A4
  Runcorn WA7 .... 23 D2
  Stalybridge SK15 .... 242 D2
  Stockport SK1 .... 240 F7
  Widnes WA8 .... 23 D3
Water Tower (Mus) CH1 .. 118 A1
Water Tower Rd L64 .... 41 F1
Water Tower St CH1 .... 237 D3
Waterbank Row CW9 .... 103 F4
Waterbridge Ct WA4 .... 26 B4
Waterfoot La SK23 .... 65 E3
Waterford Ave SK6 .... 241 F2
Waterford Ct WA4 .... 67 D4
Waterford Pl SK8 .... 34 C4
Waterford Way WA7 .... 50 B3
Watergate Row CH1 .... 237 D2
Watergate Sq CH1 .... 237 D2
Watergate St CH1 .... 237 D2
Waterhouse Ave SK10 ..... 87 F4
Waterloo Cl L65 .... 70 B3
Waterloo Gr ST7 .... 195 D1
Waterloo La WA5 .... 74 C1
Waterloo Rd Bramhall SK7 . 35 F4
  Chester CH2 .... 118 B2
  Haslington CW1 .... 191 D2
  Northwich CW8 .... 103 F4
  Poynton SK12 .... 37 D1
  Romiley SK6 .... 241 E2
  1 Runcorn WA7 .... 22 C1
  Runcorn WA7 .... 22 C2
  Stalybridge SK15 .... 242 D2
  Stockport SK1 .... 240 F5
  Widnes WA8 .... 23 D3
Waterloo St OL6 .... 242 A4
Waterloo St W SK11 .... 112 B4
Watermeetings La SK6 ..... 241 F1
Watermill Dr SK11 .... 112 C4
Waters Edge CW9 .... 78 B2
Waters Gn SK11 .... 112 B4
Waters Reach SK12 .... 36 C3
Waters Reams CH3 .... 142 A4
Watersedge WA6 .... 49 E1
Watersfield Cl SK8 .... 34 C4
Waterside Appleton WA4 .. 26 B4
  Macclesfield SK11 .... 112 C4
Waterside Cotts CW5 .... 216 C3
Waterside Dr WA6 .... 49 E1
Waterside La WA8 .... 22 B3
Waterside Mews 5 CW11 . 174 C2
  New Mills SK22 .... 38 C4
Waterside Rd Disley SK12 . 38 C4
Waterside View CW9 .... 104 C3
Waterside Way CW10 .... 128 A1
Watertower View CH2 ..... 118 C1
Waterway CH3 .... 143 D3
Waterways WA5 .... 15 C1
Waterworks La
Ellesmere Port L66 .... 68 C4
  Winwick WA2 .... 8 A4
Watery La Astbury CW12 .. 178 B3
  Winwick WA2 .... 7 F3

Watkin St Hawarden CH5 .. 116 A1
  Warrington WA2 .... 16 A4
Watkins Ave WA12 .... 1 C2
Watkinson Way WA8 .... 13 E2
Watlands Rd ST7 .... 209 F1
Watling Cres CH4 .... 141 F4
Watling Ct CH3 .... 119 E1
Watling Dr CW6 .... 123 E3
Watling St CW9 .... 103 F4
Watson Sq 20 SK1 .... 240 F5
Watson St M34 .... 241 B7
Watson's Cl CH4 .... 139 E2
Watton Cl WA4 .... 17 E2
Wavell Ave WA8 .... 22 B4
Wavells Way CH3 .... 142 A3
Waveney Dr WA14 .... 238 C6
Waverley Ave WA4 .... 26 B4
Waverley Cl SK10 .... 113 D4
Waverley Dr SK8 .... 35 D4
Waverley Rd Sale M33 ...... 242 C8
  Stockport SK3 .... 240 C3
Waverley Terr CH2 .... 118 C2
Waverton Cl
Davenham CW9 .... 103 F2
  Hough Common CW2 .... 206 C1
Waverton Cty Prim Sch
  CH3 .... 143 D3
Waverton Mill Quays CH3 . 143 D3
Waverton Rd L66 .... 69 F3
Wavertree Ave
Scholar Green ST7 .... 194 C4
  Widnes WA8 .... 23 D4
Wavertree Ct L66 .... 69 F4
Wavertree Dr CW10 .... 151 D4
Wavertree Rd CH1 .... 117 E3
Way's Gn CW7 .... 149 F4
Waybutt La Betley CW2 .... 221 E4
  Hough Common CW2 .... 221 E4
Wayfarers Dr WA12 .... 2 C1
Wayford Cl WA6 .... 49 D1
Wayside ST7 .... 193 F1
Wayside Cl WA13 .... 18 B1
Wayside Ct CH2 .... 119 F4
Wayside Dr SK12 .... 36 B2
Wayside Rd SK10 .... 112 C4
Waywell Cl WA2 .... 8 C2
Weal Stone La CH2 .... 118 C3
Weald Dr L66 .... 69 D3
Wealstone Ct CH2 .... 118 C3
Wearhead Cl WA3 .... 2 C4
Weaste La WA4 .... 17 F1
Weates Cl WA8 .... 13 F2
Weathercock La CW12 ..... 157 F2
Weaver Cl Alsager ST7 ..... 193 D2
  Biddulph ST6 .... 179 E1
  Sandbach CW11 .... 174 C4
Weaver Cres WA6 .... 49 E1
Weaver Ct SK11 .... 112 B4
Weaver Cty Prim Sch The
  CW5 .... 204 C2
Weaver Gr
Mickle Trafford CH2 .... 119 F4
  St Helens WA9 .... 1 A2
Weaver Grange CW9 .... 126 C4
Weaver La WA6 .... 49 D1
Weaver Park Ind Est WA6 . 49 E1
Weaver Rd Culcheth WA3 .. 5 D1
  Ellesmere Port L65 .... 70 B1
  Frodsham WA6 .... 49 E1
  Moulton CW9 .... 126 C4
  Nantwich CW5 .... 204 C3
  Northwich CW8 .... 103 F4
  Runcorn WA7 .... 49 D3
Weaver St Chester CH1 ..... 237 D2
  Winsford CW7 .... 126 C1
Weaver Vale Cty Prim Sch
  WA6 .... 49 E1
Weaver View Audlem CW3 . 229 F2
  Church Minshull CW5 .... 172 A3
  Northwich CW8 .... 103 F4
  Weaverham CW8 .... 77 C1
Weaver Way CW9 .... 78 C1
Weaver's La SK7 .... 35 E3
Weaverhall La CW7 .... 150 A2
Weaverham Cty High Sch
  CW8 .... 102 B4
Weaverham Forest Cty
Prim Sch CW8 .... 77 E1
Weaverham Rd
Cuddington CW8 .... 102 A3
  Weaverham CW8 .... 102 A3
Weaverham Way 4 SK9 ... 34 C2
Weaverside CW5 .... 204 C1
Weaverside Ave WA7 .... 49 F2
Webb Dr WA5 .... 6 C3
Webb's La CW10 .... 128 B1
Webster Cl CH4 .... 139 E2
Websters La L66 .... 69 F1
Weddell Cl WA5 .... 15 E4
Wedge Ave WA11 .... 1 A3
Wedgwood Ave ST7 .... 210 A1
Wedgwood Dr WA8 .... 13 D2
Wedgwood La ST6 .... 179 E1
Wedgwood Rd ST7 .... 210 B4
Wednesbury Dr WA5 .... 14 C3
Weedon Ave WA12 .... 2 A3
Weighbridge Rd CH5 .... 92 B3
Weir St ST7 .... 195 D1
Weir La WA1 .... 17 F3
Weir St Northwich CW9 ..... 103 F4
  Warrington WA4 .... 16 A1
Welbeck Cl CW10 .... 128 A1
Welbeck Rd SK14 .... 241 F6
Welch Rd SK14 .... 241 F8
Welcroft St 2 SK1 .... 240 F4
Weldon Rd WA14 .... 238 D6
Welford Ave WA3 .... 3 E4
Welford Cl SK9 .... 60 C4

Well Ave SY14 213 D2
Well Bank CW11 175 D3
Well Bank La WA16 108 B4
Well Cl L64 67 E3
Well Farm Cl SY14 213 D2
Well Field Cl WA16 80 A4
Well La Alsager ST7 193 E2
Antrobus CW9 53 D2
Biddulph ST6 179 E2
Chester CH2 118 C3
Heswall L60 41 D3
Kingsley WA6 75 E1
Little Budworth CW6 147 F4
Manley WA6 98 C2
Mollington CH1 94 C1
Neston L64 66 C3
Penketh WA5 14 C2
Prestbury SK10 87 E4
Stretton WA4 52 C4
Weaverham CW8 77 E1
Well Meadow SK14 241 D8
Well St Malpas SY14 213 D2
Mow Cop ST7 195 E4
New Mills SK22 39 D4
Winsford CW7 126 B1
Welland Cl 14 CW11 174 B3
Wellbrook Cl WA7 50 B3
Wellcroft Cl CW2 206 A4
Weller Ave SK12 36 B1
Weller Cl SK12 36 B1
Welles St CW11 175 D3
Wellesbourne Cl
Macclesfield SK10 86 C1
Neston L64 66 B3
Wellesley Ave
Ellesmere Port L65 70 B3
Haslington CW1 191 E2
Wellesley Wlk L65 70 B3
Wellfield
Preston on the Hill WA7 50 C3
Romiley SK6 241 C4
Runcorn WA7 50 C3
Widnes WA8 13 D2
Winsford CW7 127 D1
Wellfield Rd WA3 4 C2
Wellfield St WA5 15 F3
Wellington Ave L62 43 F2
Wellington Cl
Ellesmere Port L65 70 B3
Knutsford WA16 57 E2
Sale M33 242 C8
Wellington Gdns WA12 2 A2
Wellington Gr SK2 240 F3
Wellington Mill SK3 240 E5
Wellington Pl
Altrincham WA14 238 D4
Chester CH2 237 E3
Wellington Rd
Altrincham WA15 238 F6
Bollington SK10 87 F4
Broughton CH4 139 D2
Ellesmere Port L65 70 B2
Ellesmere Port L65 70 B3
Hazel Grove SK7 37 D4
Kidsgrove ST7 195 D1
Nantwich CW5 204 C2
Wellington Rd N
Ellesmere Port L65 70 B3
Stockport M19 & SK3 & SK4 240 D7
Wellington Rd S SK1 & SK2 240 F4
Wellington St Denton SK14 241 C7
Macclesfield SK11 112 B4
Newton-le-W WA12 2 A2
Northwich CW8 103 F4
Runcorn WA7 23 D2
Stockport SK1 & SK3 240 F5
Warrington WA1 16 B3
Widnes WA8 23 D3
Wells Ave CW1 191 E3
Wells Cl Cheadle SK8 34 B4
Ellesmere Port CH1 94 C4
Mickle Trafford CH2 119 F4
Warrington WA1 17 D4
Wellswood Dr CW2 205 F4
Wellswood Rd L66 69 F4
Welsby Cl WA2 8 C2
Welsh La CW7 149 E3
Welsh Rd Ellesmere Port L66 68 C2
Ledsham L66 68 C2
Puddington CH1 93 E3
Shotwick CH1 93 E3
Welsh Row Nantwich CW5 204 B3
Nether Alderley SK10 84 C3
Welshampton Cl L66 69 E1
Welshmen's La CW5 204 B4
Welshpool Cl WA5 7 E1
Welton Cl SK9 59 F2
Welton Dr SK9 59 F2
Welton Gr SK9 59 F2
Welwyn Cl WA4 17 E2
Wemyss Rd CH1 117 E2
Wendover Cl WA11 1 B4
Wenger Rd WA8 13 D3
Wenlock Cl
Macclesfield SK10 87 D1
Newcastle-u-L ST5 210 C1
Wenlock Gdns L66 69 F1
Wenlock La L66 69 F1
Wenlock Rd WA7 50 A2
Wenlock Way CH4 140 C3
Wensley Dr SK7 36 B4
Wensley Rd Cheadle SK8 239 C6
Goldborne WA3 3 F4
1 Reddish SK5 240 F8
Wensleydale Ave
Bebington L62 43 F3
Cheadle SK8 239 C6
Congleton CW12 157 D3
Wensleydale Cl WA5 14 C4
Wentworth Ave
Macclesfield SK11 111 F3
Warrington WA1 17 D4
Wentworth Cl
Northwich CW9 104 C4
Widnes WA8 13 D3
Wentworth Dr Bebington L63 43 E3
Bramhall SK7 36 A4
Kidsgrove ST7 195 E2
Wereton Rd ST7 209 E1
Werneth Ct SK14 241 E5
Werneth Low Rd SK6 241 D4
Werneth Rd SK14 241 F6
Werneth Sch SK6 241 A2
Wervin Rd Chester CH2 96 A2
Stoak CH2 96 A2
Wesley Ave Alsager ST7 193 E2
Haydock WA11 1 C4
Sandbach CW11 175 D3
Wesley C CW12 156 B1
Wesley Cl Nantwich CW5 204 C3
Neston L64 66 B4
Wesley Ct CW7 126 C1
Wesley Gdns ST7 195 D1
Wesley Pl Crewe CW2 190 B1
Northwich CW9 104 A4
Wesley St Audley ST7 210 A1
19 Stockport SK1 240 F5
Wessex Cl Shavington CW2 206 B2
Warrington WA1 17 F4
Wessex Dr CW9 104 B3
West Ave Altrincham WA14 238 A5
Crewe CW1, CW2 190 A2
Gatley SK8 239 C1
Kidsgrove ST7 194 B1
Middlewich CW10 128 B1
Northwich CW9 104 B4
Stalybridge SK15 242 D3
Warrington WA2 16 A4
Warrington, Stockton Heath WA4 16 B1
Weston CW2 207 D3
West Bank
Alderley Edge SK9 85 D4
Chester CH2 118 B2
West Bank Cty Prim Sch WA8 23 D2
West Bank Dock Est WA8 22 C3
West Bank Rd SK10 87 D1
West Bank St WA8 23 D3
West Bond St SK11 112 B4
West Cheshire Coll Arts Ctr CH1 118 A3
West Cheshire Coll Handbridge Ctr CH4 141 E4
West Cl SK10 87 F4
West Downs Rd SK8 239 F3
West Dr Gatley M22 & SK8 239 A4
Great Sankey WA5 15 D2
Heswall L60 41 D4
Neston L64 66 C3
Winsford CW7 127 D1
West Dudley St CW7 126 C1
West End CH3 121 F4
West End Ave SK8 239 A6
West End Cotts CW12 156 B1
West End Gr WA11 1 A3
West End Rd WA11 1 A3
West Gate WA8 22 A4
West Gr Alsager ST7 193 F2
Heswall L60 40 C4
Sale M33 242 B5
West Hall Mews WA16 29 E3
West Heath Gr WA13 18 B2
West Heath Sh Ctr CW12 156 A2
West Hill Sch SK15 242 C2
West House Ct SK10 86 C1
West Hyde WA13 18 B2
West La Cuddington CW8 101 F2
High Legh WA16 29 E3
Runcorn WA7 49 F4
West Lea M34 241 A6
West Lorne St CH1 237 D3
West Mains L24 21 D2
West Oak Pl SK8 239 F1
West Over SK6 241 A1
West Park Ave Denton M34 241 B6
Poynton SK12 36 A2
West Park Dr CH1 94 C4
West Quay Rd WA2 7 F2
West Rd Altrincham WA14 238 C2
Congleton CW12 156 B2
Ellesmere Port L65 70 B2
Runcorn WA7 48 B4
Weaverham CW8 77 D1
West Side Ave WA11 1 A3
West St Alderley Edge SK9 60 A1
Chester CH2 237 F4
Congleton CW12 156 B2
Crewe CW1 190 A3
Haslington CW1 191 E3
Macclesfield SK11 112 A4
Middlewich CW10 128 B1
Mount Pleasant ST7 195 D3
Stalybridge SK15 242 C2
Stockport SK3 240 D5
Warrington WA2 16 A4
West Vale L64 66 C3
West Vale Rd WA15 238 F6
West View WA2 9 D1
West View Rd WA6 101 D3
West Way
Holmes Chapel CW4 130 A2
Sandbach CW11 174 C2
Shavington CW2 206 B3
Westage La Bate Heath CW9 79 D4
Great Budworth CW9 79 D4
Westbourne Ave CW1 190 A3
Westbourne Gr M33 242 A6
Westbourne Rd Blacon CH1 118 A2
Warrington WA4 26 A4
Westbrook Ave WA4 16 B1
Westbrook Cres
Great Sankey WA5 7 D1
Warrington WA5 7 D1
Westbrook Ctr WA5 7 E1
Westbrook Dr SK10 87 E1
Westbrook Rd WA6 75 D1
Westbrook Way WA5 7 D1
Westbury Cl
Middlewich CW10 151 D4
Wistaston CW2 206 B4
Westbury Dr SK11 112 A4
Westbury Way CH4 140 C3
Westby Cl SK7 36 A4
Westcourt Rd M33 242 A8
Westdale Rd WA1 17 D4
Westend LL13 196 B4
Westenra Ave L65 69 F3
Westerham Cl SK10 87 D1
Western App CH2 118 C2
Western Ave Blacon CH1 117 E2
Ellesmere Port L65 69 F4
Macclesfield SK11 112 B3
Milton Green CH3 165 E1
Nantwich CW5 204 C2
Western Ct CH2 118 C2
Western Dr SK11 112 B3
Westfield Ave Audley ST7 209 E1
Macclesfield SK10 87 D1
Westfield Cl CH4 141 D4
Westfield Cres WA7 22 C1
Westfield Cty Prim Sch WA7 22 C1
Westfield Dr
Knutsford WA16 56 C1
Willaston (nr Nantwich) CW2 205 F4
Westfield Gr CW8 77 F2
Westfield Mews WA7 22 C1
Westfield Rd Cheadle SK8 34 C4
Mow Cop ST7 195 E4
Northwich CW9 104 A4
Runcorn WA7 22 C1
Westfields WA15 31 F4
Westfields Rise CW3 232 B1
Westford Rd WA4 16 A1
Westgate Altrincham WA15 238 E2
Sale M33 242 A6
Wilmslow SK9 60 A3
Westgate Ave CW7 126 A1
Westholme Cl CW2 206 B4
Westhouse Cl L63 43 E3
Westlands ST7 209 F1
Westlands Cl L64 41 F1
Westlands Cty High Sch CW12 156 A2
Westlands Rd CW10 128 A1
Westlands The CW12 156 B1
Westmere Cl CW2 207 D3
Westmere Dr CW1 190 C1
Westminster Ave CH4 141 D3
Westminster Cl
Middlewich CW10 128 A1
Warrington WA4 17 E1
Widnes WA8 22 A4
Westminster Dr
Bebington L62 43 E4
Cheadle Hulme SK8 35 D3
Haydock WA11 1 C4
Wilmslow SK9 60 A2
Westminster Gr
Chester CH4 141 E4
Ellesmere Port L65 70 B3
10 Winsford CW7 149 D4
Westminster Ind Pk L65 69 F3
Westminster Pl WA1 16 A3
Westminster Rd
Broughton CH4 139 D2
Chester CH2 118 C2
Ellesmere Port L65 70 B3
Macclesfield SK10 87 E1
4 Macclesfield SK11 112 B4
Westminster St
Crewe CW2 190 B1
5 Macclesfield SK11 112 B4
Westminster Terr CH4 141 E4
Westmoor Gables SK4 240 A8
Westmoreland Cl WA14 31 D4
Westmorland Ave
Kidsgrove ST7 210 C4
Widnes WA8 13 D1
Westmorland Cl SK10 86 C1
Westmorland Rd M31 11 F1
Westmorland Terr CW4 130 A2
Weston Cl Crewe CW1 190 C1
Middlewich CW10 151 E4
Weston Cres WA7 49 D3
Weston Ct WA7 48 C4
Weston Cty Prim Sch
Runcorn WA7 49 D3
Weston CW2 207 E3
Weston Dr M34 241 A7
Weston Gr CH2 118 B4
Weston La CW2 206 C3
Weston Point Cty Prim Sch WA7 48 C4
Weston Point Expressway WA7 49 D3
Weston Rd Crewe CW1 190 C1
Runcorn WA7 48 C4
Weston CW1 207 D4
Wilmslow SK9 60 C3
Weston St SK5 240 E8
Westover Rd WA1 16 C4
Westrees CW8 101 E3
Westville Dr CW12 156 A1
Westward Rd Chester CH3 142 A4
Wilmslow SK9 59 F3
Westway L60 40 C3
Westway Cres WA3 10 A3
Westwood WA7 24 B1
Westwood Ave WA15 238 F7
Westwood Ct L64 41 F1
Westwood Rd SK8 34 A4
Westy La WA4 16 C2
Wet Gate La WA13 19 E2
Wetheral Rd SK10 87 D1
Wetherby Cl Chester CH1 118 A1
Newton-le-W WA12 2 B3
Wetherby Way L66 69 E3
Wetreins La Barton SY14 197 E3
Farndon SY14 197 E3
Wetton La WA6 76 C2
Wexford Ave L24 21 E1
Wey Gates Dr WA15 32 B4
Weybridge Cl WA4 26 C4
Weybridge Dr SK10 87 D2
Weymouth Cl WA7 50 C3
Weymouth Rd WA5 6 C3
Whaddon Dr CH4 140 C2
Whaley Bridge Prim Sch SK23 65 F4
Whaley Bridge Sta SK23 65 F4
Whaley La SK23 65 E4
Whalley Ave Glazebury WA3 5 E4
Sale M33 242 C7
Whalley Cl WA15 238 F8
Whalley Dr CW6 147 D2
Whalley Gr WA8 13 E2
Whalley Hayes SK11 112 B4
Whalley Rd CW9 104 A4
Whalley St WA1 16 B3
Wharams Bank CW11 176 C3
Wharf Cl WA14 238 D7
Wharf La CW12 178 A2
Wharf Rd
Altrincham WA14 238 D7
Newton-le-W WA12 1 C1
Sale M33 242 C7
Whaley Bridge SK23 65 F4
Wharf St
Stockport SK4 & SK5 240 E7
Warrington WA1 16 B2
Wharf The WA7 50 C3
Wharfdale Cl WA5 15 D4
Wharfdale Dr L62 43 F3
Wharfdale Rd
Congleton CW12 157 D3
Crewe CW1 173 D1
Wharfe Cl CW12 156 C1
Wharfe La L65 70 A4
Wharfedale WA7 50 A3
Wharford La WA7 24 C2
Wharmby Rd WA11 1 C3
Wharton (Donefields) Ind Est CW7 127 D2
Wharton Gdns CW7 127 D2
Wharton Park Rd CW7 126 C1
Wharton Rd CW7 127 D1
Whatcroft Cl WA7 49 E3
Whatcroft La
Davenham CW9 104 C1
Lach Dennis CW9 104 C1
Wheat Croft SK3 240 F1
Wheat Moss SK11 84 A2
Wheatcroft Cl WA5 15 E3
Wheatfield Cl Barnton CW8 78 A2
Ellesmere Port L66 69 E2
Macclesfield SK10 87 E2
Romiley SK6 241 A4
Wheatfield Rd WA8 12 B3
Wheatland Rd L60 41 E4
Wheatlands WA7 23 F1
Wheatley Ave WA12 2 B3
Wheatley Rd CW1 190 C3
Wheatsheaf La CW9 53 D2
Wheatsheaf Rd SK23 65 F3
Wheelman Rd CW1 190 A4
Wheelock Cl Alsager ST7 193 D2
Wilmslow SK9 34 B1
Wheelock Cty Prim Sch CW11 175 D2
Wheelock Dr CW7 127 D1
Wheelock St CW10 128 B1
Wheelock Way ST7 195 D1
Wheldon Cl CH2 118 B4
Wheldrake Cl L66 69 D3
Whernside WA8 12 B2
Whernside Cl SK4 240 E7
Whetstone Hey L66 69 E3
Whetstone Rd ST6 179 E1
Whickham Cl WA8 12 C2
Whimbrel Ave WA12 2 B2
Whimbrel Cl WA7 49 F3
Whinberry Rd WA14 238 B7
Whinchat Ave WA12 2 B2
Whinchat Dr WA3 9 F2
Whinfell Gr WA7 49 F3
Whipcord La CH1 118 A1
Whirley Cty Prim Sch SK10 86 B1
Whirley La SK10 85 F1
Whirley Rd SK10 86 B1
Whirlow Rd CW2 206 A4
Whisterfield La SK11 109 F2
Whiston St SK11 112 B4
Whitbarrow Rd WA13 18 B3
Whitby Ave Chester CH2 118 B3
Warrington WA2 8 B1
Whitby Cl Cheadle SK8 239 C6
Crewe CW1 190 A4
Poynton SK12 36 B2
Whitby Cty High Sch The L66 70 A1
Whitby Heath Cty Prim Sch L65 70 A2
Whitby La CH1 95 D3
Whitby Rd
Ellesmere Port L65 70 B3
Runcorn WA7 23 D1
Whitby's La CW7 126 A1
Whitchurch Cl WA1 17 D4
Whitchurch Gr ST5 210 C1
Whitchurch Rd
Audlem CW3 229 E2
Broxton SY14 199 D2
Chester CH3 119 D1
Chowley CH3 183 D2
Christleton CH3 142 C4
Edge Green SY14 199 D2
Milton Green CH3 165 E2
Newhall CW3 229 E2
Royal's Green SY13 228 B1
Sound CW5 218 A4
Sound, Newtown CW5 217 F2
Waverton CH3 143 D2
Whitchurch Way WA7 49 E4
White Ave CW2 189 F2
White Broom WA13 19 D2
White Field Ave WA12 2 C1
White Friars CH1 237 D2
White Hall La CW11 173 F4
White Hall Rd ST7 194 C1
White Hart Gdns CW8 102 C2
White Hart La CW2 205 F4
White Hart St SK14 241 D8
White House Cl WA11 1 A3
White House Dr WA1 17 F4
White La CH3 142 B4
White Lodge Cl L62 43 E3
White Lodge Mews CW8 102 A2
White Park Cl CW10 128 B1
White St Macclesfield SK11 112 B3
Warrington WA1 16 A3
Warrington, Stockton Heath WA4 16 B1
Widnes WA8 23 D3
Whiteacre Rd OL6 242 A4
Whitebarn Rd SK9 85 D4
Whitebeam Ave L66 69 F1
Whitebeam Cl
Newcastle-u-L ST5 210 B1
Runcorn WA7 24 B1
Whitecroft Rd L66 69 F1
Whitecross Rd WA5 15 F3
Whitefield SK4 240 D7
Whitefield Ave WA1 16 C4
Whitefield Cl Goldborne WA3 3 D4
Lymm WA13 19 D3
Whitefield Ct WA3 4 C1
Whitefield Gr WA13 19 D2
Whitefield Rd Sale M33 242 A7
Warrington WA4 26 A4
Whitefields CH2 72 A2
Whitefriars Wlk M22 33 E4
Whitegate CH3 121 F4
Whitegate Ave WA3 4 C1
Whitegate CE Aided Prim Sch CW8 125 F4
Whitegate Cl CW10 151 E3
Whitegate Fields LL13 180 B1
Whitegate Rd CW7 125 F2
Whitegates SK8 239 D5
Whitegates Cl L64 42 C1
Whitegates Cres L64 67 F4
Whitegates Rd SK8 239 D5
Whitehall Ave ST7 194 C1
Whitehall Cl Barnton CW8 78 A2
Wilmslow SK9 60 A3
Whitehall Ct CW5 204 B3
Whitehall Dr Hartford CW8 103 E3
Shavington CW2 206 A2
Whitehall La CW6 124 C1
Whitehall Pl WA6 74 A4
Whitehall Rd M33 242 B5
Whitehaven La CW5 203 D4
Whitehaven Rd SK7 35 E3
Whitehill Prim Sch SK4 240 E8
Whitehill Rd ST7 195 D1
Whitehill St W SK4 240 E8
Whitehouse Dr WA15 32 A4
Whitehouse Expressway WA7 50 A3
Whitehouse La
Dunham Town WA14 20 B4
Nantwich CW5 204 C4
Plumley WA16 80 C3
Whitehouse Rd WA16 30 A2
Whitehouse Vale Ind Est WA7 50 C2
Whitelands Rd
OL6 & SK15 & SK16 242 A2
Whitelea Dr SK3 240 D1
Whiteleas Rd SK23 65 E2
Whiteley Pl WA14 238 D6
Whitelow Rd SK4 240 A7
Whitemere Ct L65 70 B4
Whitemore Rd CW10 151 E3
Whiteridge Rd ST7 195 D1
Whites La CW2 207 D3
Whites Meadow CH3 142 A4
Whitesands Rd WA13 18 B2
Whiteside Rd WA11 1 A3
Whitethorn Ave WA5 14 B4
Whitethorn Way ST5 210 C1
Whitewood La SY14 212 B4
Whitfield Gr WA11 1 A3

Whitfield Rd ST7 195 D1
Whitfields The SK10 87 D1
Whitley Ave Barnton CW8 78 A2
Warrington WA4 17 D2
Whitley Cl
Middlewich CW10 151 D4
Runcorn WA7 48 C4
Whitley Cty Comp Sch
WA4 52 B2
Whitley Dr CW8 103 D2
Whitley La WA16 55 D4
Whitley Rd SK4 240 B7
Whitlow Ave
Altrincham WA14 238 B8
Nantwich CW5 204 C2
Whitlow La CW9 126 C4
Whittaker Ave WA2 8 B1
Whittington Gdns CW9 104 A1
Whittle Ave
Great Sankey WA5 15 D4
Haydock WA11 1 A3
Whittle Cl CH5 116 A2
Whittle Hall La WA5 14 B4
Whittles Ave M34 241 A6
Whittles Wlk M34 241 A6
Whittlewood Cl WA3 10 A3
Whitton Dr CH2 118 C3
Wickenby Dr M33 242 A6
Wicker La Altrincham WA15 32 B4
Guilden Sutton CH3 120 A2
Wicklow Ave SK3 240 B3
Wicklow Cl L66 69 D3
Wickson La CH3, CW6 167 E2
Wicksten Dr WA7 23 E1
Widdale Cl WA5 14 C4
Widgeon Cl SK12 36 A2
Widgeon Rd WA14 238 B8
Widgeons Covert L63 41 F3
Widnes North Sta WA8 13 D2
Widnes Rd WA8 23 D4
Widnes Sixth Form Coll
WA8 12 C3
Wiend The CH2 118 B2
Wight Cl L65 70 B1
Wightman Ave WA12 2 B3
Wigmore Cl WA3 10 A3
Wigmore St OL6 242 A4
Wigsey La WA13 19 D4
Wigshaw La WA3 4 C2
Wilbraham Cl CW5 204 A4
Wilbraham Rd Acton CW5 204 A4
Congleton CW12 156 C2
Weaverham CW8 77 F1
Wilbraham's Wlk ST7 209 E1
Wilbrahams Way ST7 193 E2
Wilcott Dr SK9 59 F2
Wilcott Rd M22 239 A5
Wild Clough SK14 241 F5
Wild Goose Ave ST7 195 E2
Wild St SK6 241 A2
Wildcote Cl WA8 13 E2
Wilderhope Cl CW2 206 B4
Wilderspool Cres WA4 16 A1
Wilderspool Cswy WA4 16 B2
Wilding Ave WA7 23 D1
Wilding St CW1 190 C2
Wildings Old La WA3 9 D4
Wildwood Gr WA1 17 D4
Wilkin Croft SK8 239 E1
Wilkins La SK9 33 F3
Wilkinson Ave WA1 16 C3
Wilkinson Cl WA8 23 D3
Wilkinson Rd SK4 240 E6
Wilkinson St
Ellesmere Port L65 70 B3
Sale M33 242 D6
Warrington WA2 16 B4
Wilkinson St N L65 70 B3
Willan Rd CH1 117 E2
Willaston CE Contr Prim Sch
L64 67 F4
Willaston Cty Prim Sch
CW5 205 E3
Willaston Dr L24 21 D3
Willaston Hall Gdns CW5 205 E3
Willaston Rd L63 42 B3
Willaston Way 7 SK9 34 B3
Willbank La CW5 202 B3
Willcock Rd WA11 2 A4
Willdor Gr SK3 240 B2
Willeymoor La SY13 225 E4
William Beaumont Cty
High Sch WA2 8 A1
William Johnson Gdns L65 70 B3
William Penn Cl WA5 14 C3
William Rd Haydock WA11 1 A3
Kidsgrove ST7 195 D1
William St Chester CH1 237 E3
Chester, Hoole Park CH2 118 C2
Congleton CW12 157 D2
Macclesfield SK10 112 C4
Northwich CW9 104 A4
Widnes WA8 13 E1
Winsford CW7 126 C1
William Stockton Cty Prim
Sch L65 70 A3
William Wlk 2 WA14 238 D3
Williams Ave WA12 2 B3
Williams Cl CH2 118 B2
Williams Way SK11 111 E4
Williamson Ave SK6 241 A4
Williamson Cres SK23 65 E4
Williamson Rd SK23 65 E4
Willington La Duddon CW6 145 F4
Kelsall CW6 122 B2
Willington Rd Duddon CW6 145 D4
Kelsall CW6 122 B2
Tarvin CW6 122 B1
Willis Rd SK3 240 E2
Willis St WA1 16 B3
Willmer Cres ST7 195 D3
Willotts Hill Rd ST5 210 B1
Willoughby Cl Sale M33 242 A7
Warrington WA5 7 E1
Willow Ave Cheadle SK8 239 F2
Newton-le-W WA12 2 C2
Reddish SK5 240 F8
Widnes WA8 13 D1
Willow Bank SK8 35 D3
Willow Bank Ct M20 239 B8
Willow Bank Est WA12 2 C2
Willow Cl Chester CH2 118 B4
Lymm WA13 18 C2
Newcastle-u-L ST5 210 B1
Poynton SK12 36 C2
Runcorn WA7 49 E4
Winsford CW7 126 B2
Willow Cres Chester CH2 119 D2
Warrington WA1 17 D4
Wistaston CW2 189 F1
Willow Ct Alsager ST7 193 F2
Gatley SK8 239 A6
Higher Kinnerton CH4 161 D4
Macclesfield SK10 87 D1
Middlewich CW10 128 B1
Sale M33 242 E7
Willow Dr Blacon CH1 117 E3
Bunbury CW6 185 F4
Sandbach CW11 175 F4
Warrington WA4 16 C1
Wilmslow SK9 34 B2
Willow Gn Knutsford WA16 56 C2
Weaverham CW8 102 B4
Willow Gr Barnton CW8 78 A2
Chester CH2 119 D2
Ellesmere Port CH1 95 D4
Elton CH2 72 A2
Willow Hayes CH3 121 F4
Willow La Appleton WA4 26 B2
Goostrey CW4 107 F1
Thornton Hough L63 42 B2
Willow Lea CH1 94 C1
Willow Mews SK10 86 C1
Willow Rd Chester CH4 140 C3
Haydock WA11 1 C4
High Lane SK6 37 F4
Newton-le-W WA12 2 C2
Partington M31 11 F1
Willow Sq CW7 127 D1
Willow St CW12 156 C2
Willow Tree Gn ST7 193 F4
Willow Tree Mews SK8 239 B1
Willow Tree Rd WA14 238 D3
Willow Way Broughton CH4 139 D2
Cheadle Hulme SK7 35 E4
Prestbury SK10 87 D3
Willow Wood Cl OL6 242 B3
Willoway Rd CH3 119 D1
Willowbank Dr SK10 88 B4
Willowbrow Rd L63, L64 42 B2
Willowdale Ave SK8 239 B2
Willowdale Way CH1 94 C4
Willowgreen La CW8 77 D3
Willowherb Cl CH3 142 A3
Willowmead Dr SK10 87 D3
Willows Cl CW2 206 A4
Willows The Frodsham WA6 74 B4
Higher Wincham CW9 79 F3
Manchester SK4 240 A7
Partington M31 11 F2
Wilmere La WA8 13 D3
Wilmot Ave WA5 14 B4
Wilmot Dr WA3 2 C4
Wilmslow Ave L66 69 F3
Wilmslow Cres WA4 17 F2
Wilmslow Cty High Sch
SK9 60 A3
Wilmslow Dr L66 69 F3
Wilmslow Golf Course
WA16 59 D1
Wilmslow Grange Cty Prim
Sch SK9 34 B2
Wilmslow Old Rd
Mottram St Andrew SK10 61 D1
Wythenshawe M90 32 C3
Wilmslow Park Rd SK9 60 B4
Wilmslow Prep Sch SK9 60 A4
Wilmslow Rd
Alderley Edge SK9 60 A2
Cheadle SK8 239 D3
Cheadle SK8 239 D5
Cheadle, Handforth SK9 34 B3
Mottram St Andrew SK10 61 D2
Mottram St Andrew SK10 61 E3
Mottram St Andrew, Greendale
SK10 86 A4
Prestbury SK10 61 E3
Wilmslow SK9 34 B3
Woodford SK7 35 E1
Wythenshawe WA15 32 C3
Wilmslow Sta SK9 60 A4
Wilmslow Wlk 21 SK11 112 C4
Wilsden Rd WA8 12 A1
Wilson Cl WA4 17 E2
Wilson Cres
Ashton-u-L OL6 242 B4
Lostock CW9 80 A2
Wilson Dr CW9 126 C4
Wilson Patten St WA1 16 A2
Wilson Rd SK4 240 B8
Wilson St Hyde SK14 241 E6
Sale M33 242 B7
Warrington WA2 16 A4
Wilsons La L65 70 A2
Wilton Ave SK8 34 B4
Wilton Cres
Alderley Edge SK9 59 F1
Macclesfield SK11 111 F3
Wilton Dr WA15 32 B4
Wilton La WA3 4 A3
Wiltshire Cl
Macclesfield SK10 86 C1
Warrington WA1 17 E4
Wiltshire Dr CW12 156 C2
Wiltshire Rd M31 11 F1
Wiltshire Wlk SK10 86 C1
Wilwick La SK11 111 F4
Wimberry Dr ST5 210 B1
Wimbledon Dr SK3 240 C3
Wimboldsley Cty Prim Sch
CW10 150 C2
Wincham Ave CW9 79 E2
Wincham Bsns Pk CW9 79 E2
Wincham Cty Prim Sch
CW9 79 F3
Wincham La CW9 79 E2
Winchester Ave
Ellesmere Port L65 70 B2
Great Sankey WA5 15 E3
Winchester Cl
Shavington CW2 206 A2
Wilmslow SK9 59 F3
Winchester Ct 7 SK10 112 C4
Winchester Dr SK4 240 B6
Winchester Pl WA8 22 B4
Winchester Sq CH4 140 C3
Wincle Ave SK12 36 C1
Wincle CE Aided Prim Sch
SK11 136 C1
Wincroft Cl WA8 22 B4
Wincroft Rd WA8 22 B4
Windemere Ave CH2 119 D3
Windemere Dr CW12 156 A1
Windermere Ave
Warrington WA2 8 B2
Widnes WA8 13 D2
Windermere Cl L64 66 C4
Windermere Dr SK9 59 F1
Windermere Rd
Ellesmere Port L65 70 B1
Haydock WA11 1 A3
High Lane SK6 37 F4
Stalybridge SK15 242 D4
Wilmslow SK9 34 B2
Winsford CW7 126 B1
Wistaston CW2 189 F1
Windermere St WA8 13 D2
Windfield Gdns L66 69 E4
Windings The CW10 128 A1
Windle Ct Neston L64 41 F1
Warrington WA3 9 E2
Windlehurst Rd SK6 37 E4
Windmill Cl Appleton WA4 26 B3
Buerton CW3 230 C2
Windmill Dr CW3 229 F2
Windmill Hill Ave WA7 24 B1
Windmill Hill Ave E WA7 24 B1
Windmill Hill Ave N WA7 24 B2
Windmill Hill Ave S WA7 24 B1
Windmill Hill Ave W WA7 24 B1
Windmill Hill Cty Prim Sch
WA7 24 B1
Windmill La
Appleton WA4 26 B3
Bollington SK10 88 A3
Buerton CW3 230 C2
Christleton CH3 142 B4
Penketh WA5 14 C3
Preston on the Hill WA4 51 D3
Windmill Rd M33 242 F5
Windmill Rise CH2 118 B4
Windmill St
Macclesfield SK11 112 C3
Runcorn WA7 23 D1
Windscale Rd WA2 9 D1
Windsor Ave Crewe CW1 190 A3
Gatley M22 239 A5
Manchester SK4 240 A7
Nantwich CW5 204 C2
Newton-le-W WA12 2 B1
Sale M33 242 B8
Tarporley CW6 146 B1
Wilmslow SK9 59 F4
Windsor Cl Bollington SK10 87 F3
Cuddington CW8 101 F2
Poynton SK12 36 B2
Windsor Dr Alsager ST7 192 C2
Altrincham WA14 238 F8
Broughton CH4 139 D2
Ellesmere Port L65 70 A2
Faddiley CW5 202 C4
Haydock WA11 2 A4
Helsby WA6 73 D1
Stalybridge SK15 242 D3
Warrington WA4 17 D2
Winsford CW7 149 E3
Windsor Gr Cheadle SK8 34 C4
Romiley SK6 241 E2
Runcorn WA7 49 D4
Windsor Pl CW12 156 C1
Windsor Rd Chester CH4 140 C3
Goldborne WA3 3 E4
Widnes WA8 13 D2
Wistaston CW2 205 F4
Windsor Sq SK11 112 B2
Windsor St WA5 15 F3
Windsor Way WA16 56 C1
Windsor Wlk SK2 240 F2
Windways L66 69 E4
Windy Bank Ave WA3 3 F4
Winfield St SK14 241 F6
Winfield Way WA8 23 D4
Winfrith Rd WA2 9 D1
Wingate Rd
Bebington L62 43 F3
Manchester SK4 240 C8
Wingfield Ave SK9 59 F3
Wingfield Dr SK9 59 F3
Wingfield Pl CW7 149 D3
Winghay Rd ST7 195 E2
Winifred St WA2 16 B4
Winkwell Dr CH4 141 D3
Winmarith Dr WA15 32 B4
Winmarleigh St WA1 16 A2
Winnington Ave CW8 103 E4
Winnington Park Cty Prim
Sch CW8 103 E4
Winnington St
Northwich CW8 78 B1
Winsford CW7 126 C1
Winnows The WA7 23 E1
Winnwick Psychiatric Hospl
WA2 8 A3
Winscombe Dr CH3 119 E1
Winsfield Rd SK7 36 C4
Winsford Cl WA11 1 C4
Winsford Darnhall Cty
Prim Sch CW7 149 E3
Winsford Dr WA5 6 C4
Winsford Gr L66 69 E2
Winsford Grange Cty Prim
Sch CW7 126 A1
Winsford Greenfields Cty
Prim Sch CW7 126 A1
Winsford Handley Hill Cty
Prim Sch CW7 149 D4
Winsford High Street Cty
Prim Sch CW7 126 B1
Winsford Ind Est CW7 127 E2
Winsford Over Hall Cty
Prim Sch CW7 149 D4
Winsford Over St John's
CE Contr Prim Sch CW7 126 A1
Winsford Rd
Cholmondeston CW7 171 D1
Wettenhall CW7 170 C3
Winsford St Chad's CE
Contr Prim Sch CW7 149 F4
Winsford St Joseph's RC
Aided Prim Sch CW7 149 D4
Winsford Sta CW7 127 E1
Winsford Way CH1 117 F1
Winsford Wharton CE
Contr Jun Sch CW7 127 D1
Winsford Wharton Leaf
Lane Cty Inf Sch CW7 127 D1
Winsford Wharton Willow
Wood Cty Inf & Jun Sch
CW7 127 D1
Winsford Woodford Lodge
Cty High Sch CW7 149 D4
Winslow Cl WA7 50 B4
Winstanley Cl WA5 15 E3
Winstanley Ind Est WA2 8 A1
Winstanley Rd Neston L64 66 C3
Sale M33 242 C7
Winston Ave Alsager ST7 193 E3
Newton-le-W WA12 2 B2
St Helens WA9 1 A1
Winston Ct CH2 119 D3
Winter Gr WA9 1 A2
Winter La SY14 198 A2
Winterbottom La WA16 55 F4
Winterford La CW6 147 D1
Wintergreen Wlk M31 11 F1
Winterside Cl ST5 210 B1
Winterton Way SK11 112 B2
Winton Ct WA14 238 C2
Winton Gr WA7 24 B1
Winton Rd
Altrincham WA14 238 C2
Goldborne WA3 3 F3
Winton St SK15 242 E1
Winwick CE Aided Prim Sch
WA2 8 A3
Winwick La Croft WA3 3 F2
Goldborne WA3 3 F2
Winwick Link Rd WA2 8 B3
Winwick Rd
Newton-le-W WA12 2 C1
Warrington WA2 8 A1
Winwick St WA2 16 A3
Winwick View WA5 1 B1
Winwood Rd M20 239 C8
Wirksmoor Rd SK22 39 D4
Wirral Cl WA3 4 C2
Wirral Cres Neston L64 66 C3
Stockport SK3 240 A4
Wirral Ctry Pk Neston L64 67 E4
Willaston L64 67 E4
Wirral Ctry Pk The
Heswall L64 41 D2
Neston L64 41 D2
Wirral Ed Ctr L62 43 E4
Wirswall Rd SY13 226 B4
Wisenholme Cl WA7 49 F3
Wistaston Ave CW2 189 F1
Wistaston Berkeley Cty
Prim Sch CW2 206 A4
Wistaston Cty Jun Sch
CW2 205 F4
Wistaston Green Cl CW2 189 F1
Wistaston Green Cty Inf &
Jun Sch CW2 189 F1
Wistaston Green Rd CW2 189 F1
Wistaston Pk CW2 189 F1
Wistaston Rd Crewe CW2 190 B2
Willaston (nr Nantwich) CW5 205 F3
Wistaston CW5 205 F3
Wistaston Road Bsns Ctr
CW2 190 A2
Wistaston Westfield Cty
Inf Sch CW2 205 F4
Wisterdale Cl CW2 206 A4
Witchcroft Heath Rd
SK11 109 D2
Witham Cl CW2 206 A4
Witham St OL6 242 B4
Witham Way ST6 179 F1
Withens Cl CW8 102 B4
Withens La CW8 102 B4
Withenshaw La SK11 136 C3
Wither's La WA16 28 B3
Withers Ave WA2 16 B4
Within Way L24 47 F4
Withington Ave WA3 5 D2
Withington Cl
Northwich CW9 104 A3
Sandbach CW11 175 E4
Withinlee Rd SK10 86 B3
Withins Rd Culcheth WA3 4 C2
Haydock WA11 1 C4
Withy Cft CH3 142 A4
Withy Cl WA6 74 B4
Withy Tree Gr 1 M34 241 A6
Withycombe Rd WA5 14 C2
Withyfold Dr SK10 87 F1
Witney La SY14 213 E4
Witt Rd WA8 23 D4
Wittenbury Rd SK4 240 B6
Witter Pl CH2 237 F3
Wittering La L60 40 B4
Witterings The L64 41 F1
Witton Church Walk CE
Special Agreement Sch
CW9 104 A4
Witton St CW9 79 D1
Witton Wlk CW9 103 F4
Wivern Pl WA7 23 D2
Woburn Ave WA12 2 B1
Woburn Cl Haydock WA11 1 C4
Macclesfield SK10 87 E1
Woburn Ct SK12 36 C2
Woburn Dr Chester CH2 118 B4
Cronton WA8 12 B3
Woburn Rd WA2 8 A2
Woking Rd SK8 35 D4
Wolfe Cl WA16 57 E2
Wolseley Rd M33 242 C8
Wolsey Dr WA14 238 A1
Wolstanholme Cl CW12 156 C1
Wolverham Cty Prim Sch
L65 70 B2
Wolverham Rd L65 70 B2
Wolverton Dr Runcorn WA7 24 B1
Wilmslow SK9 34 B1
Wolvesey Pl CW7 149 D3
Wood Croft CH3 119 F2
Wood End La L64 67 F2
Wood Hey Gr 2 M34 241 A6
Wood La Appleton WA4 26 C4
Bradwall Green
CW10, CW11 152 C2
Broughton CH4 139 D2
Burton L64 67 E1
Duddon CW6 145 F4
Goostrey CW4 107 E1
Mobberley WA16 58 B4
Neston L64 66 B4
Partington M31 11 E1
Runcorn WA7 49 F2
Runcorn, Brookvale WA7 50 B3
Tattenhall CH3 167 D1
Utkinton CW6 146 A3
Weaverham CW8 102 C4
Willaston L64 43 D1
Wood La E SK10 63 D4
Wood La N SK10 63 D4
Wood La S SK10 63 D4
Wood La W SK10 63 D4
Wood Lane Prim Sch ST7 210 A1
Wood Memorial Sch CH4 140 C3
Wood Orchard La CW3 230 A1
Wood St Altrincham WA14 238 D4
Audley ST7 209 F2
Cheadle SK8 239 D6
Congleton CW12 156 B2
Crewe CW2 190 B1
Goldborne WA3 3 D4
Hawarden CH5 116 A1
Hyde SK14 241 E6
Macclesfield SK11 112 B4
Mow Cop ST7 195 E4
New Mills SK22 39 D4
Stalybridge SK15 242 C2
Stockport SK3 240 E5
Warrington WA1 16 B3
Widnes WA8 13 E1
Wood View ST7 210 A1
Wood's La CW8 101 E3
Woodacre Gr L66 69 F4
Woodacre Rd L66 69 F4
Woodacres Ct SK9 59 F3
Woodall Cl M33 242 D6
Woodall Dr WA7 23 D1
Woodavens Gr CW3 229 D1
Woodbank Cl CW2 206 A4
Woodbank La CH1 93 F3
Woodbank Rd
Ellesmere Port L65 70 A1
Penketh WA5 15 D2
Woodbine Ave M44 11 E2
Woodbine Cres SK2 240 F3
Woodbine Rd WA13 19 D2
Woodbourne Rd SK22 39 D3
Woodbridge Cl WA4 26 C2
Woodbrook SK23 65 F4

Woodbrook Ave SK14 .... 241 F6
Woodbrook Ct SK23 .... 65 F4
Woodbrook Rd SK9 .... 60 B1
Woodburn Dr L60 .... 40 C3
Woodbury Rd SK3 .... 240 B3
Woodchurch La L66 .... 69 F3
Woodclose L66 .... 44 A1
Woodcock La ST7 .... 195 E3
Woodcocks' Well CE Contr
    Prim Sch ST7 .... 195 E3
Woodcote Ave L65 .... 70 A1
Woodcote Cl WA2 .... 8 B1
Woodcote View SK9 .... 34 C1
Woodcotes The L62 .... 43 E3
Woodcott Ave CW7 .... 126 A1
Woodcott Cl CW2 .... 206 C1
Woodcott Gr 8 SK9 .... 34 C1
Woodcotthill La CW5 .... 217 D2
Woodcroft ST7 .... 210 A1
Woodend Cl CW10 .... 151 E3
Woodend La
    Hollins Green WA3 .... 10 B1
    Hyde SK14 .... 241 D5
    Mobberley WA16 .... 58 C4
Woodend Rd L65 .... 69 F3
Woodfall Cl L64 .... 67 D3
Woodfall Cty Inf & Jun Sch
    L64 .... 67 D3
Woodfall Gr L64 .... 67 D3
Woodfall La L64 .... 67 D3
Woodfield Ave SK6 .... 241 A4
Woodfield Cty Prim Sch
    CH2 .... 119 D3
Woodfield Gr Chester CH2 .. 119 D3
    Sale M33 .... 242 A8
Woodfield Rd
    Altrincham WA14 .... 238 C6
    Cheadle Hulme SK8 .... 35 D4
    Ellesmere Port L65 .... 70 B3
Woodfield Rd N L65 .... 70 B3
Woodfields CH3 .... 142 C4
Woodfin Croft SK11 .... 84 A2
Woodford Ave
    Dukinfield M34 .... 241 A4
    Goldborne WA3 .... 3 E4
Woodford Cl Crewe CW2 .... 189 F1
    Helsby WA6 .... 73 D1
    Runcorn WA7 .... 49 D3
    Warrington WA4 .... 17 E2
Woodford Court Ind Est
    CW7 .... 149 D4
Woodford La Prestbury SK10 . 61 E4
    Winsford CW7 .... 149 D4
Woodford La W CW7 .... 149 D4
Woodford Park Ind Est
    CW7 .... 148 C4
Woodford Rd Bramhall SK7 .. 35 F2
    Poynton SK12 .... 36 A3
    Wilmslow SK9 .... 61 D4
    Woodford SK7 .... 35 F2
Woodforn Ct CW7 .... 149 D4
Woodgate Ave ST7 .... 194 A3
Woodgreen La CW5 .... 171 E3
Woodhall Cl
    Great Sankey WA5 .... 15 D4
    Woodford SK7 .... 35 F2
Woodhall Gr Kidsgrove ST7 . 195 E2
    Reddish SK5 .... 240 F8
Woodham Cl CW8 .... 103 E3
Woodham Gr L64 .... 66 C3
Woodhatch Rd WA7 .... 50 A3
Woodhead Dr WA15 .... 238 F1
Woodhead Rd WA15 .... 238 F1
Woodhey La CW5 .... 202 B3
Woodhouse Cl WA3 .... 9 F2
Woodhouse End Rd SK11 .. 135 D4
Woodhouse La
    Biddulph ST6 .... 179 F1
    Buerton CW3 .... 235 E4
    Dunham Town WA14 .... 20 B2
    Warren SK11 .... 111 F1
    Wythenshawe M90 .... 33 E4
Woodhouse Mid Sch ST8 .. 179 F1
Woodhouse Park Prim Sch
    M22 .... 33 E4
Woodhouse Rd M22 .... 33 E4
Woodland Ave Crewe CW1 . 190 C2
    Lymm WA13 .... 19 D1
    Nantwich CW5 .... 205 D3
    Newton-le-W WA12 .... 2 C2
    Widnes WA8 .... 12 C1
Woodland Bank CH2 .... 96 C1

Woodland Cl SK11 .... 84 A2
Woodland Ct ST7 .... 193 E2
Woodland Dr WA13 .... 19 D1
Woodland End SK11 .... 84 A2
Woodland Gdns CW1 .... 190 B3
Woodland Rd
    Ellesmere Port L65 .... 70 A1
    Rode Heath ST7 .... 193 F4
Woodland Wlk Bebington L62 43 E4
    Runcorn WA7 .... 24 A1
Woodlands Ave
    Chester CH1 .... 118 A2
    Congleton CW12 .... 156 B2
    Kidsgrove ST7 .... 194 B1
Woodlands Cl Neston L64 .... 66 B4
    Utkinton CW6 .... 147 D4
Woodlands Cres WA16 .... 29 C2
Woodlands Ct WA15 .... 238 E5
Woodlands Cty Inf & Jun
    Sch L66 .... 69 F1
Woodlands Dr Chester CH2 . 118 C2
    Goostrey CW4 .... 107 F1
    Knutsford WA16 .... 57 D1
    Warrington WA4 .... 17 F2
Woodlands Gr CW8 .... 77 F2
Woodlands Ind Est WA12 ...... 2 B3
Woodlands Inf Sch M31 ...... 11 E2
Woodlands La
    Altrincham WA15 .... 238 E5
    Chester CH3 .... 119 D1
Woodlands Parkway
    WA15 .... 238 E6
Woodlands Rd
    Altrincham WA14 & WA15 . 238 E5
    Disley SK12 .... 38 A3
    Hartford CW8 .... 103 D3
    Huntington SK11 .... 142 A3
    Macclesfield SK11 .... 112 B3
    Neston L64 .... 66 B4
    New Mills SK22 .... 39 D4
    Sale M33 .... 242 C6
    Wilmslow SK9 .... 33 F1
    Wilmslow, Handforth SK9 .. 34 C2
Woodlands Rd E CW8 .... 103 E3
Woodlands The
    Higher Wincham CW9 .... 80 A3
    Northwich CW8 .... 78 C1
Woodlands Way CW6 .... 146 B1
Woodlark Cl CW7 .... 150 A4
Woodlea Ave CH2 .... 118 B4
Woodlea Cl L62 .... 43 E3
Woodlea Ct WA4 .... 103 E4
Woodlea Dr SK10 .... 87 F4
Woodley Fold WA5 .... 14 C2
Woodman St 2 SK1 .... 240 E6
Woodmount Cl SK6 .... 241 F2
Woodnoth Dr CW2 .... 206 B3
Woodpecker Cl WA3 .... 9 F2
Woodpecker Dr CW9 .... 103 F2
Woodridge WA7 .... 24 B1
Woodridings WA14 .... 238 B3
Woodrow Way M44 .... 11 F4
Woodruff Cl ST7 .... 195 F1
Woodruff Wlk M31 .... 11 F1
Woods Gr SK8 .... 35 D4
Woods La SK8 .... 35 D4
Woods Rd M44 .... 11 F4
Woods The WA14 .... 238 E6
Woodsfin La CH3 .... 183 F4
Woodshutt's St ST7 .... 194 C1
Woodside
    Ellesmere Port L65 .... 70 B1
    Knutsford WA16 .... 57 D1
    Lawton-gate ST7 .... 194 C2
    Siddington SK11 .... 110 A2
Woodside Ave Alsager ST7 . 193 F2
    Frodsham WA6 .... 74 B4
    Kidsgrove ST7 .... 195 D1
    Wistaston CW2 .... 189 F1
Woodside Ct CH2 .... 118 B2
Woodside Cty Jun Sch WA7 49 E4
Woodside Dr High Lane SK6 . 37 F4
    Hyde SK14 .... 241 E5
    Sandbach CW11 .... 175 E3
Woodside La Poynton SK12 . 36 C2
    Wistaston CW2 .... 189 F1
Woodside Rd Blacon CH1 ... 117 E3
    Great Sankey WA5 .... 14 B4
    Haydock WA11 .... 1 C4
    Lymm WA13 .... 19 D1
Woodside St SK22 .... 39 D3
Woodside Terr CW9 .... 104 A2
Woodslands Rd CH4 .... 141 D4

Woodsome Cl L65 .... 70 A1
Woodsome Dr L65 .... 70 A1
Woodstock Ave
    Cheadle Hulme SK8 .... 35 D4
    Newton-le-W WA12 .... 2 B1
Woodstock Cl SK10 .... 87 D1
Woodstock Dr CW10 .... 151 F3
Woodstock Gr WA8 .... 12 B1
Woodstock Rd WA14 .... 238 C8
Woodvale WA14 .... 238 C2
Woodvale Cl WA2 .... 8 C1
Woodvale Rd
    Ellesmere Port L66 .... 69 E3
    Knutsford WA16 .... 82 A4
Woodview Rd WA8 .... 22 A4
Woodville Dr M33 .... 242 A7
Woodville Pl WA8 .... 12 B1
Woodville Rd
    Altrincham WA14 .... 238 C3
    Sale M33 .... 242 A7
Woodward St CW8 .... 77 E1
Woodward Wlk CH3 .... 121 E2
Woolacombe Cl WA4 .... 16 B1
Woolaston Dr ST7 .... 193 E2
Woolden Rd M44 .... 11 D4
Woollam Dr L66 .... 69 E4
Woolley Ave SK12 .... 36 B1
Woolley Cl WA6 .... 49 E1
Woolmer Cl WA3 .... 10 A3
Woolston Ave CW12 .... 157 D1
Woolston CE Aided Prim
    Sch WA1 .... 17 E4
Woolston Cty High Sch
    WA1 .... 17 D4
Woolston Cty Prim Sch
    WA1 .... 17 E4
Woore Cty Prim Sch CW3 .. 232 A1
Woolston Dr CW2 .... 206 C1
Woolston Grange Ave WA1 .... 9 E1
Woolston Rd WA11 .... 1 B4
Woolton Ct L66 .... 69 F4
Woore Rd Audlem CW3 ...... 230 B2
    Buerton CW3 .... 230 B2
Wootton St SK14 .... 241 D8
Worcester Ave
    Denton M34 .... 241 A5
    Goldborne WA3 .... 3 D4
Worcester Cl
    Great Sankey WA5 .... 15 E3
    Kidsgrove ST7 .... 210 B4
    Romiley SK6 .... 241 A1
Worcester Pl CH1 .... 118 A2
Worcester St L65 .... 70 B3
Worcester Wlk L65 .... 70 B3
Wordsworth Ave
    Warrington WA4 .... 16 A1
    Widnes WA8 .... 22 C4
Wordsworth Cl
    8 Sandbach CW11 .... 174 B3
    Wistaston CW2 .... 189 F1
Wordsworth Cres CH1 .... 118 A3
Wordsworth Dr CW1 .... 190 C2
Wordsworth Mews CH1 ..... 118 A3
Wordsworth Sq CH1 .... 118 A3
Wordsworth Way
    Alsager ST7 .... 193 E2
    Ellesmere Port L66 .... 69 F1
Works La CW9 .... 79 F1
World Way M90 .... 33 D4
Worleston CE Contr Prim
    Sch CW5 .... 188 C3
Worleston Cl CW10 .... 151 E3
Worrall St Congleton CW12 . 156 C2
    Stockport SK3 .... 240 E3
Worsborough Ave WA5 .... 15 D3
Worsley Ave Saughall CH1 . 117 D4
    Warrington WA4 .... 16 C2
Worsley Dr CW12 .... 157 D1
Worsley Rd WA4 .... 16 A1
Worsley St Goldborne WA3 .... 3 D4
    Warrington WA5 .... 15 F4
Worth Cty Prim Sch SK12 .. 36 C1
Worthing St CW9 .... 104 B4
Worthington Ave M31 .... 11 F2
Worthington Cl
    Henbury SK11 .... 111 E4
    Nantwich CW5 .... 205 D3
    Runcorn WA7 .... 50 A4
Worthington Prim Sch
    M33 .... 242 F6
Worthington Rd
    Denton M34 .... 241 B5
    Sale M33 .... 242 F6

Worthington St SK15 .... 242 C1
Wrekin Way CH4 .... 140 C1
Wren Ave CW4 .... 129 E1
Wren Cl Crewe CW1 .... 189 F6
    Macclesfield SK10 .... 87 D1
    Runcorn WA7 .... 50 A3
    Warrington WA3 .... 9 F2
Wrenburry Cl ST5 .... 210 B1
Wrenbury Cres SK3 .... 240 C2
Wrenbury Cty Prim Sch
    CW5 .... 216 C2
Wrenbury Dr SK8 .... 239 E6
Wrenbury Hall Dr CW5 ..... 217 D3
Wrenbury Heath Rd CW5 .. 217 E3
Wrenbury Ind Est CW5 ...... 217 D2
Wrenbury Rd CW5 .... 217 D2
Wrenbury Sta CW5 .... 217 D2
Wrenmere Cl CW11 .... 174 C4
Wrenshot La WA16 .... 29 E3
Wrexham Cl Biddulph ST6 . 179 E1
    Warrington WA5 .... 7 F1
Wrexham Ind Est (Ystad
    Ddiwdiannol Wrecsam)
    LL13 .... 196 A1
Wrexham Rd Bickerton SY14 200 A4
    Bulkeley SY14 .... 184 C1
    Burland CW5 .... 203 E4
    Chester CH4 .... 141 D2
    Dodleston CH4 .... 141 D2
    Eccleston CH4 .... 162 C3
    Faddiley CW5 .... 202 B3
    Holt LL13 .... 196 A4
    Malpas SY14 .... 212 C1
    Pulford CH4 .... 162 C3
    Ridley CW6 .... 185 E1
Wright Ave CW9 .... 104 B3
Wright Cres WA8 .... 23 D3
Wright St Altrincham WA14 238 D7
    Ashton-u-L OL6 .... 242 A4
    Kidsgrove ST7 .... 194 B1
Wright Tree Villas M44 .... 11 E3
Wright's La Burtonwood WA5 .. 6 C2
    Sandbach CW11 .... 175 E3
Wrights La WA5 .... 14 A1
Wrigley La SK10 .... 86 A2
Wrigley Rd WA11 .... 1 C1
Wrinehill Rd
    Blakenhall CW5 .... 220 C4
    Wybunbury CW5 .... 220 C4
Wroxham Cl Chester CH2 .. 237 E4
    Helsby WA6 .... 73 D2
Wroxham Rd WA5 .... 14 B4
Wrynose Rd L62 .... 43 F4
Wt Bear Yd WA16 .... 57 D1
Wyatt St SK4 .... 240 E6
Wybersley Rd SK6 .... 38 C4
Wybunbury Delves CE
    Aided Prim Sch CW5 ..... 220 A4
Wybunbury
    Haymoor Green CW5 .... 205 F3
    Wybunbury CW5 .... 220 A4
Wybunbury Rd CW5 .... 205 E3
Wych House La CW10 .... 128 B1
Wych La SK10 .... 62 B3
Wyche Ave CW5 .... 204 B3
Wyche Cl CW9 .... 104 C3
Wyche Cty Prim Sch CW5 . 204 C3
Wyche La CW6 .... 185 E4
Wyche Rd CW6 .... 185 E4
Wychelm Rd M31 .... 11 F2
Wychwood WA14 .... 238 B1
Wychwood Ave WA13 .... 18 B2
Wycliffe Ave SK9 .... 60 A4
Wycliffe Rd
    Ellesmere Port L65 .... 69 F2
    Haydock WA11 .... 1 C4
Wycliffe St SK4 .... 240 D6
Wyedale L65 .... 70 A2
Wyedale Rd WA11 .... 1 B3
Wyncroft Cl L65 .... 70 A2
Wynd The CW6 .... 122 B2
Wyndham Cl SK7 .... 35 F4
Wyndham Cres L66 .... 69 F1
Wyndham Rd CH1 .... 117 E2
Wynfield Ave M22 .... 33 F4
Wyngate Rd
    Altrincham WA15 .... 31 F4
    Cheadle SK8 .... 239 F1
Wynnstay Rd
    Broughton CH4 .... 139 E2
    Sale M33 .... 242 B7
Wynter Cl SY14 .... 198 A2
Wythburn Gr WA7 .... 49 F3

Wythens Rd SK8 .... 34 A4
Wythenshawe Rd M33 ...... 242 F6

Yagol Gynradd Holt Cty
    Prim Sch LL13 .... 196 B4
Yardley Ave WA5 .... 15 F4
Yarmouth Rd WA5 .... 14 C3
Yarrow Cl CH4 .... 139 E2
Yarwood St WA14 .... 238 D3
Yarwoodheath La WA14 ...... 30 C4
Yatehouse La
    Lach Dennis CW10 .... 128 B4
    Middlewich CW10 .... 128 B4
Yates Cl WA5 .... 15 E3
Yates Rd New Mills SK22 .... 39 E4
    Thornton-le-M CH2 .... 71 F1
Yates St CW2 .... 190 B1
Yealand Ave SK4 .... 240 D7
Yeald Brow WA13 .... 18 A2
Yeardsley Ave SK23 .... 39 E2
Yeardsley Gn SK23 .... 65 E4
Yeardsley La SK23 .... 39 E2
Yeld La CW6 .... 122 C4
Yeoford Dr WA14 .... 238 B6
Yeoman Way L66 .... 69 F1
Yeovil Cl WA1 .... 17 E4
Yerburgh St CH2 .... 118 B2
Yew St SK4 .... 240 C5
Yew Tree Ave WA12 .... 2 A2
Yew Tree Bank CW6 .... 145 D3
Yew Tree Cl Broughton CH4 139 E2
    Bulkeley SY14 .... 184 B1
    Little Budworth CW6 .... 147 F4
    Macclesfield SK11 .... 112 A3
    Middlewich CW10 .... 128 A1
    Prestbury SK10 .... 87 D4
    Thornton-le-M CH2 .... 71 F1
    Wilmslow SK9 .... 60 B4
Yew Tree Ct ST7 .... 193 F1
Yew Tree Dr Barnton CW8 .. 78 A2
    Nantwich CW5 .... 204 B3
    Sale M33 .... 242 E6
Yew Tree Gr SK8 .... 239 A3
Yew Tree La Appleton WA4 . 27 E3
    Astbury CW12 .... 178 B2
Yew Tree Park Rd SK8 .... 35 D3
Yew Tree Rd Adlington SK10 . 37 E1
    Wistaston CW2 .... 206 A4
Yew Tree Way SK10 .... 87 E3
Yew Wlk M31 .... 11 E1
Yewdale Dr L66 .... 69 F1
Yewlands CW8 .... 101 E3
Yewlands Dr WA16 .... 57 E1
Yewtree Cl L64 .... 66 C4
Yewtree La SK12 .... 36 C2
Yewtree Rd WA16 .... 80 C2
York Ave Culcheth WA3 .... 4 C1
    Great Sankey WA5 .... 14 C4
    Sale M33 .... 242 B7
York Cl Biddulph ST6 .... 179 E1
    Cheadle SK8 .... 240 A1
York Cres SK9 .... 60 B4
York Ct 10 SK10 .... 112 C4
York Dr Altrincham WA14 .. 238 D1
    Mickle Trafford CH2 .... 96 C1
    Warrington WA4 .... 17 D1
    Winsford CW7 .... 149 E3
    Wythenshawe WA15 .... 32 C4
York Pl WA7 .... 23 D1
York Rd Altrincham WA14 .. 238 C1
    Connah's Quay CH5 .... 91 E1
    Ellesmere Port L65 .... 70 B3
    Sale M33 .... 242 A7
    Warrington WA4 .... 17 D1
    Widnes WA8 .... 22 B4
York St Altrincham WA15 .. 238 E3
    Chester CH1 .... 237 E3
    Macclesfield SK10 .... 112 C4
    Stockport SK3 .... 240 E4
    Warrington WA16 .... 16 B2
Yorkshire Rd M31 .... 11 F1
Yule St SK3 .... 240 D4

Zan Dr CW11 .... 175 D2
Zan Ind Pk CW11 .... 175 D2
Zinnia Dr M44 .... 11 F4
Zion St CW8 .... 103 F4

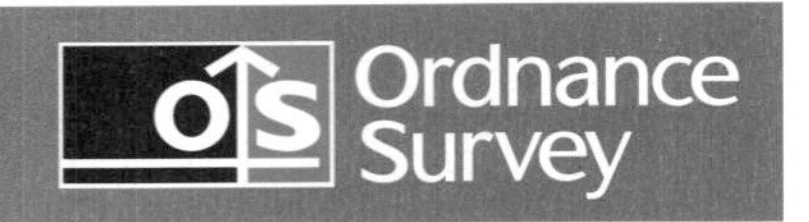

STREET ATLASES ORDER FORM

All Street Atlases contain Ordnance Survey mapping and provide the perfect solution for the driver who needs comprehensive, detailed regional mapping in a choice of compact and easy-to-use formats. They are indispensable and are ideal for use in the car, the home or the office.

The series is available from all good bookshops or by mail order direct from the publisher. Before placing your order, please check by telephone that the complete range of titles are available. Payment can be made in the following ways:

By phone Phone your order through on our special Credit Card Hotline on 01933 443863 (Fax: 01933 443849). Speak to our customer service team during office hours (9am to 5pm) or leave a message on the answering machine, quoting your full credit card number plus expiry date and your full name and address.

By post Simply fill out the order form (you may photocopy it) and send it to: **Philip's Direct, 27 Sanders Road, Wellingborough, Northants** NN8 4NL.

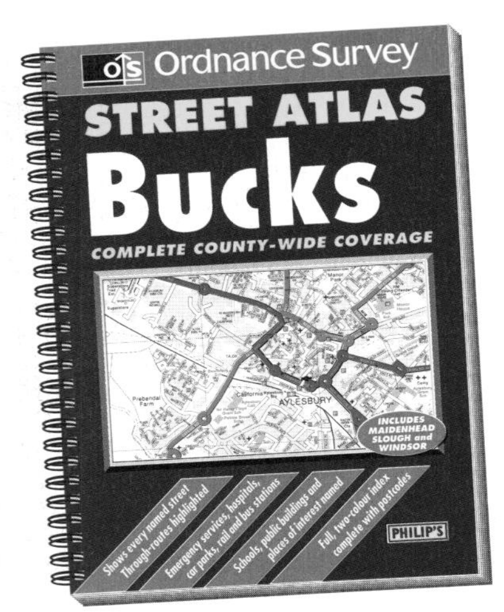

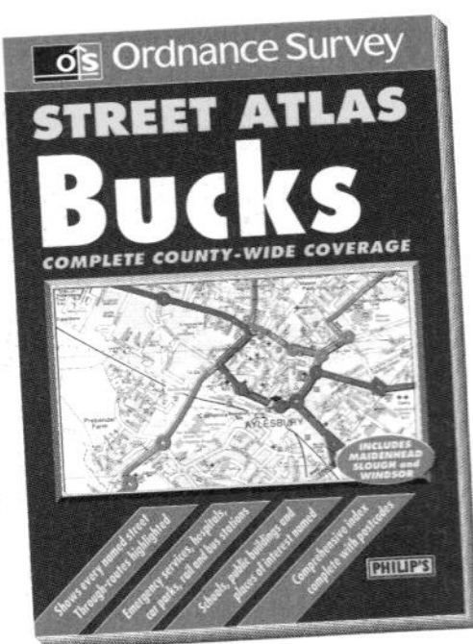

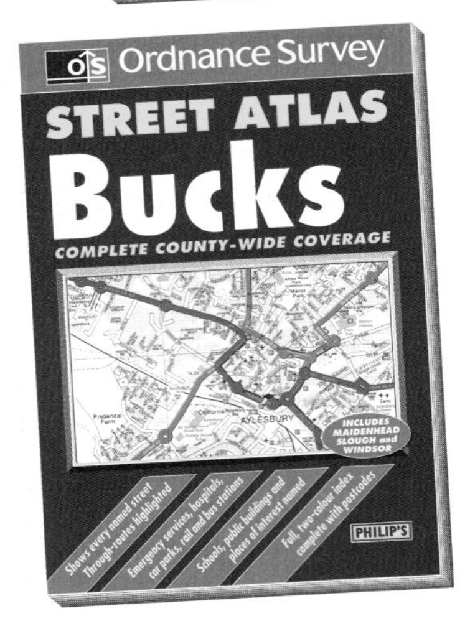

COLOUR EDITIONS

	HARDBACK	SPIRAL	POCKET	£ Total
	Quantity @ £10.99 each	Quantity @ £8.99 each	Quantity @ £4.99 each	£ Total
BERKSHIRE	☐ 0 540 06170 0	☐ 0 540 06172 7	☐ 0 540 06173 5	➤ ☐
MERSEYSIDE	☐ 0 540 06480 7	☐ 0 540 06481 5	☐ 0 540 06482 3	➤ ☐
	Quantity @ £12.99 each	Quantity @ £8.99 each	Quantity @ £4.99 each	£ Total
SURREY	☐ 0 540 06435 1	☐ 0 540 06436 X	☐ 0 540 06438 6	➤ ☐
	Quantity @ £12.99 each	Quantity @ £9.99 each	Quantity @ £4.99 each	£ Total
BUCKINGHAMSHIRE	☐ 0 540 07466 7	☐ 0 540 07467 5	☐ 0 540 07468 3	➤ ☐
DURHAM	☐ 0 540 06365 7	☐ 0 540 06366 5	☐ 0 540 06367 3	➤ ☐
HERTFORDSHIRE	☐ 0 540 06174 3	☐ 0 540 06175 1	☐ 0 540 06176 X	➤ ☐
EAST KENT	☐ 0 540 07483 7	☐ 0 540 07276 1	☐ 0 540 07287 7	➤ ☐
WEST KENT	☐ 0 540 07366 0	☐ 0 540 07367 9	☐ 0 540 07369 5	➤ ☐
EAST SUSSEX	☐ 0 540 07306 7	☐ 0 540 07307 5	☐ 0 540 07312 1	➤ ☐
WEST SUSSEX	☐ 0 540 07319 9	☐ 0 540 07323 7	☐ 0 540 07327 X	➤ ☐
TYNE AND WEAR	☐ 0 540 06370 3	☐ 0 540 06371 1	☐ 0 540 06372 X	➤ ☐
SOUTH YORKSHIRE	☐ 0 540 06330 4	☐ 0 540 06331 2	☐ 0 540 06332 0	➤ ☐
	Quantity @ £12.99 each	Quantity @ £9.99 each	Quantity @ £5.50 each	£ Total
GREATER MANCHESTER	☐ 0 540 06485 8	☐ 0 540 06486 6	☐ 0 540 06487 4	➤ ☐
	Quantity @ £12.99 each	Quantity @ £9.99 each	Quantity @ £5.99 each	£ Total
CHESHIRE	☐ 0 540 07507 8	☐ 0 540 07508 6	☐ 0 540 07509 4	➤ ☐
NORTH HAMPSHIRE	☐ 0 540 07471 3	☐ 0 540 07472 1	☐ 0 540 07473 X	➤ ☐

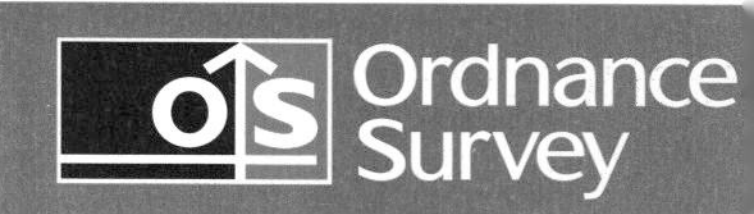
Ordnance Survey

STREET ATLASES ORDER FORM

COLOUR EDITIONS

	HARDBACK	SPIRAL	POCKET	£ Total
	Quantity @ £12.99 each	Quantity @ £9.99 each	Quantity @ £5.99 each	
SOUTH HAMPSHIRE	☐ 0 540 07476 4	☐ 0 540 07477 2	☐ 0 540 07478 0	➤ ☐
OXFORDSHIRE	☐ 0 540 07512 4	☐ 0 540 07513 2	☐ 0 540 07514 0	➤ ☐
WEST YORKSHIRE	☐ 0 540 06329 0	☐ 0 540 06327 4	☐ 0 540 06328 2	➤ ☐
	Quantity @ £14.99 each	Quantity @ £9.99 each	Quantity @ £5.99 each	£ Total
LANCASHIRE	☐ 0 540 06440 8	☐ 0 540 06441 6	☐ 0 540 06443 2	➤ ☐

BLACK AND WHITE EDITIONS

	HARDBACK	SOFTBACK	POCKET	£ Total
	Quantity @ £10.99 each			
WARWICKSHIRE	☐ 0 540 05642 1	—	—	➤ ☐
	Quantity @ £12.99 each	Quantity @ £9.99 each	Quantity @ £4.99 each	Total
BRISTOL AND AVON	☐ 0 540 06140 9	☐ 0 540 06141 7	☐ 0 540 06142 5	➤ ☐
CARDIFF, SWANSEA & GLAMORGAN	☐ 0 540 06186 7	☐ 0 540 06187 5	☐ 0 540 06207 3	➤ ☐
DERBYSHIRE	—	☐ 0 540 06138 7	☐ 0 540 06139 5	➤ ☐
EDINBURGH & East Central Scotland	☐ 0 540 06180 8	☐ 0 540 06181 6	☐ 0 540 06182 4	➤ ☐
EAST ESSEX	☐ 0 540 05848 3	☐ 0 540 05866 1	☐ 0 540 05850 5	➤ ☐
WEST ESSEX	☐ 0 540 05849 1	☐ 0 540 05867 X	☐ 0 540 05851 3	➤ ☐
NOTTINGHAMSHIRE	—	☐ 0 540 05859 9	☐ 0 540 05860 2	➤ ☐
STAFFORDSHIRE	☐ 0 540 06134 4	☐ 0 540 06135 2	☐ 0 540 06136 0	➤ ☐
	Quantity @ £12.99 each	Quantity @ £9.99 each	Quantity @ £5.99 each	£ Total
GLASGOW & West Central Scotland	☐ 0 540 06183 2	☐ 0 540 06184 0	☐ 0 540 06185 9	➤ ☐

Post to: **Philip's Direct,**
27 Sanders Road,
Wellingborough, Northants,
NN8 4NL

◆ Free postage and packing

◆ All available titles will normally be dispatched within 5 working days of receipt of order but please allow up to 28 days for delivery

◆ Please tick this box if you do not wish your name to be used by other carefully selected organisations that may wish to send you information about other products and services

Registered Office: 25 Victoria Street, London SW1H 0EX.

Registered in England number: 3396524

I enclose a cheque / postal order, for a **total** of ☐

made payable to *Reed Book Services,* or please debit my

☐ Access ☐ American Express ☐ Visa ☐ Diners

account by ☐

Account no
☐☐☐☐ ☐☐☐☐ ☐☐☐☐ ☐☐☐☐

Expiry date ☐☐ ☐☐

Signature...

Name...

Address...

....

....

....POSTCODE

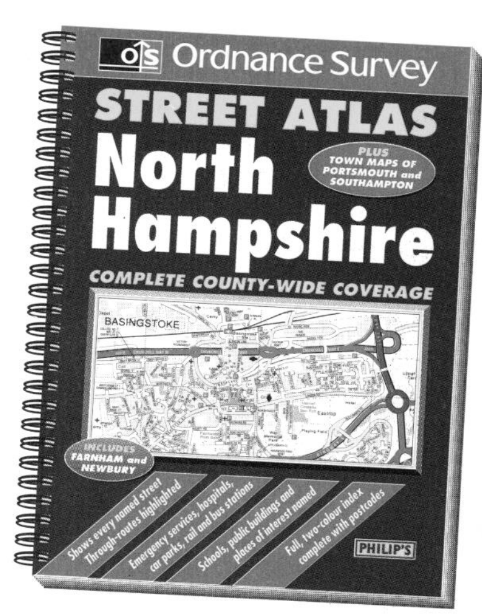
Ordnance Survey
STREET ATLAS
North Hampshire
PLUS TOWN MAPS OF PORTSMOUTH and SOUTHAMPTON
COMPLETE COUNTY-WIDE COVERAGE
INCLUDES FARNHAM and NEWBURY
PHILIP'S

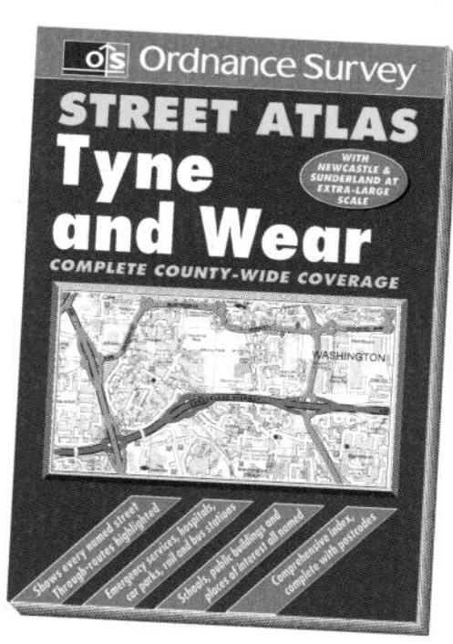
Ordnance Survey
STREET ATLAS
Tyne and Wear
WITH NEWCASTLE & SUNDERLAND AT EXTRA-LARGE SCALE
COMPLETE COUNTY-WIDE COVERAGE

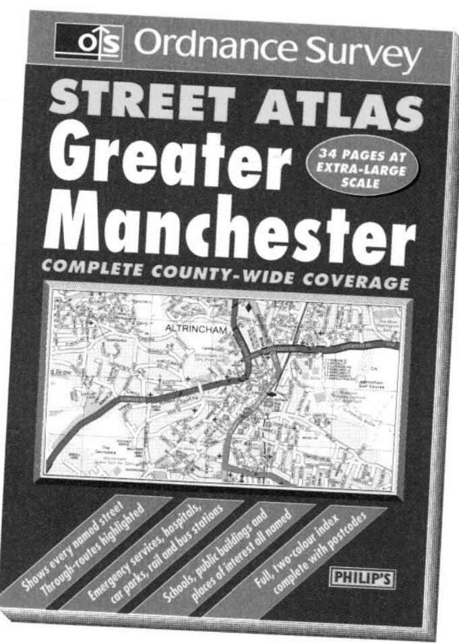
Ordnance Survey
STREET ATLAS
Greater Manchester
34 PAGES AT EXTRA-LARGE SCALE
COMPLETE COUNTY-WIDE COVERAGE
PHILIP'S

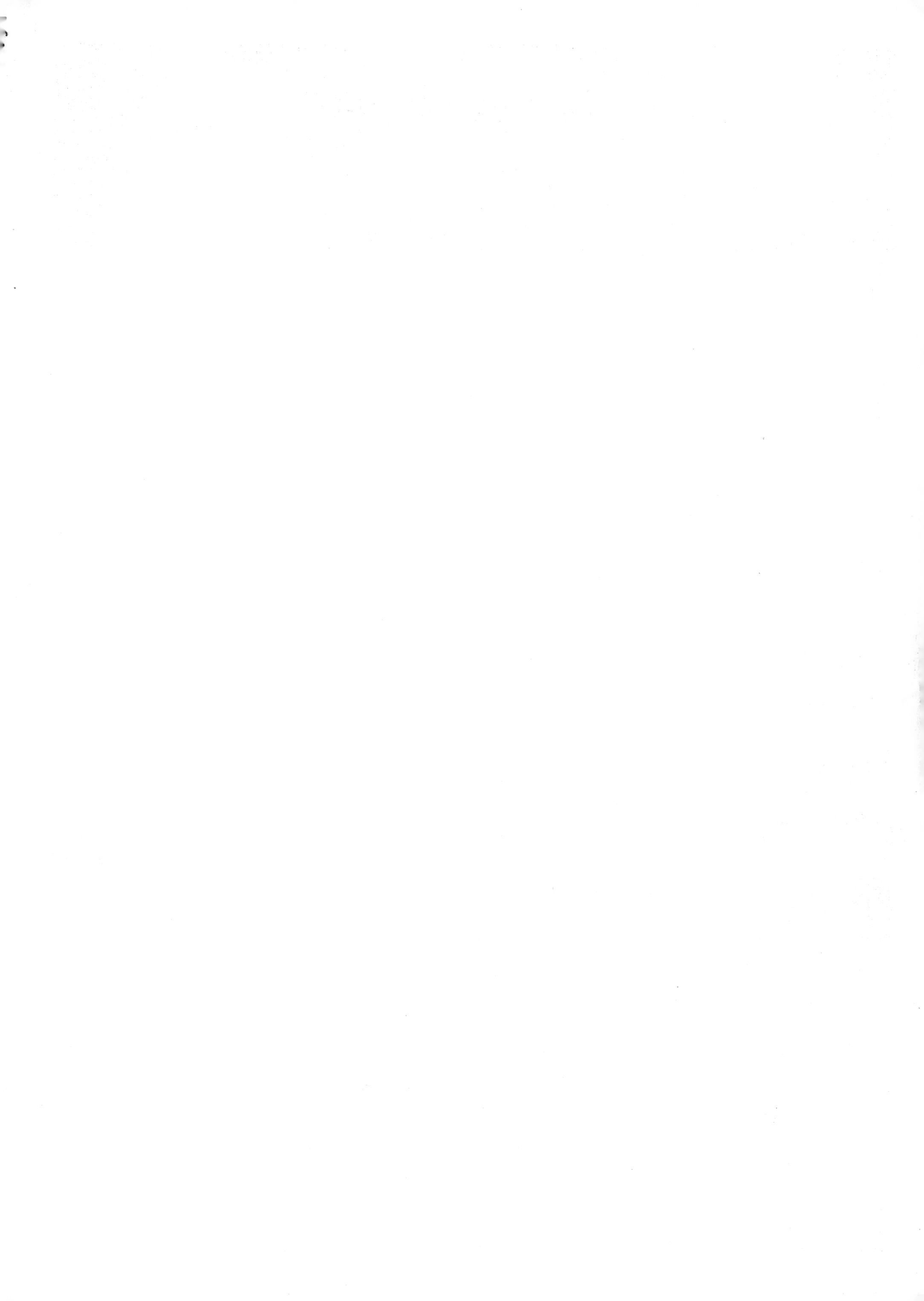